Studies in Jewish Bibliography History and Literature

in honor of

I. EDWARD KIEV

edited by

CHARLES BERLIN

KTAV PUBLISHING HOUSE, INC.
New York
1971

KTAV PUBLISHING HOUSE, INC.

SBN 87068-143-5

LIBRARY OF CONGRESS CATALOG CARD NUMBER: 70-138462
MANUFACTURED IN THE UNITED STATES OF AMERICA

To I. Edward Kiev:

Your friends and colleagues are delighted to present this Festschrift to you on the occasion of your sixty-fifth birthday.

In the more than forty years of distinguished service as the Librarian of your alma mater, Hebrew Union College-Jewish Institute of Religion in New York City, you have endeared yourself to scholars and students in the world of Jewish scholarship by your untiring efforts to assist them in their endeavors. The world of Jewish scholarship owes you a special debt of gratitude for your services to the Hebrew Union College-Jewish Institute of Religion Library in New York City.

To you, dear friend and wise counsellor, we offer this collection of essays as a token of our esteem, our affection and our gratitude.

C.B.

TABLE OF CONTENTS

תוכן

A COLLECTION OF HEBREW-LATIN APHORISMS BY A CHRISTIAN HEBRAIST

SALO W. BARON

Columbia University

Among the Oriental manuscripts of the Marciana Library in Venice a small tract of aphorisms by an unknown author is something of a bibliographical curiosity. Written in two columns in a vocalized Hebrew text, in square characters and a Latin translation, it combines certain homely lessons with a number of Christian apologetic excursuses. May a brief communication of this example of intergroup intellectual exchanges serve as a token of appreciation for a former pupil and old friend, Dr. Isaac Edward Kiev, on the occasion of his sixty-fifth birthday.

Neither in the manuscript itself nor in the description in the Library's catalogue is there any specific identification of the author. The first sentence gives the title as *Dibre Shimeon* (*Verba Simeonis*). In a superlinear correction, the word *Dibre* is replaced (without deletion) by *Mishle* ("Proverbs"), but there is no similar equivalent in Latin. The author is not identified any more closely than by saying that he was "of the Christian priests in Italy, the country which is preeminent among the nations, and the leader in the priesthood."[1] Nor is there any indication as to the time of the composition, although the Latin script may indicate a late seventeenth- or early eighteenth-century date.

The author evidently knew Latin much better than Hebrew. The occasional grammatical errors are aggravated by frequent mistakes in punctuation. Only here and there does he use words which are definitely erroneous. However, the meaning is always perfectly clear. Less obvious is the purpose of this composition or to what kind of reader it was addressed, but it undoubtedly has some readers from among Jews or Christian Hebraists in mind. Despite a number of religious polemics in the defense of Christian beliefs, one cannot classify this tract as a missionary pamphlet; it seems to pursue playful rather than practical aims.

The following excerpts in an English translation will give a fair idea of the contents of this booklet.

I

A good intellect, time, and scholarly books will bring one into the house of wisdom.

Good food and a bad stomach are bad; bad food and a good stomach are good.

It is better to converse over water than over wine.

An agnostic (epicurean) once raised a major question about the immortality of souls and the Hereafter. I told him: "Among animals there is neither knowledge of, nor a hope for, a life in the world to come. You will resemble the animals, while I shall join the great men, all of whom have believed in life in the world to come." [2]

II

A man once asked me: "If God has determined one's fate for good or evil, what purpose does prayer serve?" I replied that the divine force cannot be compared to that of fire. The latter burns, indiscriminately, the clothing of a righteous person and that of an evildoer. God, however, has a variable force at his disposal; it burns the clothing of an evildoer, but spares that of a righteous person.

Prayer and God kiss each other; where there is no prayer there is no God.

(The following aphorism is deleted in both Hebrew and Latin: The wind moves a leaf while God moves the heart of man.)

Decorous living will save man from sin.[3]

III

A wise man from among the Jewish scholars once asked me a question: "I have read in the Gospels and noted that their sayings do not agree with the intent of the Torah. And that hence Jesus, Paul, and Stephen were no Torah experts." [To which I replied] "Jesus' words in the Gospels are admirable sayings. According to Josephus, Paul was a great scholar, while Stephen, too, belonged to the sages of Jerusalem. Hence it is impossible that they were not experts in the Torah. In their days Scriptural texts differed from one another; their words varied, though not the facts. The verses in the Torah, moreover, often have double meanings, like Jeremiah's Lamentations in which he predicted the exile under Nebukadnezzar or that under Titus." Similarly what he [the Jewish scholar] said about Christians believing in matters unacceptable to reason and which transcend God's power, caused me to laugh. It is rather our reason which is subject to error. By contending that God cannot do certain things he makes Him a finite entity lacking omnipotence. But we are in no position to pass judgment on God and His power, for He is infinite in contrast to our reason which is finite and may not recognize rain falling on our heads.

God who has created everything out of nothing can certainly bring about the resurrection of the dead out of dust.[4]

IV

A Hebrew from the common people told me: "I do not know why Christians believe in Jesus who was but a hanged [crucified individual]." I replied: "Who tells us that story?" He said: "It is written in the Gospels." To which I replied: "In the same Gospels it is also written that Jesus rose from the dead and ascended to heaven."[5]

V

As may be seen from the above sample, none of the author's ethical and apologetical ideas are particularly original or penetrating. But they offer us a glimpse of what kind of debates were conducted among ordinary people, Christian and Jewish, on aspects of the Christian dogmas. That they were written in low key and without bitter accusation and invective, is actually a sign of a certain friendliness and mutual respect prevailing among the masses of the Christian and Jewish population in Venice, and some other Italian cities, in the early modern period. They confirm the general impression of fairly amicable intergroup relations emerging from contemporary records, including Simone Luzzato's well-known *Discorso*. Even many members of the lower clergy, like our Simeon, avoided the anti-Jewish fulminations of their more famous confreres from among the brimstone-spewing preachers and controversialists.

Appendix I.

~~Ex necessitate ad cerebrum~~ 1

Verba Simeonis de Sacerdotibus Chris-
Italiae
tianis qui sunt in terra, domino
gentium, ~~sacerdotum~~ principe.
Intellectus bonus, tempus, et docti
libri, sapientiae domum perducunt.
Cibus bonus in malo stomacho malus erit,
cibus malus in bono stomacho bonus erit.
est
Melius super aqua loqui, quam super
mero.
Quidam Christianus magnam mihi
obiectionem contra animae aeternita-
tem, contraque futuri seculi vitam
obiectavit, cui dixi inter iumenta,
futuri seculi spes, et notitia
non est. Tu sicut iumentum, ego
vero velut magni homines, qui omnes in vitam aeternam crediderunt.

משלי

דברי שמעון מן הכהנים
הנוצרים אשר בהארץ רבתי
בגוים שרתי בהכהנים:
שכל טוב זמן וספרי החכמים
יביאו אל בית החכמה:
אכל טוב בבטן רעה יהיה רע
אכל רע בבטן טובה יהיה טוב:
טוב לדבר על המים מדבר על
היין:
האדם מפקיד הקשה לי קושיא
גדולה על נפש נצחי ועל חיי
העולם הבא: אמרתי לו בין
הבהמות אין דעת ותקות
חיי העולם הבא: אתה תהיה
כבהמות ואני כאנשים גדולים
שכלם האמינו בחיי העולם
הבא:

Appendix II

Homo quidam mihi dixit si Deus bo-	אִישׁ אֶחָד אָמַר לִי אֱלֹהִים
num, aut malum determinauit ad	אִם גָּזַר טוֹב וָרַע לָמָּה
quid oratio? cui dixi potentia Dei	הַתְּפִלָּה: וָאֹמַר לוֹ אֵין
non est sicut potentia ignis, qui ta-	כֹּחַ אֱלֹהִים כְּכֹחַ הָאֵשׁ אֲשֶׁר
uestimenta justi, quàm uestimenta	אֲשֶׁר תִּשְׂרֹף בֶּגֶד הַצַּדִּיק
impij cremabit. Deus autem uarias	וּבֶגֶד הָרָשָׁע: אֱלֹהִים
potentias possidet, etenim uestime-	בַּעַל כֹּחוֹת מִתְחַשּׁוֹנוֹת בֶּגֶד
nta impij cremabit, uestimenta uero	רָשָׁע יִשְׂרֹף וּבֶגֶד צַדִּיק
justi conseruabit.	יְמַלֵּט:
Oratio, et Deus osculata sunt. Si	הַתְּפִלָּה וֵאלֹהִים נָשְׁקוּ:
non est oratio, nec etiam Deus.	אִם אֵין תְּפִלָּה אֵין אֱלוֹהַּ:
Ventus folium mouebit, Deus	רוּחַ תָּנוּעַ עָלָה וֶאֱלֹהִים
autem cor hominis.	יָנוּעַ לְבַב אָדָם:
Decor liberabit hominem à	הָדָר יַצִּיל אָדָם מֵחֵטְא:
peccato.	

Appendix III

Quidam doctus ex Iudeorum doctis mi:
hi obiiciebat dicens: librum Euange
lij perlegi, et animaduerti, dicta non
esse iuxta intentionem legis, et Ie:
sum, Paulum, et Stephanum scri:
pturam nesciuisse. Verba Iesu
in Euangelijs admiranda, et Pau:
li, secundum ~~iuxta~~ uerba Josephi Filij Gorion,
sicut doctissimus, Stephanus quo:
que ex doctis Hierusalem, et im:
possibile est, eos Sacram scri:
pturam non intellexisse. Te:
mporibus suis uaria Biblia
fuere, ex quibus
~~ex quibus~~

הקשה אלי חכם אחד
מחכמי היהודים לאמר
אני קראתי בספר אונגליש
וראיתי שהכתובים אינם
כפוונת התורה: וישו
ופאולו ואשטיבן אינם ב
בקיאים בתורה: ישו בא
באונגליש דבריו דברי תמהון
ופאולו כדברי יוסיפון בן
גוריון היה חכם גדול
ואשטיבן גם הוא מחכמי
ירושלם ואי אפשר שלא ה
היו בקיאים בתורה: כי
בעתם היו מקראות משת

Appendix III (continued)

כִּשְׁתַּנּוֹת וּמֵהֶן דְּבָרִים
הֲפָכִים וְלֹא הַמְּקַשִּׁים: ג
וְגַם כַּוָּנַת הַפְּסוּקִים
בַּתּוֹרָה בִּשְׁנֵי מְשָׁלִים
כְּקִנּוֹת יִרְמְיָהוּ שֶׁנִּבָּא
גָּלוּת נְבוּכַדְרֶאצַּר וּגְלוּת
טִיטוּס: וּמָה שֶׁאָמַר כִּי
הַנּוֹצְרִים מַאֲמִינִים בְּד
בִּדְבָרִים שֶׁהַשֵּׂכֶל לֹא יָ
יֵדַע אוֹתָם וְשֶׁיְּכוֹלֶת אֶל
אֱלֹהִים תּוּכַל בָּם צְחוֹק ע
עָשָׂה לִי שִׂכְלֵנוּ הוּא בַּע
בַּעַל שִׁגָּיוֹן: וכשאמר
אשר מצחקים על

ex quibus verba variant, sed non dicta.
Multę etiam periodi in scriptura
analogice dicta sunt, velut lamen=
tationes Ieremię, in quibus transmigra=
tio Nabucodonosor, et Titi intelligi=
tur. Sed et eum dixit, Christianos cre=
dere dicta, que intellectus numquam
poterit intelligere
~~intelligeret~~, nec potentia Dei in eis
~~potenti~~ blande usi, etenim intel=
lectus noster est erroris sponsus.
et quando

Appendix III (continued)

et quando dixit, Deus in eis non	וכשאמר כי אלהים לא
poterit, cum fecit indigentem	יוכל בכם יעשהו בעל תכלית
perfectione, et sine perfecta po-	ובבלי יכולת גמורה ;
tentia, sed non licet Deum iudi-	ולא טוב לשפוט אלהים
care, et secum potentiam, qui	ויכולתו שאינו בעל תכלית
non indiget perfectione, cum	עם שכלנו שהוא בעל
intellectu nostro, qui perfectio-	תכלית אשר לא ידע גשם
ne eget, dum non cognoscet plu-	שירד על ראשו ;
viam, que super caput suum	
descendet,	
Deus ex nihilo fecit omnia	אלהים מאין עשה ארץ
eo magis Resurrectionem	הכל כל שכן תחיית המתים
a pulvere mortuorum.	מעפר :

Appendix IV

Hebreus plebeius mihi dixit:	עִבְרִי מֵעַם עֶרֶב אָמַר לִי לֹא
Non intelligo quomodo Christiani	יוֹדֵעַ אֲנִי לָמָּה הַנּוֹצְרִים
possint credere in Iesu, qui sus-	מַאֲמִינִים בְּיֵשׁוּ אֲשֶׁר
pensus fuit; cui dixi: Quis tibi dixit	הָיָה תָּלוּי : וָאֹמַר לוֹ מִי
hoc; et respondens inquit: Hoc	הוּא אֲשֶׁר דִּבֵּר אֶת
scriptum est in libro Euangelij,	הַדָּבָר הַזֶּה : וַיֹּאמֶר זֶה
et dixi: In libro Euangelij etiam	כָּתוּב בְּסֵפֶר אֶוַנְגִּילִישׁ
dictum est, eum ~~resurrexisse~~ resurrexisse	וָאֹמַר גַּם בְּסֵפֶר אֶוַגִּילִישׁ
a mortuis, et ascendisse ad	נֶאֱמַר כִּי קָם מִמּוֹתָיו
Coelos.	וְעָלָה אֶל הַשָּׁמַיִם :

NOTES

1. See the first three lines of Appendix I.
2. See the continuation *ibid.*
3. Appendix II.
4. Appendix III.
5. Appendix IV. See other illustrations in my *A Social and Religious History of the Jews,* 2d ed. rev., New York, 1952 ff., esp. Vols. XIII, Chap. lvii; and XIV, Chap. lx.

APPROACHES TO RABBI NACHMAN AND HIS TALES

Abraham Berger

New York Public Library

In the summer of 1806, four years before his death of tuberculosis at the age of 38, Rabbi Nachman of Braslav announced to his followers that he had decided to tell stories.[1] "People say that stories put you to sleep. I say that they rouse you from your slumber."[2] To this very day his followers, who never acknowledged any successor to Rabbi Nachman, read these stories as Holy Writ. A "Braslaver" edition of these *Sippure Ma'asiyot* consists of the text in Hebrew and Yiddish with excerpts from commentaries. Several editions have appeared since their first publication in 1815.[3]

The reaction of the outside world was at first extremely hostile. To the rival Hasidic groups the tales appeared strange and suspect, a scandal; to the Maskilim, foolish, in barbaric Hebrew, and in poor taste. Simon Dubnow, at the end of the century, diagnosed them as the product of a man sick in body and in mind, and asserted that all search for meaning would be in vain.[4]

However, Nachman's prophecy that "My spark (*mayn fayerl*) will glow quietly till the coming of the Messiah,"[5] ready to burst into flame again, is gradually gaining ground. The Israeli critic, Eliezer Steinman, acclaims Nachman rhapsodically, not only as a great artist but as one whose ideas are relevant today.[6] Yiddish writers are welcoming him as a tutelary ancestor, and he has become the subject of essays, novels, and poetry. Israel Zinberg characterizes him as a "bleeding heart" and "sensitive soul," but notes that "we have to search for pearls and sparks among sand and rubbish."[7] Shin Niger admires the sheer creativity of the stories although still preferring to play down their symbolical character.[8] Finally, our own Yudl Mark acclaims him as one of the greatest Jewish narrators of all times: ". . . the winged scope, the delicate form and the mystical ideas . . . [are] completely original."[9]

The three authors who broke the ground for the introduction of Nachman to the Western world, or rather to a Jewry in the rapid process of westernization, are Martin Buber, Samuel Abba Horodetzky and Hillel Zeitlin. Buber's translation of the tales with a short and not very relevant introduction, was his first work in the field of Hasidism. Apparently he never went back to Nachman.[10] Horodetzky, a lineal descendant of Rabbi Nachman, devoted a great deal of his literary activity to Nachman's life and work, but was not able to penetrate into the soul of his ancestor.[11]

In many ways Hillel Zeitlin was the pioneer in our understanding of Rabbi Nachman. In newspaper articles and booklets in Hebrew and Yiddish he analyzed, discussed and preached the *Zeher* (seer, visionary) of Podolie with erudition, empathy and eloquence, treating his life, his discourses and his tales as a unit.[12]

In our own day the outstanding student of Rabbi Nachman is Joseph Weiss who, in a series of weighty articles, has opened for us new avenues to our understanding of Nachman's dialectical struggles with the problems of creation, faith and evil.[13]

It is difficult to write about Rabbi Nachman. There is hardly anyone to compare him with in the Jewish tradition. An artist who did not refine his raw creations; a thinker who denounced philosophic speculations; a mystic who could practice seclusion while surrounded by his followers; a Zaddik indulging in unlimited self-glorification and yet with dreams of falling from grace; and with it all, a resolute shepherd of a devoted flock.[14]

Nachman once told a story about a treasure in a man's own backyard; in order to find it the man first had to go to Vienna.[15] We can appreciate him better today, because we have now discovered or rediscovered Kierkegaard and Kafka, Pascal and Hölderlin, and because symbols in mythology, literature, and art are illuminated today by clinical discoveries and bold speculations.

An analysis of his tales requires an understanding of the kabbalistic language of his Discourses (*Likkute Moharan*) which, in the words of Gershom Scholem, "reveal a hyper-modern sensitivity to problems."[16] It requires a study of his inner life as revealed in the bristling and often ironic aphorisms and in his nightmares and in his dreams. The critical reader is frustrated, often despairingly so, by the sudden changes of the channels of his discourse and the shifts of associations. It is important also to be aware of the many ups and downs in his clinical chart which, in a sense, is in the very fabric of his creations.

The flourishing of the science of comparative folklore in the nineteenth century, followed by the wild craze for classification in our times, naturally stimulated the hunt for sources or parallels to Rabbi Nachman's tales. I recall many conversations with J. J. Trunk, Leo Schwarz, Simon Hazan and others on parallels in Grimm's *Tales,* in medieval folktales, *A Thousand and One Nights* and in the *Yatakas.* Motifs have wings and can penetrate many chambers, but it is the individual coloring and the imagination which makes of them a structure, a *Gestalt.* The very success of *The Road to Xanadu,* wherein John Livingston Lowes uncovered practically every word of Coleridge's *Kubla Khan* to have been in some book that Coleridge had read, has put a quietus on this type of scholarship, useful though it may be as a first step in the preparation of a concordance of the author's ideas and images.

In the tales of Rabbi Nachman we can detect echoes of the Bible (of which he was a master), Midrash *Agada,* medieval philosophic works, kabbalistic texts such as *Bahir,* Zohar and *Sefer ha-Kanah,* and Lurianic literature. But these are mere tracings in the web of his memory, the Mother of the Muses, and are utterly assimilated by the heat of his imagination.

One should not dismiss the fact that, contemporaneous with Nachman, German romanticism, with its cult of the fairy tale and the folktale, had penetrated as far as Ukrainian Uman, with whose *Maskilim* Nachman was in some kind of uneasy contact.[17] This contact, however, seems to have been only in the last few months of his life when he moved from Bratzlav to Uman.

One can follow the growth of skill and boldness in the images and structures of the *Ma'asiyot.* The first tale, the "Quest for the Lost Princess," has the appearance of a fairy tale. The story of the "Hakham and the Tam" (the Clever Fellow and the Simpleton) is written in an ironic-realistic-didactic tone. The "Burgher and the Poor Man" is clearly a Kabbalistic-Messianic allegory. The "Changelings" is a psychological wonder-tale with adventures in a forlorn forest where the son of the King and the son of the servant listen to the gossip of the planets and are awakened by the laughter of the oncoming dawn. The complicated unfolding of the tale of the "Baal Tefila" (Man of Prayer) tells of a Zaddik's retreat from civilization so that he might gain followers and carry on his war with idolatries. The last story which Nachman told just before his death was the "Ma'aseh fun Zayin Betler" (The Seven Mendicants), in which itinerant beggars entertain a pair of young orphans at their seven-day wedding feast arranged by a Beggar's Club. Each day a beggar appears and tells them a story. One of these stories will be analyzed here.

The stories were told by Rabbi Nachman in Yiddish as part of Hasidic table-talk, then memorized by Nathan or others and translated into Hebrew. When the story was told on Friday nights it could not be recorded until the following evening. Nathan often had the help of other disciples, each one memorizing the tale separately. As a result, the skeleton of the tales and the dramatic images and even the words may still accurately reflect the original.[18] However, some of the subtle nuances must have been lost in the process. Rabbi Nachman once remarked that his enemies certainly did not understand him, "and as for those who think highly of me, hardly any understand me, except Nathan and Naftali (another disciple)—a little."[19]

The "Tale of the Seven Beggars" was told in installments during two weeks in the Spring of 1810, the last year of Nachman's life. According to Nathan, on a Sabbath Eve, the 3rd of Nissan, Nachman was extremely dejected. He was worried about the critical illness of his grandchild, son of his beloved daughter Odel. His prayer session was short and during his brief table-talk he suddenly asked: "Where are we now in our story?" Nathan told him in great dread: "We are now in the third day."[20] And then Nachman began [I am now writing the tale in an abridged form. A.B.]:

On the third day the orphans were longing for the third beggar, the Stutterer, who was so helpful to them when they were very young. No sooner did they utter their wish, than he appeared. By way of explaining who he really was, he told them the following tale: At the edge of the world there is a mountain and on it a rock and on the rock a well. At the other edge of the world stands the heart of the world. This cosmic heart is a *Komah shelemah* full structure, like that of a human being with all his organs. The heart cries out to the well in great longing with alarm and supplications, and the well, in turn, is longing for the heart. But the heart of the world cannot get to the well, for were it to move from its position it would lose sight of the well and this would be the end of the life of the heart and the End of the World. And the pitiless sun is burning and punishing the heart and causes it to weaken. And the heart is also faint from its very longing. But when there is a desperate need for the heart to catch its breath, a bird appears and with its wings shields the heart from the rays of the sun. As the day is coming to its close, the heart and the well say good-bye to each other in song and music and riddles. For the well is from the higher world and has no time but what the heart offers to it as a gift. Each day may be the last day. Then appears the "great Man," the Man of True Grace and presents a day to the heart who gives it to the well, and the world continues. No day is like another day and all have different melodies and different riddles. I, concluded the stuttering beggar, go around and gather and weave deeds of grace into a day and bring it to the Man of True Grace, who presents it to the heart, who offers it to the well, and so on and so on.

The first impression the tale makes on us is one of a series of symmetries. At the same time, one feels that this symmetry is only a precarious balance in a field of insecurity. Are we in Heaven or in the Nether World, or on their borders? We feel dimly that it is a vision of Existence, of exposure to fierce and possibly hostile powers, of despair and hope.

Nathan and his friends memorized this story all day Saturday, and, out of sheer excitement over what they felt to be the crown jewel of his tales, they forgot to recollect Nachman's table-talk on that occasion. Nathan tells us that he dimly remembers that the rabbi spoke of the heart which is being persecuted.

Nachman hinted that Psalm 61 somehow stood at the source of the tale. As a matter of fact, we find in this short psalm many words which served as stimulants while he was weaving his tale. We find here the "edge of the world," "will I call unto Thee when my heart fainteth," the "rock," the "shelter of the wings," and "add days to the King's days." Even the "great Man of True Grace" is found in this psalm if we realize that this phrase is due to a pun. "Hesed we-emeth *man* yintseruhu" (Psalm 61:8) became "the hesed and emeth man will guard him," the difficult Hebrew word *man* emerges as a Yiddish "man" through the retort of his feverish imagination. Nachman often used puns in his conversations.

What is the meaning of this tale? Neither Nathan in his *Likkute*

Halakhot nor Rabbi Nachman of Cheherin in his *Rimze ha-Ma'asiyot* elaborate too much on it. Nachman told the tale "in a wonderful and awe-inspiring state of ecstasy and with wonderful dread."[20] Although the rabbi of Cheherin often finds kabbalistic or messianic allusions in other tales, here he merely quotes Nathan's didactic interpretation. The Sun, as chief of the planets, instituted by the Almighty to mark the days and the seasons, represents Time and the hustle and bustle of this world;[21] Israel, the heart of the nations,[22] is exposed to the "Oppressions under the Sun" (Ecclesiastes, 4,1). But even the other extreme, the desire for *unio mystica* with the Well, the Source of all Being, may also become dangerous. The Bird, symbol of the Torah, mediates the two extremes. In studying the Torah, one gets a respite from lustful desires and a breathing spell for the soul lost in ecstasy.[23]

Nathan, in his *Likkute Halakhot,* emphasizes that "the holy heart," although personally innocent of the "Evil under the Sun," nevertheless suffers under it, in accordance with Isaiah 53:4–5: "Surely he has borne our griefs . . . he was wounded for our transgressions. . . ."[24]

The Well is the source of all "good points" and all blessings. By prayer, studying, and longing, one may participate in the Heart's action of gaining Tikkun for the fissured world.[25]

Of great importance are the spiritual preparations for the coming of the Sabbath, the Holy Days and especially the New Year, which come with such wonderful melodies and riddles. We also share in the farewell song of the Heart.[26]

Good deeds, especially the practice of charity, is the tangible form of true grace. It is therefore incumbent upon man to practice charity, joining thus in the work of the beggar, who gathers and weaves true grace to give to the Man of True Grace, who gives it to the heart, who gives it to the Well, and so another day is born.[27]

The tale thus illustrates the cardinal principle that "the world is founded upon Torah, upon Avodah (Divine Service-Prayer) and Gemilut Hasadim (practice of charity), (Aboth I, 2). This is achieved by our mystic participation in this cosmic activity as elucidated by the Kabbalists.[28]

The note to the body of the tale also hints that the heart symbolizes King David, whose Psalm 61 was woven into the fabric of the tale. According to tradition, David originally was born "without time" and would not have lived at all had not Adam given him seventy years from his allotted one thousand years.[29] Nachman in his *Discourses* characterizes the Messiah, prefigured by King David, as being born anew each day in line with Psalm 2:7: "This day have I begotten thee." [30]

Perhaps, another interpretation of the tale is that it represents Nachman's vision of his own state: his heart afire, his lungs diseased, and himself despairing. We might call this the cosmic-organic interpretation, placing the organs of the human body and their activities in correspondence with the cosmic instruments and the Divine *Gestalt.* Nachman's struggles, spiritual and physical, correspond to the continuous struggle and harmonization of the *Sefirot* in the Divine Hierarchy.[31] The Heart, the heart of the world, corresponding to the last *Sefirah* and to the *Nefesh,* the lower part of the soul, is overheated by burning and twisting doubts.[32] It is consumed by the fire of the Sun, the negative sun (*Hamah*) which, in the words of the *Tikkune Zohar,* Nachman's favorite work, represents the Fire of Gehinnom and its evil agent, Sammael.[33] We might call this the Midnight Sun which appeared to Nachman in one of his nightmares.[34] The Bird, whose protecting wings are the wings of the Cherubim screening the Ark cover (Exodus 25:20) are represented by his own lungs, the *Ruah* part of the soul.[35] In his *Discourses,* Nachman returns again and again to the vital role of the lungs whose normal function is seen as the blowing of coolness and humidity on the overheated heart. This it draws from the Well which corresponds to *Hokhmah* (Divine Wisdom) the first breakthrough of the *Sefirot,* to the intellect (brain) in the body and the *Neshamah,* the highest aspect of the soul.[36]

The Heart of the world sends out to the Well cries of repentance and longing and alarm. His days are numbered and he yearns for more days in which to achieve his mission. Each day is not merely a day of rebirth (the Zaddik, Nachman, corresponds to the Messiah) but a day of Judgment. The fire of the Sun in the Heart is the Tempter, Accuser, and would-be Executioner. Nachman is guilty because the world's sins are his sins. His sickness proves it. He could have been cured by now but his followers do not have sufficient faith.[37] He might of course give up this earthly Gehinnom, take off his outer garment and enter *Olam ha-ba,* joining the Well, the source of blessings. He is yearning for it but cannot reach it. Will he finally reach it? In one of his dreams of that period Nachman was told by a "higher-up" Elder that he might not even have a hiding place in the real Gehinnom.[38]

Then comes the unexpected break represented by the Man of True Grace. This "great man" is not simply the intermediary who transmits the woven day to the Heart, which gives it to the Well. He is a messenger from Absolute Grace, *Rahamim Gemurim,* the highest *Sefirah* of God who announced to Moses: ". . . and I will be gracious to whom I will be gracious . . . ." (Exodus 33:19) without regard to whether the subject is worthy or unworthy.[39]

On this desperate note of hope Nachman remains suspended. Nachman is the very structure of the tale. But he is more—he is also the teller of the tale, the Stutterer who stutters out of the fullness of his melody and harmony, and his desire to communicate.

NOTES

1 *Hayye Moharan,* (Jerusalem, 1962), pp. 66–67; Nachman of Braslav, *Likkute Moharan,* (New York 1958), no. 60, 6 (referred in the text as *Discourses*).

2 Ibid., p. 16; Nathan of Nemirov, *Yeme Moharnath,* (Bene Berak, 1956), p. 12.

3 The edition used was published in New York in 1949 by the Chevra Chasidei Braslav and includes copious excerpts from *Likute Halakhot* by Nathan of Nemirov, Nachman's foremost disciple and secretary, and from *Rimze ha-Maasiyot* by Nachman of Cheherin. There is a fine Yiddish edition with an introduction and notes by S. H. Setzer, (New York, 1929) and a "secular" Hebrew edition (without the Braslaver notes) by Samuel Abba Horodezky (Berlin, 1922). In 1951 there appeared a modernized Hebrew version of the tales by Eliezer Steinman in *Kitve Rabbi Nachman,* Tel Aviv, 1951.

4 Simon Dubnow, *Geshikhte fun Hasidism* (Vilna, 1933), v. 2, p. 223.

5 Nachman of Cheherin, *Parparaot le-hokhma* on *Likkute Moharan Tinyana,* 7:7. Published together with the *Likkute Moharan,* (New York, 1958).

6 Introduction to *Kitve Rabbi Nahman,* Tel Aviv, 1951, p. 10 ff.

7 Israel Zinberg, *Di geshikhte fun literatur bay Yidn* (New York, 1943), v. 7, part 2, pp. 173–174.

8 Shin Niger (Samuel Charney), *Dertseyler un romanisten* (New York, 1946), p. 20 ff.; introduction to Jonah Speavack, *R' Nachman Bratzlaver* (Vilna, 1932), p. xxxiii–lix. Niger defends the Yiddish text of the tales as originals as against S. H. Setzer. Cf. note 18.

9 Yudl Mark, "Yiddish Literature" in Louis Finkelstein, editor, *The Jews: Their History, Culture and Religion* (New York, 1960), vol. 2, pp. 1201–02.

10 *Die Geschichten des Rabbi Nachman, ihm nacherzählt,* (Frankfurt am Main, 1906). A translation into English by Maurice Friedman was published by the Indiana University Press at Bloomington, Indiana in 1962. An early version of Nachman's tales in English is found in Meyer Levin's *The Golden Mountain* (New York, 1932), republished under the title *Classic Hassidic Tales* (New York, 1966).

11 *Rabbi Nachman von Bratzlaw; ein Beitrag zur Geschichte der jüdischen Mystik* (Berlin, 1910); *Sippure Maasiyot* (Berlin, 1922); *Torat Rabbi Nahman mi-Bratzlav* (Berlin, 1923).

12 Many of these essays were edited with a discerning introduction by his son Aaron Zeitlin under the title *Reb Nachman Braslaver, der Zeher fun Podolie* and published in New York by the Farlag Matones in 1952, as Volume I of Hillel Zeitlin's Collected Works.

13 Joseph Weiss' three most important essays relevant to our discussion are: "Ha-kushya betorat Rabbi Nahman" in *Ale Ayin* (Festschrift in honor of Zalman Schocken), (Jerusalem, 1952), p. 245–291; "Iyunim bitfisato heatzmit shel Rav Nahman mi-Braslav" in *Tarbiz* (Jerusalem, 1958, Scholem number), v. 27, p. 232–245; and "Rav Nahman mi-Braslav al ha-mahloket alav" in *Studies in Mysticism and Religion presented to Gershom G. Scholem* (Jerusalem, 1967), Hebrew section, p. 101–113.

14 A German poet once remarked that man deems himself a god in his dreams but a beggar in his reflections; Nachman, on the contrary, was the great Zaddik in his discourses and in his conduct, but in his dreams he often sees himself menaced, alienated, abased, and abandoned.

15 *Sippurim niflaim* (Bene Berak, 1961), p. 26.

16 Gershom G. Scholem, *Major Trends in Jewish Mysticism* (New York, 1954), p. 346.

17 *Sippurim Niflaim,* p. 3–7; *Hayye Moharan,* p. 81; Hayyim Liberman, "R. Nachman Bratzlaver un di Umaner Maskilim," *Yivo Bleter* (New York, 1947), v. 29, p. 201–219.

18 The suggestion was made by S. H. Setzer in his introduction to the *Sippure Maasios,* p. 33–42, that the traditional Yiddish text is really a later retranslation from the Hebrew translation of Nachman's tales as told in Yiddish. This was refuted by Shin Niger. (Cf. note 8.) However, even if the Yiddish text is a retranslation, it is still closer to Nachman's language than the Hebrew translation since, obviously, the tales were memorized in Yiddish. Some of the *Discourses* (*Likkute Moharan*) were written in Hebrew by Rabbi Nachman; others were delivered in Yiddish and rendered into Hebrew by Nathan. However, they were all revised and edited by the author. Cf. Nathan of Nemirov, *Yeme Maharnath* (Bene Berak, 1956), p. 51–52. There is no record of such a revision of the tales.

19 As a matter of fact, Nathan records that occasionally he had arguments with Naftali on some of the points of a story. On one occasion they urged Nachman to give them the true version. Cf. *Hayye,* p. 31.

20 Nachman of Braslav, *Sihot Ha-Ran,* No 151.

21 *Likkute Halakhot* on the tale.

22 *Likkute Moharan Tinyana,* No. 9; Zohar, III, 221b; Judah Halevi, *Kuzari,* II, 36.

23 *Likkute Moharan,* No. 78; Nathan of Nemirov, *Likkute Halakhot* on the Tale of the Third Day.

24 *Likkute Moharan Tinyana,* no. 8, 6; *Likkute Halakhot* and *Rimze Ha-Maasiyot* on the same tale.

25 *Likkute Halakhot* to the tale; *Likkute Moharan,* No. 34, 8; Scholem, *op. cit* p. 220 ff., 233 ff; 273–275.

26 *Rimze ha-Maasiyot,* on the tale, quoting from Nathan's *Likkute Halakhot.*

27 Ibid.

28 Scholem, *op. cit,* p. 233 ff; 268 ff.

29 Louis Ginzberg, *The Legends of the Jews* (Philadelphia, 1938), I, p, 61; V, p. 82–83.

30 *Likkute Moharan Tinyana, no. 61.*

31 *Likkute Moharan,* no. 80; Scholem, *op. cit,* p. 215 ff; Isaiah Tishby, *Mishnat Ha-Zohar* (Jerusalem, 1961), II, p. 69–124.

32 *Likkute Moharan Tinyana,* no. 46.

33 *Tikkune Zohar,* Tikkun 28, f. 24a; Tikkun 48, f. 85a.

34 *Hayye Moharan,* p. 46–47.

35 *Likkute Moharan,* no. 225, quoting Zohar III, 234a.

36 Ibid. no. 34, 6; *Likkute Moharan Tinyana,* 2, 6, ånd elsewhere.

37 *Likkute Moharan Tinyana,* no. 8, 6; *Sihot ha-Ran,* no. 157.

38 Cf. Joseph Weiss, in *Studies in Mysticism Presented to Gershom G. Scholem* (Jerusalem, 1967), Hebrew Section, p. 103 ff. Although Weiss offers a penetrating analysis of Nachman's state of mind, his identification of the "higher-up" Elder with the Shpolier Zeide (Nachman's adversary), is not convincing.

39 On *Rahamim Gemurim* as the highest *Sefirah,* cf. Joseph Gikatilla, *Shaare Orah,* gate 10.

A SIXTEENTH-CENTURY HEBREW CHRONICLE OF THE OTTOMAN EMPIRE:

THE *SEDER ELIYAHU ZUTA* OF ELIJAH CAPSALI AND ITS MESSAGE

CHARLES BERLIN

Harvard College Library

A century ago (1869), in Padua, Moses Lattes published a book[1] which brought to public attention the existence of a writer whose prodigious achievements are virtually unparalleled in the history of medieval Jewish historiography. This was the *De vita et scriptis Eliae Kapsalii,* which contained brief extracts from the historical writing of Elijah Capsali of Crete.

Scion of two famous families—the Capsalis and Delmedigos—with a long and distinguished record of scholarship and leadership in that area bounded by the metropolis of Constantinople, the island of Crete, and the peninsula of Italy, Elijah Capsali maintained and further enhanced this family tradition. For over a quarter of a century, Capsali served as leader of the Jewish community of Crete. The published ordinances[2] of the community testify to his active involvement in all aspects of communal life. In addition to this long career of public service, Capsali also managed to write two lengthy historical works—*Divre ha-Yamim* (1517) and *Seder Eliyahu Zuta* (1523), the former a history of Venice and the latter a history of the Ottoman Empire. In both there are various matters related to the history of the Jews: in the former, the Jews of Italy; in the latter, the Jews of Spain (especially relating to the Expulsion) and the Ottoman Empire.

These two chronicles are among the very few Hebrew works dealing with these topics, and—of all the chronicles that appeared in that explosion of historical writing set off by the Expulsion from Spain—are the least known and, with the exception of a few selections, remain regrettably unpublished to this day.

Capsali displays a remarkable concern for many of the necessary traits of the historian: order, accuracy, and the use of sources. In the introduction to the *Seder,* Capsali emphasizes the importance that he attached to order:

> Inasmuch as it is known that the stories, especially the stories of the kings . . . need order . . . and that with partial order they will be confused and not understood properly . . . therefore I have called the name of this book *The Order of Elijah,* because we have arranged the stories in correct, proper, and fitting order so that it is sufficiently easy for the reader to understand matters clearly and truly and they will not be as the words of a book that is sealed . . . .[3]

He was also concerned with historical accuracy; in the same introduction he promises:

> . . . I shall not write anything that is vague and sealed until its absolute verification shall become clear to me from the mouths of wise men known to their tribes . . . for every scribe and rhetorician who writes . . . and testifies about ancient matters . . . must write the truth . . . "many daughters have done valiantly, but the virtue of truth excells them all" (cf. Prov. 31:29) . . . .[4]

Similarly, in the introduction to his chronicle of Venice, he states that:

> . . . the reporting of things not in their proper order is cause for the soul of the reader (i.e., viewer) to loathe them . . . .[5]

Where he was not certain, Capsali did not hesitate to admit it:

> . . . therefore we shall not expand the narrative in this matter, for we will not prolong our account except in matters very clear to us . . . .[6]

and:

> . . . we have no desire but of stories known to us, as clear as the sun in truth, as we have designated in our opening remarks.[7]

Capsali frequently presents several explanations of certain matters and leaves to the reader the choice of the most plausible. For example, in recording the death of Sinan Pasha, Capsali writes:

> . . . Inasmuch as the truth is not clear to us whether Ghazali or the rest of the camp killed him, we have written both opinions, according to what was told to us, and you choose—not I.[8]

In describing Selim's reaction to Sinan's death, Capsali comments:

> . . . Behold I have written for you two opinions . . . select one of them. Who knows "whether they both shall be alike good" (Eccl. 11:6); grasp this one, but from the other one withhold not thy hand . . . .[9]

Rather than decide the issue himself, Capsali gives alternatives in several other places where he is not sure of the correct explanation.[10]

Capsali's use of sources also shows the traits of a genuine historian. Except for some material copied from Abravanel[11] and Ibn Daud,[12] Capsali's material on Jewish history seems to have been obtained from oral testimony. His account of the Expulsion was based on the reports of many exiles who passed through Crete.[13] Much of the general history also was based upon the oral reports of eyewitnesses. About events in Spain he learned from a R. Joseph ha-Levi Hakim and a R. Jacob; the conquest of Egypt from a R. Isaac Al-Hakim; the fall of Constantinople from his father, Elkanah; and "the stories of the kings of Turkey" from "old and knowing Turks." [14] He occasionally uses expressions like "my own ears heard, and not those of a stranger" and "my own eyes saw, and not those of a stranger." [15] He was probably his own source for information about contemporary events on Crete.

Capsali frequently alludes to the use of written secular sources. His statement in the introduction to his *Divre ha-Yamim* is very instructive:

> And now we shall begin to relate the beginning . . . of Venice . . . its rulers . . . and all that befell them as they have been verified to us from the books of the Gentiles and their chronicles . . . .[16]

There are other references to secular sources in the *Seder*. At the conclusion of his account of the reign of Mehmet, for example, Capsali mentions that the "story of the strength and courage . . . and greatness of Sultan Mehmet is written in the book of the chronicles of the kings of the Turks and in the books of the Greeks and the foreigners (*lo'azim*) and the books of Media and Persia." [17] Capsali probably knew no Persian, Turkish, or Arabic. However, he most probably did know Italian and Greek very well. Hence, in addition to Italian, he may have had access to Greek sources. The phrases: "are they not written in the book of the chronicles of the kings of Media and Persia" or "of the Turks" or "of the kings of Ishmael" are not to be taken literally; Capsali no doubt relied on Italian sources.

When compared with the contemporary Jewish attitude towards the use of secular historical works, Capsali's historical method is all the more remarkable. Joseph Caro, for example, opposed the reading of "books of wars" (i.e., secular histories); Moses Isserles, however, limited his opposition to works in foreign tongues. A later authority, Jacob Emden, was of the opinion that "the chronicles of the kings of the peoples of the world . . . there is no need at all in knowing . . . ." [18]

Moreover, Capsali's own attitude toward study—traditional and secular—is expressed clearly in a number of places in his writings, and leaves no doubt as to the primacy of traditional study in his thinking. It is seen in his recording of his father's advice to him as he set out for Italy:

> From secular studies turn aside . . . . Occupy yourself with grammar or Scripture, but your [main] occupation put in Talmud alone . . . . Talmud is for you a [foundation] stone and a pillar . . . but [place] the Kabbalah upon your head as a crown . . . this is the most valuable of them all . . . .[19]

Capsali, who numbered among his ancestors a Palestinian author of Kabbalistic works,[20] was also, himself, a student and an ardent admirer of Kabbalah. He refers to the Zohar as "distinguished" (*muflag*) and says of "the possessors of the Zohar, their doctrine is truth and their tradition is truth." [21] He refuses to believe that the messianic calculation of the Kabbalistic work *Sefer ha-Peliah ve-ha-Kanah* was wrong and proceeds to justify it.[22] His treatment of certain aspects of the history of the Jews of Spain reflects his devotion to the Kabbalah.[23] Capsali's own knowledge of the Kabbalah is reflected in the various quotations from the Zohar in his writing.[24] He reiterates the primacy of the Kabbalah in the following passage:

> "Among the tribes of Israel do I make known that which shall surely be" (Hos. 5:9), that the wisdom of the Kabbalah is the root, and its roots are planted over springs of many waters, "That it might bring forth branches and that it might bear fruit" (Ezek. 17:8), a tree of "glory to all its saints" (Ps. 149:9) . . . . Beside it [all] is vain and tasteless.[25]

Capsali further stresses the importance of rabbinic studies:

> In Mishnah sharpen your thoughts, in a diadem of beauty. "Arise, call upon thy God" (Jonah 1:6) with arranged *halakhot* and with Gemara, Tosefta, Sifre and Sifra . . . and do not please yourselves in the brood of aliens [secular studies] (cf. Isa. 2:6), only in the Torah. Do not lose everlasting life for the sake of temporal life. . . .[26]

Elsewhere Capsali presents a collection of rabbinic sayings opposing secular studies.[27]

Capsali's devotion to traditional studies—Scripture, Talmud and Kabbalah—is also seen in the style of his writing, in his traveling to Italy to study in Talmudic academies, and in his actions as leader of the Jews of Crete. Nevertheless, one cannot help but feel that Capsali's opposition to secular studies is not as uncompromising as it appears on the surface. The following passage is instructive:

> The [secular] sciences make . . . into perfumers, cooks, and bakers . . . . "Fix a period for thy study of the Torah" (*Avot* I:15) and secular studies—at random. Use them little in a crown of glory. The rest ban and rebuke greatly. Let not the miry (pun: Greek) clay take you with its eyebrows, with the smoothness of a foreign tongue.[28]

This is no demand for total abstention from secular studies but, rather, for a toleration of such studies on condition that they be subordinated to rabbinic, traditional studies. To express this view, Capsali has borrowed the phrase "perfumers, cooks, and bakers" which was used by Maimonides to express the ancillary conception of philosophy and its various branches,[29] a concept to which Capsali seems to adhere. This attitude is expressed in another passage:

> Were the people of our generation to act according to the words of Samuel, I would remain silent. . . . But to make the [secular] sciences fixed and the Torah temporary . . . this is an evil. . . .[30]

Capsali is not complaining about secular sciences *per se,* but against the reversal of the proper relationship between secular and religious studies. It was this subversion of religious studies that provoked his criticism of the secular pursuits of Spanish Jewry:

> They [the Spanish Jews] turned to secular studies and sank in the miry (pun: Greek) clay . . . and abandoned the Torah . . . and there was not "one of a city and two of a family" (Jer. 3:14) who were occupied in Talmud . . . .[31]

How, then, could Capsali, devotee of the Kabbalah and Talmud, justify his apparent devotion to historical writing, generally regarded as a secular study? How was his historical work subservient to religious tradition? Other medieval Jewish historians—e.g., Abraham Zacuto in his *Sefer Yuḥasin* and David Gans in his *Tsemaḥ David*—defended their use of secular sources as well as their writing of secular history by showing that secular history was really a part of, or identical with, the tradition, and that it had a certain pragmatic value for traditional Judaism; hence secular history should be accepted either as part of the tradition, or, at least, on utilitarian grounds.[32] Capsali, too, justifies the writing of secular history in his introduction to the *Seder*. He wrote the *Seder*

> . . . [so] that man may obtain knowledge and understanding when he hears the stories of the kings which we shall tell about the kings of the Gentiles and of the Turks . . . and we have already seen that the stories which are in the Bible [to be understood] in the obvious way, appeared [there] only so that man may get wisdom and instruction. . . .[33]

Just what "knowledge and understanding" did Capsali intend his readers to acquire from his account of the "kings of the Gentiles and of the Turks?" What religious purpose did his chronicle serve? None other than to provide the post-Expulsion generation with an account of a people—the Ottoman Turks—who were to be the divine instrument of redemption and whose whole history down to Capsali's own time was, in effect, the acting out of the messianic drama. Not only in Capsali's treatment of the three great conqueror-sultans—Mehmet, Selim and Suleiman—does the messianic message of the *Seder* become apparent; it also affects Capsali's treatment of many incidents of Ottoman history. Indeed, one is tempted to apply to Capsali, *mutatis mu-*

tandis, what has been said of an earlier Jewish chronicler, Abraham ibn Daud, whose messianic message has only recently been emphasized, that "history was a tool to him, and he would use it only to the extent that it was necessary for his purpose"; that he "was concerned with the events of the Gentile past only to the extent that they shed light on the Jewish hope for the future."[34] It is this message that Capsali alludes to in the introduction to the *Seder* when he gives as a reason for writing this chronicle the following:

> . . . so that when one looks into my stories, words, and sayings he will accept the yoke of the kingdom of God; all will know that the eyes of the Lord are looking to and fro in all the land, seeing evil men and good men, to give each one according to his ways and the fruit of his deeds, and He also watches over the nations, to cast down a nation and to raise up a nation . . . .[35]

Nor can one help but wonder whether this is what Capsali had in mind when, writing in his introduction that he has included in his chronicle some words of the Kabbalists, he wrote that "only one with expertise in this marvelous knowledge would understand these words, but he who was not experienced in this would read and think that he understands but he does not. . . ."[36]

Sultan Mehmet emerges from Capsali's account of his reign as a messianic figure. Mehmet was, of course, the conqueror of that bastion of Christianity Constantinople, whose fall was—in messianic tradition—a prelude to the ultimate collapse of Christendom.[37] That Capsali viewed Mehmet as a messianic figure is seen in his adapting to Mehmet a legend about another messianic figure, Alexander the Great. When Alexander visited Jerusalem, the legend says, the priests read to him from the Book of Daniel and Alexander understood the prophecy about a Greek destroying the Persian Empire as referring to himself. Capsali has Mehmet learn of Ibn Ezra's interpretation of the reference in Daniel 11:40–42 to "king of the north" as being the king of Constantinople (who, of course, was now Mehmet); he has Mehmet order R. Isaiah Meseni to read to him frequently from Daniel and has Mehmet even undertake the study of the Hebrew (!) language in order to be able to read Daniel himself. Capsali, in this adaptation of the Alexander legend, is thus indicating his belief that Mehmet, too, was a messianic figure, perhaps one of the world-rulers like Alexander or Cyrus, but in any event a person alluded to in the messianic prophecies of Daniel—thanks to his conquest of Constantinople.[38]

Furthermore, contemporary messianic thought identified the Ottoman sultans with the kings of Persia, especially Cyrus. Abraham ha-Levi, in his commentary on the Aramaic apocalyptic *Nevu'at ha-Yeled,* referred to the sultan as "the king of Turkey who is of the family of Cyrus, the messiah of God; . . . the king of Turkey is called Cyrus . . . because he is beloved by God as the first Cyrus and he is of his family and like him." [39] This belief is also reflected in Capsali where Mehmet's invitation to the Jews to settle in Constantinople is phrased in the language of the decree of Cyrus.[40] In keeping with such a view of Mehmet, Capsali proceeds to relate a number of anecdotes aimed at showing the good relationship between Mehmet and the Jews.

This relationship seems to have been established immediately after the conquest of Constantinople when Mehmet invited the Jews to settle in that city, gave them houses, and appointed many of them as royal physicians and officials.[40a] Capsali then reports the appointment of Moses Capsali, his great-uncle, as Chief Rabbi.[41] There follow several anecdotes illustrating the good relationship between the Sultan and the Chief Rabbi. Mehmet is said to have gone in disguise to observe Moses Capsali presiding as judge of the Jews and was very favorably impressed with him.[41a] Another anecdote tells of Moses' successful efforts—sanctioned by the Sultan—to separate Jewish youth from the immoral influence of the Janissaries.[42] On another occasion Moses is said to have used his influence on Mehmet to save some perfume merchants condemned to death by the Sultan.[43]

As further evidence of Mehmet's love for the Jews, Capsali cites the case of a Jewish official who was one of Mehmet's favorites. Sent on a mission to Venice, the Jew was robbed and murdered and the Sultan mourned his death.[44] Moreover, Mehmet's successful campaign in Wallachia is said to have been undertaken because of his desire to avenge the persecution of Jews there.[45] There follow three more stories illustrating the good relationship between Mehmet and his Jewish subjects: Mehmet and the Jewish landlady who observed the Sultan's curfew;[46] Mehmet and the Jewish musician from Spain;[47] and Mehmet at a Seder.[48]

While these stories may have been intended partly as entertainment, they also reflect Capsali's idealized image of the relationship between the Sultan and his Jewish subjects. Mehmet is pictured as a frequent visitor to the Jewish quarter; he was wandering about in the Jewish quarter when he came across the musician and the Seder.[49] The stories attribute to Mehmet an interest in matters Jewish: he was interested in a Seder service and even placed a monthly order for Jewish food.[50] Capsali's report that the Sultan wanted to learn the Jewish tongue has already been noted.[51]

Capsali's idealized image of Mehmet is further revealed in a series of anecdotes[52] concerning the cruelty and severity of Mehmet's justice. Among these anecdotes Capsali inserts an apocryphal conversation between Mehmet and Giovanni Dario, secretary of the Venetian Senate. When pressed by Mehmet as to the Venetian opinion of him, Dario replied that Mehmet's one fault was his excessive cruelty and readiness to shed blood. Capsali has Mehmet answer as follows:

> Do you think that of my own free will I kill my warriors . . . . No! for who will judge my people . . .? When I am cruel and kill ten men unlawfully to [meet the] needs of the hour, I am taking pity on the entire [people] and by this [example] the rest will see and fear and return every man from his evil path. This cruelty is, in truth, mercy.[53]

Such is Capsali's apology for and justification of the deeds of the man who "appeared to the West as the devastator of countries, the bloody king *par excellence,* the most terrible of killers of man, the hereditary enemy of Christians, the true Anti-Christ." [54] After another anecdote, Capsali says: "Many such cruel deeds did he do . . . for he was cruel to the wicked but merciful to the righteous"—a further justification of cruelty as being deserved by the wicked as punishment.[55] Elsewhere Capsali says that Mehmet carried out many such "necessary judgments," [56] thus implying his own approval of these acts of cruelty as necessities. In relating the famous story of Mehmet's page boys and the cucumbers, Capsali is not indignant at the death of the innocent page boy; rather, he proceeds to find an appropriate Biblical verse to match to the death of the guilty one.[57]

Another illustration of this idealization is seen in Capsali's account of the Ottoman conquest of the Morea, which centers about a story in which Demetrius, ruler of the Morea, gives his daughter in marriage to Mehmet.[58] A clue to the purpose of the story is provided by its appearance in Sambari's *Divre Yosef.*[59] There the story continues and has the following ending: When criticized for neglecting the affairs of state because of his new bride, Mehmet personally executes her in order to show that nothing was allowed to interfere with his duties. Now this is the familiar ending of the legend about Mehmet and his infatuation with the beautiful Irene, a Greek captive.[60] The omission of the ending in Capsali's version is understandable; the story was used by Christians to illustrate the Sultan's cruelty, while Capsali, with his idealized image of Mehmet, has omitted that part of the story which seemed damaging to the Sultan. In doing this, Capsali has converted a Christian legend aimed at condemning Mehmet into a romantic story in which Mehmet victoriously carries off a new bride. Mehmet emerges a hero instead of a villain, and, as a messianic figure, is cast in a highly idealized image of a man who can do no wrong.

The various political and military events of Mehmet's reign have messianic significance. The fall of Constantinople, divinely ordained because of the Byzantine persecution of the Jews, has already been mentioned. The conquest of the Morea, asserts Capsali, marked the complete end of *malkhut yavan*[61]—one of the four kingdoms mentioned in Daniel 8:22. Indeed, the defeat of the Greeks of the Morea was divinely ordained in order that there be no remnant of the house of the King of Greece.[62]

After discussing the fall of the Morea, Capsali deals with various other campaigns. It seems that Capsali was interested in these events only in so far as they served as a prelude to developments of greater significance. This is seen clearly in his treatment of the Ottoman campaign against Egypt. While it is not certain that Mehmet intended to attack Egypt when he mobilized his army in 1480,[63] Capsali states this as a fact because it fits in with his image of Mehmet's reign as a prelude to that of Selim. Capsali writes:

> Had he [Mehmet] lived a little longer, he would have conquered Egypt and its king; probably, [nay] almost certainly—for he had unlimited power. But what he did not have enough time for because of death, . . . there came his grandson Selim, the great king, who was like him in his splendor, and did it and enlarged the kingdom of Turkey ten times greater than in his [Mehmet's] reign . . . .[64]

Thus Selim completed what Mehmet started. This view of Mehmet's activities as prelude to the successes of the later Sultans can be seen in Capsali's remarks after relating the unsuccessful attacks on Cilli and Akkerman as well as Belgrade and Rhodes; Capsali says that their "time came" at the hands of Bayezit and Suleiman, respectively.[65] On the loss of Scutari, Capsali writes: "And from that day on the Turk captured most of the Sakboniani (i.e., Dalmatia) and left to the

Venetians a very few cities"[66]—thus marking the beginning of the loss of the Venetian territories in the Balkans. Thus—act one in the messianic drama.

In recording the history of the Ottomans during the reign of Bayezit, Capsali limits his account to four topics: the Expulsion from Spain, which receives most of his attention (chapters 40–83), and three purely "Ottoman" matters: the civil war between Bayezit and his brother Djem (chapters 37–39), the wars with Venice (chapters 84–89), and the accession of Selim (90–92). From what Capsali has seen fit to include, to emphasize and, in a sense, to omit, one can see a pattern relevant to a messianic scheme.

The event during Bayezit's reign to which Capsali devoted most of his attention was the Expulsion of the Jews from Spain and Portugal. Like many of his generation, Capsali emphasized the "redemptive character of the 1492 catastrophe."[67]

After a lengthy account of the Expulsion, Capsali reflects upon the meaning of this event. While we, says Capsali, considered the Expulsion as an evil, God intended it as a benefit:

> . . . for who knows, we may have attained at this time the kingdom [of the messiah], and salvation may have begun "when the morning stars sang together" . . . for the Gatherer of the Dispersed of Israel has gathered us together to be ready for the ingathering of the exiles. . . .[68]

He justifies the messianic calculation of the *Sefer ha-Peli'ah ve-ha-Kanah* which gave 1490 as the year of Redemption.[69] Capsali asserts that the "Expulsion which appears to the inner eye as an evil" is in reality the beginning of Redemption, for:

> . . . from that day on the Lord began to gather together the dispersed of his people, that they be ready in one place for the coming of the Redeemer; and the troubles that passed over the Jews in those times are [according to] the word of the prophet (Daniel 12:1): "and there shall be a time of trouble, such as never was since there was a nation even to that same time." Happy is he that waiteth and he will attain the time of the end; "An end is come, the end is come" (Ezek. 7:6); the Redeemer is near to come, and his days shall not be prolonged (cf. Isa. 13:22).[70]

Capsali cites another messianic tradition in the course of his account of the Expulsion from Portugal. A certain R. Joseph,[71] a member of a delegation sent by the king of Fez to the king of Portugal, had seen a Bible written "in the time of Ezra the Scribe (by) two orphan sisters"; the word *tsarah* was written in gold letters and alluded to a tradition that the messiah would come in 1530.[72]

The importance of the Expulsion in the messianic scheme may serve to explain why Capsali pays such great attention to two matters in his account: the war of succession between Isabella and her niece Joanna, and the fall of the Muslim kingdom of Granada. At the conclusion of his account of the war of succession, Capsali makes a statement which may reveal the reason for his interest:

> And the King of Aragon [Ferdinand] ruled over all of Spain and from the day that Ispan ruled in Ispania, all of Spain was not under one king, for many used to rule over her, more than seven kings . . . but now this king ruled over all of them because he was king of Aragon and he also ruled over the kingdom of his wife, [i.e., Castille] . . . and the Lord gave him the entire land, because the measure of the Children of Israel dwelling in Spain had been overfilled and the Lord wanted that there not remain in it a foot-step of a Jew; therefore God made him ruler over all the land.[73]

The unification of Spain under Ferdinand and Isabella was thus part of the divine plan for a general expulsion which, in turn, marked the beginning of the ingathering of the exiles. Therefore, Capsali would naturally be interested in the war of succession, for it resulted in Isabella's securing the throne and eventually in the unification of Spain, the necessary prerequisite for the Expulsion. This may also explain why Capsali's account is surprisingly partisan to Isabella. Capsali has apparently accepted as true the charge of the illegitimacy of Joanna, Isabella's rival, and he also mentions that Isabella was the choice of the nobles.[74] This justification of the right of Isabella to the succession, a right which has been questioned by some,[75] is probably due to Capsali's view of the unification as a prelude to the Expulsion, and Isabella's succession as a prelude to the unification of Spain —hence the rejection of the claim of Joanna. This may also explain Capsali's relating at length the story of the death of Carlos, son of John II of Aragon and Blanche of Navarre.[76] Just as the accession of Isabella to the throne of Castille was an integral factor in the unification, so, too, was that of Ferdinand to the throne of Aragon. The death of Carlos removed a popular rival[77] to Ferdinand and thus influenced the succession to the throne of Aragon and ultimately the unification.

Capsali's lengthy account of the Muslims of Granada centers about the events leading to, and culminating in, the fall of Granada.[78] Capsali's reason for including this relatively lengthy survey appears to be twofold. The first is expressly stated in the preface to this account; i.e., that the reader may see the workings of Divine Providence in the raising up and throwing down of nations.[79] In addition, the fall of Granada is connected with the Expulsion. Capsali relates that Isabella took an oath, at the prompting of a priest, to expel the Jews from Spain if God were to grant her victory over Granada.[80] The fall of Granada was thus directly related to the Expulsion.

Turning to the "Ottoman" aspects of Bayezit's reign, we see that Capsali describes the civil war between Bayezit and Djem, the latter's defeat, and his subsequent flight to Rhodes and France,[81] while he omits mention of Djem's flight to Egypt, his pilgrimage to Mecca, and his second attempt to defeat Bayezit (1481–1482).[82] Now Capsali was well aware that Djem's presence in Europe was used as a threat to keep Bayezit in check: "All the days that Sultan Zuzumi was alive, the king [Bayezit] did not have the courage to raise an army to fight the nations."[83] Upon Djem's death, Capsali has Bayezit say:

> "Certainly this is the day that I looked for; I have found, I have seen it" (cf. Lam. 2:16), because all the days that he [Djem] was alive it was not permitted to him [Bayezit] "to make war upon the nations and chastisements upon the peoples" (cf. Ps. 149:7).[84]

In describing Djem's flight, Capsali considers it stupidity on the part of the Venetians not to have offered Djem refuge, for possession of Djem, says Capsali, would have prevented the loss of the Venetian colonies of Coron, Modon, Navarino and Lepanto, and might even have restored to them Negroponte.[85] Thus, an account of Djem's European sojourn was of considerable interest, since it was an important factor in the progress of the Ottoman wars against Venice, i.e., Christendom. The wars between Islam and Christendom have, of course, obvious messianic significance.[86]

The manner in which Capsali records history after the account of the Expulsion also indicates that only matters relevant to the messianic message were of interest. The period from the flight of Djem to Europe in 1482 until the beginning of the campaign against Venice in 1499 is completely omitted and in its place is the account of the Expulsion. Similarly, after discussing the wars with Venice, the only other topic of interest to Capsali seems to be the accession of Selim. Indeed, Capsali's account of the last ten years of Bayezit's reign—he died in 1512—is not a history of Turkey or of Bayezit but rather a history of the rise of Selim[87] who, as will be shown below, was a definite messianic figure in Capsali's eyes. Thus, Capsali would be interested in such an important matter as the accession of such a figure to the throne from which he was to direct actions of great—messianic—significance.

The messianic message comes through more forcefully in the account of the reign of Sultan Selim, which is primarily a detailed account of the Ottoman conquest of Egypt with the conquerer, Selim, emerging as a definite messianic figure. Quoting an Egyptian Jewish tradition, Capsali applied to Selim the verse (Isa 19:1): "Behold the Lord rideth upon a swift cloud, And cometh unto Egypt . . ."; the word "swift" (*Kal,* 130) is the numerical equivalent (*gematria*) of a variant of the name Selim (Samekh-lamed-mem, 130).[88] Capsali continues:

> "And the idols of Egypt shall be moved at His presence" (ibid.); the meaning is that after Selim will rule over Egypt, "the idols shall utterly pass away" (Isa. 2:18) and the idols in it (i.e., in Egypt) will be cut off, and this will be in the time of Redemption. Therefore, according to this, "the time of singing is come, And the voice of the great turtle is heard in our land" (Cant. 2:12); for the Messiah, our righteousness, will swiftly come to us, because from the time of the Expulsion the Lord began to gather the dispersed of Israel . . . .[89]

Since the rule of Selim over Egypt is a sign of the time of Redemption, and of the imminent coming of the Messiah, it is no wonder that Capsali is fascinated with every detail of the conquest and included such a lengthy (chapters 110–142) account of that event in his chronicle. It should also be noted that the destruction of Egypt in "the end of days" was regarded as part of messianic doctrine.[90]

Further on, Capsali quotes[91] another tradition strengthening the messianic character of Selim as conqueror of Egypt. A verse from Micah's prophecy on the messianic king was applied to Selim: "And this shall be peace: When the Assyrian shall come into our land. . . ." (Micah 5:4). The identification of Selim with the "Assyrian" is based upon Selim's conquest of Ala ed-Daule, prince of Dhu'l-Qadr,

> . . . for it is a tradition among our elders that Ala ed-Daule is of the nation of Assyria or [at least] his lands and cities are in the portion of the king of Assyria; therefore, since the king of the Turks has conquered Ala ed-Daule and his land, from now on he [Selim] is called Assyria . . . .

What will happen to the Jews at the time of "Assyria's" entrance into Egypt is indicated in a combination of two verses: On the first of the tenth, "they overtook them by the sea" (Ex. 14:9) and "all the children of Israel had light in their dwellings" (ibid. 10:23). This is explained as referring to Selim's victory over Tuman Bey and the subsequent delivery of the Jews from the danger that threatened them in the event of an Egyptian victory. This tradition, quoted by Capsali, shows the messianic role of Ala ed-Daule, which accounts for Capsali's including in his chronicle a detailed account of a relatively minor figure.[92] Capsali is thus interested in Ala ed-Daule because this campaign justified the application to Selim of a messianic verse.

Early messianic tradition held that Rome was to fall at the hands of the Persians.[93] Later tradition identified the Turkish conquerors with the Persians.[94] It would appear that, in order to strengthen this identification, Capsali included in his chronicle an account of Selim's Persian conquests.[95] Just as the conquest of Ala ed-Daule enabled Selim to be called "Assyria" and thus meet the requirements of a messianic tradition, so, too, the conquest of Persia would tend to support the claim that the Turks were indeed the Persians whom tradition referred to as the ultimate destroyers of Christendom. Moreover, just as Mehmet was likened to Cyrus, so, too, Selim was compared with world-rulers. Of Selim, Capsali says: "His deeds are similar 'in meteyard, in weight, and in measure' (Lev. 19:35) to King Cyrus and Darius the Mede and Alexander the Greek. . . ."[96]

An apparently apocryphal story of the treasure of Kansuh al-Ghuri, the defeated Mameluke sultan of Egypt, and of the manner in which it was discovered in an abandoned city in the desert, may also have messianic implication. Selim's seizure of this treasure enables Capsali to apply to Selim the verse describing "the king of the north":

> But he shall have power over the treasures of gold and of silver, and over all the precious things of Egypt; and the Libyans and the Ethiopians shall be at his steps (Dan. 11:43).[97]

The messianic image of Selim is further emphasized by Capsali's description of Selim and his deeds in imagery reminiscent of the messianic ruler, King Solomon.[98] Capsali states explicitly that "Selim among the Turks is Solomon." [99] When Selim was routed in what was apparently some minor frontier clash, Capsali compares his flight to that of Solomon driven out of his kingdom by Asmodeus.[100] The Solomonic image of Selim is made especially clear in a number of anecdotes in which Selim's wisdom is described in terms similar to the wisdom of Solomon. That Selim's wisdom was an important factor can be seen in the fact that in the very introduction to the *Seder,* Capsali saw fit to single out this aspect of Selim's character: "the wisdom of the great king Sultan Selim, the likes of whom was not among the kings." [101] It is Selim's wisdom that enables him to recover a deposit from a Turkish shepherd who denied having it.[102] Only Selim is able to render judgment in the case of an "Ishmaelite" who tried to cheat a Turk of a reward for finding some lost jewels for him.[103] Selim foils a Jewish physician's scheme to obtain a higher stipend.[104] The expressions used by Capsali to describe Selim's wisdom are borrowed from the Biblical story of Solomon: "and the Lord gave wisdom in the heart of Selim"; (cf. I Kings 5:9),[105] "the wisdom of God was in him to do justice" (ibid., 3:28)[106] and "his wisdom increased and his greatness excelled the wisdom of all the children of the east" (cf. ibid., 5:10).[107]

In describing the execution of the Mamelukes, Capsali records a story in which a widow of one of the Mamelukes offers Selim a large sum of money to obtain permission to bury her husband's body.[108] The money, however, had been entrusted by her husband to a scribe whose name she did not know. Despite the difficulty of tracing this scribe, Selim in his wisdom finds him and recovers—for himself—the money. Capsali claims that "all Ishmael and all the elders of the land of Egypt heard of the judgment which the king had judged; and they feared him for they saw that the wisdom of God was in him, to do justice" (cf. I Kings 3:28)—a paraphrase of the popular reaction to Solomon's decision in the case of the two babies.

As in the case of Mehmet, so too in the case of Selim, the Sultan is portrayed as a good friend of the Jews. Capsali claims that Selim "loved the Jews very much because he saw that by means of them he would beat nations and kill great kings, for they made for him cannons and weapons. . . ." [109] As evidence of Selim's love for the Jews, Capsali cites a number of Selim's alleged activities on behalf of the Jews. He asserts that Selim permitted the Jews to reopen synagogues which, having been built since the Turkish conquest, had subsequently been closed by Bayezit in accordance with Islamic law.[110] Selim did this despite the transgression of Islamic law involved. An even more daring measure was Selim's permitting those Jews to return to Judaism who had been, so Capsali says, forcibly converted to Islam by the Turks.[111] Capsali relates two incidents in which Selim personally intervened on behalf of Jews. In one case, the Sultan severely punished the chief military judge for maltreating Jews;[112] in another, he executed a Turkish nobleman for striking a Jew who accidentally had thrown mud upon him.[113] Whether or not these incidents actually took place they reflect a belief that Selim, like Mehmet, was deeply interested in the welfare of the Jews. Indeed, Capsali records a story in which Selim's help to a Jew discriminates against a Turk: Selim hanged the servant-boy of a Turk for having been on the street after the curfew hour; a Jew, however, who was guilty of the same offense, was spared.[114] Another illustration of Selim's good will is the story of the Jewish exile from Spain who spilled a bucket of scented water upon Selim as the latter was passing below in the street.[115] The enraged companions of the Sultan wanted to kill the Jew and his family. Selim, however, upon learning that the Jew was a Spanish exile, pardoned him—asserting that the Jew was a stranger to Turkish customs and had only intended to honor the Sultan by his action. Capsali thus attributes to Selim sympathetic understanding of the problems of the exiles in adjusting to their new enviornment.

In yet another story,[116] the contempt of the Jews for converts to Islam is pictured as being shared by Selim. At first Selim refused to consent to the conversion of a Jewish court physician who claimed that Muhammad had appeared to him in a dream and urged him to convert to Islam. Selim knew that this was a trick in order to increase the physician's stipend, but finally assented to the conversion at the insistence of the Grand Vizier. However, Selim ordered the man to become a *darvish* with a very small stipend, for a "holy man" should not continue the practice of a worldly art such as medicine but should spend his time in prayer.

Again—as in the case of Mehmet—Capsali's idealized image of the Sultan is reflected in the manner in which he records many cruel acts of Selim, known to history as Yavuz Selim, Selim the Grim. Capsali was like those panegyrists of Selim who "represented his cruelties as just or politic acts, his tyranny as a quality necessary for the sovereign of a great empire." [117] Capsali does not hide Selim's aggression or acts of murder; he relates them, often at great length, either in a matter-of-fact manner, with no sign of reproach, or in a manner betraying his own approval or understanding of Selim's deed. Many incidents which may be viewed as derogatory to Selim are cited by Capsali with the opposite purpose in mind. Many of the stories aimed at showing Selim's love for Jews, for example, center about some act of cruelty on the part of the Sultan; such is the case in the above-mentioned story of the hanging of the Turkish servant for having violated the curfew, and the hanging of the nobleman for striking a Jew. Stories aimed at showing Selim's wisdom often involve an act of cruelty, such as the use of forged letters to provoke Egypt and to murder the Mameluke prisoners;[118] the extortion of the money from a Mameluke's widow.[119] In the case of the hanging of an "Ishmaelite" in Egypt after the conquest for using false measures and weights, Capsali admits that the death penalty was not called for, but he justifies Selim's action as being a temporary necessity in order to wipe out the prevalent lawlessness in Egypt.[120] After describing the defeat and execution of Selim's brothers, Ahmed and Korkud, both of whom he allegedly incriminated by the use of a forged letter, as well as the execution of his nephews, Capsali justifies these murders by asserting that if these relatives were alive, they would pose a constant threat of rebellion and Selim would never be able to leave Constantinople to wage war[121] (and to conquer Egypt!).

The fall of Rome was to be preceded not only by the fall of Constantinople but also by that of Rhodes.[122] Capsali was a contemporary of the latter event and was himself not far from the scene. He witnessed the arrival of refugees from Rhodes on Crete with his own eyes.[123] Indeed, he was so moved by the fall of Rhodes that he waxed poetic and composed three very lengthy *halatsot* (works in rhymed prose) describing the event.[124] Of the conqueror of Rhodes, Sultan Suleiman, Capsali writes:

> He is the tenth king of the Turks, and "the tenth shall be holy unto the Lord" (Lev. 27:32); and "in his days Judah and Israel shall be saved" (cf. Jer. 23:6), "and a redeemer will come to Zion" (Isa. 59:20).[125]

Of the conquest of Rhodes itself, Capsali says: "This victory is weightier than all the victories of the Turks."[126] Such an image of Suleiman, in a sense even more lustrous than that of the great Selim, can be understood only in the sense that the fall of Rhodes meant that the fall of Rome was next. As the prophecies concerning Constantinople and now Rhodes had been fulfilled, so it was to be hoped—even expected—that the final event, the fall of Rome and the advent of the Messiah, would soon take place. Capsali clearly expresses such a hope:

> "One thing have I asked of the Lord, that will I seek after" (Ps. 27:4): just as we have been worthy of writing the record of these matters, so may we be worthy of writing all the good which the Lord has spoken through his servants the Prophets, "for the Lord hath spoken good concerning Israel" (Num. 10:29). "Let our eye gaze upon Zion" (Micah 4:11) and the building of Ariel. Let all Israel be joined in the Ingathering of the Exiles and in the Advent of the Redeemer, the son of Padahzur, Gamaliel.[127]

In view of the importance of the fall of Rhodes in the messianic scheme, it is not surprising that Capsali gives such a long and detailed account of this one event.[128]

Shortly after the fall of Rhodes, a plague broke out on Crete, and Capsali was one of those appointed by the government to supervise measures to combat the plague.[129] It was at this time, when the Jewish community was quarantined, that Capsali wrote the *Seder*. Appended to the *Seder* are two brief works—the *Koaḥ ha-shem* and the *Ḥasde ha-shem,* the former written right after completion of the *Seder* (1523), the latter, the next year (1524). The motivation for the *Koaḥ ha-shem* was to try to account for the suffering of the Jews in the plague of 1523 within the framework of the age-old problem of the suffering of the righteous and the prosperity of the wicked.[130] This, too, may have messianic implications. The Expulsion from Spain intensified Jewish interest in this problem, some even despairing of Redemption when contemplating the contrast between Gentile prosperity and Jewish suffering.[131] Capsali may have intended this brief treatise not only as an answer to the immediate problem of the plague but also to the more general problem of exile and redemption. Indeed, at the end, Capsali alludes to this saying:

> And if we are here today, all of us in the darkness of exile, and it is dark as the night, "lo, the days came, saith the Lord" (Jer. 30:3) "and the children shall return to their own border" (ibid., 31:17) ". . . and thy God shall rejoice over thee" (Isa. 62:5)[132]

Similarly the *Ḥasde ha-shem,* an account of the deliverance of the Jews of Egypt from the hands of Ahmed Pasha, governor of Egypt who rebelled against Suleiman, serves as a reminder of divine favor towards the Jews.[133] However, Capsali's literary silence from shortly after the fall of Rhodes to the end of his life[134] may in reality be eloquent testimony to his disappointment at the failure of the messianic promise to materialize.

The author wishes to express his gratitude to Professor Isadore Twersky of Harvard University, under whose guidance he prepared his doctoral dissertation, Elijah Capsali's Seder Eliyahu Zuta. *This article is a revised version of a part of that dissertation. Page references to the* Seder *are to the edition of the text prepared as part of the dissertation, a copy of which is deposited in the Harvard University Archives.*

NOTES

1 Moses Lattes, ed., *De vita et scriptis Eliae Kapsalii* (Hebrew: *Likutim shonim mi-sefer Deve Eliyahu*) Padua, 1869; recently reprinted in a limited edition (Jerusalem, 1967/68).

2 E. S. Hartom and U. Cassuto, eds. *Takanot Kandiah ve-zikhronoteha* (Jerusalem, 1943).

3 *Seder,* 9; Lattes, 36.

4 *Seder,* 6; Lattes, 37.

5 *Divre ha-yamim* (hereafter: *DH*), 345b (British Museum MS 1059, Add. 19,971).

6 *Seder,* 42.

7 *Seder,* 401.

8 *Seder,* 406.

9 *Seder,* 407.

10 *Seder,* 308, 363–364, 401, 433, 467.

11 *Seder,* 151–153.

12 *Seder,* 169–177.

13 *Seder,* 7, Lattes, 38.

14 *Seder,* 6, 207, Lattes, 37–38, 61.

15 *Seder,* 287, 338, 363.

16 *DH,* 346a.

17 *Seder,* 139, 140.

18 Caro, Isserles and Emden, as quoted in David A. Gross' edition of part three of Joseph Ha-Cohen's *Sefer divre ha-yamim le-malkhe Tsorfat u-malkhe bet Otoman ha-Tugar* (Jerusalem, 1955), 88–89, n. 52.

19 *DH,* 372a–372b; published in part in N. Porges, "Elie Capsali et sa Chronique de Venise; pièces justificatives," *Revue des Etudes Juives,* LXXIX (1924), 37.

20 *DH,* 373b; Porges, 38.

21 *Seder,* 435.

22 *Seder,* 287–288.

23 Cf. *Seder,* 180–184, where Capsali introduces a legendary account of Nahmanides' alleged "conversion" to the study of Kabbalah.

24 E.g., *Seder,* 373, 533.

25 *Seder,* 447.

26 Capsali's *Koaḥ ha-shem,* 288b (British Museum MS 1059 (Add. 19,971), appended to *Seder*).

27 *Seder,* 448

28 *Koaḥ ha-shem,* 288b.

29 Cf. Harry A. Wolfson, *Philo* (Cambridge, 1947), I, 157.

[30] *Seder,* 448.

[31] *Seder,* 197; Lattes, 54. Some of Capsali's contemporaries, e.g., Joseph Yavets and Abraham ben Solomon of Torrutiel, went so far as to attribute the Expulsion from Spain to the pursuit of secular studies at the expense of traditional studies; cf. Joseph Yavets, *Or ha-hayyim* (Novidavahr, 1794), 3a; Abraham ben Solomon of Torrutiel, *Sefer ha-kabbalah,* cited in A. Neubauer, ed., *Medieval Jewish chronicles and chronological notes* (Oxford, 1887) I, III; cf. others cited by E. Shmueli, *Don Yitsḥak Abravanel ve-gerush Sefarad* (Jerusalem, 1963), 53. On the attitude toward secular studies in the sixteenth century, see I. Barzilay, *Between reason and faith; anti-rationalism in Italian Jewish thought 1250–1650* (The Hague, 1967), 61–71.

[32] Cf. the introduction to David Ganz, *Tsemaḥ David* (Warsaw, 1859), pt. 2; Abraham Zacuto, *Sefer Yuḥasin* (London, 1857), 231–232.

[33] *Seder,* 5; Lattes, 36.

[34] Gerson D. Cohen, *A critical edition with a translation and notes of the Book of Tradition* (*Sefer ha-Kabbalah*) *by Abraham ibn Daud* (Philadelphia, 1967), 240, 259.

[35] *Seder,* 5.

[36] *Seder,* 7.

[37] Cf. Isaac Abravanel, *Mashmi'a Yeshu'ah,* 453, printed in his *Perush 'al nevi'im u-ketuvim* (Jerusalem, 1959/60).

[38] *Seder,* 124–125. On Alexander, see V. Tcherikover, *Hellenistic Civilization and the Jews* (Philadelphia, 1959), 42–43.

[39] *Perush nevu'at ha-yeled,* 34b (Jewish Theological Seminary of America, MS Adler 1919).

[40] *Seder,* 70.

[40a] *Seder,* 70–71.

[41] *Seder,* 71–72.

[41a] *Seder,* 71; Lattes, 6–7.

[42] *Seder,* 73; Lattes, 9–10.

[43] *Seder,* 73–76; Lattes, 39–42.

[44] *Seder,* 76–77; Lattes, 42.

[45] *Seder,* 104–105, 107; published by M.A. Ha-Levi as "Ha-Rav Eliyahu Kapsali ve-sifro Seder Eliyahu Zuta," in *Minḥah le-Avraham* (*Elmaleh*) (Jerusalem, 1959), 109–112.

[46] *Seder,* 80–84; Lattes, 42–44.

[47] *Seder,* 84–87.

[48] *Seder,* 87–94.

[49] *Seder,* 84, 87.

[50] *Seder,* 92, 94.

[51] *Seder,* 125.

[52] The Janissary who stole an apple (*Seder* 117); the Janissaries who insulted a prostitute (117); the page-boys suspected of stealing a cucumber (118).

[53] *Seder,* 117–118.

[54] Cf. F. Babinger, *Mahomet II le conquérant et son temps* (Paris, 1954), 498. Cf. Robert Schwoebel, *The shadow of the Crescent: the renaissance image of the Turk 1453–1517* (Nieuwkoop, 1967).

[55] *Seder,* 117.

[56] *Seder,* 118.

[57] *Seder,* 118.

[58] *Seder,* 64–68.

[59] Joseph Sambari, *Divre Yosef,* 72a–72b (Manuscript 130 of the Library of the Alliance Israélite Universelle).

[60] Cf. Babinger, 514.

[61] *Seder,* 68.

[62] *Seder,* 68.

[63] Babinger, 492.

[64] *Seder,* 139.

[65] *Seder,* 112, 110, 122.

[66] *Seder,* 112.

[67] Cf. Gershom Scholem, *Major Trends in Jewish Mysticism* (New York, 1961), 247.

[68] *Seder,* 287.

[69] *Seder,* 287; cf. Abba Hillel Silver, *A History of Messianic Speculation in Israel* (Boston, 1959), 105–106.

[70] *Seder,* 288.

[71] *Seder,* 283.

[72] *Seder,* 283–284.

[73] *Seder,* 210. On the role of the concept of the indivisibility of Spain in the messianic thought of an earlier Jewish historian, Abraham ibn Daud, cf. Cohen, 258–259.

[74] Seder, 200.

[75] Cf. William H. Prescott, *History of the Reign of Ferdinand and Isabella the Catholic* (Philadelphia, 1872), I, 192.

[76] *Seder,* 204–205.

[77] Cf. Prescott, I, 135–141.

[78] *Seder,* 217–236.

[79] *Seder,* 218.

[80] *Seder,* 232–233.

[81] *Seder,* 144–146. Capsali refers to Djem as Zumzumi, evidently a corruption of the European Zizim; cf. J. von Hammer, *Histoire de l'Empire Ottoman depuis son origine jusqu'à nos jours* (Paris, 1836), III, 342. Joseph Ha-Cohen, *Divre ha-yamim le-malkhe Tsorfat u-malkhe bet Otoman ha-Tugar* (Amsterdam, 1733), 46a, refers to him as "Jimah, i.e., Zizimo."

[82] Cf. Hammer, III, 346–354; L. Thuasne, *Djem-Sultan* (Paris, 1892).

[83] *Seder,* 146. Cf. Sidney N. Fisher, *The Foreign Relations of Turkey 1481–1512* (Urbana, 1948), 28–50.

[84] *Seder,* 288.

[85] *Seder,* 145.

[86] Cf. Cohen, 238–239.

[87] Thus, Capsali offers an account of the strange behavior of two of Bayezit's sons who, as a result, were executed by Bayezit. Capsali may have been interested in this because their deaths eliminated two possible rivals of Selim for the throne, while his interest in Bayezit's illness was also probably due to its effect upon Selim's accession. (*Seder,* 306, 307). Even his interest in Bayezit's war with Egypt may lie in its being a prelude to the conquest of Egypt by Bayezit's "son, the mighty and terrible king Sultan Selim who will avenge his father and inherit the kingdom of Sultano with ease and will blot out Egypt . . . as we shall write . . ." (*Seder,* 305).

[88] *Seder,* 435.

[89] *Seder,* 435.

[90] Cf. Isaac Abravanel, *Yeshu'ot meshiḥo* (Königsberg, 1861), 35b.

[91] *Seder,* 446. Cf. Porges, 25.

[92] Similarly Capsali's interest in Selim's war with "Ben Hanish"—the Shiite rebel Nasir al-Din ibn Hanush—in Syria (*Seder,* 451–459) may be due to the fact that Ibn Hanush's territory included Sidon. The conquest of Ibn Hanush thus brought Sidon within the borders of Palestine-Syria, as it were, under Ottoman rule. On the messianic significance of this, cf. Isaac Abravanel's commentary on Zechariah 9:2 in his *Perush 'al nevi'im u-ketuvim* (Jerusalem, 1959/60), 224.

[93] *Yoma* 10a, quoted by Silver, 112, n.4.

[94] Cf. Abravanel, *"Mashmi'a yeshu'ah,"* in his *Perush 'al nevi'im u-ketuvim,* 401; Abravanel, *Yeshu'ot meshiḥo,* 35a.

[95] *Seder,* 338–353.

96 *Seder,* 463.

97 *Seder,* 443. Cf. Joseph ha-Cohen, *Divre ha-yamim* (1733), 65a, who reports that the treasure remained hidden.

98 On the messianic aspect of Solomon, see Frederick P. Bargebuhr, *The Alhambra: a cycle of studies on the eleventh century in Moorish Spain* (Berlin, 1968), 118, 131.

99 *Seder,* 310.

100 *Seder,* 310. Selim's capture of the fabulous throne of the King of Persia (*Seder* 350, 365) may also contribute to the Solomonic image of Selim. On the messianic significance of Solomon's throne, cf. Bargebuhr, 128–131. G. Cohen's discussion (244) of the symbolic significance in architectural curiosities brings to mind Capsali's great interest in the buildings and monuments of Venice during his stay there (May 1509–January 1514) (*DH* 416a–418b).

101 *Seder,* 5.

102 *Seder,* 324–325.

103 *Seder,* 325–327.

104 *Seder,* 328–330.

105 *Seder,* 324.

106 *Seder,* 327.

107 *Seder,* 336.

108 *Seder,* 419–422.

109 *Seder,* 327. Cf. H.H. Ben-Sasson, "Galut u-ge'ulah be-'enav shel dor gole Sefarad," *Sefer Yovel le-Yitsḥak Ber* (Jerusalem, 1960), 224–225.

110 *Seder,* 327–328. Mehmet is said to have permitted the building of synagogues after the conquest of Constantinople (Sambari, 71a). However, I have not found any reference to Bayezit's alleged closing of synagogues, although there may be an echo of anti-Jewish measures in a tale about an attempt to force a Jewish doctor to convert to Islam, cited by H. H. Ben-Sasson, "Dor gole Sefarad 'al 'atsmo," *Zion,* XXVI (1961), 28.

111 *Seder,* 328.

112 *Seder,* 328.

113 *Seder,* 331–332.

114 *Seder,* 322–324.

115 *Seder,* 330–331.

116 *Seder,* 328–330.

117 Hammer, IV, 137.

118 *Seder,* 381–383.

119 *Seder,* 419–422.

120 *Seder,* 435.

121 *Seder,* 332–335. Capsali even records a rumor, without the slightest hint of criticism, that Selim poisoned his father Bayezit (*Seder,* 318).

122 Moses ben Josephi di Trani, quoted by Silver, 113, n. 7; Abraham Ha-Levi, quoted by Silver, 130, n. 74; cf. also A. Neubauer, "Kibutsim 'al 'inyene 'aseret ha-shevatim u-bene Moshe," *Kovets 'al yad,* IV (1888), 45–46, quoted by E. Strauss, *Toldot ha-Yehudim be-Mitsrayim ve-Suriyah* (Jerusalem, 1944–51), II, 73.

123 *Seder,* 530.

124 1. "Ḥatan ve-kalah" (chapter 162), in which the Ottoman conquest of Rhodes is depicted as a marriage between Rhodes (the bride) and Suleiman (the groom); 2. "Rabot banot" (chapter 163), in which the surrender of Rhodes' insular possessions is depicted as daughters deserting their father (the Grand Master) to follow their mother (Rhodes) after her new husband (Suleiman); 3. "Mi va-mi ha-holkhim"—a *makamah* in forty stanzas beginning with "mi" and ending in "rah," rejoicing in the fall of Rhodes (chapter 164). The fall of Rhodes made a very profound impression upon Europe and inspired many such "lamenti" among European writers (cf. Carl Gollner, *Turcica: die Europäischen Turkendrucke des XVI. Jahrhunderts* (Berlin, 1961), I). It should be noted that Capsali's *Seder* includes a composition in rhymed prose —often of considerable length—after nearly

every major event recorded in the chronicle, e.g., on the fall of Constantinople, the conquests of Persia, Ala ed-Daule, Egypt, Rhodes, etc.—interesting in the light of G. Cohen's remarks about the role of poetry in Spain in helping to recapture "Jewish pride and hope." Cf. Cohen, 268.

[125] *Seder,* 481. The significance of Suleiman's being the tenth Sultan was also noted by the sixteenth-century Salonikan rabbi, Moses Almosnino; cf. his *Extremas y grandezas de Constantinopla* (Madrid, 1638), 172.

[126] Seder, 528.

[127] Seder, 481.

[128] Seder, chapters 154–164.

[129] *Seder,* 530–535.

[130] *Koaḥ ha-shem,* 271b.

[131] E.g., Joseph ibn Yaḥya, an Italian contemporary of Capsali, cited by Ben-Sasson, "Galut u-ge'ulah. . .," 219.

[132] *Koaḥ ha-shem,* 292b.

[133] Cf. *Ḥasde ha-shem,* 294b.

[134] While the exact date of Capsali's death is not known, it would appear that he died shortly after September 1549, the date of the last communal statute bearing his name. Hartom, *Takanot,* p. 141 (no. 106 dated 16 September 1549).

THE JEWISH LABOR COMMITTEE AND AMERICAN IMMIGRATION POLICY IN THE 1930'S

GEORGE L. BERLIN

Baltimore Hebrew College

INTRODUCTION

The role of Jewish communal leaders during the Nazi era and their alertness to the threat of Nazism to Jewish survival in Europe has come under severe scrutiny in recent years. In her study, *Eichmann in Jerusalem,* Hannah Arendt has contended that "wherever Jews lived, there were recognized Jewish leaders, and this leadership, almost without exception, cooperated in one way or another, for one reason or another, with the Nazis."[1] She further states that even before the war, many German Jewish leaders, although shaken to the foundations by the promulgation of the infamous Nuremberg Laws of 1935, believed that the situation must soon become stabilized. Cooperative compliance with these laws would permit the members of the Jewish community to go about their daily lives with a minimum of interference. The *Reichsvertretung der deutschen Juden,* the national council of German Jewish communities and organizations founded in September 1933, represented the Nuremberg Laws as an effort "to establish a level on which a bearable relationship between the German and the Jewish people [would become] possible."[2] Indeed, even German Zionists believed that a *modus vivendi* could be worked out with the Nazi regime obviating the need for wholesale emigration of Jews from Germany. Arendt quotes a noted Zionist's reaction to the Nuremberg Laws in the following words:

> Life is possible under every law. However, in complete ignorance of what is permitted and what is not one cannot live. A useful and respected citizen one can also be as a member of a minority in the midst of a great people.[3]

Whatever view Jewish leaders expressed on the ultimate status of German Jewry, the fact is that even before the Nuremberg Laws, American Jewish communal leadership had already become alarmed about the deteriorating condition of German Jewry, and had begun to take active measures to bring about some relief to their German brethren. As early as 1933, Jewish and liberal Gentile groups in the United States had voiced loud protests and had begun considering steps to bring pressure on the Nazi government to repudiate its anti-Semitic Jewish policies. Since the Nazis retorted by stepping up their propaganda, the ineffectiveness of these early measures soon became evident, and Jewish organizations began to consider ways of strengthening the impact of their concern and protest. Various programs were undertaken by a number of Jewish organizations in this country with a view to ameliorating the condition of the Jews in Germany.

While some of these efforts have been described, the full story of American Jewish response to the early stages of Nazism has not yet been recorded.[4] Obviously, a judicious evaluation of the role of American Jewish leadership in that period can come only after an examination of all the facts. This paper will examine the actions in the area of immigration of one such American Jewish organization: the Jewish Labor Committee (hereafter referred to as J.L.C.).

The J.L.C. was founded February 25, 1934, at a meeting attended by 1039 delegates representing the International Ladies' Garment Workers' Union, Amalgamated Clothing Workers' Union of America, United Hatters Cap and Millinery Workers' International Union, Workmen's Circle, United Hebrew Trades, Forward Association, Jewish Socialist Verband, and the Jewish Workers' Party (Left Poale-Zion). The delegates chose Baruch Charney Vladeck as chairman, David Dubinsky, president of the International Ladies' Garment Workers' Union, as treasurer, and Joseph Baskin, executive director of the Workmen's Circle, as secretary.[5] The organization's main purpose was to unify the anti-Nazi activities of the various Jewish labor organizations in the United States.[6] The reactions of the J.L.C. are especially significant, inasmuch as it represented the coordinated sentiment of the American Jewish labor force, which numbered several hundred thousand in the early and mid-1930's.[7]

I. The Immigration Problem

Large numbers of German Jews began to migrate from Germany only in the middle years of the 1930's,[8] some 350,000 Jews escaping Nazi terror through emigration between 1933 and the outbreak of the war.[9] Since the German government confiscated increasingly larger proportions of the property of these Jews, to the depression-stricken world they represented to a considerable extent an impoverished mass of people in search of a new home. Emigrants leaving Germany in 1933 were allowed to take only two hundred reichsmarks in foreign currency with them, and after 1937, this amount was reduced to ten reichsmarks. A law of May 18, 1934, inflicting a flight tax of twenty-five percent on persons owning capital of more than fifty thousand reichsmarks or having an annual income in excess of twenty thousand reichsmarks, further depleted the financial resources of the refugees. Still more deleterious to the economic well-being of the German Jewish community was a special "atonement fine" of one billion marks levied on the German Jews in November, 1938, as "reparation" for the killing of the German consular official, Ernst von Rath, in Paris by the Jewish youth, Herschel Grynszpan.[10]

II. American Restriction

The United States, like most other countries during the economically trying days of the 1930's, tightly restricted immigration to her shores. Nativist feelings in the previous decade had led to the enactment of the national-origins quota system, which, to all intents and purposes, ended the flow of immigration to this country from southern and eastern Europe.[11] While the new legislation greatly reduced the number of East European Jews entering the United States, it assigned the largest quotas to the countries of northern Europe, including Germany.

This, however, did little to alleviate the plight of the German Jewish refugees. The quotas were small and woefully inadequate to care for more than a fraction of the emigrants, especially after their number increased markedly in the late 1930's. Moreover, even these limited quotas were not filled until 1939. As late as 1937, only 17,199 immigrants entered the United States from Germany and Austria although those two countries had a combined quota of 27,370 in that year.[12] In fact, during much of the period under discussion, the number of aliens leaving the United States exceeded the number of those entering, the surplus of departing aliens over new arrivals from 1931 to 1935, numbering 79,634.[13]

Although the economic depression was undoubtedly a major factor in keeping the quotas unfilled, strict execution of the restrictive legislation of the 1920's on the part of the executive branch also played its role. On September 8, 1930, President Hoover issued an executive order to American consuls in Europe directing them to interpret strictly those provisions of the immigration laws which denied entry to any immigrant who, in the opinion of the consul, would become a public charge. In addition, the immigrant had to prove that he was both mentally and physically fit, that he had had no past criminal record, that he had no contracts of employment with any firm or individual in the United States, and that he was not an anarchist and did not advocate the forceful overthrow of the American government.[14]

Almost three years later to the day, the American Civil Liberties Union and a group of thirty-four distinguished Americans petitioned President Roosevelt to rescind the Hoover order. Granting "that in times of unemployment and depression, the government should not too widely open its doors to immigration from abroad," their statement nevertheless maintained that "a reasonable number of political and religious refugees can be cared for in this country without injury to our economic situation," and concluded that "a closed-door policy is mistaken and unsound and contrary to every tradition of American history and life." The group asked Roosevelt to direct that visas be granted to refugees under the present quota laws if it appeared probable that they would not become public charges.[15] In response to this appeal, Secretary of State Hull instructed American consuls to be lenient with refugees who had no personal dossiers, and to forego entirely the requirement of a personal dossier in cases where the immigrant involved was in immediate danger. Nevertheless, even with this relaxation, the number of refugees admitted to the United States from Germany during the first five years of the Nazi regime never filled the German quota, and although the number who could have entered under the quota by June 1939 was 183,112, the actual number admitted was only 73,322.[16]

The strict enforcement of the quota regulations reflected the anti-immigration sentiments of important segments of American public opinion during these years. A large group of congressmen and senators under the leadership of Senator McReynolds of North Carolina, including such nationally prominent figures as Senator Borah, opposed any liberalization of the immigration laws throughout the decade. Moreover, although opposing each other on most social and economic issues, the A.F.L. and conservative American businessmen joined hands to keep the gates of the United States as tightly closed as possible.[17] The prevalent feeling was summarized in the comment of a spokesman for a group of "patriotic" organizations before a Congressional committee discussing immigration: ". . . let us get all our people to work before we begin playing Santa Claus to other nations." [18]

III. The Stand of the J.L.C.

This prevailing attitude had a considerable effect on the immigration policy of the Jewish Labor Committee during these years. As the decade of the 1930's progressed, the J.L.C. was not unaware of the steady deterioration of the condition of German Jewry. Along with the A.F.L., it received reports from European labor leaders as well as from people who had visited Germany.[19] In July 1935, a meeting attended by representatives of the American Jewish Congress and the J.L.C. heard from a recently returned visitor to Germany that the Nazi regime remained firmly entrenched in power, and that "the obsessions that control the leadership remain as they were at the start." [20] The Jews of Germany, said the speaker, were "the victims of a governmental policy of extermination." Despite this candidness, none of the representatives present proposed asking the American government to lift its immigration-quota restrictions as a possible means of aiding the German Jews. While most of the speakers were from non-labor groups, and apparently feared dire economic consequences and even an outbreak of anti-Semitism if the immigration quotas were raised, there is no evidence that any Jewish labor spokesman demanded immigration reforms.[21] As a matter of fact, we have very little evidence to show that Jewish labor in America demanded immigration reform at any time before 1940. The failure of the J.L.C., which considered itself to be in the forefront of the anti-Nazi struggle, to seek this direct means of refugee aid in the 1930's can be understood only in the light of the policy of the A.F.L.[22]

IV. The A.F.L. and Immigration

Throughout the period of depression, the attitude of the A.F.L. was one of adamant opposition to any easing of quota restrictions.

Every year, from 1933 to 1939, it brought pressure on Congress to defeat any modification in the existing laws.[23]

As early as 1933, William Green had expressed his fear that immigrants would present "a serious task of assimilation." Unable to become an integral part of the American people, the immigrants could only hope to suffer in the United States and bring suffering to others.[24] More important, however, was the economic factor. As late as the very eve of the outbreak of war, the executive of the A.F.L. ruefully reported to the convention that, with ten million American workers unemployed, "any widening of the avenues of entry into this country to the peoples of other lands makes more difficult the solution of the problem of unemployment and economic stability."[25] While granting that "at no time in our history has there been such demand for the opening of our doors to the people of the world," and that the demands were "highly emotional appeals to which a justice and liberty-loving people are particularly susceptible," its report nevertheless maintained that "domestic economic and political considerations make imperative our consideration of this subject in the light of cold practical facts and the effects upon not only our economic, but our political structure as well."

At the 1935 convention of the A.F.L., the delegates of the predominantly Jewish International Ladies' Garment Workers' Union, an affiliate of the J.L.C., offered a resolution recommending the easing of immigration quotas.[26] Stating that organized labor should lend support to refugees from economic, political, and religious tyranny, the resolution claimed that such support "could not be viewed as a deviation from the traditional policies of the A.F.L." Moreover, the United States had always offered "the privilege of asylum and the protection of democracy within its boundaries" to the oppressed and persecuted. Relying on this tradition, the resolution proposed "that the A.F.L. . . . extend every possible aid to facilitate the entry of fugitives from Nazi and Fascist terror on account of trade-union activity or racial or religious affiliation."

In its report on this proposal, the committee on resolutions stated that while it was "aware of the terror and persecution inflicted upon defenseless people by the Nazi and Fascist dictatorships," nevertheless "the adoption of the resolution would run counter to the immigration laws now in existence *as a result of the activities of the A.F.L.*" (Italics mine—G.B.) It, therefore, recommended nonconcurrence and, although the voice vote taken was close enough to necessitate a vote by hand, the final vote showed that "it was clearly evident the report of the committee had been adopted" to kill the resolution.[27]

Three years later, at the 1938 convention, a delegate from the Fur Workers' Union, a largely Jewish union unaffiliated with the J.L.C., expressed his hope that "not only the doors in Palestine shall open, but also in other countries that will be able to take in a certain number of Jewish people."[28] Green responded to this by stating that "speaking for our own country we quite agree that immigrants shall be admitted here in conformity with the quota provision of our immigration laws."[29]

Following the rebuff in 1935, there is no record of any effort on the part of either the Jewish Labor Committee or any of its affiliates to pressure the A.F.L. to modify its position on immigration. As a matter of fact, as early as 1936, the J.L.C. had openly conceded that it was "physically impossible under present circumstances to transport the 450,000 Jews still remaining in Germany to other countries."[30]

V. The Evian Conference

The lack of an aggressive stand on the part of the J.L.C. becomes even more striking in face of the fact that the highest officials of the American government were not out of sympathy with the plight of the refugees. Indeed, President Roosevelt demonstrated on several occasions that he was fully aware of the gravity of the refugee problem, and that he sought a solution to it.[31] He issued the call for an international conference on refugees at Evian on July 6, 1938, with delegates from thirty-two governments attending. However, to those who had hoped for quick and decisive action the conference was a disappointment. According to one historian, "nearly all the delegates expressed their sympathy for the refugees but, with few exceptions, were very careful not to assume any obligations on behalf of their governments."[32] The one substantive achievement of the conference was the creation of a permanent Intergovernmental Committee for Refugees with the task of assuring that whatever possibilities for refugee absorption existed in the world would be realized.

Neither the J.L.C. nor any of the other organizations affiliated with the General Jewish Council sent observers to the Evian meeting.[33] The Council, however, did send a message to the American delegation expressing hope for a "speedy solution of the refugee problem."[34]

Despite lack of any resolute action, Jewish labor circles did react to the Evian conference. An article appearing in the Workmen's Circle *Call* attacked the general tenor of American immigration policy. The writer charged that through its immigration laws, America "not only has turned its back on the immigrant but has even abandoned the civilized principle of asylum for political refugees." Although recognizing some justification for a restrictive policy on economic grounds, he added that

> . . . it surely must cause every enlightened and liberty-loving American to blush with shame at the thought that the rigors of our present laws have resulted in the deportation of refugees of Fascist Italy and Nazi Germany, who had managed to escape to this country but whose entry was not in accord with our laws.

After praising Roosevelt and Hull for the initiative that they had taken in the establishment of the Intergovernmental Committee at Evian as "a step in accord with that spirit of internationalism and humanitarianism of an earlier period in American history," the article concluded with several specific proposals for American action in the refugee crisis. It suggested the elimination of the rigorous regulations governing consular visas, and called for the combination of the unused balance of the German-Austrian quota for 1937 with the 1938 quota. It is noteworthy, however, that the article did not call for legislation to revise the existing quotas.[35] On the other hand, the Labor Committee issued a declaration a few months later that was substantially different in tone from the *Call* article. It told of the Committee's satisfaction "that at this time the President and the entire administration are doing their utmost to help alleviate the hard lot of the refugees," and expressed gratitude that "America is again resuming its rightful place as a haven for the oppressed and persecuted."[36]

This ambiguous and seemingly contradictory attitude is symptomatic of the slow change that was taking place in the thinking of the J.L.C. on immigration. Like the A.F.L., it feared the detrimental results that increased immigration might have on the American economy and on American Jewry. In addition, the ideology of the Labor Committee called for the defeat of Nazi and Fascist totalitarianism in each country by a combined effort on the part of labor and progressive forces. Although these considerations remained the decisive factors in the J.L.C.'s immigration stand, a discernible change began to take place in J.L.C.'s thinking as the decade progressed. By 1939, it conceded that the heart of the refugee problem was the finding of new homes for the refugees.[37] In effect, the new position represented an abandonment of the implications of its original ideological stance, for it meant relinquishing hope for a solution through the anti-Fascist struggle in the countries of emigration. However, it was only after the outbreak of war that the J.L.C. openly broke with the A.F.L. stance on immigration.

The primary reason for this change in attitude was the alarming situation of Polish Jewry. The Jews of Poland, a large percentage of whom had been reduced to a state of poverty by economic restrictions in the 1920's and the depression of the 1930's, had been the scapegoat for Poland's economic ills. Polish Fascist groups provoked anti-Semitic outbursts and called for the elimination of Jews from gainful employment. In 1936, Cardinal Hlond, the Primate of Poland, urged a boycott of Jewish businesses. By 1938, "it was apparent that Poland's Fascist element had succeeded in transforming Smigly-Rydz into their puppet," and his government "made its preparations to crack down on—perhaps even eliminate altogether—Poland's articulate liberal, labor, and socialist organizations."[38]

The J.L.C. had become increasingly concerned with the situation of the Jews in Poland. On April 14, 1937, a delegation representing the J.L.C. and the A.F.L. presented a plea to Secretary of State Hull calling for American intervention on behalf of Polish Jewry. Charging Poland with willful violation of the minorities treaties, the representatives expressed their belief that the United States could rightfully intervene in Poland, because President Wilson had helped to establish the Polish Republic and because Americans had "contributed money and lives in order to make the independence of Poland possible."[39] In February 1938, a J.L.C. meeting in New York City decided to raise a fund of some 250,000 dollars, chiefly to aid Polish Jewry.[40]

The fact that Poland was the major center of the Jewish labor movement explains the particular concern manifested by the J.L.C. in the fate of Polish Jewry. Germany, on the other hand, had never been a bastion of Jewish labor. Whereas only 18.7 percent of Germany's Jews were engaged in industries and trade in 1933, the percentage of Polish Jewry so engaged in 1931 stood at 45.4.[41] Moreover, of those German Jews who emigrated to the United States from July 1, 1932 to June 30, 1943, only 28.7 percent were classified as laborers (skilled and unskilled).[42] Accordingly, so long as it was German Jewry that bore the brunt of the Nazi onslaught, the J.L.C. did not feel impelled to seek immigration reform. Nevertheless, even though the worsening condition of Polish Jewry began to cause a perceptible change in J.L.C. thinking on immigration, this change did not really crystallize until the war years, and in the 1930's, the old habits of mind still came to the fore. As late as 1937, a J.L.C. official wrote that "the only solution offered by all the bourgeois parties is emigration of the Jews." The Bund, on the other hand, was "the only real force among the Jewish masses" which inspired them "to fight for their rights, and for their honor as Jews and Socialists." The struggle of Polish Jewry, he concluded, "can only be won by the united efforts of the Jewish workers of Poland and the Polish Socialists and other radical elements of the population."[43] The Jews should not abandon Poland.

VI. Refugee-Saving Devices

A. *The Schacht Plan*

The establishment of the Intergovernmental Committee on Refugees by the Evian conference had important effects on Jewish emigration in the last year before the war. Shortly after the conclusion of the Evian conference, the Intergovernmental Committee entered into discussion with the German government to ascertain if some arrangement could be made whereby the Jews of Germany would be allowed to emigrate in an orderly and peaceful manner. In December, Dr. Hjalmar Schacht, president of the Reichsbank, presented a plan for Jewish emigration from Germany consisting of "certain general ideas, presented orally, and never put in writing" to George Rublee, chairman of the Intergovernmental Committee. Under it, German Jewry would be divided into three classes. The first, the wage earners, were to be given the opportunity to emigrate during the next three to four years. From their new homes they would send back money to pay for the emigration expenses of their dependents who composed the second class under the plan. Finally, the third class, made up of those Jews who were too old to leave, would be allowed to remain in Germany. The second part of the plan concerned itself with the financing of the emigration of the wage earners by means of an international loan raised from world Jewry for which Jewish property in Germany would provide security. The loan would be amortized by the expansion of German foreign trade through "additional exports over and above normal German trade under existing treaties and clearing arrangements."[44]

The reception to this plan by leading Jewish organizations was less than cordial. The administrative committee of the World Jewish Congress resolved that Jews should not accept any solution to the German refugee problem that would reward the Nazi regime's policy of expropriation and expulsion with economic advantages.[45] The Joint Boycott Council also responded sharply to Schacht's suggestions.[46] While its leading spokesman acknowledged that the German refugee problem had "assumed international dimensions," and that "it is our problem, and the responsibility for whatever may happen will rest on our shoulders," he nevertheless found the removal of the Jews from Germany "deadly wrong in principle."[47] For its part, the Jewish Labor Committee had always upheld the right of the Jews and other national minorities to maintain themselves as distinct and autonomous cultural entities within the countries of their residence. This, in fact, was one of its basic post-war demands.[48] The abandonment of Germany by its Jews meant therefore, not only the surrender of the progressive forces to the Nazis, but also the abandonment of the possibility for a distinct Jewish national cultural community in Germany. On the other hand, Tenenbaum admitted that migration was "the only possible avenue of escape from the Hell of Naziland." However, he found the idea of paying ransom for the refugees highly distasteful. In the first place, in the long run it would not benefit the German Jews, because the more ransom Germany received the more she would demand. Moreover, if Germany were to succeed in this blackmail, other Central European countries would have nothing to lose in playing the same game. Over and above all of this was the consideration that the refugees, penniless and laden with German goods, would not find a welcome in other lands. Their arrival would only serve to stir up anti-Semitism. Both business and labor groups in the countries of refuge would feel "justifiable resentment" against the refugees. Finally, wrote Tenenbaum, for the Jews to give any aid to the Nazis, even indirectly, "is tantamount to desertion of our sacred cause," and "we have no right to do that even for the sake of our refugees."[49]

B. *The Rublee Plan*

Further discussion between Rublee and Helmuth Wohlthat, an official of the German economic ministry, who succeeded Schacht as the German negotiator, removed some of the objections to the plan. The revised version was similar to the original plan in scope but differed in the proposed means of financial implementation. Referred to as the Rublee Plan,[50] it called for the emigration of some 150,000 Jewish wage earners (i.e., all men and unmarried women between the ages of fifteen and forty-five, physically and otherwise able to earn a living) during the next three to five years. After settling in their new homes, they would send for their dependents who numbered in aggregate some 250,000 people. Germany agreed to make available facilities for the occupational retraining of wage earners awaiting emigration. Old and infirm Jews would not have to emigrate. Instead, they could live quietly and without interference in Germany unless "something extraordinary" such as an attempt on the life of a Nazi official by a Jew were to occur. The same public-relief benefits available to Aryans would be open to those Jews remaining in Germany who were unable to earn their own living. In addition, recently impounded Jewish property in Germany would also serve to provide welfare benefits to these people. Thus, the Jews outside of Germany would not be called upon to support the Jews of Germany. The plan also provided for the release of Jews in German concentration camps. A trust fund consisting of at least twenty-five percent of the existing Jewish wealth in Germany was to finance the plan, and a corporation administered by three trustees, two of whom were to be Germans, would hold the property of the trust. The trust money would purchase equipment and capital goods for the emigrants. An important stipulation required that goods bought by the fund contain no imported raw materials unless Germany received the monetary equivalent of the imported raw material in foreign exchange. The Intergovernmental Committee recommended the creation of a special corporation to take charge of the purchasing and to seek financial aid from American, British, French, Dutch and Swiss Jews. Finally, the Rublee Plan allowed the emigrants to take with them all personal belongings except jewelry, art objects and similar goods that had been acquired for emigration purposes.

Although the Rublee Plan eliminated the international loan and the export provisions of the Schacht plan, there were grounds to suspect German sincerity. In the first place, like the Schacht plan, it was in no way a formal agreement. Rather, it was merely a "unilateral statement" on the part of Germany as to what she would be willing to do concerning Jewish emigration. Germany had never officially recognized the existence of the Intergovernmental Committee, and refused to make any agreement with foreign governments concerning treatment of her Jews, which she considered a purely internal affair. Moreover, the whole plan was strictly conditional upon the world's readiness to accept the refugees. However, despite the fact that these proposals did not constitute an official agreement, they had received, in the words of *The New York Times,* the "full consent and approval of the highest officials of the Reich." Accordingly, Rublee urged their acceptance and stated that if the world powers were not willing to trust Germany, they should never have convened the Evian conference in the first place.[51]

Despite Rublee's warm endorsement, the Joint Boycott Council strongly condemned the Plan.[52] There simply was not enough money in German Jewish hands to finance the project, and this lack of funds would therefore necessitate a continuous flow of Jewish money from world Jewry into Germany. Moreover, the new Plan still retained provisions that would increase Nazi exports and thus break the boycott. The corporation serving as the purchasing agent for the refugees would actually aid the export trade of Germany. The refugees required such things as furniture, tools, locomotives, and tractors. The corporation would not only purchase these goods, but negotiate the sale, allocate credit, and effect their delivery. Thus, it would become, in effect, "a clearing house for the transfer of goods . . . as a banking institution for credit operations, for the payment of the cost of the raw materials in the transfer goods." Furthermore, the need to equip whole refugee communities in the new lands meant that the twenty-five-percent trust fund would be merely "a stepping stone to much increased exports" even if there were to be no resale of the goods by the refugees. In sum, the corporation "will be a Banking and Trading Corporation for increased German exports, and at the same time would supply the Nazi treasury with much needed foreign exchange."

In addition, argued Tenenbaum, acceptance of the Rublee Plan would only give added ammunition to anti-Semites who claimed that the refugees caused unemployment in the countries of refuge which would have to "receive the refugees and the German goods in competition with home industries." He himself conceded that while "it is not true that refugees create unemployment, . . . it is undeniable that dumping of German goods under whatever form depresses the living standard of labor and does create unemployment."

Finally, according to Tenenbaum, the "universal sentiment of national exclusiveness" doomed any chances for the Rublee Plan. Moreover, it would be more difficult than ever to find new homes for the refugees, because, besides the German Jews, there were an additional 450,000 Jews in the semi-protectorate of Hungary, and some 250,000 others living in Nazi protectorates. In addition, the Nazi menace threatened the 4,000,000 Jews in Eastern Europe. Thus, Nazism could set off an exodus of millions of refugees, which the world would be totally incapable of handling. Therefore, concluded Tenenbaum, although everything should be done to alleviate the lot of the refugees, "there is no radical solution of the refugee problem except through the defeat of Hitlerism." Retention of a strict anti-Nazi boycott was one of the surest ways to accomplish this.

C. *The Coordinating Foundation*

During the spring of 1939, there was another government-initiated attempt to aid the flow of refugees from Germany. Myron C. Taylor, who had acted as special United States ambassador to the Evian conference, called upon the two Jewish members of President Roosevelt's Advisory Committee on Political Refugees, Stephen S. Wise, president of the American Jewish Congress, and Paul Baerwald, chairman of the Joint Distribution Committee, "to take steps towards the implementing of a program of orderly migration from Germany through the organization of a Coordinating Foundation."[53] Its purpose would be to coordinate the work of the various agencies and individuals engaged in improving the condition of the refugees, and in "facilitating the emigration of involuntary emigrants from Germany." Wise and Baerwald convened a meeting of seventy-five American Jewish leaders on April 15 to discuss Taylor's proposal. A subsequent meeting of this same group on June 17, decided to establish a Coordinating Foundation, and requested the Joint Distribution Committee to underwrite a sum of money of up to one million dollars for funds required by the Foundation. A directorate of twenty, consisting of ten Americans and ten Europeans, was to administer the Foundation.[54] The Foundation's goals were the following:

1) Cooperate with the League of Nations, governments, organizations and individuals working to improve conditions of persons who are subject to political and racial discrimination in Germany;
2) Endeavor to improve the conditions of the above persons who are unable to emigrate;

3) Insure orderly emigration of involuntary emigrants from the Reich;
4) Cooperate with individuals and organizations in investigations for settlement;
5) Serve as a secretarial, intermediary agency for facilitating the removal of goods and assets for use by the emigrants, but not for resale.

The Jewish Labor Committee responded negatively to both the Rublee Plan and the proposed Coordinating Foundation. Condemning the Rublee Plan for establishing "dangerous precedents" in its implied tacit recognition by world Jewry of the right to confiscate Jewish property, the J.L.C. also opposed reimbursing Germany for foreign materials contained in goods taken out of that country. The memorandum attacking the Plan suggested that it would be "more economical" if the relief agencies were to give financial aid to the refugees after they had left Germany. The strongest reason for the J.L.C.'s opposition to the plan, however, was the belief that it "will destroy the boycott against Hitler Germany, and will undermine the struggle of the labor and progressive movement against Hitlerism and anti-Semitism."[55]

The J.L.C.'s opposition to the Coordinating Foundation derived from its erroneous assumption that the Foundation would serve to finance the Rublee Plan, and it accordingly protested the Joint Distribution Committee's underwriting of the Foundation. Since the Rublee Plan was not merely a means of relief, but "a political problem which involves the interests of the Jewish people as a whole," the Joint Distribution Committee had no right to take unilateral action without first submitting its plans to other important Jewish organizations for consultation. The J.L.C. urged the Joint Distribution Committee to reverse its position "before it is too late."[56]

A delegation of representatives from the J.L.C. and the American Jewish Congress met with several officers of the Joint Distribution Committee on July 14 in an attempt to smooth out difficulties.[57] The representatives of the J.L.C. insisted upon the elimination of any right of the Foundation to engage in transfer operations, and the addition of a clause in the laws of the Foundation whereby it would be "precluded from engaging in any activities of a nature that might inure to the benefit of the German economy." The Joint Distribution Committee representatives reassured the J.L.C. delegates. Mr. Alfred Jaretzki, a lawyer and member of the executive committee of the Joint Distribution Committee, who had been involved in the drafting of the articles of incorporation of the Foundation, gave his legal opinion that the language of the articles contained nothing that would authorize the Foundation "to permit its funds to be used in any way to pay with foreign exchange for the cost of goods made or purchased in Germany." The Joint Distribution Committee spokesman gave assurances that the Foundation would be "an administrative and service agency only, and that its funds could not and would not be used for any purposes of colonization or the financing thereof."[58] Despite these assurances, the J.L.C. and Congress delegates requested the Joint Distribution Committee to exert influence so that the Foundation would adopt a clearly worded resolution to this effect at its first meeting. In addition, they urged the avoidance of any publicity "that might in any way couple the Foundation with the acceptance of the Wohlthat [Rublee] Plan."[59]

D. *Palestine*

In the face of world-wide immigration barriers, and the unlikelihood of their being lowered because of the persistence of the depression, the only refuge that seemed to hold very much hope for the German Jewish refugees was Palestine. Here, again, on the question of free immigration into Palestine, we note a strong similarity in the views of the J.L.C. and the A.F.L.

The annual convention of the A.F.L. in 1939 acknowledged the "heartrending tragedy" of the Jewish refugees in Europe, and the "just claim of the Jews to reestablish their home in Palestine."[60] It called upon the British government "to uphold the Balfour Declaration and guarantee to the refugees of an ancient race the right to a homeland of their own," and requested the British Trade Union Congress "to render every possible support in the attainment of this objective."

For its part, the Jewish Labor Committee had a rather ambiguous attitude on Palestine and Zionism. Some of its affiliates were pro-Zionist (in practice, if not in theory), while most tended to oppose Zionism.[61] As late as 1943, the J.L.C. stated that it took no stand "in regard to the ultimate constitutional status of Palestine," because "there is no unanimity among its membership on this question." At the same time, however, it declared its "solidarity with organized Jewish labor in Palestine," and supported its demands concerning Jewish immigration and colonization in Palestine.[62]

In December, 1937, Vladeck spent a five-week vacation in Palestine. Upon his return to the United States, he reported that "all this propaganda that the Jews are ruining the Arab masses economically" and the contention that "the Jews are a tool in the hands of the British imperialists" were simply untrue. In actual fact, the Arabs were profiting from the Jewish settlement, and the British were doing nothing to aid the Jews. It was "the nationalist mania which has spread like wildfire throughout the world," and not economic competition, that has caused Arab hostility to the Jews. He charged the Arab nationalist leaders with accepting aid from sources "which are openly Fascist." Although not proposing any specifics, he called upon both Arab and Jew to abandon "all accepted and time-worn formulae" and manifest a willingness to compromise.[63]

An article in the July 1939 *Call* reiterated the need for compromise. It saw the eventual solution to the Palestine problem in the establishment of "some bond of unity" between the Jewish and Arab workers of Palestine. A mutually satisfactory formula could be reached if only the world would

> Let the Jewish and Arab workers of Palestine build their common country economically, let them belong to the same unions and fight the same masters, and let them have profound respect for each other's culture, traditions and history.[64]

Despite the ambiguity of the J.L.C. on Zionism in the 1930's, the emergency caused by the 1939 White Paper evoked a clear protest against Britain. Almost a full year before the promulgation of the White Paper, a delegation of American Jewish leaders including representatives of the J.L.C., met with Secretary of State Hull, and asked him to intercede with Britain in order to obtain a more favorable immigration policy for the Jews in Palestine.[65] Reasserting this country's interest in Palestine, Hull promised to take "all necessary measures for the protection of American rights and interests in Palestine" as those rights and interests had been defined by the American British Convention of December 3, 1924.[66] At the same time, he pointed out the limits which this Convention placed on America's ability to intervene in Britain's mandatory rule. Shortly thereafter, President Roosevelt defined these limits when he wrote that under the terms of the

Convention, "we are unable to prevent modifications in the Mandate. The most we can do is to decline to accept as applicable to American interests any modifications affecting such interests unless we had given our consent to them."[67] Regulation of immigration into Palestine did not come under this category.

After the promulgation of the White Paper, the J.L.C. declared that no matter what differences of opinion existed on the question of a Jewish national home in Palestine, "on one question there can be no difference of opinion, namely on the demand for free Jewish immigration."[68] It held a special meeting of all its affiliates on August 1, 1939, to protest the White Paper. After the non-Zionist representatives stressed that their participation did not represent any concession to Zionist ideology on their part, the meeting issued a statement condemning the new British policy.[69] Proclaiming its "feeling of earnest responsibility for the fate of the Jewish masses throughout the world," the statement labeled the White Paper as "a crime against the Jewish masses who were among the most loyal fighters for social justice and democratic principles." The declaration praised the Jewish community of Palestine for its readiness to make room for thousands of refugees, and concluded with an expression of gratitude to the British Labor party, the British Trade Union Congress, and the A.F.L. for their efforts on behalf of free Jewish immigration into Palestine.[70]

E. *Haavarah*

Although the Jewish Labor Committee maintained the right of Jewish immigrants to settle in Palestine, it nevertheless opposed the Haavarah, a corporation established in 1933 for the purpose of transferring to Palestine the capital of German Jews emigrating there.[71] Representatives of the Jewish Agency, the Vaad Leumi (Jewish National Council of Palestine), the German Zionist Organization, the Anglo-Palestine Bank, and the Hitachduth Olay Germania (Union of German Immigrants) composed the Board of Directors of the Haavarah. Under the terms of a 1933 agreement between the German government and the organization, German Jews emigrating to Palestine could salvage some of their wealth in the form of German goods, which would go to Palestine with the refugees. Lasting until July 1939, this agreement transferred 105 million reichsmarks in the form of German export goods from Germany to Palestine.

The fact that the Haavarah broke the boycott was the subject of a bitter controversy in the Jewish socialist camp. Vladeck charged that while "the whole organized labor movement and the progressive world are waging a fight against Hitler through the boycott, the Transfer Agreement scabs on that fight." The Haavarah was flooding the Near East with German goods. Since there were too many goods for Palestine to absorb, the Haavarah had asked the German consul in Egypt to aid in arranging the sale of some of the excess goods in Egypt. Similar arrangements were made for other countries bordering on Palestine. Thus, charged Vladeck, Palestine was becoming "the official scab-agent against the boycott in the Near East." [72]

Labor Zionist spokesmen answered these charges. The Histadrut, the Palestine Labor Federation, challenged the opponents of Haavarah "to show an alternative method for saving the German Jews, or else they should state publicly that they prefer abandoning them to their fate." [73] The *Jewish Frontier*, a monthly then published by the League for Labor Palestine, attacked the Haavarah critics and decried the "absolute fervor with which these individuals are prepared to complete the destruction of German Jewry in the name of Boycott." [74]

F. *Alaska*

In addition to the various refugee plans connected with the Intergovernmental Committee the Jewish Labor Committee, through its membership in the General Jewish Council, also manifested interest in two other plans to alleviate the plight of the refugees. The J.L.C. archives give no information on how the J.L.C. reacted to these plans. They do, however, yield information on the reaction of the General Jewish Council with which the J.L.C. had become affiliated.

In August 1939, the United States Department of the Interior issued a report on the development of the territory of Alaska[75] which stated that current American immigration policy was having a "disastrous effect" on the population of Alaska. Although there might be some justification for the application of strict quota laws to the settled areas of the United States, the report declared that "application of the same yardstick to an under-populated territory whose future well-being depends on new immigration and new capital is extremely questionable from the standpoint of national policy." Moreover, refugees would be ideal settlers for Alaska. Forming a group that was bound together by a common tragic experience and by common ideals, they would all the more readily assume the responsibilities of a self-supporting community under circumstances where individuals who lacked common interests might tend to look to the government for aid in overcoming obstacles. Furthermore, settlers who could return to a more comfortable existence in their previous homes if they tired of Alaska were

> apt to take a critical view towards the problems of a pioneer community, whereas men and women who have definitely cut their ties with the past, who feel that they must make their new life a good life or perish in the attempt, are more likely to face the hardships and to endure the sacrifices which the fashioning of that good life demands.

The report also indicated that the population of Alaska would gladly welcome the refugees, and described the territory as a melting pot for three races—Eskimo, Indian, and Caucasian, which was uniquely free from prejudice.

In the same month that this report appeared, the General Jewish Council also dealt with the Alaskan question. Senator Tydings, chairman of the Senate Committee on Territories, expressed interest in supporting legislation that would call for refugees to help colonize and develop Alaska. Felix S. Cohen, an official of the Department of the Interior, sent a letter requesting a statement of opinion on the proposed Alaska legislation to Arthur S. Meyer, chairman of the Council's Policy and Program Committee.[76] Cohen wrote that Tydings was hesitant about urging the legislation because of his fear that the Zionists would oppose it. He asked Meyer if, without committing the Council to support of the bill, he could indicate to Tydings "a sympathetic interest in any legislation which might contribute even a partial solution to the problem of refugee settlement." Meyer communicated this request, along with a copy of a letter to Tydings that he had drafted, to Isaiah Minkoff, the Labor Committee's representative on the Policy and Program Committee.[77] Meyer informed Tydings that the Alaska legislation was "of great interest to the General Jewish Council." He wrote that he assumed that the legislation was concerned primarily with Alaskan development and that it would not be solely or even primarily a refugee measure. He did, however, offer the cooperation of the Council, and expressed the hope that the legislation might make "some contribution to a partial solution of the refugee problem."

In March 1940, a bill introduced in Congress provided for the chartering of Alaskan development corporations, which would open new industrial and agricultural projects in that territory.[78] Refugees unable to enter the United States under the existing quotas could go to Alaska under the more lenient rules that governed admission of ministers, students, and those in special professional categories. They would not become American citizens until they had resided continuously in Alaska for a period of five years, and had been reclassified as quota immigrants. The bill called for stringent regulation of the refugees. It set age limits of sixteen to forty-five. Moreover, the United States Public Health Service had to certify the physical and mental well-being of each settler. Finally, the bill provided that the settlers could not engage in occupations that would compete with American industry.

The General Council manifested little enthusiasm for this proposal despite its rather modest aim. In May, the Alaskan Development Committee, the promoter of the bill, complained that the General Council had not as yet given its support to the proposed bill, and declared that this lack of action "is seriously affecting this committee's efforts" to muster public support for the bill. The proposed legislation had already gained the backing of an impressive list of people including representatives of the Departments of State, Interior, Commerce and Labor, the mayor of Seward, Alaska, and Dr. Clarence E. Pickett of the American Friends Service Committee. The Alaskan Development Committee now wanted a statement of endorsement from a leading Jewish organization. Such a statement was crucial for friendly non-Jewish groups "who, having a sympathetic relationship to the Jewish groups, feel constrained against action without the approval of the latter agencies." The Development Committee warned that lack of Jewish support for the bill might result in the drafting of a substitute bill that would exclude Jewish immigrants from Alaska by limiting immigration there to Scandinavians or people from other countries with little or no Jewish population.[79]

The General Council refused to back the proposal out of fear that it would increase anti-alien feelings in the United States. Prominent supporters of the bill tried to allay these fears. Nathan Margold, an Interior Department official, wrote to Ambrose Doskow, the chief attorney of the Council, that the Department had received more than seven thousand letters on the bill and that "not more than a dozen or so have been in any way critical." Expressing agreement with the Council's desire to avoid giving the impression that the bill "is simply a Jewish affair," Margold nevertheless maintained that Jewish organizations should not "lean over backwards so far that they are in effect opposing the bill." [80]

This lack of active Jewish backing combined with strong nativist opposition to defeat the bill. Senator McReynolds, leader of the opposition, charged that "those foreigners would deprive the American citizens of their daily bread." Anthony Dimand, the Alaskan delegate to Congress, declared that Alaskans would oppose the legislation because they felt entitled to the same treatment as the rest of the United States. The bill was eventually "relegated to the archives of Congress" and soon forgotten.[81]

G. *The Wagner-Rogers Bill*

Among the thousands of refugees from Germany were many children whose plight aroused much humanitarian sympathy in the United States and Britain. In November 1938, the World Movement for Care of Children was founded in London to help transfer refugee children below the age of eighteen to Britain for temporary refuge, where arrangements would be made for their reemigration to permanent homes before they reached their eighteenth birthday. By the end of August 1939, this agency had cared for some 13,060 children.[82]

The plight of the refugee children was also the subject of concern in the United States. In 1939, Senator Wagner of New York and Congresswoman Rogers of Massachusetts cosponsored a bill that would provide for the admission into the United States of ten thousand German refugee children of all faiths in 1939, and another ten thousand in 1940. Admission of these children was conditional upon the assurance that they would receive adequate care from respected citizens or private organizations. The bill excluded these children from the German refugee quota. At the same time, Clarence E. Pickett founded the Non-Sectarian Committee for German Refugee Children with the purpose of implementing the bill by assuming the responsibility for placing the children in foster homes of their own faiths throughout the United States.[83]

The Wagner-Rogers bill aroused humanitarian sentiment and received considerable public support. Public officials, religious and labor groups including the A.F.L., and the General Jewish Council expressed approval of the bill.[84]

On the other hand, this proposed legislation also aroused stiff opposition. At the very time that the Senate Immigration Committee was considering the Wagner-Rogers bill, it was also weighing another bill supported by the American Legion, calling for the suspension of all immigration into this country. Opponents of the Wagner-Rogers bill objected that the bill was inhumane because it would separate children from their parents. They further charged that the bill contained no adequate safeguards against the children becoming public charges. Worst of all, if the bill passed, the parents would eventually also be brought to the United States. A representative of the Allied Patriotic Societies of New York told the Congressional committee that the bill was "just part of a drive to break down the whole quota system —to go back to the condition when we were flooded with foreigners who tried to run the country on different lines from those laid down by the old stock." [85]

The opponents eventually won through the insertion of an amendment that counted the children against the quota. Although bitterly opposed to this amendment, Wagner was powerless to prevent its being attached to his bill. The General Council also opposed the amendment and stated that, if adopted, it would defeat the whole purpose of the bill.[86]

VII. White House Meeting of the Intergovernmental Committee

President Roosevelt continued to manifest a lively interest in the refugee problem, even after the outbreak of hostilities. A month after the beginning of the war, he convened a meeting of the Intergovernmental Committee at the White House. Addressing the participants, the President spoke of a twofold refugee problem. He stated that it had become quite clear since 1938 that private organizations would no longer be able to deal satisfactorily with the growing number of refugees. The immediate task was the permanent settlement of the 200,000-300,000 prewar refugees. The world had to "clear the decks" of this old issue because the war would present it with a far greater challenge. Predicting that the war would add ten to twenty million men, women, and children to the refugee lists, Roosevelt called on the Committee to conduct extensive surveys to determine "definitely and scientifically this geographical and economic problem of resettling several million people in new areas of the earth's surface." As for the prewar refugees, no one could expect of Britain or France more than a "continuance of their sympathy and interest" since they were bogged down in war. The neutral nations had to shoulder this burden. The President concluded his speech with the following declaration:

> It is not enough to indulge in horrified humanitarianism, empty resolutions, golden rhetoric and pious words. We must face it [the refugee problem] actively if the democratic principle based on respect and human dignity is to survive, if world order, which rests on security of the individual, is to be restored. Remembering the words written on the Statue of Liberty, let us lift a lamp beside new golden doors and build new refuges for the tired, for the poor, for the huddled masses yearning to be free.[87]

Although Roosevelt did not offer to raise the American quotas, his initiative in convoking the Evian conference and the White House meeting of the Intergovernmental Committee demonstrate a sympathetic attitude towards the refugees. Moreover, even had he proposed quota reform legislation, it is almost certain that Congress would have cast it into oblivion. Nevertheless, the fact remains that representatives of the Jewish Labor Committee never asked the President to lend his support to any such program.

Conclusion

In the 1930's, the J.L.C. was a very important organization in the American Jewish community. This organization laid claim to represent the largely Yiddish-speaking, East European-born Jewish working masses, who were still a potent force in Jewish life in the 1930's.[88] The process by which the children of Jewish workers became middle class and professionals, begun already in the 1920's and to reach its peak in the years following World War II, had not yet eaten away significant numbers from the working class. Moreover, the acceleration of this process as a result of the war could not have been foreseen in the 1930's and, therefore, the J.L.C. thought that it would continue to represent a large constituency in American Jewry, and acted under this assumption. It conceived of itself as the American branch of the world-wide Jewish socialist movement. As socialists, the J.L.C. saw in Nazism a threat to everything progressive and liberal, and believed that that threat should be met by a combination of all progressive and liberal forces. In America, its logical ally was the A.F.L.

This ideological stance greatly affected the actions of the J.L.C. The most striking example of how this labor orientation affected its actions during most of the decade, and how, on the other hand, the critical situation in Europe pushed ideological considerations into the background late in the decade is in the area of immigration. Throughout the decade, the J.L.C. failed officially to call for a revision of the American quota laws. The negative attitude of the A.F.L., and the J.L.C.'s fear that a flood of refugees would have a harmful effect on the American economy and that this, in turn, would lead to anti-Semitic outbreaks, were the reasons for this attitude. This opposition also precluded giving any serious consideration to accepting the refugee barter plans that were worked out between the German government and the Intergovernmental Committee of the Evian conference. Had these plans been accepted, many Jews might have been saved. Schacht himself claimed that "had the plan been carried through, not a single German Jew would have lost his life."[89] Obviously this statement cannot be taken at face value. In the words of a historian of the period:

> Is one really to believe that Hitler would have financed Jewish emigration during the war merely to honor the Schacht loan or that the allies would have accepted Jews from the Reich throughout the wartime blockade? And even if the Allies accepted some 300,000 Jews, who were under Hitler's rule in January 1939, what of the subsequently occupied territories where over four millions perished?[90]

The Jewish Labor Committee rejected the barter plans, because it feared that they would strengthen anti-Semitism in the United States and that they would break the boycott. Nevertheless, despite the unreliability of the word of the Nazi government, and despite the effect on the boycott, had the transfer plans received a more enthusiastic reception by Jewish organizations, it is possible that more Jewish lives would have been saved. Yet, from a historical perspective, we must conclude that the Jewish Labor Committee as well as other American Jewish organizations could hardly have done much more than they did. It seems apparent that the Jewish Labor Committee was not satisfied with American immigration policy in the 1930's, and that it withheld official protest as long as it did only with reluctance and feelings of guilt. Powerless to fight against the prevailing stream of economic turbulence of the 1930's which carried all along with it, the J.L.C. remained silent. Bound by its ideology and its labor orientation and close ties with the A.F.L., the Jewish Labor Committee could not really be expected to have pursued a different line of action as long as the masses of European Jewish workers were not in immediate danger.

NOTES

1 Arendt, Hannah. *Eichmann in Jerusalem* (New York, 1963), 111.

2 *Ibid.*, 35.

3 *Ibid.*, 35–36.

4 On the anti-Nazi boycott movement see Katz, Benedict, *Crisis and Response* (Columbia University M.A. thesis, Department of Sociology, 1951, unpublished); Tenenbaum, Joseph, "The Anti-Nazi Boycott Movement in the United States," *Yad Washem Studies* (Jerusalem, 1959), III, 141–159.

5 *New York Times*, April 15, 1934, 10.

6 "The Jewish Labor Committee." 1938. (*Archives of the Jewish Labor Committee.*) This pamphlet contains a full statement of the goals of the J.L.C.:

> 1) To help Jewish workers develop and apply a consistent program and policy on all important questions of, and pertaining to, Jewish life; 2) To fight for the protection of the civil, political, and religious rights of the Jewish masses in all countries and to encourage and to aid all progressive and democratic elements throughout the world in their struggle against fascism, Nazism, reaction and anti-Semitism; 3) To aid in the reconstruction and rehabilitation of Jewish life on a productive basis; 4) To fight for the right of free immigration in all countries, including Palestine; 5) To work in closest contact with the organized Jewish and non-Jewish labor movement in the struggle against fascism and anti-Semitism; 6) To aid Jewish and labor refugees and other victims of fascist persecution; 7) To acquaint the general labor and progressive movement of America with the plight of the Jews in the fascist and semi-fascist countries, with their struggle for the right to live and to work, and to enlist the support of all liberal forces in this struggle; 8) To impress upon the Jewish masses that they must fight hand in hand with the general forces of democracy and social advancement, that the struggle against anti-Semitism is part of the general struggle against fascism and reaction, and that they must support all liberal and labor victims of fascist aggression; 9) To carry on and to intensify the boycott against Nazi-made foods and services.

7 Lestschinsky, Jacob, "The Economic Development of the Jews in the United States," *The Jewish People Past and Present* (New York, 1955), I, 403.

8 Before the autumn of 1935, responsible Jewish leaders in Germany did not advise emigration. However, their policy changed with the promulgation of the Nuremburg Laws in September 1935, for "these laws brought home to the German Jews the fact that emigration was their only salvation." Wischnitzer, "Jewish Emigration from Germany, 1933–1938," *Jewish Social Studies*, II (1940), 28.

9 Greater Germany consisted of Germany, Austria, and the Sudeten Region of Czechoslovakia. In 1933, the number of professing Jews in this area was 721,654. At the start of World War II, the number was 286,000, a decline of 435,054 compared to the 1933 figure. Of these, about 350,000 had emigrated, while about 85,000 had died. Mark Wischnitzer, *To Dwell in Safety* (Philadelphia, 1948), 221.

10 Tartakower, Arieh, and Kurt R. Grossman, *The Jewish Refugee* (New York, 1944), 34.

11 Higham, John, *Strangers in the Land* (New Brunswick, 1955), 308 ff.

12 Wischnitzer, *To Dwell in Safety*, 205.

13 Reitlinger, Gerald, *The Final Solution* (New York, 1961), 24.

14 Bernstein, John L., "Migration of Jews in Recent Years," *American Jewish Yearbook*, XXXVIII, 1936–1937, 124, 127.

15 *Asylum for Refugees Under our Immigration Laws—Views of Some Distinguished Contemporaries and Leaders of Public Opinion of Earlier Days on Asylum*

and Their Application to German Political and Religious Refugees. Prepared for the Committee of Ten by Mrs. Carrie Chapman Catt, September 9, 1933.

16 Tartakower and Grossman, *The Jewish Refugee,* 88.

17 Leuchtenburg, William, E. *Franklin D. Roosevelt and the New Deal* (New York, 1963), 286. For a history of the A.F.L.'s attitude on immigration, see Higham, *Strangers,* 71–72; 112; 305–306; 316; 321.

18 *New York Times,* April 21, 1939, 6.

19 Upon his return in 1937, Rabbi Jonah B. Wise wrote to the J.L.C. "that the situation of the Jews in Germany has reached its lowest ebb," and he proposed that the "young and mobile" be removed from Germany. Letter from Rabbi Jonah B. Wise to Benjamin Gebiner of the J.L.C. April 8, 1935. *Archives of the J.L.C.*

20 Quoted from the "Address Delivered by Louis Lipsky, Acting President of the American Jewish Congress at the Joint Conference of the American Jewish Congress and the Jewish Labor Committee to Plan Action to Halt the Hitler Menace," July 22, 1935. *Archives of the J.L.C.*

21 Brody, David. "American Jewry, the Refugees, and Immigration Restriction (1932–1942)" *Publications of the American Jewish Historical Society,* XLV (June 1956), 219–247. Brody analyzes the lack of enthusiasm for immigration reform among the various groups in the American Jewish community. He contends that the Jewish labor groups represented in the Jewish Labor Committee were an exception to this rule. Desiring to foster a distinctive Yiddish culture, the Labor Committee welcomed more immigrants to the United States. Although, as we shall see, its semi-articulate beginnings go back several years earlier, this desire for more immigrants became manifest only after the outbreak of the war. What is clear is that during the decade of the 1930's, the Labor Committee did not call for legislative reform that would have enabled more immigrants to enter this country.

22, 23 *Report of the Proceedings of the Fifty-Third Annual Convention of the American Federation of Labor,* LIII (1933), 103, 428–430; LIV (1934), 550; LVI (1936), 129; LVIII (1938), 167; LVX (1939), 135.

24 *Ibid.,* LII (1933), 464.

25 *Ibid.,* LIX (1939), 416.

26 "Resolution Proposing U.S. Offer of Asylum for Nazi and Fascist Refugees." *Report of the Proceedings of the Fifty-fifth Annual Convention of the American Federation of Labor,* LV (1935), 603.

27 *Ibid.,* 603.

28 *Ibid.,* LVIII (1938), 507.

29 *Ibid.,* 507.

30 Report of the executive committee of the J.L.C. January 7, 1936. *Archives of the J.L.C.*

31 In 1939, Roosevelt ordered that visitors' visas that had been granted to an estimated 15,000 German Jewish refugees be extended to allow them to remain in this country as long as necessary.

32 Tartakower and Grossman, *The Jewish Refugee,* 412. The call to the conference issued by the State Department stated that "it should be understood that no country would be expected or asked to receive a greater number of immigrants than is permitted by its existing legislation." *American Jewish Yearbook,* XL, 1938–1939, 97. For a detailed account of the Evian Conference, see S. Adler-Rudel, "The Evian Conference on the refugee question" *Leo Baeck Institute Yearbook,* XIII (1968), 235-273.

33 The General Jewish Council, founded in 1938, was an organization whose purpose was to coordinate the defense work of the American Jewish Committee, American Jewish Congress, Bnai Brith, and J.L.C.

34 *Contemporary Jewish Record,* I, September, 1938, 123.

35 Workmen's Circle *Call,* VI, July, 1938, 5–6.

36 *Call,* VII, January, 1939, 10.

37 "The German Refugee Transfer Plan Memorandum," submitted by Dr. Joseph Tenenbaum. Undated. *Archives of the J.L.C.*

38 Sachar, Howard M. *The Course of Modern Jewish History* (New York, 1963), 361.

[39] *American Jewish Yearbook,* XXXVIII, 1936-1937, 197.

[40] *Ibid.,* XXXIX, 1937-1938, 230.

[41] Lestschinsky, Jacob, "The Economic and Social Development of the Jewish People," *Jewish People Past and Present,* I (New York, 1955), 379.

[42] Tartakower and Grossman, *The Jewish Refugee,* 372.

[43] *Call,* V, December, 1937, 4–5.

[44] *New York Times,* January 11, 1939, 11.

[45] *Ibid.,* January 17, 1939, 1.

[46] In 1935, the J.L.C. and the American Jewish Congress formed the Joint Boycott Council whose purpose was to organize and maintain a boycott of German goods.

[47] "Refugee Barter Memorandum Submitted by Dr. Joseph Tenenbaum." December 13, 1938. *Archives of the J.L.C.*

[48] "Post War Demands for the Jews Submitted by the Jewish Labor Committee to the American Jewish Conference." August 29, 1943. *Archives of the J.L.C.*

[49] "Refugee Barter Memorandum."

[50] Details of the plan were given in *The New York Times,* February 14, 1949, 1 and 12.

[51] *Ibid.,* 12.

[52] "Refugee Barter Memorandum."

[53] The following is based on the letter from Joseph C. Hyman, executive director of the Joint Distribution Committee, to Isaiah Minkoff of the J.L.C. July 28, 1939. *Archives of the J.L.C.,* and "The American Jewish Joint Distribution Committee Inc., Minutes of the Meeting of the Executive Committee." July 17, 1939. *Archives of the J.L.C.*

[54] The American representatives were former ambassador John W. Davis, Owen D. Young, former ambassador David Hennen Morris, former New York governor Nathan L. Miller, Rufus Jones, chairman of the American Friends Service Committee, Paul Baerwald, Stephen S. Wise, Joseph M. Proskauer, Lewis L. Strauss, and Lessing Rosenwald.

[55] Letter from Adolph Held to the Joint Distribution Committee. July 12, 1939. *Archives of the J.L.C.*

[56] *Ibid.*

[57] Proceedings of the meeting are reported in "Joint, Minutes of the Executive Committee," July 17, 1939. *Archives of the J.L.C.*

[58] Cable from Lewis Strauss to the Joint Distribution Committee quoted in "Joint, Minutes of the Executive Committee." July 17, 1939. *Archives of the J.L.C.*

[59] All efforts along the lines of the transfer proposals were ended by the outbreak of war. Tartakower and Grossman, *The Jewish Refugee,* 418.

[60] *Proceedings of the Fifty-ninth Annual Convention of the American Federation of Labor,* LIX, 1939, 679.

[61] Halperin, Simon. *The Political World of American Zionism* (Detroit, 1961), 157–175.

[62] "Post War Demands."

[63] *American Jewish Yearbook,* XXXIX, 1937–1938, 239–240.

[64] *Call,* VII, July, 1939, 7.

[65] For this and the following see *American Jewish Yearbook,* XLI, 1939–1940, 200.

[66] For the significance of the Convention, see ESCO Foundation for Palestine, *Palestine, a Study of Jewish, Arab and British Policies* (New Haven, 1947) II, 1111–1112.

[67] The terms of the Anglo-American Mandate Convention of December 3, 1924 called for: a) nondiscriminatory treatment in matters of commerce; b) nonimpairment of vested American property rights; c) permission for American nationals to establish and maintain educational, philanthropic, and religious institutions in Palestine; d) safeguards with respect to the judiciary "and, in general, equality of treatment with all other foreign nationals." Press release issued by the Department of State, October 14, 1938. *Archives of the J.L.C.*

68 "Resolution of the Jewish Labor Committee Concerning the London Conference." Undated. *Archives of the J.L.C.*

69 Jewish Telegraphic Agency Bulletin, August 3, 1939.

70 Official declaration issued by the J.L.C. at a special protest meeting held on August 1, 1939. *Archives of the J.L.C.*

71 Tartakower and Grossman, *The Jewish Refugee,* 443; and Thompson, Dorothy, *Refugees, Anarchy or Organization* (New York, 1938).

72 *Call,* IV, January, 1936, 3.

73 *American Jewish Yearbook,* XXXVIII, 1936–1937, 195.

74 *Jewish Frontier,* January, 1936, 5.

75 The Report of the Department of the Interior is quoted in the *J.T.A. Bulletin,* August 16, 1939.

76 Letter from Felix S. Cohen to Arthur S. Meyer, July 31, 1939. *Archives of the J.L.C.*

77 Letter from Arthur S. Meyer to Isaiah Minkoff, August 2, 1939. *Archives of the J.L.C.*

78 *J.T.A. Bulletin,* March 6, 1940. Also, "Projects for Jewish Mass Colonization," *Jewish Affairs,* I, November, 1941, 8.

79 Letter from Beatrice B. Schalet, secretary of the Alaskan Development Committee, to the General Jewish Council, May 17, 1940. *Archives of the J.L.C.*

80 Letter from Nathan Margold to Ambrose Doskow, May 18, 1940. *Archives of the J.L.C.*

81 "Projects for Jewish Mass Colonization," 8.

82 Wischnitzer, *To Dwell in Safety,* 200.

83 *American Jewish Yearbook,* XLI, 1939–1940, 195, and *The New York Times,* April 21, 1939, 6.

84 Report of the Public Relations Committee to the General Jewish Council, September 16, 1939. *Archives of the J.L.C.*

85 *New York Times,* April 23, 1939, 1 and 34.

86 *J.T.A. Bulletin,* July 12, and July 14, 1939.

87 The speech is quoted in full in the *J.T.A. Bulletin,* October 18, 1939.

88 Glazer, Nathan, "Social Characteristics of American Jews" in Finkelstein, Louis, ed., *The Jews,* (Jewish Publication Society, 1960) II, 1711 ff.

89 Reitlinger, *The Final Solution,* 21.

90 *Ibid.*

MAIMONIDES' ATTITUDE TO MIDRASH

WILLIAM G. BRAUDE

Congregation Sons of Israel and David
Providence, Rhode Island

Dedicated with affection to I. Edward Kiev, whose heart and mind are attuned to Scripture's polyphony.

The principal presupposition in Midrashic discipline, the Babylonian Abaye (fourth century) sets forth as follows:

אחת דבר אלהים שתים זו שמעתי כי עז לאלהים (תהלים סב:יב). מקרא אחד יוצא לכמה טעמים ואין טעם אחד יוצא מכמה מקראות. דבי ר׳ ישמעאל תנא: וכפטיש יפוצץ סלע (ירמיה כג:כט). מה פטיש זה מתחלק [מן הסלע] לכמה ניצוצות אף מקרא אחד יוצא לכמה טעמים (סנהדרין לד.).

> God speaks once. From that one utterance of His I draw at the very least two inferences, such being God's strength. Thus a single verse may be construed as conveying innumerable meanings, whereas identical meaning is never conveyed by several verses. Indeed in the school of R. Ishmael it is taught: Even as from a hammer striking a rock there issue innumerable flashes of fire, so from a single verse flash forth innumerable meanings.[1]

The fundamental presupposition that a single verse has a multiplicity of meaning is expressed elsewhere even more sharply, and with greater boldness: זכור ושמור שניהם בדבור אחד נאמרו מה שאי אפשר לפה לומר ולא לאוזן לשמוע (ירוש׳ נדרים פרק ג׳ הלכה ב׳).
"The words *Remember the Sabbath day* (Exod. 20:8) and *Observe the Sabbath day* (Deut. 5:12) were uttered by God at one and the same time, something which a mortal's voice cannot do, or a mortal's ear apprehend."[2]

Maimonides knew, it goes without saying, the Rabbinic theory that each of God's words is charged with a profusion of meaning. Nevertheless, in a well-known chapter in his *Guide* (*3*, 43), wherein he deals with the year's holidays, he seems to disregard and even wave aside the principle that multiple meaning inheres in each verse—indeed in each word—in Scripture. He waves aside this principle as he sets forth what, in his opinion, are the true reasons for the observance of the Sabbath and of each of the festivals. The reasons he gives are what we might call rational ones. Thus when he comes to the Feast of Tabernacles, he says: "It is kept in the autumn, as stated in the Torah: *When thou hast gathered in the labors out of the field* (Exod. 23:16); that is to say, when you rest and are free from pressing labors." Then, by way of wishing to demonstrate the reasonableness of the Festival's being set in the autumn of the year, Maimonides quotes Aristotle: "This was the general practice of religious communities in ancient times . . . The . . . sacrifices and gatherings used to take place after the harvesting of the fruit. They were, as it were, offerings given because of leisure." By quoting Aristotle, Maimonides seems to say to the reader: You see, in observing Tabernacles you are part of a goodly and universal company. Then Maimonides goes on: "In addition it is possible to live in the Tabernacle during that season, there being neither great heat nor troublesome rain."

At this point Maimonides comes to a matter more troublesome to him than rain is for people dwelling in booths. The troublesome matter, which he does not identify, is a congeries of Rabbinic interpretations of the four species which make up a lulab cluster. These four are, in Rabbinic commentary, said to symbolize God, the Matriarchs, the Patriarchs, the great Sanhedrin or the entire people of Israel.[3] To one who prefers the so-called plain meaning of a text, the devices which the Rabbis use to arrive at the interpretations just mentioned, devices such as employment of key terms whose meaning is cognate, plays on words, and so on, appear farfetched. Indeed in this very chapter wherein Maimonides deals with the holidays, he characterizes the unspecified Rabbinic interpretations of a lulab cluster's four species as farfetched.

To use his own words—Englished for me in part by my friend Leon Nemoy: "As for the lulab cluster's four species, the Rabbis have mentioned something in the way of reason for them, in the manner of *derashot,* whose nature (lit. "way, road") is known to him who comprehends Rabbinic discourse, namely, that *derashot* as used by the Rabbis are analogous to poetic anecdotes, and are not [to be understood] as representing the [true] meaning of a particular text. People, [however], fall into two schools of thought as to *derashot:* one school imagines that the Rabbis intend a Midrash to be the [actual] explanation of the meaning of a particular text; the other school deprecates *derashot* and regards them as humorous or laughable stories, since it is obvious and clear that the *derashah* is not the actual meaning of the text. The former school strives mightily to clarify what they regard is the accuracy of *derashot* and to defend them, for they think that this is indeed the [actual] meaning of the text, and that the status of *derashot* is equal to that of traditional [legal] decisions. Neither school comprehends that *derashot* are analogous to poetic anecdotes whose matter is not hidden from one possessed of intelligence. This procedure was well-known at the time of the Rabbis, and everyone made use of it, in the same way as poets use poetic sayings. For example, Bar Ḳappara teaches: In the verse *Thou shalt have a paddle* [*yated*] *upon thy weapon* [*'azenecha*] (Deut. 23:14) do not read *'azenecha,* 'thy weapon,' but *'oznecha,* 'thy ear.' The verse tells you that whenever you hear a reprehensible thing, you should put your finger into your ear, pad your ear so to speak" (B. Keṭuboṭ 5a). "Now," says Maimonides, "I wonder whether the ignorant persons [who take *derashot* as literal interpretations of the text], believe that Bar Ḳappara, the author of this saying, gave it as the true interpretation of the text, as the meaning intended by the precept, namely, that *yated,* 'paddle,' means a finger, whereby the padding of *'oznecha,* of a man's ears is to be effected. The truth is that Bar Ḳappara employed the text as a witty poetic conceit in order to teach an excellent lesson he sought to convey through the use of a Biblical text. In the same way you must understand Bar Ḳappara's use of the phrase 'Do not read thus, but thus,' wherever it occurs in Midrashim." [4]

Here Maimonides seems to regard Midrashic lessons based on texts of Scripture as not inhering in the words of Scripture, but as superimposed upon them. And the relevant implication for the theme of Tabernacles with which Maimonides deals follows clearly: The Rabbinic assertion that the four species symbolize God, the Matriarchs, the Patriarchs, the great Sanhedrin or the entire people of Israel is, so Maimonides implies, not read out of but read into the precept to take during Tabernacles the *ethrog,* the palm tree's branch, the myrtle, and the willows of the brook. The true meaning of the precept's intent—Maimonides asserts—is to symbolize by the four species the rejoicing at our departure from the wilderness, *a place with no grain or figs or vines or pomegranates, where there is not even water to drink* (Num. 20:5), into a country full of fruit trees and rivers. Accordingly—and I quote Maimonides' own words—"for the purpose of commemorating our arrival into a fertile land, we take the fertile land's most delicious fruit—the fruit that is most fragrant as well as the land's most beautiful leaves and greenest verdures."[5]

If what I have set forth thus far—namely, that Midrash is no more than a poetic anecdote—represents Maimonides' true view of Midrash, the Midrashic method could not be used by him as proof for traits or accomplishments in the lives of certain Biblical worthies; could not be used by him to demonstrate the particular characteristics of certain laws; could not be used by him as authority for certain theological principles; and finally could not be used by him as evidence for the history of law.

In what follows I shall endeavor to show that with utter inconsistency, Maimonides uses the Midrashic method for filling in biographical details in the life of David; for proving men's proneness to sexual transgressions; for demonstrating the provisional character of miracles; and finally for deducing from Scripture that six commandments were given to Adam. I shall then suggest the reason for Maimonides' inconsistency and in conclusion state what I believe to have been Maimonides' true attitude toward the Midrashic method.

Now to the particulars of my exposition:

Item 1. The filling in of biographical details in the life of David. The twenty-third chapter in the Second Book of Samuel gives the names of David's heroes and some of their deeds of derring-do which for all the obscurity in phrasing still ring forth with the thunder of armor. The recital of the heroes' names begins in the eighth verse of that chapter with the words: *These are the names of the mighty men whom David had: Josheb-basshebeth a Tachkemonite, chief of the captains.* This reading, or translation of the Hebrew, I may say in passing, is supported by the marks of cantillation. Maimonides, however, basing himself on R. Abbahu's reading of verse 8 in II Samuel 23—a reading as bold and as farfetched as Bar Kappara's behest to pad up both ears with one's fingers—suggests that the verse intimates that David was both prophet and chief of the seventy elders of the Sanhedrin. For, says Maimonides, Scripture describes David as יושב בשבת תחכמוני, *josheb-basshebeth,* seated in the place of one whose vision, power, and humility are such that God Himself says to him *Taḥkemoni* (=*tehe komoni* תהא כמוני) "Have thou power like unto Mine so that when even I, your God, issue a decree, thou mayest set it aside."[6]

Note that in this instance Maimonides distorts the plain meaning of the text in Samuel into having it say something which the writer had not intended to say. To demonstrate certain excellencies of David, Maimonides uses rhetorical devices which he previously characterized as witty poetic conceits—uses such devices to demonstrate that David was not only a warrior, but a prophet and legist as well—indeed head of the Sanhedrin.

Item 2. The proof from Scripture for man's proneness to sexual transgression. Maimonides says: "There is no prohibition in the whole of Scripture which the generality of the people experienced greater difficulty in observing than the interdict of forbidden unions and illicit intercourse. Indeed, the Sages declared that when Israel was given the commandments concerning forbidden unions, they wept and accepted these injunctions with grumbling and wailing, *weeping in their families* (Num. 11:10), i.e., weeping on account of the sexual constraints put upon them in family relations."[7] In this instance, the comment of the Sage, R. Nehorai, based on *weeping in their families*, a comment which Maimonides quotes with approval, is likewise a bold and farfetched departure from the sense of the verse in Numbers where the *weeping in their families* took place not because of hitherto unknown regulations concerning sexual behavior, but rather because, petulantly, the people of Israel in the wilderness grew weary of the manna. Of course, in support of R. Nehorai's interpretation, it may be argued that the hint of sex in the phrase *weeping in their families*, Maimonides found in the statement made earlier in the same chapter namely, that *the people fell a-lusting . . . and wept* (Num. 11:4). By the same token one may argue in behalf of Bar Ḳappara's assertion that the paddle among the weapons has reference not merely to digging a hole into which excrement is to be put out of reach, but also to digging into one's ears to make certain that obscenity, the excrement of the tongue, is put out of reach. Still, with regard to the craving for illicit intercourse, Maimonides apparently regards R. Nehorai's comment on the sexual overtones in *weeping in their families*, the farfetched character of this particular interpretation notwithstanding, as a reading out of, not a reading into the text.

Item 3. Miracles, though extraordinary, are nevertheless in a certain respect events set in nature from the beginning. For, says Maimonides, according to the Sages, "When God created that which exists and stamped upon it the existing natures, He put it into these natures, that all the miracles which are to occur would be produced in them at the time when they do occur." [8] With regard to the theory that miracles are, so to speak, built in, Maimonides quotes R. Jonathan's comment concerning a stipulation God had made with the sea at the time of its creation, the stipulation being that on one occasion it should divide, part in two, before the Israelites. The proof for such a stipulation from the very beginning of the sea's existence, R. Jonathan draws from the verse וישב הים לפנות בקר לאיתנו (שמות יד:כז)=לתנאו. "When the morning appeared, the sea returned to its strength, in keeping with the stipulation set for it." [9] Again a farfetched reading of the verse in Exodus.

Item 4. The proof from Scripture that to Adam were given six commandments, namely, prohibition of idolatry, of blasphemy, of murder, of adultery, of robbery, and the behest to establish courts of justice. Concerning these six, Maimonides says, "It is evident from the general tenor of Scripture that *Adam* was bidden to observe these commandments." [10] What Maimonides characterizes as "the general tenor of Scripture" is as wild a Midrashic foray as I know. R. Levi is the one responsible for the extraordinary stretching of what at first appears to be the rather simple statement that *The Lord God commanded Adam, saying: Of every tree of the garden thou mayest freely eat, but of the tree of knowledge, of good and evil, thou shalt not eat of it* (Gen. 2:16–17). R. Levi seems to regard the wordiness and formality of this passage as intimating matters not stated explicitly. Hence, R. Levi construes the passage as follows: God prohibited the worship of things foul, and prescribed reverence for the true God, respect for justice, for man's life, for chastity and for property.[11] By intense use of the Midrashic method, the commandments I mentioned may be extracted from the words in the text. Yet the farfetched meaning thus extracted Maimonides unhesitatingly characterizes as "the general tenor of Scripture." If R. Levi's Midrashic foray on the commandments given to Adam is evident from the general tenor of Scripture, then why does Maimonides dismiss as poetic conceit the assertion that a lulab cluster symbolizes God, the Matriarchs, and so on? Why, too, does he regard as mere poetic conceit Bar Ḳappara's assertion that by the paddle prescribed for a camp in an army on the march, Scripture also implies the paddle's use to stop one's ears, to pad them so to speak, against obscene or reprehensible talk? My answer is brief :Maimonides intended his *Guide* to help people whose faith in the words of the Rabbis was shaken by Karaite polemics, people who were strongly influenced by the rationalism then current in the world. So, not to lose these people whose faith had been so shaken, he sought to define the Midrashic method which they regarded as bizarre, as being in fact no more than poetic conceit.

Maimonides in his own writing thus followed the principle "The Torah must speak in a language which men—even those who have gone astray from the Torah—can understand." [12]

Maimonides' own view of the Midrashic method, he set forth by implication in the statement: "As to importance there is absolutely no difference between verses such as *His wife's name was Mehetabel, the daughter of Matred* (Gen. 36:39) and *Timna was concubine to Eliphaz* (ibid., 36:12); and verses such as *I am the Lord thy God* (Deut. 5:6) and *Hear, O Israel, the Lord our God, the Lord is One* (ibid., 6:4)." [13] If Maimonides had in truth regarded *derashot* as no more than witty poetic conceits, he could not have spoken of these four verses as being alike in importance.

His real attitude toward *derashot* is seen in the eloquent statement: "It is proper that we judge the *derashot* [which appear to us bizarre] in the scale of merit, examine them closely and not reject as farfetched anything in them. Should an utterance of the Sages appear to us farfetched then we must train ourselves in the disciplines of wisdom until we come to understand the Sages' intent in a particular utterance, assuming of course that our minds are capable of understanding that great utterance of theirs . . . after all [unlike the Sages of former years], each of us is afflicted by four faults—*four sore judgments* (Ezek. 14:21)—our intelligence is weak, our lust is strong, our quest for wisdom laggard, and our longing for lucre lively . . . whereas all that the Sages had to say is clear, precise and contains no dross (parenthetically, hostile minds may look upon poetic conceits as a form of dross) whatsoever." [14]

Who knows? In citing Bar Ḳappara's advice that when one hears reprehensible things one should put one's finger into his ear, so to speak pad his ear, Maimonides may have intended a self-castigating kind of humor. He may have subtly addressed this particular advice to a reader who shared his own belief concerning the multiplicity of meaning in every verse in Scripture, meaning which by the sundry devices of Midrash is to be mined and dug out. To such a devout reader, Maimonides put up a kind of semaphor by way of saying: You who see clearly, who is not perplexed, heed this: For the sake of those who have strayed from the ways of Torah, I characterize *derashot* as witty poetic conceits—a thing which I consider reprehensible. Therefore, you, O reader, who sees clearly and is not perplexed, instead of heeding the reprehensible thing circumstances constrain me to say, follow Bar Ḳappara's advice: put your finger in your ear, pad it, so to speak.

You my reader, who sees clearly, attend to what I am about to say: "The bidding of the holy spirit is discerned in Scripture through any one of ten modes of expression: through mantic seizure, through vision, through flow of prophetic speech, through divine utterance, through a solitary word, through a precept, through an oracle, through a proverb, through metaphor or through riddle." [15]

You my reader are therefore to regard Bar Ḳappara's utterance concerning the padding of one's ear—with which the discussion began—as a combination of metaphor and riddle by means of which he who sees clearly will detect the urgent yet gentle bidding of the holy spirit.

NOTES

1 B. Sanhedrin 34a.

2 P. Nedarim 37b, 3.2.

3 Pesikta de-Rav Kahana, ed. Mandelbaum, p. 414–416.

4 *Guide 3,* 43.

5 *Ibid.*

6 B. Mo'ed Ḳaṭan 16b cited in Commentary on Abot, chap. 4, ed. Harav Kook, p. 121.

7 Sifre, Num. 90, B. Shabbat 130a, and B. Yoma 75a cited in The Book of Holiness, Laws concerning Forbidden Intercourse, 22.18; *Yale Judaica Series, 16,* p. 145.

8 *Guide 2,* 29, Pines-Strauss tr. p. 345.

9 Gen. Rabbah, 5:2, ed. Theodor-Albeck, p. 35; *Guide 2,* 29.

10 The Book of Judges, Laws Concerning Kings and Wars, 9.1; *Yale Judaica Series 3,* p. 231.

11 Gen. Rabbah 16:6, ed. Theodor-Albeck, p. 149–50. The intimations for the six precepts may be found in the following words and phrases of Gen. 2:16–17: *Commanded* intimates a prohibition of idolatry, of worshiping that which is foul צו=צואה ; *The Lord* intimates reverence for the true Sovereign; *God,* the attribute of justice, implies a behest to set up courts of justice; *Adam,* literally "concerning man," intimates that the life of man must be preserved and that his blood may not be shed; *saying* (a term which in the form *ma'amar* [literally "a say"] denotes the marriage contract) proscribes unchasity; *of every tree of the garden thou mayest freely eat*—except, of course, the tree of knowledge and the tree of life—intimates the prohibition of taking that which belongs to another. Cf. Midrash on Psalms, *Yale Judaica Series, 13,* vol. 2, p. 417–18.

12 B. Berakot 31b.

13 Introduction to Pereḳ Ḥeleḳ, ed. Harav Kook, p. 145. See B. Sanhedrin 99b.

14 Preface to the Mishnah, ed. Harav Kook, p. 70–71.

15 Genesis Rabbah 44:6. Cf. Abot de R. Nathan, ch. 34, *Yale Judaica Series, 10,* p. 142.

EZRA STILES AND THE POLISH RABBI

ARTHUR A. CHIEL

Congregation B'nai Jacob, Woodbridge, Connecticut

The Reverend Ezra Stiles, proud holder of a degree of Doctor in Divinity, University of Edinburgh, 1765, was ever keenly interested in broadening his knowledge of matters Hebraic and Judaic. He kept a close eye for any visiting rabbis to his beloved Newport, where he served as a Congregationalist pastor from 1755 to 1778. His unflagging curiosity was well rewarded. Between 1759 and 1775, Stiles made the acquaintance of some six rabbis:

1759 - Rabbi Moses Malki
1772 - Rabbi Moses b. David
1773 - Rabbi Hajim I. Karigal
1773 - Rabbi Tobiah b. Jehudah
1774 - Rabbi Bosquila
1775 - Rabbi Samuel Cohen

Each of the rabbis spent several weeks in Newport as guests of the then thriving Jewish community. Stiles delighted in their company. He listened attentively to their preaching at the Newport Synagogue. He hosted them graciously and held learned discourse with them in his home, in the synagogue, and in the Redwood Library. After each encounter, Stiles would make careful note of their discussions in his *Literary Diary*. It is his entries concerning the Rabbi Tobiah which are considered in this paper.

Stiles' entry of November 19, 1773 reads:

> Went to the Synagogue and was introduced to a new Rabbi from Poland.[1]

He obviously extended an invitation to the newcomer at this, their first meeting. Three days later the rabbi was guest at his home. This is indicated by an entry of November 22, 1773:

> Visited this Afternoon by Rabbi Tobiah Bar Jehuda late from near Cracow in Poland Aet 48. We had much convers[a] on the Zohar and particularly the X Saphirots. He said that the Sapher Haujtzirah was now in the same state as in Abrahams Time; that Rabbi Akiba made no change in it—only he selected it as a part of a larger Book called the Sapher Razael, which was communicated by the Angel Razael to Adam, from Adam to Seth, who delivered it to Enoch, he to Methuselah, he to Noah, he to Shem & Shem delivered it to Abraham.[2]

Jewish mysticism had held Stiles' interest for several years before Rabbi Tobiah's coming. He had had discussions of Kabbalistic matters with Rabbi Moses bar David and very extensive explorations with Rabbi Karigal. In fact, Stiles had troubled to correspond with a London book dealer to arrange for the purchase of the *Zohar,* which he accomplished in 1772.[3] Well before his acquisition of the Zohar he had made inquiry into Jewish mysticism, assuming it to hold intimations of the Trinity.[4]

That Rabbi Tobiah, in turn, found the Reverend Stiles a worthy companion is attested to by the fact that he called on Stiles again, the day following their first encounter. Writes Stiles in his entry of November 23, 1773:

> The Rabbi visited me again or came to my house but I was not at home. In the Evening I visited him at Mr. Tauro's—and supped with them, the only Time I ever happened at Meal with a Jew. Just before they sat down to supper, Water was bro't by the Maid, in a white earthern Bottle which stood in a Vase or Bason: they two washed their hands, taking up the bottle and pouring the Water on the hand. I asked if this was טבל (because the Baptists say this word denotes total not partial Immersions) they said yes—& quoted a passage of the Talmud that none can eat till they had thus washed themselves in which I recollect the word טבל was twice

repeated. I did not wash, but sat down & eat with them. After sitting each in a whispering voice said Grace for himself. The Rabbi said, that in the days of Messiah, it would be allowed to the Jews to eat Swines Flesh—. I said that Abraham, Isaac and Jacob when they come with Messiah, would not eat Food as formerly; he said they would.— I said Circumcision must cease—he said not—I added Childbearing must cease when the World was full as it would be in Messiahs day, and then there would be no more to circumcise and so it must cease. I added we were then talk[g] on the Dur[a] of the K[m] that it could not be perpetual in this State of Man, but would continue only to the Conflagr[a] & Remov[a] &c New Heavens & new Earth.—He said these Inquiries bewildered & lost us in the Incomprehensibility of Futurity, & that it was best to leave them to God. He had with him a Book of an eminent Jew that flourished at Metz 600 years ago R. [Name not recorded by Stiles] He was a great Rabbin, & great Philosopher, and a great Physician. He read sundry passages in him, which together with the Cmts gave me some Idea of the Rabbinical Philosophy. — I asked him the Value of a couple of Pearls I had & of the dimensions I described; he said if good, 500 Ducats, which is about £100. Sterlg. I asked him whether he believed in any Thing of that whimsical Notion the אבן של פילוסוף —he said yes & added that he had himself beheld actual Fragment[a] of base metal into Gold—but that though it was possible, it was folly to pursue it, for that it required 6 oz Gold to furnish Matter eno' to make one qu. oz. I asked him the Composition, he said Sal amoniac &c. He discoursed of Aben Ezra and Maimonides &c. He said R. Simon Ben Johai lived & wrote in Babylon & so in Chaldee as the Targums.—I tho't he had lived at Tiberias. I asked whether there were yet to be found any Writings (besides the Script) of the Period from Moses to Malachi? He ans—they were all lost and destroyed by the Romans—. I s[d] the School of Elijah at Babylon was not affected by the Roman Desolations, but subsisted from the Times of Ezra till 1000 years after the Destruct of 2[d] Temple, and was as eminent for Literature as Jerusalem, & part[y] that the great Hillel was educated there, & Onkelos lived there—Was not this a Repository of an Antient Books? He said all the Books of the Antiquity I spoke of, were lost, except so far as Excerpta might be interwoven in the Babylon Talmud, which was the principal Remains of the Babylon Rabb Literature. He said there were 280 Hocamin or Rabbis in Poland, eight of which superintended the Whole. He is a great Cabbalist and Philosopher; which two Branches of knowledge are far more to his Tast than the Talmud. He has a son of about 13 years age—when aet. 12 he had read thro'

> the Talmud. This Rabbi was educated and spent 26 years in Amsterdam, whither he was sent aet. 8. He told me he was of the Family and ninth Descendant of R. *Selomoh Ishaaci* the celebrated Commentator who died A.D. 1180. Commonly called *Jarchi* but improperly.[5]

As is evident, it was a wide range of Jewish matter which Stiles covered with Rabbi Tobiah bar Jehudah. They were themes close to Stiles' heart and mind—baptism, the advent of Messiah, and even alchemy! The writer will return to Rabbi Tobiah's alchemy proclivity at a further point in this paper, as a clue to the rabbi's past, before his coming to America.

Stiles, then, heard Rabbi Tobiah from the Newport Synagogue's pulpit a second time. He writes in his *Diary* of November 27, 1773:

> The Rabbi preached today as he did last Saturday.[6]

Three days later, on November 30, 1773, there is a further entry:

> Spent the evening at Mr. Touro's in company with Rabbi Tobiah and Mr. Levy a London Jew Convert to Xtianity. We discoursed on Daniel LXX Weeks &c. His (the Rabbi's) Interpretation not satisfactory.[7]

This was an interesting foursome which had gathered in the Touro home: Stiles, the Congregationalist minister, Isaac Touro, *Hazzan* of the Newport Synagogue, Rabbi Tobiah, the wandering preacher, and David Levy, the convert to Christianity. From a later Stiles' *Diary Entry*,[8] it emerges that Levy had immigrated from London to Boston, and studied with Judah Monis, another convert to Christianity, who, on his conversion, was appointed Instructor in Hebrew at Harvard. As Stiles' entry reveals, the evening's discussion centered on the "Seventy Weeks" text in the Book of Daniel (9:24–27). It is a text on which had arisen heaps of Messianic calculations and interpretations. Naturally, Stiles, the Christian advocate, would find a Jewish interpretation unsatisfying. He would return to the challenging text on many future occasions.

Stiles' final entry in his *Diary* concerning the visiting rabbi appeared on December 4, 1773:

> Went to the Synagogue and heard R. Tobiah Bar Jehudah preach in Dutch—his Sermon 56 minutes.[9]

But Stiles the keen researcher and prolific note-taker, in an addendum dated December 7, 1773 in his *Hebrew-Aramaic Notebook,* recalled yet another fragment of information gathered from the rabbi:

> R. Tobiah Bar Jehudah told me that the Sapher Jatzirah was a part of the Book of Rozel ספר רזיאל w[h] the Angel Rozel gave to Adam which with Adam & other Writings came to Seth, Seth delivered it to Enoch; Enoch delivered it with his Additions to Methuselah—& he to Noah—Noah to Shem—Shem (who he said was Melchizedek) to Abraham. Ab[m] selected that upon the Creation in a Volume by itself. It came from Ab[m] to the Patriarchs and is now in being in a Quarto Volume. I have since seen & perused it.[10]

In all likelihood Stiles was shown the *Book of Raziel* published in Amsterdam in 1701. Rabbi Tobiah erred in lumping together the much earlier *Sefer Yetzirah* with the *Book of Raziel.*

As in the instance of the other rabbis who visited Newport, Ezra Stiles carried on, from November 19th to December 7th 1773, an intensive dialogue with Rabbi Tobiah Bar Jehudah.

What, then, of the question earlier posed, of Rabbi Tobiah's enthusiasm for alchemy? Here we arrive at a conjecture as to the Rabbi's esoteric proclivity. It is based on a paper presented before the Jewish Historical Society of England by Professor Cecil Roth.[11] Titled, *The King And The Cabbalist,* the presentation by Roth sheds light on the colorfully complex personality of Samuel Jacob Hayyim Falk, the so-called "Baal Shem" of London. Born in Poland about 1710, Falk indulged in a mystic-alchemistry enterprise in Westphalia, for which sorcery he was banished from that land. To avoid prosecution he fled to England. In London, he came to be known as Doctor Falk and he drew to himself a coterie of Jewish and non-Jewish devotees.

In his treatment, Professor Roth cites a passage from the writings of John Archenholz which describes the person of Falk and his mystic preoccupation. Archenholz points up the far-flung fame of Falk to the degree that

> A royal prince who eagerly searches for the philosopher's stone desired to visit him a few years ago.[12]

Further, Cecil Roth draws extensively from a manuscript-diary[13] of the Polish Jew, Zevi Hirsch Kalisch, Falk's personal attendant. In a 1747 entry, Zevi Hirsch reveals that on a certain Friday

> at one o'clock after midnight the Sage went alone into his room and remained there about two hours and afterwards called R. Tobias and R. Isak Zamoscz and me into his room. . . .[14]

There followed a series of strange doings carried on by Falk, which included a Ram's Horn, Divine Names inscribed on a table, lighted tapers of varying sizes. To all of this elaborate rite, Rabbi Tobias was very much a partner.

If the assumption is correct that Stiles' Rabbi Tobiah of 1773 is the "R. Tobias" of Falk's company, at the time of their association he would have been a young man in his twenties. Rabbi Tobiah, like Falk and his sundry *gabbaim,* was a Polish Jew, he from Cracow, they from Kalisch and Zamoscz, Falk from Podhayce, altogether an interesting *landsmanschaft* indeed. But it was this association which could well account for Rabbi Tobiah's observation, twenty-six years later, to Stiles, on the matter of his having seen the transmutation of "base metal into gold." *Falk had been the man with the Philosopher's Stone!*

But, then, the question remaining—what of the fact that Rabbi Tobiah had informed Stiles only of his Polish and Dutch sojourns; no mention of England? Here we are indebted to the minutes of New York's Spanish-Portuguese Congregation. These fill the lacuna in this matter:

> 1st of Hesvan, year 5534 (October 18, 1773)
> At a meeting of the Parnasim and Adjountos it was agreed that Ribi Tobiyah from London haveing been maintained Two weeks at the Kahal expences and haveing applied for assistance he intending for Philadelphia it is agreed to give him Eight dollars and pay Mrs. Hays account accordingly.[15]

So Rabbi Tobiah had been to London Town, after all, and was very likely, too, an associate of the renowned Dr. Falk.

A final point out of Stiles' *Diary,* nearly four years later after his encounter with Rabbi Tobiah, reveals that the Newport Congregationalist minister had his misgivings on the matter of alchemy. On rereading his own entries of previous years he was overcome by a dread concern:

> Interspersed among my miscellaneous Writings may perhaps be found Things respecting the Rosacrucian Philosophy, which may induce some to imagine that I have more Knowledge of that matter than I really have. I have no Knowledge of it at all; I never saw Transmutation, the aurific Powder, nor the Philosophers Stone; nor did I ever converse with an Adept Knowing him to be such. The only Man that I ever suspected as a real & true Adept was Rabbi Tobias of Poland, but he evaded my Interrogatories & communicated to me nothing—I believe he was only a conjectural speculative Philosopher.[16]

But, then, Rabbi Tobiah had dared to say that he had "himself beheld" it and that "it was possible." His reservation was that the alchemy process was merely economically unprofitable.

NOTES

1 *Literary Diary,* Volume IV, The Beinecke Rare Book and Manuscript Library, Yale University.

2 Ibid.

3 *Literary Diary,* Volume III, Entry: October 29, 1772: This day I received from London the Zohar, a Hebrew Folio Volume of 800 or 770 pages, Sultzbac Edit. 1684 and published at Nuremberg.

4 *Literary Diary,* Volume 1, March 28, 1769: Wrote a letter to Rev. Chauncy Whittlesey on the import of יהוה and the Trinity in the Zohar.

5 *Literary Diary,* Volume IV.

6 *Literary Diary,* Vol. IV.

7 Ibid.

8 *Literary Diary,* Vol. IV, December 2, 1773.

9 Ibid.

10 Stiles, *Hebrew-Aramaic Notebook,* Beinecke Rare Book and Manuscript Library, Yale University.

11 Cecil Roth, *Essays And Portraits In Anglo-Jewish History,* Jewish Publication Society, Philadelphia, 1962.

12 Ibid., p. 142.

13 The diary is in the Elkan Adler Collection of the Jewish Theological Seminary.

14 Roth, *Essays and Portraits,* p. 144.

15 P.A.J.H.S., Vol. 21, p. 116.

16 Stiles, *Literary Diary,* Vol VII.

THE REBELLIONS DURING THE REIGN OF DAVID

An Inquiry into Social Dynamics in Ancient Israel

MARTIN A. COHEN

Hebrew Union College—Jewish Institute of Religion

New York

1. *The Problem*

Like other great men King David had no lack of enemies. The eruption of three rebellions during his reign testifies to a pervasive discontent beneath his tenuous union of Israel and Judah. Absalom's rebellion chased him ignominiously from Jerusalem, and later across the Jordan; Sheba's revolt stunned him into an admission that it was worse than Absalom's. The third rebellion, Adonijah's, was nipped in the bud, but prospectively it was no less terrifying.

It is axiomatic that revolts are not fed by contented men. No leader, however persuasive or charismatic, can generate a successful uprising unless social conditions are propitious. If revolts are to become revolutions, discontent with conditions of life must rankle among large segments of the populace. They must lay their troubles at the doorstep of the regime and must conclude that their plight can be mitigated by nothing short of force. At the same time, power elements opposed to the regime must be willing to provide support for the rebellion in return for the hope of eventual increased control of the society.[1]

Yet, the biblical account treats the rebellions as if they were entirely the product of self-seeking leaders, conceived full-blown, like Athene from Zeus' head. It leaves the impression that there were no substantial grievances; that the people were lured or cozened into these revolts; that even close associates, like Absalom's two hundred companions, bovinely followed him "in their simplicity."[2]

A close look at the biblical narratives dealing with the rebellions (II Sam. 9–20 and I Kings 1–2; and the events, if not the present form, of II Sam. 24 and 21.1–14) suggests that this approach was deliberate. This narrative has a complex history of transmission and redaction, going back from its present Deuteronomistic casing to an original author, contemporary with the events described.[3] Who this author was is not known; he has been identified with Ahimaaz,[4] Abiathar,[5] and Zabud,[6] son of the prophet Nathan. But one fact is clear. From the first writing, down to and perhaps including, the final stages of its retouching, the narrative was the work of men sympathetic to David. Even if the Deuteronomists themselves were not the servants of his dynasty, they depended upon the ideology it had created. This means that the authors and revisers of the narrative, however much they might have wished to write objectively, were in no position to do so. They were all spokesmen for the Davidic house. They could not therefore take the liberty of dilating on the rebels' grievances or interpreting events embarrassing to the dynasty.

Embarrassing enough were the bald facts of the history of David's monarchy—David's affair with Bathsheba and his dexterous disposal of Uriah; his delivery of Saul's sons to the Gibeonites; the prolonged absence of the heir apparent, Absalom, from the court, hardly explained as a banishment for the murder of Amnon, for this act was not unjustified; and, of course, the scars of the rebellions themselves.

Events like these could easily have played into the hands of the adversaries of the Davidic dynasty, and it is not difficult to imagine what damaging interpretations they might have concocted. They might have seized on the fact of the rebellions to dispute David's reputation for equity and justice. They might have insisted that Absalom's long removal from the court betrayed the king's cruelty or perhaps even fear of his son; and they could point to the fact that in Absalom's restoration popular pressure was in far greater evidence than paternal love. They might have claimed that David's delivery of Saul's seed royal to the Gibeonites smacked of perfidy. From David's dallying with Bathsheba they might have cast a cloud of discomfort, if not illegitimacy, on Solomon and his successors. And on the basis of David's treatment of Uriah they might have tried to persuade the populace that the founder of Judah's throne, far from being a saint, was nothing but an unprincipled rogue.

It is because of such possible claims that our narrative had to be written. In Solomon's days the throne had to justify the reign of

David. Although the facts of David's public life were too notorious to be suppressed or altered, they could be presented by a skillful writer in such a way as to cloak David's image in the most favorable possible light.

The first author of the narrative was an image builder, and his successors followed his lead. Without concealing the irrepressible facts of David's life, they perpetuated the exalted picture of David that has become traditional in Judaism and Christianity.

The narrative, known as the Court History, Family History [of David], or History of the Throne Succession, might more felicitously be called the "Apology for the Throne of David" or, as we shall call it, simply the Apology.

2. *The Data*

The three rebellions are linked by a single theme—the struggle between the premonarchical elements in Israel-Judah and the bureaucracy created by David.

This fact is clearest from the third rebellion, where Adonijah is supported by Joab and Abiathar, and Solomon by Zadok and Benaiah. Both Zadok and Benaiah were bureaucratic appointments. There is no evidence to connect them with power sources outside the palace, and the Bible first mentions them in connection with David. Zadok may even have been the Jebusite high priest in Jerusalem at the time of its capture by David. Both Benaiah and Zadok were wholly dependent upon the king. In any crisis their loyalty to the monarch would be insured.

On the other hand, both Joab, as commander of the united militias of Israel and Judah, and Abiathar, as the leading Shilonite priest, had connections with power sources antedating the monarchy and responsible for its creation.[7]

The political positions of both Solomon and Adonijah coincided with those of their respective backers. Like Benaiah and Zadok, Solomon was David's man, his claim to the throne resting entirely on his father's appointment. On the other hand, Adonijah could claim the monarchy on primogeniture. The Bible pointedly mentions that Adonijah was David's oldest son, "born after Absalom," implying that he was the heir apparent.[8]

The defection to Adonijah of Joab and his armies—for without his armies the defection would have been meaningless—as well as of

Abiathar and his sources of support, suggests a break between the old power in the provinces and the new power concentrated in Jerusalem.

Substantiating this analysis is the fact that in addition to Benaiah and Zadok, Solomon was joined by other bureaucratic elements: Nathan, the court prophet; David's elite guard, the *gibborey-hayyil;* and the mercenary Cherethites and Pelethites.

Why this alignment took place is not explained in the Bible.

The account of the second rebellion discloses a similar alignment of forces. On first glance the rebellion may appear as a secession by Israel from its union with Judah.[9] The Apology crisply states that "all the men of Israel went up from following David, and followed Sheba, the son of Bichri," while "the men of Judah followed their king steadfastly." Sheba, described as "a man of the hill country of Ephraim," belonged to the tribe of Benjamin and was politically, if not familially, close to the house of Saul. He may have represented opponents of David who longed for the pre-Davidic political structures of the North.[10]

The revolutionaries' declaration, "We have no portion in David, neither have we inheritance in the son of Jesse," verbalized the rebels' conviction that David had failed to show them justice and implied the utter hopelessness of any attempts at peaceful redress of their grievances.

The Apologist lingers on the murder of Amasa and Sheba rather than on the details of the revolt.[11] But what he does disclose suggests that the combined armies of Israel and Judah, and their officers, allied themselves against David!

(1) At the time of the revolt the commander of these armies was Amasa, a Judite from Jezreel and a nephew of David!

(2) At the onset of the rebellion David ordered Amasa, whom he had appointed commander of the armies in Joab's place after Absalom's rebellion, to convoke the men of Judah within three days. Israel's troops were apparently already lost to Jerusalem or were considered lost. Amasa went off, "but," says the Apology cryptically, "he delayed beyond the set time which had been appointed him."

(3) At this juncture David exclaimed that Sheba could now cause more harm than Absalom did.[12]

(4) David dispatched a group of mercenaries, the "servants of the king," under Abishai, in pursuit of Sheba,[13] and then sent

the Cherethites and the Pelethites, along with Joab and "his men." Joab's "men" might have been defectors from the ranks of the Judite forces or, more likely, his personal guard. The term could not have referred to the armies of Judah, the "men of Judah" whom Amasa went to fetch, for these, at the time, were Amasa's men and not Joab's.

(5) Joab overtook Amasa "at the great stone which is in Gibeon." This was within the territory of Benjamin, the very seat of the rebellion!

(6) Joab killed Amasa with impunity.

(7) Joab then rallied around him all the men assembled there, calling out "Whoever favors Joab and whoever is for David, let him follow Joab."[14] Since Joab would hardly have had to use such persuasion with David's mercenaries, or to men previously committed to David or himself, it is likely that he was addressing troops of the national armies of Israel-Judah that remained under Amasa to fight against David.

(8) Not until this juncture did Joab begin his victorious campaign against Sheba.

This hypothesis would explain David's anxiety over Sheba's strength, as well as Joab's role in bringing David victory once Amasa was out of the way.

In Absalom's rebellion the cleavage between the Old Guard and the New appears in greatest clarity.

For purposes of analysis the narrative is divisible as follows:

(1) The conspiracy (II Sam. 15:1–6).
(2) The eruption of the rebellion (15:7–37).
(3) Other conspiracies (16:1–15).
(4) Espionage and counterespionage (16:2c–17.23. Also 15: 32–37).
(5) The great battle and Absalom's death (17:24–18:15).
(6) The restoration of national unity (18:16–19:44).

It is significant that two revolutionary leaders, Saul's son, Meribaal, and the Saulide Shimei, each seeking power for himself, joined Absalom for the sake of overthrowing the common foe. As we might have suspected from an enemy of David, Shimei accused the king of spilling "all the blood of the house of Saul."[15]

Absalom's ranks were swelled by men from both Judah and Israel. The Apology declares that "Absalom stole the hearts of the men of Israel," and "the hearts of the men of Israel have gone after Absalom," but the name "Israel" signifies Israel-Judah.[16]

Various facts point to the broad involvement by Judites in the revolt: (1) Absalom himself was a Judite. (2) He was anointed king in Hebron, the old capital of Judah. (3) Accompanying Absalom to Hebron were two hundred Jerusalemites. There is little probability that they were all from the Northern kingdom. We may reasonably assume that they came from the royal court, where Judites were present in large, if not preponderant numbers. (4) Absalom's entourage included a leading Judite, the Gilonite priest Ahibaal (Ahithophel), formerly a highly respected advisor of David.[17] (5) Hushai advised Absalom to gather together "all Israel . . . from Dan to Beersheba," [18] a phrase which in David's time and in a military setting, must be understood in its literal sense. (6) In his flight from Jerusalem David relied on his mercenaries. He fled, says the Apology, with "all his servants . . . and all the Cherethites, and all the Pelethites and all the six hundred Gittites who had followed after him from Gath." [19] It also asserts that he was accompanied by "all the people" in his flight, but fails to specify who and how many they were.[20] It clearly does not say "the army," Joab's force. About this force the Apology maintains a baffling silence.

Yet, at the same time, the account mentions, almost parenthetically, that Absalom had removed the Judite Joab from his position over *the army*—that is the combined armies of Israel and Judah—and replaced him with Amasa, also a Judite! [21] Then, at the end of the rebellion, when David wishes to regain the favor of the defectors, we read that he promises to retain Amasa as head of the army, and he keeps his promise. Amasa continues as army commander until Joab murders him and resumes his former position.[22] It, therefore, seems natural to conclude that the armies of Israel and Judah abandoned David and joined Absalom in his revolt.

Whether Abiathar also defected to Absalom is moot. A cursory reading of the Apology creates the impression that Abiathar remained loyal to David, carrying the ark at his behest and receiving intelligence from David's counselor, Hushai. On closer scrutiny the impression fades. In this section of the narrative Zadok is twice mentioned without Abiathar. When David decides to return the ark to Jerusalem, he issues his command to Zadok alone, though later we read that Abiathar joined Zadok. Furthermore, in speaking to Zadok alone, the king utters a confusing sentence: "Do you (singular) see? Return (singular) to the city in peace, along with Ahimaaz, your (singular) son, *and Jonathan, the son of Abiathar, your* (plural) *sons with you* (plural)." The awkward insertion of a reference to Abiathar and his son suggests an alteration of the text.

This suspicion is heightened by an examination of II Sam. 15.24, where Zadok bears the ark alone. In its midst, is a mystifying reference to Abiathar:

והנה גם צדוק וכל הלוים אתו נשאים את ארון ברית האלהים ויצקו את ארון האלהים ויעל אביתר עד תם כל העם לעבור מן העיר

A rabbinic tradition sees Absalom's rebellion as initiating the decline of Abiathar's office. According to the rabbis, both Abiathar and Zadok consulted the Deity; Zadok was answered favorably, while Abiathar received no answer at all. David, realizing that the Holy Presence had forsaken Abiathar, replaced him with Zadok. The rabbis understand the word ויעל to connote Abiathar's removal.[23]

Abiathar disappears until Adonijah's rebellion, when we find him to have been sharing his old position with Zadok.

Exactly what happened to Abiathar in Absalom's rebellion cannot be reconstructed with certainty. Quite possibly Abiathar's "going up" was really a defection, allowing David the opportunity to elevate Zadok.

Aside from Abiathar's dubious role, the familiar pattern is visible in this rebellion. David and his bureaucratic structure are pitted against a coalition of Old Guard elements, comprising Saulides and other Northerners, as well as the national armies of Israel-Judah. Again, the Apology does not explain the reasons for the alignments.

The peculiar circumstances surrounding both the conclusion and the inception of the revolt merit detailed consideration.

With respect to the conclusion, it is apparent that David did not achieve a spectacular triumph. If Absalom's death brought on the despair and strife characteristic of revolutionary factions which have lost their cohesive leader, it did not melt their resolve. If "all Israel fled, everyone to his tent,"[24] the flight was certainly not permanent.

This is obvious from the fact that the rebellion did not end in a rout of the rebels and the punishment of their leaders, but in compromise. David even restored the revolutionaries to favor. Meribaal returned to court after abjectly pleading for forgiveness and blaming his defection on his servant, Ziba.[25] Shimei, who spat upon and cursed David, also received David's pardon. When Joab's brother, Abishai, suggested that Shimei be put to death, he was severely rebuked by the king.[26] In addition, the people of Israel and Judah were permitted to welcome back their king. The army returned to David, commanded not by Joab but by the rebel Amasa!

Why the rebels did not regroup and continue the fight is nowhere analyzed, but it is reasonable to assume that, with the defeat of their armies and Absalom's death, they could not see the possibility of victory or were unwilling to face an internecine struggle for the leadership of their motley forces. The fact is that they did make peace. Not long afterwards many, if not most of them, reappeared as revolutionaries under Sheba.

Far more mystifying is the introductory section of the narrative of Absalom's rebellion. It purports to reveal something about Absalom's development of a revolutionary nucleus to the point where he could have himself proclaimed king at Hebron. According to the Bible, or at least the Septuagint,[27] four years elapsed between Absalom's first desire for the throne and his open break with David. Yet, during this period, the Bible pictures Absalom as aspiring to become not king, but "a judge in the land," and his judicial activity is the only one it mentions.

Also perplexing is the description and procedure of Absalom's court. Absalom, says the Apology, would arise[28] early in the morning and go to the "way of the gate" of the city—patently Jerusalem—to await litigants bringing cases to the king. As a man approached, Absalom would call to him and ask his city; and when the reply came that the man was from "such and such a tribe in Israel," Absalom forthwith proclaimed his case to be just, lamenting that "there is no man deputed by the king to hear you." In this way, according to the Apology, Absalom lured the loyalty of large numbers of men, indeed "the hearts of the men of Israel."

This sketchy account pullulates with anomalies:

(1) The Apology implies that Absalom never opposed the petitions of the plaintiffs.

(2) His favorable decisions resulted not from pondering the substance of a case, but from learning that the petitioner came from "one of the tribes of Israel."

(3) The number of people coming directly to the king seems to have been so large that, by wooing them, Absalom could steal "the hearts of the men of Israel." One may ask why these men did not seek redress for their grievances in local courts or, if the cases belonged in the capital, in a Jerusalem court

under the king's jurisdiction? Why did they bring them to the king? Rulers, even in peaceful times, rarely preside over a court of claims all day. More regularly, they delegate judicial authority to functionaries, though they may reserve for themselves the right of final decision.

(4) Though Absalom frankly and repeatedly explained to the hordes of provincial plaintiffs that the king had deputed no one to hear their claims, this apparently did not become known, and people kept coming to Jerusalem—and leaving as Absalom's allies.

(5) Strangest of all facts are Absalom's unaccountable wish to be a judge and the Apology's stress on the improvised courtroom as the breeding place for the revolt.[29]

The questions raised by these facts can all be answered on the basis of the element common to all the rebellions—the struggle between Old Guard interests, harking positionally back to premonarchical days, and the structures of David's bureaucracy.

3. *The Context of David's Reign*

The question arises as to which of David's policies could have provoked resentment sufficient for Old Guard leadership and large segments of the populace to join in successive rebellions.

The evidence points to the characteristic policy of David's reign—the centralization and consolidation of the separate regions or tribes of Israel and Judah into a tightly unified and efficient state and, as a necessary corollary, the concentration of all possible political power in the office and person of the king. The results of this policy become apparent from a comparison of the monarchies of Saul and Solomon.

In Israel, the monarchy was less a child of love than of military force. Threatened with annihilation by the Philistines, the leadership of the loosely federated tribes decided, not without hesitation, to unite the separate militias under a supratribal leader. As authority figure for the new organization, and hence as their spokesman and subordinate, the tribal leaders selected Saul.[30]

The elders could not have been insensitive to the danger that a supratribal institution might accumulate sufficient power to subordinate them completely. Yet they had no viable alternative to its creation. If they demurred for long, they faced the danger of enslavement by the Philistines.

The elders took precautions to restrict the monarchy's opportunities for power building. They selected Saul from a weak tribe and confined his activity to the military sphere. Even Saul's armies remained the militias of the tribes, the peasant militia, as Max Weber happily called them,[31] officered by the Old Guard, or at least men loyal to it. It is reasonable to assume that as a group these officers were prepared to follow Saul's command as long as it appeared in the interest of the united tribes. The Bible does not speak of Saul's acquiring a mercenary army. He certainly possessed none at the beginning of his reign.

To contain ambitions aroused by his new office, the elders subordinated Saul to their seer-priests, the interpreters of Yahweh. Since they were supported by the tribal leaders they could be depended upon to hear Yahweh's word in accordance with Old Guard needs. The Old Guard, therefore, had Saul anointed by the seer-priest, Samuel. When Saul later moved to extend his power, they had Samuel depose him in Yahweh's name.

Very likely the elders, aware of its potential dangers, conceived of the monarchy as an *ad hoc* institution, subject to review at the successful conclusion of the war. Significantly, the incumbent of the new position at first appears to have borne not the title "king" (*melekh*) but "leader" or "military leader" (*nagid*).[32] His function is described as that of a *shofet*. In Saul's day as in previous centuries, the word *shofet* denoted a military leader.[33]

The prolongation of the Philistine war afforded Saul licit opportunities to improve his straitened position. It retained him in the public eye and enabled him to lure the primary loyalties of many of his soldiers away from their respective tribes. He achieved this unimpeachably by bestowing distinctions on the *gibborey-hayyil*. The elders could not have failed to recognize Saul's growing advantage and the danger of losing the war to him even if they vanquished the Philistines. Since the need for military unity remained, they could hardly return to their ineffective premonarchical structures. Their best alternative was to replace Saul with a relatively powerless supratribal leader. But if they deposed Saul publicly they risked civil war and Philistine conquest. They, therefore, chose to retain Saul, but to shift the real source of authority to a new leader. This is the background of their conspiracy with David.

In stunning contrast, the monarchy transferred by David to Solomon had become absolute. David triumphantly demonstrated this by appointing Solomon not by law or custom, by consultation or compromise, but simply by fiat. David had become the state, and Solomon, at least in the early years of his reign, could reap the benefits of this achievement.

By Solomon's reign, the old armies had been superseded as the military arm of the State by mercenary troops wedded to the crown. The old seer-priesthood had lost its status with the removal of Abiathar from royal priesthood.[34] The old tribal leaders had relinquished their last vestiges of real autonomy. Solomon even effaced their old boundaries and rezoned their lands into twelve administrative districts, each under an officer of the crown.[35] The demise of the old autonomy had to be accompanied by the abrogation of local laws and customs interfering with Jerusalem's policies of centralization. It is likely that one such change involved the establishment of a uniform solar calendar for the entire land.[36]

The process of centralization facilitated the imposition of two obligations to the monarch unheard of in Saul's day—a levy of taxes and a levy of men. The taxes went to support a massive bureaucracy, descending from the king to the nine- or ten-man royal council, the twelve district officials, a host of lesser officials, and, at the bottom, the mercenary armies and the legion of workers impressed into the royal corvée.[37] With the help of this cheap labor and rationalized organization, Solomon engaged in his extensive construction projects, capped by the Temple, the palace, store cities, and a fleet to bring wealth and luxuries from the remote corners of the known world. The biblical writer insists that the bondservants came from subjects "who were not of the children of Israel," and that the Israelites served the king as "his soldiers and aides and his generals and his captains, and officers of his chariots and horsemen."[38] But this defense obliquely reveals that the children of Israel were also marshaled into service.

4. *The Genius of David*

David attained kingship over Israel, de jure, when its elders selected him to replace Saul. When Saul discovered the conspiracy, David was compelled to take refuge in his native Judah. The paucity of David's troops testifies convincingly to the fact that he was not accompanied by hosts from the North.[39] Their plot exposed, the leaders of Israel closed ranks with Saul to avoid plunging their nation into internecine war.

David's resumption of his climb to power reveals the extent of his genius. After his flight, his life falls into two epochs, divided by his selection as king over the combined territories of Israel and Judah. The details of the first period revolve mainly around his relationship with the house of Saul:

(1) His reaction to the death of Saul and Jonathan.
(2) The "long war" against Israel, in which "David waxed stronger and stronger, and the house of Saul waxed weaker and weaker."
(3) Abner's bid for union with Judah.
(4) The bid for union by Baanah and Rechab.
(5) The bid for peace and union by the elders of Israel.

These events are all intimately connected.

It was in the interest of Judah, now united, to embark on an expansionist policy for the sake of its own protection and survival. As the first step in this direction, Judah set out to incorporate its war-torn neighbor to the north. The threat this posed to Israel accounts for the outbreak of warfare between David and Ishbaal. The fact that the monarchs could devote their attention to warfare with one another and the failure of any other nation to intervene indicate that at the time both Israel and Judah were free from threats of absorption or annihilation by outside powers. The Philistines, after their impressive victory at Gilboa, did not capitalize on their advantage and apparently could not. They disappear from the biblical scene until David becomes monarch of the United Kingdom of Israel and Judah. When they return to fight it is to avoid enslavement by David and not to crush his state.[40]

The theory that David, as King of Judah, was an ally or vassal of the Philistines cannot be supported. On the assumption that the Philistines equaled or surpassed David in strength, it would be impossible to explain their delay in moving against him.[41]

In order to achieve maximum benefit from a possible incorporation of its neighbor, it was in Judah's interest to win the war at the least possible cost to Israel's men and materiel. With this end in mind, Judah's best tack would be to attain military advantage and then sit back and watch its enemy deteriorate politically. The pursuit of this tactic by Judah would account for the Bible's suspension of its narrative of the warfare immediately after recording Judah's attainment of military advantage.[42] It would also explain the inception of the period of instability in Israel's government that led eventually to the elders' suit for peace.

Political prudence would dictate a policy of restraint for anyone seeking maximum benefit from such a period of instability. David's patience was remarkable. He did not intervene in Israel's affairs until he was asked to do so by the elders of Israel. And then he came in not as a foe, but as a savior.

Political considerations can also explain Abner's treason. With the tide of battle decisively against the North, Abner could fight to the last man or seek a peace that might permit the North to retain some measure of its dignity. Abner and the members of the power group behind him chose David over a hero's grave. Abner, therefore, deposed Ishbaal and went to Hebron to bargain with David (II Sam. 3:17 ff.).

In return for his offer to capitulate, Abner doubtless sought the retention of some of Israel's prerogatives, and a position in David's administration. The post for which Abner was best qualified was that of supreme commander of the combined armies of Israel and Judah.

Abner's murder by Joab can also be explained politically. Without much ingenuity, David's opponents could have laid the crime at the doorstep of the palace. They might have observed that it was in David's interest to rid himself of Abner. Abner had proved to be a traitor, a dethroner of a monarch, and hence incapable of being trusted. Furthermore, with Abner out of the way, the North would deteriorate more rapidly, thus enhancing David's bargaining power. They might also have noted that Joab was neither punished nor reprehended for his crime. Since he had a grudge against Abner, and an interest in preventing him from joining David's camp, he might have been instructed to dispose of Abner and accept David's painless reprimand.[43]

Political considerations can also explain David's public displays of mourning for Abner, Ishbaal, and even the slain heroes of Gilboa.[44] Regardless of how David may have felt about these men personally, the political wisdom of his public mourning and his execution of the regicides can hardly be placed in doubt.

Enervated by internal strife and reconciled to political subordination, the elders of Israel coming to Hebron to offer their nation to David contrasted strikingly with their counterparts who enthroned Saul and then selected David as his replacement. At Hebron Israel's elders were cast not as kingmakers, but as suppliants. Like other disadvantaged leaders, they came imploringly to a mightier force, pledging their readiness to join and support it. They were prepared to compromise with the integrity of their polity in return for the preservation of some part, however small, of the material and political advantage that Israel had attained.

In accepting their offer of union, David won a far less costly victory than he would have attained in attempting to impose this union by force.

Once Israel and Judah were joined David, not unnaturally, turned his attention to securing his new borders and consolidating his kingdom. The major steps taken by David for the achievement of this goal were:

(1) David's conversion of the erstwhile Jebusite stronghold of Jerusalem into the capital of his new state.[45]

(2) His transfer there of the ancient Shilonite ark, thus tying it to his dynasty.

(3) His assumption of the role of chief priest in the procession which brought the ark into Jerusalem,[46] signifying that henceforth he would be the ultimate determinant of Yahweh's will.

(4) His struggle to control the traditional priesthood with its strong loyalties among the people and ties to traditional sources of power. The retention of the priesthood and restoration of Abiathar to his position appear to have been part of the arrangement worked out by David and Israel's elders in Hebron before the union of their two states. It would have been best for the monarchy to remove the old priesthood completely. Unable to do so, David moved to neutralize its power through the appointment and retention of Zadok. It was Solomon who removed the traditional priesthood at a time when the monarchy in Israel-Judah was approaching or had already achieved absolutism.

(5) David's struggle for military autonomy. It was also in David's interest to wean himself from dependence upon the national armies, rooted in Old Guard sources of power and hence always a potential threat to the monarchy. David was in no position to dissolve these forces. But he did begin to build armies of mercenaries, among them the Cherethites and Pelethites, the "six hundred," the "thirty," and the *gibborey-hayyil*.[47] The highest post among David's own troops was given to Benaiah, and David sought to raise his position to equivalence with Joab's. This parity was not attained until late in David's reign or early in Solomon's. When Solomon had Joab put out of the way he

did not fill the vacancy but left Benaiah as the highest ranking military figure.[48]

(6) Finally, as the culmination of David's efforts, his preparations to conduct a census throughout Israel-Judah.

The account of the census in II Sam. 24, enveloped in the Deuteronomic ideology and form, hinges on three extractable historical facts: David's initiation of the census; a popular reaction against it, explained as "unconstitutional," or, in accordance with the ideology of the day "sinful"; and the popular interpretation of a plague occurring around the time of the census as a punishment for David's wrongdoing.

The Deuteronomic writers and redactors, unable to suppress or alter these notorious facts transmitted by tradition, sought to do the best they could with them. They tried to protect David by attributing the idea of the census to Yahweh, much to the embarrassment of the later Chronicler, who shifted the blame to Satan.[49] They could not change the negative image of the census itself. It was a wrongdoing, a sin requiring punishment. But since it was not fully David's fault, David is given a choice of three punishments. The Deuteronomic writers thus created a paradox: Yahweh orders David to conduct the census and David, in obeying, sins. Further complicating matters, but bringing the account to a happy and Deuteronomically desirable conclusion, the Deuteronomists explained that the plague was stayed when David offered sacrifices to Yahweh on Araunah's threshing floor. This was the traditional site of the Jerusalem Temple, regarded by the Deuteronomic writers as Yahweh's chosen dwelling.[50]

The question which naturally arises is: "What was unconstitutional or sinful about David's census?" As the highest interpreter of the national ideology David would not have admitted to its unconstitutionality. Nor would he have taken such a step unless he deemed it beneficial to his polity. The claim of unconstitutionality would obviously have been raised by his opponents in the Old Guard. A census in Israel would facilitate the collection of taxes and the drafting of men for the king's corvée, enhancing the strength of the monarchy at the expense of the Old Guard and the populace. The Old Guard and their supporters therefore naturally regarded David's action as a sin.

David apparently discontinued this census, but eventually others were taken. In Solomon's time the census was no longer considered a sin.[51]

5. *The Direction of the Rebellions*

While one may choose to view the three rebellions as unconnected, it is equally possible to regard them as the three successive stages of Old Guard reaction to David's policies of consolidation. With the failure of the third rebellion, the Old Guard's power was broken and the monarchy proceeded to tighten its grip over Israel's social and economic life.[52] The failure of the Old Guard cannot be attributed to poor judgment on the part of its leadership. Circumstances beyond its control had brought about the situation which eventually spelled its doom.

The elders of Israel who first decided to establish the supratribal office that became the monarchy were not oblivious to its inherent dangers; nevertheless, they established it, for the dangers in not creating it were even greater. So too, the later elders of Israel who brought the olive branch to King David recognized that of the alternatives they faced none would assure them a return to their palmy past. The one they chose at least had the possibility of allowing them to retain a portion of this past. Their readiness to throw their support behind David implies the monarch's willingness to guarantee a measure of their status and power. Such an arrangement is reflected in the continuation of representatives of the Old Guard priesthood and army in the royal cabinet. With his superior military and political position David, of course, held the upper hand in the new coalition.

Barring a national catastrophe, the Old Guard could not upset this balance of power. All they could hope for was a retention of their position. The monarchy, more favorably situated, could move to increase its power at the Old Guard's expense. This appears to have been the monarchy's program. The resulting tensions and struggles explain the three outbreaks of violence.

We cannot assume that the Old Guard precipitately rushed to armed rebellion at the monarchy's first attempts to constrict its power. A civil war could only reduce its own power and surplus. We must assume that the Old Guard repeatedly sought peaceful redress for its grievances before resorting to force. It is possible to understand the enigmatic account in II Sam 15:1–16 as the transition between the last efforts for a peaceful reconciliation and the inception of the first rebellion.

(1) One cannot harbor the naive assumption that the king or his court in Jerusalem concerned itself with all the people's cases. It

would have been more likely for this court to have dealt with extraordinary cases.

(2) The plaintiffs are described not as Judites or Israelites, but as individuals belonging to "one of the tribes of Israel," a term recalling the premonarchical political structures.

(3) It is unlikely that all or even many of the men who eventually joined the rebellion brought their cases to Jerusalem. It would be much more natural to assume that the plaintiffs were leaders of groups, and that by attracting them Absalom could win over their retainers and "steal the hearts of the men of Israel."

(4) The most natural complaint which men of "the tribes of Israel" could be expected to bring to Jerusalem would involve the royal encroachment on their prerogatives. This would explain why David suspended his court.

This explanation, to be sure, is highly hypothetical and conjectural, as all explanations of II Sam. 15:1–16 must be, for want of sufficient data. However, it does account consistently and coherently for all the details in this section.

In each of the revolts, the men of the Old Guard appear to have sought the retention of the maximum possible amount of power and surplus. It was in their interest to maintain the united monarchy, with guarantees of their prerogatives, for the united monarchy offered them the possibility of greater power and surplus than a smaller, independent unit of their own creation. The Old Guard, therefore, appealed to aggrieved men in both Israel and Judah and secured Absalom, David's heir presumptive, as their leader. Evidently, there was some uncertainty as to whether David would respect the principle of primogeniture. This would have afforded Absalom sufficient inducement to revolt, and would explain Absalom's desire to be made a *shofet* in the land. The *shofet* had been a rallying point of autonomous groups of tribes concerned with mutual defense. Though not a king, he was a source of unity and stability. By stating that he wished to be a *shofet*—not a *melekh*—Absalom proclaimed that under his regime the tribes or regions would find the kind of unity they had anticipated when the monarchy was first established.

The failure of Absalom's revolt demonstrated that David and his mercenary troops were too strong to be dislodged. Old Guard elements in both Israel and Judah then fomented a second rebellion, apparently aimed at the creation of a new state including territory from both Israel and Judah and isolating David and his forces in a small pocket around Jerusalem.

This rebellion likewise failed. The Old Guard, recognizing that they could not hope to secure their independence in the immediate future, faced two alternatives: a fight to the death or full subordination to the New Guard. The Old Guard leaders chose to accept the yoke of David's earthly kingdom.

They still had alternatives. They could passively resign themselves to absolutism or join with sympathetic elements in the New Guard to place some measure of restraint on David's will. Not unnaturally they chose the latter alternative, and this eventually led to the third rebellion. In supporting Adonijah they upheld the binding principle of legal transfer of monarchical power, while David's side championed the monarch's right to choose his successor arbitrarily.

Had Adonijah's rebellion succeeded, it would have marked an arrest, but not a reversal, of the policy of centralization, and would have given some small measure of comfort to the Old Guard. But with its failure David moved swiftly toward absolute power.[53]

NOTES

I wish to acknowledge with gratitude the assistance and encouragement given to me in the preparation of this paper by Professor Harry M. Orlinsky, currently president of the Society of Biblical Literature.

1 A. Meusel, "Revolution and Counter-Revolution," *Encyclopedia of the Social Sciences,* Vol. XIII (1937), p. 367; Gaetano Mosca, *The Ruling Class* (trans. by Hannah D. Hahn, New York: 1939), p. 65; N. S. Timasheff, *War and Revolution* (New York: 1965), p. 68. Cf. also P. A. Sorokin, *The Sociology of Revolution* (Philadelphia and London: 1925), p. 367; G. S. Pettee, *The Process of Revolution* (New York: 1938), pp. 10 and 33; and Chateaubriand's classical *Essai historique, politique et moral sur les révolutions anciennes et modernes,* (London: 1815), especially p. 19.

On the ideals and symbolism of revolutions see E. Sapir, "Symbolism," *Encyclopedia of the Social Sciences* Vol. VII (New York: 1930), pp. 492–495. See also C. D. Burns, *The Principles of Revolution* (London: 1920), p. 110; G. Ferrero, *The Principles of Power* (trans. by T. R. Jaeckel, New York: 1942), p. 135; and S. Jankélevitch, *Révolution et tradition* (Paris: 1947), pp. 19 f., 26 f. and 196 ff.

2 II Sam. 15:11.

3 See, e.g., R. H. Pfeiffer, *Introduction to the Old Testament* (New York: 1948), pp. 353 ff., and O. Eissfeldt, *The Old Testament: An Introduction* (trans. P. R. Ackroyd, Oxford: 1965), pp. 137 ff., 265 f., See also K. Budde, *Die Bücher Samuel* (Tübingen-Leipzig, 1902), pp. xvii f., and *Geschichte der althebräischen Literatur* (Leipzig: 1906), pp. 35 ff.; L. Rost, *Die Überlieferung von der Thronnachfolge Davids* (Stuttgart: 1926), pp. 82 ff.; O. Eissfeldt, *Die Komposition der Samuelisbücher* (Leipzig: 1931), pp. 34 ff.; M. Noth, *Überlieferungsgeschichtliche Studien* I (Halle [Saale]: 1943), pp. 61 ff.; and R. A. Carlson, *David, The Chosen King* (Uppsala: 1964), p. 430.

4 A. Klostermann, *Die Bücher Samuelis und der Könige* (Nördlingen: 1887), pp. xxxii f.

5 B. Duhm, *Das Buch Jeremia* (Tübingen: 1901), p. 3.

[6] Vriezen, T. C. "De Compositie van de Sameül Boeken," *Orientalia Neerlandica,* (Leiden: 1948), pp. 167 ff.

[7] See M. A. Cohen, "The Role of the Shilonite Priesthood in the United Monarchy of Ancient Israel," *HUCA* XXXVI (1965), pp. 63, 86 ff., 94 ff. See also R. Halevi, "חדושי פולחן של דוד המלך" in בית מקרא IV (39), (1970), pp. 91 ff. Halevi, however, does not understand my terms "Old Guard" and "New Guard."

[8] I Kings 1:6. In II Sam. 3:2–5 we find a list of David's oldest sons, Amnon, Chileab (of whom nothing further is said), Absalom, Adonijah, and Shephatiah and Ithream (neither of whom is again mentioned in II Sam.) From I Sam. 25:42 f. it is possible to conclude that one or more of these sons were born before David was ensconced in Hebron. II Sam. 5:13–16 lists David's sons subsequently born in Jerusalem. Cf. I Chr. 3.1 ff.

On primogeniture in the Ancient Near East, see G. R. Driver and J. C. Miles, eds., *The Babylonian Laws,* Vol. 1 (Oxford: 1952), p. 331, and I. Mendelsohn, "On the Preferential Status of the Eldest Son," *BASOR,* 156 (1959), pp. 38–40.

[9] So, for example, S. A. Cook, "Notes on the Composition of 2 Samuel," *AJSL,* XVII (1899), p. 166; A. Lods, *Israel* (New York: 1932), p. 365.

[10] II Sam. 20.1 f., 21. Gen. 46.21 and I Chron. 7.6 mention Becher as a son of Benjamin, while Becorath in I Sam. 9.1 is an ancestor of Saul. Modern commentators have observed this. Cf., for example, O. Thenius—M. Loehr, *Die Bücher Samuels* (Leipzig: 1898), p. 246; A. F. Kirkpatrick, *Samuel II* (Cambridge: 1897), p. 185; and H. W. Hertzberg, *I and II Samuel* (trans. J. S Bowden, Philadelphia: 1964), p. 371.

[11] It is because of the Apologist's handling of the rebellion that the real conflict appears overshadowed and commentators like Hertzberg, *op. cit.,* p. 373, are led to conclude erroneously, that "things never get to the point of a battle." The Apologist presents Sheba's rebellion as a coda to Absalom's. On this see the commentators, for example, K. Budde, *Samuel,* pp. 295 f.

[12] II Sam. 20.4 ff. The term "the people," (perhaps better, "the troops") found frequently in this narrative, refers to David's followers. The people as a whole in all probability flocked to Sheba's side. The Apologist's inadequate account of the campaign against Sheba has the further effect of suggesting that Sheba had little support. See, for example, J. Bright, *A History of Israel* (Philadelphia: 1959), p. 189. However, for all his art, the Apologist could not suppress the details that imply a massive uprising.

[13] As is regularly recognized, the "mighty men" are professional soldiers. Cf. W. McKane, *I and II Samuel* (London: 1963), p. 278.

[14] II Sam. 20.6 ff.

[15] II Sam. 16.3, 7f. Cf. Targum Jonathan, *ad loc,* and Kimhi, *ad loc.* Cf. also O. Thenius, *op. cit.,* p. 224, and A. F. Kirkpatrick, *op. cit.,* p. 160. On David's involvement in the death of Saul's sons (II Sam. 21.1–14) see J. Prado, "El exterminio de la familia de Saul (2 Sam. 21.1–14)," *Sefarad,* XIV (1954), p. 43.

See also H. Cazelles, "David's Monarchy and the Gibeonite Claim (II Sam. 21.1–14)," *PEQ,* LXXXVII (1955), pp. 165 ff., and A. Kapelrud, "König David und die Söhne des Saul," *ZAW,* LXVII (1955), p. 198.

[16] So, e.g., H. W. Hertzberg, *op. cit.,* p. 337. But a few scholars, like S. A. Cook, *op. cit.,* p. 159, claim that "it was Judah alone which took part in the rebellion." For a balanced view and a recognition of the role of men from both Israel and Judah in the revolt see R. Pfeiffer, *An Introduction to the Old Testament* (New York: 1948), p. 354; J. Bright, *op. cit.,* p. 188 and M. Noth, *The History of Israel* (London: 1958), pp. 200 f.

[17] The name Ahithophel is a derisive distortion. It is likely to have been originally "Ahijah," as in I Chron. 11.36. On this and the name Ahibaal see B. Mazar, "The Military Elite of King David," *VT,* XIII (1963), pp. 314 ff. Ahibaal may have been the grandfather of Bathsheba. Cf. II Sam. 11.3 and 23.34, and J. Bright, *op. cit.,* p. 188, n. 59. Giloh was located in Judah. Cf. Josh. 15.51. It is usually identified with

Khirbet Jala, a ruin seven miles to the northwest of Hebron; cf. M. Rehm, *Die Bücher Samuel* (Würzburg: 1949), p. 101.

[18] II Sam. 17.11.

[19] II Sam. 15.18.

[20] S. R. Driver, *Notes on . . . The Books of Samuel* (Oxford: 1913), p. 319, observes, in commenting on II Sam. 16.15, that "throughout the narrative כל העם are regularly with David. כל איש ישראל are with Absalom."

[21] II Sam. 17:25. Amasa may well be identical with Amasai, chief of the thirty, in I Chr. 12.18.

[22] II Sam. 19.14 ff.

[23] II Sam. 15.24 ff. and Rashi and Kimḥi *ad loc.*

[24] II Sam. 18.17.

[25] II Sam. 19.27. The commentators, agreeing, seek to exonerate Meribaal and to lay his alleged participation in the uprising to Ziba's slander. Cf., for example, H. P. Smith, *op. cit.,* p. 347 and A. F. Kirkpatrick, *op. cit.,* p. 159. Politically, the backing of Meribaal by power elements of the North who were aware of continuing widespread affection for Saul's regime, makes sense. It would have been natural for them to think of using the Saulides as a foil to David. The fact of Meribaal's deformity, mentioned by Smith, Kirkpatrick, and others as factors militating against his monarchical ambitions, is of little consequence. Whether Meribaal could have become monarch is a moot question. It would have depended on the success of Absalom's revolt and then a counterrevolution under Meribaal.

[26] II Sam. 19.22 ff.

[27] See S. R. Driver, *op. cit.,* p. 311. Jewish tradition, following the MT, views the forty years as beginning with the rise of the monarchy in Israel. See, e.g., Kimḥi and Gersonides, *ad loc.* See also commentators like B. Wolf, *Das Buch Samuel* (Frankfurt a.M.: 1923), p. 120.

[28] For the frequentative והשכים cf., S. R. Driver, *op. cit.,* p. 310. Also B. Wolf, *op. cit.,* p. 118.

[29] The commentators offer little help here. Invariably they attempt to show the rampant injustice in the land or to explain that David, burdened with responsibilities, could no longer adequately discharge his duties as a judge. Cf., for example, Targum Jonathan *ad loc.,* O. Thenius, *op. cit.,* pp. 215 ff., A. F. Kirkpatrick, *op. cit.,* p. 149; H. W. Hertzberg, *op. cit.,* pp. 336 f.; and W. McKane, *op. cit.,* p. 249.

[30] M. A. Cohen, *op. cit.,* pp. 67 ff. Cf., A. Alt, "Das Königtum in den Reichen Israel und Juda," in *Kleine Schriften zur Geschichte des Volkes Israel,* Vol. II (Munich: 1953), pp. 116 ff. (*Essays on Old Testament History and Religion* [Tr. by R. A. Wilson, Oxford: 1966], pp. 313 ff.)

[31] M. Weber, *Ancient Judaism* (trans. H. H. Gerth and D. Martindale, Glencoe, Illinois: 1952), p. 53.

[32] On the relationship of the word נגיד to נוקד and the consequent association of the new position with the old pastoral society, see J. J. Glück, "Nagid-Shepherd," *VT,* XIII (1963), pp. 144–150.

[33] See H. M. Orlinsky, "The Tribal System of Israel and Related Groups in the Period of the Judges," *Oriens Antiquus* V (1966), p. 13, note 6.

[34] I Kings 2.26. Cf. G. Mendenhall, *op. cit.,* p. 57. Solomon, though able to have Joab killed, even in the sanctuary (I Kings 2.5, 28 ff.), was not in a position similarly to remove Abiathar, though Abiathar is called an איש מות in the text. If this fact shows nothing else, it demonstrates the continued respect, potentially generative of power, held by the Shilonite priesthood.

[35] I Kings 4.7 ff. Regarding Judah, cf. F. M. Cross, Jr. and G. E. Wright, "The Boundary and Province Lists of the Kingdom of Judah," *JBL,* LXXV (1956), p. 224: "It now appears highly probable that Judah was first divided into administrative provinces during the reign of David." On the boundaries of Solomon's kingdom see A. Alt, "Israels Gaue unter Salomo," *Kleine Schriften* II (Munich: 1953), pp. 76–89.

[36] J. Morgenstern, "The Chanukkah Festival and the Calendar of Ancient Israel," *HUCA,* XXI (1948), pp. 380 ff.

[37] I Kings 4.1–20, 9.24 and *passim*. Cf. I. Mendelsohn, "On Corvée Labor in Ancient Canaan and Israel," *BASOR*, CLXVII (1962), p. 33.

[38] I Kings 9.22.

[39] I Sam. 21.11 ff., especially 22.2.

[40] II Sam. 5.17 ff.

[41] A. Alt, "The Formation of the Israelite State," *Essays on Old Testament History and Religion*" (Garden City, New York: 1966) p. 286, does not appear to recognize this fact.

[42] II Sam. 3.17 f.

[43] II Sam. 3.29 contains a stylized curse, composed in the light of what ultimately happened to Joab, not through supernatural means, but through the instrumentality of Solomon, prompted by his father. See also II Sam. 3.39.

[44] Some, like O. Eissfeldt, *The Old Testament: An Introduction*, p. 281, regard the words of David's dirge in II Sam.1 to be original.

[45] II Sam.5.7.On Jerusalem and its conquest see M.H.Ben Shalosh תולדות ירושלים בימי בית ראשון in ספר ירושלים I (Tel Aviv: 1956), pp. 112 f.; A. Alt, "Jerusalems Aufstieg," *Kleine Schriften* III (1959), pp. 253 f.; and, on its military significance, Y. Yadin, "Some Aspects of the Stategy of Ahab and David (I Kings 20, II Sam. 11)." *Biblica*, XXXVI (1955), p. 344: See also Y. Yadin, תורת המלחמה בארצות המקרא (Ramat Gan: 1963), pp. 236 f. Cf. also M. Noth, "Jerusalem und die israelitische Tradition," *Oudtestamentische Studiën*, VIII (1950), pp. 31 ff.

[46] II Sam. 6.1 ff. On the significance of the ark, see, e.g. E. Nielsen, "Some Reflections on the History of the Ark," *VT*, VII (1960), pp. 61–74; M. Haran, "The Nature of the 'Ohel Mo'edh'" in Pentateuchal Sources" *JSS*, V (1960), pp. 50–65, and "Shiloh and Jerusalem: The Origin of the Priestly Tradition in the Pentateuch," *JBL*, LXXX (1962), pp. 14–24. See now also J. G. Vink, "The Date and Origin of the Priestly Code in the Old Testament," *Oudtestamentische Studiën* XV (1969), p. 130.

[47] See K. Elliger, "Die dreissig Helden Davids," *PJB*, XXXI (1935), pp. 29–75, especially p. 75; and, for a different view on several issues, B. Mazar, *op. cit.*, pp. 310–320.

[48] I Kings 2.5 and 2.8 ff.

[49] I Chron. 21.1.

[50] For a parallel, see E. A. Speiser, "Census and Ritual Expiation in Mari and Israel," *BASOR*, CXLIX (1959), pp. 17 ff. The census there "is linked to new land grants and relatively recent political structures" (p. 25).

[51] The account of David's census and the ensuing pestilence may be, as some scholars have pointed out (cf. R. H. Pfeiffer, *op. cit.*, p. 353), a sequel to the story of the ark in II Sam. 6.1–23. This is to be understood in literary terms. For the Deuteronomic redactors there was a link between the movable ark and the stationary Temple. However, the historical fact of the census (as opposed to later tendentious interpretations) is not to be understood as having occurred at the time of the transference of the ark to Jerusalem. On Araunah's threshing floor, see B. Mazar, "David's Reign in Hebron and the Conquest of Jerusalem," *In The Time of Harvest: Essays in Honor of Abba Hillel Silver* (New York: 1963), p. 237. It is often stated that the census lists in Num. 1.26 are derivatives of this Davidic census.

[52] See G. Mendenhall, "The Census Lists of Numbers 1 and 26," *JBL*, LXXVII (1958), p. 53: "The cultural discontinuity which attended the establishment of the state under David and Solomon may actually have been more farreaching than that which accompanied the 'Conquest' of Palestine." See also W. F. Albright, *The Archaeology of Palestine and the Bible* (Harmondsworth: 1960): "Israel was still a rather primitive agricultural and pastoral state in the time of Saul and David, though it must have been making great strides towards a more complex industrial and mercantile level before the death of David about 960 B.C." On the changes generated by sociocultural systems, see P. A. Sorokin, *Social and Cultural Dynamics* (Boston: 1957), especially p. 639; V. Pareto, *The Mind and Society* (trans. A. Bongiorno and A. Livingston, New York: 1935), IV, SS. 2063–2079. Cf. A. M. Grompone, *Filosofía de las revoluciones sociales* (Montevideo: 1932), p. 57.

The idea of S. A. Cook (*op. cit.,* pp. 159, 176 f.) that the rebellions by Absalom and Sheba occurred before David became monarch over all Israel finds little support among scholars and less substantiation in the evidence.

[53] M. Weber, *op. cit.,* p. 46, though failing to reconstruct all the details of the rebellions, is not far off the mark when he points out that the uprisings of Absalom and Adonijah correspond to opposition to urban domination found in the peasant tribes. Weber says nothing about Sheba in this regard. Cf. A. Lods, *op. cit.,* p. 368, where he says that David "succeeded . . . in bringing Israel . . . into the circle of the great powers"; and M. Noth, *op. cit.,* p. 196: "David's political organization was the first great independent power structure on Palestinian-Syrian soil of which we have knowledge."

JEWISH BOOKPLATE LITERATURE: AN ANNOTATED BIBLIOGRAPHY

PHILIP GOODMAN

To I. Edward Kiev, friend and colleague, who encouraged the writer to collect Jewish bookplates.

The study of bookplates yields fruitful results for art specialists and historians. The former are interested in exploring the various graphic techniques employed and the symbolism frequently found on ex libris. Students of history discover that bookplates reveal genealogical and biographical data on individuals as well as pertinent information for the development of chronicles of libraries and other institutions. Hence it is not surprising that a fairly substantial literature has developed that deals with bookplates, and a number of general and specialized bibliographies have been published for the benefit of devotees of this subject. On the other hand, the literature on ex libris of Jewish interest is rather limited and until now there has not appeared a listing of more than several items, with one exception to be noted below. The compiler of this bibliography makes no pretensions to completeness. He takes comfort in the pretext provided in *Pirke Avot* (2.21): "It is not your duty to complete the work, but neither are you free to desist from it . . ." He anticipates that others will eventually add to this bibliography.

Special attention is called to the catalog *Exhibition of Jewish Book Plates.* Containing the largest listing of Jewish ex libris—over eight hundred—currently available, the catalog was prepared by the late Abraham Weiss of Tel Aviv, although his name does not appear as editor. The exhibition for which the catalog was issued was held in

Jerusalem in 1956 and attracted masses of visitors including the late Yitzchak Ben-Tzvi, President of the State of Israel, and many other dignitaries. Weiss, who arranged the exhibition from his personal collection, succeeded in creating tremendous interest in Jewish ex libris throughout Israel. A bibliography (see "Bibliografia") of seventy-one entries, limited to articles on the exhibition and reviews of the catalog, has been published. With a few exceptions, the items recorded in this bibliography are not repeated here. Weiss' collection of ex libris is now housed in the Museum of the Printing Arts in Safed.

This writer's collection of 7,000 bookplates of Jewish interest has been in the Klau Library of the Hebrew Union College-Jewish Institute of Religion, Cincinnati, since 1968. Appreciation is herewith expressed to Professor Herbert C. Zafren, Director of Libraries, and Dr. Israel O. Lehman, Curator of Manuscripts and Special Collections, respectively, of the HUC-JIR for their generous assistance in the compilation of this bibliography.

N.B.: Periodical articles, made available as reprints, are marked with an asterisk.

1. Barreira, João, "Ex-Libris Decorativos" (Ornamental Ex Libris), *Archivo Nacional de Ex-Libris,* vol. 1, no. 1 (1927), pp. 14–15.

   A description of the bookplate of Isaac Mendes of London, the first known dated (1746) ex libris of a Jew. See Navarro, below.

2. "Bibliografia" (Bibliography), *Hed Hadfus,* no. 11 (March, 1957), p. 54.*

   59 articles on the exhibition of Jewish bookplates held in Jerusalem, March 29–May 13, 1956, and reviews of *Taarukhat Tve-Sefer Yehudiyim,* see below, which appeared in periodicals throughout the world. The items in this bibliography are, with a few exceptions, omitted from the present listing.

3. "Bibliografia" (Bibliography), *Tav ha-Sefer* [Supplement, ed. by A. Weiss, to *Hed Hadfus,* December, 1958], Institute for the Art of Printing, no. 1 (1959), p. 7.

   A continuation of no. 2, containing 15 items.

4. "Bookplate Collection Acquired," *Some Recent Acquisitions and Other Matters,* vol. 18, no. 1 (March, 1969), p. 1.

   Announcement by the Klau Library of the Hebrew Union

College-Jewish Institute of Religion, Cincinnati, of its acquisition of the Philip Goodman Collection of Jewish Bookplates, consisting of over 7,000 items.

5. "Book-Plate of Mr. Elkan Adler," *Journal of the Ex Libris Society,* vol. 13, part 10 (October, 1903), p. 152, opp. p. 145. 1 illus.

   A description and reproduction of Elkan Nathan Adler's bookplate.

6. "Bookplates Symbolize Learning," *Jewish News* (Detroit), vol. 20, no. 8 (November 2, 1959), p. 8.

   Reproduction of a panel of twenty Jewish ex libris that was part of a portable exhibit of books and visual materials circulated by the Jewish Book Council of America, sponsored by the National Jewish Welfare Board. The reproduction was syndicated and appeared in many English-Jewish weeklies.

7. "Book-Plates of the University of California," *Journal of the Ex Libris Society,* vol. 14, part 2 (November, 1904), p. 168. 1 illus.

   A description and reproduction of the bookplate of Temple Emanu-El, San Francisco, for the books donated by the congregation to the University.

8. Brieger, Lothar, "Bücherzeichen" (Bookplates), in his *E. M. Lilien: Eine Künstlerische Entwickelung um die Jahrhundertwende* (Berlin-Wien, Verlag Benjamin Harz, 1922), pp. 91–108. 27 illus.

   A detailed exposition of the ex libris artistry of Lilien (1874–1925), called the "father of Jewish bookplates."

9. Davidovitch, David, "Yosef Budko, Oman ha-Ex-Libris ha-Yehudi" (Joseph Budko, Artist of the Jewish Ex Libris), *Tav ha-Sefer* [Supplement . . .], *supra,* pp. 1–3. 8 illus. English summary, p. 16.

   The article describes the distinctively artistic and Jewish qualities of the bookplates of Budko, a master of graphic techniques.

10. Eisenstein, Judah D., "Sefarim: Hotem Baal ha-Sefer" (Books: A Book Owner's Seal), in his *Otzar Yisrael* (New York, 1912), vol. 7, pp. 279–280. 4 illus.

    A short article on bookplates.

Exhibition of Jewish Book Plates. See *Katalog le-Taarukhat Tve-Sefer Yehudiyim.*

11. "Ex Libris," *Philo-Lexikon: Handbuch des Jüdischen Wissens* (Berlin, 1935), cols. 180–181. 2 illus.

A short item.

12. Fingesten, Peter, "Michel Fingesten (1883–1943)," *Boekcier: Tijdschrift van de Stichting Nederlandsche Exlibris-Kring,* vol. 3, no. 4 (October, 1948), pp. 37–39.

An evaluation of a prolific ex libris artist by his son.

13. Fortlage, Arnold, and Schwarz, Karl, "Ex Libris," *Das Graphische Werk von Hermann Struck* (The Graphic Works of Hermann Struck), (Berlin, Paul Cassirer, 1911), pp. 99–103.

A descriptive listing of 18 bookplates by the artist. One ex libris illustration on p. 51.

14. "Fré Cohen," *Boekcier,* no. 1 (January, 1946), pp. 3–6.

A necrology including a checklist of bookplates designed by the deceased artist.

15. Friedeberger, Hans, *Joseph Budko* (Berlin, Verlag für jüdische Kunst und Kultur, 1920). 24 p.

An evaluation of Budko's ex libris is found on pp. 12–13.

16. Ginsberg, Louis, "Bookplate Art of Efraim M. Lilien," American Society of Bookplate Collectors and Designers *Yearbook 1958* (1960), pp. 19–26. 3 illus.

An appraisal of the ex libris work of Lilien with a checklist of forty-nine bookplates by the artist.

17. Goldschmidt, Henry, "Marco Birnholz—70 Jahre" (Marco Birnholz—Age 70), *Aufbau,* August 12, 1955, p. 14.

A tribute to the late bookplate collector.

18. Goldstein, Maksymiljan, and Dresdner, Karol, "Exlibrisy i Plakaty" (Ex Libris and Posters) in their *Kultura i sztuka ludu zydowskiego na ziemiach polskich* (Lwow, Nakladem Maksymiljana Goldstein, 1935), pp. 103–112. 17 illus.

An account of Polish Jewish bookplates starting with that of Dr. Majer Hinckler of Lublin, 1668, as well as of other European ex libris from the collection of Goldstein.

19. Goodman, Philip, "American Jewish Bookplates," *Publications of the American Jewish Historical Society,* vol. 45, no. 3 (March, 1956), pp. 129–216. 64 illus. Reprinted in 300 copies.

A documented article dealing with American college bookplates with Hebrew inscriptions; ex libris for Judaica and Hebraica collections in college and public libraries; bookplates of major Jewish libraries; several bookplates of various institutions and ex libris of American Jews.

Reviewed by Leah Yablonsky Mishkin, *Chicago Jewish Forum,* vol. 2 (Winter, 1957–58), pp. 124–126; by C. Vilh. Jacobowsky, *Judisk Tidskrift,* vol. 29, no. 10 (October, 1956), pp. 274–277*; by C. Vilh. Jacobowsky, *Jodisk Samfund,* vol. 28, no. 3 (March, 1957), pp. 6–10*; by Federico Luzzatto, *Ex Libris: Amici dell' Ex Libris,* vol. 3, no. 2 (March–April, 1957), pp. 8–9; by Federico Luzzatto, *La Rassegna Mensile di Israel,* vol. 23, no. 4 (April, 1957), pp. 187–189.

20. ——, "Biblical Bookplates," *Brooklyn Jewish Center Review,* vol. 37, no. 8 (October, 1955), cover and pp. 12–13. 7 illus.

A review of a group of bookplates with biblical themes.

21. ——, "A Bookplate of Marco Birnholz," *Fuller Library Bulletin,* no. 19 (July–September, 1953), p. 2. 1 illus.

A note on the late bookplate collector and on one of his ex libris executed by Uriel Birnbaum.

22. ——, "Bookplates of Jewish Interest," *Antiquarian Bookman,* vol. 9, no. 19 (May 10, 1952), cover and p. 1725.* 10 illus.

A rationale for collecting Jewish bookplates.

23. ——, "Jewish Bookplates of Dutch Interest," *Boekcier,* vol. 9, no. 2 (April, 1954), pp. 21–26.* 5 illus.

This review of bookplates of and by Jews with Dutch interest reveals the attachment of Jews to the traditions of Judaism and the mores of Holland. While the article is in English, there are summaries in Dutch and French.

24. ——, "Love of Books as Revealed in Jewish Bookplates," *Jewish Book Annual,* vol. 12 (1954), pp. 77–90.* 11 illus.

Through a study of selected bookplates there is revealed the Jewish attitude on such subjects as lending and stealing of books, the pride of book possession and book production. Bookplates of authors and bibliophiles are also described.

25. ——, "Love of Learning as Reflected in Bookplates," *Jewish Heritage,* vol. 2, no. 2 (Fall, 1959), pp. 17–19.

A brief article featuring six reproductions with detailed captions.

26. ——, "Love of Zion as Reflected in Bookplates," *An Exhibition of Zionist and Israeli Bookplates from the Jewish Bookplate Collection of Philip Goodman* (New York, Theodor Herzl Institute, 1957), pp. 5–9. 7 illus.

A description of bookplates of artists and book owners who used them to convey their yearning for the Land of Israel. The article is featured in an exhibition catalog.

27. ——, "Marco Birnholz—Ex-Librist," American Society of Bookplate Collectors and Designers, *Year Book 1952/1953* (1955), pp. 14–25. 11 illus.

The biography of one of the world's outstanding collectors of bookplates as reconstructed from his personal ex libris.

28. ——, "Musical Motifs in Jewish Bookplates," *Jewish Music Notes,* April, 1953, p. 3.* 3 illus.

A description of some ex libris of Jews with musical themes starting with that of David Friedlander, engraved by Daniel N. Chodowiecki in 1774.

29. ——, "Zeh Sifri" (This is My Book), *Dvar le-Yeladim,* vol. 24, no. 13 (Dec. 2, 1953), pp. 194–195. 7 illus.

Similar to "Love of Zion as Reflected in Bookplates," *supra.*

30. Hedman, Dolf, "Judiska Exlibris" (Jewish Ex Libris), *Nordisk Exlibris Tidsskrift,* vol. 9, no. 3 (1957), pp. 100–105.* 14 illus.

A discussion of Jewish bookplates from different countries.

31. Hirsch, Helen, "And You Shall Keep Me Until the Fourteenth Day . . . ," *The Jewish Times* (Baltimore), vol. 71, no. 16 (Dec. 17, 1954), pp. 19–21. 4 illus.

This article is substantially the same as Harold S. Loeb's "Artistic Jewish Book-Plates." See below.

32. Hirschfelder, M., "E. M. Lilien," *Ost und West,* vol. 1 (1901), pp. 521–522.

A description of the bookplates of Richard Fischer made by Lilien.

33. ——, "Zwei Neue Lilien'sche Ex-Libris" (Two New Bookplates by Lilien), *Ost und West,* vol. 1 (1901), pp. 821–824.

Descriptions of bookplates of Dr. Emil Simonsen and Reuben Brainin.

34. Hirschler, Paul, "Ex Libris," *Jüdisches Lexikon* (Berlin, Jüdischer Verlag, 1928), vol. 2, cols. 564–565. 13 illus.

A brief article.

35. Hofmann, Else, "Der Sammler Apotheker Marco Birnholz: Eigenblatter" (The Collector Chemist Marco Birnholz: His Own Plates), *Österreichische Kunst,* vol. 6, no. 6 (June 15, 1935), pp. 8–10. 12 illus.

An exposition of some of the many bookplates created by outstanding artists for Birnholz.

36. Horodisch, Abraham, *Die Exlibris des Uriel Birnbaum gefolgt von einer Selbstbiographie des Künstlers* (The Ex Libris of Uriel Birnbaum with an Autobiography of the Artist), (Amsterdam, Erasmus Antiquariat, 1957). 107 p. 36 illus.

An analysis of 36 bookplates designed by Birnbaum. English summaries.

37. ——, "Joseph Budkos Jüdische Exlibriskunst" (Joseph Budko's Jewish Ex Libris Art), *Soncino-Blätter,* vol. 3, no. 1 (July, 1929), pp. 73–79.* 16 illus.

A description of Joseph Budko's ex libris style and a check list of fifty-one bookplates he designed.

38. Horodisch-Garman, Alice, *Book Plates in Pen and Ink: Twenty-one ex libris and a monogram for a bibliographer's library* (New York, Aldus Book Co., 1954). 16 p. 21 plates.

An album of different bookplates for Abraham Horodisch's bibliophilic library designed by his wife; with an introduction.

39. Jablin, Julian N., "Some Book-Plates of Reform Interest," *American Judaism,* vol. 9, no. 1 (Rosh Hashanah, 1959), pp. 16–18. 10 illus.

Bookplates of rabbis and lay leaders of the Reform Jewish movement are described.

40. Jacobowski, C. Vilh., "Al ha-Ex-libris ha-Yehudi be-Artzot ha-Skandineviot" (On the Jewish Ex Libris in the Scandinavian Countries), *Tav ha-Sefer* [Supplement . . .], *supra,* pp. 4–5. 4 illus. English summary, p. 16.

The author estimates that there are about 200 bookplates of Jews in Scandinavia but only a few with Jewish themes which he describes.

41. Jacobs, Joseph, "Book-Plates," *The Jewish Encyclopedia,* vol. 3, pp. 313–315. 6 illus.

A brief article.

42. "Jewish Bookplate Collection Goes on Tour," *JWB Circle,* vol. 7, no. 9 (November, 1952), p. 2.

A news item describing a circulating exhibit of 60 Jewish bookplates from Philip Goodman's collection. The item was syndicated and published in various English-Jewish weeklies.

43. "Jewish Bookplates," *World Over,* vol. 14, no. 2 (November 14, 1952), p. 9. 7 illus.

Reproductions of bookplates, with detailed captions, from the collection of Philip Goodman.

44. "Jewish Book-Plates," *Journal of the Ex Libris Society,* vol. 13, part 6 (June, 1903), p. 88. 1 illus.

A reprint of the article on bookplates by Joseph Jacobs from *The Jewish Encyclopedia.*

45. "Jewish Book-Plates," *Journal of the Ex Libris Society,* vol. 13, part 9 (September, 1903), p. 141.

A letter from J. [sic] Solomons.

46. "Jewish Bookplates Collection to Be Shown Here," *New York Herald Tribune,* October 11, 1952, p. 26. 1 illus.

A short news item and a reproduction of the bookplate of Leo M. Brown, by Ephraim M. Lilien.

47. Jones, Louise Seymour, "Brave Utensils," in her *The Human Side of Bookplates* (Los Angeles, Ward Ritchie Press, 1951), pp. 103–109.

The burning of books in history and, particularly, Hitler's book bonfires as related to bookplates. Attention is called to the desirability of collecting the bookplates of Jewish authors whose books were burned.

48. *Journal of the Ex Libris Society,* vol. 14, part 4 (April, 1904), p. 59; *ibid.,* part 6 (June, 1904), p. 84; *ibid.,* part 7 (July, 1904), p. 109; *ibid.,* vol. 15, part 1 (January, 1905), p. 16; *ibid.,* parts 2–3 (February–March, 1905), p. 26; *ibid.,* parts 4–5 (April–May, 1905), p. 43. 13 illus.

Reproductions of Jewish bookplates will be found on the pages listed above.

49. *Katalog le-Taarukhat Tve-Sefer Yehudiyim* (Catalog for an Exhibition of Jewish Bookplates), (Jerusalem, Graphic Archives and Museum, 1956). XVI, 99 p. 24 plates. 74 illus.

English title: *Exhibition of Jewish Book Plates.* This bilingual (Hebrew-English) catalog records 812 Jewish bookplates which comprised the most outstanding exhibit of this kind ever held as it reflected the development of Jewish ex libris in all styles, from their beginnings to the present. Abraham Weiss, who supplied the bookplates from his collection, contributed "The Jewish Book-Plate" (pp. VII–XI, in English; pp. 5–8, in Hebrew), and Z. J. Plaschkes wrote "Physicians' Ex-Libris" (p. XII, in English; p. 9, in Hebrew). Text includes advertisements (pp. 10–24, 82, 84–98).

Reviewed by Philip Goodman, *In Jewish Bookland,* February, 1957, p. 4; by C. Vilh. Jacobowsky, *Jodisk Samfund,* vol. 28, no. 3 (March, 1957), pp. 6–10*; by C. Vilh. Jacobowsky, *Judisk Tidskrift,* vol. 29, no. 10 (October, 1956), pp. 274–277.* 7 illus.

50. Kohut, George Alexander, *Bookplates: Some Modern Examples by Edwin R. Schwabacher* (New York, 1909). [24 p.] 14 illus.

"A few remarks on the selection of bookplates" by Kohut. Reproductions of bookplates including some of Jews.

51. Kolb, Leon, ed., *The Woodcuts of Jakob Steinhardt* (San Francisco, Genuart Co., 1959), n.p.

The Subject Index, p. 24, lists 10 ex libris illustrated in the book.

52. *Kolektzie Eks-Libris Tzugeshikt fun Gershon Epstein fun Offenbach* (A Collection of Ex Libris sent by Gershon Epstein from Offenbach), (1948).

An album of 1,350 photostats of ex libris housed in the archives of the YIVO Institute for Jewish Research.

53. Kronfeld, Gershon, "Ex Libris," *Hadapas* (March, 1936), p. 4. 3 illus.

A sketch on the origin of bookplates.

54. Landman, David, "Bookplates," *Universal Jewish Encyclopedia,* vol. 2, pp. 456–458. 17 illus.

An encyclopedic article.

55. Lehman, Israel, "Text and Symbolism in the Jewish Bookplate," *AJL* [Association of Jewish Libraries] *Bulletin,* vol. 3, no. 2 (May, 1969), pp. 11–13.

A discussion of typical themes on bookplates.

56. Levussove, M. S., *The New Art of An Ancient People: The Work of Ephraim Mose Lilien* (New York, B. W. Huebsch, 1906). 51 p.

Includes a description of Maxim Gorky's bookplate (p. 35).

57. "E. M. Lilien," *Österreichische Exlibris-Gesellschaft,* vol. 7 (Christmas, 1909), pp. 52–56. 5 illus.

An evaluation of Lilien and his ex libris work.

58. *E. M. Lilien: Sein Werk* (E. M. Lilien: His Work), Introduction by Stefan Zweig (Berlin and Leipzig, Schuster and Loeffler 1903). 349 p.

Reproductions of 21 bookplates.

59. Lilien, E. M., *Verzeichnis Der Radierungen von E. M. Lilien* (Vienna, Halm & Goldman, 1919). 45 p.

    Lists ten bookplates.

60. Loeb, Harold S., "Artistic Jewish Bookplates," *The American Hebrew,* vol. 113, no. 7 (June 29, 1923), pp. 137, 146. 5 illus.

    A description of a number of interesting bookplates.

61. "Marco Birnholz eifriger Ex-Libris Sammler" (Marco Birnholz —Ardent Ex Libris Collector), *Staats-Zeitung und Herold,* August 15, 1955, p. 6.

    A tribute to Birnholz on his seventieth birthday.

62. Meijer, J., "Ex Libris," in his *Encyclopaedia Sefardica Neerlandica* (Amsterdam, Portugees-Israelietische Gemeente, 5710), part 2, pp. 130–133. 8 illus.

    The article deals primarily with Dutch Jewish bookplates.

63. Meyer, Hermann, "Ex Libris," *Encyclopaedia Judaica* (Berlin, Verlag Eschkol, 1930), vol. 6, cols. 863–866. 6 illus.

    A brief article.

63a. Minayev, Yevgeni, "Exlibris," *Sovetish Heimland,* vol. 9, no. 12 (December, 1969), pp. 138–139. 3 illus.

    The author mentions that, during the two hundred years prior to the October Revolution, only 8,000 bookplates were made, but that since then 40,000 ex libris have been created. Attention is called to several artists who designed bookplates with Yiddish legends, notably, Shlomo Yudovin who executed sixteen ex libris, and Gershon Krovtsav who made many more; both artists used the wood-engraving technique.

64. *Misifrei* (From My Books) (München, Grafpresse-Privatdruck, 1950). 4 p. 10 plates.

    An album containing reproductions of bookplates of prominent Jews. Introduction by Heinrich Graf.

65. Navarro, A. de Gusmão, "Notas varias sobre os Ex-libris estrangeiros" (Sundry Notes on Foreign Ex Libris), *Archivo Nacional de Ex-libris,* vol. 1, no. 1 (1927), pp. 11–14. 2 illus.

    Deals with the ex libris of the Mendes da Costa family, including the first known dated (1746) bookplate of a Jew, Isaac Mendes of London, and that of Alexander Teixeira de Mattos of Amsterdam.

66. "New Book-Plates by Miss May Sandheim," *Journal of the Ex*

Libris Society, vol. 13, part 6 (June, 1903), pp. 88–89. 1 illus.

A description of Herbert Bentwich's bookplate.

67. Oldham, Ellen M., "Early Jewish Books Printed in America," *The Boston Public Library Quarterly* (April, 1953), pp. 83–96. 2 illus.

A description of an exhibit held at the Boston Public Library which included bookplates from the collections of the late Fanny Goldstein and of the late Dr. Cecil Roth.

68. Oliver, Vere Langford, comp., *West Indian Bookplates: Being a First List of Plates Relating to Those Islands: Supplement to vol. III of Caribbeana,* (London, Mitchell Hughes and Clarke, 1914). 100 p.

Includes descriptions of bookplates of ten Jews who lived in Jamaica (pp. 43–44, 56–57).

69. Plaschkes, Z. J., "Marco Birnholz—Rokeah ve-Ex-librist" (Marco Birnholz—Pharmacist and Ex Librist), *Hed Hadfus,* no. 10 (September, 1955), p. 70.* 1 illus.

A tribute to Birnholz on his seventieth birthday.

70. Pless, Will, "Die Graphikerin Nina Brodskij" (The Graphic Artist Nina Brodskij), *Aus Alter und Neuer Zeit: Illustrierte Zweiwochenschrift des "Israelitischen Familienblattes,"* no. 50 (September 5, 1929), supplement to no. 36, p. 394. 2 illus.

A critique of the artist who designed bookplates.

71. Radbill, Samuel X., "The Pediatrician Chooses a Bookplate," *Abraham Levinson Anniversary Volume: Studies in Pediatrics and Medical History,* ed. by Solomon R. Kagan, (New York, Froben Press, 1949), pp. 307–309.

A description of the bookplate of Dr. Abraham Levinson.

72. "Recent Book-Plates," *Journal of the Ex Libris Society,* vol. 6, part 7 (July, 1896), p. 113. 1 illus.

Description of Dr. Hermann Adler's bookplate.

73. Regener, Edgar Alfred, "Exlibris," in his *E. M. Lilien: Ein Beitrag zur Geschichte der Zeichnenden Kunste* (Berlin-Leipzig, F. A. Lattman in Goslar, 1905), pp. 147–164. 7 illus.

This essay includes detailed descriptions of many Lilien bookplates.

74. Rubens, Alfred, "Anglo-Jewish Coats of Arms: Being a List of Armorial Bearings in Current Use in Great Britain up to the year 1900: accompanied by a list of Armorial Bookplates," *Anglo-Jewish Notabilities: Their Arms and Testamentary Dis-*

positions (London, The Jewish Historical Society of England, 1949), pp. 75–128.* 96 illus.

An important descriptive listing of 215 bookplates.

75. ——, "Early Anglo-Jewish Artists," *Transactions of the Jewish Historical Society of England,* vol. 14 (1940), pp. 91–129.*

This monograph contains references to nine Anglo-Jewish artists who made bookplates.

76. Schwarz, Karl, "Ex Libris," *Ha-Entziklopediah ha-Ivrit: Kelalit, Yehudit ve-Artzisraelit* (Jerusalem-Tel Aviv, 5711 [1951]), vol. 3, cols. 290–292. 5 illus.

A short article.

77. Schwencke, Johan, *De Nederlandsche Ex Libris Kunst* (The Dutch Ex Libris Art) (Maastricht, Boosten & Stols, 1929). 203 p.

References to Jewish bookplates and artists will be found on pp. 77, 78, 94, 95, 100–101.

78. ——, "Grafisch Werk von Fré Cohen," (The Graphic Work of Fré Cohen), *De Vrouw en Haar Huis,* vol. 29, no. 11 (March, 1935), pp. 572–577. 2 illus.

An account of the artistic work of Fré Cohen including bookplates.

79. ——, *Het Portret-exlibris* (The Portrait Ex Libris) (Zaandijk, De Getijden-Pers, 1951). 40 p.

Includes a detailed description of Lilien's bookplates for Reuben Brainin (pp. 14, 18–19), and work of D. A. Bueno de Mesquita (p. 39) and Paul Citroen (p. 40).

80. ——, "Joden" (Jews), in his *De Bloei van de Nederlandse Exlibriskunst in de Laatse vijfentwintig jaar* (Amsterdam, De Bezige Bij, 1967), pp. 64–67.

Descriptions of Jewish bookplates.

81. ——, *Tweehonderd Nederlandse Grafische Kunstenaars* (Two Hundred Dutch Graphic Artists) (Amsterdam-Antwerp, Wereldbibliotheek, 1954). 171 p. 200 illus.

Among the two hundred short biographies of Dutch bookplate designers of the past 50 years, the following are Jewish: Paul Citroen, Fré Cohen, Dora van Creveld Geldzahler, Henri Friedlaender, Alice Horodisch-Garman, D. A. Bueno de Mesquita, H. J. Bueno de Mesquita, S. Jessurun de Mesquita, Leonard Pinkhof.

82. Seeligmann, Sigmund, "Joodsche Boekmerken" (Jewish Book-

plates), *De Vrijdagavond,* vol. 1, no. 20 (August 8, 1924), pp. 309–311.

An article on Dutch Jewish bookplates by a collector.

83. Solomons, Israel, "Jewish Book-Plates," *Journal of the Ex Libris Society,* vol. 13, part 10 (October, 1903), pp. 149–150.

The author of this article is the first known collector of Jewish bookplates; his collection has been in the library of the Hebrew Union College-Jewish Institute of Religion, Cincinnati, since the 1920s.

84. ——, "Jewish Book-Plates," *The Jewish Chronicle,* no. 2255 (June 21, 1912), pp. 18–20.* 5 illus.

An interview with Solomons who explains the symbolism of his own bookplate and the contents of his collection of 500 ex libris. Reprinted with thirteen illustrations of bookplates.

85. ——, "List of Jewish Book-Plates," *Journal of the Ex Libris Society,* vol. 14, part 2 (February, 1904), pp. 25–26; *ibid.,* part 4 (April, 1904), p. 58; *ibid.,* part 5 (May, 1904), p. 75–76; *ibid.,* part 6 (June, 1904), p. 92.

85a. ——, "Notes on Jewish Book-Plates," *Journal of the Ex Libris Society,* vol. 14, part 2 (February, 1904), p. 27; *ibid.,* part 4 (April, 1904), p. 61; *ibid.,* part 5 (May, 1904), p. 74; *ibid.,* part 6 (June, 1904), p. 96.

These notes apply to the above "List of Jewish Book-Plates."

86. "Taarukhat Tve-Sefer Yehudiyim" (Exhibition of Jewish Bookplates), *Hed Hadfus,* no. 10 (September, 1955), p. 71.*

A full page announcement of an exhibition to be held in Jerusalem.

87. "Taarukhat Tve-Sefer Yehudiyim" (Exhibition of Jewish Bookplates), *Hed Hadfus,* no. 11 (March, 1957), pp. 49-53. 11 illus.

A report on the exhibition held in Jerusalem, March 29–May 13, 1956, and the activities associated with it. This article is followed by excerpts from periodical comments on the exhibition.

88. Veth, D. Giltay, *Dutch Book Plates: A Selection of Modern Woodcuts & Wood Engravings* (New York, Golden Griffin Books Arts, 1950). 53 p. 83 illus.

In this account of bookplates by Dutch artists, Bueno De Mesquita and Alice Horodisch-Garman are included (pp. 43–46).

89. Vilhena, João Jardin de, "Ex-libris estrangeiros que se Relacionam com Portugal" (Foreign Ex Libris and Their Relationship with Portugal), *Archivo Nacional de Ex-libris,* vol. 1, no. 1 (1927), pp. 7–11. 1 illus.

    The article deals with the bookplates of David Henriques de Castro, M. de Pinto and Mendes da Costa.

90. Weiss, Abraham, "Avraham Horodish ve-Tve ha-Sefer Shel Uriel Birnbaum" (Abraham Horodisch and the Bookplates of Uriel Birnbaum), *Tav ha-Sefer* [Supplement . . .], *supra,* pp. 6–7. 3 illus.

    A discussion on the bibliophile Horodisch, the artist Birnbaum, and the latter's bookplates which the former published.

91. ——, "Ex Libris," *Moladti le-Noar vele-Am,* vol. 20 (5715), pp. 264–266. 4 illus.

    A short article written for youth.

92. ——, "Mah Zeh Ex Libris?" (What Is an Ex Libris?), *Ha-Aretz Shelanu,* vol. 4, no. 31 (April 21, 1954), p. 7. 5 illus.

    A brief exposition on bookplates with references to Jewish ones.

93. ——, "Mordecai Birnholz—Ben Shivim" (Marco Birnholz—Age Seventy), *Hed Hadfus,* no. 10 (September, 1955), p. 70.* 2 illus.

    A tribute to the ex libris collector on the occasion of his seventieth birthday.

94. ——, "Shefa u-Pizur be-Yetzirat Shlomoh Yedidiah" (Abundance and Dissipation in the Work of Shlomoh Yedidiah), *Olam Hadfus,* vol. 5, no. 9 (September, 1962), n.p.* 5 illus.

    This appreciation of Yedidiah (Seelenfreund—1875–1961) includes an examination of several bookplates designed by the artist in his original style.

95. ——, "Tve-Sefer le-Zikaron" (Memorial Bookplates), *Hed Hadfus,* no. 10 (September, 1955), pp. 68–69.* 6 illus.

    A descriptive essay about Jewish bookplates made to memorialize departed ones that are frequently found in institutional libraries.

96. ——, *Tve Sefer Yehudiyim* (Jewish Bookplates), Safed, Museum of Printing Art; Tel Aviv, Ha-Histadrut ha-Klalit Shel ha-Ovdim ha-Ivrim be-Eretz Yisrael and Ha-Igud ha-Artzi Shel Poale ha-Dfus, 1961. 16 pages. 16 illus.

A brief sketch, reprinted in part from *Hed Hadfus,* no. 9 (January, 1954), pp. 42–43.

97. ——, "Tve Sefer Yehudiyim be-Artzot ha-Brit (Jewish Bookplates in the United States), *Hed Hadfus,* no. 11 (March, 1957), pp. 55–56.* 5 illus.

This essay deals to a large extent with "American Jewish Bookplates," by Philip Goodman.

98. ——, Tve-Sefer Yehudiyim: Ex Libris (Jewish Bookplates: Ex Libris), *Hed Hadfus,* no. 9 (January, 1954), pp. 42–43.* 7 illus.

An historical sketch. Reprinted in *Olam ha-Sefer* (April, 1954), pp. 25–27 (4 illus.); in revised form, *Mahanaim,* no. 106 (Tamuz, 5726), pp. 166–171 (18 illus.).

99. ——, "Vili Geiger—Ben Shemonim" (Willi Geiger—Age Eighty), *Tav ha-Sefer* [Supplement . . .], *supra,* p. 11. 3 illus.

An appreciation of the German anti-Nazi graphic artist who designed ex-libris for Jews.

100. Werff, P. Hillebrand, "In Memoriam: Lodewijk Lopes Cardozo," *Boekcier,* vol. 6, no. 3 (July, 1951), pp. 29–30. 5 illus.

A memorial tribute to an ex libris artist.

101. Werner, Alfred, "The Tragedy of Ephraim Moses Lilien," *Herzl Year Book: Essays in Zionist History & Thought,* vol. 2 (1959), pp. 92–112.

This appreciation of Lilien from the Zionist point of view includes references to his bookplate work, pp. 105, 108.

102. Westheim, Paul, "Hermann Struck," *Ex Libris Buchkunst und Angewandte Graphik,* vol. 19, no. 1 (1919), pp. 13–15.

An evaluation of the prolific bookplate artist.

103. Wertheim, Joh. G., "Het grafisch oeuvre von Alice Garman" (The Graphic Work of Alice Garman), *Nieuw Israelietisch Weekblad,* no. 17 (January 1, 1954), p. 7. 2 illus.

A concise evaluation of the artist.

104. "West Indian Book-Plates: Jewish Book-Plates," *Journal of the Ex Libris Society,* vol. 13, part 10 (October, 1903), p. 150.

A letter from William Remington.

105. Wolf, Albert, "Jüdische Ex-Libris" (Jewish Ex Libris), *Monatsschrift für Geschichte und Wissenschaft des Judentums,* vol. 42 (1898), pp. 522–524.

Probably the first article ever written on Jewish bookplates with the exception of a description of one bookplate (see "Recent Book-Plates," *supra*).

106. Zeitlin, William, "Ein Chassidisches (?) Exlibris!" (A Hasidic (?) Ex Libris!), *Mitteilungen zur jüdischen volkskunde,* vol. 12, no. 4 (1909), p. 122.

A humorous Hebrew inscription reported to be found on books in White Russia.

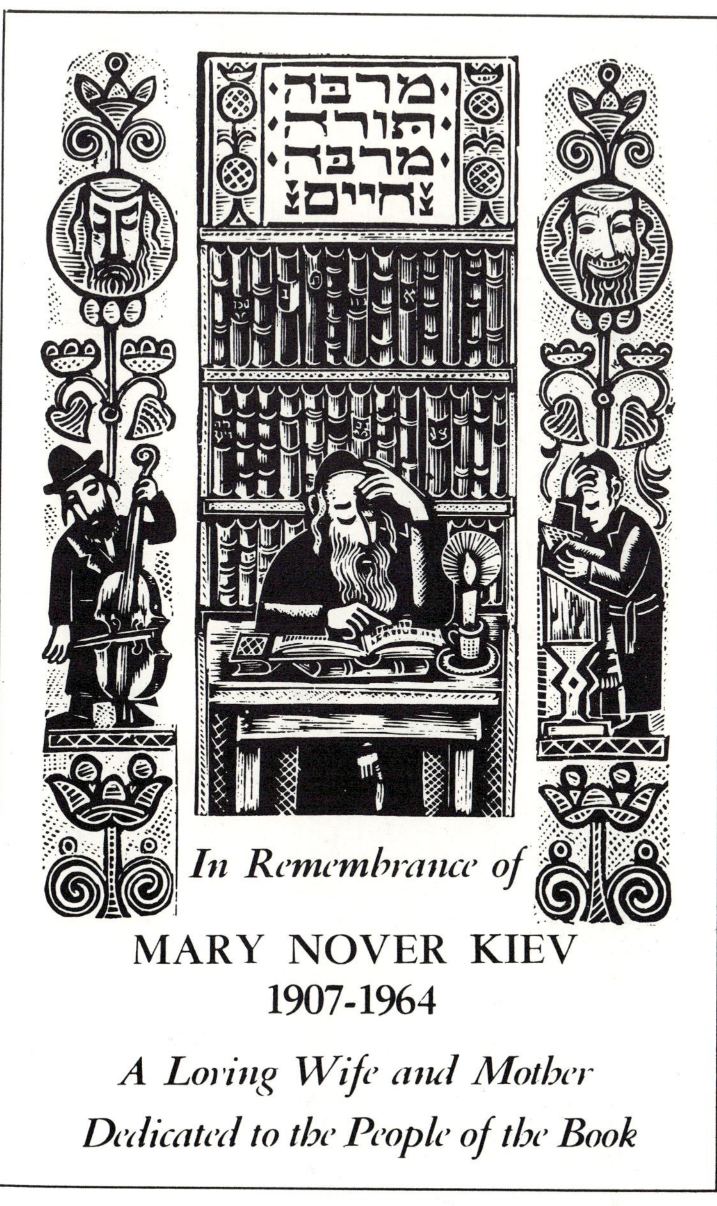
מרבה
תורה
מרבה
חיים
In Remembrance of
MARY NOVER KIEV
1907-1964
A Loving Wife and Mother
Dedicated to the People of the Book

Mary N. Kiev by Ilya Schor

Credit for illustrations:
The Philip Goodman Bookplate Collection of the Hebrew Union College-Jewish Institute of Religion, Cincinnati.

Elkan Adler by
Emma D. Goitein

Moses Marx by Joseph Budko

Joshua Loth Liebman
by Joanne Bauer-Mayer

Marco Birnholz
by Uriel Birnbaum

Israel Solomons
designed by Tobias Lewis

S. Shapira by S. Yudovin

Leo Winz by Ephraim M. Lilien

Lazarus Goldschmidt, *ipse fecit*

AHAD HA-AM AS BIBLICAL CRITIC—A PROFILE

ALFRED GOTTSCHALK

Hebrew Union College-Jewish Institute of Religion

I

Ahad Ha-Am had a great reverence for the Bible, since he considered it to be the bedrock out of which Judaism was built. Fully schooled in its contents and in the commentaries and master commentaries which comprised traditional Jewish biblical scholarship, he was at ease in its complex thought-molds and its exegesis. His veneration for the Holy Scriptures, upon which he drew so heavily in the development of his own philosophy of "Spiritual Zionism," did not preclude a critical approach to biblical materials, however, as well as to the highly selective use of the researches of the biblical scholarship of his day.

When it is taken into account that Ahad Ha-Am was a confirmed agnostic, it becomes clear that his attitude toward the Bible and its exegesis flows from other than traditional religious considerations. He regarded reverence for the past and its religious heritage a vital psychological attitude, even when its vast body of belief is no longer deemed tenable in the modern world. Criticism of the Bible meant, for Ahad Ha-Am, the constructive use of those aspects of biblical thought which would enable modern Judaism to survive in its historic continuity.

The attitudes of reverence for tradition and of criticism of tradition abide in tension in Ahad Ha-Am's thought and are held together by the mortar of "Spiritual Zionism." The founder of the philosophy of "Spiritual Zionism" entertained the belief that the literary creations of the Jewish people were the product of the Jewish "national spirit," brought into being to assure the national survival of the Jewish people. With this notion as a premise for the investigation of the Jewish past, the Bible and tradition must be viewed both as inevitable consequences of the creativity of the "national spirit" and as its objects of reverence.

The *Tanakh,* Ahad Ha-Am maintained, exercises a certain "hypnos" upon us, tying us to it through a close and unique feeling which transcends the generations.[1] Ahad Ha-Am's *feeling* about the Bible was certainly a factor which prevented him from engaging in that rigorous discipline of biblical studies which characterizes modern biblical scholarship. His emphasis on feeling, as well as his reluctance to engage in the kind of critical inquiry which was characteristic of the *Wissenschaft* school, was due also in part to his rejection of objective canons of scientific inquiry which conceivably might have led him from his primary concern of finding a solution for the plight of Judaism. Since Ahad Ha-Am proceeded to project such a solution in a somewhat doctrinaire manner, he used the results of biblical scholarship selectively and without particular concern for inner consistency. Leon Roth is undoubtedly correct when he observes:

> Ahad Ha-Am *used* ideas he found ready to his hand in order to enable him to master and systematize the problems of his age and environment. He *used* ideas he found. He did not examine them over-minutely first; and he did not worry overmuch if they were—ultimately—not sound and—ultimately—incompatible with one another.[2]

If the Bible, the historic repository of Jewish national feeling and consciousness, was to have value as the fundamental buttress of his system, Ahad Ha-Am most likely felt that in essential respects he had to keep the *textus receptus* free of that penetrating criticism which might have interfered with his philosophic predispositions and the conclusions which were already inherent within them. In this respect he is guilty of being orthodox, but for reasons different from those of his orthodox religious confreres. Another reason for Ahad Ha-Am's anticritical attitude to such problems as textual emendations, documentary hypotheses, and philological problems, is that he felt these researches to be inconclusive and confusing. A telling synopsis of his views on such subjects of criticism as mentioned above may be obtained from his observations on the Bible curriculum offered at the Hebrew Gymnasium of Jaffa. The Gymnasium which was founded by the Hilfsverein der deutschen Juden, a philanthropic organization for the assistance of Jews in Eastern Europe and the Near East, was Germanic in its pedagogical methodology.[3] While the Gymnasium ultimately adopted Hebrew rather than German as the language of instruction and became more Zionistically oriented, it was under the Hilfsverein influence that Ahad Ha-Am made a tour of inspection of it. He published the results of his visit in *Hashiloah* in 1912. In his review, Ahad Ha-Am apologizes for what will be a scathing critique of the school, since he wished no harm to such a young and fragile institution as the Gymnasium. The truth, however, must be told.[4]

Ahad Ha-Am, among others, attended the lectures of Dr. Mosensohn who, alone among his colleagues, publicly set forth his methodology. According to Ahad Ha-Am, Dr. Mosensohn taught that, until the present time, *Tanakh* research was not carried on as an independent course of study. Jewish biblical scholarship was the peg upon which generations fastened the creativity of their spirit until finally the Bible's original natural luster was lost. The time is now ripe, claimed Dr. Mosensohn, to return to study the *Tanakh* itself. The *Tanakh,* Dr. Mosensohn held, was the sole source to which a poor, despoiled and driven people, such as the Jews, could look for a different life—one of freedom and honor.[5] To accomplish this, it was necessary to study each period, hero or sage in proper order and in proper context, so that all the particulars and minutiae surrounding the subject could be integrated and made to yield a complete picture.[6] For this purpose, Dr. Mosensohn held, the *Tanakh* was to be divided into four divisions for purposes of study: (1) the historical Books of the Bible; (2) the Books of the Prophets; (3) the books of poetry and metaphor; and (4) the Books of Law. According to the present order of the books of the *Tanakh,* these divisions are intermeshed. What is required is to sort out the literature of the same genre and to present it to the student in its sequential unfolding. It is necessary first to begin with the historical materials, then the prophetic and so on. For example, in the Prophetic books as in the historical, there are intertwined within the same book early and later materials which, in fact, are as far removed from each other as are East and West. What is required, proceeded Dr. Mosensohn, is the restoration of material to its proper source and time so that each prophet will be fully and clearly portrayed and the interconnected chain of ideas among the prophets fully understood in relation to their historical causes and settings. In order to achieve clarity in the prophetic literature, for example, so that all difficulties in meaning can be reconciled, it may be necessary to correct or change a letter, a word, or even a full sentence. The poetic literature is methodologically to be studied in the same way and according to the same principles.[7]

Ahad Ha-Am, seeking to test the effectiveness of this method of instruction, questioned students in the professor's class and found them knowledgeable in certain areas. When Ahad Ha-Am asked one of the more alert students to read a passage from one of the Prophets, the student hesitated and offered the excuse that he had studied the book during the previous year and had forgotten it. Ahad Ha-Am showed his astonishment at the student's level of performance only to have the student reflect, "How is it possible to remember? Everything is so completely mixed up!" Ahad Ha-Am concluded that while the students knew about the prophets, they did not know the Prophetic books.[8] This incident, Ahad Ha-Am observes, opened his eyes. The multiplicity of corrections, deletions and emendations, all undertaken in the hope of achieving clarity, led instead to ambiguity and confusion. He adds the further caustic observation that part of the students' training in methodology required the rewriting of a Prophetic book in accordance with the schema laid down by the professor. This was to include all of the rearrangement of passages and the professor's proposed emendations. Ahad Ha-Am observes that if the student lost his notebook, all of the copies of the *Tanakh* extant in the world were of no avail to him, while a knowledge of German and Professor K. Marti's *Commentary on the Old Testament* might rescue him. Marti's work alone, even without the aid of an instructor, would make it possible for the student to recreate his notebook, as though Marti's work constituted the revelation at Sinai.[9] Ahad Ha-Am concluded that if knowledge of the *Tanakh* was to be the basis of a nationalist education, such an education could not rest

> . . . on a castle suspended in the air . . . The basis of a nationalist education must be solely the *Tanakh* as it is, as it has been transmitted for more than two thousand years through the inner depths of our national life, serving as its foundation, through all the generations.[10]

It is clear from the above illustration of Ahad Ha-Am's attitude toward the scientific study of the Bible that he believed such study to be inimical to his program. What was required in biblical studies was the cultivation of a love for the Bible and a knowledge of it as it was traditionally transmitted. What differentiates Ahad Ha-Am from the strict traditionalist is the use to which this kind of biblical knowledge and reverence for the Bible is to be put. For the fundamentalist Christian or Jew the Bible is a hallowed, immutable document because it is God's timeless revelation to man. Ahad Ha-Am was anything but a fundamentalist. For him, the Bible was the prime document reflecting the activity of the Jewish "national spirit." The Bible, in a sense, was the blueprint of the evolution of the Jewish national existence. Criticism of a radical nature could only revise the lines of that blueprint, blur its outlines and undermine its authority. Carving the Bible up, as Dr. Mosensohn had done, led in fact only to confusion. Since confusion is not conducive to reverence, love or awe, Ahad Ha-Am apparently concluded that the *textus receptus* presented fewer problems toward the furtherance of his program than did the new scholarship. Particularly in light of his general viewpoint of the evolution of Judaism, it was easier to explain the prelogical or the miraculous elements in the Bible as stemming from the nation's spiritual childhood than to perform drastic surgery on the biblical text itself. The Bible, in Ahad Ha-Am's system, was a static document to be spiritually and dynamically interpreted. He required that it be respected but not that its theological ideas be believed. He reserved to himself the right of the liberal interpreter of the Bible, to make selective use of its contents. If Ahad Ha-Am is a critic of the Bible, it is in this sense that his criticism must be understood.

II

The world of scientific criticism against which Ahad Ha-Am reacted, and which he accused the followers of the *Wissenschaft* school of imitating, was essentially the creation of middle- and late-nineteenth-century German biblical scholarship. What characterized this scholarship, by and large, was its rejection of the traditional view that the Holy Scriptures contained a timeless revelation of God to the world. This revelation was viewed as immutable and categorically binding upon the believer. The modern biblical criticism that had been set in motion challenged this doctrine of revelation. Holy Scripture soon came to be viewed as the literary record of man's slow growth in his understanding of moral imperatives and of the divine. From the middle of the nineteenth century onward, the contents of the Bible were viewed as reflecting the evolutionary process and in some instances as being tied to the rectilinear mode of development.[11] Such a supposition carried with it implicitly a dateline on the contents of the Bible. The latter came to be viewed in terms of their primitivism or sophistication as the nineteenth-century critic understood "primitivism" and "sophistication."

A prime example of this approach may be found in the work of Karl Heinrich Graf (1815–1869) who, in a letter to Eduard Reuss (1804–1891) in October 1862, contended that the middle section of the Pentateuch was post-exilic in its entirety.[12] In his work, *Die geschichtlichen Bücher des Alten Testament: Zwei historisch-kritische Untersuchungen* (Leipzig: 1866),[13] Graf concluded that the Priestly Document (P) was a post-exilic work to be assigned to and connected with the age of Ezra in the fifth pre-Christian century. This dating was arrived at because the document contained a universal history, an extensive legal code, concerned with and dominated by priestly interests and was formal and precise in its style and "given to stereotyped expressions." [14] Far from being the most ancient source of the Pentateuch, it was really the latest.[15] This theory transferred, so to speak, Mosaic law from the beginning to the end of Jewish history. Graf's thesis, a particular expression of the documentary hypothesis, impressed Abraham Kuenen (1828–1891), who had earlier come to a similar conclusion.[16] Kuenen differed with Graf, however, on the splitting up of the *Grundschrift* into a pre-Yahwistic *Grundschrift* and what Graf had called "the pseudo-*Grundschrift*." Both documents, Kuenen reasoned, had to be either early or late. Kuenen believed that the entire *Grundschrift* was post-exilic.[17]

Julius Wellhausen (1844–1918), whom Ahad Ha-Am had referred to as an important source of modern biblical scholarship,[18] enlarged and developed Graf's viewpoint.[19] Wellhausen's *Prolegomena zur Geschichte Israels* [20] depicts the religious development of the Old Testament with masterful strokes and lays bare with impressive clarity the complex literary and critical problems of the Old Testament.[21] What is particularly germane to our discussion is the likeness of approach between Ahad Ha-Am and Wellhausen regarding some salient aspects of the history of the religion of Israel. The question of dependence of Ahad Ha-Am on Wellhausen is difficult to gauge. Were it not for the unusual reference to Wellhausen in one of his letters, the association of these two names, in light of Ahad Ha-Am's outspoken anti-critical attitude, would have, on the face of it, escaped us. The similarity in thought between the men lies in their schematization of ancient Jewish history, in their placing a high value on the prophetic movement and a low estimation on the cultus, and their common emphasis on an evolutionary development of ancient Jewish thought.[22]

In his *Prolegomena zur Geschichte Israels,* Wellhausen reconstructed the history of Israel as beginning with the Exodus, not the patriarchs. An evolutionary hypothesis precluded that the patriarchs could have held the lofty monotheism mirrored in the Book of Genesis. The patriarchal narratives were the creation, therefore, of late Judaism.[23] Only with the Exodus from Egypt did the history of Israel commence.[24] Moses' religion was not monotheism but monolatry.[25] The cultus grew out of life:

> Hier ist alles lebendig und im Fluss; wie Jahve selber, so arbeitet auch der Mann Gottes im lebendigen Stoff, praktisch, in keiner Weise theoretisch; geschichtlich, nicht literarisch.[26]

From these beginnings Israel's religion became more complex. The prophets pushed the religion to a new crest of development by the growth of monolatry into ethical monotheism.[27] Righteousness became the basic requirement of religion.[28] The Deuteronomic Reformation, growing out of prophetism, centralized the cultus in Jerusalem which in turn led to the Priestly Code.[29] The codification of the ritual law was post-exilic, carried out during the period of Ezra and Nehemiah.[30] While the Graf-Wellhausen hypothesis was broadly attacked, the general overview of the hypothesis dominated biblical scholarship for half a century. There is much in the hypothesis that compelled assent. Yet, remove from it the presuppositions of evolutionary development, add to it the archeological evidence since the turn of the century, focus upon it the remarkable researches of Gunkel, and the hypothesis begins to weaken. The *evolution* of the religious thought of the Bible, through these researches, became much more complex and far less arbitrary than heretofore supposed.

Ahad Ha-Am was at one with Wellhausen in describing the period prior to the prophets as one which was characterized by polytheism, in which the phenomena of nature became gods and the world was peopled with as many deities as there were good and bad forces in nature.[31] Ahad Ha-Am projects a double polytheism—one natural, the other national—which corresponded to the needs of life in this primitive period. The national god was appealed to in times of trouble and war, and was called "the God of their fathers." When the danger was past, the people reverted again to the everyday gods of nature.[32] The prophets, however, spoke of the one God. Their message fell on deaf ears until after the destruction of the Temple, when historical circumstances established the monotheistic idea firmly in the heart of the people. Coupled to it was the hope for national restoration and the return to Palestine.[33] For Ahad Ha-Am, prophecy is the distinguishing characteristic of the Hebrew "national spirit." Out of Jewish tradition, as well as Wellhausen's scholarship, Ahad Ha-Am knew that Moses initiated the major religious and historical thrust of Judaism. In his essay, "Moses," Ahad Ha-Am reiterates the traditional belief that Moses was the "lord of the prophets"; that tradition states, "And there arose not again in Israel a prophet the likes of Moses." [34]

III

Ahad Ha-Am further agrees with Wellhausen on the religious coloration of the pre-Mosaic period in regard to the patriarchs. Ahad Ha-Am is virtually silent on the patriarchal period which would suggest he considered it of little importance. This is noteworthy, since the promise of Canaan to Abraham is crucial for the Zionist idea.

On the question of the role of the priest in ancient Jewish society, Ahad Ha-Am has much to say. Without going into any analytical discussion of the Priestly Code and its relationship to preexisting documents of the Bible, Ahad Ha-Am places a negative value on priestcraft. Nevertheless, priestcraft had a purpose and was of use in the mediation of the prophetic ideas and ideals. For Ahad Ha-Am, the prophet is the radical man, the initiator of a primal force. By definition, the prophet is an extremist. An absolutist in truth-telling, he epitomizes truth in action. The prophet stands for the ideal of a society based on absolute righteousness.[35] The prophetic ideals require accommodation and compromise to get them to work in society. This task falls to the priest.[36] The priest accommodates the prophet's teaching; he develops laws, rituals, and institutions to make the prophetic ideals function in the lives of men.[37] In a most insightful essay, entitled "Priest and Prophet," [38] Ahad Ha-Am notes that one of the differences between prophet and priest is that the priest seeks "not what *ought* to be, but only what *can* be."[39] This treatment of the priesthood as a secondary force in society presupposes the preexistence of the prophetic community, hence the idea that the prophets produced the teaching of the priests.[40]

Ahad Ha-Am clearly accepts the dateline of the Graf-Wellhausen school, as well as its emphasis in favor of prophetism. Ahad Ha-Am also shares Wellhausen's denigration of the appearance of the Law and its marking the end of the "law of freedom" in religion and the cultus.[41] The Law, a creation of the "national spirit," was a necessary implement in the survival of post-exilic Judaism.[42] Ahad Ha-Am also accepts the notion that there was a basic hostility between prophet and priest. "The prophets were accordingly 'men of strife' to the priests more so than to the general body of the people."[43] The priest stands for order and status quo. The prophet stands for change and upheaval. Ahad Ha-Am makes no clear distinction which prophets, other than Moses, he has in mind. This is further complicated since some prophets, e.g., Jeremiah and Ezekiel, were also priests.

Ahad Ha-Am further follows the Graf-Wellhausen school when he asserts that the centuries that elapsed between the end of the prophetic period and the rise of the Maccabeans was essentially dominated by the priestly class.[44] Ahad Ha-Am distinguishes between Hebraism, which is especially exemplified by Moses, the prophets, and Judaism which is the handiwork of the Pharisees.[45] In his close adherence to the critical school of scholarship, Ahad Ha-Am is virtually in total agreement with the Jewish "reformers" whom he castigates for this very same position. Ahad Ha-Am, however, differs from them and from Wellhausen in his nationalist emphasis. The prophets were not solely universalists. They were also Jewish particularists.[46] While the prophets emphasized Israel's mission, they did not predicate the success of the mission to bring absolute morality to the world on the basis of a permanent dispersion. It was not, as the "reformers" maintained, a question of either universalism or particularism, but of both.[47] A further difference between Ahad Ha-Am and Wellhausen and his school was that the former's concerns were polemical and practical while those of the latter were primarily historical and critical. Temperamentally both thinkers responded to the same values but the uses to which these values were to be put were worlds apart. Ahad Ha-Am, for example, was a staunch defender of the Pharisees as being successors to the prophetic tradition. They were the revivers of Hebraism. For Wellhausen they were the progenitors of a legalism based on separatism. Ahad Ha-Am thought separatism indispensable to Jewish survival and, therefore, endorsed the Pharisees who were the architects of a system of thought and action which purposed to provide a historic identity and continuity for Judaism. In the last days of the Second Commonwealth when all seemed lost ". . . the political Zealots remained sword in hand on the walls of Jerusalem while the Pharisees took the Scrolls of the Law and went to Yavneh. . . ."[48] As the prophets, the Pharisees believed in the unity of the people, land and ideals, flesh and spirit. It is in these ruminations of Ahad Ha-Am that we sense a distinct pulling away from the *Wissenschaft* School, from Wellhausen, academic discipline, and the universalist aspirations of the early "reformers." Unlike the historical-critical school, Ahad Ha-Am used biblical criticism and its findings to develop a philosophy of Jewish nationalism and culture. He employed the findings of scholarship to create a scaffolding of fact which he then filled in with the brick and mortar of spiritual and cultural Zionism. Ahad Ha-Am's uniqueness lies in the plausibility of the total structure of thought and action he created. His proclivity toward *historismus,* in which facts are conditioned by existential necessities, is best illustrated in his midrash on Moses. In this essay Ahad Ha-Am makes the distinction between archeological truth and historical truth.

> Not every archeological truth is also an historical truth. Historical truth is that, and that alone, which reveals the forces that go to mold the social life of mankind.[49]

Real history, for Ahad Ha-Am, reflects only those elements which have become forces in human life. It is therefore the Moses of the imagination, the Moses who has become the ideal, who is the historical reality of the Jewish people. For Ahad Ha-Am the canons of criticism and evaluation are then always conditioned by the uses to which they are put. Biblical criticism and *Die Wissenschaft des Judentums* must serve the program of cultural and spiritual renovation of the Jewish people. Knowledge of the Jewish past must shed light on the Jewish present. It must attempt inductively or deductively to present a solution to the *tzoret ha-yahadut* as well as to the *tzoret ha-yehudim.*

NOTES

[1] *Kol Kitbe Ahad Ha-Am* (Dvir Co., Ltd., Tel Aviv: 1956), p. 408.

[2] Leon Roth, "Back To, Forward From, Ahad Haam?" *Conservative Judaism,* XVII, Nos. 1–2 (Fall 1962–Winter 1963), p. 29.

[3] Ahad Ha-Am, *Essays, Letters, Memoirs,* tr. Leon Simon (Oxford, East and West Library: 1946), p. 347, note 55.

[4] *Kol Kitbe,* p. 417.

[5] *Ibid.,* pp. 417–418.

[6] *Ibid.,* p. 418.

[7] *Ibid.*

[8] *Ibid.*

[9] *Ibid.* Cf., K. Marti, *Kurzer Hand-Commentar zum Alten Testament* (Tübingen: 1897–1903).

[10] *Kol Kitbe,* p. 419.

[11] Note, for example, the comment on K. H. Graf, that "His standard of judgement was to a great extent the law of linear evolutionist development." Simon J. DeVries, "The Hexateuchal Criticism of Abraham Kuenen," *JBL,* LXXXII, Part I (March 1963), 43.

[12] Hans Joachim Kraus, *Geschichte der historischkritischen Erforschung des Alten Testaments* (Duisburg-Ruhrort: Verlag der Buchhandlung des Erziehungsvereins Neukirchen Kreis Moers: 1956), p. 224. Reuss also had believed that "P" was the latest source of the Pentateuch. *Ibid.,* p. 227.

[13] The book was published in 1865 but carried 1866 as its publication date. DeVries, *JBL, ibid.*

[14] Herbert F. Hahn, *Old Testament in Modern Research* (Philadelphia: Muhlenberg Press: 1954), p. 5.

[15] *Ibid.*

[16] DeVries, *JBL, ibid.,* pp. 41–42, 43.

[17] *Ibid.,* pp. 43–44.

[18] *Iggerot Ahad Ha-Am,* ed. Aryeh Simon (rev. and enlarged ed.; Dvir Co., Ltd., Tel Aviv: 1956), II, p. 18.

[19] Kraus, *Geschichte,* p. 236.

[20] A first edition of the work appeared in 1878 under the title, *Geschichte Israels.* Kraus, *ibid.,* p. 236.

[21] *Ibid.*

[22] Kraus, in his *Geschichte,* p 240, points to four major influences on Wellhausen: (1) The source criticism with regard to the Urkundenhypothese from Astruc to Hupfeld; (2) The work of Reuss, Graf and Kuenen on the historical priority of the legal and priestly materials; (3) The efforts of DeWette and Ewald in creating, out of the source criticism, a composite picture of the history of Israel; (4) The Hegelian philosophy of history received through Vatke, The confluence of these influences are to be found as *Forschungstendenzen* in Wellhausen's *Prolegomena to the History of Israel,* p. 240. It is particularly with reference to Vatke's evolutionary schematization that Wellhausen and Ahad Ha-Am share some common points of view.

[23] J. Wellhausen, *Prolegomena zur Geschichte Israels* (3rd ed.; Verlag Georg Reimer, Berlin: 1886), pp. 330–340.

[24] *Ibid.,* p. 367.

[25] J. Wellhausen, *Israelitische und jüdische Geschichte* (3rd ed.; Verlag Georg Reimer, Berlin: 1897), pp. 30–31.

[26] Wellhausen, *Prolegomena,* p. 362.

[27] Wellhausen, *Israelitische und jüdische Geschichte,* pp. 110–111.

[28] *Ibid.,* p. 111.

[29] *Ibid.,* pp. 132–134.

[30] Wellhausen, *Prolegomena,* pp. 427–428.

[31] *Kol Kitbe,* p. 79.

[32] *Ibid.*

[33] *Ibid.*, pp. 79–80.

[34] *Ibid.*, pp. 343–344.

[35] *Ibid.*, pp. 90–91.

[36] *Ibid.*, p. 91.

[37] *Ibid.*

[38] Published 1893.

[39] *Kol Kitbe,* p. 91.

[40] *Ibid.*, p. 92.

[41] *Ibid.*, pp. 41–44.

[42] *Ibid.*, p. 272.

[43] *Ibid.*, p. 92.

[44] Ahad Ha-Am, *Selected Essays,* tr. Leon Simon (The Jewish Publication Society of America, Philadelphia: 1912), Leon Simon's "Introduction," p. 19. Cf., *Kol Kitbe,* pp. 350–352.

[45] Ahad Ha-Am, *Selected Essays,* pp. 22–23.

[46] *Kol Kitbe,* p. 92.

[47] *Ibid.*

[48] *Ibid.*, p. 351.

[49] Ahad Ha-Am, *Selected Essays,* p. 307.

SOME NOTES AND CONCLUSIONS ABOUT THE PUBLISHED TOTALS OF THE SOVIET CENSUS OF JANUARY 15, 1959,

by Y. KANTOR

Translated and Annotated by

A. A. GREENBAUM

University of Haifa

INTRODUCTORY NOTE

Yaakov (in the Soviet spelling, Yankev) Kantor was one of the two leading Jewish demographers and statisticians in the Soviet Union, publishing—in both Yiddish and Russian—a number of books, articles, and pamphlets on the structure and dynamics of the Soviet Jewish population. In the late 1920's he paid special attention to colonization of Jews on the land. Kantor also wrote political and pedagogical books and tracts. His most important works are: *Natsional'noe stroitel'stvo sredi evreev v SSSR* ("National construction among the Jews in the U.S.S.R."), Moscow: 1934; and, *Ratnboyung in der idisher svive* ("Formation of Soviets in Jewish Areas"), Kiev: 1928.

The results of the 1939 Soviet census have been analyzed from the Jewish point of view by Lev Zinger, whose fate during the purge of the late forties is unknown. After the "thaw" Kantor published the attached preliminary article on the 1959 census, and at the time of his death was writing historical sketches on Soviet Jews in the war against Hitler. These last writings appeared in Warsaw—whether for political reasons or because a suitable Soviet outlet was lacking, we do not know. Kantor, who had been born at Pinsk in 1886, died in Moscow in 1964.

The article here translated appeared in the original Yiddish in the Warsaw journal *Bleter far geshikhte,* v. 15 (1962–63), pp. 142–154. This, Kantor's last demographic study, is admittedly sketchy, and (especially towards the end) somewhat apologetic and repetitious. An examination of the statistics also revealed numerous errors—corrected by us where possible—probably due in part to transmission problems. Nevertheless we feel that, because of the pioneer nature of the work as well as the author's inside knowledge of the situation, the article should be made available to a wider audience. A full translation is also pertinent because parts of the article are sometimes quoted out of context in the current polemics on the status of Soviet Jewry.

We must first note that the census totals published thus far are restricted largely to the demographic structure of the population. Occupational structure is dealt with only in part. Secondly, we have little data about nationality breakdown. Nevertheless it is already possible to draw some conclusions about the Jewish population of the U.S.S.R.

A. Number and demographic distribution of the population.

The total number of Jews in the U.S.S.R. came to 2,268,000 persons in the last census. In the light of Jewish population dynamics for all the Soviet census years this result shows up as follows (in thousands):

TABLE 1

Population	Census of 1926	Census of 1939	Census of 1959	Increase 1926–39		Decrease 1939–59	
				Absolute	%	Absolute	%
Number	2,681	3,020	2,268	339[1]	13.0[2]	752	25.0

Instead of the 1926–1939 population increase of 13.0[2] we note a 1939–1959 decrease of 25%. The Jewish population even decreased compared with 1926, when the territory of the Soviet Union was much smaller.

However, the numerical decrease of the Jewish population since 1939 is in reality much greater than 752,000. The data of the 1939 census represent the Soviet Union in the boundaries that existed before there united with it the republics of Lithuania, Latvia, and Estonia, part of Moldavia (Bessarabia), the Western Ukraine, and

Western Belorussia. According to some computations, the Jewish population of these areas in 1940 was about 800,000. This means that the actual decrease consisted of not 752 but 1,552,000 persons.

Even this is not all. If we want to know the real decrease of the Jewish population for these years, we must add the natural increase of the population for 1939–1959. We know that the general population of the Soviet Union grew by 9.5%[3] in the 1939–1959 period, while in the twelve years from 1926 to 1939 it grew by 16%. This means that under normal conditions, the expected increase for twenty years would be about 27%. Therefore, the wartime deprivations caused the natural population increase to be one-third of what it should have been. If we assume that for the Jewish population, as well, the war caused the natural increase to decline to the same extent —i.e., a third of what we would expect under normal conditions— then the increase for the twenty years would have been 6.6% rather than 20%; in other words, an increase of about 150,000. In this way the actual decrease of the Jewish population turns out to be 150,000 + 1,552,000, or 1,700,000.

This means that, had the Jewish population of the U.S.S.R., like the rest of the population, suffered only from wartime deprivations, it should have consisted of about 4,000,000 persons on January 1, 1959.

There are, however, only 2,268,000—a gap of 1,700,000. This opens for us a possibility of determining with some degree of accuracy the number of Jews murdered in the Soviet Union by the Hitlerite beasts. When we deduct from the number 1,700,000 those Jews who denied their ancestry at the census (children of mixed marriages, and those who listed themselves as non-Jews) as well as a certain number of repatriates who were in the Soviet Union at the time of the census,[4] we are left with about 1,500,000 to 1,600,000 killed by Hitler.[4a] More precise figures can unfortunately not be given because nobody is engaged in producing such statistics.[5]

It is well to take a look at the distribution of Soviet Jews by sex. There were 1,103,000 men and 1,165,000 women.[6] It is interesting to see that at a time when the proportion of women in the general population grew considerably in comparison with 1939—obviously as a result of the wartime killing of men in large numbers—the Jews have a reverse situation: the percentage of women decreased compared with 1939. The participation of Jewish males in the war was not less than that of other men; and surely their percentage of battle deaths was not smaller than that of other men. The fact that, nevertheless, the percentage of women among the Jews now almost equals that of men is a result of the Hitlerite exterminations. It is evident that women and children became victims of the exterminations more frequently than men. The latter were largely in the army and thus able to escape the relentless slaughters which the Hitlerite murderers carried out.

The distribution of the Jewish population by republics, as well as the changes in this respect in the 1926–1959 period, are shown in Table 2.

Table 2

The number of Jews by republics and their proportion in each[7]

Republic	1926 Number (In Thousands)	1926 % of General Population	1939 Number (In Thousands)	1939 % of General Population	1959 Number (In Thousands)	1959 % of General Population
R.S.F.S.R.	589	0.5	948	0.9	875	0.7
Ukraine	1,574	5.4	1,533	4.9	840	2.0
Belorussia	407	8.2	375	6.7	150	1.9
Azerbaidzhan			41	1.3		
Georgia			42.5	1.2	52	1.3
Armenia			0.5	0.05		
Turkmenistan			3	0.2		
Uzbekistan	111		51	0.8	94	1.2
Kirghizia			2	0.1		
Tadzhikistan			5	0.3		
Kazakhstan			19	0.3		
Latvia					37	1.7
Lithuania					25	0.9
Moldavia					95	3.3
Estonia					5	0.5
Total U.S.S.R.	2,681	1.82	3,020	1.78	2,268	1.1

What does this table tell us? Firstly, about one hundred thousand Jews are found in the republics whose census figures do not show that they contain Jews (e.g., in Azerbaidzhan, for which the 1939 census shows 52,000[7a] Jews, who did not suffer from Hitler). This is due to the fact that in these republics the 1959 census only lists those national minorities constituting a large number; in Azerbaidzhan, for example, only those who number at least 90,000 are shown.[8] Secondly, the proportion of Jews to the general population decreased in all republics when compared with 1939. This is true even of the R.S.F.S.R., into which there is a natural migration of Jews and where many retained their domicile after the evacuation; yet the Hitlerite slaughters in its western and southern regions (Smolensk, Orel, Rostov, etc.) caused a reduction of the Jewish proportion in the R.S.F.S.R. as well.

What part of the Jewish population resides in each of the major republics? This is shown in Table 3.

TABLE 3

Republic	Percentage of Soviet Jewish population residing in republic in			Increase or decrease of percentage for	
	1926	1939	1959[9]	1926–39	1939–59
R.S.F.S.R.	21.8	31.4	38.5	+ 9.6	+ 7.1
Ukraine	60.4	50.8	37.0	− 9.6	−13.8
Belorussia	15.7	12.4	6.7	− 3.3	− 5.7
Other republics	2.1	5.4	17.8	+ 3.3	+12.4
Total	100	100	100		

The table shows that, in 1926, 60% of the U.S.S.R.'s Jewish population lived in the Ukraine, and in 1939 more than half were still there. In place of this we find a little more than one-third there now, while in Belorussia there are not more than 7% in place of the previous one-fifth. In the R.S.F.S.R., on the other hand, there now resides almost 40% of the Jewish population as against 22% in 1926. In the other republics we now have, in place of the 1926 percentage of 2%, a notable 17.8% [9] or nearly one-fifth, of which 10% are in the Caucasian and Central Asian republics. In the Baltic republics and in Moldavia there are no more than 7%. This distribution of the Jewish population through the Union republics had great importance for the language affiliation of the Jewish population in the 1959 census.

How is the Jewish population distributed among urban and rural settlements? Since the nationality breakdowns for this have unfortunately not yet been published, it is difficult to determine the urbanization of the Jewish population with any degree of accuracy. We can, however, consider it fairly certain that the percentage of rural dwellers is quite negligible. In 1939, 87% of the total Jewish population was in the cities and only 13% in rural areas. Since then basic changes have taken place in this category. The ruin brought upon the Jewish colonies of the Southern Ukraine and the Crimea by Hitler's legions, as well as the extermination of the Jewish population in the small towns of the Ukraine and Belorussia—many of which had been counted as rural settlements—resulted in the fact that very few Jews now live in rural areas.

B. Distribution of the population by language affiliation.

The 1959 census proves that the Jewish population of the U.S.S.R. has made great strides towards linguistic assimilation in the 1926–1959 period. In 1926 Yiddish was listed as their language by 76.1% of the Jewish population in the Ukraine, 96.7% in Belorussia, and 50% for the Union as a whole. In 1959 no more than 20.8% listed Yiddish [10] —i.e., only a fifth instead of the previous half.

We must, however, make a few points to clarify this problem. We lack the relevant data from the long-settled areas of Jewish life: the Ukraine, Belorussia, Moldavia. But we can say with certainty that much closer ties to their language prevail among the Jews in these regions. We know, for example, that in Lithuania 69% of the Jews, and in Latvia 48%, recorded Yiddish as their language. We can therefore surmise that the percentage of those who recorded Yiddish as their national language in the Ukraine, Belorussia, and Moldavia can be explained to a considerable extent by the lack of clarity on this point during the census. How was one to interpret, "rodnoi iazyk" (native tongue)? The census instructions said nothing about it, and many understood it to mean the language of everyday life; in any case the registrars so interpreted it. As a result not a few who speak and read Yiddish, and even appreciate Yiddish books and the Yiddish theater, recorded their language as Russian, because at work, in the street, and sometimes also at home they speak mostly Russian. I know of numerous such cases.

The fact that almost one-half the Jewish population lives in the R.S.F.S.R. and in the Caucasian and Central Asian republics obviously has considerable bearing on the language problem. At any rate, it cannot be gainsaid that the Jewish population has advanced far on the road to linguistic assimilation. Nor should this surprise us. In Soviet Russia each of the national minorities is undergoing a dual, parallel process: assimilation on the one hand, and consolidation of its nationality on the other. The factors which favor assimilation are:

1.) Growth of mixed marriages, as illustrated by the following table:

TABLE 4

Mixed marriages as a proportion of total marriages in selected republics.

Republic	1926	1939
Ukraine	7.5%	19.1%
Armenia	1.0%	7.4%
Kazakhstan	4.0%	7.0%

This process increased in 1959.

2.) The process of diminution of the national population's proportion in its own republic, as shown by the following: The proportion of Uzbeks in Uzbekistan fell from 65% to 62% in the 1939–1959 period, [Kazakh's] in Kazakhstan from 38% to 30%, [Kirghiz] in Kirghizia 52% to 41%, and similarly in other republics. In other words, there is an ongoing process of intermingling by all nationalities, and especially by Russians with the local nationality.

3.) The effect of the Russian language, theater, cinema, and of Russian culture generally on the masses. This influence is growing stronger year by year.

Despite the above we see that, with respect to the national language, an opposite phenomenon parallels the weakening of the tie to that language, and this phenomenon grows with each new census. For example, in 1939, 97.8% recorded the national language as their own language in Uzbekistan, a percentage which increased to 98.4% of the national population in 1959. The same was true in Kirghizia, Azerbaidzhan, and especially in the Bashkir A.S.S.R. There, 53.8% recorded their language as Bashkirian in 1926; in 1959 the number was already 61.9%.

This phenomenon results from the fact that, together with the factors favoring assimilation and in opposition to them, there are created powerful factors making for consolidation, and for supporting and strengthening indigenous national culture. Such are the schools of all kinds, newspapers, journals, theaters, libraries, museums, even departments of academies, and so on. In these areas a new type of Soviet citizen is being created, who harmonizes his national culture with the influence of the totality of Russian progressive culture, enriching and broadening thereby also his national culture.

It is regrettable that Jews are one of those national minorities which have now been for several decades without such factors for supporting and strengthening their culture—since the days of the increased cult of the person. Under such conditions, factors favoring assimilation necessarily obtain the upper hand. However, one should and, indeed, must emphasize that it would be entirely wrong—even under the conditions of the cult of the person—to accuse the government of a special policy with respect to the Jews. In 1938 there were liquidated, together with the Jewish cultural institutions, also those of the Polish, German, Lithuanian, Estonian, and all other national minorities which had ties to the West. This was a result of the spy mania which then reached its high point.[11]

C. About the number of Jewish specialists and students in the U.S.S.R.

The occupational structure of the U.S.S.R.'s population by nationality has not yet been published by the Central Statistical Administration. Therefore we do not yet have precise knowledge of the social structure of the Jewish population in the U.S.S.R. In the Central Statistical Administration's *Vysshee obrazovanie* ("Higher Education") 1961, however, the published data about the number of specialists and students in the Soviet Union include incomplete information about distribution by nationality. This already makes it possible for us to get an idea of the changes in recent years in the social structure of the Jewish population. It is important to take cognizance of the fact that the data bear the date, December 1, 1960.[12]

Jewish specialists in the U.S.S.R. were as follows: With middle-level education 136,400; with higher education 290,700; total 427,100. What is the percentage of specialists among all employed Jews in the U.S.S.R.?

If we assume that the percentage of employed persons for the

Jews is the same as for the population as a whole, i.e., 48%,[12a] the number of employed Jews would be 1,086,000, of whom 427,100 are specialists. This means that 40% of all employed Jews are specialists employed in the Socialist economy. If we add to them the 77,000 students in the institutions of higher education in the U.S.S.R. (without those studying in the middle-level professional schools such as technicums, etc.) the result is that more than half of all employed Jews are specialists or studying to be specialists. The Jews, whose numerical proportion currently given them eleventh place in the Soviet Union, occupy third place among all the peoples of the country in terms of the number of specialists among them.

TABLE 5

The national breakdown of specialists in the U.S.S.R. with middle-level and higher education employed in the national economy (in thousands).

Nationality	Number	Percentage of the specialist population
Russians	5,509.3	63.7
Ukrainians	1,338.4	15.2
Jews	427.1	4.9[13]
Belorussians	257.7	2.9
Georgians	155.1	1.8
Tatars	133.8	1.5
Armenians	130.0	1.4
Azerbaidzhanians	97.4	1.1
Uzbeks	95.7	1.08
Kazakhs	76.1	0.9
Lithuanians	74.1	0.8
Estonians	48.3	0.5
Moldavians	31.7	less than 0.5
Tadjiks	23.7	" " "
Turkmen	20.4	" " "
Total U.S.S.R.	8,783	

While before the revolution, traders, agents, and all other kinds of *luftmenshn* ("people living on air") constituted 55% of the Jewish population, today more than 50% of them are specialists. The other half also consists of working people: workers, salaried employees, pensioners, soldiers, peasants, and craftsmen (before the war more than 600,000 were workers). True, even now the social structure of the Jewish population is very different from that of the general population; but what a change! The Jewish population can rightfully boast of such a social structure, which bespeaks great cultural attainments and much benefit for Socialist construction.

This is demonstrated with especial clarity by the fact that, according to the number of specialists with middle-level and higher education per thousand of population, the Jews are first in the country and possibly first among the peoples of the world. It is true that if we took the number of specialists per thousand of urban population, the difference would not be so great; but the relevant data are unfortunately unavailable.

TABLE 6

The number of specialists per thousand of population for the larger nations of the U.S.S.R.

Russian	population	50	persons
Ukrainian	"	51	"
Belorussian	"	33	"
Georgian	"	58	"
Latvian	"	45	"
Lithuanian	"	32	"
Armenian	"	47	"
Jewish	"	180	"

The Jews thus constitute 1.1% of the population but 4.9% [13] of all specialists; and show, per thousand, more than three times as many specialists as the Russians, Ukrainians, and Georgians, and more than four times as many as the other nations of the Union.

Of great interest is the distribution of Jewish specialists by republics, and the percentage they form of the specialists in each republic. Unfortunately such data is available only for specialists with higher education.

What can we learn from this table? First of all, Jewish specialists are found in all republics—even in those for which the census lists no Jews—and they frequently constitute a larger percentage than among the urban population. They occupy a noteworthy place in Socialist construction of all republics. And these are, incidentally, only the specialists with higher education. Unfortunately, it is not yet known how many specialists with middle-level education are among them, but we can guess that the number is considerable.

TABLE 7

The number of specialists with higher education in the various republics (in thousands).

Republic	Total number of specialists in republic	Jewish specialists	Percentage of Jewish specialists
R.S.F.S.R.	2,083.3	160.7	7.7
Ukraine	685.9	83.6	12.2
Belorussia	110.2[14]	12.1	11.0
Uzbekistan	108.9	8.6	8.0
Kazakhstan	124.8	4.2	3.4
Georgia	106.7	1.8	1.7
Azerbaidzhan	73.2	4.1	5.6
Lithuania	37.2	1.8	4.9
Moldavia	33.3	6.2	18.6
Latvia	40.8	3.6	8.8
Tadzhikistan	23.3	1.2	5.2
Armenia	41.1	0.2	0.5
Turkmenistan	22.5	0.48	2.1
Estonia	24.2	0.87	3.7
Kirghizia	29.8	1.1	3.7

We have a similar picture for the number of Jewish students in the Union's institutions of higher education. Of the total number of students (2,395,500) in the country, 77,571, or 3.2%, are Jews. One might think that this percentage is hardly different from that obtaining in Czarist Russia. But when we consider that in 1909–10 there were not more than 7,241 Jewish students, constituting not more than 0.001% or 21 per thousand of the Jewish population [16] in the Czarist empire, we now find the 77,571 students to be 3.5% of the Jewish population, or more than 7% of all employed Jews.

The large share Jews have in higher education of the Union is brought into stronger relief if we compare it with the share of the other peoples per thousand of population.

TABLE 8 [17]

Number of students by nationality (in thousands).

Nation	Population of particular nation in U.S.S.R.	Number of students of particular nation in higher education	Number of students per thousand of particular nation
Russians	114,114	1,480	13.0
Ukrainians	37,253	343	9.2
Belorussians	7,913	64	8.1
Uzbeks	6,015	54	9.0
Tatars	4,968	40	8.1
Kazakhs	3,622	41	11.3
Aberbaidzhanians	2,940	28	9.5
Armenians	2,787	37	13.3
Georgians	2,692	48	17.8
Lithuanians	2,326	28	12.0
Jews	2,268	77	34.0
Moldavians	2,214	12	5.5
Letts	1,400	16	11.4
Tadzhiks	1,397	12	8.8
Turkmen	1,002	9	9.0
Estonians	989	13	13.1
Kirghiz	969	10	10.3

The all-Union totals are 208,827,000 persons including 3,295,000 students (11.5 per thousand). But since the number of students is listed as of December 1, 1960, and the population figure was taken by us from the 1959 census, the actual number of students per thousand of population for all nations should be somewhat less than the one we have shown. In any case we see from the above figures that the number of Jewish students per thousand is about three times as high as that of any other nation.

How are Jewish students distributed by republics, and what percentage of each republic's student body do they constitute?

TABLE 9

The number of students in particular republics.

Republic	Number of students in republic	Of whom are Jews	Percentage of Jewish students	Percentage of Jews in particular republic
R.S.F.S.R.	1,496,097	46,555	3.1	0.7
Ukraine	417,748	18,673	4.4	2.0
Belorussia	59,296	3,020	5.1	1.9
Moldavia	19,217	1,225	6.4	3.3
Lithuania	26,713	413	1.6	0.9
Uzbekistan	101,271	2,902	2.8	1.2
Azerbaidzhan	36,017	906	2.5	......
Latvia	21,568	800	3.7	1.7
Tadzhikistan	19,959	391	2.0	......
Georgia	56,322	910	1.7	1.3
Kirghizia	17,379	263	1.5	......
Kazakhstan	77,135	837	1.1	......
Armenia	20,165	52	......	......
Turkmenistan	13,151	104	......	......
Estonia	13,507	126	......	......

Thus the proportion of Jewish students is higher in every republic than the proportion of Jews in the republic's population. In this connection it is of interest that in all republics, even in those with a very small number of Jewish students, the number of Jewish students per thousand of the republic's Jewish population is much higher than the general number of students per population in the republic. This is shown by Table 10.

The largest number of Jewish students per thousand is thus found in the R.S.F.S.R., but in all republics it is greater than that of the general population. We must note, however, that the difference would not be great if we compared the percentage of students only to the urban population in each republic.

TABLE 10

Number of students, general and Jewish, per thousand of population (in thousands).

Republic	Population of republic	Students in republic	Of whom are Jews	Number per thousand for General Population	Number per thousand for Jewish Population
R.S.F.S.R.	117,534	1,496	46.5	12.7	53.1
Ukraine	41,869	418	18.7	10.0	22.3
Belorussia	8,055	59.3	3.0	7.3	20.0
Uzbekistan	8,106	101.3	2.9	12.3	30.9
Georgia	4,044	56.3	0.9	13.8	17.0
Lithuania	2,711	26.7	0.4	9.8	16.0
Moldavia	2,885	19.2	1.2	6.8	12.6
Latvia	2,093	21.5	0.8	10.3	21.6
Estonia	1,197	13.5	0.13	11.3	25.0

NOTES

[1] In original: 348.

[2] In original: 16%.

[3] We assume the author here is discounting the increase of population brought about by the annexations of 1939–40; otherwise the percentage of increase from the 1939 total of 170.6 million to the 1959 total of 208.8 million is much higher than 9.5%.

[4] Refugees who held Polish or Rumanian citizenship were allowed to opt for repatriation after the war.

[4a] This number should be revised slightly upward because the Georgian and Bukharian Jews were counted among the 2,268,000 Jews. (Author's footnote.)

[5] It is possible that the author himself did some work on the subject after this was written—see his last writings mentioned in our introductory note.

[6] The U.S.S.R. summary census volume published in 1962 shows a somewhat greater preponderance of women: 1,237,000 women as against 1,031,000 men. Kantor seems to have used less precise preliminary figures.

[7] In table 2 and 3 and the discussion based on them the author treated the R.S.F.S.R. figure for 1926 as that of Belorussia and vice versa. We have corrected this and many other errors by using in the main the following works: L. Zinger, *Dos banayte folk* (Moscow, 1941), p. 35 f.; Solomon M. Schwarz, *The Jews in the Soviet Union* (Syracuse, 1951), p. 15; *Narodnoe khoziaistvo SSSR v 1960 g.* (Moscow, 1961), p. 17 f.; and M. Altschuler's summary statistical pamphlet *The Jews in the Soviet Union Census* (Jerusalem, 1963).

[7a] This should probably read 41,000—see table 2.

[8] Since the above was written, the census breakdowns for the union republics have been published and show the smaller Jewish populations as well. They have been summarized in Altschuler's pamphlet (see previous note), and are: Azerbaidzhan, 40.2; Armenia, 1.0; Turkmenistan, 4.1; Kirghizia, 8.6; Tadzhikistan, 12.4.

[9] Original has 37.4 for the Ukraine and 17.4 for "other republics." Percentages of increase and decrease have been adjusted.

[10] It should be noted that those Jews considering other Jewish dialects as their national language are not included in this percentage. These Jews—mainly Georgian, Bukharian, and "mountain Jews"—when added to the Yiddish speakers bring the total percentage of those "considering the language of the nationality as their national language" to 21.5—a figure erroneously shown as 21.1 in some Soviet statistical handbooks.

[11] What the author states here is substantially true; the sudden closing of Polish, German and other schools in January, 1938 is mentioned by Markoosha Fischer, *My Lives in Russia* (New York, 1944), p. 191 f. However, Kantor by implication exaggerates the extent of the 1938 purge for the Jews, probably to avoid mentioning the near-total and clearly anti-Jewish purge of 1948–49, discussion of which was and still is a delicate problem in the Soviet Union. After the purges of the 30's a number of Jewish institutions were still able to carry on, inter alia, those in Birobidzhan, the newspapers outside of Moscow, and the Jewish department of the Ukrainian Academy.

[12] In text: December 15, 1961.

[12a] In reality it should be smaller, because farming leads to heavy employment of women, and the Jews have now almost no peasantry left. (Author's footnote.)

[13] By error the number is given as 471,100, and the percentage as 6.0.

[14] The Belorussian and Uzbekistan numbers have been given erroneously as 110.0 and 106.9; many of the percentages in Kantor's table were incorrect as well.

[15] Of the total population?

[16] Possibly this should read: 2.1 per thousand, as the number in the text is much too high.

[17] There are quite a few typographical and other errors in this and the next two tables, which we have corrected.

JEWISH CEREMONIAL ART: A BASIC BIBLIOGRAPHY

JOSEPH GUTMANN

Wayne State University

The study and collecting of Jewish ceremonial art are of recent origin. Only in the late nineteenth century, when interest in the cultures of primitive peoples led to the collection of their art and the establishment of ethnographical museums, did collections of Jewish art objects and the establishment of Jewish museums also begin. Although the first Jewish Museum was founded at Vienna in 1895 and others, like those at Warsaw, Prague, Frankfurt am Main, and Berlin soon followed, two major exhibits had previously been devoted to Jewish ceremonial art—one in Paris at the Trocadéro in 1878 (*Collection de M. Strauss. Description des objets d'art religieux hébraïques exposés dans les galeries du Trocadéro, à l'Exposition universelle de 1878*) and another at London's Royal Albert Hall in 1887 (*Catalogue of the Anglo-Jewish Historical Exhibition, Royal Albert Hall, London, 1887*).

The pioneer in the scientific exploration of Jewish ceremonial art was a German Catholic, Heinrich Frauberger, Director of the Industrial Arts and Crafts Museum in Düsseldorf. In 1895, when an architect sought his advice about a design for a grilled enclosure around a Jewish grave, Frauberger found he could be of little help in suggesting appropriate Jewish symbols because there were no studies or resource people available on the subject. The incident persuaded Frauberger to begin collecting Jewish ceremonial objects, and led him in 1897 to help establish the first society dedicated to preserving, studying and researching Jewish art objects. Thus in 1900, there appeared at Frankfurt am Main the first volume of *Mitteilungen der Gesellschaft zur Erforschung jüdischer Kunstdenkmäler* and, shortly thereafter, the *Notizblatt* of the society, which had gathered around it a competent body of scholars to embark on the scientific study of Jewish ceremonial art.

Although seventy years have passed since this auspicious beginning and many private and public collections of Jewish ceremonial art have sprung up (and continue to spring up), especially in the United States and Israel, no comprehensive study of the entire field exists and only a handful of scientific articles, catalogues and monographs have been produced. Few young scholars have been attracted to this field and such diligent, devoted students as Franz Landsberger and Mordechai Narkiss are no longer with us. In an attempt to encourage further research in this neglected field of Judaica, the major, recent scientific studies in this discipline will be briefly listed.

My own *Jewish Ceremonial Art* (Thomas Yoseloff, New York: 1964) is actually the only volume available which attempts to survey the complex history of ceremonial art from antiquity to the present day. Leo A. Mayer's *Bibliography of Jewish Art* edited by Otto Kurz (Magnes Press, Jerusalem: 1967) is an indispensable tool for research in this field. Many catalogs of public auctions of private collections, such as those of the Parke-Bernet Galleries, O'Reilly's Plaza Art Galleries, and Astor Birnbaum Galleries have been issued within the last twenty years, but the information given on the objects for sale is frequently unreliable and of little help in furthering the scientific study of Jewish ceremonial art. In this connection, it should be noted that many spurious objects are finding their way into private and public collections. The serious student is advised to read carefully the following articles: Cecil Roth, "Caveat Emptor Judaeus," *Commentary* (March 1967), pp. 84–86; Otto Kurz, "Forgeries of Jewish Ritual Lavers," *Eretz Israel,* VII (1964), pp. 54*–55*; and Joseph Gutmann, "Is there a Place for Art in the Synagogue?" *Central Conference of American Rabbis Journal,* XIII (1965), pp. 30–33.

Some years ago, Stephen S. Kayser and Guido Schoenberger prepared a model catalog to the collection of the Jewish Museum of the Jewish Theological Seminary in New York: *Jewish Ceremonial Art* (Jewish Publication Society of America, Philadelphia: 1959). In the best tradition of German scholarship are the catalogs to the Judaica exhibitions held at the Historisches Museum, Frankfurt am Main and Kölnisches Stadtmuseum: *Synagoga. Jüdische Altertümer, Handschriften and Kultgeräte* (Ner Tamid Verlag, Frankfurt am Main: 1961) and *Monumenta Judaica. 2000 Jahre Geschichte und Kultur der Juden am Rhein* (Melzer Verlag, Köln: 1964). The ceremonial collections in such outstanding museums as the Musée Cluny, Paris; Joods Historisch Museum, Amsterdam; Bezalel National Museum (now the Israel Museum) in Jerusalem, and the Jewish ceremonial objects in German and Swiss museums are thoroughly researched in their catalogs. The magnificent objects in private and public Italian collections are pictured in Silvio G. Cusin, *Art in the Jewish Tradition* (Adei-Wizo, Milan: 1963). Italian ceremonial objects are also depicted in Umberto Nahon's *Torah Scroll Ornaments* (American Israeli Paper Mills at Hadera, Jerusalem: 1966, Hebrew and Italian), and "Ceremonial Art from Italy," *Ariel,* 8 (1964), pp. 33–36 with eight plates. The illustrations in *From the Beginning, Archaeology and Art in the Israel Museum, Jerusalem* by Karl Katz, P. P. Kahane and Magen Broshi (Reynal and Co., New York: 1968) and in the catalog to the exhibition *Israël à travers les âges* at the Petit Palais, Paris, in 1968 are important for studying ceremonial objects still extant in Israel. The finest and richest collection of Jewish ceremonial art is now housed in Prague's State Jewish Museum. No published, scientific catalog of this vast collection exists, but some of its objects are illustrated in *Prague Ghetto in the Renaissance Period,* edited by Otto Muneles (The State Jewish Museum, Prague: 1965); *Schicksal des Jüdischen Museums in Prag* by Hana Valovková (Artia, Prague: 1965); *Historica Hebraica,* exhibition catalog, Jüdisches Gemeindehaus Berlin (Berlin: 1965); and *Die Kunst der Synagoge* by Renate Krüger (Koehler and Amelang, Leipzig: 1966).

For a survey of the role Jews played as artisans in different countries from ancient times to the end of the eighteenth century, Mark Wischnitzer's *A History of Jewish Crafts and Guilds* (Jonathan David, New York: 1965) is to be recommended. Such recent studies as those by Bernhard Brilling, "Geschichte des jüdischen Goldschmiedegewerbes in Schlesien," *Hamburger mittel- und ostdeutsche Forschungen,* VI (1967), pp. 163–221; "Zur Geschichte des jüdischen Goldschmiedegewerbes in Prag, Die erste jüdischen Goldschmiede," *Zeitschrift für die Geschichte der Juden* V/1 (1968), pp. 21–26 and Josef Hráský, "La corporation juive d'orfèvrerie à Prague," *Judaica Bohemiae,* II/1 (1966), pp. 19–40, and "Die Kennzeichnung von Edelmetallen,"

Judaica Bohemiae, II/2 (1966), pp. 97–106 offer important new data on Jewish goldsmiths. The studies by Jeanette W. Rosenbaum, *Myer Myers, Goldsmith 1723–1795* (Jewish Publication Society of America, Philadelphia: 1954), and Guido Schoenberger, "The Ritual Silver made by Myer Myers," *Publication of the American Jewish Historical Society,* XLIII/1 (1953), pp. 1–9, are basic for information about this colonial American Jewish craftsman. Equally significant are studies of English Jewish ceremonial art like *Treasures of a Temple. A descriptive catalogue of the ritual plate, mantles and furniture of the Spanish and Portuguese Jews' Synagogue in Bevis Marks . . .* (Taylor's Foreign Press, London: 1951; A. G. Grimwade, "Anglo-Jewish Silver," *Transactions of the Jewish Historical Society of England,* XVIII (1953–55), pp. 113–125; and Jonathan Stone, "English Silver Rimmonim and their Makers," *Quest,* I (1965), pp. 23–29. Guido Schoenberger's study "Der Frankfurter Goldschmied Johann Matthias Sandrart . . .," *Schriften des Historischen Museums Frankfürt am Main,* XII (1966), pp. 143–70, is the first scholarly essay devoted to Jewish ceremonial objects created by an important non-Jewish craftsman.

On the origin and development of Jewish ceremonial objects used in connection with home and synagogal observances, the following studies deserve to be mentioned:

On Torah Decorations:

Franz Landsberger, "The Origin of European Torah Decorations," *HUCA,* XXIV (1952–53), pp. 133–50; Franz Landsberger, "A German Torah Ornamentation," *HUCA,* XXIX (1958), pp. 315–30; Joseph Gutmann, "Priestly Vestments, Torah Ornaments and the King James Bible," *Central Conference of American Rabbis Journal* (January 1969), pp. 78–79, 104; David Davidovitch, "Torah Binders—An Extinct Custom and Artistic Tradition," *Museum Haaretz, Bulletin No. 4* (1962), pp. 25–34.

On Torah Curtains:

Franz Landsberger, "Old-Time Torah Curtains," *HUCA,* XIX (1946), pp. 353–87 and Hana Volavková, *The Synagogue Treasures of Bohemia and Moravia* (Sfinx, Prague: 1949).

On the Ner Tamid and Decalogue:

Joseph Gutmann, "How Traditional are our Traditions?" *Central Conference of American Rabbis Journal* (April 1968), pp. 59–61.

On the Sabbath:

Franz Landsberger, "The Origin of the Ritual Implements for the Sabbath," *HUCA,* XXVII (1956), pp. 387–415; Mordechai Narkiss, "The Origin of the Spice Box known as the 'Hadass' ", *Eretz-Israel,* VI (1960), pp. 189–98 (Hebrew with English Summary).

On Hanukkah:

Franz Landsberger, "Old Hanukkah Lamps," *HUCA,* XXV (1954), pp. 347–67 and the important monograph by Mordechai Narkiss on *The Hanukkah Lamp* (Bnai Bezalel Publishing Co., Jerusalem: 1939, Hebrew with English Summary).

On the Jewish Wedding:

Joseph Gutmann, "Wedding Customs and Ceremonies in Art," *The Jewish Marriage Anthology,* ed. by Philip and Hanna Goodman (Jewish Publication Society of America, Philadelphia: 1965), pp. 175–83, 347–50; Mordechai Narkiss, "An Italian Niello Casket of the Fifteenth Century," *Journal of the Warburg and Courtauld Institutes,* XXI (1958), pp. 288–95; Franz Landsberger, "Illuminated Marriage Contracts," *HUCA,* XXVI (1955), pp. 503–44; and the handsome volume by David Davidovitch, *The Ketuba, Jewish Marriage Contracts through the Ages* (E. Lewin-Epstein, Tel Aviv: 1968).

On Burial:

Isaiah Shachar, "Burial Society Glass," *Bezalel, Bulletin of the Bezalel National Museum,* II (1963), no pagination (Hebrew with English Summary).

On the Mezuzah:

Franz Landsberger, "The Origin of the Decorated Mezuzah," *HUCA,* XXXI (1960), pp. 149–66.

This bibliography,* though not exhaustive, has been compiled as a small token of my appreciation to a great librarian, Dr. I. Edward Kiev, in the hope that others will emulate his noble example and encourage young scholars to pursue serious research.

---

* Many articles cited in this bibliography are reprinted in *Beauty in Holiness, Studies in Jewish Customs and Ceremonial Art,* edited by Joseph Gutmann, Ktav Publishing House, Inc. (New York: 1970).

S. B. SCHWARZBERG (1865–1929)—
HEBREW PUBLISHER AND BIBLIOGRAPHER

JACOB KABAKOFF

Lehman College of the City University of New York

Samuel Benjamin Schwarzberg, who represents a unique figure in the annals of American Hebrew publishing activity, attempted almost single-handedly to carry out far-reaching publishing and bibliographical projects. Although his plans did not see fulfillment and ended largely in frustration, he tried valiantly to arouse the Hebrew-reading public to its responsibility to perpetuate the Hebrew literary heritage in this country. After engaging in several publishing ventures, he devoted himself to the monumental task of preparing a reader's guide to the whole of Hebrew periodical literature. On the basis of his literary remains, which are to be found in the library of the Jewish Theological Seminary of America, we are able to trace more fully the course of his activities.

Schwarzberg was born in Lipno, district of Plock, Poland, in 1865.[1] Following his marriage during the early 90's he settled in Warsaw where he published several volumes, including works by Isaac Leib Peretz, Mordecai Aaron Günzburg and others, as well as a new edition of the siddur, *Tefillat Yisrael,* with a commentary by Jacob Zebi Mecklenburg. To some of the volumes he added prefaces and introductions.

Arriving in this country in 1897, Schwarzberg sought to continue his publishing activity. The Hebrew *maskilim* in America had founded a Hebrew monthly literary review entitled *Ner ha-Ma'arabi* ("The

Western Light") in 1895. Among the editors listed in the first issue were Abraham Baer Dobsevage, Menahem Mendel Dolitzky, Abraham Hayyim Rosenberg, Moses Reichersohn and Gerson Rosenzweig. The magazine appeared sporadically under the sponsorship of the Society for the Advancement of Hebrew Literature in America and had financial difficulties. Beginning with issue 7 in 1896 its sponsorship was assumed by the Ohale Shem Association, and the editorship passed into the hands of Adolph Moses Radin and A. H. Rosenberg. The sponsorship reverted to the Society for the Advancement of Hebrew Literature in America and, beginning with volume 1, number 12, 1897, Schwarzberg is listed as editor.

Schwarzberg's hand as editor and publisher is clearly evident in the magazine beginning with volume 2, number 1, July 1897. In his leading editorial, entitled "To The Readers," he indicated his reasons for accepting responsibility for the magazine. He was motivated by a desire to afford the writers and scholars who had come to America with a suitable organ of expression that would appear regularly. The magazine, he stated, would continue not only to publish the writings of leading European Hebrew writers but would give special emphasis to American Jewish life. The first issue under his editorship inaugurated a section called "Jews and Judaism in America." Articles by Judah David Eisenstein on the colonies of the Russian Jewish immigrants and by Mordecai Ze'ev Raisin on George Washington and the Jews appeared side by side with contributions by such well-known European Hebrew writers as Mordecai David Brandstaetter, Solomon Mandelkorn and Solomon Rubin.

Schwarzberg continued his efforts in behalf of *Ner ha-Ma'arabi* until the end of the year and published 4 issues. In the fourth issue, dated December 1897, he penned an article entitled "Let Us Search Our Ways," in which he appealed for the strengthening of Jewish national education and the support of the Hebrew language and literature. He expressed the hope that the encouraging report on the first Zionist Congress rendered by the American delegate, Dr. Shepsel Schaeffer, at a meeting of the Ohale Shem Association would serve as an impetus in this direction. Schwarzberg's hopes, however, were soon dashed to the ground. He had poured energy and funds into the magazine but to no avail. His mood at that time is evident from a letter which he sent to M. Z. Raisin on February 21, 1898, in which he stated that he would still try to maintain the magazine but that he could not continue to do so at his own expense and at the expense of his family.[2]

Keenly disappointed, Schwarzberg was led to publish a sharp indictment of the Hebrew readers and the Jewish public under the title *Tikkateb Zot le-Dor Aharon* ("This Shall Be Written for the Generation to Come"), N.Y., 1898, 33 pages. He subtitled his pamphlet, "A faithful description of the state of our literature in the new land and the attitude of the People of the Book to it." He viewed his failure as sad testimony to the condition of our people not only in America but in Europe as well. Regarding the *Ner ha-Ma'arabi* he wrote:

> We had thought that if in a land such as this and in a city as large as this we would work unceasingly and tirelessly to give our people a monthly journal for literature and scholarship, to which the most prominent Jewish writers and scholars would contribute, it was inconceivable that such a monthly journal, the only one of its kind in the U.S., would not find enough supporters in order to become firmly established, even though its editor would not live in luxury (page 8).

Schwarzberg revealed the many difficulties he had encountered in obtaining support and subscribers. He obtained help from such men as Gustav Gottheil, Mayer Sulzberger, Isaac M. Wise and Gotthard Deutsch. In Philadelphia he had received twenty-two subscriptions, but less were forthcoming from Baltimore and other cities; and the Society for the Advancement of Hebrew Literature in America had done little to help. Schwarzberg castigated American Jews for sinking into materialism and for failing to uphold their cultural and spiritual values. His pamphlet is a powerful condemnation of an immigrant generation that was far too preoccupied with its problems of adjustment to foster Hebrew literature and scholarship. Many of his fellow-*maskilim,* like Wolf Schur, editor of *ha-Pisgah,* and Ephraim Deinard, who reviewed the pamphlet, felt that while the author was justified in his criticism, he had adopted too extreme a tone and had praised the Reform Jewish leaders at the expense of the East European immigrants.[3]

Following the demise of *Ner ha-Ma'arabi,* Schwarzberg became a bookdealer on the East Side of New York. One of the prominent European contributors to the magazine had been Dr. Solomon Rubin. In 1904, we find Schwarzberg renewing his publishing activity with the issuing of a brochure by Rubin, entitled *Ha-Adam Etz ha-Sadeh* ("Man is the Tree of the Field," N.Y., 15 pages). In a postscript he indicated that Dr. Rubin had assigned to him the lifetime publication rights to his writings and he warned against any infringement of these rights. Three years previously, in 1901, Schwarzberg also published Dr. Rubin's volume *Hidot ha-Olam* ("Riddles of the World," 76 pages) in Cracow, the author's city of residence.

Schwarzberg's tenacity and single-mindedness concerning the role of Hebrew literature and scholarship did not slacken despite his setbacks and disappointments. He was sustained throughout the years by his unbounded admiration for the exemplars of Hebrew learning whose works he sought to bring to the attention of the reading public. His extremism led him to believe that only Jewish scholarship in the Hebrew language was authentic and that all other forms led to assimilation.

A vivid characterization of Schwarzberg's temperament was offered by Mordecai Danzis, who knew him in his later years. Danzis wrote:[4]

> His image rises before me. He was a thin man of average height, with a shiny bald pate and a gaunt, expressive face. His bushy-browed, gray eyes would flash and he would wave his delicate hands during the course of his flowing conversation.

Schwarzberg never forsook his dream of establishing a publishing house for the dissemination of Hebrew literary and scholarly works. At the end of World War I, when the Jewish centers of learning overseas were at a standstill, he felt that the time was propitious in America for a major effort. Mustering whatever support he could gather, and with the encouragement of his friends Mordecai Danzis and Abraham Goldberg, he issued a prospectus concerning his proposed publishing house "Ashkoloth." The twelve-page printed brochure bears the following legend: "Prospect/ Kol Mewasser/ le-Tehiat Hokmat Yisrael we-Sifruta/ Al-yede Hevrat/ 'Ashkolot.' " ("Prospectus—Tidings Concerning the Rebirth of Jewish Scholarship and its Literature by the Ashkolot Society"). The address is given as Ashkoloth, Inc., 159 East Broadway, New York. The prospectus bears no date of publication but it appears to have been issued in 1918. It states that the aim of the new publication society was to restore the glory of the Hebrew book at a time when literary activity in Europe had come to a halt. It would thus impart a new role and purpose to American Jewry and attest to its vitality.

The purposes of Ashkolot were defined as follows:

> The Ashkolot publishing society has collected books, brochures and articles by the greatest Jewish scholars and the best thinkers and researchers . . . their publication will greatly enrich our cultural treasures and will be a source of amazement and joy to every book-lover and student of Jewish studies. . . .
>
> In addition to publishing the works of authors whose rights it has acquired, the Ashkolot publishing house is prepared to reprint old and rare items which are unknown even to most people who deal with literature and which have a scientific and universal value that will never grow old. . . .

The prospectus indicates that the backers of Ashkolot had decided to issue shares in the sum of $10.00 each, and it appealed to the public to support the venture by acquiring them. In its concluding section it listed the names of thirty-eight scholars whose scattered writings were to appear in collected form. Schwarzberg's literary and scholarly tastes are revealed in the list. The names include such nineteenth-century European Hebrew scholars as Meir Ish Shalom, David Oppenheim, Elijah Ben Amozeg, Senior Sachs, Samuel Joseph Fuenn, Mordecai Plungian and Jakob Reifmann, among others. It is evident that Schwarzberg's primary purpose was to save from oblivion their writings which were scattered in numerous periodicals and learned journals.

The subject areas that were to be covered by the publishing activities of Ashkolot included the following:

1. Studies of antiquity and history.
2. Biblical researches.
3. Studies in the development of the Oral Law.
4. Studies in the development of religion, culture, and literature.
5. Studies in philosophy and kabbalah.
6. Biographies of great spiritual figures and historical personages.
7. Hebrew travel literature, including all which has already appeared in book form and which is still scattered in periodicals.
8. Hebrew polemical literature, much of which is unknown to the public.
9. Shorter works of scientific value, over 200 in number, which have not appeared in book form.

Also listed are six works which were said to be in press and which were to appear first. They included the writings of David Neumark,

Hayyim Oppenheim, Isaac Hirsch Weiss, Eliezer Zebi Zweifel, and Solomon Rubin, and a collection of three travel books. Each volume, consisting of 192 pages, was to be printed in a new Hebrew type face specially prepared for the publishing society. The price of the volumes was uniformly set at $1.25 each and advance subscribers to all 6 could acquire them for a total of $5.00.

Efforts were made to give wide circulation to the prospectus, to sell shares and obtain subscribers. A copy of an undated letter addressed to lovers of Jewish scholarship and literature and appealing for the support of Ashkolot has been preserved in the Ephraim Deinard collection at the library of the Jewish Theological Seminary of America. The signatories of the letter include Peter Wiernik, chairman, Israel Matz, treasurer and Mordecai Danzis, secretary. The letter states that many leading American Jews were among the directors of the new publishing venture. Nevertheless, little headway was made and the project died a-borning.

After the cessation of *Ner ha-Ma'arabi* Schwarzberg had given vent to his frustration in a brochure. The failure of his dream to establish a publishing house led him to seek literary expression for his wounded spirit once again. Among his literary remains there are to be found the printed sheets of his unpublished work entitled *Mi-Ma'amakim* ("Out of the Depths," N.Y., 1919). The work was to consist of three parts but only sixty-four pages of the first part were set in type (pages 47–50 are lacking). The verse "And set a mark upon the foreheads of the men" (Ezekiel 9:4), which appears on the title page, indicates the mood in which the author penned his book.

The first part of *Mi-Ma'amakim* is entitled "A Question to Jewish Scholars." In page after page of trenchant words and sharp invective Schwarzberg castigates the Jewish scholars who had forsaken Hebrew for other languages. He considers their action an unpardonable sin against the Jewish people and upholds the honor of the East European Jewish scholars who wrote in Hebrew and were thus assured a place in our literary history. Among the men he singles out for mention and praise are Krochmal, Rapaport, Schorr, and Pinsker.

In rambling fashion and intemperate language Schwarzberg also discusses the low state of modern Hebrew literature. He condemns many of its authors for their imitativeness and lack of religiosity. He finds a sense of irresponsibility concerning Jewish values not only among some of the leading European Hebrew writers but also among representatives of the Palestinian school of authors. In short, he delivers himself of a bitter diatribe against the builders of modern Hebrew literature. Why Schwarzberg failed to publish this work is left unexplained. Perhaps he had second thoughts about its volatile tone.

In line with his lifelong ambition to preserve the scholarly contributions of Hebrew authors and to provide a reference tool to their scattered writings Schwarzberg devoted himself for many years to the preparation of a reader's guide to Hebrew periodical literature. His aim was to record in alphabetical fashion all that had been published since the days of the *Me'assfim*. His literary remains contain bundles of thousands of slips on which he recorded his references in a fine hand. In many instances he included annotations as well. In one place he notes that he had already indexed over 300 periodicals and collective volumes and that he had gathered references on more than 1,000 contributors. In addition to the material in Hebrew publications, he also included Hebrew articles printed in periodicals that appeared in other languages as well.

In reply to a query about the aim of his work, Schwarzberg wrote as follows:

> The aim of my work is to record all the articles and poems, the letters and epigrams, as well as published manuscript materials, from the days of the *Me'assfim* to the latest newspapers and collective volumes.
>
> But the main aspect of my work is one which has been unparalleled to date, namely to give the contents of every article and letter and of the many items appearing under the headings 'Notes' and 'Comments,' in most of the newspapers and volumes. Since the reader cannot know from the entries about their contents, I have listed every note, etc. as an individual item.
>
> My purpose is to make of my index a volume that will aid anyone who is dealing with any subject.

Schwarzberg's bibliographical slips cover the entire range of Hebrew periodical literature and include entries for both renowned and lesser known figures. For several men, like Jakob Reifmann, Adolph Jellinek and Isaac Samuel Reggio, fairly extensive listings were prepared. The full listings which he endeavored to compile came to fill a desideratum which is still with us.

An example of Schwarzberg's method of annotative listing may be seen in his published bibliography of the writings of Senior Sachs (1815–1892), who made many contributions to the study of medieval

Hebrew literature.[5] Following a lengthy introduction on the quality of nineteenth-century Hebrew scholarship and on the work of Sachs, Schwarzberg describes his method of listing and proceeds to present his bibliography of Sachs' books, the periodicals he edited and his articles arranged chronologically by year of publication. In all, 268 items are listed in this comprehensive survey.

The Sachs bibliography appeared in 1929, the year of Schwarzberg's passing. Regrettably, the other comprehensive bibliographies which he had prepared did not see publication. Among his literary remains there is the manuscript of a full-scale bibliography of Baer Goldberg (1800–1884), the author of many articles and studies on Jewish history and Hebrew literature. From the printer's notations on the manuscript it is evident that it was set in type.[6] The bibliography encompasses 282 items and includes not only Goldberg's books, translations, and works which he edited, but also his numerous articles. Also listed are Goldberg's letters to such scholars as Solomon Buber and Reifmann, which had been published posthumously.

Among Schwarzberg's papers is found an introductory note to the Goldberg bibliography which casts further light on his aims. He wrote:

> This article is a chapter of the book on which I am working in order to record all the books, brochures and pamphlets dealing with all branches of Jewish and general scientific study; also the articles, stories, poems, etc.—including those left in manuscript and published in recent times—which are scattered in periodicals, collective volumes, annuals, monthly publications, quarterlies and daily newspapers.

He indicated that on the basis of his book the readers would come to know what our authors had accomplished since the rise of modern Hebrew literature and would be in a position to trace its development. Finally, he stated that he was submitting his chapter on Goldberg, on the advice of Isaac Rivkind, because Goldberg had been unjustifiably neglected more than all the other scholars of his generation.

Schwarzberg also prepared a bibliography of the writings of Zebi Hirsch Chajes (1805–1855), which was intended for the memorial volume in honor of the latter's grandson, Zebi Perez Chajes, but which was never published. Among Schwarzberg's papers is found only the title page of this bibliography together with an introductory note by the author indicating that he took pride in presenting it to the readers of the volume.

A Hebrew postal card from Dr. Viktor Aptowitzer, one of the editors of the Chajes memorial volume, was addressed to Schwarzberg, care of the Jewish Theological Seminary, regarding this bibliography. The postal card, which is dated August 19, 1928, reads as follows:

> The Honorable Mr. Schwarzberg,
> Dear Sir:
> Mr. Dr. Joshua Bloch—New York, was good enough to inform me that you have a bibliography of the writings of Rabbi Zebi Chajes. It is clear, as Mr. Bloch has also indicated, that the place for this bibliography is in the memorial volume for Rabbi Zebi Perez Chajes, the grandson of Rabbi Zebi Chajes. May I therefore request that you submit your article to the publication committee of the memorial volume.

Schwarzberg's projected bibliographical volume roused the interest of various scholars and bookmen both in this country and abroad. A Hebrew letter from A. H. Rosenberg, a former editor of *Ner ha-Ma'arabi* and its printer, inquires concerning his progress on the work. In a postscript to the letter, dated August 3, 1921, Rosenberg asked: "Are you making plans for the publication of your unique volume?"

The Hebrew poet, Hayyim Nahman Bialik, who headed the Dvir Publishing Co. in Tel Aviv, also evinced interest in Schwarzberg's project. In volume 4 of his collected letters we find three items concerning Schwarzberg. On July 7, 1928, Bialik addressed a letter to Dr. Joseph Marcus. He enclosed a preliminary bibliography of the writings of Jakob Reifmann with the request that it be submitted to Schwarzberg for his additions. Bialik indicated that he needed this information for a literary project in which he was engaged.[7] Bialik had intended to publish an edition of Reifmann's collected works.

Schwarzberg apparently wrote to Bialik informing him of the scope of his projected bibliographical work. Bialik, in turn, replied that his Dvir Publishing Co. might be interested in sponsoring its publication. He wrote Schwarzberg on September 28, 1928, as follows: [8]

> Your suggestion appeals to me, and I am prepared to carry it out. Please submit to me the bibliographical listing of Reifmann's writings and Dvir will publish it. If the experiment succeeds, perhaps we will

continue with it and fulfill your plan regarding the large bibliographical book by combining the brochures into a complete unit, as you suggest.

Writing to Dr. Joseph Marcus again on January 17, 1929, Bialik inquired why he had received no reply from Schwarzberg concerning the Reifmann bibliography. He stated that since he had agreed to publish it as a separate brochure he wondered why he had not heard from the author.[9]

We find Bialik writing to Dr. Marcus once more on June 29, 1930, asking this time where he could obtain a copy of the Freidus memorial volume containing the late Schwarzberg's bibliography of the writings of Senior Sachs.[10] Schwarzberg had passed away, forlorn and forgotten, on April 27, 1929. During his last years he resided with his son, who was connected with the Yiddish theater. Because of this connection, Maurice Schwartz, of the Yiddish stage, was among those who eulogized him. In the Hebrew weekly *Hadoar* only a brief obituary appeared.[11]

NOTES

1 For biographical entries on Schwarzberg see: Benzion Eisenstadt, *Hakme Yisrael ba-Amerika,* New York: 1903, p. 103, and G. Kressel, *Lexicon ha-Sifrut ha-Ivrit ba-Dorot ha-Aharonim,* Merhavia, Israel: 1967, vol. II, column 900. Daniel Persky devoted 3 articles to him in *Hadoar,* as follows: vol. XXXII, no. 21, March 28, 1952; vol. XXXIV, no. 37, Aug. 27, 1954; vol. XXXIV, no. 38, Sept. 10, 1954.

2 See his letter to Raisin in *'Iggerot Soferim 'Ibrim,* edited by M. Z. Raisin, B'klyn, New York: 1947, p. 296.

3 Schur's review appeared in *ha-Pisgah,* vol. VI, no. 4, Nov. 11, 1898. Deinard published his review in the volume *Sifrat Zion,* New York: 1899, p. 52.

4 In his letter to Daniel Persky, included in the latter's article "S. B. Schwarzberg and His Contribution to Our Literature," *Hadoar,* vol. XXXII, no. 21, March 28, 1952.

5 In *Studies in Jewish Bibliography and Related Subjects in Memory of Abraham Solomon Freidus,* New York, 1929, Hebrew section, pp. 44–119.

6 According to Dr. Joshua Bloch, who was a member of the committee on publications of the Alexander Kohut Memorial Foundation, this bibliography was intended for the Chajes memorial volume, which was eventually published by the Foundation in 1933. Dr. Bloch indicated to me that Schwarzberg had received some financial support towards his work from the Foundation.

7 See *'Iggerot H. N. Bialik,* edited by F. Lachower, Tel Aviv: 1938, vol. 4, p. 138.

8 *Ibid.,* p. 164.

9 *Ibid.,* p. 201.

10 *Ibid.,* vol. 5, 1939, p. 89.

11 Vol. IX, no. 25, May 10, 1929.

SUPPLEMENT III: JUDAICA AMERICANA PRINTED BEFORE 1851

NATHAN M. KAGANOFF

American Jewish Historical Society

INTRODUCTION

Since Dr. A. S. W. Rosenbach first published his *American Jewish Bibliography* in 1926, two supplements have appeared, one by Dr. Jacob R. Marcus in 1954, and the second by Edwin Wolf 2nd in 1958. These three compilations brought the total known number of American imprints published before 1851 to 1155.

For the past decade the American Jewish Historical Society has made a conscientious effort to collect these early American imprints. The following listing is limited to items found in its Library. We have excluded materials of a purely peripheral nature such as were included in the first two compilations. One can note in the 199 items of the following list the very large percentage of ephemeral material and items published by Jewish institutions. Many shed much new information on the American Jewish experience before the Civil War period. It must also be noted that this listing is in no way intended to be definitive. Without doubt future research will discover a large amount of material still unearthed.

1795

1. The / Counterfeit Messiah; / or / False Christ, / of the / Jews at Smyrna; / in the Year 1666. / Written by an English Person of Quality / . . . Keene-(Newhampshire;) / Printed by C. Sturtevant, jun. & Co. . / For Amos Taylor. / 1795. / 36 pp. 17 cm.

2. KEACH, BENJAMIN
The / Travels / of / True Godliness: / From the beginning of the World to / this present Day. / . . . The Ninth Edition, corrected, with some / Additions, by the Author. / . . . Newark—Printed by John Woods, for / Benjamin Gomez, Bookseller and Stati- / oner, No. 97, Maiden-Lane, N. York. / [1795] 144 pp. 13 cm.

3. ROWE, ELIZABETH
Friendship in Death: / in / Twenty Letters / from the / Dead to the Living. / . . . By Mrs. Elizabeth Rowe. / New-York: / Printed by Tiebout & O'Brien, / for Benjamin Gomez, No. 97, Maiden-Lane, / 1795. / xii + 300 pp. 18 cm.

4. The / Wonderful Life / and most / Surprising Adventures / of that Renowned Hero, / Robinson Crusoe, / . . . New-York: Printed by Hurtin & Com- / mardinger, for Benjamin Gomez / 1795 / 132 pp. 14 cm.

1800

5. SOLOMON, SAMUEL
A / Guide to Health; / or, / Advice to Both Sexes, in / Nervous and Consumptive Complaints: / . . . By S. Solomon, M.D. / Fifty-third Edition. / Printed for the Author: / and / sold by R. Bach, No. 128, Pearl-Street, New-York; / and Others. / Price One Dollar. / Printed by J. Clarke, Underbank, Stockport, England. / [1800?] 293 pp. 21 cm.

1803

6. AARON, MOSES
The / Merchant: / A Satire. / By Moses Aaron, / A Jew. / . . . New-York, / Printed for the Booksellers, / December, 1803. / 7 pp. 17 cm.

1805

7. NEW YORK. CONGREGATION SHEARITH ISRAEL.
Sir, / You are requested to attend a Meeting of / the Congregation of Shearith Israel on o'clock . . . / By Order of the Parnass & Assistants, / June 1805. Isaac M. Gomez, Clk. / 1 p. 18 cm.

1806

8. NEW YORK. KALFE TZEDAKAH MATON BESETER.
To the Contributors of the Charitable Fund of / קלפי צדקה מתן בסתר / We, the Committee appointed on the 22nd day of December, 1805, / to draft and report such amendments, alterations and additions, to the / rules and regulations . . . / We beg leave to lay before you an enlarged plan of Charity. / . . . January 7, 1806. / 1 p. 34 cm.

1809

9. NEW YORK. CONGREGATION SHEARITH ISRAEL.
מי לה׳ אלי To the Electors and Members of ק״ק שארית ישראל / The time is now arrived that a regulation can be made, so that the תפלה in / Shool can be בכונה ובזמנה and without the erroneous interruption of such / a number of מ״ש . . . . New York, Feb. 14th, 5569. / 1 p. 13 cm.

10. ———
New-York, March 8th, 1809. / You are hereby invited to attend the sale of Men and Women's Seats / . . . By order: / Isaac M. Gomez, Clerk. / 1 p. 18 cm.

1811

11. NEW YORK. CONGREGATION SHEARITH ISRAEL.
New-York, January 2, 1811. / You are requested to attend a Meeting of the Con- / gregation Shearith Israel . . . / N. Phillips, Clerk. / 1 p. 18 cm.

12. ———
New-York, 18th Oct. 1811. / Sir, / In compliance with the annexed letter, and in conformity with the 4th section / of the Bye-Laws, you are requested to attend a meeting . . . / 1 p. 18 cm.

13. ———
New-York, October 21st, 1811. / Sir, / As I learn the Parnass will not publish my letter to the Trustees of K.K.S.I. you have / herewith a copy of the same . . . / Jacob Abrahams. . . . / 1 p. 18 cm.

14. ———

Sir, / You are requested to attend a meeting of the Congregation of Sheerith Israel, on Sunday the / 19th January next . . . / New-York, 25th December 1811. / 1 p. 18 cm.

1812

15. Mordecai, Samuel

A Discourse / delivered at the / Synagogue in Richmond, / on the / First Day of January, 1812, / a day devoted to / Humiliation & Prayer, / In consequence of the loss of many / valuable lives, / caused by the burning of / the Theatre, / On the 26th December, 1811. / By Samuel Mordecai. / Richmond: / Printed by John O'Lynch, / 1812. / 8 pp. 16 cm.

16. New York. Congregation Shearith Israel.

Sir, / You are requested to attend a semi-annual meeting of the electors of the / Congregation of Sheerith Israel . . . M. Gomez, Clerk. / April 26, 1812. / 1 p. 18 cm.

17. ———

Statement / Exhibited at the Semi-annual Meeting of the / Congregation Sheerith Israel, held 3d May, / 1812. / . . . M. Gomez, Clerk. / New-York, April 26, 1812. / 12 pp. 20 cm.

18. ———

Sir, / Pursuant to instruction from the Board of Trustees, I hereby present you / with a Resolution . . . M. Gomez, Clerk. / New-York, May 6, 1812. / . . . Resolved, that any congregator, or congregators, who shall, or may be twelve / months in arrears . . . shall / not . . . be entitled to vote . . . / 1 p. 26 cm.

1813

19. New York. Congregation Shearith Israel.

Statement / Exhibited at the Semi-Annual Meeting / of the / Electors of the Congregation / Sheerith Israel, / Held the 16th day of May 1813, conformable to the / 4th Section of 7th Article of the By-Laws / . . . M. Gomez, Clerk. / . . . 6 pp. 23 cm.

1815

20. NEW YORK. CONGREGATION SHEARITH ISRAEL.
Conditions / and / Terms / Of Leasing the Seats in the Synagogue, on Monday the 10th day of July Next . . . / . . . Moses Gomez, Clerk. / New York, June 23, 1815. / 1 p. 34 cm.

1816

21. PHILADELPHIA. CONGREGATION MIKVEH ISRAEL.
Order of Service / for Sabbath Evening פרשת יתרו 5576, being the celebration / of depositing a ספר תורה in the היכל of ק״ק מקוה ישראל . . . 1 p. 22 cm.

1818

22. NEW YORK. CONGREGATION SHEARITH ISRAEL.
Conditions / and / Terms / Of leasing the Seats in the Synagogue, on Monday, the 13th day of April . . . Moses B. Seixas, Clerk. / New-York, April 8, 1818. / 1 p. 34 cm.

1819

23. NEW YORK. CONGREGATION SHEARITH ISRAEL.
New York, July 18, 1819. / At a Meeting of the Trustees of the Congregation Shearith Israel, the following / Recital was adopted: / . . . Moses B. Seixas, Clerk. / . . . 4 pp. 25 cm.

1821

24. Review / of the / Opinion of the Supreme Court / of the United States, / in the case of / Cohens vs. Virginia: / Originally published in the Washington (City) Gazette / to which is added, / a Letter / From a gentleman, eminent for his legal and scientific / attainments . . . Steubenville, O. / Printed by James Wilson. / 1821. / 78 pp. 21 cm.

1823

25. MARYLAND. CITIZENS.
To the Honorable the General Assembly of Maryland. / The Memorial of the subscribers, Citizens thereof, / respectfully represents: / Your Memorialists are of that class of the Citizens of Maryland, long subjected to the pressure / of political disqualifications . . . your Memorialists humbly pray at your hands, that the Bill / before you may be confirmed. / [Baltimore? 1823] 2 pp. 26 cm.

1825

26. HARBY, ISAAC.
A discourse, / Delivered in Charleston, (S.C.) / on the 21st of Nov. 1825, / before the / Reformed Society of Israelites, / . . . on their First Anniversary. / By Isaac Harby, a Member. / . . . Charleston: / Printed by A. E. Miller, / 4, Broad-street. / 1825. / 40 pp. 21 cm.

27. SIMON, ERASMUS H.
. . . To / the friends of Israel. / . . . New York, June 7, 1825. / . . . 3 pp. 25 cm.
Resignation of Simon from the Board of the American Society for Meliorating the Condition of the Jews.

1826

28. JACKSON, S. H.
Proposals / for Printing, by Subscription, / מאור עינים / or / Hebrew Student's Assistant, / being the / Hebrew Pentateuch, / With the literal translation of each word in English, / above the Hebrew word. / . . . New York, December 1st, 1826. / 5 pp. 23 cm.

29. JOWETT, WILLIAM
Christian Researches / in / Syria and the Holy Land, / in / 1823 & 1824. / In Furtherance of the Objects / of the / Church Missionary Society. / By / Rev. William Jowett, M.A. / . . . From the London Edition. / Boston: / Published by Crocker and Brewster, Cummings, Hilliard, & Co. / Lincoln and Edmands, Timothy Bedlington, Richardson / and Lord, Charles Ewer, R.P. & C. Williams. / New-York: John P. Haven, C. & G. Carvil. / 1826. / 364 pp. 19 cm.

30. NEW YORK. CONGREGATION BNAI JESHURUN.
Circular. / . . . Glad Tidings to the Faithful. / . . . We . . . have been chosen by the Congregation / (בני ישורון) the Children of Jeshrun, to solict . . . free-will / offerings . . . 1 p. 21 cm.

1827

31. New York. Hebra Hased va Amet.
New-York, Dec. 26, 1827. / At a meeting of the Committee, appointed . . . / . . . for the purpose of taking into / consideration the expediency of extending the views . . . / . . . But the Committee desirous to form / a new Society for charitable purposes . . . respectfully invite such individuals / to attend a meeting . . . 1 p. 9 cm.

1830

32. Levy, Benjamin.
United States of America. / State of Louisiana. / Printed by Benjamin Levy, New-Orleans. / By Jacques Dupré, / Acting Governor of the State of Louisiana. / These are to certify, That / whose name subscribed to the instrument of writing herein annexed / Given at New-Orleans, under my hand, and seal of the / State . . . / By the Governor: / . . . Secretary of State. / 1 p. 26 cm.

33. Moses, Myer.
The / Commercial Directory, / and / a Digest / of the / Laws of the United States, / Relating to Commerce; / . . . By Myer Moses. / New-York: / Printed by Ludwig & Tolefree, / Corner of Greenwich and Vesey-Sts. / 1830. / 280 pp. 25 cm.

34. New York. Congregation Bnai Jeshurun.
Circular. / Whereas it is incumbent upon us, to comply with the divine injunctions . . . Resolved that each member of the Board be authorised to receive proposals from any / person or persons indebted to this Congregation . . . H. Nathan, Clerk / to the Congregation Bnai Jeshurun. / 1 p. 14 cm.

35. New York. Hebra Hased va Amet.
The Committee appointed by the Hebra Hased ve Emet to confer with the Committee of Hebra / Gamelut Hased, having performed that duty, submit the following Preamble and Resolutions / . . . Isaac B. Seixas, Chairman Committee . . . [New York; n.d.] 1 p. 26 cm.

36. NEW YORK. LOMDI TORAH SCHOOL.
אחינו בני ישראל . . . In consequence of the above the Trustees of the ק״ק אנשי חסד have founded a school under the name and title of לומדי תורה . They therefore solicit of every Lady or Gentleman . . . to subscribe . . . / New-York, Feb. 21st 5590. / 1 p. 25 cm.

1832

37. HEBRA TERUMAT HAKODESH.
With the Help of the Lord! Amen. / To the worthy members of the several holy Congregations of Israel in America . . . Sol'n Seixas, Sec'ry. / New-York, 1st November, 1832. / 1 p. 28 cm.
Call to establish the Hebra Terumat Hakodesh

38. LEVY, BENJAMIN.
United States of America, / State of Louisiana. / Printed by Benjamin Levy, New-Orleans. / By A. B. Roman, / Governor of the State of Louisiana. / These are to certify, That whose name subscribed to the instrument of writing herein annexed / . . . By the Governor: / Secretary of State. / 1 p. 25 cm.

39. NEW YORK. CONGREGATION SHEARITH ISRAEL.
A Meeting of the Electors of the / Congregation Shearith Israel, will be held / . . . for the purpose of / taking into consideration, a proposition, to / . . . making Sale of the Property / owned by the Congregation in Mill- / street and Beaver-street . . . Bernard Hart, Clerk. Jan. 18, 1832. / 1 p. 13 cm.

1833

40. HOWLAND, FREEMAN P.
A / Sermon / Delivered before the / Palestine Missionary Society, / at their / Twelfth Annual Meeting, / Held at / Scituate, Mass. June 19, 1833. / By Freeman P. Howland, / . . . Boston: / Printed by Perkins & Marvin. / 1833. / 19 pp. 20 cm.

1834

41. Drake, W. E.
The Prophet! / A / Full and Accurate Report / of the / Judicial Proceedings / in the / Extraordinary and Highly Interesting Case / of / Matthews, alias Matthias, / charged with having / Swindled Mr. B. H. Folger . . . By W. E. Drake, Congressional and Law Reporter. / New-York: Printed and Published by W. Mitchell, 265 Bowery, . . . / 1834. / . . . 16 pp. 24 cm.
Matthias claimed to be chief High Priest of the Jews.

42. Hebra Terumat Hakodesh.
New York, March, 5594. / Circular. / The undersigned having been appointed a Committee to address a Circular for the purpose of obtaining / members and contributions in aid of the Society (Terumat Hakodesh,) . . . 2 pp. 25 cm.

43. New York. Congregation Shearith Israel.
Divine Worship will commence on / Friday afternoon . . . in the middle story / room of the building on the corner of / White and Centre streets, . . . [New York. 1834] 1 p. 12 cm.

44. ———
New York, 16 May, 1834 . . . 7 Iyar, 5594. / The Trustees of the Congregation Shearith Israel, in this City, / have erected a new Place of Worship in Crosby Street . . . we request the favor of your company on that interesting occasion. / . . . 1 p. 11 cm.

45. ———
Conditions and Terms / of / Leasing the Seats / in the / New Synagogue / of the / Congregation Shearith Israel, / . . . Bern'd Hart, Clerk. / New York, May 21, 1834. / 1 p. 32 cm.

46. ———
New York, 2d June, 1834. / Sir, / The Trustees of the Congregation Shearith Israel, have assigned to you / the Mitzva of carrying the Seaphar on the Circuit, on the / evening of the Consecration of the New Synagogue . . . 1 p. 14 cm.

1836

47. HARDY, ROBERT SPENCE.
Travels / in / The Holy Land, / and other places / mentioned in the Scriptures; / in 1832-33. / By Rev. R. Spence Hardy. / New-York: / Thomas George, Jr. Spruce Street. / 1836. / 64 pp. 26 cm.

48. NEW YORK. CONGREGATION SHEARITH ISRAEL.
Circular. / Sir:-The Following will come under consideration at a meeting of the Electors . . . / . . . Attest-N. Phillips, Clerk. / New-York, 7th August 1836. / 1 p. 26 cm.

49. ———
New York, Oct. 17th, 1836 / At a Meeting of the Trustees of the Congregation / Shearith Israel, the following Resolutions were adopted. / Resolved. That the present Lessees of Seats, in Synagogue, / shall have the privilege of retaining them . . . N. Phillips, Clerk. / 1 p. 13 cm.

50. ———
Sir. / A meeting of the Electors of the Congregation Shearith / Israel, will be held . . . N. Phillips, Clerk. / Dec'r. 25th 1836. / 1 p. 6 cm.

1837

51. CHARLESTON. K. K. BETH ELOHIM.
New / Constitution / of the / Hebrew Congregation / of / Kaal Kadosh Beth Elohim, / or / House of God. / Charleston: / Printed for the Congregation by B. Levy. / June, 1837. / 22 pp. 19 cm.

52. NEW YORK.
The undersigned have been appointed an Executive Committee, for the purpose / of raising funds to aid and assist persons, recently arrived from foreign countries . . . September 3d. 1837. / 1 p. 28 cm.

53. PARAMARIBO.
Paramaribo, den 1837. / De Inwijding van het Kerkgebouw der Nederlandsche / Israëlitische Gemeente . . . 1 p. 25 cm.

54. WARE, HENRY.
The / Feast of Tabernacles. / A Poem for Music. / By Henry Ware, Jr. / . . . Cambridge: / Published by John Owen. / 1837. / x + 38 pp. 17 cm.

55. WARE, HENRY.
The / Feast of Tabernacles. / an / Oratorio. / The Music by Charles Zeuner. / The Words by Henry Ware, Jr. / Performed at the Odeon / by the / Choir and Orchestra / of the / Boston Academy of Music. / [1837] 12 pp. 19 cm.

1838

56. NOAH, MORDECAI M.
Our Way Across The Mountain, Ho! / Words by Charles Mackay, Esq., / Composed & Respectfully Dedicated to / M. M. Noah, Esq. / (of New York) / As a slight token of grateful remembrance of early kindness to a stranger / by / Henry Russell. / Boston: Published by Parker & Ditson 135 Washington St. / Corner of School Street. / . . . 1838 . . . 7 pp. (score) 34 cm.

57. RICHMOND. CONGREGATION BETH SHOLOM.
קהל קדוש בית שלום: / To our Israelitish Brethren residing in the State of Virginia. / Gentlemen: / It is well known that our congregation has for many years been des- / titute of a regular Hazan . . . / . . . We have among us, on a visit from the City of Philadelphia, the Reverend Jacques J. Lyons . . . / Richmond, April 14th, 5598. / 1 p. 16 cm.

1839

58. MORDECAI, LAURA.
You are respectfully requested to attend the Funeral of / Miss Laura Mordecai, / . . . Thursday, July 4, 1839. / Bailie & Gallaher, prts. / 1 p. 7 x 15 cm.

59. NEW YORK. CONGREGATION SHEARITH ISRAEL.
Sir, / A meeting of the Electors . . . / . . . will be held . . . / . . . for the purpose of affording the Parnass an / opportunity of presenting . . . an application from the Rev. / Jacques J.

Lyon for the office of Hazan . . . / Sept. 4, 1839. / N. Phillips, Clerk. / 1 p. 11 cm.

60. RICHMOND. CONGREGATION BETH SHOLOM.
קהל קדוש בית שלום / To our Israelitish Brethren in Virginia. / Whereas, it hath pleased the Almighty to favor us with the services of the / Rev. Jacques J. Lyons . . . / Richmond, Sept. 1, 5599. / 1 p. 19 cm.

1840

61. BENRIMO, S.
S. Benrimo. / Respectfully informs his friends and / the public in general; that he / has opened his store at / 473 Pearl St. / for the sale of / Sausages, Smoked and Salt Beef, / . . . Board-ind. / [New York? 1840?] 1 p. 13 cm

62. CHARLESTON. SOCIETY FOR RELIGIOUS INSTRUCTION OF JEWISH CHILDREN.
At the Examination of the School, the first Anniversary celebration . . . / . . . which took place in Charleston, South-Carolina, on the 5th of April, 1840. The following / Resolutions were proposed . . . / Sarah C. Moise, Secretary & Treasurer. / 1 p. 25 cm.

63. COHEN, PHILLIP F.
Phillip F. Cohen. / Cosher Sausage / and / Smoked Beef Manufacturer, / No. 167 Elizabeth-Street, / (in the Basement.) / New-York.) / [1840?] 1 p. 5 x 8 cm. (business card)

64. FREY, JOSEPH SAMUEL C. F.
Joseph and Benjamin: / A / Series of Letters / on the / Controversy / between Jews and Christians: / . . . By Joseph Samuel C. F. Frey, / . . . Seventh Edition. / New-York: / Printed and Published by / Daniel Fanshaw, / 148 Nassau-Street. / 1840. / 2 vols. 19 cm.

65. NEW YORK. CONGREGATION ANSHE CHESED.
New York, April 12th, 5600. / Sir, / The Trustees . . . have assigned to you / the Mitzva of carrying the ספר on the Circuit, in the evening of the / Consecration of the New Synagogue . . . 1 p. 11 x 20 cm.

66. NEW YORK. CONGREGATION SHAARE ZEDEK.
חנוך בית הכנסת שערי צדק / The Synagogue Sahari Tsadek, / No. 472 Pearl Street: / Near Chatham Street, / will be consecrated on the 9th day of February next. / . . . 1 p. 5 x 8 cm. (admission card)

67. NEW YORK. HEBREW ASSISTANCE SOCIETY.
Circular. / To meliorate the condition of our fellow-beings . . . / Hence it has been deemed advisable to establish the "New-York Hebrew / Assistance Society" . . . / New-York, 2d. March 5600. / . . . 1 p. 21 cm.

68. ———
Circular. / To meliorate the condition of our fellow-beings . . . / Hence it has / been deemed advisable to establish the "New York Hebrew / Assistance Society," . . . / New York, 2d March, 5600. / 1 p. 20 cm.
A variant print.

69. ———
Constitution / of the / חברה לעזרת עני ואביון / New-York / Hebrew Assistance Society. / . . . Printed by S. H. Jackson, / At the Hebrew and English Printing Office, 146 William-Street [1840] 12 pp. 17 cm.

70. NEW YORK. HEBREW LITERARY AND RELIGIOUS LIBRARY ASSOCIATION.
Hebrew Literary / and / Religious Library Association. / Rules and Regulations for the Hebrew School. / . . . [1840?] 1 p. 19 cm.

71. ———
You are respectfully invited to attend a / Meeting . . . Alex. Kursheedt, Chairman. / A.R.B. Moses, Secretary. / 1 p. 11 cm.

72. NEW YORK. ISRAELITES.
Sir, / You are respectfully requested to attend a Meeting / of the Israelites of the City of New York . . . for the purpose of uniting in an expression of sentiment, / on the subject of the Persecutions of our Brethren in Damascus. / . . . August 14th, 1840. / 1 p. 8 cm.

73. PALACHE, J.
Miss J. Palache / Begs leave to inform the members of the Jewish community, that she will / open a School for Children of the Jewish Faith . . . [1840?] 1 p. 10 cm.

74. WILLSON, JAMES R.
Hebrew Literature: An / Introductory Lecture / delivered at the opening of the / Alleghany Institute, / By James R. Willson, D.D. / Nov. 2nd, 1840. / Newburgh: / J. D. Spalding, Printer. / 28 pp. 21 cm.

1841

75. ALBANY. CONGREGATION BETH JACOB.
Sir, / The President and Trustees of the Congregation / Beth Jacob, respectfully invite you to attend the Conse- / cration of Synagogue . . . / Simeon Newburgh, Clerk. / Albany May 17th, 5601. / 1 p. 10 cm.

76. ———
Consecration, May 25, 5601. 4 P.M. / Beth Jacob, / No. 8 Rose Street, / Albany. / 1 p. 4 x 7 cm. (admission card)

77. CHARLESTON. K. K. BETH ELOHIM.
Charleston, March 1841 / You are Respectfully invited to attend the Consecration of the New Synagogue / of Beth Elohim . . . 1 p. 12 cm.

78. NEW YORK. CONGREGATION SHAAR HASHAMAYIM.
חנוך בית הכנסת שער השמים / The Synagogue Shaar Hashamoyem, / In Attorney, between Rivington & Stanton Streets, / Will be consecrated on the 10th of September inst. / עש״ק כ״ד אלול תר״א / . . . 1 p. 7 x 9 cm. (admission card)

79. NEW YORK. HEBREW ASSISTANCE SOCIETY.
Report of the Board of Managers / of the / New York Hebrew Assistance Society, / January, 1841. / . . . 2 pp. 19 cm.

80. NEW YORK. HEBREW BENEVOLENT SOCIETY.
חברה משיבת נפש / Hebrew Benevolent Society. / New-York, December 7th, 1841. / Sir, / The Hebrew Benevolent Society,

of the City of New York, / design to commemorate their 19th Anniversary . . . 1 p. 30 cm.

81. ———
Hebrew Benevolent Society. / Anniversary / Dinner, / Washington Hotel, December 15th, 1841. / . . . 1 p. 6 x 9 cm. (admission card)

82. ———
Bill of Fare / of the Dinner for the Anniversary of the / Hebrew Benevolent Society . . . Washington Hotel, New-York, December 15th, 1841. / 1 p. 29 cm.

83. ———
Programme. / . . . 1 p. 9 cm. (program card for dinner)

84. New York. Hebrew Literary and Religious Library Association.
The Course of Lectures before the Hebrew Lit- / erary and Religious Library Association, / will be resumed . . . / . . . Lecture by Montgomery / Moses Esq. / . . . Gershom Nathan, Secretary. / New York, January, 1841. / 1 p. 12 cm.

85. New York. Hebrew School Fund.
First Annual Ball / in aid of the / New York Hebrew School Fund / Association, / . . . Wednesday Eve'g, March 10th, 1841 / Admit a Gentleman and two Ladies. / . . . 1 p. 7 x 10 cm. (admission card)

86. New York. Society for the Education of Poor Children.
Report / of the Committee of the Society / for the Education of Poor Children / and / Relief of Indigent Persons / of the / Jewish Persuasion. / and / Plan and Estimate for a School. / New York: / Thompson & Hart, / Printers, 106 Broadway, (Entrance in Pine Street.) / 1841. / 8 pp. 23 cm.

87. Richmond. Congregation Beth Sholom.
„קהל קדוש בית שלום" / To our Israelitish Brethren in Virginia. / Brethren: / Whereas, by the dispensation of an all wise Providence, our Congregation is destitute of a Hazan . . . It is

known to all, that the Rev. E. J. Lyons . . . Richmond, Ellul, 5601. / Sept. 6th, 1841. / 1 p. 25 cm.

88. ———

To the Contributors of / קהל קדוש בית שלום / A Meeting of the Contributors of the Congregation will be held this afternoon . . . It being also desirable to obtain the services of the Rev. E. J. / Lyons . . . Richmond, Sept. 26, 1841. / Tisri, 11, 5602. / 1 p. 11 cm.

89. ———

קהל קדוש בית שלום / To our Israelitish Brethren in Virginia. / Gentlemen: / Whereas, it is well known by all our brethren, that this once happy Congregation / is at present thrown into a great degree of dissatisfaction and discontent, in not having their choice / of a Hazan . . . It is well known to all, that at present the Rev. El. J. Lyons, of Surinam, is / amongst us . . . Richmond, Nov. 1, 5601. / 1 p. 18 cm.

90. Two hundred / Pictorial illustrations / of the / Holy Bible, / and / Views in the Holy Land, / . . . Second series. / New York: Robert Sears, 122 Nassau Street. / Boston: Saxton & Pierce, 133½ Washington Street. / Philadelphia: R. S. H. George.—Baltimore: W. N. Harrison. / and Sold by the Booksellers Generally. / 1841. / 383 pp. 23 cm.

1842

91. THE HEBREWS' MAGAZINE

Prospectus of a Monthly Magazine, / to be published in the City of Richmond, / devoted to / Hebrew and Miscellaneous Literature, Useful and Entertaining Knowledge, / and to be entitled / The Hebrews' Magazine / and Jewish Miscellany. / . . . T. K. Lyon. / Richmond, Va., 23d Shebath, 4602. / 2d. Feb. 1842. / 1 p. 16 cm.

92. NEW YORK. CONGREGATION SHEARITH ISRAEL.

At a meeting of the Congregation Shearith Israel, held July 31, 1842, the following / resolution was adopted: / . . . 2 pp. 26 cm.

93. NEW YORK. HEBREW ASSISTANCE SOCIETY.
חברה לעזרת עני ואביון / Anniversary Ball / New-York Hebrew Assistance Society, / Niblo's Saloon, / Wednesday December 7th 1842. / Gentlemen's Ticket. / 1 p. 7 x 11 cm. (admission card)

94. ———
Ladies' Ticket / חברת לעזרת עני ואביון / Anniversary Ball / New-York Hebrew Assistance Society, / Niblo's Saloon, / Wednesday December 7th 1842. / 1 p. 7 x 11 cm. (admission card)

95. ———
Anniversary Ball / of the / Hebrew Assistance Society. / Order of Dancing. / . . . [New York: 1842] 1 p. 8 cm.

96. NEW YORK. HEBREW BENEVOLENT SOCIETY.
Hebrew Benevolent Society / New York, December 1st, 1842. / Sir, / This Society intends to celebrate its 21st Anniversary by a Dinner . . . 1 p. 18 cm.

97. ———
21st Anniversary Dinner, / December 14th, 1842. / Hebrew Benevolent Society, / Bill of Fare. . . . 1 p. 12 cm.

98. NEW YORK. SOCIETY FOR THE EDUCATION OF POOR CHILDREN.
. . . A Special Meeting of this Society will be held . . . / M. H. Cardozo, Sec'y. / New York, June 13th, 1842. / 1 p. 6 cm.

99. NORDHEIMER, ISAAC.
אוצר לשון הקדש / Prospectus / of a / Complete Hebrew and Chaldee / Concordance to the Old Testament, / . . . New-York, January, 1842. / . . . University Press, / John F. Trow, Printer. / 3 pp. 28 cm.

100 THE OCCIDENT.
Prospectus / for issuing a semi-monthly magazine, to be called / The Occident, / and / American Jewish Advicate, / . . . Philadelphia, Ab 6th, 5602. / July 13, 1842. . . . 1 p. 26 cm.

101. PHILADELPHIA. UNITED HEBREW BENEFICENT FUEL AND SAVING SOCIETY.
Circular. / The Board of Managers / . . . Report . . . Philadelphia, February 28th, 1842. / 1 p. 26 cm.

102. RICHMOND. CONGREGATION BETH SHOLOM.
קהל קדוש בית שלום / Brethren of the House of Israel, / Residing in this City and its Adjacent Counties: / It is not through vain presumption . . . Richmond, Aug. 8, 1842. / Ellul 2d, 5602. / 1 p. 15 cm.

103. SOCIETY FOR THE RELIEF OF THE POOR OF THE HOLY LAND.
You are requested to attend a meeting . . . / J. B. Kursheedt, / Acting Secretary . . . [New York: 1842] 1 p. 13 cm.

1843

104. THE FIRST FRUITS OF THE WEST.
Announcement. / To the Jewish Public of Jamaica. / The existence of a National Organ among the Jews of Jamaica, having, of late, been ardently desired, the / establishment of such a publication has, for some time, been contemplated. . . . Kingston, Jamaica, 10th Hesvan, 5604.—November 3, 1843 / 2 pp. 27 cm.

105. NEW YORK. CONGREGATION RODOPH SHOLOM.
חנוך בית הכנסת רודף שלום / The Synagogue Rodoph Sholom, In Attorney, between Stanton & Houston- sts, / Will be Consecrated on the 3d. of February, Instant. / . . . 1 p. 5 x 8 cm. (admission card)

106. NEW YORK. HEBRA HASED VA AMET.
Hebra Hased Vaamet. / New York, April 3, 1843. / Sir,- / Your attention is particularly requested to the following report. . . . 1 p. 28 cm.

107. NEW YORK. HEBREW ASSISTANCE SOCIETY.
Hebrew Assistance Society. / New-York, February, 1843. / In presenting their Annual Report . . . 3 pp. 25 cm.

108. NEW YORK. SOCIETY FOR THE EDUCATION OF POOR CHILDREN.
Report / of the / Committee / of / the Society / for / the Edu-

cation of Poor Children / and / Relief of Indigent Persons / of the / Jewish Persuasion. / J. M. Elliott, Printer, 33 Liberty-Street. / 1843. / 12 pp. 18 cm.

109. THE OCCIDENT.
Prospectus / of / The Occident; / and / American Jewish Advocate. [Philadelphia: 1843] 4 pp. 24 cm.

110. WINES, E. C.
E. C. Wines / Proposes to repeat, in New York, sometime during the month of April, / (Provided 300 subscribers to the course are obtained by the 10th of the Month,) his / Four Lectures / on the Civil Government of the Hebrews, / . . . [New York? 1843] 1 p. 25 cm.

1844

111. MORDECAI, M. C.
(Circular.) / Charleston, S. C. May 20th, 1844. / The Citizens of Charleston, without distinction of Party, and with unexampled unanimity, have at a Public / Meeting declared their decided wishes in favor of the immediate Annexation of Texas to the Union . . . Very respectfully, your obedient servants, / C. G. Memminger, / Henry Bailey, / W. C. Gatewood, / M. C. Mordecai. / 1 p. 26 cm.

112. NEW YORK. CONGREGATION BNAI JESHURUN.
ק״ק בני ישורון / Trustee-Room, Elm st. Sept. 11th, 5604. / Sir, / . . . Resolved, That this Board will neither sell nor let, the / Seats in the Synagogue, to any persons, other than electors, / . . . for the ensuing year, until / the Suits now pending in the Court of Chancery, and Supreme / Court, shall have been disposed of . . . / Edward Heilbuth, Clerk. / 1 p. 14 cm.

113. NEW YORK. ESRATH YETHAMIM VE-ALMONOTH MUTUAL ASSISTANCE SOCIETY.
State of New-York. / No. 34. / In Assembly, / January 19, 1844. / . . . An Act / To incorporate the Esrath Yethamim Ve-almonoth / Mutual Assistance Society for Hebrew widows and / orphans. / . . . [Albany: 1844] 2 pp. 31 cm.

114. NEW YORK. MENDELSOHN BENEVOLENT SOCIETY.
State of New-York. / No. 22. / In Assembly, / January 15, 1844. / . . . An Act / To incorporate the Mendelsohn Benevolent Society / of the city of New-York. / . . . [Albany: 1844] 2 pp. 31 cm.

115. NEW YORK. SHAAREH TIKVAH BENEVOLENT SOCIETY.
State of New-York. / No. 27. / In Assembly, January 16, 1844. / . . . An Act / to incorporate the Shaareh Tikvah Benevolent So- / ciety in the city of New-York. / . . . [Albany, 1844] 2 pp. 31 cm.

1845

116. The Jew. / . . . New-York: / Published by Harper & Brothers, / No. 82 Cliff-Street. / 1845. / 173 pp. 22 cm.
"This volume is a very free version of a work, bearing the same title, which has attained to a high degree of popularity on the Continent."

117. PRIDEAUX, HUMPHREY.
The / Old and New Testament / Connected, / in / The History of the Jews, / and / Neighbouring Nations; / . . . By Humphrey Prideaux, D. D. / Dean of Norwich. / Fifteenth American, From the Twentieth London Edition. / . . . New-York: / Harper & Brothers, 82 Cliff Street / 1845-1848. 2 vols. 24 cm.

1846

118. HEBRA TERUMAT HAKODESH.
Hebra Tarumot Hakodesh. / Extract from the Constitution—Section 5. / . . . The Hebra Tarumot Hakodesh has received recent intelligence that our Brethren in the Holy Land / are suffering from the horrors of Famine . . . / New-York, 18 Kislef, 5607. / 1 p. 15 cm.

119. NEW YORK. CONGREGATION SHEARITH ISRAEL.
Sir, / The Annual meeting of the Electors . . . / will be held . . . / N. Phillips, Clerk. / 17th July, 1846. / 2 pp. 25 cm.

120. New York. Shaaray Tefila Society.
State of New-York. / No. 338. / In Assembly, March 19, 1846. / An Act / To incorporate the Shaaray Tefila Society of New- / York. / . . . [Albany, 1846] 2 pp. 28 cm.

121. Phillips, Philip.
Digest of Class / decided by the / Supreme Court of the State of Alabama, / from / Minor to VII. Alabama Reports Inclusive, / . . . By P. Phillips, / Counsellor at Law. / . . . Mobile. / 1846. / xii + 629 pp. 24 cm.

1847

122. Charleston. Hebrew Benevolent Society.
Circular. / Charleston, S. Ca., February 8th, 1847. / Sir: In consequence of the frequent drafts of poor and afflicted Israelites upon the / Treasury . . . 1 p. 25 cm.
Invitation to Subscription Ball.

123. Huie, James A.
The / History of the Jews / from the / Babylonian Captivity / to the Present Time . . . With a preface by / William Jenks, D. D. / Boston: Published by M. A. Berk. / 1847. / 476 pp. 20 cm.
Variant edition with different introduction and preface.

124. Josephi, E.
Mr. & Mrs. E. Josephi's / compliments to / Mr. / and requests the pleasure of your / company . . . at their / infant son's berith . . . / New-York, Nov. 12th 1847. / 1 p. 18 cm.

125. Lyons, Ellis.
Education. / Rev. Ellis Lyons, proposes to establish in the City of Richmond, a daily School for young La- / dies and Gentlemen . . . Richmond, Nov. 30th, 1847. / 1 p. 26 cm.

126. New York. Congregation Benai Israel.
The President and Trustees of the / New Netherland Congregation, "Benai Israel," / invite your attendance at the Consecration . . . / May 12th, 5607-1847. / 1 p. 10 cm.

127. ———

Consecration of the New Synagogue / of the / Netherland Congregation, / "Benai Israel," / Thursday, May 20, 5607. / Admit / Mr / 1 p. 5 x 8 cm. (admission card)

128. NEW YORK. CONGREGATION SHAARAY TEFILLA.

קהל קדוש שערי תפלה / The Gates of Prayer. / Trustee-Room, April 21, 5607. / The Trustees of this Congregation hereby notify you that the Seats in the New Syna- / gogue in Wooster Street, will be disposed of . . . 2 pp. 28 cm.

129. ———

ק"ק שערי תפלה / Congregation "Gates of Prayer." / . . . The Committee of Arrangements beg to inform you that the new Synagogue, / "Gates of Prayer," will be consecrated . . . / New-York, 1st June, 4607-1847. / 1 p. 19 cm.

130. ———

Synagogue "Gates of Prayer," / Wooster-Street, between Spring and Prince. / Admit / To the Consecration, / On Friday, 25th of June. / . . . 1 p. 7 x 9 cm. (admission card)

131. ———

Programme of Music / for the consecration of the / Synagogue "Gates of Prayer," / Composed expressly for the occasion by Mr. Edward Woolf. / . . . 1 p. 16 cm.

132. ———

ק"ק שערי תפלה / Trustee Room, Wooster Street, / New-York, August 6th, 4607,-1847. / At an adjourned Meeting . . . / Resolved, That the Seats in the Synagogue be rated . . . / Aaron S. Solomons, / Secretary C.S.T. / 1 p. 13 cm.

133. NEW YORK. CONGREGATION SHEARITH ISRAEL.

New-York, 4th Nissan, 4607. / Sir, / At a Meeting of the Trustees . . . / the following was adopted.— / Resolved. That no Seat in our Holy Place of / Worship, shall hereafter be leased to any person, / married contrary to our religious laws . . . / N. Phillips, Clerk. / 1 p. 13 cm.

134. ———
Sir, / The Annual Meeting of the Electors . . . / will be held . . . / N. Phillips, Clerk. / 17th July, 1847. / 2 pp. 25 cm.

135. NEW YORK. FEMALE HEBREW BENEVOLENT SOCIETY.
The Female Hebrew Benevolent Society respectfully requests the favor / of your company to a dinner . . . / New York, Nov. 18th, 1847 / . . . 1 p. 25 cm.

136. NEW YORK. GERMAN HEBREW BENEVOLENT SOCIETY.
Charity is our Motto, Benevolence our Design! / New York, November 1, 1847. / Sir, / By the heading of our circular you will at once perceive the object of our Association, / which is about celebrating its fourth Anniversary dinner . . . 1 p. 27 cm.

137. ———
Fourth / Anniversary Dinner, / of the German / Hebrew Benevolent Society / on Tuesday Nov 16th 1847 . . . [Printed by] Doty & Bergen / 1 p. 7 x 10 cm. (admission card)

138. NEW YORK. HEBREW AND CLASSICAL SCHOOL.
Hebrew and Classical School, / No. 41 Mercer Street, (between Broome and Grand Sts.) / New York. / E. Block, Principal. / In the establishment of this School, the Principal offers to the Jewish inhabitants of New York . . . / New-York, Nov. 17, 1847. / 1 p. 26 cm.

139. ———
Prospectus. / The undersigned proposes to establish in the City of New York, A Hebrew Classical School . . . / E. Block. / New York, August 30, 1847. / . . . 1 p. 12 cm.

140. NEW YORK. HEBREW BENEVOLENT SOCIETY.
חברת משיבת נפש / Hebrew Benevolent Society. / New-York, October 25th, 1847. / Sir, / This Society intends to celebrate its Twenty-Sixth Anniversary, by a Dinner, / . . . 1 p. 25 cm.

141. ———
Hebrew Benevolent Society / 26th / Anniversary Dinner / at

the Apollo Saloon B-Way / Tuesday Nov. 9th 1847 / . . . 1 p. 6 x 9 cm. (admission card)

142. NEW YORK. HEBREW UNION SCHOOL SOCIETY.
Hebrew Union School Society. / New-York, November 19th, 1847. / Sir, / The festivity to which you are most respectfully invited . . . 1 p. 25 cm.

143. ———
Dinner and Ball / in aid of the / Hebrew Union School Fund, / On Thursday, December 2nd, 1847, / . . . Tickets to admit a Gentleman and Lady . . . 1 p. 5 x 9 cm. (admission card)

144. NEW YORK. LADIES HEBREW BENEVOLENT SOCIETY.
Ladies' / Hebrew Benevolent / Society. / December 2d 1847. / 1 p. 5 x 9 cm. (admission card)

145. NEW YORK. MISSES PALACHE'S BOARDING AND DAY SCHOOL.
The Misses Palache's / Boarding and Day School, / for Young Ladies of the Jewish Faith, / No. 97 Thompson-Street / New York. / Terms . . . [1847?] 1 p. 26 cm.

146. NOAH, MORDECAI M.
Gleanings / from / A Gathered Harvest, / By M. M. Noah. / New-York: / H. Long & Bro., 32 Ann Street. / 1847. / 216 pp. 18 cm.

147. RICHMOND. HEBREW SCHOOL FUND.
Hebrew School Fund Ball, / in aid of the / Hebrew School Fund of the City of Richmond. / The pleasure of your company . . . Wednesday / Evening, February 10th, 1847, at the City Hotel. / . . . Lyon, Print. / 1 p. 16 cm.

1848

148. BEHRMAN, D.
Choice Groceries for Passover, / פסח / at D. Behrman's New Store, / 172 Bowery / Opposite Delancy Street, New-York . . . / Jackson, Cheap Printer, 190 Houston Street, and 203 Bowery. / 2 pp. 220 cm.

149. CINCINNATI. CONGREGATION BNAI JESHURUN.
. . . The Congregation will feel honored by your acceptance of the enclosed invita- / tion . . . / Cincinnati, August, 5608-1848. / 1 p. 25 cm.

150. ———
Synagogue "Bnai Jeshurun," / Lodge Street, bet. 5th & 6th. / Admit / to the Consecration, / on Friday, 22d September. . . . 1 p. 7 x 10 cm. (admission card)

151. HART, EMANUEL B.
To the Electors of the Fifth Ward. / . . . For Congress we present for your suffrages, your own favorite, devoted, inflexible and vigilant / champion, Emanuel B. Hart, . . . [New York: 1848] 1 p. 25 cm.

152. HEBRA TERUMAT HAKODESH.
New York, July 5608. / Sir, / The Committee appointed by the Society . . . for the purpose of making an Extra Collec- / tion in behalf of our distressed brethren in the Holy Land, owing to the dreadful famine which prevailed / there, have the pleasure of reporting the collection and transmission of the sum of / Dollars, / . . . J. B. Kursheedt, / S. I. Isaacs, Sim. Abrahams. / Committee. / 1 p. 25 cm.

153. JEHOSHUA, ABRAHAM.
The following is a translation by Professor Roy, of the city of Brooklyn, / of the Rabbi's Certificate from the city of Jerusalem . . . / I . . . / testify that the Wine before me is the pure blood of the grape, without any / mixture of intoxicating liquor. . . . / Abraham Jehoshua, / Head Sagan (ruler) in the Synagogue / of the City of Jerusalem. / . . . [New York: 1848] 1 p. 20 cm.
(Circular enclosed in catalog of sale of wine, etc. sold at auction in New York on June 30, 1848)

154. LINDO, A. A.
A Retrospect of the Past, / As connected with and preparatory to a faithful exposition intended to be given of the Divine Will / and Dispensation disclosed in the Sacred Books received as

authority by Jews. By A. A. Lindo, / an Israelite. Cincinnati: Robinson & Jones. 1848. / . . . Notices of the Cincinnati press . . . [Cincinnati? 1848] 2 pp. 26 cm.
(A prospectus)

155. New York. Bachelors' Hebrew Benevolent Loan Association.
New York, January 31st, 1848. / The Committee of the Bachelors' Hebrew / Benevolent Loan Association, respect- / fully solicit the honor of your and Ladies' company, at a Ball / . . . 1 p. 6 cm. (invitation)

156. ———
First Ball / In aid of the Funds / of the / Bachelor's Hebrew Benevolent Loan Association, / . . . Monday Eveg 21st Feb., 1848 / Gentlemen's ticket . . . 1 p. 6 x 9 cm. (admission card)

157. ———
First Ball / Of the Bachelors Hebrew / Benevolent Loan Association. / . . . Record of engagements. / [New York: 1848] 1 p. 8 cm.

158. ———
. . . Dear Sir, / The pleasure of you and your Ladies' company is respectfully solicited at the Second An- / nual Ball . . . / to be given on Tuesday, Jan. 9th, 1849, . . . 1 p. 20 cm. (invitation)

159. New York. Congregation Shaaray Tefilla.
קהל קדוש שערי תפלה / The Gates of Prayer. / Trustee-Room. Nov. 7, 5608. / The Trustees of this Congregation hereby notify you, that the Seats in the new Syn- / agogue in Wooster Street, will be disposed of on Sunday, Nov. 21, 5608, at half past /two o'clock on the following / Terms and Conditions. / . . . 2 pp. 33 cm.

160. New York. Congregation Shearith Israel.
Sir, / The Annual Meeting of the Electors of the Congregation Shearith Israel, / will be held at their Meeting Room, on

Sunday, 30th inst., . . . / N. Phillips, Clerk. / 17th July, 1848. / 2 pp. 25 cm.

161. ———
. . . New York, 10 Hesvan, 5609. / Whereas Rabbi Yeckiel A. Cohen has been commissioned . . . / to apply to the Jewish / people of the United States for assistance to build a synagogue in the Holy City . . . / N. Phillips, Clerk. / 1 p. 18 cm.

162. NEW YORK. HEBREW BENEVOLENT SOCIETY.
חברת משיבת נפש / Hebrew Benevolent Society. / New York, November 18th, 1848. / Sir, / This Society intends to celebrate its twenty-seventh anniversary, / by a Dinner . . . / to which you are respectfully invited. . . . 1 p. 25 cm.

163. NEW YORK. ISRAELITES.
A Meeting / of the / Israelites of New-York, / Will be held at for the / purpose of expressing their sympathy with . . . / the now persecuted and imprisoned Dr. Jordan, of Kurhessen, / . . . [New York: 1848] 1 p. 20 cm.

164. NEW YORK. SOCIETY FOR THE EDUCATION OF POOR CHILDREN.
. . . New York, December 1st, 1848. / The Anniversary Dinner and Ball of this Society will take place . . . / . . . S. M. Judah, President. / H. Hendricks, Vice President. / T. I. Tobias, Treasurer. / 1 p. 18 cm. (invitation)

165. NEW YORK. TEMPLE EMANUEL.
Admit / / To the Consecration of the / Temple "Imanu-El," / Chrystie St., between Hester & Walker, / on Friday April 14th, / . . . 1 p. 7 x 9 cm. (admission card)

166. ———
Auswahl / deutscher Gesänge / zum Gebrauche im / Tempel / der / Imanu-El Congregation / in / New-York. / Nebst Anhang. / New-York. / Druck und Verlag von J. Mühlhäuser, / No. 237 Division St. / . . . [1848?] 82 pp. 18 cm.

167. PHILADELPHIA. HEBREW EDUCATION SOCIETY.
Circular / Philadelphia, June 29th, 1848. / Dear Sir, / The

Subscribers, appointed a committee at a town meeting of Israelites, assembled to promote a system of Religious / and General Education among us . . . / In accordance with this object, a Constitution and by-laws to / form a Hebrew Education Society for the City and County of Philadelphia, were adopted at a meeting held on the / 28th day of June last, and we earnestly invite you herewith, to be present at the meeting . . . / . . . A. Hart, / Chairman of Committee. / . . . 1 p. 32 cm.

168. TOBIAS, DR.
The Greatest Discovery / of the Age. / Dr. Tobias' / Venetian Liniment, / A Sure and Speedy Remedy / For Rheumatism, Cuts, Burns Scalds, Cramp, / . . . For Sale at Dr. Tobias' office, No. 1 Murray Street, / near Broadway, New York. / . . . 4 pp. 25 cm.

169. WINES, E. C.
Professor Wines's Lectures / on the / Civil Polity and Laws of the Ancient Hebrews / New York, January 11th, 1848. / . . . Programme. / . . . Van Norden & Amerman, Printers, 60 William-st., N. Y. / 1 p. 31 cm.

1849

170. THE ASMONEAN.
The Asmonean / On the 12th day of תשרי, 5610 . . . / will be published, a Journal of Literature and News, / . . . Published for the Proprietors, by / R. Lyon. / 151 West Sixteenth street, New-York. / 2 pp. 26 cm (prospectus)

171. Israels Herold. / Adar 5609. New-York, März 1849. Prospectus. . . . Gedruckt bei J. Mühlhäuser, 237 Division-Strasse. / 2 pp. 33 cm.

172. NEW YORK. BACHELOR'S HEBREW BENEVOLENT LOAN ASSOCIATION.
2d Ball / In Aid of the Funds of the / Bachelor's Hebrew Benevolent Loan Association / . . . Tuesday Evening, 9th Jany 1849. / Gentlemens ticket. / 1 p. 6 cm. (admission card)

173. ———
M / The honor of your / and Ladies Company is / respectfully solicited to attend the / Third Annual Ball, / . . . Tuesday Evening, December 18th, 1849. / . . . 1 p. 16 cm. (invitation)

174. ———
Hebrew Bachelor's Ball. / Programme. / . . . 2 pp. 8 cm. (heart-shaped dance card)

175. NEW YORK. CHEBRA BIKUR CHOLIM UND KADISCHA.
New York, December 9th, 1849. / . . . Sir: / Die Chebra Bikur Cholim und Kadischa will celebrate / their first anniversary by a Society Dinner . . . 1 p. 25 cm.

176. NEW YORK. CONGREGATION SHAARAY TEFILLA.
Order of Service / at the / Synagogue "Gates of Prayer," / Wooster Street, / on Friday, August 3d. 5609-1849. / the day / Appointed by the President of the United States as a / day of Fasting, Humiliation and Prayer. / . . . M. S. Moss, Sec'y. / July 27th 5609. / 1 p. 18 cm.

177. NEW YORK. CONGREGATION SHEARITH ISRAEL.
Sir, / The Annual Meeting of the Electors of the Congregation / Shearith Israel, will be held at their Meeting Room, on Sunday, / 5th August next, . . . / N. Phillips, Clerk. / 17th July, 1849. / 2 pp. 25 cm.

178. NEW YORK. HEBREW BENEVOLENT SOCIETY.
Grand Musical Festival / in aid of the / Hebrew Benevolent Society! / Will take place, at the / Broadway Tabernacle, / on / Tuesday evening, March 20th, 1849 / On which occasion the following Eminent Artists will appear: / . . . accompanied by the Grand Orchestra of the Italian Opera, / . . . 1 p. 31 cm.

179. PHILADELPHIA. CONGREGATION HOUSE OF ISRAEL.
ק"ק בית ישראל / Congregation House of Israel, / . . . The Committee of Arrangements beg to inform you, that the new / Synagogue, "House of Israel", will be consecrated . . . on Wednesday, the 28th instant . . . Philadelphia, 6th March

(5609) 1849. Young, Printer, Black Horse Al. / 1 p. 25 cm. variant print.

180. ———
Synagogue House of Israel, / Crown St. between Race & Vine and 4th & 5th. / Admit / to the Consecration, / on Wednesday, 28th of March. / . . . Young Pr. / 1 p. 6 x 9 cm. (admission card)

181. PHILADELPHIA. HEBREW EDUCATION SOCIETY.
Circular. / Your attention is respectfully solicited to the subjoined proceedings of the School Directors, and / the report which they presented . . . Isaac Leeser, Chairman. / . . . Nov. 5th, 1849. / At a meeting of the Board, held on the 17th of June, it was Resolved, that a school or schools be established . . . 2 pp. 26 cm.

182. RAPHALL, MORRIS J.
Stuyvesant Institute. / Sillabus of / A Course of Six Popular Lectures / on the / Poetry of the Hebrews, / . . . by the Rev. Morris J. Raphall, M. A., Ph.D., . . . / Isaacs & Solomons, Job Printers, (Sign of the Golden Ledger), 53 Nassau-St. / 1 p. 21 cm.

1850

183. ABRAHAMS, SIMEON.
Programme / of / Masonic Celebration / of the / M. W. Grand Lodge / . . . Dec. 27th, A. D. 1850 . . . / . . . A Procession / Will then be formed, under the direction of / R. W. Simeon Abrahams Esq., Grand Marshall / . . . [New York: 1850] 4 pp. 20 cm.

184. BUFFALO. CONGREGATION BETH EL.
Congregation 'Beth-El'. / . . . The Committee of Arrangements beg leave to inform you that the Synagogue, / 'Beth-El,' will be consecrated . . . 1 p. 26 cm.

185. ———
Synagogue "Beth El", / Pearl-Street, Buffalo. / Admit / To the Consecration, / . . . 1 p. 7 x 9 cm. (admission card)

186. JOSEPH, GERSHOM.
Joseph, Rochon & Co. / General Agents & Commission Merchants, / Pueblo del San José, / Sacramento City & San Francisco, / California. / . . . [New York? 1850?] 1 p. 7 x 11 cm. (business card)

187. NEW YORK.
סליחות ליום כפור / . . . Jackson, Cheap Printer, New-York. [1850] 1 p. 33 cm. Order of Selihot to be recited on Yom Kippur.

188. NEW YORK. BNE JESHURUN HEBREW INSTITUTE.
New York, February 12th, 1850. / ק"ק בני ישרון / Sir; / You are requested to attend a special meeting of this Con- / gregation . . . for the / purpose of receiving the Revised Report of the School Committee . . . Henry Goldsmith, / Sec'ry C. B. I. / Isaacs & Solomons, Printers. / 3 pp. 33 cm.

189. NEW YORK. CHEBRA BIKUR CHOLIM UND KADISCHA.
Whoever practices Benevolence and virtue, attains a Long Life, / Riches and Honor. / Foundation Feast . . . on Tuesday, the 1st January, 1850. / . . . 1 p. 7 x 11 cm. (admission card)

190. NEW YORK. CONGREGATION ANSHE CHESED.
ק"ק אנשי חסד / Congregation "Anshi Chesed," / Norfolk-Street, between Stanton & Houston. / The undersigned Committee have the honor of informing you, that the new Synagogue / of the Congregation Anshi Chesed, will be consecrated . . . on / Thursday, May 16th . . . New York, April 5610-1850. / . . . 1 p. 21 cm.

191. ———
Consecration of the / New Synagogue / of the Congregation / Anshi-Chesed / Norfolk St., between Stanton & Houston, / on Thursday May 16th, / . . . Admit / . . . 1 p. 6 x 10 cm. (admission card)

192. NEW YORK. CONGREGATION SHEARITH ISRAEL.
Sir, / The Annual Meeting of the Electors of the Congregation / Shearith Israel, will be held at their Meeting Room, on Sunday, 28th / July next, . . . / . . . N. Phillips, Clerk. / 17th July, 1850. / 2 pp. 32 cm.

193. NEW YORK. HEBREW BENEVOLENT SOCIETY.
Twenty-Ninth Anniversary / of the / Hebrew Benevolent Society / . . . on Thursday Evening, Nov. 7, 1850. / . . . 1 p. 7 x 11 cm. (admission card)

194. NEW YORK. UNIVERSITY.
University of the City of New-York. / Commencement. / Wednesday, June 26th, 1850. / . . . Wm. L. S. Harrison, Book, Card and Job Printer, 2 Ann St., near Broadway / . . . 10 . Dissertation-Unemployed time. . . Isaac Hendricks, / New York City / . . . 3 pp. 26 cm.

195. NEW YORK. YOUNG MEN'S HEBREW BENEVOLENT ASSOCIATION.
Italian / Opera House, / Astor Place. / Benefit / of the / Young Men's / Hebrew / Benevolent Association / . . . Tuesday Evening, Dec. 3rd, 1850 / . . . P. J. Joachimssen, Chairman, 118 Nassau Street; . . . 1 p. 54 cm.

196. Order of Distribution of the Funds Collected in the United States, and Neighboring / Countries, for the Poor of the Holy Land. / In order to avoid any difficulties . . . / we have concluded and resolved to fix the following rate of distribution for / now and hereafter:- / . . . M. M. Noah, [et al.] New York, 8th Adar, 5610. Isaacs & Solomons, Printers, New York. / 1 p. 25 cm.

197. RAPHALL, MORRIS J.
Syllabus / of a course of six lectures / on the / Post Biblical History of the Jews, / to be delivered at the / Broadway Lecture Room, / . . . By the Rev. M. J. Raphall, M.A. Ph.D / . . . To commence on Thursday, April 25th, 1850. / . . . 1 p. 19 cm.

198. RICHMOND. HEBREW & ENGLISH INSTITUTE.
Fourth Annual / Hebrew School Fund Ball, / in aid of the / Hebrew & English Institute of the City of Richmond. / . . . on Wednesday Evening, February 13th, 1850. / . . . 1 p. 16 cm. (invitation)

199. SYRACUSE. SOCIETY OF CONCORD.
Syracuse, April 8, 1850. / The Members of the Society of Concord . . . / to their charitable friends throughout the State and Union. / In behalf of the Holy Hebrew Religion which we profess, we appeal to you . . . 1 p. 25 cm.

AN INNOVATOR OF HAGGADAH ILLUSTRATION—CYRIL KUTLIK

GUIDO KISCH

University of Basel, Switzerland

The Bratislava *Juedisches Familienblatt* of April 20, 1932 (Vol. VII No. 8, pp. 96-7) contains an essay by Alfred Tolnai entitled "A Slovak Illustrator of the Haggadah." The essay deals with a unique Haggadah which may well be the first to contain illustrations that deviate sharply from earlier conventional ones. These illustrations were the creation of a Slovak artist of the Augsburg Confession, Cyril Kutlik. At only nineteen years of age Kutlik was commissioned by the Prague publisher Samuel W. Pascheles to create the twelve illustrations which adorn this Haggadah. The young Slovak illustrator was the son of Bogdan Kutlik, a Protestant minister in Křižlice. In his description of the individual Haggadah illustrations, Tolnai points out that several represent scenes not depicted by earlier artists. He also discusses other works by Kutlik whose interest in biblical subjects continued and later culminated in his most mature painting, "The First Victim of Death" (the death of Abel).

Tolnai deserves credit for having rescued from oblivion the memory of this talented and ingenious Haggadah illustrator whose artistic career was ended prematurely by his death at the age of thirty-one. Although each of the illustrations bears the signature and the date 1888, Kutlik's name is not even mentioned on the title page of the Haggadah he illustrated. This reveals how little importance publishers in those days attached to the role of book illustrators. To the best of this author's knowledge Kutlik's early attempt to create a modern picture cycle for the text of the ancient Passover story has gone unmentioned even in the abundant modern literature on the history of Haggadah illustrations. This is so despite the fact that this edition of the Haggadah is already listed as item No. 776 in S. Wiener's *Bibliographie der Haggada* (St. Petersburg, 1902). Thus, one can read in the *Encyclopaedia Judaica* (Vol. VII, 1931, p. 812):

> In the nineteenth century the most popular Haggadah prototypes—the Venetian woodcut Haggadah of 1629 and the Amsterdam copper engraving Haggadah—were reproduced in cheap printed editions. French editions published in the 1850's and 1860's include small-sized Haggadot with color illustrations in the style of the Romantic School, but these illustrations are few and rather crude; there are no picture cycles.

The encyclopedia entry lists Joseph Budko's etchings of the year 1917 as the earliest attempt at modern Haggadah illustration.

There is no doubt that the readers of Tolnai's essay would have been interested in seeing Kutlik's pictures, for in the light of the artistic conceptions and the state of the illustrative techniques of the eighteen-eighties, they were certainly of historical interest in their own right. They marked the beginning of a new era in the development of Haggadah illustration, an art which has come into full flower only as a result of the technical advances since the beginning of the twentieth century. Cyril Kutlik appears to have been the first nineteenth-century artist to break away from the conventions of traditional Haggadah illustrations, which had been faithfully reproduced and reprinted for hundreds of years. He was the first to apply his own artistic ideas and style to the creation of a contemporary picture cycle. Today there exist countless artistically embellished editions of the Haggadah. The more felicitous the illustrations, the more effectively they function to familiarize their readers, particularly children, with the ancient texts and stories of the Haggadah. The situation was different eighty years ago, when the old heirloom Haggadot with their precious artistic ornamentation had become scarce. Some of them had become worn with age; others had found their way into the art collections of Jewish and non-Jewish museums, and into libraries, public and private. Thus the creation, in the late eighteen-eighties of a Haggadah adorned with modern illustrations which conformed to the artistic taste of the era stands out as a bold and remarkable achievement.

However, attempts to identify this interesting illustrated Haggadah were unsuccessful and, for unknown reasons, Tolnai's essay contains no bibliographical information which might have provided a clue to its identity. Even so knowledgeable a student of the history of Haggadot as Isaac Rivkind, in his bibliography relating to the Passover Haggadah (*Kiryat Sefer,* Vol. XII, 1935/36, p. 365 f.), was unable to make this identification and accepted Tolnai's vague reference to ". . . the twelve illustrations which enrich the Passover Haggadah in question."

The author of this article has admired Kutlik's illustrations on Seder nights since his earliest childhood, and has no difficulty in answering the question posed. The Haggadah to which Tolnai refers is the one published in 1889 by my late father, Dr. Alexander Kisch, who occupied the pulpit of the Meisel Synagogue in Prague from 1885 to 1917. This edition is worthy of note, not only for its illustrations, but also for its original "new German rendering of the time-honored Hebrew text." Furthermore, it contains annotations in which my father recorded many an explanation which he had personally heard from his teacher, the great scholar Zacharias Frankel of Breslau (cf. Guido Kisch, *Alexander Kisch, 1848-1917, eine Skizze seines Lebens und Wirkens, zugleich ein Beitrag zur Geschichte der Juden in Prag,* private publication, Prague, 1934).

While this article was primarily intended to clear up a long standing bibliographical mystery, it is hoped that it may also help the illustrations executed by the Slovak artist Cyril Kutlik attain their rightful place in the history of modern Haggadah illustration.

Although the volume of literature on the Haggadah has grown to considerable proportions in recent times, it has to date failed to take note of this, the earliest modern illustrated Haggadah. A case in point is Cecil Roth's valuable study, "The Illustrated Haggadah" (*Studies in Bibliography and Booklore,* Vol. VII, 1965, p. 54), which lists the names of many modern Haggadah illustrators, but makes no mention of Cyril Kutlik. While it may be true that the illustrations executed by this young Slovak artist cannot compare in quality with those by artists of the caliber of Joseph Budko, Jacob Steinhardt, Fritz Kredel or Arthur Szyk, Kutlik's name should not be forgotten in the history of Haggadah illustration. He deserves credit for having created the first original and modern picture cycle for the most popular Jewish liturgical book since the well-known edition published in 1526-27 by the Prague printer Gershom Cohen. His illustrations made a clean break with earlier traditional clichés, and attempted to conform with the artistic tastes and standards of his day. They were also used to adorn the similar edition of the Kisch Haggadah with a translation into Czech by Moric Kraus (Prague, 1889).

סֵדֶר

הַגָּדָה שֶׁל פֶּסַח

Die Peßach-Hagada,

Gebete und Gebräuche am Familientische für die beiden ersten Peßach-Abende. Mit 12 künstlerisch ausgeführten Illustrationen. Der althergebrachte hebräische Text mit

neuer deutscher Uebersetzung

und Erläuterung versehen

von

Phil.-Dr. **Alexander Kisch,**

Rabbiner und Prediger in Prag.

Der Sederabend.

Eigenthum und Verlag von Samuel W. Pascheles.

Buch-, Kunst- und Musikalienhandlung und hebr. Verlag.

Prag 1889.

Title Page of the Kisch Haggadah

A BIBLIOGRAPHY OF HEBREW PRINTING IN DYHERNFURTH 1689–1718

MOSES MARX

Hod Hasharon, Israel

Edited with an introduction, by Herbert C. Zafren

Moses Marx lived two professional lives during most of his pre-retirement years: he earned a living largely by being Head Cataloger at the Hebrew Union College in Cincinnati; and he worked an even longer week of evenings, weekdays, holidays, and other "spare" time on an impressive variety of bibliographical projects. Being a perfectionist, he published little of his work. But large arrays of material exist in various stages of completion, ranging from the nearly complete Bibliography of Hebrew Printing in the Fifteenth and Sixteenth Centuries, through his pet bibliographies of Hebrew printing in Germany, to notes on Hebrew printing wherever it might be.

Years ago I suggested to Mr. Marx that he publish sections of his material on German-Hebrew printing while spending greater energies on the fifteenth and sixteenth centuries; and I even "threatened" to dress them up a bit and publish some myself. This small section of the early years of Dyhernfurth printing is the partial fulfillment of my "threat." Mr. Marx's notebooks have long fascinated me, and they stimulated some of my recent work on Shabtai Bass and Dyhernfurth printing. At every step I was using his bibliography and his notebooks of facsimiles, extending them some and building on them; and now, in this volume, I am delighted to present the Marx bibliography as the basis of my own article on Bass's typography which itself derives much from my master's work.

My thanks go to Mr. James Neiger and Dr. Simon Cohen of the Hebrew Union College Library Staff who were of great help to me in the preparation of the manuscript and the checking of all the references. I must take final responsibility for the editing, the format, and the decisions about what to include and what to omit.

Mr. Marx prepared this bibliography many years ago and added to it after its initial preparation. His work was in draft form, there were naturally some inconsistencies of form and content, and his notes were all in German. In order to retain the character of the original compiler, the bibliography remains basically in the form that Mr. Marx developed, it remains in German, and I have added only a small number of entries, notes, and references. At every turn, when I tried to improve the format or style, I found even more strenuous objections to the "improvements" than to the original concept. Thus, the bibliography remains essentially as Mr. Marx developed it, with a little dressing up.

The bibliography, and a bibliography of works on Dyhernfurth, was to serve as the basis of a short history of printing there. Since the current list is only a small part of the total Dyhernfurth bibliographic history which Mr. Marx prepared, I thought it best to limit the literature to the works cited in abbreviated form in the references in the entries. Some other literature, cited infrequently, will be found only in the appropriate entries. Books and articles on Shabtai Bass and on Dyhernfurth, some of which were suggested by Mr. Marx's unpublished notes, are to be found in my companion article in this volume, "Dyhernfurth and Shabtai Bass: A Typographic Profile."

Following the list of references and other abbreviations comes the bibliography itself arranged by date: within each date, the arrangement is alphabetical by title, except that Bible and standard liturgies precede other books. Works without date, but before the period of joint publishing by Bass and his son, appear after 1711 and before 1712. Other works without date appear after 1718. There are cross references as appropriate. Entry numbers were added for easy reference; because doubtful items are included (and for other reasons), the last number does not indicate an accurate total of books published.

Each entry follows this format: Date, title (language when necessary), author, editor, related information, and collation; notes; references and some locations in American libraries. Except for HUCL, some of the locations have not been verified and have even been reported as "not found on shelves"; an asterisk identifies the items that have been looked for and not found. Because the size designations are not always clear, I have added the approximate size in centimeters for the books I examined. It should be noted that no effort is made to gather all information from all sources, but rather to give the essentials and references to further information. Thus there are no notes on typesetters, pressmen, and others because they are all brought together conveniently by Brann in a footnote on pp. 518–520. Much other detailed data can be obtained by going to the references.

Abbreviations of References

Al. בית הספר. *Catalog... hebräischer und jüdischer Bücher, Handschriften,... nachgelassen von Giuseppe Almanzi... Jacob Emden... M. J. Lewenstein...und Anderen...*, redigirt von M. Roest. Amsterdam, 1868.

Bj. Benjacob, I. A. אוצר הספרים... [Wilna] 1880.

Br. Brann, M[arkus] "Geschichte und Annalen der Dyhernfurther Druckerei." *Monatsschrift für Geschichte und Wissenschaft des Judenthums* 40 (1896), 474–480, 515–526, 560–574.

I.R. Bibliothek der Israelitischen Religionsschule zu Frankfurt am Main. *Katalog*. Frankfurt am Main, 1909.

Pin. [Pinner, Ephraim Moses] כתבי יד [ספרי דפוס, שמות הצדיקים וימי מיתתן... Berlin, 1861]

R. Roest, M[eyer] *Catalog der Hebraica und Judaica aus der L. Rosenthal'schen Bibliothek*. 2 volumes. Amsterdam, 1875.

Rt. [Roest, Meyer] *Anhang*. יודע ספר. *Bibliographisches Verzeichnis eines grossen Theiles der L. Rosenthal'schen Bibliothek...* [Amsterdam, 1875].

S.vB. Seeligmann, Sigmund. Catalog der... Sammlung hebräischer u. jüdischer Bücher... von N. H. van Biema in Amsterdam [also Hebrew title... רשימת ספרים]. Amsterdam, 1904.

SBB. *Studies in Bibliography and Booklore.*

Ser. Steinschneider, M[oritz] "Jüdisch-Deutsche Literatur, nach einem handschriftlichen Katalog der Oppenheim'schen Bibliothek (in Oxford) mit Zusätzen und Berichtigungen." *Serapeum* 9 (1848), 313–336, 344–352, 363–368, 375–384; 10 (1849), 9–16, 25–32, 42–48, 74–80, 88–96, 107–112; Register. 10 (1849) 54–59, 68–70. [Also] "Jüdische Litteratur und Jüdisch-Deutsch. Mit besonderer Rücksicht auf Ave-Lallemant." *Serapeum* 25 (1864), [33]–46, [49]–62, [66]–79, [81]–95, [97]–104; 27 (1866), (Ser.) 1–12; 30 (1869), [129]–140, [145]–159.

St. Steinschneider, M[oritz] *Catalogus librorum hebraeorum in Bibliotheca Bodleiana...* 3 volumes. Berlin, 1852–1860.

Str. Straalen, S. van. *Catalogue of Hebrew books in the British Museum acquired during the years 1868–1892.* London, 1894.

U. [Unger, Christian Theophil] "Index librorum in Silesia typis Dyrenfurtensibus ab anno Christi 1690 ad annum 1710 evulgatorum." *Neuer Büchersaal* 9, 691–712; 14, 91–107.

Wie. Wiener, Samuel. קהלת משה. *Bibliotheca Friedlandiana. Catalogus librorum impressorum hebraeorum in Museo Asiatico Imperialis Scientarum Petropolitanae asservatorum*... 8 no. (א—ל) *Saint Petersburg*, 1893–1936.

Wolf. Wolf, Johannes Christophorus. *Bibliotheca Hebraea*... 4 volumes. Hamburg, 1715.

Z. [Zedner, Joseph] *Catalogue of the Hebrew books in the library of the British Museum.* [London] 1867.

Other Abbreviations

Anm.	Anmerkung
Bd.	Band
Bl. (Bll.)	Blatt (Blätter)
ca.	circa
Ed.	Edition
Gr.	Groschen
h. K.	ha-Kohen
h. L.	ha-Levi
H.	Harvard College Library, Cambridge
HUCL	Library, Hebrew Union College–Jewish Institute of Religion, Cincinnati
HUCL-N	Library, Hebrew Union College–Jewish Institute of Religion, New York
JTSL	Library, Jewish Theological Seminary, New York
L.	Rabbi Schneersohn Library of Lubawitz, Brooklyn
LC	Library of Congress, Washington, D.C.
No.	Nummer
NYPL	New York Public Library
S.	Siehe, Seite
s.a.	sine anno (no date)
s.a.e.l.	sine anno et loco (no date, no place)
s.l.	sine loco (no place)
Tl.	Teil
Thlr.	Thaler
u.	und
UCLA	University of California, Los Angeles
Vgl.	Vergleiche
YIVO	Yivo Institute for Jewish Research, New York
YU	Library, Yeshiva University, New York.

1. 1689, 28. Av—3. Elul.

בית שמואל

Samuel ben Uri Schraga ben Jehuda Loeb aus Woydyslaw (s. Kelilat Jofi, 1, 81b, ff.; 2, 58b).

1, 159 bll. 2° (30 cm.).

Veröffentlicht zum Preise von 1 Thlr., 10 Gr.

Auf Josef Caro ben Efraim אבן העזר.

Br. 520; U 696—697; St. 1489/5940, 76; Z. 341; Bj. 76/394; Wie. 178/1382; Al. 245; Jüdisches Lexikon, 2, 223, Faksimile des Titelblatts.

HUCL, JTSL, LC, YU.

2. 1689, ערב ראש השנה (14 September).

דברי דוד... על רש״י שעל חמשה חומשי תורה

David h. L. ben Samuel. Editor: Moses ben Isak Sprinzes ben Oser aus Krzeminiec, Schwiegersohn von Jesaja h. L. ben David ben Samuel [author] (s. Kelilat Jofi, 1, 48a–77b; Buber, Ansche Schem, 56/135). Co-editor: Aron h. L. ben Jakob.

1, 79, (3) Bll. 2° (29 cm.).

Br. 521; U. 696; St. 886/4844; Z. 202; Bj. 103/59; Wie. 257/2097; S.vB. 453.

HUCL, NYPL, YIVO, YU.

3. 1689.

מענה לשון (Juedisch)

Elieser Liebermann Sofer ben Jehuda Loeb Rofe aus Prag in Mainz.

12 Bll. 8°.

Br. 521; St. 966/5010, 18 (vgl. 5010, 22).

4. 1689.

ענוי נפש ורפואתו

Anonym. [Mordechai ben Moses]

8°.

Aus einem Akrostichon in der Fürth ca. 1722 Ausgabe dieses Titels ergibt sich Mordechai ben Moses als Verfasser. (s. St. 1670/6249).

Ueber Tod und Strafen im Jenseits.

Br. 522; Bj. 439/329.

5. s.a. [1689]

שערי ציון

Natan Nata Hannover ben Moses.

48 Bll. 4°.

Preis: 4 Stück für 10 Gr.

Br. 521–522; W. 1, 923; (St. 2046/6637, 18, Anm.).

6. 1690.

[סדר תפלות]

Ritus Polen, Reussen, Deutschland, Böhmen und Mähren.

Mit grammatischen Noten des Sabbatai ben Isak Przemyslaw; Tikkune Schabbat, Jozerot, Psalmen (mit besonderem Titelblatt; St. 105/651), Ma'amadot, Kinnot, Minhagim (mit besonderem Titelblatt), Ascher ben Jechiel, Orchot Chajim.

422 (?) Bll.

Br. 522; U. 100; St: 333/2199.

7. 1690.

מים חיים, דרושים [חלק א]

Chajim h. L. Horowitz ben Josua (Moses Aron).

70 Bll. 4° (19 cm.).

Tl. 2: S. no. 64, 1703.

Br. 522; U. 703; W. 1, 373; St. 827/4688, 1; Z. 290; Bj. 324/1115.

HUCL, JTSL, LC, NYPL, YIVO.

8. 1690.

מנהגים

Isak Tyrnau.

Ritus Polen, Reussen, Litauen, Böhmen, Mähren und Deutschland.

17 cm.

Teil des Gebetbuches, no. 6, 1960?

Nach dem Faksimile des Titelblatts von A. M. Habermann zur Verfügung gestellt.

9. 1690.

עיר מקלט

David ben Arje Loeb aus Lida (s. Kelilat Jofi, 1, 68a; 2, 59a f., 70a; Buber, Ansche Schem, 54/137).

(1–7, 6^2, 9–16, 21–44, 43–54 =) 52 Bll. 4°.

Preis: 7 Gr.
Br. 522; U. 702; St. 878/4826, 13; Z. 198; Bj. 440/358.
HUCL, JTSL, LC, NYPL, UCLA, YIVO, YU.

10. 1691.

סליחות עם פירוש

Ritus Gross- und Klein-Polen, Reussen und Mähren.
2°.
Der auf dem Titelblatte angekündigte Kommentar ist im Buche nach Brann nicht vorhanden. Z. erwähnt das nicht.
S. no. 78, 1705.
Br. 524; U. 94; St. 436/2860; Z. 464; Bj. 421/396.

11. 1691.

ברכת המזון

[50] Bll. 4° (19 cm.)
JTSL.

12. 1691, 1. Siwan.

בית הילל

Hillel ben Naftali Hirz ben Samuel in Kempen. (s. Kelilat Jofi, 2, 56b f.). Editor: Moses ben Hillel ben Naftali Hirz in Kempen
Bd. 1:1, 134; Bd. 2:1, 49 Bll. 2° (31 cm.).
Preis: 1 Thlr.
Auf Josef Caro ben Efraim יורה דעה und אבן העזר.
Br. 523–524; U. 98; W. 1, 351; St. 1488/5940, 64; Z. 334; Bj. 72/310; R. 570; Rt. 256; Wie. 163/1276; Al. 230.
H, HUCL, JTSL, LC, YIVO, YU.

13. 1691.

חקי משפט מטור חושן משפט

Moses Jekutiel Kaufmann h. K. ben Avigdor aus Krotoschin.
8°.
Vgl. no. 55, 1701.
Preis: 8 Gr.
U. 709; I. R. 891 (vgl. 890).
YU*.

14. 1691.

ילקוט דוד... לקוטים ממפרשי התורה... ממדרשים וגמרא

David Spitz Posner ben Naftali in Krotoschin. Editor: Vater des Verfassers, Naftali Hirz Spitz ben Moses.
376 Bll. 4° (20 cm.).
Preis: 8 Gr.
Br. 524; U. 704; St. 863/4810; Z. 202; Bj. 222/225; Wie. 591/4822; S. v.B. 1074.
HUCL, JTSL, LC, NYPL, YU.

15. 1691.

לב שמח

Abraham Allegri.
4°.
Br. 524; Bj. 254/30 (2°).

16. 1691.

קרבן שבת, חיבור על קצת דינים של שבת מלוקטים מפוסקים ומספרי קבלה ובדרושים...

Bezalel ben Salomo aus Kobryn in Sluzk.
1, 51 Bll. 4° (19 cm.).
Br. 524; St. 800/4594, 7; Z. 95; Bj. 536/570; S.vB. 2913, 1.
HUCL, LC, NYPL.

17. 1692.

סדר תפלות

Deutscher und polnischer Ritus.
Br. 524; Alexander Marx, Zeitschrift für hebräische Bibliographie 11 (1907), 124.
JTSL.

18. 1692.

תיקוני שבת עם פירוש מנחת יעקב... עם המלת הזרים פ׳ בל״א...

Isak Luria ben Salomo.
Kommentar von Jakob h. L. ben Rafael aus Posen.
1, 37 Bll. 4°.
Br. 524; U. 704; W. 2, 1470; St. 471/3115; 1248/5605, 1; Z. 471; Bj. 670/903, Liberman, Kirjath Sepher, 38/39, 405.
JTSL, L.

19. 1692.

ברכת אברהם

Gebete.
8°.
Br. 525; St. 481/3199; Bj. 87/639; Ser. 324/30.

20. 1692.

זמר לספר תורה

Se'ew Wolf Naumberg ben Baruch, Vorbeter in Gross Glogau.
Gesang zur Einweihung einer Torarolle. Beginn:
אשירה שירת דודי אלי רועי מעודי. . .
4 Bll. 8°.
Br. 525; St. 2576/7160; Bj. 160/215.

21. 1692.

מגני ארץ . . . על הש״ע מטור אורח חיים . . .
Josef Caro ben Efraim.
Mit dem Kommentar von Moses Isserles (ben Israel), David h. L. ben Samuel מגן דוד und Abraham Abele Gumbiner ben Chajim מגן אברהם.
(3), 342 Bll. 2° (31 cm.).
Preis: 4 Thlr.; auf gutem Papier 5 Thlr.
Br. 522–523; U. 697; St. 1484/5940, 26; Z. 355; Bj. 585/704; Pin. 10/79.
HUCL, JTSL, YIVO, YU.

22. 1692.

מנהגים (Juedisch)

Nach dem Hebräischen von Isak Tyrnau.
56 Bll. Illustriert. 4° (19 cm.).
Br. 525; St. 600/3828; Ser. 376/149.
HUCL.

23. 1693.

חמשה חומשי תורה עם חמש מגילות והפטרות...
Mit Targum, Raschi, Sifte Chachamim, Ba'al ha-Turim, Toldot Aharon.
(6), 1–342 (Pentateuch), 343–368 (Megillot), 335 [*sic*]–362 (Haftarot) Bll. 4° (20 cm.).
Abdruck der Ausgabe Amsterdam, 1680, bei Uri Phoebus.
Megilloth und Haftaroth haben besondere Titelblätter.
Preis: 3–4 Thlr.
Br. 525; U. 705–706; St. 108/669; 669a auf grossem Papier; Bj. 635/284; R. 179; Rt. 2381.
HUCL, YIVO.

24. 1693.

מחזור

S. no. 63, 1703.
Br. 524; St. 382/2498; vgl. 383/2506 (1703).
JTSL.

25. 1693.

ברכת המזון (Hebräisch und Juedisch)

Illustriert. 4°.
Jewish Theological Seminary, Register, 1930–31, p. 189.
JTSL*.

26. 1693.

אהבת עולם

Salomo Algasi ben Abraham.
124 Bll. 2° (31 cm.).
Preis: 18 Gr.
Br. 525; U. 697; St. 2278/6894, 2; Z. 712; Bj. 18/354; Wie. 32/266; Al. 5235; S.vB. 48.
HUCL, JTSL, LC, NYPL, YIVO, YU.

27. sa. [1693]

מאמר העיתים. . . הוא מאמר השביעי לספר עשרה מאמרות

Menachem Asarja aus Fano ben Isak Berechja.
Editor, Jonatan ben Jakob aus Ofen.
4°.
Br. 525–526; 1723/6342; 23; Z. 530; Bj. 453/643; S.vB. 1283.

28. 1693.

מנורה (Juedisch)

Gebete.
8°.
Jede weitere Auskunft fehlt. Vielleicht enthält das Buch ausser dem in Leuchterform gedruckten Psalm 67 einige jüdische Gelegenheitsgebete, wie Ed. Prag, 1696 (s. bei St. 494/3250).
Br. 525; U. 104.

29. 1693.

מראה להתקשט בו

Elchanan K"z ben Isachar (Elchanan Jentel's Schammasch, Chasan und Sofer aus Prossnitz.

1 Bl. 2° (39x28 cm.).

Ethischen Inhalts.

St. 923/4931, 2; Jacob R. Marcus, עטישע ייווא בלעטער ,וואנטשפיגלען 21 (1943) 201–214.

HUCL

30. 1693.

עמודיה שבעה, דרושים

Bezalel ben Salomo aus Kobryn in Sluzk.

72 Bll. 4° (20 cm.).

Preis: 8 Gr.

Br. 525; U. 704; St. 799/4594, 3; Z. 95; Bj. 443/430; Al. 1534; S.vB. 1964.

HUCL, JTSL.

31. 1693.

פרקי רבי אליעזר

32 Bll. 4° (19 cm.)

Preis: 6 Gr.

Br. 525; U. 704–705; St. 634/4015; Bj. 498/1204; S.vB. 2125.

HUCL, JTSL, LC, UCLA.

32. 1693.

ר[אשית]" ח[כמה] תוצאות חיים . . . קיצור . . . ראשית חכמה

Elia de Vidas ben Moses.

121 Bll. 32° (10 cm.)

Preis: 4 Gr.

Br. 526; U. 710; St. 952/4973, 13; Z. 231; Bj. 628/226.

HUCL.

33. 1693.

שערי ציון

Natan Nata Hannover ben Moses.

40 Bll. 4°.

D. Simonsen–Kopenhagen, bei Brann, 568 (s. שערי ציון, s.a.).

34. 1694.

[חמשה חומשי תורה, מגלות, הפטרות]

Mit Moses Saertels ben Isachar, באר משה.

4°.

Preis: 16 Gr.

Br. 562; U. 706; St. 108/674.

35. 1694

כתבי קבלה

Simson Ostropoler.

4°.

Bj. 249/354.

36. 1694.

מאמר העיתים

Menachem Asarja aus Fano ben Isak Berechja.

8 Bll. 4° (19 cm.)

Ausgabe 1693, mit neuem Titelblatt.

St. 1723/6342, 24.

HUCL.

37. 1694.

צוואת ר' ישראל ב"ר אליעזר פרנס ק"ק ליסא

1 Bl. 2°.

נדפס במצות האשה יקרה מרת מירל שתי' אשת האלוף ר' שבתי בעל המדפיס נכד כמ"ר ישראל הנ"ל [המחבר]

Br. 565; U. 103–104; St. 1165/5457, 1; Bj. 507/42.

Jewish Quarterly Review, Old Series, 3, 482.

38. 1695.

הטבת חלום

Juedische Ausgabe von פתרון חלומות von Salomo Almoli ben Jacob. Moses ben Isak aus Brezesc, וידוי גדולה.

32 Bll. 8°.

Preis: 3 Gr.

Br. 564; U. 708–709; St. 635/4025; 490/3236: Add. zu. col. 2283; Bj. 503/1328.

39. 1695.

(Hebräisch und Juedisch) שחיטה ובדיקה

Jakob Weil.

Compendium, juedisch von Alexander ben Mordechai.

12 Bll. 8°.
Vermutlich identisch mit Alexander Rein: שחיטות ובדיקות.
Br. 564; St. 1265/5631, 69; Bj. 571/385; Str. 199; Ser. 47/286.

40. 1696.
[סדר תפלות]
Polnischer und deutscher Ritus.
Jozerot, Psalmen (St. 110/687), Ma'amadot.
456 Bll. 12°.
Br. 562; St. 335/2209.

41. 1696.
[סדר תפלות]
Tl. 1 mit Jozerot etc.; Tl. 2 Psalmen (St. 110/686), Kinot etc.; Tl. 3 Minhagim von Isak Tyrnau und dem Kommentare dazu von Eljakim Gottschalk ben Chiskija (St. 968/5019), etc.
236, 104, 28 Bll. 8°. 3 Teile.
Br. 562; St. 335/2208.

42. 1696.
שבעים ושתים פסוקים (Juedisch)
Liturgie.
4°.
Br. 563; St. 503/3308; Ser. 46/282.

43. s.l., 1696, 17. Siwan.
בית יעקב . . . פתרונים על חדושי דינים . . . והם דרך שאלות ותשובות
Jakob aus Zausmer ben Samuel in Sandomierz.
(2), 3–128, (8) Bll. 2° (30 cm.)
Preis: 12 Gr.
Sehr fehlerhafter Druck.
Die Unterschrift des Setzers Chajim ben Katriel aus Krakau beweist Dyhernfurth als Druckort.
Br. 564; U. 698–699; St. 1268/5636; Z. 305; Bj. 73/332; R. 521; Wie. 165/1291; Pin. 158; S.vB. 2457.
H, HUCL, JTSL, NYPL, UCLA, YIVO, YU.

44. 1697.
[סדר תפלות]
Polnischer Ritus.
Mit Jozerot, Psalmen mit juedischer Uebersetzung (St. 111/695), etc.
344 Bll. Schmal 12°.
Preis: 1 Thlr.
Br. 562. St. 336/2217.

45. 1697.
(Juedisch) [איין שיין נייא טייטש מעשה בוך]
Editor: Jonatan ben Jakob aus Ofen.
8 Bll. 4°.
Br. 563; St. 614/3904; 1432/5868, 1; Bj. 398/176.

46. s.l.e.a. [1697.]
קסת יהונתן
Jonatan ben Jakob aus Ofen.
Auszüge aus ספר החסידים, של"ה, etc.
20 Bll. 4° (20 cm.)
Datum der Aprobation.
Br. 563; U. 703–704; St. 1432/5868, 2; Z. 327; Bj. 531/423; R. 560; Rt. 1801; Al. 1797; S.vB. 2272.
HUCL, JTSL, LC, NYPL, UCLA.

47. 1700.
[תהלים ומעמדות]
12°.
Aus einer Siddur Ausgabe?
Preis: 6 Gr.
Br. 563; U. 709; St. 113/711; 338/2223.

48. 1700.
שער התקונים [ליל שבועות וה"ר]
12°.
Preis: 4 Gr.
Br. 563; U. 709–710; St. 464/3057; Bj. 601/1067.

49. s.a. [1700]
אורים ותומים
Abraham ben Abraham aus Adrianopel.
Zauberbuch, chiromantische Deutungen, etc.
56 Bll. 8°.
Br. 564; St. 518/3392: 1728; Z. 14: 1700?;

Bj. 30/598; R. 20: 1700?; Rt. 110; Wie. 68/536.
JTSL*.

50. 1700, 3. Tammus.
התחלת יצחק
Isak ben Jakob שלומים aus Dubno.
8°.
"Anweisung in Briefen die Namen der Adressaten akrostich zu verherrlichen."
Br. 564; U. 102–103; St. 1127/5360, 2.

51. s.l., 1700, 27 Tischri.
לב טוב (Juedisch)
Isak ben Eljakim aus Posen.
75 Bll. 2° (28 cm.).
U. und Wolf, und nach ihnen Brann verzeichnen eine Ausgabe 1701, die St. für nicht existierend hält.
Preis: 16 Gr.
Br. 563; U. 698; W. 3, 555; St. 1109/5344, 6.
JTSL, NYPL, YU.

52. s.l., 1700.
מנחת ערב [תקון קריאת שמע שעל המטה]
Nach der Anordnung des Jehuda ha-Chassid.
12°.
Br. 563; St. 467/3087; Bj. 343/1549.

53. 1700.
צאינה וראינה
Jakob ben Isak aus Janowo.
Editor: Salomo aus Lokacz (Lokaczer).
148 Bll. 2°.
Preis: 16 Gr.
Br. 562; U. 697–698; St. 1218/5545, 17.

54. 1701.
תפלת יום כפור קטן להשבית השטן
Mit juedischer Uebersetzung von Natan, Vorbeter aus Prossnitz.
8°.
Br. 563; St. 423/2774.

55. 1701, 18. Elul.
חקי משפט משלחן ערוך מטור חשן משפט. . .
Israel Samuel Clefara ben Salomo.
Mit Kommentar von Moses Jekutiel Kaufmann h. K. ben Awigdor aus Krotoschin in Koethen.
114 Bll. 8° (15 cm.)
Vgl. no. 13, 1691.
Preis: 8 Gr.
Br. 564; St. 1172/5477, 5; 1381/5793, 4; Z. 392; Bj. 232/473.
HUCL, LC.

1701.
לב טוב
S. no. 51, 1700.

56. 1701.
[שחיטות ובדיקות]
Jakob Weil.
4°.
Preis: 3 Gr.
Br. 564; U. 707.

57. 1702.
[תהלים]
15 Bll. 16°.
Teil eines Gebetbuches? Vielleicht no. 60, 1703?
Br. 566; St. 115/724.

58. 1702.
[סליחות]
Litauischer Ritus.
8°.
Br. 567; U. 101; St. 437/2867; W. 2, 1385.

59. 1702. Siwan.
מגני ארץ . . . על הש"ע מטור אורח חיים
Josef Caro ben Efraim.
(4), 338, 2 Bll. 2° (32 cm.)
Preis: 4 oder 5 Thlr.
Mit den üblichen Kommentaren und der Erstausgabe der Glossen von Menachem Auerbach ben Meschullam Salman Fischhof aus Wien in Krotoschin.
Br. 569–570; U. 697; St. 1484/5940, 27; 28; charta alba; 29: charta alba maxima; Bj. 585/704; Al. 984; Str. 107.
H, HUCL., JTSL., LC, YU.

60. 1703.

[סדר תפלות]

Deutscher Ritus.
Preis: 12 Gr.
Hierzu die Psalmen, no. 57, 1702?
Br. 567; U. 797; St. 340/2247.

61. 1703.

[סדר תפלות]

Deutscher Ritus.
48°.
Br. 567.

62. 1703.

[תיקוני שבת]

[4°?]
Bj. 670/903.

63. 1703.

[מחזור]

Ritus Polen, Reussen etc.
264 Bll. 8°.
Mit Erklärung der "schweren Wörter."
Br. 567; St. 383/2506; Titel 1693; Approbation 1703. (Vgl. 382/2498.)

64. 1703, Tewet.

מים חיים שני

Chajim h. L. Horowitz ben Josua (Moses Aron).
2, 68 Bll. 4° (19 cm.).
Preis: 10 Gr.
Tl. 1 erschien 1690; s. no. 7.
Br. 570; U. 703; W. 1, 373; St. 828/4688, 2; Z. 290; Bj. 324/1116; Al. 1084; S.vB. 1471.
HUCL-N, JTSL, NYPL, YU.

65. 1704.

[חמשה חומשי תורה. מגלות. הפטרות.]

Mit Moses Saertels באר משה am Rande.
4°.
Preis: 16 Gr.
Br. 566; U. 706; St. 117/735 (dub.).

66. 1704.

טייטש עשרים וארבע (Juedisch)

Auszug aus den historischen Büchern der Bibel, von Chajim ben Natan. Verkürzte Ausgabe.
21 Bll. 4°.
Preis: 12 Gr.
Nachdruck der Ausgabe Prag, 1674.
Br. 566; U. 707; St. 177/1186; Bj. 640/343; Ser. 108/356.

67. 1704.

(Hebräisch und Juedisch) [תהלים. מעמדות]
8°.
Aus einem Siddur?
Br. 566; St. 117/742 (dub.).

68. 1704.

[סדר תפלות]

Deutscher Ritus.
4°.
S. Siddur 1705, no. 75.
Br. 567; U. 708; St. 341/2254.

69. 1704.

[סליחות]

2°
Br. 567–568.

[תקון ליל שבועות וה"ר]

8°.
70. 1704.
Br. 568; W. 2, 1470 (s. St. 464/3057).

71. 1704.

מענה לשון

Elieser Liebermann Sofer ben Jehuda Loeb Rofe aus Prag in Mainz.
93 Bll. 12°.
Br. 568; St. 965/5010, 9.

72. s.a. [1705]

[תהלים]

Mit der juedischen Uebersetzung von Elia Lewi Bachur ben Ascher.
10 Bogen, die Seite zu 19 Zeilen. 8°.
Hebräischer Satz vom Siddur 1705, 8° no. 73.
St. 120/754.

73. [1705.]

[סדר תפלות]

Deutscher und polnischer Ritus.

Mit Hoscha'anot, Ma'ariwim mit juedischer Uebersetzung, Dewarim sche-bikeduscha, Jozerot, Selichot, Psalmen (St. 120/752, 12°!; Br. 566), Techinnot juedisch, etc.

44 1/2 Bogen (356 Bll.?) 8°.

Am Ende ein Leuchter.

Br. 567; St. 342/2261.

74. 1705.

[סדר תפלות]

Mit Neumondgebeten, sowie mit שערי ציון von Natan Nata Hannover ben Moses. Hebräisches und juedisches Vorwort vom Editor Mordechai ben Israel.

8°.

Preis der Scha'are Zion, die auch allein verkauft wurden, 10 Gr. für 4 Stück.

Ist der Siddur mit dem vorhergehenden identisch?

Br. 568; St. 2046/6637, 18; 342/2262; Bj. 604/1134.

JTSL (שערי ציון).

75. s.l., 1705.

[סדר תפלות]

Deutscher Ritus.

4°.

Mit Haggada, Psalmen (St. 120/753), Ma'amadot etc.

St. 341/2260: Fragment, gehört vielleicht zu dem Siddur 1704, no. 68.

76. 1705.

[מחזור]

Deutscher Ritus (?)

Mit Kommentar oder juedischer Uebersetzung?

2°

Br. 567; W. 2, 1337; St. 383/2509: Ed. suspecta. s. Ed. 1707.

77. 1705.

[מחזור]

Mit Kommentar.

8°.

Br. 567.

78. 1705.

סליחות עם פירוש

Ritus Böhmen, Polen, Mähren, Oesterreich.

Kommentar von Mordechai ben Jehuda.

89 Bll. 2°.

Preis: 1 Thlr.

Vermehrte Auflage der Ausgabe 1691, no. 10.

Br. 568; U. 698, 94; W. 2, 1384; St. 438/2869; 2869a: charta alba magna.

79. 1705.

דרך הנשר (Hebräisch, Aramäisch, Juedisch und Deutsch)

Daniel Springer, Professor des Hebräischen am Evangelischen Gymnasium in Breslau.

Des Adlers Weg. Trauerlied auf den Tod des Kaisers Leopold.

2°.

Preis: 3 Gr.

Der deutsche Teil ist in Breslau gedruckt.

Br. 570–571; U. 699–700; St. 2651/7266; Bj. 118/457.

80. 1705.

Druck des Titelblatts und des Vorworts zu den vom Superintendenten Tobias Linck (oder Linke?) (s. W. 1, 394 und 3, 277) ins Hebräische übersetzten Gebeten.

Der Text wurde nicht gedruckt.

Br. 571; U. 710–712, 97–98.

81. 1706.

[חמשה חומשי תורה. מגלות. הפטרות]

Mit Targum und Raschi auf Pentateuch und Megilloth.

סמנים לקריאת הפרשיות, 3 S.

Preis: 1 Thlr. und 8 Gr.

Br. 566; U. 706; St. 120/756.

82. 1706.

ספר המעשה

354 Ma'assijot, gesammelt aus Talmud und Midrasch, von Ascher Anschel ben Leiser, Chasan.

4°.

Br. 570; St. 613/3899; Bj. 353/1793; Ser. 379.

83. 1707.

[מחזור]

Polnischer Ritus.

Mit Kommentar. Ferner שערי ציון von Natan Nata Hannover ben Moses. Editor: Josef, Sohn des Druckers.

2 Bde. Bd. 1: 144; 2: 110 Bll. 2°.

Preis: 2–5 Thlr.

St. ist der Ansicht, dass die Ausgabe 1705 auf Konfusion mit dieser begründet ist.

Br. 567; U. 698; St. 383/2512; 2512 b: charta maxima.

84. 1707.

דברי נתן

Kommentar von David ben Moses aus Zülz, Bibliothekar bei David Oppenheimer in Prag.

Von diesem Kommentar auf מגלה עמוקות, wurden die Approbationen von David Oppenheimer und Gabriel ben Jehuda Loeb in Nikolsburg gedruckt.

Nicht mehr erschienen.

Br. 571; U. 99–100.

85. 1707.

מאזני צדק

Kommentar auf die Psalmen von Isak Zoref ben Isachar Berl aus Krakau (s. D. Kaufmann, Die letzte Vertreibung, 171–172).

Mit Kommentar רוממות אל von Mose Alschech.

(6, 187) Bll. 8°.

Preis: 10 Gr.

Auf Kosten von Moses Austerlitz ben Josef aus Nickolsburg (s. oben, Kaufmann, 171) und seines Bruderssohns Isachar Berl.

Br. 566–567; U. 709; W. 2, 1323; St. 121/764; 1159/5440, 2; Bj. 642/386; B. Zuckermann, Catalog der Seminar-Bibliothek [Breslau], 48.

HUCL, UCLA.

86. 1708.

[סדר תפלות]

Polnischer Ritus.

Mit Kiddusch ha-Chodesch, Semirot etc.

29 Bogen (348 Bll.?). 12°.

Br. 567; St. 344/2280.

87. 1708 [Ausgabe 1709?]

[סליחות]

8°.

1702 und 1709: 8°; 1704 und 1705: 2°.

"Selichoth [Dyhernfurth, 1708. 8°]... in der Offizin des Sabbatai... gedruckt, enthält manche Gebete, welche sich nicht in den gewöhnlichen Ausgaben befinden." Dukes, Moses ben Esra, 73, Anm.

88. 1708.

שנות חיים

Josef Chasan. Kommentar auf die Babot. Editor: Sohn Chajim ben Josef Chasan aus Smyrna.

2°.

Von ca. 120 Bogen waren die ausgedruckten 100 bei einer Feuersbrunst, nach Pessach 1708, zu Grunde gegangen.

Br. 571; U. 702–703.

89. 1709.

[סדר תפלות]

Deutscher und polnischer Ritus.

4° und 8° [?]

Preis: 4°; 12 Gr.–1 Thlr; 8°: 3 Gr.

Br. 567 nimmt das für 2 Ausgaben: eine in 4°, eine in 8°; U. 707 and 708; St. 345/2288: Format "4 et 8".

90. 1709.

[מחזור]

Mit juedischer Uebersetzung. Kommentar von Awigdor Eisenstadt ben Moses aus Krakau.
8°.
Br. 567; St. 392/2566: dub.; St. erwähnt Ritus, Uebersetzer und Kommentar nicht.

91. 1709.

[סליחות]

Ritus Gross- und Klein-Polen, Böhmen und Mähren.
8°.
Preis: 8 Gr.
Br. 568; U. 698; St. 438/2874.

92. 1709.

סדר ברכת המזון דאש איז עברי טייטש בענשן
Illustriert. 4°.
Preis: 4 Gr.
Br. 569; U. 707; W. 2, 1271; St. 408/2643.

93. 1709.

שומרים לבקר
8°.
Preis: 3 Gr.
Br. 569; U. 698, 96–97; St. 457/3014.

94. 1709.

איין שיין מעשה בוך
4°.
Preis: 6 Gr.
Br. 570; U. 707.

95. 1710.

[חמשה חומשי תורה]
4°.
Preis: 16 Gr.
Wahrscheinlich Nachdruck der Ausgabe 1704; enthält aber auch des Druckers grammatisches Vorwort zu באר משה.
Br. 566; U. 706–707; St. 123/781: fict.?

96. 1710.

[שער התקונים לליל שבועות וה"ר]
12°.
Preis: 4 Gr.
Br. 568; U. 709–710; St. 465/3065: dub.; s. St. 464/3057.

97. 1710.

ארץ צבי
Verfasser: Efraim. Editor: Sohn Zwi Hirsch ben Efraim.
8 Bll. 8°.
Br. 570; U. 103; St. 2751/7416, 1; Bj. 54/1011; Wie. 118/957.

98. 1711.

[חמשה חומשי תורה. תרגום אונקלוס ופירוש"י]
4°.
Wahrscheinlich Neudruck der Ausgabe 1706, no. 81.
Br. 566; St. 124/793: dub.

99. 1711–?

[לוח]
Alljaehrlich.
12°.
U.104–105; Brann, Der hebraeische Buchdruck in Breslau, Jahrbuch zur Belehrung und Unterhaltung (ed. M. Brann) 39 (1891): 79–80. [Issued with Jüdischer Volks- und Haus-Kalender... 1892.]

100. 1711.

פרקי אבות
Mit juedischer Uebersetzung.
4°.
Br. 569; U. 708; St. 237/1502.

Sine anno, 1689–1711

s.a.

תהלים
S.: no. 72, 1705.

101. s.a. [1700?]

סדר תפלות מכל השנה
314 Bll. 16°
Str. 144.

102. s.a. [1706?]

סליחות כמנהג בית הכנסת הישנה

Ritus Prag.

2°.

Br. 568; U. 698: 1706; St. 438/2871: dub.

103. s.l.e.a.

סדר יום כפור קטן להשבית קטרוג של שטן

8°.

U. 103; W. 2, 1378/483; St. 423/2774, Anm.

104. s.a. [1689–1701]

[תחנה]

Editor: Sabbatai Bass.

8°.

[Eine schöne תחנה, sie kommt aus Palästina.]

Br. 563; St. 480/3187: 1689–1701; Ser. 77/304.

s.a.

אורים ותומים

S.: no. 49, 1700.

s.a.

מאמר העתים

S.: no. 27, 1693.

105. s.a.

סגולות ורפואות

Zwi Hirsch Chotsch ben Jerachmiel ben Abi Esri Selig.

3 Bll. 8°

Br. 573; U. 708; St. 2754/7426, 5, Anm. JTSL*.

s.l.e.a.

קסת יהונתן

S.: no. 46, 1697.

s.a.

שערי ציון

S.: no. 5, 1689.

106. s.a.

שערי ציון

Natan Nata Hannover ben Moses.

4°.

Für Josef ben Sabbatai.

Setzer: Menachem Man ben Isak Jakob aus Prag, der in den Jahren 1689–1693 als Arbeiter in Dyhernfurth bekannt ist.

Falls diese Ausgabe mit der vorhergehenden undatierten identisch sein sollte, wäre das für jene von Wolf angegebene Datum 1689 wohl unrichtig, da Josef, des Druckers Sohn, der nicht vor 1707 in die Erscheinung tritt, wohl in dem genannten Jahre noch nicht das Alter für selbständige Geschäfte erreicht gehabt haben dürfte.

Simonsen bemerkt zu seiner Ausgabe 1693 des Sha'are Zion, dass auf dem Titelblatt "auf einem in der Mitte des untern Rahmenstücks freigemachten Platz mit den Worten שנת תנ"ג לפ"ק (= 1693) die Jahreszahl angegeben" sei. "Es zeichnen auf Blatt 40b hintereinander die oben S.518, Anm. 3 [in Br.] sub Nr. 11, 15 (als Drucker), 5 und 18 (hier also zum ersten Mal genannt) aufgezählten Personen. Wenn nun auch die Möglichkeit nicht ausgeschlossen ist, dass es sich um ein nachgeschossenes (vgl. Oelsner, R. Sabbathai Bassista und sein Prozess, S. 21, No. 12) und nachträglich datirtes Exemplar der von Unger und Wolf erwähnten Ausgabe handelt, so muss doch vorläufig mein Exemplar als eine zweite Quartausgabe gelten. Für die nachträgliche Datirung spricht die durch den Augenschein bestätigte Tatsache, dass der Raum für die Jahreszahl innerhalb des Rahmenstückes ohne Zweifel erst nachträglich freigemacht ist. Die dritte Dyhenrfurther Quartausgabe ist durch ein undatiertes Exemplar der Bodl. vertreten, welches St. 2046, 18 bespricht und inhaltlich zwar mit der zweiten identisch, mit dieser aber darum garnicht zu verwechseln ist, weil es im Auftrag des Joseph b. Schabatai angefertigt und von dem oben S. 523 in der Anm. sub Nr.

12 genannten Menachem Man, der 1689–1693 in D. auftritt, gesetzt ist. Die Möglichkeit, dass das Exemplar der Bodl. zu der von Unger und Wolf erwähnten undatirten Auflage gehöre, halte ich wegen der Nennung Josephs für ganz ausgeschlossen."

Dazu bemerkt Brann, dass die genannten Schwierigkeiten sich durch die Annahme beheben liessen, dass Sabbatai bei Beginn seiner Tätigkeit das Buch habe herstellen, und dann den Satz zu jederzeitiger Wiederverwendung für neue Auflagen habe stehen lassen. "Nichts hindert anzunehmen, dass Joseph 1711 oder 1712 nach der Uebernahme der Druckerei eine neue undatierte Auflage von dem alten Satz habe anfertigen lassen".

Br. 568–569; U. 702–703; St. 2046/6637, 18: 1689–1711; Bj. 604/1134: 1705.

Sabbatai Bass durch seinen Sohn Josef

107. 1712.

[סדר תפלות]

Polnischer Ritus.

28 Bll. 12°.

St. 347/2305.

108. 1712.

(Juedisch) חכמות המספר

Moses Katzenellenbogen ben Chajim aus Eisenstadt.

Arithmetik.

104 Bll. 8° (13 cm.)

St. 1800/6458, 2; Z. 411; Bj. 190/615; Ser. 335/71.

JTSL.

109. 1712.

נתיב הישר

Naftali Hirsch h. L. ben Jonatan aus Pinsk.

Korrektor: Salomo Aschkenasi ben Moses.

(3), 2–44, 24? Bll. 2° (31 cm.).

Wolf 1, 918; St. 2025/6612, 1; Z. 606; Bj. 405/348.

HUCL, JTSL, YIVO.

110. 1712–1713.

(Hebräisch und Juedisch) [מחזור]

Polnischer Ritus.

138, 107 bll. 2°.

St. 385/2526.

111. 1714.

תהלים עם מעדמות

Mit Kommentar von David Kimchi.

151 Bll. 4°.

Teil des Gebetbuches, 1714, no. 112?

Rivkind, SBB 1, 204.

L; NYPL.

112. 1714.

[סדר תפלות]

Mit Kommentar. Psalmen mit David Kimchi (s.: St. 127/814).

4°.

St. 350/2325.

113. 1714.

מנהגים

Isak Tyrnau.

Ritus Polen, Mähren, Reussen und Deutschland

4°.

Teil des Gebetbuches, 1714, no. 112?

Rivkind, SBB 1, 204.

L.

114. 1715.

[שלחן ערוך מטור אורח חיים]

Josef Caro ben Efraim.

Angehängt: סדר התפלות ותיקון שבת, ohne Punkte, 32 Bll. 12°. obl.

St. 1485/5940, 35; 36: charta alba; Bj. 585/706.

YU*.

115. 1716.

[סדר תפלות ותקוני שבת]

Paraschijot, Volksmedizin ("guter AnspTach"), Kalender 5476–5525 etc.

12°.

St. 351/2334.

116. 1716.

[מחזור]

Ritus Polen.
12°.
St. 387/2532.

117. 1717.

[סדר תפלות]

Deutscher und polnischer Ritus. Mit Paraschijot.
228 Bll. 48°.
St. 352/2337.

118. 1718.

[סדר תפלות־מנהגים]

4°.
St. 352/2341, nach W. 3, 86.

119. 1718.

מלמד שיח (Hebräisch-Jüdisch)

Eljakim ben Jakob Melammed, Kantor aus Komorna.
Glossar zu Pentateuch und Megilloth.
8°.
St. 969/5021, 4; Bj. 335/1376.

Sine anno, 1689–1718

120. s.a.

[סדר תפלות]

Deutscher Ritus.
12°.
Br. 574.

121. s.a.

סדר ברכת המזון וקריאת שמע, זמירות וברכת לבנה, ברכות הנהנין

32 Bll. Breit 24°.
Br. 569; U. 105; St. 409/2655: 1690–1721.

122. s.a.

סדר יום כפור קטן להשחית קטרוג של שטן

8°.
Vgl. ed. 1701.
U. 103; St. 425/2786.

123. [1693? oder später]

סדר היוצרות

24 Bll. 4°.
Das Buch hat Amsterdam, 1682; vgl. Zafren.
Zafren beweist in Hebrew Union College Annual 40/41, 555–580, dass dieses Buch in Dyhernfurth gedruckt wurde.

124. s.a.

תחנות ובקשות

Gebete für Montag und Donnerstag, mit juedischen Zugaben.
8°.
Br. 569; St. 512/3359: 1689–1714.

125. s.l.e.a.

תחנות ובקשות (Juedisch)

8°.
Das gleiche, nur juedisch.
St. 512/3360; Ser. 92/340.

126. s.a.

דברים שבקדושה

Jakob h. L. Horowitz ben Abraham ben Sabbatai. Durch Josef Jekutiel Salman Deutsch ben Jakob.
Gebete für den Privatgottesdienst.
12 Bll. (St.) 12°.
Br. 573–574; St. 1215/5541, 1; Bj. 107/57.

127. s.a.

וידוים

24°.
Preis: 2 Gr.
U. 710.

128. s.a.

רחמי יוסף (Juedisch)

Gebete.
4°.
Br. 574; St. 483/3211; Bj. 546/135.

129. s.l.e.a.

רחמי יוסף

8°.
Wie vorige no. 128.
Br. 574 nach Bj. 546/135; St. 483/3210 bezweifelt Dyhernfurth.

130. s.a.

תלמוד מסכת מכות

2°.

Preis: 6 Gr.

Br. 573; U. 98; St. 260/1747: 18. Jahrhundert.

131. s.l.e.a. [17. Jahrhundert?]

תלמוד מסכת סוכה

2°.

St. 273/1911 (Dyhernfurth?)

132. s.a.

תלמוד מסכת קדושין

Br. 573; U. 699.

Index of Hebrew Titles

THE HEBREW EXERCISES OF GOVERNOR WILLIAM BRADFORD

Isidore S. Meyer

American Jewish Historical Society

Specimens have been preserved of the Hebrew exercises written by William Bradford (1589/90–1657), the second governor of the Plymouth Plantation, which were written first in 1650 and subsequently in 1652. Set down three decades after the landing of the Pilgrims at Cape Cod, they are inscribed, unnumbered, in the first folios of his history "Of Plimmoth Plantation," in which he states that his aim and desire were:

> . . . to see how the words, and phrases lye in the holy texte, and to discerne somewhat of the same, for my own contente.[1]

The second manifestation of that interest is to be found in *A Dialogue Or 3[d] Conference betweene some yonge-men borne in New-England; And some Ancient-men, which came out of Holand, and Old England, concerning the church,* and is published here *in toto* for the first time.[2]

In his history, Bradford recorded the vicissitudes of his church which was dedicated to the "Congregationall Way," from its origins in England to its transference to Holland, because of persecution in England;[3] and, finally, he describes the migration of the Pilgrim Fathers from Holland to the New World—to New English Canaan in 1620, three and one-half centuries ago—and the history of their new settlement, the Plymouth Plantation, during the early years of its founding. Here, on New England's shores, the Pilgrims hoped that, unhampered—devoid of dissension, strife and discrimination against them, and in freedom—they could maintain and continue their ecclesiastical form of congregational self-government, and preserve intact their way of life and of worship with a free conscience.

Peter Gay, in his *A Loss of Mastery: Puritan Historians in Colonial America,*[4] evaluating the writings of the Anglicans and the Puritans, notes how they used their views of history against each other, and how both employed history against the Roman Catholics. As Englishmen, they laid claim to privileged status, for:

> . . . like the children of Israel (whom Englishmen admired as their spiritual ancestors even if they would not have them in their midst), the English had erred in the wilderness and come at last into the promised land.[5]

Gay perspicaciously defines Bradford's view of history as being:

> . . . a Protestant version of the Protestant theology of history, which was itself a sectarian view of the reigning Christian view.[6]

This range of vision is reflected not only in Bradford's historical account as a leading Pilgrim participant-observer in England, Holland, and New England, but in his other writings, as well: his two *Dialogues* that have come down to us—the first,[7] and the third—and his poems, composed during the last decade of his life.[8] As indicated above, his prime concern was to perpetuate and to further the Congregational Way of life, of church governance, and of worship.

The themes of Bradford's first conference (or *Dialogue*) between the young men born in New England and the older men who came to New England out of Holland and Old England, written in 1648 (the second one is no longer extant), of the third one written in 1652, and the subject matter of his poems, as well, present his Separatist interpretation of the Protestant Reformation; describe the history of the peregrinations of the Pilgrims and their church, from British beginnings to their removal into the Netherlands and their transplantation to Plymouth Plantation, and offer a reasoned appeal to the generation born in the New World to appreciate what their forebears had endured in order to set up their permanent habitation in the Massachusetts wilderness.

The third *Dialogue,* which also contains the Hebrew exercises, according to Charles Deane "cannot be wholly devoid of interest and value in an historical point of view,"[9] although it is primarily an ecclesiastical discussion, for it does present Governor Bradford's views concerning the Christian religious sects of his own day.

The first chapter of Book I of his *History,* written about the year 1630 and shortly thereafter, presents the Pilgrims' interpretation of the Reformation in England from the mid-sixteenth century down to 1607, the origin of their church in their native land, and their earnest endeavors, despite wars, opposition, imprisonment, banishment and other "hard usages" to see that "the truth prevail" and "the churches of God revert to their ancient purity and recover their primitive order, liberty and beauty."[10] The first book carries the story as far as their arrival at Cape Cod and the exploration of the terrain. The second book of the *History* covers the events until 1647, to which is appended a list of the pioneering passengers of the *Mayflower,* which brought them to their new place of habitation, and was written in the year 1650.[11]

The *Dialogues* of 1648 and 1652, respectively, and his poems written during the concluding years of his governorship, fit into the framework of Bradford's concern about the future of his community in perpetuating the Pilgrim way of life after the many hardships it had undergone in establishing itself in the New World. They are Bradford's literary legacy to his compatriots and coreligionists. In a sense, his thoughts seem to encompass, in their totality, a farewell address to the generation of the children of the pioneering Pilgrims in this new land.

During the period between 1648 and the years that followed, a period of transition, certain major changes had taken place on continental Europe and in the British homeland. The Peace of Westphalia (1648) marked the end of the Thirty Years' War and, in England, the civil wars had terminated with the ascendance to power of the Puritans under Oliver Cromwell, the Commonwealth and the Protectorate. In Massachusetts, there had earlier been certain challenges to the Puritan way of life, moral lapses and dissensions raised by recalcitrant individuals. Thus, if the younger generation could be informed and instructed by an outstanding senior member of the community, about its history, from the very beginning until their own day, they might be inspired through such guidance to live undisturbed by the religious dissension and physical harassment from which they had sought to escape, to find peace in their new homeland. Here, they then could continue to perpetuate their religious and theological ideals. The founding fathers of Plymouth Plantation had left the Old World for that reason, and it was this heritage of the Congregational Way that Bradford wished to transmit to future generations.

With regard to Bradford's motivation in writing the first *Dialogue,* Bradford Smith observes:

> The failure of the beloved community, he [Bradford] felt, was partly due to the fact that the young men born in New England had no contact with the rich heritage of suffering, sacrifice and scholarship out of which it had grown.[12]

Recording the events of 1642 in his *History,* of the wickedness which had broken forth in the colony, Bradford begins the thirty-second chapter as follows:

> Marvilous it may be to see and consider how some wickednes did grow and breake forth here. . . .[13]

These included controversies, discontent, and dissension over church matters as well as moral lapses. In the autumn of 1645, Edward Winslow wrote a letter to Governor John Winthrop of the Massachusetts Bay Colony, in reference to Winslow's opposition to a proposition that had been introduced at the General Court of Plymouth which would have permitted the toleration of other religions. He wrote:

> I utterly abhorred it as such as would make us odious to all christian commonwealths. . . . The sum of it was to allow and maintain full and free tollerance of religion to all men that would preserve the civill peace and submit to our government, and there was no limitation or exception against Turke, Jew, Papist, Arian, Socinian, Nicholayton, Familist or any other &c. But our Governor[14] and divers of us having expressed the sad consequences would follow especially myselfe[15] and Mr. [Thomas] Prence,[16] yet not withstanding it was required, according to be voted: But the Governor would not

> suffer it to come to vote, as being that indeed would eate out of the power of godlines, &c.
>
> By this you may see that all the trouble of N[ew] E[ngland] are not at the Massachusetts. The Lord in mercy looke upon us, and allay this spirit of division that is creeping amongst us.[17]

The notion of tolerating other religions was viewed by the older men as a dangerous innovation and was shelved by parliamentary tactics as is intimated above by Winslow.[18] The proposition was not brought to a vote by Bradford. In 1646 Winslow left for England, as is recorded in the last chapter of Bradford's *History:*

> This year Mr. Edward Winslow went into England, upon this occation: some discontented persons under the govermente of the Massachusetts sought to trouble their peace, and disturbe, if not innovate, their govermente, by laying many scandals upon them; and intended to prosecute against them in England by petitioning and complaining to the Parlemente.[19]

Winslow cleared them of any blame or dishonor.[20]

* * *

The first *Dialogue,* as already mentioned above, was held, or written, soon after, in 1648. Bradford endeavored to clarify the true and simple meaning of the designation, Separatists or Independents, and their relation to the Church of England. He preferred the designation, the Congregational Way, which rejected:

> . . . a National Church, combined together of all in the land promiscuously under hierarchical government of archbishops, their courts and canons so far differing from the primitive pattern of the Gospel.[21]

In seeking an understanding of, and precedents for, the primitive structure of the early Church, particularly before the time of the Emperor Constantine, Bradford endeavored to go back to the Greek New Testament and to the propaedeutic Hebrew Scriptures, and to the basic tenets of the Reformation. Bradford gives an account of the ministers and elders[22] who had served the Pilgrims in England and in the Netherlands, and information about their Church during its sojourn in Amsterdam and in Leyden.[23] To the query of the young men in regard to the common assertion that the Separatists held none to be true churches, except their own, and that they condemned all other churches in the world, even some in New England, Bradford replied that:

> . . . it is a manifest slander upon them; for they hold all the Reformed Churches to be true churches . . .

and although some were not of the best mold

> . . . there has been intercommunion with them reciprocally. . . .[24]

In the first *Dialogue,* the author indicates that a rabbinic source, even though drawn from a secondary source, if it can serve as a precedent to support the governance and practices of the "Congregational Way," which is essentially democratic insofar as it relates to the appointment by the individual congregation of its ordained pastor and elders, it will be drawn upon. Thus, Bradford refers to the Code of Maimonides in citing a reference to the Rambam in John Speed's *Cloud of Witnesses,* to support the manner in which the Pilgrim community engaged its ordained ministers, its instructors, and its elders, and in which it set forth their qualifications.[25] Two of their most eminent leaders in Holland, according to Bradford, were John Robinson, who preached a fast-day sermon to the Pilgrims before they were ready to leave Holland three hundred and fifty years ago,[26] and the learned Hebraist and student of rabbinic literature, Henry Ainsworth (1571–*c.*1622).[27] Some of Ainsworth's works were in Bradford's library,[28] and his version of the Psalms was regularly used by the Pilgrims.[29] In the preface to his *Annotations,* Ainsworth praised Rabbi Moses ben Maimon, who abridged the Talmuds and whose work gave added light on the external practice of the ordinances of Moses in the commonwealth of Israel, "which the Rabbines did record and without whose helpe, many of those legal rites (especially in Exodus and Leviticus) will not be easily understood." [30]

The Pilgrim congregation which moved to Leyden found a great center of Hebraic studies there, at its University; it was at Leyden that Elder William Brewster and his partner, Thomas Brewer, maintained their Separatist press for a few years, and engaged in licit and illicit printing of books in English, Dutch, and Latin. They published such works as those of John Dod, Robert Cleaver, Francis Johnson, and Thomas Cartwright, which appeared in 1617.[31] Thus, Bradford, between the ages of nineteen and thirty, had been exposed to an environment in which biblical studies had been cultivated through men of learning, through the press and university at Leyden where the Pilgrims lived upon their removal from Amsterdam in 1609. When they left Leyden to migrate to the New World it was with the hope that they would be able to live there in peace, in their own community, undisturbed by religious disputations, theological differences and wars of religion.[32]

* * *

The text of the second *Dialogue,* or conference, with the young men born in New England, as has already been stated above, is lost. The first conference had ended with Bradford's words, as follows:

> . . . for this time, desiring the Lord to make you grow up in grace and wisdom and the true fear of God that in all faithfulness and humility you may serve him in your generations.[33]

According to one estimate, about one hundred English communities lined the coast of New England from Maine to Long Island Sound in 1660, forty years after the landing of the Pilgrims on the shores of Massachusetts. The population had grown from ninety-nine at Plymouth to 25,000 in 1660 (including Plymouth Plantation, the Massachusetts Bay Colony, and Maine) with a total English population in New England of 36,800.[34] During this period there had been some rifts among them. A few more settlements had been added to Plymouth Plantation at a distance away from the original location of Plymouth itself.[35] Bradford was greatly concerned over the loss of Plymouth colonists who set forth to establish new communities separate from the mother colony. With the expanding population and the appearance of diversity in religious and theological outlook among the newcomers and others, Bradford was worried about the preservation of the Congregational Way which, as he viewed it, emulated the original primitive Church that had functioned during its first three centuries of existence before the advent of the Emperor Constantine.

The third *Dialogue,* that of 1652, was written five years before Bradford's death. It contained a harsh, blistering reproof of the Roman

Catholic Church,[36] a sharp censure of the abuses of the Anglican prelacy and church structure,[37] a milder criticism of the Presbyterian system,[38] and a complete justification of the Congregational Way.[39] In defense of the latter, he drew heavily from John Cotton's *The Way of Congregational Churches Cleared* (London, 1648). As a starting point of his discussion, Bradford asserted that Congregationalism was in agreement with the original Scriptures and with the example of the first Christians, and set down the basic principle of Protestant doctrine, the "Sufficiency of the Scriptures."[40] In the beginning of his peroration on the fruits of the Congregational Way, he notes his reliance on John Cotton's viewpoint:

> . . . it hath been proved that our congregational discipline is the same (for substance) wherein the primitiue churches walked for the first 300 years (to wit, during all the time of the primitiue persecuitons) I conceive without arrogance, (saith he) acknowledge the fruits of their discipline to be ours.[41]

Their strict censure kept them pure; they were martyrs; and it was the neglect of the Congregational Way and the usurpation of bishops and presbyters in the days of Constantine that brought about the decline. It was through the vigilancy of that way of discipline that either prevented or removed and healed this decline. Bradford avers:

> We have suffered this hazardous & voluntary banishment into this remote wilderness, for conscience sake.

He urges:

> . . . loue among our selus; . . . spiritual watchfullness one ouer an other, the like union & comunion of members in one misticall body in a simpathy of affections in such a fraternitie as is described, Psa[lm] 133. a liuely tipe of a true church of Christ . . . We haue the rather noted these things, and not necligently loose what your fathers haue obtained with so much hardshipe. . . .[43]

Referring to the harassments suffered by the Pilgrims and the civil wars in England, Bradford noted how the privileges they had won were lost in former ages, and the misery that ensued.

> . . . and how longe & with what difficulty it was, before they could in any purity be recovered againe . . . It would require much praier,

> zeale, holiness, humilitie, vigilance and love, & peace, with a spirite of meeknes, that liberty be not abused, and by prid & faction turned into licentiousness [Gal. 5:1; 2 Thes. 5:12–13; Heb. 13:17]. . . . We had thought to have given you some of their cheefe grounds breefly, from the Scriptures. . . .[44]

These grounds had been sufficiently handled in many books, and Bradford urged the young men

> . . . that upon examination, you, you shall find the scriptures which they lay there grounds upon, to be taken in their true, and native, genuine sence, agreeing with the best and most godly expositors, viz., most of those shineing lights that God hath reased up in the Reformed Churches & before. . . .

Bradford expressed the hope that to the end of their days, the young men would help propagate the Congregational Way, and that they, the young men, take their leave of the ancient men, craving "the continuance of your prayers for us." The discourse ends with Rom. 16:27 in the original Greek, and with the Greek word **ΤΕΛΟΣ** [End].[45]

* * *

One, therefore, would have to read the entire text of Bradford's third *Dialogue* for a clear picture of the controversy of the Pilgrims with the churches that they opposed, and an image of the one that they favored. Although he was not a profoundly learned linguist, one finds allusions to and citations of passages, phrases, and words in Latin, Hebrew, and Greek, to support his thesis about the origins of the primitive church, its role and destiny. But it is only in the Hebrew exercises at the beginning and end of his manuscript that one notes Bradford's great interest in Hebrew, the language to which he devoted time in his old age. It was because of his lack of knowledge of that "holy tongue," that he set down his apology in one of the opening flyleaves of his history of the Plymouth colony, as mentioned above.[46] Bradford was an autodidact and, in examining the original manuscript of the text of the third *Dialogue,* one senses his yearning to express himself in the language of the learned men of his generation.

* * *

At the beginning of the third *Dialogue*, the young men, in their quest for truth about the great controversies that had arisen in later times

> about the Church and the Gouermente thereof; and much trouble and disturbance hath growne in the world thereby, and doth still remaine to this day . . . we humbly craue your best judgment and aduise. We conceiue this, this controuersie lyes chiefly amongest 4 sorts of men,
>
> The Papists,
> The Episcopacie,
> The Presbiterians, and
> The Independants, as they are called.

The Ancient-men reply:

> We shall in the first place co̅mend this necessarie consideration unto you (which we desire you may carrie all along with you in this whole controuersie) that the true church and the proper gouermente of the same is to be known by the scriptures. . . .

And at the top of this page of the manuscript, Bradford wrote:

> In sacrosancta scriptura existat fundamentum ecclesiae dei.

It was only by this rule that the church and its government had been sufficiently described by the apostles and evangelists, Bradford asserts.[47]

In challenging the claims of the papacy and the Roman Catholic Church, its authenticity, its universality, its hierarchy, its system of governance, its infallibility, his attack is most vitriolic and, at the very beginning of the discussion of this theme, Bradford says:

> Extra bibliam non est veritas infallibilis.[48]

The "Epicopacie" or the Anglican prelacy is "strang from the scriptures," and its lordly hiercharchy was unlawful and a departure

> . . . from the rule of holy scriptures, and according to popish patterne yet we acknowledge that many of their personnes were men of worth for virtue & learning, for pietie and godliness, and many exelent parts, some of them blessed martires. . . .[49]

Bradford cites Calvin and other Reformers as authorities for his anti-prelacy views. The lordly "hierarchie" of the Episcopalian prelacy has no diocesan or metropolitan jurisdiction from Scriptures. The Hebrew term אֲדֹנִי, the Greek κύριος, the Latin *Dominus,* the Dutch *Here,* the French *Monsieur,* do not always imply power and authority and sole rule and government over others, but often, and more usually, import no more "but *M*r or *Sir,* in our sense and phrase and maner of speaking." It is "a sacrilege and tyranus usurpation," for a Lord Bishop to claim through it to lordly spiritual power.[50] The episcopal pedigree is of a much later date.

* * *

As for the "Presbiterians," Bradford esteemed the Reformed Churches under their government, believing that they were "for the main rightly constituted and reformed according to the word of God," in accordance with the principles set down "in the first times of Reformation"; and what required mending "hath been left unreformed at first" and had "seldom been mended afterwards but rather grown worse, as too much experience hath showne."[51] Bradford objected to their system of ascending classes and synods, and to their claim to superior power and jurisdiction one over the other. He reviewed the situation in England and analyzed the chief grounds advanced by

> . . . the Assembly of Deuines, or others that joyne with them in setting up this Presbyteriall gouernment now in our owne countrie, in England. . . . Againe we find not in scriptures the name of classes, prouinciall, sinods, nationall sinods, or assemblies, general councels . . . Much lese doe we find in the scriptures one presbyterie to be sett over an other. . . .[52]

Based upon the views of the Reverend Henry Burton, the Ancient-men assert:

> All those perticuler churches which the apostles planted were all absolute authority amongst themselues respectively and equall to one another . . . Thus you may see the churches of the Independant are not (besids the scriptures, which is the surest anchor-hold,) voyd of antiquitie . . . The framing and squaring of the gouerment of the church, according to the nations of the world, hath been the ground of much errour and mischeefe.

If the Presbyterians in England pursue a similar policy they are to be criticized in the words of II Kings 17:34 and Isaiah 8:20. For Bradford maintained: "Consuetudo sine veritate vetustas erroris est"; and: "Quod verum est, serum non est."[53]

In the section dealing with the Congregational Way,[54] he drew upon the Reverend John Cotton as well as the Reverend Henry Burton. The name "Independents" ascribed to the Puritans "is not a name of choyse" of their own but is "a title imposed by others which are their opposits." In matters of civil government, they

> . . . doe professe dependencie upon magistrats for civill gouerment & protection, dependencie upon Christ . . . and they maintain correspondencie with all sister churches by way of consociation, consultation, comūnion, comūnication, mutuall consolation, supportation [in which] the liberties of each church [is] preserued entire. . . .[55]

"In the second century of years," Bradford continues:

> the church gouernment was administered not in a Classical but in a Congregationall-way . . . the synods left the power of chosing, calling, ordaining ministers, of censuring offenders and of absoluing penitents, to the single churches, each one enjoying power within them selues. The help which neighbour churches yielded to one another, was not *cum imperio & subjectione* . . . but out of brotherly loue & care, & desire of mutuall edification. . . .

In support of this thesis, Bradford quotes the Latin text relating to friendly association, or consociation, within the Church from the anti-Romanist Magdeburg Centuries as follows:

> [Caeterum,] si quis probatos autores hujus seculi perspiciat; videbit formam gubernationis propemodum **δημοκρατίας** similem fuisse.[56]

In other words, the form of government in which the Church was fashioned was a *democratic* one and, as mentioned above, the government of each church was based upon equality and independent governance. This was the purpose of the congregational system of self-government, the fruits of which were alluded to by Bradford[57] before introducing his Hebrew exercises[58] on the remaining pages of his manuscript.

* * *

Bradford had pointed out that, through negligence, they might lose the privileges that the fathers of the young men had "obtained with so much hardship."[59] These privileges had been lost in former ages with evil and misery following thereupon, and the young men could see

> how longe & with what difficulty it was before they could in any purity be recouered againe. They were lost by slouth . . . and by pride & ambition in the bishops & elders. But it had cost much blood & sweat in the recouerie; and will do no lesse care and pains in keeping of them. It will require much praier, zeale, holiness, humilitie, vigilancie and love, & peace, with a spirite of meeknes, that liberty be not abused and by prid[e] & faction turned into licentiousness.[60]

For there could be no edification in church if there were no love, peace, and brotherly forbearance, and it was upon the evidence of Scriptures and the writings of diverse and excellent men, learned, godly and very judicious that Bradford had drawn for support of his *Weltanschauung.* Based upon these grounds, and upon close examination by the young men, they would find guidance in the Bible and in the work of its expositors:

> . . . viz. most of those shineing lights that God hath reased up in the Reformed Churches & before. . . .[61]

Bradford then expressed the desire that the Lord should guide them

> in his trueth and to establish you in the same, unto the ende of your dayes, and that you may help to propagate the same, to the generations to come, till the coming of the Lord. . . .[62]

The young men, in turn, thanked him for his labor of love and craved the continuance of their senior mentor's prayers for them so that they might act accordingly, and then took humble leave of him. Bradford then ended his third *Dialogue* by citing the Greek text of Rom. 16:27—to which we have alluded above.[63]

* * *

(The supplementary pages at the beginning of the manuscript, five in all [nos. 1 through 5], and the concluding nine pages [nos. 6 through 14] of the manuscript are appended here in facsimile. Some of the Hebrew verses or phrases are identified by Bradford and some of the others by the present writer.)

(1) The opening page that serves as the cover of the manuscript, bears the date 1652, and informs us that it is William Bradford's book. The verse is from Proverbs 21:30.

William Bradford his

Booke.

Aº 1652

אין חכמה ואין תבונה ואין עצה
לנגד יהוה

Ther[illegible] no wisdom, neither understanding
nor [illegible]nsell, againest the Lord. pro. 21. [illegible]

(2) Hebrew alphabet and vowels with an English transcription.

א	Aleph	A.	
ב	beth	Bh	
ג	gimel	gh	
ד	daleth	dh	
ה	He	H.	
ו	vau	v.	
ז	zaijn	s. or z.	
ח	Cheth	Ch.	
ט	Teth	T.	
י	iod	I	
כ	caph	Ch.	
ל	Lamed	L.	
מ	mem	m.	
נ	nun	N.	
ס	samech	ſ. acutum	
ע	ain	ſ. or h.	
פ	[illegible]	ph.	
צ	Tzadi	TZ.	
ק	koph	K. x. grecorum	
ר	Resh	R.	
ש	Schin	Sh.	
ת	Tau	th.	

The Ebrew Letters

The vouels longe

Kametz.	אָ	A mixt
Tzere.	אֵ	E. clear.
Chirek.	אִי	I. longe
cholem.	אֹ	o
Shurek.	אוּ	u. as. 8.

short vou:

pathach.	אַ	a pure
sægol	אֶ	E. mixt
Chirek short.	אִ	I. short
Kametz. cha:	אָ	[illegible]
kibbutz	אֻ	y. mixt [illegible]

Chateph pathach.	אֲ	A.
Chateph sægol	אֱ	E.
Chateph Kamet[illegible]	אֳ	O.

Sheua an[illegible] אְ

proper vou[illegible]

(3) Greek alphabet with the English transcription.

Α α — ἄλφα — Alpha — a — greek

Β β ϐ — βῆτα — beta — v. vel. b.

Γ γ — γάμμα — gamma — g

Δ δ — δέλτα — delta — d

Ε ε — ἐψιλὸν — Epsilon — e. breue

Ζ ζ — ζῆτα — zeta — z

Η η — ἦτα — Eta — e. Longum

Θ θ — θῆτα — theta — th

Ι ι — ἰῶτα — iota — i

Κ κ — κάππα — cappa — k c

Λ λ — λάμδα — Lamda — l

Μ μ — μῦ — my — m

Ν ν — νῦ — ny — n

Ξ ξ — ξῖ — xi — x

Ο ο — omicron — ὀμικρὸν — o. paruum

Π π ϖ — πῖ — pi — p

Ρ ρ — ῥῶ — Rho — r

Σ σ ς — σίγμα — sigma — ſ

Τ τ — ταῦ — tau — t

Υ υ — ὑψιλὸν — ypsilon — u

Φ φ — φῖ — phi — ph

Χ χ — χῖ — chi — ch

Ψ ψ — ψῖ — psi — ps

Ω ω — ὠμέγα — omega — o. [illegible]

(4) In a later hand, dated January 7, 1826, with information where the manuscript was found, in a collection belonging to the Old South Church in Boston and deposited in the Library of the Massachusetts Historical Society, signed by A. Bradford.

Jan 7. 1826. This Mss. was found among some old papers taken from the remains of Rev. Mr. Prince's collection, belonging to Old South Church in Boston, & by consent deposited in Library of Massa.tts Historical Society -

A. Bradford

(5) This page was reproduced in facsimile by Deane, *op. cit.,* p. 407. Above the title that appears on this page are three lines in Hebrew consisting of the following citations from Psalms 26:8; 16:5, and 26:5.

יְהוָה אָהַבְתִּי מְעוֹן בֵּיתֶךָ וּמְקוֹם מִשְׁכַּן כְּבוֹדֶךָ

יְהוָה מְנָת חֶלְקִי

psa: 16. 5.

ר. ר. psa: 26. 5. שָׂנֵאתִי קְהַל מְרֵעִים

A Dialogue

Or 3[d] conference, betweene some yonge-men borne in New-England; And some Ancient-men, which came out of Holand, and old England, concerning the church.

[illegible] gouermente therof. ר.ר.ר.

— yonge-men —

Gentle-men, we hope you wi[illegible] pardon our bouldnes, in that we haue Impor-tuned you to giue us meeting once more in this kind, for our Instru[illegible] on, & establishmente in the truth. We find that many, and great are the controuersies, which haue risen in thes[e] later times, about the church, and ye gouermente therof; and much troub[le] and disturbance hath growne in the

(6) A list of Greek and Roman authors who met untimely and strange deaths.

and was banished.

The untimely, and strang deaths of many of the heathen poets, and comedians

Æschilus, his brains were dashed out wth the fall of a torteis; which an eagle let fall upon his bald-pate.

Euripides, was torne in peeces by doggs; as he went home in the night.

Sophocles, dyed suddenlly on the stage by vaine joye; as was conceived.

Philippides, dyed in ye same maner, being a famous comedian.

Theodoctes; a play-poet, was smiten of God with blindnes, for inserting some pasages of the old testament into one of his Tragedies.

Menander, a comedian (& insanus mulierum amatur) was drowned, as he was swiming, & washing him selfe.

Terence, the eminentest Latin-comedian, was drowned, as he returned out of Greece with 108 of Menanders comedies, which he had translated.

Plautus, an elegant latine comicall-poet, had got a masse of money by his playes; and lost it all, by marchindise, and was inforced to grind in a mill.

Antiphanes, ye cōposer of 365 comedies; being casually struck with a pear, dyed suddenly. And Eupolis was drowned.

(7) Citations of passages and phrases from:

Amos 6:4.
Isaiah 19:4.
Psalms 25:2.
Psalms 125:4.
Psalms 51:11.
Jeremiah 5:25.
Proverbs 11:31.
Proverbs 16:6.

אֵילִים כָּרִים מִצֹּאן
ate the rames out of the
flocke. Amos. 6. 4.

בְּיַד אֲדֹנִים קָשֶׁה
In ye hands of hard Lords.
Isa. 19. 4

אֱלֹהַי בְּךָ בָטַחְתִּי אַל אֵבוֹשָׁה
O my god I trust in the, let me not
be ashamed. psa. 25. 2.

psa. 125. 4 הֵיטִיבָה יְהוָֹה לַטּוֹבִים
doe good O Lord to the good

psa. 51 הַסְתֵּר פָּנֶיךָ מֵחֲטָאָי
hid away thy face, from my sine

וְחַטֹּאותֵיכֶם מָנְעוּ הַטּוֹב מִכֶּם
And your sines, haue with-houlden
good things, from you. Jer. 5. 25

הֵן צַדִּיק בָּאָרֶץ יְשֻׁלָּם אַף כִּי־רָשָׁע
Behold, ye righteous shalbe recompensed in
the earth; much more ye wicked-siner pro. 11

pro. 16. 6. בְּיִרְאַת יְהוָֹה סוּר מֵרָע
By ye feare of the Lord men depart from
evill.

(8) Citations of passages and phrases in two columns:

Left column	*Right column*
Numbers 32:14.	Psalms 19:9.
Proverbs 15:20.	Psalms 19:10.
Isaiah 9:2.	Psalms 19:8.
I Kings 21:10.	Nehemiah 9:13.
Genesis 22:12.	Psalms 119:137.[64]
I Chronicles 29:28.	Psalms 18:31.
Psalms 24:4.	Ecclesiastes 12:9.[65]

תַּרְבּוּת אֲנָשִׁים חַטָּאִים׃ an Increase of sinfull men. Num: 32. 14.	פִּקּוּדֵי יְהוָה יְשָׁרִים ~~the statutes~~ ye precepts of Lord are right. psa. 19. 9.
בֵּן חָכָם יְשַׂמַּח אָב A wise sone maks glade his father. pro. 15. 20.	יִרְאַת יְהוָה טְהוֹרָה the fear of ye Lord is clean v. 10.
כְּשִׂמְחַת בַּקָּצִיר As ye joye in harvest.	תּוֹרַת יְהוָה תְּמִימָה the Law of Jehovah is perfecte. v. 8.
אֲנָשִׁים בְּנֵי־בְלִיַּעַל men ye sones of belial.	חֻקִּים וּמִצְוֹת טוֹבִים good Statuts, & commandoments. Nem: 9. 13.
יְרֵא יְהוָה אַתָּה thou feares god, gen. 22. 12.	יָשָׁר מִשְׁפָּטֶיךָ thy Judgments are right. psa. 119. 138.
שְׂבַע יָמִים עֹשֶׁר וְכָבוֹד saciate with dayes, riches and honour. 1. Chr. 29. 28.	הָאֵל תָּמִים דַּרְכּוֹ god, his way is perfecte. psa. 18. 31.
נְקִי כַפַּיִם וּבַר לֵבָב Innocent in hands, and pure in hart. psa: 24. 4.	לִמַּד דַּעַת אֶת הָעָם He taught the people knowledge. Eclo. 12. 9.

(9) *Left column*

Joshua 24:10.
Isaiah 30:27.
Leviticus 26:41.
—— —— ——
Ezekiel 16:4.
Genesis 6:8.
Deuteronomy 25:19.

Right column

Zechariah 1:13b.
II Kings 17:13.
Jeremiah 25:15.
Exodus 31:18, or
Deuteronomy 9:10.[66]
Zechariah 3:3.
Kings 1:40.
Jeremiah 22:10.

ויברך. ברוך אתכם

And blessing, hee blessed you. Jos: 24. 10.

כאש אוכלת

like consuming fire. Isa. 30. 27.

לבבם הערל

their vncir= cumcised harts. Leu: 2.6. 41.

[illegible]

לא כרת שרך

thy nauell was not cute. Eze. 16

ונח מצא חן

and Noah found grace.

מכל איביך

from all thy enemies.

דברים נחמים

comfortable words. Zac: 1. 13.

ביד כל נביאי

by the hand of all the prophets. 2. kings. 17. 13

את כוס היין החמה

the cup of ye wine of furie Jer: 25. 15.

כתבות באצבע אלהים

writen with ye finger of god. 31. 18.

לבוש בגדים צואים

clade with filthy garments Zac: 3. 3.

והעם מחללים בחללים

1. kings. 1. 40.

and ye people piped with pips.

בכו בכו להלך

weeping, weepe for him, that goeth out. Jer: 22. 10.

(10) Citations of passages and phrases from:

Isaiah 32:5.
Isaiah 62:4.
I Samuel 2:36.
Deuteronomy 28:44.

לא־יקרא עוד לנבל נדיב ולכילי

לא יאמר שוע Isa·32·5·

A nigardly-foole shall no more be called liberall, nor the Churle said to be bountifull·

לא־יאמר לך עוד עזובה ולארצך

לא־יאמר שממת כי לך יקרא חפצי

Isa: 62·4· בה ולארצך בעולה

It shall no more be said unto the forsaken; neither shall it be said any more to thy land desolate; but thou shalt be caled Hephzi-bah, and thy land Beulah·

להשתחוות לו לאגורת כסף וככר־לחם

Shall bow-downe to him, for a peece of siluer, and a morsell of bread ·1·sam·2·36

הוא יהיה לראש ואתה תהיה לזנב

He shall be the head, & thou shalt be ye taile·

deu 28.44

(11)

Genesis 43:8.
I Samuel 6:5b.
Joshua 1:8b.
Genesis 3:23b.
Genesis 3:11.

גם אנחנו

ונקומה ונלכה ונחיה ולא נמות גם

אתה גם טפנו gen: 43. 8.

and we will arise and goe. that we may
Live, and not dye, both we, and thou,
and also our Little-ones.

אלהיכם ומעל כם

אולי יקל את ידו מעליכם ומעל ארצ

peradventure he will lighten his hand fro
of you, and from of your gods, and from
of your land. 1. sam. 6. 5.

אז תצליח את דרכך ואז תשכיל

for then thou shalt ~~thy~~ make thy way
prosperus, and then thou shalt have
good successe. Josh: 1. 8.

ם

לעבוד את האדמה אשר לקח מש

to till the ground, from whence he was
taken. gen. 3.

מי הגיד לך כי עירם אתה gen. 3. 11

who tould thee that thou was naked.

(12) Citations of passages and phrases in two columns:

Left column

Psalms 60:1.
[a psalm of prayer].[67]
Psalms 33:4.
I Kings 5:11.
Psalms 12:4.
Proverbs 27:17.
Psalms 11:1.

Right column

II Samuel 14:5, or I Kings 7:14, 17:10.
[Cf. Judges 11:1].[68]
I Samuel 2:4.
Psalms 119:1.
Psalms 34:19.[69]
Genesis 24:31.
Proverbs 3:35.

מכתם לדוד ללמד

A goulden song of David to teach. psa. 60

מזמור להתפלל

a psa of praire.

ישר דבר יהוה

Right is ẏ word of Jehovah

בכל הגוים סביב

In all ẏ nation about.

לשון מדברת גדלות

a tongue speaking great things. psa. 12

ברזל בברזל יחד

Iron sharpeneth iron. pro: 27. 17.

נודי הרכם צפור

flie to your mountaine as a birde. psa. 11. 1.

אשה אלמנה

a widow woman.

בן זונה

the sone of a whore.

קשת גברים חתים

the bowes of ẏ mightie are broken. 1 sam 2. 4

אשרי תמימי דרך

blessed are ẏ perfect in way, psa 119.

ואת דכאי רוח יושיע

psa. 34. 18. and saueth, such as are of a contrite spirite

בוא ברוך יהוה

come in thou blessed of the Lord, gen. 24

כבוד חכמים ינחלו

the wise shall inherite glorie. pro. 3. 35

(13) *Left column*

Genesis 24:42.[70]
Ezra 10:12.[71]
I Kings 17:15.
Genesis 1:28.
Habakkuk 3:11.
Psalms 7:4.
Genesis 4:7.

Right column

Cf. Ecclesiastes 12:10.[72]
Ezekiel 22:18.
Psalms 60:5.
Canticles 1:8.
Canticles 2:5.
Psalms 133:2.
[Psalmes of praise].[73]
Proverbs 20:29.[74]

אלך ...

...alk, or goe

ויענו כל-ה...

... ye whole con=
...egation answer
... Ezra·10·12·

ותאכל והיא...

...e, & she did eate

וירדו בדגת הים

...nd haue dominion
ouer ye fish of ye sea

שמש ירח עמד

the sunne & moone
stood stil·hab.3·11

אם יש-עול בכפי

... iniquitie be in
my hands·psa·7·
4·

לפתח חטאת רבץ

gen·4·7·

sine lieth, or couch
at ye doore·

...ים אמת

words of truth

סיגים כסף

dross of siluer

יין תרעלה psa·60·3

wine of horrour

היפה בנשים

O thou fairest among
women; cant·1·8

חולת אהבה

sicke of loue·

כשמן הטוב

like ye good oyle

מזמור להלל

psalmes of praise

תפארת בחורים

the glorie of young
men·pro·20·

(14) Because of its faded condition and torn corners, this last page of the manuscript is difficult to decipher. Through the slightly exposed corners of this page one sees some letters on the second page preceding it. This last page consists of two columns and a fragmentary third column which may have been an extension of part of a page no longer extant. The page is made up of two-word phrases and one phrase of three words.

Left column	*Right column*
Top blank faded space	כּוֹס מָלֵא[?] the cup of blessing, or pri [?]
אֵל־גִבּוֹר strong God	* אִישׁ עָשִׁיר a rich man
גֵּר־בֶּן־בְּרִית a proselite, sone of ye covenant	** עָשִׁיר גָּדוֹל great riches [*sic!*]
גֵּר צֶדֶק a proselite of righteousness	אֶרֶץ חֵפֶץ a land of desire, or delight
הֲבֵל הֲבָלִים vanitie of vanities [Ecclesiastes 1:2a]	אֹרֶךְ יָמִים length of days
זִקְנֵי יִשְׂרָאֵל elders of Israel	אִישׁ לָשׁוֹן a man of tongue
מְנָת שׁוּעָלִים portion of foxes [Psalms 63:11]	לֶחֶם שְׂעֹרִים barly bread
אִישׁ דָּמִים a man of bloods [Psalms 5:7]	עֶבֶד עֲבָדִים a servant of servants

As for the fragmentary third column on the right, two words, torn and out of context are discernible:

* שְׂפָתַ[?] of [?] lips	** שְׁמֶךָ [?] thy [name].

כוס ברכה the cupp of Blessing, or pr...	[illegible] a ...
איש עשיר a rich man	אל גבור ...strong god
עשר גדול great riches	גר ברית a proselite, sonne of ye couenant
ארץ חפץ a land of desire, or delight	גר צדק a proselite of righteousnes
ארך ימים Length of days	הבל הבלים vanitie of vanities
איש לשון a man of tongue	זקני ישראל elders of Israel
לחם שערים Barly bread	מנת שועלים portion of foxes
עבד עבדים a servant of servants	איש דמים ... man of bloods.

As the historian of Plymouth Plantation, and as its guardian, Bradford saw a close similarity between the pilgrimage to the New World and the Exodus of the Israelites from Egypt to the Promised Land; he believed that God's hand was operative in the settlement and in the affairs of the Pilgrims as it had been in the days of Moses and during the sojourn of the children of Israel in the wilderness, in Canaan, and, in later times, in the return of the remnant of the children of Israel to the Holy Land under Ezra. Applying these historical analogies drawn from Hebrew Scripture through the system of historical typology, and not limiting it alone to the allegorical, Bradford viewed Plymouth Plantation, as a new "state of Israel," the antitype of ancient Israel—of the former Hebraic type.[76] Since the Congregational Way of Plymouth Plantation served as the antitype of Israel in Canaan, Bradford's selection and presentation of his Hebraic exercises towards the end of his life, in addition to his numerous references to the peregrinations of the ancient Israelites and of their governance and experiences, supported his theory that that Way was based upon "the primitive" sources of the Hebrew Scriptures. It was also undergirded by the Greek Testament and by the doctrines of the anti-Romanist historians, theologians, and theoreticians of the Protestant Reformation. In his poetry, including the verses written in 1654, Bradford also indicated how the Pilgrims were reliving, by analogy,[77] the experiences of Israel from the time of Abraham down through the Exodus, their establishment in Canaan during the period of Joshua and the Judges, and subsequent periods of their history. This is sensed clearly in his poetry as well as in his prose. In his *History* and in his *Dialogues* he counseled those were to follow—the young men born in New England—to be true to the ancient yet newly reestablished Congregational Way. He admonished them not to neglect and fall away from the heritage and legacy of their forebears who, through trial and tribulation, had endeavored to establish a Puritan *Israel redivivus,* the model, visible church-state, the true Christian theocratic antitype of the one that had preceded it centuries before in ancient Canaan.[78] Bradford's epitaph, engraved on his monument in 1835 bore three Hebrew words affirming his faith that the Lord was the One who sustained him throughout his lifetime;[79] and, in Latin,[80] a reassertion of his concern for the future of the English colony that he had helped to establish upon a firm and permanent foundation during its formative years from 1620 until he passed away in 1657. It read:

> What our fathers with so much difficulty secured, do not basely relinquish.

* * *

Three and a half centuries after the landing of the Pilgrims at Plymouth, it is appropriate to be reminded of the analagous Hebraic antecedents and experiences that served as a beacon of encouragement to William Bradford and the others who braved the Atlantic Ocean to plant the first settlement in the New English Canaan.[81]

NOTES

[1] They were reproduced in a note by the present writer in the *Publications of the American Jewish Historical Society* [=*PAJHS*], Vol. XXXVIII, no. 4 (June, 1949), pp. 289–303, and consist of eight pages, containing approximately over 1,000 Hebrew words: 879 words together with eight names of the Deity and twenty-five biblical passages in the original Hebrew. The third page [*ibid.*, p. 296] shows the oft-quoted apology of Bradford for not having a sufficient knowledge of that ancient language, and his reasons for setting down these Hebrew words. For the date, 1650, in which they were written, see *Of Plymouth Plantation, 1620–1647* by Samuel Eliot Morison, [=Morison], (New York, 1952), pp. xxvii–xxviii.

[2] The text of the third *Dialogue* was edited by Charles Deane [=Deane] and published in the *Proceedings of the Massachusetts Historical Society* [=*PMHS*] *for the Years 1869–1870* Vol. XI (Boston, 1871), pp. 396–464, in which one page containing Bradford's Hebrew handwriting is reproduced (p. 407). Two pages at the beginning of the manuscript contain the Hebrew and Greek alphabets as well as the long and short vowels to aid in Hebrew pronunciation. At the end there are eight pages (and possibly some may be wanting) which contain passages from Hebrew Scriptures, phrases and vocabulary with English translation. See *infra*, pp. 250-277, where they are reproduced.

[3] See *History of Plymouth Plantation, 1620–1647* by William Bradford (Boston, 1912), 2 vols., edited by Worthington C. Ford [=Ford], Vol. I, p. 25, for the reason for their migrating to the Netherlands:

> Yet seeing them selves thus molested, and that ther[e] was no hope for their continuance ther[e], by a joynte consent they resolved to goe into the Low-Countries wher[e] they heard was freedome of Religion for all men. . . .

[4] In the *Jefferson Memorial Lectures at the University of California* (Berkeley) in 1966 [first edition, Vintage Books (New York, 1968)], see "William Bradford, Caesar in the Wilderness," chapter 2, pp. 26–52.

[5] *Ibid.*, p. 7. Cf. *The New England Mind: The Seventeenth Century*, by Perry Miller (Cambridge, Mass., 1954), and "Conscious Art in Bradford's *History of Plymouth Plantation*," by E. F. Bradford in the *New England Quarterly*, Vol. I, no. 2 (April, 1928), pp. 133–157. According to the latter, in his *History of Plymouth Plantation* Williams Bradford's citations were in a proportion of five from the Old to two from the New Testament. Bradford used the Genevan English version.

[6] Gay, *op. cit.*, p. 33.

[7] "A Dialogue, or the Sume of a Conference betweene some Yonge-Men, born in New England, and sundry Ancient-Men that came out of Holand and Old England," endeavors to uphold the good name of the Pilgrims and their Church and its representative leaders in Amsterdam and in Leyden during their stay in the Netherlands. This first *Dialogue* is published in *The Chronicle of the Pilgrim Fathers of the Colony of Plymouth,* by Alexander Young [=Young], 2nd edition (Boston, 1844), pp. 409–458; *New England's Memorial,* by Nathaniel Morton, sixth edition (Boston, 1855), and *Plymouth Church Records (1620–1859), Part I* [*Publications of the Colonial Society of Massachusetts*], Vol. XXII (Boston, 1920), pp. 115–141.

[8] On his poetry, see Deane, pp. 465–482, and his note on p. 465 for data on the poems, where reference is made to Bradford's last will which was presented for probate on June 3, 1657, a month after Bradford's death, wherein Bradford commended his "little book with a black cover, wherein is A Word to Plymouth, A Word to Boston, A Word to New England, with sundry useful verses." For the earlier publication of a fragment of Bradford's poetry, see the *Collections of the Massachusetts Historical Society* first series, Vol. III (1794), pp. 77–84. On Bradford's will, see, in particular, "Governor Bradford's Will and Inventory," by George Ernest Bowman, *Mayflower Descendant,* Vol. II (Boston, 1900), pp. 228–234.

[9] Deane, pp. 397–398.

[10] Morison, p. 3.

[11] *Ibid.,* pp. 441–447, and Ford, Vol. II, pp. 401–411.

[12] *Bradford of Plymouth* by Bradford Smith, (Philadelphia and New York, 1951), pp. 297–298.

[13] Ford, Vol. II, pp. 308–341; Morison, pp. 316–323 and Appendix X, pp. 404–413. There was concern over the Islanders of Aquidneck, i.e., the Rhode Islanders. Roger Williams was already at Providence, and two years later, in 1644, obtained the Providence Plantations Patent from Parliament. Other dissenters were Anne Hutchinson, who settled at Portsmouth, William Coddington, at Newport and Samuel Gorton who would soon establish a fourth settlement of sectaries (*ibid.,* p. 317 n.). On "Religious Diversity," see *The Puritan Frontier Town—Planning in New England Colonial Development, 1630–1660* by William Haller, Jr. [=Haller] in *Studies in History, Economics, and Public Law, Number 568,* Columbia University Press (New York, 1951), chapter 5:

> Puritan churches had the delicate and difficult duty of maintaining themselves as institutional oases of Saints amid a wilderness of original sin. (*Ibid.,* p. 84.)

On Roger Williams' views concerning his distinction between the respective roles of the religious ministry and civil magistracy vis-à-vis Puritan theocracy and theology, see, "Roger Williams: An Essay in Interpretation," by Perry Miller in *The Complete Writings of Roger Williams,* Vol. VII (New York, 1963), pp. 5–25; and *Roger Williams, John Cotton and Religious Freedom: A Controversy in New and Old England,* by Irwin H. Polishook (Englewood Cliffs, N. J., 1967), particularly the discussion of their respective differing views on the separation of Church and State and the moral validity and universal force of Mosaic laws (excluding the ceremonial laws which were no longer binding on Christians). Christian commentators viewed the Hebrew Scriptures as a precursor or propaedeutic to the New Testament (*ibid.,* pp. 32–33). Roger Williams' typology, distinguishing between the physical "type" of the former and the spiritual "antitype" of the latter, maintained that the church order of the Jews must never be taken as a literal pattern for any other epoch. To Cotton, the Mosaic laws of moral equity, its judicial laws, were a moral force and an eternal force that were eternally binding on all rulers (Matthew 5:17). Polishook, *op. cit.,* pp. 85–86. See *infra,* p. 286, n. 76, the differing view on Williams' and Cotton's typological views, in which Sacvan Bercovitch corrects Miller's views.

[14] William Bradford.

[15] Edward Winslow served as Governor of Plymouth Plantation in 1633, 1636, and 1644, and several times as Assistant (Ford, Vol. II, pp. 157, 226, 367, and 174 n., 196 n., 242 n., 294 n., and 342 n.).

16 Thomas Prence, who had served as Governor of Plymouth Plantation in 1634 and 1638, and several times as Assistant (*ibid.,* pp. 174, 263, and 196 n., 242 n., 274 n., 294 n., 342 n.) later served as Governor (1657–1673). *Saints and Strangers* by George F. Willison (New York 1945), Appendix B, p. 455.

17 *The Publications of the Prince Society: The Hutchinson Papers,* Vol. I (Albany, N.Y., 1865), pp. 172–175. There was evidence of discontent among certain classes of people in New England who were excluded from a share in the government. See *New England's Jonas Cast Up in London (1647)* by Major John Child, with an Introduction by W. T. R. Marvin (Boston, 1869), p. vi. The proposition seems to have been favored by Miles Standish, John Brown, Timothy Hatherley and Edmund Freeman (*ibid.,* p. xx, n. 38). The transaction regarding this petition does not appear in the records of the General Court of Plymouth Colony. Cf., *Orthodoxy in Massachusetts (1630–1650): A Genetic Study* by Perry Miller (Gloucester, Mass., 1965), p. 297.

18 "Governor Edward Winslow," by Winslow Warren, *PMHS, 1918–1919,* Vol. LII (Boston, 1919), p. 328. It was opposed by another Assistant, William Collier. The petition was submitted by William Vassall. Edward Winslow believed that Vassall was the author of all but the preface of Mayor John Child's pamphlet, mentioned above, *New England's Jonas Cast Up in London.* Vassall died in Barbados in 1655. Winslow's trip to England was to answer the pamphlets of Samuel Gorton and Major Child. See *Simplicity's Defence Against Seven-headed Policy,* by Samuel Gorton (1646); Child, *op. cit.;* and Winslow's *Hypocrosie Unmasked* (London, 1646) and his *New England's Salamander . . .* (London, 1647).

19 Ford, Vol. II, p. 391; Morison, p. 346.

20 Ford, Vol. II, p. 393; Morison, p. 347. Winslow never did return to New England (*ibid.,* p. 347, n. 4).

21 Young, pp. 414–415.

22 He mentions Robert Brown, who later fell into "apostasy" (the Separatists refused to be called Brownists, *ibid.,* pp. 441–444); Francis Johnson, who swerved and fell (*ibid.,* pp. 445 f.); John Smith, an eminent man and a good preacher "but his inconstancy and unstable judgment . . . soon overthrew him" (*ibid.,* p. 450); John Robinson, the anti-Arminian pastor in Leyden, who was much esteemed and revered (*ibid.,* pp. 451–452); and Richard Clifton, an aged man, who remained in Amsterdam. John Robinson and Henry Ainsworth appear to have been the pastors whom Bradford regarded as the most admired and respected by the Pilgrims. Before describing the Church in Amsterdam and in Leyden, he makes the observation:

> We perceive God raiseth up excellent instruments in all ages to carry on his own work, and the best of men have their failings sometimes, as we see in these our times, and that there is no new thing under the sun (pp. 454–455).

23 *Ibid.,* pp. 455–456.

24 *Ibid.,* pp. 456–457.

25 Bradford refers to, *A Cloud of Witnessès, and They the Holy Genealogies of the Sacred Scriptures* (London, 1620) by John Speed, for his information on the laws which describe who may minister, teach, and judge in the community, and the qualifications of training and character they must possess. He refers to Maimonides' Code and to the Gospel. For the relevant passages see the *Code of Maimonides* (*Mishneh Torah* or *Yad ha-Ḥazakah*), *Book Eight: The Book of Temple Service* [*Yale Judaica Series: Volume XII*] (New Haven: Yale University Press, 1957), translated by Mendell Lewittes; "Treatise II, Laws concerning vessels of the Sanctuary and those who minister therein," Chapter 3, paragraph 1, p. 50; Chapter 4, paragraph 1, p. 53; *Book Fourteen: The Book of Judges* [*Yale Judaica Series: Volume III*] (New Haven, 1949), translated by Abraham M. Hershman, "Treatise One, Laws concerning the Sanhedrin and the penalties within their jurisdiction," Chapter 2, paragraph 1, p. 3; paragraphs 6, 7 and 8, which deal with the qualifications of judges, pp. 8–9; and the first book of the *Code,* the *Book of Knowledge,* [ספר המדע] in the laws pertaining to the study of Torah [הלכות תלמוד תורה],

Chapter 3, paragraph 1, which states that any Israelite may attain the crown of Torah, if he qualifies.

26 His text was Ezra 8:21, as Bradford records it:

> So being ready to departe, they had a day of solleme humiliation, their pastor taking his texte from Ezra 8:21. *And ther[e] at the river, by Ahava, I proclaimed a fast, that we might humble our selves before our God, and seeke of him a right way for us, and for our children, and for all our substance.* (Ford, vol. I, p. 121; Morison, p. 47.)

With the downfall of the Bishops and the breaking of their power (1640–1660), and with the execution of Archbishop Laud (1645) in England, Bradford in 1646, added a subsequent portion of his story on the reverse side of some of the pages in the first chapter of his *History:*

> A late observation, as it were by the way, worthy to be noted. Full litle did I thinke, that the downfall of the Bishops with their courts, cannons, and ceremonies, &c. had been so neare, when I first begane these scribled writings [which] was about the year 1630, and so peaced up at times of leasure afterward. . . .

He expressed his joy over the change of events by quoting Psalm 126:1, 3, 5, and 6:

> When the lord brougt againe the captivite of Zion, we were like them that dreame. . . . The lord hath done greate things for us, whereof we rejoyce . . . They that sow in teares shall reap in joye. They wente weeping, and carried precious seede, but they shall returne with joye, and bring their sheaves. . . . (Ford, Vol. I, p. 15; Morison, p. 351.)

27 Bradford, in the words of John Cotton, described Ainsworth as follows:

> Mr. Ainsworth, a man of modest and humble spirit, and diligently studious of the Hebrew text, hath not been unuseful to the church in his Exposition of the Pentateuch, especially of Moses and his rituals. We have heard some, eminent in the knowledge of tongues, of the University of Leyden, say that they thought he had not his better for the Hebrew tongue in the University, nor scarce in Europe. He had an excellent gift of teaching and opening the Scriptures. . . . (Young, pp. 448 f.)

Ainsworth's works appeared in several editions. In the London edition of 1626, we find bound together (with a title page bearing the date 1627) the following works: *Annotations upon the Five Books of Moses; The Booke of Psalms;* and the *Song of Songs, or, Canticles.* As for his regard for the Pentateuch, he cites, on the title page, Deuteronomy 33:4: "Moses commanded us a Law, the Inheritance of the Church of Iacob," and Malachi 4:4: "Remember the Law of Moses my servant, which I commanded him in Horeb for all Israel; with Statutes and Iudgements." In his annotations, he is selective and draws upon postbiblical Greek, Chaldee, Apocryphal, and rabbinic sources such as Maimonides' *Code* (the *Mishneh Torah*), his *Commentary on the Mishnah;* the *Midrash Rabbah,* and such commentators as R. Bechai, R. Menahem, Kimḥi, and others.

Ainsworth defends his use of rabbinic sources by maintaining that, although he does not accept all of the comments of the rabbis, scholarly Christian expositors had made use of rabbinic sources before, and he was following in their tradition in the quest for a better understanding of Hebrew Scriptures. This apologia is described on its title page as: "An Advertisement to the Reader, touching on some obiections made against the sincerity of the Hebrew text, and the allegations of the Rabbis in these former annotations." He discusses the *Keri* and *Chetib* and states that the Hebrews cannot be accused that they have corrupted the Scripture, but the Hebrew text remaineth as it was in the Apostles dayes. . . .

In referring to the work of "R. Iudah hannasi," the "Thalmud Ierusalemi," and the "Thalmud Babeli," he describes Maimonides' reworking of them in his *Code* as follows:

These longsome volumes were after abridged by Moses sonne of Maimon (called Maimony, and Rambam) who lived 1200 years after our Lords birth, and he set down in plainer Hebrew, the expositions, canons and traditions according to which they had interpreted the Law of God given by Moses and practised the same, omitting the discourses, fables, disputes, &c. wherewith the Thalmud is referred. And this Maimon is of such esteeme among the Iewish nation, that of him it is said, From Moses (the Prophet) to Moses (son of Maimon) there was none like this Moses.

Ainsworth justifies what he has done because he only drew upon the works of Jewish expositors and teachers for the "many profitable things [that] are found in them for the opening of the Scriptures," and that "the Apostles also in alleging sometimes the testimonies, doe teach us that their writings are not wholly to be despised. . . ." Following this, on the title page of his *Annotations upon the Booke of Psalmes* (London, 1626), he cites II Samuel 23:1–2 and Luke 24:44. The final book in this volume to which we have thus far referred, contains the title page of *Solomons Song of Songs in English Metre and Annotations* (London, 1626) with reference to Eph. 5:32, 23, 25–27. It must always be borne in mind, therefore, that the Puritans *never* dissociated the Gospels from the earlier Hebrew Scriptures, the latter having propaedeutic value and being useful to them for historico-analogical purposes in undergirding their own Church structure and governance. They were primarily concerned with fashioning their own ecclesiastical institutions and government in consonance with the "primitive" Church, and with their typology, both allegorical and linear- historical. See *infra,* p. 286, n. 76.

Ainsworth was in touch with rabbinic scholars in Holland. Between 1606 and 1618, three Jewish congregations had been established there. During this period, Hugo Grotius prepared his *Remonstrantie,* concerning Jews and Marranos who had settled in Holland at the end of the sixteenth and at the beginning of the seventeenth centuries. Grotius recommended that they be allowed freedom of religion and recommended certain necessary safeguards for the legal toleration of the Jews. See "Hugo Grotius' *Remonstrantie,*" by Jacob Meijer, *Jewish Social Studies,* Vol. XVII, no. 2 (April, 1955), pp. 91–104, and his *Remonstrantie nopende de ordre dije in de landen van Hollandt ende Westvrieslandt dijent gestelt op de Joden naar het manuscript in de Livraria D. Montezinos,* uitgegeven en ingeleid door Dr. J. Meijer (Amsterdam, 1949). Cf. Bradford's negative attitude towards such legal toleration, *supra,* p. 241, as well as the liberalizing attitude of Roger Williams. For references to the resettlement of the Jews in Puritan England under Oliver Cromwell, see *Magna Bibliotheca Anglo-Judaica: A Bibliographical Guide to Anglo-Jewish History* by Cecil Roth (London, 1937), pp. 47–65, and *Three Hundred Years: A Volume to Commemorate the Tercentenary of the Re-settlement of the Jews in Great Britain, 1656–1956,* published for The Tercentenary Council and *The Jewish Chronicle* (London, 1957), Part One, pp. 9–48.

28 See *supra,* p. 280, end of n. 8.

29 See *The Music of the Pilgrims: A Description of the Psalm-book Brought to Plymouth in 1620* by Walden Selden Pratt (Boston, 1921). The Psalm book, published in Amsterdam, was that of Henry Ainsworth, the title page of which is reproduced by Pratt, *ibid.,* p. 4, and which reads:

The Book of Psalmes: Englished both in Prose and Metre, . . . by H. A. "Ephe. 5:18.19. Be ye filled with the Spirit: speaking the yourselves in Psalms, and hymnes, and spiritual songs & making melodie in your hart to the Lord." Imprinted at Amsterdam. By Giles Thorp, A° D° 1612.

A copy of this edition was in Elder Brewster's library (Ford, Vol. I, p. 122 n.). Ainsworth had fled to Amsterdam in 1593 and this first edition was intended for fugitive Separatist congregations. This Psalter appeared in later editions in 1617, 1626, 1639, 1644, and 1690.

30 See the letter of John Pory, August 28, 1622, to Bradford and Brewster in praise of "Mr. Ainsworths elaborate work upon the 5 books of Moyses" (Ford, vol. I, p. 280); and the Rev. Charles Chauncy's reference to Ainsworth's views on the legal interpretation of Leviticus 18:6–19 (Ford, vol. II, p. 324). Cf. also, in addition to Chauncy's views, those of the Rev. John Reyner and the Rev. Ralph Partridge (*ibid.*, pp. 315–328).

31 See *The Pilgrim Press: A Bibliographical and Historical Memorial of the Books Printed at Leyden by the Pilgrim Fathers,* by Rendel Harris and Stephen K. Jones, with a chapter on "The Location of the Pilgrim Press in Leyden," by Dr. Plooij (Cambridge, England, 1922), Appendix II, Collations, pp. 72–87, items 3 (in English), 4 (in Dutch), 7 (in English) and 8 (in Latin), respectively. Dod and Cleaver wrote an exposition of the Ten Commandments with a methodical short catechism, containing briefly all the principal grounds of the Christian religion; Johnson, *A Christian Plea;* and Cartwright, a Latin commentary on the Book of Proverbs.

Earlier, in Leyden in 1593, there had been published John Udall's English translation of Pierre Martini's מפתח לשון הקדש (*Mafteaḥ Lashon ha-Kodesh*) *That is the Key of the Holy Tongue: Wherein is conteineid, first the Hebrew Grammar (in a manner) woord for woord out of P. Martinius, Secondly, A practize upon the first, the twentie fift, and the syxtie eyght Psalmes according to the rules of the same Grammar, Thirdly, A short Dictionary conteining the Hebrue woords that are found in the Bible with their proper significations, All Englished for the benefit of those that (being ignorant in the Latin) are desirous to learn the holy tongue;* by Iohn Udall. Imprinted in Leyden, By Francis Raphelengius, CIↃ·IↃ·XCIII (A copy of this grammar in the Rare Book Division of The New York Public Library bears the autographs of Increase Mather and William E. Stoughton.)

32 See *The England and Holland of the Pilgrims* by Henry Martyn Dexter and Morton Dexter (Boston and New York, 1905), Book VI, "The Pilgrims in Leyden," pp. 471–593; and *The Pilgrim Fathers from a Dutch Point of View* by D. Plooij (New York, 1932), pp. 24–81.

33 *New England Memorial* by Nathaniel Morton, sixth edition (Boston, 1855), p. 356.

34 Haller, pp. 13 and 16 n.

35 *William Bradford of Plymouth* by Albert H. Plumb (Boston, 1920), pp. 92–93.

36 See Deane, pp. 408–428.

37 "Of the Episcopacie," *ibid.*, pp. 428–441.

38 "Of the Presbyterians," *ibid.*, pp. 441–456.

39 "Of the Independents, or Congregationall Way," *ibid.*, pp. 457–464, which includes the final section, "Of the Fruits of Congregationall Discipline in the Primitive Times," *ibid.*, pp. 460–464.

40 *Ibid.*, p. 398, in Deane's introduction.

41 *Ibid.*, pp. 460 f.

42 *Ibid.*, pp. 462–463.

43 *Ibid.*

44 *Ibid.*, pp. 463–464.

45 *Ibid.*, p. 464.

46 See *supra,* p. 237, and p. 279, n. 1.

47 Deane, p. 407.

48 *Ibid.*, p. 408. The discussion on the Catholic Church ends on p. 428.

49 *Ibid.* The discussion on the Episcopalian Church, which continues to p. 441, points out how the Anglicans became a national church and differed from the principles of "the liberty of the gospell and practiss of some other Reformed Churches."

50 *Ibid.*, pp. 434–435.

51 *Ibid.*, 441. The Presbyterian system is analyzed; the differences between it and the prelacy, and between the Congregational Way are delineated (pp. 441–456).

52 *Ibid.*, pp. 443–446.

53 *Ibid.*, pp. 446–456.

54 "Of the Independent or Congregationall Way," *ibid.*, pp. 457–460. "Of the Fruits of Congregationall Discipline in the Primitive Times," *ibid.*, pp. 460–461.

55 *Ibid.*, pp. 457–458. Bradford refers to John Cotton as his authority on the antiquity of the Independent or Congregational Way and government in answer to Robert Baylie. "The way of God is the old way" (Jer. 6:16), and other verses from Matthew, Corinthians, and Acts are cited to support this thesis.

56 See *"De Gubernatione Ecclesiae ejusq̃, rerum & personarum," Historiae Ecclesiasticae, Volumen Primum, Centurias Quattuor, Primas complectens* (Basel, 1624), pp. 94–117; in particular on the policy of mutual reciprocity, the section entitled "De Consociatione Ecclesiarum & mutuis inter officiis."

57 See *supra*, pp. 244 and 248, where we refer to the section, "Of the Fruits of Congregationall Discipline."

58 Deane, pp. 460–464, did not reproduce these exercises.

59 *Ibid.*, p. 463.

60 *Ibid.* In support of this, Bradford refers to the following passages in the New Testament: Gal. 5:1; 2 Thess. 5:12–13, and Heb. 13:17.

61 Deane, p. 464.

62 *Ibid.*

63 See *supra*, p. 245.

64 Incorrectly designated by Bradford as verse 138.

65 It should read Ecclesiastes 12:9. instead of 21:9. The number 21 should be transposed to read 12.

66 Instead of the feminine plural כְּתֻבּוֹת , it should read כְּתֻבִים , the masculine plural.

67 Bradford's own wording.

68 It reads בֶּן־אִשָּׁה זוֹנָה .

69 Incorrectly designated as verse 18 by Bradford.

70 The phrasing אָנֹכִי הוֹלֵךְ occurs in several places in Hebrew Scriptures, in which certain serious and critical events are described such as Jacob's promise to God upon awakening from his dream; Joshua's farewell words of counsel towards the end of his life, to the Israelites whom he had led into the Promised Land; and David's parting words of advice before he dies (cf. Gen. 28:20; Josh. 23:14; and I Kings 2:2), which seem to be analagous to similar situations in the life of Bradford from the time he leaves England until he settles in the New English Canaan, and in his words of counsel and admonition concerning the future of Plymouth Plantation towards the end of his life.

71 Was Bradford inwardly expressing the hope that the entire community would affirm its acquiescence to what he had counseled as had occurred under similar circumstances in the days of Ezra: "Then all the assembly answered with a loud voice, 'It is so; we must do as you have said.' "

72 It should read דִּבְרֵי אֱמֶת instead of דְּבָרִים אֱמֶת .

73 Bradford's own wording.

74 The allusion to these words was most appropriate for a dialogue between the young men and the ancient men. Cf. the entire chapter 20 of Proverbs for its rules on proper conduct.

75 We wish to thank Prof. L. D. Geller, Director of the Pilgrim Society of Plymouth, Massachusetts, for making available to the present writer as clear a photograph as possible of this last page of the extant manuscript which is on loan from the Massachusetts Historical Society of Boston, Massachusetts and is now housed there. The "Bibliographic Essay," by Dr. George D. Langdon, Jr., in *Occasional Papers in Old Colony Studies,* No. 1 (July, 1969), published by Plimoth Plantation, Inc., was very helpful in the preparation of this paper. We wish also to thank the

Massachusetts Historical Society for making available to us several years ago a microfilm of the entire manuscript of the "Third Dialogue or Conference" of William Bradford from which enlargements were made that are here reproduced in facsimile. We wish also to express our appreciation to its Director, Dr. Stephen T. Riley and his staff for the many courtesies and the cooperation extended to us.

76 "Typology in Puritan New England: The Williams-Cotton Controversy Reassessed," by Sacvan Bercovitch, in the *American Quarterly,* Vol. XIX, no. 2, part 1 (Summer, 1967), pp. 166–191, corrects Perry Miller's views that the clash between Roger Williams and John Cotton, the Puritan, was not between a typologist and a Puritan, but between two types of typology. Williams followed the allegorical or spiritual typology, whereas Cotton and those who agreed with him—the historical or literal typology as well as the spiritual or allegorical typology. Frequently, as Bercovitch points out, the two methods were juxtaposed: the individual's accomplishments as allegory, and the collective body of New England as history. "The two methods sometimes appear separately and sometimes along one another in the same work" (*ibid.,* p. 188), and that Cotton proposed that "the acts both of Israel and of New England are simultaneously, literal and spiritual." On Bradford's use of Cotton's approach, see *ibid.,* p. 186, note 42. On recent studies of typology as applied by the Puritans, see Michael McGiffert's survey of "American Puritan Studies in the 1960's," *William and Mary Quarterly,* 3rd series, vol. XXVII, no. 1 (Jan., 1970), pp. 54–58.

77 See the fragment of Bradford's "A Descriptive and Historical Account of New England in verse," *Collections of the Massachusetts Historical Society for the Year 1794* (1st edition, 1794; 2nd edition, 1810), pp. 77–84. The fragment here begins:

Famine once we had—
But other things God gave
us in full store,
As fish, ground nuts, to
supply our strait,
That we might learn on
providence to wait;
And know, by bread man lives
not in need,
But by each word that doth
from God proceed. . . .

He cautions: "Where godliness abates, evil will succeed"; and that "Another caution of our declining here,/Is a mixt multitude, as doth appear," as had happened in the wilderness when "they were punished at 'Kibrath Hatavah'." He recalls: "How when the elders and Joshua was dead," the Israelites forgot "What God had done, and wrought for Israel, and turned aside and did not abide in his truth. But in the next age did generate;/I wish this may not be New England's fate."
He concludes:

O my dear friends, and children
whom I love,
To cleave to God, let these few
lines you move,
So I have done, and now will
say no more,
But remember, God punished
them sore.

He then refers to Judges 2:7, 11–12 and 14–15, and adds a line in Latin:

Melius est peccatum cavere,
quam emendare.

Thus he counsels that it is better to avoid transgression than to amend one's ways through punishment. For other specimens of Bradfords verses and his poem, "A Word to New Plymouth," see Deane, pp. 465–482. The verses bear the following Hebrew superscription:

Psa[lm] 46:12 :יְהוָה צְבָאוֹת עִמָּנוּ מִשְׂגָּב־לָנוּ אֱלֹהֵי יַעֲקֹב סֶלָה .
and underneath it:

> Spes una homine nec morte reliquit.
>
> Some observations of God's merciful dealings with us in this wilderness, and his gracious protection over us these many years, Blessed be his name.
>
> Firma fides turris est fortissima.

These verses were written in 1654, three years before the author died; he expresses here his gratitude for divine protection, and asserts, that the message of the Psalmist is a hope that never leaves man even in death; that a firm faith is the strongest fort and source of protection. The earlier fragment, published in 1794, also occurs here in the fully extended version of the poem, published by Deane in 1871 (*ibid.,* pp. 468 ff.).

Bradford also was the author of a poem relating to Boston, and of another *Epitaphium Meum,* which were verses dealing with his preparedness and fittedness for death, which begins:

From my years young in days
 of youth
God did make known to me
 his truth
And call'd me from my native
 place
For me to enjoy the means of
 grace,
In wilderness he did me guide,
And in strange lands for me provide
In fears and wants, through
 weal and woe
A pilgrim, passed to and fro. . . .

Chronicles of the Pilgrim Father by Nathaniel Morton (New York, 1910), p. 173.

78 S. Bercovitch, *op. cit.,* p. 183.

79 According to *Epitaphs from Burial Hill, Plymouth, Massachusetts, from 1657 to 1892* by Bradford Kingman (Brookline, Mass., 1892), p. 1, the three words read: יְהוָה עֵזֶר חַיַּי.

("The Lord is the help of my life.") David Philipson, who visited Plymouth's ancient burial ground at the beginning of this century could not decipher the middle word of this Hebrew inscription. The first word, the Tetragrammaton, and the last word חיי were clearly readable; the middle word was not completely visible since it had eroded. He conjectured that it was מעוז [strength] and that it read originally:

יהוה מעוז חיי

("The Lord in the strength of my life"), the words taken from Psalm 27:1. Apparently Philipson was unaware of the earlier reading, published by Kingman. See "The Hebrew Words on the Tombstone of William Bradford" by David Philipson *PAJHS,* Vol. XXII (1914), pp. 186–187.

80 The Latin inscription on the north side of the tombstone, according to Kingman reads:

Qua patres difficillime/
adepti sunt nolite turpiter/
relinquere.

[81] The Hebraic exercises can only be understood in the light of Bradford's typology as related to the Gospels, and the teachings of the theologians and theoreticians who supported his views of the Protestant Reformation in his quest to reestablish the primitive basis of the Congregational Way. He merely indicated that he wished to go back to the primitive original Hebraic and Greek sources, to the Hebrew Scriptures and the Greek Gospels, and to the period before the Emperor Constantine; and to sources as interpreted, for example, by Matthias Flacius and his Magdeburg colleagues, by John Calvin, and by the representative Puritan teachers such as John Cotton, and the early teachers of the Pilgrims such as John Robinson, Henry Ainsworth and others. It is pointless to interpret them in the spirit of polemics or apologetics. Cf. the present writer's "Hebrew at Harvard (1636–1760)," *PAJHS*, Vol. XXXV (1939), pp. 146–147, n. 4, and *The Puritan Mind* by Herbert W. Schneider, (New York, 1930), pp. 26–27. Bradford never divorced or separated one from the other when one critically reads and examines his history, his prose, and his poetry.

CHRISTIAN INFLUENCE ON EARLY GERMAN REFORM JUDAISM

MICHAEL A. MEYER

Hebrew Union College—Jewish Institute of Religion
Cincinnati, Ohio

When Christianity emerged from the matrix of Judaism nearly two thousand years ago, it brought with it a rich heritage of religious ideas and practices. The early Jewish-Christian community was no more than a sectarian offshoot of Judaism, a variant form which became wholly distinct from it only as Christianity grew into the larger pagan world. But as the daughter faith gradually became the dominant religion, it increasingly moved away from its Jewish origins and isolated the Jewish community on the periphery of Christian society. It came to regard itself as the true Israel, even as the Jewish people continued to see itself as perpetually chosen by God, destined to preserve its religious identity by complete faithfulness to the covenant. Under such circumstances the exponents of one faith could have little considered and conscious desire to borrow religious ideas and forms from the other. Only when situations of relatively free contact arose—as for example in Renaissance Italy or in seventeenth-century Holland—did the situation of mutual abhorrence give way to a new relationship whereby Jews began to look more favorably upon some of the religious forms developed through the centuries by Christianity. This process gained momentum when, in the course of the eighteenth century, Western Christianity in some circles underwent a process of rationalization causing it to accept the Enlightenment's insistence upon the validity of other faiths and giving it more common ground with Judaism. Thus, especially in Germany, some 1900 years after Christianity had departed from Judaism, the milieu was created for the first major influence of Christian practices upon Judaism, and certain of the Jews of Germany began to consider seriously whether Judaism in the modern world did not need to reshape itself according to the contemporary model of Christianity.

It is the purpose of this article to explore the evolution of Christian influence as it was exercised upon Reform Judaism in Germany during the first half of the nineteenth century. I shall limit myself principally to forms rather than theology, since the latter category, in Judaism at least, has remained highly individual. My interest lies in those elements which were taken over by the Jewish community as a whole, or rather by that portion of it which was most concerned with confronting the new world now visible to the Jewish community outside the ghetto. The thesis which I shall try to support is that during the first three decades of the nineteenth century the tendency among Jewish reformers was to take over Christian practices as acceptable and desirable modern forms in which to clothe the content of Judaism, but that by the thirties and forties, for various reasons which I shall endeavor to explicate, there was a reaction within the Reform leadership against the earlier tendency and a reevaluation of the entire form-content relationship.

In order to explain the course of developments within Reform Judaism it is necessary, first of all, to devote brief attention to the history of the Protestant Church in Germany during the same period. For Church historians, the Age of Enlightenment is generally considered an age of Christian decline, a trough which separates the spiritual vigor of the Reformation from the renewed creativity of the nineteenth century. During this period Protestantism in Germany subjected itself to the dictates of *Aufklärung;* its dogmas were submitted to the scrutiny of reason; eudaemonism—the ideal of happiness—replaced concern for individual redemption. The pulpits of Berlin and other centers of German Enlightenment no longer resounded with the preaching of orthodox doctrine or with expressions of deep spiritual conviction. Preachers, instead, delivered even-tempered moral addresses or provided practical advice for living. Reformation hymnody, which had remained vibrant in the Pietistic era, gave way to the singing of flat, moralizing verses. Enthusiasm for the unique truth of Christianity was dissipated by the Enlightenment view that non-

Christians as well might achieve salvation. The "neologians," the most thoroughgoing rationalists among the enlightened clergy, were interested above all in inculcating virtue and good taste. They regarded Jesus principally as moral paradigm and spoke little of the Cross. Spiritual leadership in large measure passed out of the hands of the clergy to the popular philosophers and moralists, who in more than five hundred moralistic weeklies published during the eighteenth century, set forth a model of the good life based on the psychological needs of the individual.

When a Christian revival followed in the early nineteenth century, it rejected this heritage of the Enlightenment. Under the profound influence of Schleiermacher, and intimately linked with the Romantic movement, the new Protestant theology in Germany staked out an independent realm for itself and rejected the earlier dependence upon philosophy. Enlightenment religion came to be seen as shallow if not entirely misplaced, unhistorical and unresponsive to the inner realm of feeling.[1] By 1821 Christian religiosity had rebounded so forcefully that Schleiermacher could claim that the educated of that day—unlike those of twenty years earlier—were more likely to err on the side of hyper-piety than that of hyper-rationalism.[2] In the first third of the nineteenth century Christianity in Germany succeeded in regaining most of the influence it had lost in the previous generation.

The period of the *Aufklärung,* which church historians have come to regard as an ebb in the Protestant tide was, on the contrary, regarded by Jewry as a mighty wave of progress. In the eighteenth-century stress on the eternal truths of natural religion, in the highlighting of morality rather than dogma, and in the willingness to neglect historical revelation, a rapidly acculturating element of the Jewish community found a common ground with Christianity and reason to hope for a happier and closer coexistence. These Jews therefore felt it incumbent upon themselves to bring the Jewish religion more directly into line with a freer and more flexible Christianity. Thus there arose a new willingness to be influenced by Christion forms and to disregard Jewish historical precedent, even as the church was breaking some of its links with the past.[3]

When Protestantism reversed itself in the nineteenth century and returned to tradition, Jewish leaders could only regard this shift as a great step backward, especially as it was accompanied by the reimposition of political and economic disabilities. At first many of them regarded the rejection of Enlightenment rationalism in Christianity as only temporary, and assumed that the tendency toward an increased stress of Christian differences from Judaism would soon abate. By the thirties, however, Reform Judaism was itself becoming historically conscious and beginning to rethink its attitude toward the acceptance of Christian practices.

There were various Protestant forms which served as models for Jewish reform in Germany. Our purpose cannot be to make an exhaustive study of each of them, but only to trace their influence, most briefly, over the first half of the nineteenth century in order to determine whether there was a common pattern. I shall deal in sequence with the architecture of the synagogue, the role of the rabbi, the sermon, the nature of the worship service, and religious education.

Christian influence upon synagogue architecture [4] is not a modern phenomenon. Throughout the Middle Ages Jewish houses of worship were patterned on styles prevalent in the various countries of Jewish habitation. In Muslim lands synagogues bore a distinct resemblance to contemporary mosques; in Christian lands to the local churches. In Muslim Spain, for example, the elevated Torah reading desk was apparently modeled after the Arabic *mimbar;* in medieval Germany we know of at least one synagogue which employed stained-glass windows. Even the use of such seemingly indigenous symbols as the Eternal Light and the tablets of the Ten Commandments within the synagogue may have been influenced respectively by the practice of Catholic and Protestant churches in the premodern period.[5] Until the last century, synagogues in Central and Western Europe were designed by non-Jewish architects who, quite naturally, chose the models with which they were most familiar. Variations were introduced to avoid the use of patently inappropriate elements, such as the cruciform floor plan of the churches, and to provide for the specific requirements imposed by the nature of Jewish worship.

Thus when Israel Jacobson built the first "Reform" synagogue, or "temple," [6] as he called it, in Seesen, Westphalia (completed in 1810), he did not break with precedent by employing a Christian architect who modeled the interior after the local Andreas Church. What made Jacobson's temple different was only the provision for three items closely associated with Christian religious practices: a bell tower complete with church bells, an organ, and a raised pulpit directly in front of the ark and facing the congregation. The novelty lay not in the choice of a foreign architectural model, but in the reflection of Jacobson's new conception of Jewish worship.

Israel Jacobson desired to make his temple as little specifically Jewish in appearance as possible because he wanted Christians as well as Jews to feel at home in it. But a generation later, when intellectual and social acculturation had begun to wear away Jewish identity for large numbers of German Jews, preservation of uniqueness rather than the alignment with Christian example became the more prominent concern. Consequently we find a determined desire not to imitate the architecture of the contemporary church, and a serious consideration of how to make the synagogue building distinctively Jewish. For the first time there are Jewish architects engaged in synagogue construction, and one sees congregational leaders and professionals discussing just how a synagogue in its overall architectural design, not just in its interior arrangements, can be given a peculiarly Jewish character. It is now felt that the synagogue should awaken historical memories. The Temple of Solomon is considered as model though it was built according to a Phoenician design; the Moorish style, setting the synagogue sharply apart from the church, comes to be favored by some architects in Germany as representative of the Jews' Oriental heritage. In Cassel protracted discussion over the choice of a synagogue style during the 1830's leads finally to the selection of a form intended to represent the pre-Gothic architecture which was thought common to both early churches and synagogues in the late Roman period.[7] The absence of any indigenous Jewish architectural tradition necessarily frustrated the search for any definite single model.[8] But whatever the solutions reached, the tendency by mid-century was clearly to seek architectural precedent in some phase of the Jewish past.

A second area of Christian influence in the early nineteenth century was that of the role of the clergy. In the Jewish tradition of preceding centuries the rabbi's task principally had been that of legal authority and teacher. In Ashkenazic Jewry his role had not included the preaching of weekly sermons nor the functions of a pastor. He spoke to the congregation in Judeo-German, generally on a Talmudic subject, and only twice a year; he shared such obligations as visiting the sick with every other member of the community. At the turn of the nineteenth century the rabbinate in Germany consisted of men trained to this traditional role and quite unwilling and, indeed, incapable of preaching a vernacular sermon or of assuming the other specific functions of Christian clergy. Yet that group within the Jewish communities of the larger cities which desired forms of worship more appropriate to the Christian environment also sought a new kind of leadership. We thus find a number of young Jewish men who become *Prediger* for the newly established Reform services in Berlin and Hamburg and gradually also in more traditional congregations. They become for the Jewish community the equivalent of the Protestant clergyman, taking on the same sermonic and pastoral duties. They exist side-by-side with rabbis who retain their consultative role in matters of Jewish ritual law.

The new Jewish preachers don the garb of their Christian contemporaries—the clerical robe and collar bands [9]—supplemented by the Jewish prayer shawl and black silk cap; they receive doctoral degrees at German universities to supplement the extensive traditional Jewish education obtained in youth. Gradually this new generation of Jewish leaders succeeds to rabbinical positions as well, when the need is felt to place all aspects of spiritual leadership into the hands of individuals trained both in Jewish law and tradition and in secular disciplines.[10]

By the 1830's there was thus a new type of rabbi who could preach from the pulpit and discuss philosophy and history as well as argue points of Jewish law. The question then arose whether to continue with the title of "preacher," which did indeed represent the principal function, or to return to the use of "rabbi," though it now meant a very different role. It is significant in terms of our thesis to note that the title "preacher" gradually disappeared, to be joined to or replaced with "rabbi" by even the most extreme reformers. In order to justify their expanded role with its wide range of clerical functions, these new rabbis sought precedent in Jewish tradition for the far-reaching spiritual leadership of the rabbi while at the same time attempting to differentiate the modern rabbi from the Protestant minister.[11] When Samuel Holdheim assumed leadership of the Reform congregation of Berlin, he not only chose to be called "rabbi," but he declared that he regarded his new role principally as that of a teacher and only secondarily as that of a preacher and pastor.[12]

The Reform rabbis at mid-century, both in outlook and in role, were certainly far more similar to many of their fellow Christian clergy than to the traditional rabbis of earlier times.[13] Yet here, too, as in synagogue architecture, there was a desire to reestablish a link with tradition. It was done by reassuming the title of "rabbi" and, at least in one instance, by interpreting it to mean "teacher."

If we proceed now to the influence of the Christian sermon, we shall discover a similar course of development.[14] In the eighteenth century the Protestant homily in Germany became more of a moralistic discourse than a preaching of the Gospels. As acceptability to reason became an indispensable criterion of judgment, the more extreme of the neologians reduced the Christian message to those elements considered free of super-rational dogma. They chose to discuss only that portion of their tradition which they themselves and their congregants found credible. The Bible served them mainly as a source of illustrations for the truths of natural religion and examples of the moral, and hence happier life.[15] The first modern Jewish preachers in Germany were drawn to this kind of sermon because it had little Christological character and was therefore easily adaptable to the Jewish service. Even if the respective liturgies would remain very different, the sermon could provide a common form for Jewish and Christian worship. The pulpits would give clear evidence that Jewish spiritual concerns were very much the same as those of Christians. And, not unimportantly, the political and social acceptability of the Jews would thereby be advanced.

The earliest Jewish sermons of the new type in Germany were thus predominantly in a universal vein. They dealt with such matters as the proper use of time, religiosity and morality, and the like.[16] At first the younger generation, coming of age in the twenties, likewise looked to Christian models and shied away from topics too specifically Jewish. They chose quotations from the Bible rather than rabbinic literature.[17] Their listeners could think of no higher expression of esteem than to compare them to the more famous Christian preachers of the day. But Christian preaching was not to continue in its eighteenth-century course. In the early nineteenth century it began to react to the "flat *Kanzelberedsamkeit*" of the earlier period and turn instead either to the utterance of personal faith in Christian mysteries, as in the case of Schleiermacher, or to the renewed expounding of Christian dogma, as in the now resurgent orthodoxy. The rationalistic discourse was no longer highly regarded in a Christian world much under the influence of romanticism. Its Jewish counterpart, however, modeled after the older form, could obviously not adapt itself to the new, more Christian type of sermon. Yet neither were the Jewish congregations willing to give it up entirely, for the German sermon, after initial opposition by the orthodox, was making steady headway wherever governments allowed its use. It was ever more widely accepted as an important part of the Jewish service.

As the Christian sermon began to draw more heavily from its own tradition, its Jewish equivalent was set adrift. Since especially in Reform-minded circles there was no desire to give it up, the attempt was made to disclose a native Jewish homiletical tradition. When Leopold Zunz, the founder of scientific study of the Jewish past, published his classic *Sermons of the Jews* in 1832, he was desirous not only of proving to a reactionary Prussian government that Jewish sermons were not a radical, politically subversive innovation, but also in showing his fellow Jews that they possessed their own tradition, however much the midrashim of earlier times might differ from the Jewish sermons of that day. Two years later the reformer Ludwig Philippson established a Jewish homiletical journal devoted to the development of a specifically Jewish type of sermon. In the following decade, as the sermon found its way into more and more synagogues, Jewish preachers made distinct efforts to define their task. They agreed in rejecting slavish imitation of the Christian model and chose instead to build somehow on the traditional homily, the *derasha,* though purified of timebound dross. To base Jewish homiletics on those of another religion, one writer argued in 1840, would be to set the building on a foundation which it simply did not fit; inevitably the structure would collapse.[18] It was Gotthold Salomon, one of the preachers at the Reform Temple in Hamburg, who is credited with being the father of a new, specifically Jewish modern homiletics.[19] By mid-century a regular German sermon, but now drawing freely from rabbinical as well as biblical tradition, was widely accepted in Jewish congregations. Its adoption by the synagogues of Germany had been unquestionably due to the Protestant example, but its form and content were now far more distinctly Jewish.

Aside from the German sermon, a number of other Christian practices influenced the Jewish Reform service. Some of them remained throughout the period and were never questioned, others underwent the same process of Judaization which we have already noted above. A third category consisted of those elements of Christian worship which were scarcely or not at all adopted during this half-century but which did find subsequent acceptance in Reform circles.

The conviction that a proper worship service should be decorous was a Christian sentiment which, to the best of my knowledge, was never questioned by early Reform and which spread to more traditional Jewry as well. Over the centuries Ashkenazic Jewish prayer had become a highly individual matter, each participant in the service responding or not to the prayer leader as the spirit moved him. Congregants talked freely to one another on topics sacred and secular, milled about, feeling very much at home in the synagogue, sometimes achieving great spontaneity and exuberance, but hardly creating an atmosphere of reverence. To outsiders it seemed chaotic. And to the reformers, no doubt with the dignified solemnity of the church service in mind, such free reign of expression and such informality seemed destructive of true worship as they now conceived it.[20] When reconsideration of Christian forms came in the thirties and forties, the reformers' insistence on decorum was not diminished; it was however justified by attributing it to "the German sense of order" rather than the imitation of Christian practice.[21]

The use of an organ in the service was another lasting innovation of early German Reform. But unlike decorum it did not spread to orthodoxy, which opposed its introduction bitterly. Much ink was spilled between reformers and traditionalists over the entire course of our period in arguments as to whether any musical instrument, and specifically an organ, might, according to Jewish law, be played in the synagogue. The issues of this legal discussion do not concern us here.[22] What is of consequence for our purpose is that the organ, unlike the sermon, did not allow of Judaization. Aside from *halakhic* arguments regarding its permissibility, the reformers who wanted the instrument in the synagogue could only try to justify its use historically with the precedent of similar musical instruments in the ancient Temple and, as Zunz noted, the fact that an organ had existed "for centuries" in a synagogue in Prague.[23] But there was no getting away from the intimate association of the organ with the church and this bothered the more conservative reformers.[24] Abraham Geiger, the principal leader of the more radical group, however argued that the "pressing need" to elevate the service by music and song here justified the adoption of a Christian form. The best Geiger could do in its defense was to refer once again to the playing of an organ-like instrument in the ancient Temple and to ask whether it was not desirable for the Jews now to reclaim their inheritance, with appreciation to Christianity for perfecting its use through the centuries.[25]

Unlike the organ, the ceremony of confirmation lent itself to Judaization. It was widely adopted by German Reform, at first as an individual ceremony for boys and then for groups including girls. It, too, became permanent in Reform Judaism and its acceptance was also clearly the result of Protestant influence. At first the ceremony in Judaism was very similar to its Protestant model. It, too, included a confession of faith by the confirmand as part of the ritual.[26] But once again, after a lapse of some years, serious questions about Jewish confirmation were raised by the reformers themselves. The value of the ceremony, pedagogically and religiously, drove out any consideration of its rejection. But it was frankly admitted that Judaism contained no precedent for confirmation, the Bar Mitzvah ceremony representing only a distant analogy. Judaization therefore had to proceed by eliminating those aspects of the ceremony which were held to be foreign to Judaism and by reinterpreting its significance. Thus Solomon Herxheimer argued in 1835 that since a Jew becomes a member of his faith by birth, and circumcision is not an equivalent of Christian baptism, confirmation could not represent the consummation of entry into Judaism. Moreover, a confession of faith was entirely foreign to the Jewish religion. However, as a solemn examination in Judaism and as a pledge of Jewish loyalty, Herxheimer found confirmation both acceptable on the basis of Jewish tradition and eminently desirable, especially at a time when children were exposed to much anti-religious thought. In the view of the reformers the Christian ceremony of confirmation thus became a means for preserving Judaism.[27]

Certain Christian forms, however, did not find acceptance in German Jewish Reform during the first half of the nineteenth century, although they made headway later in the left wing of the movement in Germany and in the United States. These included worship without a head-covering, sitting together of men and women, and Sunday services. During the period of our discussion such departures were, with few exceptions, judged too radical.[28]

The last illustration of our thesis lies in the area of religious instruction. Here it was the Protestant catechism which served modern Jewish educators in Germany as a model for the transmission of religion.[29] Judaism as a faith based on certain articles of belief had not been taught in the traditional Jewish schools where the curriculum was limited to the study of sacred texts. Jewish educators, and in some cases governments,[30] were interested that Jewish youth become familiar with the tenets of their faith in the same manner that Christian children learned the essentials of theirs. As Judaism of the early nineteenth century was almost totally bereft of any pedagogical model of this type, it was only to be expected that the catechism should be adapted for Jewish use. Of course Jewish content was substituted for Christian: the principles of Maimonides or Albo for those of Luther, along with the Ten Commandments which were common to both. Yet some objections were raised to the adoption of the catechism—in this case from the very beginning. Some educators regarded catechizing as against the spirit of Judaism, or pointed out that, in their opinion, Judaism, unlike Christianity, possessed no *Glaubenslehre,* no system of beliefs.[31] But the form of question and answer was at this time considered a most effective means for presenting Jewish teachings and commandments. On this account it was employed by some of the orthodox as well as by the reformers. But whereas especially the earlier catechisms tended to stress the common core of morality in all religions, the later ones often placed more emphasis on specifically Jewish doctrines. An ultimate stage in this respect was reached slightly beyond our period, in 1859, when a Jewish educator published a *Catechism of Doctrines Differentiating Judaism from Christianity.*[32] A Christian form was thus employed to point out which Christian doctrines were foreign to Judaism. But the catechism as such did not become a permanent form of Jewish instruction. It disappeared gradually after our period, apparently less out of reaction to its Christian origins than because the form was no longer considered pedagogically effective.

After an examination of these individual areas of influence, it remains to summarize and to account for this changing Jewish attitude toward the adoption of Christian forms in terms of the overall development of Reform. Until the late eighteenth century Christian exclusiveness supported a Jewish attitude to religious assimilation best characterized by the biblical dictum: "You shall not walk in their statutes" (Lev. 18:3). But as Enlightenment influence on Christianity made it more congenial to Judaism and the achievement of political equality for the Jews became a real possibility, Jewish attitudes markedly changed. Christianity, in its late eighteenth-century form no longer seemed so hostile or strange. The new Europe could encompass Judaism and Christianity as variant forms of a rational faith. But it was widely felt that Judaism would have to make certain adjustments in order to become a religion in the modern sense. If it was to become one of the religious denominations of Germany, and not an entity apart, Judaism would have to adopt certain forms, found in the church, but considered proper to all religions. The earlier reformers thought that some adjustment to the Christian model was expected of them and their own aesthetic and religious sensibilities, conditioned by exposure to Christian practices, drove them in the same direction.[33] They seldom found reason to oppose pouring Jewish content into Christian forms. In fact, unlike the orthodox, they regarded this transfusion as the best way to preserve the contents of Judaism in a Christian environment.

That this attitude was significantly altered in the thirties and forties must be explained by the course of developments both outside and within Judaism. As Christianity returned to its separate theological path in the early nineteenth century and, in the spirit of romanticism looked to its historical rather than its rational foundations, it continued to exercise an influence on Judaism, but in this case a separative rather than an imitative one. The reformers who in their earlier enthusiasm had favored the use of Christian forms began to turn to Jewish history and seek links between their efforts and Jewish tradition. As we have seen, in some cases this led to the attempt to find Jewish precedent for a Christian form, in others to eventual rejection of the form, and in still others to efforts at Judaization. In 1820 such forms as the modern sermon and the textbook of religion were strange to Judaism. They had to be learned from Christianity. But once the form was mastered, it was possible to depart significantly from the model.

By the 1830's and 40's there was a great desire to do so. For the new generation was trying to regain its balance. It looked to the Jewish past, increasingly cognizant that religious forms as well as content grow out of historical traditions from which they cannot arbitrarily be severed. This is a sentiment not limited in this period to the conservative reformer Zacharias Frankel, who developed a "positive-historical" approach to Judaism, but is found generally in German Reform. The synagogue, Geiger argued in 1835, must develop out of itself and its own tradition if it is to face the world with dignity. Nothing is to be gained by giving up all the unique elements in Judaism and imitating Christianity (*Christeln*) in the vain hope of thereby gaining full acceptance in society. Judaism must maintain its "religious independence."[34] Even among the radical reformers of Berlin the unreflective simulation of Christianity had fallen into disrepute. It was argued that mere change of forms—the addition of choir and preacher, German prayer, and choral singing—would not cure the disunity (*Zerrissenheit*) within a Jewish community divided on the significance of its own tradition. The exposed nakedness could not be covered by "the foreign dress of Christianity."[35] These reformers also raised the objection that using contemporary Christian forms creates the false impression that Judaism is thereby modern and thus directs attention away from the unresolved problems posed by biblical criticism.[36]

Yet if this rejection of imitation was deemed necessary for maintaining the religious independence of Judaism, it was also seen as creating the possibility of a more fruitful relationship between the two faiths. In 1843 Sigismund Stern, a lay leader in Berlin, summed it up: "Judaism, which for a time thought itself drawing nearer to Christianity because it was departing from its own character, is now drawing nearer to it in truth, but *with an awareness of its own personality. . . .*"[37] That awareness, which had been dimmed during the period of its origins, was what Reform in its second generation was trying to achieve.

NOTES

1 Luther Reed, *The Lutheran Liturgy* (Philadelphia: 1947), pp. 139–54; J. A. Dorner, *History of Protestant Theology* (Edinburgh: 1871), II, pp. 293, 467; Karl Kahnis, *Der innere Gang des deutschen Protestantismus* (Leipzig: 1860), pp. 30, 228; and especially F. W. Kantzenbach, *Protestantisches Christentum im Zeitalter der Aufklärung* (Gütersloh: 1965).

2 F. Schleiermacher, *Über die Religion* (3d ed.; Berlin: 1821), pp. xiii–xiv.

3 A good example is David Friedländer, *An die Verehrer, Freunde und Schüler Jerusalems, Spaldings, Tellers, Herders und Löfflers* (Leipzig: 1823).

4 On this subject in general see R. Wischnitzer, *The Architecture of the European Synagogue* (Philadelphia: 1964); A. Grotte, *Deutsche, böhmische und polnische Synagogentypen* (Berlin: 1915).

5 J. Gutmann, "How Traditional are out Traditions?" *Central Conference of American Rabbis Journal,* April 1968, pp. 59–61.

6 Wischnitzer (p. 176) thinks that the name "temple" was inspired by the French Reformed churches which were also called "temples." However, Jacobson more likely had in mind the Temple of Solomon. See his specific reference to it in *Sulamith,* III, 1 (1810), pp. 311–12. The building is discussed in detail in N. Friedland, *Zur Geschichte des Tempels der Jacobsonschule* (Seesen: 1910).

7 R. Hallo, *Kasseler Synagogengeschichte* (Kassel: 1931), pp. 43–66.

8 See, for example, the revealing article by the Jewish architect Max Fleischer, "Über Tempelbau," in the Viennese Jewish weekly *Die Neuzeit,* XIV (1884), pp. 134–37, 154–56.

9 The use of the clerical robe and collar bands (*Bäffchen*) by Jewish clergy was, however, neither a Reform innovation nor limited to the reformers. Rabbis wore

them as early as the seventeenth century. Illustrations may be found in Alfred Rubens, *A History of Jewish Costume* (London: 1967), pp. 175–94. On the subject in general see Leopold Löw, "Die Amtstracht der Rabbinen," *Gesammelte Schriften* (Szegedin: 1898), IV, pp. 217–34.

10 The higher level of general education demanded of the new generation of rabbis paralleled developments in the Christian community where higher educational standards and greater professionalism were characteristic of the Protestant clergy after the Prussian Church Union of 1817. See R. M. Bigler, "The Rise of Political Protestantism in Nineteenth-Century Germany," *Church History,* XXXIV (1965), p. 436; Kahnis, p. 235.

11 David Rothschild, "Über den geistlichen Charakter des Rabbiner-Amtes," *Zur Judenfrage in Deutschland,* II (1844), pp. 199–210.

12 Samuel Holdheim, *Antrittspredigt* (Berlin: 1847); *idem, Geschichte der Entstehung und Entwicklung der jüdischen Reformgemeinde in Berlin* (Berlin: 1857), pp. 173, 179. In Vienna, however, I.N. Mannheimer kept the title of "preacher" and allowed matters of Jewish law to remain in the hands of a traditional rabbi. Unlike Holdheim, Mannheimer regarded his pastoral duties to be of greater significance than his teaching or preaching. See "Zwei interessante Briefe Mannheimer's," *Monatsschrift für Geschichte und Wissenschaft des Judentums,* XX (1871), pp. 279–81.

13 See, for example, the duties outlined for the rabbi of Sondershausen in *Allgemeine Zeitung des Judentums,* X (1846), pp. 37–40.

14 On this subject see the two important articles by Alexander Altmann: "Zur Frühgeschichte der jüdischen Predigt in Deutschland," *Leo Baeck Institute Year Book,* VI (1961), pp. 3–57; and "The New Style of Preaching in Nineteenth-Century Jewry," *Studies in Nineteenth-Century Jewish Intellectual History,* ed. A. Altmann (Cambridge, Mass.: 1964), pp. 65-116. For earlier developments in Italy, see Ellis Rivkin, "The Sermons of Leon da Modena," Hebrew Union College Annual, XXIII[2] (1950–51), pp. 295–317.

15 Reed, p. 147; Kantzenbach, pp. 88–98; Dorner, II, p. 468.

16 The best example is provided by the sermons written, but not delivered, by David Friedländer: *Reden der Erbauung gebildeter Israeliten gewidmet* (Berlin: 1815 and 1817).

17 Even Leopold Zunz in his *Predigten, gehalten in der neuen Israelitischen Synagoge zu Berlin* (Berlin: 1823). See also the personal testimony of I. M. Jost, *Geschichte des Judentums und seiner Sekten* (Leipzig: 1859), III, p. 333.

18 M. Kayserling, *Bibliothek jüdischer Kanzelredner,* II (1872), pp. 40–42; Holdheim, *Geschichte,* p. 180; J. A. Fränkel, "Zur Geschichte der Homiletik," *Literaturblatt des Orients,* I (1840), p. 557.

19 *Allgemeine Zeitung des Judentums,* VII (1843), p. 621; Kayserling, I (1870), pp. 154–55.

20 For a consideration of the *Synagogenordnungen* promulgated by German governments to maintain decorum, often at the behest of Jewish leaders, see: Jakob J. Petuchowski, *Prayerbook Reform in Europe* (New York: 1968), pp. 105–27.

21 *Zur Judenfrage in Deutschland,* II (1844), p. 66.

22 For a survey of the literature, see the unpublished Hebrew Union College prize essay by Meir Ydit, "The Controversy Concerning the Use of the Organ During the 19th Century in Europe and in America."

23 L. Zunz, *Die gottesdienstlichen Vorträge der Juden* (Berlin: 1832), p. 476.

24 See, for example, the remarks in the 1830 letter of I. N. Mannheimer in *Monatsschrift für Geschichte und Wissenschaft des Judentums,* XX (1871), pp. 334–35. The Jewish composer, Meyerbeer, in 1855 made the interesting suggestion that if instrumental music was to be used in the service it would be more appropriate to compose it for flute and trumpet, as in Solomon's Temple, than for what he regarded as "a purely Christian instrument" (*Allgemeine Zeitung des Judentums,* XXVIII [1864], p. 541).

[25] A. Geiger, "Die Begleitung des gottesdienstlichen Gesanges durch die Orgel," *Jüdische Zeitschrift für Wissenschaft und Leben,* I (1862), pp. 89–98.

[26] E. Kley, "Zur Konfirmation der Mädchen," *Predigten* (Hamburg: 1819), pp. 47–65.

[27] S. Herxheimer, "Über die synagogische Zulässigkeit und Einrichtung der Konfirmation," *Wissenschaftliche Zeitschrift für jüdische Theologie,* I (1835), pp. 68–96. J. Heinemann very early chose to call a similar ceremony he instituted in his school in Berlin "Religionsfest" in order thereby to differentiate it from the Christian ceremony (*Jedidja,* II, 1 [1818], pp. 207–16).

[28] Even the radical *Reformgenossenschaft* in Berlin, when it held its first New Year services in 1845, had separate seating of the sexes and provided head coverings for the worshippers (*Zweiter Bericht der Genossenschaft für Reform in Judentum* [Berlin: 1846], pp. 10–11). By 1849 the Sunday service of this congregation had supplanted its Saturday morning worship but was justified by its rabbi only as an "unfortunately" necessary concession to insure attendance. Holdheim called it "the most painful operation which we have had to perform on the deathly ill patient" (Holdheim, *Geschichte,* pp. 180–84, 209).

[29] See Jakob J. Petuchowski, "Manuals and Catechisms of the Jewish Religion in the Early Period of Emancipation," *Studies in Nineteenth-Century Jewish Intellectual History,* pp. 47–64.

[30] In Denmark in 1814 the government made systematic religious instruction and confirmation a requirement for obtaining economic and civil equality. I. N. Mannheimer was engaged as "royal catechist" for Danish Jewry (M. Rosenmann, *Isak Noa Mannheimer* [Vienna: 1922], pp. 30–31).

[31] *Sulamith,* I, 1 (1806), 51n; *ibid.,* IV, 1 (1812), pp. 246–54.

[32] Emanuel Hecht, *Katechismus der Unterscheidungslehren des Juden- und Christenthums* (Hoppstädten: 1859).

[33] An excellent example of this point of view is the article by David Fränkel, "Die Lage der Juden alter und neuerer Zeiten," *Sulamith,* I, 2 (1807), pp. 353–86. See also Israel Jacobson's speech at the dedication of his temple in *Sulamith,* III, 1 (1810), pp. 303–17.

[34] A. Geiger, "Das Judentum unserer Zeit und die Bestrebungen in ihm," *Wissenschaftliche Zeitschrift für jüdische Theologie,* I (1835), pp. 1–12.

[35] S. Stern, *Die Aufgabe des Judentums und des Juden in der Gegenwart* (Berlin: 1845), pp. 109–12, 180.

[36] A. Rebenstein [Aaron Bernstein], "Unsere Gegenwart," *Zur Judenfrage in Deutschland,* II (1844), pp. 65–102.

[37] S. Stern, "Das Judentum als Element des Staats-Organismus," *ibid.,* I (1843), p. 138. Emphasis in the text is Stern's.

STUDIES IN THE HISTORY OF THE EARLY KARAITE LITURGY: THE LITURGY OF AL-QIRQISĀNĪ

LEON NEMOY

Dropsie University

Fragmentary and meager as is our knowledge of the early history of Karaite life and thought, it is ample compared with what we know about the history of the early Karaite liturgy [1] prior to the adoption of the official Karaite prayer book compiled in the second half of the thirteenth century by Aaron ben Joseph (Aaron the Elder).[2] Our first ray of light came with the publication by the late Jacob Mann of fragments dealing with liturgical matters from Anan's *Sēfer ha-miṣ̌wōt.*[3] But—and that is a very important point to remember—Anan was only the titular, and not the actual, founder of Karaism, and his arrangement of the liturgy represents only one of the several liturgical orders which must have been current among the non-Rabbinite schisms of the second half of the first millenium after Christ. Moreover, the text published by Mann is fragmentary, and the information conveyed by it, while of capital importance, is not at all free from gaps and uncertainties.

A second important source became available with my publication of the code of Karaite law composed in the second quarter of the tenth century by Ya'qūb (Jacob) al-Qirqisānī, one of the greatest minds of the golden age of Karaite literature (ninth-eleventh centuries).[4] Among other, not strictly legal, matters, al-Qirqisānī's code contains a full exposition of his order of the liturgy,[5] and fortunately the text of this section has reached us complete. Even more fortunately, al-Qirqisānī not only was not an Ananite, but vigorously and outspokenly opposed Anan in many aspects of law and ritual.[6] His order of the liturgy is therefore not just a retelling or modification of Anan's order, but a thoroughly independent scheme of his own.

More than a quarter of a century has elapsed since al-Qirqisānī's chapters on the liturgy have been published, and all along I had hoped that they would catch the eye of a specialist in liturgical history who would make them accessible to readers unfamiliar with the Arabic language, and would supply them with a detailed commentary of his own. Regrettably this has not happened, and so this is my excuse for offering the following part-paraphrase part-translation [7] of the liturgical order of al-Qirqisānī for the reader's attention. Needless to say, neither these prefatory remarks nor the few footnotes are meant to be exhaustive; but perhaps they will serve to arouse at last the interest of a serious student of liturgical history (which I most assuredly am not) and lead him to make a more extensive and detailed study of the whole subject.

What arrangements the pre-Ananite schismatics had made for themselves in regard to their liturgy, we do not know, and Anan's order is the earliest of which we have some documentary evidence. He, like other early non-Rabbinite sectarians, subscribed to the principle that prayer should consist entirely of citations, predominantly psalmodic, from Scripture, and that the Rabbinite practice of introducing poetic hymns (*piyyūṭīm*) and prose prayers of their own composition is a sinful innovation. But he did not stop there. The entire order of Rabbinite worship appeared to him to be a wicked deviation from the only true and divinely ordained service, that of the Temple in Jerusalem.

To be sure, Anan readily admitted that since the Temple was no longer in existence and the Children of Israel were dispersed in exile, an exact restoration of the worship of the Temple was physically impossible, since it was based upon the statutory animal sacrifices, and these could no longer be offered in proper ritual purity. Prayer, then, had to take the place of these sacrifices, but in all other aspects, he thought, the divine service should be, as far as possible, an exact counterpart of the Temple ritual.

Just as the Temple was the only place wherein public sacrifices could be lawfully offered, so should each man, thought Anan, set aside a special place, a sort of private chapel—he called it *ḥāsēr,* "courtyard"[8]—for prayer, and should keep this place, like the Temple, ritually clean and undefiled by the presence of unclean or non-Ananite persons. To parallel the two daily sacrifices in the Temple, two prayers only should be offered, in the morning and in the evening, thus excluding the Rabbinite third, afternoon, prayer, the *Minḥāh.* The daily lessons from the Torah, which were to be the actual substitutes for the discontinued sacrifices, are to be read only by men of priestly descent, because it was their lineal ancestors, the priests, who had actually performed the offering of animal sacrifices in the Temple. By the same token, the Song (Psalm) of the day (*shīr ha-yōm*) is to be recited only by men of Levitic lineage, thus continuing the function performed by their ancestors in the House of God in Jerusalem. Again, the Holy Ark containing the Scrolls of the Law was to be honored by kneeling before it and bowing to the ground, as was its prototype, the Holy of Holies in the Temple.

This was indeed a logical arrangement, but like many other ordinances promulgated by Anan it met with immediate opposition. His principle that prayer *equaled* sacrifice was met with the objection that while prayer did indeed *take the place* of sacrifice in the absence of the Temple, it was not its equivalent, for a valid sacrifice must be offered by a priest in the Temple, whereas a prayer may be offered by any person anywhere, so long as that person and that place are ritually clean. The same distinction, argued Anan's opponents, applied to the Holy Ark, since it was merely a substitute for, and not the equivalent of, the Holy of Holies in the Temple, and therefore to kneel and bow before it, in each of the individual synagogues, was a procedure perilously akin to idolatry. And many schismatics found fault also with Anan's limitation of the number of prayers to two, and saw no harm in adopting the Rabbinite *Minḥāh,* so long as it was offered at what they thought was the proper time of the day, that is, at midday or thereabouts, and not late in the afternoon as is the Rabbinite custom. No doubt the schismatics felt uncomfortable praying only twice a day, when they observed their Rabbinite cousins offering three prayers, and their Muslim fellow-citizens five prayers, daily.

The result of this opposition to Anan's order of the liturgy is displayed also in al-Qirqisānī's liturgical order. Anan's courtyard theory is rejected. The *Minḥāh* is adopted without hesitation, with the proviso that it must be observed as a noontime prayer. The assignment of certain prayers to men of priestly or Levitic descent is rejected, as is the adoration of the Holy Ark. But the rigid limitation of public prayer to citations from Scripture is retained in all its severity (the later official Karaite prayer book abolished it by introducing a mass of hymns by both Karaite and Rabbinite authors), although al-Qirqisānī, exceedingly sensible man as he was, warns the reader that this does not apply to private prayer, in which man may converse with his Maker in any terms that his heart may suggest to him. As to the choice and order of the individual Psalms assigned to each prayer in daily and holy-day services, the situation is somewhat unclear, for on the one hand our text of Anan's liturgy is fragmentary, while on the other al-Qirqisānī does not discuss such supplementary matters as occasional prayers, benedictions, etc.

In another place,[9] I had occasion to suggest that it is high time to place Karaite studies upon a more realistic basis, with greater regard to the political, economic, and psychological factors which played an important role in the birth and development of this sect. But it is perhaps in liturgical matters, better than in any other aspect of Karaite expression, that the human side of the early schismatics is so clearly discernible. It is a rather moving sight to observe these profoundly devout and sincere men, struggling desperately to do what they believed to be right, in defiance of the entire mainstream of Jewish tradition, at the cost of hardship and discomfort to themselves, and too often in the face of logic and common sense. And there is no better illustration of this, I think, than their stubborn insistence on shackling that most intimate expression of religious feeling—man's direct dialogue with God—with the tight handcuffs of Biblical psalmody, which, magnificent though it is, could not possibly satisfy completely the souls of men living in the midst of a civilization a thousand years removed from the one which gave birth to the Psalter.

CHAPTER XV

On the duty of praying.

The duty of praying is inherent in the Second Commandment, where the reference to other gods, *thou shalt not bow unto them, nor serve them* [10] (Exod. 20:5), necessarily implies that one should bow down unto the One God and serve Him; and any service accompanied by bowing down can mean nothing but prayer. The same idea is expressed in other Scriptural verses, for example, Deut. 11:16 and Exod. 23:24–25.

Some of "our coreligionists" (*baʿḍu asḥābinā*) infer the duty of praying from Deut. 12:5, *even unto His habitation shall ye seek* (*tidreshū*), by taking the verb *dārash* to mean "to pray," as in Ps. 34:5, *I sought* (*dārashtī*) *the Lord*—that is, I prayed to Him—*and He answered me,* and in 2 Chron. 15:13, *whosoever would not seek* (*yidrōsh*) *the Lord . . . should be put to death,* that is, whosoever fails to pray is guilty of a mortal sin. Similar proof-verses are found also in the Prophets, for example, in Jer. 29:12, *And ye shall call upon Me, and go and pray unto Me, and I will hearken unto you.*

Some say that men used to pray from the time of Adam to that of Enosh, when, according to Gen. 4:26, *men ceased*[11] *to call upon the name of the Lord,* meaning to pray to Him. In any case, the Patriarchs certainly used to pray, for we find it said of Abraham (Gen. 12:8), Isaac (Gen. 26:25), and Jacob (Gen. 33:20) that each one of them erected an altar and *called upon the name of the Lord,* that is, prayed to Him. Moreover it may be inferred from Gen. 19:27 that Abraham prayed in the morning, from Gen. 24:63 that Isaac prayed in the afternoon, and from Gen. 28:11 that Jacob prayed in the evening, showing that the Patriarchs observed three prayers daily.

The Writings also provide proof, in the story of Daniel, of the sublimity of the duty to pray, since Daniel, by refusing to pray to anyone but the One God (Dan. 6), exposed himself to mortal danger, which shows that prayer is one of those cardinal duties that man is obligated to uphold even at the cost of his own life.

CHAPTER XVI

Number and times of prayer.[12]

Many in Israel (*kathīr min al-ummah*) are agreed on the necessity of two daily prayers, in the morning and in the evening, corresponding to the two daily sacrifices prescribed in Exod. 29:39. The generality of the sectarians (*jumhūr al-jamā'ah*)[13] and the Rabbinites, however, require three daily prayers, the two just mentioned, and a third they call *Minḥāh,* which should properly be called midday prayer, although they defer it until late afternoon, perhaps because most people cannot spare the time for it at noon. Indeed a certain Rabbinite[14] has acknowledged in a work of his (*fī kitābin lahu*) that the *Minḥāh* is the midday prayer, and has stated that during the period of the kingdom only the two, morning and evening, prayers were observed, and that it was only after the destruction of the First Temple that the prophets introduced the midday prayer which is the *Minḥāh.* Benjamin al-Nahawandi,[15] too, subscribed to this view.

His own view, al-Qirqisānī continues, is that three prayers are required, in accordance with Dan. 6:11, *and he kneeled upon his knees three times a day and prayed,* from which it is evident not only that Daniel customarily prayed thrice daily, but also that the duty to pray at midday is even more stringent than the duty to pray in the morning and in the evening, since Daniel could observe the latter two orisons in the safe privacy of his own home, whereas at midday, when he was in attendance upon the king at the royal palace, he had to pray in full view of everyone present and in open defiance of the king's edict. A much earlier proof-verse is David's statement in Ps. 55:18, *Evening, and morning, and at noonday, will I complain and moan,* that is, will I pray. To be sure, one of the opponents of the midday prayer has objected that in Ps. 119:62 we are told that David prayed at midnight—are we to assume then that this adds a fourth daily prayer? The answer is that in the former verse from Daniel the noonday prayer is associated with the two prayers which are assuredly obligatory, whereas in the latter verse the midnight prayer is mentioned alone, and must therefore have been purely supererogatory (*nāfilah*).

The proper times for the three prayers are as follows: morning prayer, between daybreak and sunrise; evening prayer, between sunset and full darkness, which is the time of the day called "twilight" in Scripture; and noonday prayer, properly due at midday, when shepherds take their siesta (*yaqīlu*) and people generally take their noontime nap, but permissible at any time between the beginning of the second quarter of the day and the end of third quarter.[16] To these, on Sabbaths, holy days, and New Moons, the supplementary prayer, *Mūsaf,* should be added.

CHAPTER XVII

The content of prayer.[17]

All Israel except for the Rabbinites agree that prayer should consist exclusively of the recital of the Psalms of David and similar Scriptural prayers. In fact even the Rabbinites admit this, for they begin their prayers with the blessing "Who hath chosen His servant David, and was pleased to accept his sacred poesy."[18] Moreover they open the Eighteen Benedictions with the verse (Ps. 51:17) *O Lord, open Thou my lips,* and conclude the same with the verse (Ps. 19:15) *Let the words of my mouth . . . be acceptable before Thee,* the pronoun in both cases obviously referring to David, and not to any other author. Yet so great is their hatred and contempt for those who disagree with them in this respect that they are said to have thought at one time of abolishing the Psalter by consigning all copies of it that they could lay their hands on to the flames.[19]

A certain champion of the Rabbinites[20] cited some Scriptural verses in support of their view. For example, Ezra 6:10 speaks of Israelites praying for the prosperity of King Darius and his sons—surely no Psalm refers to that Persian king. 1 Kings 8:38 speaks of *what prayer and supplication soever be made by any man,* clearly implying that prayers may in the future be composed by other persons than David. Ps. 68:27 exhorts us *Bless ye God in full assemblies . . . from the fountain of Israel,* this fountain being nothing else than those of the Sages of Israel who had composed hymns in praise and glory of the Lord, such as Yannai, Eleazar [ha-Qalir], and Phinehas.[21]

These arguments, however, are but stratagems (*iḥtiyāl*), the product of Rabbinite blindness of heart (*'amā al-qalb*) and corruption. Surely it should be crystal clear to every sensible person that the limitation of prayer to the Psalter applies only to the statutory formal orisons, and not to supererogatory or occasional prayers. Indeed these arguments work both ways: true, there is no prayer for the prosperity of King Darius in the Psalter, but neither is there one in the Eighteen Benedictions or in any other of the Rabbinite liturgical compositions. And if everyone may pray in his own way, why insist on the Eighteen Benedictions, or why demand that prayer be in the Hebrew language and in no other, seeing that so many in Israel know little Hebrew or none? As for *the fountain of Israel* signifying the Sages, that is quite true, but the Sages referred to are those who had received and transmitted the rules of prayer from the prophets, not those who made up prayers of their own.

CHAPTER XVIII

The direction of prayer (*qiblah*).[22]

All Israel agree that when praying one should face in the direction of Jerusalem. The only exception is Mīshawayh al-'Ukbarī,[23] who is reported to have held that one should always face westward, regardless of where one may be, so that a person praying in Egypt would stand with his back to the Holy City. As for the Samaritans, who turn towards Shechem—some say, Mount Gerizim—they need not be considered here, since they do not venerate Jerusalem nor recognize the prophets.

A number of Scriptural verses support the direction in prayer toward Jerusalem, particularly Dan. 6:11, where we are told that the windows of Daniel's praying chamber were open toward Jerusalem, clearly implying that he used to gaze out of them as he prayed.

In support of the westward direction, Mīshawayh cited Num. 3:38, *And those that were to pitch before the Tabernacle eastward, before the Tent of Meeting, towards the sunrising,* from which he concluded that the entrance to the Tent of Meeting and the courtyard faced eastward, and that the Holy of Holies was situated westward of it. Since the Temple was built on the same plan, the same applied to it also. Hence it follows that the congregation in prayer faced westward. This view is refuted, however, by numerous Scriptural passages showing that once the Temple in Jerusalem was built, prayer was addressed in the direction of it, that is, toward the Holy City, the point of the compass varying with the locality where a person happened to be.

CHAPTER XIX

Refutation of those who think that prayer may be offered only in a certain appointed place.

Anan asserted that a person should set aside a special place for prayer, and should keep it ritually clean and holy, out of bounds for unclean persons and those not of the Ananite persuasion,[24] including women, even when they are not unclean.

His followers refer for proof to the verse (1 Chron. 16:29) *Worship the Lord in the beauty of holiness,* which signifies, according to them, in a special place beautiful by reason of holiness. They point out further that their Karaite opponents agree that an unclean person may not pray until he has become clean again, and this is only another way of saying that prayer may take place only where there are no unclean persons. Their opponents also agree that the supplicant may not have his footwear on while praying, and the only support for this rule is the fact that no footwear was worn by those who entered the

Sanctuary in Jerusalem. The logical conclusion, therefore, is that prayer is allowed only in a place that is kept as holy as was the Sanctuary. Moreover we are repeatedly told of the Patriarchs that they had built special altars not for sacrifice but for prayer, for example, *And he builded an altar there, and called upon the name of the Lord* (Gen. 26:25), that is, obviously, prayed to Him. When altars were built for sacrifices, Scripture says so expressly, as in Gen. 8:20, referring to the altar built by Noah and mentioning the burnt offerings brought by him on it. And finally, prayer is repeatedly called "sacrifice" or "incense" in Scripture (for example, Ps. 51:19, 141:2)—just as sacrifices may not be offered except in an appointed place kept clean and holy, so should prayer be offered only in a clean and holy place set aside for it. As for the exclusion of even clean women, it follows from 2 Chron. 8:11, *No wife of mine shall dwell in the house of David . . . because the places are holy whereunto the Ark of the Lord hath come.*

These arguments, in al-Qirqisānī's judgment, are not cogent. As for the phrase *in the beauty of holiness,* it cannot mean anything other than "in the Holy City," and it cannot imply that prayer may not be offered anywhere else, which would be obviously absurd. Nor does it follow that man is authorized to sanctify a place for prayer in the same manner as God had sanctified Jerusalem, for if this were so, man would be equally authorized to sanctify holy days or sacrifices not authorized by Scripture—if man is not free to sanctify time, neither is he free to sanctify place. As for the prohibition of prayer by unclean persons, it is, while devoid of Scriptural proof, based on the consensus of all Israel; and this does not mean that anything else, equally devoid of Scriptural proof, must be true, even when it is not supported by popular consensus. The same applies to the matter of footwear. As for the exclusion of women even when they are clean, the verse quoted specifies the reason for it, namely the presence of the Ark of the Covenant, hence it does not apply to any other occasions. Moreover, excluding women at all times is the same as exempting them from prayer altogether, which is patently contrary to many Scriptural accounts. What the verse means is that women were forbidden to abide permanently in the house of David by reason of their being subject to periodic uncleanness.[25] As for altars built for prayer only, that is indeed so, but all it signifies is that just as an altar might be built for prayer, so may a synagogue (*kanīsah*) be erected so that people could assemble therein for the recitation of Scriptural lessons and for public prayers, and this has nothing to do with holiness and the exclusion of unclean persons.

In short, "Anan—may Allah be pleased with him—was indeed a leader, an exemplar, and a principal (*imām wa-qudwah wa-muqaddam*) in religious and secular learning, but he was not a prophet. Rather, though he was a man skilled in speculation and research (*naẓẓāran baḥḥāthan*), he was not immune from mistake and error, and this fact is evident from a number of places in his utterances."[26] No man may sanctify a place, or a day, or a sacrifice not sanctified by God himself, and while prayer is analogous in *some* respects to sacrifice—in that it may not be offered by an unclean person and must be preceded by ablution of hands and feet and by the removal of footwear—it is not analogous to it in *all* respects. Hence prayer may be offered in any clean place.

CHAPTER XX

Definition of prayer, its conditions, and what should be done in the matter of it.[27]

1. We do not find in Holy Writ any exact definition of prayer, nor are we told the particular Psalms that should be recited as prayer at particular times and on particular days—we can only arrive at this knowledge by deduction of what seems to us to suit the particular occasion or time. The same is true of the conditions of prayer and of what should be done in the matter of it—we arrive at the knowledge thereof by way of sufficient (*muqni'ah*) arguments immune from refutation, and not by way of decisive (*qāṭi'ah*) proofs.

Now we find in the sacred record that prayer stands upon three things: thanksgiving (*hōdā'āh*), prayer proper (*tefillāh*), and supplication (*teḥinnāh*), this being evident from Solomon's prayer *When Thy people Israel . . . turn again to Thee, and give thanks unto Thy name, and pray and supplicate unto Thee* (1 Kings 8:33).

Give thanks[28] refers to thanksgiving, and goes back to the Psalm *O give thanks unto the Lord, for He is good, for His mercy endureth for ever. O give thanks unto the God of gods,* etc. (Ps. 136: 1-2), as well as to other Psalms, as we shall mention later on.

2. *And pray* refers to prayer, and goes back to the Psalm *A prayer of the afflicted, when he fainteth* (Ps. 102:1), and we shall later explain the interpretation thereof, showing that it is the Psalm of the

people of the exile and refers to them.

And supplicate refers to supplication, and goes back to the Psalm *Accept my supplication, O God, according to Thy mercy* (Ps. 51:3). We shall explain its interpretation later on, in a way that will confirm what we have just said about it.

This should be followed by the lesson of the sacrifice, and this in turn should be followed by the Psalm treating of the particular season, that is, the Psalm called by Anan and his followers "Song" (*shīr*), meaning the Song of the particular season or day. After this should come the Psalm *Who can express the mighty acts of the Lord?* (Ps. 106:2), which likewise speaks of thanksgiving,[29] and thanksgiving is necessary at the conclusion of prayer, as it is at the commencement thereof, as it is said in Daniel (6:11) *and he kneeled upon his knees three times a day, and prayed, and gave thanks,* thanksgiving thus following prayer.

These five Psalms are, in our judgment, the mainstay and basis of prayer, upon which one should lean.

3. After Psalm 136 and before Psalm 102 one should, in my opinion, recite the Psalm *Praise, of David. I will extol Thee, O my God, the King* (Ps. 145:1), since it goes on to say *Every day will I bless Thee, and I will praise Thy name for ever and ever* (Ps. 145:2). This is confirmed by, *and to stand every morning to give thanks and praise the Lord, and likewise at even* (1 Chron. 23:30), where *to give thanks* refers to *O give thanks unto the Lord* (Ps. 136:1), and *praise* refers to *Praise, of David,* which is followed by *and I will praise Thy name.* Likewise, as the Song dealing with the particular season, one should recite two Psalms, as I will explain later on.

Thus what one should lean upon, according to my order of prayer, in the morning and in the evening, is seven Psalms, in accordance with *Seven times a day do I praise Thee because of Thy righteous ordinances* (Ps. 119:164). As for other Psalms in the Psalter, it should not be hidden from anyone which ones of them are suitable to be added, for this may be learned from the liturgies instituted by Anan and others.

4. Let us now return to the explanation of what we have said above about thanksgiving (Ps. 136). There is an analogous Psalm that should serve as the commencement of prayer, namely the one cited in 1 Chron. 16:8, *O give thanks unto the Lord, call upon His name.* This is evident in several ways: Firstly, from the preceding verse *Then . . . did David place at the head in giving thanks unto the Lord,* which is

followed by *O give thanks unto the Lord, call upon His name,* thus stating that David had made this prayer the commencement of his praising and extolling; secondly, because it contains praise as well as thanksgiving, since it ends with *And all the people said: Amen, and praised the Lord* (1 Chron. 16:36), and it mentions also song (verses 9 and 23) and singing for joy (verse 33). Now Scripture states that thanksgiving in prayer must be accompanied by praise, as it is said *and to stand every morning to thank and praise the Lord* (1 Chron. 23:30), and it also mentions singing for joy in both morning and evening prayers, as it is said, *So that they that dwell in the uttermost parts stand in awe of Thy signs; Thou makest the outgoings of the morning and evening to sing for joy* (Ps. 65:9). These verses serve as additional proofs of the duty of praying.

5. Thanksgiving and praise should be offered while standing upright upon one's feet,[30] as is evident from the aforequoted verse *and to stand every morning to thank and praise the Lord* (1 Chron. 23:30), where *stand* implies standing upon one's feet.

We have already mentioned that after *O give thanks* (Ps. 136:1) and *Praise, of David* (Ps. 145:1) there should follow *A prayer of the afflicted* (Ps. 102:1), which is the prayer proper, and this should be offered while one kneels upon his knees[31] and raises his hands upwards.[32] This kneeling and hand-raising at the prayer proper is supported by Scriptural tradition, for example, by what is stated concerning Solomon's prayer that *he kneeled down upon his knees before all the congregation of Israel, and spread forth his hands toward heaven* (2 Chron. 6:13); and of the conclusion of his prayer we are told that *when Solomon had made an end of praying all this prayer and supplication unto the Lord, he arose from before the altar of the Lord, from kneeling on his knees with his hands spread forth toward heaven* (1 Kings 8:54). We are likewise told in the Book of Nehemiah[33] that *I fell upon my knees, and spread forth my hands unto the Lord my God* (Ezra 9:5). Indeed God himself, in reproving the people of Israel, says *And when ye spread forth your hands, I will hide Mine eyes from you* (Isa. 1:15), followed immediately in the same verse by *Yea, when ye multiply prayer, I will not hear.* We read also of Daniel that *he kneeled upon his knees* (Dan. 6:11), and of Solomon that he said *and shall spread forth his hands toward this House* (2 Chron. 6:29). And we read further *Lift up your hands to the Sanctuary* (Ps. 134:2), *I have spread forth my hands unto Thee* (Ps. 88:10), *When I lift up my hands toward Thy holy Sanctuary* (Ps. 28:2), *Let us lift up our heart with our hands unto God in the heavens* (Lam. 3:41), and *If thou set thy heart aright, and spread forth thy hands toward Him* (Job 11:13).

6. Raising one's hands toward heaven should be accompanied by raising also one's eyes heavenward, as it is said *Mine eyes fail with looking upward* (Isa. 38:14), and *O my God, I am ashamed and blush to lift up my face to Thee, my God* (Ezra 9:6).

Prayer should be recited in a voice that is audible,[34] as it is said *what time I cry in the night before Thee* (Ps. 88:2), followed in the next verse by *Let my prayer come before Thee,* and again, *I will lift up my voice unto God and cry* (Ps. 77:2). And in a number of passages we are told that *Moses cried unto the Lord, saying* (Exod. 17:4, etc.). So also of David we read *Maschil of David, when he was in the cave, a prayer. With my voice I cry unto the Lord, with my voice I supplicate unto the Lord* (Ps. 142:1-2).

This controverts the opinion of the Rabbinites that prayer should be inaudible,[35] which they base on the story of Hannah, of whom we are told that *her voice could not be heard* (1 Sam. 1:13). This opinion of theirs [is mistaken],[36] seeing that her silence was deemed unseemly, wherefore the priest thought that she was intoxicated, as it is said in the same verse *therefore Eli thought she had been drunken,* for which he upbraided her. The true reason for her acting thus was her bitterness, as it is said *and she was in bitterness of soul* (1 Sam. 1:10), and it is the wont of one who is laden with heaviness and bitterness to be unable to raise his voice.

7. The proof that *A prayer of the afflicted* (Ps. 102:1) is the prayer of the people of the exile lies in the fact that "the afflicted" is the term used for Israel, as it is said *And I will leave in the midst of thee an afflicted and poor people* (Zeph. 3:12), and *For Thou dost save the afflicted people* (Ps. 18:28).

When he fainteth (Ps. 102:1) is explained by the references to the Children of Israel as they were led into exile, namely, *when they faint as the wounded in the broad places of the city* (Lam. 2:12), and *that faint for hunger* (Lam. 2:19).

And poureth out his complaint (Ps. 102:1) is analogous[37] to Hannah's saying *I poured out my soul before the Lord* (1 Sam. 1:15), meaning I prayed.

For my days are consumed like smoke (Ps. 102:4) is analogous to *How long wilt Thou fume against the prayer of Thy people?* (Ps. 80:5).

And my bones are burned as a hearth (Ps. 102:4) is analogous to *the fire hath devoured both the ends of it, and the midst of it is singed* (Ezek. 15:4).

My heart is smitten like grass, and withered (Ps. 102:5) is analogous to *Ephraim is smitten, their root is dried up* (Hos. 9:16).

For I forget to eat my bread (Ps. 102:5) is analogous to *The young children ask bread* (Lam. 4:4).

By reason of the voice of my sighing (Ps. 102:6) has the same meaning as *Her priests sigh* (Lam. 1:4), *She herself also sigheth, and turneth backward* (Lam. 1:8), and *They have heard that I sigh* (Lam. 1:21).

My bones cleave to my flesh (Ps. 102:6) is analogous to *Their skin is shriveled upon their bones* (Lam. 4:8).

I am like a pelican of the wilderness, I am become as an owl of the waste places (Ps. 102:7) has the same meaning as *As for Ephraim, their glory shall fly away like a bird* (Hos. 9:11).

Like a sparrow that is alone upon the housetop (Ps. 102:8) is analogous to *How doth the city sit solitary* (Lam. 1:1), and *And Ephraim is become like a silly dove* (Hos. 7:11).

Mine enemies taunt me all the day (Ps. 102:9) has the same meaning as *We are become a taunt to our neighbors* (Ps. 79:4).

They that praised me[38] *do curse by me* (Ps. 102:9) is obviously analogous to the commonly used oath[39] "If what I say is not so, may I become a Jew!" and also to *I called for my lovers, but they deceived me* (Lam. 1:19).

For I have eaten ashes like bread (Ps. 102:10) has the same meaning as *O daughter of my people, gird thee with sackcloth, and wallow thyself in ashes* (Jer. 6:26).

And mingled my drink with weeping (Ps. 102:10) is analogous to *Thou hast fed them with the bread of tears, and given them tears to drink in large measure* (Ps. 80:6), and *My tears have been my food day and night* (Ps. 42:4).

Because of Thine indignation and Thy wrath (Ps. 102:11) is analogous to *And hath rejected in the indignation of His anger* (Lam. 2:6).

For Thou hast taken me up, and cast me away (Ps. 102:11) is analogous to *and the Lord rooted them out of their land . . . and cast them into another land* (Deut. 29:27).

My days are like a lengthening shadow (Ps. 102:12) is analogous to *our days on the earth are as a shadow, and there is no abiding* (1 Chron. 29:15).

And I am withered like grass (Ps. 102:12) is analogous to *How long shall the land mourn, and the herbs of the whole field wither?* (Jer. 12:4).

The Psalmist then proceeds to speak of deliverance, by saying *Thou wilt arise, and have compassion upon Zion* (Ps. 102:14), and further *This shall be written for the generation to come* (Ps. 102:19), meaning that these prayers shall be written down so that the people of the exile shall recite them, as it is said in the same verse *and a people which shall be created shall praise the Lord,* that is, shall extol Him with this prayer.

So much for the meaning of the prayer called *A prayer of the afflicted,* the which is clear and evident.

8. As for the prayer which follows *A prayer of the afflicted* (Ps. 102:1), that is, *Accept my supplication, O God, according to Thy mercy* (Ps. 51:3), some of our coreligionists think that it should be likewise recited while kneeling on one's knees, in the same manner as *A prayer of the afflicted* is recited kneeling, while others think that it should be recited while bowing down.[40] This prayer, too, refers to some of the things mentioned in *A prayer of the afflicted,* such as the exile and the cessation of sacrifices, as it says *For Thou delightest not in sacrifice, else would I give it* (Ps. 51:18), and indeed expressly mentions prayer unaccompanied by sacrifice, as it says *The sacrifices to God are a broken spirit* (Ps. 51:19); and follows this with the mention of the return, of the building of the future Temple, and of the sacrifices that will be offered in it, as it says *Do good in Thy favor unto Zion . . . Then wilt Thou delight in the sacrifices of righteousness, in burnt offering and whole offering* (Ps. 51:20–21).

As for the preceding verse, *Restore unto me the joy of Thy salvation* (Ps. 51:14), it refers to the holy spirit which shall be infused into the people of Israel, as it is said *I will pour out My spirit upon all flesh* (Joel 3:1), and the same is implied in *And take not Thy holy spirit from me* (Ps. 51:13).

So also the clean heart which God shall renew in the righteous ones, mentioned in *Create me a clean heart, O God* (Ps. 51:12), has the same meaning as *A new heart also will I give you* (Ezek. 36:26).

Against Thee, Thee only, have I sinned (Ps. 51:6) is analogous to *And in that day thou shalt say, I will give thanks unto Thee, O Lord, that Thou wast angry with me* (Isa. 12:1).

And blot out all mine iniquities (Ps. 51:11) has the same meaning as *I have blotted out, as a thick cloud, thy transgressions* (Isa. 44:22).

So much for this prayer, which is *Accept my supplication, O God.*

9. These two prayers are the ones of which it is said *and pray and supplicate* (1 Kings 8:33), and again *then hear Thou in heaven their prayer and their supplication* (1 Kings 8:45).

After the Psalm beginning *Accept my supplication* (Ps. 51:3) and ending *Then will they offer bullocks upon Thine altar* (Ps. 51:21) one should recite the lesson of the sacrifice, as it is said *So will we render for bullocks the offering of our lips* (Hos. 14:3).

This should be followed by the prayer of the season, which is called by Anan "Song." We shall presently specify the prayer of each season, as it appears to us.

After this should come the thanksgiving, as we have stated before, which is the Psalm *O give thanks unto the Lord, for He is good . . . Who can express the mighty acts of the Lord!* (Ps. 106:1–2), since it contains the promise given to us that we shall admit our sins and the sins of our fathers, as it says *We have sinned with our fathers* (Ps. 106:6); this has the same meaning as *And they shall confess their iniquity, and the iniquity of their fathers* (Lev. 26:40).

As for the lessons of the sacrifices accompanying prayer, they are well known, having been set forth by Anan and others.[41]

10. As for the seasonal prayers, called by Anan "Song," he appointed a separate Song for morning and evening of each day of the week, and most of our coreligionists have followed him in this matter. We, however, are not of this opinion. In our view, there should be one seasonal prayer for the morning, and another for the evening, of all the days of the week.

As for the morning, the likeliest Psalm is *A prayer of Moses the man of God* (Ps. 90:1), for several reasons. Firstly, because it is the prayer of the man who had brought to us the commandments of the Lord of the two worlds,[42] and provided us with our faith. Therefore our prayer is his prayer.

Secondly, because this prayer refers to several matters contained in *A prayer of the afflicted* (Ps. 106:1), such as the exile, the return caused by repentance, and the reward. As for the exile and the wrath, it says *For we are consumed in Thine anger . . . Thou hast set our iniquities before Thee . . . For all our days are passed away in Thy wrath* (Ps. 90:7–9). As for the repentance and the forgiveness, it says *Return, O Lord, how long? And let it repent Thee concerning*

Thy servants. O satisfy us in the morning with Thy mercy . . . Make us glad according to the days wherein Thou hast afflicted us (Ps. 90: 13–15). And as for the reward, it says *And let the graciousness of the Lord our God be upon us* (Ps. 90:17).

Thirdly, this prayer mentions morning twice,[43] and we have already stated that a prayer should be appointed according to the suitability of its content.

11. As for the evening prayer, it is, in our opinion, *A Psalm of David. Lord, I have called Thee; hasten unto me* (Ps. 141:1), since it says *Let my prayer be set forth as incense before Thee, the lifting up of my hands as the evening sacrifice* (Ps. 141:2).

As for the midday prayer, we commence it with the thanksgiving of *O give thanks unto the Lord, for He is good* (Ps. 136:1), and follow it with *A prayer of the afflicted* (Ps. 102:1), as explained before, but we do not recite the Psalm *Accept my supplication, O God, according to Thy mercy* (Ps. 51:3), because it mentions sacrifice, and there is no sacrifice prescribed for noontime. For this Psalm we therefore substitute the supplication of *A prayer of David. Incline Thine ear, O Lord, and answer me* (Ps. 86:1), because it says *Accept my supplication, O Lord, for unto Thee do I cry all the day* (Ps. 86:3), and because it too treats of the sublime matters of imploring forgiveness, seeking mercy, and the like.

After this comes the seasonal prayer, namely *For the leader, with string music, Maschil of David. Give ear, O Lord, to my prayer* (Ps. 55:1–2), because it says *Evening, and morning, and at noonday, will I complain and moan* (Ps. 55:18), for complaint signifies prayer, as in the aforequoted verse, *and poureth out his complaint before the Lord* (Ps. 102:1).—This Psalm should be recited also in the other two, that is, the morning and the evening prayers, after the two seasonal Songs, which are *A prayer of Moses* (Ps. 90:1) and *A Psalm of David. Lord, I have called Thee; hasten unto me* (Ps. 141:1), since it mentions praying at all the three seasons of the day.—This is followed by *Who can express the mighty acts of the Lord?* (Ps. 106:2).

So much for the prayers of the three daily seasons, which are evening, morning, and noon.

12. As for the supplementary prayer (*Mūsaf*) of the Sabbath, it is evident that it too is one of the Mosaic prayers, namely *A Psalm, a Song, for the Sabbath day* (Ps. 92:1).[44]

As for the prayer of the New Moon, it is likewise clear that it is

Sing for joy unto God our strength (Ps. 81:2), since it says *Blow the horn of the New Moon* (Ps. 81:4); and also *Bless the Lord, O my soul. O Lord my God, Thou art very great* (Ps. 104:1), since it says *Who appointedst the moon for seasons* (Ps. 104:19).

For the Song of the New Moon, as well as for the rest of the holy days except the Feast of Weeks, Anan appointed *Maschil of Asaph. Why, O God, hast Thou cast us off for ever?* (Ps. 74:1), since it says *Thine adversaries have roared in the midst of Thy holy seasons*[45] (Ps. 74:4), and also *They have burned up all the holy seasons of God in the land* (Ps. 74:8). It says also *They have set up their own signs for signs* (Ps. 74:4), meaning that they have abolished the holy seasons which Thou hast required and hast caused the moon to serve as a sign thereof, as it is said *and let them be for signs, and for seasons* (Gen. 1:14), and have set up their own signs for them. As I live, this Psalm is indeed appropriate as prayer for the holy days save the Feast of Weeks, inasmuch as the latter is determined not by the moon, which serves as sign and mark for the other seasons, but by calculation.

13. As for those other than Anan[46] (*ghayru 'Ānān*), they appointed a different prayer—that is, a different Psalm—for each day of the holy days.

For the first day of Passover they appointed *O give thanks unto the Lord, call upon His name* (Ps. 105:1)—the same phrase occurs in Scripture also outside of the Psalter[47]—to be recited in the evening together with the Passover sacrifice. For the second day they appointed *For the leader, for Jeduthun, a Psalm of Asaph. I will lift up my voice unto God, and cry* (Ps. 77:1–2), since it contains the story of the exodus from Egypt, for it says *Thou hast with Thine arm redeemed Thy people . . . The waters saw Thee, O God, the waters saw Thee, they were in pain* (Ps. 77:16–17), referring to the dividing of the sea, and also *Thou didst lead Thy people like a flock* (Ps. 77:21).

For the third day they appointed *Maschil of Asaph. Give ear, O my people, to my teaching* (Ps. 78:1), which treats of the same, namely in the verse *Marvelous things did He in the sight of their fathers in the land of Egypt, in the field of Zoan* (Ps. 78:12), followed by *How He set His signs in Egypt* (Ps. 78:43), and so forth, to *And He led them safely, and they feared not, but the sea overwhelmed their enemies* (Ps. 78:53). For the fourth day they appointed *Give ear, O Shepherd of Israel* (Ps. 80:2), since it says *Thou didst pluck up a vine out of Egypt* (Ps. 80:9).

For the fifth day they appointed *When Israel came forth out of Egypt* (Ps. 114:1); for the sixth day, *Hallelujah. Praise ye the name of the Lord, give praise, O ye servants of the Lord, ye that stand in the House of the Lord* (Ps. 135:1–2), since it says *Who smote the first-born of Egypt . . . He sent signs and wonders into the midst of thee, O Egypt* (Ps. 135:8–9); and for the seventh day, *Then sang Moses and the Children of Israel this Song* (Exod. 15:1).

14. For the day of the Waving of the Sheaf[48] they appointed *God, accept our supplication, and bless us* (Ps. 67:2), since it says *The earth hath yielded her increase* (Ps. 67:7), referring to the commencement of the gathering of the crop.

For the day of the Feast of Weeks they appointed *Lord, Thou hast been favorable unto Thy land* (Ps. 85:2), since it says *Yea, the Lord will give that which is good, and our land shall yield her produce* (Ps. 85:13), referring to the commencement of the gathering of wheat.

For the second supplementary prayer[49] they appointed *Let God arise, let His enemies be scattered* (Ps. 68:2), since it says *O God, when Thou wentest forth before Thy people . . . the earth trembled* (Ps. 68:8–9), which refers to the giving of the Torah; and also *For the leader, Al-tashheth, a Psalm of Asaph, a Song. We give thanks unto Thee, O God, we give thanks, and Thy name is near* (Ps. 75: 1–2), since it says *When I take the appointed time* (Ps. 75:3).

For the day of the Memorial of Shouting[50] they appointed *O clap your hands, all ye peoples* (Ps. 47:2), since it says *God is gone up amidst shouting* (Ps. 47:6); and also *O come, let us sing for joy unto the Lord, let us shout for the Rock of our salvation* (Ps. 95:1); and also *A Psalm. O sing unto the Lord a new Song, for He hath done marvelous things* (Ps. 98:1), since it says *With trumpets and sound of the horn shout ye before the King, the Lord* (Ps. 98:6); and this is followed by *The Lord reigneth, let the peoples tremble* (Ps. 99.1) and *A Psalm of thanksgiving. Shout unto the Lord, all the earth* (Ps. 100:1).

15. For the day of the Sin Offering of Atonement[51] they appointed *The heavens declare the glory of God* (Ps. 19:2), *Of David, Maschil. Happy is he whose transgression is forgiven* (Ps. 32:1), *A Psalm of David, to make memorial. O Lord, rebuke me not in Thine anger* (Ps. 38:1–2), *For the leader, for Jeduthun, a Psalm of David. I said, I will take heed to my ways* (Ps. 39:1–2), *I waited patiently for the Lord* (Ps. 40:2), *O God, the heathen are come into Thine inheritance* (Ps. 79:1), *Of David. Bless the Lord, O my soul, and all that is within me*

(Ps. 103:1), *Bless the Lord, O my soul. O Lord my God, Thou art very great* (Ps. 104:1)—both these last two Psalms being included, because each one of them contains an admission of sins and iniquities, intentional and unintentional; also *Hallelujah. Praise God in His Sanctuary* (Ps. 150:1), since it says *with the shout of the horn* (Ps. 150:3), as it is said *in the Day of Atonement shall ye make proclamation with the horn throughout all your land* (Lev. 25:9).

For the second supplementary prayer[52] they appointed *Save me, O God, for the waters are come in even unto the soul* (Ps. 69:2), *As the hart panteth after the water brooks* (Ps. 42:2), *A Psalm of David, when he was in the wilderness of Judah* (Ps. 63:1), and *O God of my praise, keep not silence* (Ps. 109:1), since all these Psalms speak of fasting and thirst.

16. For the first day of the Feast of Tabernacles they appointed *The Lord is my light and my salvation—whom shall I fear?* (Ps. 27:1), since it says *For he concealeth me in His tabernacle* (Ps. 27:5). For the second day, *In Thee, O Lord, have I taken refuge, let me never be ashamed* (Ps. 31:2), since it says *Thou concealest them in a tabernacle from the strife of tongues* (Ps. 31:21). For the third day, *In Judah is God known* (Ps. 76:2), since it says *In Salem also is set His tabernacle* (Ps. 76:3).

For the fourth day, *O thou that dwellest in the covert of the Most High, and abidest in the shadow of the Almighty* (Ps. 91:1), since it says *He will cover*[53] *thee with His pinions, and under His wings shalt thou take refuge* (Ps. 91:4). For the fifth day, *Give ear to my words, O Lord, consider my meditation* (Ps. 5:2), since it says *And Thou shalt shelter*[54] *them* (Ps. 5:12). For the sixth day, *Deliver me, O Lord, from the evil man, preserve me from the violent man* (Ps. 140:2), since it says *Who hast screened*[55] *my head in the day of battle* (Ps. 140:8). For the seventh day, *For the leader, of David the servant of the Lord, who spoke unto the Lord the words of this song . . . and said, I love Thee, O Lord, my strength* (Ps. 18:1–2), since it says *He made darkness His hiding place, His tabernacle round about Him* (Ps. 18:12). We have already stated that the subject matter of all these Psalms is suitable for the occasion of each day.

For the Eighth Day of Assembly[56] they appointed *Out of my straits I called upon the Lord* (Ps. 118:5), since it says *Order the festival procession with boughs*[57] (Ps. 118:27).

All the aforementioned Psalms are to be recited following the Psalm *Why, O God, hast Thou cast us off for ever?* (Ps. 74:1), except on the Feast of Weeks, when this latter Psalm is not to be recited.

17. As for the manner of commencing and concluding prayer, it involves no uncertainty, since it is uniform among all our coreligionists, and therefore needs no discussion on our part.[58]

As for the conditions of prayer, they are as follows: man should come forth before the Creator with his heart free of sin and his thought free of evil and disobedience, for prayer offered otherwise is not acceptable, as it is said *If I had regarded iniquity in my heart, the Lord would not hear* (Ps. 66:18), meaning that when the heart harbors deception—which is implied by *iniquity*—prayer is not accepted. This is followed by *But verily God hath heard* (Ps. 66:19), meaning that when there is verity and truth, God hears it and receives the prayer. And it is said also *If thou set thy heart aright, and stretch out thy hands toward Him* (Job 11:13), that is, the stretching out of the hands, which is prayer, should be preceded by the preparation and the settlement of the heart. This is followed by *If iniquity be in thy hand, put it far away* (Job 11:14), which is analogous to *If I had regarded iniquity in my heart,* that is, the removal of deceit from the heart should be accompanied by its removal from the hand and the whole body, for prayer requires cleanness of both body and heart from injustice and disobedience, as it is said *Although there is no violence in my hand, and my prayer is pure* (Job 16:17). Such inner cleanness should be accompanied also by outer cleanness,[59] that is, by the cleansing of the body from physical uncleannesses and impurities, for prayer is held to be analogous to incense, as David says *Let my prayer be set forth as incense before Thee* (Ps. 141:2)—just as incense is holy, so is prayer, and uncleanness may not be mixed with holy things.

18. The least uncleanness is ordure and its like, and Scripture has declared that he who does not cleanse himself therefrom by ablution is not clean, as it is said *There is a generation that are pure in their own hearts, and yet are not washed from their ordure* (Prov. 30:12). This is confirmed by the Creator's command that ordure be kept outside the encampment—that is, the encampment of the people of Israel—in order to prevent any uncleanness from being present within it. And not only must it be kept without the encampment, but it must also be covered, and he who does not observe this rule is liable for an *unseemly thing* (Deut. 23:15), meaning a shameful deed, and is displeasing to the Creator. Thus also Aaron and his sons were commanded,[60] whenever they wished to enter the Tent of Meeting, to wash their hands and feet. This being so, it is incumbent upon him

who wishes to pray to wash his hands and feet after he has cleansed himself of ordure in the most thorough fashion.

It is for the violation of the aforementioned rules that God reproved the Children of Israel and informed them that He will not accept their prayer, by saying *And when ye spread forth your hands, I will hide Mine eyes from you* (Isa. 1:15), and explaining this by the next sentence *Yea, when ye multiply prayer, I will not hear*, the reason for which then follows, namely *your hands are full of blood,* meaning all their disobedient acts. And thereafter it is said *Wash you, make you clean, put away the evil of your doings* (Isa. 1:16), that is, by washing and purifying, both outer and inner. The same is also the implication of our previous citation of *and my prayer is pure* (Job 16:17).

19. Man should come forth to prayer with humility and submission, wearing[61] long shirt and trousers, so as to cover his body, especially his private parts, as is evident from God's command to the priest—since each man acts in prayer as his own priest—to wear four garments, namely, long shirt, trousers, girdle, and *headtires,* as it is said *And for Aaron's sons, thou shalt make long shirts, and thou shalt make for them girdles and headtires . . . And thou shalt make for them linen trousers* (Exod. 28:40–42), the purpose of it being *to cover the flesh of their nakedness* (Exod. 28:42), on account of their entering into the holy place. This being so, he who desires to pray is even more in need of donning trousers. As for the *headtires,* we are told that their purpose was *for splendor and for beauty* (Exod. 28:40), which is something the rest of the people do not have any need for; what they do need is something analogous, namely covering the head with part of the clothing that they are wearing.

20. Praying should be done while standing upon the bare ground, with nothing between the foot and the ground, neither carpet or anything like it, nor footwear, such as boot, or sandal, or the like. This is evidenced by two proofs. First, by God's command[62] to Moses and Joshua to remove their footwear when on holy ground, for it is impossible that, as the Rabbinites claim, the footwear of both these goodly saints and excellent prophets should have happened to have been made out of hides of unclean animals.[63] Rather God commanded them to preserve the sanctity of holy places by removing their footwear, so that any one treading upon them should be bare of foot, which is one of the marks of humility and submission. This is one of the two proofs of the requirement to be barefoot while praying.

The second proof is the Tabernacle, in two ways. Firstly, God commanded Moses to make the several appurtenances of the Tabernacle, and among them there is no mention of a carpet or anything like it; and the same applies to the Temple built by Solomon. Secondly, God commanded the making of several kinds of garments for Aaron and his sons, to cover their bodies from head to foot, yet among them there is no mention of footwear, such as sandal, or boot, or the like. We thus learn that prayer must be recited while standing barefoot upon the ground, with nothing of the aforementioned kind between the foot and the ground.

21. No one can claim that there is anything blameworthy, shameful, or forbidden among the several conditions of prayer mentioned above. Rather even those who do not require them acknowledge that they are good and fitting. Hence he who does observe them is more to be praised than he who does not.

There is here another matter that we must mention, which none of our predecessors has mentioned, as it has been introduced only recently by some people of our time. Since they did introduce it, we are in duty bound to mention it.

CHAPTER XXI

On commencing prayer with the superscriptions of the Psalms.

1. Some of our modern (*al-muḥdithīn*) coreligionists are of the opinion that it makes no sense to commence prayer with the superscriptions of Psalms, and that he who does so does not, in effect, pray, but merely states the fact that someone else had prayed thus and so. Thus, they say, when one commences prayer by reciting *A Psalm of David* (Ps. 3:1, etc.), or *A Psalm of Asaph* (Ps. 50:1, etc.), or *A Prayer of Moses* (Ps. 90:1), he merely states that Moses had prayed thus and so by saying this and that, which does not constitute prayer. Rather, since it is the supplicant himself who is praying, he should commence with the beginning of the prayer proper, without prefacing it by the statement that So-and-so did pray, or praise, or say thus and so.

The Ananites, on the other hand, regard this view as exceedingly disgraceful, and accuse its adherents of dropping the names of the prophets from prayer.

2. We ourselves, in the light of our own judgment, say that the Psalms which constitute prayer fall into two categories. One category is such as lends itself to being ascribed by the supplicant to himself and being adopted by him, for example, such Psalms as contain admission of sins, plea for pardon, forbearance, and forgiveness, request for one's needs, praise of the Creator, and commendation, glorification, and description of His works and His might. In the case of Psalms of this kind, the supplicant may, if he so wishes, commence with the name of the author of the particular Psalm, on the basis of his conviction that "even though these prayers are compositions of So-and-so, yet I admit what he had admitted, and seek what he had sought." Or, if he prefers, he may omit the superscription and commence with the prayer proper, without mentioning the author's name. For it is the prayer proper which is the soul of the recital (*nafs al-qawl*), and not the mention of its author. With this category of Psalms, the supplicant is thus free to exercise his choice.

3. The second category comprises Psalms in which the Psalmist speaks of his own merit, righteousness, beneficent works, and obedience. In such Psalms, it is much preferable to commence with the superscription which assigns the particular Psalm to its author, to the effect that it is he who says this, and that what he says is true with reference to his own self, whereas we recite it merely in order to follow his example, inasmuch as he had used it for his own prayer. And as for what he had said about his own self, that applies to him only, and not to us, since it is he who is worthy of it, whereas we are unworthy.

Therefore, in such Psalms, anyone who omits the name of the author and fails to assign the particular Psalm to him, by commencing with the Psalm proper—which is the soul of the prayer, containing the aforementioned declaration of the author's merit—is in effect ascribing this merit and this obedience to himself, and this cannot be permitted. Consequently those who prohibit commencing prayer with the heading of the Psalm, that is, its superscription, must not, in my judgment, use any of such Psalms for their prayers, but should use only Psalms of the other category.

Here endeth the discussion of prayer and its particulars.

APPENDIX

Schematic table of the
Liturgy according to
al-Qirqisānī.

Daily prayer

Morning and evening

Pss. 136 (or 1. Chron. 16:8 ff.), 145, 102, 51

Lesson (from the Torah) of the (morning or evening) sacrifice

Song of the day: Ps. 90, morning; Ps. 141, evening

Pss. 55, 106

Midday

Pss. 136, 102, 86

Song of the day: Ps. 55

Ps. 106

Sabbath

Supplementary prayer (*Mūsaf*): Ps. 92

New Moon

Pss. 81, 104

Song of the day: Ps. 74 (so Anan)

All Holy Days (except Pentecost)

Song of the day: Ps. 74 (so Anan: to be recited before the Psalms listed below)

Passover

Song of the day: Ps. 105, first day; Ps. 77, second day; Ps. 78, thirdy day; Ps. 80, fourth day; Ps. 114, fifth day; Ps. 135, sixth day; Exod. 15:1–19, seventh day

Waving of the Sheaf

Song of the day: Ps. 67

Pentecost (Feast of Weeks)

Song of the day: Ps. 85

Second supplementary prayer (*Mūsaf*): Pss. 68, 75

New Year's Day

Song of the day: Pss. 47, 95, 98, 99, 100

Day of Atonement

Song of the day: Pss. 19, 32, 38, 39, 40, 79, 103, 104, 150

Second supplementary prayer (*Mūsaf*): Pss. 69, 42, 63, 109

Tabernacles

Song of the day: Ps. 27, first day; Ps. 31, second day; Ps. 76, third day; Ps. 91, fourth day; Ps. 5, fifth day; Ps. 140, sixth day; Ps. 18, seventh day

Eighth Day of Assembly

Song of the day: Ps. 118

NOTES

1 The bibliography on this subject is virtually nonexistent. The Rev. George Margoliouth published the Arabic introduction to the liturgy of the Karaites in Damascus, from a British Museum manuscript dated 1700 (*JQR*, XVIII/1906, 505–527; with English translation); it represents, of course, a late order similar to the official printed liturgy. P. Selvin Goldberg's *Karaite Liturgy and its Relation to Synagogue Worship* (Manchester, 1957) is a handy comparative study of the official Karaite prayer book and the Rabbinite liturgy, but the author was unable to make use of the early Arabic literature of the Karaites and was not aware of al-Qirqisānī's order (cf. my review of the book, *JQR*, L/1959–60, 277–278). For works on the Rabbinite liturgy which touch *en passant* upon the Karaite liturgy, see the "Select bibliography" in Goldberg's book, pp. 127–128.

2 This is the prayer book still used (with the addition of hymns of later composition) by the Karaites of today. Two earlier prayer books are also known, which did not gain universal acceptance among the Karaites. One was compiled by an unknown scholar, the other by Joseph, father of Aaron the Elder. Manuscripts of these two prayer books were still available in the second half of the 15th century. Cf. J. Mann, *Texts and Studies*, II, 705, 1158; L. Nemoy, *Karaite Anthology* (New Haven, 1952), pp. 271 ff.

3 *Journal of Jewish Lore and Philosophy*, I/1919, 329 ff. Short references to liturgical matters are found also in the fragments of Anan's work published by Harkavy (*Studien und Mitteilungen*, VIII, St. Petersburg, 1903) and Schechter (*Documents of Jewish Sectaries*, II, Cambridge, 1910).

4 *Kitāb al-anwār wal-marāqib*, ed. L. Nemoy, New York, 1939–43, 5 volumes.

5 *Ibid.*, III, 603–636, Chapters XV–XXI of the Sixth Discourse. So far as I am aware, this is the only Jewish liturgy as yet discovered which consists entirely of Biblical psalmody.

6 See below, the last paragraph of Chapter XIX, and note 26.

7 For the sake of brevity, Chapters XV–XIX are given here in summarizing paraphrase, while Chapters XX–XXI, which set out the order of the liturgy, are translated verbatim and in full.

8 *Kitāb al-anwār*, I, 53; *HUCA*, VII/1930, 384. The term is, I suppose, borrowed from the Court of Israelites in the Temple of Jerusalem, where the commonalty stood during worship (cf. Maimonides, *The Book of Temple Service*, tr. M. Lewittes, New Haven, 1957, plan facing p. 498); see Mann, *JJLPh*, I/1919, 344, note. Such a parallel, however, would properly apply to the communal synagogue, the exilic substitute for the Temple, rather than to an individual's private chapel. See below, Chapter XIX, and note 24.

9 *JQR*, XL/1949-50, 307 ff.

10 Biblical citations are given according to the Jewish Publication Society's (JPS) version, 1917, with such minor modifications as seem to be required by the context.

11 JPS: *began*; but al-Qirqisānī obviously interprets *hūḥal* as derived from *ḥallēl* (Arabic *ḥalla*), "to untie, undo, release from a duty or an obligation."

12 Cf. Goldberg, pp. 1 ff.

13 The precise meaning of *al-jamā'ah* seems to vary, sometimes signifying the

whole of Jewry (*jamā'at al-ummah*), Rabbinites and non-Rabbinites together; sometimes only the several non-Rabbinite sectarians (perhaps *jamā'at aṣḥābinā*); and sometimes the majority of Jewry, that is, the Rabbinites alone. Here the addition of "and the Rabbinites" clearly limits the meaning of the word to non-Rabbinite sectarians.

[14] Probably Saadiah Gaon.

[15] Lived in the 9th century, and stands next to Anan in the official Karaite hierarchy of *patres synagogae*.

[16] That is, approximately, 9 A.M. to 3 P.M.

[17] Cf. Goldberg, pp. 96 ff.

[18] This sentence, which is not found in the traditional Rabbinite prayerbook, occurs in the fragment of a Palestinian liturgy published by Alexander Scheiber, *HUCA*, XXII/1949, 307–320.

[19] I do not know the source of this rather amazing tradition. If none is known at present, I can only caution the reader not to jump to the conclusion that al-Qirqisānī is mistaken or, worse, deliberately misleading. He rarely is, and the preceding note shows how risky such hasty conclusions may be.

[20] Presumably again Saadiah Gaon.

[21] The earliest known composers of *piyyūṭīm*, of the 6th, 7th, and 8th (?) centuries, respectively.

[22] Cf. Goldberg, pp. 30 ff.

[23] Sectarian teacher of the 9th century. For the latest discussion of him and of his followers, the Mishawites, see Z. Ankori, *Karaites in Byzantium*, New York and Jerusalem, 1959, pp. 372 ff.

[24] Note that what follows is a discussion of the views of the Ananites, and not of those of Anan himself, so that it would appear that al-Qirqisānī knew only that Anan had instituted the liturgical "courtyard," and did not see Anan's definition of it or his arguments in support of it—presumably he had no access to the pertinent chapters of Anan's *Sēfer ha-miṣwōt*. Cf. above, note 8.

[25] Menstrual and puerperal.

[26] This is one of the mildest of the numerous criticisms voiced by al-Qirqisānī against Anan. His sharpest is "I wish I knew whether he (Anan) was talking in his sleep or was out of his mind when he said this." Cf. my paper in *Jubilee Volume in Honor of Bernhard Heller*, Budapest, 1941, p. 259.

[27] Cf. Goldberg, pp. 59 ff.

[28] Here begins the exposition of the daily prayers.

[29] The preceding verse reads *O give thanks unto the Lord, for He is good.*

[30] Cf. Goldberg, pp. 11 ff.

[31] Cf. Goldberg, p. 19.

[32] Cf. Goldberg, pp. 14 ff.

[33] The Books of Ezra and Nehemiah were then regarded as one book.

[34] Cf. Goldberg, pp. 28 f.

[35] Cf. B. Ber. 31a; P. Ber. 4:1; B. Ber. 24b.

[36] The text here is somewhat awkward, *wa-qawluhum fī dhalika inna dhalika minhā*. Perhaps it should be emended to the more logical *wa-qawluhum fī dhalika fāsid idh dhalika minha*. The meaning remains the same in either case.

[37] All the following analogies, which obviously refer to the Children of Israel, are meant to demonstrate that Psalm 102, too, refers to them.

[38] JPS: *They that are mad against me;* but the following parallel *my lovers* shows that al-Qirqisānī derived *mehōlālay* from *hallēl*, "to praise."

[39] Used, of course, by non-Jews (Muslims).

[40] Cf. Goldberg, pp. 18 f.

[41] More's the pity that al-Qirqisānī does not specify them.

[42] The present world and the next.

[43] Rather three times, Ps. 90:5, 6, 14.

[44] For the ascription of Psalm 92 to Moses, cf. Midrash Tehillim 90 (English tr. W. Braude, New Haven, 1959, II, 87).

[45] JPS: *Thy meeting place*; but Anan and al-Qirqisānī evidently read *mō'adekā* as a plural, and construed it in the sense of "seasons, holy days." The same applies to the following quotation from verse 8.

[46] Meaning apparently the other sectarian teachers after Anan.

[47] Isa. 12:4 and I Chron. 16.8; literally, "that is, the phrase which is in the Psalter."

[48] Lev. 23:10 ff.

[49] In addition to the *Mūsaf* of the Sabbath (above, Section 12)?

[50] That is, New Year's Day; cf. Lev. 23:24.

[51] That is, the Day of Atonement; cf. Num. 29:10.

[52] See above, note 49. The Day of Atonement is called in Lev. 23:32 *Sabbath of rest* (*Shabbāt Shabbātōn*), which Mīshawayh al-'Ukbarī (see above, note 23) interpreted as "double Sabbath," and concluded that it must always fall on the Sabbath day (*Kitāb al-anwār,* I, 58; *HUCA,* VII, 390).

[53] In Hebrew *yāsek,* from the same root as *sukkāh,* "booth, tabernacle."

[54] In Hebrew *tāsēk*; see above, note 53.

[55] In Hebrew *sakkōtāh*; see above, note 53.

[56] That is, the eighth day of the Feast of Tabernacles; cf. Lev. 23:36.

[57] The festal booth is constructed with boughs and branches of trees.

[58] Again, more's the pity that al-Qirqisānī does not go into details.

[59] Cf. Goldberg, pp. 33 ff.

[60] Exod. 30:18 ff.; 40:30 ff.

[61] Cf. Goldberg, pp. 47 ff.

[62] Exod. 3:5; Josh. 5:15.

[63] I do not know the source of this tradition. It is not mentioned by Kasher, *Tōrāh shelēmāh,* VIII, 128 ff. (to Exod. 3:5), who quotes only the usual explanation that shoes, by coming in contact with dust and grime, unavoidably become unclean.

SOME EARLY TRADITIONS CONCERNING YOḤANAN BEN ZAKKAI

JACOB NEUSNER

Brown University

Traditions concerning sayings and deeds of Yoḥanan ben Zakkai took shape as early as the first decade before his death and as late as the fifteenth century A.D. It would stand to reason that sayings appearing in early collections are apt to be earlier than those first redacted later on. To be sure, the time in which a saying is first found implies nothing at all about the credibility or historical veracity of the saying, for early and late, none is demonstrably an eyewitness account written down by a reliable observer. We may, nonetheless, assume that sayings and stories clearly attributed to Tannaim are apt to be both more reliable and earlier than similar materials attributed to Amoraim or not specifically assigned to any authority at all.

Further, I cannot accept the unexamined opinion held in rabbinical circles, both scholarly and traditional, that all of rabbinical material was somehow sent floating into the air, if not by Moses, then by someone in remote antiquity (the Men of the Great Assembly or the generation of Yavneh, for instance). The material remained universally available until some authority snatched it down from on high, placed his name on it, and introduced it into the processes of named tradition and transmission. By this thesis nothing is older than anything else. The dictum, "There is neither *earlier* nor *later* in the Torah," thus is imagined to apply to the Oral Torah.

On the contrary, I suppose that in most instances, when a rabbi quoted a tradition, he did so, if he could, in the name of the authority from whom he had heard it. There are admittedly some important exceptions to this rule, for instance Rabbi Judah the Prince's statements in the Mishnah, which stand without authority, because it was common knowledge that when he did not specify an authority he was quoting his teacher, R. Meir. Anonymous statements in other major collections are similarly attributed, more or less reliably, to the major figures supposed to stand behind those collections. But apart from such cases, where a rabbi makes a statement without quoting his authority, we must ask why. And the most likely suppositions are (1) it represents a conclusion which he himself reached by some process of reasoning from Scripture or observation of other traditions; or (2) he has forgotten from whom he heard it—in which case he probably does not consider it of great importance (or else he thinks it so important that he has convinced himself he must have heard it from somebody, though he never has); or (3) he heard it from somebody not worth citing—if so he probably does not consider it authoritative; or (4) he has some special reason for omitting the name of the authority. Of these various reasons it seems probable that the first was by far the most common.

Hence it is important to see which sayings were said by earlier masters, which by later ones. We may thereby trace the growth of the traditions on Yoḥanan as some were invented, others taken up by the rabbis and made authoritative. Whether or not traditions about Yoḥanan were passed on for centuries until finally included in a given document, we *do* know for sure that traditions redacted earlier were approved of, therefore became *normative,* earlier. We can in other words be certain that a source appearing in an early Tannaitic midrash was *approved of* by the school which produced that midrash. We thereby gain some slight insight into what seemed important to men of a particular time and place to say about Yoḥanan or in his name. That is not much certainty, to be sure, but it provides a point of analysis hitherto ignored.

That does not mean that we shall ever have certain knowledge about the growth of the traditions as a whole. But that is not important, for we can never have that, and might as well not waste time trying to find out what the sources themselves do not contain *ex hypothesi.* It is sufficient to know when and where things were first given the shape in which we now have them. That itself permits us to make consequential statements about the formation of the extant, authoritative legends on Yoḥanan ben Zakkai. We thus can very reliably trace the growth of the normative tradition, in the end the only one we have.

We shall here examine elements of the earliest stratum of the tradition. In part I, I shall suggest that sayings first found in Tannaitic midrashim edited in the Schools of Ishmael and 'Aqiva, in fact, are based on an antecedent tradition, to be attributed to Yoḥanan or to his own circle of immediate disciples. In the second, I shall similarly postulate the existence of sayings of Yoḥanan ben Zakkai which earlier circulated in a form different from that which comes down to us.

I

A saying of Yoḥanan concerning the taboo against touching the altar with iron occurs in early midrashic collections produced by both the School of R. Ishmael and the School of R. 'Aqiva, the latter in two versions. It seems likely that a tradition common to the two schools in fact antedates both of them, hence derives from the earliest stratum of Yoḥanan materials.

Ishmael:

1. *For If Thou Lift Up Thy Sword Upon It.* In this connection R. Simon b. Eleazar used to say, "The altar is made to prolong the years of man and iron is made to shorten the years of man. It is not right for that which shortens life to be lifted up against that which prolongs life."

R. Yoḥanan b. Zakkai says: (a) "Behold it says: *Thou shalt build . . . of whole stones* (Deut. 27.6). They are to be stones that establish peace. Now, by using the method of *qal vaḥomer,* you reason: The stones for the altar do not see nor hear nor speak. Yet because they serve to establish peace between Israel and their Father in heaven the Holy One, blessed be He, said:

(b) "*Thou shalt lift up no iron tool upon them* (*ibid.,* v. 5). How much the more then should he who establishes peace between man and his fellow-man, between husband and wife, between city and city, between nation and nation, between family and family, between government and government, be protected so that no harm should come to him."

(*Mekhilta de R. Ishmael,*
Baḥodesh 11, ed. and trans.
J. Z. Lauterbach, II, p. 290.)

Comment: This is not described as "in the manner of the *ḥomer*" but explicitly as a *qal vaḥomer.* I do not think, though, that *kemin ḥomer* means simply, "in the manner of an argument *a forteriori,*" since other exempla of the *homer* method contain no hint of an argument *a forteriori.* Here the "whole stones" with the "iron" homilies are fused together. Below they appear as separate sayings.

'Aqiva:

2. (a) This is what Rabban Yoḥanan ben Zakkai says: "What was the reason iron was prohibited more than all [other] metals [for use in building the tabernacle (Ex. 20:25)]?" Because the sword is made from it, and the sword is a sign of punishment, but the altar is a sign of atonement. A sign [means] of punishment is removed from something which is a sign [means] of atonement.

(b) "And is this not a matter of a *qal veḥomer?* Stones, which neither see nor hear nor speak—because they bring atonement between Israel and their father in heaven, the Holy One blessed be he said [concerning them] *Thou shalt lift upon them no iron tool* [Deut. 27:5], sons of Torah, who are an atonement for the world, how much the more so that any of all the harmful forces which are in the world should never touch them."

(*Mekhilta of R. Simeon b. Yoḥai, Yitro* 20:22, ed. Epstein-Melamed p. 157 1. 29–31, 1–4.)

Comment: We have two separate sayings. The first is Yoḥanan's, that metal is prohibited because the sword is made of metal and is a sign of punishment, while the altar is a sign of atonement. The second saying is the *qal veḥomer,* that as stones should not be injured because they bring atonement, so sons of Torah should all the more so be free of injury from harmful forces. The *qal veḥomer* has nothing to do with Yoḥanan's observation, and need not be directly attributed to him, though it occurs in all formulations of this passage.

3. Rabban Yoḥanan ben Zakkai says, "Behold it says, [*With*] *whole stones* [*'avanim shelemot*] *will you build the altar of the Lord your God* [Deut. 27:5]—Stones which make peace [*shalom*], and behold it is a matter of *qal veḥomer:* Stones which do not see and do not hear and do not speak, because they bring peace between Israel and their father in heaven. Scripture says that *you shall not lift up iron*

over them [Deut. 27:6], a man who brings peace between a man and his wife, between one family and another, between one city and another, between one province and another, between one nation and another—how much the more so that punishment should not come near to him. . . ."

(*Sifra Qedoshim, Pereq* 10:4,
ed. I. H. Weiss, p. 92b.)

Comment: The exegesis in an 'Aqivan collection is nearly identical with the Ishmaelean version. The Scriptures are different. There it is "why is iron prohibited" and here it concerns the play on words of "whole stones—stones which make peace." "Atonement" becomes "peace," "sons of Torah" become "peacemakers." The structure is otherwise the same; the thought is the same ("Peacemakers or those who atone for the world should come to no harm"). The details are somewhat different. Yet, as I said, the differences are not very considerable.

I suspect that Yoḥanan would have said something about the altar/altar-stones in the form of a *qal veḥomer.* The context was Deut. 27:5 and 27:6. The play on words concerning the "whole stones" was dropped in the 'Aqivan *Mekhilta;* the stress on "iron" of all metals was omitted here.

Strikingly, the Ishmaelean version is close to this one. Both versions elide the "whole-stones" play on words and the *qal veḥomer* involving an iron tool. We have no way of knowing which of the versions preceded the other. Both schools preserved a single account but the 'Aqivans preserved another in addition. I do not know why the 'Aqivans were eager to preserve Yoḥanan's praise of peacemakers, but we can have no doubt that they did.

Some anterior version must have been available to both schools. That anterior version would derive from circles close to Yoḥanan himself. In a period of less than a few decades between Yoḥanan's death and the formation of the schools of Ishmael and 'Aqiva, a group of Yoḥanan's disciples must have put into final form materials which were subsequently made use of by *both* schools. I should regard the account common to both schools as deriving from such a circle of tradents, and thus imagine it is a very old story.

This supposition is likely to be valid if the following conditions are also valid: (1) if both documents actually come from the schools to which they are attributed; (2) if the present form was edited *ca.* 200, if not somewhat earlier; and, most important, (3) if they were not expanded since that time. Then the story stands in both by A.D. 200 and was known to teachers in both schools. The common source of the story would have come substantially earlier than the founding of the two schools, *ca.* 100–120. In that case, as I said, the story is certainly part of the corpus of Yoḥanan-sayings edited by the time of Yavneh. However, two possibilities require further specification. First, it may be that the parallels indicate posterior insertion in both midrashim from some outside source, not necessarily earlier than the two schools' traditions at all. Second, later scribal contamination of one midrash may have led to the insertion of material from the other, or, similarly, one midrashic collection may have made reference to the other. This second possibility is especially likely if the material stands in the same place, either in exegesis of the same verse, or in the same contexts before and after, in both midrashim. No. 1 and Nos. 2–3 manifestly provide exegeses of a common verse, Deut. 27:5–6. The Ishmaelean and 'Aqivan *Mekhiltas* obviously may have depended on one another, likely the latter on the former. But No. 3 concentrates on Deut: 27:5–6, while No. 1 pertains to the parallel in Exodus. Hence the second possibility does not apply to this parallel. We cannot come to firm conclusions, because the history of the texts is not known to us. We cannot be sure that the conditions specified above—that the present text was not expanded since its editing *ca.* A.D. 200, that the documents actually come from the schools to which they are attributed, that the present form was in fact edited *ca.* A.D. 200 and not many centuries later—we cannot be sure that these conditions have been met. So these conclusions must be regarded as tentative hypotheses. Since regnant opinion is that posterior insertions were not made; that later scribal contamination of a substantial order did not take place; that the documents actually did come from the schools to which they are attributed, I therefore suppose that No. 1 and No. 3 do antedate the schools of Ishmael and 'Aqiva.

We may safely go a step further and designate as deriving from Yavneh *all* materials occurring in substantially similar form in materials ascribed to the two schools; obviously, as Ishmaelean, materials unique to that school, hence not necessarily later than Yavneh but probably from a circle at Yavneh not acceptable to the 'Aqivans; as 'Aqivan, materials unique to that school, within the same limitation. It would be tempting to suppose that materials unique to one or the other school were later than materials common to both. It is consequential, since we have no documents edited at Yavneh, to recognize that within documents edited later on may be found materials which probably did come from Yavneh.

II

In addition to sayings directly attributed to Yoḥanan ben Zakkai, we find a number of traditions supposedly stated by him but only referred to in later times. These traditions exist only in the oblique references of disciples and subsequent students. The first group of such references all pertain to sayings redacted "on that day" on which Gamaliel II was deposed at Yavneh. The second comes from Usha, approximately a half-century later.

On That Day

4. *All that is in it will be unclean* (Lev. 11:33). Rabbi 'Aqiva says, "It does not say *unclean,* but *will be unclean*—to render unclean other objects, teaching concerning the second loaf that it renders the third unclean. . . ."

Rabbi Joshua says, "Who will remove the dust from between your eyes, O Rabban Yoḥanan ben Zakkai, for you would say that another generation is destined to declare clean the third loaf, for which [exegesis] there is no Scriptural [proof] in the Torah, and behold 'Aqiva your disciple brings Scriptural [proof] from the Torah that is unclean, for it is said, *And all that is in it will be unclean* (Lev. 11:33)."

(*Sifra Shemini, Parasha* 7:12,
ed. I. H. Weiss, p. 54a)

Comment: It is natural for 'Aqivans, responsible for the Sifra, to preserve a record of how Yoḥanan's outstanding student had conceded the superiority of 'Aqiva's exegetical method to Yoḥanan's. It is striking that 'Aqiva is called by the 'Aqivans "Yoḥanan's disciple." This is consistent with the preservation of several favorable accounts of Yoḥanan in the ʿAqivan circles. I think it clear that the ʿAqivans wanted to underscore their master's relationship to Yoḥanan. If so, perhaps ʿAqiva's disastrous politics was at issue; Yoḥanan had advised against the first war, ʿAqiva for the second. Yet, the disciples would have stressed, the wisdom of the master was not lost upon his "disciple" ʿAqiva, who was not only a true heir to his master's prescience, despite his poor guess about Bar Kokhba, but even superior to the master in exegetical abilities. If that was the ʿAqivans' intent—and it is purely conjectural to suggest so—then Joshua's saying would have been useful.

But standing by itself, Joshua registers an ironic observation, that Yoḥanan had suspected that some day someone would say pretty much what ʿAqiva now maintained. The implication may be that the master, prescient as always, would not have been pleased.

Eliezer's and Joshua's Yoḥanan-traditions certainly were at the outset edited in their respective schools and by their immediate disciples. This pericope would therefore represent a third stage in the process of transmission: (1) Actual event or saying; (2) Joshua's preservation of the tradition; (3) ʿAqivans' rendition of Joshua's comment on ʿAqiva's exegesis.

Clearly the teaching, and there certainly *was* one, had to begin with something like this formulation:

> Rabban Yoḥanan ben Zakkai said, "The third loaf is [capable of rendering other loaves] unclean, though there are reasons to think the contrary."

An alternative theoretical formulation would be:

> Rabban Yoḥanan ben Zakkai said, "Some future generation is likely to declare the third loaf [incapable of transmitting] uncleanness."

In that form, or something like it, the teaching would probably have been handed on at first. But if this modest conjecture is correct, then it is noteworthy that no such saying actually *was* handed on in Yoḥanan's name in preserved materials. It was suppressed, so the only exemplum we have is in the form as given here, namely, R. Joshua said, "Who will remove the dust . . ."

The earlier recension, if it existed, would thus have been replaced by this one, and then was dropped. The teachings of Yoḥanan reach us through the medium not only of his disciples, but also of the 'Aqivans (and others) later on, who chose to preserve only parts of Yoḥanan's disciples' teachings about their master, and to revise even these parts to conform to later opinions.

5. R. Joshua [b. Hananiah] and R. Judah b. Bathyra testified that the widow of one which belonged to an *Isah* family was eligible for marriage with a priest; [and] that the members of an Isah family are qualified to bear testimony as to which [of themselves] is unclean or clean, and which must be put away and which may be brought near. Rabban Simeon b. Gamaliel said, "We accept your testimony, but what shall we do, for Rabban Yoḥanan b. Zakkai decreed that courts may not be set up concerning this. The priests would hearken to you in what concerns putting away but not in what concerns bringing near."

6. R. Joshua said, "I have received as a tradition from Rabban Yoḥanan b. Zakkai, who heard from his teacher, and his teacher from his teacher, as a Halakhah given to Moses from Sinai, that Elijah will not come to declare unclean or clean, to remove afar or to bring nigh, but to remove after those [families] that were brought nigh by violence and to bring nigh those [families] that were removed afar by violence."

(*Mishnah 'Eduyyot* 8:3, 7
trans. H. Danby, pp. 435–37.)

Comment: These two accounts come from Joshua's school. Simeon b. Gamaliel II lived long after Joshua, so the story concerns Simeon I. The colloquy is therefore set in Jerusalem before 70, which is unlikely. Yoḥanan said Pharisaic courts had no power over whom the priests marry, though they would listen to the strict Pharisaic rulings when against priestly liaisons. Can we suppose that the story actually took place in such circumstances? How can we envision a situation in which Joshua and Judah b. Bathyra were offering testimony before Simeon in the *absence* of Yoḥanan then still alive! Is it possible, moreover, that Joshua would *not* have known what his master had decreed, but that Simeon b. Gamaliel *would* have known the teaching? It is further farfetched to suppose it is Simeon b. Gamaliel II who flourished after A.D. 140, when both Joshua and Judah b. Bathyra (I) were long since dead, as I said.

No. 6 seems to me a far more reliable tradition. Joshua here quotes his master. The teaching is unequivocal, and since no teacher is assigned to the tradition other than Yoḥanan, we may suppose Yoḥanan's failure to attribute the tradition to Hillel was on account of his being the first to say it.

Nos. 5 and 6 are so similar in concept as to raise the suspicion that two separate sayings are not actually before us at all. It seems more likely that Yoḥanan made a single statement, much like the one in No. 6. It was transposed into a testimony-story in No. 5. But if this is the case, the original story continued without variation, and the second, subsidiary account circulated alongside.

7. On that day . . . they voted and decided that Ammon and Moab should give Poorman's Tithe in the Seventh Year.

And when R. Jose the son of the Damascene came to R. Eliezer in Lydda, he said to him, "What new thing had ye in the House of Study to-day?'

He said to him, "They voted and decided that Ammon and Moab must give Poorman's Tithe in the Seventh Year."

R. Eliezer wept and said, *"The secret of the Lord is with them that fear him, and he will show them his covenant!* (Ps. 25:14). Go and tell them, Be not anxious by reason of your voting, for I have received a tradition from Rabban Yoḥanan b. Zakkai, who heard it from his teacher, and his teacher from his teacher, as a Halakhah given to Moses from Sinai, that Ammon and Moab should give Poorman's Tithe in the Seventh Year."

(*Mishnah Yadaim* 4:3,
trans. H. Danby, p. 783)

Comment: As above, the *on that day* pericopae refer to Yoḥanan's disciples and their approval of decisions taken in Gamaliel's absence. It is as if the *on that day* materials emphasize not only the active approval of Yoḥanan's disciples on the occasion of Gamaliel's deposition, but even more important, their emphasis that everything done "today" merely serves to reaffirm the heritage of their master. Since Yohanan was probably replaced at Yavneh by Gamaliel, it was a pointed, important assertion.

It is obvious that Yoḥanan originally said something like this:

> Rabban Yoḥanan ben Zakkai said, "Ammon and Moab give Poorman's Tithe in the Seventh year."

Alternatively:

> Rabban Yoḥanan ben Zakkai in the name of his teacher, and his teacher in the name of his, as a law given to Moses at Sinai, said, "Ammon and Moab . . ."

In either case, the saying of Yoḥanan never survived in that form. We should not know it had not Eliezer quoted it. And Eliezer quoted it only when he was able to do so—when Gamaliel II had temporarily fallen from power. What happened, therefore, is that in that brief period it was possible to include in the official traditions sayings which formerly had been suppressed, or which the disciples were unable earlier to introduce into the corpus of accepted law. Those materials were not afterward suppressed again and therefore we have them. But the original sayings were never allowed to exist in the form in which Yoḥanan had first handed them on.

It is further striking that Yoḥanan's name was sufficient assurance for the revolutionary synod. "Do not doubt you are right, for Yoḥanan said so." The contrary was that until now, Yoḥanan's opinion would have been equally reassuring—if it could have been announced and preserved. It was not.

The assembly actually knew nothing of Yoḥanan's view. Therefore it had to vote on the issue. It was afterward reassured its vote was correct. Some sorts of privy traditions on Yoḥanan obviously were preserved by Eliezer, but he did not teach them publicly or even privately. He kept alive the memory of Yoḥanan's words, and when able, brought them to the attention of others who formerly had not known them. They revered Yoḥanan's memory, so that when the opinions were made known, they were found to be welcome reassurance.

Yet, as I said, even though Gamaliel II was unable to wipe out the decrees of "that day," including the language in which they were preserved, he was still able to make certain Yoḥanan's original words never were preserved in the form in which they were originally redacted.

Usha

8. They may cover a lamp with a dish so that it shall not scorch a rafter, and [cover] animal droppings to protect a child, or a scorpion so that it shall not bite. R. Judah said, "Such a case once came before R. Yoḥanan b. Zakkai in 'Arav, and he said: 'I doubt whether he is not liable to a Sin-offering.' "

(*Mishnah Shabbat* 16:7,
trans. H. Danby, pp. 114–115)

9. A man may broach a jar to eat dried figs therefrom provided that he does not intend to make a utensil of it. They may not pierce the plug of a jar [on the Sabbath]. So R. Judah. But the Sages [or, R. Yosi] permit it.

They may not pierce it at the side; and if it was pierced already a man may not put wax on it [on the Sabbath] since he would [need to] smooth it over.

R. Judah said, "Such a case once came before Rabban Yoḥanan b. Zakkai in 'Arav, and he said, 'I doubt whether he is not liable to a Sin-offering.' "

(*Mishnah Shabbat* 23:3,
trans. H. Danby, p. 119)

Comment: Nos. 8 and 9 exhibit identical form:

1. Sabbath law—cover lamp or scorpion with dish
 —broach a jar to eat figs but not pierce plug of a jar.
2. R. Judah: Case came to Yoḥanan in 'Arav.
3. Yoḥanan's Decision: liable to sin-offering. Judah b. Ilai (*ca.* A.D. 120–180), a disciple of 'Aqiva, and preserver of Eliezer b. Hyrcanus' traditions in 'Aqivan circles, cited Yoḥanan's case as precedent-setting support for his view. In No. 8 no contrary view is stated.

We cannot guess at the original form of Yoḥanan's saying, if any, on Sabbath laws. It may be that a brief pericope existed, in which were preserved Yoḥanan's Sabbath-precedents. If so it probably covered more Sabbath-laws than those pertaining to covering lamps and opening jars, two matters which are not related and do not exhibit similar principles of law. But if such a collection of 'Arav-cases existed, it would have been formulated long before Judah b. Ilai, who merely alluded to, but did not cite its contents *verbatim*. We may suppose that the pericope began "Once a case came before Yoḥanan . . . in which so-and-so had happened. Yoḥanan ruled . . ." From such a tradition, Judah b. Ilai would have cited a sentence which would originally have read, "He may be liable to a sin-offering." Judah would then have put the words back into direct discourse: *"I doubt* whether he is . . ."

All this is entirely conjectural, but represents one way in which the tradition on Yoḥanan's 'Arav-cases would have reached Usha and then would have been revised in the generation preceding the editing of the Mishnah. After Judah b. Ilai, it obviously was *not* again revised, but preserved in the form Judah—but *not* Yoḥanan or his 'Arav disciples (e.g. Ḥanina b. Dosa)—gave it.

THE JEWISH WOMAN IN MEDIEVAL MARTYROLOGY

SHLOMO NOBLE

YIVO Institute for Jewish Research

In his discussion of the crusading movement, the eminent historian, Salo W. Baron states that "its victimization of Jews . . . also affected members of the weaker sex. In fact, women played a significant role . . . in the self-sacrificing deeds of the martyrs."[1] Speaking of the massacres of 1096, Julius Aronius says: ". . . As frequently in such cases, here too the women excelled in readiness for sacrifice and steadfastness of faith."[2] Because I wanted to determine this role of the Jewish women and the degree of their excellence of faith, I have analyzed the lists of victims in Sigmund Salfeld's *Das Martyrologium des Nurnberger Memorbuches* (Berlin 1898).

Salfeld's lists cover the period of 1096–1350. As he himself notes in the introduction (p. xix), there may be some repetition of names in them. However, their major shortcoming, for my purpose, is the indeterminateness of the sex of by far the largest part of the victims. The records generally read: "So and so and his wife and their children." When more specific, they state "and their five children." In very rare instances are the children named. The large number of child victims thus remains unidentifiable as to sex.

The total of identifiable male victims figuring in these lists is 2,664 and of females—2,533. These figures are highly revealing. Enjoying the shelter of their homes and less exposed to the perils of the roads,[3] the women nevertheless account for practically the same number of victims as the men. The factor of recognizability should also be borne in mind. The Jewish woman was far less identifiable as Jewish than the man; distinguishing marks were introduced somewhat later in the period and were not always scrupulously observed. If, nevertheless, the percentage of female victims was so high, clearly the vaunted medieval chivalry was a myth or did not apply to Jews.

In a sense, the cold martyrdom of the Jewish woman began with the fall of the Second Judean Commonwealth and the violent dispersion of the Jews. "The mother of the seven"[4] was cast in the dual tragic role of Jew and woman and the two were complementary in agony. The "exceedingly beautiful" wife of R. Moses, of the famous four captives on the sea who, valuing her honor above life and who, upon assurance from her husband that those who drowned would be "brought back from the depths of the sea," leaped into the waters, was not unique.[5] An earlier Talmudic source speaks of four hundred young people, who under similar circumstances preferred death to dishonor.[6] The story of the captive daughter of R. Ishmael the High Priest, "peerless in her beauty in the whole world" who was about to be mated to her brother and upon recognizing him expired, became the subject of a medieval poem that found its way into the Dirge for the Ninth of Av. Even in Italy, where the condition of the Jews was comparatively good, the tenth-century poet, Amittai son of Shephatiah, contrasts the lot of the Jewish woman with that of the non-Jewish in the following words: "Other women spend their time in revels and song, but the dolorous daughters of Judah and Israel are always in wailing and lamentation" (Brody and Wiener, *Mivehar hashira haivrit,* p. 47). Lamenting the anti-Jewish disorders in Palestine, in 1012, the Spanish poet Joseph ibn Abitor stresses in elegiac strains the tragic plight of the Jewish woman . . . "Weep for the chaste matrons, scrupulously guarding their purity, who were made pregnant by the seed of Ham . . ."[7] Significantly, several such plaints come to us from that period—and all from Palestine. In a report on conditions in Jerusalem in the eleventh century we read: "They took the maidens . . . to do with them according to their will. . . ." In a letter from Jerusalem, toward the end of the eleventh century we are told: "The women and the maidens [going out] into the market place to seek their livelihood, are ravished." Paradoxically, hate destroyed the Jewish woman in those years; love did no less. Some two centuries later, at the time of the Second Crusade, the poet R. Joel, son of Isaac the Levite, denounces the lust of the adversary in biblical idiom: "His soul did cleave unto

Dinah, daughter of Leah."[8] Similarly, the poet R. Joseph son of Asher, who flourished in Chartres around 1190, declares plaintively: "My enemies have crushed the breasts of my sister."[9]

The finest hour of the Jewish woman came in 1096 and the years following, in the period of the Crusades, when *kiddush hashem* became a social phenomenon and assumed community dimensions. As early as 1007 she gave a demonstration of her mettle. Robert the Pious, king of France, gave the Jews of his realm the choice of conversion to Christianity or destruction by the sword. "At that time there arose noble women and took hold of one another's hands, saying: 'Let us go to the river and drown ourselves, so that the name of God be not desecrated through us, for the sacred is trodden down in the mire of the streets and our treasures are burned in fire and altogether death is better for us than life.' "[10] Eighty-nine years later this scene was repeated in countless communities of the Rhineland. The primacy goes to Speyer. "And there lived a prominent and pious woman, who killed herself for the sanctification of the Name. She was the first in all of the communities to slay herself."[11] Worms followed suit. "A worthy woman lived there and her name was Minna. She hid in the cellar of a house outside the city. And there gathered unto her all the people of the city and said to her: 'Behold you are a woman of valor—know now that God no longer wants to save you. The dead lie naked in the streets and there is none to bury them. Defile yourself (a pejorative expression for baptism).' And she answered and said: 'Far be it from me to deny the God in heaven. For His sake and for His sacred Torah slay me. Delay no more.' Thus was killed the renowned in the gates."[12] Mainz did not disgrace her sister communities in the Rhineland. "There the women girt their loins with strength and slew their sons and their daughters and then themselves. . . . The tender and delicate woman slaughtered her darling child. . . . Maidens and brides peered through the windows and cried in a loud voice: 'See, O Lord, what we do for the sanctification of Your great Name.' "[13] Events in other places are variations on the same theme.

The above accounts of the Jewish woman's role are the work of the chroniclers of the period. The liturgic poets do not lag behind them in their exaltation of that role. The poet R. Abraham relates: "Compassionate women strangle their children . . . the brides bid farewell to their bridegrooms with a kiss and rush off to be slaughtered."[14] Eulogizing the thirty-two martyrs of Blois, of 1171, the poet R. Hillel, of Bonn, significantly points out the number of women among them: "As the women are led to the stake /they urge one another to make haste/ seventeen is their count by the staff/ with gladness and rejoicing they enter into the king's palace." [15] The poet R. Shlomo, son of Abraham, holds up as an example the young woman who answered the crusaders' request for her conversion by spitting on the cross.[16]

Not only are the women credited with taking the initiative in sanctifying the Name of God, they are also singled out for rare resourcefulness and adroitness in attaining their ends. Knowing the greed of the adversaries, they would cast out to them through the windows money and silver and other valuables to keep them busy with picking up the treasure so they could complete the slaying of their children.[17] Another delaying tactic of the women was to hurl stones at the adversaries through the windows, which they would then hurl back at them till "their bodies became one bloody mess." [18] Dreading most the seizure and subsequent baptism of their children, the women would resort to all kinds of stratagems to frustrate the plans of the adversaries.[19] In some instances they would tie their children to their bodies and thus be burned together with them.[20] Several centuries later, on the threshold of the modern period, a Jewish woman claimed to possess magic powers of invulnerability and urged her assailant to test them. He fired his harquebus, and she fell dead.

It was also the women who were the first to perceive the nature and true significance of the onslaught and to alarm their menfolk accordingly. Quite early it dawned upon them that the aim of the crusaders was to extirpate Judaism rather than exterminate the Jew. The Augustinian interpretation of the Psalmist's sentence (59:12), "slay them not . . . bring them down," gained acceptance in the Christian community. God Himself, as it were, is made privy to this plan.[21] "They oppress us and vex us, slay and hang . . . to make us forget the living God, to learn their Mass . . ." [22] The dominant faith resolved to brook rivalry no longer. It directed its blow at the fountain and source of Judaism.[23] Some crusaders, the chronicler tells, found a Scroll of the Torah and tore it to shreds. The women broke out in a lament over the desecration of "the Holy Torah, the perfection of beauty, the delight of the eyes" and roused their husbands to such "holy zeal for God and the Holy Torah" that they fell upon one of the crusaders and slew him.[24]

The rôle of the Jewish woman in this titanic struggle between two unequal forces was not lost on the adversaries, either. Reluctantly they admitted failure of their enterprise, but blamed it on the Jewish women, who "enticed their husbands to repudiate the crucified" and proceeded to vent their rage on them.[25] In general, the Jewish women were reputed to excel their men in contempt for Christian sanctities. The chronicler of Cologne tells of an alleged desecration of icons by some Jews, in which the Jewish women took a leading part.[26] Ecclesiastic legislature took note of the role of the Jewish woman and singled her out for particularly harsh treatment. The infamous yellow badge imposed upon the Jews by Pope Innocent III fixed the minimum age for male wearers at thirteen and for females at eleven.[27] The pointed hat was obligatory for women long after men had been freed from it.[28] Frequently, ridicule was resorted to, thus the Jewish women were made to wear sandals of unmatched colors—one black and one red. And the obscene suggestion of the Avignon synod of 1326, imposing a coiffure with horns on Jewish women over twelve years of age, was not lost on the least subtle. The decree of the Council of Paris of 1213, prohibiting Christian midwives from assisting at Jewish childbirths at times jeopardized the life of the Jewish woman.[29] Similarly, the prohibition of nursing Jewish children was aimed mainly at the Jewish woman.[30]

There are also other indications of the extraordinary devotion of the medieval Jewish woman to her faith. Her share in apostasy was most likely much smaller than that of the Jewish male. There are no statistics on the subject, but acquaintance with the literature of the period strongly points to this conclusion. The cases of women requiring *halizah* from converts are frequent. The instance of a man who "had been saved from the error of Jewish blindness," feuding with his wife, who remained a Jewess, over the possession of their four-year-old son, which Pope Gregory IX was called upon to adjudicate, may have been representative of many other instances of similar religious breaks.[31] In speaking of the paucity of Jewish conversions in medieval England, Joseph Jacobs mentions only seven cases in a given period. Of these only one was a Jewess.[32] Attempting to explain why a number of Jews figure in the official records of England under their mother's name rather than their father's, he advances the possibility of apostasy of the father.[33] That number is fairly large. Significantly, when in 1096 the community of Trèves was forcibly converted, upon the cessation of the persecution the converts immediately reverted to Judaism, except for one person. This was a male and, surprisingly, the rabbi.[34] Caesarius of Heisterbach tells the story of the spiritual adventures of a Jewess who converted, and he quite ingenuously places this story in his

Dialogue on Miracles.[35] Toward the end of this tragic period, in reviewing the Jewish agony in Spain, R. Joseph Yaavez pays magnificent tribute to the Jewish women: they led the way of the sanctification of the Name followed by their husbands.[36]

Perusal of the pertinent literature of the period brings out a striking and curious fact. In no other comparable body of Jewish writings—excluding of course the genrist love lyric—is there so much stress on the physical charms of the Jewish woman as in these writings. In this critical hour the Jewish men suddenly cast away their traditional reticence and unabashedly celebrated not only the moral valor of their women, but their physical beauty as well. This endowment of the Jewish woman is pointed up deliberately and with great care. For the chronicler's purpose it would have sufficed merely to record the heroic deed of a certain woman without the additional descriptive phrase, "and she was of beautiful form and fair to look upon and very attractive to all beholders." [37] Such simple characterizations abound in the chronicles and in the liturgic poetry.[38] There is even a suggestion of romance in the relations between the Count of Blois, Thibaut V, and a Jewish woman, Pulcelina.[39] In one instance, we are told, the brutish crusaders were so overawed by the exquisite beauty of a young woman that they refused to harm her.[40] Time and again the Jewish women are described as going to their voluntary death as if going to the wedding canopy. In this ambience the rapture-ravished idiom of the Song of Songs is a natural. In this chivalrous tribute to the Jewish woman we may see an attempt at compensation for her supernumerary suffering *qua* woman.

Some of the poets individualize and sublimate these characterizations to the rank of symbol. R. Moses, son of R. Elazar, speaks of the victims as "beautiful women, shaped like Keziah and Jemimah," the proverbially beautiful daughters of Job.[41] R. Eliezer of Worms, author of *Rokeah,* eulogizing his thirteen-year-old daughter, a victim of the crusaders, and enumerating her virtues, suddenly apostrophizes: "Oh, maiden beautiful!" [42] Great significance attaches to the aforementioned poem by R. Joel of Bonn.[43] The line "his soul did cleave unto Dinah, the daughter of Leah" is entirely biblical, save for the words "the daughter of Leah," where the original has the daughter of Jacob. Quoting the Bible, then, what prompted our poet to make the change? Assuredly, we shall not be far from the truth if we say that he wanted thereby to give recognition to the place and the new historic role of the Leahs—as women and as Jews—in Jewish life.

The inspiration for the assumption of this role came to the Jewish woman from both life and letters. For Jewish life in those centuries, specifically the life of the woman was on a high ideal plane. Even with due allowance for exaggeration, the characterization of his martyred wife, Dolca, by R. Eliezer of Worms provides an exalted image of Jewish womanhood. She lived a life of good deeds, principally devoted to the advancement of the study of the Torah. "She mended the clothes of the students" and in her short life "sewed together about forty Scrolls of the Torah."[44] Before her untimely death she purchased parchment for the writing of books. The wife or R. Eliezer saw the importance of the education of women and acted accordingly. And this education began at the tender age of four.

Literature provided a powerful stimulus to the heroic deed. The story of the *akedah,* the sacrifice of Isaac, moved in those days to a position of centrality and assumed a new meaning in Jewish life.[45] And although the principal characters in the drama are men, the role of the women is not negligible. "The one hundred outcries which mother Sarah cried out then" determined the number of *tekiot,* the notes of the shophar sounded on Rosh Hashanah.[46] Sarah's tent was designated as the repository of the ashes of the son to be sacrificed.[47] In the second half of the tenth century *Yosiphon* appeared, a version of ancient Jewish history in a sublimate key, which immediately came to enjoy an enormous popularity,[48] and even came to exert an influence on liturgical poetry. The image of the Jewish woman is exalted in this book; she is raised to the position of the heroine of Jewish history.[49] She manifests an aristocratic aloofness from the cares of workaday life, a profound contempt for self-interest, a boundless devotion to her people and stoic defiance of death and suffering. Queen Esther expresses her contempt for the royal crown on her head and for her royal garments "so long as her nation is in exile";[50] the wife of the treacherously slain Simon the Hasmonean, urges her son to disregard her tortures and to avenge his slain father; [51] Miriam, wife of Herod, walks calmly to her death "as if to a house of mirth, despising death . . . and thereby manifesting the glory of her family and the splendor of her ancestors"; [52] Berenice, sister of King Agrippa II pleads pathetically with Procurator Felix for her people,[53] and the women of Jodephath ascend the walls of the fortress beside the men for a final stand against the foe [54]—all these provide shining examples for their sisters of a later generation. And they outstripped their predecessors in number and in quality of deed.

NOTES

[1] Salo W. Baron, *A Social and Religious History of the Jews* (New York: 1957) vol. IV, p. 96.

[2] Julius Aronius, *Regesten zur Geschichte der Juden im fränkischen und deutschen Reiche bis zum Jahre 1273* (Berlin: 1902) p. 81.

[3] Although the role of the Jewish woman in the economic life of the period seems to have been not insignificant. See Joseph Jacobs, *The Jews of Angevin England* (New York: 1893) p. 86 and *passim.* Because of the limited area, the comparatively short space of time—two centuries—with which the book deals and the availability of ample materials, the study provides many details on Jewish economic activity in England. The situation, in this respect, was not dissimilar in other Western European and Mediterranean Jewish settlements. See also Robert Hoeniger, *Das Judenschreinbuch der Laurenzpfarre zu Köln* (Berlin: 1888).

[4] *Pesikta Rabati,* cited from B. Halper, *Post-Biblical Hebrew Literature* (Philadelphia: 1921) p. 39.

[5] Abraham ibn Daud, *The Book of Tradition,* ed. Gerson D. Cohen (Philadelphia: 1967) p. 64.

[6] *Gittin,* 576. Not all Jewish women, however, were of such heroic cast. Zipiah, daughter of Hai, meekly submitted to the embraces of Mohammed, after he put her husband, the poet Cnana, to death on a trumped-up charge (Shimeon Bernfeld, *Muhamad* [Warsaw: 1898] p. 127 n.)

[7] Hayim Shirman, *Hashira haivrit bisfarad uviprovans* (Jerusalem: 1954) vol. I, p. 64.

[8] A. M. Haberman, ed., *Sefer gezerot ashkenaz vezarfat* (Jerusalem: 1945) p. 109.

[9] H. Brody and M. Wiener, *Mivehar hashira haivrit* (Leipzig: 1922) p. 246.

[10] Haberman, *op. cit.*, p. 19.

[11] A. Neubauer and M. Stern, *Hebräische Berichte über die Judenverfolgungen während der Kreuzzüge* (Berlin: 1892) p. 2.

[12] *Ibid.,* pp. 50-51.

[13] *Ibid.,* p. 7.

[14] Haberman, *op. cit.,* p. 62.

[15] *Ibid.,* p. 138.

[16] *Ibid.,* p. 171.

[17] Neubauer and Stern, *op. cit.,* p. 9.

[18] *Loc. cit.*

[19] Leopold Zunz, *Die synagogale Poesie des Mittelalters* (Frankfurt am Main: 1920) p. 41.

[20] Haberman, *op. cit.,* p. 224.

[21] *Historians and Historical Schools* (Jerusalem: 1962) p. 47.

[22] Zunz, *op. cit.* p. 16 also pp. 32 and 204.

[23] Haberman, p. 20.

[24] Neubauer and Stern, *op. cit.,* p. 10.

[25] *Ibid.,* p. 27.

[26] Aronius, *op. cit.,* p. 315.

[27] Solomon Grayzel, *The Church and the Jews in the 13th Century* (Philadelphia: 1933) p. 69.

[28] *Loc. cit.,* n. 125; cf. also Baron, *op. cit.,* vol. IX, pp. 31 and 253.

[29] Grayzel, *op. cit.,* p. 307.

[30] *Ibid.,* p. 331.

[31] *Ibid.,* p. 181.

[32] Joseph Jacobs, *The Jews of Angevin England* (New York: 1893) p. 339.

[33] *Ibid.,* p. 155.

[34] Aronius, *op. cit.,* p. 90.

[35] *The Dialogue on Miracles,* quoted from Jacob R. Marcus, *The Jew in the Medieval World* (New York: 1938) pp. 142–144.

[36] Joseph Yaavez, *Or hahayim* (Amsterdam: 1781) p. 12 a.

[37] Shimeon Bernfeld, *Sefer hademaot* (Berlin: 1929) vol. I, p. 120.

[38] *Ibid.*, pp. 169, 184, 202, 203; vol. II pp. 57, 73; Haberman, *op. cit.*, p. 195; Zunz, *op. cit.*, p. 16.

[39] Bernfeld, *Sefer hademaot,* vol. I, p. 233.

[40] *Ibid.*, p. 191.

[41] Haberman, *op. cit.*, p. 221.

[42] *Ibid.*, p. 166.

[43] See n. 8.

[44] Haberman, *op. cit.*, pp. 165–167.

[45] Cf. Shalom Spiegel, *The Last Trial* (Philadelphia: 1967).

[46] *Ibid.*, p. 75.

[47] *Ibid.*, p. 148.

[48] Baron, *op. cit.*, vol. VI, p. 195.

[49] On the impact of *Yosiphon* on the following generations see Gerson D. Cohen, "Maase Hanah veshiveat baneha basifrut haivrit," *Sefer hayovel likhvod Mordekhay Menahem Kaplan* (New York: 1953) pp. 109, 118, 121.

[50] David Günzburg, ed., *Josippon* (Berdichev: 1896–1913) p. 31.

[51] *Ibid.*, p. 87.

[52] *Ibid.*, p. 150.

[53] *Ibid.*, p. 185.

[54] *Ibid.*, p. 204

OBSERVATIONS ON MAIMONIDES' *GUIDE FOR THE PERPLEXED*

HERBERT PARZEN

Theodor Herzl Institute, New York City

Moses Maimonides, unquestionably the outstanding talmudic scholar and Jewish philosopher-theologian of the Middle Ages, finished his *Guide for the Perplexed*[1] about 1195[2] in Egypt. He created therein a rational rapprochement between Judaism and the science of his epoch by his unique method of homonymy and allegory[3] in interpreting pertinent sections of the Bible and midrashic statements. The *Guide* has been received by certain religious circles in American Jewry as a contemporaneous chart that might help them to overcome their theological difficulties. Its popularity among the neo-Orthodox and elements of Conservative Judaism, loyal to the Tradition and conversant with the currents of present-day culture, is due to their sense of religious and intellectual kinship with the author as well as their self-identification with him because of the abuse heaped on him by generations of extreme traditionalists.[4]

Disappointed with the corrosive effects of emancipation, enlightenment and democracy on Judaism and discouraged with the results of the various ventures to vitalize the Jewish religion by modern innovators, they turned to him for guidance because he was unswervingly loyal to the belief in the Divine origin of the Torah[5] and, despite his respect for the human mind, did not permit reason to have full rein in theology.[6] They, therefore, use the *Guide* as a suggestion —not a pattern—for designing a panacea for the bewildered of this era, for they recognize the abyss which separates medieval cosmology and cosmogony, let alone the sciences underlying them, from modern conceptions. They are encouraged, too, by the fact that Maimonides wrote the book for the religiously perplexed, educated Jews—the grouping to which they, also, belong—and not for the "infidels and heretics" who "do not believe in the existence of God and, much less in prophecy" nor for the multitude of "fools" and the "ignorant."[7] Modern educated Jews, however, need to realize that the *Guide* must be applied selectively and reasonably to their problems. Just as its reasoning was based on the scientific data of its era, so must their scientific knowledge share in shaping their faith.

At the outset it is desirable to point out that many generations of educated Jews in the past have looked upon Maimonides as the inspired architect of a creative highroad to the existent sciences. Moreover, recent generations of yeshivah students first perceived the reality of reason and its beneficence through the solitary window provided by the *Guide;* it also served as the portal through which they stepped into the wide world of intellectual ideas devoted to the exploration of all fields of knowledge. Moses Mendelssohn[8] and Solomon Maimon[9] of the eighteenth century were only the forerunners of a motley host of talmudic students and scholars who were goaded by the *Guide* to master Western thought. True, numbers of them stumbled and fell into the morass of disloyalty and denial; it is also true, however, that many more steadfastly created, articulated or redirected the modern thrusts in Jewish civilization.

In sum, Maimonides established the precedent for sanctioning scientific research to overcome the obstacles obstructing the search for an efficacious synthesis of Judaism and general learning. He validated the intellectual discipline as a positive part of Jewish scholarship. Yet, he was a modest, tolerant man usually ready to consider with respect serious objections to his opinions or decisions by fellow scholars. He was not at all interested in provoking disputes though he was intolerant of fools.[10] As a matter of fact, he went out of his way in the *Guide* to placate the extreme traditionalists as far as possible, by his treatment of the *Mercabah,* his explanation of the purposes of the *mitzvot* and his rejection of total reliance on reason in religious matters. Yet it was his affirmation of the prerogative to assign to the intellect a significant role in theology[11] which chiefly caused the clamorous controversies after his death. In the end he was victorious. His antagonists failed to attain their goal since they conceded that mature men were entitled to read his work. In reality, Maimonides repeatedly emphasizes in the *Guide* that it was written exclusively for the mature intellectual élite which had mastered talmudic literature and the mathematical and physical sciences. In addition, he points out that the presentation of the material in the book is so organized that only ripe scholars would be able to grasp the issues he is exploring and defining.[12]

After this prelude it is imperative to pose the question whether Maimonidean premises, methodology, and the resultant synthesis are conclusive for modern Jewish religionists in quest of an adequate and appealing adjustment between Jewish faith and modern thought.[13] This is indeed a crucial question.

Fundamentally, Maimonides, despite his exalted attainments as a scholar of Jewish and general culture was, to a considerable degree, a medieval man, a son of his epoch. The medievalists were predominantly religious in their outlook on life. The Synagogue, the Mosque and the Church dominated their respective societies. Theology was the queen of wisdom; other branches of learning were considered her handmaidens, and were cultivated to sustain, to serve, and to shield her prerogatives. In fact, science and philosophy were studied "to demonstrate the rationality of the universe as a revelation of God" and, at the same time, to validate the dogmas of the several religious disciplines. Just as this purpose of scholarship prevailed among Christian schoolmen and Islamic scholars so was it, generally, followed by Jewish philosophers, including Maimonides, all of whom were authorities in Rabbinics.[14] It is significant that the appearance of the *Guide* coincided with the dominant influence of Aristotle in Andalusian Spain, and was followed two generations later by Thomas Aquinas' *Summa,*[14a] which purposed to harmonize Christian theology with Aristotle's philosophical system and was considerably influenced by the *Guide.*

Even so, Maimonides was a unique thinker in the medieval theological world. For he held fast to the rule that "the properties of things cannot adapt themselves to our opinions but that our opinions must be adapted to the existing properties." Hence his proof, according to him, for the existence of God, His unity and His incorporeality was adapted to "the laws of nature" and the "properties" of the universe as envisioned by the metaphysics of his time. Generally, however, he did not free reason altogether from its subservience to theology and dogmatics; on occasion he did grant it equality.[15]

Moreover, medieval theologians, Jewish and non-Jewish, harmonized faith with Aristotelian metaphysics and Greek thought in general as a result of their lack of historical perspective. They were, therefore, uncritical "in the matter of historical facts and relations." Thus Maimonides assumed, in all probity, that the Prophets originated or, at least conceived independently, the intellectual disciplines of the Greeks. He taught that in the course of time they were forgotten among Jews partly because of circumstance and partly because of neglect. The Exile, especially, caused their demise because of the oppression and resulting insecurity. Besides, speculative studies were not open to all men; the sages revealed the "Secrets of the Law"—as metaphysics and the physical sciences were denominated—only to a select few, and orally. Consequently this secret wisdom was, in due course, lost by default. Only a few hints and allusions have been preserved in the Talmud and the Midrash. The Prophets themselves utilized figurative language in speaking of this secret wisdom to keep it from the uninitiated and the ignorant who, as a result, have become accustomed to accept these figures of speech literally. Thus arose the exoteric and the esoteric interpretations of their visions.[16] Maimonides by means of unique and pervasive use of "homonymous and hybrid terms" as well as the allegorical interpretation of anthropomorphisms in the Bible, sought to recover the secret wisdom, partly at least, for the properly trained enlightened minority—"religious men trained in our holy Law who consciously fulfill their moral and religious duties and, at the same time, have been successful in their philosophical studies."[17]

Parenthetically, the Rabbis resorted to similar dialectics to provide Divine sanction and origin for the Oral Law, and the Cabalists had recourse to the same sort of argument to establish the Divine inspiration and provenance of mystic lore.[18]

In any case, Maimonides, by these means, converted portions of the Scriptures into a textbook of metaphysics, and the Jewish tradition into a rational religious philosophy.

Obviously, Maimonides' assumptions and procedures are no longer tenable. There has been an on-going revolution in human thought. History has become an integral part of cultural consciousness. Basically, Western thought is history-centered—irrespective of its logic or morality—pluralistic and flexible in form; not absolute and authoritarian but experimental and libertarian in orientation. As a consequence, the status of religion in society has altered. Science is now not only regnant but dominating. Religion as a source of truth has been dislodged to a subsidiary position; it is indeed frequently obliged to initiate adjustment to the contemporaneous scientific culture. The human mind has free rein. Reason is entirely emanicipated, free to examine existing institutions at will, certainly in the free world. It is sovereign, and not theology based on Revelation. Accordingly, the law of change has replaced the rule of dogma in human thinking.

The Synagogue, naturally, is confronted with this all-pervasive revolution. To survive, let alone to thrive, it has been obliged to seek accord with the modern intellectual environment. There is general agreement that the search has not yet succeeded in finding a wholly rewarding accommodation. But the quest goes on, as it must, in order that Judaism be cherished by Jews who are not only progressively attuned to, but also zealously championing the scientific spirit. Besides, to ignore, ostrich-like, the omnipresent intellectual revolution or to compartmentalize the mind into two sealed cubicles—one reserved for reason and the other for faith—without reciprocal communication, does not abolish the revolution. Facts are stubborn—they cannot be wished away. How, then, can the answer of the sage of the twelfth century, no matter how scintillating and scientific his *Guide* appeared in the past, be meaningful for the twentieth-century educated Jew who is a religionist, committed to preserve the values of the Jewish tradition? How can he find therein at least a modicum of self-fulfillment?

Actually, Maimonides has something to teach the modern Jew even though the *Guide* can no longer direct him to an adequate answer to his perplexities. Clearly, Maimonides was an observant religious Jew and learned in rabbinic lore as well as a philosopher, who insisted that reason has an exact role to play in religious thought, despite the fact that the human mind (or intellect) is finite and cannot find an answer to all questions in regard to God and His rule in the world.[19]

As a matter of fact he had little respect—contempt is probably nearer the truth—for the Jew uneducated in current philosophic thought. As will be indicated in due course, he considered the erudite talmudist less "perfect" than the talmudic scholar with philosophical training. Indeed, he could not conceive of worship without a reasoned understanding of God.

Actually, he was an independent, self-confident, systematic scholar. He was as critical of some of Aristotle's theories as he was of those of traditional scholars, who, for example, were complacent regarding the "corporeality" of God. This analytical venturesomeness is apparent in his readiness to discard the traditional dogma "creation out of nothing" in favor of the Aristotelian theory of the "eternity of the world," if the latter had conformed to his logical configuration. Only because he determined that the difficulties in proving the theory of "eternity"—basically associated with mechanical necessity including the mechanical laws of the causation of motion of the celestial spheres—outweighed those of the "creation" concept, did he reject Aristotle's thesis and adopt the *creatio ex nihilo* theory; he frankly admitted that his religious convictions played a part, but not an exclusive part in his preference.[20] In sum, he sought to build a rational foundation for the retaining of the traditional dogmatic formulations in the Jewish faith as far as feasible. Irrespective of the validity of his rationale for modern times, the fact is that he did philosophize and theorize, speculate and reinterpret the basic religious doctrines in accordance with his scientific knoweldge, in order to formulate a guide for the bewildered of his epoch. It is this application of thought, and the courage required for that effort, which must be emulated by the religious teachers of our age in order to erect a bridge between religion and modern thought in the broadest sense of these terms. It is largely due to him that the process of harmonization has become a part of the Jewish tradition. In this respect his guidance is not a minor matter.

Even his justification of placing limitations on reason is valuable to the religionist of today. Certain aspects of Judaism—the biblical miracles, for example—he regarded as "extra-rational." They took place as the result of the will or wisdom of God; therefore, they are beyond human cognition. To the present-day religionist, too, extreme rationalism in religion is repugnant. It has been found wanting: Emotion and intuition are currently considered constructive channels for religious experience. Thus Maimonides' "extra-rational" concept may well be introduced into the religious life of educated Jews in order to make their faith more profound, more devotional and awesome, encouraging, at the same time, a degree of humility to counteract somewhat the arrogance of modern man.

It is noteworthy, but not surprising, that a substantial section of the third book of the *Guide* is devoted to the Law, the legislation in the Torah which, according to Maimonides, has its source in Divine Wisdom. Accordingly, all Jewry—the common people and the learned—accept the doctrine that every precept has a purpose, an aim, a cause.[21] In general the Law has two objectives: "the well-being of the soul and the well-being of the body." The first is attained by correct opinions or truths, communicated to the people according to their capacity. The Unity, Eternity and Incorporeality of God, for example, are among these truths some of which are, therefore, "imparted allegorically," because the common people would not understand them in plain language.

The second purpose, the well-being of the body, is obtained by the establishment of humane social relations, the suppression of "violence and injustice," and by teaching "such good morals as will create a good social state."[22]

He applies this reasoning to the sacrifices. For the moment it is sufficient to point out that to him, the sacrificial cult was "of great use" as a deterrent to idolatry in that it was transferred to the worship of the true Deity. However, Maimonides' problem was "why one offering should be a lamb whilst another is a ram and why a specific number of animals should be provided on fixed occasions?" His answer: "Those who trouble themselves to find a cause for any of these detailed rules are . . . void of sense. . . . Those who believe that these detailed laws originate in a certain cause are as far from the truth as those who assume that the whole Law is useless. . . . Divine Wisdom demanded it, or if you prefer, say that circumstances made it necessary . . . ; and as regards the Law it appears to be impossible that it should not include some matter of this kind. . . ." He consequently formulated this rule: "The assertion of the Rabbis that there are reasons for all commandments . . . refer to the general purpose of the commandments, and not to the object of every detail."[22a]

Moreover, while the well-being of the soul as expounded by Maimonides is "first in rank," that of the body is "anterior in nature and time." Thus, there is general agreement among the sages and the philosophers that the prerequisite for the well-being of the soul is a sound body. In sum, a healthy society wherein man's wants are supplied—"food, shelter, sanitation and the like"—is essential for the development of the spiritual and intellectual life, *attained by "knowledge arrived at only by speculation or established by research . . . it alone is the source of eternal life."*[22b] (Italics supplied.)

To validate his thesis that the Law has the designated twofold purpose, he proceeds to divide the 613 precepts into fourteen classes and demonstrates the object of the commandments in each grouping.

Our interest is in the first two. They deal with the knowledge, the fear, and the love of God as the fundamental principles of the faith, and the eradication of idolatry, respectively.[23] In a sense they complement each other.

He, however, prefaces them with a general rule which conforms to the golden mean: "It is impossible to go suddenly from one extreme to the other; it is, therefore, according to the nature of man, impossible for him suddenly to discontinue everything to which he has been accustomed." Accordingly, though God bid Moses to make Israel "a kingdom of priests and a holy nation" by means of the knowledge of God yet, in accordance "with His wisdom and plan" He did not command the people to abandon all their idolatrous obeisances to which they adhered before the Sinaitic Revelation; He rather permitted the people to utilize them in His service in order to wean them from the errors of idolatry and the evil practices connected with it. Examples of such survivalist institutions were the building of the Tabernacle and, later, the Temple, the ordaining of a priesthood limited to one specific family, the offering of animal sacrifices, the burning of incense, etc.

Other idolatrous exercises, such as witchcraft, in all its manifestations, including astrology (which, incidentally, was quite popular in Maimonides' times not only among the populace but was also accepted by many prominent talmudic scholars)[24] which enabled idolatry to flourish aforetime, were entirely interdicted in the Law. As a result, in accord with the Divine plan, the traces of idolatry were blotted out, and the truly great principle of our faith—the Existence, the Unity and the Incorporeality of God—was firmly established.[25]

Maimonides seems dissatisfied both with his reasoning and with the inclusion of the sacrificial cult among the other idolatrous practices, especially as a considerable number of them are altogether prohibited.[26] He consequently feels the need for further clarification. So he seeks to strengthen his standpoint with a comparison: The banning of the sacrifices "in those days would have made the same impression as a prophet would make at present if he called us to the service of God and told us in His name that we should not pray to Him, not fast, not seek His help in time of trouble; that we should serve Him in thought, and not by any action."[27]

The implication is clear that no one would listen to this prophet just as the people would not have listened to Moses had he demanded the discontinuance of the sacrificial cult—another illustration of the power of custom or habit in the life of man.

Nevertheless, he has emphasized that the Law distinguishes between the sacrificial cult as a form of worship and that of prayers and supplications. "The primary object of the commandments about sacrifice" is the eventual overthrow of idolatry, while prayers are "nearer to the primary object and indispensable for obtaining it," that is, the recognition of the existence of God and His Unity and His glorification. This accounts for the reason that worship by means of animal sacrifices had "not been made obligatory for us to the same extent as before" Sinai, although they are offered in the name of and to God they are limited in place, in personnel, and time. Prayers and supplications, on the other hand, "can be offered everywhere and by every person." As a consequence, the Prophets frequently rebuked the Israelites for "being over-zealous . . . in bringing sacrifices." Thereby they distinctly proclaimed "that the object of the sacrifices is not very essential and that God does not require them." [28]

To minimize further the importance of the sacrificial cult he cites Jeremiah VII: 22–23. He explains the verses in two ways: the first reiterates the cited arguments: the sacrifices were ordained as a means of worship to deter idolatry and to promote, at the same time, the knowledge of God. But, according to Jeremiah, the people ignored the chief purpose and emphasized the means rather than the end desired.

The second explanation, however, is a unique Maimonidean statement: The first commandments after the Exodus, were given at Marah (Ex. XV: 25–26). These first precepts "distinctly" omitted—and it is so handed down by tradition—any reference to burnt offerings and sacrifices." According to the traditional interpretation only "Sabbath and civil laws" were revealed at Marah. Consequently, he holds that sacrifices are only of "secondary importance." [29]

This laborious defence of the sacrificial cult is, in reality, an apology. Apparently Maimonides was not too much concerned with its fate.

It is a remarkable phenomenon that Maimonides repeatedly and with clarity differentiates between the fear of God—a form of perfection induced by the fulfillment of the Law—and the love of God—synonymous with the knowledge of God—the highest form of perfection envisioned by the Law. In his own words:

> The two objects, love and fear of God, are acquired by two different means. The love of God is the result of the truths taught in the Law, including the true knowledge of the Existence and Unity of God, while fear of God is produced by the practices prescribed in the Law.[30]

This differentiation is of paramount import, especially in his discussion of wisdom, which, in Hebrew, is of course a homonym. His favorite definition of *ḥokhma* is true knowledge of the Law in a double sense: The first is the result of the study of the Law as sanctioned by tradition—the rabbinic method—without understanding the proofs for the truths of the faith which are attainable only by philosophical methodology. The second is the "real" wisdom attained by philosophical study; it enables man to demonstrate "by proof" those truths which Scripture teaches by way of tradition. It is a truism, according to Maimonides, that "real" wisdom and knowledge of the Law are treated as separate subjects even by the Rabbis. For wisdom is "the means of proving the lessons taught in the Law by correct reasoning."[31]

Furthermore, he posits in conformance with the views of the philosophers, that man may attain four kinds of perfections. For our purposes the third and fourth are pertinent. The former encompasses moral perfection, "the highest degree of excellency in man's character," which is the aim of "most of the precepts." But, as he frequently suggests, it is only a preparation, a stepping-stone for the final "true perfection of man"; therewith he acquires "the highest intellectual faculties" leading "to true metaphysical opinions as regards God," and the knowledge of His Providence, and the manner in which it influences His creations in their production and continued existence."[32] This perfection constitutes the final goal of man. "It gives him immortality, and on its account he is called man."[33]

It must be emphasized that Maimonides apparently was of the opinion that "immortality" and "eternal life" are exclusively reserved for those sages who know God and not merely serve Him. And that the knowledge of God is attainable only as a result of metaphysical studies, whereas serving Him is the consequence of the study and observance of the precepts. This is a startling theory, frequently repeated; it certainly is not in rapport with traditional doctrine. He even went so far in this regard—by means of his exegetical method—as to maintain that Scripture and the Sages hold the same view—*ḥokhma,* wisdom, "denotes the highest aim of man, the knowledge of

God . . . and the religious acts prescribed in the Law, viz., the various kinds of worship and the moral principles . . . do not constitute the ultimate aim of man . . . for they are but preparations leading to it. . . ."[34] As proof he cites Jeremiah, IX: 22–23 and a midrash in *Bereshit Rabbah*,[35] interpreted according to his methodology.[36]

Maimonides certainly was an intellectual aristocrat, intolerant of "fools" and the "ignorant." Therefore, he demanded excellence and devotion in the study of Bible and Talmud. For thorough knowledge of these literatures were absolutes—essential and prerequisite for the study and understanding of science and philosophy. Supreme perfection was unattainable without morality as taught in the traditional literature. Thus, "true wisdom"—the topmost rung in the ladder of human perfection—is acquired by the "imitation of God" and the "knowledge of God." To him they were really one discipline.

Maimonides' conception of Divine Providence, and its relation to the individual human being, is intriguing. It differs in part from that of Aristotle, who held that Providence relates only to the species on earth and not to any individual creature of the species, and, in part, from the Islamic theologians whom some of the Geonim followed (especially the Mutazellites[37] who, though they believed in man's free will, held that Providence extended "over all things"). He, however, posited that Divine Providence in the "sublunar world" extends exclusively to the individual members of the human species, and depends on the individual's merit; he, accordingly, accepted man's "absolute free will." He admits that his theory is not amenable to demonstrative proof but on his conception of the "spirit of Scripture, the prophetic writings and, generally, the views of the sages."[38]

In association with this thesis he affirms, as noted, the principle of the free will of man and the justice of God in imposing reward and punishment; he excludes consequently, the "afflictions of love," upheld by some scholars but not supported by any Scriptural text. He clarifies his view with this illustration: A ship has gone down with all aboard. This may be by mere chance; but it is not due to chance that those particular individuals were on board. It is due to the will of God and is in accordance with the justice of His judgment, "even though our mind is incapable of understanding its method."[39]

He, nevertheless, proceeds to clarify his philosophical reasoning which brought him to that conclusion: "Divine Providence is related to and closely connected with the intellect because Providence can only proceed from an intelligent being, from a being that is itself the most perfect Intellect. Those creatures, therefore, that receive part of that intellectual·influence will become subject to the action of Providence in the same proportion as they are acted upon by the Intellect."[40] Accordingly, the relation of Divine Providence to human beings is not identical. It, therefore, follows that even "among the pious and good men" it varies according to their piety and uprightness as well as among "the ignorant and disobedient"—some may even be ranked as "irrational beings," "like unto the beasts."

He insists that this belief has the sanction both of reason and traditional doctrine. Indeed this concept that God provides for every human being in accordance with his deserts is "one of the fundamental principles on which the Law is founded."[41]

In conclusion, he argues that philosophy likewise has been concerned with this question and has come to similar conclusions: "Those who possess the faculty of raising their souls from virtue to virtue obtain, according to Plato, Divine protection to a higher degree."

This assumption—as Maimonides has noted—was not accepted by some philosophers, including Aristotle, who erroneously argued that Divine Providence extends only to species, and not to individuals. They were mistaken. "For only individual beings have real existence and individual beings are endowed with Divine Intellect; Divine Providence acts therefore upon these individual beings." In sum, "the intellect which emanates from God unto us is the link that joins us to God."[42]

It is quite clear that Maimonides by this theory, validates his characteristic conclusion: The philosophically trained scholars gain the Providence of God in the fullest measure because their intellectual faculties are more vitally attuned to God than those of the talmudic scholars engrossed only in the study of the Law; albeit they are rewarded commensurately. For the true intellectual man is, by Maimonides' definition, a man of wisdom of the highest order—moral and pious, learned in the traditional literature and trained, additionally, in science and philosophy. Indeed, this type of intellectual is the truly pious man; and "God protects him in this world till he is removed to eternal life."[43]

This definition and discussion have certainly something significant to say today to the Jewish religious community.

This distinction among men, as far as the protection of God is concerned, is lucidly portrayed in the famous simile describing the relationship between the King in his palace and his subjects. Therein mankind is divided into six classes according to their nearness to the Regal presence:

1) The subjects "in our country and abroad": those beyond the borders of the King's dominion who do not have regard for the sovereignty of God, have not even seen "the face of the wall of the house." They are without religion, irrational, inhuman. Since they have the human form and shape as well as a mental faculty "above that of the monkey, they are below mankind and above monkeys."

2) The King's subjects in the country, "with their backs turned towards the palace, possess a religion, belief and thought, but hold false doctrines" due to erroneous personal speculation or teachers who misled them. This group is *"worse that the first class and under certain circumstances it may be necessary to execute them and extirpate them in order that others should not be misled."* (Italics supplied.)

3) The masses of religious people who "desire to reach and to enter the palace but they have never yet seen it": They *constitute the multitude that observe the divine commandments but are ignorant."* (Italics supplied.)

4) The King's subjects, devoted to the exclusive study of the practical law, who "arrive at the palace but go round about it": These talmudic scholars "believe traditionally in true principles of faith, and learn the practical worship of God." However, *they are not trained in philosophical treatment of the principles of the Law and do not endeavor to establish the truth of their faith* by *proof."* (Italics supplied.)

5) There are those subjects "who have come into the antechamber" of the palace: they have undertaken to "investigate the principles of religion." These scholars have studied not only the Mathematical sciences and Logic but also Physics. However, they remain "in the hall."

6) There are the "wise men" who have mastered Metaphysics and have entered "the innermost court." They have *"succeeded in finding a proof for everything that can be proved";* they have *"a true knowledge of God, so far as a true knowledge can be attained;"* and they *"are near the truth, wherever an ap-*

proach to the truth is possible." They have gained the goal—they are in the palace in which the King lives.[44] (Italics supplied.)

This gradation of the Jewish community is significant on several scores. This ladder to human perfection, a reiterative theme, is conceived in the mind of a medieval man. In spite of the fact that he ranks philosophy as the ultimate study for the acquisition of true wisdom and for the topmost rung in the hierarchy of the perfect, he still regards it as a stay to theology. His attitudes towards heretics and the common people are also cases in point. His condoning of the extermination of heretics is curious, if not startling. For he, himself, not only lived in the shadow of this accusation, but the Jewish people, throughout the Middles Ages, likewise suffered unabatedly on its account. His antipathy towards the "ignorant" Jewish masses, faithful to their faith, however they understood or misunderstood it, is the stereotyped reflection of the historical contempt of the learned for the *am ha'aretz.*

Maimonides adds a personal "note" to the parable for the guidance of his disciple Joseph ibn Aknin for whom the *Guide* was written. It is suggestive for the understanding of his subjection of philosophy to theology. He provides Aknin with a disciplined training program to attain perfection which, in effect, would make the student an ascetic—complete concentration of mind and heart on prayer, observance of the commandments and study in order to become attuned to the contemplation of God and His works. To achieve this goal "retirement and seclusion" are emphasized; association with others discouraged "to cases of necessity." These are, "when you eat, drink, bathe, talk with your wife and little children or when you converse with other people."

Incidentally, Maimonides admits that this discipline is very exacting, so much so that only four men—the Patriarchs and Moses—were able to carry it out fully and attain supreme perfection.[45] He himself, necessarily, had not achieved this degree of wisdom, though it is quite likely that he practiced this regimen to a feasible degree.

Strangely enough this educational process for obtaining perfection is not so very different from that of the mystics. It is, therefore, not surprising that outstanding Jewish mystics, Abraham Abulafia[46] and Moses de Leon,[47] were students of the *Guide,* and others created and spread the legend that Maimonides became a mystic towards the end of his life.[48]

Another aspect of Maimonides' training program for perfection and for forging a link between the Jew and his God is instructive in that it defines the difference between the "fear of God" and the "love of God."

When this discipline has definitely affected the practitioners "they will be filled with fear of God, humility, and piety, with true, not apparent, reverence and respect for God." Their conduct will be modest even during intercourse with their wives and they will restrict their speech"—another emphasis on ascerticism. In short, fear of God is the result of action in accord with the "postive and negative precepts."

However, the truths which the Law embodies, the knowledge of the Existence and Unity of God—in contrast to the commandments—evokes the love of God, "as we have shown repeatedly." His own words: "The two objects, love and fear of God, are acquired by two different means. The love is the result of the truths taught in the Law, including the true knowledge of the existence of God; whilst fear of God is produced by the practices prescribed in the Law." [49]

He repeats this doctrine in a different context, in his discussion of wisdom. A person with a true knowledge of the Law is wise in a two-fold sense, for the Law teaches him "the highest truth [about God] and good morals [as a result of the observance of the precepts]". However, those truths are conveyed "by way of tradition, not by a philosophical method." Hence, "the knowledge of the Law and the acquisition of true wisdom" *are presented in the biblical writings and by the Rabbis* (italics supplied) "as two different things." Thus tradition, according to Maimonides, accepts the thesis that real wisdom demonstrates by proof those truths which the traditional literature posits. "It is to this kind of wisdom . . . that Scripture refers when it extols wisdom and the high value of this perfection. . . ." [50]

As usual he substantiates this doctrine with his interpretation of citations from the Bible and the Midrash, and concludes: "This proves that our sages distinguished between the knowledge of the Law, on the one hand, and wisdom on the other, as the means of proving the lessons in the Law by correct reasoning."

In sum, he has tradition confirm his theories.

The implication of this distinction, so clearly put by the author and so important in his theological system, deprives the non-philosophically trained Jew, no matter how observant and learned, of the highest type of religious experience, the love of God, the knowledge of God, and excludes him from the ranks of the truly wise—and the rabbinic authorities sanction this position. That these ideas provoked anger if not hostility in the talmudic camp of his time and subsequently, need not be gainsaid; it is a part of the historical record.

These theories, however, should be helpful to the perplexed religious Jews of today searching to sustain their faith in the modern scientific climate in that these doctrines provide ample precedent that a philosophical conception of God in contemporaneous terms—and not merely a generalized emotional abstraction of a superman—is prerequisite for a relevant Jewish piety.

Modern scholars fully recognize that Maimonides was an extraordinary personality with an exceptional mind that had mastered the Judaic, philosophic and scientific learning of his time; that he was a devout Jew with sagacious religious insights and unafraid to pioneer uncharted courses for the understanding of Judaism, and a consistently systematic scholar who successfully synthesized, by means of his unique talents, reason and faith, religion and philosophy for his age. His *Guide* reflects his ideals and his personality.

Yet he was, as has been indicated, a medieval thinker, necessarily so; yet he transcended his environment in that he insisited that religious truths like all truths require demonstrable proofs. That the *Guide,* in spite of the author's careful efforts to conciliate in some respects the traditional authorities of his age, inevitably aroused their hostility can easily be explained—apparently extreme religious traditionalists are more or less alike in this respect throughout the generations.

Actually, it is not reasonable to expect the theology of the *Guide* to solve the complexities of Jewish religionists of this age which is so utterly unlike the Middle Ages. Nevertheless, the book has served and still serves as a challenge—that Judaism cannot and should not become intellectualy isolated or arid, that only educated men, in the broadest sense of the words, can guide the perplexed religious men to a clear relationship between religion and secular knowledge; that ignorance of scientific and intellectual accomplishments is not a qualification for piety. These challenges are Maimonides' legacy to Jewish history.

NOTES

[1] The references to the *Guide* can be found in the English translation by M. Friedlander (London, 1910). (Henceforth referred to as M.F.) Roman numerals refer to the section of the book, Arabic to the chapters.

[2] This date is followed in accordance with Prof. Alexander Marx's findings: "The Correspondence Between the Rabbis of Southern France and Maimonides

about Astrology," *Hebrew Union College Annual* (Cincinnati, 1926), p. 331 and note 33. (Henceforth referred to as Marx.)

[3] MF, *op. cit.,* I: 1–30, pp. 13–39.

[4] Silver, Daniel Jeremy, *Maimonides Criticism and the Maimonidean Controversy, 1180–1240,* pp. 148–198 (Leiden, 1965); Rosenthal, J., "The Anti-Maimonides Controversy in the Light of History," (Hebrew) in *Maimonides, His Teachings and Personality, Essays on the Occasion of the 750th Anniversary of His Death,* Edited by Dr. Simon Federbush (New York, 1956), pp. 37–57. (Henceforth referred to as Maimonides).

[5] Zeitlin, Solomon, *Maimonides, A Biography* (New York, 1955), p. 145; MF. *op cit.,* II:33, pp. 219–223.

[6] MF. I: 31–32, pp. 40–42.

[7] *Ibid.,* Introduction, pp. 1, 4 and 8.

[8] *The Jewish Encyclopedia.* Vol. 8, pp. 479–485.

[9] *Idem.* pp. 266–269.

[10] Marx. *op. cit.,* p. 329. In fact the entire paper corroborates this description.

[11] MF., *op. cit.,* I:48, pp. 100–102.

[12] *Ibid.,* pp. XXXIX and 2–3.

[13] Marx, *op. cit.,* p. 325; Baron, Salo, "Maimonides Significance to Our Generation" (English) in *Maimonides,* pp. 7–21; Zeitlin, Solomon, *op. cit.,* pp. 110–155.

[14] MF., *op. cit.,* I:50, pp. 67–68.

[14a] *The Jewish Encyclopedia,* Vol. II, pp. 38–39.

[15] M.F., pp. 41, 43, 277. This theme is frequently restated.

[16] *Idem,* Introduction, pp. 1–9. See also the chapters on Prophecy, II:32–33, pp. 219–223.

[17] *Ibid.,* I:1–46, pp. 13–63.

[18] Scholem, Gershon, G., *Major Trends in Jewish Mysticism* (New York, 1954), especially the Fourth Lecture, pp. 119–155.

[19] Husik, Isaac, *A History of Medieval Jewish Philosophy* (New York, 1916), pp. 266 and 274; MF., *op. cit.,* I:72, p. 119.

[20] MF. *op. cit.,* II: 14–25, pp. 174–199; also Husik, Isaac, *op. cit.,* pp. 268–274.

[21] MF., *op. cit.,* III: 25–28, pp. 307–314.

[22] *Ibid.,* III: 34–49, pp. 328–380.

[22a] *Ibid.,* III: 26, p. 311.

[22b] *Idem.,* III: 51, pp. 386–387.

[23] *Ibid.,* III: 35, p. 329.

[24] Marx, *op. cit.,* pp. 331–358. The entire paper deals with the question of astrology and clearly indicates its prevalence among scholars. See also MF. III: 30, pp. 320–32, "On Worship of Stars."

[25] MF. III: 32, pp. 322–327.

[26] *Ibid.,* III: 37, pp. 332–337.

[27] *Ibid.,* III: 32, p. 323. As a matter of fact the Midrash provides a similar justification for the preservation of the sacrificial cult—to wean the people from their accustomed sacrifices to the Egyptian gods. *Vayikrah Rabba,* 22:8.

[28] *Idem.* p. 325.

[29] *Idem.* p. 326.

[30] *Ibid.,* III: 52, pp. 391–392. The specific question is at the end of the chapter on p. 392.

[31] *Ibid.,* III: 54, pp. 393–394.

[32] *Idem,* p. 397.

[33] *Idem.,* pp. 394–395.

[34] *Idem.,* p. 396.

[35] *Midrash Bereshit Rabba,* Ch. 35 at end.

[36] Friedlaender, Israel, *Past and Present* (Cincinnati, 1919), pp. 193–216.

[37] MF. *op. cit.,* I: 71–76, pp. 107–144.

[38] *Ibid.,* III: 17, p. 286.

[39] *Idem.,* p. 287.

[40] *Idem.*, p. 288.

[41] *Ibid.*, III: 18, pp. 289–290.

[42] *Idem.*, p. 290.

[43] *Ibid.*, III: 51, p. 386.

[44] *Idem.*, pp. 384–385.

[45] *Idem.*, pp. 386–387.

[46] Scholem, Gershon G., *op. cit.*, p. 126.

[47] *Idem.*, p. 197.

[48] Dienstag, I. J., "Maimonides as Viewed by the Cabalists," *Maimonides* pp. 99–135.

[49] MF. III: 52, pp. 391–392. Maimonides concludes this discussion with "Note this explanation." It indicates the importance he assigns to this distinction.

[50] *Ibid.*, III: 54, pp. 394–395.

"TALMUDIC HUMAN SACRIFICES": EGYPT 1890

Moshe Perlmann

University of California, Los Angeles

The blood accusation, though mainly recorded in Christian countries, made its appearance from time to time under Islamic régimes, mostly among Christian communities. Thus it turned up several times in nineteenth-century Egypt.[1]

One of these episodes occurred in 1890, so to speak, in absentia: the Egyptian agitation was connected with an actual case in Damascus where, in April of that year, a six-year-old Armenian Catholic boy, Henry ᶜAbd al-Nur, had disappeared. When the child's body was found in a well, the Jews were accused, a medical commission examined the body, submitted a report, and the matter resounded in the press. From a British consular report to Sir Evelyn Baring (the future Lord Cromer) we learn of discussion of the Damascus case in the Cairo press and, in particular, about the anti-Jewish blood libel in the newspaper *al-Maḥrūsa*. The publisher-editors of this paper were (as were most journalists in Egypt at that time) Syrians, and were "under the aegis of the French flag." They owed money to a Jew, and as a result of nonpayment, their household furniture was impounded. The paper published violent articles on the Damascus case. The Jews of Cairo and Alexandria made representations to the authorities. The British document mentions the danger of excitement, especially among the Syrians and the Jews. "The former seem to regard as an article of faith that the blood of Christians is indispensable in the preparation of unleavened bread for Passover . . . ." The Syrians had been imbued with Jew-hatred since the Damascus Affair of 1840. The mood of the Muslim mob is not predictable. It is high time, concludes the report, to call a halt, e.g., through a governmental warning to the Syrian journalists. (Indeed, a Greek mob attacked Jews in Port-Said when a child strayed into a Jewish home.)[2]

Seventy-two years after the event, in 1962, the case is revived. In a series of *National Books* (*Kutub Qaumiya*) a volume appeared entitled *The Talmudic Human Sacrifices* (*al-ḏabā 'iḥ al-basharīya al-talmūdīya*), edited by ᶜAbd al-ᶜĀṭī Jalal (assisted by ᶜAbd al-Raḥīm Surur) (Cairo, published by *al-Dar al Qaumiya li-l-taba ᶜa wa-l-nashr,* 146 pages).

In his Introduction (pp. 3–8) dated June 1962, A. A. Jalal mentions that in preparing his drama, *The Jerusalem Tragedy,* he read up on Roman-Jewish and Christian-Jewish relations, and came across a French volume on Jewish human sacrifices, as well as an Arabic book on the subject. The Arabic volume was dated November 15, 1890 and was the work of Habib Faris. The badly preserved copy had been in the possession of a descendant of the author. It proved impossible to find another copy in the libraries. "It seems worthwhile to reissue this booklet now when the Jews are loud-mouthed about their role as builders of civilization and pioneers of humanity, the people whom God destined to lead man from darkness toward light. It is a clear indictment supported by documents and proofs: the Jews declare bloodshed permissible, they deem it a religious duty sanctioned in the Talmud. Murder, bribery, corruption . . . , the Jew considers them all permissible in order to attain his goal."

The author of the volume, Habīb Fāris, wrote in *al-Maḥrusa,* a newspaper that was published first in Alexandria, and later in Cairo, daily except Thursday and Sunday by Salem Naqqash, and later by Yusuf Asᶜaf and ᶜAziz Zand, and finally by Ilyas Ziyada. His subject was the Damascus blood accusation of 1890, the case of Henry ᶜAbd al-Nur slaughtered by the Jews to draw blood for the Passover Wafers. The Jews are always eager to buy up and destroy such works. That is, presumably, the reason why only one imperfect copy has been preserved. Indeed, the issues of *al-Maḥrusa* in which the chapters originally appeared, are missing in the libraries.[3]

Mr. Jalal hoped to republish in French and in Arabic the writings of two French authors on Jewish crimes. Such books, he felt, were sorely needed in the new nations of Asia and Africa. The reader is urged to distinguish between the divine Torah and the Talmud. The Torah contains the Pentateuch followed by the Psalms of David, Solomon's Song of Songs and Ecclesiastes; the Talmud is of a different nature.

"The Talmudists believe they are a race apart from the rest of mankind. Those not of the Jewish persuasion are considered by them to be as senseless animals, or servants or retainers of the Jews. Indeed, heaven and earth were created for the sake of the Jews alone. They are God-like upon earth. God bewails and mourns the destruction of the Temple." Jews are enjoined to treat wickedly the other nations, nay to kill the children, drain blood, and to seize the wealth of non-Jews.

Some Jews believe and follow these tenets.

Yet one Jewish scholar in eighth-century Baghdad, David ᶜAnan, and his followers, the Karaites, rejected the Talmud.

Mr. Jalal corrected numerous slips and barbarisms in the text.

This editorial preface is followed by the author's foreword (pp. 9–10) which is a plea to the Sultan ᶜAbd al Hamid, that paragon of justice, to respond to the outcry of the innocent. This appeal to the Sultan's justice recurs throughout the book.

The innocent victim makes his appeal.

"An Ottoman boy by birth, born of a father and mother of a stock that had been Ottoman for generations, sincerely devoted to the Ottoman dynasty, I was kidnaped by wicked stiff-necked and hard-hearted people. I shouted, cried, called for my mother. . . ." (p. 13)

In particular, the Damascus governor, ᶜAsim Pasha, is taken to task: he sought to hush-hush the affair. This was due to Jewish pressure (pp. 21, 23, 24, 28, 29, 83).

'While our enemies invoked the aid of foreign powers, we did not resort to that. Yet we are told we are enemies of the state" (p. 23). We learn, however, that the victim's mother did turn to foreign powers, in particular to their queens; and the consuls of Britain, Italy, and Greece were asked to report (p. 81) to their governments. The mother's poem of grief is also reproduced (pp. 33-35).

Evidently, some pressure was exercised against *al-Maḥrusa,* which led Faris to use the argument of the freedom of the press (pp. 40 ff). Doubts or negative opinions expressed in other publications also come under attack (p. 70).

The blood accusation, says Faris, is true beyond doubt. In 1240 the Jews were forced to confess, during the Paris disputations that their literature contained objectionable passages on Jesus, Mary, and the Church; on the virtue of killing Christians; that a contract with a Christian was not binding.

Yet "we do not accuse all Jews" (49). Some Jews are innocent of slaughtering innocent victims, and may well be unaware of such events (pp. 60, 67). But the truth of the blood accusation is too deeply ingrained (only the shroud will change old habit; *'ada fi-l-badan la yughayyirha illa-l-kafan*) (p. 62).

Proofs? There are hundreds of thousands. A violent passage by one Lotharus (?) (a teacher-monk?) is adduced (p. 67).

The Damascus doctors' report is discussed (pp. 69 ff). The list of the physicians included: military physicians (a Britisher, a Greek, Ottoman Greeks, Muslims, an Ottoman Jew) and civilians (two Italians, five Ottomans, a Roumanian, two Arabs of British citizenship, and a Greek).

The blood accusation is deeply entrenched in the people, in their minds and hearts, and is widely commented on in the press. It has a perpetual record. How can this agreement of peoples in many lands, and throughout centuries, be wrong? (p. 98). *La dernière bataille* by the author of *La France Juive* is mentioned as a source (p. 97). An individual may err but such a wide consensus could not. A list is given of medieval European cases, and of recent cases in the Near East [Aleppo 1810, Corfu 1812, Beirut 1824, Tripoli 1834, Rhodes 1839, and above all the Damascus Affair of 1840 (pp. 116-136), Alexandria 1840, Izmir 1881 (pp. 144 f.).]

Proof from the Talmud is to be adduced. Here an editorial footnote is inserted:

"Regrettably we have not yet come across the author's talmudic documentation, and hope that those who possess it will publish it for the public weal" (p. 136).

However, a sequel with illustrations is promised (p. 146).

As to the "proofs" in the present volume, they are confined to a retort to a Jewish journal (p. 87):

> Let them read a section in Sanhedrin, Aboda Zara, Erubin etc.; and what R. Jacob wrote in the *Tur;* the Mishna; the commentary of Maimonides on the Talmud; Shulhan Arukh, Hoshen Mishpat; and the writings of Moshe Abulafia, (pp. 95, 104), father of the Damascus rabbi Isaac Abulafia.

(Moshe Abulafia, in fear of torture, converted to Islam during the

Damascus Affair, in 1840. He is mentioned here as Muhammad Effendi Abulafia). The author argues that innocent Jews should, instead of protecting the guilty Jews, stand up in defense of the sufferers, the victims, and their families. The author's heart bled when he read about the suffering of a Jewish child in Russia; why would not Jews show similar feelings when a non-Jewish child is martyred by Jews? How would Jews feel if their young ones were exposed to such horrors? (pp. 84, 114).

When a Jewish reader asked the editors of the monthly *al-Muqtataf* for their opinion, they wrote that after several years' study and after comparing the arguments and counter-arguments, they concluded that the accusation was baseless, especially as it could not be traced to the Jews' religious literature (pp. 64, 66, 70; *Muqtataf*, v. 14, p. 688).

Nothing daunted, the author proceeds with his arguments. At the harbor a box with jars of blood was received, detained, and finally spirited out by a Jew. The rabbis sell the precious blood, and make a nice profit, too (pp. 142 f.). On the other hand, twenty Jewish maidens in Istanbul were so struck by the news of the 1890 Damascus case that they petitioned for conversion to Christianity (p. 111). Yes, the author had read that the blood accusation originally appeared as one directed against the early Christians but he brands this as a Jewish fable (p. 48).[4]

Formerly often suppressed, such pamphlets along with *Mein Kampf,* seem to have recouped their freedom of circulation.

NOTES

1 Cf. J. M. Landau in *Sefunot* v. *V* 415 ff. (Jerusalem 1961) and his *The Jews in Nineteenth-century Egypt* (Hebrew; Jerusalem 1967), especially pp. 21–29 and 169–178. *Sefunot* also contains an article by U. Heyd on the blood libel in 16th–17th-century Turkey.

2 Landau, *Sefunot V*, pp. 450–456.

3 Sarkis, *Dict. Enc. de bibliogr. Arabe* (Cairo 1930) p. 741 registers the first edition: Habib Afandi Faris, *Ṣirākh al-barī fi būq al-hurrīya wa-l-ḏabā'iḥ al talmūdīya,* 1891, p. 176 (Outcry of the innocent through the trumpet of freedom, and the talmudic sacrifices).

4 It must be remembered that 1891 saw blood-libel trials in Germany and in the Austrian Empire.

THE METHODOLOGY EMPLOYED BY THE HEBREW REFORMERS IN THE FIRST REFORM TEMPLE CONTROVERSY (1818–1819)

Moshe Pelli

University of the Negev

The first reform-temple controversy of 1818 [1] was the culmination of some forty years of fermentation in religious thought among Jewish thinkers in Germany. Elsewhere I have attempted to trace the causes of this fermentation to the deistic writings of the eighteenth-century European Enlightenment.[2] I have also shown, previously, some reform tendencies that had taken place in German Jewry in the 1780's and the 1790's[3] which, I believe, gave rise to some attempts in the beginning of the nineteenth century to introduce reform הלכה למעשה into the religious services.[4]

In this paper I shall endeavor to analyze and evaluate the methodology employed by some of the major participants in the controversy on the reform side, namely, Eliezer Liebermann,[5] M. I. Bresselau,[6] Aaron Chorin,[7] and some rabbis.[8] For reasons of limitation, David Caro,[9] who merits special attention, was excluded from this study.

Significantly, a great proportion of the argumentation on the part of the Hebrew writers who sided with the reform faction was based on the traditional Halachah. While this tendency could be expected of the rabbis among them, such as Rabbi Aaron Chorin, Rabbi Shem Tov Samun of Livorno (Leghorn), Rabbi Yehudah Aaron Hacohen, it is also to be found in Eliezer Liebermann and M. I. Bresselau. One may thus conclude that the Hebrew reformers of the early nineteenth century, very much like their predecessors in the late eighteenth century, were still deeply implanted in the old, traditional school of thought in Judaism. Somewhat related to this conclusion is another which I previously arrived at with regard to the early manifestations of religious reform among the Hebrew writers of the Haskalah, namely, that the Hebrew reformers had had some hope for a rapport with the traditionalist rabbis.[10]

From the Halachah, the Hebrew writers took the argument of קל וחומר , i.e., inference from the minor to the major. Arguing for playing the organ in the synagogue, a focal point of disagreement between the traditionalist rabbis and the reformers, Rabbi Shem Tov of Livorno uses this method as follows: If one is allowed to play a musical instrument in honor of flesh and blood (e.g., during weddings) should he not be allowed to do the same for the honor of God?[11] The same argument is presented by Liebermann,[12] who also uses the argument of inference from the major to the minor to enhance praying in German.[13] A change in a forbidden custom (*shinui*) is enough to make it legally permissible; thus an Italian rabbi advises placing the organ in the women's section of the synagogue, and argues that the player should play the organ in a different manner.[14]

Reliance on precedents is widely maintained by the Hebrew reformers as a legal ground for reform. Liebermann cites several precedents where the organ had been played regularly without any objection.[15] The use of the organ on Sabbath eve at the famous *Altneuschule* in Prague is mentioned by Liebermann,[16] while Rabbis Chorin and Recanate cite other precedents.[17] Similar precedents in favor of reform are cited regarding the issue of introducing the Sphardi pronunciation into the services abolishing, as the reformers proposed, the silent prayer of *Shmone 'Esre,*[18] and with regard to the question of *lo titgodedu*[19] (that is, whether any deviation whatever is permissible in a given locale).

This very method of citing precedents in order to advocate reform is in its very nature *anti*-reform, for it does not arrive at the suggested reform through methods such as the inference from the minor to the major or any of the other methods mentioned above, but rather through citing existing customs practiced elsewhere. As a result, it does not necessarily advocate the empowering of contemporary institutions or individuals with the license to change religious ordinances, practices, or customs held in veneration and observed for generations. However, it should be noted that although principles were important to the preachers of reform, the enactment of what they proposed was even more important, regardless of the means. Moreover, it is safe to assume that some of the so-called Hebrew reformers regarded most of their proposals as correcting customs that had been corrupted, and as restoring old, forgotten practices, rather than as instituting completely new and foreign customs.

That this assumption is correct we can see from some of their other arguments. Regarding the use of the organ, Rabbi Shem Tov maintains that "this thing has its origins and roots in Israel with our holy forefathers [who used] to sing and play to praise and glorify with all kinds of songs [instruments]."[20] On the controversial issue of not calling the people to the Torah by their names, Liebermann comments that "this too is nothing new under the sun," and he cites a responsa item where the custom is mentioned.[21] Similarly, he maintains that by eliminating part of the *Kedushah* on Sabbath ("Az bekol ra'ash gadol . . ."), the reformers actually restored the *Kedushah* to its original form: "Some man, whose name is unknown to us, instituted it [the addition], and we are not obligated to follow his words at all, for this version is not part of the *Kedushah* at all."[22] In the same vein, he argues that the Sphardi pronunciation as practiced by the Spanish and Italian Jews is the correct pronunciation, and that the reformers are in effect restoring the correct accent and eliminating the wrong, corrupted one.[23]

Of a slightly different nature is Rabbi Kunitz's argument *shekvar pashat haminhag,*[24] that is, since the [wrong] custom became prevalent it should be legalized by the religious authorities; this in effect demands of the rabbis legalizing reforms that have already taken place.

A popular method used by the Hebrew writers is that of defining a given prohibition in such a way as to delimit its scope in a manner favorable to reform. Thus Rabbi Shem Tov maintains that the prohibition to play an instrument after the destruction of the Temple refers only to worldly occasions; however, for religious purposes it is indeed permissible.[25] And Rabbi Jacob Ḥai Recanate limits the religious restriction to the song or tune and not the instrument;[26] that is to say, one may not play a special tune which is used at religious services by gentiles, and also the very instrument itself which is used by gentiles at church; however, any other musical instrument, such as an organ which is not used for gentile religious services, may be used in the synagogue. In the presentation of his argument, Rabbi Recanate shows some common sense which borders on *epikorsut;* according to his argumentation, if the restriction is not limited as suggested above, similar restriction should apply in other such instances. For example, one should not light wax candles in the synagogue, for the gentiles are using wax candles in the churches.[27] By using for analogy a common and necessary object, Rabbi Recanate attempts to drive home the point that organ playing is as necessary in the synagogue as wax candles. Rabbi Shem Tov also makes the same argument: "Are we going to refrain from everything that the gentiles are doing?"[28] To the (relatively speaking) modern mind of the Italian rabbi, it seems an absurd idea which one cannot entertain; therefore, via analogy, playing the organ in the synagogue, too, is permissible beyond any doubt. Somehow, no one among the Hebrew reformers has the sensitivity to notice the imitative implication of introducing the organ into the synagogue. However, one should not be surprised, for imitation of the surrounding culture for various reasons, the discussion of which goes beyond the scope of the present paper, was actually in the mind of the Hebrew enlighteners.

Liebermann, too, uses this method of delimiting the borders of a given restriction so that it favors reform, (such as playing the organ in the synagogue, and the injunction of *lo titgodedu*); so does Rabbi Chorin.[29] Worth mentioning is the attempt of both reformers to do away with the general injunction *Uveḥukotehem lo telechu* ["Neither shall ye walk in their ordinances"], limiting it so as to refer only to pagan nations, and then proclaiming that the European nations, which believe in one Deity (a generality which has not been elaborated upon), are not pagan; thus it is not forbidden to imitate their practices.[30]

Related to this category of halachic-oriented delimitation of a restriction is the attempt to discuss *ta'amei hamitzvot* (reasons for precepts). Although this discussion by itself is not necessarily indicative of an anti-traditionalist trend, for it has been in vogue throughout Jewish history, yet now it acquires a pro-reform twist. Thus it is a completion of a cycle started by the early Hebrew *maskilim* in Germany toward the end of the eighteenth century, and their covert goal in discussing *ta'amei hamitzvot* became crystallized.[31] The nineteenth-century Hebrew *maskilim* take an additional step beyond the discussion of the reasons for the precepts; they maintain that the reason for a given precept is no longer meaningful, and thus both precept and reason are no longer binding.[32] Playing the organ on Sabbath was originally forbidden, writes Eliezer Liebermann, lest the player try to repair the instrument; now that Jews do not know how to repair this instrument, there is no doubt that it is permissible to play the instrument even on the Sabbath.[33] Similarly, the cantillations were originally intended to help understand the Bible; now that the singing actually makes understanding even more difficult, we are not obligated to hold to the cantillations, and the reform practice of reading the Bible instead of intoning it becomes justified.[34]

It is of importance to note that all of the reform arguments concerning the Halachah are accompanied by long quotes from religious authorities of the traditionalist rabbinate.[35] My previous contention that the Hebrew reformers were very much implanted in the traditional school of thought, and that they attempted some rapport with the traditionalist rabbis thus gets additional support.

Aside from the halachic argumentation, the Hebrew reformers developed other methods in their demand for reform, some of which bear a more modern or contemporary coloring as might be expected of *maskilim* who had been rather willing to absorb the *Weltanschauung* of European culture.

Reflecting the religious deterioration that took place among the Jews in Germany in the beginning of the nineteenth century, the Hebrew reformers quite often utilized the argument of necessity. As the Hebrew reformer M. I. Bresselau puts it: "Halo 'et la'asot la'Adonai, heferu brito." ["Now is the time to act for God, for they violated His covenant"].[36] This is a paraphrase of the Psalms verse used in *Gitin* and *Brachot* to explain why, at times of necessity, the rabbis instituted a decree which deviated from the written law.[37] Should it be necessary—said the rabbis—for the sake of preserving the Jewish religion, even biblical laws may be temporarily changed.

Thus Liebermann advocates "Tefilah bechol lashon" ["prayers may be said in any language"],[38] that is, praying in the vernacular, in German. The lack of knowledge of Hebrew is given as a reason which necessitated the change. Playing the organ in the synagogue will attract people to come who otherwise would have refrained from attending the services, explains Rabbi Shem Tov; therefore, it is a necessity, he maintains, and *mitoch shelo lishmah ba lishmah* ["doing something not for its own sake would eventually bring one to do that thing for its own sake"].[39] The lack of participation in public prayers is also underscored by both Rabbi Moshe Kunitz and Eliezer Liebermann as reason for change.[40] Playing musical instruments in the synagogue will attract people, writes Kunitz, and the introduction of these instruments to the Jewish services is tantamount to *Kidush shem shamayim barabim,*[41] that is, sanctifying the name of God in public. Liebermann adds to this, that those attracted to the synagogue as a result of the beautification of the services would become, in the long run, God-fearing Jews; if they do not, eventually their descendants might.[42] The urgent need to find some way to appeal to the young generation is expressed by Bresselau as the sole reason for the changes introduced in the reform temple.[43]

Concurrently, we find arguments concentrating on esthetics, wisdom, and grammar. Rabbi Aaron Chorin objects to reading the Torah with cantillations because it is not esthetic, and because it dishonors the Torah.[44] He stresses *Kavanah,* i.e., intention and devotion in praying, the prerequisite of which is understanding. The principal part of praying, according to Chorin, is wisdom and understanding; it is thus proper to cut short the length of the service on weekdays, he maintains, as long as whatever is part of the service is said with *Kavanah.*[45] Chorin and Liebermann also use grammatical arguments to prove that the Sphardi pronunciation is the correct one, and that the reformers were right in abolishing the corrupted Ashkenazi pronunciation and introducing the Sphardi one.[46]

While there is nothing inherently "reformist" in the above contentions, the results of these contentions, indeed, took a reform characteristic. Further, they are indicative of the long struggle of the Hebrew writers of the Haskalah in the preceding decades to modernize the Jewish religion. I believe these contentions also prove the continuous line of thought and of goal from the Hebrew reformers of the late eighteenth century to the reformers of the first quarter of the nineteenth century. And finally they show how highly influenced were the Hebrew reformers by the surrounding culture.

The last point is clearly evident in their writings. There is no attempt to conceal the fact that the Hebrew reformers, though to a lesser degree than their German Jewish counterparts, set the gentile religious practices as an example for the ideal way of worship. This tendency was manifested in two ways. The direct approach is used by Rabbi Kunitz. Arguing that silent prayer exists in every nation in the form of private prayer, Kunitz maintains that the silent prayer among the Jews too should be in private and not in public, thus supporting the reform to eliminate the silent *Shmone 'Esre*.[47] Overtly, and without any hesitation, Kunitz declares: "Thus to the observer there is nothing strange about it [silent prayer] to differentiate between Israel and the nations." [48] He even supports his contention by an analogy with the Catholic confession which is conducted also in private and in secret.[49]

The indirect approach, as used by Chorin, Liebermann, and Bresselau, points out that a change is necessary in a given custom because that custom brings dishonor and disrepute to the Jews in the eyes of the non-Jews (or: among the nations). To quote it in the original, *"Hayinu ḥerpah bagoyim."* [50] Thus the services should be orderly, as proposed by the reformers, and certain changes should be introduced in order to eliminate any occasion for chatting or screaming among the worshippers. Liebermann goes as far as to say that the non-Jews who visit the synagogue mock at the Jews as a result, and comment: "This is not a house of God, but a madhouse or a saloon." [51] In all fairness to the reformers, it should be noted that they were not the first to introduce this approach; one can find precedents in the responsa literature where similar criticism was expressed.[52] However, that degree of sensitivity as to *Lamah yomru hagoyim* ["what (or, why) would the nations (or, the non-Jews) say?"], and the intensity and frequency of such an argument in the literature of the Haskalah is indeed characteristic of that generation of Jews in Germany.

The underlying a priori assumption of the Hebrew reformers (excluding the Italian rabbis enlisted by Liebermann to support the reformers) is the same as that of the early reformers of the late eighteenth century; as we shall see, it has many expressions, yet it may be summarized as follows: Irreverence toward the past and what it represents in traditional Judaism, skepticism with regard to accepted traditions, and disregard of the authority of the religious and legal (halachic) institutions of the Jews.

Like their predecessors in the Haskalah literature, the nineteenth-century writers attempt to remove the authoritative halo of infallibility from the Jewish sages and legislators of antiquity. Replying to an argument against reform, Liebermann writes: "Why did not our holy forefathers practice [a given custom suggested by the reformers] in the generations of yore? . . . Speaking like this is not wise. Have we not found that the last generations became wiser and increased in knowledge in a few things which were unknown to the early generations?" [53] He thus concludes that the authority of talmudic legislators is limited, and he cites their own words as authority to prove his point.[54] More eloquent is M. I. Bresselau when he asks rhetorically: "Will you not go right or left from the road which your fathers, men of renown, had walked? Your fathers, where are they? And the prophets, would they live forever?"[55] By stating that the fathers of the Jewish people were not immortal, Bresselau attempts to persuade his contemporaries that the customs which the forefathers instituted are as immortal as they. The equation of the dead legislators with the live customs which they had enacted creates some disharmony in the mind of the reader; in his search for the harmonious equation, the reader envisions the covert equation alluded to by Bresselau. Either live customs should equal live legislators—which is impossible—or, actually, therefore, dead legislators should equal dead customs, which is a possibility, indeed the very suggestion of Bresselau.

Liebermann goes one step further, expressing his doubts as to the grounds on which a custom was said to have been enacted by an ancient legislator in Judaism; "Who heard the voice of Moshe Rabenu, may he rest in peace, concerning the tune which he sang for Zarka and Segol, and the like; or whether he ordered anybody: thus you should sing Zakef Katan, and thus Zakef Gadol?"[56] Now, even though this is a logical argument, and it is well said, its implications are far-reaching. For it carries with it a complete denial of the fundamental of any historical religion, namely, tradition. It destroys the very essence of tradition by demanding that tradition prove what it says. In effect it comes very close to expressing disbelief in a given tradition.

No wonder then that the reformers make it their business to examine the authenticity and actual origin of certain customs. No longer do they accept customs as holy just because they are old.[57] This way they reject the silent prayer of *Shmone 'Esre,* and the custom of praying only in Hebrew.[58]

Following the scrutinizing of customs, the Hebrew reformers arrived at the conclusion that no custom, be it even an authentic one, can stay forever.[59] A custom is dependent on its time and place and is limited to both;[60] different times and different places have their own customs. Thus the contemporary Jews in Germany, says Liebermann, do not have to read the Torah with the cantillations which had been composed in other places and other times.[61] A few years later Rabbi Chorin is to develop this theme even further maintaining that the modern time and locale require, in effect, of the Jews that they change some traditions of antiquity and adapt themselves to the new environment (with regard to the tradition of wearing a hat).[62] Elaborating on the above-mentioned contention on the dependence of customs on their times and places, Bresselau is of the opinion that even traditional customs held for a thousand years and regarded now to be as binding as the written law have their limits and are bound to be changed so as to fit the new environment.[63]

Another method, widely used by the European deists of the previous century, is to point out that there has not been a *single* custom, which will indicate that it is universally recognized by all Jews and thus is a true custom, but rather there have been a number of customs in a given instance.[64] Why is it that the custom held by the Sphardi community is wrong and the custom observed by the Ashkenazi community is necessarily right? It follows that the Ashkenazi rabbis who fought against reforming of certain traditions are in no way the sole possessors of the truth. In every generation, writes Bresselau, there were those who claimed that the Torah had been given only to them as a heritage; whereas Moses actually gave the Torah to the whole of Israel. Yet whoever does not follow their own way and their own interpretation of the law has been persecuted by them.[65] Thus the reformers came to the denial of the authority of the rabbis. As David Caro was a major spokesman for this denial of authority, the discussion of it is excluded from the present paper.

In addition, a number of techniques in style, approach, and presentation, commonly used by the Hebrew reformers under study, would give us a better insight into the mind of these advocates of religious reform. Liebermann quite often uses the personal approach by relating in a vivid style his own feelings, emotions, and thoughts concerning his participation at reformed services.[66] It is a powerful way to attempt to persuade the undecided; much more appealing than the dry argumentative nature of the halachic discussion which dominates this literature on both sides of the fence. Equally effective is his story with a moral,[67] or the use of a clever midrash,[68] which proves his point. Liebermann, as well as Bresselau, tends to describe vivaciously the disorder, noise, and complete chaos that typify the traditional service at a synagogue of the old school.[69] This description is contrasted with the quiet, orderly, and civilized service at the reform temple.[70] The Hebrew reformers are very eager to spell out some of the ridiculous mistakes which are mouthed by worshippers who are not familiar with the Hebrew language; the examples used by these writers point out that instead of praising God the worshippers, in effect, curse him.[70a] Conclusion: this desecration should be stopped, and praying in the vernacular, as proposed and practiced by the reformers, should be instituted.[71]

Generality is used by Liebermann;[72] false analogy based on a word or a term—by Chorin;[73] change in legal terminology, in a way favoring reform, is utilized by Liebermann.[74] Almost all of the writers under study use the technique of oversimplification; "Any further discussion is superfluous," they are accustomed to say;[75] or: "It is simple," thus avoiding, at times, detailed discussion of a complicated issue.[76] In another technique, reformers such as Liebermann and Chorin would approach a controversial issue in two steps; they would start the discussion in a favorable manner toward the traditionalists; at first it seemed as though the reformers and the suggested reforms were completely wrong, but it turns out to be the reverse, that is to say, the reformers are right.[77] The technique is reminiscent of the talmudic *Hava 'amina,* yet I think it is used for polemical purposes. By putting himself on record right at the outset that he sympathized with the traditionalists (as Liebermann has it: I always rejected those seeking innovations, and I was never happy in the company of reformers who change the customs of our holy fathers . . .),[78] the writer gains the confidence of his traditionalist audience, and keeps their attention until he makes his point in favor of reform.

*

Although we have covered in the present study only a small portion of the literature on the first reform-temple controversy, I believe the following comments are appropriate:

The great part of the argumentation is based on the Halachah; this tends to indicate that although the reformers were influenced by the outside culture, they were still very much involved spiritually, intellectually, and emotionally with the traditional way of life.

There are also two conflicting tendencies to be found with the reform argumentation. According to one, the Hebrew writers under study desired only restoration of old customs which have been forgotten or else corrupted long ago; according to the other, they were undermining the very foundations of historical religion; the authenticity of tradition, and the authority of its legal institutions. This is indicative of the divergence of opinion that existed among the writers. A cumulative study like this finds each writer at a different stage of his personal process of reform which, in most cases, started as the desire to restore customs to their original form, and later develop into the demand for complete reform. However, both tendencies, I think, indicate the relationship of the authors under study to the Hebrew *maskilim* of the previous century. One notices the lack of serious discussion concerning the implications of the proposed reform. Some of the arguments at times are superficial (such as a grammatical argument).[79] Only occasionally would the Hebrew reformers dwell on the consequences resulting from the omission of Hebrew.[80] Many of them do not discuss the possibility of teaching all the prayers in Hebrew as a solution. They never, as far as I know, try to understand the meaning and the consequences of imitating foreign religious customs; only one touches upon the question of what the suggested reform may do to Judaism, only to wave it aside by saying: Just go to the reform temple and judge for yourself.[81]

NOTES

The author expresses his thanks to the Research Institute of the University of Texas at Austin for the grant which made this paper possible. The paper was presented at the annual meeting of the American Academy of Religion in Boston, October 25, 1969.

1 The first reform temple was initiated in 1815 in Berlin by Israel Jacobson; a similar reform service was conducted at the same time and in the same city in the house of Jacob Herz Beer. The Hamburg temple (1818) was in effect the second temple. Although the arguments for religious reform in *Nogah Hatzedek* (Dessau, 1818) and *'Or Nogah* (Dessau, 1818) were originally intended to support the Berlin reform (as is also evident from the dates of the books as well as the dates of the various answers) and not the Hamburg reform, the publication of the books close to the opening of the Hamburg temple is the reason for their inclusion in the controversy known as "the first reform-temple controversy." Graetz believes the answers were intended by Jacobson to support the Hamburg temple (*Divrei Yemei Hayehudim,* IX [Warsaw, ?], p. 278).

2 See this writer's paper *The Impact of Deism on the Hebrew Literature of the Enlightenment in Germany* (mimeograph).

3 "Intimations of Religious Reform in the German Hebrew Haskalah Literature," *Jewish Social Studies,* XXXII (January, 1970).

4 Several attempts had been made even before the Berlin reform by Israel Jacobson; some innovations in religious services were introduced in newly established Jewish modern schools. See: David Philipson, *The Reform Movement in Judaism* (New York, 1931), pp. 12–21; Simon Bernfeld, *Toldot Hareformatzion Hadatit Beyisra'el,* I (Warsaw, 1908), pp. 59–62 [Hebrew]; Mordechai Eliav, *Haḥinuch Hayehudi Begermania* (Jerusalem, 1960), p. 99 [Hebrew]; Jacob Rader Marcus, "Reform Judaism and the Laity, Israel Jacobson," *Central Conference of American Rabbis,* XXXVIII (1928), pp. 386 ff.

5 Contrary to reports by Graetz (*Divrei Yemei Hayehudim,* IX, p. 278) and Yekutiel Greenwald (*Liflagot Yisra'el Be'ungaria* [Deva, Romania, 1929], pp. 8–9), Liebermann did not convert. See Joseph Klausner, *Historia Shel Hasifrut Ha'ivrit Ḥahadashah,* I (Jerusalem, 1960), p. 282, and J. Tzevi Zehavi, *Tenu'at Hahitbolelut Beyisra'el* (Tel Aviv, 1943), pp. 27–28. Liebermann was enlisted by Jacobson to solicit favorable rabbinic responsa with regard to the reforms enacted in Berlin.

6 Author of *Ḥerev Nokemet Nekam Berit* ([Dessau], 1819), publisher (with S. Fraenkel) of the Hamburg reform prayer book *Seder Ha'avodah* (Hamburg, 1819), and one of the leaders of the Hamburg reform temple.

7 See this writer's "Ideological and Legal Struggle of Rabbi Aaron Chorin for

Religious Reform in Judaism," *Hebrew Union College Annual,* XXXIX (1968), pp. 63–79 [Hebrew].

[8] Rabbis Shem Tov Samun, Jacob Ḥai Recanate, Yehudah Aaron Hacohen, and Moshe Kunitz.

[9] Author (under the pseudonym Amitai Ben Avida Aḥitzedek) of *Berit 'Emet* (Constantinople [Dessau], 1820), in which he defends the reforms introduced in Hamburg against the traditionalist rabbis (whose views were published in *'Ele Divrei Haberit*). In part two of his book, entitled *Berit Hakehunah,* or *Techunat Harabanim* (character of the rabbis), David Caro vehemently attacks the institute of the rabbinate, and draws a *maskil's* ideal image of the rabbi and his duties. For reasons of limitation, our discussion is limited to the following books: *Nogah Hatzedek, 'Or Nogah* and *Ḥerev Nokemet Nekam Berit.*

[10] The *maskilim* were trying to approach the rabbis, and to communicate with them; see *Hame'asef,* 1786, p. 131 (Elijah Morpurgo's call to the rabbis), *ibid.,* 1790, pp. 301, 310 (Aaron Wolfssohn's call to the rabbis for certain religious reforms). Naphtali Herz Wessely, too, expected the rabbis to accept his challenge and explain their attacks on his *Divrei Shalom Ve'emet.* See "Rav Tuv Levet Yisra'el," *Divrei Shalom Ve'emet,* II (Berlin, 1782), pp. 39a–b.

[11] *Nogah Hatzedek,* p. 3.

[12] *'Or Nogah,* I, p. 17.

[13] *Ibid.,* p. 4: The inference is from *Birkat Kohanim,* which is so strict (*hamur,* i.e., more important, major) that the Ineffable Name, the Tetragrammaton (*shem hameforash*), had been pronounced in it at the Holy Temple. Even this major, or strict, blessing could have been said in the vernacular (*bechol lashon*) were it not for a special limitation, or exclusion, which in effect specified that *Birkat Kohanim* should be said in Hebrew [i.e., *ko tevarchu*]. Thus—Liebermann concludes—any minor prayer may be said in the vernacular.

[14] *Nogah Hatzedek,* p. 7: "Vehamenagen gam ken yeshane 'et ta'mo." Yehudah Aaron Hacohen was born in Jerusalem. Rabbi Shem-Tov Samun is using a similar argument, basing it on Rashi, as follows: the prohibition of singing in a synagogue refers only to a synagogue which is an exact replica of the holy Temple; *ergo,* the use of the organ is permissible for it is not a replica of a musical instrument played in the holy Temple (*ibid.,* pp. 5–6). Regarding the authenticity of Rabbi Samun's responsa: The editors of *'Ele Divrei Haberit* (Altona, 1819) publish a letter of the Italian Rabbi, and in a note they remark: "Mize nir'e ba'alil ki sheker he'id haḥonef bishmo vehotzi la'az 'al 'oto hatzadik" (*ibid.,* p. 69). However, nowhere does Rabbi Samun himself deny that he had written the responsa in *Nogah Hatzedek,* nor does he claim that his answer had been forged. The only thing he writes is a generality, namely, "Kol hameshane yado 'al hataḥtonah" (*ibid.*). In addition, Shmuel ben Moshe Hacohen, *dayan* of Livorno, who testified to the authenticity of Samun's writings (*Nogah Hatzedek,* p. 6), is also one of the signatories of the letter from Livorno published in *'Ele Divrei Haberit,* p. 68. He does not deny the authenticity of Samun's letter either.

[15] *'Or Nogah,* I, p. 17.

[16] *Ibid.:* "And to this day they welcome the Sabbath with musical instruments, and the music continues till one-half hour into the night (i.e., on Sabbath), the players being Jews."

[17] *Nogah Hatzedek,* p. 21: "And till this day there are [Jewish] communities which are accustomed to sing *Lechah Dodi* in the *Kabalat Shabat* service accompanied by musical instruments" (Chorin). *Ibid.,* p. 12: Rabbi Recanate cites the case of Corfo, where traditionally the *Kri'at Shma'* has been sung; he uses the terms *shir* ("sing") and *nagen* ("play an instrument" as well as "sing") indiscriminately. From the context, however, one may conclude that he refers only to singing without musical instruments. From the point of view of reform, his argument is rather weak, for it says in effect that because there has been an old tradition, the rabbis abode by it. Not being a reformer himself, Rabbi Recanate does not sense that point of his argument. However, the result is the same, namely, that singing is indeed allowed and is prac-

ticed. The traditionalist claim that one may not sing—and as a result, not play a musical instrument—after the destruction of the Temple is thus proven wrong. Recanate also cites another example of playing an instrument upon the approval of the local rabbinic authority (*ibid.,* p. 11).

18 *Ibid.,* p. 27. Rabbi Kunitz argues that seven-eighths of contemporary Jewry use the Sphardi pronunciation; they all call on the Name of God using the Sphardi pronunciation, and he advises the Jews of Berlin to join the majority so that "God will listen to your prayers as he has listened to the voice of these brethren of ours." Kunitz thus infers that the corrupted Ashkenazi pronunciation is not liked by God. His argument is based on both the practice of the majority and on the authority of God. Interestingly enough, Kunitz is attempting to prove that the suggested pronunciation is not foreign to German Jewry at all, for [controversial] Rabbi Nathan Adler of Frankfurt conducted the services using the Sphardi pronunciation. To support his argument for the elimination of the silent prayer of *Shmone 'Esre,* Liebermann cites several legal precedents enacted by rabbinic authorities. One of them is Maimonides' son, Abraham, who wrote that his father had established the practice of saying the *Shmone 'Esre* aloud, thus eliminating the silent part of it (*'Or Nogah,* I, pp. 9–13).

19 *Ibid.,* pp. 21–22. Liebermann mentions several locales where divergence of religious practices did, indeed, exist among the Jews.

20 *Nogah Hatzedek,* pp. 4–5.

21 *'Or Nogah,* I, p. 21.

22 *Ibid.,* p. 13.

23 *Ibid.,* pp. 19–20. Liebermann refers to the Ashkenazi pronunciation as a "stammering language" (*leshon 'ilgim*), and asks rhetorically: Since "pure-hearted people's eyes were opened [i.e., they realized, or saw, that they ought] to alleviate the obstacle and correct that which had been corrupted, are we going to consider them as defectors (deserters) from religion (*porshei min hadat* = "non-believers," heretics)?"

24 *Nogah Hatzedek,* p. 28.

25 *Ibid.,* pp. 3, 6.

26 *Ibid.,* pp. 10–11.

27 *Ibid.,* p. 10. Rabbi Recanate thus concludes: Surely no legal authority has had the intention of forbidding the playing of the organ for this reason (namely, that the gentiles, too, play the organ) as long as the organ is not used for idolatry (*'avodah zarah,* which in this contex may mean also any non-Jewish worship).

28 *Ibid.,* p. 4: "'Atu [Aramaic interrogative] kol ma'ase she'osim hagoyim 'anaḥnu lo na'ase?"

29 *'Or Nagah,* I, p. 15. Liebermann argues that the rabbinic restriction on instructing a non-Jew to play the organ applies only when the instruction is given on Sabbath; however, to instruct a non-Jew before the Sabbath that he should play the instrument on Sabbath is indeed permissible, "and no [legal] proof is needed for that." Nevertheless, he finds it necessary to rely on the authority of *Magen Avraham.* Regarding the injunction of *lo titgodedu,* Liebermann delimits it to a given religious court [*bet din*]; however, two religious courts, even in one locale, may disagree on religious matters and practices. He supports his claim on the authority of Sh. Ch. (*Siftei Cohen,* known by the abbreviation "SHaCH," *ibid.,* p. 21). Liebermann further argues that the injunction of *lo titgodedu* is applicable only in cases of disagreement regarding matters of *'Isur* and *Heter* (legal prohibition and permission respectively), where it might appear as though there does not exist a single unified law (*umiḥazi kishtei torot*). However, difference in customs (such as the customs proposed by the reformers) is not included in *lo titgodedu* (*ibid.*). Rabbi Chorin delimits the injunction to apply only to either a single court, or even to two religious courts in the same locale (in deviation from Liebermann); however, *lo titgodedu* does not apply to customs (*Nogah Hatzedek,* p. 22).

30 Liebermann maintains that "it is known that the peoples of this [our] time are not pagans (*'ovdei 'avodah zarah*); furthermore, music is not necessarily typical of

pagan worship, or for that matter of any non-Jewish worship, therefore, it is not included in *"Uvehukotehem"* (*'Or Nogah,* I, p. 15). Chorin is of the same opinion (*Nogah Hatzedek,* p. 21).

31 Some of the eighteenth-century Hebrew reformers arrived at the conclusion that the *mitzvot* were only a means to an end: to remind one of the fundamentals of religion—doing that which is good and righteous (Mordechai Gumpel Schnaber [George Levison], *Tochaḥat Megilah* (Hamburg, 1784), p. 9b; Saul Berlin, *Besamim Rosh* (Berlin, 1793), *siman* 251, pp. 77a–b. Should these goals be achieved without the *mitzvot*—wrote Schnaber—perhaps they ought to be eliminated completely (*Tochaḥat Megilah,* p. 9b).

32 "Laze 'en 'anu meshu'abadim linginah zo" (Liebermann, *'Or Nogah,* I, p. 20).

33 *Ibid.,* p. 14.

34 *Ibid.,* p. 20.

35 For example: Joseph Caro (*Nogah Hatzedek,* p. 3); Rashi (*ibid.*); Maimonides (*ibid.,* p. 6); *Magen Avraham* (p. 16); ReMA (p. 23); ROSH (*'Or Nogah,* I, p. 9), etc.

36 *Ḥerev Nokemet Nekam Berit,* p. 5.

37 Psalms, 119:126; *Gitin,* p. 60a; *Brachot,* at the end.

38 *'Or Nogah,* I, pp. 8–9. Polish Jews are excluded from this, in Liebermann's opinion, since they do not face this problem; they are familiar with the Hebrew language.

39 *Nogah Hatzedek,* p. 6.

40 *Ibid.,* pp. 27–28; *'Or Nogah,* II, p. 19.

41 *Nogah Hatzedek,* p. 23.

42 *'Or Nogah,* II, p. 19.

43 *Ḥerev Nokemet Nekam Berit,* pp. 5, 9.

44 *Nogah Hatzedek,* p. 24.

45 *Ibid.,* pp. 16, 20–21.

46 *Ibid.,* p. 24 (Chorin); *'Or Nogah,* I, p. 18 (Liebermann).

47 *Nogah Hatzedek,* p. 27: "Shebechol 'am ve'am timtza [or, timatze] tefilat laḥash pratit."

48 *Ibid.*: "Ve'en zarut bah lehevdel yisra'el miben ha'amim be'ein kol ro'e."

49 *Ibid.* Even when he criticizes the reformers for conducting public services only once a week, Kunitz gives as an example the Christian churches which, according to him, are open twice daily (*ibid.,* p. 28); cf. Liebermann in *'Or Nogah,* II, p. 22.

50 *Nogah Hatzedek,* p. 20. Chorin cites the disorder and noise that typify a Jewish service: "When a stranger, who does not know the custom of these ignorant people, comes, and observes this great confusion and big noise, he would not believe that this crowd is occupied with a holy matter and prayer." The same argument is used by Chorin several times in his responsa (*ibid.,* pp. 24, 26).

51 *'Or Nogah,* II, p. 20, in footnote: "Umah gam shekedei bizayon veḥerpah hi lanu neged ha'amim haba'im life'amim levet hakneset veshome'im kol gadol venora, 'omrim: 'en ze bet eloḥim, ki 'im bet meshuga'im 'o shotei shechar." Cf., a similar argument by Bresselau, *Ḥerev Nokemet,* p. 7.

52 *'Or Nogah,* I, p. 13, citing Maimonides.

53 *Ibid.,* p. 22. It is important to note that Liebermann is trying to contradict the traditionalist assumption that new discoveries and newly acquired knowledge in the sciences and other mundane and secular disciplines have no bearing on Judaism. He claims that not only is this [wrong] assumption against reason and against self-evident truths [*mefursamot*], but this assumption is against the authoritative opinion of the talmudic sages.

54 *Ibid.* Citing the talmudic discussion in *Ḥulin,* p. 6b, regarding "makom hiniḥu lo 'avotav lehitgader bo" and "mikan letalmid ḥacham she'amar devar halacha she'en maziḥim 'oto" (see Rashi's commentary in the cited source).

55 *Ḥerev Nokemet,* p. 6: "Ha'im min haderech 'asher darchu bo 'avotechem me'olam 'anshei hashem, mimenu lo tasuru yamin usmol? 'avotechem 'aye hem? vehanevi'im hale'olam yiḥyu?"

[56] *'Or Nogah,* I, p. 20: "Mi shama' kol moshe rabenu 'alav hashalom be'eze nigun nigen zarka vesegol vechadome, 'o 'im tzivah leshum 'adam: kach tenagen zakef katan vechach zakef gadol?"

[57] *Ibid.,* II, pp. 7–8. Liebermann first maintains that there are old customs which had been instituted by fools (*ksilim*) or by ignorant people (*bur ve'am ha'aretz*), and that there are some customs which came from "women weaving in the moon [light]." In addition, Liebermann makes it quite clear that even customs which had been enacted by wise people should be re-evaluated: "Hahiskilu 'avotam bedarkam ve'im hetivu 'asher 'asu."

[58] And in Aramaic. *Ibid.,* I, p. 10. Liebermann rejects the silent prayer; *ibid.,* p. 3: praying in the vernacular is advocated by him, employing the same method.

[59] It is best pronounced by Bresselau in *Ḥerev Nokemet,* p. 6: "Mah tevahalu 'al pichem, ki haminhag ḥayah 'elef shanim pa'amayim, 'al ken 'amad ta'mo bo vereḥo lo namar vechatorah ye'ase" [why do you hurry to enunciate (cf. Ecclesiastes, 5:1) that the custom lives (or, endures) twofold a thousand years, therefore, its taste remained in it, and its scent is not changed, and it should become like the Torah (law; as binding as the biblical law)].

[60] *Ibid.:* "Halo ted'u, halo tishma'u, halo havinotem, ki 'et umikre yikre 'et kulam, vehaminhag beshanoto 'et ta'mo, beshiga'on yinhag" (Have you not known? Have you not heard? Have you not understood? that the custom, when its reason is changed [or, when a custom is changing its behavior, for it no longer fits the changing times. Bresselau is using a play on words based on Psalms, 34:1], this custom [if practiced in the old way], would appear insane [again, a play on words based on II Kings, 9:20]).

[61] *'Or Nogah,* I, p. 20: "Therefore, we are not obligated to this melody (cantillations), and only the generations of antiquity (*dorot harishonim*) which intoned everything in this melody (*'asher kol divrehem hayu binginah kazo*), therefore, they read the scroll of the Torah also in this melody; however, we now, in our generations and in our lands, our intonation is different. Therefore, it is incumbent upon us (*mitzvah 'aleinu*) to read [the Torah] in accordance with the intonation chanted by everybody."

[62] See this writer's article on Rabbi Chorin (footnote 7), pp. 73–74.

[63] See note 59.

[64] *'Or Nogah,* I, p. 13. Liebermann argues that the *Kedushah* on Sabbath is not known "in all the lands of the Occident, Spain and the Land of Israel," i.e., among Sphardic Jews.

[65] *Ḥerev Nokemet,* pp. 10–11: "Uvechol dor vador 'omdim hamitkadshim vehamiṭaharim bilvavam leimor ki rak lahem levadam nitnah morashah zot hatorah, 'asher sam moshe le'einei kol yisra'el-va'asher lo yiten 'al pihem vekidshu 'alav milḥamah."

[66] E.g., *'Or Nogah,* II, p. 19: ". . . How sweet and pleasant is such a voice [or, sound, of the congregation chanting the *Shma' Yisra'el* together] . . . believe me, my brethren! By God! When I heard it, I could not restrain myself from tears, rivers of weeping (i.e., tears) from the source of my heart's happiness flooded my cheeks." "On my soul! All my life I have never felt such a spiritual enthusiasm as I felt then; and so will testify everyone who has truth as his objective."

[67] To prove his point (that there are people who do not understand the meaning of their prayers, and therefore—as Liebermann maintains—the vernacular should be substituted for Hebrew) the Hebrew reformer tells an anecdote of a learned Jew (*'ish rabani*) at a time of drought who was praying in the synagogue repeating a single verse while weeping excessively. Someone overheard him repeat the verse: "Ve'atzar 'et hashamayim velo yihye matar" (And he will shut up the heaven, that there be no rain" [Deuteronomy, 11:17]). Having been asked the reason for saying that [inappropriate] verse, the "learned" Jew replied: I prayed that God should *squeeze* the skies and that he should not leave any rain *there* but pour it onto the earth (" 'atzar" means both "stop" and "squeeze"; italics are mine), *'Or Nogah,* I, p. 8.

[68] *Ibid.*, p. 6.

[69] *Ibid.*, II, p. 20: "This one screams, and this one yawns; one begins the prayer, and one ends his prayer" (Liebermann); *Ḥerev Nokemet,* pp. 6–7: "One will cause the beam to fall, raising his voice . . . while blinking his eyes and scraping the floor with his feet . . . the second has a roar like a lion . . . the third is chirping like flying birds . . . their songs are songs of drunkards. . . ." Cf. similar description by Liebermann, *'Or Nogah,* II, p. 21.

[70] *Ibid.*, I, in the unpaginated introduction.

[70a] *Ibid.,* II, p. 16 (Liebermann); *Nogah Hatzedek,* p. 18 (Chorin).

[71] See footnote 38.

[72] *'Or Nogah,* I, p. 6: "After seeing that *all* the legal authorities permit prayers in the vernacular . . ." (Italics are mine).

[73] *Nagah Hatzedek,* p. 23. In his attempt to prove that the silent prayer of *Shmone 'Esre* should be eliminated, Chorin quotes Rabbi Moshe Isserles (ReMA) to the effect that if the time is pressing (*'im hasha'ah deḥukah*), the cantor should say the *Shmone 'Esre* aloud with the congregation. Concludes Chorin: "There is no more pressing a time than now" (Ve'en lecha sha'ah deḥukah yoter mizot). His argument is fallacious, for he takes a specific legal case in which a legal term is used (*hasha'ah deḥukah,* i.e., the hour is getting too late for a given practice, and it is necessary to hurry), and applies it—in its figurative and broad meaning (time is getting short; it is high time), and at the same time expects the legal result to apply too.

[74] *'Or Nogah,* I, p. 14. The term *'isur* (prohibition) is substituted by the term *ḥashash 'isur* (questionable prohibition, that is, a prohibition which is debatable, open to question) before any justification for the change in legal term has been put forth.

[75] *Ibid.*, p. 8; *Nogah Hatzedek,* p. 28.

[76] *'Or Nogah,* I, pp. 8, 21; *Nogah Hatzedek,* pp. 3, 4 ("umah lanu leha'arich bidvarim pshutim"), 6, 10, 15.

[77] *'Or Nogah,* I, p. 14: "Regarding . . . the (playing of the) organ, since it appears to me as somewhat a great sin, and is considered an iniquity and a[n act of] rebellion [against God], we are compelled to lengthen our discussion in this matter. . . . Now, at first observation we shall decree on this musical instrument a definite prohibition, a conclusive prohibition as a result of a few prohibitions which are dependent on it." After a lengthy discussion Liebermann makes a complete about face. See also *ibid.*, pp. 9–10; and *Nogah Hatzedek,* pp. 22–23 (Chorin).

[78] *Ibid.*, pp. 9–10.

[79] *Nogah Hatzedek,* p. 24. Chorin argues that by listening alone one may conclude that the Ashkenazi pronunciation is corrupted.

[80] Although both Chorin and Liebermann advocate praying in the vernacular, they still insist that certain prayers be said in Hebrew. Interestingly enough, their arguments in this matter sound anti-reform (it should be added that there are some other anti-reform arguments in the works under study especially with regard to the frequency of the services). Chorin's statement is indicative of some ambivalence in the attitude of the Hebrew reformers toward the reforms. He writes: "it is not in our hands to change them (*Kri'at Shma'* and *Shmone 'Esre*) to another language, for these prayers are traditional. . ." (*Nogah Hatzedek,* p. 17). He also touches upon the role praying in Hebrew has in the hope for *Ge'ulah,* and its symbolic importance: "And it (praying in Hebrew) would serve as a true sign of our belief in *Kibutz Galuyot* ("the ingathering of the exiles"), that we hope that the crown of our kingdom would return to us, and that our Holy Temple be rebuilt, and there we shall offer before him (God) our requests in the Hebrew tongue which is well established in our heart in a safe place" (*ibid.*, p. 18). Chorin further dismisses the argument of *necessity* in this case, since these Hebrew prayers are easy to learn (*ibid.*). Liebermann, too, demands that certain prayers be said in Hebrew only, and he mentions *Kri'at Shma'*. His reason: These are very holy and elevated prayers, and it is more appropriate to say them "in the language of the heritage of our holy fathers" (*'Or Nogah,* I, p. 23). Both reformers are of the opinion that the said

prayers be taught in Hebrew; Liebermann adds that parents should teach "our holy tongue" to their children (*ibid.*, p. 24).

[81] *Ibid.*, II, p. 17. Liebermann refers to those traditionalist Jews who do think that changes in antiquated customs and habits are right and correct, and that indeed there is nothing wrong in them as such; yet these people consider the changes as dangerous to religion, for these changes could cause other changes to follow. Here the Hebrew reformer touches upon one of the most important issues of religious reform in Judaism. Yet he uses it only for his polemics, avoiding any serious discussion, or else is not aware of the seriousness of the issue. His solution for those people is: Come, my friends, to the reform house of God, and judge for yourselves as to the good intention of the reformers. . . .

A RECTIFICATION OF THE DATE OF JUDAH MESSER LEON'S DEATH*

ISAAC RABINOWITZ

Cornell University

The dated superscription of an unpublished document in the Baron David Guenzberg Collection of the Moscow Lenin Library,[1] considered in the context of other literary and bibliographical evidence, allows the death of 15th-century Italy's most eminent Jewish humanist, Judah Messer Leon of Mantua and Naples, to be fixed within fairly close chronological limits. The amplified evidence, as will be shown, denies and refutes a speculation that has now become the dominant scholarly view, namely, that Judah Messer Leon is to be identified with the Messer Leon who was publicly beheaded in Moscow on April 22, 1490 for having failed to cure the mortal illness of Ivan Ivanovich, son of the Grand Duke Ivan III Vassilivich.[2]

I

We now have attestation of the fact that Judah Messer Leon's death occurred no later than the 8th of Tishri, 5260, which corresponds to September 12, 1499. His name, followed by the initial letters of one of the pietistic formulae used only when reference is made to a deceased person, appears together with this date in the head-note to the document mentioned above, Guenzberg MS 1053c. The document proper consists of the text-form of the certificate of *semikha*, or rabbinical diploma, conferred by David Messer Leon, Judah's son, upon Judah Sarephatti and upon Solomon b. Perez Sarephatti Bonfoi. The superscribed note, in text and translation, is as follows:

1. סדר הסמיכה אשר סמך הרב הכולל כמהר"ר מסיר דוד בכמוהר"ר
2. יאודה הנקרא מסיר/ ליאון זלה"ה להרב כמה"ר יהודה צרפתי
3. ולבן הרב הגאון כמהר"ר פרץ צרפתי זלה"ה / המכונה בונפוי הובא לי הצעיר ברכיה בכמה"ר יאודה רושו זלה"ה מעיר /
4. מונישטירייו היום יום ה' ח' לתשרי שנת היוצר יחד לבם לפ"ג

1. "Order of the *semikha* which the widely-learned[3] Rabbi, o[ur] h[onored] t[eacher], the R[abbi], R[abbi] Messer David, s[on of] o. h. t. the R.R. Judah,
2. called Messer/ Leon (r[emembered be he] f[or the] l[ife of] the w[orld to] c[ome]), conferred upon the Rabbi, o. h. t. R. Judah Sarephatti,[4] and upon the son of the Rabbi, the Gaon, o. h. t. the R. R. Perez Sarephatti
3. (r. f. l. w. c.), surnamed Bonfoi[5]: it was brought to me, the insignificant Berechiah, s[on of] o. h. t. R. Judah Russo[6] (r. f. l. w. c.), from the
4. city of/ Monesterio[7], today, Thursday, the 8th of Tishri, of the year [numbered by letters in the verse] *He that fashioneth the hearts of them all* [Ps. 33:15], 5260 b[y the] l[arger] s[pecification]."

No earlier documentation than that given above of the date by which Judah Messer Leon was known to have died has thus far been published. The earliest previously available indication of the *terminus post quem non* refers to the year 1505: this date appears in a scribal addendum to the Parma MS of *'En haq-Qore,* David b. Judah Messer Leon's commentary on Maimonides' *Guide,* on folio 2b of which David mentions his father with addition of the *post mortem* formula, ז"ל.[8]

II

Judah Messer Leon could hardly have died before the printing of Jacob Landau's legal code, the *Agur*, for both he and his son David furnished approbations for the book.[9] Since Landau himself is known to have corrected the work as it was being printed, he would certainly have followed his usual practice and written the abbreviation of some *post mortem* pietism after Judah's name if the latter's death had occurred before the printing of the book was finished.[10]

Now several considerations impel us to conclude that the *Agur* cannot have been printed before 1490; indeed, the work probably did not appear before 1491 or 1492. In the first place, as stated, David Messer Leon was included by Landau among the group of rabbis and *ḥakhamim* whom he invited to write approbations of his book: he would hardly have done this prior to David's *semikha*, which we know was conferred upon him publicly on his 18th birthday, Sabbath Hanukkah, 5250 = November 21, 1489.[11] Secondly, R. Joseph Colon is cited several times in the *Agur* with the formula זצ"ל following his name, and he is known to have died *ca.* 1490.[12] Thirdly, study of the characteristics of the Hebrew type-font used in the *Agur* points to a date possibly as late as 1493 for the volume's publication.[13]

The evidence afforded by the date of the printing of the *Agur* is wholly consonant with, and corroborates, that of the responsum on the study of philosophy and the sciences which Jacob Provenzali addressed to David Messer Leon. This document, in which Judah Messer Leon is referred to as alive, is dated in the year 1490.[14]

III

On the basis of the facts presented above, Judah Messer Leon's death must have occurred between 1490 and 1499. Other evidence, however, is available to show that this event must be set at a date closer to 1499 than to 1490: this consists of some bio-bibliographical data drawn from those of David Messer Leon's extant works known to have been written before his father's death.

There are three such works: (1) a commentary on Lamentations (Paris MS 676[8]: brief notice by H. Zotenberg, *Cat.*, Paris 1866); (2) *Magen David* (Montefiore MS 290: partially published by S. Schechter, REJ xxiv [1892], 110–138); and (3) *Ma'amar Shebhaḥ han-Nashim* (Guenzberg MS 782 and Parma MS 1395[2]: brief excerpt [wrongly attributed to Judah Messer Leon[15]] published by A. Neubauer, REJ X [1885] 94–97).[16] *Magen David* is a kabbalistic work; *Ma'amar Shebhaḥ han-Nashim* is a commentary on Prov. 31:10–31, prefaced by a long and learned defence of the study, by Jews, of the arts of rhetoric and poetry. All three were written by David while his father was yet living: *Shebhaḥ han-Nashim*, the latest of the three since it quotes the other two,[17] refers to Judah with addition of the *ante mortem* formula יצ"ו. It is probable that the sequence of the three books is that in which I have listed them, since in *Shebhaḥ han-Nashim* (p. 24). David adds the words "which I recently wrote" to a citation of the *Magen David* (...בס׳ מגן דוד שחברתי מקרוב).

In these three extant works, David refers to at least six other books of his that have not come down to us.[18] Among these is *Menorath Zahabh*, cited in all three; of this he says in *Shebhaḥ han-Nashim* (p. 30) that he wrote it "six years ago" (....בס׳ מנורת זהב שחיברתי זה ו׳ שני׳). Speaking in *Shebhaḥ han-Nashim* of another, *Abbir Ya'aqobh* (devoted, in part at least, to music [p. 14]), he adds the words "which I have just written" (...ובס׳ אביר יעקב שחברתי עתה [p. 30]).

We are thus apprised that David Messer Leon wrote at least nine books during a six-year period which must have elapsed some time before his father's death. If, then, the speculation that dates Judah Messer Leon's death on April 22, 1490 is correct, David Messer Leon would have been 18 years old when he wrote the last of these nine, *Shebhaḥ han-Nashim*, and only 13 years old when he wrote *Menorath Zahabh*. A fecundity *so* precocious, unlikely in itself, is nowhere attested of David Messer Leon; the six-year period in question certainly endured considerably beyond April 22, 1490.

Corroboration of this conclusion is readily available from what David tells us about himself in *Shebhaḥ han-Nashim* and *Magen David*. At the outset of the former volume he says: "Saith the insignificant David, s[on of] o[ur] h[onored] t[eacher], the R[abbi], R[abbi] Judah, h[is] R[ock] and [Redeemer] p[rotect him], called Messer Leon: Some time ago, I departed from Madness Land[19] and *without the camp* made my *dwelling* [Lev. 13: 46] *to feed in the gardens and to gather lilies* [Song of S. 6:2]. By virtue of the fact that I was free from worldly preoccupations — although my soul was *desolate, faint all the day* [Lam. 1:13]. . . . — the circumstances born of the time *smote me, wounded me* [Song of S. 5:7], *beat me, but I knew it not* [Prov. 23:35]. The *waters* of tribulations would have *flowed over my head* [Lam. 3:54], *if it had not been the Lord who was for me* [Ps. 124:1]. For because of His compassion upon me, the Lord gave bountifully of His abundant wisdom and of His *willing spirit*, and *upheld* [Ps. 51:14] me, *cleansed me* [*ibid*. v. 4], to make many compositions after my departure. And I made many studies in Torah, Scriptural verses, and philosophy alike; and fashioned many verses, too, in the Hebrew language, and in the Christian tongue[20] during periods of leisure."[21] We learn from this passage that several, at the very least, of the nine works written by David over the six-year period were composed subsequent to his departure from "Madness Land"; one of these several was certainly *Magen David*, which, he tells us in *Shebhaḥ han-Nashim*, he wrote "recently." Now *Magen David* was written in some place where there were Karaites[22] — hence not in Italy — and at a time, subsequent to "the tribulations of the expulsion", when David Messer Leon had adopted the practice of accepting fees for his rabbinical services.[23] Thus we see that "Madness Land" is David's designation of an actual locale, one from which he claims to have been driven to the place(s) outside Italy where he wrote "many" of the nine works (at least) mentioned above. We note, too, that the "departure from Madness Land" of *Shebhaḥ han-Nashim* was referred to as "expulsion" in the somewhat earlier *Magen David.*

The chronological, geographical and other facts adduced above permit David Messer Leon's "expulsion" (גרוש) - "departure" (נסיעה) to be identified with only one historical episode. Following upon Charles VIII's entry into Naples, February 22, 1495, the Neapolitan populace, aided by the French, attacked and plundered the Jews, thousands of whom fled the city; most of these refugees found their way into the European territories of the Turkish Empire.[24] Accordingly, the "many" works stated by David Messer Leon in the latest of them, *Shebhaḥ han-Nashim*, to have been written subsequent to his "departure" from "Madness Land" (the Neapolitan kingdom) must have been written in and after 1495. Now since we know that these "many" works include at least three — *Magen David, Abbir Ya'aqobh*, and *Shebhaḥ han-Nashim*, in this order — and since we must allow sufficient time for David's settling in his new locale and for the composition of the books, we cannot be far wrong if we assign the last-named work to the year 1497 or 1498.

Where did David — and probably his father, too — settle after departing Naples and Italy in 1495? We cannot be altogether certain, but to judge by the superscription of David's *hattarat hora'ah*, quoted above, it was very likely "the city of Monasterio" (Monastir) in what is now Yugoslavia; and it may have been here that Judah Messer Leon, the celebrated author of the *Nopheth Ṣuphim*, died. Wherever he died, however, he was not the physician who was executed in Moscow on April 22, 1490. Such an identification is necessarily excluded by the date of *this* Judah's death, which, as shown in this paper, certainly occurred between some time in the year 1497 and early September of the year 1499.

NOTES

* From time to time, in the course of preparing a critical edition and English translation of Judah Messer Leon's most significant book, his biblically illustrated treatise on the rhetorical art (*Sepher Nopheth Ṣuphim: The Book of the Honeycomb's Flow*), I have come upon various problems in connection with this author's life and works. The present treatment of one such problem will, I hope, be considered a not inappropriate token of regard for an old friend who is an outstanding devotee of Jewish books and their lore.

1 The 2-page document is listed by A. I. Katsh, *Catalogue of Hebrew Mss. Preserved in the U.S.S.R.*, N.Y, 1957, p. 14; it is MS 1053c of the Guenzberg Collection. Thanks are herewith expressed to President Katsh and to the authorities of the Moscow Lenin Library for making a photograph of the document available to me.

2 The speculation was first advanced as a tentative hypothesis by V. Colorni, "Note

per la biografia di alcuni dotti ebrei vissuti a Mantova nel secolo XV," *Annuario di Studi Ebraici*, I, Rome 1935, pp. 175-6. Repeated as a possibility by C. Roth, *History of the Jews in Italy*, Philadelphia 1946, p. 203, the hypothesis has now passed as a commonly accepted fact into S. W. Baron's monumental standard work, *A Social and Religious History of the Jews*, X, New York and Philadelphia 1965, p. 289.

[3] For this meaning of the term הרב הכולל, cf. David Messer Leon's polemical legal essay on *semikha*, edited by S. Bernfeld under the title כבוד חכמים, Berlin 1899, p. 65: .... שמי שהוא חכם כולל בשאר החכמות עם התלמוד הוא יותר ראוי לסמיכה מהתלמודי הפשוט. As in the signature to the present document, David elsewhere calls his father, Judah Messer Leon, החכם הכולל; see S. Schechter, "Notes sur Messer David Léon tirées de manuscrits," *Revue des études juives*, XXIV (1892), p. 120.

[4] This may be the Judah Sarephatti mentioned in Sassoon, *Ohel David*, I, no. 799 (510b), and in Hirschfeld, *Cat.*, no. 371 (p. 117); cf. Conforte, *Qore ha-Doroth*, Berlin 1846, 39a (1. 6 from bottom).

[5] This "son of.... R. Perez Sarephatti... Bonfoi" is the *musmakh* named on p. 2, 11. 7-8 of our document, R. Solomon. He is known as the corrector (מגיה) of the 1484 edition of Solomon ibn Gabirol's *Mibhḥar ha-Peninim*, and of the edition of Beḥai ibn Paquda's *Ḥobhoth ha-lebhabhoth* printed at Naples in 1489; see J. B. de Rossi, *Annales hebraeo-typographici sec. XV.*, Parma 1795, p. 177, and M. Steinschneider, *Cat. Bodl.*, pp. 2319 and 780. Both Solomon and Perez Sarephatti Bonfoi figure in David Messer Leon's *pesaq-din* (כ"ח, pp. 12, 16, 64), the former as *ḥazzan* of the Valona Pugliese congregation, the latter as at one time Rabbi there; cf. Schechter, *op. cit.*, pp. 130–131, 133.

In view of the historical importance attaching to David Messer Leon's essay and his views on *semikha*, it may be of interest to transcribe the concluding and more important portion of the text of his *hattarat hora'ah* (p. 2, 11. 5–15):

5. אליכם אישים אקרא ודברי לכם ינעם כי הרימותי בחור מעם
6. סמכתי ידי עליו בסמיכה בשמחה להלבישו מלכות ולכסותו
7. בשמיכה ויקרא מורינו ורבינו הרב ר' שלמה בן מורינו הרב רבי
8. פרץ ז"ל צרפתי בונפוי תמיד בספר תורה ובכל דבר
9. שבקדושה כי לא יאתה המלוכה יורה יורה ידין ידין יחייב יפטור
10. יזכה יחייב יתיר יאסור יתעסק בטיב גטין וקידושין
11. וחליצות ינדה יחרים כתועפות הרים נוה האל עושה
12. פלא תצרנהו תסובבנהו תבוננהו בעדותיך יחיה לפניך
13. באמונת עתך לשלמה אלהים משפטיך נאם דוד
14. הקטן בן הרב החסיד הכולל החכם כמהר"ר יאודה נקרא
15. מיסיר די ליאון ז"ל.

On the social and historical role of the *semikha*, see now M. Breuer, הסמיכה האשכנזית, in *Zion* XXXIII (1968), 15–46.

[6] Although a R. Berechia Russo (רוסו) is listed by Conforte, *op. cit.*, 51a, he is scarcely to be identified with the writer of our superscription. We do not know where this Berechia was when he received the text-form of David Messer Leon's *hattarat hora'ah* from Monastir. If he was at Arta (near Valona) he may have been a scion of the Russo (רוסו) family known to have settled there, or if at Lepanto, he may have been a connection of the R. Moses Russo (רושו) who was one of the Italian rabbis of that community; see Rosanes, דברי ימי ישראל בתוגרמה, Jerusalem 1930, pp. 113 and 229.

[7] I.e. Monastir, today Bitola in Yugoslavia; cf. Rosanes, *op. cit.*, pp. 109 and 152–

153, and Bernfeld, כ"ח, p. XII. David Messer Leon (and his father, too) may well have been at Monastir for some years before the former took up residence first at Saloniki and then at Valona.

8 According to P. Perreau, "Hebräische Handschriften in Parma," *Hebräische Bibliographie* (המזכיר), VIII (1865), p. 65, note 5.

9 The *Agur* was the first printed Hebrew book to carry such approbations, the second to be printed in its author's lifetime; cf. J. Bloch, *Hebrew Printing at Naples*, N.Y. 1942, 22-23, and J. L. Teicher, "Notes on Hebrew Incunables," *Journal of Jewish Bibliography*, IV (1943), 56–59. The text of Judah Messer Leon's approbation is given in the *Jewish Encyclopaedia*, N.Y. 1904, II, 27, David's in Teicher, *op. cit.*, 58. Judah Messer Leon is not only notable as one of the initial approbationers of a printed Hebrew volume, but holds even greater distinction as writer of the very first Hebrew book to be printed in its author's lifetime, his *Nopheth Ṣuphim*, printed by Abraham Conat at Mantua, 1475-6. For a description of this incunabulum, see Moses Marx, "A Catalogue of the Hebrew Books Printed in the Fifteenth Century Now in the Library of the Hebrew Union College," *Studies in Bibliography and Booklore*, I (1953-4), no. 36, p. 36.

10 Judah's signature appears at the foot of his approbation as הקטן יהודה מסיר ליאן; David's is signed דוד הקטן מקטני התלמידים בן כמהר"ר יהודה הנקרא מסיר לאון (citations above, note 9).

11 The date has been correctly worked out by Rosanes, *op. cit.*, p. 85, on the basis of data furnished by David Messer Leon in כ"ח. Accordingly, David was born at Venice Dec. 10, 1471, as stated by Cassuto, *Enc. Judaica*, Berlin 1928–34, X, 787.

12 Graetz, *Gesch.*, Leipzig 1890, VIII, 281–282 (based on the chronology of Colon's controversy with Moses Capsali); cf. Teicher, *op. cit.*, and the articles in *Kirjath Sepher* VI and VII referred to therein.

13 M. Fava and G. Bresciano, *La Stampa a Napoli nel XV Secolo*, Leipzig 1912, II, 208–209; cf. Teicher, p. 59, and Bloch, *op. cit.*, p. 23, where it is stated that the *Agur* "probably represents the last Hebrew book printed in Naples."

14 The text is printed in Eliezer Ashkenazi, *Dibhre Ḥakhamim*, Metz 1849, 63–75; see the opening lines, p. 63. Even if, as suggested by Cassuto in *E.J.*, this responsum was "gänzlich oder z. T. gefälscht," there is no reason to doubt the accuracy of the date or the fact that Judah Messer Leon was then alive.

15 Neubauer's incorrect attribution of *Ma'amar Shebhaḥ han-Nashim* to Judah instead of to David Messer Leon also appears in M.A. Shulvass, *Jewish Life in Italy during the Renaissance* (Hebr.), N.Y. 1955, p. 216, and in C. Roth, *The Jews in the Renaissance*, N.Y. 1965, p. 312.

16 In addition to the published excerpts of these works I have been able to consult the Parma MS of *Shebhaḥ han-Nashim*, a microfilm of which was kindly supplied me by the authorities of the Biblioteca Palatina; Parma 1395[1], incidentally, is a copy of the Conat incunabulum of Judah Messer Leon's *Nopheth Ṣuphim*. On *Shebhaḥ han-Nashim*, see additionally the remarks by M. Steinschneider, "Zur Frauenliteratur," in A. Habermann's convenient reprint, Jerusalem 1968, 57–62.

17 The Lamentations-commentary is cited p. 19, *Magen David* p. 24 (my numbering of the pages of Parma MS 1395[2]).

18 *Menorath Zahabh; Segullath Melakhim* (cited in *Lam.*-com.); *Migdal David* (not listed by Cassuto in *E.J.* X; cited in *Magen David* according to Schechter, *op. cit.*, p. 125); a commentary on the *Semag* (Schechter, *ibid.*); *Abbir Ya'aqobh*; and his

Halaṣa be-Sippure ham-Meliṣim, a poetic treatment of tales written by poets (p. 45 of *Sh. han-N.*; also pp. 1 and 40).

19 Doubtless Naples in the time of troubles that ensued after 1492; see below.

20 Italian is certainly meant, perhaps Latin as well.

21 The Hebrew text of the passage, transcribed from the Parma MS:

אמר דוד הקטן בכמהר"ר יהודה יצ"ו הנקרא מיסיר ליאון : הנה מאז נסעתי מארץ ההוללה, ובדד ישבתי מחוץ למחנה לרעות בגנים וללקוט שושנים. ובהיות כי היתי פנוי מעסקי העולם — עם כי נפשי שוממה, כל היום דוה, עד דוד הגדיל ביגונות ומחשבות משתנות — הכוני פשעוני [צ"ל : פצעוני] ילידי הזמן, הלמוני בל ידעתי. צפו מי' הצרות על ראשי לולי ה' שהיה לי ; כי לחמלתו עלי ה' השפיע משפע חכמתו ורוח נדיבתו, ויסמכני טהרני לעשות חבורים רבים אחר נסיעתי. ועשיתי חקירות גדולות בין בתורה בי[ן] בפסוקים בין בפלוסופיא, גם חרוזים רבים בלשון עברי ובלשון נוצרי בעתות הפנאי.

Cf. the somewhat variant text of a portion of this passage quoted from the end of *Tehilla le-David* by Bernfeld, *op. cit.*, p. XXIII.

22 Schechter, op. cit., pp. 126–127: ... ובפרט להיותם עומדים בכאן ובינינו קראים ...

23 *Ibid.*, p. 127 bottom: ... גם אני נוהג ... לקחת פרס אחר צרות הגרוש...

24 See the account in B. Netanyahu, *Don Isaac Abravanel*, Philadelphia 1953, pp. 67 ff., especially the references in the notes to the Hebrew account of Elijah Capsali.

THE ORDER OF THE BOOKS

NAHUM M. SARNA

Brandeis University

It would seem to be incontestable that the threefold division of the Hebrew Scriptures into Torah, Prophets and Hagiographa reflects the historic process whereby these three corpora became canonized.[1] There is also plenty of evidence to show that in early times, and throughout the Talmudic period, it was not customary for the scribes to write the entire Bible continuously as a single roll.[2] For obvious, practical, reasons such a gigantic roll would have been thoroughly unwieldy, if not unusable, and was not encouraged by the rabbinic authorities.

According to a report in the Palestinian Talmud,[3] R. Meir permitted the writing of the Torah and the prophets "as one,"[4] while the Sages disallowed this, though permitting the Prophets and Hagiographa "as one." Another version of this dispute, this time in the Babylonian Talmud,[5] reports that R. Meir permitted the "fastening together" of the Torah, Prophets and Hagiographa "as one."[6] R. Judah required each corpus to be kept distinct, while the Sages insisted on a separate roll for each of the several Books. It is further related by R. Judah that a certain Boethus b. Zonin possessed all the Prophets "fastened together as one," something that was done at the direction of R. Eleazar b. Azariah. A variant tradition, however, denies this. Rabbi (Judah Ha-Nasi) testified that the rabbinic authorities had, indeed, once declared valid a copy of the entire Scriptures "fastened together."[7]

Clearly, the normal practice was not to combine several Books into single volumes, but to restrict rolls to individual works. This state of affairs is exactly what prevails in the Dead Sea Scrolls, and what is reflected in halakhic discussions regulating the placing of rolls from the different sections of the Canon on top of one another.[8]

In the light of all this it is pertinent to inquire into the meaning of "order." If the three corpora that constitute canonized Scripture were not combined into a single roll, and if even the prophetic Books were only exceptionally so combined, but were regularly kept individually distinct, as it is certain the Hagiographa almost always were, then what is meant, from a practical standpoint, when one speaks of the "order" of the threefold canon? In what way did this order find tangible expression?

It is well known that the earliest source for the arrangement of the Books of Scripture is an anonymous Tannaitic statement appearing in the Babylonian Talmud which separately lists the "order" of the Prophets and Hagiographa.[9] The sequence given diverges startlingly in many respects from that current in our printed Bibles. The Amoraim questioned and attempted to rationalize some of the more unusual features of the list, but they did not cavil against the concept of a fixed, standard, arrangement. Again, it is appropriate to ask, what is meant by priority in order when each Biblical Book existed as a separate roll?

It might be suggested, of course, that the problem arose when the codex-form came to supplant the roll.[10] Here, the problem of sequence would, indeed, inevitably arise and an authoritative ruling would need to be laid down for scribal instruction.[11] However, a study of the history of the use of codices among Jews demonstrates decisively that this explanation has to be ruled out.

In the first place, if the references to the order of the Books were to the codex-form, it would be inexplicable that such a revolutionary development would pass unmentioned in Talmudic literature and would not have its own technical term or have engendered discussion or formulation of the halakhic consequences.[12]

Moreover, the above-mentioned anonymous *Baraitha*[13] that records the order of the Books cannot be later than the end of the second century C.E., and most likely reflects a much earlier tradition. The codex-form had, by the end of the Tannaitic period, become dominant among Christian communities, but it did not really establish itself in the pagan world before the fourth century C.E. Among Jews it was even at this time not in vogue and the use of the roll for the sacred books was still stubbornly adhered to. In fact, it was the adoption of the codex-form for the Scriptures that was one of the distinguishing features of the Christian communities and that differentiated Christian from Jewish practice.[14] By the time Jews finally yielded to innovation, the differing traditions relative to the sequence of the Books had long crystallized.

Clearly, some explanation other than the need to collect more than one Book onto a single roll or the complete Scriptures into a codex must be found to account for the emergence of a fixed order. It is not a question of the considerations that conditioned a particular arrangement, but a problem of the very meaning of the concept of order itself. Fortunately, recent studies in cuneiform literature, taken together with information long at hand concerning the practices of the Hellenistic book world, afford an opportunity to present a fresh approach to the issue.

Two processes may be discerned at work in the world of the Mesopotamian scribes. A clear and unmistakable trend toward standardization in respect to the classical literature develops, and the growth of archives and libraries takes place. These two phenomena need not necessarily have operated originally in tandem, but it cannot have been long before they interacted to create mutually complementary stimuli to the acceleration of both processes.

The impulse toward canonization (in the secular sense of the word) manifested itself in the emergence of a recognized corpus of classical literature and in the tendency to produce a standardized text, a fixed arrangement of content and an established sequence in which the works were to be read or studied. Tablets would be grouped into series and often subseries, each being properly numbered.[15]

The growth of collections of cuneiform tablets (or of papyrus rolls) must, of necessity, have generated rationalized and convenient methods of storing materials in such a way as to facilitate identification and expedite usage. This would be particularly true of a systematically assembled library like that of Ashurbanipal (668–627 B.C.E.) which, it is estimated, contained about fifteen hundred tablets. The techniques adopted and developed in this royal collection must surely have become the model for librarians throughout the cuneiform world.

Generally speaking, the tablets were equipped with informative, identifying colophons, or they were indexed at their rims. They were topically arranged in series, each series apparently having been stored together either in built-in bookcases or in buckets. The bundles were frequently tied together with strings, and tags or dockets were attached to indicate the contents. Of particular interest for assessing the establishment and significance of a fixed sequence is the oft-found scribal practice of including the incipit of the next tablet or series at the end of the preceding item. The existence of catalogues is further proof, if any be needed, of the fixation of order within a given collection, and when these catalogues also contain the serial catch-lines, and when they have been found in duplicate copies, there cannot be any doubt that the concept of a standardized order of classical works became part of the Mesopotamian scribal-bibliographic tradition. This tradition was nurtured as much by archival and library needs as by pedagogic considerations which answered the requirements of the curriculum of the scribal schools.[16]

The bibliographic techniques developed in Mesopotamia spread throughout the Near East and undoubtedly exercised a profound influence upon the classical and Hellenistic world, although the channels of transmission cannot yet be determined with certainty. Libraries, private and public, had existed in the classical world as early as the sixth century B.C.E., and they became quite widespread throughout the Greek mainland and Asia Minor in the succeeding two centuries.[17] Since the extreme limit of a Greek papyrus roll was about thirty-five feet, it would be difficult to keep together several works belonging to a single genre or credited to a single author. Hence, collectors resorted to the devices invented by the Mesopotamian scribes. In addition to the informative colophon, they used the book-boxes or buckets for storage in such instances and attached to each roll an identifying tag of papyrus or vellum. They also compiled a list of the works held within each bucket.[18]

Our most detailed information about the quest for established order of literary compositions comes, of course, from the greatest library of all antiquity, the crowning glory of the Hellenistic world, the great museum-library of Alexandria.[19] Founded during the first decade of the third century B.C.E., the main collection could boast, just a half-century later, of four hundred thousand "mixed rolls" containing two or more separate works, and ninety-thousand "unmixed" (i.e., single) rolls, while the outer library contained forty-two thousand eight hundred single rolls.[20] By the year 41 B.C.E., the library had grown to no less than seven hundred thousand volumes to which were added the two hundred thousand stolen from Pergamum by Marcus Antonius to present to Cleopatra.[21]

A collection of nearly a million volumes would very soon degenerate into a state of utter chaos without an ordered system of storage, classification and cataloging.[22] Accordingly, the manuscripts were distributed throughout ten great halls, each hall representing one of the divisions of Hellenic learning. Then they were housed in the *armaria,* the book-lockers that lined the walls. The key to retrieving the myriads of rolls was the great classification system and the one-hundred-twenty volume catalogue, the famed *Pinakes* developed by Callimachus c. 310–240 B.C.E.). The most significant result of the work of this great bibliographer and of the labors of the "grammarians," the scholars of the museum-library, was the production of the "Alexandrian Canon," the authoritative, standardized corpus of the great writers of the past, arranged according to certain principles of order.[23]

The impact of Hellenism upon Jewish civilization was many-faceted and enduring and has long received the attention of the scholarly world. In particular, the influence of the Alexandrian grammarians, their professional practices and technical terminology, upon the Jews of Palestine has recently been thoroughly established and documented in great detail.[24] It must be remembered that Palestianian Jewry was part of the common Mediterranean civilized world and it occupied a strip of land which was at once the crossroads and meeting point of the Near Eastern and Hellenic traditions. It must be taken for granted that in the libraries of the Jewish communities throughout Palestine in Second Temple times and subsequently,[25] as well as in the archives and library of the Jerusalem Temple itself, the established time-honored library practices and bibliographic techniques of Mesopotamia and the Hellenistic world were fully operative.

It is the suggestion of this writer that the Tannaitic discussions anent the order of the Scriptural Books derive from precisely the aforementioned traditions. The three corpora of the Biblical Canon would be stored in the libraries each in its own section, and the individual Books that made up each corpus would be placed in the *armaria* in their appropriately assigned order and shelf-listed accordingly. It might be said, in fact, that the Biblical codices, when they finally emerged, simply reflected and preserved the orders of shelving and cataloging current in the ancient Jewish libraries. What the original, underlying, principles of arrangement were that determined the place and sequence of the books on the library shelves is another matter and beyond the scope of the present study.

NOTES

1. It should be noted that there is good reason to believe that the Hagiographa were never really formally canonized as a complete corpus.

2. The length of rolls varied in the ancient world. The Egyptian Harris Papyrus I (BM 9999) is 133 ft. long. Greek papyri were much shorter, rarely exceeding 35ft. See, F. G. Kenyon, *Books and Readers in Ancient Greece and Rome* 2d. ed. Oxford, 1951. pp. 53f.

3. P. Megillah III, i 73b

4. כותבין תורה ונביאים כאחת

5. Baba Bathra 13b; cf. M. Soferim III, i, iii.

6. מדביק... כאחד

7 מדובקים כאחד

8. Tosephta Megillah IV (III) 20 (ed. Zuckermandel, p. 227, ll. 2f; ed. Lieberman, III, 20, p. 359, ll. 64-66); B. Megillah 27a; P. Megillah, III, i, 73b.

9. B. Baba Bathra 14b ת״ר סדרן של נביאים... סדרן של כתובים

10. Cf. H. E. Ryle, *The Canon of the O.T.,* London, 1909, p. 236.

11. See the discussion in C. D. Ginsburg, *Introduction to the Massoretico-Critical Edition of the Hebrew Bible*. Ktav, N.Y., 1966, pp. 1-8.

12. The later Hebrew technical term for the codex, מצחף , is a loanword from Arabic and is not found before the Geonic period. v. E. Ben Yehuda, *Thesaurus,* VII, p. 3248, s.v. S. Lieberman, *Hellenism in Jewish Palestine,* N.Y. 1962, pp. 204, has pointed out that in rabbinic literature פנקס is sometimes identical with codex. This refers, however, to the primitive sense of writing tablets being fastened together. They were certainly used for records or notes and even if extracts of the Biblical books were recorded in this form, certainly the consecutive inscription of more than one very short book would be out of the question.

13. V. supra n.9.

14. For the revised history of the codex, see C. H. Roberts, *Proceedings of the British Academy,* XL (1954), pp. 169-204. Cf., also F. G. Kenyon, *Books and Readers in Ancient Greece and Rome,* Oxford, 1951, pp. 40, 65, 96-101, 110-115; *idem, Our Bible and the Ancient Manuscripts,* N.Y. 1958, pp. 41-43; D. Diringer, *The Hand-Produced Book,* N.Y., 1953, pp. 132f., 161-163, 203; Lieberman, *op.cit.* pp 202-208.

15. These phenomena have been explored in detail by W. W. Hallo, *IEJ,* 12 (1962), 13-26; *JAOS,* 83 (1963), 167-176; 88 (1968), 71-89.

16. See the preceding note as well as, A. Leo Oppenheim, *Ancient Mesopotamia,* Chicago, 1964, pp. 14f., 17-20, 240f. and the literature cited on p. 370, nn. 15-16. Of particular importance is M. Weitemyer, *Libri* 6 (1955-56), pp. 217-238.

17. G. H. Putnam, *Authors and Their Public in Ancient Times,* N.Y. London, 1894; Kenyon, *Books,* etc. *op. cit.,* esp. pp. 24, 38, 81; E. A. Parsons, *The Alexandrian Library,* Amsterdam-London-N.Y., 1952, pp. 3-50.

18. Kenyon, *op. cit.,* pp. 62, 64f.; H. Hunger *et al., Geschichte der Textüberlieferung etc.,* Zurich, 1961, pp. 44-46. J. A. Goldstein, *The Letters of Demosthenes,* N.Y. London, 1968, pp. 9f., 19, 267.

19. For a comprehensive description of the Alexandrian library see Parsons, *op.cit.*

20. *Ibid.,* p. 204.

21. *Ibid.,* pp. 24-31.

22. *Ibid.,* pp. 204-218

23. *Ibid.,* pp. 224-231.

24. S. Lieberman, *Greek in Jewish Palestine,* N.Y., 1942; *Hellenism in Jewish Palestine,* N.Y., 2d. ed. 1960.

25. On Jewish libraries in the Roman empire see J. Juster, *Les Juifs dans l'Empire romain,* I (Paris, 1914), p. 474f.

BIBLIOGRAPHISCHES AUS DER GENISA

A. SCHEIBER

בית המדרש לרבנים, בודפשט

I. Maimuni als Bibliophile

Aus der klassischen Periode der Genisa kennen wir Bibliotheken, die im Besitze von Ärzten waren.[1] Sie enthielten sowohl hebräische wie arabische Bücher.[2] Sie beweisen, dass die jüdischen Ärzte im Mittelalter nicht nur Praktiker waren, sondern dass es unter ihnen auch Männer von wissenschaftlichem Interesse und hoher Gelehrsamkeit gab.

Wir haben von Ärzten Kenntnis, die sich auch mit Buchhandel befassten.[3]

Zum bibliophilen Ärztetypus möchten wir einen neueren Beitrag liefern.

Es handelt sich um einen Brief aus der Genisa in Cambridge (T.-S. Misc. Box 28[140]). Er ist auf Papier, in Quadratschrift, auf beiden Seiten geschrieben.

Mosche b. Levi, der Diener, schreibt an seinen gewesenen Herrn, Mosche, den Arzt. Er war mit seinem Herrn sehr zufrieden, hoffte auch 10 Zuz (Silberlinge)[4] von ihm zu erhalten, verliess ihn aber dennoch, denn er schämte sich, dass der Arzt oftmals sich selbst half und sich Wasser zum Händewaschen holte. (Bemerkenswert, dass der jüdische Arzt bereits im Mittelalter sich häufig die Hände wusch.)

Der Diener scheint auch die Büchereinkäufe des Arztes besorgt zu haben. Aus dem Brief ergibt sich, dass er ihm einen Talmudband verkaufte, der die Traktate Joma, Sukka und Jom Tov (Beza) enthielt und das ספר קנין. Dieses wird mit Samuel b. Chofnis Werk identisch sein.[5] Vom Erlös der Bücher hatte er noch je einen halben Silberling zu bekommen. Dies möchte er von seinem gewesenen Herrn erhalten. Vielleicht war dies der Anteil, der vom Verkauf ihm gebührte.

Auf grund der Charakteristik des Dieners müssen wir den Arzt mit Maimuni identifizieren. Die hochwertigen Beifügungen können sich nur auf ihn beziehen. Auch seine Söhne werden erwähnt (Zeilen 12–15.).

Der vollständige Text des Briefes lautet folgenderweise:

T-S. Misc. Box 28[140]

[1a]

שלום רֿב וג׳
והאיש משֿה וכ׳
כי ארֿך ימֿים וכ׳

גביר רופאים עטרת החכמים
אביֿ [ה]שרים וגזע התמים:
וגם נדיב וגם צדיק וישר
וירא מנעוריו ובמרומים
שמו משה כמשה
איש אלהים אשר הריד אמרים הנעימם
יהי האל בעזרך שר ותרום
ותצליח בכל לילות וימים
חמודיך יהו לעד ברוכים
וגם ישבו עלי כסא אבותם
בחייך והם ששים שלמים
לקיים תחֿת אבותיך וכ׳
העבד ישתחוה לפני מושב אדוניו
וישאל מטוב שימשוך על[י]ו חוט
חסדו וידינו בכל מעשיו לכף
זכות כמו [של]מדנו מהדרתו
היקרה אל תדין את חבירך
אלא לכף זכוֿת וכך אמרו חכמֿ
זֿל דע מה למעלה ממך וכו׳
והעבד לא בא אצל רבו והני[ח]
ביתו אלא כדי שימצא
מה שיהיה בו תחייתו ו[כו׳]
ואין העבד שוטה שידבר
דבר ולא ישלימו אבל חש

1 שלום] תה׳ קיט, קסה. 2 והאיש] במ׳ יב, ג. 3 כי] משלי ג, ב. 4 עטרת] שם, יד, כד. 8 משה] לפניו כתוֿב ״כמומש״ ונקוד עליו. 9 איש] תה׳ צ, א. 15 תחת] שם, מה, יז. 20 אל תדין] אבות א, ו. 22 דע] שם, ב, א. 27 חש] למלא השורה.

שלום [illegible]
והאיש [illegible]
[illegible]

גביר רופאים עטרת החכמים
[illegible] ישרים ונרעה [illegible]
ונדיב נדיבים וגביר [illegible] [illegible]
[illegible]
שמו משה [illegible]
איש אלהים אשר [illegible]
יהי האל [illegible]
והצליח בכל [illegible]
[illegible] [illegible] ברכות
וגם ישבע [illegible] בפסח [illegible]
[illegible] והם שנים שלמים
לקיים [illegible]
העבד ישתחוה לפני מושב
וישאל מטוב שישגיח על [illegible]
[illegible] בכל [illegible]
[illegible]
[illegible]
[illegible]
[illegible]
[illegible]
[illegible]
[illegible]
[illegible] שיהיה [illegible]
[illegible] שיעבר
[illegible]

היום [illegible] ואיש [illegible]
[illegible] בכל שבוע [illegible]
[illegible]
[illegible]
בכבוד והטרחתי על השר [illegible]
קשר הטריח על עצמו [illegible]
השבוע [illegible]
הטורח שהטריח השר על עצמו
[illegible]
העבד [illegible]
[illegible]
[illegible] בכל שיהיה [illegible]
השר על [illegible]
[illegible]
[illegible] הספרים מן
שאר [illegible] ויום טוב
[illegible] ספר [illegible]
[illegible] ושלום [illegible]
[illegible]
[illegible]
[illegible] על נדיבו [illegible]
[illegible] העבדים

[1b] חשב בלבו ואמר אולי יבוא לידי
עשרה זוזים בכל שבוע אולי יהי׳
בהם עזר במזונות שאני צריך
להם לא בא לידי אלא חסדי השר
בלבד והטרחתי על השר וגם
השר הטריח על עצמו כל [י]מי
השבוע שהייתי אצלו ומפני רוב
הטורח שהטריח השר על עצמו
ברחתי כי נכלמתי וכמה פעמים <שאל>
העבד קיתון מים כדי לרחיצת
ידים ולא מצאתי ולבסוף אני עבד
לאדוני בכל שאהיה בו וחסדי
השר עלי כחסדי הבורא וסוף
נישאר לעבד אצל אדוניו מאת
דברי מכירת הספרים מן
שאר דמי יומא וסוכה ויום טוב
חצי זוז ומשאר דמי ספר קנין
חצי זוז וחס ושלום לאדון שיחסיר
את עבדו ממון ואין העבד חי
אלא בחסדי רבו ונדיב נדיבות
יעץ והו<א> על נדיבות יקום
צעיר העבדים
משה ב[י]ר לו[י] שלום

37 קיתון] דלי, עי׳ ש. קרויס ב-LW שלו, עמ׳ 540–541.
43 יום טוב] הוא ביצה. עי׳ למשל נ. אלוני בקרית ספר כרך לח, תשכ״ג, עמ׳ 550, שורות 11, 12, 16 ; א. שייבר, שם, כרך מד, תשכ״ט, עמ׳ 548, שורה 25. 44 ספר קנין] לשמואל בן חפני, עי׳ בהקדמה. 47 ונדיב] ישׁ׳ לב, ח.

Im Sommer 1970 fanden wir in Cambridge ein mit derselben Hand geschriebenes anderes Exemplar dieses Briefes, bzw. ein Fragment desselben, das einen viel besseren Text darbietet. Das obige wird das Impurum, das untere das endgültige Konzept gewesen sein. Offenbar sind beide die eigene Handschrift des Dieners.

Seine Signatur ist: T-S. 6. J. 10[9]. Papier, 1 Blatt, 8.5 x 12 cm. Mit seiner Hilfe vermochten wir ein ausgelassenes Wort ergänzen (Zeile 36.). Wegen der vielen Abweichungen halten wir es für notwendig, das Ganze mitzuteilen.

T.-S. 6. J. 10[9]

[1a] העבד ישתחוה לפני מושב אדוניו
וישאל מטובו שימשוך עליו חוט
החסד וידינו בכל מליו ומעשיו
לכף זכות כמו שלמדנו מהדרתו
והוי דן את כל האדם לכף זכות ועוד
אל תדין את חבירך אלא לכף זכות
וכך אמרו חכמ ז״ל דע מה למעלה
ממך וכול׳ והעבד לא בא אצל רבו
והניח ביתו אלא כדי שימצא מה
שיהיה בו מחייתו ואין העבד שוטה
שידבר דבר ולא ישלימו אבל חשׁ
חשב בלבו ואמר אולי שיבוא לידי
עשרה זוזים בכל שבוע אולי אמצא
בהם עזר במזונות שאני צריך להם
והעת עת בצורת לא בא לידי אלא
חַסְדֵי השר בלבד והטרחתי על השר
[1b] וגם השר הטריח על עצמו כל ימי
השבוע שהייתי אצלו ומפני רוב
הטורח שהטריח השר על עצמו
ברחתי כי נכלמתי וכמה פעמים
שאל העבד קיתון מים כדי לרחיצת
ידים ולא מצאתי ולבסוף אני עבד
לאדוני בכל מקום שאהיה [ב]ם וחסדי
השר עלי כחסדי הבורא המקום יפיל
שכרו ויהיה בעזרו ועוד העבד ישאל
מרבו לארוך רחמיו עליו ויודיעו
כי נשאר לו ע[וד] מדמי השלוש מסכתות
חצי זוז ומדמי ספר קנין חצי זוז
והיה זוז ואין לעבד משיאכל
אבל עיניו לחסדי אדוניו שתשגרו
לי כמו הצדקה כי אני שקלתי ושכר
........[ונד]יבותו ידועה

II. Die Auslösung eines Buches aus der Beute von Rhodus

Die Kreuzfahrer eroberten 1099 Jerusalem.[6] Auch Kaufleute von Rhodus schlossen sich ihnen an und waren bei der Eroberung Jerusalems zugegen. Dort mochten sie das Buch erbeutet haben, von dem im folgenden die Rede sein wird.

Es ist möglich, dass es einen anderen Hintergrund hat. Am 28. Oktober 1099 berührte eine venezianische Flotte Rhodus auf ihrem Wege nach Palästina.[7] Auf ihrem Rückwege mochte sie in Rhodus einen Teil der erbeuteten Sachen in den Kauf bringen, darunter dieses hebräische Buch.

Ein kleines Pergament-Fragment liegt uns vor (T.-S.N.S.298^{26}). Es war der Deckel des Traktats Baba Kamma. Der darauf angebrachte Text verrät, dass es 1071/72 in Jerusalem für Ebjatar Hakkohen kopiert wurde. Elijahu Hakkohen löste es auf der Insel Rhodus aus der Kriegsbeute aus.

Der Auslöser ist vielleicht identisch mit dem Elija, den Benjamin Tudela erwähnt als einen der drei Vorstandsmitglieder des vierhundert Seelen zählenden Judentums von Rhodus: "[ובה כמו א]רבע מאות יהודים. ובראשם ר' אבא ור' חננאל ור' אליה".[8]

Indem Elijahu Hakkohen diesen Talmudtraktat ankaufte, ging er im Sinne der jüdischen Lehre vor, die die Auslösung des Buches ebenso zur Pflicht machte wie die der Gefangenen: "אין פודין את השבוים אלא בכדי דמיהן. יש חילוק אם חכם הוא וצדיק וצריכים לו רבים שאני וכן ספרים, אם ספר שיש בו חידושים ואין במדינה כיוצא בו הרי פודין ביותר".[9]

Der einstige Eigentümer des Buches war Ebjatar b. Elijahu Hakkohen, der letzte Gaon der palästinensischen Akademie,[10] der über den um seine Würde entbrannten Streit seine berühmte Megilla schrieb.[11] Das Talmud-Exemplar wurde in Jerusalem für ihn kopiert, wahrscheinlich bevor die Seldschuken die Stadt eroberten und er — samt seinem Lehrhaus — gezwungen war, nach Tyrus zu gehen.[12]

Das Titelblatt ist folgendes:

T.-S. N.S. 298^{26}

נעתק לאביתר ה[כה]ן

שנת דֹתֹתֹלֹבֹ בירושלים

סלה סימן טוב וחיים

וברכות שמים

וארץ

פדיתיו מן השלל באי רודוס אני אליהו הכ[הן]

סימן טוב אמת

*

Noch ein Buch kennen wir in der Genisa aus Ebjatars Besitz, wie die Einschreibung davon zeugt (Cambridge, Or. 1081, 1^{24}): אמין. אביתר הכהן אשר נקרא שם יי' עליו בן גאון נין גאון זצ"ל.

In derselben Form kommt sein Name auch in anderen Quellen vor (T-S. 12.J. 29; 13. J. 2^{7}; 20. 126; 24. 49.).

I. Edward Kiev, der verdienstvolle Forscher der jüdischen Bibliographie, den ich 1963 auch persönlich kennen lernte in New York, wird gewiss willkommen heissen diese zwei Genisatexte, die hinsichtlich des hebräischen Buches neue Daten bringen. Hat doch die Erforschung dieses Gegenstandes sein Leben ausgefüllt. Möge er es noch lange tun können zum Nutzen der jüdischen Wissenschaft!

Bemerkungen

1 *W. Bacher*: La bibliothèque d'un médecin juif. REJ. XL. 1900. pp. 55–61 (dazu: *S. Poznanski*, ibid., pp. 264–267); *E. J. Worman*, JQR. XX. 1907/8. pp. 460–463; *D. H. Baneth*, Tarbiz. XXX. 1960/1. pp. 171–185. Cf. *S. Shaked*: A Tentative Bibliography of Geniza Documents. Paris–The Hague, 1964. pp. 73, 162, 184.

2 *S. D. Goitein*: Medical Profession in Cairo Geniza Documents. HUCA. XXXIV. 1963. pp. 185–186.

3 *S. D. Goitein*, ibid., p. 183; The oldest documentary Evidence for the title Alf Laila wa-Laila. Journal of American Oriental Society. LXXVIII. 1958. pp. 301–302; Kirjath Sepher. XLIV. 1968. pp. 125–128.

4 *S. D. Goitein*: A Mediterranean Society. I. Berkeley–Los Angeles, 1967. p. 368.

5 *N. Allony*, Kirjath Sepher. XLIII. 1967/8. p. 131, Zeile 51.

6 *A. Scheiber*, HUCA. XXXIX. 1968. pp. 163–75; *M. Benvenisti*: The Crusaders in the Holy Land. Jerusalem. 1969.

7 *C. Torr*: Rhodes in Modern Times. Cambridge, 1887. pp. 4–7; *J. Starr*: The Jews in the Byzantine Empire 641–1204. Athen, 1939. p. 232. Auch Reisende von Ägypten nach Konstantinopel berührten Rhodus: *S. D. Goitein*: A Letter from Seleucia (Cilicia). Speculum. XXIX. 1964. pp. 298–303; A Mediterranean Society. I. p. 214.

8 ספר מסעות של ר' בנימן ז"ל. Ed. *M. N. Adler*. London, 1907. p. 17. Neueste Literatur bei *H. G. Reissner*: Benjamin of Tudela on Ceylon. Zeitschrift für Religions- und Geistesgeschichte. VI. 1954. pp. 151–155.

9 ספר חסידים. Ed. *R. Margulies*. Jerusalem, 1957. p. 503. No. 926; *A. Sternberg*, Bar Ilan. Annual of Bar-Ilan University. VI. 1968. p. 260; *A. Bashan*: שבייתם ופדיונם של ספרים בהלכה ובמציאות־ההיסטורית. Taggim. I. 1969. pp. 5–21.

10 *J. Mann*: The Jews in Egypt. I. Oxford, 1920. pp. 187–198; Texts and Studies. I. Cincinnati, 1931. pp. 346–352; Enc. Hebr. I. 1960. col. 152.

11 *S. Schechter*: Saadyana. Cambridge, 1903. pp. 80–104. No. XXXVIII; *W. Bacher*: Ein neuerschlossenes Capitel der jüdischen Geschichte. JQR. XV. 1903. pp. 79–96; *A. Marx*, PAAJR. XVI. 1947. pp. 197–198.

12 *S. Assaf*: תקופת הגאונים וספרותה. Jerusalem, 1955. p. 101.

RASHI'S *COMMENTARY ON THE PENTATEUCH AND ON THE FIVE SCROLLS*, VENICE, BOMBERG, 1538

MENAHEM SCHMELZER

Jewish Theological Seminary of America

The Hebrew Union College Library in Cincinnati owns a very rare printed edition of Rashi's *Commentary on the Pentateuch and on the Five Scrolls*.[1] There are only three other copies known of this book; one in the British Museum,[2] another in the Schocken Institute in Jerusalem, and a third in a private collection in the same city.[3]

The late Isaiah Sonne, in an article on the text-criticism of Rashi's *Commentary on the Pentateuch*, has called attention to this rare, 1538 edition and to its many interesting features.[4] An examination of the volume, indeed, reveals some new information and at the same time raises some questions relating to the activity of Daniel Bomberg's famous Venetian printing house.

On the title page we read:

פירוש רש״י על התורה ועל
חמש מגילות נדפס שנית עם רב העיון ע״י
השר דניאל בומבירג מאנווירש״ה
בשנת רצ״ח לפ״ק
פה ויניציאה

The book, in small quarto, contains 197 leaves. At the end there is the following colophon, in rhymed prose:

בהיות כי כל השכנים אשר סביבותי ישנים ושבחי לא יגידו ועל טובי לא יעידו לשבח את עצמי אתעורר אף שאמר המשורר יהללך זר ולא פיך אקרא מלת ולא במשיכה ועם פיך אותו לא אחבר [5] והישר אדבר ואגיד מישרים ודברי אמת נכרים הנה כאשר

זממתי ובלבי הסכמתי להדפיס הספר הזה שהוא באור תורתנו הקדושה מהנשר הגדול הרב המובהק רבינו שלמה יצחקי ז״ל כי באמת על כל דברי התורה הזאת פירוש זולת פירושו לא יאות וכל המפרשי׳ שפירשום ודרשום נחשבים כנגדו כקליפת השום כי כל התלמוד הארוך היה לפניו כשלחן ערוך [6] לכן פירוש המצוות ודקדוקם לא יצאו מתחת ידו רקם ועליו אמרו המושלים בדרך מליצה אלו המלים כל פרש״תא תרמוס לאשפתא חוץ מן פרש״נדתא ופר״תא [7] והנה אף כי נדפס הספר הזה כמה פעמים בכל המקומות אשר נמצא שם בית דפיסה אכן לרוב טובו ותועלתו ושאין מי יעמוד בלתו ספו תמו מן הארץ וכל מבקשיו לא ימצאונהו ואני בראותי כי כן ולעמוד בלתו לא יתכן שנסתי את מתני לרגל המלאכה אשר לפני ואמרתי עת לעשו׳ לה׳ והסכמתי להדפיסו אף הפעם והשתדלתי בהגהתו בעיון רב וקבצתי העתקו׳ היותר מוגהות וטובות מן המחוקקות ומן הנכתבו׳ אך מצאתי בהם שנוי והפרדה שניין דא מן דא יש׳ שבא בארוכה ויש שבא בקצרה וזה לסיבת מיעוט ידיעת המגיהים ושלא הבינו עצתו ומה טובו שמו בו דברים אשר לא צוה ולא עלו על לבו וכן קם אחד מבני שונצי״ן חשב עצמו ראש וקצין והתפאר לאמר כי הוא ידפיס פירוש רבינו שלמה שבכל העולם לא יהיה דומו וכל שלפניו נחקקו ונכתבו מאפס ותהו לו נחשבו והנה ראיתי את אשר כבר עשהו והב״ל הביא גם הוא ובמקומות אין חקר העיד עדות שקר ובמקצת מקומות חשב לתקן המעוות והוא עות את המתוקן ויצא משפטו מעוקל והוא לא פנים קלקל ובדרך הזה הלכו שאר המגיהים ואני לא עשיתי כן מפני יראת האלהים ועוד יתרון לפירושי זה על פירוש השונצי״ן כי הוא לא הדפיס רק פירוש חמשה חומשי תורה לבד ואנכי הוספתי עליו פירוש של חמש מגלות ואת כלם הגהתי ושפטתי משפט צדק עד שלא נמצא שם בדק ובמקומות שהיתה ידיעתי קצרה מלהבין ראיה או סברא על בינתי לא נשענתי ושאלתי מה שלא הבנתי ועל הרוב על דברי רבי אליהו המדקדק נסמכתי ובו יתדותי תמכתי כי במקרא ובפירושי׳ יש לו יד ושם והוא ידע ולא אשם ובכן אודה לאל אשר עד הנה הגיעני והחייני וקיימני להשלים הספר הזה עד תומו ולהעביר חסרונו ומומו כן יהיה עוד בעזרי להגיה בתלמוד כאשר החלותי ועד הנה נדפסו מסכתות ששה היינו בבא קמא בבא בתרא שבועות חגיגה תענית מגילה ואגיע בע״ה להגיה עד תשעה ויהיו נקיות מכל טעות ורשעה כאשר עיינתי בהעתקות מוגהות וצודקות אשר למדו בהם ראשי ישיבות בעיון רב ובחשיבות והנה היתה השלמת הספר הזה בחדש תשרי שנת רצ״ט לפר״ק פה וויניציה בבית השר דניאל בומבירגי יר״ה אנכי המגיה הצעיר מבית אבי יהודה המכונה ליביא ב״ר יצחק הלוי המכונה אייזק קולפא מורנקבורט.[8]

After this lengthy and interesting colophon we find a poem by Elijah Levita:

ויהי כאשר ראה רבי אליהו הלוי האשכנזי את המלאכה והנה היא עשויה כהלכה מערכה לקראת מערכה לא נעשה כן בכל ממלכה ולא נשאר בה טעות או מבוכה וישם על המגיה ברכה ויפתח את פיו בשירה ערוכה וישא משלו ויאמר ככה

את ליב״א קולפ״ה יודה כל פה — כי טוב עושה הוא תוך עמו
לבו תואב אל ספרי בין — אל כל אחד קורא בשמו
יתן למבקש למודו — וספרים אתו אינימו

הוא המשביר אל כל העם   יפתח אוצרו ואסמו
ובתוכו כל ספרי משנה   גם המקרא עם תרגומו
לו פירושים גם מדרשים   מה טוב לאכול את פרימו
ובסדורים ובמחזורים   ימציא כל עם מנהגימו
יש נחקקים יש נכתבים   יש נקשרים בעבותימו
המה לרוב אך מקרוב   נעדר פירוש שלשלמה
היצחקי הרב בקי   על כל אדם תטוף נואמו
כל הגולה שותה מימיו   כל ישראל לוחם לחמו
ופעמים רבים נדפסו   אכן תמו אזלו למו
לכן בחר ליב״א הנזכר   גם הפעם בדפוס שמו
הוא הגיהו והכינהו   שלם מראשו עד תומו
כי בספרים הראשונים   הסופרים שנו את טעמו
יש הוסיף בו יש גרע בו   יש בשגגה יש באשמו
אך זה נמצא בלתי שמצה   מעולם לא נעשה דומו
רובו הגיע הוא עצמו   גם לפעמים ידי עמו
אותו הכשיר בעל השיר   ובראשי בתיו חותמו
ובשם האל צור ישראל   היום היה יום תשלומו
ששת תשרי בשנת פטר״י   ליצירת אל את עולמו
וויניצייה בית דניאל   ולאנווירשה שב למקומו [9]

Jehudah ben Isaac ha-Levy of Frankfort, called Loeb Kulpa, the corrector of this Rashi edition, was active in the Hebrew printing of Italy. His name appears in a number of books printed in Venice and in Mantua between the years 1538 and 1561.[10] M. Horovitz mentions him briefly among sixteenth-century Frankfort scholars.[11]

From a study of the colophons signed by Kulpa we can gain some knowledge, although fragmentary, of his life and work. He originates from a well-known family in Frankfort. The Kulpas (Kulps), a branch of the Gehlhaeuser family, are traced back by Alexander Dietz to the sixteenth century. Members of this family were affluent and some were known as learned and active men in the community. The first bearer of the Kulp name appears in 1592 with a certain Loeb (Jehudah) Kulp, the son of Samuel Gehlhaeuser.[12] The corrector of the 1538 Rashi edition bears the same name—apparently it was common in that family—and now the beginnings of the Kulp family can be dated at least some fifty years earlier than the date offered by Dietz. Kulpa was involved in many branches of the book business. Elijah Levita seems to refer to his activities as a book dealer who had in his stock a wide assortment of manuscripts and printed books.[13] Whether the printed books were all products of Bomberg's press or included also other books cannot be determined.[14]

As a corrector, Kulpa started his work prior to the printing of Rashi. In his colophon to this book he mentions six tractates of the Talmud which he had already corrected and printed. Elijah Levita also seems to refer to his previous work as a printer.[15]

The richest information about Kulpa is to be found in a number of books printed by him and his associate, Jehiel ben Jekuthiel ha-Cohen Rapa,[16] between the years 1544 and 1548. In 1544 they worked for the Christian printers, the Brothers dei Farri and, from 1545, for Marc Antonio Giustinian. The books printed by them are listed by M. Steinschneider,[17] R. N. Rabinowitz [18] and D. W. Amram.[19] Kulpa, the initiator of the enterprise, and his partner Rapa, announce their plans in the following words:

בהיות כי ראה ראינו כי הזמן הולך וסוער עלינו ולומדי התורה הולכים ומתמעטים... לכן אנחנו השותפים אשר בשמינו רשומים.. קנא קנאנו לה׳ צבאות... והקרה ה׳ לפנינו איש גדול ורם מבחר הנוצרים והדרם.. ובלשונינו הקדוש ידו גברה... הוא השר והאדון נקרא בשם מארקו אנטוניאו יושטיניאן ובראותו כי כמה שנים אנחנו עמלים בתקונים לעשות אותיות וכלים ובעזר האלהי מעולם לא מצאנו בעל מלאכה שנצחנו עם כי לטורח גדול ורב ההוצאה לא השגחנו והשכיל והבין ענינינו כי יש לנו שכם אחד על אחינו המדפיסים אשר היו לפנינו... ולכן את בן משק ביתו צוה להדפיס כל הספרים אשר עד הנה היו נסתרים.. ואף כי זה הספר נעשה במלאכה חדשה וכל התחלה קשה..[20]

The administrator of Giustinian's firm (בן משק ביתו), probably Cornelio Adelkind, also speaks about the partners:

בהתעדן מאד מאד גבירי הנעלה בלשון הקדש לדבקה בו... פקד עלי... לחבר לולאות הזריזות בקרסי המפעלות להשתדל לתת התחלות להדפיס כל מיני הספרי׳ רבי התועלות והיו למאורות ברקועים פחי הדפוסיות באותות חרותות בעט ברזל ועופרת חקוקות בכתיבות היותר מאושרות ויפות ונְיירות ישרות ביותר מעולות וטובות אשר מעולם לא היו בפעל נדפסות... ויד הנכבדים באמצע כהן ולוי הנלוים להצדיק את הרבים... רבי יהודה הלוי ורבי יחיאל הכהן השותפים... מי בכם אוהבי התורה ולומדיה... והכינו עצמכם להשיג ממנו בקוצר זמן כל חפצכם עם התלמוד ערוך כלו והעשרי׳ וארבע קטן כגדול עם כל המתיחס לו ורב אלפס עם חדר שכלו יחפש וכל חפץ מחופש משאר החבורים חדשים גם ישנים בשכבר נדפסו או לא נדפסו....[21]

From the above it is evident that the partners were for many years engaged in improving printing machinery and types and had introduced a new method in typography.

In addition to his technical and business skills, Kulpa had scholarly interests, too. Already in the 1538 edition of Rashi he describes his method of establishing the text by using many manuscripts and printed editions. In the colophon to the same book he also mentions his efforts in the printing of Talmud tractates. For the publication of these texts he claims to have used "correct and true copies such as those being studied by the heads of Yeshiboth." (ההעתקות מוגהות וצודקות אשר למדו בהם ראשי ישיבות). Kulpa's introduction to the 1548 Venice edition of *Halakhoth Gedoloth* was recorded as a proof of his scholarship by R. N. Rabinowitz and M. Horovitz.[22] In this introduction Kulpa tackles the problematic authorship of the book, reviewing the conflicting opinions of early Rabbinic authors.

In 1547 he published a commentary to the Pentateuch, culled from the Pentateuch commentaries of Rashi, Nahmanides, Abraham ibn Ezra, and David Kimhi. In addition to this interesting and useful anthology of selected comments, Kulpa included in his book notes to the Masorah and the order of the 613 precepts. He also planned to append at the end an index of all the Biblical passages mentioned in the Talmud.[23]

It is to be assumed that Kulpa, during his association with the Bomberg, dei Farri, and Giustinian printing houses helped in the publication of numerous other books though his name is not explicitly mentioned in them.

Some of the information contained in the colophon of the 1538 Rashi edition adds to the complexity of problems relating to the activities of the Bomberg press. Though the history of Bomberg's press was dealt with frequently [24] we are still in the dark in regard to the chronology of events and to many aspects of the work done under Bomberg's auspices.[25] From 1516 to 1533 there is a continuity in Bomberg's work. This period can be divided into two: The "golden age" of his activities, between 1516 and 1525, when the most important editions, e.g., that of the *Biblia Rabbinica*, of the Babylonian and Jerusalem Talmud, and of important Rabbinic texts were printed, and the second period, from 1525 to 1533, when mainly second editions, frequently unchanged, were produced.

Bomberg resumed his activities in 1537 and issued a few minor books again until 1539. In the latter year the only anti-Jewish book ever to be printed by Bomberg was published.[26] According to Elijah Levita's poem in the 1538 Rashi, dated Tishre 6, 5239 (1538), Bomberg returned to his native city of Antwerp.[27] Two years later Levita again refers to Bomberg as having stopped his work, "and he will not work again."[28] However, there are quite a large number of books printed between the years 1543 and 1548 bearing Bomberg's imprint.[29]

A special problem is presented by the different editions of the Talmud on which Bomberg's name appears. R. N. Rabinowitz was at a loss to explain the confusion of dates, sequence, number, and designation of editions of the Babylonian Talmud after the first one.[30] He also refers to the contradiction relating to the printing of the Jerusalem Talmud.[31] According to Rabinowitz's suggestions it seems likely that tractates of the Talmud with the imprint 1538–9 were actually printed between 1526 and 1531 and that in 1538–9 Bomberg removed the old title pages and printed new ones with the current date. Rabinowitz admits that he cannot find a reason for this fact and for the lack of Bomberg's activity between 1533 and 1538.[32] About a hundred years have passed since Rabinowitz expressed his aforementioned views and we are still in no better position to solve these problems. In fact, the 1538 Rashi colophon only adds to the confusion. Kulpa mentions there that he had finished the careful correction of six tractates of the Talmud: *Baba Kama, Baba Bathra, Shebuoth, Hagiga, Taanith* and *Megilla*, and that he plans to print an additional three (unnamed) tractates. Indeed, we know of the tractates *Baba Kama, Hagiga, Taanith, Megilla, Makkoth, Moed Katan* and *Aboth*, bearing the imprint date 1538–9. Rabinowitz lists also an undated second (or third?) edition of *Baba Bathra* and *Shebuoth*.[33] This brings the total of tractates from 1538–9 to nine (including the two undated ones), thus equaling the nine tractates mentioned by Kulpa (six finished in 5238=1537/8 and three more in preparation at the beginning of 5239 = 1538). This, and the fact that four of the tractates bearing the imprint 1538 and the other two undated ones are all mentioned by Kulpa, tend to invalidate Rabinowitz's view that no real printing of these tractates took place in 1538–9. On the other hand, a cursory examination of three editions of tractates *Aboth* (1521, 1526, 1539), *Moed Katan* (1521, 1526, 1538/9) and *Makkoth* (1520, 1529/30, 1538/9) shows that there is no significant textual difference between the second and third(?) editions.[34]

Similar problems arise in connection with the 1538 edition of the Rashi text. Kulpa boasts in his colophon about the superiority of his text in relation to all previous editions. He also mentions Elijah Levita's assistance in the establishment of the text. He especially singles out the 1525 Soncino Rashi as being full of mistakes.[35] Now, on the title page, we read that this is the second Bomberg edition of Rashi. The first one was printed in 1522, i.e., three years before Soncino's. A comparison between the three editions shows that the first and second Bomberg editions are almost identical, and that of Soncino is different from the two. Is there any merit then in Kulpa's claim of presenting a new text? Similarly why does he claim that his edition is far better than Soncino's because it also contains Rashi on the Five Scrolls, when the commentary on the Five Scrolls is already printed in the first, 1522, Bomberg edition? Furthermore, the two texts are again identical.[36] Is it possible that Kulpa, counting on the naivité of his contemporaries was only praising his ware without actually doing any work in presenting a new text?

In view of our limited knowledge of the events in Venetian Hebrew publishing in the fifteen-twenties and fifteen-thirties no definitive answer can be given to the many questions relating to apparent contradictions, conflicting designations, and sequence of editions of the period.

A thorough new investigation, and the possibility of discovering hitherto unknown documents perhaps in the archives of Venice only can throw much needed new light on this very important period of early Hebrew publishing history.[37]

Notes

[1] I wish to express my thanks to Prof. H. Zafren for providing me with a microfilm copy of the book.

[2] Cf. M. Steinschneider, Supplement to *CB*, p. 506; Van Straalen, p. 225.

[3] I am grateful to Mr. A. Rosenthal of the Schocken Institute in Jerusalem for calling these copies to my attention.

[4] י. זנה, לביקורת הטכסט של פירוש רש״י על התורה *HUCA*, v. 15, p. 40 (Hebrew section).

[5] On this well-known, humorous interpretation of Proverbs 27, 2 cf. Eshtori Farhi, כפתור ופרח, ch. 44, ed. J. Blumenfeld, v. 2, p. 833; Ratner, אהבת ציון וירושלים, v. 12, p. 231; cf. also *Zohar*, v. 3, f. 193b and N. S. Libowitz, פניני הזהר, pp. 23-4.

[6] Cf. Moses ibn Danon, כללים, ms. JTS, Rab. 959, f. 101a–b and ms. JTS, Rab. 955, f. 68a:

כת׳ גברא רבא על ר״ת וז״ל שאני ר״ת דרב גובריה והיה כרש״י ור״ח ובה״ג והיה כאחד מהם ואולי יותר מהם בחריפות ובקיאות לפי מה שנראה ממה שחידש בתלמוד וכל חכמי ישראל הנמצאים היום כלם כקליפת השום וכגרגיר שומשין נגד אחד מתלמידיו הקטנים וכו׳ ;

cf. also Responsa of R. Isaac bar Sheshet, no. 394:

המאור הגדול רבינו שלמה זכר צדיק לברכה גלה עמוקות התלמוד מני חשך לא עממוהו כל סתום ובזולת פירושו היה כדברי הספר החתום והמאור השני רבינו יעקב איש תם אשר כמוהו בפלפול לא נהיה מאחר שהתלמוד נחתם תלמוד ערוך בפיו וכו׳

The first statement is quoted, the second is mentioned by Azulay in his שם הגדולים, s. v. R. Jacob ben Meir, י׳ no. 241.

[7] This saying is found in a slightly different version in Moses ibn Danon's כללים, Ms. Oxford, no. 850, f. 14b (this section is missing in the two JTS mss. mentioned in the preceding note). Azulay, op. cit., s.v. Rashi, ש׳ no. 35 quotes it from Ibn Danon's work. Cf. Aptowitzer, *Bitzaron*, v. 2, p. 324 note 1; Wellesz, *Rasi*, Budapest: 1906, p. 111, 187 (in Hungarian); A. Geiger, פרשנדתא, p. 5.

[8] Part of this colophon is quoted by Sonne, ibid. See also: M. Marx, in *HUCA*, v. 11, p. 481.

[9] On Elijah Levita in general and on his role in Bomberg's publishing house see: G. Weil, *Elie Levita*, Leiden: 1963 (where this poem is not mentioned). A few lines of the poem are quoted by Steinschneider, ib. Reference to the last line is made by A. Freiman, in *ZfhB*, vol. 10, p. 34; D.W. Amram, *The Makers of Hebrew Books in Italy*, p. 193; J. Bloch, *Venetian Printers of Hebrew Books*, p. 14; Ch. B. Friedberg, תולדות הדפוס העברי באיטליה, p. 66 note 16; I. Mehlman, in ארשת, v. 3, p. 98.

[10] Cf. Steinschneider, CB, col. 2937; Nepi-Ghirondi, תולדות גדולי ישראל, p. 182; Mortara, מזכרת חכמי איטליא, p. 33 (Levi Jehuda ben Isac); Rabinowitz, מאמר על

הדפסת התלמוד (ed. A. M. Haberman), p. 53, note: Friedberg, op. cit., p. 67–68; Amram, op. cit., p. 201, 253; Bloch, op. cit., p. 17; A. Yaari, *Kirjath Sepher*, v. 15, pp. 377–380; I. Sonne, *ib.*, v. 16, pp. 134–7; the rejoinder by Yaari, *ib.*, pp. 137–9 and the latter's דגלי המדפיסים, pp. 129–131.

[11] In his *Frankfurter Rabbinen*, v. 1, p. 23.

[12] Alexander Dietz, *Stammbuch der Frankfurter Juden*, pp. 102–3, 174–4. Dietz's assumption that the Kulps were not Levites (ib., p. 103) is contradicted by the fact that our Jehudah Kulpa always signs his name as Ha-Levy.

[13] See above in his poem, ll. 4–8.

[14] A book-list of Daniel Bomberg's firm, compiled after 1541, contains books from Bomberg's press as well as books printed in Constantinople and Bologna, cf. *ZfhB*, v. 10, pp. 38–42.

[15] In his poem, l. 13.

[16] On Rapa cf., Steinschneider, *CB*, col. 2933 and the works by Rabinowitz, Friedberg, Amram, Yaari, Sonne and Bloch quoted in note 10. Cf. also Friedberg, op. cit., p. 23, note 7; Y. T. Eisenstadt, דעת קדושים, St. Petersburg: 1897–98, p. 136. On the role of the Rapa and Kusi families in introducing Hebrew printing to Italy cf. A. Friedmann in *Journal of Jewish Bibliography*, v. 1, pp. 9–11.

[17] See above, note 10.

[18] See above, note 10.

[19] Op. cit., p. 201.

[20] In the colophon to ביאור על התורה להרמב״ן, Giustinian, Venice: 1545. It also appears in other books printed by them, cf. Rabinowitz, op. cit., p. 52 note 11, where excerpts from this colophon are quoted; on the phrase: מעולם לא מצאנו וכו׳ see Responsa of R. Simeon Duran, I, 72.

[21] *Ibid.* On the identity of בן משק ביתו see the works by Yaari and Sonne cited in note 10.

[22] See above, note 10 and 11.

[23] ארבעה ועשרים עם באור כל מלה קשה . . . נעתק אות באות מלשון גדולי המפרשים . . . והם רש״י והרמב״ן וראב״ע ורד״ק ז״ל . . . ובחתימת כל הכ״ד ספרים יהיה מורה מקום מכל הפסוקים הנדרשי׳ והמבוארי׳ בתלמוד. . .

Cf. Steinschneider, *CB*, col. 23, no. 123; Zedner, p. 17; Van Straalen, p. 26; Roest, בית הספר, p. 175, no. 2425. According to all these bibliographies the title page reads: ארבעה ועשרים. The same title appears in the copy seen by Sonne. See the latter's comments on this book in the *Alexander Marx Jubilee Volume*, Hebrew part, pp. 218–219. However, in the copy at the Library of the Jewish Theological Seminary the title page is different; it reads: חמשה חומשי תורה וחמש מגילות והפטד(!)ות עם באור כל מלה קשה וכו׳ ובחתימת החומש וחמש מגילות יהיה מורה מקום וכו׳.

Apparently, the printers, after realizing that they will not be able to complete the entire Bible, changed the title page of some copies.

[24] See the bibliography in *Encyclopaedia Judaica*, vol. 4, col. 930.

[25] Mehlman, ארשת, v. 3, pp. 93–98, establishes the date of the first book printed by Bomberg as 1511 instead of the generally accepted date of 1516.

[26] ibid. [27] l. 22.

[28] Cf. Elijah Levita ni his introduction to his תשבי, Isny: 1541.

[29] Cf. *ZfhB*, v. 10, pp. 86–88. Incidentally, an interesting testimony to the rather chaotic conditions of Hebrew printing in Venice in the 1540's is the edition of *Midrash Rabba*, Venice: 1545. There are copies of this book with Bomberg's title-

page and others with that of Giustinian. Cf. *Bereshit Rabba*, ed. Theodor-Albeck, introduction, p. 129; *ZfhB*, v. 9, p. 61–62, 159; *Kirjath Sepher*, v. 4, p. 227.

[30] Op. cit., pp. 43–45; cf. also Rivkind, *Alexander Marx Jubilee Volume*, Hebrew section, pp. 410–414.

[31] Op. cit., p. 44. [33] Ibid. [32] Ibid.

[34] The third edition of *Aboth* contains a number of misprints in passages where the first and second editions are correct; e.g. f. 2a: אז תבין ירתא (!) ה׳; 2b: הצריך מן העינים (!) (read: (הענינים); 5c: כעבדים שאינם מקוים להטהבה (read: (להטבה); 9c: שלא תעשה התובה (! (read: (התורה).

[35] See above, note 8.

[36] A few examples will show the almost complete identity of the two Bomberg texts versus the Soncino text (the passages are taken from Genesis, 25. 19ff., the text being used by Sonne, *HUCA*, v. 15, p. 49–56 (Hebrew part), for his model of a new edition of Rashi on Pentateuch:

Bomberg 1538	*Bomberg 1522*	*Soncino 1525*	
ומשנולד יצחק עד שמתה שרה שלשים ושבע היו ובת צ׳ היתה כשנולד ובת קכ״ז כשמתה שנאמ׳ ויהיו חיי שרה וגומר הרי ליצחק ל״ז שני׳ ובו בפ׳ נולדה רבקה המתין לה עד. שתהא ראוי׳ לביאה שלש שנים ונשאה	ומשנולד יצחק עד שמתה שרה ל״ז היו ובת צ׳ היתה כשנולד ובת קכ״ז כשמתה שנאמר ויהיו חיי שרה וגומר הרי ליצחק ל״ז שנים ובפ׳ (!) נולדה רבקה המתין לה עד שתהא ראוי׳ לביאה שלש שני׳ ונשאה	ומשנולד יצחק עד שמת׳ שרה ל״ז שנה היו בת צ׳ היתה כשנולד ובת קכ״ז כשמתה שנ׳ ויהיו חיי שרה וגו׳ הרי ליצחק ל״ז ובו בפרק נולדה רבקה המתין לה שתהא ראויה לביאה שלש שנים ונשאה	20.
ויעתר לו, לו ולא לה	ויעתר לו, לו ולא לה	ויעתר לו, ולא לה	21.
לדרוש את ה׳, להגיד לה מה תהא בסופה	לדרוש את ה׳, להגיד לה מה תהא בסופה	לדרש את ה׳, להגיד מה תהא בסופה	22.
ואין זו שיבה טובה שהבטיחו הקב״ה לפיכך קצר הקב״ה ה׳ שני׳ משנותיו שיצחק חי קפ׳ שנה וזה קע״ה	ואין זו שיבה טובה שהבטיחו הקב״ה לפיכך קצר הקב״ה ה׳ שנים משנותיו שיצחק חי קפ׳ שנה וזה קע״ה	ואין זו שיבה טובה שהב־טיחו הקב״ה לפיכך קצר ה׳ שנים משנותיו של יצחק חי ק״פ וזה קע״ה	30.
הנה אנכי הולך למות, אמר עשו מה טיבה של עבוד׳ זו	הנה אנכי הולך למות, אמר עשו מה טיבה של עבודה זו	הנה אנכי הולך למות, אמר מה שכר של עבודה זו	32.

[37] It was only after this article was set in type that Meir Benayahu's important book, *Copyright, authorization and imprimatour for Hebrew books printed in Venice* (Jerusalem 1971, in Hebrew), appeared. Therefore, it was not possible for me to make use of his materials and conclusions. However, it should be pointed out that Benayahu's suggestion that Judah Kulpa converted to Christianity around the year 1545 (p. 23, note 2), is not convincing. Cf. the colophon to ס׳ יחוס הצדיקים, Mantua 1561:

והוגה בעיון רב ע״י כמ״ר יהודה הלוי יצ״ו בכמ״ר יצחק הלוי זצ״ל מברנקבורט המכונה ליבא קולפה אשכנזי

It is obvious that an apostate could never have been referred to in this manner.

CONTEMPORARY HEBREW LITERATURE: SOURCE OF UNTAPPED VALUES

EISIG SILBERSCHLAG

Hebrew College, Brookline, Massachusetts

In our sloganized society value itself has become a slogan. In education the slogan for the past few years was, and still is, excellence. And John W. Gardner, former Secretary of Health, Education and Welfare and present chairman of the Urban Coalition in Washington —an organization of businessmen attacking problems of cities—has written an excellent book on *Excellence*. Even violence on campus is alleged to be a precondition of excellence. Value is also in the run; a close second. The late Clyde Kluckhohn, who was Professor of Anthropology at Harvard University, has properly diagnosed the weakness of our civilization when he said that "in the long run the Achilles heel of the West is in the realm of ideas and values. . . . We lack a system of general ideas and values to give meaning to human life in the mid-twentieth century."[1] Perhaps these two slogans, excellence and value, should be married and appear under the joint name: valuable excellence or excellent value. The adjective component will naturally play the humbler, qualifying role as all good adjectives should. Or should one say like all good adjectives should?

The word "value" is Rome's gift to the English language. It derives from a root *valere* which means to be strong (hence valiant), to be worth. It has invaded many branches of science and invested them with multiple meaning. In economics it is identical with price, in music it points to the duration of a note (thus a quarter note has the value of two eighth notes), in daily use it is equal, roughly, to importance. Professor Horace Kallen has underlined the essential qualities of value: they usually point to someone or something—to a person or an item "about whose prosperous survival and growth we are actively concerned."[2] This is the dynamic aspect of values: it demands a constant vigil about them, otherwise they may be attenuated or they may deteriorate altogether. Sociologists like Alfred McClung Lee speak of "multivalent man," i.e., man belonging to many groups —family, professional association, club—and adjusting his values to a particular group at a particular time and place.

To isolate value out of a mass of literary artifacts and to place it in the context of modern civilization—that is our task. It has been done by Leo Baeck in his *Essence of Judaism*[3] and, in recent times, by the controversial English rabbi, Dr. Louis Jacobs. Baeck dwelt on the essence of Judaism as the faith without an intermediary between man and God, as "the faith that confronts man continually and directly with the moral decision, with God's mystery . . .[4] as the great chain of tradition in which each generation confronts tradition. . . ."[5] Jacobs, who published his book on *Jewish Values* more than a half-century after Baeck, constructed a decalog of his own: 1. Study; 2. Love and fear of God; 3. Sanctification of the Name; 4. Trust in God; 5. Holiness; 6. Humility; 7. Love of neighbor; 8. Compassion; 9. Truth; 10. Peace.[6]

Both Baeck and Jacobs formed their sets of values on the basis of classical Judaism, that is Judaism as it existed prior to the American and French Revolutions; Baeck from a neo-liberal point of view, Jacobs from a neo-orthodox vantage point. Others, like Professor André Neher[7] reemphasize religion as the preservative factor of Judaism. Still others try to reinterpret aspects of Judaism: Joseph Weiss,[8] mysticism; Jacob Taubes,[9] beliefs and opinions in nineteenth-century theology; Nathan Rotenstreich,[10] neo-nationalism. This frantic search for values—and it is not only a Jewish, but a worldwide search—may be merely an infinite regret for the loss of an Infinite Being. In one of his rare excursions into our age, Professor Harry A. Wolfson warned against "the gentle art of devising deities." And he mentions, among some current substitutions, "man's aspiration for ideal values."[11] This is more than a caveat: it is an indictment couched in a memorable phrase. For, especially in America, there is a brisk and frantic trade in panaceas which last a day and give way to others. The authorized and the unauthorized, the educated and the half-educated shout their new values, even new religions: psychoanalytic modernizations of the Nietzschean "death of God," existentialist theology, death of secularism, ecstatic theology.

Contemporary Hebrew literature emphasizes values which differ both from Baeck and Jacobs. As an integral part of world literature it shares some of the current values of the literatures of the world, but it contributes its own coloration to them and it offers some values which are peculiar to its people. Like all major contemporaneous literatures of the West, Hebrew literature is a literature of alienation.[12] This theme was, for centuries, a *Jewish* theme. *Golah*-exile—was alienation. And when Ezekiel Kaufmann, the sociologist and biblical scholar, joined these two concepts in a multi-volumed work *Golah we-Nekar* (Exile and Alienation), he seemed to allude to a tautological entity. For the concept of exile symbolized the unassimilated and unassimilable life of the Jew, ethnical alienation par excellence. With the establishment of the state of Israel the concept of alienation assumed new significance for Jews. It was no longer a sociological designation for a situation of an entire people; it was a name for the isolation of the individual in a faceless, technological society. At that point, it intersected with alienation which, for peoples and literatures of the West, was a forgotten phenomenon.[13] And at that point poets like Yehiel Mar (1921–1969) and Wystan Hugh Auden and Allen Ginsberg meet; Mar, in his frantic search for the other—any other, any thou; Auden in his capitulation to technology; Ginsberg in his cult of the bizarre ego. All three of them abandon traditional poetics for new devices in form and format, in theme and content. Consciously or unconsciously they intimate or indicate that the driving force of our civilization—technology—is also the major cause of our dehumanization, alienation, decline.[14]

Hebrew poets of former generations built on biblical or rabbinic associations: the knowledge of the source-texts, the Bible and the Talmud, was taken for granted. Mar still weaves biblical phrases into the texture of his poetry with exemplary skill. In a poem entitled "Summer 1966" he produces two interesting lines:

> And all the girls stream to the sea,
> Yet my heart is not full.

Readers of the Bible will immediately spot the allusion to *Ecclesiastes* 1:7:

All the rivers run into the sea,
Yet the sea is not full . . .

This is conscious manipulation of an ancient philosophical aperçu for purposes of ironic allusion to modern frivolity and futility. But Mar can also allude to a Churchillian phrase like "their finest hour" as if it were a well-known lingual source in Hebrew.

It is, perhaps, not without significance that one of the better-known younger poets, Nathan Zak, may be characterized as the master of uncertainty. His hesitant vocabulary, his many "perhapses" and "ors" and "ifs," are not merely personal idiosyncrasies; they are the symptoms of a generation. When such a poet chooses "Ḥoni the Circle-Drawer" for the theme of a poem, it is not to recreate the obvious background and foreground of an ancient Rip Van Winkle; it is to resuscitate the imaginative and imaginary experience of Ḥoni, the prototype of alienation.[15]

Hebrew and non-Hebrew contemporary poets, as well as French and Hebrew existentialist novelists Sartre and Camus, Aaron Meged and the youngest of the lot, Amalia Kahana-Karmon, focus the tragicomedies of modern youth in the Near East including Israel, in Europe, in America. This youth drifts in an uncharted sea of void values. In this country they were the beat generation, the beatniks in the previous decade; they are the alienated or the hippies or the SDS in this decade; they march, riot, picket, parade, participate in anti-segregation sit-ins, teach-ins, love-ins, be-ins, mill-ins. And they include the tried repertoire of beatniks: coffee-shops, sex, marijuana, LSD (lysergic acid diethylamide), long hair, eccentric or extravagant forms of dress or rather undress. Lest it be thought that this is an indigenous phenomenon exclusive to this country with a celebrated habitat in the Haight Ashbury section of San Francisco,[16] it should be immediately stressed that a few years ago "city authorities of Elat in southern Israel ousted a colony of 200 beatniks by burning the wooden shacks they had set up on the beach."[17] And even in Japan the so-called *futenzoku,* the crazy tribe, have occupied a tiny park near the railroad station at Shinjuku, the Tokyo equivalent of Greenwich Village, to the annoyance of the police and the established social order. A new international set has come into being: it cherishes identical non-values.

But—a very important qualification—contemporary Hebrew poets draw same positive values out of their alienated selves. Hayyim Guri, a native of Israel and a poet of considerable stature, called "Kelulot" (Espousals) the second part of his book *'Ad 'Alot ha-Shaḥar* (Before Dawn). The title is a metaphor: the bride to be conquered is the desert of the Negev. Intense identification with Israel is also evident in the very popular play of Yigal Mossenson *be-'Arbot ha-Negev* (In the Plains of the Negev). It characterizes the entire war literature which was born out of the struggle for Israel's independence; it nourishes S. Yizhar, the best spokesman of that heroic age in a series of stories and, especially, in his voluminous novel *Yeme Ẓiklag.*[18]

As a matter of fact, the literary conquest of the land of Israel preceded the establishment of the State of Israel. As far back as the days of the first *'Aliyyah,* the first modern wave of immigration in the eighties of the previous century, the landscape of Palestine was being absorbed by such writers as Moshe Smilansky (1874–1953) and Zev Jawitz (1847–1924). It was intensely assimilated into the fabric of Hebrew literature in the twenties and thirties of this century. Heavenly Jerusalem and mystical Zion gave way to an earthy Jerusalem and to old-new place-names like *Petaḥ Tiḳwah*[19] and *Rishon le-Ẓiyyon*[20] which generated a symbolism of their own. There was a marked change of feeling for ancient place-names. And there was a change of attitude to the Palestinian landscape. Since Biblical times there was no "landscape per se" in Hebrew literature but rather "theological landscape": earth as the Lord's earth, mere text and pretext of divine power. Palestinian landscape was de-theologized by writers from Eastern Europe. Like their fellow Jews they came to settle and live in a realistic land rather than to die in the Holy Land.[21] And it is no mere accident that Mikveh Yisrael, the agricultural college, was founded as early as 1870 by the *Alliance Israélite Universelle.* David Ben-Gurion, somewhat hyperbolically, remarked at a lecture at Mikveh Yisrael: "The State of Israel was not founded in 1948 . . . the origin of the State is here. . . ."[22] To put it tersely: alienation is an old concept but identification with his own native land and landscape as a sequel of alienation is a new concept with the Jew. The reverse is true of the non-Jew.

The logical culmination of the Jew's identification with his land and landscape was the establishment of the State of Israel. But the establishment of the State of Israel was preceded by the most painful experience of Jewry: the holocaust. The link between the two dominant events of contemporary Jewry is obvious to all trained and untrained observers. What is not obvious is the climate of cultural decay which preceded the holocaust in German-speaking countries, in Germany and in Austria, and the impact of the holocaust on Hebrew literature.

The climate of decay which produced the holocaust is not the proper concern of our investigation. Let it be said in all brevity, however, that it was Friedrich Nietzsche who advocated a dangerous transvaluation of all Judaeo-Christian values at the end of the nineteenth century. The lesser-known Max Scheler observed the dissolution of traditional values and, already in 1915, published the first edition of his essays, *The Subversion of Values*.[23] German and Austrian writers of the first decades of this century—Hofmannsthal and Kafka and Karl Kraus, Musil, Brecht, and Broch—are full of apocalyptic intimations. They have anticipated a private rather than objective correlative of corrosion to the erosion of human rights in the totalitarian state. They have been the prophets of despair.

But if civilization means anything at all, it is primarily freedom from violence. The holocaust is a long lapse from civilization to barbarity. And a catastrophe of such dimensions cannot possibly be converted into an immediate literary masterpiece: it is *sui generis,* it postulates an attitude to life which is perhaps adumbrated in the words of Rabbi Isaac Nussenbaum in the Warsaw ghetto:

> This is the time of *Ḳiddush ha-Ḥayyim,* the sanctification of life, and not for *Ḳiddush ha-Shem,* the holiness of martyrdom. Previously the Jewish enemy sought his soul, and the Jew sacrificed his body . . . now the oppressor demands the Jew's body and the Jew is obliged therefore to defend it, to preserve his life." [24]

Memoirs, documentaries, poems and plays have explored the theme of the holocaust partially; outside Hebrew literature we may note the eight novels by Elie Wiesel, from *Night* to *A Beggar in Jerusalem, O The Chimneys* by Nelly Sachs, *The Deputy* by Rudolph Hochhut, *The Wall* by John Hersey, *The Last of the Just* by André Schwarz-Bart, and *Trot fun Doyres* (March of Generations) by Peretz Markish, the Yiddish poet who was killed by Stalin's executioners in 1952. Special Jewish and non-Jewish research institutes are exploring that tragic period scientifically.[25] There is even a periodical, *Yalḳut Moreshet,* which is devoted exclusively to its documentation and research: some poignant fragments of human misery in the forms of diaries and letters are constantly coming to light in and outside its pages.[26] Single events of overwhelming significance are researched again and re-evaluated in the red light of documentary evidence: the uprising in the Warsaw ghetto, the extermination of 33,771 Jews—according to the low figures of German sources—in the ravine of Babi Yar on the outskirts of Kiev on September 29 and 30, 1941. And the Eichmann trial by the Jerusalem District Court encouraged a new wave of books and articles on the holocaust.

In Jewish literature the most poignant expression of the sorrows of the holocaust was the poetical oeuvre of the martyred poet, Yitzhak Katznelson (1885–1944) in whose memory one of the research institutes of the holocaust was founded: The Ghetto Fighters' House in Memory of Yitzhak Katznelson in Kibbutz Loḥame ha-Getaot near Haifa. No other document has the poignancy and immediacy of Katznelson's poems which were written in Warsaw, in Vittel, in Drancy, in Yiddish, mostly, in Hebrew occasionally. A whole book of poetry by Uri Zvi Gruenberg is consecrated to the theme of the holocaust *Reḥobot-on-the-River* (*Reḥobot ha-Nahar*). Students of the Bible know that it is a place-name associated with princes of Edom,[27] and that in Hebrew literature Edom symbolizes Rome, then Roman Christianity, finally Christianity in general. The place-name may therefore be regarded as an indictment of the Christian world.[28] The impact of the indictment can be felt even in a feeble translation of a few verses:

> Nations have slain us with merciless wrath
> And ruined our remnant in the valley of woe.
> The beautiful sky and the pasture below
> Is terror to us. The violin's voice
> Is a rending of heart. If whitest snow
> Were to fall, we would think it was black
> Like black stripes on the prayer-shawl's field
> Of our father who is dead.
> For now has come true what we dared not dread.[29]

Reḥobot ha-Nahar presupposes a spiritual experience and solidifies it into a value. For the Jew can never be the same after Dachau, Birkenau, and Ravensbruck, after Maidanek, Auschwitz, Treblinka, and the dozens of extermination places all over Europe. He is holocaust-branded. And, perhaps for generations to come, he will live with that experience both as a *memento mori* and a *memento vivere.*

The younger writers who are survivors of concentration camps, like Aaron Appelfeld, carry the traumatic experience with them to their work. In a poignant story like "The Road to Myself," Appelfeld describes the growing up of a refugee, perhaps himself, in Israel. Like other refugees, he has acquired the art of fighting the enemy without, but "we knew that the enemy was entrenched within us, that he ambushed us from there." That enemy was memory. Uri Orlev (1931–), a holocaust child who came to Palestine in 1945 and became sabraized, singes his stories with holocaust embers in *Ḥufshat ha-Ḳayiẓ ha-Aḥaronah* (The Last Summer Vacation). Aba Kovner describes, in a narrative poem *Aḥot Ḳetanah* (Little Sister), the education of a Jewish girl in a Catholic convent and the inability of the girl to face life after liberation. A similar theme pervades Leah Goldberg's play *Ba'alat ha-Armon* (The Chatelaine). Impotent vengeance in the camps is the burden of Baruch Avivi's stories. Liberation comes too late, liberation does not liberate. In story, poem and play the holocaust creates a new dimension for the human beings who have experienced it—directly or indirectly.

Hayim Gouri, who was born in Tel Aviv and spent his youth in the military organization *Palmaḥ* during the Second World War, was a stranger to the holocaust. But his confrontation with Eichmann at the trial in Jerusalem, twenty years after the holocaust, changed his outlook. In *Mul Ta ha-Zekukit* (The Glass Cage), a report on the trial, he achieved complete identification with holocaust-branded Judaism. In *'Isḳat ha-Shoḳolad* (The Chocolate Deal) he novelistically transformed his experience as organizer of displaced Jews for illegal immigration—so-called *'Aliyyah Bet*—to former Palestine. The work involves two friends who are imprisoned in their holocaust experiences—in Auschwitz memories. One tries to escape total despair, one accepts defeat by his own personal history. The novel *ha-Nissayon ha-Nosaf* (The Added Experience) by Yonat and Alexander Sand is a sort of interior monologue of a woman, Martha, whose basic experience was the holocaust and whose added experience was the new life which she brought to the world in Israel. What is particularly interesting is the total lack of Jewish identification on the part of the heroine. She suffers as a Jew in an ethnic sense, she comes to Israel by chance and she throws in her lot with her people unconsciously. The lot of the individual as an individual and the lot of the individual as an ethnic molecule in an ethnic compound of tragic proportion—this dichotomy lends to the book a special significance.

In summation: the holocaust is an apocalyptic event in Jewish history; holocaustism is a tragic value of the modern Jew.

The last years of the mandatory government, the establishment of the State of Israel, and the subsequent war of independence, found their echoes in three notable novels: Moshe Shamir's *Hu Halak ba-Sadot* (He Walked in the Fields), Nathan Shaham's *Shib'ah me-Hem* (Seven of Them) and S. Yizhar's *Days of Ziklag*. There was an accelerated process of the in-gathering and acculturation of exotic exiles: Yemenites and Iraqi Jews, Kurdish and Persian, Syrian and Lebanese, Moroccan and Algerian, Tunisian and Egyptian Jews. Hopefully, the result will be a new society in Israel and a strengthened feeling for the totality of Jewry—*Kelal Yisrael*—in the near future.

Interestingly, the logic of social and historical events is often anticipated by literary artifacts. Already before the First World War Yemenites made their way into Hebrew literature. David Shimoni was not only their first poet; he was also the first observer of their quaint idiom and patriarchal behavior in a playlet *Night in a Vineyard,*[30] which was published before the First World War. After the First World War Hayyim Hazaz, one of the most popular novelists of Israel, interpreted the exotic Yemenites in two novels: *Ha-Yoshebet ba-Gannim*[31] and *Yaish*. In the first, he depicted three generations of Yemenites in Israel; in the second, he traced the life of an individual, Yaish, in his native Yemen. In both he probably contributed to a better understanding of that exotic Jewry than any living author (and that includes writers of Yemenite origin like Mordecai Tabib and Zekariah Nissim who cannot compete with his maturer talent).

Another prolific writer, a native of Old Jerusalem and a Sephardic Jew by the name of Judah Burla (1887–1969), has succeeded in portraying a whole gallery of Oriental Jews in his novels. And not only Jews among themselves but in their relations to the Bedouin and the Fellahin, to the sheik and the nomad of Arab origin. It may be said without exaggeration that the neglected world of Oriental Jewry was resuscitated through the literary efforts of Burla and Hazaz, their forerunners and their successors. Their endeavor enriched our concept of the totality of Israel: it made Jewish interdependence and interrelationship a matter of existent actuality rather than a matter of romantic aspiration. This totalism is a new, a third value, in addition to the two previous values, alienism and holocaustism.

It is taken for granted that Oriental Jewry, more primitive and more naive than Ashkenazic Jewry, is also more religious. While the older generation of Oriental Jews is rigidly orthodox, the younger generation is almost as lax in observance as the younger generation of European, American, and Israeli Jews. But our crisis of religion is merely a link in the chain of the world-wide crisis which dates back to the days of the high Renaissance. It was toward the end of the fifteenth century that an emergent anthropocentrism dislodged an entrenched theocentrism, that, to put it simply, a passionate concern with man replaced a fanatic pursuit of God. Jews were not unaffected by the critical attitude of the Italian Renaissance to matters of religion. But amidst prevalent doubt and confusion they clung, on the whole, to ancestral ways. Even in this century of cynicism and extreme sophistication and bizarre alienation a truly religious vein runs through contemporary Hebrew literature. This is the notable paradox of secularized Jewish life and letters. The Hebrew language itself, like all ancient languages, is not only rich in religious idiom; it is textually and texturally religious. And the world expects from that language and that people a religious revival. It is a justified expectation. Ḥasidism, for instance, was not only the great efflorescence of religion among Jews two hundred years ago; it proved to be—through the interpretetive genius of a Buber—a message of faith to the Gentiles. In contemporary Hebrew literature Agnon, the Nobel Prize winner, is not alone in reconstructing the world of Ḥasidism with touching piety and loyalty. Poets like Samson Meltzer and S. Shalom and even Uri Zvi Gruenberg, E. Steinman in numerous essays, Harry Sackler in sensitive plays and stories, Yohanan Twersky in a number of novels, have wistfully turned their talents to the ḥasidic world. But Agnon, in his *In the Heart of the Seas* and *The Bridal Canopy*,[32] is the paramount poet-in-prose of Ḥasidism. Modern Jewry borrowed from him a dimension of faith.

The revival of Ḥasidism is not the only religious contribution of contemporary Hebrew literature. Saul Tschernichowsky (1875–1943) sought to achieve a religious stance—diametrically opposed to that of Agnon—with a daring leap into Jewish history. True Jewishness, as far as he was concerned, was not only pagan in origin; it outpaganed pagans with the cult of Astarte, the Semitic Venus, and all the attendant manifestations of uninhibited sexuality. In the justly famous poem, "Before the Statue of Apollo," he claimed a hidden kinship between the Greek God and the ancient Hebrew God before he was bound "by the straps of phylacteries." All this mythologizing power of the poet evoked nostalgia for a forgotten past, a proto-

Israelism.[33] It is in total contradiction to theories of an Ezekiel Kaufmann who claims, for Jews, a monotheistic creed from the very roots of their nationhood. But while the scholarly theories of a Kaufmann rarely carried weight outside the halls of academe, Tschernichowsky's proto-Israelism inspired a whole generation with passionate interest in a presumably idolatrous Israel. He also exercised a strong influence on another poet, Zalman Shneour (1886–1959), whose *Luḥot Genuzim* (Apocryphal Tablets) is a long poetic recreation of a past which never existed. And it is undoubtedly the poetry of Tschernichowsky and Shneour and the quest of Berdyczewski for a revaluation of Jewish values which led to a bizarre coterie in Israel: the "Canaanites."

The so-called "Canaanites" or "Young Hebrews" reject Diaspora Jewry—past and present—as irrelevant to contemporary Israel. The more than 1800 years which followed Bar Kokhba's revolt are dismissed by them as an embarrassing episode. Hebrews, born in Israel, aspire to Hebrew values which are conceived in narrowest terms and which may be characterized as militant biblicism. Jews outside Israel are strangers and foreigners. This dichotomy is fortunately the faith of the few. But they have powerful adherents in the literary and political circles of Israel, and they have powerful antecedents in the works of Tschernichowsky, Shneour and Berdyczewski.[34]

To sum up again: loss of traditional ways resulted in a feverish search for religious substitutes: neo-Ḥasidism, proto-Israelism and Canaanism. They all share a taste for history. They are all imbued with a quality which might best be characterized as unconscious historicism. And this is a fourth value, in addition to alienism, holocaustism, and totalism.

Conscious historicism in contemporary Hebrew literature is almost purely secular. In one of the few idylic sections in that grim book on the holocaust, *Reḥobot ha-Nahar,* its author identifies himself with a boy in the reign of the Hasmonean warrior-king, Alexander Yannai (103–76). Together with his father he watches the splendid procession of the sovereign and the nobles and the peasants into the Temple. And, contrasting the subsequent miseries and contemporary woes with the ancient glory, he allows himself to be seduced into hope that the people will turn their ploughshares into swords and inaugurate a robust dawn for themselves. This idealization of a virile king who fought constant battles of conquest and violent civil wars could not but lead to a complete reversal of the Isaianic dream. And it is perhaps more than a literary coincidence that a young novelist, Moshe Shamir, has published a historical novel[35] and a play about Alexander Yannai. The Dead Sea Scrolls undoubtedly led to a renewed interest in the king. The title of Shamir's play *Milḥemet Bene Or* (*The War of the Sons of Light*) is a conscious imitation of the Scroll which was published by Yigael Yadin in a sumptuous edition.[36] It was an English scholar who identified Yannai, erroneously in the estimation of most scholars, as *Kefir ha-Ḥaron* (*Lion of Wrath*), in one of the Scrolls in the commentary on the Book of Naḥum.[37]

Interest in Jewish history verges on fetishism in Shamir's *Weltanschauung:*

> The bridge which the younger literature seeks to build between ourselves and our great past does not resemble bridges of yore. We lost the religious, physical ties with the heritage of our people. Instead we raise historic ties. All those wonderful things which our predecessors regarded as slices of life, essential experiences, eternal principles—the prayer book, the traditional holidays, the typical modes of thought, the world of the Halakha, the customs—all these are history as far as we are concerned, and their value is only the value of a historical heritage.[38]

Not only Shamir but writers who recreated other epochs in Jewish history, novelists like Twersky and Churgin, playwrights like Sackler and Shoham, sought out the great religious periods of our people. They may have felt that lasting works must indicate ways of spiritual transformation to individuals and peoples, that history and religion complement each other in Hebrew literature.

A final word about a final value: Hebrew. Unlike modern languages, it is veined with religious associations. Two examples will suffice. Science is a secular word in English; *Madda'*, its Hebrew equivalent, is also a deeply theological expression. When Maimonides called the introductory book to his great code *Sefer ha-Madda'*, he did not mean the Book of Science but the Book of Knowledge [of God.] Again an example from everyday speech; "welcome" is a secular expression; the Hebrew equivalent *Barukh ha-Ba,* "Blessed be he who comes," is part of a biblical verse.[39] These examples can be easily expanded into the size of a hefty volume. But they make the point: Hebrew is a religious language. And when the Communist regime began to liquidate Hebrew as a reactionary, anti-revolutionary language—and that meant a religious language—it was right in its reasoning though wrong in its anticivilizational, antihumanistic drive.

Even the secularization of modern life did not affect the essential character of the Hebrew language. Between Anglo-Saxon and English there is a chasm; between the language of Isaiah in the eighth century B.C.E. and the language of Bialik in the twentieth century there is a strong bond: in grammar and in idiom they are almost identical. Only the vocabulary is quantitatively larger than it was twenty-six centuries ago. If proof were needed for the essential unity of the Hebrew language, it was given by the pioneer of spoken Hebrew, Eliezer Ben Yehudah (1857–1922). The monumental Hebrew dictionary in sixteen volumes, initiated by him and completed by Professor N. H. Tur-Sinai [Torczyner], testifies on every page to the marvelous continuity of the language. Almost eighty years elapsed from the initial labors of Ben Yehudah on the dictionary to its completion by Tur-Sinai. But they gave the Hebrew language its most important chronicle of words from their emergence in pre-biblical times to their resurrection and continuation in our time.

It is in the realm of neologisms and new, startling word-combinations that the modern Hebrew writer made his most lasting contributions. He was, of course, not the only architect of language. The people in the cities and on the farms coined new expressions for new needs. Children at play were coining words. Since 1890 a Committee on Language, *Va'ad ha-Lashon,* functioned in former Palestine both as watchdog over the evolving language in spoken form and as creator of words in new and old fields of human endeavor. That Committee evolved into the Academy of Hebrew Language: it has performed and is still performing a valuable service to the people.

But the most important single factor in the development of the Hebrew language is the Hebrew writer. It is he who adapted Hebrew to modern use and recreated it as a tool of infinite suppleness and subtlety. It is he who enriched its vocabulary to such an extent that it became a modern language with an infinite variety of expression. It is he who made the common and the uncommon words which are on everybody's lips today. Thus no less a person than Bialik created the words for import, *Yebu,* and export, *Yeẓu.* And Tschernichowsky was responsible for hundreds of terms in medicine, botany and zoology. Shlonsky, the poet who made his debut in the twenties, was so inventive in new coinages and in new word-combinations that no less a poet than Shneour called him facetiously *Lashonsky,* Mr. Language.[40] He really deserves the sobriquet. For like Hebrew writers in Eastern Europe a century ago he has an almost fetishistic attitude to the

Hebrew language. But he is infinitely more inventive and imaginative in his translations and in his original poetry. In a recent interview, occasioned by his new version of Alexander Pushkin's *Yevgeni Onegin,* he paid a handsome compliment to the hidden resources of Hebrew:

> I like to struggle with the language, with the sentence, with the word. And when I am victorious and when I feel that I have found the proper expression, I smile and say to myself: Shlonsky, it is not you. It's she—it's the Hebrew language which is victorious.[41]

The language is female in Hebrew. And this fact accounts for the endearments lavished on her beauty by Hebrew writers who, until recent times, were 99% and some fractions, male. A responsible appreciation of the Hebrew language for this generation was made by a young novelist, Amos Oz:

> You compose a Hebrew sentence, combine a few Hebrew words: a palaceful of echoes and secondary echoes answers you . . . I and people like me stand before a difficult experience with no similarity in the entire history of Hebrew literature. We have to write in a language which, on the one hand, belongs to us more than to former generations and, on the other hand, belongs to us less than to former generations because its treasures were opened before them day by day in an ever-living reality.[42]

What Amos Oz is saying amounts to a sound appreciation of the language situation vis-à-vis the creator of language: the untutored Hebrew writer is at a disadvantage, the learned Hebrew writer is overwhelmed by the associational wealth of the Hebrew language. Still, it is no exaggerated claim: the Hebrew writer has converted a sacral language into a secular language of a modern state. It is still a powerful link between the ethnic groupings of Jewry: a *lingua franca,* an international medium of expression that binds the Jew from Bokhara and the Jew from Warsaw into a fraternal community. It is also taught in the universities of America as a modern language. Now that it is a living language again, it is right to remember that the Hebrew writer is not only one of the architects of the State of Israel; he is also the creator of its modernized language—a value of unimaginable spiritual significance for modern Jewry.

This is an expanded version of a paper given at Brandeis University, on February 7, 1967 under the auspices of the Philip W. Lown School of Near Eastern and Judaic Studies.

NOTES

[1] See his excellent paper "The Scientific Study of Values and Contemporary Civilization," *Zygon* I[3] (September, 1966), p. 233. It was originally read at a meeting of the American Philosophical Society on April 26, 1958. Subsequently it was published in the *Proceedings of the American Philosophical Society CII*[5] (October, 1958) and reprinted in *Zygon.*

[2] See his *Philosophical Issues in Adult Education* (Springfield, Illinois, 1963), p. 26.

[3] The book was first published in 1905 under the name *Das Wesen des Judentums.* In essence it was a reply to the popular book of Adolf von Harnack on the *Essence of Christianity.*

[4] Leo Baeck, *This People Israel: The Meaning of Jewish Existence* translated by Albert H. Friedlander (New York, 1964), p. xvii. In German it was published in 1955 under the name, *Dieses Volk: Jüdische Existenz.* It is the culmination of Baeck's work: reaffirmation of Jewish faith in terms of personal and ethnic experience. Written in the concentration camp of Theresienstadt in the so-called "Protectorate," it marks the fifty-year-long road "from essence to existence, from nineteenth-century optimism to twentieth-century existentialism."

[5] *Ibid.,* p. xviii.

[6] Louis Jacobs, *Jewish Values* (London, 1960), p. 8.

[7] See his *"Yahadut wa-ʿArakehah-Motivim," Gesher* (December, 1965) pp. 12–15.

[8] See his *"Ḥasidut Shel Mistiḳah wa-Ḥasidut Shel Emunah"* in *ʿErke ha-Yahadut* (Tel Aviv, 1952), pp. 81–90.

[9] See his *"Emunot we-Deʿot be-Teologiyyah Shel ha-Meah ha-TeshaʿEsreh," Ibid.,* pp. 91–106.

[10] See his *"Ha-Maḥshabah ha-Leumit ha-Ḥadashah", Ibid.,* pp. 107–116.

[11] See his *Religious Philosophy* (Cambridge, Mass., 1961), p. 271.

[12] Many forms of alienation are listed and discussed in a recent article: alienation from oneself, alienation from the opposite sex, alienation of man from man, alienation of man from society, alienation from work, alienation from nature, alienation from God. See Henry Winthrop, "Alienation and Existentialism in Relation to Literature and Youth," *The Journal of General Education XVIII*[4] (January, 1967), pp. 290–293. Alienated youth is not only the popular subject of radio and television programs; it dominates sometimes entire or almost entire issues of serious periodicals. See the special issue of *School and Society* (April 15, 1967). As a characteristic of Young America alienation has been exhaustively treated by the Yale psychiatrist Kenneth Keniston in his book, *The Uncommitted: Alienated Youth in American Society* (New York, 1965). Far-seeing scholars have begun to project a post-alienation era. See especially Ernest Becker, *Beyond Alienation* (New York, 1967). And Vienna, in its post-Freudian, post-Adlerian era, proclaims a new psychotherapy—logotherapy—for modern futilitarianism. See Viktor E. Frankl, *Man's Search for Meaning* (Boston, 1963), a translation of his book in German: *Ein Psychologe erlebt das Konzentrationslager.*

[13] The concept of alienation flourished in medieval times: man was regarded as a "wayfarer in a strange world." See the excellent study of Gerhart B. Ladner, "Homo Viator: Medieval Ideas on Alienation and Order," *Speculum* XLII[2] (April, 1967), p. 256. Two major texts in the Hebrew Bible furnished the basis for two forms of alienation in the medieval world: *Exodus* 20:3 and *Psalms* 39:13: "You shall have no other gods before me" and ". . . For I am a stranger among you, a sojourner, as all my fathers were." Since the words "other gods" in *Exodus* read *deos alienos* and "a sojourner" *peregrinus* in the Vulgate, alienation was regarded (1) as "a failure to love God" with Satan himself as chief *alienus,* alien; (2) as a pilgrimage on this earth or, as the anonymous author of the Epistle to Diognetus expressed the lot of Christians, "They dwell on earth, but they are citizens in heaven" *Ibid.,* pp. 235–236.

[14] An interesting parallel has been drawn recently: "The relatively low esteem of technology may have been as much reason for the ruin of the [Roman] Empire as an over-emphasis on technology may be an important cause of our decline." See Sir Llewellyn Woodward, "Will Civilization Survive?" in *Journal of Historical Studies* I, no. 1 (Princeton, New Jersey, Autumn 1967), p. 12.

[15] Nathan Zak devotes two poems to Ḥoni in his volume of verse *Kol he-Ḥalab we-ha-Debash* (Tel Aviv, 1966) pp. 42–43; 70.

[16] There are even hippie-Hasidim who have a House of Love and Prayer within a half-hour's walk from Haight Ashbury. They combine dance, song, and prayer with hippie practices: occasional drugs, strumming the guitar and "doing their thing." See *The Jerusalem Post* (July 7, 1969), p. 13.

[17] Herbert R. Lottman, "A Baedeker of Beatnik Territory," *The New York Times Magazine* (August 7, 1966), p. 53. On Elat as a center of Israeli beatniks, see Jewish New Year 5727 Picture Supplement of *Ha-Areẓ*, p. 23.

[18] This is the major novel of the War of Independence. The other two wars, in 1956 and, especially, in 1967, inundated the literary market with journalistic reportage. But not one important story or novel, poem or play reflected the desperate struggles of the fifties and sixties.

[19] *Petaḥ Tiḳwah*—a door of hope—is mentioned as an apposite to *'Emek 'Akor* —Valley of Troubling—in Hosea 2:17: "And I will give her her vineyards . . . and the valley of 'Akor for a door of hope. . . ." The settlers in the eighties of the nineteenth century considered their native home—Eastern Europe—a true "Valley of Troubling." And so did Eliyyahu Margalit, the hero of Solomon Zemah's novel which appeared as late as 1921. The real and the fictional characters were eager to wrest a new reality from the context of ancient symbolism.

[20] *Rishon le-Ẓiyyon*—the first to Zion—is mentioned in Isaiah 41:27. The settlers undoubtedly favored the interpretation of the medieval commentator David Kimhi on the two Hebrew words: *"Rishon she-Yavo le-Ẓiyyon me-ha-Galut . . ."*—"the first who will come to Zion from exile."

[21] See my "Hebrew Literature's Homecoming," *Jewish Social Studies* XVIII[3] (July, 1956), pp. 181–182.

[22] Quoted in *The Alliance Review* XXIII[43] (Spring, 1969), p. 32.

[23] A fourth edition under the original title *Vom Umsturz der Werte* appeared in Bern in 1955.

[24] See *Judaism* II[2] (1962), pp. 106–107.

[25] See Jacob Robinson, "Research on the Jewish Catastrophe," *The Jewish Journal of Sociology* VIII[2] (December, 1966), p. 201.

[26] Recently, Professor Abraham I. Katsh discovered, translated and edited *Scroll of Agony: The Warsaw Diary of Chaim A. Kaplan* (New York, 1965). It was also translated into Hebrew and into several European languages: German, French, Swedish, Portuguese. Additional chapters appeared in *Bitzaron* LIX[2] (November-December, 1968), pp. 61–68; *ibid.*, (January-February, 1969), pp. 109–115 and *ibid.*, (March, 1969), pp. 150–154.

[27] *Genesis* 36:37; 1 *Chronicles* 1:48.

[28] Critics, unaware of the biblical *Reḥobot ha-Nahar,* have recourse to fanciful theories about its interpretation and meaning. See, for instance, Sholom J. Kahn, "Uri Zvi Greenberg—Poet of Kingship," *Ariel* 13 (1966), pp. 47–48.

[29] The original in Uri Zvi Gruenberg, *Reḥobot ha-Nahar* (Jerusalem and Tel Aviv, 1951), p. 347. The translation is mine.

[30] *Ha-Shiloaḥ* XXV (Odessa, 1911), pp. 7–21; 105–114.

[31] The novel was translated into English—with some sizable omissions—by Ben Halpern under the title *Mari Said* (New York, 1956). The Hebrew title is taken from the *Song of Songs* 8:13: "Thou that dwellest in the gardens." It also undoubtedly alludes to the Aramaic translation and interpretation of the two Hebrew words, ". . . the Lord of the Universe will say to the congregation of Israel at the end of days: You, congregation of Israel, you are like an insignificant garden among the nations and you dwell in the house of study. . . ." Thus two facts, the insignifi-

cance of Jewry in exile and the love of study which is characteristic of Jewry, are fixed in the title of Hazaz's book. But there they refer to a segment rather than the totality of Jewry.

32 The long short-story, *In the Heart of the Seas,* is available in an English translation by I. M. Lask (New York, 1948). *The Bridal Canopy,* also in Lask's translation, was published by Doubleday, Doran and Co. (New York, 1937).

33 On proto-Israelism see E. Silberschlag, *Saul Tschernichowsky: Poet of Revolt* (Ithaca, New York, 1968), pp. 36–41.

34 Kurzweil's study of Canaanism "Mahutah u-Meḳorotehah Shel Tenu'at ha'Ibrim ha-Ẓeirim", *Luah ha-Areẓ* (Tel Aviv, 1952), pp. 107–129, is available in an English version of Theodore Friedman in *Judaism* (January, 1955), pp. 3–15.

35 The novel is available in an English translation by David Patterson under the title *King of Flesh and Blood* (London, 1958).

36 *The Scroll of the War of the Sons of Light Against the Sons of Darkness,* edited with commentary and introduction by Yigael Yadin; translated from the Hebrew by Batya and Chaim Rabin (Oxford, 1962).

37 See J. J. Allegro, "Further Light on the History of the Qumran Sect," *Journal of Biblical Literature* LXXV, Part II (June, 1956), p. 92 ff. For an illuminating discussion of the pros and cons of Allegro's identification of "the lion of wrath" with King Alexander Yannai, see Millar Burrows, *More Light on the Dead Sea Scrolls* (New York, 1958), pp. 213–218.

38 Moshe Shamir, "The Renaissance" in the daily *'Al ha-Mishmar,* (April 26, 1957).

39 *Psalms* 118:26.

40 See Dov Sadan, *Ḳe'arat Egozim* (Tel Aviv, 1953), p. 196.

41 Raphael Bashan, *Reayon ha-Shanah 'Im Abraham Shlonsky, Ma'ariv* (August 26, 1966), p. 14. The first translation of Pushkin's *magnum opus* by Shlonsky appeared in Tel Aviv in 1937. The new translation is equipped with a formidable commentary of over 100 pages. See Alexander S. Pushkin translated by A. Shlonsky (Jerusalem, 1966), pp. 485–611. Nabokov who, like Shlonsky, is inordinately proud of his translation of *Yevgeni Onegin* into English, has added two volumes of commentary to his translation which appeared in 1964.

42 *Moznayim* (July, 1966), p. 134.

DAVID KIMḤI AND THE RATIONALIST TRADITION II: LITERARY SOURCES

FRANK TALMAGE

University of Toronto

The cross-fertilization of culture and the interfusing of disciplines so characteristic of Provençal Jewish learning are nowhere more evident than in the biblical commentaries of Rabbi David Kimḥi. Although they are not quite a primer of philosophy, the uninitiated might find his curiosity piqued by the philosophical material while the adept might find striking new relevance in a biblical passage. Kimḥi's relation to philosophical literature and his treatment of various topics of that literature have been treated in an earlier study.[2] As a contribution to the study of the history of culture in the period, we propose to outline Kimḥi's rationalist sources and his use of philosophical literature.

The sources dealt with may be treated under six headings: (a) The *Sefer Yeẓirah* (b) literature of the geonic period (c) the twelfth-century neo-Platonists (the Spanish philosophers) (d) Maimonides (e) Post Maimonideans (f) non-Jewish sources. Rabbinic literature, though not to be considered a rationalist source, figured heavily in Kimḥi's philosophizing. His treatment of it generally followed that of Maimonides and will consequently be discussed under that rubric.

(a) *Sefer Yeẓirah.*

The earliest "rationalistic" work to demand our attention is the *Sefer Yeẓirah* or *Book of Creation*. That ancient tract, the purpose and origins of which still remain shrouded in mystery, was accepted in the Middle Ages as a source of knowledge in the fields of linguistics, metaphysics, and mysticism.[3] Kimḥi's citations of the *Yezirah,* although limited in number, are nonetheless representative in that they range from a problem of phonetics to the esoteric. Our author was acquainted with several commentaries to the *Yezirah,* among them being that of pseudo-Saadia which he cited in the name of R. Saadia Gaon, that of Isaac Israeli (Dunash b. Tamim-Jacob b. Nissim),[4] the remarks of Judah Halevi in the *Kuzari,*[5] and the commentary of Judah b. Barzilai Albargeloni.[6]

Our author presented the *Yezirah* first as an authority for cosmology and physics.[7] It is in this context that a rather strained interpretation from the Israeli commentary[8] was cited together with a remark in the name of R. Saadia Gaon. The text of the *Yezirah* which Kimḥi presented here reproduces the explanation of the word *tohu* which is found in the Babylonian Talmud.[9] This phrase does not appear at all in Saadia's text of the *Yezirah* but it is to be found verbatim in that of Pseudo-Saadiah.[10] One might conclude from this that Pseudo-Saadia on the *Yezirah,* or as Epstein would have it, proto-Pseudo-Saadiah, was already before Kimḥi, who considered it the work of the Gaon.[11]

The *Yezirah* was cited twice in the *Mikhlol.* On one occasion Kimḥi remarked the existence of the *resh degushah,* which the *Yezirah* presupposes, citing Ali ben Judah the Nazirite[12] who testified to its use in Tiberias.[13] The purpose of the other citation is to demonstrate that although the *Yezirah* takes the letters *alef, mem,* and *shin* as the three *matres* (*immoth, ummoth*), one is justified in calling *alef, waw,* and *yod, matres* since the former are *immoth ha-ᶜolam,* while the latter are *immoth ha-sippur.*[14] Such a statement, coming as it does in a grammatical work, illustrates the currency and authority of the *Yezirah* in this period.[15]

In his philosophical commentary to Ezekiel, Kimḥi reproduced the passage in the *Sefer Yezirah* which incorporates the phrase "and the living creatures ran and returned." [16] He did not however provide any comment or amplification. On the other hand, he lent an esoteric flavor to Zechariah 2:4 by connecting the seven-branched candelabra with the seven "double" letters (*kefuloth*) of chapter four of the *Yezirah* and included an explanation drawn from the *Kuzari.*[17]

The probable influence of Judah ben Barzilai's commentary to the *Yezirah* can be seen in Kimḥi's emphasis on the correspondence of the throne of glory (*kisse ha-kavod*) to the holy sanctuary (*hekhal ha-*

qodesh)[18] or even on their identity.[19] This point was developed at great length by Judah ben Barzilai in his commentary.[20]

(b) *Literature of the Geonic Period.*

Geonic literature played an important role in forming Kimḥi's attitude towards rabbinic Midrashim. Our author cited R. Samuel ben Hophni to the effect that, while the Rabbis may hold a certain opinion, "the[ir] words cannot be accepted wherever there are grounds for objection on the part of the intellect."[21] This attitude of certain Geonim[22] to the aggadah was readily adopted.

> We expound the *haggadoth* as is proper and correct, grasping their true meaning and scientific allusions, as our predecessors the Geonim, such as R. Sherira, R. Hai, and R. Isaac Alfasi, and the other pillars of the world . . . taught us. We live according to their word and rely on them and on no one else in questions of *haggadah*.[23]

There are however very few places in the commentaries where such interpretations are presented and even these are not entirely accepted by Kimḥi.[24] Clearly then, it was not the geonic interpretations themselves that were important to Kimḥi but rather the license to indulge in interpretations of this type.

Kimḥi did not cite the literature of the Geonim or of the geonic period extensively. Some rationalistic interpretations of R. Saadia Gaon were cited in the commentaries in addition to the above remarks. However, Saadia left a marked impression on Kimḥi in the latter's discussion of epistemology and the biblical precepts.[25]

Another eleventh-century writer cited by Kimḥi was Isaac Israeli. That our author had a special interest in this scholar can be seen from the fact that he requested a translation of Isaac Israeli's *Book of Elements* from his friend Abraham ben Samuel Halevi ibn Hasdai.[26] This is especially noteworthy in the light of the rejection of Israeli by both Maimonides and Samuel ibn Tibbon.[27] Israeli was cited by name only twice[28] and the statements probably come from his commentary to the first chapters of Genesis known as the *Sefer Yezirah* or the *Yishrezu ha-mayim* which was cited by Ibn Ezra.[29] As has been mentioned Kimḥi drew from the commentary of Israeli to the *Sefer Yezirah*.[30]

(c) *The Spanish Philosophers.*

The eleventh and early twelfth centuries represent a highly creative period in the development of Jewish philosophy. The introduction of neo-Platonism, on which was based the systems of Ibn Gabirol, Ibn Zaddik, Judah Halevi, Abraham bar Hiyya, and Abraham ibn Ezra, laid the groundwork for the edifice of Maimonides, the *Guide for the Perplexed.* Maimonides knew most of the literature of this period and was of course extensively influenced by it. His debt to Ibn Ezra is exceptionally great and has not yet been adequately assessed. Despite the fact that Maimonides drew upon his predecessors, however, he never spoke at length concerning the period as a whole or its representative thinkers.[31]

David Kimḥi, on the other hand, did not draw heavily on these thinkers—with the exception of Abraham ibn Ezra. Baḥya ibn Pakuda, for example, was mentioned only once in passing.[32] Kimḥi did occasionally see fit to utilize the *Improvement of the Qualities of the Soul* or the *Tiqqun middoth ha-nefesh* of Solomon ibn Gabirol in order to provide a scientific explanation or perhaps a moralizing statement. Thus in explaining the passage "a wild ass used to the wilderness that snuffs up the wind in her desire" (Jeremiah 2:24), Kimḥi remarked that the drawing of wind is necessitated by the running of the beast. For support, he cited "the great sage, R. Solomon ibn Gabirol" who wrote "that the sense of smell is alluded to in the verse 'the race is not to the swift' (Ecclesiastes 9:11) because running involves the inhalation of air to circulate and fan the natural heat in the body. Inhalation takes place by means of the olfactory sense and were it not for the nose, there would be no breathing." [33] In connection with the verse, "He guides the humble in justice, and He teaches the humble His way" (Psalms 25:9), Kimḥi remarked that the "sage R. Solomon ibn Gabirol explained that the humble attain the will of the Creator through the trait of contrition and acquire bliss and learn His way as stated [in the above verse]." [34]

In the allegorical commentary to Ezekiel 1:5, Kimḥi used the expression "microcosm" ("*ᶜolam qatan*) which, according to the context in which it is found, seems to be drawn from Ibn Gabirol. The concept of man as a microcosm was the theme of a work by Joseph ibn Zaddik which Kimḥi knew and cited but once. To Genesis 2:7, Kimḥi brought a lengthy explanation as to why man was created from earth as discussed in the *Microcosm.*[35]

Our author's apparent neglect of Judah Halevi is somewhat more surprising. To judge by the number of citations, the original and profound *Kuzari* left only a barely visible mark on the commentaries. The "Sage, the *Kuzari*" provided an occasional physiological or scientific explanation.[36] To Isaiah 6:3, for example, Kimḥi brought Halevi's remark concerning the applicability of the term 'holy" (*qadosh*) to God.[37] The remark of the Judah Halevi mentioned in the *Shorashim*[38] does not appear in the *Kuzari* and may possibly be taken from another Judah Halevi, especially since Kimḥi seemed to prefer to call the author of the *Kuzari* by the title *"he-ḥakham ha-kuzari."* In addition to these references, however, Halevi's influence can be noted elsewhere in Kimḥi's writings, especially in the latter's discussions of Providence and prophecy, in which Kimḥi shared Halevi's ethnocentrism.[39]

The exegesis of another twelfth-century scholar, the noted astronomer and mathematician, Abraham bar Hiyya Savasorda, was cited on several occasions. For Jeremiah 9:23, Kimḥi cited "R. Abraham bar Hiyya who is styled *Sahib el-shurta.*" [40] Savasorda's well-known discussion of the terms *bara', yazar,* and *ᶜasah* in reference to the creation was echoed by Kimḥi,[41] and Poznanski was of the opinion that he borrowed his interpretation of Genesis 3:14 and 3:15 from the *Megillath ha-megalleh.* Similarly his discussion of Isaiah 43:7, especially the eschatology there presented, bears a very strong similarity to that work.[42] Kimḥi cited several astronomical observations of Bar Hiyya,[43] among them that the number of visible stars is 1098, which is in contradiction to the *Heshbon mahalekhoth ha-kokhavim* which cites the number as 1022.[44] Kimḥi most certainly made use of the *Hegyon ha-nefesh,* the *Yesode ha-tevunah u-migdal ha-'emunah,* and probably of the *Megillath ha-megalleh.*

The one exception to Kimḥi's relative neglect of the twelfth-century neo-Platonists is Abraham ibn Ezra. Our author's debt to Ibn Ezra's philology and general exegesis alone is considerable.[45] This is no less true with respect to the sciences and philosophy. Indeed, the influence of Ibn Ezra upon our author in these areas was almost as profound as that of Maimonides. From Ibn Ezra, Kimḥi drew scientific observations and rationalist interpretations of all sorts.

Kimḥi's cosmology and cosmogony, for example, were largely though not exclusively drawn from Ibn Ezra, as R. Hayyim ben Israel in his book *Gan ᶜeden* observed.[46] Ibn Ezra is cited frequently[47] and with approval[48] in the creation story with respect to discussions of the spheres,[49] the role of the angels in creation,[50] and so forth. It may be noted here that Kimḥi seemed to have studied Ibn Ezra's commentary to the first chapters of Genesis especially well. Our author incorporated without acknowledgment Ibn Ezra's explanation of the decree of death upon Adam and the sin of the builders of the tower of Babel.

The first states that Adam would have died in any event, but that the Lord punished him with a death earlier than had been originally ordained. The second defines the sin of Babel as the desires of its inhabitants to remain together rather than to populate the earth as the Lord desired.[51] The purpose of the tower therefore was to serve as a marker of their settlement lest any of the members stray too far. No one, both Ibn Ezra and Kimḥi maintained, could be foolish enough to think he could build a tower by which he could ascend to heaven. It is interesting that these two ingenious explanations incurred the wrath of Naḥmanides as being the overzealous creations of "those of little faith" and "devotees of literalism." [52] By his choice of such material, Kimḥi thus branded himself as a member of these camps as had been brought out in the Maimonidean controversy.

To be sure, our author might take issue with Ibn Ezra's rationalistic interpretations. The latter's explanation of "good and evil" as sexual awareness[53] and his explanation of the serpent episode[54] did not appeal to Kimḥi. Such rejections, however, appear minor when viewed in the light of Kimḥi's extensive dependence on Ibn Ezra.

Cosmological remarks of the latter appear elsewhere in the commentaries. In explaining the passage "the work of Your fingers" (Psalms 8:4), Kimḥi cited Ibn Ezra's connection of God's ten "fingers" with the ten spheres as a support for his own explanation. As an alternate explanation, our author cited Ibn Ezra's explanation of "the upper chambers in the Heavens" (Amos 9:6) according to which the heavens represent air while the upper chambers are the three other elements. Relevant astronomical observations were drawn from Ibn Ezra such as Kimḥi's remarks concerning the Pleiades and Orion mentioned in Amos 5:8.[55]

Ibn Ezra also served as a source for biological and physiological information.[56] At Genesis 30:14, Kimḥi shared Ibn Ezra's rejection of the notion that mandrakes induce conception, a theory advanced to explain Rachel's desire for her nephew's flowers. Again, Kimḥi drew on an analogy which declares that "the heat of the sun in the world is like the heat of the heart in the body as science has proven." [57]

Interpretations which do not involve a particular science but which have a rationalist tone or employ philosophic terminology are shared with Ibn Ezra. Kimḥi's citations of Ibn Ezra's remarks in his explanation of Psalm 139, for example, give a rationalist tone to his comments.[58] Ibn Ezra's rationalist lexicography,[59] his motifs (such as the "point within a circle" image),[60] and his classification of the commandments[61] may be mentioned in this connection.

Kimḥi's attitude toward Ibn Ezra's so-called esoteric explanations or *sodoth* is enlightening. Kimḥi made the following observation: "The sage R. Abraham ibn Ezra wrote that the definite article in the phrase 'the man' (*ha-'adam*) has a *sod,* that is, according to my opinion it refers to the human species which is governed by the definite article."[62] This rather commonplace interpretation of the *sod* is consistent with Ibn Ezra's own use of the term in many places.[63] While he often employed it in the sense of "inner meaning," it was frequently taken as an equivalent for *yesod* (foundation). Thus when Ibn Ezra talks about the *sod* of the commandments, he is referring to their fundamental rationale rather than something mysterious or esoteric. Similarly, in commenting on *husad* of II Chronicles 3:3, Kimḥi compared the word *sod* to *yesod,* for "counsel is to action as a foundation is to an edifice" (*ki ha-ezah we-ha-sod la-ma ᶜaseh ka-yesod la-binyan*).

Kimḥi's attitude to Ibn Ezra's *sodoth* is revealed by the following. Ibn Ezra stated that there was a *sod* behind Jonah's fleeing from the Lord. Kimḥi, without mentioning Ibn Ezra, remarked that Jonah had no intention of fleeing before (*mi-pene*) the Lord, for he knew this to be impossible. He thought, however, that by leaving the Holy Land he could escape his prophetic mission which came from before (*mi-lifne*) the Lord. This exegesis of the unusual prepositional form *mi-lifne* was apparently what Ibn Ezra had in mind but which he refrained from expressing.[64]

Kimḥi did of course recognize and respect "esoteric" elements in Ibn Ezra's commentaries. Concerning one remark of Ibn Ezra, Kimḥi stated: ". . . this is sufficient for the wise for we are not to explain it further,"[65] while elsewhere he stated "and how good is his explanation to the wise."[66]

Kimḥi's affinity for Ibn Ezra may be attributed to certain similarities between the two. On the one hand, they were both primarily biblical exegetes and they both counted themselves members of the literalist or *peshat* school of exegesis. On the other hand, they both used science and philosophy as aids in exegesis and seldom employed the biblical text as a mere starting point for a philosophical discourse. Ibn Ezra of course went deeper than Kimḥi and was far more difficult. Kimḥi drew, however, on what he felt was suitable for his own commentary and his own audience.

Kimḥi generally neglected Maimonides' immediate precursor and the first Jewish Aristotelian, Abraham ibn Daud (d. 1180?). Nowhere in the commentaries did Kimḥi refer to or draw on the *'Emunah ramah* of that author. On the other hand, Kimhi did know and make use of Ibn Daud's important chronicle the *Sefer ha-qabbalah.* He offered the interpretation of the "sage R. Abraham Halevi of Toledo who composed the *Sefer ha-qabbalah*" which explained the two sticks of Zechariah (11:14) as a reference to the dissension between the brothers Hyrcanus and Aristobulus during the second commonwealth.[67] Kimḥi's notion that gentiles came to offer gifts at the dedication of the second Temple may be based on a similar report in the *Sefer ha-qabbalah.*[68]

(d) *Maimonides.*

In a sense, practically the entire section dealing with Kimḥi's treatment of philosophical topics and exegesis could be included in a discussion of Maimonides as a source in David Kimḥi's writings. Maimonides was certainly Kimḥi's chief master in rationalist studies as the latter himself testified. It was Maimonides who "taught us and illuminated our eyes about [many things] concerning which we walked in darkness before he came." [69]

Maimonides was widely quoted throughout the commentaries,[70] often as authoritative[71] but sometimes as simply an alternative explanation. On occasion Kimḥi cited Maimonides' interpretation approvingly, but for one reason or another provided his own[73] which might itself be Maimonidean in origin.[74] Our author might also paraphrase Maimonides, embellishing and expanding his words.[75] Instances of these which could not be included in the discussion of the larger topics are listed below.

There are many places throughout the commentaries where Kimḥi introduced Maimonidean views without citing Maimonides by name. Some of these are particularly significant in that one can see how readily some of Maimonides' views were accepted and considered normative.

For example, in reference to the sacrifices, Kimḥi wrote:

> It is possible that it is as Rabbi Moses of blessed memory said concerning the daily sacrifices and the building of the Temple for divine service, namely that their purpose is to transfer the foreign notions (*ha-deᶜoth ha-zaroth*) and the idolatrous temples to the service of God so that all idolatry be abolished from them.

Kimḥi brought this notion from the *Guide* III:32, at the end of a long discussion on the sacrifices, in connection with the verse: "For I spoke not unto your fathers, nor commanded them in the day that I brought them out of the land of Egypt, concerning burnt-offerings or sacrifices. But this thing commanded I them, saying, 'Obey My voice, and I will be your God, and you shall be My people' " (Jeremiah 7:22–23).

It is instructive to see how much more of Kimḥi's explanation not specifically attributed to Maimonides is, nevertheless, derived from him.

Kimḥi	Maimonides
There are those who say that . . . the first commandment was [that] ordained at Marah as it is said: "There He made for them a statute and an ordinance" (Exodus 15:25).	This passage has been difficult in the opinion of all those whose words I read or heard; they ask, "How can Jeremiah say that God did not command us about burnt-offering and sacrifice, seeing that so many precepts refer to sacrifice . . .?" The first commandment after the departure from Egypt was given at Marah, in the following words, "If you will diligently hearken unto the voice of the Lord your God, and will do that which is right in His sight, and will give ear to His commandments" (Exodus 15:26). "There He made for them a statute and an ordinance and there He proved them" (Exodus 15:25).

Kimḥi	Maimonides
This is to be explained as the Rabbis said, "Sabbath and civil laws were commanded at Marah," and He did not command concerning burnt-offerings or sacrifices. One might also explain that the main object of the commandment [of sacrifices] was not the burnt-offerings and the sacri-	According to the true traditional explanation, Sabbath and civil laws were revealed at Marah . . . thus . . . the first laws do not refer to burnt-offering and sacrifice which are of secondary importance. Jeremiah says [in the name of God] that the primary object of the precepts is

fices themselves but "Obey My voice . . . and you shall be My people" (Jeremiah 7:23), and on this condition He gave them the Torah.

this, "Know Me and serve no other being; I will be your God, and you shall be My people" (Leviticus 26:12).

Then follows a passage, the purpose of which is to minimize the emphasis on sacrifices as much as possible, and which is similar, if not in letter, certainly in spirit to Maimonides.

Kimḥi

Indeed there is no mention in the entire Ten Commandments which are the quintessence of the Torah any mention of burnt-offerings or sacrifices. Even when there is mention of the sacrifices, [God] did not command [Israel] explicitly to offer a sacrifice but rather said, 'When any man of you brings an offering unto the Lord . . .' (Leviticus 1:2), i.e., if he bring it of his own free will, he should do such and such.

Maimonides

[The sacrifices] had not been made obligatory for us to the same extent as it had been before. Men were not commanded to sacrifice in every place, and in every time, or to build a temple in every place, . . . All the restrictions [placed on sacrifice] served to limit this kind of worship, and keep it within those bounds within which God did not think it necessary to abolish sacrificial service altogether.

Kimḥi

The daily offerings which He commanded them are in honor of the Temple and were incumbent upon the community (*zibbur*). Individuals, however, were not commanded to offer sacrifices as they were commanded to do justice, etc. An individual was commanded to offer a sacrifice only if he should sin unintentionally.

Kimḥi then closed with some rationalizations of sacrificial precepts.

Kimḥi

He commanded the burning of the inner parts of the sacrifice

Maimonides

(Cf., *Guide* III: 46 near end and *Kuzari* II:26.)

(*'emurim*) to cause the sinner to repent, to crush the bestial desires since their origin is in the fat and blood (*helev we-dam*).

. . . and to be careful that he does not err in a commandment, not to speak of transgressing it wilfully.

If a person sins in ignorance, he is blameable, for if he had been more considerate and careful, he would not have erred.

This same trend of thought is to be found in the commentary to Chronicles where the main purpose of the Temple, which is likened to an angelic advocate (*malakh meliz*), is said to be prayer.[76]

Among other Maimonidean influences which are to be observed, one of the most striking is the utilization of Maimonides' views concerning the origin of idolatry. In the code, Maimonides had propounded the theory that idolatry had originally developed out of a desire to serve the one God, for the heavenly bodies were considered the agents or emissaries of the Lord, and to honor them would be to honor Him. In the *Guide,* he went a step further and discussed the "theurgic" nature of idolatry, seeing in it more than the mere fetishism ascribed to it in the biblical view.[77] Kimḥi, in commenting on the disputed verse concerning the generation of Enoch (Genesis 4:26), presented an analysis similar to that of Maimonides in the *Mishneh Torah,* while in a lengthy excursus on Isaiah 40:21, he commented:

> Idolators do not believe that a particular piece of stone or wood or gold or silver created the world or is the lord of the world. Let no one imagine that there is anyone in the world foolish enough to believe this. Rather they were first made [in dedication] to the name of a particular star or heavenly image and [they] . . . imagined that they cause the power of the star to descend on the image. Thus by worshipping the image, they worship the star and it is proper to worship stars since they govern the lower world.

Yet Kimḥi was not satisfied to stop at this point and maintained that if "the former [generations] erred in their opinion (*be-da^{c}tam*) the latter [generations] erred ignorantly (*mi-beli da^{c}ath*)." He then proceeded to describe the gradual degeneration of idolatry into complete fetishism, so that it was thought that "an image made of stone, wood, or anything else causes benefit or harm precisely because it is made in a particular form."

Most apparent throughout the commentaries is the influence of Maimonidean lexicography. The definition of *ḥesed* as an excess or extreme of good or evil, which had its origins in Ibn Ezra[78] and was developed by Maimonides,[79] was cited frequently. It is defined with such expressions as "an excess of good" (*yithron ha-tov*),[80] or as "an excess of a thing" (*yithron ha-davar*).[81] Thus the *ḥasid* is he who does good to his fellow to a greater degree than is expected (*lifnim mi-shurath ha-din*).[82] As an example of exemplary behavior, Kimḥi remarked that "everyone who is silent upon hearing his reproach should properly be called a *ḥasid*."[83] Similar to the definition of *ḥesed* are those of "blessing" (*berakhah*) and curse (*me 'erah*) shared by Kimḥi with Maimonides. These are defined also as an excess or deficiency of good respectively.[84]

Kimḥi followed Maimonides in certain etymologies of biblical words. For example, the former related the word *qeri* (contrariness) to the word *miqreh* (chance) as Maimonides (and Ibn Ezra) had done. According to this, the sinner or he who walks contrary (*be-qeri*) to the Lord, feels that his chastisement is not from God but is only accidental (*be-miqreh*).[85] Again the word *nissayon* (trial) is derived not from the verb *nissah,* to try, but from the word *nes,* banner or standard. On the basis of this etymology, it can be shown that the command to sacrifice Isaac did not have as its object a test of Abraham, but rather a demonstration of Abraham's faithfulness to God to future generations.[86] This interpretation, although it has its source in the Midrash,[87] occupied an important place in the *Guide* in connection with Maimonides' discussion of the concept of the trial of man by God.

Another interesting etymology of Kimḥi's might be connected with his relationship to Maimonides. The word *mishneh* in the expression *mishneh torah* is related in the *Shorashim* to the root *shny* and an anonymous source is cited relating it to *shnn.* In the commentaries, Kimḥi adopted this latter interpretation, thereby implying that the meaning of the expression is not "a second law" but the "expounding of the law" (*limmud ha-torah, perush ha-torah*).[88] The adoption of this interpretation may well be connected with the reluctance of many to refer to Maimonides' code as the *Mishneh Torah* because such a name was allegedly so presumptuous. Kimḥi's change of roots removes this connotation.[89]

Among the many other things for which our author was indebted to Maimonides, we may mention here Kimḥi's attitude toward anthropomorphisms. They are treated, of course, as metaphors and are declared to be parabolic (*derekh mashal*), metaphoric (*derekh ha-ᶜavarah*), or "after the fashion of human speech" (*ᶜal leshon bene 'adam*).[90] This method of explaining anthropomorphisms was of course much older than Maimonides.[91] Yet it was he who presented the most detailed and elaborate exposition of these principles. Much of the first part of the *Guide for the Perplexed,* indeed, expounds individual, apparently anthropomorphic expressions in the light of rationalistic exegesis. It is this unique contribution of Maimonides which Kimḥi adopted in his own writings in various places. Thus God's *zelem* in which man was created, is declared to be the intellect,[92] while His *temunah* refers to man's intellectual acquisition of His being.[93] God's feet (*raglayim*) refer to His role as a Cause (*sibbah*),[94] and His heart (*lev*) is understood as the intellect (*sekhel*).[95]

The name of God Himself could be thus treated. The word *elohim* can be used with other words to magnify (*le-hagdil*) something.[96] The exposition of the tetragrammaton as related to God's other names is similar to that of Maimonides[97] as is his interpretation of God's ways (*darkekha*) which are said to refer to "the nature of all things and their relationships to each other . . . together with His government of all things in general and in particular." [98]

A major contribution of Maimonides to Kimḥi's exegesis was the former's use of Midrash and Targum in philosophical discussions. While Kimḥi was not dependent exclusively on Maimonides in this area, R. Moses was certainly his chief motivation and source in this "rationalistic" treatment of rabbinic literature. This material may then properly be presented in this context.

Targumim

The reading of esoteric and philosophical material into the Targumim began in the post-talmudic period when the influence of the Muslim philosophical schools made themselves felt. The Targum was regarded as a trustworthy authority especially in dealing with the problem of anthropomorphism.

R. Saadia Gaon declared:

> With regard to Tradition, we find that the Sages of our people, who are the trustworthy guardians of our religious heritage, whenever they come across such metaphors, never translated them in anthropomorphic terms, but paraphrased them in a manner which conformed to the fundamental principle. They were the disciples of

> the Prophets and understood their words. Had they thought that these words had an anthropomorphic meaning, they would have rendered them in their literal sense. But they knew on the authority of the Prophets, apart from the judgment of their own reason, that those anthropomorphic expressions were intended to convey certain sublime and exalted ideas, and so they translated them according to what they knew was the true meaning.[99]

On this basis, Maimonides devoted considerable space to the relationship of the Targumim to biblical anthropomorphisms. In a tone similar to that of Saadia, he observed:

> Onkelos the Proselyte, who was thoroughly acquainted with the Hebrew and the Chaldaic languages, made it his task to oppose the belief in God's corporeality. Accordingly, any expression employed in the Pentateuch in reference to God, and in any way implying corporeality, he paraphrases in consonance with the context.[100]

Concerning a targumic paraphrase, Maimonides commented: "Consider this well, and you will observe with wonder how Onkelos keeps free from the idea of the corporeality of God, and from everything that leads thereto even in the remotest degree."[101]

Unlike Naḥmanides, who declared that anthropomorphism was not of principal concern to the translators,[102] Kimḥi accepted and affirmed the views of Maimonides in this regard. He therefore commented:

> In many places the Torah speaks in human language concerning the Creator and attributes to Him sight, hearing, a sense of smell, a hand, or a foot after the fashion of man. All these terms are metaphoric [and are used] to enable people to understand [more easily]. In every instance, Onkelos, translator of the Torah, and Jonathan ben Uzziel, translator of the prophetic books, removed these attributes from the Creator. In [Jeremiah 14:10], Jonathan referred that which was said of God to Israel, for he wanted to remove even metaphoric attributes from Him.[103]

Commenting upon the verse "should I leave my wine, which cheers God and man?" (Judges 9:13), Kimḥi remarked:

> Jonathan translated "for from it libations are made before the Lord in which great men (*ravravin*) rejoice." Jonathan, peace be

> upon him, removed [the notion of] happiness from the exalted Creator as he removed all other attributes from Him, for there is no happiness or sadness in relation to Him. The Torah speaks of Him in human language and that which is said of Him in human language is metaphorical. Thus Onkelos translated the words "and he was saddened to His heart" (Genesis 6:6) by the words "and he intended in His word (*memra'*) to shatter their might according to His will." He thereby removed the expression of sadness from Him.[104]

Kimḥi followed Maimonides in an observation on the words "and His soul was grieved for the misery of Israel" (Judges 10:16). He remarked: Jonathan left [these words] untranslated in order to remove the attributes from the exalted Creator as we have written. He found no way to explain it so he refrained from translating it."[105]

Maimonides was aware of the fact that the Targumim did not always react to a passage in accordance with the general principles which he set forth, and consequently attempted to reconcile these discrepancies.[106] Naḥmanides, on the other hand, used these passages in rejecting the Maimonidean interpretation of the Targum's paraphrastic renderings of biblical anthropomorphisms. Yet he made no attempt to explain the relationship of the Targumim to this problem but satisfied himself by remarking that it is known to those versed in the qabbalah (*yodᶜe HeN*).[107]

Kimḥi, too, was aware of these problems but declined to discuss them as Maimonides had done. Rather, in a remark very similar to that of Naḥmanides, he commented that the solutions to these problems are "a secret known to those versed in science (*mevine maddaᶜ*),"[108] referring of course to those learned in philosophy rather than qabbalah.

Kimḥi once again followed Maimonides in utilizing Targum Jonathan for support in dealing with problems other than anthropomorphism. In the philosophic commentary to the first chapter of Ezekiel, Kimḥi remarked that "the Targum of Jonathan tends towards our interpretation" in translating the Hebrew *ruaḥ* as *raᶜawa* (will).[109] The employment of the Targum in the explanation of the *Merkavah* had its origin in Maimonides' discussion of the subject.[110]

It is interesting to observe that Kimḥi so took it for granted that the Targum was aware of the inner meaning of a text, that he took pains to point out those places where Jonathan maintained his reticence, and remarked: ". . . Jonathan introduced nothing in this verse."[111]

Midrash and Talmud

At the close of the talmudic period, much of the material in aggadic literature proved to be a source of difficulty and embarrassment to Jewish scholars. Karaites in the geonic period and Christians afterwards mocked the anthropomorphisms and other "absurdities" in the aggadah. A changing intellectual climate and the assimilation of foreign modes of thought created a situation in which many of these legends and statements "no longer squared with [the Rabbis] convictions." [112] Under these conditions, many sought refuge in the talmudic dictum, "one does not derive any [binding] conclusions from aggadoth." [113] Certain Geonim in the tenth and eleventh centuries declared that certain of the aggadoth were only fanciful conceits,[114] while Naḥmanides told his Christian adversaries that these tales and legends were *sermones* without binding authority.[115]

It was soon learned however that the aggadoth need not be treated as a delinquent stepchild of rabbinic literature. Certain of the Geonim, notably R. Hai and R. Samuel ben Hofni, attempted to approach this material in a rational spirit and thereby saved it from abuse. The rules and principles of rabbinic exegesis were classified and explained with a view to providing a better understanding of midrashic material. Even more striking, however, is the fact that R. Hai Gaon attempted to understand aggadoth metaphorically and declared, for example, that certain miracles which were said to have been performed for the Sages occurred in an inner vision.[116]

Thus did the Geonim lay the foundation for later attitudes toward the aggadah. Maimonides freely interpreted this material in a philosophic framework and declared that they were parabolic or figurative (*mashal, ᶜal derekh meliẓah*).

> . . . the method (of aggadic interpretation) is well known to those who are acquainted with the style of our Sages. They use the text of the Bible only as a kind of poetical language (*bi-demuth melizath ha-shir*) [for their own ideals], and do not intend thereby to give an interpretation of the text. . . . Our Sages employ biblical texts merely as poetical expressions, the meaning of which is clear to every reasonable reader.[117]

It was due to Maimonides' development of this theme that the use of Midrash as a source of proof texts for philosophical views, and the reading in of such views into the Midrash, became common in post-

Maimonidean literature. Abraham Maimonides, Samuel ibn Tibbon, and Jacob Anatoli, for example, were notable for their activity in this area. Ibn Tibbon proposed to write a commentary on the aggadoth which has not, however, come down to us.[118]

Throughout Kimḥi's writings, one can point to a number of places (both in the philosophical commentaries and elsewhere) where the Midrash was treated in this fashion. Many of these references have their parallel in the writings of his contemporaries and the influence of Maimonides is clearly discernible throughout. It is noteworthy, however, that when he was criticized for his liberal interpretations of the aggadoth, Kimḥi appealed not to Maimonides but to the Geonim.

> We expound the haggadoth as is proper and correct, grasping their true meaning and scientific allusions as our predecessors the Geonim, such as R. Sherira, R. Hai, and R. Isaac Alfasi, and the other pillars of the world and the rocks of the earth taught us. We live according to their word and rely on them in questions of haggadah and on no one else.[119]

Furthermore, of all the instances in which Kimḥi gave a philosophical interpretation to the aggadic Midrash, he cited Maimonides only twice although the influence of the latter is evident elsewhere. At Genesis 28:13, Kimḥi presented a passage from Midrash *Tanhuma* cited in the *Guide* and paraphrased Maimonides' observations.[120] Then in the philosophical commentary to Genesis, Kimḥi explained a Midrash in the light of Maimonides' interpretation of it in the *Guide*.[121]

Kimḥi's relegation of Maimonides to the background in the question of aggadic interpretation can be easily understood in the light of what has been said above. He would naturally want to refer back to the earliest possible authority in order to establish a tradition of rationalistic interpretation of the Midrash from which not only he, but presumably Maimonides also, could draw. As we have seen, however, geonic interpretations of aggadoth were cited very rarely in the commentaries and even these were not accepted *in toto*. Kimḥi therefore relied on the Geonim for their principles of interpretation rather than for the interpretations themselves, which were drawn principally from the *Guide* and other works of Maimonides.

Maimonides' method in his use of Midrash was varied. In indicating the esoteric character of a midrashic text he often found it sufficient to allude to an inner meaning without stating it in detail. He therefore commented:

> You must know that their words which I am about to quote are most perfect, most accurate, and clear for those for whom they were said. I will therefore not add long explanations, lest I make their statements plain, and I might thus become a revealer of secrets.[121a]

This principle of reticence was not consistently maintained by Maimonides however. One consequently finds him elaborating on what he feels is the true esoteric meaning of a midrashic text. At times also, he might use a Midrash as a proof text in a philosophical discussion.

Kimḥi's own approach to a rationalistic interpretation of Midrash follows these three aspects of Maimonides' method. Kimḥi would frequently use the same Midrashim which Maimonides had employed in the *Guide,* but, of course, he often selected his own texts for interpretation or support. Accordingly, Kimḥi's "rationalist" approach to Midrash may be categorized as follows: (a) allusion to an esoteric meaning, (b) philosophical interpretation of a midrashic text, and (c) use of a Midrash as a proof text.

(a) Allusion to an esoteric meaning of a Midrash can be found at several places in the commentaries. After citing a Midrash, Kimḥi might remark: ". . . and how excellent is this for those who understand."[122] Again: "The Rabbis wrote concerning the inner meaning . . . and understand this, for how excellent is their parable . . . and this is firmly established for him who understands."[123]

Several such Midrashim which were alluded to in the general commentary were discussed in full in the philosophical commentaries.

(b) Certain of the interpretations alluded to by Maimonides were presented in full by Kimḥi. In the thirtieth chapter of the second part of the *Guide,* Maimonides referred to a series of Midrashim, each of which is

> a remarkable passage most absurd in its literal sense; but as an allegory it contains wonderful wisdom, and fully agrees with real facts, as will be found by all those who understand all the chapters of this treatise.

One such passage is the following:

> "The tree of life extends over an area of five hundred years' journey, and it is from beneath it that all the waters of the creation sprang forth," and they added the explanation that this measure referred

> to the thickness of its body, and not to the extent of its branches, for they continue thus, "Not the extent of the branches thereof, but the stem thereof has a thickness of five hundred years' journey."

Now in order to prove that the absurdity of this Midrash is only apparent, Kimḥi provided the following explanation:

> . . . That is to say, the distance from the earth to heaven is [a] five hundred years' [journey] as the Rabbis said[124] and as the scientists (*hakhme ha-mehqar*) have said. It is the intent of the parable in this passage to say that the body refers to the attainment of natural science, which is terrestrial, by the human mind. The foliage refers to what is above the heavens including a knowledge of astronomy and of the intelligences. As for their saying that the waters of creaation divided underneath it, this refers to the creatures which were created on the sixth day of creation from the sphere of the moon downward as we explained in the esoteric commentary.[125]

In addition to explaining Maimonides' texts, Kimḥi was anxious to find others suitable for philosophical exegesis. "See what our Rabbis wrote concerning this matter," wrote Kimḥi after the fashion of Maimonides, "and understand how their opinion agrees with that of the investigators (*hakhme ha-mehqar*)." To Genesis 1:2, Kimḥi brought the following Midrash from Genesis Rabbah. "The upper world and the lower world were created simultaneously—the upper alive and the lower dead." [126] From the Midrash, Kimḥi learned that

> the four elements are dead bodies (*gufim*) with no will or choice but just the nature with which they were endowed. If one of them leaves its natural place under compulsion, it will return to its [original] place in a straight line when the compelling force is removed.

In his commentary to Genesis, Kimḥi remarked "and some of the Sages said, 'The Garden was created before the creation of the world . . . and this is according to the inner meaning.' " [127] Exactly what this inner meaning is was made plain in his philosophical commentary *ad locum*. There we learn that the Garden is a metaphor for the Active Intellect.

In the Isaiah commentary, he remarked that

> the meaning of the *derash* [that six things were created before the creation of the world] is not as most students understand it. The

explanation is that they were created *in potentia* before the creation of the world for these things are the goal (*takhlith*) of the world.[128]

On occasion, Kimḥi would cite a Midrash which had been interpreted by Maimonides but would give his own interpretation instead of the Master's. The rabbinic dictum that "the Patriarchs are the Chariot (*merkavah*)" was taken by Maimonides to mean that "they had attained a true conception of the Deity."[129] Kimḥi who cited this midrashic statement at Genesis 17:22 and 35:13 with the comment "how excellent is this to the perceptive," explained it in the prologue to the philosophical commentary on Ezekiel. There he remarked that it refers to the fact that the patriarchs' "intellect governs and guides them, and then the spirit of the Supreme Rider (i.e. the Active Intellect) descends on them."[130]

Indeed in one place, Kimḥi neglected an interpretation of Maimonides and rationalized a Midrash on the basis of the remarks of R. Nissim ben R. Sherira Gaon.[131]

(c) Kimḥi, as Maimonides before him, occasionally brought a Midrash as a proof text for a rationalistic interpretation. Sometimes he would choose a text identical to that employed by Maimonides, as when he wished to illustrate the preordained nature of miracles,[132] the intellectual superiority of Adam,[133] and the fact that the three angels who came to Abraham existed only in a prophetic vision.[134] On the other hand, he might choose a text other than that chosen by Maimonides. For example, in order to show that the visions of Ezekiel and Isaiah were substantially the same, Kimḥi cited the rabbinic statement that "this was seen while the Temple was standing, the other when it no longer stood. It is as if the number of the wings decreased."[135] On the other hand, Maimonides made the statement that "Isaiah saw all that had been seen by Ezekiel: Isaiah is like a townsman that sees the king, Ezekiel like a countryman that sees the king."[136]

From these illustrations, it is clear that Kimḥi did more than borrow from Maimonides in his treatment of Midrash. At times he would enlarge on a Maimonidean theme or he might reinterpret material entirely. However, despite any departures from the Master, it is the latter's method and approach which are central to Kimḥi's discussions so that departures from Maimonides were the exception rather than the rule. Kimḥi generally followed Maimonides so closely that even the latter's ambiguity was reflected in the commentaries.

Kimḥi raised the question as to whether the word *'adonay,* addressed to Abraham's three angels (Genesis 18:2), is to be considered sacred or profane. He weighed the considerations on both sides but came to no conclusion. Maimonides himself accepted the *derash* that Abraham spoke to the leader of the three men, implying that the word is to be understood as profane.[137] In the *Mishneh Torah,* however, Maimonides accepted it as sacred according to the halakhah.[138]

The above discussion plus that in the following sections serves to indicate the role Maimonides played in Kimḥi's own thinking and literary activity. To Kimḥi, as we have seen, Maimonides was the Master in philosophic studies, just as he was to generations of Jewish scholars, and it was Kimḥi's function to introduce and interpret the *Guide* to an audience which might not otherwise have had access to it. This required, as has been indicated, a process of modification and adaptation. One must remember, too, that Kimḥi used many other sources and indeed sometimes preferred their opinions to those of the Master. Nevertheless, despite any alteration and new dress to which R. Moses was subjected, the spirit and indeed most of the content of Kimḥi's rationalism was truly Maimonidean.

(e) *Post-Maimonideans.*

Of the post-Maimonidean thinkers, only one, Samuel ibn Tibbon, can be clearly connected with David Kimḥi. Ibn Tibbon, the prominent translator and interpreter of Maimonides, bore a special relation to David Kimḥi in that the two were personal friends and were wont to share their ideas in learned conversation. Some ten years younger than Ibn Tibbon, Kimḥi lamented the latter's death and the loss of his intellectual companion.[139] Kimḥi's true debt to Ibn Tibbon cannot be determined since citations of him in the commentaries are few, while Ibn Tibbon wrote one original work and that not before 1221.[140]

Kimḥi cited Ibn Tibbon's interpretation of Jeremiah 17:12. The latter stresses God's providence on earth, a favorite theme with Kimḥi, and Kimḥi mentioned that Samuel was the only one to interpret the verse in context. He was also cited at Genesis 3:6.

One may note other similarities. Ibn Tibbon saw the visions of Isaiah and Ezekiel as representations of the gradual development of the human intellect.[141] This theme can be clearly seen in Kimḥi in the interpretation of Jacob's dream[142] and traces of it are present in the allegorical commentary to Ezekiel. Ibn Tibbon and Kimḥi also shared, among other things, the view that chapter six of the Book of Isaiah was not Isaiah's first prophecy.[143]

(f) *Non-Jewish Sources:*

Statements relating to the natural sciences[144]—astronomy,[145] physics,[146] physiology,[147] and psychology[148]—are common in the commentaries. Such references were intended only as aids in exegesis, for it was not our author's intention that his commentary develop into an encyclopedia of the sciences. At one point, after recommending the study of anatomy, he remarked:

> Were we to discuss, in this work, the nature of the limbs and their functions and the various faculties and their functions, our work would be too drawn out. He who is eager for this, however, will find it in the words of the sages.[149]

Here Kimḥi tried to avoid the type of philosophical expatiation so harshly criticized by Ibn Ezra,[150] while like the latter he sparingly presented that which he considered pertinent. Some of this knowledge was gleaned from Jewish writers as has been indicated above. As sources for many of these remarks, however, Kimḥi would cite "the investigators" (*hakhme ha-mehqar,*[151] *baᶜale ha-mehqar,*[152] *hakhme ha-nissayon*),[153] "the astronomers" (*baᶜale ha-tekhunah,*[154] *hakhme ha-tekhunah*),[155] "the sages (*hakhamin*),[156] "the natural scientists" (*hakhme ha-toladah*),[157] or the "ancients" (*ha-qadmonim*).[158] Aristotle alone is mentioned by name.[159] One wonders whether all of these remarks were obtained second-hand from Hebrew authors or whether Kimḥi had read any non-Jewish technical material directly. In all probability, our author had little access to non-Jewish sources. His Arabic was not sufficiently fluent to enable him to read a scientific text, nor are there grounds for believing that he could handle one in Latin. It is quite possible, of course, that he saw some of the many Hebrew translations of such texts which were produced in his lifetime.[160] Both the anonymity and the nature of the material in question, however, would seem to indicate that these references were taken from knowledge current among enlightened Provençal Jews and found in the Hebrew writers, such as Israeli, Bar Hiyya, Ibn Ezra, Maimonides, and so forth.

NOTES

1 See most recently I. Twersky, "Aspects of the Social and Cultural History of Provençal Jewry," *Journal of World History,* XI (1968), 185–207.

2 "David Kimhi and the Rationalist Tradition," *HUCA* XXXIX (1968), 177–218.

3 Cf. G. Scholem's article "Jezira" in *EJ,* IX, 104–111, G. Scholem, *Reshith ha-qabbalah we-sefer ha-bahir* (Jerusalem, 1962), 1–69; A. Epstein, *Mi-qadmoniyoth ha-yehudim* (Jerusalem, 1957), 38–53, 179–225.

4 Gen. 1:2.

5 Zech. 4:2.

6 Jer. 17:2, Ps. 132:2.

7 Gen. 1:2 (four references), Ps. 89:13 (in support of Ibn Ezra who described the six corners of the world).

8 Dunash ibn Tamim, *Perush le-sefer yezirah* (ed. Grossberg, London, 1902), 53 *et passim.*

9 Babylonian Talmud, Hagigah 12a.

10 Ps.-Saadiah on *Yezirah,* I:11.

11 Cf. Lambert's edition of Saadia's commentary, *Le Commentaire sur le Sefer Yesira* (Paris, 1891), 85f. (Arabic section). On Pseudo-Saadiah, cf. A. Epstein, *Mi-qadmoniyoth ha-yehudim* (Jerusalem, 1956–7), 211f. and bibliography. It is to be noted that Kimhi took the expression *awir she-'eno nithpas* as a generic term for air rather than as referring to a specific type of air. Cf. Scholem, *Reshith ha-qabbalah we-sefer ha-bahir,* 47.

12 H. Malter, *Life and Works of Saadia Gaon* (Philadelphia, 1921), 21, 33.

13 *Mikhlol* (Lyck, 1862), 81b. On the *resh degushah,* cf. Dunash ibn Tamim, *Perush,* 21; *Diqduqe ha-te'amim* (Leipzig, 1879), 7f.; Saadia, *Commentaire,* 46; M. H. Segal, *Yesodoth ha-fonetiqah ha-'ivrith* (Jerusalem, 1928), 31, 111.

14 *Mikhlol,* 78a; cf. Segal, *Yesodoth,* 101.

15 Cf. Dunash ibn Tamim, *Perush,* 19f.

16 Ez. 1:14.

17 *Kuzari* IV:25.

18 Jer. 17:12.

19 Ps. 132:2.

20 Judah ben Barzilai, *Perush le-sefer yezirah* (ed. S. J. Halberstamm, Berlin, 1885), 231ff.

21 I Sam. 28:24.

22 Cf. S. Baron, *Social and Religious History of the Jews* (Phil., 1958), VI, 175ff.

23 *Qovez,* 3d.

24 See especially Gen. 5:3, I Sam. 28:24.

25 Cf. Talmage, *HUCA* (1968), 181ff.

26 Cf. *Sefer ha-yesodoth* (ed. S. Fried, 1906) pp. 1–42 (introd.), 2 (text).

27 *Iggeroth ha-RaMBaM* (Amsterdam, 1712) 14b.

28 Gen. 1:2, 1:10.

29 Introd. to Pentateuch Commentary. Cf., on the Israeli work, *Ha-tehiyah,* I (1849–50), 39–41.

30 Gen. 1:2.

31 In a letter to Samuel ibn Tibbon, Maimonides catalogued those thinkers and works with which he was familiar. Cf. *Iggeroth ha-RaMBaM,* 14b.

32 Ps. 35:10.

33 Jer. 2:24; *Tiqqun middoth ha-nefesh,* introd.

34 Ps. 25:9; *Tiqqun,* I:3.

35 *ᶜOlam qatan,* (ed. Horowitz, Breslau, 1903), 19–25.

36 Gen. 1:2 (*Kuzari,* IV:25); Jer. 10:16 (*Kuzari* V:21); cf. Hos. 2:1 (*Kuzari,* II:2), Kimhi's functional description of the brain in the allegorical commentary to Ezekiel (1:5) and as in the introduction to Ps. 119 is similar to *Kuz.* V:12.

[37] Isa. 6:3 (*Kuz.* IV:3).

[38] *S.v. Lwn.*

[39] *HUCA* XXXIX (1968), 187ff.

[40] The citation is based on material in *Hegyon ha-nefesh,* 7a; cf. *Megillath ha-megalleh,* 53. Cf. J. M. Millás-Vallicrosa, "La Obra Enciclopédica *Yesode Ha-tebuna W-migdal Ha-emuna* de R. Abraham Bar Hiyya Ha-Bargeloni," *HUCA,* XXIII (1950–51), pt. 1, 663.

[41] Gen. 1:21.

[42] *Megillath ha-megalleh;* 66. Cf. S. Poznanski, *Perush ᶜal Yehezqe'el u-tere ᶜasar* (Warsaw, 1909–11), introd., XXIV.

[43] Ps. 147:4 (*Hegyon,* 7a ff.).

[44] J. M. Millás-Vallicrosa, *La Obra Sefer Hesbon mahlekot ha-kokabim* (Barcelona, 1959), 102.

[45] Cf. F. Talmage "A Study of David Kimhi," unpublished Ph.D dissertation, Harvard University, 1965. 74f.; H. Cohen, *The Commentary of David Kimhi on Hosea* (New York, 1929), xxxvi f.

[46] Cited by A. Geiger, *Qevuzath ma'amarim* (Berlin, 1877), 42.

[47] Gen. 1:1 (twice), 1:3, 1:5, 2:8.

[48] Cf. especially Gen. 1:6.

[49] Gen. 2:2.

[50] Gen. 2:4 (from Ibn Ezra on Gen. 1:1).

[51] Gen. 2:17; 11:1. Cf. G. Van Rad, *Genesis* (Philadelphia, 1961), 145f.

[52] Cf. comm. of Nahmanides, *a.l.*

[53] Gen. 2:17.

[54] Gen. 3:1.

[55] Cf. also Ps. 19:2, 19:5, 89:13.

[56] Hos. 7:9. Cf. Gen. 2:3.

[57] Gen. 1:26, 2:4, 2:17.

[58] Cf. esp. Ps. 139:15, 16, 18.

[59] Zech. 12:1 (explanation of the word *ruah*).

[60] Gen. 1:8, Isa. 40:22, Ps. 8:2. The Karaite Aaron ben Joseph in his *Mivhar* (Eupatoria, 1835, 8a–b) made use of the image which in essence parallels Maimonides' "palace metaphor." Cf. W. Bacher, "Abraham Ibn Esras Einleitung zu seinem Pentateuch Komm.," *Sitzungsberichte d. phil.-hist. Klasse d. Wiener Akademie,* LXXXI (1875), 371.

[61] See below.

[62] Gen. 2:8.

[63] Cf. the title of his work *Yesod mora' we-sod torah.* It is to be noted that these two words are used interchangeably in the writings of the Judean desert sect. Cf. IQS 6:19, 8:10 and elsewhere.

[64] Jonah 1:2.

[65] Gen. 22:12 (based on Ibn Ezra at Gen. 18:21).

[66] Gen. 4:1, cf. *Yesod mora',* XII.

[67] Zach. 11:4. (*Sefer ha-qabbalah,* ed. Prague, 1795, 76). Cf. *Shorashim s.v. hbl;* M. Schloessinger, *JE,* VII, 260.

[68] Hag. 2:6 (*Sefer ha-qabbalah,* 76b).

[69] Gen. 1:6. Much use was made of Maimonides in dealing with the cosmogony, where material was brought from *Guide,* II:30. On Gen. 1:6, he questioned Maimonides' interpretation of the separation of the waters although he modified his criticism. Cf. Gen. 1:1, 2, 3.

[70] For a list of references, see Cohen, *Commentary to Hosea,* xxiii.

[71] Jos. 6:26 (*Guide* III:50), Isa. 6:2 (probably from *Guide* I:43), Zech. 14:4 (*Guide* I:28), Zech. 14:9 (*Guide* I:61), Joel 3:1 (*Guide* II:40), Ps. 16:8 (*Guide* III:51), Ps. 19:2 (*Guide* II:5). Maimonides is cited anonymously at Jos. 3:11.

[72] Joel 3:3 (*Guide* II:29); Zech. 14:5 (*Guide* I:22).

[73] Jud. 10:16 (*Guide* I:41), Ps. 4:5 (*Guide* I:50, 59).

[74] Isa. 3:3 (*Guide,* I:37), Jer. 9:23 (*Guide* III:54).

75 Gen. 28:13 (*Guide* II:10).

76 II Chron. 6:18.

77 *Hil. cAkum,* I; *Guide* III:29.

78 W. Bacher, *Die Agada in Maimunis Werken* (Leipzig, 1914), 58, n.2.

79 *Guide* III:53; *Comm. to. Mish.,* Avoth V:7.

80 Gen. 24:27; cf. Jos. 2:12, Hos. 4:1, 10:12.

81 Ps. 145:10.

82 Ps. 4:4.

83 Ps. 16:10.

84 Gen. 12:3; cf. Bacher, *Die Agada,* 58, n. 2.

85 Amos 9:10, *s.v. qry;* cf. Ibn Ezra on Lev. 26:27.

86 Gen. 22:1; *Guide* III:36.

87 Genesis Rabbah LI:I.

88 Jos. 8:32, II Chron. 34:22.

89 Cf. I. Twersky, "Beginnings of Mishneh Torah Criticism," in A. Altmann, *Biblical and Other Studies* (Cambridge, Mass., 1963), 173, n. 55.

90 Gen. 6:10, 8:1, 9:15, Isa. 40:12; Zech. 9:8; Mal. 2:17, 3:16.

91 On the problem see L. Ginzberg, "Allegorical Interpretation", in *JE,* I, 403–11; S. Rawidowicz, *"Becayath ha-hagshamah la-RaSaG we-la-RaMBaM," Kenesseth,* III (1938), 322–77.

92 Gen. 9:6. (*Guide* I:1); cf. Gen. 1:26, 11:5.

93 Ps. 17:15. Cf. *Guide* I:3, but *Guide* I:37 (on *panim*).

94 Hab. 3:5 (*Guide* I:28). Cf. Zech. 14:4.

95 Gen. 8:21 (*Guide* I:39).

96 Gen. 10:9, 30:8; Jon. 3:3; I Chron. 12:22. *Elohim* with a plural verb is explained as *pluralis maiestatis* (*derekh kavod*) (Gen. 35:7) or as "the language of the polytheists" (Gen. 20:13).

97 Hos. 12:6; cf. Ps. 8:2 (*Guide* I:61, II:6).

98 Ps. 25:4 (Ex. 33:18) (*Guide* I:54).

99 *'Emunoth we-decoth,* II:3. Translation from A. Altman, *Three Jewish Philosophers* (New York, 1960), 87f.

100 *Guide,* I:27 (Friedlander, 35f.).

101 *Guide,* I:28 (Friedlander, 37).

102 *Comm. to Pent., Gen.* 46:21.

103 Jer. 14:9.

104 Jud. 9:13. At Mic. 5:4, Kimhi considered Jonathan a bit over-zealous. He remarked: ". . . and Jonathan translated 'and we shall appoint over us (*calana*) seven kings and eight great men' and I am surprised at the way in which he translated *calaw* as *calana* for it is possible to explain *calaw* as 'with him' (*cimmo*), i.e. with the King Messiah [and not 'with God']."

105 Cf. *Guide* I:41. Similarly Persian translators of the Koran left anthropomorphisms in the original Arabic. See S. Rawidowicz, *"Becayath ha-hagshamah la-RaSaG we-la-RaMBaM", Knesseth* III (1937–8), 326f., n. 1.

106 *Guide* I:27 *et passim.*

107 See above, n. 115. On the problem in general, cf. M. Kadushin, *The Rabbinic Mind,* (New York, 1952), 325–336.

108 Jud. 9:13.

109 *Phil. Comm.,* to Ezek. 1:20.

110 *Guide,* III:2; cf. *Guide,* I:40.

111 *Phil. Comm.* to Ezek. 1:10, 13, 14, 17, 19, 20.

112 Baron, *History,* VI, 176.

113 Palestinian Talmud, Pe'ah II:6.

114 Baron, *History,* VI, 175ff. H. Graetz, *Divre yeme yisra'el,* (Warsaw, 1890–9), IV, 14, n. 4.

115 Cf. S. Liebermann, *Sheqicin,* (Jerusalem, 1939), 81f.

116 See above, n. 113.

117 *Guide* II:43 (Friedlander, 343f.).

[118] J. Anatoli, *Malmad ha-talmidim* (Lyck, 1866), 616; Samuel ibn Tibbon, *Ma'amar yiqqawu ha-mayim,* (Pressburg, 1837), 9. Both Ibn Tibbon and Maimonides (*Guide,* introd. and *Comm. to Mish.,* Sanhedrin. ch. X) proposed to write commentaries on the aggadoth. For Abraham Maimonides on this subject, see *Qovez,* II, 40d.

[119] *Qovez,* III, 3d.

[120] *Guide,* III:6.

[121] Gen. 2:9, *Guide,* II:30.

[121a] *Guide* II:30.

[122] Gen. 2:9.

[123] Gen. 3:1.

[124] Babylonian Talmud, Pesahim 49b.

[125] Gen. 2:9.

[126] Genesis Rabbah II:2.

[127] Genesis Rabbah XV:3.

[128] Isa. 22:11; cf. Samuel ibn Tibbon, *Ma'amar,* 15f.

[129] *Iggereth Teman* (ed. A. S. Halkin, New York, 1952), 70.

[130] Cf. Nahmanides on Gen. 17:22, 35:13.

[131] Gen. 5:3. This Midrash is considered in the *Guide,* I:7.

[132] Gen. 2:9 (*Guide* III:29); cf. Gen. 3:13 (*Guide* III:23).

[133] Gen. 1:14 (*Guide* II:30).

[134] Gen. 18:1 (*Guide* II:6, 42).

[135] Introd. to *Phil. Comm.* to Ezek.

[136] *Guide* III:6.

[137] *Guide* I:42, Genesis Rabbah XLXIII.

[138] *Hil. yes. ha-torah,* VI:9: cf. Babylonian Talmud, Shevu'oth, 35b.

[139] *Qovez,* III, 3d, 4a.

[140] M. Steinschneider, *Hebr. Ueber.,* (Berlin, 1893), 200.

[141] G. Vajda, "Samuel b. Judah Ibn Tibbon's *Ma'amar Yiqqawu Ha-mayim,*" *JJS,* X (1959), 143.

[142] Gen. 28:13.

[143] Isa. 6:1; *Ma'amar,* 26.

[144] Ps. 19:7, 148:1.

[145] Astrology was not stressed by Kimhi but he would give an occasional reference to the role of the stars in mundane affairs. Cf. Gen. 1:16, Amos 4:7, Hab. 3:6, Ps. 33:6.

[146] Gen. 1:1 (cf. *Guide,* II:13); Gen. 1:2; at Isa. 40:12, Kimhi discussed the fifth element of Aristotle (cf. *Guide,* I:72, *De Caelo,* I:3); at Ps. 33:7, the notion of the four elements was read into the text by Kimhi.

[147] Gen. 30:39, Isa. 2:22, Jer. 2:24 (from Ibn Gabirol), Ps. 116:16, 139:3.

[148] Gen. 2:7, Hab. 3:10, I Chron. 28:9.

[149] Ps. 139:14.

[150] Int. to *Pent. Comm.*

[151] Gen. 1:1, 1:6, 1:9, 2:7, 2:9, 9:1; Ez. 10:12, Ps. 102:27, 104:30; *Phil. Comm.* to Genesis, 2:22; *Shorashim s.v. bhy.*

[152] Gen. 1:16, 1:26.

[153] Gen. 1:25.

[154] Gen. 1:16.

[155] Isa. 40:26.

[156] Jer. 9:23, Ps. 145:17, 148:4.

[157] Ps. 148:8.

[158] II Sam. 1:10. See also the list in Cohen, *Comm. on Hosea,* xxvi.

[159] Isa. 40:12.

[160] See C. H. Haskins, *Studies in the History of Medieval Science,* (Cambridge, 1924), 96; P. Duhem, *Le Système du Monde,* (Paris, 1913), 298ff.; E. Renan, in *Hist. Lit.* XXVII, 571–623; C. Singer in L. Finkelstein (ed.), *The Jews,* (Philadelphia, 1949), II, 1048.

LETTERS FROM STEPHEN S. WISE TO A FRIEND AND COLLEAGUE: MORTON MAYER BERMAN

CARL HERMANN VOSS

Jacksonville, Florida

Stephen Samuel Wise (1874–1949), known throughout his active career to millions of people in the United States and abroad, had acquaintances in the tens of thousands; among them he could list many hundreds of loyal friends (plus a public figure's usual quota of enemies) and could count scores of men and women as devoted disciples. One of the foremost of his friends and followers was Morton Mayer Berman, a member of the first class of graduates of the Jewish Institute of Religion in 1926. After a year's study at the Hebrew University in Jerusalem as the first Guggenheimer Fellow of the J.I.R., Berman served for two years as rabbi of Temple Emanuel in Davenport, Iowa, returning to New York in 1929 to serve as director of field activities of the J.I.R., and, a year later, to become also assistant rabbi of the Free Synagogue. From 1937 to 1957 he was rabbi at Temple Isaiah Israel in Chicago, with leave (1943–46) to serve as Navy chaplain, attached to the Sixth Marine Division (he was awarded the Bronze Star in the Okinawa Campaign). In 1957 the Berman family settled in Israel, where he was an executive of the Keren Hayesod in Jerusalem, and is now an honorary director. Berman is also an assistant editor of Encyclopedia Judaica.

As with an untold number of people, Stephen Wise carried on an extensive correspondence with Morton Berman. Excerpts of letters from Wise to Berman over a period of twenty-two years reveal the love and concern, compassion and sympathy, guidance and counsel he gave in abundance to so many individuals—comrades in the Zionist movement, like Theodor Herzl and Louis D. Brandeis, Chaim Weizmann and David Ben-Gurion; preceptors like Richard Gottheil and Thomas Davidson, Israel Abrahams and Solomon Schechter; Presidents Theodore Roosevelt, Woodrow Wilson and Franklin D. Roosevelt; authors Israel Zangwill and Ludwig Lewisohn; colleagues of the rabbinate such as Maximilian Heller and Henry Pereira Mendes, Abba Hillel Silver and Philip S. Bernstein; many non-Jews like Jenkin Lloyd Jones and Charles Parkhurst, John Haynes Holmes and John Howard Melish; fellow-Democrats George Foster Peabody, Edward M. House, Josephus Daniels and Newton D. Baker; Negro leaders Booker T. Washington, Robert Moton, and Roy Wilkins; labor chieftains Samuel Gompers, William Green, John L. Lewis and Philip Murray, and a host of others: rich and poor, great and obscure, known and unknown. This vast array only highlights, I believe, the importance of these paragraphs, so representative and characteristic and, thus, so significant, which I have chosen from among Stephen Wise's hitherto unpublished letters to a single person: his former student and longtime co-worker, Morton Berman. Here may be seen Wise's genuine personal interest and unfeigned affection for every single person with whom he came in touch. Here are humor and sadness, love and compassion, tragedy and sorrow, drama and jest.

New York, N.Y.
September 20, 1927

I have just been home for a few days [from attendance in Zürich at the Conference on Rights of Jewish Minorities and the World Zionist Congress in Basle] and I am delighted to have your letter. In the first place, it is amusing, and there are very few things that come to me that bring me any amusement. In the next place, it is serious, and I like that. Of course, you won't permit yourself to be disturbed by the fact that there are Balkan divisions between different groups in the community! That is always so. There are a few things in my life that I look back to which give me satisfaction, and one of them is the feeling that twenty-five years ago and more I was enabled to do just what you are going to do, namely, bridge rivers of division that flowed between the various elements of the community [at Temple Beth Israel in Portland] in Oregon.

New York, N.Y.
January 26, 1928

I owe you an apology for failing to answer before this your letter of about a fortnight ago. I put it aside, only because I wanted to write to you in longhand, but I find that, after all, I cannot do so, and must write to you in this way [by dictation to a secretary].

I understand perfectly the spirit of your note. I am a little disappointed to think that the conflict [concerning freedom of the pulpit in discussion of social issues, civil rights, Zionism, etc.] should have come, as it has come, or seem to be coming. I thought that the Adolph Ochs of Davenport [E. P. Adler, head of the newspaper syndicate and later to become Berman's close friend] was a more enlightened person than his New York prototype. But I suppose the type and types are the same.

One thing let me say to you and no more, for I cannot judge the problem from afar. Be as patient as you can be where no principles are involved; but if the principle of freedom of speech is involved, then be magnificently and gloriously impatient! The difficulty is that for two or three generations in America, and for generations in the German-speaking countries, the rabbi had no status. He enjoyed a certain amount of meaningless respect as a scholar, but that was all. Now, however, that some of us insist upon being taken seriously in our application of religion to the facts of every-day life, the congregations will not endure it, and yet, that is not an accurate way of putting it. It is usually a few men of place and power and fortune who misrepresent the congregations and who are against us—and only they. You know that my own Executive Council is something of an exception, though not wholly so; but the truth is that the greatest disaster to American Israel lies in the character and the conduct of the Board of Trustees who represent neither the rabbi nor the congregation but imagine themselves to be sent from Heaven to superimpose their judgment upon the congregation, and their will upon the rabbi.

It is a parlous situation, and you will have to fight it. Don't give up unless you must. To surrender your post is always an admission. I do not mean that you are to hang on if the congregation does not want to keep you; but don't go just because one or two or three powerful men, who misrepresent both the congregation and the spirit of Jewish idealism, are against you.

Forgive me for saying to you what I would have liked to have written in longhand: don't grow bitter! The harder the fight, the sweeter you must be. I mean exactly that. In the horrid controversy which raged with [Louis] Marshall [hon. sec'y., Temple Emanu-El,

N.Y.C.] twenty years ago and more [1905–06], I never once lost my temper, though he did all he could to destroy me without quite succeeding.

Keep in touch with me. Let me hear how things develop. If you can avoid reaching an ultimate decision until you have talked things over with me in this way, it might possibly be better. Please know that I have confidence in you and that I know you will do the right thing—the thing that commends itself to your conscience. I will always have the most affectionate interest in all you say and do.

Hotel Krafft-am-Rhein
Basel
July 16, 1931

I am going to treat you as one of my children, for once in any event, seeing that you were almost filial in your kindness to me during the [World Zionist] Congress [when Wise collapsed from fatigue after an address] . . . . I am mighty glad you left. It was a very dull Congress and there is a great deal of bitterness and resentfulness. Nobody is happy excepting [Nahum] Sokolow [successor to Chaim Weizmann as president of the World Zionist Organization],* and no one looks unhappier than the new members of the Executive.

Prague
August 15, 1933

. . . My heart has been sick since landing in Europe. We have lived with the refugees for weeks, first in London, then Paris, then Geneva, and now we are surrounded by them in Prague. A constant stream comes to my door-step. The situation in Germany cannot be told in human speech. One would have to learn the vocabulary of hell, in order to describe it, even approximately. Every day some new decree, devastating and exterminating!

I cannot go into the details about what you [as director of placement for the Jewish Institute of Religion] wrote about places for the boys, but the only grain of satisfaction I have had in many a day has been to learn that some of our supremely gifted graduates have found places worthy of them.

* Wise wrote to his children, James and Justine:

. . . So much has happened and yet so little may be told, excepting that last night (Sunday) the whole thing came to a climax. I could have wept for Weizmann, because after all, fifteen years of work, good, bad, and indifferent, were ended by a vote of censure. He deserved it and I voted for it. At the same time, it was a sad spectacle. . . .

Letter in Stephen Wise Archives, Brandeis University, Waltham, Mass.

Hotel Montana
Lucerne
August 27, 1935

Busy as I am, and I am in the midst of the [19th Zionist] Congress, in which my golden voice—Heaven save the raucous mark—still goes unheard; yet I must write to you to tell you how much I appreciated all the information you were good enough to give me with regard to the status of our men. I am jubilant over the fate of our three Hillelites [i.e. appointments to posts of the Hillel Foundation], and you seem to have done awfully well by the other men, though 40 West [68th Street, N. Y. C., address of the Jewish Institute of Religion] moves me to wonder how you found time between marriage ceremonies to think of "placing rabbis." *

. . . The Congress goes well. It is less bitter than the [Basle] Congress [in 1931] you attended . . . and altogether I think good will come out of this Congress.

The German delegates are terribly fearful of what I may say [about the Nazi regime and the persecution of Jews in Germany]. You will be amused to hear that I may read my address in German instead of speaking it in English.

* On June 20, 1937 Abram Leon Sachar, national director of the B'nai B'rith Hillel Foundations at American universities, wrote to Wise:
. . . I continue to be amazed at the personal interest that you take in these young people [J. I. R. graduates and students] when your mind and heart are so fully bound up with national and international considerations.
Letter in Stephen Wise Archives, Brandeis University, Waltham, Mass.

Park Lane Hotel
London
July 6, 1936

It has been terribly disappointing to me to find that I must be anchored for the present in London rather than be in Roumania where I was to have been yesterday at a public meeting [to secure support for the World Jewish Congress and the choice of a delegation]. This week, beginning to-day, should have been given to Roumania, and the following week or ten days to Poland. But all plans have gone awry and I am detained in London for sufficient and alas! very bad reasons, the nature of which I cannot discuss in writing, excepting that it is bound up with the Palestine situation. I have no plans excepting to remain here until things are better or worse. I am hopeful, of course, that they may be better. A stiff fight is being made, and [Chaim] Weizmann and [David] Ben-Gurion are leading it with wisdom, resourcefulness and courage.

. . . I feel more strongly than ever, in the light of what I have heard in London, that the Yishuv [the Jewish community in Palestine] is bearing its trouble with the highest of all heroism, the heroism of self-discipline, which moves the tens of thousands of young, hardy, unafraid Jews to refrain from reprisal and vindictiveness. In that magnificent self-discipline of our young brothers, we have a real symptom of capacity for nation building. . . .

. . . The situation in Europe is very grave. Nothing in my judgment saves the world from war, excepting the unreadiness of the nations that have been humiliated by the failure of sanctions and the general unwillingness of England to wage another frightfully costly win-or-lose war. There is a sense of defeat and humiliation in the air. . . .

There was a way to avert the disaster that now threatens; but it has become too late to pursue it, namely, for the civilized nations of the earth—England, France, and America—to serve common notice upon Germany. But the nations are doing all over again what they did until 1914, namely, let Germany decided when der Tag should be.

Geneva
August 7, 1936

. . . I haven't spoken of the [World Jewish] Congress because I am going to . . . send you in two or three days a fairly full report of what is going on. Perhaps you will listen in tomorrow afternoon when I am to hold forth through an International Broadcast. But you will be at a baseball game with your son or spending your income in some other equally riotous way.

Geneva
August 10, 1936

The [World Jewish] Congress has begun and it is well begun.

I do appreciate your kindness in telegraphing about the broadcast. I can hardly believe it, so unimaginative am I—or so incredulous. That you could really hear in Manhattan what I was saying in a room in Geneva! That broadcast helped to kill my later speech which went very badly, due to the fact, among other things, that [Nahum] Goldmann took the world Jewish situation as his problem and handled it magnificently, almost with the power of [Max] Nordau [Zionist leader of earlier decades], and left me only the Congress.

The sessions have begun and the Congress moves on fairly well, but the accursed spirit of party divisiveness is manifesting itself; and too many of the big guns have stayed away, including [Menahem] Ussischkin, who calmly asked me to run down to South Africa [on behalf of the Jewish National Fund] but would not come from Carlsbad for the Congress.

New York, N.Y.
September 18, 1937

Happy to learn about the Yom Kippur service [at Temple Isaiah Israel in Chicago where Berman had become the spiritual leader], the crowds and the appeal. I think if you got 4,000 [in the two services], you got more than we did [at the Free Synagogue]. We have settled down into a congregation of simple, humble folk, and the large and generous givers of other years are gone.

New York, N.Y.
November 4, 1937

. . . I feel pretty good and rather happy this morning, not only because of the triumph of the entire Fusion Ticket [on behalf of which Wise campaigned actively], including [Mayor Fiorello] LaGuardia and [District Attorney Thomas] Dewey, but also over the fact that I won a few pounds of candy for Mrs. Wise. I bet on 200,000 plurality in Brooklyn, and I was right. I bet on 400,000 in Greater New York, and it is 450,000 or more. You would have been amused if you could have heard the conversation between Fiorello and me at City Hall in the afternoon on Election Day. Nervous as three kittens, I asked him why he was "tzoppling." He answered "because I do not know what is going to happen." I tried to reassure him, and I told him he would run between 400,000 and 500,000. His answer was "I never was elected that way, and you do not know anything about it." I have not yet had an apology from him, but I expect it.

New York, N.Y.
January 20, 1938

. . . [I] note what you say about [Abba Hillel] Silver's address. I read bits of it and it seemed very fine. He is very able. There is no doubt about that. My answer to those who wonder why I chose him [to be Wise's successor as national chairman of the United Palestine Appeal] is: "No one has deeper grievances against him than I. He has stepped on no man's face harder than my own, which may account for its battered appearance. But Palestine comes before personal grievances." Even some of his bitterest foes, like C - - - - - - and S - - - - - - -, are agreed that he has access to non-Zionists and semi-Zionists which no one, not even I, can have. As a non-Congressist [Silver did not belong to the American Jewish Congress], he is not as unloved a figure as he would otherwise be in the sight of the assimilationists. . . .

You think I can easily get $18,000 to clear the year's deficit? I will send you a copy of the letter which has gone out to the membership [of the Free Synagogue]. We have been reduced to the device of starting the budget year three months earlier. That is how well off we are.

I am desperately worried about the [Jewish] Institute [of Religion]. If we don't get $10,000 this year from the graduates, I shall seriously consider discontinuing the Institute. That is not for publication, but will have to be done. There is no other way. We can give ourselves two years to wind up, admit no more students, give the professors an extra year's salary, and then "good-night." I have no right to go on, even though I stay alive, unless I have some assurance that the work can be carried on. At present I am not. . . .*

* In both instances, the Free Synagogue and the Institute, Wise's appeals to the membership and the graduates, respectively, were successful.

New York, N.Y.
July 29, 1938

. . . I note what you say about the situation [in Berlin and Vienna] with respect to the overcrowded consulates [where long lines of Jews waited through day and night for a chance to see the American consul to secure visas to the U. S. A.], and I agree with you. When you return, I think we can take it up together in Washington, you, as an eye-witness, and I, as a friend of the Secretary [of State, Cordell Hull] and his and our Chief [President Franklin D. Roosevelt]. Don't you think that would be the best way? I think it will work out best in the end.

Of course, [the] Evian [Conference on Refugees] is a terrible disappointment. I would like to send you a letter about it from an eye witness, Nahum Goldmann; but Goldmann appreciates two things: the high disinterested service of Myron Taylor [the President's personal representative], and [chairman of the President's Committee on Political Refugees, James G.] MacDonald, of course, and, too, the supreme service and initiative of the Great Boss [President Roosevelt].

New York, N.Y.
August 8, 1938

We are appalled at what is happening in Italy [where Mussolini had announced full support for Hitler and his objectives]. There seems to be no end of it. I never felt more like *Tisha B'Av* [mourning for the Destruction of the Temple in 70 C. E.] than yesterday. It is an ineffable and illimitable sorrow that has come to our people. But we must keep our heads up and morally our fists clenched.

New York, N.Y.
September 9, 1938

I have just gotten in today from Lake Placid, where Louise and I had a joyous week with the two little Stephens [Stephen Andrews Wise, Jim's son; and Stephen Wise Tulin, Justine's son], the bigger one rough, the little one tough. They are both terribly like your own little *Gazlan* [affectionate term of "little gangster" or "petty thief," referring to the Berman child, John Simon].

What you write about Russia interests me of course immensely. The difference between Russia and the rest of Europe seems to me that in Russia there are Jews without Judaism, and in the rest of Europe there is to be Judaism without Jews. It is hell. I would not dare to say this in the presence of Syd [Sidney E. Goldstein, associate rabbi of the Free Synagogue and a pacifist] or William Jennings Bryan or Jesus, but I confess to you that I am almost afraid war will not come. The world is being continuously enervated and impoverished by submitting to the little Austrian swine blackmailer. But then you know more about these things than I do, coming as you do fresh from Europe.

New York, N.Y.
October 12, 1938

I suppose you know that we are working like Trojans here in order to prevent the tragedy of shutting out Jews from Palestine. [Solomon] Goldman [president of the Zionist Organization of America] has taken hold magnificently of the situation, and we are working day and night. Tomorrow we shall present our case to the British Ambassador, and the following day to the Secretary of State [Cordell Hull]. I have no doubt that we may also yet have a chance to present the case fully to our understanding and sympathetic President [F.D.R.].

New York, N.Y.
January 18, 1939

I am still "tzoppling" about going to London [for the prospective Round Table Conference of Jews and Arabs]. Of all the d.f. errands that ever were, this is the d.f.'est. We are walking into a trap without even the partial satisfaction of having our eyes blindfolded. It is naive to go into a trap blindfolded. It seems idiotic to go into one with eyes open. We shall reach an impasse as soon as the conference begins, or before. The conditions laid down by the *momzer* [bastard] Mufti [Haj Amin el-Husseini] are absolutely intolerable: no immigration—and they who never assented to the Balfour Declaration now say, "it is crystallized." Second, of course—no land sales! We [members of the Zionist Executive] are meeting today to talk it over.

New York, N.Y.
January 27, 1939

Just a word before I sail tomorrow morning on the S. S. *Champlain* [for the conference of Arabs and Jews in London]. I tried, I confess, up to the last hour to avoid the necessity of going, because I think we are going to be caught "hook, line and sinker"; but I suppose I have got to go! [Chaim] Weizmann said this morning over the [transatlantic] telephone that I need only stay a week or two and have part in initiating the discussions; and then I can return.

I want to be in Washington for a few weeks during the Conference [For Refugees], where I think I can be of more help.

London, England
February 2, 1939

Your wireless a delightful surprise after Hitler's hideous harangue. . . .

What a job ahead for Bob Szold and me [as American delegates to the Round Table] and above all for [Chaim] Weizmann [as president of the World Zionist Organization]. We shall not renounce, though they may superimpose. Hitler's speech may affect things still more adversely.

New York, N.Y.
March 31, 1939

. . . I know that we fought a good fight [at the Round Table Conference in London], not good enough, but I think we made, throughout, . . . a dignified presentation of our case. . . . The attitude of the [British] government was overwhelming [in opposition to the Zionist point of view].

. . . You will be glad to hear that if the situation has been temporarily saved, it is due solely to L.D.B. [Louis D. Brandeis] and F.D.R. [President Roosevelt]. If the situation is permanently saved and there is be no rotten pro-Arab anti-Jewish decision, I think Sol [Solomon Goldman, president of the ZOA] and I will have some part in it. I had an appointment with the Chief [F.D.R.], and I took Sol along, and I think I got him to see that he must take one further step.

New York, N.Y.
April 18, 1940

Have as happy a Pesach [Passover] as the tragic moment permits. I do not know when I have been more worried and more sorrowful in all my life. . . .

New York, N.Y.
May 10, 1940

. . . I can hardly believe that I can jest about anything when I remember I had a pain in my heart as I read the appalling news this morning of the invasion of Belgium, Holland and Luxembourg! That means two things—Germany is not against the Jews but against civilization. It means, too, that the ultimate conflict will be with us. God help or damn, as He chooses, the idiotic pacifists who would expose us to the fate of Belgium, Holland, Finland, Norway!

New York, N.Y.
November 12, 1940

I had a delightful time on Sunday evening, speaking at Ford Hall [five days after the reelection of President Franklin D. Roosevelt], where a year ago I had announced that on Sunday, November 10th, I would speak on "Why America Chose a Third Term President for the First Time." Note the past tense—"chose." We had a very good time. I bore out their faith in my power of prophecy.

New York, N.Y.
May 16, 1941

I suppose you may have heard that we did not go to Cincinnati [for talks concerning the prospective merger of the Jewish Institute of Religion and Hebrew Union College]. I had to call it off at the last moment because the Palestine situation, alas ten thousand times, is become so critical that I had to spend Tuesday in Washington—and I believe not ineffectively, as far as getting heavy supplies for Jewish soldiers in Palestine is concerned—and I felt that I could not get out of reach of Washington, [Chaim] Weizmann, [Louis D.] Brandeis, and others. . . . In a day or two I shall write to [Julian] Morgenstern [president of Hebrew Union College], suggesting another date.

New York, N.Y.
February 15, 1943

I am glad . . . about the [Commencement] Exercises [of the Jewish Institute of Religion]. They were really fine; and even I, incredibly modest that I am, must admit that my address was fair, not as good, of course, as yours was two years ago, but then you are a scholar and a gentleman. What am I, nebich [poor thing]? Just a little beggar for big causes. I think that it is so good a phrase I shall have it put on my *Mazavah* [tombstone]. . . .

I note that you are going to be in St. Louis Wednesday night and that you and [Maurice] Perlzweig [of the World Jewish Congress] are to present the case of the [American Jewish] Congress before the Welfare Fund meeting. There are many things to stress as you say, one being the Inter-American Jewish Conference. After all, we were the first to bring together the Jews of all the Americas from Argentina to Canada into an Inter-American Jewish Conference. The really big thing we are doing—and you know it, for you know [Jacob] Robinson [of the World Jewish Congress]—is the Institute of Jewish Affairs. Within a few weeks we shall publish *Ten Years of Hitler* (*The Black Decade,* as the OWI [Office of War Information] calls it). I think the publications of the Institute have been magnificent throughout.

I suppose you can't say too much about whatever has been done; and, God knows, it is little enough for the creatures whom Hitler's extermination policy is aimed at. Yesterday we met—I mean, we of the Planning and Coordinating Committee [of the Inter-American Jewish Conference], under the chairmanship of Herman Shulman, a corking good lawyer associated with David Podell; and I insisted on calling in [Henry] Monsky [president of B'nai B'rith], [Joseph M.] Proskauer [president of the American Jewish Committee], and [James G.] Heller [president of the Central Conference of American Rabbis] in crder to determine what can be done to stay the hand of Hitler. But, alas, if nothing can be done, then the United Nations ought to undertake in some degree to implement their declaration.

The children could be rescued. The United Nations could guarantee the support of all refugees who managed to escape into the neutral countries, and there are still five of them outside of Argentina—Turkey, Sweden, Switzerland, Spain and Portugal. England could admit and, I think, is prepared to admit any refugees that can reach the British Isles. I have for a long time dreamed of the possibility that Harold Ickes [U.S. Secretary of the Interior] suggested, namely, that a goodly number of refugees be permitted to land in some such place as the Virgin Islands, there to remain until the end of the War with our government or Jewish organizations meeting the expenses of such settlement. They are to remain unemployed and unproductive but saved from Hitler Europe. We would undertake to try to include the Roumanian proposal [to deliver Jews for cash], which may or may not be a fake, designed to win the good will of the United Nations (whose triumph is now foreseen, even by such stupid creatures as the prime ministers of Bulgaria, Roumania, and Hungary. Of course, no Hungarian can really be stupid, as you know, even though the Hungarians, like the writer, do not compare with Litvaks, like the recipient of this letter, in acuteness, astuteness, *genavesche chochme* [thieving wisdom], etc.)

New York, N.Y.
March 15, 1943

I cannot tell you how much I appreciate your note [for Wise's 69th birthday]. I am delighted to think that you were installing one of our boys, Albert Troy, in Aurora, while we were having a lovely party which was distinguished by a gift of the boys who not only gave me $69 for my birthday (remember it was only my 47th when I first celebrated my birthday at the Institute) but had a testimony from the Red Cross that they had given 69 pints of blood in my honor.

New York, N.Y.
March 24, 1944

. . . How very fine was your contribution to the [Jewish] Institute [of Religion] dinner [in honor of Wise's 70th birthday]. Of all the dinners it was the smallest numerically but, to me, the most welcome and the finest, just because we had no outsiders and only our own. Your address was fine and I hope that as soon as possible you will let us have it so that we may include it in a volume containing all the addresses.

The [American Jewish] Congress-Zionist [Organization of America] dinner was really a magnificent function. I am to have a colony [Kfar Shmuel] named for me, although I am still alive (if they get to work at it) and a community center for which a corporation gave $10,000. This, too, is to bear my name.

New York, N.Y.
July 5, 1944

. . . You saw what the Republican Convention said about Palestine. Now I must see to it that the statement of the next [Democratic Party] Convention be made even better than the Republican. I shall move earth, if not heaven, to get a decision from the two gentlemen [F. D. R. and his as-yet-unchosen vice-presidential running mate] who are to have the power of making it before the election.

New York, N.Y.
July 8, 1946

I have had a tough time [with illness] these last few days. I made up my mind to go to Palestine. I was to sail tomorrow on the [S.S. *Queen*] *Mary*. My doctors will not permit me to fly, darn it. The British Embassy in Washington telephoned to London and a visa was refused me. I shall say in a "blast" to be issued today or tomorrow they did not want me to put aside the Iron Curtain and tell the truth about them.

New York, N.Y.
April 1, 1947

Yes, I think the HUC [Hebrew Union College] is eager to come to some arrangement with us. We have something to gain but we have also much to lose. The non-sectarian character of the JIR [Jewish Institute of Religion] is its distinction and its glory. Can that non-sectarian character be maintained if we tie ourselves up with the Reformism of HUC, even though [Maurice] Eisendrath [president of the Union of American Hebrew Congregations] comes very near to seeing eye to eye with us. I wish a half-dozen of us, including you, Jack [Jacob P. Rudin, rabbi, Great Neck, Long Island], could sit down and talk this thing through. . . .

New York, N. Y.
December 22, 1947

I know how you must have felt about Louise [Waterman Wise, who had died on December 11th]. You are right. Quoting your message, "she was a great woman in every sense of the word and takes her place among the noblest of Israel's daughters." I wish she might have seen your word about Jim's [James Waterman Wise's] address at the Chanukah Breakfast.

The [American Jewish Congress] Convention is postponed for very good reasons. It will interest you to learn that pressure is being brought to bear upon Justine to become the President of the Women's Division. She has not reached a decision. I wish to God she might feel that she ought to take over this heritage of service.

New York, N.Y.
May 17, 1948

. . . May I say *Chag Semeach* ["happy holiday"] to you. What days these are! Within seventy-two hours: proclamation [of the new state of Israel], recognition [by the United States of America], election of [Chaim] Weizmann [as the first president of Israel].

New York, N.Y.
February 25, 1949

. . . I am very glad that you reached the decision that I preach for you [at the] Friday [evening service of Temple Isaiah Israel in Chicago], and meet with the Decalogue [Society of lawyers to receive the Award of Merit] Saturday, and leave for home the same night. I have been so wretched lately I am wondering whether I can keep any engagements, although I devoutly hope that I can keep all of them.

I spent all last week at the Lenox Hill Hospital getting checked-up. I appear to be able to do everything but regain my strength.

New York, N.Y.
March 25, 1949

. . . I must tell you that I am afraid there can be no [American Jewish] Congress meeting in Chicago for me in May. I am going to Boston today [to visit Brandeis University and to speak at the Ford Hall Forum], because I promised months ago I would. And then I am through. The doctors say that they cannot guarantee I will stay alive unless I quit. I was to have been in Detroit for a great meeting of Rabbi Morris Adler's on Wednesday night, and an [American Jewish] Congress [75th birthday celebration] luncheon; but it is off. Two things are still before me: the finishing of the autobiography, and a visit to Israel. Frankly, I am very doubtful that I will get to Israel, but in the Divine Mercy I may be permitted to go. I am terribly sorry I cannot go to Chicago, but it is out of the question. If I made a great improvement during April and May, I might be able to come in June, but that is a rather remote possibility.

Three weeks later, Stephen Wise's secretary, Mrs. Florence Eitelberg, wrote to Morton Berman:

New York, N.Y.
April 18, 1949

I had your letter several days ago, but under the conditions didn't feel like replying. However, as you may have heard over the radio, Dr. Wise has made a slight gain; that was yesterday. Today he has held that gain, and that is something for which to be very, very grateful in the light of his most grave condition last week. However, he is still on the critical list, and we are all just praying that he continues to gain.

On April 19th Stephen Wise died.

A PUTATIVE CEYLON RITE

Myron M. Weinstein

Library of Congress

In the standard reference works of Hebrew bibliography one finds inventoried a liturgy described as the rite of Ceylon. The existence of such a rite would appear rather surprising in light of the paucity of data regarding Jewish settlement on that island. Thus, the subject clearly invites investigation.

We shall select as a convenient starting place Meijer Roest's Catalog of the Bibliotheca Rosenthaliana.[1] This is due as much to Roest's implicit mastery of Amsterdam imprints—among which the *editio princeps* and the *editio secunda* of this liturgy are numbered—as to his detailed treatment of books which exhibit deviations from the norm.[2] His entry (v. 1, p. 700) is disappointing, however:

> Ceylon. *Gelegenheitsgebete.*
>
> **סדר תפלות שבחות ושירים לימי שמחת תורה וחופת נעורים, ולזמן מילת זכרים, וסדר מילה וטבילת עבדים וגרים, ולשמחה ימי הפורים, ויום תרועה תקיעה ושברים, ולסליחת עון ביום הכפורים . . . כפי מנהגי אנשי שינגילי יצ״ו וקהל קדוש בקוגין . . .**
>
> אמשטרדם ור״י אדברה נא שלום לפ״ק [*Amsterdam, Joseph, Jacob und Abraham, Söhne des Salomo Proops*, 1757.] 8⁰.
>
> (2) und 78 Bll. — Zedn. S. 455.
>
> **סדר תפלות לימי שמחת תורה וחופת נעורים . . . כפי מנהגי אנשי שינגילי . . .** [Herausgegeben von J. *ben* D. Heilbronn.]
>
> אמשטרדם ה׳תקכ״ט ליצירה *Amsterdam, Joseph, Jacob und Abraham, Söhne des Salomo Proops*, 1769.] 8⁰.
>
> (1) und 100 Bll. — Zedn. S. 455.

We are left, obviously, to infer that the מנהג שינגילי is the Ceylon rite, that it is followed by the Jews of קוגין [3] (Cochin), and that the matter is, moreover, beyond cavil.

Since Roest cites Zedner as his authority, a look at the *Catalogue of the Hebrew Books in the Library of the British Museum*[4] is in order. The situation there is no more satisfactory, for under the heading "Ceylon. Occasional Prayers" Zedner has entered the same two Proops' editions without further comment. He has, in fact, augmented the list with a Leghorn 1849 liturgical work that does not mention the *Minhag Shingli*[5] on its title page at all. From the BM *Catalogue* this identification has been disseminated further (e.g., Ephraim Deinard, *'Atiḳot Yehudah,* Jerusalem, 1915, p. 44, and perhaps, also, Alfred Freimann, *Seder Ḳidushin ve-Nisu'in,* Jerusalem, 1944/5, p. 304).

But Roest cannot in the final analysis be dependent upon Zedner. Six years before the appearance of the BM *Catalogue* he had already described the Amsterdam 1757 liturgy, a copy of which was found in the Isaac da Costa collection he was listing,[6] as containing the prayers of the Jews of Ceylon and Cochin China.[7] As Roest makes clear in this *Catalogue* his indebtedness to Steinschneider (p. 119), the suspicion arises that both he and Zedner have borrowed in this matter from *CB.* We repair, then, to the catalog of the Bodleian Library.[8]

One is surprised by the absence of entries for these liturgical works among the prayer books proper (Anonyma, v. 1). The geographical index at the end of v. 3 (p. LL), however, directs us to our goal: Steinschneider has mentioned these liturgies in passing in a long bibliography on the Jews of Cochin placed, artificially, *s.v.* "Wessely, Hartwig." There (v. 2., col. 2723), he asserts: "Liber precum ibid. laudatus, primum, A. 1757, dein 1769 excusus, est ritus Ceylan (שינגלי, non Senegal, ut *Delitzsch* p. 51, *Dukes,* Litbl. V,451 . . . et adhuc *Polak* l.c. p. 390 sub China!) et Cochin."[9] In fact, Steinschneider had—by implication—already asserted the equivalence of Shingli and Ceylon in his article "Jüdische Literatur" in the Ersch and Gruber *Allgemeine Encyklopädie* (Leipzig, 1850) v. 27, p. 460. After the explicit identification of Shingli in *CB,* he was to return to it in print—so far as we are able to discover—just once more in his last half-century. This mention occurs in the caustic review of Franz Delitzsch's translation of *Romans,* which Steinschneider published in *HB,* 17 (1877), p. 3. There, in a sentence rich as ever in corrections of his contemporaries, he seems silently to withdraw the identification of שינגילי as Ceylon; he speaks now of the rite of Cochin and "Singali."[10]

Of the literature brought together by Steinschneider in *CB s.v.* "Wessely," we find only one author who equates Shingli with Ceylon (or, rather, with the "Ceylonese"). That is P. J. Bruns, in his article "Von den Juden in Cochin," which appeared in the *Repositorium für die neueste Geographie, Statistik und Geschichte,* 1 (1792), pp. 383–400. In translating Ezekiel Rahabi's letter of 1767 to Tobias Boas, Bruns (p. 385) renders the line: ורובם היו בכרנגינור הנקרא מאגודירא פטנם וג״כ קורין שינגלי

"Die meisten waren zu Crangonoor, genannt Magodirapatnam, welchen Namen ihr auch die Schingaleser (Ceyloneser) geben." In his note on the passage (pp. 391–392) Bruns states that though "Büsching's *Magazin für die neue Historie und Geographie* (v. 14 [1780], p. 130) gives "Chingel" or "Chingely" (the second form used by Barkey in Büsching's *Magazin* is, in fact, "Chingily" after Gravezande whose article he was translating) as another name for Cranganore, he believes he is able to defend his translation on grammatical grounds. Though Rahabi omits the word אותה in his sentence, its meaning is clear. It cannot bear the interpretation which Bruns would give it. But whatever the fancied grammatical grounds on which the identification was to be defended, what is it that led Bruns—and by suggestion probably Steinschneider, as well—to identify שינגילי with the Ceylonese precisely? We shall return to the question after a brief survey of Jewish contacts with Ceylon.[11]

We commence on a rather negative note: It is not the case that any known Hebrew work from Cochin has anything whatever to contribute to knowledge of the ancient history of Ceylon (or India, for that matter). This asseveration is a needed corrective to a misguided attempt by Sir James Emerson Tennent in his history of *Ceylon* (London, 1860), v. 1, pp. 396–397, n. 2, to invoke the aid of a late eighteenth-century Hebrew manuscript from Cochin to buttress a point about the extent of South Indian control in Ceylon in the fourth Christian century. This manuscript may be Trinity College Ms. Wright 150, that is now unlocated. Enough of it, however, is quoted and "translated" in Charles Forster's fantasy, *The One Primeval Language* (London, 1854), v. 3, pp. 294–339, to make clear its character and affiliations.[12] It is one of a group of synthetic histories from late eighteenth–early nineteenth-century Cochin consisting of extensive extracts, largely from European authors, poorly harmonized. The very point on which Tennent thought the manuscript could speak, namely, the extent of the reign of an Indian king "from Goa to Colombo," may be safely discounted. On the one hand this phrase has been borrowed—probably indirectly—from a marginal annotation in Mosseh Pereyra de Paiva's *Notisias dos Judeos de Cochim* (Amsterdam, 1687), p. 9, which is itself useless for anything other than the contemporary situation observed by the author, and the events of the immediate past. On the other hand, the date of the king in question—the bestower of a grant upon Joseph Rabban—seems now, after fluctuating widely among various writers on the subject, to have been fixed in the late tenth century.[13] This ruler has, in fact, no relevance to the history of fourth-century Ceylon.

None of the ancient sources appears to mention Jews in Ceylon.[14] The situation is different for the medieval period. For it, documentary evidence from the Genizah is available to prove the presence of Jews on the Island and thus to confirm, in a general way, the reliability of specific reports to this effect by two Arab geographers and probably by Benjamin of Tudela, as well.[15] Not one of these three authors reached Ceylon, however.

The earliest reference[16] is that of Abū Zaid al-Ḥasan al-Sīrāfī, *ca.* A.D. 915, in his supplement to an anonymous work of A.D. 851 (ascribed by some to a merchant named Sulaymān). This author writes of a large number of Jews and adherents of other faiths in Ceylon, the king permitting free exercise of every religion.[17]

Both of the other literary sources date to the twelfth century. The geographer Idrisi, *ca.* A.D. 1154, relates that in the capital the king had a council of sixteen ministers consisting of four of his own faith, four Christians, four Muslims and four Jews. Religious disputations between followers of the various beliefs were held, and the scholars of each of these faiths taught their own religion.[18]

There is some uncertainty when we come to the account of Benjamin of Tudela, *ca.* 1170, whether it is Ceylon at all that is described in what is taken to be the relevant passage (or, conceivably, the two relevant passages). In the first, there are difficulties with the place name, the designation of the inhabitants and the cult ascribed to them, the distance from the previous station on the itinerary—which is certainly Malabar—and the size of the Jewish population quoted. This figure, which is given as 23,000 in the edition of A. Asher as well as in several manuscripts, is much more plausibly shown as some 3,000 in a British Museum manuscript used as the basis for Marcus Nathan Adler's collation.[19] Even this reduced number is thought by the authors of the *EJ* article and H. G. Reissner to be highly inflated.[20] No concrete data about this Jewish community are conveyed by Benjamin, unfortunately.

The documentary material from the Genizah bearing on Ceylon concerns—so far as we are aware of it—the individual affairs of Near Eastern merchants trading across the Arabian Sea and the immigration of Moroccan silversmiths—apparent refugees from the Almohad outbreaks—to Ceylon encouraged by a Jewish official in Aden. As the relevant material is to appear in Professor S. D. Goitein's forthcoming "India Book," a collection of 332 Genizah documents relating to the

Egypt-India trade of the eleventh and twelfth centuries, further details may be anticipated.

H. G. Reissner has credibly surmised that the complete absence of sources for Jewish contacts with Ceylon from the end of the twelfth century to the advent of the European powers at the beginning of the sixteenth century reflects the failure of Jewish communities, in places entirely dependent upon foreign trade, to survive the decline of such commerce.[21] That the Portuguese did not encounter Jews in Ceylon upon their arrival in 1505 is the fair inference from the silence of Portuguese sources, which do, in contrast, convey some information about Jews in India.[22] For the Dutch period, which begins with the expulsion of the Portuguese in the middle of the seventeenth century, there is again silence from the sources, broken by two specific reports that Jews were not to be encountered.[23] The contrary impression conveyed by a Dutch church historian has been found to be without probative worth.[24] Not directly pertinent, but of possible interest, is the fact that Hebrew was taught for a brief period in the 1750's to the students at the Dutch Reformed Seminary in Colombo by a former Jew—a strange personality—L. I. J. van Dort.[25]

Despite the ouster of the Dutch by the British in the last decade of the eighteenth century, numbers of Dutch subjects continued to arrive in Ceylon, among them possibly some Jews.[26] Of greater moment here is what is perhaps the earliest nineteenth-century scheme—albeit abortive—for Jewish settlement. This is associated with the name of Sir Alexander Johnston, the second Chief Justice of British Ceylon—later President of the Ceylon Council—and beyond question one of the most appealing personalities to have been connected with the British colonial administration.[27] Sent by the Governor in 1809 to advise the British Government on its future course in the Island, he proposed among other things that Jews from Asia and Africa be encouraged to establish settlements near the pearl-fishery coast and the major towns of Ceylon, the settlers to be assured of land grants on easy terms, honors and distinctions, and protection. Johnston had been led to this proposal by the commercial achievements of the Jews of Cochin and the excellent reputation which they had won for industry, integrity and loyalty. The scheme, he writes, was approved by Viscount Castlereagh, Secretary of State for the Colonies, but the latter's resignation from his post prevented its implementation.[28] These plans yielded no issue, and when Jacob Saphir reached the Island in 1860 in search of coreligionists he encountered only the

Worms brothers—pioneer tea and coffee planters and Rothschild cousins—though it is likely that other Jewish settlers had also been attracted[29] by the coffee rush.

Maurice and Gabriel Worms—their mother was Jeanette Rothschild, oldest child of Mayer Amschel and Güttele—arrived in Ceylon via London in 1841–42 and established themselves in the coffee business. They thrived—following the Rothschild fraternal formula—with Maurice, the younger brother, managing the firm's plantations from their Rothschild estate near Kandy, and Gabriel attending to the mill and their shipping and banking interests from Colombo. In 1848 Governor Torrington selected Gabriel Worms provisionally to fill a vacancy on the Legislative Council of Ceylon. The appointment was disallowed in London, however, because denization did not confer the full rights of a British-born subject on one of alien birth (the brothers hailed, of course, from Frankfurt). This led, curiously, to the passage of an ordinance by the Council—without awaiting advice from London as to its legality—naturalizing Gabriel Worms and, ostensibly, permitting him to hold a seat on the Council. The Queen's approval was conveyed early the following year. It is not clear what transpired next.[30] There are, in fact, seemingly contradictory accounts in the published literature as to whether Worms was ever seated.[31] This occurred, significantly, during the very years that his cousin, Baron Lionel de Rothschild, first attempted to occupy the seat in Parliament to which he had been elected. The brothers liquidated their holdings on the Island in 1865 and returned to England, where Maurice succumbed soon afterwards. Gabriel survived until his eightieth year in 1881. The Messrs. Worms are credited with an important role in Ceylon's agricultural and commercial development.[32]

In 1906, Elkan Adler could report even less success than Saphir in locating coreligionists. He was, in fact, distinctly disappointed to find that "the synagogue," marked on a map of Colombo in an excellent location, proved upon investigation to be nothing more than the villa of a local official.[33] Israel Cohen's fleeting visit in 1920 proved again the absence of a Jewish community.[34] Later that decade some Russian Jewish merchants and tradesmen reached Ceylon by way of Harbin.[35] They do not appear to have struck roots. In the early thirties we hear of an Iraqi Jew living in Kandy.[36] On the eve of the war, a group of German and Austrian Jews found their way to Ceylon, some seeking to reach Australia. Suggestions made in England to open the Island to Jewish refugee settlement in lieu of Palestine fell on deaf ears. In vain did Herbert Loewe apprise the British public—in a letter to the London *Times* (2/28/39)—of Sir Alexander Johnston's plan of 130 years earlier. Governor Caldecott pleaded unemployment and the depressed state of trade as a bar to mass immigration. He recommended, however, that "Jews of eminence" be admitted as permanent residents. Internment awaited most of the arrivals.[37] In independent Ceylon very few persons of Jewish extraction were to be found domiciled. Numbered among them was the German remnant—including a Buddhist monk—and several English wives.

Such are the paltry data which a far-ranging investigation of the subject has turned up. It is evident that if a Ceylon *Minhag* were to exist it would go back to the early medieval period. As such it would be of considerable interest. But if it is a Ceylon rite that the Cochin Jews transmit in the *Minhag Shingli,* one would expect to find this stated in their tradition. No such tradition exists. Quite the contrary, "Shingli" is, as we shall see, connected with a very specific site in India by the Cochin community. How, then, did Bruns and Steinschneider come to associate it with Ceylon? One may attempt a reply with a fair degree of assurance: It is not merely the physical proximity of Ceylon to Cochin that suggested this association; it is the orthographic-phonetic similarity between a gentilic used for the people of Ceylon, "Singhalese," and the place name "Shingli" which suggested it. The derivation of "Singhalese" need not detain us. It is thought to go back to a Sanskrit form from which most of the names for the Island, including "Ceylon" itself, are ultimately descended.[38] Evidence that this similarity is responsible for the identification can be found in the travel account of Jacob Saphir—who does not consciously connect the two—for he spells both שינגולי.[39] It is obvious, of course, that Saphir could not have influenced Steinschneider in *CB* since his Volume 2 did not appear until the 1870's. (That Steinschneider influenced Saphir is entirely excluded). In fact, this similarity was noticed independently of both, in all likelihood, and in another context by Aaron Ze'ev Aešcoly.[40]

Is it possible, notwithstanding, that Steinschneider is right in *CB* in taking Shingli to be Ceylon? There is no such possibility. Steinschneider failed, apparently, to notice a *piyyut* in the 1769 liturgy (l. 60b) which makes it clear that Shingli is a city—despite a reference to a king—not an island.[41] Moreover, he chose to ignore the fact that in some of the secondary literature he had collected, Shingli was not only assumed to be a city, but was already identified as

"Cranganore."[42] This identification is, in fact, unanimously supported by Cochin opinion,[43] which can hardly be dismissed despite the manifest weakness of some of Malabar tradition.

It is beyond the scope of the article and the competence of the writer to provide an exhaustive account of what is known of the ancient city of Cranganore. We may, however, conclude with a summary calculated to show that the equation of Shingli with Cranganore is hardly open to serious question.

The site of Cranganore lies some twenty miles north of Cochin in the State of Kerala on the southwest coast of India (Malabar). It is now silted up, but it was once a leading world port. For there is small doubt that it was Cranganore which classical antiquity knew as "Muziris," and which is described in some detail in the *Periplus of the Erythraean Sea*.[44] The history of Jewish association with Cranganore cannot be reviewed. Little enough of it is certain, in any case. Suffice it to say that local tradition holds the earliest Jewish settlement in Kerala to have been there—whatever the date of that may have been—and in Cranganore or its environs Jews lived continuously for many centuries, possibly—but this is far from assured—in an autonomous quarter or principality.[45] It is, perhaps, least open to doubt that Jews abandoned the city totally in the sixteenth century—whether this was the effect of Muslim or Portuguese attack, the combination of both in succession, or other causes is not of moment here—never to return.[46] It is not by accident that the traditions of the Christians of St. Thomas ascribe the beginnings of the Syrian Church in Malabar to the Cranganore area, and early Muslim penetration of the southwest coast may also have occurred there.[47] One encounters an embarrassment of riches in searching for material in the various Indian literatures, for the city and its environs figure under a variety of names. Into this we cannot enter, except to say that but for a single instance no name that possibly designates Cranganore appears immediately cognate with "Shingli."[48]

The situation is reversed in regard to medieval and postmedieval travelers' notices of Malabar. Here a succession of accounts in various languages may reflect differing forms of the name "Shingli." In the Arabic geographic literature, one finds "Sinjlī," "Sinjī," "Shinklī," and "Jinkalī," or the like.[49] Benjamin of Tudela's גנגלה, where he records some 1,000 Jews resident, may possibly be in Malabar.[50] David Ha-re'uveni's שינגולי appears certainly to be in Malabar, as does also Moses di Rossi's סנייל.[51] Chinese annals record a mission from the countries of the South to the Mongol court, including a representative from "Sêng-ki-li."[52] In European accounts, there is Friar Jordanus' "Singuyli," Friar Odoric's "Cyngilin," "Ziniglin," "Singulir," "Singulum," or "Sigli" (quoted differently in different manuscripts), and John de Marignolli's "Cynkali." Any or all of these place names may conceivably be a reflex of what appears in the Hebrew form as שינגילי,[53] etc.

Though Jews are mentioned at the place in question in some of these accounts, that does not yet constitute proof of the identity of Shingli and Cranganore. In the absence of Hebrew manuscripts from Shingli that might shed light on the matter,[54] we shall fall back on two Syriac manuscripts from the Malabar Coast now at the Vatican, the two oldest Syriac mss. to survive the auto-da-fé of heretical literature of the Church of St. Thomas.[55] A direct transcription into Hebrew characters may be used since the perfect correspondence of the Syriac and Hebrew alphabets permits an uncluttered transliteration of the place names. The colophon of the first manuscript (*Cod. Syr. Vat.* No. XXII), executed in A.D. 1301,[56] states that it was written in the "royal, renowned and famous city of שנגלא in Malabar, in the country of India . . ." The colophon of the second (*Cod. Syr. Vat.* No. XVII), written 209 years later, records that it was completed in the "blessed and famous city of שנגלא [57] which was called קרונגלור [58] in Malabar, in the country of India . . ." There can be no question of this proof of identity.

In light of the foregoing, it is clear that the "Ceylon rite" must be expunged from catalogs which continue to show it, e.g., those of the British Museum, the Bibliotheca Rosenthaliana, and Hebrew Union College. One may propose for emulation, rather, the improvement in the Bodleian catalogs where Arthur Ernest Cowley—between the appearance in 1906 of Volume 2 of its *Catalogue of . . . Hebrew Manuscripts* (with the Index he had prepared equating Shingli and Ceylon, p. 534) and the issuance in 1929 of its *Concise Catalogue of . . . Hebrew Printed Books*—may have realized the untenability of the equation. He seems to have abandoned it, in any event, in the later volume (p. 550), for he wisely confines himself to describing the Proops' 1757 and 1769 liturgies as intended for the "use of Cochin."[59]

NOTES

[1] *Catalog der Hebraica und Judaica aus der L. Rosenthal'schen Bibliothek,* (Amsterdam, 1875), 2v. The Amsterdam 1966 reprint reproduces the *Catalog* not entirely unamended. The Ceylon heading is untouched.

[2] Cf. Lajb Fuks' article "Meijer Roest Mz., De Eerste Conservator van de Bibliotheca Rosenthaliana" in *Studia Rosenthaliana,* 1 (1967), p. 9.

[3] The spelling of this Hebrew place name is discussed by the present author in another article.

[4] London, 1867, p. 455. In the partly corrected reprint of the *Catalogue* (Norwich, 1964), Zedner's entry is left undisturbed.

[5] We shall transcribe the place name spelled in Hebrew שינגילי as "Shingli." Variant Hebrew spellings encountered are: שינגלי (Wessely, Steinschneider, Kahana, Assaf); שינגולי (Saphir, Neubauer, Aešcoly); שנגילי (Gravezande, Neubauer-Cowley); שינגילא (R. N. Rabinowitz); אלשנכלי (Dinur); שינקאלי (Fischel); סינגילי (Adler). The following romanized forms have been recorded (as transcriptions from the Hebrew): Cingali (Forster); Chingel (Gravezande, Barkey, Bruns); Chingely (Bruns); Chingli (Baer); Chingily (Gravezande, Barkey); Shingly (Ernakulam elders, Simon, Koder, Brown, Segal, Woodcock); Shinkali (Fischel); Shinkli (Fischel); Sangli (Kahana); Senagal (*India and Israel*); Senegal (Delitzsch, Dukes, Eisenstein, L. Rabinowitz); Sengale (Winter-Wünsche); Sengali (Winter-Wünsche); Sengili (Zunz); Sengli (Idelsohn); Singali (Steinschneider); Singili (Kuster-Sike, Gravezande, Benjamin, Frankel, Roest, Oppert, Kaufmann, Adler, Marx, L. Rabinowitz); Singoli (Adler); Sinjoli (L. Rabinowitz). It is apparent from this enumeration that certain authors have employed more than one form of the place name. We leave aside for the moment equivalents with which this place name has been identified. (The place in question is not to be confused with צינגולי , the Italian town of Cingoli). [Add: סינגלי (Goldschmidt); Chingili (Krauss); Shingali (Fischel)].

[6] *Catalogue de la collection importante de livres et manuscrits hébreux . . .* (Amsterdam, Muller, 1861), v. 2, p. 80, no. 2211.

[7] To resolve a confusion among certain Hebrew bibliographers it is necessary, lamentably, to state that the Jews of Cochin hail from India (Kerala) and not from Vietnam (Cochin China), as Roest has it here, or, indeed, from China! The error occurs first, apparently, in W. Spottiswoode's English version of Steinschneider's Ersch and Gruber article, *Jewish Literature* (London, 1857), pp. 242, 258. It reappears two years later in the index to the English edition of I. J. Benjamin's travels, *Eight Years in Asia and Africa* (Hanover, 1859), p. xiv. It is perpetuated by Alexander Marx in *Soncino-Blätter,* 2 (1927), p. 114, who also knows, however, of Jews from Cochin, India (*ibid.,* and *REJ,* 89, 1930, pp. 293–304). Joshua Bloch, in *Jewish Life in Oriental Countries,* (New York, 1927), p. 7—and presumably in the exhibit of which this publication is the catalog—assigned some of the prayer books of the Cochin liturgy to Cochin China and subsumed the area under China. (Already in *CB* Steinschneider noted that I. G. Polak had misplaced the Cochin Jews in China, v. 2, col. 2723). They are back again in China via the *Jewish Book Annual,* 19 (1961–62), p. 27. Isaac Baer Levinsohn in *Te'udah be-Yisrael,* 4th ed., (Warsaw, 1901), p. 46 makes the same mistake.

[8] *Catalogus librorum hebraeorum in Bibliotheca Bodleiana* (Berlin, 1852–60), 3 v.

[9] Misprints in Steinschneider's page-reference citations of each of these works are to be corrected as follows: Franz Delitzsch, *Zur Geschichte der jüdischen Poësie* (Leipzig, 1836), "p. 57"; Leopold Dukes in *Literaturblatt des Orients,* 5 (1844), "cols. 373–4"; G. I. Polak in his Dutch translation of Menahem Amelander, *Seërith Jisrael* (Amsterdam, 1855), "p. 590."

[10] The reference is not an unequivocal retraction as it provides only a pronunciation of the Hebrew place name and not an identification—for where, after all, is "Singali"? Zunz (*Ritus,* p. 57), to whom Steinschneider refers Delitzsch for correction as to the nature of the rite, uses the form "Sengili." Delitzsch writes "Senegal," but he cannot have believed this "Senegal" to be in Africa as is apparent from his note.

11 The omitted word is supplied in the parallel passage in Cambridge manuscript Oo.1.49. We may also notice here that J. Perles in *MGWJ*, 9 (1860), p. 355, asserts that the Jews of Shingli are the Jewish inhabitants of Ceylon. His source for this cannot be Graetz (*Geschichte*, Berlin, 1853, v. 4, p. 472) as a footnote appears to imply, since Graetz says merely that there are white and black Jews resident on Ceylon (and in Malabar).

12 Forster has created several new Indian dialects in the course of studying the manuscript. It is beyond peradventure of a doubt that what he renders as "the tongue of Al-Nadiz" (pp. 294, 306) reads in the manuscript לשון אולנדז , "the language of the Hollander," i.e., Dutch. (The same Portuguese-influenced form occurs in other Hebrew mss from Cochin.) What he renders as "the Bisnagi," is part of the name of the French historian, Jacques Basnage de Beauval. His "the Cingali" is, of course, the place name which is the subject of the present paper. It has been entered in our enumeration of romanized variants.

13 George Woodcock, *Kerala* (London, 1967), pp. 123–124.

14 For the sources, cf. the University of Ceylon, *History of Ceylon* (Colombo, 1959–60, v. 1, pts. 1 & 2), v. 1, chap. 4. Reference to a supposed mention of Jews there in the sixth-century *Topographia christiana* of Cosmas Indicopleustes is, apparently, a slip (cf., Ludwik Sternbach, "India as Described by Mediaeval European Travellers: Jewish Dwelling Places" in *Bhāratīya Vidyā*, n.s. 7, 1946, p. 27). Cf. *EJ*, *s.v.* "Ceylon," v. 5, col. 114 (art. by Herbert Loewe and Mark Wischnitzer).

15 In light of the Genizah material, there are no grounds for the scepticism expressed in the University *History of Ceylon*, v. 1 pt. 2, p. 578, as to the presence of Jews on the Island at that time. On the Genizah material, cf. Elkan N. Adler in the *Jewish Chronicle*, 6/1/1906, pp. 34–35; *idem*, *Jewish Travellers* (London, 1930), pp. 100–02; *Fragments from the Cairo Genizah in the Freer Collection* (New York, 1927), pp. 45–47; Solomon D. F. Goitein, "From the Mediterranean to India" in *Speculum*, 29 (1954), p. 191; *idem*, *A Mediterranean Society* (Berkeley and Los Angeles, 1967), v. 1, pp. 50–51. Cf. also *idem*, "The Jewish India-Merchants of the Middle Ages" in *India and Israel*, 6/1953, pp. 36–37.

16 The tale about a Jew who carried astronomical books from Ceylon to Baghdad in the eighth or ninth century (cf., E. N. Adler, *Jewish Travellers*, *op. cit.*, p. xii) is disposed of by D. Pingree in *Journal of Near Eastern Studies*, 27 (1968), p. 101.

17 *Relation des voyages* . . . (Paris, 1845) 2 v. (ed., J. T. Reinaud; Arabic text ed. by L. M. Langlès under the title *Silsilat al-tawārīkh*), v. 1, p. 128; v. 2, pp. 122–23. Hanns G. Reissner's assertion that Abū Zaid visited the Island ("Jews in Medieval Ceylon" in *The Ceylon Historical Journal*, 3, 1953–54, p. 138—this article also appeared in a slightly contracted form in *Eastern World*, 5, 1951, pp. 14–16 as well as in *India and Israel*, 9/1951, pp. 22–25)—is seemingly based upon faulty information in the Renaudot edition of Abū Zaid. Cf. Reinaud, *op. cit.*, v. 1, p. xv. The ascription to Sulaymān (A.D. 851) of the earliest reference to Jews on the Island in *EJ*, v. 5, col. 114 rests upon a confusion of the first two parts of the unique ms. which contains both texts (cf., *'Aḫbār aṣ-Ṣīn wa l-Hind; Relation de la Chine et de l'Inde*, Paris, 1948, ed. J. Sauvaget, p. xv).

18 *India and the Neighbouring Territories in the Kitāb nuzhat al-mushtāq fī ikhtirāq al-'āfāq of . . . al-Idrīsī* by S. Maqbul Ahmad (Leiden, 1960), p. 28.

19 *The Itinerary of Rabbi Benjamin of Tudela* (London, 1840–41), ed. A. Asher, v. 1, ע׳ צ״ב, p. 141, and v. 2, pp. 185–89; *The Itinerary of Benjamin of Tudela* (London, 1907), ed. M. N. Adler, p. 65–66, ע׳ נ״ט. Adler indicates (*loc. cit.*) that this 20,000 difference in population is achievable by a mere shift in the numeral marker, i.e., כ״ג vs. כג׳ , on the part of a manuscript copyist. As to the reliability of Benjamin's population statistics, cf. also Salo Wittmayer Baron *A Social and Religious History of the Jews*, 2nd ed., v. 3 (New York, 1957), pp. 283–84; on Benjamin's trustworthiness, cf. *ibid.*, v. 6 (New York, 1958), pp. 435–36. A new edition of the *Itinerary* is promised by Zvi Ankori.

20 Reissner, *The Ceylon Historical Journal*, 3 (1953–54), p. 139, and *idem*, "Benjamin of Tudela on Ceylon," *ibid.*, 3 (1953–54), pp. 229, 232. (This article was published as well in *Zeitschrift für Religions- und Geistesgeschichte*, 6, 1954, pp.

151–55). The preposition "on" in the title is ambiguous. Reissner does not contend that Benjamin journeyed to the Island.

[21] *The Ceylon Historical Journal,* 3 (1953), pp. 143-44.

[22] There is no reason why Jacob Saphir should not be right in reporting—opaquely—that the offspring of Marrano families, still conscious of their descent, could yet be met with on the Island at the time of his visit in the 1860's (*Even Sapir,* Mainz, 1874, v. 2, p. 95). Their presence in Portuguese India appears not to have been negligible (cf. *Encyclopaedia Hebraica, s.v.* "Goa," and Cecil Roth, *A History of the Marranos* (Philadelphia, 1959), pp. 394–95, n. 11. On the other hand, the significance which Saphir attaches to the use of biblical names by the Ceylonese (*loc. cit.*) is, of course, wildly erroneous.

[23] Johann Jacob Schudt, *Jüdischer Merckwürdigkeiten* (Frankfurt am Main, 1717), Teil 4, Contin. 1, p. 13; Jacob Canter Visscher, *Letters from Malabar* (Madras, 1862) p. 114: "Jews are found here [Malabar], and in many other places on the vast coast of India. . . . They are not, however, to be met with in the neighbouring islands, nor at Java, Sumatra, Celebes, Amboyna, Banda, or Ceylon." Visscher's original Dutch work, of which the Madras edition is a translation, appeared in 1723.

[24] In his history of the Reformed Church in the Indies under the Dutch East India Company, C. A. L. van Troostenburg de Bruyn writes of the existence of a synagogue on Ceylon (*De Hervormde Kerk in Nederlandsch Oost-Indië onder de Oost-Indische Compagnie, 1602–1795,* Arnhem, 1884, pp. 582–83). A close scrutiny of the cited sources discloses that this conclusion is an inference based upon Roest's entry of the Amsterdam 1757 liturgy in the da Costa *Catalogue,* no. 2211. Cf., *supra.* We have already indicated Roest's likely dependence upon Steinschneider in this matter, and Steinschneider's probable indebtedness, in turn, to Bruns. How "Shingli" came to be identified with Ceylon in the first place we shall suggest below.

[25] Cf. van Troostenburg de Bruyn, *op. cit.,* p. 516; Walter J. Fischel in *Journal of the American Oriental Society,* 87 (1967), pp. 240–42.

[26] *EJ, s.v. "Ceylon,"* v. 5, col. 115.

[27] Cf. H. W. Tambiah "The Alexander Johnstone [!] Papers" in *The Ceylon Historical Journal,* 3 (1953), pp. 18–30. He is largely responsible for the introduction of universal popular education and the restoration of religious liberty, as well as for the abolition of slavery on the Island. He conducted extensive investigations of the history and laws of the Sinhalese, Tamil and Muslim communities of Ceylon. Back home in England at a later stage of his career he was an advocate of native rights in the colonies. Cf. *The Dictionary of National Biography* (London, 1937–38), v. 10, pp. 940–41.

[28] Cf., Francis Henry Goldsmid, *The Arguments Advanced against the Enfranchisement of the Jews* (London, 1833), 2nd ed., pp. 41–43. The letter which contains this information is available in Hebrew translation in W. J. Fischel's *Ha-yehudim be-Hodu* (Jerusalem, 1960), pp. 201–203. Neither the Public Record Office in London nor the National Archives in Nugegoda, Ceylon—to each of which acknowledgements for its help are made—has been able to trace the documents in question. (The various inquiries of Sir Alexander Johnston on the history and "character" of the Jews of Asia, undertaken as chairman of the correspondence committee of the Royal Asiatic Society, seem similarly to be lost.) Sir Alexander was also interested in encouraging Parsee settlement in Ceylon. Cf. Tambiah, *op. cit.,* p. 29.

[29] The *Jewish Chronicle,* 10/8/1869, p. 13.

[30] Ceylon National Archives: 5/35/71; 4/45/247; 5/35/175; 4/46/538; 5/35/207; 4/46/359. Grateful acknowledgement is made to the Archives for these data.

[31] According to John Ferguson in *Pioneers of the Planting Enterprise in Ceylon* (Colombo, 1894), [1st series], p. 55, Worms took the oaths with covered head and was seated (apparently at the outset of this affair). In a biographical sketch of the brothers prepared by one of their relatives which is appended by Ferguson (*op. cit.,* p. 52) it is stated, however, that Gabriel Worms was unable to take his seat as the

Jewish disabilities had not been removed. Cf. also the *Jewish Chronicle*, 11/5/1858, p. 4. Perhaps this refers only to a permanent seat. (An examination of the documents in the case [C.O. 54/251 ff. 200–207; 54/252 ff. 192–198, 200; 54/266 ff. 145–146 *d*, 148–149 *d*] received in facsimile from the Public Record Office—to which our thanks —after the article had gone to press discloses that the Queen's approval of the ordinance was given with the understanding that Gabriel Worms' naturalization would not be construed to remove his disqualification to hold a seat on the Council. In the opinion of the Law Officers of the Crown, the Governor and Legislative Council of Ceylon could not pass an ordinance removing the disqualification "arising from the condition of alienship," but Worms was "not disqualified in consequence of his professing the Jewish Religion, provided he take the oaths required from a member of the Council." The Worms' affair is not discussed in the literature on the removal of Jewish disabilities, e.g., in H.S.Q. Henriques' *The Jews and the English Law* [London, 1908].)

32 Saphir, *loc. cit.;* Tennent, *op. cit.*, v. 2, p. 250; Lucien Wolf, *Essays in Jewish History* (London, 1934), p. 213; Ferguson, *op. cit.*, is a laudatory sketch of the brothers. Tennent, too, is lavish with praise.

33 The *Jewish Chronicle*, 5/11/1906, p. 16. Adler was not the last to be misled by this legend. Sir Sidney Abrahams, Chief Justice of Ceylon from 1936 to 1939, was another prominent Jewish victim. According to Messrs. C. de Saram and A. L. Dassenaike—to whom our thanks—the building was dubbed "the synagogue" as a "joke," it having once, before the 1860's, been the property of an allegedly Jewish judge. Grateful acknowledgement is made to Dr. Abraham M. Hirsch for calling attention to this matter.

34 *The Journal of a Jewish Traveller*, (New York, 1925), p. 31.

35 Mark Wischnitzer, *Die Juden in der Welt* (Berlin, 1935), p. 298.

36 *Israel's Messenger*, 3/1/1932, p. 13; 1/1/1933, p. 22.

37 *Ceylon News:* 8/8/1938, pp. 5, 12; 10/10/1938, pp. 2–3, 18; 11/28/1938, pp. 16, 20; 1/9/1939, p. 15; 9/11/1939, p. 4; 1/1/1940, p. 4; the London *Times:* 11/19/1938, p. 11; 2/28/1939, p. 15; 10/16/1939, p. 7.

38 Cf. *Journal Asiatique*, 5. série, 9, pp. 76–77; Henry Yule and A. C. Burnell, *Hobson-Jobson*, (new ed. by W. Crooke), 2nd ed. (Delhi, 1968), *s.v.* "Ceylon," and "Singalese, Cinghalese." Variant spellings in several European languages all display the characteristic elements.

39 *Even Sapir, op. cit.;* cf., e.g., pp. 62 and 94.

40 Cf. his *Sipur David Ha-re'uveni* (Jerusalem, 1940), p. 230.

41 Per contra, the responsa of RaDBaZ and Castro call Cochin an island. However, in common usage Cochin designates a complex of islands and mainland area. The geographic situation is somewhat different at Cranganore.

42 *Verhandelingen*, Zeeuwsch Genootschap der Wetenschappen, 6 (1778), p. 535; cf. also pp. 533–34; *Ha-me'asef*, 1790, p. 259; Delitzsch, *op. cit.*, p. 57, n. 1.

43 Rahabi in *Ha-me'asef, loc. cit.;* N. E. Roby in *Otsar Yisrael*, v. 9, p. 130; A. I. Simon in *The Songs of the Jews of Cochin* (Cochin, 1947), p. 13; S. S. Koder in *India and Israel*, 11/1949, [p. 21?] and *ibid.*, 5/1951, p. 31.

44 According to Arthur C. Burnell in *The Indian Antiquary*, 3 (1874), p. 334, the area opposite Cranganore across the backwater is the only place on the southwest coast of India corresponding to the description in the *Periplus*. Cf. *The Periplus of the Erythraean Sea*, ed. W. H. Schoff (New York etc., 1912), pp. 44, 205–208, *passim*.

45 On the Jewish history of this city, cf. *EJ*, *s.v.* "Cranganore," v. 5, cols. 685–86 (art. by Herbert Loewe and Mark Wischnitzer); S. S. Koder, *op. cit.;* Woodcock, *op. cit.*, pp. 120–27; J. B. Segal, "The Jews of Cochin and Their Neighbours" in *Essays Presented to Chief Rabbi Israel Brodie*, (London, 1967), Eng. volume, pp. 390–91. The two-column article in *EJ* accomplishes the considerable feat of avoiding mention of "Shingli." Since Herbert Loewe was certainly aware of the problem (a chapter in his projected work on the Jews in India was to be entitled "The Names of Cranganore") is one to assume that his silence denies a connection? One could wish for a more explicit rejection.

[46] On the abandonment of Cranganore, cf. W. J. Fischel "Cochin in Jewish History" in *PAAJR*, 30 (1962), pp. 39–40; Moses Gaster's assertion that an auto-da-fé against the Jews was lit in Cranganore (and Cochin) at the beginning of the eighteenth century is in error (cf. *Transactions of the Jewish Historical Society of England*, 7, 1911–14, p. 305). The mistake is based upon a sermon preached by the Portuguese Archbishop of Cranganore at an auto in Lisbon—not Cranganore—in 1705. Besides, so far as is known, no Jews resided at Cranganore in the eighteenth century, and the Dutch were then in control at Cochin. The error is corrected in the *Transactions*, 12 (1931), pp. 53–56, 77.

[47] Leslie Wilfrid Brown, *The Indian Christians of St. Thomas* (Cambridge, 1956), p. 52; Muhammad Firishtah, *History of the Rise of the Mahomedan Power in India* (London, 1829), v. 4, pp. 531–32. Cf. *ibid.*, pp. 537–38 on the abandonment of Cranganore by the Jews.

[48] Cf. *Quarterly Journal of the Mythic Society*, 19 (1928), pp. 93–100; *Bulletin of the Rama Varma Research Institute:* 1 (1930), pp. 33–36; 2 (1933), pp. 64–71; 7 (1939), pp. 60–61; 8 (1940), pp. 35–47, 92–120; 10 (1942), pp. 15–16. The last of these cites as a Malayalam place name for a port north of Cochin "Changala." According to H. Gundert, a nineteenth-century authority on Dravidian linguistics, "Shingli" derives from "Tiruvan-jiculam" (River-Harbor). This he identifies with Cranganore, in any case. Thanks are expressed to Mr. E. T. Narayanan for his help with Malayalam.

[49] Ahmad, *op. cit.*, pp. 103–105; S. Muhammad Husayn Nainar, *Arab Geographers' Knowledge of Southern India* (Madras, 1942), pp. 75–77; *JRAS*, n.s. 4 (1869–70), p. 345.

[50] The geographer Carl Ritter took it to be at the southern end of Ceylon (and thus Benjamin's second mention of Ceylon and its Jews). Cf. Asher's edition of the *Itinerary, op. cit.*, p. 189. M. N. Adler professed ignorance (cf. his edition of the *Itinerary, op. cit.*, p. 67). E. N. Adler, following G. Oppert, believed it to be Cranganore, *Jewish Travellers, op. cit.*, p. 372. In the *Jewish Chronicle* of 5/11/1906, p. 16 he had, however, identified סינגילי as "Similla."

[51] Cf. Aešcoly's edition of David Ha-re'uveni, *op. cit.*, and Adler, *Jewish Travellers, op. cit.* p. 376. On Di Rossi, cf. David Kaufmann in *JQR*, o.s. 9 (1897), pp. 491–499 and L. Rabinowitz, *JQR*, n.s. 48 (1958), pp. 376–79.

[52] *T'oung Pao*, 2nd series, 15 (1914), pp. 440–41; Henry Yule, *Cathay and the Way Thither* (London, 1913–16), 2nd ed., v. 1, p. 82; cf. also *ibid.* v. 2, pp. 132–35, and v. 4, p. 78.

[53] *The Wonders of the East by Friar Jordanus* ed. by H. Yule (London, 1863), pp. 40–41; *Les voyages en Asie au xive siècle du Odoric de Pordenone* ed. by H. Cordier (Paris, 1891), pp. 99, 107–108. Most of the texts are conveniently cited in *Hobson-Jobson, op. cit., s.v.* "Shinkali, Shigala." Cf. also *s.v.* "Cranganore." They are thoroughly treated by Sternbach, *op. cit.*, pp. 13–16, 23–24.

[54] The only positive references discovered to Hebrew mss. from Cranganore-Shingli are to Torah scrolls at Parur in the seventeenth century in Pereyra de Paiva's *Notisias*, p. 7, and a mention in Cambridge manuscript Oo.1.33—itself apparently from the eighteenth century—of a Shingli manuscript from which it, or an ancestor, was partly copied (cf. *JQR*, o.s. 6, 1894, p. 138). Ezekiel Rahabi's reply of 1767 to Tobias Boas' eleventh question (cf. *Ha-me'asef*, 1790, p. 262) is highly significant in this regard. Bodleian Ms. Opp. 227 requires further study.

[55] Cf. J. B. Chabot "L'autodafé des livres syriaques du Malabar" in *Florilegium . . . dédiés à Melchior de Vogüé* (Paris, 1909), pp. 613–23.

[56] Through a curious error, Domenico Ferroli's *The Jesuits in Malabar* (Bangalore City, 1939), v. 1, pp. 63 and 79 dates it two centuries too late.

[57] The Vatican catalog, S. E. and J. S. Assemani, *Bibliothecae Apostolicae Vaticanae codicum manuscriptorum catalogus* (Rome, 1756–59), Pars I, Tomus II, p. 64 reads שיגלא . This, however, appears to be an error (caused by the similarity of "yud" and "nun" in certain Syriac hands), which is perpetuated in W. H. P. Hatch's *An Album of Dated Syriac Manuscripts* (Boston, 1946), pp. 231 and 284, cf.

also p. 226. It is corrected in S. Giamil, *Genuinae relationes* . . . (Rome, 1902), p. 586, n. 1, and A. Mingana's "The Early Spread of Christianity in India" in *Bulletin of the John Rylands Library,* 10 (1926), p. 502, (b). "Shigala" given in *Hobson-Jobson* as an alternative to "Shinkali," *q.v.,* derives from the Assemani reading in Cod. No. XVII and is, thus, a phantom.

58 This is a common Syriac spelling for Cranganore, reflecting the vernacular pronunciation. Cf. Mingana, *op. cit.,* p. 485, n. 3. From this Syriac evidence it becomes apparent that "Shingli" is not a specifically Jewish name for Cranganore, as is implied or asserted in some of the relevant literature. Indeed, it is passing strange that Cranganore is not once called "Shingli" in the *Notisias.*

59 The *Jewish Encyclopedia,* too, would profit by removal of the rubric "In Ceylon" from the article on "Marriage Ceremonies" (v. 8, p. 344). The authors of the article have unwittingly copied the Malabar rite twice, once from Salomon Rinmon's *Mas'ot Shelomoh* (Wien, 1884), pp. 156–159, and again from Saphir's *Even Sapir, op. cit.,* v. 2, pp. 74–83. That the error has not been spiked is evidenced by its recurrence in contemporary works, e.g., in the *Catalogue of the Sassoon Collection,* 1st portion (London, Sotheby, 1970), pp. 66, 68, and in *The Passover Haggadah,* edited by Nahum N. Glatzer (New York, 1969), pp. 103-04. The latter is dependent in turn on Ernst Daniel Goldschmidt's *Die Pessach-Haggada* (Berlin, 1936), pp. 105-06. Goldschmidt, in his Hebrew text, *Hagadah shel Pesah* (Jerusalem, 1960), p. 98 has meanwhile retreated to the noncommittal סינגלי . Johanna Spector, who comes to the subject from the field of ethnomusicology rather than Hebrew bibliography, has, however, managed to escape this pitfall (cf. Fifth World Congress of Jewish Studies, Jerusalem 1969, Ḥaṭivah D, *Taktsirim,* p. 12).

ADDENDA TO
YAARI'S *BIBLIOGRAPHY OF THE PASSOVER HAGGADAH* FROM THE LIBRARY OF CONGRESS HEBRAICA COLLECTION

Compiled by
THEODORE WIENER
Library of Congress

The following bibliography includes 31 Haggadot listed neither in Yaari nor in the six supplements to his work (A. M. Habermann in *Kirjath Sepher*, XXXVI (1961), 419–22; N. Ben-Menahem in *Aresheth*, III (1961), 442–65; IV (1966), 518–44, and in *Sinai*, LVII (1965), 56–67; Harry J. Hirschhorn, *Mah Nishtana* (1964), and my own in *Studies in Bibliography and Booklore*, VII (1965), 90–129. In addition, amplifications, corrections and/or variants to 31 Yaari entries are presented. Both the catalogued and uncatalogued parts of the Library of Congress Hebraica collection were searched.

1770

1. The הגדה של פסח, containing the ceremonies and prayers which are used and read by all families... of the Israelites, the two first nights of Passover: faithfully translated from the original Hebrew... by A. Alexander and assistants. London, printed... by W. Gilbert, 5530 [1770]

lxxvii p. illus. 18 cm.

Same title page as Yaari 167, but different pagination. Ends with נשמת, without אדיר הוא and חד גדיא.

1809

2. סדר הגדה על פסח, זכרון יציאת מצרים... ווין, געדרוקט פאן ג. הראשאנצקיא, תקס"ט [1809]

24 l. 18 cm.

1825

3. סדר ההגדה לליל שמורים, מפורש במאמר אפיקומין למורינו הרשבץ. מדויק היטיב ומסודר יפה ומתורגם אשכנזית מאתי וואלף היידנהיים. Hagadah ווין, גידרוקט פאן א. שמיד, 1825.

44 l. 20 cm.

Variant of Yaari 467.

1846

4. ספר חקת הפסח, והוא הגדה של ליל פסח עם כמה מעלות טובות תפלו'... ודינים... וביאורים בלשון ערבי בלשון צח... נדפס שנית. כלכתה, בבית ובדפוס אלעזר בן מארי אהרן סעדיה עראקי הכהן, בשנת ושמרתם את היום הזה לדרותיכם חקת עולם לפ"ק [1846]

46 l. 16 cm.

1848

5. סדר הגדה של פסח עם עברי טייטש באותיות גדולות מאד ובנייר יפה ובדוי שחור גם אלע דינים פון פסח.

Lemberg, Gedruckt bei F. Grossman, תר"ח [1848]

[40] p. 20 cm.

1849

6. סדר הגדה של פסח.

Service for the two first nights of Passover, according to the custom of the German and Polish Jews. London, S. Solomon, 5609–1849.

26 l. 22 cm.

Hebrew and English. Yaari 683?

1868

7. סדר מרבה לספר והוא הגדה של פסח. Vortrag für beiden Abende des Uiberschreitungsfestes mit Beifügung aller Gebräuche. Ganz neu in's Deutsche übersetzt von M. I. Landau. Prag, Druck von S. Freund's Witwe & Comp., 1868, 63 pp. illus. 20 cm.

1879

8. הגדה של פסח עם עברי טייטש... אויך... פירוש מוט... משלים פון... דיבנער מגיד... לעמבערג, בדפוס של א. נ. זיס, בשנת לשנה הבאה בני חורין לפ"ק

Hagudy. Lemberg A. N. Süs, 1879.

[16] l. 23 cm. Yaari 1151?

1883

9. הגדה של פסח.

Die beiden Pessachabende. Uebersetzt von R. J. Fürstenthal. 6. Aufl. Prag J. B. Brandeis, 1883.

63 p. illus. 20 cm.

1885

10. הגדה של פסח עם אותיות גדולות ובדיו שחור ועל נייר יפה. מור האבון דא גושטעלט אלע דינים פון דעם חיי אדם אונ אלעס כסדר כדי מען זאל נושט דארפון זוכען. וגם נוסף עליו ברכת המזון והלל וספירה, הכל על מקומו. קאלאמעא, אויפלאגע דעס אלטער טייכער, תרמ"ה.

Hagada. Kolomea, Druck von M. Bilous, 1885.

[36] p. 19 cm.

1885

11. הגדה של פסח, ערצעהלונג פון איזראעלס אויסצוג אויס עגיפטען פיר דיאביידען ערש־טען אבענדע דעס פסח־פעסטעס מיט איינער דייטשען איבערזעטצונג.

Hagada. Wien, J. Schlesinger, 1885.

[62] p. illus. 20 cm.

1886

12. סדר הגדה של פסח.

Erzählung von dem Auszuge Israels aus Egypten, an den beiden Pessach-Abenden. New York, Lewine & Rosenbaum, 1886–5646.

70 p. 20 cm.

1889

13. סדר הגדה של פסח... עם עברי דייטש, גם אללע דינים פאן פסח, עם... פירוש מהרב אליעזר בעל מעשה רוקח והרב שאול אמסטר־דם... טארנאוו, דבורה שטראם.

Tarnow, Gedruckt von J. Styrna, 1889.

36 p. 21 cm.

1894

14. סדר הגדה לליל שמורים... מתורגם ענגליש.

Service for the first two nights of Passover. New ed., thoroughly rev. Vienna, J. Schlesinger, 1894.

64 p. illus. 19 cm.

1901

15. סדר הגדה של פסח... מיט ספורים אויף עברי טייטש... (א) ספורי הפלאות. (ב) ספורי יציאת מצרים מאת משה מזאלישין. (ג) משלי יעקב מאת המגיד מדובנא. (ד) דאס בענטשן מיט עברי טייטש. (ה) סדר ספירת העומר. (ו) שיר השירים...

Wien, J. Schlesinger, 1901.

64 p. illus. 22 cm.

1901

16. סדר הגדה של פסח עם העתקת עברי טייטש המדוברת בינינו ועם פירוש ומשלים מהרב המ"מ מדובנא על עברי טייטש... ווילנא, 1901.

32, 304–305 p. illus. 22 cm.

"שיר השירים" : p. 304–305.

1905

17. סדר הגדה של פסח, זכרון ליציאת מצרים, מיט אללען דינים אונד מנהגים אין דייטשער שפראכע.

Wien, J. Schlesinger, 1905.

40 p. illus. 19 cm.

1907

18. הגדה של פסח עם ספורי נפלאות ועברי טייטש... אלע דינים פון דעם חיי אדם... שיינע פירוש מיט דיא גוטע משלים מהמגיד מדובנא על עברי טייטש... לעמבערג, הירש שלאג, תרס"ז.

Lemberg, Druck V. Kübler, 1907. [8] l. 24 cm.

1908

19. סדר הגדה של פסח עם פירוש משלי יעקב. (א) ספורי הפלאות. (ב) ספורי יציאת מצרים מאת משה מזאלישין. (ג) משלי יעקב מאת המגיד מדובנא... ניו יארק, די יוראפיאן היברו פובלישינג קאמפ., בדפוס החדש של מ. לעמפערט.

30 p. illus. 23 cm.

Cover title:

סדר הגדה של פסח עם העתקת ע"ט המדוברת בינינו ועם פירוש ומשלים מהרב המ"מ מדוב־נא...

New York, The European Hebrew Publishing Co., 1908.

1908

20. סדר הגדה של פסח עם העתקת עברי טייטש המדוברת בינינו ועם פירוש וחדושים מהרב המ"מ מדובנא ונעתק על עברי טייטש... ווילנא, האלמנה והאחים ראם, תרס"ח, 1908.
28 l. illus. 22 cm.

1909

21. סדר הגדה של פסח.
Hagada na Paschę czyli Opowiadania o wyjściu Israelitów z Egiptu. Modlitwy i obrządki na dwa pierwsze wieczory Paschy. Przetłómaczył i przypiskami opatrzył Salomon Spitzer... Kraków, nakładem i czcionkami J. Fischera, 1909.
96 p. illus. 17 cm.

1916

22. הגדה של פסח.
Hagadah mit durchgesehenem Texte, von B. Koenigsberger. Berlin, L. Lamm, תרע"ו, 1916.
48 p. 15 cm.

1921

23. הגדה של פסח באותיות גדולות ובהירות עם דיני בדיקת חמץ ודיני הסדר בליל פסח. מוגה על פי חקי הדקדוק עם מפסיקים, מתגים... מקפים. חרל"פ.
New York, Hebrew Pub. Co., 1921.
45 p. 23 cm.

1934

24. הגדה של פסח.
Hagadah for Passover. New York, Fairmont Creamery Co. [1934]
[64] p. illus. 18 cm.
Hebrew and English.
On inside cover: Abridged five-year calendar, English dates of important Jewish holidays, 5694–5698.

1935

25. הגדה של פסח, מעשה חכמים ומעשה אלפס, פירושים פון פינף־און־צוואנציג גאונים און דרשנים אין א קלאהרען אידיש... ניו יארק, פערלאג מיימון, תרצ"ה, 1935.
58 p. illus. 18 cm.

1942

26. הגדה של פסח באותיות גדולות ובהירות עם דיני בדיקת חמץ ודיני הסדר בליל פסח. מוגה על פי חקי הדקדוק עם מפסיקים, מתגים... מקפים. חרל"פ.
Form of service for the first two nights of Passover, with revised English translation. [New York] Hebrew Pub. Co. [1942, c1921]
44, 45 p. illus. 24 cm.
Cover: Compliments of Yeshivas Ohel Torah, 1897–1942.
Accessioned at L.C. December 18, 1942.

1943

27. Passover Hagadah with English instructions.
הגדה של פסח מצוירת עם אותיות גדולות ועם הערות בעברית ובאנגלית. הגיה חיים מרדכי ברכר. ניו יארק, כתב
New York, Ktav, c1943.
48 p. 24 cm.

1955

28. הגדה של פסח. עם מדור מיחד לילדים "והגדת לבנך." ערוך על־ידי ש"ס. תכן, עטר וציר צ. לבני. תל־אביב, יבנה [תשט"ו, 1955]
55, 55 p. illus. 27 cm.

Added t.p.: Passover Haggadah, with a special section for children "Vehigadeta levincha" (And thou shalt narrate it to thy son). Edited and prepared by Shas (S .Skolsky) and translated by I. M. Lask. Designed, ornamented, and illustrated by Z. Livni.

no date

29. הגדה של פסח.
Service for the first nights of Passover. With a revised English translation and copious explanatory notes by Joseph Loewy and Joseph Guens. Illustrations reproduced from... drafts of M. Kunstadt. Budapest, Schlesinger, Jos.
64 p. 31 cm.

no date

30. סדר הגדה של פסח עם העתקת עברי טייטש . . . ועם פירוש ומשלים מהרב המ"מ מדובנא על עברי טייטש, עם . . . ציורים . . . ניו יארק, י. ספירשטיין.

32 p. 22 cm.

no date

31. הגדה של פסח ; ערצעהלונג פון איזראעלס אויסצוג אויס עגיפטען פיר דיאביידען ערש־טען אבענדע דעס פסח־פעסטעס, מיט איינער ד״יטשען איבערזעטצונג אונד איללוסטראטיא־נע׳

Hagada. Wien, M. Hirschler & Sohn. [32] p. 21 cm.

Without German translation.

Editors and Translators

Alexander, A. 1
Fürstenthal, R. J. 9
Guens, Joseph 29
Koenigsberger, B. 22
Landau, M. I. 7
Lask, I. M. 28
Loewy, Joseph 29
Spitzer, Salomon 21
היידנהיים, וואלף 3

Illustrators

Kunstadt, M. 29
Livni, Z. 28

Commentaries

חקת הפסח 4
מעשה אלפס, מאת בן־ציון אלפס 25
מעשה חכמים 25
משלי יעקב, מאת יעקב מדובנא 15, 19
ספורי הפלאות, מאה משה מזאלישין 15
ספורי יציאת מצרים, מאת משה מזאלישין 15, 19
ספורי נפלאות, מאת משה מזאלישין 18

Commentators

אליעזר בעל מעשה רוקח 13
אלפס, בן־ציון 25
יעקב מדובנא 15, 16, 18, 19, 20, 30
משה מזאלישין 15, 18, 19
שאול אמסטרדם 13
שמעון בן צמח דוראן (רשב״ץ) 3

Translations

English 1, 6, 14, 24, 26, 28, 29
German 7, 9, 12
Judeo-Arabic 4
Judeo-German (including Yiddish and German in Hebrew characters) 3, 5, 8, 11, 13, 15, 16, 18, 19, 20, 25, 30
Polish 21

Places of Publication

Berlin 22
Budapest 29
Calcutta 4
Cracow 21
Kolomea 10
Lemberg 5, 8, 18
London 1, 6
New York 12, 19, 23, 24, 25, 26, 27, 30
Prague 7, 9
Tarnow 13
Tel Aviv 28
Vienna 2, 3, 11, 14, 15, 17, 31
Vilna 16, 20

Amplifications, corrections and/or variants to Yaari

Yaari 119 (1741)
Full text and collation

הגדה סדר של פסח, דאש מוז מן ווישן דאש איין מצוה איז אונטר דענן מצות דיא אונז קינדר ישראל גיבאטן האט דאש מן זאל אונזרי קינדר דיזי נאכט ארצילן פון יציאת מצרים וואש אונז הש״י האט פר ניסים ונפלאות גיטאן וויא ער אונז אויז לנד מצרים האט ארויז גצוגין אלז וויא דא שטיט אין פסוק (והגדת לבנך ביום ההוא) דאש איז טייטש דוא זאלשט דיינן קינ־דר זאגן וואש דא איז גשעהן איז אונזר עלטרן דא זיא אויז גאנגן זיין אויז מצרים. פון דעשט וועגן הבן אונזרי חכמים די הגדה מתקן גווזן צו זאגן דיזי נאכט. ווייל אבר בעונות הרבים אין דען דור דז מיינשט לייט מנש פרשונן ניקש פר שטינן מכל שכן ווייבר אונ׳ קינדר די פר שטינן פשיטא ניקש אונ׳ ווייל דיא עיקר מצוה איז דיא הגדה צו פר שטין וואש גשעהן איז : דרום האבן מיר גטראכט, אונ׳ דיא הגדה פון לשון הקודש אויף טייטש גבראכט. דרום זאל איין איטליכר דרינן לייאן. דר ווערט זיך ערפרייאן. בזכות זה ובא לציון גואל אמן.

פיורדא, בשנת כל המרבה לספר ביציאות מצ־
רים לפ"ק [1741]
[1], 16 l. illus. 32 cm.
Judeo-German translation up to במתי חד and אחד מי יודע, אדיר הוא ; also מעט גדיא Includes also פירוש אברבנאל and פירוש על פי הסוד Without printer on t.p.

Yaari 255 (1794)
שנת בקשו פניו לפ"ק instead of תקנ"ד

Yaari 341 (1806)
Same as variant listed by Ben-Menahem in *Sinai*, no. 5, but different pagination: [1] 47 l. instead of [1] 46 [1] l.

Yaari 388 (1815)
עם פירוש אשכנז instead of עם פירש אשכנז
[1] 23–36 l. instead of 15 l.

Yaari 530 (1833)
Full text and collation

סדר ההגדה לליל שמורים, מדויק היטיב ומ־
סודר יפה מאת וואלף היידנהיים. פרעסבורג,
געדרוקט בייא א. עדלען פ' שמיד, 1833.
26 l. 20 cm.
"Contract zum Verkaufe des Chametz": leaf 26.

Yaari 618 (1842)
Full text and collation

סדר הגדה של פסח... והצגנו בו גם תפלת
קבלת שבת ותפלת ערבית... ירושלים, ע"י
המדפיס ישראל בהרב אברהם ב"ק, בשנת
למען תזכור את יום צאתך מארץ מצרים כל
ימי חייך לפ"ק [1842]
[30]l. 16 cm.

Yaari 789 (1858 or 9)
First four lines of title:

סדר הגדה לליל שמורים
עם שלשה באורים יקרים...
instead of הגדה...

Yaari 887 (1864)
full text and collation

סדר ההגדה ללילי פסח, עם העתקה והוראת
הדינים והמנהגים בלשון הללנדית.
Hagadah, voordragt op de beide eerste avonden van het Paasch-feest, in het nederduitsch vertaald en met vele ophelderingen voorzien door G. A. Parser. Amsterdam, I. Levisson, 5624—1864.
102, iv p. 19 cm.

Yaari 899 (1864)
[2] l., 64 p., 1 l., instead of [2] l., 63 p., [1] l.

Yaari 937 (1865)
homiletischer instead of homiletischen. 52 l., 9 p. instead of 63, 9 p.

Yaari 945 (1866)
30 (i.e. 36) l. instead of 30 l.

Yaari 1019 (1870)
Full text and collation

סדר מרבה לספר והוא הגדה של פסח.
Vortrag für die beiden Abende des Uiberschreitungsfestes mit Beifügung aller Gebräuche. Ganz neu in's Deutsche übersetzt von M. I. Landau. Prag, G. Schmelkes, 1870.
63 p. illus. 19 cm.

Yaari 1042 (1872)
63 p. instead of 32 l.

Yaari 1091 (1875)
שנת אשירה נא לידידי לפ"ק instead of תרל"ה

Yaari 1135 (1878)
Full text and collation

קצור הגדה לליל פסח,
Family service for the eve of Passover, Hebrew and English, by M. Jastrow. Philadelphia, 1878. 27 p. 20 cm.
Hebrew text abridged.

* Yaari 1236 (1884)
ולשמך אזמרה לפ"ג instead of תרמ"ד

Yaari 1285 (1887)
London, Ann Abrahams & Son.
39 l., 41–49 p. instead of 44 l.

Yaari 1290 (1887)
שנת אמרות טהורות לפ"ק instead of תרמ"ז

Yaari 1338 (1889)

78 p. instead of 73 p.

Yaari 1438 (1893–5654)

114 l. instead of 112 l.

Yaari 1562 (1899)

33 l. instead of 53 l.

Yaari 1631 (1903)

[24], 56 l. instead of 46, 112 p.

Yaari 1655 (1904)

תרס״ד instead of שנת בונה ירושלים ה׳ לפ״ק

Yaari 1663 (1904)

תודת שנת זאת חקת הפסח לפ״ג instead of תרס״ד

Yaari 1714 (1906)

ליל התקדש חג instead of סדר ליל התקדש חג
תרס״ו instead of שנת אסתר המלכה לפ״ק

Yaari 1736 (1907)

144 p. or 72 l., instead of 114 p.

Yaari 1777 (1910)

תר״ע instead of בשנת שירה לה׳ נסי לפ״ק

Yaari 1800 (1911)

34 l. 23 cm.

Yaari 1969 (1923)

Full text and collation

סדר הגדה לחג הפסח עם פירוש. . . לב שמח, חברו חנוך העניך אבד״ק אלעסק. . . זלאטשוב, נ. א. וואגשאהל, תרפ״ג [1923]

64 l. 24 cm.

Yaari 2210 (1935)

תורת instead of תודת

Yaari 2691 (1958)

full text and collation

סדר הגדה של פסח.

The Haggadah of Passover; line by line with a new translation into English by Saadyah Maximon and a supplement on the story of Passover by Charles B. Chavel. Illustrated by Siegmund Forst. New York, Shulsinger Bros. [1958]

63, 32 p. illus. 32 cm.

Added t.p.: A supplement to the Haggadah of Passover: Passover, the timeless story of Israel's oldest festival... by Charles B. Chavel...

PRIVILEǦOS DEL PODEROZO REY KARLO [*1740*]; A NEAPOLITAN CALL FOR THE RETURN OF THE JEWS, AND ITS LADINO TRANSLATION

YOSEF HAYIM YERUSHALMI

Harvard University

During a recent stay in Madrid I had the good fortune to acquire an exemplar of the original printed charter issued in 1740 by Charles IV, king of the Two Sicilies, inviting the Jews to return to the Neapolitan and Sicilian territories. I confess that, at the time, I regarded this purchase merely as an opportunity to enhance my collection with a rather choice item. Beyond that I would perhaps have a good story to tell to friends, of how I had found the document in an unlikely place, and had bought it at a bargain price.

It was only upon returning to Cambridge that I became aware of another item directly related to my new acquisition, which has impelled me to write the present study. By the kind of coincidence which sometimes warms the heart of a bibliophile, it turned out that the Houghton Library at Harvard University possesses an excessively rare Ladino translation of that very charter of Charles IV, printed in the same year. While I shall describe and analyze both the original and the translation, the latter is of special interest. It offers us, not only an intriguing addition to Ladino bibliography, but a curious sidelight on the events themselves.

The Recall of the Jews to the Kingdom of the Two Sicilies

In the wake of the Spanish Expulsion the Jews were expelled from the island of Sicily on January 12, 1493, and from the kingdom of Naples in

May of 1551. Henceforth no official Jewish residence was tolerated in either place. Toward the very end of the seventeenth century, it is true, a mild attempt was made to grant licenses to some Jews to come and trade in Naples, but the few who arrived were expelled in 1702 and again in 1708.[1]

The only serious effort at the resettlement of the Jews occurred after the end of Spanish domination over Naples and Sicily and their union under Charles IV of Bourbon in the so-called Kingdom of the Two Sicilies. Preparations were begun in 1739. The Marchese di Salas, charged with the execution of the plan, had a study made of the legal status of the Jews in the Venetian, Roman, and Tuscan territories, consulted learned theologians, and even had a few Jews brought from Leghorn to answer questions concerning Jewish religion, commerce, and relations to converts.[2] On February 3, 1740, the recall of the Jews to the Kingdom of the Two Sicilies was officially proclaimed in the charter which is the object of our present concern.

Though it has been characterized as "hedged about by numerous restrictions in a bigoted medieval spirit,"[3] the charter of Charles IV is very much an eighteenth-century document, suffused with the mercantilistic theories of the age as they were applied to the Jews. The interest of the king is clearly reflected in the charter itself. He wanted to attract Jews because he shared the widespread belief that they would enrich the country by their economic activities. It was a belief which had been fostered by the Jews themselves since the seventeenth century in arguments that sometimes fell on willing ears. If mercantilistic theory predicated the welfare of the state on increasing its wealth through commerce, the Jews, it was urged, are par excellence the commercial leaven that was required. This had been the argument of the Venetian rabbi Simone Luzzato when he pleaded for toleration of the Jews in his famous *Discorso circa il stato de gl'Hebrei* of 1638. It was in the forefront of Manasseh ben Israel's *Humble Addresses* to Oliver Cromwell asking for the readmission of the Jews to England, and beginning, significantly, not with theological or humanitarian arguments, but with a chapter on "How Profitable the Jewes Are." It was at the heart of John Toland's pamphlet of 1714 on *Reasons for Naturalizing the Jews in Great Britain and Ireland on the Same Foot with Other Nations* ("What a paltry fisher town was Leghorn, before the admission of the Jews? What a loser is Lisbon, since they have been lost to it?").[4]

It is unnecessary, of course, to assume that Charles IV was even aware of these and similar works. Such theories were "in the air" in the eighteenth century. Charles must have known, however, that the Jewish resettlement in France since the sixteenth century, beginning with Marranos who had kept a Christian façade, but by now openly Jewish, was due to a policy based on the economic advantage to be derived from the presence of these "marchands portugais." And in Italy there was always the example of Leghorn itself, whose thriving commercial life was attributed not only by Toland, but by many others, to the presence of a dynamic Jewish community. Naples and Sicily, lagging far behind the rest of Italy in economic development, might well appear in the king's eyes to require an infusion of Jewish merchants in order to revive their former vitality.

That such considerations were indeed uppermost in Charles' mind may be seen from his preamble to the charter of 1740. After avowing the divine obligation of a sovereign to procure the welfare of his people, he continues:

> Because of which, having clearly recognized the distress in which our beloved peoples, residing in our kingdoms and states, find themselves; and that this originates principally in the lack of Commerce which, for various reasons, is debilitated and destroyed among our same most dear peoples, no less between citizens as between natives and foreigners; We have therefore, with supreme care and diligence, applied the greatest attention of our Royal heart to seek the appropriate and valid means to revive and cause trade to flourish in all our kingdoms and states, both internal as well as external.
>
> And since, by the felicitous experiences of other Christian and Catholic princes in their states, it has been discerned clearly by one and all that the Hebrew Nation, which is uniquely and totally devoted to commerce, is a sufficiently proper instrument to make the peoples, who are badly instructed therein, to learn the true arts through which impetus is given to navigation and extends itself from one region to the other, however remote and distant, for such reason, following the example and footsteps of other wise and pious Catholic Princes, we have determined and resolved to introduce and admit the Hebrew Nation into our kingdoms and states, conceding to all the Merchants, and to other Hebrew persons living, whether in the West or in the East, or in any country whatever, without any exception, by virtue of our Letters Patent, the graces, privileges, immunities, franchises, exemptions and prerogatives recorded below. . . ."[5]

Though the preamble speaks blandly of "the felicitous experiences of other Christian and Catholic princes," a close examination of the articles which follow reveals the pervasive influence of one particular place: Leghorn. There can be no question but that the details of Charles' charter were derived, and in many instances incorporated almost verbatim, from the charter issued for Pisa and Leghorn on July 10, 1593 by Ferdinand I, Grand Duke of Tuscany.[6] That epoch-making proclamation, which turned Leghorn into a free port and laid the foundations for its subsequent growth and prosperity, had invited for settlement "Merchants of whatever Nation, Easterners and Westerners, Spaniards, Portuguese, Greeks, Germans, Italians, Hebrews, Turks, Moors, Armenians, Persians, and others." Significantly, however, most of the provisions were specifically relevant to the Jews alone, according them a range of privileges and liberties unknown in any other part of Italy. It is only when we realize the close connection between Charles IV's Neapolitan charter of 1740, and that of Ferdinand de' Medici almost a century and a half before, that we understand the project itself. Charles wanted for Naples and Sicily what had been achieved for Leghorn, and he was willing to use the same means to bring it about.[7] The visit to Naples of the Jewish delegation from Leghorn, to which we alluded above, was thus obviously the result of more than a random choice. They had been summoned to provide information on their life and legal status, while the charter was still being deliberated, because Leghorn was to be the model for Naples in every respect. They, in turn, could not have missed the opportunity to impress on Charles that if he wished his kingdom to attain the commercial eminence of their city by attracting the Jews, he must be prepared to offer them comparable inducements. This the charter of 1740 certainly did, and in describing the document we shall take note of the parallels.

The Italian Original

The charter was printed in Italian and sent to the Neapolitan agents, representatives, and ambassadors abroad. We know definitely that copies reached Paris, Strasbourg, Metz, Bordeaux, Ancona, Rome, Mantua, and Ferrara.[8] For bibliographical purposes the document may be described as follows:

> [Arms of Charles IV]/ CARLO/ PER LA GRAZIA DI DIO,/ RE DELLE DUE SICILIE, / DI GERUSALEMME, & c. / *Infante delle Spagne, Duca di Parma, Piacenza,/ Castro & c. Gran Principe Ereditario/ di Toscana & c./* Proclama, o vero Banno, con il quale si concede/ alla Nazione Ebrea un Salvocondotto, perche/ possa venire a trafficare, ed a stabilire il/ suo Domicilio nelli Regni delle due/ Sicilie, e loro dipendenze./ [11 lines of the text follow immediately, beginning with a woodcut initial].
>
> 27 1/2 X 20 cm. 6 fols., unpaginated, last side blank. Signatures: A, A_2, A_3.
> Dated at end: ". . . Napoli a di 3. Fe-/Braro 1740./ (L.S.) CARLO./ *Giuseppe Giovachino di Montealegre.*

The text itself, following the preamble we have quoted, consists of 37 articles of varying length. A summary of their contents will demonstrate

CARLO

PER LA GRAZIA DI DIO, RE DELLE DUE SICILIE, DI GERUSALEMME, &c.

Infante delle Spagne, Duca di Parma, Piacenza, Caſtro &c. Gran Principe Ereditario di Toſcana &c.

Proclama, o vero Banno, con il quale ſi concede alla Nazione Ebrea un Salvocondotto, perche poſsa venire a trafficare, ed a ſtabilire il ſuo Domicilio nelli Regni delle due Sicilie, e loro dipendenze.

NOn meno per li dettami impreſſi nel fondo degli animi noſtri, che per l'eſpreſſe Divine leggi, le quali da ogn' uno ſi poſſono oſſervare nelle Sagre Scritture, la maggiore, e più indiſpenſabile obbligazione di qualunque Sovrano, conſiſte nel procurare con ogni ſtudio, e diligenza la ſalute, il vantaggio, ed il benefizio delli Popoli commeſſi alla ſua cura dalla Divina Providenza: Per la qual coſa, avendo Noi chiaramente conoſciuto le ſtrettezze, nelle quali generalmente ſi trovano coſtituiti li noſtri dilettiſſimi Popoli Abitatori delli noſtri Regni, e Stati; e che queſte principalmente naſcevano

A dalla

that, considering the time and place, the concessions to the Jews were by no means inconsiderable, and in some respects quite remarkable:[9]

I. Full safe-conduct is given to all Jewish merchants and other Jews to come to the king's realms, whether temporarily or for settlement, with or without their families, for a period of fifty years dating from January, 1740. At the end of that time a grace period of five years is granted, during which the Jews may liquidate their assets and recover their debts, in whatever form they desire. Ships, horses, and carriages will be provided for their departure. They may take with them all their goods, assets, and Hebrew books. All efforts will be made to secure free passage for them through territories of other princes, whether by land or by sea.[10]

II. In an obvious, albeit oblique, reference to the Marranos, the king notes that in the past it frequently occurred that when Jews came from their countries of origin into new lands, some people, motivated by envy, hatred, or excessive zeal, accused them of "enormous and grave crimes and misdeeds." Inquiries were made into their former lives when they feigned to be Christians. In order to remove any occasion for denunciations which may place the lives of such Jews in jeopardy, and following the example of such Catholic states as Ferrara, Venice, and Florence, the king promises that should any Jews be accused of having committed those crimes in another country, he will not permit any minister, magistrate or tribunal to molest them.[11] Moreover, the same will obtain for any criminal or civil case pending in another land.[12] All the aforementioned Jews and their families are assured the free exercise of the ceremonies, rites, ordinances and customs of their Hebrew law. Jews are, however, prohibited from engaging in usury.

III. All Jews are exempt from the jurisdiction of the Consuls of the Arts. Litigation between a Jew and a Christian shall be adjudicated by special judges appointed by the king.

IV. Those Jews who establish their domicile in the kingdom are to enjoy, with regard to both domestic and foreign trade, the same privileges and immunities as the other citizens of the city in which they live. Jews who merely visit the kingdom on temporary business are to be accorded the privileges enjoyed by the most favored foreign nations.

V. All household goods and personal effects, no matter where they were bought, are free of all taxes and customs duties, general laws to the contrary notwithstanding.[13]

VI. The Jews shall have a Delegate in the city of Naples, and two in Sicily (at Palermo and Messina). Those at Naples and Palermo shall be members of the Tribunal of Commerce. They shall judge all cases between Jew and Christian, as well as those between Jews which involve major penalties graver than imprisonment or exile. All other cases between Jews are to be judged by their own officials (*massari*). Appeals can be brought before the crown.

VII. If Jews have sexual relations with Christians, Turks or Moors, they shall be judged by their Delegate, with the fines increasing upon each offense.[14]

VIII. If any Jew be falsely sued or accused, his adversary shall have to indemnify him for any expenses, damages, or interest he may have suffered.[15]

IX. Should any accident befall a Jew so that he be bankrupt and remain in debt, the merchandise, letters of credit, and other goods belonging to his business correspondents shall not be disturbed, detained or confiscated.[16]

X. If the Jews are not pleased to have the dowries of their wives accorded the same status as those of the women of the realm, they may have them continue to be treated according to the laws of the places from which they came.[17]

XI. Anyone who impounds Jewish merchandise must justify the action within one month or release the goods.[18]

XII. Any pledge or security given by a Jew must be held by the officials of the city, even over the protests of the other party.

XIII. The Jews may possess any books, printed or in manuscript, whether in Hebrew or in other languages, provided that they are reviewed by their Delegates.[19]

XIV. Jewish doctors, whether physicians or surgeons, can treat any person who wishes to submit to their cure. However, in treating a Christian patient, either a Christian doctor must also be present, or the Jew must swear before the Delegate of the Jews that, when called to a Christian who is critically ill, he will clearly warn the sick man, his family, and all those present of the danger.[20]

XV. A Jew can receive the doctorate at faculties of medicine in the form and manner practiced at Pisa, Padua and Rome, on condition that the degree is awarded behind closed doors without pomp or sensation, and that he take the Hippocratic Oath.[21]

XVI. When forty families shall have settled in Naples, Palermo or Messina, they shall be permitted to open a synagogue. In other towns the required number shall be twenty, and until that is reached, they shall remain within the jurisdiction of the synagogue in the nearest of the aforementioned three cities. The synagogues shall be built on plots enclosed by walls. They shall not be built with magnificent exteriors.[22] All Jews must be registered in the books of the Delegates.

XVII. Should a Jew die without heirs, he may leave his property to whomsoever he desires. In the absence of a will, the Jewish officials shall dispose of it according to Jewish law and custom.[23]

XVIII. All important business transactions must be attested by a written contract signed by buyer and seller, and authenticated by a notary or by witnesses. Such formalities are not required for ordinary and minor transactions.[24]

XIX. The business records of Jews shall be accorded the same confidence as those of other merchants and artisans.[25]

XX. The Jews shall not be disturbed on Sabbath days, nor on their other festivals, provided that at the beginning of each year the Jewish officials shall provide the Hebrew calendar in Italian, which will then be posted at the customshouses and other appropriate places.[26]

XXI. The officials of the Jewish synagogues shall have authority to judge and impose penalties according to Jewish law in all civil and criminal cases between Jews, without interference from the Delegates, up to and including the penalty of imprisonment or exile. If the Jew feels he has been unjustly condemned he may appeal to the royal authority. Cases involving more severe penalties must come before the Delegates, and appeals from their sentences may be brought before the Supreme Magistrates of Commerce.[27]

XXII. No one shall dare take away or accept a Jew below the age of thirteen for baptism. Beyond that age it is licit, and the convert is entitled to his due inheritance from his Jewish parents after they have died.[28]

XXIII. Jews may own slaves, provided they are not Christian. Should a Turkish or Moorish slave of a Jew become a Christian, he is to be set free, and his owner is to be indemnified with a just price.[29]

XXIV. Butchers may not raise their prices for meat sold to Jews. The Jews may open their own slaughterhouse for their own use. The Jewish slaughterer, or his agent, may import animals, paying the same tax as other citizens.[30]

XXV. Jews have the same privileges as all native merchants and can engage in all commercial arts. They must not, however, peddle old goods in the city. Still, they may buy and sell such goods privately in their own shops and homes. Jews are not obliged to wear any sign distinguishing them from others. They can buy immovable property, except fiefs and other rights which would give them authority over Christians.[31]

XXVI. Jews, whether domiciled or visitors, have the same right as citizens or members of favored nations to bear all licit arms, to wit: a sword within the city, a long pistol while traveling, and a shotgun for hunting.[32]

XXVII. In cases brought before the Delegates, Sub-delegates and other officials, Jews are expected to pay the same court fees as others.[33]

XXVIII. All captains of the guards and soldiers are to carry out the orders of the Delegates and Sub-delegates, as well as of the Jewish officials, in affairs concerning the Jews, with no payment other than that which is customary.[34]

XXIX. As stated earlier, the charter is valid for fifty years. At the end of this time, if they are not told to leave, the privileges are automatically renewed for fifty years more.[35]

XXX. In any city or place where Jews live they may buy one or more fields in which to bury their dead. These shall be enclosed by walls. Anyone who desecrates a Jewish cemetary shall be punished.[36]

XXXI. Once they have paid the customs and other taxes, both the persons and the merchandise of the Jews and their associates coming from abroad are assured protection from any molestation even without an explicit safe-conduct.[37]

XXXII. Jews shall not be required or coerced to give lodging to soldiers or to support them with any of their goods.[38]

XXXIII. No one may presume to annoy or molest Jews, and those who do so shall be severely punished.[39]

XXXIV. Jews may hire Christian nurses for their children, but such nurses cannot live in the home except by special permit. Jews may employ Christian servants, males over the age of 25, and females over 35. These too cannot live in the house except by special permit.[40]

XXXV. At the port of Naples six storehouses are to be set aside for the Jews, free of rent. In other ports similar provisions are to be made according to the proportion of Jews and their share in commerce.

XXXVI. The first forty families to settle in Naples, Palermo, and Messina, and the first twenty in other places, shall constitute themselves as a council from which their board of officials is to be elected.

XXXVII. All the above articles are to be observed in good faith, and they are always to be interpreted in favor of the Jews. The provisions of the charter supercede all contrary laws, statutes and usages.[41]

The Ladino Translation

Shortly after the charter was printed, some copies must have reached Constantinople. There it was translated from Italian into Judeo-Spanish (Ladino), and was published in the same year.

This translation is, in the first place, of the very highest bibliographical interest. Its rarity is attested by the fact that it has remained unknown to bibliographers. It is not to be found in Kayserling's *Biblioteca*,[42] nor in any bibliography of Ladino. More significantly, it is not even listed in Abraham

פריוויליג'וש

דיל פודירוזו ריי

קארלו

ריי די לאס טיירראס אי סיפֿאראדים אינמינטאדאס אין איסטי קואדירנו ·
אנדי פור גראסייא דיל דייו דה ליסינסייא קי וינגאן אה מוראר גודייוס אין
טודאס סוס טיירראס קון סוס בואינוס פריויליג'וס אסיגוראדוס אי בעה״י סון
ביין אסיגוראדוס קי לה פאלאברה די איל ריי נו סי רימודה די נינגון מודו :
קי טאנביין איסטה קון אינקומינדאנסה די פרוקלאמה או בירו באנדו · קידי
דיזיר קון גזרות וחרמות · אי סיירטו קי איס דיל דייו ב״ה קי מונג'וס דיזיאן
אמוראר אין איסטאס טיירראס פורקי סון מויי בואינאס בינדינג'אס די פרוטו
אי סינבראדו אי פארה טודו מודו די טראטו פורקי איסטה אין מידייו דיל
מונדו אנדי די לה אונה פארטי איסטה סירקה די טורקייא · קי איס
לישוס די אבלונייא טריזי אוראס פור מאר ·· די זלת אוטרה פארטי איסטה
סירקה די אפריקה שיפינטה מילייאס לישוס · די אוטרה פארטי סירקה די לה
איטאלייא טודה · פור מאר אי טיירה קון שי קירי אינפורמאר בירא אין לה
קארטי די לה גאוגראפייא ·

שי קופיאין דילה מיזמה דילה איטאלייאנה אקי אין קושטאנטינה

איסטאנפאדו אין

קושטאנדינא

בדפוס הח״ר יונה המדפיס

שנת השקיפה ממעון קדשך לפ״ק

in Conſtantinople

Yaari's superb and comprehensive bibliography of the Hebrew press in Constantinople, which records not only Hebrew but also Ladino imprints.[43] The Harvard copy is at present the only one known to exist.[44]. It bears a new frontispiece which, as will be immediately obvious, is not present in the Italian original:

> **פריויליג׳וש/** דיל פודירוזו ריי/ **קארלו/** ריי די לאס טייראש אי סיב׳דאדיס
> אינמינטאדאס אין איסטי קואדירנו./ אנדי פור גראסייא דיל דייו דה ליסינסייא קי
> וינגאן אה מוראר ג׳ודייוש אין/ טודאש סוש טייראש קון סוש בואינוש פריוויליג׳וש
> אסיגוראדוש אי בעה״י שון/ ביין אשיגוראדוש קי לה פאלאב׳רה די איל ריי נו סי
> דימודה די נינגון מודו./ קי טאנביין איסטה קון אינקומינדאנסה די פרוקלאמה או
> ב׳ירו באנו. קירי/ דיזיר קון גזרות וחרמות. אי סיירטו קי איש דיל דייו ב״ה קי
> מונג׳וס דיזיאן/ אמוראר אין איסטאש טייראש פורקי סון מויי בואינאש בינדיג׳אש
> די פ׳רוטו/ אי סינבראדו אי פארה טודו מודו די טראטו פורקי איסטה אין מידיין
> דיל/ מונדו אנדי די לה אונה כארטי איסטה סירקה די טורקייא. קי איש/ ליש׳וש
> די אב׳לונייא טריזי אוראש פור מאר. די לה אוטרה פארטי אישטה/ שירקה די
> אפ׳ריקה שישינטה מילייאש ליש׳וש. די לה אוטרה פארטי סירקה די לה/ איטאלייא
> טודה פור מאר אי טיירה קין שי קירי אינפ׳ורמאר בירה אין לה/ קארטי די לה
> ג׳אגראפ׳ייא./ שי קופייו די לה מיזמה דילה איטאלייאנה אקי אין קושטאנטינה/
> אישטאנפאדו אין/ **קושטאנדינה/** בדפוס הח״ר יונה המדפיס/ שנת **השקיפה**
> ממעון קדשך לפ״ק/ in Constantinople.
>
> [20 X 14 cm. 6 fols., unpaginated. Text begins on verso of frontispiece. Printed in "Rashi" characters.]

Transliteration:[45]

> Privileğos del poderozo rey Karlo, rey de las tieras y sivdades enmentadas en este kuaderno, onde por grasia del Dio da lisensia ke vengan a morar ğudios en todas sus tieras kon sus buenos privileğos asegurados y *b*[*e*]-*e*[*zrat*] *h*[*a-Shem*] *y*[*itbarakh*] son bien asegurados ke la palavra de el rey no se demuda de ningun modo, ke tanbien está kon enkomendansa de proklama o vero bano, kiere dezir kon *gezerot va-ḥaramot*, y sierto ke es del Dio *b*[*arukh*] *h*[*u*] ke munchos dezean a morar en estas tieras porke son muy buenas, bendiğas de fruto y senbrado y para todo modo de trato, porke está en medio del mundo, onde de la una parte está serka de Turkia, ke es leshos de Avlonia [*sic*] treze oras por mar; de la otra parte está serka de Afrika, sesenta milias leshos; de la otra parte serka de la Italia toda, por mar y tiera. Kien se quiere informar verá en la karte [*sic*] de la ğografía. Se copió de la mizma dela italiana aki en Kushtantina. Estanpado en Kushtandina *bi-defus he-ḥ*[*akham*] *R*[*ab*] *Yonah ha-madpis, shenat HASHKIFAH mi-me 'on kodshekha li-f*[*rat*] *k*[*atan*] in Contantinople.

Translation:

> Privileges of the mighty King Charles, king of the lands and cities recorded in this pamphlet, in which, by the grace of God, he gives license that Jews come to live in all his lands, with all their good privileges assured, and *with the help of God, Blessed be He*, they are well assured that the word of the king shall not be altered in any manner, for it is also given with the commitment of a proclamation or true ban, that is to say with *decrees and sanctions*, and certainly this comes from God, *be He blessed*, for many desire to live in these lands because they are very good, blessed with fruit and grain, and for all manner of trade, since it is in the middle of the world, where from one part it is near Turkey, thirteen hours away from Avlona[46] by sea; from the other part it is near Africa, sixty miles away; from the other part it is near all of Italy, by sea and land. He who wishes to inform himself will see it in the geographical map. Copied from the Italian of the same, here in Constantinople. Printed *at the press of the sage Rabbi Jonah the printer in the year "LOOK FORTH from Thy holy habitation"* [= 1740] *according to the minor reckoning*, in Constantinople.

As the examples we shall give in the Appendix will show, the text of the charter is translated fully and accurately. Undoubtedly the close kinship of Italian and Spanish facilitated this, to the degree that occasionally the Italian form of a word is unwittingly retained. Being in Judeo-Spanish, the normal number of Hebrew words are, of course, also present. Only at times is there a slight interpretation placed on the meaning of the Italian original, in order to make it more obvious. The most interesting example occurs in Article II, which assures the Jews that they will not be prosecuted for having feigned to be Christians elsewhere. This was naturally of supreme interest to Sephardic Jews, and especially to the many former Marranos among them. Thus, where the Italian text merely states that in the past certain persons have sought "to cause to *inquire* against the aforesaid Jews," the Ladino translation states more explicitly: "to cause the *Inquisition* to *torture* them."[47]

We have no way of knowing the precise circumstances under which the translation was published, though its purpose is clear. Ladino was the vernacular of masses of Sephardic Jews in the Ottoman Empire, and only in such a translation could the charter be widely publicized among them. But was it translated at the instigation of Neapolitan agents in the Turkish capital? Or was it done on the initiative of some enterprising Jews, eager to explore the new vistas which it seemed to open? Of this the Ladino pamphlet reveals nothing.

Nor does it record the name of the translator. It does, however, give us the name of the printer, and he is a personage concerning whom, thanks to Yaari's researches, we now know a great deal.

Jonah b. Jacob Ashkenazi, originally from Galicia, became the greatest Constantinopolitan Hebrew printer of the eighteenth century. The press he founded in 1710, and which was continued by his sons and grandson until 1778, made of Constantinople a world center of Jewish printing in that period. Most significant for us is the fact that in the decade and a half prior to his death in 1745, R. Jonah published, not only Hebrew books, but a series of important works in Ladino. Indeed, Yaari credits him with a major share in the revival of Ladino, and in laying the foundations for modern Ladino literature.[48]

But perhaps here we also have a clue as to the translator of the charter of Charles IV. Apart from the *Privileğos,* R. Jonah published thirteen other books in Ladino.[49] Of these, six were original works and seven were translations. All the seven Ladino translations were the work of the same man: Abraham ben Isaac Assa.[50] It would seem that he was the "house translator" for R. Jonah's press. This being so, one is tempted to suggest that he was also the translator of the charter. However, all of Abraham Assa's known Ladino translations were made from Hebrew texts, and since we have no proof that he knew Italian, our identification must remain tentative.

Aftermath

The historical value of the Ladino pamphlet lies in its being the only actual document of Jewish response to the charter available. The words of its frontispiece show that, at least in some Jewish quaretrs, there was considerable excitement about the project. From other sources we hear of the arrival of English, French, Dutch, German, and Italian Jews in the Kingdom of the Two Sicilies.[51] However, the glowing hopes of the king, and whatever Jewish enthusiasm had been aroused, were soon to be dashed to the ground. The experiment ended in total failure. It had really been doomed before it began.

For Charles had either naively or deliberately ignored two crucial factors: the fanaticism of the clergy, and the rank prejudice of public opinion. The truly sweeping privileges contained in the charter were bound to bring both to a pitch of hysteria, and Charles was soon to learn that Naples was, after all, not Leghorn.

Even while the charter was being deliberated some alarm had been expressed from Rome and from Spain. Once it was published, a storm of protest broke out within the kingdom itself, constantly fanned from abroad. An anonymous and vicious pamphlet, attacking Jews, Judaism and the charter, appeared almost immediately. In 1742, as the clamor began to mount, immigration was halted. The next year, under coercion from the Archbishop of Naples, many clauses in the charter were severely qualified. The mob continued to be inflamed by harangues from the pulpits. By February the twenty Jewish families who had settled in Naples were reduced to four or five.

The king had necessarily bowed to the pressures upon him from every quarter, but he would still be derided as "Infans Carolus Iudaeorum" until every one of the few remaining Jews was banished from the kingdom. Still, it was not until September 18, 1746 that the formal edict of expulsion was promulgated.[52] The reasons set forth in the edict were more propaganda than fact, obviously intended to placate the masses. Blame for the expulsion was heaped entirely on the Jews themselves. The privileges of 1740, so the edict stated, had been given in good faith, but the king had been disillusioned in his hopes. The few Jews who had come arrived without funds, capital, credit, or any talent for commerce save their avidity to enrich themselves through inordinate usury and other illicit means. The instability of their fortunes has always originated in their despicable conduct, as have the variable laws of sovereigns which have been issued, sometimes in favor and sometimes to the detriment of a nation which clings too much to its superstitions, and which cannot long coexist without prejudice to human society. In view of the notorious inconvenience to commerce, to order, to religion, to the quiet and edification of the citizens of the realm, deriving from the pernicious residence of the Jews, they are to depart within nine months. The king added that no one must molest them, under threat of severe punishment. The charter of 1740 having been annulled, nothing further was said concerning means of transportation or safe-conduct through other countries. The experiment begun six years earlier was ended, as abruptly as it had been initiated. Nothing, in essence, had changed. Against the millennial background of Italian Jewish history, the recall of the Jews to the Kingdom of the Two Sicilies is no more than a minor and abortive episode. Its failure may serve as a vivid reminder of the intransigence of anti-Jewish attitudes in the eighteenth century.

APPENDIX

The following selections have a dual purpose: to offer some examples of the Ladino translation of the charter of Charles IV, and to illustrate the dependence of the latter on the Leghorn charter of 1593. In the Ladino texts I have corrected the more obvious typographical errors.

— 1 —

Naples: Art. II

Ma perchè spesse fiate nelli trascorsi tempi si è veduto, che trapassando gli Ebrei dalle Regioni nelle quali erano nati, ed allevati, in altre Regioni, e Paesi novelli; taluni, o accietati dall'invidia della felicità de'loro traffichi, o commossi da emolazione, e da odio, o per un falso, ed inconsiderato zelo, o per altre varie passioni, e motivi, accusavano, ed accagionavano gli Ebrei nelle novelle Regioni trapassati, di delitti, e di malefici enormi, e gravi, anzi enormissimi, e gravissimi commessi atecedentemente in altri Paesi, ed in altri Stati; cercando ancora di fare inquirere contro delli sudetti Ebrei, e delle loro famiglie, come se altrove avessero menata la loro vita in abito di Cristiano, e fingendosi Cristiani, o facendosi per tali riconoscere, e nominare; Perciò per togliere Noi ogni qualunque occasione a sì fatte scandalose denuncie, ed accuse, che mettono gli Ebrei, e le loro famiglie in evidentissimo pericolo di perdere la vita, o la robba: e sequendo in ciò Noi le prudenti leggi prattiche, e costumi, che su tal proposito altre volte, ed al presente sono state praticate, e si praticano in Ferrara, in Venezia, in Firenze, e nelli Stati di altri Saggi, e Pii Principi Cristiani, e Cattolici, anche coll'approvazione della Santa Sede, e che quando entrammo gloriosamente nel possesso del Reame di Sicilia, trovammo già per espressa legge stabilito nel Porto, e nella città di Messina; Dichiariamo, che per qualunque accusa, o denuncia che si facesse contro degli Ebrei, e delle lor famiglie dimoranti, e trafficanti nelli nostri Regni, anche in nome di alcun Principe; per le quali venissero incaricati delli sopra espressi delitti commessi in altri Stati fuori delli nostri, non permetteremo, che sieno in guisa alcuna molestati, ed inquisiti da qualunque Ministro, Magistrato, Foro, o Tribunale, e sotto qualunque pretesto, o titolo: Promettendo ancora alle sudette persone Ebree, ed alle loro famiglie, le quali verranno a fissare il loro domicilio, o a trafficare nelli nostri Regni, e Stati, che saranno libere, esenti, e sicure per le persone, beni, e mercanzie loro da qualsivoglia procedura, e molestia per debiti Civili, e Criminali, che si pretendesse aver contratto fuori delli Stati nostri, delli quali debbiti, e delitti dal tempo, che saranno entrati nelli nostri Stati, e Regni, e nominati, e riconosciuti per Ebrei dalli Massari della loro Scuola dimoranti nelle Città, e Luoghi delli nostri Regni, facciamo loro libero salvocondotto, e concediamo libertà reale, e personale, non volendo, che in verun modo Giudice alcuno, Foro, Tribunale, Magistrato, ò Ministro per li sudetti pretesi debbiti, e delitti possano fare procedura, atti o sentenza alcuna in pregiudizio delli sudetti Ebrei, e delle loro famiglie, per quanto tengono cara la nostra Real grazia, e temono d'incorrere nella nostra Reale indignazione; anzi vogliamo, che se mai per errore, o per altra causa facessero il contrario, ogni loro atto, procedura, e sentenza sia *ipso jure* nulla, e di niun vigore, non ostante qualunque cosa in contrario: Concediamo perciò a tutte le antecedentemente mentovate persone, e famiglie Ebree l'uso libero in tutti li nostri Regni, e Stati delle loro Cerimonie, Riti, Ordini, e Costumi della loro legge Ebraica, purchè ciascuna di esse persone si faccia riconoscere dalli Delegati da deputarsi da Noi; proibendo però a tutti gli Ebrei, ed alle for famiglie l'esercizio dell'usure manifeste, e palliate, o in qualsivoglia modo coperte, e denominate.

Ladino

פירו פורקי מונג׳אש ויזיש סי ב׳ידו אין לוש טיינפוש פאסאדוש קי פאסאנדו לוש ג׳ודייוש די לאש שיב׳דאדיש אין קי אב׳יאן סידו נאסידוש אי קרייאדוש אה אוטראש שיב׳דאדיש אי טייראש נואיב׳אש אלגונוש או סייגוש פור לה אינבידייא די לה פ׳לישידאד די סוש ניגושייוש או מובידוש די סילו אי אודייו או פור און פ׳אלסו אי פ׳ינג׳ידה קנאה או פור אוטראש פאסייוניש אקוזאבאן אה לוש ג׳ודייוש אין לאש נואיב׳אש סיב׳דאדיש וינידוש די דיליטוש אי מאליפ׳ישייוש גראנדיש אי גראב׳יש קי אבייאן אקומיטידו אין לאש אוטראש טייראש אי אישטאדוש בושקאנדו טאנביין די אזיר קי לה אינקיסיסייון טורמינטאסי אה אילייוש אי א סוש פ׳אמייאש קומו סי אין דיג׳אש טיראש אוב׳ייסין איג׳ו שו ב׳ידה קומו קרישטייאנוש אי אזיינדושי ריקונושיר אי נומבראר פור טאליש: פור אישטו פארה קיטאר לה אוקאשייון אה אישטאש אישקאנדאלוזאש דינונשייאש אי אה קוזאש קי פוני אלוש ג׳ודייוש אי סוש פ׳אמייאש אין פיליגרו די פדריר לה וידה אי לה אזיינדה אי סיגיינדו אין איסטו נוש לאש לייש אי אוזאנשאש קי סוברי איסטי פארטיקולאר אוטראש ויזיש או אל פריזינטי סי פלאטיקארון אי סי פלאטיקאן אין פ׳יראר־ה אין ויניצייא אי אין פ׳לורינשייא אי אין איסטאדוש די אוטרוש פרינסיפיש קריסטייאנוש קון לה אפרובאסייון די לה סאנטה סידי אי קי קואנדו אינטרימוש אין איל פוסיזו דיל ריינו די סיסילייא טופימוש ייא פור דיקלארדה ליי אישטאבלישידו אין לה שיב׳דאד די מיסינה: דיקלאראמוש קי פור דינגונה אקוזה או דינונסייא קי שי איזיישי קואינטרה לוש ג׳ודייוש אי שוש פ׳אמייאש מוראנטיש או ניגושייאנטיש אין נואישטרוש ריינוש אפ׳ילו אין נומברי די אלגון פרינסיפי קי ויניסין קולפאדוש די לוש דיג׳וש דיליטוש אה קומיטידוש אין אוטרוש אישטאדוש פ׳ואירה דילוש נואישרוש נו פירמיטירימוש קי שיאן אינג׳יריאדוש די דינגון מינישטרו ני מאג׳ישטראדו פור נינגונה אישקוזה פרומיטיינדו

טאמבין אה דיג׳וש איב׳ריאוש קידאן ליבריש אי סיגורוש פור סוס פירסונאש בייניש אי מירקאנסיאס די קואלקיר מוליסטייא ני דאנייו פור דיב׳דאש סיויליש או קרימינאליס קי סי פריטינדיישי אביר איג׳ו פ׳ואירה די נואיטרוש איסטאדוש די לאש קואליס דיב׳דאש אי דיליטוש איל טיינפו קי אינטראראן אין נואיסטרוש ריינוש אי סיראן נומבראדוש ריקונוסידוש פור ג׳ודייוש די לוש ממונים די סו קהלה מוראדוריש די לאש סיב׳דאדיש די נואישטרוש ריינוש ליש אזימוש ליבריש סאלב׳ו קונדוטו אי ליש דאמוש ליבירטה ריאל אי פירשונאל נו קיריינדו קי נינגון ג׳ואיז ני בית דין או מיניסטרו פור לאש פריי־טינדידאש דיב׳דאש אי דיליטוש פואידאן אזיר אלגון דאנייו או דאר גזרה אין פריג׳ואזייו די דיג׳וש איבריאוש פור איל אמור די נואיסטרה ריאל גראשייא אי פור טימור די נו קאייר אין נואיסטרה דיסגראסייא אנטיס קירימוש קי סי פור יירו או פור אוטרה קאב׳זה איזייסין אל ׳קונטראריו טודה סו דיטירמינאשייון או אילאס או גזרה סיאה די נינגון ב׳אלור אאון קי אייגה קוזה קי לו אינפידה: קונסידימוס פור טאנטו קי אטודאש לאש דיג׳אש פ׳אמייאש איב׳ריאש איל אוזו ליברי אין טודוש נואישטרוש ריינוש די סוש סירימוניאש אי סדרים אוזאנסאש אי אורדיניש די סו ליי איב׳ראייקה קון קי קאדה אונה די דיג׳אש פירסונאש סי אגה ריקונוסיר די נואיסטרוס דיפוטאדוש פרואיביינדו אה טודוש לוש איבריאוש איל איזירסיסייו דיל רבית מאניפ׳ישטו או אין קואלקיר מודו איב־קוב׳ירטו.

Leghorn: Art. III

Vogliamo ancora, che per detto tempo non si possa esercitare alcuna inquisizione, visita, denunzia, o accusa contro di voi, e vostre famiglie, ancora che per il passato siano vissute fuori del dominio nostro in abito come Cristiani, o avutone nome, e potrete venire, stare, abitare, e conversare in detta nostra Città di Pisa, e Livorno, trafficare negli altri luoghi del Dominio nostro liberamente, e usare in essi tutte le vostre cerimonie, precetti, riti, ordini, e costumi di Legge Ebrea, o altre, secondo il costume a piacimento vostro, purchè ciascuno di voi ne faccia denunzia all'infrascritto Giudice da noi da deputarsi, come a Venezia, e Ferrara s'osserva, e proibendovi di esercitare le usure manifeste, o palliate, o in altro qualsivoglia modo.

— 2 —

Naples: Art. IX

Vogliamo ancora, che se mai accadesse qualche accidente sinistro ad alcuno Ebreo, in maniera che mancasse, fallisse, o andasse in rovina, il che Iddio non voglia, e perciò restasse Debitore; in tal caso, le mercanzie, lettere di cambio, o altre robbe, e merci spettanti alli loro Corrispondenti, e Commissionari non debbano venire aggravate, impedite, o sequestrate per detta Causa, purche si provi l'identità delle sudette cose, che appartengono alli Corrispondenti, o alli Commissionari.

Ladino

קירימוש טאמביין קי שי אקונטישיישי אלגון מקרה אה אלגון ג׳ודייו די קיב׳ריטה או שימיג׳אנטי קי דייוש נו קירה אי קידאשי דיבדור אין טאל קאזו לאש מירקאנסייאש ליטראש די קאמבייו או אוטראש רופאש אפארטיניסיינטיס אשוש קונרישפונדיינטיש נו דיואן שיר אגראבאדאש ני סיקריסטאדאש פור דיג׳ה קאבזה קון קי סי פרואיבי קי דיג׳אש קוזאש אפארטיניסיין אלוש קוריספונדיינטיש או אלוש קומיסייונארייוש.

Leghorn: Art. XIII

Se per qualsivoglia sinistro accadesse, qualcuno di voi fallisse, o andasse male, e in rovina, che Dio non voglia, e restasse debitore a'particolari, in tal caso le robe, mercanzie, lettere di cambio, o altro de'vostri committenti, e rispondenti non vogliamo che venghino aggravati, impediti, o sequestrati per detto conto, se non secondo che per gli Ordini è disposto.

— 3 —

Naples: Art. XIV

Vogliamo parimente che li Medici Ebrei, tanto Fisici, quanto Cerusici, senza altro impedimento possano medicare qualsisia persona, che voglia sottoporsi alla lor cura, con condizione però che medicando persone Cristiane, o debbano farlo in compagnia d'altro Medico, o Cerusico Cristiano, o veramente debbano aver prestato giuramento innanzi alli Delegati, o Sottodelegati della Nazione Ebrea; che nel caso, che veggano un'Infermo Cristiano in pericolo di morte, debbano chiaramente, precisamente, ed accuratamente avertire l'Infermo, e li suoi assistenti, o famiglia del pericolo in cui si ritrova costituito, acciò proveda alli bisogni della sua Coscienza, ed interessi.

Ladino

קירימוש טאמביין קי לוש מידיקוש איבריאוש טאנטו פ׳יזיקוש קומו סירוג׳אנוש סין דינגון אינפידימיינטו פואידאן קוראר קואלקיר פירשונה קי קירה פונירסי דיבאש׳ו די סו קורה קון פארטידו קי קוראנדו קריסטייאנוש דיבה סיר אין קונפאנייא די אוטרו מידיקו או ג׳יראח קריסטייאנו או דיואן דאר שבועה דילאנטרי לוש דיליגאדוש קי קואנדו מיראן און אינפ׳ירמו קריסטייאנו אין פיליגרו די מואירטי דיואן קלארה מינטי אי קון קוידאדו אקאוידאר[?] איל אינפ׳ירמו אי שוש אסיסטינטיש או פ׳אמייא דיל פיליגרו אין קי סי טופה פארה קי פרוב׳י אה איל הכרח די סו קונסינסייא אי אינטיריסיש.

Leghorn: Art. XVIII

Vogliamo che gli vostri Medici Ebrei tanto Fisichi, come Cerusichi, possino curare, e medicare non solo voi, ma ancora qualsivoglia Cristiano, et altra persona non ostante.

— 4 —

Naples: Art. XV

Permettiano ancora, che li Professori Ebrei possano dottorarsi nelle sudette facoltà mediche nella forma, e maniera, che si prattica in Pisa, Padova, ed in Roma, con condizione, che la funzione si faccia a porte Chiuse, e senza pompa, o strepito, e che nell'atto del dottorarsi debbano fare quel giuramento, che communemente si chiama d'Ippocrate.

Ladino

דאמוש ליסינסייא טאמביין קי לוש פרופיסורש איבריאוש פואידאן אדוטוראשי אין דיג׳אש פ׳אקולטאדיש מידיקאש אין לה פ׳ורמה קי שי אוזה אין פיזה פאדובה אי רומה קון פארטידו קי לה פ׳ונסייון שי אגה קון פואירטה שיראדה אי סין פונפה או איסטריפיטו קי אין טיינפו דיל אדוטוראמיינטו דיואן דאר שבועה קי שי לייאמי די אבוקראט.

Leghorn: Art. XIX

Vogliamo, che tutti i vostri, come di sopra possino studiare, e addottorarsi.

— 5 —

Naples: Art. XX

Vogliamo ancora, che li giorni del Sabbato, ed altri giorni festivi Ebraici siano a riguardo degli Ebrei feriati, nè in tali giorni si possa agitar Causa alcuna ad Essi appartenente, o sieno Attori, o sieno Rei; Con condizione però, che nel principio di ogni anno, debbano li Massari Ebrei formare il Calendario in lingua Italiana; il quale si doverà affigere nelle Dogane, e negli altri luoghi opportuni.

Ladino

קירימוש טאנביין קי לוש דייאש דיל שבת אי אוטרוש דייאש די פ׳יישטה די לוש ג׳ודייוש שיאן פארה לוש ג׳ודייוש פ׳ירייאדוש אי אין טאליש דייאש נו שי פואידה מיראר ג׳וזגו אפארטיניסיינטי אה אילייוש או שיאן אטוריש או שיאן קולפאדוש קון פארטידו פירו קי אין פרישיפייו די קאדה אנייו דיואן לוש ממונים פ׳ורמאר איל קאלינ־דארייו אין לינגואה איטאליינה איל קואל שי דיוירה אפיגאר אין לאש דואנאש אי אין אוטרוש לוגאריש אפרופייאדוש.

Leghorn: Art. XXIV

Vogliamo ancora, che i vostri giorni di Sabato, ed altri festivi Ebraici, oltre alli Feriati della Città di Firenze siano inutili, et feriati, ne si possa in tali giorni agitare, piatire, nè n pro, nè in contra di voi, o di altri ammettendoli ex nunc, e dichiarandoli feriati, et inutili.

—6—

Naples: Art. XXII

Ordiniamo, e commandiamo, che niuno ardisca di togliere agli Ebrei, o di accettare alcuno della lor famiglia maschio, o femina sotto titolo che voglia farsi Cristiano, se non passano l'età di anni tredici, conforme è stabilito, e pratticato in altri Stati Cattolici; ma passata detta età, se alcuno Ebreo maschio, o femina vorrà abbracciare la Sagro Santa Religione Cattolica, non potrà esiggere la legittima dalli lor Padri, e Madri ancor vivi; non di meno costoro non potranno per testamento, o per altro atto privarnelo, anzi venendo a morire il Padre, o la Madre, l'Erede sarà tenuto a dare la porzione debita deli'Eredità de'suddetti Padri, o Madri, al figlio già fatto Cristiano.

Ladino

אורדינאמוש אי קומאנדאמוש קי נינגונו טינגה אוזאדיאה די קיטאר ג׳ודייוש או די ריסיויר אלגונו די סו פ׳אמיאה מאג׳ו או אימברה קון איסקוזה די אזירסי קריסטייאנו סי נו פאסה לה אידאד די טריזי אנייוש סינון סי אוזה אין אוטרוש איסטאדוש קריסטייאנוש פירו פאסאדה דיג׳ה אידאד סי אלגון איב׳ריאו מאג׳ו או אימברה קירה אבראסאר לה ליי קאטוליקה נו פודרה דימאנדאר לה אירידאד די סוש פאדריש או מאדריש אאון ביב׳וש ני מינוש אישטוש פודראן פור צואה או פור אוטרו צד דיש׳ארלוש סין איללייא סינו ב׳יניינדו אה מוריר איל פאדרי או לה מאדרי איל אירידירו סירה אוב׳ליגאדו אה דאר לה פארטי דיוידה די לה אירידאד אל איג׳ו קריסטייאנו.

Leghorn: Art. XXVI

Proibendo a ciascuno dei nostri Cristiani, che non ardischino torvi, nè raccattarvi alcuno di vostra Famiglia maschio, o femmina per doversi far battezzare, e farsi Cristiano, se però non passano anni tredici di età, e quelli maggiori mentre che saranno, e staranno nelli soliti Catecumeni, o altrove alla loro quarantina per battezzarsi possino essere sovvenuti, e parlati da loro Padre, e Madre, o altri Parenti, che avessero; volendo che qualsivoglia Ebreo, o Ebrea, che si facesse Cristiano, o Cristiana, essendo figlio, o figlia di Famiglia non siano tenuti, nè obbligati il Padre, nè la Madre darli legittima, o porzione alcuna in vita loro, e che tali Battezzati non possino fare testimonianza in casi di Ebrei.

—7—

Naples: Art. XXVI

Concediamo ancora licenza agli Ebrei così trafficanti, come domiciliati in varie Città, e Luoghi, che possano come gl'altri Cittadini, e come Nazione privilegiata portare tutte le armi lecite, cioè spada in Città, pistole lunghe da sella in viaggio, e schioppi quando anderanno alla caccia, colla dovuta licenza però di coloro, alli quali spetta il concederla alli Cittadini.

Ladino

קונסידימוש לישינשייא אלוש איבריאוש קי פואידאן קומו לוש דימאש שיבדאדינוש אי קומו נאשייון פריוילִיזידאדה לייאר טודה לאש ארמאש לישיטאש ג׳ואי אישפאדה אין לה שיב׳דאד אי פישטולאש לארגאש די סייא אין וייאג׳י אי טופ׳יק קואנדו איראן אה קאסה קון לה לישינשייא פירו דילוש קי ליש אפארטיניסי איל דארלה אלוש שיבדאדינוש.

Leghorn: Art. XXX

E più vi concediamo, che tutti i Capi di casa possino portare, e usare tutte le sorte di Armi non proibite, e difensive ordinarie per tutti li Stati nostri, eccetto però nella Citta di Firenze, Siena, e Pistoia.

Notes

[1] The texts of the edicts of 1702 and 1708 are to be found in the *Nuova collezione delle prammatiche del Regno di Napoli*, vol. IV (Naples, 1804), tit. LXXVII ("De expulsione Hebraeorum, sive Judaeorum"), pramm. iv and v, pp. 101f.

[2] For these and other details see Nicola Ferorelli, *Gli ebrei nell'Italia meridionale dall'età romana al secolo XVIII* (Turin, 1915), pp. 244f.

[3] Cecil Roth, *The History of the Jews of Italy* (Philadelphia, 1946), p. 351.

[4] Luzzato's *Discorso*, available in a Hebrew translation by D. Lattes, with introductions by M.A. Schulwass and R. Bachi, as: *Ma'amar 'al yehudey Veneẓia* (Jerusalem, 1950), especially ch. IV; M. ben Israel's *Humble Addresses*, reprinted in Lucien Wolf's edition of *Menasseh ben Israel's Mission to Oliver Cromwell* (London, 1901), pp. 81ff.; Toland's *Reasons*, together with a German translation, in H. Mainusch's ed. of the text (*Gründe für die Einbürgerung der Juden in Grossbritanien und Irland* [Stuttgart, 1965]).

[5] Fol. 1r-v of the original printed charter described below. The entire charter is reprinted, though with occasional errors, in *Nuova collezione*, loc. cit., pramm. VI, pp. 102–10.

[6] Ferorelli shows no awareness of this relationship.

[7] He was not the only one to have thought of emulating the success of Leghorn in this manner. The Duke of Savoy tried, in 1648, to set up a free port at Villa Franca (Villefranche) near Nice, with special Jewish privileges, as did Genoa in the same year (Roth, *Italy*, 344, 350). Though there are some parallels, neither experiment was as thoroughgoing as that of Charles IV in 1740.

[8] Ferorelli, *op. cit.*, p. 248.

[9] In the notes which follow, all references to the parallels in Ferdinand I's charter of 1593 are to the text reprinted in the *Collezione degl'ordini municipali di Livorno, corredata delli statuti delle sicurtà, e delle più importanti rubriche delli statuti di mercanzia di Firenze* (Leghorn, 1798), pp. 237–56: "Privilegi concessi sotto dì

10. Giugno 1593. per lettere patenti a tutti i Mercanti di qualsivoglia Nazione, che si porteranno ad abitare in Pisa, e Livorno." [Abbreviated hereafter as: *Leghorn*, followed by the number of the article, of which there are forty four in all].

The same volume contains also an important documentary appendix on the subsequent laws concerning the Jews ("Regolamenti ebraici," pp. 301–36).

[10] Cf. *Leghorn*, no. I. There the term is twenty-five years, but with the same five year grace period.

[11] *Leghorn*, no. III. In *Leghorn* no. VI there is an added provision, not incorporated into the Neapolitan charter, that they may continue to assume Christian names at their own convenience: "Vi concediamo, che voi possiate trafficare... per tutte le Città... et altri luoghi delli Stati nostri, e navigare per Levante, Ponente... et altrove sotto nome vostro, e sotto nome di Cristiano, o altri, che a voi piacerà..." For the texts of Naples no. II and Leghorn no. III, see *infra*, Appendix, no. 1.

[12] *Leghorn*, nos. II, IV.

[13] *Leghorn*, no. IX.

[14] For the first offense, no more than 50 ducats; for the second, 100. Further offenses to be punished by the decision of the Delegate. Cf. *Leghorn*, no. XI, where the same sums are stated in *scudi*.

[15] *Leghorn*, no. XII.

[16] *Leghorn*, no. XIII. For the texts see *infra*, App., no. 2.

[17] Though no other details are given here, we may speculate, on the basis of the parallel clause in the Leghorn charter (no. XIV), that the question concerned both the priority of the woman's claim over other liens, and the exemption of the dowry from certain taxes. Unlike the Neapolitan charter, that of Leghorn offers no choice in submitting Jewish dowries to local regulations.

[18] *Leghorn*, no. XV.

[19] And not by the Holy Office. *Leghorn*, no. XVII, states simply: "Vi concediamo licenza, e facoltà di poter tenere libri d'ogni sorte stampati et a penna in ebraico, et in altra lingua." A later note adds: "È in osservanza compatibilmente alle regole generali di buon governo."

[20] *Leghorn*, no. XVIII, grants the permission to treat Christian patients with no restrictions whatever. For the texts see *infra*, App., no. 3.

[21] *Leghorn*, no. XIX, merely states that all may study and receive the doctorate. The texts, *infra*, App., no. 4.

[22] Cf. *Leghorn*, no. XX, where there is no mention of numbers, jurisdiction, nor the restriction on ostentation. On the other hand, there is an explicit provision that the Jews must not proselytize.

[23] *Leghorn*, no. XXI.

[24] *Leghorn*, no. XXII. No mention of witnesses.

[25] *Leghorn*, no. XXIII.

[26] *Leghorn*, no. XXIV. No mention of calendars, but this may well have been the practice at Leghorn by the eighteenth century. The texts, *infra*, App., no. 5.

[27] *Leghorn*, no. XXV, had stated the competence of the Jewish elders in general terms, and had given them the right to impose exile. Later ordinances spelled out further details. They are summarized in the law of August 5, 1650 (*Collezione degl'ordini municipali di Livorno*, pp. 304–06).

[28] *Leghorn*, no. XXVI. A vexing problem for Italian Jewry in the eighteenth century. See Cecil Roth, "Forced Baptisms in Italy," *JQR*, XXVII (1936–37), 117–36. "No-

where in Italy were the Jews so amply protected against baptism by force as they were in Leghorn" (*ibid.*, 118). For the texts see *infra*, App., no. 6.

[29] *Leghorn*, no. XXVII, has merely: "Vi concediamo che li vostri schiavi non possino avere libertà." But a later note adds: "Sono state introdotte posteriormente diverse cautele." We may assume that those subsequent provisions were of the kind now specified in the Neapolitan charter.

[30] *Leghorn*, no. XXVIII.

[31] *Leghorn*, no. XXIX, lacks the clauses concerning Jewish peddling and authority over Christians.

[32] *Leghorn*, no. XXX. The texts, *infra*, App., no. 7.

[33] *Leghorn*, no. XXXII.

[34] *Leghorn*, no. XXXIII.

[35] *Leghorn*, no. XXVI, where twenty-five years are specified.

[36] *Leghorn*, no. XXXVII. No walls are mentioned.

[37] *Leghorn*, no. XXXIX.

[38] *Leghorn*, no. XL.

[39] *Leghorn*, no. XLI.

[40] *Leghorn*, XLII, with no restrictions or qualifications. But, as a later note declares, such were added later.

[41] *Leghorn*, XLIII–XLIV.

[42] Meyer Kayserling, *Biblioteca Española-Portugueza-Judaica* (Strasbourg, 1890), does list a Portuguese translation of the charter by Francisco Xavier de Oliveira (p. 79): *Carta ao Senhor Isaac de Souza Brito com os Privilegios concedidos em Napoles e Sicilia a Naçao Hebrea, trad. do original italiano em Napoles no anno de 1740*, published in the Hague in 1741. I have not succeeded in locating a copy. Obviously Kayserling did not see one either, for he merely recorded the entry he found in Diogo Barbosa Machado, *Bibliotheca lusitana* (Lisbon, 1741–59), II, p. 296. There is, nevertheless, every indication that such a translation was actually made. Its author, who achieved fame as the "Cavaleiro de Oliveira," had been in the Portuguese diplomatic service, but became a Protestant abroad and was burned in effigy by the Lisbon Inquisition. Outspoken in his Jewish sympathies, he even urged the readmission of professing Jews to Portugal. Since he was in personal correspondence with Barbosa Machado, we may assume that the latter was well informed as to his writings. On his relations with Isaac de Souza Brito see António Gonçales Rodrigues, *O Protestante Lusitano* (Coimbra, 1950), pp. 89, 102.

[43] Abraham Yaari, *Ha-defus ha-'ibri be-Kushta* (Jerusalem, 1967).

[44] It was acquired some years ago from A. Rosenthal Ltd., Oxford, England. See the firm's *Catalogue 61: Biblioteca Sefardica*, compiled by Dr. Maurice L. Ettinghausen, no. 592, p. 35.

[45] I follow the scheme outlined in Henry V. Besso's *Ladino Books in the Library of Congress: a Bibliography* (Washington, 1963), pp. 42ff. Hebrew words are italicized, and Hebrew abbreviations are completed in square brackets.

[46] On the Western coast of Greece, which was, of course, part of the Turkish empire at the time.

[47] For the texts see *infra*, App., no. 1.

[48] Yaari, *op. cit.*, p. 46.

[49] Ibid., nos' 324, 327, 338, 340, 343, 375, 376, 379, 384, 393, 398, 399, 402. The last three

bear the names of his sons, but were printed while he was still alive and active at the press.

[50] In the decades after R. Jonah's death he published four more Ladino translations (Yaari, *op. cit.*, nos. 407, 421, 442, 457), three of them at the same press. See on him Yaari, "Abraham ben Yiẓḥak Assa u-mif-'alo ba-sifrut ha-sefaradit-yehudit," (Abraham b. Isaac Assa and his activity in Judeo-Spanish literature), *Kirjath Sepher*, X (1933–34), 378–80; XIII (1936-37), 533f.

[51] See Ferorelli, *op. cit.*, pp. 248ff.

[52] The complete text in *Nuova collezione delle prammatiche del Regno di Napoli,* IV, tit. LXXVII, pramm. vii, pp. 110f.

DYHERNFURTH AND SHABTAI BASS: A TYPOGRAPHIC PROFILE

HERBERT C. ZAFREN

Hebrew Union College—Jewish Institute of Religion, Cincinnati

The history of Hebrew typography[1] cannot yet be written. A vast quantity of bibliographic and literary data exists; and scattered in the literature of Hebrew bibliography there are facts about type, ornaments, title pages, and other typographic appurtenances. The encyclopedia articles generalize, and the monographs gather together stories, facts, notions, mistakes, theories. But when one gets right down to it, he finds that the generalizations are based more on observation and "feel" than on organization and analysis of data; that the facts, theories, and mistakes are not easily isolated from each other; that the building blocks of knowledge are scattered, blurred and unorganized. There are, of course, exceptional islands of firm information about the printing history of one place or another,[2] but so much basic work remains to be done that the general history of Hebrew typography cannot yet be written with any authority.

It is the purpose of this essay to provide reliable typographic data for a small unit of typographic history: one printer in one place. There is no special reason that Shabtai Meshorer Bass and Dyhernfurth have been selected; but it was convenient that I had access to the manuscript bibliography of this printer by Moses Marx, to whom I am indebted in many ways, and it is a manageable unit with which to try to chart a method in an uncharted field. It is, perhaps, also fitting that this first typographic survey concern itself with Shabtai Bass, the father of Hebrew bibliography. If and when a large number of printers are similarly profiled—perhaps with the data stored and made manipulatable and retrievable through the use of a computer rather than the all too limited memory of any scholar—there will be a data pool which will be able to serve the historian in ways well beyond the merely typographical.

As I envision it, a profile of a printer should be composed of the following elements:

I. A *bibliography* of the known printed works from his press—the artifacts;

II. A careful *list* of those works which were examined by the investigator so that the work may be checked and expanded by others;

III. A *bibliography* of the secondary literature on the place and printer;

IV. A *record* of all title page cuts;

V. A *record* of the type faces and sizes;

VI. A *record* of the metal ornaments;

VII. A *record* or description of the ornamental and illustrative cuts;

VIII. A *description* of other distinguishing features, if any (e.g., signatures, watermarks in the paper used, etc.); and

IX. A *listing* of special problems, with or without solutions.

Whether these elements need be, or can be, absolutely complete is open to question. At this point, I feel that categories IV and VI above should be represented by a facsimile or a reference to a readily available facsimile for each device located (because they are of potential artistic interest), that the type faces should have representative facsimiles, and that some descriptions of the illustrations may serve instead of facsimiles. After a reasonable amount of data from different times and places are published, it may be possible to develop a terminology and techniques of exact description that will obviate the necessity of publishing a full corpus of facsimiles.

The "bibliographies" enumerated above are basic but not an integral part of the profile. The rest of the record can at least be begun well before a complete bibliographical record is available; the secondary literature is meant only as a guide for further study and an eventual history. The list of the items which have been examined is most essential, because it reveals the current state of the profile. As more of the "artifacts" are examined, the profile is corrected or corroborated, and the bibliography is augmented. Thus, the profile grows more nearly complete and new data are systematically added to the old. The right time to publish is when a substantial cross-section has been studied—when the point of diminishing returns may have been reached. More experience with this kind of publication is necessary before the optimum point can be identified better. I think that this point has been reached in my study of Shabtai Bass and Dyhernfurth.

I

The bibliography of Hebrew books published by Shabtai Bass and his son is contained in another article in this volume: Moses Marx, "A Bibliography of Hebrew Printing in Dyhernfurth, 1688–1718." It should be mentioned that some of the books in that bibliography are ascribed to Dyhernfurth without certainty. These doubtfuls might, indeed, be examined closely utilizing the data presented later in this article; perhaps the doubt can thus be resolved by a more nearly certain decision in one direction or the other.

II

The following works are the artifacts that were examined closely for relevant data. All are in the Cincinnati Library of the Hebrew Union College–Jewish Institute of Religion, from whose copies the figures were made, unless otherwise noted. All are complete except as noted. The twenty-nine volumes represent close to one-fourth of the works printed by Shabtai Bass alone and with his son and seem to comprise a sufficiently large sample upon which to proceed.

אהבת עולם	1692	
בית הילל	1691	
בית יעקב	1696	
בית שמואל	1689	
ברכת המזון	1691	(Courtesy of Library, Jewish Theological Seminary of America, New York—hereafter JTSL)
דברי דוד	1689	
חכמות המספר	1712	(Courtesy of JTSL)
חקי משפט	1701	
ילקוט דוד	1691	
לב טוב	1700	(Courtesy of JTSL; lacks last leaf)
מאזני צדק	1707	(Courtesy University of California, Los Angeles; HUCL copy lacks title page)
מאמר העיתים	1694	
מגני ארץ	1692, 1702	
מים חיים	1690	
מים חיים שני	1703	(Courtesy of JTSL and Library, Hebrew Union College–Jewish Institute of Religion, New York)
מנהגים	1690	(Title page only, courtesy of Mr. A. M. Habermann, Jerusalem), 1692, 1714 (Title page only, courtesy of Rabbi H. Liberman, Rabbi Schneersohn Library of Lubawitz, Brooklyn)

מראה להתקשט בו 1693—hereafter מראה

נתיב הישר 1712 (Lacks last two leaves)

סדר היוצרות 1693? or after (Microfilm of JTSL copy at HUCL)

עיר מקלט 1690 (Lacks leaves 9–12, 17–24)

עמודיה שבעה 1693

פרקי רבי אליעזר 1693

קסת יהונתן [1697]

קרבן שבת 1691

שפתי חכמים = חמשה חומשי תורה 1693—hereafter Pentateuch

תוצאות חיים (= ר[אשית]״ ח[כמה] תוצאות חיים) 1693

III

The secondary literature on Shabtai Bass and on Dyhernfurth (of the Bass period) is not very voluminous, and it is repetitious. The standard Jewish encyclopedia articles in various languages provide the basic data, while more bibliographic data on the books with which Shabtai Bass was involved (as author, editor, or publisher) can be found in some of the references in the Marx bibliography referred to in Section I above. The following list is suggestive, not definitive; further material can be found in the literature cited in the individual items:

Bernstein, Mardoqueo. ביבליאגראפיע בכלל—ביבליאגראפיע ביי יידן און יידישע ביבליאגראפיע. In Ephim H. Jeshurin, 100 יאר מאדערנע יידישע ליטעראַ־טור... New York: Educational Committee Workmen's Circle, 1965. Pages 24–30 deal with Shabtai Bass.

Brann, Markus. *Das bibliographische Handbuch des Schabtai Bass in der lateinischen Uebersetzung Clanners*. Breslau: T. Schatzky, 1882. This appeared as an article on Manuscript 477 of the Breslauer Stadtbibliothek in *Deutscher Volks-Kalendar und Jahrbuch* 30 (Brieg, 1882): 105–117.

Brann, Markus. "Geschichte und Annalen der Dyhernfurther Druckerei." *Monatsschrift für Geschichte und Wissenschaft des Judentums* 40 (1896): 474–80, 515–26, 560–74. Mr. A. M. Habermann informs me that there is also a 34-page offprint of this series of articles.

Brilling, Bernhard. "Auras in Niederschlesien als Sitz einer jüdischen Druckerei." *Zeitschrift für die Geschichte der Juden in Deutschland* 6 (1935): 24–28. Almost exactly the same as Brilling's "Die jüdische Buchdruckerei in Auras."

Brilling, Bernhard. "Die jüdische Buchdruckerei in Auras (Niederschlesien)." In *Festschrift für A. Freimann*... pp. 97–100. Berlin: Soncino-

Gesellschaft, 1935. Concludes that some books without place or date and even some that say Dyhernfurth may have been printed by Shabtai Bass in Auras.

Erik Max. ...די געשיכטע פון דער יידישער ליטעראטור. Warsaw: Kultur-Liga, 1928. Considers Shabtai's involvement with the Bible translation into Judaeo-German, pages 233–36.

Friedberg, B. ... תולדות הדפוס העברי בערים האלה שבאירופה: ...דיהרנפורט Antwerp: 1937. Shabtai in Amsterdam: page 24. The Dyhernfurth press: pages 55–64.

Habermann, A. M. "רבי שבתי משורר בס." יד לקורא 3 (1953): 157–63. An encyclopedia-like summary, with some literature cited in footnotes.

Oelsner, Ludwig. *R. Sabbathai Bassista und sein Prozess. Nach gedruckten und ungedruckten Quellen.* Leipzig: O. Leiner, 1858.

Rabin, Israel. "Aus Dyhernfurths jüdischer Vergangenheit." (Sonderdruck aus dem *Breslauer Jüdischen Gemeindeblatt* Nr. 2 (1929). 10 p. Short, general survey of printing in Dyhernfurth.

Raphael, Isaac. "ר' שבתי באס, הביבליוגראף העברי הראשון". In his ראשונים ואחרונים. תל־אביב: אברהם ציוני, תשי"ז, pp. 169–200. This is a much expanded and partly revised version of Raphael's (Werfel's) article in סיני 8 (1941): 229–233 and 9 (1941): 373–376. A very general introduction, mostly biographical; it contains many quotations from Shabtai's introductions and other writings.

Slatkine, Mendel. ראשית בכורי הביבליוגרפיה בספרות העברית, הספר שפתי ישנים מר' שבתי משורר בס. Tel-Aviv: 1957/58.

Zafren, Herbert C. "The Value of Face Value." *Hebrew Union College Annual* 40-41 (1969-1970): 555-580. This article, among other things, delves into Shabtai Bass's personality and motivations as well as the relationship of his typographic equipment to that used in Amsterdam.

IV

The Title Pages in Wood or Metal

T[itle] p[age] 1: A woodcut characterized by an eagle spreading its wings along the lowest quarter of the woodcut.[3] It was used for Isaac Tyrnau's מנהגים in 1690.

T[itle] p[age] 2: A woodcut characterized by a man standing at the top holding two rows of musical notes.[4] Used first in 1692 for מנהגים and סדר תיקוני שבת; it was used again in 1693 for פרקי רבי אליעזר and עמודיה שבעה; in 1703 for מים חיים שני; and in 1714 for a Psalms edition and another edition of the מנהגים. Shabtai also used it for an edition of סדר היוצ־

רות, which falsely represents itself as having been printed in Amsterdam in 1692 by Uri Phoebus ben Aaron ha-Levi.[5]

T[itle] p[age] 3: Figure 1. Used first in 1692 for מגני ארץ, it was used again in 1701 (לב טוב), 1702 (מגני ארץ), and 1712 (נתיב הישר).

T[itle] p[age] 4: Figure 2. This appears only in the Pentateuch of 1693.

T[itle] p[age] 5: Figure 3.[6] This appears in the חמש מגילות section of the 1693 Pentateuch as well as in the הפטרת.

Not all of the Dyhernfurth title pages are one-piece cuts as described above. Most, in fact, are title-page borders, that is, frames made up of type ornaments set in decorative patterns. For examples of this kind of title page, see Figures 4 and 6.

T[itle] p[age] 6: Strictly speaking, the border for the broadside מראה להתקשט בו,[7] is neither a one-piece cut nor a design composed of type ornaments. It is rather four woodcuts with mitred, but seemingly unattached, joints that make up the border.

V

The Metal Types (heights measured in hundredths of an inch)

A word of caution is necessary in introduction to the type faces and sizes that were used by Shabtai Bass in Dyhernfurth. The faces have no really distinguishing names, and I have used the traditional "square" and "rabbinic" (or "Rashi") and the not so traditional "Yiddish" (for "Weiberteutsch"); the numbering is arbitrary.

Measurement of type — as indeed of ornaments and woodcuts as well — is a difficult matter. Although letters may come from the same mold and, therefore, be exactly the same size, they may appear to be of different sizes or actually measure as different sizes, several hundred years after printing. Appearance is affected by the measure and the amount of leading; and actual size is determined by such factors as the condition of the type; the expansion, contraction, or wrinkling of the paper; and the amount of inking or bleeding.

Ordinarily one would measure ten or twenty lines of unleaded type and calculate an average to determine the size of the type. The Hebrew faces that we are concerned with offer problems of ascenders, descenders, vocalization, and various leading, among other things, that make normal measurement difficult. Furthermore, such measurement yields the body size of the type, without revealing the size of the face; different face sizes can be on the same body size. At this stage, it seemed important to me to recognize *differences* in face sizes (because there are no face names beyond the generic), and I preferred to risk the problems of measuring the so-called "x-height" of letters (excluding those that have ascenders and descenders). Therefore, the sizes below represent my approximate measurements of letters like ב and פ with a rule graduated in hundredths of an inch and read through a 5× magnifier. (The approximate millimeter equivalents are not measurements; they are taken from tables of equivalents.) The measurements cannot be absolute because of the variables mentioned above, but one size can be relatively differentiated from another.

One further point: when an elongated מ is referred to, it is always the final letter (ם).

S[quare] 1 (.25″ = 6.3 mm.): Represented by the words דברי דוד in Figure 4, this type appears in every book examined except עמודיה שבעה, פרקי רבי אליעזר, תוצאות חיים, קסת יהונתן and חכמות המספר.

S[quare] 1 (vocalized): Only in לב טוב (1700).

S[quare] 2 (.15″ = 3.8 mm.): Represented by the words טורי זהב and others in Figure 4, this type appears in every book examined. By 1690 the letters א and ל appear in elongated form in עיר מקלט; the letters א, ה, ל, מ, and ת are elongated in מים חיים the same year. The same elongated letters appear in other books from time to time.

S[quare] 2 (vocalized): The first appearance is in ברכת המזון (1691), with further occurrences in סדר היוצרות (1693?), מראה (1693), the Pentateuch of 1693, לב טוב (1700), and מאזני צדק (1707). The letters א, ל and ת are elongated in 1691; ה and מ are added to these in 1963 (מראה).

S[quare] 3 (.105″ = 2.7 mm.): Represented by the words אין זה כי אם... in Figure 4, this type appears in every book examined except מים חיים, עיר מקלט and קרבן שבת. Letters ה and ת appear elongated in בית שמואל and דברי דוד (both of 1689); ל is added in מנהגים (1690); א appears in קסת יהונתן (1697); מ, in מאזני צדק (1707).

S[quare] 3 (vocalized): This type appears only in מנהגים (1692), סדר היוצרות (1693?) and מאזני צדק (1707). In סדר היוצרות, א, ה, ל, מ, and ת appear elongated.

S[quare] 4 (.07″ = 1.8 mm.): Represented by the three lines before the place of publication in Figure 4, this type appears in every book examined except בית יעקב, מראה, תוצאות חיים, פרקי רבי אליעזר, and קסת יהונתן. The letters א, ה, ל, מ, and ת appear elongated in the first Dyhernfurth book and frequently thereafter.

S[quare] 4 (vocalized): The only appearance is in מנהגים of 1692. The elongated letters also appear in this vocalized text.

S[quare] 5 (.055″= 1.4mm.): Represented by the vocalized text in Figure 5, this type appears in the Pentateuch of 1693, in תוצאות חיים of the same year, and in מאזני צדק (1707). In the last the מ and ת appear elongated.

S[quare] 5 (vocalized): The only appearance is in the Pentateuch of 1693 (Figure 5). The letters א, ה, ל, מ, and ת appear elongated.

R[abbinic] 1 (.08″ = 2.0mm.): Represented by the big block of thirteen lines (Figure 4), this type appears in all the examined books of 1689 and 1690, in בית הילל and ילקוט דוד of 1691, in מגני ארץ (1692), in סדר היוצרות (1693?), in מראה and the Pentateuch of 1693, and in no later books.

R[abbinic] 2 (.075″ = 1.9mm.): Represented by most of the text of Figure 6, this type appears in מראה and the Pentateuch of 1693; סדר היוצרות (1693?); בית יעקב (1696); חכמות המספר (1712); and in up to four lines each of קסת יהונתן (1697), חקי משפט (1701), and מגני ארץ (1702).

R[abbinic] 3 (.065″ = 1.7mm.): Represented by the words . . . בדפוס המשובח in Figure 4, this type appears in every book examined except ברכת המזון, מראה, חכמות המספר, and מנהגים (1714).

R[abbinic] 4 (.055″ = 1.4mm.): Represented by the commentary sections of Figure 5, this type appears in קרבן שבת (1691); מגני ארץ (1692); תוצאות חיים, אהבת עולם, and the Pentateuch (all of 1693); חקי משפט (1701), מגני ארץ (1702), מאזני צדק (1707).

Y[iddish] (.07″ = 1.8 mm.): Represented by the text above and to the top left of the illustration in Figure 26, this type appears in ברכת המזון (1691), מנהגים (1692), לב טוב (1700), and חכמות המספר (1712).

Ro[man] 1 (Upper case — .12″; lower case — .085″): Represented by the Latin of Figure 42 (אהבת עולם), this type appears also on the title page of מים חיים (1690), מגני ארץ (1692), and עמודיה שבעה (1693).

Ro[man] 2 (Upper case — .10″; lower case — .075″): The only appearance is the Latin text of Figure 41.

I[talic] 1 (Upper case — .13″; lower case — .09″). The only appearance is in the words "Cum Licentia Superiorum" in the Pentateuch of 1693 (Figure 41).

I[talic] 2 (Upper case — .10″; lower case — .075″): Represented by the three Latin words of Figure 4, this type appears also in בית שמואל (1689) and בית הילל, ברכת המזון, and ילקוט דוד (all of 1691).

VI

The Metal Ornaments

Ornaments 1, 2, 3, and 4 are the four ornaments, from left to right, on the left border of Figure 4. Ornaments 5 and 6 are the hands in Figure 7. Ornament 7 is the topmost of the six rows of ornaments at the bottom of Figure 4. Ornament 8 is the row of ornaments in Figure 7. Ornament 9 is the fourth row from the bottom of Figure 4. Ornaments 10–19 are all in Figure 6. Ornaments 10, 11, and 13 are the top three rows; Ornament 12 is the third row from the bottom; Ornaments 14 and 15 are the right and left-pointing hands with the top line of text; Ornaments 16 and 17 are in the fourth and fifth rows from the bottom; Ornament 19 is the rightmost row; Ornament 18 is the second row from the bottom.

Ornament 1:
Floral arabesque (.22″ x .185″), appears in 1689 (דברי דוד, בית שמואל), 1690 (עיר מקלט, מים חיים), 1691 (קרבן שבת, ילקוט דוד, ברכת המזון, בית הילל), 1692 (מנהגים, אהבת עולם), 1693 (פרקי רבי אליעזר), 1694 (מאמר העיתים), and 1700 (לב טוב).

Ornament 2:
Floral arabesque (.16″ x .14″), appears in 1689 (דברי דוד, בית שמואל),, 1690 (מים חיים), 1691 (קרבן שבת, ילקוט דוד, ברכת המזון, בית הילל), 1692 (אהבת עולם), 1693 (פרקי רבי אליעזר), and 1700 (לב טוב).

Ornament 3:
Border with two rules on each side (.23″ x .14″ including rules), appears in 1689 (דברי דוד, בית שמואל), 1690 (מים חיים), 1691 (בית הילל), 1692 (אהבת עולם), 1693 (פרקי רבי אליעזר), 1694 (מאמר העיתים), and 1696 (בית יעקב).

Ornament 4:
Flower and curved leaf (.20″ x .12″), appears in 1689 (דברי דוד, בית שמואל), 1691 (קרבן שבת, ילקוט דוד, ברכת המזון, בית הילל), 1693 (תוצאות חיים), and 1700 (לב טוב).

Ornament 5:
Hand, thumb up, pointing to left (.21″), appears in 1689 (בית שמואל, דברי דוד), 1690 (עיר מקלט, מים חיים), 1696 (בית יעקב), and 1703 (מים חיים שני).

Ornament 6:
Hand, thumb up, pointing to right (.22″), appears in same books as Ornament 5 and 1691 (קרבן שבת) and 1700 (לב טוב).

Ornament 7:

Arabesque (.17″ x .16″), appears in 1689 (דברי דוד ,בית שמואל), 1690 (מים חיים ,עיר מקלט), 1691 (ברכת המזון ,בית הילל), 1693 (Pentateuch), 1696 (בית יעקב), 1700 (לב טוב), and 1703 (מים חיים שני).

Ornament 8:

Geometric design (.23″ x .22″), appears in 1689 (דברי דוד ,בית שמואל), 1690 (מים חיים), 1691 (קרבן שבת ,ברכת המזון ,בית הילל), 1692 (מנהגים), 1693 (פרקי רבי אליעזר ,אהבת עולם), and 1694 (מאמר העיתים).

Ornament 9:

Wheel with single rule on each side (.13″ x .13″) appears in 1689 (בית שמואל ,דברי דור), 1690 (מים חיים), 1691 (ברכת המזון ,בית הילל), 1693 (אהבת עולם, Pentateuch), 1700 (לב טוב), and 1712 (נתיב הישר).

Ornament 10:

Flower with wheel-like petal (.34″ x 26″), appears in 1696 (בית יעקב), 1697 (קסת יהונתן), 1700 (לב טוב), 1703 (מים חיים שני), and 1712 (חכמות המספר ,נתיב הישר).

Ornament 11:

Clover leaf (.11″ x 10″), appears in 1696 (בית יעקב), 1697 (קסת יהונתן), and 1712 (נתיב הישר).

Ornament 12:

Wheel (.13″ x .13″), appears in same books as Ornament 12 and in 1700 (לב טוב).

Ornament 13:

Arabesque with single rule (.14″ x .11″), appears in 1696 (בית יעקב), 1700 (לב טוב), and 1712 (חכמות המספר).

Ornament 14:
Hand, thumb up, pointing to right (.15″), appears in 1696 (בית יעקב) and 1701 (חקי משפט).

Ornament 15:
Hand, thumb up, pointing to left (.14″) appears in 1696 (בית יעקב), and 1703 (מים חיים שני).

Ornament 16: 
Arabesque with dotṣ in the curves (.19″ x 13″) appears in 1696 (בית יעקב), 1697 (קסת יהונתן), 1700 (לב טוב), and 1707 (מאזני צדק).

Ornament 17: 
Arabesque without dots (.20″ x .13″) appears in 1696 (בית יעקב) and 1700 (לב טוב).

Ornament 18:
Arabesque with three dots at narrow end (.31″ x .15″), appears in 1696 (בית יעקב), 1697 (קסת יהונתן), 1700 (לב טוב), and 1712 (חכמות המספר, נתיב הישר).

Ornament 19:
Floral arabesque (.24″ x .19″), appears in 1696 (בית יעקב), 1697 (קסת יהונתן), and 1707 (מאזני צדק).

VII

The Cuts

(In "Woodcuts," the horizontal measurement is given first)

Woodcut A (Figure 7), a heavy rule over two lighter rules and a floral design (5.30″ x .76″), appears in 1689 (דברי דוד ,בית שמואל),1691 (בית הילל), 1692 (אהבת עולם), and 1702 (מגני ארץ).

Woodcut B (Figure 10; 2.62″ x 1.95″) appears only in 1689 (בית שמואל).

Woodcut C (Figure 11; 1.65″ x 1.17″), appears in 1689 (בית שמואל) and 1693 (Pentateuch, end of Haftarot).

Woodcut D (Figure 12; 1.88″ x 1.10″), appears only in 1689 (בית שמואל).

Woodcut E (Figure 13), a basket of flowers (2.24″ x 2.00″), appears in 1689 (דברי דוד ,בית שמואל).

Woodcut F (Figure 14), the same basket with upper right corner flower broken off (2.15″ x 1.97″), appears in 1690 (עיר מקלט ,מים חיים), 1691 (ילקוט דוד ,בית הילל), and 1703 (מים חיים שני).

Woodcut G (Figure 15; 4.00″ x 3.03″), appears in 1690 (עיר מקלט), 1691 (קרבן שבת ,בית הילל), and 1703 (מים חיים שני).

Woodcut H (Figure 16; 2.56″ x 2.00″), appears only in 1691 (ילקוט דוד).

Woodcut I (Figure 17; 6.17″ x 1.43″), appears only in 1692 (מגני ארץ).

Woodcut J (Figure 18; 1.78″ x 1.03″), appears only in 1693 (Pentateuch).

Woodcut K (Figure 19; 1.79″ x 1.05″), appears only in 1693 (Pentateuch).

Woodcut L (Figure 20; 2.16″ x 1.62″), appears only in 1693 (Pentateuch, end of Genesis).

Woodcut M (Figure 21; 2.32″ x 1.30″), appears only in 1693 (Pentateuch, end of Exodus).

Woodcut N (Figure 22; 2.05″ x 1.98″), appears only in 1693 (Pentateuch, end of Leviticus).

Woodcut O (Figure 5; 4.73″ x 1.45″), appears only in 1693 (Pentateuch, חמש מגילות).

Woodcut P (Figure 23; 2.06″ x 1.74″), appears only in 1693 (Pentateuch, end).

Woodcut Q (Figure 24; 1.01″ x 1.36″), appears only in 1702 (מגני ארץ).

Woodcut R (Figure 25; 1.54″ x 1.42″), appears only in 1702 (מגני ארץ).

Woodcut S (Figure 9; 2.11″ x 2.42″), appears only in 1703 (מים חיים שני).

Woodcut T (.27″ x 4.24″), appears only in 1689 (Figure 4, third line from bottom—whole line; דברי דוד ,בית שמואל) and, broken to 2.92″' in 1702 (מגני ארץ) and 1707 (מאזני צדק).

Woodcut U (Figure 8; .27″ x 2.88″), appears in 1702 (מגני ארץ), alongside Woodcut T, on preliminary leaf 4b, and in 1707 (מאזני צדק).

Woodcut V (Figure 45; .30″ x 2.31″), appears only in 1707 (מאזני צדק).

The woodcuts above are primarily decorative as distinct from the woodcut illustrations below. The two volumes that have many illustrations are ברכת המזון (1691) and (1692); in fact, many of the cuts are used in both books and/or more than once in the same book. Illustrations 1–12, those that appear in both, are represented by facsimiles: the others are only described briefly.

(In Illustrations, the vertical measurement is given first)

Illustration 1 (Figure 26; 2.28″ x 2.03″), Havdalah (1691, 21a; 1692, 2a and 24b).

Illustration 2 (Figue 27; 2.35″ x 1.44″), Kiddush (1691, 32b and 43a; 1692, 8b).

Illustration 3 (Figure 28; 2.29″ x 1.97″), Sanctifying New Moon (1691, 4a; 1692, 10b and 52a).

Illustration 4 (Figure 29; 2.92″ x 2.02″), Burning(?) leavened bread (1691, 34a; 1692, 14a).

Illustration 5 (Figure 30; 2.68″ x 2.45″), Candle lighting (1691, 1b and 35a; 1692, 5b and 16b).

Illustration 6 (Figure 31; 2.30″ x 2.00″), Seder scene (1691, 1b, 24a, and 49a; 1692, 17a).

Illustration 7 (Figure 32; 4.48″ x 2.13″), Chase — יקנה״ז (1691, 31b; 1692, 17a).

Illustration 8 (Figure 33; 2.28″ x 1.98″), Kaparot (1691, 27b; 1692, 37b).

Illustration 9 (Figure 34; 2.31″ x 2.03″), Lighting menorah (1691, 4b and 22b; 1692, 49a.

Illustration 10 (Figure 35; 2.28″ x 2.03″), Purim merriment (1691, 5a and 23b; 1692, 52b).

Illustration 11 (Figure 36; 2.28″ x 2.00″), Wedding (1691, 24b; 1692, 54a).

Illustration 12 (Figure 37; 2.30″ x 2.00″), Circumcision (1691, 25b; 1692, 54b).

Illustration 13 (2.60″ x 1.72″), Man on a chair, illustrating Zemirot singing (1691, 7a).

Illustration 14 (2.46″ x 1.07″), Man standing, illustrating מעשה ברבי אליעזר in the Passover Hagadah (1691, 35b).

Illustration 15 (2.75″ x 1.18″), Man with book illustrating the Wise Son (1691, 36a).

Illustration 16 (2.52″ x 1.32″), Warrior illustrating Wicked Son (1691, 36b).

Illustration 17 (2.73″ x 1.22″), Man and young child (1691, 36b).

Illustration 18 (1.30″ x 2.60″), Three men in a boat (1691, 37a).

Illustration 19 (2.26″ x 1.95″), Women and many children illustrating fertility (1691, 38a).

Illustration 20 (2.80″ x 1.22″), Man working (1691, 38b).

Illustration 21 (1.33″ x 3.87″), Building with bricks (1691, 38b).

Illustration 22 (1.80″ x 4.89″), Killing of male infants (1691, 39a).

Illustration 23 (1.77″ x 2.31″), The Temple (1691, 41b and 49b).

Illustration 24 (1.44″ x 4.09″), The Red Sea (1691, 41b).

Illustration 25 (2.81″ x 1.23″), Woman and Paschal Lamb (1691, 42a).

Illustration 26 (2.74″ x 1.21″), Man holding Matzah (1691, 42a).

Illustration 27 (1.65″ x 1.04″), Wanderer (1691, 42b).

Illustration 28 (2.84″ x 1.04″), Moses, with rod, and rays emanating from head (1691, 42b).

Illustration 29 (1.46″ x 3.43″), Elijah heralding the Messiah (1691, 44b).

Illustration 30 (2.88″ x 1.15″), King David (1691, 45b).

Illustration 31 (2.76″ x 2.60″), Preaching from the pulpit (1692, 11b and 37a).

Illustration 32 (2.60″ x 2.47″). Flour mill (1692, 12a).

Illustration 33 (2.80″ x 2.57″), "Koshering" utensils for Passover (1692, 12b).

Illustration 34 (2.66″ x 2.48″), Searching for leavened bread (1692, 13a).

Illustration 35 (2.67″ x 2.53″), Baking matzah (1692, 15a).

Illustration 36 (2.63″ x 2.76″), Barbershop scene illustrating Lag Ba'omer (1692, 26a).

Illustration 37 (2.78″ x 2.43″), Moses and the Tablets (1692, 27a and 41a).

Illustration 38 (2.55″ x 2.73″), Three men sitting on synagogue(?) floor illustrating Tish'ah Be'av (1692, 29b).

Illustration 39 (without frame, 1.62″ x 1.08″), Man, alone, blowing shofar (1692, 31a).

Illustration 40 (2.53″ x 2.72″), Man blowing shofar in synagogue with group of people (1692, 34b).

Illustration 41 (2.56″ x 2.43″), Man and sukkah (1692, 41b).

Illustration 42 (2.51″ x 2.43″), Two men with lulav, etrog, etc. (1692, 42b).

Illustration 43 (2.56″ x 2.41″), Two men, one without head, illustrating superstition that if one does not see his shadow (i.e., the shadow of his head) on Hoshanah Rabbah, he will not live through the year: "דען האט גישלאגן דער טראפף, דש ער האט קיין קאפף" (1692, 45b).

Illustration 44 (2.53″ x 2.40″), Table set with fruit illustrating Hamishah Asar Bishvat (1692, 50b).

Illustration 45 (2.52″ x 2.76″), Man using set of scales on a table illustrating Parashat Shekalim (1692, 51a).

Illustration 46 (2.55″ x 2.78″), Moses's arms being supported as he watches battle illustrating Parashat Zakhor (1692, 51b).

Illustration 47 (2.52″ x 2.76″), Burning of cow on altar illustrating Parashat Parah (1692, 52a).

The next twelve illustrations are zodiacal introductions to the months of the year in the 1692 מנהגים. Each is divided into two parts, the left representing the sign of the zodiac, the right illustrating the words which are printed just above or below the name of the month. Figure 38 shows two samples of these charming cuts.

Illustration 48 (.90″ x 1.57″), Nisan — Aries, עת הזמיר הגיע (10b).
Illustration 49 (.88″ x 1.54″), Iyyar — Taurus, ונטעתם לכם כל עץ מאכל (25b).
Illustration 50 (.90″ x 1.59″), Sivan — Gemini, ואקח את אביכם מעבר הנהר (26b).
Illustration 51 (.87″ x 1.57″), Tammuz — Cancer, מעת דגנם ותירושם רבו (28b).
Illustration 51 (.86″ x 1.55″), Av — Leo, ונתתי עשב לבהמתך (28b).
Illustration 52 (.85″ x 1.56″) Elul — Virgo, וקצרו לפי חסד (31a).
Illustration 53 (.88″ x 1.57″), Tishri — Libra, חדשו וזרעו לכם לצדקה (33a).
Illustration 54 (Figure 38; 86″ x 1.59″), Marheshvan — Scorpius, איש עובד אדמה (48a).
Illustration 55 (Figure 38; .89″ x 1.56″), Kislev — Sagittarius, איש יודע ציד (48a).
Illustration 56 (.88″ x 1.56″), Tevet — Capricornus, וטבוח טבח והכן (49b).
Illustration 57 (.87″ x 1.57″), Shevat — Aquarius, ולפני קורתו מי יעמוד (50a).
Illustration 58 (.84″ x 1.53″), Adar — Pisces, ואשר יבא ביער לחטוב עצים (51a).

Though two well illustrated books use fifty-eight separate cuts, some perhaps offering glimpses into the life of the period as well as providing excellent material for comparison with the book art of other times and places, the rest of the books show little of significance.

Illustration 59 (Figure 39; 2.61″ x 1.38″), Ladder of Jacob's dream, representing a crude "map" of Palestine (1689, דברי דוד, 13b).
Illustration 60 (Figure 40), Play on author's name (1691, ילקוט דוד, 2b). Rather crude rules, sometimes no straighter than those of Illustration 60, are used also in 1690 (title pages of מים חיים and עיר מקלט, as well as most of the pages of the latter).
Illustration 61 (Figure 41; 4.67″ x 5.38″), Menorah (1693, Pentateuch, preliminary leaf 2a).
Illustration 62 (1.61″ x 1.62″), A checkerboard-type square (8 x 8 units) with six diamond shapes worked into the inner 6 x 6 unit square (1712, חכמות המספר, 1b).
Illustration 63 (.70″ x .46″), Diamond, as above, in six units — 3 x 2 (1712, חכמות המספר, 1b).
Illustration 64 (1.50″ x 1.64″), Illustration of Pythagorean theorem by means of three square grids of 5 x 5, 4 x 4 and 3 x 3 units (1712, חכמות המספר, 2b).

VIII

Other Distinguishing Features

It is conceivable that certain other characteristics of the printer or place are sufficiently distinctive to warrant mention or even emphasis. Examination of the Dyhernfurth books from this point of view does not reveal very much. The watermarks in the paper are very difficult to discern, the margins are undistinctive, the rules are common. One should call attention to the fact that Shabtai Meshorer Bass used musical notes frequently in his books and even used the word תגן in a chronogram for two 1693 publications (מראה, Pentateuch); otherwise the chronograms seem undistinctive as well. Shabtai was quite egocentric,[8] not only in the use of musical references in his books, but also in his use of his own name; consequently, a book lacking any indication that it is from his press should not casually be ascribed to him.

Arabic numerals appear in these Dyhernfurth books as do Roman and Italic type. In the חכמות המספר, the numerals are, in fact, a major factor in the book. The numerals are so difficult to describe and differentiate and so unlikely to be a determining factor in any typographic problem that it is sufficient merely to mention them.

One of the uses of numerals along with letters may, however, indeed be distinctive, namely, in signatures. The signatures of the Dyhernfurth books use numerals and Hebrew letters in various combinations, but they do not (with the one exception noted in IX, D below) use Latin letters. Thus, if an item uses Latin letters in its signatures, one should suspect that it may not have been printed in Dyhernfurth. The Dyhernfurth typesetters were not comfortable with Latin—even the words "Cum licentia superiorum" are spelled wrong several times (see Figures 4 and 42). They were apparently not comfortable with numerals either; they often printed two digits backwards (e.g., 12 as 21).

IX

Problems—and Some Solutions

A. What I have called Title page 2 appeared in a book, סדר היוצרות, the title-page text of which states that it was published in Amsterdam in 1682. A study of the types and ornaments of Amsterdam Hebrew printing of that time, among other things, led me to conclude that the סדר היוצרות could not have been printed in Amsterdam in 1682. A similar study of Dyhernfurth, of which this article is the record, convinced me[9] that

סדר היוצרות was printed in Dyhernfurth about 1693 or later. These studies also suggested that systematic study might present and solve other problems of detail and perhaps have wider-ranging value as well.

B. Does a perusal of the data suggest any trends in the early printing history of Dyhernfurth? For one thing, Shabtai Bass began to print in 1689 with a full repertoire of types (S1-4, R1 and 3, and I2), ornaments (1–9), and woodcuts (A-E and T). Only in 1690 did he use a one-piece cut for a title page, but by 1693 he had all he was going to use. He used one illustrative woodcut in 1689 (דברי דוד), blossomed forth with illustrated books in 1691 and 1692, and added little thereafter. By 1693 he had also used almost all the woodcut ornaments he ever used. In 1691 he introduced types R4 and Y which he may have had earlier; in 1693 he introduced types S5, R2, and I2 and many woodcut ornaments. The business was apparently successful in the first few years. By the time he introduced ten more ornaments in 1696 (בית יעקב) he had practically completed his inventory of types, ornaments, and woodcuts.

C. It has been suggested by Brann[10] that the title page of בית יעקב was not printed in Dyhernfurth because of the dissatisfaction of the author with the quality of the printing in the book. The reason given is the lack of place and publisher on the title page. "Proof" is added in the "fact" that the ornamental border seems not to appear other than on this title page.[11] While it may be true that the exact configuration of the type ornaments that went into this title page (Figure 7) does not appear in any other book, the ornaments do appear in a variety of other Dyhernfurth prints after 1696. Furthermore, the type on the title page is Dyhernfurth type *in toto*. If only Brann had compared the types of the rest of the book, he would have seen that they are the same as those of the title page. Also, Ornament 18 appears both on the title page and within the book. In this case, a closer look at the book itself would have tended to negate the theory that the book and the title page were printed in separate places; a typographic profile proves the title page compatible with Dyhernfurth. Only the discovery of the same type *and* the same ornaments in some other printing place would allow the question to be reopened.

D. But there is a book printed in Dyhernfurth that has, in one large section, spurious types and ornaments; but no one, to my knowledge, has previously raised the possibility that this section was *not* printed in Dyhernfurth. Figure 43 shows the bottom of the penultimate leaf of אהבת עולם, in which is the only occurrence in Dyhernfurth—if indeed

Dyhernfurth!—of three types and three typographic ornaments. Figure 44 shows a signature within the same section with a Roman type.

1. S[quare] 6 (.18″ = 4.6mm.), serves as the running title on each page. In Figure 43, this type is in the words. . . תם ונשלם.
2. S[quare] 7 (.085″ = 2.2mm.), serves as the introductory word(s) to each paragraph. In Figure 43, the words in this type are כי אל ארצי ואל מולדתי.
3. R[abbinic] 5 (.065″ = 1.7mm.), serves as the text. Although this is seemingly the same size as Rabbinic 3 which is used in the rest of the book, there are differences. A twenty-line measurement of each shows a total *body* size of 3.33″ for R5 and 3.20″ for R3. There are face differences also. In R3, for example, the left vertical of the ע is quite straight; in R5, it slants from left to right as it goes down. The slants of the top of the צ are different in the two fonts. The ב in R5 has a practically straight vertical; in R3, the vertical has a marked indention in the middle. The slant on the top of the א is quite a bit more pronounced in R3 than in R5.
4. Ro[man] 3 (Figure 44; upper case — .11″; lower case — .08″). This might be the same as Roman 1; there is very little to compare and the inking varies greatly.
5. Ornament 20: Arabesque (.35″ x .16″), occurring fifteen times in the one ornamental line.
6. Ornament 21: Wheel (.16″ x .14″?), occurring once in the line.
7. Ornament 22: Arabesque (.16″ x .075″), occurring once, like Ornament 14, but smaller.

Several points need to be made about this section of אהבת עולם that begins on leaf 63 and goes through leaf 124:

a. The three ornaments appear here and in no (other) Dyhernfurth book (including the first 62 leaves and the last leaf of this one).
b. No ornaments used in undoubted Dyhernfurth books appear in this doubted section.
c. Four types appear here and in no (other) Dyhernfurth books.
d. No types used in undoubted Dyhernfurth books appear in this doubted section.
e. No (other) Dyhernfurth book has Latin type in its signatures.

There seems no question that this section of the book was printed elsewhere. My candidate for place of printing is Frankfurt on the Oder in the press of Johann Christoff Beckmann, since the three spurious (for Dyhernfurth) Hebrew types and the three spurious ornaments can be found in books from this press at this time.[12] Further study might also reveal that the Roman type is the same as well.

E. A few words about "Cum Licentia superiorum." This legal phrase appears in almost every book published in Dyhernfurth through 1692, the exceptions being מנהגים (1690), קרבן שבת (1691), and מנהגים (1691). It appears in 1693 only in the Pentateuch; and it does not appear at all after 1693.

F. It is often impossible to date books without date, and to date relatively those that have the same date. Among other things, one seeks evidence in the relative newness or the signs of use of the type, the ornaments, and especially the woodcuts. For example, there is little doubt that the הפטרת part of the Pentateuch of 1693 was printed after the חמש מגילות, since both use the same woodcut title page frame; and the frame shows obvious deterioration from a small crack in the earlier to a significant one in the latter (Figure 3). It is questionable whether this frame could be used again after its use for the הפטרת.

It is possible, using a similar analysis and a bit of luck to propose that מים חיים predated עיר מקלט in 1690. Both books use Woodcut F, the basket with a flower broken off. But in the copy of מים חיים that I examined, there is a light impression of the very part that broke off, suggesting that this break took place during the printing. It would not be surprising to find copies of the book in which Woodcut E, the complete basket of flowers, is present instead of Woodcut F. But never again was Woodcut E used because it became Woodcut F.

The woodcut of title page 2 also underwent change, in this case intentional; and the change once again suggests the priority of one book over another. The two books that use this woodcut in 1714 are an edition of Psalms[13] and an edition of מנהגים. It has been pointed out[14] that the מנהגים is the only occurrence of this woodcut with words related to the music; presumably it is the tune to יגדל אלהים חי because these words appear (in type S4). Since the woodcut was incised and damaged to make space to set the type for the three words, the Psalms, which is still undamaged, was probably the prior printing.

Although it is not essential to the discussion, a book published in Dyhernfurth in 1727, the יון מצולה of Nathan Nata Hannover is pertinent here.[15] The very same woodcut, as seen in the developing crack in the upper right quadrant, is used. But this time, there is no יגדל. There is evidence of some letters in the same two lines, but nothing is very clear. Apparently holding letters in the space gouged out of the wood was not an easy matter.

CONCLUSION

This is not the place to argue the independent value of the history of printing, its value to general history, to economic history, to intellectual history, to social history, to art history. Suffice it to say, the obvious point to be made is that whatever the value of typographical history, the writing of it, in small units or in large sweeps, can only be enhanced if the data that comprise the facts are systematically gathered, recorded, organized, compared, analyzed, and interpreted, that is, made available for the creation of hypotheses and for testing them. Towards this goal, this small but tightly controlled body of the printing facts of Dyhernfurth from 1689 to 1714 is presented.

NOTES

[1] A definition of typography is not easy because the word has been used broadly as equivalent to the broadest sense of "bibliography," narrowly as "the craft of printing" or "the design of a book," and as various things in between. My use of the word will best emerge from context; basically I use "typography" to refer to the elements that go into the printed artifact (type, ornaments, woodcuts and other illustrations, etc) that identify it and relate it to other printed artifacts. Thus the history of typography is the chronicle of the relationships of printed artifacts to each other and to the people and times which produced them.

[2] A model bibliography, including a full set of facsimiles of typographic elements, is Josef Prijs's *Die Basler hebräischen Drucke (1492–1866)*. (Ergänzt und herausgegeben von Bernhard Prijs.) (Olten: Urs Graf Verlag, 1964 [c 1965]).

[3] A facsimile is published by A. M. Haberman, שערי ספרים עבריים (Safed: Museum of Printing Art, 1969), p. 50, Fig. 36.

[4] Fig. 2 of my article "The Value of Face Value", *HUCA* 40–41 (1969–1970) : 555–580; also Habermann, . . . שערי, p. 108, Fig. 92.

[5] See my article (note 4 above) for full documentation on the occurrences of this title page and for the proof that Shabtai actually printed the סדר היוצרות.

[6] Abraham Yaari, דגלי המדפיסים העבריים (Jerusalem: Hebrew University Press Association, 1943), p. 48, Figs. 77–77a, shows part of this title page and of T.p.4 above.

[7] A facsimile is published by Jacob R. Marcus, with his article, עטישע וואנטשפיגלען, ייווא בלעטער 21 (1943) : 204–5.

[8] Elaborated on in my article (see note 4 above), pp. 560–564.

[9] *Ibid.*, whole article.

[10] Markus Brann, "Geschichte und Annalen der Dyhernfurth Druckerei," *Monatsschrift für Geschichte und Wissenchaft des Judentums* 40 (1896) : 564.

[11] *Ibid.*: "Dafür scheint auch die sonst nicht vorkommende Randverzierung zu sprechen."

[12] As examples, see פרי מגדים, עולת יצחק, and צפנת פענח חדש (Frankfurt, 1691, 1692, and 1694 respectively). The second has the three types and two of the three orna-

ments on its title page (see facsimile in *Studies in Bibliography and Booklore*, 1 (1954): 151); and all, including the third ornament, appear internally. The three types and the three ornaments appear in the other two books as well.

[13] This edition is at the New York Public Library, Jewish Division, and at the Rabbi Shneersohn Library of Lubawitz. It is not listed in II of this article because I used it only briefly at an early stage and could not write with authority about it.

[14] Isaac Rivkind, עיטור ספרים, *Studies in Bibliography and Booklore* 1 (1954): 204 and 202 (צלום ב׳).

[15] Miss Dora Steinglass of the Jewish Division of the New York Public Library kindly supplied an enlarged photostat of the title page for me to study. A facsimile is in M Balaban, *Z Historji Żydów w Polsce* (Warsaw: 1920), p. 113.

טוב וישר
ה

ספר

נתיב הישר

לפני׳ כל המשכ׳לים לדרוש כתובי׳ הוא מוכפר ·
כל בדר וסדר בכמה דרכי׳ כמיכות כמספר .
וחלק ב׳ נקרא דרך ישרה כחלק ל״ב דרושי׳
ורגלי׳ אגדה וימי׳ נוראים ומדרשי׳ תמוהים · אל
השערה קלוגים : אשר חיבר הראש הרבני
התורני הדרשן כמוהר״ר נפתלי הירש בן
מוהר״ר יהונתן כנ״ל ז״ל מק״ק פינטש יצ״ו ·
חתן הגאון הגדול כמוהר״ר אלחנן בהגאון
כמוהר״ר משה ואב ז״ל : שהי׳ אב״ד
ור״מ בק״ק אליק יצו :

נדפס פה דיהרן פארט

בדפוס של האלוף מהור״ר שבתי יצ״ו
משורר מפראג :

ע״י בנו האלוף המרומם כהר״ר יוסף יצו

עיניכם תסור בנתיב
הישר ויהי׳ דרש סמיכות
למיסור לפ״ק

Fig. 1. T p 3 (also Type: S1, S2, S3, S4, R3).

Fig. 2. T p 4: Main title page of Pentateuch, 1693.

הפטרת
מכל השנה
כמנהג כל קהלות הקדש
בשבתות וימים טובים׳ כמנהגי כל
קהלת קדושות בכל
תפוצות ישראל
וברכות ההפטרה לפניה ולאחריה׃
וסימני ההפטרות בנגינים :
בבית בענות האלוף מהור״ר שבתי משורר יצו
פה דיהרן פארט

Fig. 3. T p 5: Part of Pentateuch, 1693 (also Type: S1, S2, S3, S4, R2, R3, R4).

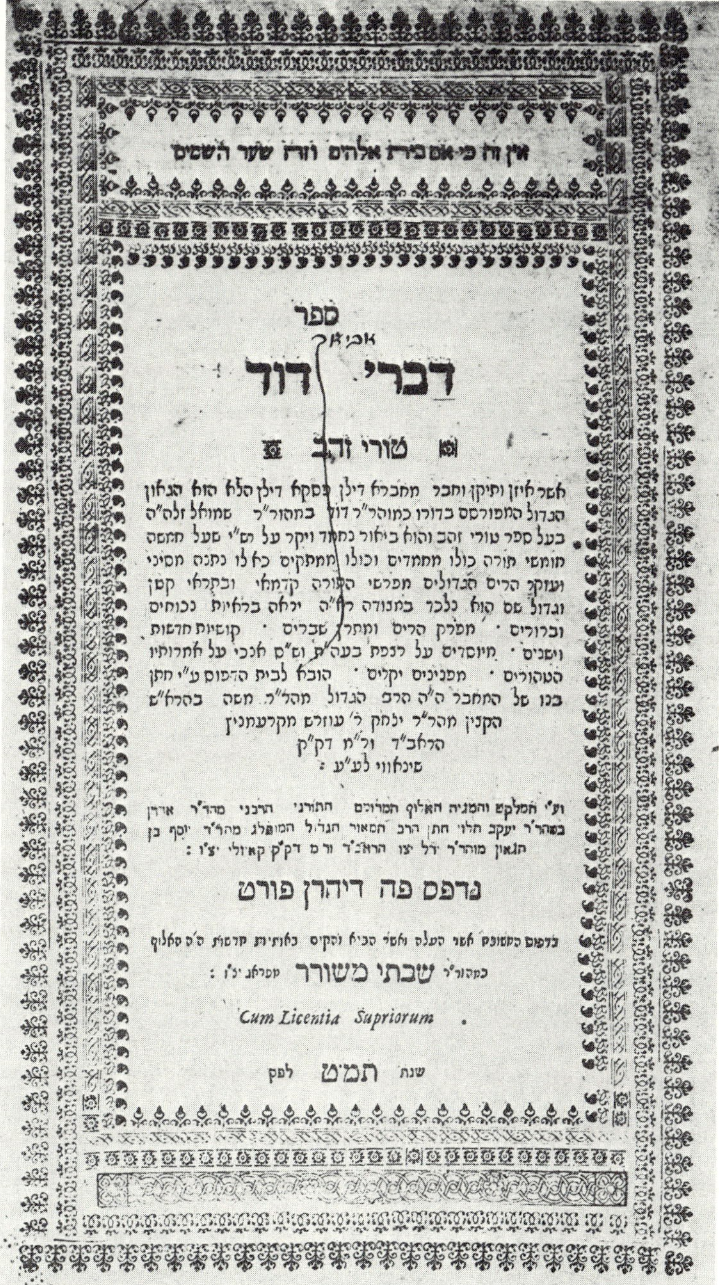

אין זה כי אם בית אלהים וזה שער השמים

ספר

דברי דוד

טורי זהב

אשר איזן ותיקן וחבר מחברא דילן בפסקא דילן הלא הוא הגאון
הגדול המפורסם בדורו כמוהר"ר דוד בהמור"ר שמואל זלה"ה
בעל ספר טורי זהב והוא ביאור נחמד ויקר על הש"ע בעל חמשה
חומשי תורה כולו חמודים וכולו ממתקים כי לו נתנה מסיני
ועזקי הרים הגדולים מפרשי התורה קדמאי ובתראי קטן
וגדול שם הוא נלכד במצודה לה"ה ילאה בראיות נכוחים
וברורים · מפרק הרים ומתרץ שברים · קושיות חדשות
וישנים · מיוסדים על רצפת בעה"ת וש"ס אכבי על אמרותיו
הטהורים · מפנינים יקרים · הובא לבית הדפוס ע"י חתן
בנו של המחבר ה"ה הרב הגדול מהו"ר משה בהרא"ש
הקצין מהו"ר יצחק ר' עוזרש מקרעמניץ
הראב"ד ור"מ דק"ק
סינאווי לע"ע :

ועי' המלקט והמגיה האלוף המרומם התורני הרבני מהו"ר אהרן
בהו"ר יעקב הלוי חתן הרב המאור הגדול המופלג מהו"ר יוסף בן
הגאון מוהו"ר ידל יצו הראב"ד ור"מ דק"ק קאזלי יצ"ו :

נדפס פה דיהרן פורט

בדפוס המשובח אשר הועלה ואשר הכין והקים באותיות חדשות ה"ה האלוף
כמהו"ר שבתי משורר מפראג יצ"ו :

Cum Licentia Supriorum .

שנת תמ"ט לפק

Fig. 4. Type: S1, S2, S3, S4, R1, R3; Ornaments: 1–4, 7, 9.

תולדת אהרן

שיר השירים א

שפתי חכמים

רשי

Fig. 5. Type: S5, S5 (vocalized), R4 (also S2 [vocalized], S3); Woodcut O.

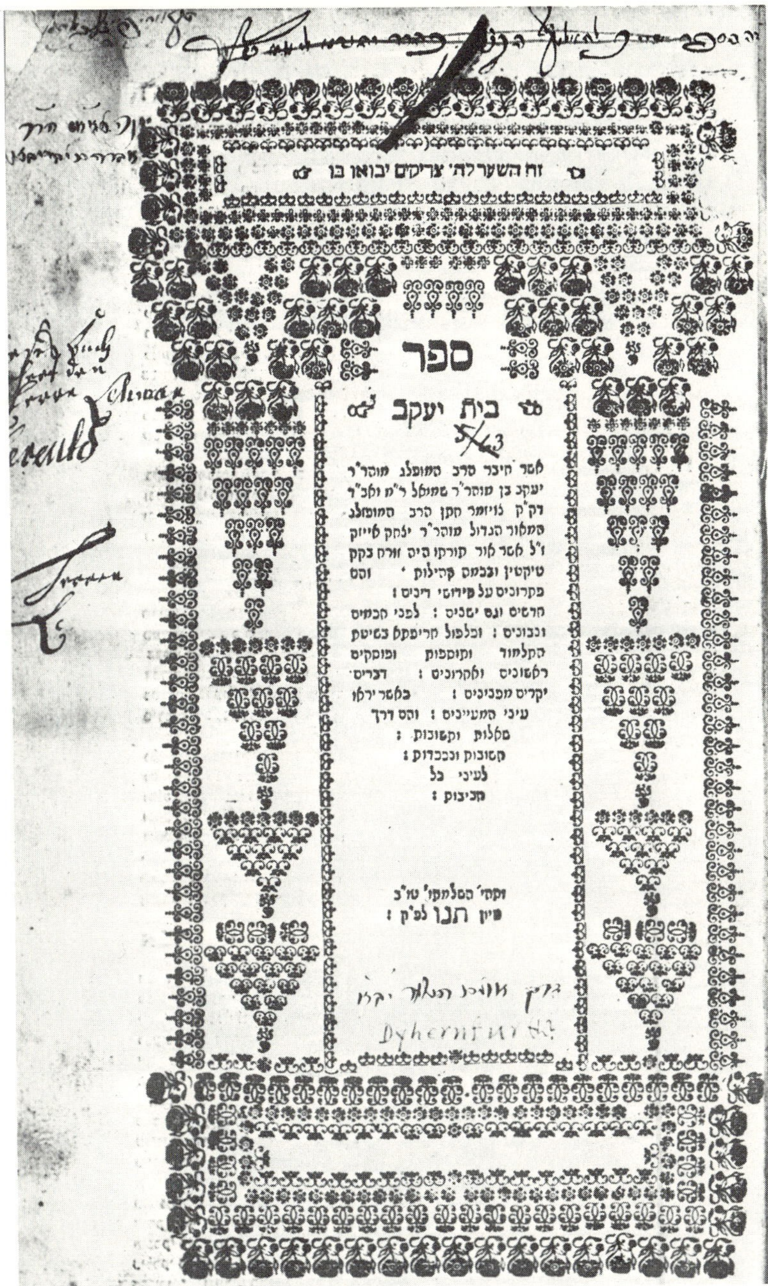

זה השער לה' צדיקים יבואו בו

ספר

בית יעקב

אשר חיבר הרב המופלג מוהר"ר
יעקב בן מוהר"ר שמואל ר"מ ואב"ד
דק"ק צוזמר חתן הרב המופלג
המאור הגדול מוהר"ר יצחק אייזיק
ז"ל אשר אור תורתו היה זורח בקק
טיקטין ובכמה קהילות . והם
פתרונים על פירושי דינים :
חדשים וגם ישנים : לפני חכמים
ונבונים : ובפלפול חריפתא בשיטת
התלמוד ותוספות ופוסקים
ראשונים ואחרונים : דברים
יקרים מפנינים : באשר יראו
עיני המעיינים : והם דרך
שאלות ותשובות :
חשובות ונכבדות :
לעיני כל
הניבות :

וקמי' השלמתו' טו"ב
פיון תנו לפ"ק :

Fig. 6. Type: R2 (also S1, S2, S3); Ornaments: 10–19.

ה ומה בשורש הא' כיינו העליונים שהרינס כנ"ל ·
ה לכן כאומר כתוספ' כאורה א"ן צריך לותוספ ליון דיש שלשה
א"צ'ן וכיון דבהכל יש כ' א"צ'ן מהילה נולדו עמו שכ
ות ובראה שהוא נ"כ כדרך שעברתי דרש"י לא דריש אתי'ן אם לא
א וכן אל כשו"ה לשם רק שלומשה לא יכריע לוס נושו
לא יפנה כנ"ל :
ו לפתם התרגום כתב ליום דינא כנ"ל ·
ו אף הן וכן פי' רש"י בפ' נח כנ"ל :
ר נח בח"ד ואמר רש"י בהעתם' לפניו כדי שיראו

סדר מקץ בה"ד זה נכורו של יוסף כנ"ל :
סדר ויגש בד"ה הפני פיים על זה
כנ"ל · ומסכרא הוא את כנ"ל · שם
זה דבאו לבוכים כנ"ל :
בד"ה פ' שני ושם א"ל כן כנ"ל ·
בד"ה כששכון לא כואת שהוא ראוי לאביו כנ"ל :
סדר עקב בד"ה ומכן מתרגם עד י"כ היא סוף
דיבור ותיבת לכי ששמע לכם הוא
תחילת דבור בפני עצמו ·

ע"י הפועל במלאכת הקודש הזעיר מנחם נקרא
מן בן כמר יצחק יעקב ז"ל מק"ק פראג :

ע"י הפועל הראשון ושם · העוסק במלאכת הקודש :
המחבר האותיות · כ"מ נס ולא נרמות :
פ"ס בן כה"ר כפריאל · וצעיר מק"ק קראקא ראש
קהלת ישראל :

ועל ידי הפועל במלאכת הקודש הפרעסן צייר משה בר צבי ז"ל מנהרשי איסטריין :

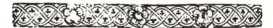

Fig. 7. Ornaments: 5, 6, 8; Woodcut A (also Type S2, S4, R1, R3).

Fig. 8. Woodcut U.

Fig. 9. Woodcut S.

Fig. 10. Woodcut B.

Fig. 11. Woodcut C.

Fig. 12. Woodcut D.

Fig. 13. Woodcut E.

Fig. 14. Woodcut F.

Fig. 16. Woodcut H.

Fig. 15. Woodcut G.

Fig. 17. Woodcut I.

Fig. 18. Woodcut J.

Fig. 19. Woodcut K.

Fig. 20. Woodcut L.

Fig. 21. Woodcut M.

Fig. 22. Woodcut N.

Fig. 23. Woodcut P.

Fig. 24. Woodcut Q.

Fig. 25. Woodcut R.

Fig. 27. Illustration 2.

קומט דאז ער מאג קומן דא רופן מיר אין דאז ער,
זאל קומן · אין טייל זאגן עס איז גוט צום (זכרו׳)
ווען מן אופט נענט (אליהו הנביא) ·אם סבת צו נכט ·
אך האבן מיר גלערנט דאז (אליהו הנביא) אעל״ז זיך
אונטר דען (עץ הדעת) אי (גן עדן) אונ טרייבט דיא (זכות)
פון ישראל דז זיא דען סבת האבן גהלטן · אונ׳ מן ניט
אן איין קערן דיא גלייך אז איין פאקיל איז · אונ׳ נעמט
איין (כוס) מיט ווין אין דיא הנט אונ׳ אן אלט סטענדיג
(הבדלה) מיט פולר סטים אונ׳ זאגט אזא :

הנה אל ישועתי אבטח ולא אפחד כי עזי וזמרת יה יי ויהי
לי לישועה׃ ושאבתם מים בששון ממעיני הישועה׃ ג׳ ב׳ ׃
ליי הישועה על עמך ברכתך סלה׃ יי צבאות עמנו משגב
לנו אלהי יעקב סלה׃ ליהודים היתה אורה ושמחה וששון
ויקר׃ סברי מרי׃ מרנן ורבנן׃
ברוך אתה יי אלהינו מלך העולם בורא פרי הגפן׃
אונ׳ שיט אויז ווין אויף דר ערדן אי דיא (ברכה) אויז איז ·
נאך דער (ברכה) דרך אן ניט אויז סיטן · דען עס איז
אב זג אין

דער בעל הבית הבדלה אלט אזו גאר
סטוק אונ׳ גוויט אונ׳ ליכט צו אלות אונ׳
אעסים טובים זייני קינדרך :

Fig. 26. Type: Y (also S2, S4, S4 [vocalized]); Illustration 1.

Fig. 28. Illustration 3.

Fig. 29. Illustration 4.

Fig. 30. Illustration 5.

Fig. 31. Illustration 6.

Fig. 32. Illustration 7.

Fig. 33. Illustration 8.

Fig. 34. Illustration 9.

Fig. 35. Illustration 10.

Fig. 36. Illustration 11.

Fig. 37. Illustration 12.

איש עובר אדמה

ראש חדש מרחשון

ראש חדש מרחשון) איז אלי יאר צווייא טאג (ראש חדש) · און פאסט (שני וחמישי ושני) דאס אין גלייך אויז קומט פאר (ראש חדש כסליו) · דען אין ספארט ביז דיא טעג נאך קורצטן זיין אים דעם חדש דעם סבת דר פאר זאגט אין אים (מי שבירך) דעם קהל (בעבור שיקבלו עליהם להתענות שני וחמישי ושני) · (אין די מנהגים פון רבי אייזק טירנא כנהג פולן אונ׳פיהם שרייבט ער · און גירעכנט דעם תענית שני וחמישי ושני דער נעהסט שבת נאך ראש חדש מרחשון · נאך אשרי אין יהללו זאגט) אונ׳ וויא און ארט אונ׳סליחות זאגט איט אלי זלן אונ׳ ... און פאסט ווערסטו פערדן אוז ביסיידליך נאך פסח גשריבן אונ׳ וויא און שני וחמישי ושני טוט נאך פסח זא טוט אין אך אזא נאך סוכות :

איש יודע ציד

ראש חדש כסליו

ראש חדש כסליו) איז אונטר וויילן צווייא טאג · אונטר וויילן איין טאג · און היבט אן צו זאגן אים (כסליו ותן טל ומטר לברכה) אין (שמונה עשרה) : אונ׳ היבט אן דעם זעכציגסטן טאג אים אובנט נאך דער (תקופת תשרי) :

Fig. 38. Illustration 54–55 (also Type: S2, S3, S4, Y).

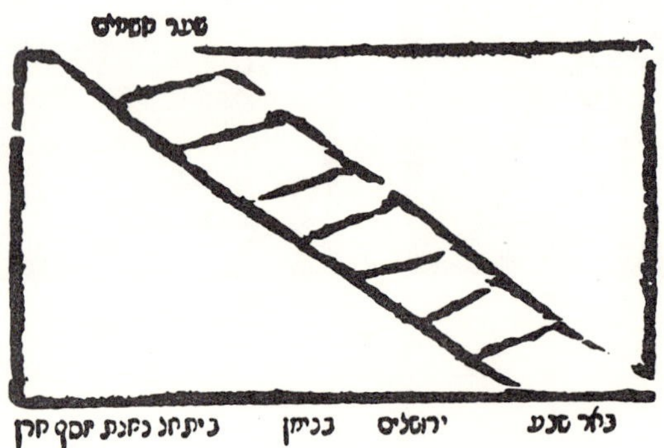

Fig. 39. Illustration 59 (also Type: R3).

Fig. 40. Illustration 60 (also Type: S1, S2, S4).

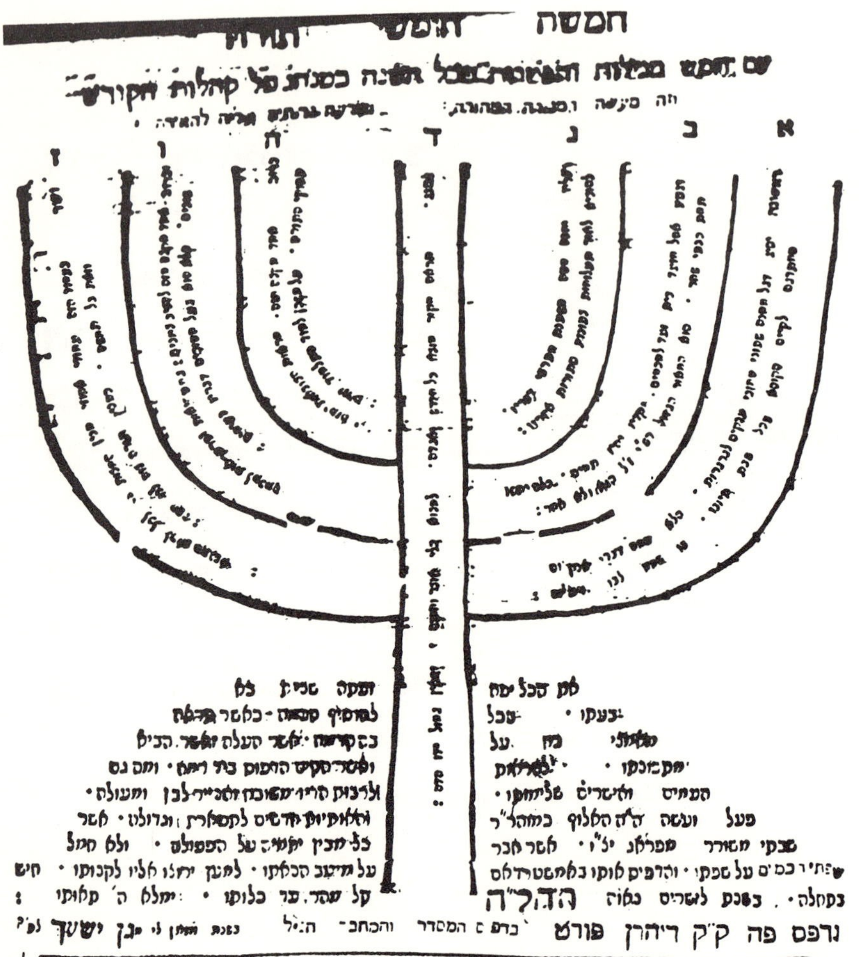

חמשה חומשי תורה

נדפס פה ק״ק דיהרן פורט

Cum Licentia Superiorum

Et

PRivilegio ſpeciali Præpotent Dn Dn Ordin. & Statuum Generalium Hollandiæ & Weſtfriſiæ, Hagæ Comitis die 6 Februarij Anno 1688 Philippo Aaroni Levi Typographo Amſteledamenſi ad quindecim Annos Clementiſſimè indulto, dehinc autem juſto titulo, in bene nominatum Sabbathay Baſiſta, ab eodem Levi, coram Notario & Teſtibus die 20 Martij 1691 Amſtelodami tranſlato, impreſſus

Fig. 41. Illustration 61 (also Type: S2, S3, S4, R2, R3, I1, Ro2).

נדפס פה ק״ק דיהרנפורט

בדפוס המשובח האלוף כמהור״ר שבתי משורר יצ״ו :

Cum Licenria Super,

לפרט עד שמצאתי את שאהבה נפשי לפ״ק :

Fig. 42. From title page of אהבת עולם (1692) (Type: S2, S4, Ro1).

ואשביעך בה אשר תקח אשה לבני מארצי והדר אשר לא תקח
אשה מבנות הכנעני אנכי ירא׳ בעיני כי בעל הטעמים הטעים
הענין בשיס טעם מהפך במלת תקח לרמוז כי למה שהוא
בדין העושה שליח לקדש לו אשה פלונית והלך השליח וקדשה
לעצמו מה שעשה עשוי לזה התחיל בחלוקת אשר לא תקח
לכלול בשבועתו ולומר לו שהאשה הראויה לבני לא תקח
לעצמך ותעשה רמאות בדבר :
כי אל ארצי ואל מולדתי · יש לדקדק ייתור
לבני ליצחק ובמדרש בפ׳ עם בני עם יצחק
דרשו עם בני אע״פ שאינו יצחק עם יצחק אף על פי שאינו בני

Fig. 43. Spurious Type (S6, S7, R5) and Ornaments 20–22.

כמה שאמרתי דבגזה יהיה טל דממילא אתי ולא כמה שאמרתי
דבארץ יהי חורב דהא טל לא מעכר אבל עכשו אגפה בגזה
לבדה והוא נסיון גדול שאע״פ שבכל הארץ ממילא שיהיה טל
ואנבה הגזה גם כן צריך להיות הטובה מכל מקום יהא הנסיון
בגזה שיהא עליה חורב · ואתי שפיר דקדוק אחר שאמר
בכתוב יהי נא חורב אל הגזה ועל כל הארץ יהיה טל גבי ארץ
אמר יהיה דמשמע בהויתו יהיה דהא לא מעכר ובחורב הגזה
אמר יהי נא חורב שמתפלל שישנה הטבע וכן משמע מלשון נא
פירוש בעת יהיה חורב מש״כ לעולם דטל לא מעכר וראיתי ברש״י
ז״ל שדרך כזה ושמח לבי :
יח א 1 S אמנם

Fig. 44. Spurious Type (Ro3, S7, R5).

Fig. 45. Woodcut V.

A SUGGESTED SOURCE FOR SOME OF THE SUBSTITUTE NAMES FOR YHWH

FRANK ZIMMERMANN

Reconstructionist Rabbinical College

By the common consent of scholars, the Tetragrammaton in the masoretic text was originally pronounced as Yahweh. The Hebrew text itself, however, never gives evidence other than a perpetual reading *adonai* of the letters in YHWH, or where necessity requires because of a conjuncture of *adonai* and YHWH, to read the letters as *elohim*. The oldest witness to the Hebrew text, the Greek translators as found in the uncials A and B, give no hint through any transliteration how it was articulated except to render YHWH by *kurios* "lord." This signifies that they read the Hebrew *adonai* "lord" uniformly and as a matter of course.[1]

In an early period, then, YHWH became replaced by *adonai* whereas other words as *el, shaddai, elohim, elyon* kept their vocalization and did not take on substitutes. The reason is obvious. Yahweh is the personal name of the god. These other names are either attributive or generic. *Elyon* is the "exalted one," rt. *alay; elohim* has a plural ending based on *eloha,* itself a broken plural founded on *el; shaddai* meaning "powerful one," and *el* "the covenanting one" from Arabic *alla* (with *teshdid*) as I had occasion to point out elsewhere.[2] However, YHWH as the name of the tribal god—a *shem,* reflecting character, nature, a palpable powerful extension of himself—became subject to substitution and modification.

We turn to the question: how did the word *adonai* come to be employed as a replacement for YHWH?

Now the term *adon,* applied to YHWH honorifically, was undoubtedly borrowed from the common speech of the people very much like *kurios, dominus, Herr,* and *Lord.* The everyday life provided the form, the modality of address. A man invoking another would simply address him by his name: Gen. 49.8, יהודה אתה יודוך אחיך ; Exod. 5.4 למה משה ואהרן תפריעו את העם ממעשיו . If more formality or respectful language was called for, the term *adoni* was prefixed: Num. 11.28 אדוני משה כלאם I Kings 18.7 האתה זה אדוני אליהו II Kings 4.16 אדוני איש האלהים.

The same mode obtained in invocation and prayer to YHWH. One could call upon YHWH directly, or one could be more ceremonial about it: a petitioner in his distress would supplicate YHWH directly:

> Ps. 3.2 יהוה מה רבו צרי
> invocatively Jud. 5.31 כן יאבדו כל אויביך יהוה
> I Sam. 3.9 דבר יהוה כי שומע עבדך
> II Kings 5.18 יסלח נא יהוה לעבדך

If he were worshipping more formally, he would prefix the word *adon,* at first it was *adoni Yahweh,* then *Adonai Yahweh* as I shall explain.

Words for "master, lord" would keep the singular form, Gen. 24.12 אדוני אברהם but very early such words acquired a plural formation, the plural of majesty in the common speech. Thus ויקח אדוני יוסף Gen. 30.20; דבר האיש אדוני הארץ Gen. 42.30; וסכרתי את מצרים ביד אדונים קשה Is. 19.4. Similarly with other words as *ba^cal* e.g. אם בעליו עמו Ex. 22.14; וחמור אבוס בעליו Is. 1.3.

At first, the worshipper would undoubtedly use *adoni Yahweh* which, if I do not have direct evidence for this, is suggested by the singular *adon* in other connections: שלש פעמים בשנה יראה כל זכורך אל פני האדן יהוה Ex. 23.17 and similarly Ex. 34.23. Comp. further Ps. 114.7 מלפני אדון חולי ארץ and of course the familiar examples of Isaiah's usage האדון יהוה צבאות 1.24; 3.1; 10.33; 19.4 and interestingly Mal. 3.1 האדון אשר אתם מבקשים .

But YHWH being the god who demanded and received homage more than any one, the singular gave way to the plural, the plural of majesty, so that in contrast to *adon,* the plural came to be employed ואם אדונים אני איה מוראי Mal. 1.6; הודו לאדוני האדונים Ps. 136.3 כי קדוש

היום לאדונינו Neh. 8.10; Is. 51.22 כה אמר אדוניך יהוה and even for a foreign god והנה אדוניהם נפל ארצה Jud. 3.25.

It is interesting that there was no prohibition against writing the name of YHWH but only against its utterance. Why should there be a prohibition against articulating the name of YHWH? By analogy, I should say that the same psychology that operated in ancient Egypt, for example, was prevalent in Israel. One may cite the example of the supreme god Re in a text dated in the Nineteenth Dynasty (1350–1200 B.C.E.) wherein Re has a secret name, and by this name he retains power universally over gods and mankind. He has other names; but this secret name Re keeps severely to himself. The goddess Isis desired to secure power for herself and it was urgent that she learn this hidden name. From spittle that the god Re had cast upon the ground, Isis kneaded some lime from the spittle and the soil to create a formidable snake who bit the god Re. The divine god almost expired from the cold chills and the high fever occasioned by the venomous bite. So he revealed his secret name and said to Isis: "Let thy ears be given to me, my daughter Isis, that my name may come forth from my body into thy body. Isis then cast a spell and thereby expelled the poison from Re."[3] We are impressed with the power and substance that a divine name has.

In a similar fashion, the name Yahweh, with its magic potency, would be in the hands of one who had control and manipulation of the name with its correct pronunciation, a formidable weapon of "sacred electricity" in Robertson Smith's phrase. It would be employed to work miracles, to destroy one's enemies, ward off harmful spirits, and demons of disease and death. It was very important that the name with its correct pronunciation not fall into improper hands. The latter rabbinic literature provides some clues as to the thinking that prevailed. A teacher could convey the pronunciation of the Tetragrammaton only to select pupils.[4] Abba Sha'ul declared that one could not have a portion in the world to come if one articulated the name of Yahweh as the letters represent it. Apparently there is a connection with the preceding statement relating to one who uttered incantations over a diseased person, that is, employing the name of YHWH for the purpose.[5]

Still there was a problem of the priestly benediction in public where the name was articulated, and in the public reading of the scroll of the Torah where enunciation was required. An ingenious solution, I believe, was hit upon. The public reader, in seeing the phrase, *adonai Yahweh,* uttered the first word by mouth and read Yahweh with his eye. He read *adonai* and implied Yahweh. It need hardly be mentioned that the prohibition of taking Yahweh's name in vain (Ex. 20.7) played its role in shaping up this regulation as other scholars have advanced. Conclusion: *Adonai* is not a substitute for Yahweh but part of a title.

Circumventions for avoiding the name of Yahweh manifest themselves within the Hebrew Bible itself. One may cite the case of the nameless son of the Israelite woman who suffered stoning because he cursed the Name ויקב בן האשה הישראלית את השם ויקלל without the specific mention of YHWH. We may note again v. 16 ונקב שם יהוה, מות יומת, but at the end of the verse the name is avoided again כגר כאזרח בנקבו שם יומת ... if an alien curse the Name, he shall be put to death. Seemingly the writer wished to avoid the repetition of the name. Observe too that the passage provenes from the P document, a matter of some moment as we shall see.

Associatively, in I Sam. 3.13 we are told that the sons of Eli were evil-doing, and Eli is to be punished אשר ידע כי מקללים להם בניו ולא כהה בם because he knows that his sons curse themselves (?), and he does not reprove them. "Themselves" is an obvious error for God. The Masoretes say that a *tiqqun soferim* is in place here and *li/lahem* should be read. The LXX correctly gives us the reading (Driver, S. R., *Notes to Samuel,* 44). Some scribe however consciously or unconsciously sought to substitute and tone down the brazen imprecation.

Very arresting is a passage in Amos 6.10. The context reads: And if ten men remain in one house, they shall die; and when a man's kinsman, or the one who burns a memorial for him shall take him up to bring the bones out of the house, and shall say to him in the innermost parts of the house, Is there still anyone with you? He shall say, No one; and the other shall say, Hush, you should not mention the name of YHWH.

ואמר לאשר בירכתי הבית העוד עמך ואמר אפס ואמר הס כי לא להזכיר בשם יהוה.

The difficulty is evident because the latter statement implies that YHWH's name was spoken. It should be obvious I think that the original wording had YHWH's name and the text read אפס יהוה which translated would be exclamatory: Nothing, by God! as if in oath while the other man responded: Don't mention YHWH's name, implying: His is the power which caused the earthquake; he did the damage; don't mention his name for fear power may be loosed again.

The construction אפס יהוה was shocking to some scribe as the expression could mean "Yahweh is of no account." This usage is found elsewhere in *Baba Batra* 111a where there is a similar expres-Rab Nitai thought to carry through a procedure according to the opinion of Rabbi Zechariah ben Hakazzab. Said Samuel to R. Nitai: According to whom? According to Zechariah? The opinion of Zechariah is not important. Zechariah is out! אפס זכריה .[6] And so in our Amos passage, Yahweh was omitted because of the sensibility of the scribe and his apprehension of profaning YHWH's name, in אפס י־הוה.

With the Second Commonwealth, the employment of Yahweh declined although Ezra, Nehemiah and Chronicles use the term freely. Substitutes for YHWH appear in Daniel as שמיא 4.23; עליא 4.29,31; חי עלמא v. 31; מלך שמיא 4.34; מרא שמיא 5.23. I Macc. uses the term "heaven" for the Deity. Surrogates proceeded apace with גבורה , מעלה ,שמים ,עליון.

I want to deal however with two perplexing ones: מקום "place" and שכינה "resting-place" as well as the term ברוך Aramaic בריכא. How is it that מקום "place" was used for God, as well as שכינה, a feminine?

The prophet who had the most profound and farreaching influence on the course of exilic Judaism was Ezekiel. Combining within himself the gift of prophecy as well as the ritual discipline and the legal training of a *Kohen,* he has been rightly called the father of Judaism. Many scholars would maintain that the priestly circles, about 400 B.C.E., who informed the whole compass of the Hexateuch with the supplement and redaction of the Priestly document owe their direction and doctrines to the profound stamp of Ezekiel on their minds.

For post-exilic Judaism, it was his words, his teaching, his impress that proved overriding and lasting, more than any other prophet.

C. 1–3.15 recount the episode of Ezekiel's revelation with all the overwhelming impact, and numinous terror in the presence of that awesome vision of Yahweh, his chariot, the wheels, the *kerubim* and the pinioned beasts with their intelligent eyes. Ezekiel was then transported to give Yahweh's message to the exiles:

ותשאני רוח ואשמע אחרי קול רעש גדול ברוך כבוד יהוה ממקומו

Qol here is to be taken in the sense of voice as the Greek translator (**λεγόντων**) and the Targum קל זיע סגי דמשבחין ואמרין imply, of celestial beings who were uttering "Blessed be the Glory of Yahweh from his place." *Because the words were in close association with the word YHWH in this divine revelation, and since YHWH was for-*

bidden to be pronounced, the words surrounding YHWH acquired because of their proximity the significance and potency of a quasi-divine appellative. Thus מקום because of the context became a surrogate for YHWH. Simon b. Shetaḥ employed the term in the first century B.C.E.[7]

שכינה as a surrogate for YHWH came through via the Aramaic. The Targum as a representative of synagogue exegesis translates ממקומו as אתר בית שכינתיה . The term שכינה could very easily be both Hebrew and Aramaic, but שכינתא, with its feminine formation in Aramaic undoubtedly supplied the Hebrew with its feminine ending. At any rate it is clear that because of its sacred association it acquired currency as a name for YHWH.

We should expect that כבוד mentioned in the verse would be similarly employed. Actually כבוד became better known as יקרא דיי׳ in Aramaic and, in essence, became a surrogate for God's name. Thus in Isa. 6.5 כי את המלך יהוה צבאות ראו עיני the Targum translates יקר שכינת מלך עלמיא avoiding the Tetragrammaton. יקרא דיי׳ is found frequently in the Targums and New Testament scholars will remember several instances where δοξα appears as a separate essence, as in John 1.14, Hebrews 9.5 χερουβειν δοξης. יקרא דיי׳ came through in an unexpected quarter. The mystics of the Middle Ages picked it up for their purpose and the יקרא "splendor, glory" became a characteristic feature of this thought and writing.

The word ברוך as a title for God had a limited development. In Mark 14.61 the High Priest asked Jesus the probing question, "Are you the son of the blessed?" which Matthew 26.23 varies with the more explicit "Are you the son of God"?[8] Where did this word "blessed" come to be a name for God? The answer may be supplied very appositely from my hypothesis. The authority for *barukh* came from its being uttered by the heavenly beings in the divine revelation to Ezekiel.

This idea that words contextual and contiguous to YHWH's name in a divine revelation became the basic surrogates for his name receives confirmation from another parallel and example. When Isaiah had his first revelation as reported in Isa. 6, and the celestial beings called to one another קדוש קדוש קדוש יהוה צבאות the word קדוש, by association with the name YHWH and sanctified by the utterance of the seraphim, became later another surrogate in the phrase קודשא בריך הוא the Holy One, blessed be He. הַקָּדֹשׁ as a divine substitute is the Hebrew equivalent (*Sifre,* ed. Friedman 33a; Dalman, *Words of Jesus,* Eng. trans. p. 202).

NOTES

1 There is no need in this paper to discuss the reproduction of Yahweh in the other Greek translators as Aquila, Symmachus and Theodotion. Comp. further JBL, IV, 1967, 477.

2 VT, XII, 1962, 190f.

3 Comp. Pritchard, ANET, 13.

4 b. Qiddushin 71a.

5 b. Sanhedrin XI.1.

6 רב ניתאי סבר למעבד עובדא כרבי זכריה בן הקצב אמר ליה שמואל כמאן כזכריה אפס זכריה.

7 Ta'anit 3.8 מה אעשה לך שאתה מתחטא לפני המקום

8 ὁ υἱὸς τοῦ εὐλογητοῦ ‖ ὁ υἱὸς τοῦ θεοῦ

מחקרים במדעי
היהדות

ספר יובל

לכבוד

יצחק קיוב

מחקרים במדעי היהדות

ספר יובל

לכבוד

יצחק קיוב

מוגש לו ע"י חבריו ומעריציו
כאות הוקרה לציון יובלו הס"ה
ולציון ארבעים שנה של עבודה
פוריה בשדה הספרנות היהודית.

בעריכת

יהושע ברלין

ניו־יורק

„כתב"

תשל"ב

תוכן

For Table of Contents of English Section, see p. vii.

מדרש לחנוכה בכתב־יד עברי מאויר של הספריה הלאומית בפריס

ישראל אדלר
בית הספרים הלאומי והאוניברסיטאי
ירושלים

המדרש המתפרסם כאן לפי כתב היד Heb. 1459 של הספריה הלאומית בפריס [1] מהוה נוסחה נוספת לאגדות סביב נושא הספור על יהודית ואשר לרובם רק קשר רופף עם ספר יהודית שבכתובים אחרונים [2].

בחינת הרכבם של ספורי אגדות אלה מעלה שיש בהם שני חלקים עיקריים: א׳) הספור על התנקשות בחיי מנהיג אויב — ובצוע ההתנקשות כאן לאו דוקא מעשה ידי אשה — הבאה כתגובה על מקרה של איום בהזדקקות ל־jus primae noctis. חלק זה של המדרש, המובא בכל המקורות בקשר עם חנוכה, זיקתו לספר יהודית רחוקה ביותר; ב׳) ספור על התנקשות אחרת בחיי מנהיג אויב — ובצוע ההתנקשות כאן תמיד מעשה ידי אשה — אשר זיקתו לספור שבספר יהודית נראית לעין אם כי שֵם גבורת הספור אינו מוזכר בו תמיד.

אפשר למיין את המקורות המביאים ספור אגדה על הנושא הנ״ל לפי הרכבו של הספור הכולל את החלק הראשון בלבד, את החלק השני בלבד או צרוף של שני החלקים יחד. והרי כמה ציונים למקורות בהתאם למיון זה:

א. מקורות הכוללים את החלק הראשון בלבד: מגלת תענית, פרק ו׳ [3], אשר שם גבורת הספור האנונימית הנה בתו של מתתיה; המדרש לחנוכה המובא אצל ילינק, **בית המדרש**, חלק ו׳ (וינה, 1878), ע׳ 1—3, אשר בו גבורת הספור נקראת בשם חנה בת מתתיה; **ביוצר לשבת ב׳ של חנוכה**, אשר שם היא מופיעה בשם חנה; **בפירוש ר׳ נסים בן ראובן גירונדי** על הלכות האלפסי למסכת שבת, פרק ב׳ [4], אשר שם גבורת הספור האנונימית הנה בתו של יוחנן. אפשר לכלול בסוג זה גם את נוסח הספור המופיע **בכל־בו** [5] אשר שם גבורת הספור נקראת בשם יהודית בת יוחנן כהן גדול. אמנם מעשה ההתנקשות לא בא כאן על רקע גזירת ה־jus primae noctis כי אם כתגובה על תאוות ״מלך יוון״ לאשה ״יפת תואר מאוד״, אך הצד השוה שבין הספור כאן לזה שבמקורות הקודמים שמעשה ההתנקשות בא בהם כתגובה על מקרה מסוים של איום בחלול

כבודה של בת ישראל בעוד שבמקורות סוג ב׳ אותו מעשה בא כ י ז מ ה, ללא גורם אישי, מצד גבורת הספור.

ב. מקורות הכוללים את החלק ה ש נ י ב ל ב ד: מלבד הטקסטים המהוים עבוד של ספר יהודית בלבוש עברי כמו זה שמובא אצל ילינק, **בית המדרש**, חלק ב׳ (ליפציג, 1853), ע׳ 12—22, שייכים לסוג זה הספור על ״נערה מבנות הנביאים״ שבחבור יפה מן הישועה מאת נסים בן יעקב מקירואן [6] והטקסט, הקרוב מאוד לקודם, המובא אצל ילינק **בית המדרש**, חלק א׳ (ליפציג, 1853), ע׳ 130—131, אשר גם בו גבורת הספור הנה נערה ירושלמית אנונימית ״מבנות הנביאים״.

ג. בסוג שלישי זה מוצאים הרכב של שני החלקים הנ״ל המופיעים בספור, זה בצד זה, או משולבים יחד. שייכים לסוג הזה המדרש לחנוכה המובא אצל ילינק, **בית המדרש**, חלק א׳ (ליפציג, 1853), ע׳ 132—136 ונוסח המדרש שבכתב יד שלנו, הדומה בעקרו לחלקים המקבילים של הטקסט המובא אצל ילינק, כדלהלן:

נוסח כתב היד שלנו קרוב לטקסט של ילינק החל מן הפסקא השניה שבעמוד 132 (״דרש מרי בר מר...״) עד לסוף הפסקא שבעמוד 134 (״ובא לציון גואל״) ובתוספת שלוש השורות האחרונות שבעמוד 136. ההבדלים העיקריים (מלבד ״שנויי נוסחאות״) בין שני הטקסטים הנם כדלהלן: פ ת י ח ה: מדרש שונה של אותו פסוק (״כי נר מצוה״ וכו׳); ח ל ק א׳ ש ל ה ס פ ו ר: בכתב היד שלנו גבורת הספור נקראת בשם [יהודית] [7] בת מתתיה בן יוחנן כהן גדול, בטקסט של ילינק הנה אנונימית, בתו של יוחנן כהן גדול; ח ל ק ב׳ ש ל ה ס פ ו ר: בכתב היד שלנו חלק זה של הספור ה מ ש ו ל ב עם החלק הראשון (גבורת הספור כאן זהה עם זו של החלק הראשון), הרבה יותר מפותח מאשר בטקסט המובא אצל ילינק, אשר שם החלק הזה ב א ב צ ד ו של החלק הראשון ללא קשר אורגני עמו (גבורת הספור שם, אלמנה בשם יהודית, אינה זהה עם זו שבחלק הראשון).

[דף 20, ב:]

חנוכה. כי נר מצוה וכו׳ ארז״ל כי נר מצוה [זה חנוכה] ותורה אור זה מתן תורה. כי לעולם ביום שחל להיו׳ עצרת בו ביום יבוא להיות יום חנוכ׳. תנו רבנן בימי מלכות יון הרשעה גזרו שמד על ישר׳ שלא יעסקו בתור׳ ולא ישימו בריח בבתיהם וכל מי שיהיה לו שור שיכתוב בקרן השור אין להם חלק בי״ אלהי ישר׳ ושלא ישמרו את השבת ושלא יקריבו קרבן ושלא ימולו ומי שישא אשה שיעבירנה קודם לפני השר תחלה ויבעול אותה ואח״כ תחזור לבעלה. נהגו בדבר זה ג׳ שני׳ וח׳ חדשים עד שנשאת בתו של מתתיה בן יוחנן כ״ג וכשנתחברו לסעודה הסירה תכשיטיה וקרעה בגדיה ולבשה סמרטוטי׳ ונכנסה אליהן. כיון שרא׳ אותה יהודה אחיה כך העיר עליה חימה ואמ׳ לה אין את מתביישת מן העם הזה. אמרה לו מוטב שאתבייש לפני אחיי ועמי משלא אתביי׳ לפני ערל וטמא והלא תזכרו מה עשו שמעון ולוי על דינה אחות׳ מפני שטימא אותה שכם. באותה שעה נתמלאו חימה וקנאה ויועץ יהודה עם אחיו שידקרוהו בחרב. מה עשה יהוד׳ הביא הדס וכל עצי בשמים וכל ריח טוב והציען מביתו עד בית השר. כיון שרא׳ אותם השר שעשו לו כל אותו הכבוד אמ׳ הללו הם הגדולי׳ הנכבדים

שבישר׳ וכבר נכנסו שמחים ראוי לכבדם. באותה שעה הוציא כל שריו וגדוליו לחוץ ונשאר הוא ויהודה ואחיו ועשה הב״ה למען שמו ונתן כח ביהוד׳ ואחיו ודקרו את השר בחרב ורדפו ישר׳ את היונים מעכו עד נמירי׳ ומיד חזרו ישר׳ לעסוק בתורה ולקיים המצות ולחזור בתשובה ונתבטלה הגזירה. והיו ישר׳ אשר בירושלם באימה ובפחד גדול חושבים כי נהרג יהודה ואחיו במלחמה. ונכנס מתתיה לבית המקד׳ לעבוד עבודת[ו ?] ויצאת ב״ק מבית קדשי הקדשי׳ נצחו טליא דאזלו לאגח׳ קרבא באנטוכיא. כיון ששמע מלך יוונים שהרגו בני מתתיה את השר שלו קבץ כל חילותיו ובא וחנה על ירושלם ברחוק מיל. והיו ישר׳ באימה ופחד גדול ובבכי ותענית וחזרו בתשובה לפני ה׳ והיו עוסקי׳ בתורה יומם ולילה. והיה שם עם מלך היווני׳ הגמון אחד חכם [דף 21, א:] ונסתכל באצטגנוני׳ ואמ׳ למלך אדוני המלך כל זמן שישר׳ הן ומחזי׳ במצותיה׳ אין שום [בריה] יכולה להזיק להם. מיד נתמלא חימה עליו וכפהו [צ״ל: וכפתו? או, בהתאם לתיקון בשוליים: וכפהו תחת ידיו?] בידיו ותלאהו בהם חי כדי שלא ימות במהרה אצל שערי ירושלם. והיו רואים אותו כל ישר׳ מבפני׳ מן החומה כשהיה תלוי ושאלו אותו מן המגדל על מה עשו לו כך. א״ל בשביל שלמדתי זכות על ישר׳. מה עשתה יהודית בת מתתיה שהית׳ יפה עד מאד כיון שראת׳ צער ישר׳ מסרה עצמה לשמים ואמרה אלך אני בעצמי לערל הזה שאני בטוחה במקום שיעשו לי נס ואהרג את הערל הזה ויושיע את ישר׳ על ידי. ותעש לה חרב שתי פיות ותשם אותו במנעלה והגיעה עד שערי ירושלים ואמרה לשוערים שיפתחו לה. אמרו שמא חשקת אחד מעבדי המלך. אמרה ח״ו אלא אני בוטחת ברחמי ה׳ שיעזרוני ואהרוג את הצורר הזה. ונשבעה להם באמונת שמים ופתחו לה ולשפחתה. ותלכנה בדרך עד שהגיעו לפני המלך וכשראה המלך את יפיה נשאה חן בעיניו ויאמ׳ לה מי את ומאין תבא. אמרה לו אנכי מבנות הנביאי׳ ושמעתי מאבי כשהיה חי שתלכד העיר ביד מלך גדול ואין מלך חשו׳ כמותך וכששמעו ישר׳ את הנבואה הזאת אחזה בשרם פלצות ועתה הנה באתי אליך לבשרך ואני שואלת מאתך שתחיה את אמי ואת אחיי ואת כל בית אבי. אמ׳ לה המלך אנכי אעשה כדברך ואמלא כל משאלותיך והנה חותמי בידך ובלבד שאקחך לאשה. ותאמ׳ לו אדוני המלך ואנכי לא אהיה כאחת שפחותיך ואם תצוה עלי להיות שפחת׳ לא אסור ממצותך ימין או שמאל אבל אודיע לך כי אני טמאה והיום נשלמו ימי לבוני וכתו׳ בתורתינו לטבול במים וכדי שאטהר אני צריכ׳ לעשות טבילה קודם שאשכב עמך ואחר אעשה כדבר המלך. אך צוה מעתה בכל מחנותך ויעבירו קול בכל קהלך שאם יראו הלילה ב׳ נשים יורדות למעיין שלא יגעו בהם ולא יזיקו׳ ולא ילכו אחריהן לראות מה הן עושות. וארד אני ואמתי ואטבול להשלים חפצך. מיד שמח המלך מאד על רוב יפיה ועל חכמת דבריה ועל אמריה ויותר על הבשורה ונשבע לה לקחתה לו לאשה ולשום כתר מלכות בראשה ושאחר שילכוד ירושלם ישים אותה גברת על כל הגבירות

[דף 21 ב:]

בשכר הבשורה. ויצו המלך ויעבירו קול במחנה לאמר איש ואשה אל יעשו שום דבר לשתי הנשים הללו. ומרוב השמחה אסף את כל שריו ויעש את כל שריו ואת גדוליו משתה גדול לכלם וישתו ויאכלו וישכרו עמו וגם המלך נשכר מאד. ויאמר לה המלך לעת הערב גושי הלום וחבקיני ונשקיני כדי שאהיה בטוח בך[?]. אמרה אדוני המלך יש לי בשת מהיושבים כאן אבל צוה ויוציאו כל איש מעלינו. ויצו המלך להיעשות. כיון שיצאו כלם התחיל לחבקה ולנשקה ותיישנהו על ברכה עד שנרדם מרוב השכרות וכשראתה כך העלמה כיונה לבה ודעתה ונשאה עיניה לשמים שיעזרנה. מיד הוציאה חרבה ממנעלה וכרתה ראשו ותשימהו בדוד אחד ותצא עם שפחת׳ ותלך האשה לדרכה ולא דברו להם מטוב ועד רע כי מצות המלך היא עד שהגיעו לשערי ירושלם. ותקרא אל השוערים ותאמר לאמר פתחו לי כי ה׳ ברחמיו עזרני והרגתי את הרשע והנה ראשו בידי. ולא האמינו לה השוערי׳ ותאמר להם הנה השר התלוי חי אצל השער והוא יכיר אותו. ויגיעו עד ההגמון והראהו הגלגלת ויכירה ויאמר ברוך ה׳ אלהי ישר׳ אשר סגר אותו בידכם והושיעכם בידו עתה ידעתי כי גדול מכל האלהי׳. באות׳ שעה פתחו לה. וכששמעו כך מתתיה ובניו ואנשי ירושלם נאספו כלם ויצאו מן העיר ונפלו על האויבים והיו קורא׳ בקול גדול שמע ישר׳ י׳ אלהי׳ י׳ אחד. ויעש לו יהוד׳ מגן אחד וחרות עליו שם מפור׳ היוצא ממי כמוכ׳ באלהי׳ ה׳. וכשמו[ע] כך אישי המלחמה הלכו אצל אדוניהם והנה אדוניה׳ נופל ארצה מבלי גלגלת. ויעזבו את אהליהם ואת כל אשר להם המחנה כאשר היה וינוסו לנפשם. ויהרגום בני ישר׳ מכה גדולה מאד ויכנעו כל הגוים תחת יד ה׳ ישר׳ ולא יספו עוד לצאת ראשם ותלך יד בני ישר׳ הלוך וקשה. וישמחו למחר ואח״כ באו לדביר ה׳ ויפנו את ההיכל ויטהרו את המקדש וידליקו נרות בבית המקדש וקבעו ח׳ ימים בהלל. כאשר בדקו ולא מצאו שמן שלא נגעו בו היוני׳ וטימאוהו רק פך אחד של שמן שהיה מונח בחותמו של כ״ג ולא היה בו רק כדי להדליק לילה אחת ונעשה בו נס והדליקו בו את המנורה ח׳ ימי׳. ולכן קבעו לדורות לעשו׳ אלו הימי׳ בהלל והודאה ולהדליק נרות בכל ליל זכרון לנסי׳ שנעשו לאבותי׳.

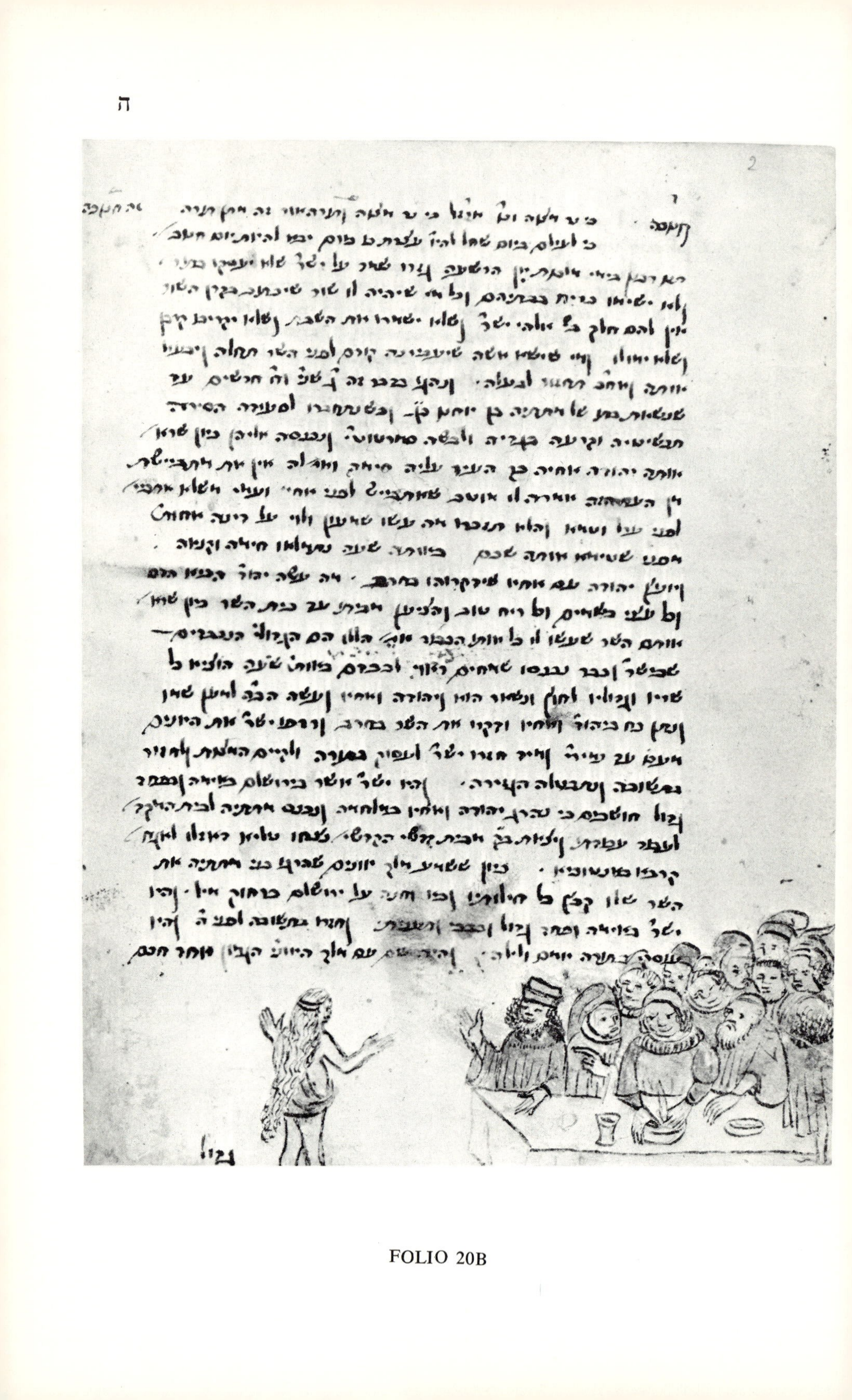

FOLIO 20B

FOLIO 21A

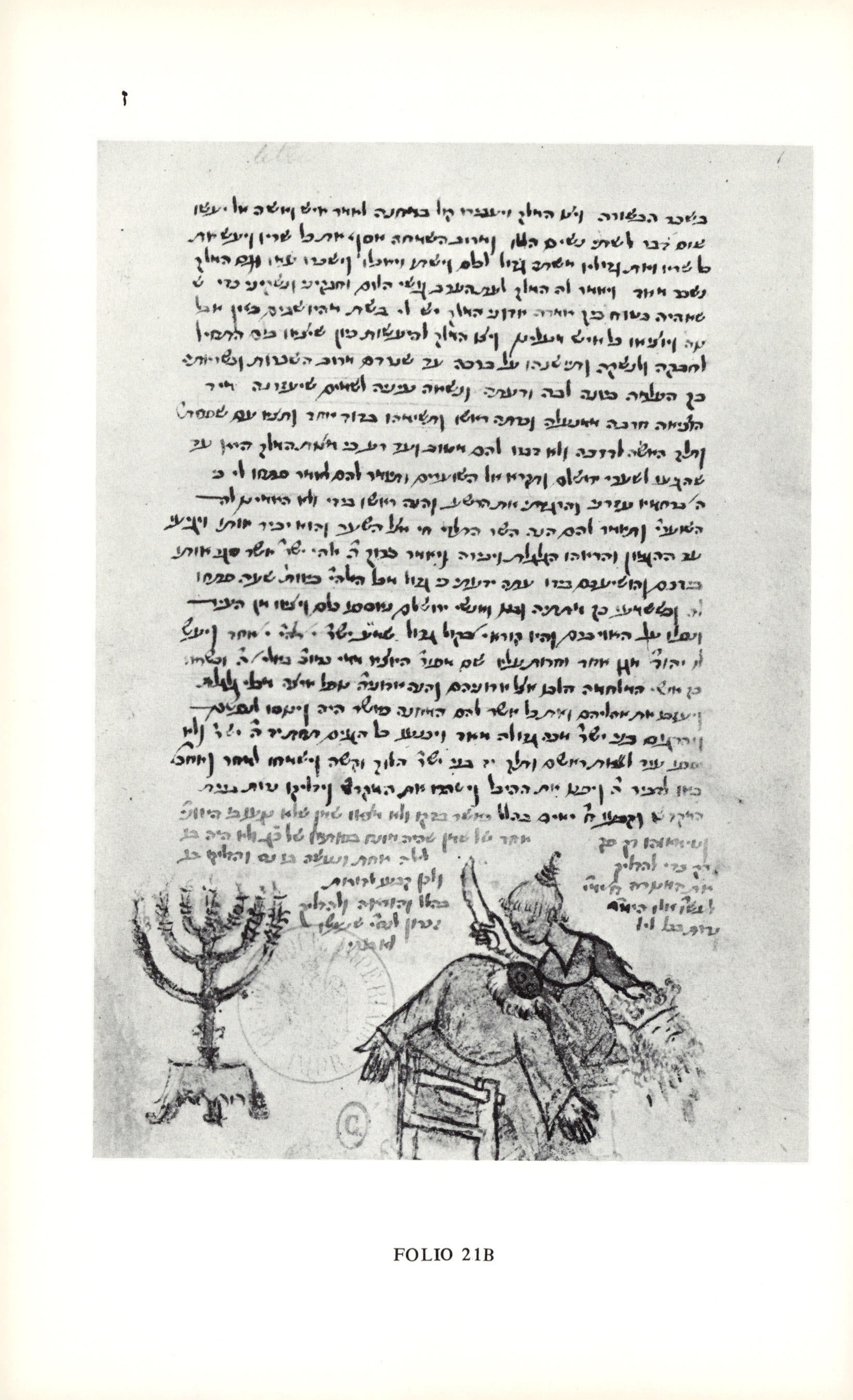

FOLIO 21B

הערות

[1] כ״י זה שייך לקבוצה קטנה של כתבי יד עבריים הנספחים לדפוסים של הספריה הלאומית בפריס ושבגלל סבה זו נעלמו מעיני עורך הקטלוג של כתבי היד העבריים של ספריה זו. במאמרי *Manuscrits hébraïques dans les imprimés de la Bibliothèque nationale* בתוך *Révue des études juives*, 4e série, t. II, 1962, p. 194–200 אפשר למצא תאור ביבליוגרפי מפורט גם של כתב יד זה. אסתפק כאן בציון שכה״י, הנספח לדפוס מ ש ל ה ק ד מ ו נ י (Res. Ya. 12), הנו כ״י אשכנזי מן המחצית השניה של המאה ה־16 והוא כולל מלבד המדרש לחנוכה את הספור (בצורת מקאמה) ב ג י ד ת ה ז מ ן. שנים מתוך עשרים וארבעת הציורים שבכתב היד מוקדשים לטקסט של המדרש לחנוכה והנם אולי מעשה ידיו של ״משה הסופר״ החותם את שמו בסוף החלק הראשון של כתב היד.

[2] ראה צונץ־אלבק, ה ד ר ש ו ת ב י ש ר א ל . . ., ירושלים, תשי״ד, ע׳ 60 וע׳ 299, הערה 25; S. Krauss, *La fête de Hanoucca* בתוך *Revue des études juives*, כ׳ 30 (1895), ע׳ 24 וכו׳ ובמיוחד הע׳ 37—43; I. Lévi, *Hanoucca et le jus primae noctis* בתוך כתב העת הנ״ל, הכרך הנ״ל, ע׳ 220—231; A. M. Dubarle, *La mention de Judith dans la littéraire ancienne juive et chrétienne*, in *Revue biblique*, vol. LXVI (1959), pp. 514–549.

[3] מהדורת ש. ש. פיגנזהן, וילנה, ראם, תרפ״ה, ע׳ 26.

[4] ״הלכות חנוכה״, דף י׳ ע״ב במהדורת וילנה, ראם, 1881—1886.

[5] דפוס ויניציאה, שכ״ז, דף מג ע״ב, טור ב׳.

[6] תרגום עברי מן המקור הערבי על ידי ח. ז. הירשברג, ירושלים, תשי״ד, ע׳ 53—56.

[7] שם גבורת הספור, יהודית, מתגלה רק בחלק השני של הספור.

זכרונות נשכחים
[מתוך הגנזך של ד״ר מרדכי וישניצר ז״ל]

שלמה אידלברג
מכללת שטרן
ישיבה אוניברסיטה

ד״ר מ. וישניצר [1] ההיסטוריון הנודע בחקר תולדות יהודי רוסיה ופולין היה אישיות רבת פנים. נוסף להיותו איש ציבור מובהק, עסק גם בעריכה ובמו״לות. בישיבתו בברלין יסד בשנות העשרים הוצאת ספרים בשם ״רמון״. יחד עם אשתו גב׳ רחל וישניצר הוציא לאור כתב עת בשם ״רמון״. תוכן כתב־העת היה מאמרים בהיסטוריה, מחשבה ספרות אומנות. המאמרים שנושאם היה אמנות נערכו ע״י גב׳ רחל וישניצר ואילו שאר הנושאים נערכו ע״י ד״ר מ. וישניצר, תחילה יחד עם ברוך קרופניק (קרוא), ולאחר מכן עם משה קליינמאן. הצורה החיצונית של חוברות אמנות הדורה ביותר, ובנוי מושך את הלב. כדרך עורכים נהלה מערכת ״רמון״ חליפת מכתבים עם סופרים רבים ביניהם גדולי הסופרים והמשוררים של הזמן ההוא. בידי ד״ר וישניצר היה אוסף גדול של מכתבים ואגרות. עקב הנדודים והטלטולים שעברו על משפחת וישניצר נשאר רק מעט מהקורספונדנציה העשירה הזאת. פרופ׳ רחל וישניצר הואילה בטובה להרשות לי להשתמש באגרות אשר נשארו לפליטה. ותודתי נתונה לה ע״כ.

א. אגרות מאת מרדכי דוב (ג׳ורג׳) לאנגר [2]. מ. ד. לאנגר סופר ומשורר צ׳כי ועברי, בן למשפחה אמידה ומתורבתת, אשר גדל בסביבה מתבוללת, (אחיו פרנצישק לאנגר היה רופא ידוע וסופר ומבקר אמנותי צ׳כי מפורסם) [3].

מ. ד. לאנגר בעל נפש נרגשת וכשרוני להפליא לא מצא את מקומו בסביבה של צעירי פראג, התרחק מהם. תהפוכות חייו הביאוהו להדבק בחסידות, ישב כשנתיים בחצר הרבי מבעלז, לבש בגדי חסיד וגדל זקן ופיאות. למד בכוחות עצמו עברית והגיע לכלל כתיבת שירים בלשון עברית. אח״כ נסוג אחור מרעיונותיו הדתיים, התקרב לפרנץ קאפקה [4] ואף למדוהו עברית. התהלך כריע עם מאקס ברוד שעודד אותו בעבודותיו הספרותיות.

נוסף להתענינותו בספרות כללית, עברית וחסידות התקרב מ. ד. לאנגר לחקר הפסיכואנאליזה. וכתב בשטח הזה מאמרים מדעיים. התקרבותו לציונות הביאוהו לביקור

בארץ לפני מלחמת העולם השניה, ביקר אבל לא השתקע בה. בפרוץ מלחמת העולם השניה זכה להגיע לשערי הארץ, ברם כוחותיו לא עמדו לו הוא חלה, ושכב בבית חולים בת״א ולמרות הסעד והעזרה שקיבל מידידיו ומוקיריו בארץ מת מחוליו גלמוד וערירי.

1. ד״ר מ. וישניצר ניסה להפיץ את ה״רמון״ בין דורשי עברית ותרבותה באירופה ובאמריקה. בין הסופרים שהזמין להשתתף היה מאכס ברוד שישב אז בפראג. ברוד שלח לעורך ג׳ שירים שכתב ריעו מ. ד. לאנגר והמליץ להדפיסם ב״רמון״. נראה שהעורך הבטיח להדפיס שיר אחד. במכתב מח׳ אייר תרפ״ב מודה לאנגר לד״ר וישניצר על ההבטחה, מאידך הוא תוהה ושואל: ״מה חסרון שאר השירים״? הוא גם תאב לדעת מתי יופיע השיר הנבחר.

2. מדבריו בגלויה שנכתבה בששי לשני 1923 נכרת חוסר סבלנות, לאנגר חוזר ושואל מתי יידפס שירו. הוא מזהה את שם השיר: ״כגווע פנימה״. לאנגר מרמז שביאליק וברוד שניהם זכרו לטוב את השיר הזה. הוא גם מודיע שעתיד להופיע ספרו "Die Erotik der Kabbala" ומציע לשולחו כשי״ל אל מערכת רמון על מנת שיכתבו בקורת על ספרו. (הספר י״ל ב־1923).

3. בגלויתו משני לשלישי 1923, דורש לאנגר במפגיע מד״ר וישניצר שיודיעו מתי יידפס השיר ב״רימון״. הוא גם מודיעו שאליעזר שטיינמן הדפיס שנים משיריו בכ״ע ״קולות״ ששטיינמן ערך אז בורשה[5]. השיר היפה והעדין ״כגווע פנימה״ לא נדפס ב״רמון״, גם בקורת על ספרו של לאנגר לא נמצא בחוברות ״רמון״. אבל שיר זה נדפס אח״כ בשני ספרי שיר של מ. ד. לאנגר: בחוברת ״פיוטים ושירי ידידות״ פראג תרפ״ט, ובחוברת ״מעט צרי״ שי״ל ע״י דבר, ת״א, תש״ג.

מתוכן הגלויה הזאת נראה שד״ר וישניצר ביקש מלאנגר לעזור לו בהפצת ה״רמון״ לאנגר מודיעו שמצב הפצת ספרים עבריים בפראג אינו מעודד ביותר: ״היות והקוראים עברית מעטים ודלים״. מאידך מרמז לאנגר, אשר רצה מאוד ששירו יראה אור ב״רמון״, שאם שירו יידפס, הוא יעביר לוישניצר כתובות פרטיות של אנשים והסתדרויות ויתכן שיימצאו מעונינים ברכישת ה״רמון״. לא נודע לי תוצאות ההתכתבות הזאת וכן גם הטעם למה לא נדפס השיר הזה ב״רמון״.

ב. אגרת מאת אהרן גורלאנד.

ד״ר א. גורלאנד[6] סופר חוקר והוגה דעות נולד בוילנה למשפחה מכובדת. כסטודנט נסע להשתלם בשויצריה. שם הצטרף לתנועה הציונית והיה מבין חברי נחמן סירקין. גורלאנד בעל נפש סוערת חפש מפלט בפילוסופיה — כתב ספר על הרמן כהן — ובעיקר מקום בחברה הגועשת של תקופת המהפכה וחידוש רעיונות פוליטיים, ברם קשה היה לו למצוא מקום מנוחה. הוא נדד על פני ארצות שונות, חזר משויצריה לרוסיה, מרוסיה הגר לאנגליה, מאנגליה לארה״ב, שם גם הצטרף ללגיון העברי. אחרי המלחמה ישב זמן מה ביפו והשתתף ב״האמת״. משם עבר לקהיר שבמצרים, ומשם חזר לוילנה, ומווילנה לברלין. בשבתו בברלין השתתף ב״מילגרוים״ שהוציא וישניצר לאור יחד עם ״רמון״ העברי (ראה מאמרו ב״מילגרוים״ II, חוב׳ ב׳). בשנות העשרים התהלכו בברלין סופרים יהודים רבים, ביניהם שהושפעו מהמהפכה הקומוניסטית, מהם עזבו את ברלין והתישבו ברוסיה הסוביטית. ביניהם היה ד״ר גורלאנד שאחרי נדודיו הרבים לא זכה לקבל עליו את הרעיון הציוני שחלם עליו רבות בימי נעוריו. על חייו ברוסיה ועל אחריתו

לא נודע דבר. אגרתו לד״ר וישניצר כתובה ברוח שקטה ובקבלת גזר־דין, כעובד במחלקה לכת״י עבריים שבספריה ע״ש לנין במוסקבה.

4. במכתבו של גורלאנד מ־21.6.28 הוא שואל פרטים מד״ר וישניצר על כתב יד של הספר ״מציב גבולות עמים״ ליוסף הכהן בעל ״עמק הבכא״. מהשאלות ניכר שגור־לאנד היה אז טירון בחקר ספרי יוסף הכהן (את הפרטים המעטים שמזכיר הוא לקח מהאנציקלופדיה היהודית (הגרמנית והרוסית).

ספר ״מציב גבולות עמים״ הוא בעצם עיבוד שעיבד יוסף הכהן מהתרגום האיטלקי של ספרו של יואנס אובאנוס בוֹאֶמוּס, שענינו נושאים גיאוגרפיים־היסטוריים, שנכתב בלאטינית וי״ל באוגסבורג בשנת 1520 (יש גם תרגום אנגלי של הספר). עיבודו של יוסף הכהן נמצא בכ״תי בכמה העתקים במוזיאון הבריטי (ר׳ הקטלוג הכללי של ב. מ., עמ׳ 343), וכן נמצא העתק במחלקה לכ״י שבספרית באטלער של אוניב. קולומביה X893 — K82.

ג. מכתב מאת יצחק צבי ברוֹדוּצקי באירקוטסק [7]

המכתב מאת י. צ. ברודוצקי לא נכתב אל ד״ר וישניצר, אלא לעורכי האנציקלופדיה [8] ״אשכול״ שוישניצר היה מעורכי המאמרים שנכתבו על מזרח אירופה. נראה שהמערכת שלחה את המכתב לד״ר וישניצר ונשאר באוספו הפרטי.

י. צ. ברוֹדוּצקי נולד בסלוצק, לאחר שלמד שנים בישיבות שונות נדד ע״ג קהילות שונות ובתחילת המאה הכ׳ הגיע לאירקוטסק שבסיביר. שמש גם כמורה ושוחט ומשנת 1908 היה השמש של ביה״כ הגדול שבאירקוטסק שבין מתפלליו היו אנשים בעלי עבר שונים שנתגלגלו לאירקוטסק הן כמחפשי הון ומסחר והן כגולים פוליטיים שנשתקעו שם. ברודוצקי בשבתו באירקוטסק התענין בתולדות היהודים בסיביר. אסף חומר וידיעות על כך ופרסם מאמרים בעתונות בשלוש לשונות: עברית, אידיש ורוסית וחתם על גביהם שמו בתוספת תוארו ״שמש דמתא אירקוטסק״.

5. במכתבו מי״ז באלול תרפ״ו הוא מעיד על הגחלת שבערה עדיין בין יהודי סיביר המזרחית. הוא גם מוסר על ההתענינות הרבה שיש לו וליהודים אחרים במקומו, בעניני יהדות. דבריו היפים נכתבו בפשטות ובתמימות ישרה. הוא גם מיעץ לעורכים: ״כי ישימו לב לבאר ולתאר כל ביוגרפיה בלי שום טנדנציה כחל ושרק רק האמת תהא נר לרגלם״. ומודיע שהוא מוכן לקבל על עצמו שלא על מנת לקבל פרס לכתוב ערכים על הקאנטוניסטים, סובאטניקים, וסתם גולים יהודים שהוגלו לסיביר. בדבריו הוא מזכיר על הצעת שני מלומדים ד״ר י. ל. כצנלסון (הסופר בוקי בן יגלי) ופרופ׳ מַרקוֹן, להוציא אנציקלופדיה עברית, וברודצקי שלח בזמנו אליהם חומר על תולדות יהודי סיביר ולא ידוע לו מה היה סופו של חומר זה. כמו כן לא ידוע לנו אחריתו של אדם מופלא זה אשר ישב בירכתי סיביר, ואף בתקופת השלטון הקומוניסטי כל מאויי נפשו היה לאסוף ידיעות על תולדות היהודים בחבל ארץ הזה.

בזה אני מסיים את רשימת האגרות שהיו לפני מתוך צער על שרוב החומר הארכיוני של ד״ר מ. וישניצר אבד ואיננו.

[1] על אישיותו ופעולותיו של ד"ר מ. וישניצר ראה ז. שזר, אור אישים, כרך א', עמ' 180 ואילך, וד"ר נ. מ. גלבר, "ד"ר מ. וישניצר" בס' "חכמת ישראל במערב אירופה", בעריכת ד"ר ש. פדר־בוש, כרך ב', עמ' 109 ואילך.

[2] ר' דב סדן, אבני זכרון, עמ' 243 ואילך. וגם מאמרה של מרים זינגר על מ. ג. לאנגר, ב"מעריב" מיום 4.11.69, עמ' 27.

[3] למרות שפ. לאנגר היה מתבולל הוא כתב הקדמה נוגעת ללב להוצאה האנגלית של הספר "תשעה שערים", שאחיו מרדכי דב כתבו בצ'כית. שם ההקדמה נדפס ב־My Brother Jiri. Langer, M. G., *Nine Gates, Chassidic Mysteries*. D. Mc-Kay Co. 1961 הספר י"ל בגר־מנית בשם: Neun Tore במינכן 1957. ההקדמה נכתבה ע"י גרשם שלום.

[4] ב"פיוטים ושירי ידידות" הקדיש מ. ד. לאנגר שיר למותו של פרנץ קאפקה, בשם "למות המשורר" ומתחיל בתיאור אימת המוות "אכן התור הגיע החבילה מתפרדת".

[5] ורשה תרפ"ג, שנה א', חוב' ג, ה, ו'.

[6] על ד"ר א. גורלאנד, ר' בלעקסיקון של זלמן רייזען, ווילנא 1926, חלק א', ע' 552. וכן בלעקסי־קון היהודי, חלק ב', נ. י. 1958, עמ' 197 (שני הערכים אינם מעודכנים).

[7] על י. צ. ברודוצקי, ראה בלעקסיקון של ז. רייזען, כרך א' ע' 393.

[8] הכוונה לאנציקלופדיה "אשכול". בעריכת יעקב קלצקין, הופיעו בעברית שני כרכים בלבד: א. 1929 ו־ב. 1932.

ר׳ מרדכי אליעזר וועבר ז״ל: חייו וספריו

נפתלי בן־מנחם
ירושלים

נולד בעיירה קטנה באונגאריה, Petroveselo, בשנת תקפ״ב [1822], עלה לירושלים בשנת תרל״ה [1875], בערך, ונפטר בה ביום כז בתמוז תרנ״ב [22.7.1892] [1], בן שבעים.

אביו, ר׳ דוד, היה סוחר ובנו מספר עליו[2]: הגם שהיה עני בלא נכסים ולא היה רב לעדתו ולא מורה, היה משגיח על העדה... אהבת תורה ואהבת ת״ח ואהבת רבו הגאון חת״ס [חת״ם סופר] זצוק״ל אינו בנמצא בין סוחרים כמו אבא מארי ז״ל, ולהיפך שנאה של רשעים בעלי עבירה ופרעדיגער [מטיפים] ג״כ קשה למצוא דוגמתו בין אנשי העולם שאינם רבנים והמשרה על שכמם. עוד מספר הבן עליו, ששימש ״גבאי ארץ־הקודש כל ימיו וחיבב את אה״ק עד כלות הנפש. והנוסע לאה״ק או אורח הגון מאה״ק היה כבבת עיניו בחיבה״. הוא היה מקפיד שבנו יחידו, ר׳ מרדכי אליעזר, לא ילמד חלילה ״לימודים אחרים״ ושלא ילבש ״מלבושי נכרים״ ומובן, ש״ספרי דעססא [3] והמאספים היו כחמץ בפסח בבית״. קפדן היה האיש ומטיל מוראו על כל הקהילה, ש״אם היה בעל דרשן אומר תיבה אחת שלא כהוגן והיה נראה כאילו נוטה חוץ לשיטה היה מוכרח לירד מתוך הדרשה״, כלומר: הכריח אותו לירד מן הבמה, שאין רחמים בדין. האב ציווה על בנו יחידו לעלות לירושלים ולחיות בה.

בליל ראש־חודש שבט תר״ח [5.1.1848] נהרג ר׳ דוד על־ידי מתקוממים סרבים שהתנפלו על כמה יישובים יהודים באונגאריה. בנו מספר: נרצח כאחד הקדושים בגמרו ספר תהלים ברגע שהשלים לומר ׳כל־הנשמה תהלל׳ [4]... ואחרי יסורין קשים ומרים ועינויים נוראים שחטו אותו כטבוח את השה ר״ל ואני הייתי בחדר הסמוך נחבא אל תחת המטה... שמעתי את גסיסת אאמו״ר ז״ל במר נפשי ומה היה כחי לעשות. ומה בצע היה לאאמו״ר ז״ל אם גם אותי הרגו. ואהי כאבן דומם ונתייאשתי בעצמי [5].

ר׳ מרדכי אליעזר למד בישיבתו של ר׳ שלמה זלמן אולמאן, בעל ״ יריעות שלמה״ [6], במאקאווא [7]. חמש שנים למד בישיבה זו, שהיתה אחת הישיבות המפורסמות באונגאריה, וכששב לביתו השיאוהו אבותיו עם בת הרב פינחס ליב פריעדען מקאמארן [8].

בשנת תרי״ב [1851] עלה על כס הרבנות הראשונה בעיר מולדתו, פעטראוואסעלא,

ואחר שנה הסכימה גם קהילת אדא [9] להתאחד עם גליל פעטראוואסעלא ולמנותו רב. ר׳ מרדכי אליעזר אומר: קבלתי עלי סבל עול הרבנות, אך שמרתי בקרבי את פקודת אאמ״ו הקדוש... אשר יסרני בחוזק יד ללכת לאה״ק ת״ו, אך ממשלת אשתי עלי, ונישאות יד מו״ח ז״ל, לא נתנו לי אז עדן רשות לפצות פה ולהרים עין להתהלך בגדולות ונפלאות... אך רוחי בקרבי שחרתי רק למלאות פקודת אאמ״ו ז״ל ומאסתי את כבוד הרבנות ואת עמליה, וכל התנהגות ברבנות היה בעיני לצנינים [10], וחבבתי את ההתבודדות [11], וכל זאת לא נפל דבר ארצה ולא מנעתי מלהיות צופה נאמן, לשמור את הרבנות ככל חוקותיה ומשפטיה.

בינתיים נולדו לו בנים והוא הביא להם מלמד מיוחד מקראקא, הריהו הרב משה יוסף יוקר ז״ל, ששימש אחר־כך רב בז׳פניק [12] ״יקר רוח וחסיד אמתי״. מלמד זה שימש כנראה מלמד לא לבנים בלבד, אלא גם לאב שהכניסו לעולם החסידות. הוא מודה: טעמתי מיערת דבש חסידותו ויאורו עיני, ותאלצני נפשי לרעות בגני שעשועי החסידים ועל משכנות רועיהם, וברוב נסיונות נסעתי לצאנז, וכאשר נפתחו עיני ליהנות מזיו כבוד הדר תפארת קדושת אדמו״ר הרב הגאון הקדוש דברי חיים ז״ל, רוחי הציקתני, ותהום נפשי להסתופף בצלו אשר חמדתי, וכל משך איזו חדשים אשר שבתי לרבנות לא נחה רוחי ולא שקטה נפשי מרוב השתוקקות לשמוע הלפידים אשר מפי הקדוש יהלכון. אך נהייה זו אחר החסידות גרמה כנראה שהזניח את תפקידיו בקהילות, שהתמרמרו על כך, וחותנו, הרב פ״ל פריעדען, הצדיק אותן. הוא מתאונן: ״שלום בית ושלום העדה הקדושה הי״ו נעדר ממני״. ביקש לנסוע לארץ־ישראל כדי לצאת מתוך עמקי הצרות המרובות שבהן היה נתון, אך אשתו במרמה ובתחבולות הפרה עצתו עד שבאלול תר״ל אסף את כל כוחותיו והחליט לעלות, אך ״לא הרחקתי נדוד עד איזו פרסאות נתחרטה אשתי ותאמר אלי שהיא תשוב אל בית אביה ואני אתהלך באשר אתהלך״. הוא נשאר אפוא נבוך ושט בארץ. איש לא אסף אותו אל ביתו. מרוב דאבון־נפש חלה ושכב למעלה משׁשה שבועות. הוא לא רצה להיפרד מאשתו ונסע לצאנז. כאן נתבקש לנסוע לוואלאווא [13] הסמוכה לסיגט ולשמש בה רב. הוא קיים פקודת ר׳ חיים האלברשטאם, רבה של צאנז, ונסע לוואלאווא, אך היתנה עם קהילתו, שלא ישמשה אלא שלוש שנים בלבד, שבדעתו לעלות אחר־כך לירושלים. נראה שבוואלאווא פקדו אותו ייסורים נוראים, שהוא אומר: ״סבלתי שלשה שנים בכל האופנים שיש הגלות בעולם, ברוך הנותן עצמה לאין אונים״.

ב״מזמור לתודה״ שבראש ספרו ״תמורת תודה״ (ירושלם תרמ״ז) הוא מספר על רבנות זו בוואלאווא דברים קשים: ״שנאתי וברחתי מן הרבנות ושבעה עשר שבועות הייתי בגולה נבוך בסבך הדאגות, לא ידעתי אנה ואנה. פניתי לימין ואין עוזר, לשמאל ואין מאסף אותי הביתה. עד כי נכמרו רחמי אדמו״ר סבא קדישא זצוק״ל עלי וספחני אל אחד הכהונות... ונכנסתי לגלות המר אשר למדתי שם פירוש השיר ׳למוליך עמו במדבר׳, ארץ אשר במסכנות יאכלו לחם אשר ממרחק יביאו. ואין שם חריש ואין קציר, מחוז כלו ביער ועץ עושה פרי לא יצמח ולא יועיל. החיות ישאגו, הדובים ינהמו, הזאבים לטרף יארובו, וחזירי יער יכרסמו הארחות והשבילים שבין כפר לכפר, ההרים הרמים והנשאים מסכים מבדילים שלא תזרח השמש שבעה חדשים בשנה, ואורו עליהם לא יהל. שלש שנים וחצי נרדפתי בגלות ההרים והיערות ובעמקי תהומות״. הרי זה תיאור נאמן של כפרי מאראמאראש.

בשנת תרל״ה עלה לירושלים ואף־על־פי שהחליט לחיות כאן בבדידות ״כצפור בודד, מתבודד בחדרי, לא מפני קדושה כי אם חמותי ראיתי ונתברר לי כי טוב היות האדם לבדו לעצמו ולא להתערב בשום עסק וענין״, לא נח ולא שקט ועורר סערות בירושלים ובארץ כולה.

על שתי סערות הוא מספר בעצמו ב״מדבר קדמות״:

א. נעניתי להפצרה להיות בורר ופסקתי על־פי תשובת זכרון יוסף[14], שלא היה פקפוק על הפסק. עד היום לא נמתקו המרירות אשר כים נגרש התגעשו עלי.

לצערנו איננו יודעים מהו עניין זה, שגרם כנראה לסערת־רוחות גדולה בירושלים.

ב. כאשר נפרץ גדר ראשונים אודות לימודי לשונות... התאספו תלמידי חכמים של כולל אונגארין לעמוד בפרץ, ואני נמנתי עם רבותי וחבירי לדבר מצוה זו, רק אני נלכדתי בפח הצרות ואותי שמו למטרה לחציהם השנונים ויורו עלי הרובים וישטנוני תחת רדפי טוב וימררו את חיי.

על אסיפה זו של כולל אונגארן סופר ב״הקול״, שנה ג, תרל״ח, עמ׳ 156: קפץ על הבמה איש אחד המתימר בשם רב ׳מאדא׳ במדינת אונגארין. הרב הזה לפנים נמנה את פושעים חלקו ובין המתקנים (רעפארמער) התחשב ואחרי ימים כבירים הואיל האיש הזה ללכת אל איש המופת ויתן כסף רב כופר פדיון נפשו ובכן בזה סר עונו וחטאתו כפרה ועתה נספח אל המתקדשים והמטהרים. האיש הזה אחרי עלותו הבמתה קרא בגרון נחר את הקריאה הזאת: אחי ועמי! יום צרה ותוכחה היום, יום ענן וערפל, ומדוע אתם מחשים? התאספו יחד ורוצו אל ׳כותל המערבי׳, לכו אל ׳הר הזיתים׳ לעורר שם את ישיני עפר מתרדמתם, קדמו את פני הרעה בטרם תעשה לה כנפים, התקבצו ועברו בחוצות ירושלם באש ובדם! הרגו איש את אחיו ואת קרובו! הפכו את העולם לתוהו ובהו! הכו ואל תחמולו, אל תיראו כי ה׳ הוא הנלחם לכם וזרועו תאמצכם לעשות את חיל[15].

על שמועה זו שהרב וועבר נמנה לפנים עם ״מתקנים״ שמענו גם מפי ר׳ שלמה גאנצפריעד במחברתו ״מכסה לאוהל״ (לעמבערג תרמ״ד), שב״מבחר ימיו היה מסית ומדיח לדעת ה׳ בעיר מאַל בבאטשקא, ולאחר שמילא כרסו בנבלות וטרפות וספרי מינים אשר באיה לא ישובון, יצא ללקט עצמות תחת שולחנו של הגאון הקדוש בעל ד״ח [דברי חיים]״.

ועיין להלן ברשימת ספריו של הרב וועבר, מס׳ 4.

ג. הסערה הגדולה ביותרר עורר בספרו ״מלחמת חובה״ (ירושלם תרמ״ב; שם תרמ״ה), שבו יצא להגן על כבודו של ר׳ חיים האלברשטאם, בעל ״דברי חיים״, שר׳ שלמה גאנצפריעד, בעל ״אהלי שם״, אונגוואר תרל״ח, פגע בו[16]. עיין להלן מס׳ 2—3.

להלן רשימה מדויקת של ספריו שכולם יקרי־מציאות הם ובקושי רב אפשר להשיגם.

1] קונטרס נ ו ב ל ה ע ל י ם (צעקת הדל מרדכי אליעזר וועבר בה״ק מוהר״ר ז״ל מלפנים ראבד״ק אדא באונגרין)...

צפת, שנת ב ר ך ב נ י ך ב ק ר ב ך [תרכ״ח, אבל הנכון תרל״ח, 1878]. ד דף. 4°.

המחבר מעתיק בין השאר שתי רשימות מתוך שלוש שנתפרסמו ב״הקול״ (שנה ג, גל׳ 21—23, י, טו, יט אדר־ב תרל״ח), שבהן סופר עליו, שהוא מעורר מהומות בירושלים נגד הצעת משה מונטיפיורי להנהיג לימוד הלשון הערבית בבתי תלמוד־תורה בירושלים. המחבר יוצא בדברים חריפים ביותר נגד ״הקול״ ונגד מונטיפיורי.

הקונטרס פותח: ב"ה מב לעומר שנת ברך בניך בקרבך: פעה"ק צפת ת"ו. אין ספק שהפרט משובש.

עיין: חבצלת, שנה ה, תרל"ח, גל' 34—39: אודות הקונטרס "נובל העלים" אשר יצא לחֹושך בעיר צפת מאת הרב מאדא. עיין גם: גליה ירדני, העיתונות העברית בארץ־ישראל, תל־אביב תשכ"ט, עמ' 76; ג' קרסל, מבחר כתבי ישראל דב פרומקין, ירושלים תשי"ד, עמ' סד; א"ר מלאכי, הרב אהרן שמחה בלומנטאל — בתוך "שערי שמחה", מאת הרב א"ש בלומנטאל, ניו־יורק תשכ"ז, עמ' ג.

"נובל העלים" לא נרשם על־ידי א' יערי ב"הדפוס העברי בצפת" שבספרו "הדפוס העברי בארצות המזרח", חלק א, ירושלים תרצ"ז, אבל נרשם על־ידי פרידברג ב"בית עקד ספרים", כרך ג, עמ' 713, מס' 123: דברי ריב נגד העתון שערי ציון [!]: צפת תרל"ח.

אגב: המכתב מירושלים שנתפרסם ב"הקול" חתום: יליד ירושלים. מקובלני שזהו מכתבו של אבא דייטש, צעיר ברוך־כשרונות שנפטר בדמי ימיו, בשנת תר"ם.

2] מלחמת חובה; נגד עלילות הבל, מן אויב שקר אשר יצא לקרב [ר' שלמה גאנצפריעד בספרו "אהלי שם", אונגוואר תרל"ח] על ס' דברי חיים [לר' חיים האלברשטאם, זאלקווא תרכ"ד] בבזיונות ובקונטרס הלז נבעו שקריו, נחשפו טעותיו... [מאת] דולה ומשקו מתורת רבו דלנו... אל אוהבים נשלחתי...

[ירושלם, דפוס פרומקין], שנת אל תדברו גבהה גבהה [תרמ"ב, 1882]. כז, [1] דף. 4°.

המחבר העלים את שמו וגילה אותו בהוצאה השנייה. עיין להלן, מס' 3.

ר' חיים בראדי אומר על "מלחמת חובה": שמץ דבר חכמה לא נמצא בכל המחברת הזאת רק אולת פרוח תפרח כראש על תלמי לוחותיו ובזה רצה לחלל כבוד זקן שקנה חכמה ולהפריח אוהל ישרים (אוצר הספרות, שנה ג, תרמ"ט—ן, תולדות אנשי שם, עמ' 58).

3] מלחמת חובה... אך שוטני דחקוני ולחצוני, ועל ידי מדקרות פיות ומכתבים אלצוני ואוהבי הד"ח [הדברי חיים] בנחת יעצוני, למען יאירו זהרי ד"ח אצוני, להסיר כל היתול וכל דיבור שנון [שבמהדורא קמא], אך עצה וגבורת חכמה למלחמה הזאת, לזאת אני נחפז משני צדדים להדפיס המלח [המלחמת חובה] עוד פעם, ואחרי כי כבר גדל עונשי אשר הענישוני הא"ש [ה"אהלי שם"] ואחוזת מרעהו, מנשא, ולקחתי כפלים בכל חטאתי אני מפרסם את שמי מרדכי אליעזר ועבר בהק' מוהר"ד ז"ל אשר היה עול הרבנות על שכמי בקהלות קדושות אדא, מאַל, פעטראוואסעלא, בעטשע, פולדוואר יע"א הי"ו, וזה אחד עשר שנים זכיתי בעזה"י להסתופף בצל קדושת ההר הטוב הר הקודש ירושלם תובב"א והבוחן עשתונותי רואה כי מראש בסתר דברתי לכבוד שמים, ולכבוד שמו ית' ויתע' אני מתראה ממחבואי, ובעליון שמתי מחסי, ואמתו צנה וסוחרה וכו'...

ירושלם, דפוס יצחק גאשציני, בשנת ואוהביו כצאת השמש בגבורתו [תרמ"ה, 1885]. [2], יט, [1] דף. 2°.

מעבר לשער מכתב ר' שלמה האלבערשטאם, ווישניצא, א תצא תרמ"ד, אל המחבר. ר' שלמה האלבערשטאם הוא נכדו של ר' חיים האלבערשטאם. נולד בדזיקוב בשנת תר"ז

[1847], נפטר בנויהיים שבגרמניה בראש־חודש תמוז תרס״ה [1905] והובא לקבורה בבובוב. מכתביו לרמ״א וועבר נתפרסמו שנית בספר ״ארזי לבנון״, מאת ר׳ אלימלך אליעזר ארנברג, ירושלים תשכ״ז, עמ׳ פז—צ.

ח״ד פרידברג, בית עקד ספרים, כרך ב, עמ׳ 611, מס׳ 1998, רושם: מלחמת חובה... עם עדות שושנים. עיין גם: אהל ברוך, מאת ברוך שטרויס, לונדון תשי״ט, עמ׳ 192, מס׳ א 3340. אמנם ״עדות שושנים״ קשור בפולמוס זה, אך לא יצא יחד עם ״מלחמת חובה״. עיין: שושנה הלוי, הספרים העבריים שנדפסו בירושלים, ירושלים תשכ״ג, עמ׳ 145, מס׳ 464.

הוצאה זו של ״מלחמת חובה״ שימשה גם תגובה על ״מכסה לאוהל״ של ר׳ שלמה גאנצפריעד, שצירף אל ״קיצור שלחן ערוך״, לעמבערג תרמ״ד.

4] עדות שושנים... יצאנו לישע הרב... מו״ה מרדכי אליעזר וועבער נ״י... אשר בעבור תום לבבו... לתקן את ההשגות, ודברי דופי, של ספרי אהלי שם... על בעל דברי חיים [ר׳ חיים האלברשטאם מצאנז]... ולא השביע נפשו הרב... מו״ה שלמה [גאנצפריעד] נ״י מק״ק אונגוואר, זה שנתים... וימרמר את חייו... עתה הדפיס עלה קטנה (מכסה לאוהל) מחוברת אל ספרו קצש״ע [קיצור שלחן ערוך]... ודבר עתק על הרב רמ״א נ״י בעל מלחמת חובה... עשינו עצמנו לשלוחי מצוה, להדפיס את כל כתבי תעודות אשר אספנו... ולהזהיר... את אור כבוד הרב רמ״א נ״י... הק׳ ישראל יהודא בהרב... מו״ה שלמה זצלה״ה מקראשנוב, הק׳ שמשון בר״מ מתושבי ירושלים...

ירושלים, חש״מ, [תרמ״ה, 1885]. [3] דף. 2°.

כולל ״העתק מכסה לאוהל אות באות״ ומכתבים בשבחו של ר׳ מרדכי אליעזר מראשי הקהילות שבהן שימש ברבנות ומרבנים שונים.

הקונטרס נדפס על־ידי ר׳ מרדכי אליעזר עצמו כפי שכותב ב״אופל ובחן״ שהוציא.

5] אופל ובחן על מכסה לאהל [מאת ר׳ שלמה גאנצפריעד] (הוציאו לאור... מחדש... ונפוץ בכל עה״ק... והגזימו לשלוח לחו״ל... לזאת נאלצתי לצאת... ולפרסם אגרת אחת מאונגוואר... מבי דינא רבא... כי הרב... מוהר״ש [ר׳ שלמה גאנצפריעד] ז״ל לא ידע מאומה מן הדפסת המכסה, רק זייפן ושקרן אחד הדפיסו... הק׳ מרדכי אליעזר וועבר מק״ק אדא מתגורר פעה״ק)...

(ירושלם), חש״מ, [תר״ן, 1890]. [2] דף. 2°.

כולל גם מכתבי רבנים נגד ״מכסה לאוהל״.

דף [1, ג]: בחורף אשתקד... בפ׳ תרומה, הוציאו לאור עלת המכסה [לאוהל]. עיין שושנה הלוי, הספרים העבריים שנדפסו בירושלים, ירושלים תשכ״ג, עמ׳ 171, מס׳ 598 א, ש״מכסה לאהל״ נדפס בירושלים בשנת תרמ״ט. מכאן שהקונטרס הנוכחי נדפס בשנת תר״ן. עיין גם: נ׳ בן־מנחם, בשערי ספר, ירושלים תשכ״ז, עמ׳ 155—156.

מן הראוי להביא כאן את דבריו של ר׳ חיים בראדי ז״ל, נכדו של ר׳ שלמה גאנצפריעד: ועתה לשמע אוזן שמעתי כי האיש ההוא [ר׳ מרדכי אליעזר וועבר], הרבה ספות רעה על רעה בהדפיסו מכתב מהרב וכו׳ מו״ה ישראל יהודא מיטעלמאנן ז״ל שהיה דיין דק״ק אונגוואר, אשר בו כתב לאמר: כי ״המכסה לאהל״ רק זייפן כתבו ואינו כתב ידו של אא״ז [ר׳ שלמה גאנצפריעד] ז״ל כי לא היה אז שפוי בדעתו,

וגם ההסכמה מכבוד אמו״ר הרה״ג מו״ה חיים צבי מ״ה [מאנהיימער] ז״ל הנדפסה שם מזויפת היא, כי לא הי׳ דרכו לתת הסכמות על עלים; ולא די כי טח עיניו מראות כי ההסכמה נכתבה עוד בשנת תרל״ח בעת שנדפס האהלי שם ועליו נתנה, ולא על המכסה כי הוא נכתב רק אחרי כן — עוד עור עיני חכמים אשר נתנו לו הסכמותיהם להפיץ דבריו על פני תבל, ולאסור איסר לבל יהין איש לשום עיניו על דברי ״המכסה״. והנה מלבד כי הכתבי יד נמצאים עוד אצלי, ואוכל להוכיח כי גם הסכמת אמו״ר ז״ל וגם ה״מכסה לאהל״ כתבי ידי החתומים תחתיהם המה, שאול אשאלה את הגונב לבבות, למה הסתיר מכתבו של הדיין מו״ה רי״י מ״מ [ר׳ ישראל יהודא מיטטעלמאנן] עד הנה, עד אחרי מותו? היש מענה בפיו? ואם יש זיוף בדבר מי הזייפן אם לא הוא בעצמו? עד כאן דברי ר׳ חיים בראדי במאמרו על ר׳ שלמה גאנצפריעד ב״אוצר הספרות״, שנה ג, תרמ״ט—ן, תולדות אנשי שם, עמ׳ 58—59.

6] ספר ערך דל; ענף עץ ע״ב״ת [ערכין, בכורות, תמורה] כמפורש במדבר קדמות [הקדמה]. טפחתי ורביתי הדל באלפי. וקטן מכל מלפי. מרדכי אליעזר וועבר... מלפנים בירחי קדם, רבצתי תחת משא רבנות בעזה״י בק״ק אדא, מאַל, פעטראוואסעלא, בעטשע, פולדוואר... ע״י נסיבות... נסעתי ממקהלות הק׳ הנ״ל לחנות בהר שפר...

ירושלם, דפוס יצחק גאשצינני, שנת ואוהביו כצאת השמש [תרמ״ה, 1885]. [5], כ, [1] דף. 2°.

הסכמות ר׳ משה יהושע יהודא ליב דיסקין ור׳ שלמה האלבערשטאם שנדפסו גם ב״עץ אבות״. עי׳ להלן.

דף [2—5]: מדבר קדמות. הקדמה שבה מספר על תולדותיו.

דף א—כ, א: ערך דל על מסכת ערכין. דף כ, ב—[1]: ג׳ שו״ת ממורי ורבותי, ר׳ שלמה זלמן אולמן, מאקא, ור׳ יוסף שאול הלוי נאטנזאהן, לבוב. התשובה הראשונה, של ר׳ ש״ז אולמאן, נכללה ב״יריעות שלמה״, ווילנא תרס״ה, סי׳ ב.

7] ספר עץ אבות; ביאור על האגדתא שבמסכת ערכין ועל פרקי אבות (פרק א—ג). אשר ספחתי לספר עץ ע״ב״ת לחלק שני. קטונתי מכל חסדי ה׳ עלי מרדכי אליעזר וועבר... אשר נתקתי אהלי זה ארבע עשרה שנה להתגורר על ההר הטוב הר הקודש קרתא דשופריא. קרתא קדישתא ירושלם...

ירושלם, דפוס יצחק גאשצינני נגמר בעזה״י חית לירח בול שנת ואוהביו כצאת השמש בגבורתו [תרמ״ה, 1885]. [1], ח, י—כ, [1] דף. 2°.

הסכמות: ר׳ משה יהושע ליב דיסקין, ירושלם; ר׳ שלמה האלבערשטאם, ווישניצא.

[1] דף: נגד ״חדשים מקרוב באו... הנסיון של אכרים... הלהוטים... אחרי קניית אדמה״.

8] ספר עץ אבות; אשר חנני ה׳ פירושים על פרקי אבות (פרק ד—ה) ומאמרי חז״ל במסכתת בכורות לספח לספר ״עץ עב״ת״ דברי אגדה המושכים את הלב. אני הדל באלפי, קטן מכל מלפי, בלעית טובא קולפי, קטונתי מכל חסדי ה׳ עלי, מרדכי אליעזר וועבר... זה ששה עשר שנה הציקתני רוח ממרום עפ״י פקודת אבותי נ״ע לחבק ולחונן אבני אה״ק ולהתאבק בעפרה וזכיתי לנתק אהלי לקרתא דשופריא...

ירושלם, דפוס אלחנן טענענבוים, בשנת קחו מזמרת הארץ [תרמ״ז, 1887]. [2], יז דף. 2°.

ח״ד פרידברג, בית עקד ספרים, ג, עמ׳ 807, מס׳ 1001, רושם: ״באורים על מסכת אבות והאגדות במסכת ברכות... (42 עמ׳)״.

9] ספר תמורת תודה [על מסכת תמורה]; ענף שני מן ״עץ עב״ת״ אשר שתלתי ונטעתי בעזה״י, [י]זכני השי״ת להקדיש ימים לתורתו לבד, ולהקריב זבחי רוחי הנשברה על יקוד אש אהבת הש״י ותורתו, חלף קרבנות תודה עבור רבואות נסים ונפלאות אשר הרבה השי״ת עלי חסד. הכינותי בעניי... מרדכי אליעזר וועבר...

ירושלם, דפוס אלחנן טעננבוים, בשנת עזי **וזמרת** יה ויהי לי לישועה [תרמ״ז, 1887]. [4], לד דף. 2°.

הסכמות: ר׳ משה יהושע יהודא ליב דיסקין, ירושלם, ור׳ שלמה הלברשטאם, ווישניצא, תרמ״ז.

נראה שלספר זה כיוון חיים המבורגר בספרו ״שלשה עולמות״, חלק שני. ירושלים תש״ו, עמ׳ 13, בכתבו: בעת ההיא סדרתי לדפוס את הספר לחמי[!] תודה (על ערכין תמורה ומעילה) שחבר הרב מרדכי אליעזר וועבר... (נתן לי בשליק אחד — 30 מא״י — בעד כל עמוד כתב יד).

10] ספר בכור דל [על מסכת בכורות]; ענף שלישי המשלים את עץ עב״ת אשר שתלתי ונטעתי... וכניתי שמו בכור דל על שם הכתוב ורעו בכורי דלים (ישעיה יד למ״ד). ותיבת דל ראשי תיבות של שמות אאמו״ר הק׳ מוה״ר דוד ז״ל ואמי... מרת ליבלא נ״ע... הכינותי אני הפעוט מרדכי אליעזר בהרב הקדוש מו״ה דוד וועבר זצלל״ה...

ירושלם, דפוס שמואל הלוי צוקערמאן ושותפיו, בשנת כי עת לחוננה [תרמ״ט, 1889]. [5], [כג]—מא דף. 2°.

[דף 5, ב]: שני מכתבים [הסכמות] מר׳ משה יהושע יהודא ליב דיסקין, ירושלם.

בראש הספר ״קדמת אשור״. הקדמה.

מספרי הדפים הם המשך של ״זמרת הארץ ושמים״ שנרשם להלן לא של ״עץ אבות״ כפי שרשמה שושנה הלוי בספרה ״הספרים העבריים שנדפסו בירושלים״, עמ׳ 168, מס׳ 578.

בסוף הספר, דף מא, ב, אומר המחבר: ע״י משגה טעו המדפיסים להסמין הדפים של בכור דל אחר הזמרת. ואני בעניי נותן משפט הבכורה והקדימה להבכור... אך המעוות לא יוכל לתקון. וסימני הדפין אין אופן לשנות כי אם ע״י הדפסה חדשה. ועל הראשונות אני מתדחק... ואין [!] אוסיף לחץ על הדחק ואין לי להשען כי אם על הכלל גדול אין מוקדם ומאוחר בתורה...

ח״ד פרידברג, בית עקד ספרים, כרך א, עמ׳ 148, מס׳ 880, רושם בטעות: חדושי מסכתות[!]... 23 דף. אחריו: פנחס יעקב הכהן, אוצר הבאורים והפירושים, לונדון תשי״ב, עמ׳ 215, מס׳ 74.

ברשותי טופס של ״בכור דל״ שממנו נשמטה מן השער השורה האחרונה: בדפוס ר׳ שמואל הלוי צוקערמאן ושותפיו הי״ו.

11] ביאור על פרק שירה... ונקרא שמו זמרת הארץ ושמים... [מאת] מרדכי אליעזר בהרב הקדוש מו״ה דוד וועבר זצלל״ה...

ירושלם, [דפוס צוקערמאן ושותפיו], בשנת כי עת לחוננה [תרמ״ט, 1889]. [1], כב דף. 2°.

דף יז—כב: תשלום עץ אבות, על פרקי אבות.

פנחס זעליג הכהן שווארטץ, שם הגדולים מארץ הגר, חלק ג, קליינוואררדיין תרע״ה, דף טז, ב, רושם בטעות: זמרת השמים והארץ; ביאור עפרק״א ועל פרק שירה; ח״ד פרידברג, בית עקד ספרים, כרך א, עמ׳ 337, מס׳ 571 רושם: דרוש על פרקי שירה: ירושלם תרמ״ח... (16 דף) [17].

[1] ב״מדבר קדמות״ שבראש ספרו ״ערך דל״, ירושלם תרמ״ה, הוא אומר: הנה עשר שנים אני מתגורר באה״ק. בספר ״מרא דארעא ישראל״, מאת מ״מ גערליץ, ירושלים תשכ״ט, עמ׳ לד, שעלה בשנת תרכ״ח. אין ספק שיש כאן טעות. עיין: אשר ליב בריסק, חלקת מחוקק, חוב׳ ו׳ [תרס״ז], דף א, ב־ב, סי׳ כ.

[2] ב״מדבר קדמות״, שם.

[3] משה מנדלסזון מדסוי.

[4] תהלים קנ,ו: הפסוק האחרון של תהלים.

[5] עיין על ״שערוריה״ זו באונגאריה: יקותיאל יהודה גרינוואלד, טויזנט יאר אידיש לעבן אין אונגארן, ניו־יארק 1945, עמ׳ 63—66.

[6] על יורה דעה, חלק א—ב, וויען תרי״ד — מארגיטא תרצ״ו; שאלות ותשובות, ווילנא תרס״ה, 1904; על סוגיות הש״ס, מונקאטש תרע״ג. עי׳ גם תשובות אליו ב״יריעות שלמה״ סי׳ ב (תרט״ז), ז (תרכ״ב), י (תרי״ב), כ (תרט״ז), כג (תרי״ג), כו (תר״ך).

[7] נולד בשנת תק״ס [1800] ונפטר במאקאווא [Makó] ביום יא בטבת תרכ״ג [2.1.1863].

[8] נולד בבאנהארט [Bonyhád] ונפטר בקאממארן [Komárom], טז סיון תרל״ג [11.6.1873]. ידוע ספרו ״דברי פני אריה״, וויען תרי״ט, 1859. בעל ״שם הגדולים מארץ הגר״, חלק ב, מונקאטש תרע״ד, דף כט, ב, קורא לו בטעות ״פריעדמאנן״.

[9] Ada. בשם זה ״רבה של אדא״ נתפרסם בירושלים ורבה של צאנז קרא לו ״רב אדא בר אהבה״. עיין: פנחס זעליג הכהן שווארטץ, שם הגדולים מארץ הגר, חלק ב, דף ז, ב, סי׳ קז; ר׳ חנניה יום טוב ליפא ברוין, תפארת חיים, גראסווארדיין תש״א, עמ׳ 9.

[10] בשערי ספריו נאמר: רבצתי תחת משא רבנות בעזה״י בק״ק אדא, מאל, פעטעראוואסעלא, בעטשע, פולדוואר. ב״מדבר קדמות״: בתשרי תרי״ב נתנו לי נזר רבנות מכל הגליל, ק״ק בעטשע, ק״ק מאל וק״ק פולדוואר גליל נכבד. כולם יישובים קטנים בגליל אחד.

[11] הוא מדגיש פעמים רבות שרצונו לחיות בהתבודדות, אך נראה שהיה זה רצון בלבד, שתמיד הוא נמצא בתוך קלחת־ציבורית מפעפעת. גם בבואו לירושלים הוא אומר: ״ואני פעה״ק ת״ו כצפור בודד, מתבודד בחדרי... כי טוב היות האדם לבדו לעצמו ולא להתערב בשום עסק וענין״, אף על פי כן אפפוהו סערות שונות ולהתבודדות לא הגיע.

[12] Rzepiennik. רזפניק על־יד Tarnowa.

[13] היא Ökörmezö.

[14] זכרון יוסף, מאת ר׳ יוסף שטיינהארט, פיורדא תקל״ג—תקל״ד. וודאי שאין זו המחלוקת שעליה מספר חיים המבורגר בספרו ״שלשה עולמות״, חלק ב, ירושלם תש״ו, עמ׳ צו—צט.

[15] עיין גם: מימים ראשונים, כרך א, חוברת יא, אפריל 1935, עמ׳ 324.

[16] בשאלות ותשובות דברי חיים, חלק שני, לבוב תרל״ה שתי תשובות אליו: יורה דעה, סי׳ קי: לכבוד ידידי הרב המאה״ג החריף ובקי החסיד המפורסם כו׳ מוה׳ מרדכי אליעזר ני׳ אבד״ק אדא יע״א במדינת הגר. שם, אבן העזר, סי׳ ד: לידידי הרב המאה״ג הירא ושלם החסיד המפורסם... עי׳ עכשיו גם: הרב יהודה רובינשטיין, תולדות הגאון רבי שלמה גאנצפריד זצ״ל — המעין, כרך יא, תשל״א, גליון ג, עמ׳ 10—11.

[17] ראיתי ב״חלקת מחוקק״, חוברת ו, דף ב, א, שמזכיר בין ספריו של רמ״א ועבר גם ״קונטרסי יונת אלם״ ואיני יודע מהם. עיין גם: אגרות רבי עזריאל הילדסהיימר, כינס וערך מרדכי אליאב, ירושלים תשכ״ו, עמ׳ קב, הע׳ 216.

משנה תורה להרמב"ם

ביבליוגראפיה של הוצאות

ישראל יעקב דינסטאג

ישיבה אוניברסיטה

הקדמה

רשימה ביבליוגר'אפית זו של היד החזקה, היא חלק־המשך הביבליוגראפיה הכללית והמקפת את כל חיבורי הרמב"ם ומשנתו. חלק ממנה על באור מלות ההגיון הופיע ב"ארשת", ספר ב (תש"ך), עמ' 7—34; אגרת תימן, שם ג (תשכ"א), עמ' 48—70; ספר המצוות, עומד להופיע ב"ארשת" כרך ה.

בניגוד לרשימות הנ"ל שבהן כללתי מלבד ההוצאות, גם תרגומים, פירושים ומחקרים, רשמתי פה רק הוצאות שלמות (או שבדעת המו"ל היתה כוונתו לכך ואולם מפני טעמים שונים לא נגמר בדפוס). חלקים בודדים, אנתולוגיות, לקוטים וקיצורים לא נכנסו ברשימה זו. כל אלו ביחד עם תרגומי המשנה תורה, פירושים, מחקרים ומפתחות המדפיסים והמגיהים, אי"ה, במקום אחר.

תודתי העמוקה נתונה למנהלי הספריות ועוזריהם שהמציאו לי הוצאות היד החזקה, ביחוד האוניברסיטה העברית, מוסד הרב קוק, והיכל שלמה, מכון שוקן בירושלים; ספרית רמב"ם בתל־אביב; היברו יוניאון קוליג', הסמינר התיאולוגי, הספריה הציבורית ישיבה אוניברסיטה ויוו"א בניו־יורק ואוניברסיטת הרברד.

עבודתי זו מוקדשת לזכרו של החוקר והביבליוגראף, ר' יצחק ריבקינד ז"ל, חובב ספרים וספרנים שהתעניין בביבליוגרפיה שאני עורך על הרמב"ם ועודדני בנאמנות בהמשכת עבודתי זו.

ר"ם (1480)

1. [משנה תורה. איטליא לפני שנת ר"ם]

על ידי המדפיסים שלמה ב"ר יהודה ועובדיה ב"ר משה. 2°. [350] דף.

שמותיהם של העוסקים בהדפסת הספר לא צוינו בסוף הספר, אלא באמצעו, בסוף הספר השביעי שהוא ספר זרעים שבו נאמר: "ותכל מלאכת הקודש השבעה ספרים

שנ גאולת עולם תהיה ללויים ישרא׳ שירש את אבי
אמו לוי הרי זה גוא׳ מלויי אעפ׳ שאינו לוי הואיל והערי׳
או השרות של לויים גוא׳ לעולם שדין זה תלוי במקומות
אלו ולא בבעלים ולוי שירש את אבי אמו ישרא׳ גוא׳ כישרא׳
ולא כלויים שלא נאמר גאולת עולם תהיה ללויים אלא בערי
הלויים כל שבט לוי מוזהרין שלא ינחלו בארץ
כנען וכן הן מוזהרין שלא יטלו חלק בבזה בשעה שכובשין
את הערים שנאמר לא יהיה לכהני׳ הלויי׳ כל שבט לוי חלק
ונחלה עם ישרא׳ חלק בבזה ונחלה בארץ וכן הוא אומר
בארץ לא תנחל וחלק לא יהיה לך בתוכם בבזה וכן לוי
או כהן שנטל חלק בבזה לוקה ואם נטל נחלה בארץ
מעבירי׳ אותה ממנו יראה לי שאין הדברי׳ אומרין
אלא בארץ שנכרתה עליה ברית לאברהם ליצחק
וליעק׳ וירשה בניה ונתחלקה להם אבל שאר
כל הארצות שכובש מלך ממלכי ישראל
הרי הכהני׳ והלויי׳ באותן הארצו׳ ובביזתן
ככל ישרא׳ ולמה לא זכה לוי בנחלת
ארץ ישרא׳ ובבזתה עם אחיו מפני
שהובדל לעבוד את ה ולשרתו
ולהורו׳ דרכיו הישרו׳ ומשפטיו
הצדיקים לרבים שנא׳ יורו
משפטי׳ ליעקב ותורתך
לישרא׳ לפי הובדלו
מדרכי העול לא
עורכין
מלחמה כשאר
ישרא׳ ולא נוחלין
ולא זוכין לעצמן
בכח גופן אלא הם חיל
ה׳ שנא׳ ברך ה׳ חילו והוא
ברוך הוא זוכה להם שנ׳ אני
חלקך ונחלתך ולא שבט לוי
בלבד אלא כל איש ואיש מכל באי
העולם אשר נדבה רוחו אותו והבינו
מדעו׳ להבדל לעמוד לפני ה׳ לשרתו
ולעבדו לדעה את ה׳ והלך ישר כמו שעשהו
האלהים ופרק מעל צוארו עול החשבונות הרבי׳
אשר בקשו בני האדם הרי זה נתקדש קודש
קדשים ויהיה ה׳ חלקו ונחלתו לעולם ולעולמי
עולמים ויזכה לו בעולם דבר המספיק לו כמו שזכה
לכהנים וללויים הרי דוד עליו השלום אומ׳ ה׳ מנת חלקי
וכוסי אתה תומיך גורלי

נגמר ספר שביעי והוא
ספר זרעים

והלכותיו שבע ופרקיו חמשה ושמונים

הלכות כלאים

עשרה פרקים

הלכות מתנות עניים

עשרה פרקים

הלכות תרומות

חמשה עשר פרקים

הלכות מעשרות

ארבעה עשר פרקים

הלכות מעשר שני ונטע רבעי

אחד עשר פרקים

הלכות בכורים ושאר מתנות כהונה שבגבולין

שנים עשר פרקים

הלכות שמטה ויובל

שלשה עשר פרקים

בריך רחמנא דסייען מריש ועד כען

ותכל מלאכת עבודת הקדש חשבעה ספרים הראשונ׳ על
ידי המחוקקי׳ שלמה בר׳ יהודה ועובדיה בר׳ משה ה׳ יזכינו
להתחיל ולהשלים החצי האחרו׳ וספרי׳ אחרי׳ לחיים ולש״ו

כל המצות קידוש חמץ

חמו״ד [איטליא (רומא?)], שלמה ב״ר יהודה ועובדיה ב״ר משה, [קודם ר״ם]. רמב״ם, משנה תורה.

S. l. e. a. [Italia (Roma?)], Salomo b. Jehuda et Obadia b. Moses, [ante 1480]. Moses Maimonides, Mischne Tora.

St. p. 1869, no. 6513, 1. Fr. p. 13, no. 44. Pr. 7340.

A 17, 3

ROME BEFORE 1480.

הראשוני" על ידי המחוקקי' שלמה ב"ר יהודה ועובדיה ב"ר משה. ה' יזכנו להתחיל ולהשלים החצי האחרו' וספרי אחרי' לחיים ולשלו'". "אמר מעתיק המימוני הזה כמתנצל אלו האחד ועשרי" פרקים אשר מתחלת ספר טהרה עד כאן לא היה לנו כי אם העתק אחד ולכן ראוי למעיין להשתדל להגיהם אבל הספר הזה בכללו מתחלתו ועד סופו היה לנו ד' או ג' העתקות זולת אלו האחד ועשרים פרקים כאשר זכרתי" (ספר טהרה, סוף פרק כ"א) (פרופ. משה לוצקי, רשימת של ההוצאות השלמות של ספר משנה תורה להרמב"ם ז"ל. במשנה תורה, הוצאת שולזינגר. כרך ה', מספר א').

מספרי ההלכות הקטנות בכל פרק הנדפסים בהוצאות הרגילות לא נמצאים בהוצאה זו (לוצקי, שם).

נדפס באותיות מרובעות בשני עמודים על כל דף.

פקסימיליות אצל פריימן: אוצר מלאכת הדפוס, מספר 3, A 17 ולוצקי שם.

במהדורה זו נשמט מהלכות טומאת מת, חלק מפרק י"ז,וראש פרק י"ח. לאחר שהבחינו המדפיסים בדילוג זה הדפיסו את החסר על סרט נייר והדביקוהו לתחתית העמוד שם (לוצקי שם). ראה הערתינו בסוף מהדורת הצילום שיצאה בשנת תשט"ו, להלן מספר 41.

הוצאה זו נמצאת באוניברסיטה העברית, שוקן, סמינר התיאולוגי, ניו־יורק, היברו יוניאון קוליג', סינסינטי וישיבה אוניברסיטה.

ראה: Moses Marx: Catalogue of the Hebrew Books Printed in the 15th Century Now in the Library of the Hebrew Union College, *Studies in Bibliography and Booklore* 1 (1953), p. 40, No. 49. Steinschneider Cat. Bod. p. 1869.

בסוף כדאי להעיר שהמנוח ר' ישעיה זנה מטיל ספק אם הוצאה זו נדפסה באיטליה (רומה) כי "אותיות המשנה התורה גוון פרובינצאלי להן, והולכות ומתקרבות למטבע ספרדית" ("טיולים במקום שהמציאות והספר — היסטוריה וביבליוגרפיה — נושקים זה את זה" בספר היובל לאלכסנדר מארכס, ניו־יורק תש"י, עמ' ריב, הערה 7). עיין י. אבידע: לתולדות הדפוס בישראל ודפוסי ספר "משנה תורה" להרמב"ם ז"ל, סיני, כרך 34 (תשי"ד), עמ' ש"ז—ש"י.

ר"ן (1490)

2. [משנה תורה]

שונצינו: גרשון ב"ר משה שונצינו ר"ן. °4. [380] דף.

קולופון: ותשלם כל המלאכה מלאכת ה' היא הי"ד החזקה אשר עשה משה לעיני ישראל ותהיא השלמתה ביו' ר"ח ניסן שנת נ"ר [ר"ן] מצוה ותורה פה שונצינ"ו אשר במדינת לומב"רדיאה... נאם... אליעזר ברבי שמואל זצ"ל. בלי פירוש.

בספריה הציבורית וספרית הסמינר בניו־יורק; בספרית קולומביה חסר בראשו ובסופו.

עיין הברמן: המדפיסים בני שונצינו 42—43; Israel Adler, "Les Incunables Hébraïques de la Bibliothèque Nationale", Paris, 1962, p. 32–34; Moses Marx, *Studies in Bibliography and Booklore* 1 (1953), p. 40; Steinschneider; Ibid,

Freimann, Thesaurus, A 55; לוצקי, מספר ב׳. פקסימיליות שונות אצל פרימן ולוצקי, שם (עם תאור מפורט).

F. R. Goff, p. 322 (Heb. 77; [H 571]).

על שינויי־דפוס בעותקים שונים של הוצאה זו, עיין י. ריבקינד, קרית ספר 4 (תרפ"ז), עמ׳ 275—276. עיין י. אבידע וי. זנה, שם עמ׳ ר"כ;

Abraham Berliner, "Aus meiner Bibliothek, Beiträge zur hebräischen Bibliographie u. Typographie". Frankfurt a.M., J. Kaufmann, 1898, p. 32–33.

תוכן הקדמת המדפיס ושירו:

"לקול קורא וצורח בגרון
אזור גבר חלציך וקומה
חקוק ספר אשר הונח בארון
חזור נזר וכתר למקומה
בתוך גלות וזעם עת וחרון
בתולת ישרא"ל מי מקימה
הלא הגות בתורת אל וזכרון
שמירתה תבטל אף וחימה
לאורה נ ראה ישע וגרון
מהרה חוש וכל קדם וימה
תמלא ב ספריך ויתרון
פעליך במיעוט התנומה
הכינותי כתוב ספר וכשרון
מלאכתי רצה נותן נשמה
גשנו נא ראות ישע ישורון
שלח לנו משיחנו ברמה.

אמר צעיר המחוקקים בכתב אמת משפטים צדיקים גרשם מן הח"ר משה זלה"ה איש שונצינו נדרשתי לאשר שאלוני ונמצאתי לאשר בקשוני הגדולים אשר בארץ שופטי ארץ וגודרי פרץ רועי עדר ה׳ צבאות וצאן מרעיתו לוחמים מלחמת ה׳ ותורתו לילה ויום עומדים על משמרתו ויאמרו לכה אתנו ניעצך והיטבנו לנפשך נלבישך מגן וצינה וכובע ישועה בראשך מכל פגע ותמורת הזמן להצילך ועשית לך שם גדול משם המחוקקים היו לפניך עת לעשות לה׳ הפרו תורתיך ואתה תאזור מתניך וקמת וחקקת בעט המהיר ספר הרב הגדול מרנא ורבנא הגאון האלקי רבי׳ משה ב"ר מיימון משנה תורה עטרת צבי וצפירת תפארה לבוש מכלול נימוסי משנה וגמרא תלמוד בבלי וירושלמי ספרי וספרא לכל היד החזקה ולכל המורא הגדול אשר עשה משה משמרת למשמרת סייג לתורה אשר נזר הסדר המעולה על ראשו וכתב הלשון הבהירה בה ירוץ כל קורא בספריו וכל עין מאירה ומלאת כל הגולה על ימינה ועל שמאלה מהספר היקר הזה אשר לא יסולה בזהב אופיר וחוילה יען זה ממה שלא יעלם היות מן המחוייב לכל ירא ה׳ וחרד על דברו צופה לחזות בנועמו ולאור באורו להיות הספר הזה בביתו ולהגות בו יומם ולילה עם הלמוד בשאר ספרי הקדש משיבי טעם מפיקי מאמרים כזוהר הרקיע מזהירים על כן אמרתי אקומה נא ואסובבה בבתי נכאת הספרים המדוייקים ואקח לי

משם העתק ספר הרב הגדול ז״ל ובעט מחוקק מהיר חנני ה׳ אחקקנו ועל ראשי עטרות אענדנו וביד המשכילים ומבינים מדע אגיהגו וקורא לו ספר מדוייק אשר פי ה׳ יקבנו והוא ית׳ בחמלתו ורחמיו חדשים לבקרים יעזרני להשלים הספר הנכבד הזה עם שאר ספרי הקדש מעולפים ספירים אשר באורם נראה אור ובם נחיה לדור דורים וזכות מאור הגולה הרב הגדו׳ ז״ל מגלה נסתרים אשר ספרו אחקוק וארביצנו בכל פינות ועברים יעמוד לי למחסה מכל צרים וצירים ותפילתו תעמוד לנו עת נריד בשיחנו ונהים תפלה למש״ה איש האלהים״.

בסוף השיר חתום גרשם.

גליון 29 דף ג׳ וג, ב שונים מבחינה טיפוגראפית מן הצילום שבאוצר של פרימן, סימן A 55,6.

רנ״א (1491)

3. [משנה תורה. ספרד או פורטוגאל: משה בן שאלתיאל רנ״א 1491 ?]. 4°.

בסימנר התיאולוגי, ניו־יורק נמצא ספר מדע, אהבה וזמנים (הלכות קידוש החודש לא נגמר) וחסר בראשו. [159] דף.

עיין: לוצקי, שם, סימן ג׳;

A. Marx, "Library Report", *Register of the Jewish Theological Seminary*, 1931–1932, p 158; Frederic R. Goff, "Incunabula in American Libraries", New York, 1964, p. 322 (Heb. 78); A. Freimann, "Hebr. Inkunabul" Frankfurt a.M. 1920, N. 46, p. 14; Schwab 91; Freimann Thesaurus 32; Steinschneider: Cat. Bod. p. 1871.

ר״ס ? (1500)

4. [משנה תורה. ספרד בר״ס לערך ?]

חמו״ד ושהמ״ד. 4°.

הוצאה בלתי ידועה ונדפסה באותיות מרובעות. עמוד אחד על כל דף. מספר השורות ל׳.

מהוצאה זו מצויים דפים בודדים במקומות שונים:

(א) בסמינר התיאולוגי בניו־יורק 26 דף מספר המדע ואהבה ועוד קטע מספר אהבה ז׳ דף.

(ב) בקמברידג׳ בין קטעי הגניזה, דף אחד המכיל הלכות קריאת שמע א, ד—ו, ט—יג (סימנו: T.-S.N.S. (10) 171)

(ג) ב־Bibliotheca Judaica Simonseniana, 6 דפים.

(ד) הסמינר התיאולוגי בבודפסט 4 דף וכוללים ה׳ קריאת שמע ב, ז עד ה׳ תפלה ב, ד (על פי אלכסנדר שייבר: דפים נוספים מאינקונבולום אחד של המשנה תורה, קרית ספר, כרך 39 [אדר תשכ״ד], עמ׳ 280; לוצקי, שם מספר ה׳).

פקסימיליות בפריימן: אוצר מלאכת הדפוס. מספר B 36; לוצקי שם (סימן ה—ו).

רס״ה ? (1505)

5. [משנה תורה להרמב״ם. קושטאנדינא, רס״ה—רע״ד לערך].

או״מ גדולות, שני טורים לעמוד. שני הספרים הראשונים: ספר מדע וספר אהבה. 2°.

אז לא אבוש בהביטי אל כל מצותיך

כל המצות

שניתנו למשה בסיני בפירוש ניתנו שנאמר
ואתנה לך את לוחות האבן והתורה והמצוה
תורה זו תורה שבכתב והמצוה זו פירושה וצונו
לעשות התורה על פי המצוה ומצוה זו היא
הנקראת תורה שבעל פה כל התורה כתבה
משה רבינו קודם שימות בכתב ידו ונתן
ספר לכל שבט ושבט וספר אחד נתנו
בארון לעד שנאמר לקוח את ספר התורה הזה
ושמתם אותו וגו' והמצוה שהיא פירוש
התורה לא כתבה אלא צוה בה לזקנים
וליהושע ולשאר כל ישראל שנאמר את כל
הדבר אשר אנכי מצוה אתכם אותו תשמרו
לעשות וגו' ומפני זה נקראת תורה שבעל פה
אף על פי שלא נכתב' תורה שבעל פה למדה
משה רבינו כולה בבית דינו לשבעים זקנים
ואלעזר ופנחס ויהושע שלשתן קבלו ממשה
וליהושע שהוא תלמידו של משה רבינו מסר
תורה שבעל פה וצוהו עליה וכן יהושע כל
ימי חייו למד על פה וזקנים רבים קבלו
מיהושע וקבל עלי מן הזקנים ומפנחס
ושמואל קיבל מעלי ובית דינו ודוד קיבל
משמואל ובית דינו ואחיה השילוני מיוצאי
מצרים היה ולוי היה ושמע ממשה והיה קטן
בימי משה והוא קיבל מדוד ובית דינו

ואליהו קיבל מאחיה השילוני ובית דינו
ואלישע קיבל מאליהו ובית דינו ויהוידע
הכהן קיבל מאלישע ובית דינו זכריה קיבל
מיהוידע ובית דינו והושע קיבל מזכריה
ובית דינו ועמוס קיבל מהושע ובית דינו
וישעיה קיבל מעמוס ובית דינו ומיכה קיבל
מישעיה ובית דינו ויואל קיבל ממיכה ובית
דינו ונחום קיבל מיואל ובית דינו וחבקוק
קיבל מנחום ובית דינו וצפניה קיבל מחבקוק
ובית דינו וירמיה קיבל מצפניה ובית דינו
וברוך בן נריה קיבל מירמיה ובית דינו ועזרא
ובית דינו קבלו מברוך בן נריה ובית דינו
בית דינו של עזרא הם הנקראים אנשי כנסת
הגדולה והם חגי זכריה ומלאכי ודניאל וחנני'
ומישאל ועזריה ונחמיה בן חכליה ומרדכי
ובלשן וזרובבל והרבה חכמים עמהם תשלום
מאה ועשרים זקנים האחרון מהם הוא שמעון
הצדיק והוא היה מכלל המאה ועשרי' וקיבל
תורה שבעל פה מכולם והוא היה כהן גדול
אחר עזרא אנטיגנוס איש סוכו ובית דינו
קיבלו משמעון הצדיק ובית דינו ויוסי בן
יועזר איש צרידה ויוסף בן יוחנן איש
ירושלים ובית דינם קבלו מאנטיגנוס ובית
דינו ויהושע בן פרחיה וניתאי הארבלי ובית

א ב

SONCINO 1490.

בית הספרים הלאומי בירושלים ע"פ א. יערי: הדפוס העברי בקושטא, מספר 34 שמתארו כ"תופס יחיד בעולם" ומזהה אותו עם ההוצאה שנרשמה אצל וואכשטיין, חלק ב', 289 בלוית פקסימיל של עמוד אחד בגודל טבעי. הטופס היה לנגד וואכשטיין ונרשם אצל פרימן, שם, B 41 .

רס"ט (1509)

6. החבור הגדול הנקרא / משנה תורה לרב רבינו / משה בן הרב הדיין רבי / מימון ז"ל כולל יד ספרי' / וזה לך סמנים במשקל /
במדע אהבתך לזמנים
ובנשים קדושתך פליאה
זרעים מעבודתך קרבנותך
תטהר מנזיקים בקנייה
שנים עשר רמזתים לך והנה
במשפטי' ושופטי' יד מלאה
[קושטנטינא: ר' דוב ור' שמואל נחמיאש. רס"ט]. 2°. או"מ ואו"ר.
פגינציה:
ספר המדע מד דף;
ספר אהבה נו דף;
ספר זמנים קעו דף;
פירוש הלכות קדוש החודש לר' עובדיה עם שער מיוחד [20] דף;
ספר נשים צח דף;
ספר קדושה. [1], ב־ק' דף;
דף [1] מכיל שער מצוייר.
ספר הפלאה כד דף;
ספר זרעים מד דף (בדף מד כבר מתחיל ספר עבודה);
ספר עבודה מ דף (בדף מ כבר מתחיל ספר קרבנות);
ספר קרבנות יח דף (בדף יח כבר מתחיל ספר טהרה);
ספר טהרה סה דף;
ספר נזיקין, קנין, משפטים ושופטים. רנה, [4] דף.

הקולופון: מה נכבד היום אשר נגלה אלינו כבוד המלך י"י צבאות כי נגלו לפני עמו ועבדיו אנשים בני עליה אשר נדבה רוחם אותם להקים סוכת התורה הנופלת להגדילה ולהאדירה. כי בעונותינו שרבו ברוב הצרות הצרורות אשר עפפונו סבונו גם סבבונו תורתינו התמימה נתדלדלה בדלותינו ונתמעטה במיעוטינו ולולי ה' שהיה לנו כמעט שנשתכחה תורה מישראל כי אין דורש ואין מבקש לשמוע בלמודים הגיעו ימיב אשר נאמר צור תעודה חתום תורה בלמודי. גם הספרים המקודשים, ובתי הנפש והלחשים, ספו תמו מבלהות הגירושים וחמת המציקים מאז הֹמֹטיר ה' האלה והמגרעת על גלות ירושל' אשר בספרד כי מכלי אל כלי הורקנו, ובגולה הלכנו, יגענו ולא הונח לנו, ושאון מי הצרות הקורות אותנו תמיד השחירו פני עדתינו כשולי קדירה, מעת הוסרה מגבירה, ופרקה נזמה ותלייתה, ותלבש בגדי אלמנותה, וראינו כל המון ישראל

יושבים בשלים מלמודה של תורה מפני שצוק העתים וטרדות הזמן לא יתנום השם רוחם ואף אם יספיק להם הזמן יהיו מתניהם מועדים מפני חסרון מציאות הספרים, ואם באולי ימצאו מי זה ערב אל לבו לגשת לקנות לו ספר היד החזקה או המגיד משנה או ההגהות או ההשגות, כי כל אחד מהספרים האלה היה נמכר בדמים יקרים וכשל כה הסבל. כל אלה היו סבות עצומות לפרוק האנשים מעליהם עול הלמוד ונשארים רעבים גם צמאים על התורה ועל העבודה. ועתה הראנו י״י אלדינו את כבודו ואת גדלו כי קרא ה׳ בשם שני אחים מחוקקים ר׳ דוד ור׳ שמואל ן׳ נחמיאש אשר לא ימצא בישראל חרש ואומן וחושב כמוהם אשר נתן ה׳ חכמה ותבונה בהמה לדעת לחקוק על הספר בדיו בעט ברזל ועופרת והמה בחכמתם הקימו מלאכת הדפוס על מכונה ועל ידם בעזרת העוזר ברוך הוא מתרבי׳ הספרים בישראל, ששון ושמחה ישיגו ואיש פני רעהו יחד, מה טוב ומה נעים שבת אחים גם יחד. והאל׳ים הרועה אותנו השפיע והופיע עלינו והקרה לפנינו... אנשים עברים מחשובי עמנו המה הנכבדים והמפוארי׳ כר׳ יוסף ן׳ מובחר ספרדי וכר׳ משה הלוי אשכנזי יצ״ו המכונה די מדונא, אשר נשא לבם אותם לתמוך ידי עושי המלאכה ונכנסו בממונם והונם בעובי קורת המצוה הגדולה הזאת לכבוד התורה לתמכה ולסעדה. ונחה עליהם רוח ה׳ רוח עצה וגבורה להמציא לפנינו בדמים מועטים ספרים מפוארים יקרי המציאות אשר כל מבקש ה׳ ימצא בהם מרגוע ושם ינוחו יגיעי כח, ונחה שקמה הסכמתם לעשות בכתיבה אשורית ספר היד החזקה הנקרא משנה תורה שחבר המאור הגדול הרמב״ם שמו, וה׳ עמו. ומנגד סביב לאהלו יחנו בכתיבה מפוארה המגיד משנה וההגהות מימוניות בספרי הדינים הנהוגים. וביתר הספרים השגות הרב הגדול הראב״ד כי בהמה יהיה שמן חלקנו, וחפץ ה׳ יצלח בידינו. האמנם בקצת מהספרים הנהוגים לא הגיע לידינו מגיד משנה וחפשנו אותו בכל אלפי יהודה ולא מצאנוהו. והחברים המפוארים האלה לא רצו להוציא מתחת ידם דבר בלתי מתוקן ושמו בספרים ההם תמורת המגיד משנה חבורים אחרים מפוארים וגדולי התועלת להאיר מחשך עיני המעיינים, כי באמונה הם עושים, יהי נועם ה׳ עליהם, ובמעשה ידיהם יכוננם.

ואני הצעיר אברהם בן לאדוני כמ״ר יוסף בן יעיש זלה״ה בראותי יקר תפארת כתב חמדת הדת הלז אשר לא יערכנו זהב וחלי כתם, העירותי לב עושי המלאכה ותומכיה, נושאיה ונותניה, ודברתי על לבם דברים טובים דברי נחומים, לחזק את ידיהם בהשלמת המבוקש הנורא הלז וי״י עזרני להביא אל היש ולהוציא כלי למעשהו, וגם שמתי עיני ולבי בהגהת הספר וסידורו כיד אלי׳ הטובה עלי עם החכמי׳ אנשי המשמר אשר שלטה ידם בהגהת קצתו. לכן אנשי לבב שמעו לי ותבא עליכם ברכת טוב, לכו שברו הספר היקר הלז אשר כל עצי עדן החבורים שנחקקו עד היום לא דמו אליו בגודל וכבוד. וכסף משנה קחו בידכם כי משנה שכר שכיר עבדו אתכם ואשרי שיאחז הספר הזה לגורלו וחבלו, כי מה׳ היתה לו.

והיתה השלמת הספר הנכבד הזה בחדש אדר ראשון שנת הרס״ט ליצירה בקוסטנטינא העיר הגדולה אשר תחת ממשלת... המלך סולטן בייזיט ירום הודו ותנשא מלכותו בימיו ובימנו תושע יהודה וישראל ישכן לבטח אוי״ר.

הדף האחרון כולל שני שירים בשבח הספר עם סיומו בדפוס: שיר לר׳ דוד בר׳ יוסף ן׳ יחייא, תחילתו: אליכם עוברי דרך ראו אם יש כחמדתי; שיר לר׳ יוסף ביבאס, תחילתו: ישישים עם נערים הללו שם י״י כי שמו נשגב לבדו. אחריהם: סימן

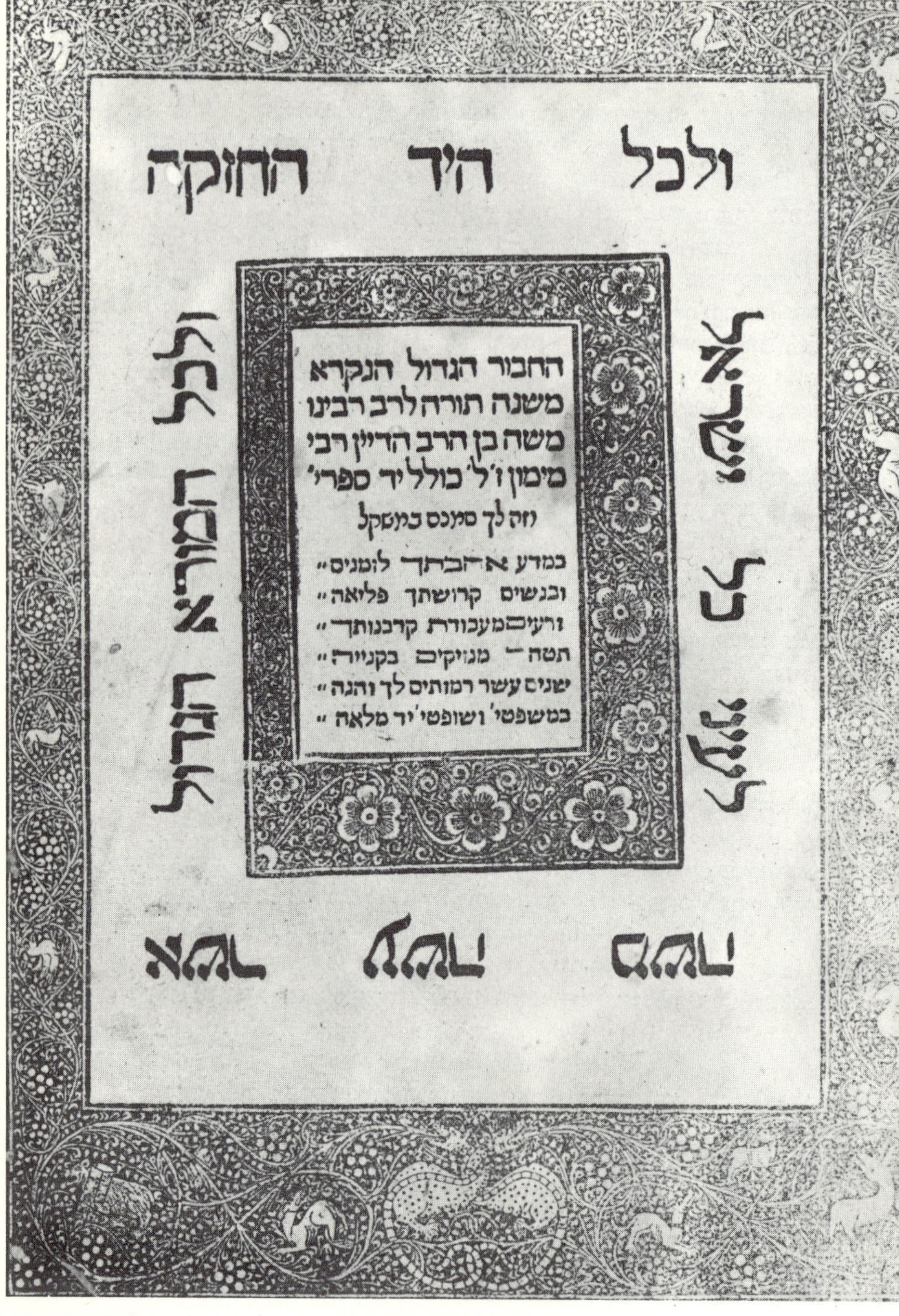

ולכל היד החזקה

ולכל המורא הגדול

אשר עשה משה

לעיני כל ישראל

החבור הגדול הנקרא
משנה תורה לרב רבינו
משה בן הרב הדיין רבי
מימון ז׳ל׳ כולל יד ספרי׳
וזה לך סימנס במשכל

כמדע א־הבתך לזמנים״
ובנשים קדושתך פליאה״
זרעים מעבודת קרבנותך״
תטה־ מנזיקים בקניה״
שנים עשר רמותים לך והנה״
במשפטי׳ ושופטי׳ יד מלאה״

CONSTANTINOPLE 1509.

שעשה יוסף ביבאס לי"ד ספרי הרמב"ם ז"ל: תדע באהבתך זמן נשיך, לקדוש בהפלאה זריעתך, עובד להקריב טהרת נזק קנה, משפט בשופט י"ד בחזקתך.

השער מוקף שתי מסגרות מקושטות, אחת גדולה ואחת קטנה. מסביב לשער: ולכל היד החזקה ולכל המורא הגדול אשר עשה משה לעיני כל ישראל.

הוצאה זו היא הראשונה המכילה פירושים והשגות:

(א) השגות הראב"ד (בתוך פירושי "מגדל עוז" ו"מגיד משנה" ולא כחטיבה בפני עצמה — עיין ר' יהודה אבידע, סיני, ל', תשי"ב, עמ' קלח—קמ).

(ב) הגהות מיימוניות מה"ר מאיר הכהן, תלמיד מהר"ם מרוטנברג (שנדפסו בקיצור בהוצאות האחרות עד שהדפיסוהו שוב בשלמות בהוצאת המשנה תורה "אל המקורות" בשנת תשי"ד, עיין להלן). על הבעיות הביבליוגראפיות הכרוכות בהוצאות שונות על ה"הגהות מיימוניות", ע' פרופ' אפרים א. אורבך: "בעלי תוספות", עמ' 435—436.

המנוח הרב י. ל. מימון התלונן על המדפיסים בוויניציאה רפ"ד שאחר שנודע להם "כי מחבר ההגהות הוא אשכנזי ולא ספרדי, קיצצו בו הרבה כי אי אפשר היה להשמיטו כליל" (סיני, כרך 50, תשכ"ב, עמ' שסו [= מדי חודש בחדשו, תשכ"ב].

(ג) מגיד משנה לר' דון וידאל די טולושא על ספר זמנים, נשים, קדושה, נזיקין, קנין ומשפטים.

(ד) מגדל עוז לר' שם טוב ב"ר אברהם גאון על ספר אהבה.

(ה) פירוש על ד' פרקים הראשונים של הלכות יסודי התורה ממחבר בלתי ידוע [הריטב"א — ר' יום טוב ב"ר אשבלי]. על הבעיות הביבליוגראפיות בענין השגות הראב"ד, עיין פרופ' א. א. אורבאך, קרית ספר לג (תשי"ח), עמ' 360—375; (לוצקי, שם, סימן ז'; א. יערי: הדפוס העברי בקושטא, ירושלים, תשכ"ז, עמ' 63—66; בקורת על יערי מאת א. מ. הברמן, קרית ספר מג (תשכ"ח), עמ' 164; ר' יהודה אבידע, סיני 30 (תשי"ב) עמ' קלח—קמ; 31 (תשי"ב), עמ' רמז—רמח; 34 (תשי"ד), עמ' שז—שי).

תיאור פירוש הלכות קדוש החדש לר' עובדיא שנדפס גם בפני עצמו, אצל יערי שם, עמ' 64, 66. המדפיס השאיר מקום לדיאגרמות, שבחלק מן הטפסים ניתוספו ביד, ובחלק מהם נשארו המקומות חלקים (הברמן, שם).

נמצא באוניברסיטה העברית, ספרית שוקן, ספרית רמב"ם בתל-אביב, הסמינר התיאולוגי, ניו-יורק (גם על קלף), ר"ש ליברמן, לודוויג ג'סלסון, ניו-יורק.

רפ"ד (1524)

7. ההודאה לממציא כל מחוייב המציאות שהגיענו להתחיל כן יגיענו להשלי' לחקוק בעט ברזל ועופרת חיבור משנה תורה אשר חיבר אחד קדוש רבינו משה בן הדיין ר' מיימון הספרדי זצ"ל עם המגדל עוז שחיבר הרב ר' שם טוב ב"ר אברהם בן גאון ספרדי זצ"ל ועם המגיד משנה שחיבר אחד נגר ובר נגר זצ"ל ועם ההגהות מיימוניות שחיבר אחד אוריין בר אוריין זצ"ל כל אילין רבוותא קהו קהוותן ופרקו פירוקין וציינו ציינים בכל פרטי החיבור הזה מגמרא דילן ומתלמודא דבני מערבא ומכולהו רבוותא: וכל אלו החיבורים מזוקקים שבעתים מסוקלים ממוקשי הטעיות עם עיונא סגין ונברר הסולות מהתוך הסובין ע"י ה"ר דוד פיציגט"ון יצ"ו מגיה ההעתק וע"י הצעיר מצעירי הצאן

יעקב ב״ר חיים ן׳ אדוניהו מגיה אח״כ בדפוס במצות השר דניאל בומבי״רגי מאנויר״שא שנת רפ״ד לפ״ק בויניציאה. 2°.

או״מ ורש״י.

כרך א: מדע־קדושה. [2], ב־שפ״ט, [6] דף.

[2] דף: שער וראשית דבר מר׳ דוד ב״ר אליעזר הלוי שחסר ברוב העותקים שהיו לפני.

[6] דף: נספח: מגיד משנה מהלכות אישות (״אחר שהדפסנו נשים וקדושה והפלאה הגיע לידנו מה שהיה חסר במגיד משנה בדף רס״ו בפרק שני״).

כרך ב: הפלאה—שופטים. [1], שצ״ד—תשס״ז דף.

[1] דף: שער כרך ב (שחסר ברוב העותקים שבדקתי), בלי מקום ושנת הדפוס. קולופון: והיתה השלמתו יום כ״ה לחדש תמוז רפ״ד פה ויניציאה... במצות דניאל בומברגי... נאם... יעקב ב״ר חיים ן׳ אדוניהו.

ספר ״מגדל עוז״ נדפס בהוצאה זו מלבד ספר אהבה גם על עוד ספרים אחדים שלא נמצא להם בהוצאת קושטא הנ״ל (יהודה אבידע, סיני 30 (תשי״ב), קל״ח; 34 (תשי״ד), ש״ז—ש״י). השגות הראב״ד נותנו בשלימותן ב״מגדל עוז״ ו״מגיד משנה״ ולא כחטיבה בפני עצמה.

נוסח השער של כרך ב׳:

מיימוני

ישתבח הבורא הנותן לכל קץ תכלה שהגענו עד פה לחקוק בעזק׳ דגושפנקא חיבור משנה תור׳ שחבר הנשר הגדול הרמב״ם זצ״ל עם פירוקי וציוני הריטב״א [צ״ל: ר׳ שם טוב ב״ר אברהם ן׳ גאון בעל ״מגדל עוז״] שהשי׳ על הראב״ד בהשגותיו ועם נימוקי וציוני ההנגר בעל המגיד משנה ועם ההגהות והציונין מחבר האוריין תלמיד מהר״ם ז״ל: כל אלו החיבורים מזוקקים ומסולקים ממוקשי הטעיות מוגהים ע״י האלוף הרב המובהק רבי דוד פיצגטון י״ץ פעם ראשונה בהעתק ועל ידי אני קטן התלמידי׳ יעקב ב״ר חיים ן׳ אדוניהו ליבל אח״כ פעם שנית בבי׳ הדפוס ועיינתי בהו סגין דמסתפינא טובא מהא דאמרי׳ פ״ב דכתובות אל תשכן באהלך עולה זה ספר שאינו מוגה ואין להבדיל בין תורה שבכתב לתורה שבע״פ כי מאז הושמה בספר אין בין זה לזה כאשר כתב הרא״ש דאם נמצא טעות בגמרא או בספר מפוסקים יבא להתיר האסור ולאסור את המותר ולזכו׳ את החייב ואין עולה גדולה מזו ועוד דהא חזינא לרמב״ן ז״ל בחידושיו בב״ב היותו מתעצם לתקן ספרי׳ מסברא וגם הרשב״א ז״ל בתוספותיו במסכת ברכו׳ והרביצו אלה על אשר כן יעשה ועוד דהא חזינא לר״ת ז״ל אשר כל התורה כולה היתה ראויה ליכתב מפיו ועכ״ז הניח לו רב ואשר עשו חכמי התלמוד חסורא מחסרא או האחרונים להיישיר הגירסות אשר היו גאוני ועמודי עולם כל שכן וכ״ש אנן יתמי דיתמי וכמחט סדקית לסבר׳ חלילה וחלילה ללכת בגדולות האלה לחסר או להוסיף אות אחת מהכרעת הלב חס לי ולזרעא דאבא אמנם בשומי ה׳ נגדי שלא יכשלו בני אדם בפעולתי עשיתי התנצלותי והייתי נקי מאלהים ומישראל.

(שטיינשניידר, שם; לוצקי שם, סימן ח׳; וואכשטיין ב׳, 113, מספר 293).

ש״י (1550)

8. ההודאה לממציא כל מחוייב המציאות שהגיענו להתחיל כן יגיענו להשלים לחקוק בעט ברזל ועופרת חיבור משנה תורה אשר חיבר אחד קדוש רבינו משה בן הדיין ר׳ מיימון הספרדי זצ״ל, עם המגדל עוז שחיבר הרב ר׳ שם טוב ב״ר אברהם בן גאון ספרדי זצ״ל, ועם המגיד משנה שחיבר אחד נגר ובר נגר זצ״ל ועם ההגהו׳ מיימוניות שחיבר אחד אוריין בר אוריין הוא תלמיד מהר״ם זצ״ל כל אילין רבוותא קהו קהוותן ופרקו פירוקין וציינו ציונים בכל פרטי החיבור הזה מגמרא דילן ומתלמודא דבני מערבא ומכולהו רבוותא: וכל אלו החיבורים מזוקקים שבעתיים מסוקלים ממוקשי הטעיות עם עיונא סגין ונברר הסולת מתוך הסובין ע״י הרב המובהק האלוף ה״ר דוד פיציגטו״ן יצ״ו מגיה ההעתק פעם ראשונה וע״י הגאון מהר״ר מאיר מפדו״אה וע״י בנו גדול מרבן שמו יהודה פעם שנית וגדול כבוד האחרון הזה מן הראשון באשר נתוסף עתה הספר מצות שחבר הרב המחבר עם השגת הרמב״ן שהשיג על הי״ד שרשים שעשה הרב על מניין המצוות וגם נתוספו עתה קצת חדושים חדשו האלוף מורינו הרב רבי מאיר ובנו הנ״ל עם עיון רב:

נדפס במצות השר מאניי״פיקו מיסי״ר אלווי״זי בראגדי״ן בן האדון מאניי״פיקו מיסי״ר פי״רו בראגדי״ן: שנת חמשת אלפים ושלש מאות ועשרה לבריאת עולם בשנה רביעית לאדונינו הדוכוס פראנצי״סקו דונ״ה יר״ה אמן. בויניציאה.

כרך א: מדע — קדושה. [2], ג—שפ״ט דף. קודם לו: ספר המצוות (עם שער קצר של ספר המצוות): [2], ג—מ״א דף. בטפסים אחרים שער הנ״ל מהמשנה תורה נכרך בראשו.

כרך ב: הפלאה — שופטים. [1], שצ״ד—תשס״ז, [2] דף.

מעבר לשער של כרך א׳ דברי מהר״ם מפדובה:

מאת ה׳ היתה זאת

להעיר לב השר מסי״ר אלווי״זי בראג״דין בן השר מסי״ר פי״רו ברא״גדין להציב י״ד להדפיס שנית משנה תורה של הרמב״ם וטרם החל מלאכתו קרא אלי מאיר קצנאי״לנבוגן להגיה חשכי הספר לסקל מסילותיו ולהרים המכשולות מקרבו. אמרתי מי הקדימני ואשלים את אשר חסר הלא הוא הגאון נ״י כמהר״ר דוד פיצגט״ון ז״ל אשר בדרכיו נוגה אור האיר כל מאפל בראשונה ומי יבא אחר המלך אשר כבר עשהו. הלא הבאים אחריו יחשבו כנמושות לקוטי בתר לקוטי שבתי ואמרתי כבר אמרו אינו דומה מי ששונה פרקו מאה פעמים לשונה פרקו מאה ואחת לכן אי אפשר שלא הניח לי הגאון הנ״ל מקום להתגדר בו. לזה שמעתי לקול האדון מסי״ר אלווי״זי הנ״ל ואף גם זאת שנסתי מתני לעיין היטב כיד ה׳ הטוב עלי בקצת מקומות שנמצאים בספר סתימות ודברי׳ תמוהים למעיינים בו והיתה יד ה׳ וחזקתו על בני ינִיק וחכים האלוף יהודה יצ״ו שהיה לי לעזרת ה׳ בקושיות ופירוקים בכל מקום שמצאנו שם מילתא דתמוה כתבנו בהעתק אשר ממנו נדפס בגליון בחוץ מה שנראה לנו ולסימן שמאתנו יצא כתבנו שם אמר המגיה והצבנו עליו יד פושטת אצבעה ורומזת על המקום אשר שב אליו. והנני מעיד עלי שמים וארץ שלא קראתי בספר כמי שקרא להגיה בלבד אך למדתי כל הלכה והלכה בעסק רב והיו לפני שלשה ספרים להגיה מתוכן. ולא תקנתי דבר מלבי ואם היה נראה בעיני טעות באיזה מקום ולא מצאתיו לתקנו מתוך הספרים כתבתי בגליון שנר׳ שטעות

הוא. ובפנים הנחתיו כמו שהיה. אמנם במגיד משנה לא יכולתי להפיק הרצון כי לא היה לפני שום העתק אחר רק הנדפס ראשונה אך כאשר מצאתי בו איזה טעות או דלוג ועלה בידי לתקנו מתוך התלמוד או תוספתא שהביא תקנתי אותו. ובמגדל עוז היה יותר נמנע לתקן בו הקלקולים לחסרון ספרים שלא מצאנו שום ספר ממנו וגם דרכי נתיבותיו אינם סלולים בנתיבות אשר כמו בעל המגיד אשר מטוב סדורו ופלפולו הישר היה נקל למצא לפעמים החסרון לתקנו באופן ניאות. ועלה ברוחי בראשונה להוסיף בספר מראה מקום בתלמוד לרשום מקום מוצא הדברים בדפים שבתלמוד ונחמתי אחרי כן ומאסתי בזה לאשר מי יגיד לי ומי יפיס שלכל אדם יהיה לפניו התלמוד ערוך במניין דפים אילו אולי לקצת בני אדם חביב לפניהם ללמוד מתוך הספרים הישנים כמוני היום. או אולי היום ולמחר יהיו נדפסי׳ במקומות אחרים בסדר אחר. בכן הנחתי הספר בדבר הזה כמו שהיה. וכן בהגהו׳ צדקו דברי הגאון מהר״ד דוד פיצגט״ון ז״ל שלא להשים בתוכו רק הגה׳ מיימוני לכן הוספתי רק מעט מזער עליהם שהיה נראה לי צורך בהם. ולאשר כתב המחבר מניין המצוות בהתחלת הספר והם כחלום בלא פתרון למי שלא ראה י״ד שרשים שהקדים הרב בספר מניין המצות שלו לכן בחרנו להשים עם הספר הזה הספר מצות שחיבר הרב עם הי״ד שרשים ההם כי ימצא בהם המעיין לפעמים תועלת גם בעיקר ספר הי״ד. ולזה שמנו גם כן בצדם השגת הרמב״ן אשר השיג על קצת שרשים אילו. נאם הטרוד מאיר בכמ״ר יצחק ז״ל קצנא״ילנבוגן.

נוסח השער של כרך ב:

חלק שני. ברוך הנותן ליעף כח אשר הגיענו להשלים החלק הראשון ולאין אונים עצמה ירבה להשלים גם את החלק השני הזה מן חבור מ ש נ ה ת ו ר ה אשר חבר רבינו משה בן הדיין רבי מיימון הספרדי זצ״ל עם השגת הראב״ד ועם המגדל עוז שחיבר הריטב״א ז״ל ועם המגיד משנה ועם הג״הות מיימוניות שחבר תלמיד מהר״ם זצ״ל. וכל אלו החבורים מזוקקים שבעתים מסוקלים ממוקשי הטעיות... ונברר האוכל מתוך הפסולת ע״י הגאון כמהר״ר דוד פיצגטון אשר הגיה ההעתק פעם ראשונה וע״י הגאון מהר״ר מאיר מפדואה וע״י בנו גדול מרבן שמו יהודה פעם שנית וגדול כבוד האחרון הזה מן הראשון באשר נתוסף עתה הספר מצות שחבר הרב המחבר עם השג׳ הרמב״ן שהשיג על י״ד שרשים שעשה המחבר על מניין המצוות. וגם נתוספו עתה קצת חדושים חדשו האלוף מהרב מאיר ובנו הנ״ל עם עיון רב.

נדפס במצות השר מאניי״פיקן מיסי״ר אלוויז״י בראגד״ין בן האדון מאניי״פיקן מיסי״ר פיר״ו בראגדי״ן. שנת חמשת אלפים ושלוש מאות ועשרה לבריאת עולם... בויניציאה.

מעבר לשער: תוכן ההלכות של ספר הפלאה.

בסוף כרך ב׳, דף תשס״ז, ב:

כתב התנצלות הועתק מלשון מסיר א״לויזי בראגא״דין ללשון הקדש

אחרי זכני ה׳ ית׳ להשלים ספר המיימוני

על ידי עושי המלאכה אלי דבר יגונב איך היושט״יניאן בהקדמה בספר המיימוני שלו הדפיס דברי׳ חבר אחד מעבדיו שנתן דופי בספרי זה באומרו שכל ההגהות אשר באו בגליון על שם המגיה נעשו שלא כהוגן כי אין ראוי לשום אדם בדור הזה להשיג על

דברי הרב הגדול המחבר. והיושטיני"אן או שלוחו העבד הנזכר הרחיב לדבר באלה והנה לאשר היתה עצתו נמהרה ונכספה גם כלתה נפשו לתת דופי בספרי ולהתכבד בקלון חברו לאמר שלי טוב משלו בא לכלל טעות כי האשל הגדול הרב רבי מאיר מפד"ואה הוא המגיה כבר היה נשמר מזה וכל אשר עשה הוא לכבוד ולתפארת אל הרב המחבר. וברוב פלפולו העמיד דברי המחבר על מכונם כדי שלא יקשו דבריו על המעיין לכן גלה כל סתום. וכאשר לפעמים לא היה יכול להפיק רצונו ליישב היטב כתב רק לעורר לב המעיין שיתבונן היטב ואמר שצריך עיון וכל זה נתברר לי על ידי עושי המלאכה והמופת יוכיח והאותיות יגידו לכל אשר יקרא בהם יתנו עדיהם ויצדקו. ולא ימלט מחלוקה או העבד הזה לא קרא ולא ראה ההגהות ההם וחבר הדברים במצות אדונו מס"יר מאר"קו אנט"וניו אשר קבל שמע שוא כי הוא לא מבין לשון הקדש ולא מכיר לשון עברי. או אותו העבד קרא אותם ולא הבינם וחבר דברים למי שיקרא ההקדמה לבד ולא יגיע לעיין תוכן הדברים. אמנם כל בן מדע אשר יקרא הדברים בעצמם ויבינם יעיד שכבוד ספרי זה במקומו יעמוד אשר הגיה אותו גדול היהודים הרב רבי מאיר מפד"ואה ושמו נודע בשערים ועמו אשר הוליד בדמותו הבחור המהולל בפי כל בנו רבי יהודה. ועוד רוח בכנפי העבד הנזכר לאמור שנמצא חכם אשר התחיל לעשות הפלה על דברי המגיה. אל יתהלל בדברי שקר ואם אמת יהגה החכם ההוא הרואה ואינו נראה שהתחיל להפיל לפי דבריו ימצא אחריו הפלה דהפלה. ובעט שקר חקק העבד הנזכר לאמר שאדונו הדפיס הספר לתועלת היהודים כדי שלא יהיו מוכרחים לקנות משלי וימצאו לקנותו משלו בזול. כי אדרבה כל כוונתו לסבב שיהיה יחידי במלאכה זו ויכוף היהודים ברצונו ויתעשר מהם וכן בהנהגתו הבלתי ראויה עם הבומ"בירגי סבב שפסקו מלהדפיס והזיק בזה מאד ליהודים כי מלאכתם היתה טובה מאד בכל דבר וכאשר פסקו מהדפיס נחדלו הספרים הטובים וגם נתיקרו הספרי' וכל מחשבתו למנוע אף אותי מהדפיס ולא יעלה בידו כי בעזרת האל בקרב ימים מועטים אתחיל להדפיס אף התלמוד באופן שלם בנייר טוב שכולו שוה מעניין אחד ולא בניירים מתחלפים ומוגה כהוגן הפך משלו וכן העשרים וארבע הגדול ורב אלפס. ולא איש דברי' אנכי כי יהיו נשלמים באמת וטרם יקרא כל איש אני אענה אותו הנה הוא קחנו ולך. ויזולו הספרי' ובשכר זה כל היהודים אלי ירוצו לקנות ולמלאת חפצם. וידעתי שאדון העבד הזה כאשר יראה התחלתי להדפיס העשרים וארבע ורב אלפס ירוץ גם הוא אל המערכה לעשות המלאכה ולא מקודם כאשר עשה עמי במיימוני ובזאת אדע שתתנו לי שבח שבסבתי יהיו הספרים בזול.

אלה דברי אני אלווי"זי בראגד"ין בן לאדוני מס"יר פ"ירו בראגד"ין:

ואני המעתיק מוסיף מעט על דברי מס"יר אלווי"ז בראגד"ין. נראה בעין שהעבד הקטן אשר כתב הקדמת המיימוני מהיושטינ"יאן אין לו ער בחכמים ולא עונה בתלמידים רק מכת המדברים תועה הוא. הלא כמה וכמה תשובות נמצאים בתשובות הרשב"א ור"י בר ששת ורבינו קלון ובכל דור ודור שנתעסקו בזה להקשות ולתרץ בדברי הרמב"ם ובעקבותם הלך אף הרב רבי מאיר וככה ראוי והוגן לכל מגיה ספר לעיין היטב וליישב הדברים הסתומים בספר והעבד הקטן הנזכר אולת ידבר שהמגיה יראה ולא יבין ויאמר גמרא גמור וזמרותא תהא יפה שתיקתו מדבורו שמו אשר קרא לעצמו נאה לו עבד קטן והטעה את רבו כי האגרת שהביא לראייה אינן מן העניין כי עניינו הוא על מי שידבר תועה על דברי המחבר ויאמר שדבריו סותרים זה את זה. כלל העולה

מי שירצה לעמוד על האמת לא יפנה אל ההקדמות הכוזבות כי קליפות הם. אך יזרוק הקליפות ויאכל תוכו וישבע מטובו:

[2] דפים האחרונים: [1]: שני שירים: היכל דביר נאה מגדל וגם ארמון. (דאווידסון: אוצר ב׳, 138; מספר 524); ספר נקרא משנה תורה כניו בא לכל הי״ד (דאווידסון, ג׳, 245 מספר 230);

[2]: דגל המדפיס וקולופון: נדפס במצות השר אלוויז״י בראגדי״ן... שנת חמשת אלפים ושלש מאות ועשרה לבריאת עולם... בויניציאה.

בספרית היברו יוניאון קוליג׳ בצינסינטי; בעותקים של הסמינר התיאולוגי והספריה הציבורית בניו־יורק חסרים בראשו ספר המצוות.

בשאלת ההתחרות בין בית־דפוס זה ובין בית־דפוס יוסטיניאן בויניציאה שגם כן התחיל להדפיס באותה שנה את ספר המשנה תורה, עיין הערתנו בסוף הערך הבא.

(לוצקי, שם סימן ט׳; הרב אבידע, שם עמ׳ קמ, קמ״ב; י. זנה, שם עמ׳ ריד, רט״ז).

ש״י (1550)

9. משנה תורה, הוא ספר הי״ד שחיבר הרב הגדול רבינו משה בן הדיין רבי מיימון הספרדי זצ״ל: עם המגדל עוז ועם המגיד משנה ועם ההגהות מיימוניות נדפס מחדש מוגה ומדוייק ברוב העיון מתוך ספרים קדמונים נמצאים בדפוס וכתיבת יד מעויינים ומוגהים מחכמים גדולים אנשי שם ע״י הגאון ראש הגולה מהר״ר דוד פיציגטון ז״ל: וע״פ העתקות של הרב הגדול בדורו מהר״ר עזריאל דיינה ז״ל:

עוד הוספנו הרבה הגהות שמצאנו בספרים ישנים וקדמונים מגדולי עולם. גם נתחדש על הנדפסים בתחלה חיבור מנין המצות שחיבר הרמב״ם ז״ל שהוא עקר גדול לזה הספר. גם זה לעומת זה ההשגות אשר השיג הרמב״ן ז״ל על החיבור הנז׳ למען יהיה שלם בתכלית השלימות לא יחסר בו. עוד הוספנו בו מראה מקום מהדינים בפוסקים מסומן כל דין בגיליון באיזה סימן מהטור ומהסמ״ג נזכר. גם בכל מקום שיזכיר המגיד משנה או המגדל עוז מסכתא או פרק מסומן על דגלו לאותות באיזה דף נמצא. עוד נדפס עמו המפתחות שנדפסו לפנים ולא נתפשטו בגלילות אלו שהם הכרחיות מאוד למצוא כל דין בקלות:

גם הסכמנו להדפיס באחרונה מה שכתב בגיליון חכם אחד וראש מרבני פדוואה הרב רבי מאיר חדשים לבקרים שכתב מלבו בדפוס המיימוני אשר הדפיס מחדש הברגאדי״ן והכניס ראשו בין הקדמונים גדולי עולם אשר נועצנו עם חכמים ושלימים קרובים ורחוקים וייעצונו באמת שלא להדפיסם תוך הספר בשמא ואולי לא יצדקו להרבה לומדי תורה כאשר יתבאר לכל מעיין בהקדמה אחת מעבר לדף זה אך אמנם הדפסנום להפיק רצון כל אדם ולעשות כרצון איש ואיש:

פה ויניציאה. בבית... מארקו אנטוניינו יושטינייאן. 2°.

חלק א: ספר המצוות; ספר המדע — קדושה. ש״י.

[1], ב—כ״ו [צ״ל: מ״ו], א, י—שפט, [5] דף. [1] = שער; ב—מו: הקדמה למשנה תורה; ספר המצוות והשגות הרמב״ן (עד דף מד, א); סימני הלכות; דף א: המשך סימני הלכות; דף י—שפט: ספר מדע—קדושה; [5] דף: דגל המדפיס (1 דף), וד׳ האחרונים: הגהות מְהר״ם מפדואה (״אלו הם התוספות שהוסיף וכתב מדעתו הרב מהר״ר מאיר מפדואה״).

ושאבתם מים בששון ממעיני הישועה

לכל היד החזקה ולכל המורא

הגדול אשר עשה משה לעיני כל

ישראל ונגש משה לבדו אל יי

והם לא יגשו והעם לא יעלו עמו

שהודאה למצוה כל מחוייב המצוות שהגיעו להתחיל בן יגיעו להשלים
לחקוק בעט ברזל ועופרת חיבור משנה תורה אשר חיבר אחד קדוש רבינו
משה בן הדיין ר׳ מיימון הספרדי זצ״ל עם המגדל עוז שחיבר הרב
ר׳ שם טוב ב״ר אברהם בן גאון ספרדי זצ״ל ועם המגיד משנה שחיבר
אחד נגר ובר נגר זצ״ל ועם ההגהו׳ מיימוניות שחיבר אחד אוריין
בר אוריין הוא תלמיד מהר״ם זצ״ל כל אילין רבוותא קהו קהוותן
ופרקו פירוקין וביינו ביונים בכל פרטי החיבור הזה מגמרא דילן
ומתלמודא דבני מערבא ומכולהו רבוותא: וכל אלו החיבורים
מזוקקים שבעתים משוקלים ממוקשי הטעיות עם עונבא
סנון ונברר הסולת מתוך המורסן ע״י הרב
המובהק האלוף ה״ר דוד פיטגטון יצ״ו
מנוה הפעם ראשונה
וע״י הגאון מהר״ר מאיר מפדואה וע״י בנו גדול מרבן שמו
יהודה פעם שנית וגדול כבוד האחרון הזה מן הראשון
באשר נתוסף עתה הספר מצות שחבר הרב המחבר עם
השגות הרמב״ן שהשיג על הי״ד שרשים שעשה
הרב על מניין המצות
גם נתוספו עתה קצת חדושים חדשו האלוף מורינו
הרב רבי מאיר ובנו הנ״ל עם שנון רב:

נדפס במצות השר מאלויזיקו מיסיר אלוויזי ברגדין בן האדון מאלויזיקו מיסיר פ״רו ברגדין:

שנת חמשת אלפים ושלש מאות ועשרים לבריאת עולם בשנה רביעית לאדונינו
סדוכוס פראנציסקו דונא ירה״ה אמן ·

בוויניציאה

VENICE (BRAGADIN) 1550.

בסוף הדף האחרון: "על ידי הגבר הוקם על המלאכה קורניליו אדי"ל קינ"ד".

חלק ב: הפלאה — שופטים. שי"א.

[1], שצ"ד — תשס"ז, [5] דף. [1] דף: שער חלק ב'; שצ"ד — תשס"ז: גוף הספר; [5] דף: הגהות מהר"ם מפדואה ודגל המדפיס.

נוסח השער של חלק שני:

משנה תורה חלק שני

חיבר הנשר הגדול רבינו משה בן הדיין רבי מיימון הספרדי זצ"ל ישתבח הבורא הנותן לכל קץ תכלה שזיכנו להגיע עד כה לחקוק בעוזקא דגושפנקא חיבור משנה תורה זה עם פרקי וציוני הריטב"א שהשיב על הראב"ד בהשגותיו ועם נימוקי וציוני הנגר בעל המגיד משנה. ועם ההגהות והציונין שחבר האוריין תלמיד מהר"ם ז"ל:

עוד נתחדש ונתוסף על הנדפסים מקדם מראה מקום מהדינים בפוסקים מסומן כל דין בגיליון באיזה סימן מהטור והסמ"ג נמצא. גם בכל מקום שיזכיר המגיד משנה מסכתא או פרק מסומן על דגלו לאותות באיזה דף נזכר. מוגה ומדוייק ברוב העיון מתוך ספרים קדומים נמצאים בדפוס ובכתבי־יד מעויינים ומוגהים מחכמים גדולים אנשי שם ע"י הגאון ראש הגולה מהר"ר דוד פיציגיטון ז"ל פעם ראשונה בהעתק וע"פ העתקות של רב גדול בדורו מהר"ר עזריאל דיינ"ה זצ"ל באחרונה.

פה ויניציאה

בבית בן משק בית האדון מארקו אנטוניו יושטינייאן שמנה לחדש שבט שנת שי"א לפ"ק ממשלת השררה יר"ה תגדל ותנשא מלכותם אמן:

מעבר לשער: "אמרתי אחכמה והיא רחוקה ממני; נאם העבד הקטן אוהב הנאמן בן משק בית האדון מארקו אנטוניאו יושטיניאן המכיל דברי זלזול על הוצאת בראגאדין. דברי זלזול אלה חוזרים בכותרת שלפני הגהותיו של מהר"ם מפאדובה: אלה הן התוספות שהוסיף וכתב מדעתו הרב מהר"ר מאיר מפדובה [עד כאן באותיות גדולות] בכותבו אמר המגיה עם היד פושטת אשר פשט ושלח ידו במלאכי אלהים בדפוס המיימוני של הבראגאדין והדפסנום פה כדי שכל חכם ותלמיד ילמוד ויעיין בהם ואם טובות וישרות הם יקיימם ויאשרם ואם לאו ישיג עליהם כראוי לפי שכלו; גם כי לכדי נכתבו וכמאן דליתי דמי, כי כל ארץ תימן [?] ומערב הסכימו להעבירם מעל הספר כי אם באולי מטעם שטעה הרב הנז[כר] ואם מטעם שבא לבאר דברים יבינם אפילו בר בי רב דחד יומא..." בצדק מעיר הרב אבידע, שממנו העתקנו את הנ"ל, "לא רק שגנבו ושמו בכליהם דברי הר"ם מפדובה ז"ל אלא שעטרום בדברי זלזול, מלבד דברי הזלזול שלא חשכו מעבר לשער של חלק ב'" (הרב י. אבידע: לתולדות ההוצאות הראשונות של י"ד ספרי משנה תורה להרמב"ם ז"ל, סיני 30 (תשי"ב), עמ' קמ"ב).

עיין ישעיהו זנה בספר היובל מארכס, ניו־יורק, תש"י עמ' רי"ד, רט"ז; לוצקי, סימן י'.

הוצאה זו שבאה מיד אחר הוצאת בראגאדין גרמה שהרמ"א יצא עם פסק דין לאסור הפצת הוצאת יוסטיניאן (שו"ת הרמ"א, סימן י). תוצאות התחרות שבין בראגאדין ויושטיניאן היו חמורות בשביל הדפוס העברי באיטליה, כי גרמה לסגירתו בויניציאה למשך עשר שנים (שי"ד — שכ"ג). עיין, זנה, שם, עמ' רי"ד; א. מ. הברמן: המדפיסים בני ר' יעקב פרענצוני בוויניציאה, ארשת א (תשי"ט), עמ' 63; Cecil Roth: Venice, p 253–258.

ועיין עכשיו: מאיר בניהו: הסכמה ורשות בדפוסי ויניציאה, ירושלים, תשל״א, עמ׳ 23—30, 339.

של״ד (1574)

10. משנה תורה היא היד החזקה להרמב״ם זצ״ל עם השגות הראב״ד ז״ל ומגיד משנה ועם כסף משנה לגאון המופלא כמהר״ר יוסף קארו נר״ו [בכרך הרביעי: זצ״ל] וחדשנו בו התמונות השייכות בפירוש הלכות קדוש החדש ועוד הוספנו על ההלכות הנזכרות פירוש מהר״ר לוי ן׳ חביב ז״ל הכל הוגה עם רוב העיון והשקידה בהעתק הבא מצפת תוב״ב וגם בהעתק מעויין ומוגה מישיבת מצרים ועם תוספת כמה חסרונות שהיו במגיד משנה ובהשגות בדפוסים הראשונים והוספנו עליו מפתח גדול ורחב ידים עיני כל אליו ישברו ולחם משנה ילקטו יום יום ועוד הוספנו באחרונה מפתח אחר על סדר אלפא ביתא מצאנו בבית מדרשו של הרב המובהק כמוהר״ר ברוך עוזיאל חזק זצ״ל וזה החלנו לעשות במצות השר מיסיר אלוויסו בראגאדין על יד הקטן מאיר פרינץ... [חלק ד׳ ע״י אשר פרינץ], פה ויניציאה.

ד׳ כרכים. 2°.

חלק א: מדע — זמנים. של״ד. [22], שי״ו דף. [22] דף: שער, הקדמה, מנין המצות ומפתחות והשיר ״במדע אהבתך״. כרך זה נגמר בדף שי״ו, עמ׳ א.

חלק ב: נשים — קדושה. של״ד. [10]. ריט [צ״ל: רי״ח] דף. [10] דפים הראשונים: השער ומפתח להרמב״ם ופרטי דיניו. על דף רי״ט, עמ׳ א: קולופון: ותשלם המלאכה... יום ג׳ ר״ח טבת של״ה לפ״ק; עמ׳ ב: חלק.

חלק ג: הפלאה — טהרה. של״ד. [20], תנ״א, [1] דף. [20] דפים הראשונים: השער ומפתח להרמב״ם; [1] דף האחרון: תוכן ספר טהרה.

חלק ד: נזיקין — שופטים. של״ו. [10], רצ״ז, [9] דף. [10] דף: מפתח להרמב״ם ופרטי דיניו על סדר הספרים; [9] דף: מפתח להרמב״ם על סדר אלפא ביתא״. ודף הקולופון.

קולופון: והיתה השלמת הספר הנכבד והנורא הזה יום ד׳ כ״ט מרחשון של״ו לפק כבודך יי.

מעבר לשער החלק הראשון: אמר המגיה, למה שקדם היות כל מצוה נקראת על שם גומרה, ובפרט במלאכת הדפוס שסופו מוכיח על תחלתו, והיה הקונטריס הראשון למשמר אחרון למלאכה, חלה עלי חובת ההודאה לאל המרומם על כל ברכה ותהלה שזכנו להשלים הספר הזה לשלום עם כל השלמיות שנתוספו בו כי עיני כל תחזינה משרים מה נשתנה למעליותא החבור הנורא זה בצאתו לאור מחדש מאשר כבר עשוהו הדפוסים הראשונים. ואם כי הרב האלוף כמהר״ר אברהם מנחם פורטו הכהן יצ״ו התחיל בהגהה זו, וכבר נשלמה על ידו המחצה ממנה, הנה עתה כי נקראתי להשלימה למה שפנה הרב הנזכר אל אשר היה שמה הרוח ללכת, יצאתי בעקבותיו לכל המלאכה לעשות אותה בתכלית התקון האפשרי. המחברים יזהירו כזהר הרקיע והמסייעים בהדפסה מצדיקי הרבים ככבבים לעולם ועד, ובראשם הרב המובהק כמהר״ר משה פרווינצאלי יצ״ו, שהוא במנטובה ומצודתו פרושה בצפת תוב״ב לזרז הרב המופלא בעל הכסף משנה להועיל בו את הרבים, זכות השר הבראגדין לעולם תהיה, שנתן לכסף מוצא ומנה איש אמונים זקן ביתו ראש המדפיסים כמ״ר מאיר פרינץ י״ץ, להיות נצב על האומנים

משנה תורה

הוא ספר הי״ד שחיבר הרב הגדול רבינו
משה בן הדיין רבי מיימון הספרדי זצ״ל:

עם המגדל עוז ועם המגיד משנה ועם ההגהות מיימוניות נדפס
מחדש מוגה ומדוייק ברוב העיון מתוך ספרים קדמונים נמצאים
בדפוס וכתיבת יד מעויינים ומוגהים מחכמים גדולים אנשי שם
ע״י הגאון ראש הגולה מה״ר דוד פיצינטון ז״ל: ועם העתקות
של הרב גדול בדורו מה״ר עוריאל ריינה ז״ל:

פה ויניציאה

Purchased in Russia.

VENICE (GIUSTINIAN) 1550.

ולסדר המלאכה בשלם שבפנים. והיה לנו לעינים איש אשר רוח דעת ויראת ה' היא אוצרו, בר אוריין ובר אבהן, הקצין כמה"ר מנחם עזריה מפאנו, פקיד מהגאון המופלא מהר"י קארו נר"ו ובית דינו שהשליטוהו על החבור הלז לסדר אופן הדפסתו ולהזהר עוד שלא יבוזו זרים יגיע הרב הנזכר בהדפיסו פעמים אחרות עולה קמשונים וחרולים. האל המאזרנו חיל יתן עז ותעצומות לכל העוסקים במלאכת שמים, עוד ינובון בשיבה וצאצאיהם יחדו ירננו. תפלה לעני כי יעטוף אני הוא קטן התלמידים צעיר הרופאים חזקיה בכמ"ר יצחק מפאנו זצ"ל.

בסוף הכרך הרביעי: אמר המגיה, אני אמרתי בחפזי להפיק רצון השר הבראגדין אשר צוה עלינו זה כמשלש חדשים להשלים החלקים שהיו מסויימים בעת ההיא, כי דרך המדפיסים השלמים לאחר את הקונטריס המוקדם עד סוף המעשה והיה לעד על תחלת המחשבה הטהורה שקמה וגם נצבה במציאות הפועל המשתלם, למען לא ישלחו בעולתה לשונם לידור ולא לשלם, והיה הטוב ההוא אשר יוסיפו מחדש על החבורים לתהלה ולשם ולתפארת יגמרו עליו את ההלל לראש אשמורות כעל אשר כבר עשוהו והלא דין הוא לכל ברכות השבח וההודאה, שלא תחול מצותן עובר לעשייתן. כמעט שעברנו מחקי המדפיסים לעשות נחת רוח למאהבי השר הנזכר שחשקה נפשם לחזות בנועם הספר הנורא הזה בחפזון שכינה, עדין לא לקחה אזננו שמץ מהלקח ארון האלקים הרב המופלא כמוהר"ר יוסף קארו זצ"ל, שנתבקש בישיבה של מעלה יום ה' י"ג ניסן של"ה והיתה מנוחתו כבוד. וגם אחרי כן היתה יד ה' בזקן ונשוא פנים, הוא הראש במלאכת הדפוס שלא הניח כמותו כמ"ר מאיר פארינצו ז"ל, שנפטר אל בית עולמו יום ה' יח תשרי של"ו וחיים לרבנן ולכל ישראל שבק, תנוח נפשו במשכבו בשלום, כי הפליא עצה להגדיל תורה, וכל כוונתו היתה לשמים לזכות את הרבים. ואחריו היה בסומכי ידינו המפואר כמר אשר פרינצו, אחיו יצ"ו, המקום יסייע בידו וביד שאר אחיו למלאת מקום אחיהם הנפטר ז"ל להאיר עיני ישראל במלאכת הדפוס כאשר עם לבבם ואנחנו נברך יה כעל כל אשר גמלנו כרחמיו וכרוב חסדיו להתחיל ולהשלים לשלום עם כל השלמיות שנתוספו בספר הנפלא הזה, לא נעשה כן לכל ההדפסות, ועיניכם הרואות כי אמרנו מעט ועשינו הרבה. ראו כי הדפסנו בסוף הספר מפתח כולל קטן הכמות ורב האיכות בסדר אלפא ביתא מצאנוהו שגיא כח להועיל למעיינים לנחותם הדרך להשיג מבוקשם, מוצאו מבית מדרשו של הרב הזקן הגדול בדורו כמוהר"ר ברוך עוזיאל חזק זצ"ל. האל המאזרנו חיל יזכה אותנו ואת כל ישראל ללמוד וללמד לשמור ולעשות את כל דברי התורה הזאת ובה נחזה בטוב ירושלם במהרה בימינו אמן.

לאחר דברי המגיה בא "שיר ידידות לאיש חמודות אשר יצק מים על ידי הרב זצ"ל בעל הכסף משנה ושמו בראשי שטין נגש והוא נענה". התחלת השיר היא: "אומץ גבורות אל אשר עמקו".

בהוצאה זו העתיקו בפעם הראשונה את השגות הראב"ד כחטיבה בפני עצמה לכל הספרים והיא הראשונה שבה מצויינת כל ההלכות הקטנות (הרב יהודה אבידע, סיני, כרך 30 (תשי"ב), עמ' קל"ח—ק"ם; עיין י. זנה, שם עמ' רי"ז; לוצקי, סימן י"א. על אדות הציורים המופיעים בכרכים השונים, עיין א. מ. הברמן: המדפיסים בני ר' יעקב פרענצוני בוויניציאה, ב"ארשת", א (תשי"ט), עמ' 79 שבמחקרו (עמ' 77—79) נתעזרנו בתיארנו.

עיין עכשיו על הדפסת "כסף משנה" בס' "הסכמה ורשות" למאיר בניהו, ירושלים, תשל"א, עמ' 29, 152, 339, ו־342.

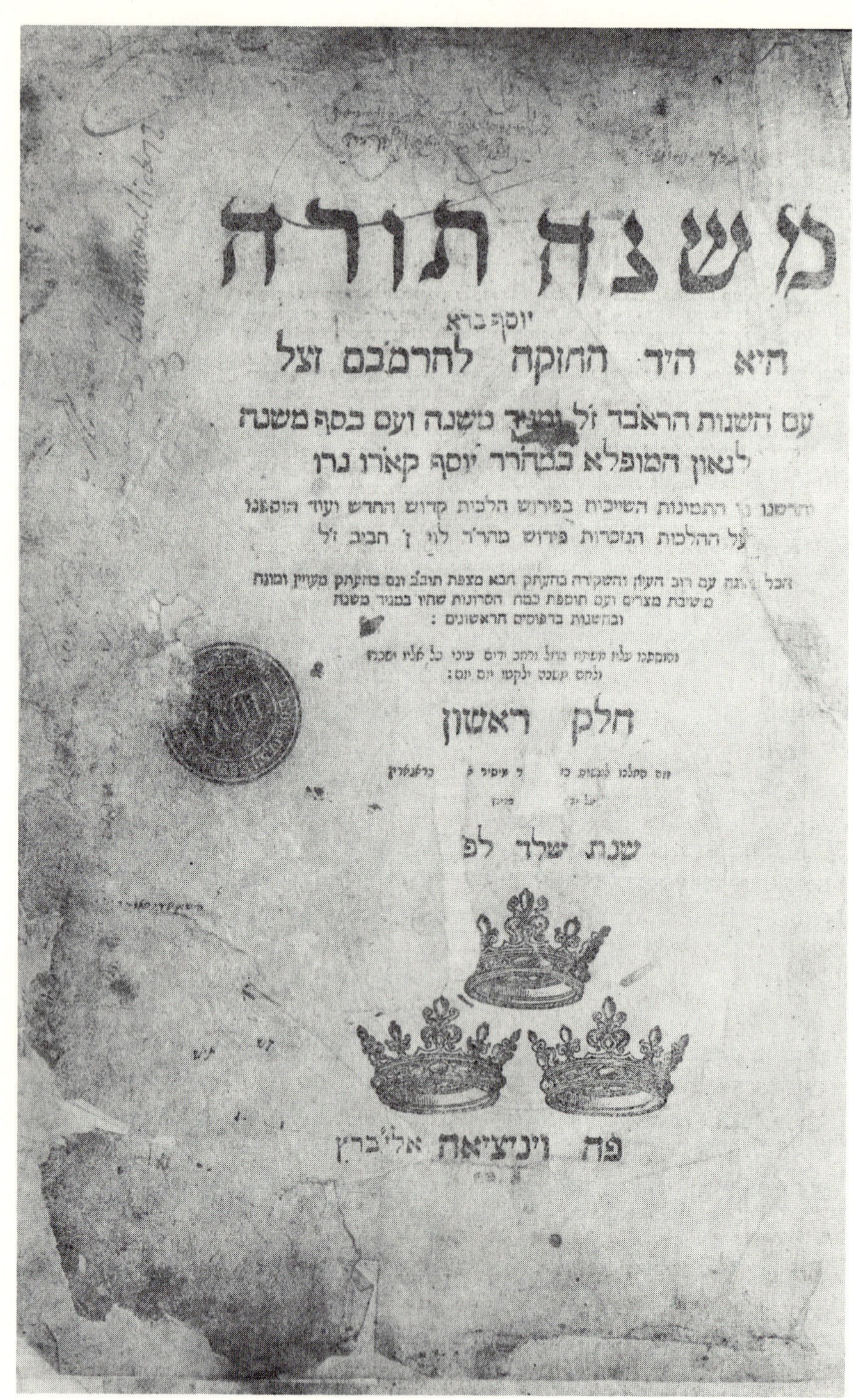

משנה תורה

היא היד החזקה להרמב״ם ז״ל

עם השגות הראב״ד ז״ל ומגיד משנה ועם כסף משנה

לגאון המופלא כמהר״ר יוסף קארו נר״ו

והרשמנו גם התמונות השייכות בפירוש הלכות קדוש החדש ועוד הוספנו

על ההלכות הנזכרות פירוש מהר״ר לוי ן׳ חביב ז״ל

הכל מוגה עם רוב העיון והחקירה בהעתק הבא מצפת תובב״א וגם בהעתק מעוין ומוגה

מיטבת מצרים ועם תוספת כמה חסרונות שהיו במגיד משנה

ובהשגות בדפוסים הראשונים :

חלק ראשון

שנת שלד לפ

פה ויניציאה אלו״ברין

VENICE 1574.

תס"ב (1702)

11. משנה תורה הוא היד החזקה להנשר הגדול רבינו משה בר מימון... עם השגות הראב"ד ז"ל, ופירוש הרב מגיד משנה. וגם הכסף משנה לגאון המופלא... יוסף קאר"ו זצ"ל: ועוד נתחברו לטהורים האלה המגדל עוז. והגהות מיימוניות: ועל הלכות קידוש החדש פירוש רבינו עובדיה ומהר"ר לוי ן' חביב. עם כל הצורות השייכות בין להלכות אלו. בין להלכות שבת וסוכה [ובשער של חלק שלישי: וחדשנו בחלק הזה התמונות השייכות להבנת כלאי זרעים וכלאי הכרם]. ושמנו אותם בסוף הספר בקונטרים לבדו: [ובשער של חלק רביעי: ובחלק הזה נרשמו התמונות השייכות להלכות מכירה ושותפין כל אחת ואחת במקומה] וזה מוסיף על הראשונים מורה מקום מהש"ס הבבלי על דברי הרב המגיד והכסף משנה מלבד מורה מקום הטור והסמ"ג על דברי רבינו המחבר זצ"ל: ועשינו עליו שתי מפתחות גדולות ורחבות: אחת על סדר הפרקים [בשערים של חלק ב—ד נוסף: "בכל חלק וחלק"] ואחת [בשערים של חלק ב—ד נוסף: "בחתימת חלק הרביעי"] על דרך אלפא ביתא. והיה למעיינים לעינים למצוא בנקל מבוקשו איש על דגלו. [ובשערים של חלק ב—ד: והוספנו עליו בסוף כל אחד מחלקיו כיאור נפלא על ספר משנה תורה הזאת מהרב המובהק כמוה"רר אברהם די בוטון אשר עיני כל אליו ישברו ולחם משנה ילקטו יום יום]. והכל נעשה יפה בעתו. מוגה ומנופה בעשרים נפה בעיון גדול ובשקידה... על ידי החכם הנעלה כה"ר דוד נוניש טוריס נר"ו [ובשערים של חלק ב—ד: שלמה יהודה ליאון נר"ו]: ד' כרכים. באמשטרדם: בדפוס וכמצות הבחור הנחמד עמנואל בן הישיש הנכבד כה"ר יוסף עטיאש זצ"ל. שנת מכתב אלהים הוא לפ"ק [תס"ב 1702]. 2°.

Com Previlegio

כרך א: מדע — זמנים. [9], שכ"ז, [4] דף.

שער מקוצר נוסף בראשו, מקושט; הקדשה בפורטוגיזית:

Ao illustre e megniffico senhor Mosseh Machado.

הסכמות רבני אמשטרדם: שלמה די אוליוירה (כ"ז אייר, תנ"ט; כ"א מנחם, תס"ג תאריך זה הוא אחר שנת דפוס של הרמב"ם: תס"ב; שלמה בן יעקב אאיליון (תס"א); מעשה יהודה בן קלונימוס הכהן (כ"ט אייר, תנ"ט; ט' אלול, תס"א).

כרך ב: נשים — קדושה. [2], רכ"ז, [4] דף.

כרך ג: הפלאה—טהרה. [2], שס"ח, [9] דף.

כרך ד: נזיקין — שופטים. [1], ש"ט, [13] דף.

בדף האחרון, עמוד ב': נשלם הספר... כמצות ובבית הבחור... עמנואל בן הישיש הנכבד יוסף רפאל בן הקדוש אברהם עטיאש אשר נשרף על יחוד קדושת השם יתברך בעיר קורדווא, בשבעה עשר בתמוז שנת חמשת אלפים ארבע מאות ושבעה ועשרים לבריאת העולם.

הספר "לחם משנה" נכרך לפעמים בסוף כל כרך עם שער מיוחד ולפנים בפני עצמו בכרך אחד. על זה — במדור הפירושים על המשנה תורה, אי"ה, במקום אחר.

תצ"ט (1739)

12. משנה תורה הוא היד החזקה להנשר... רבינו משה בר מימון... עם השגת הראב"ד... פירוש הרב מגיד משנה וכסף משנה להגאון... רבינו יוסף קארו...

משנה תורה
הוא
היד החזקה
להרמבם זצ״ל
עם השגות הראב״ד ז״ל ופירוש
המגיד הכסף משנה
עוז והגהות מיימוניות
חלק ראשון
באמשטרדם
משנה
תורה
ברפוס ובמצות הבחור הנחמד עמנואל
הישיש הנכבד כה״ר יוסף עטיאש
שנת והמכתב מכתב אלהים הוא ל״פ

AMSTERDAM 1702.

ומגדל עוז והגהות מימוניות ופירוש רבינו עובדי' והרב המוסמך מהר"ל ן' חביב על הלכות קידוש החדש עם כל הצורות השייכות להלכות אלו ולהלכות שבת וסוכה. ועם מורה מקום על דברי הרב המגיד וכסף משנה. גם שתי מפתחות... אחת על סדר הפרקים ואחת על דרך אלפא ביתא... כפי אשר נדפס באמשטרדם... ספר לחם משנה וספ' משה למלך הראשון מהגאון... אברהם די בוטון... והשני מהגאון... יהודה רוזאנים... גם... ניתוסף מה שנשמט מהראשונים תשובת הכסף משנה על השגת הראב"ד שבמנין המצות וגם סימנים הלכות שברמב"ם הוצבנו גם בכל הפירושים הנ"ל. יעסניץ (בדפוס ר' ישראל ב"ר אברהם). 2°.

חלק א: מדע — זמנים, לסדר **וכתב לו את** משנה התורה הזאת על ספר [תצ"ט]. [9], רל"ד, ק"ב. [3] דף; [2] דפים: צורות השייכות להלכות קדוש החודש. הסכ' הר' יעקב הכהן מפראג, יהושע מקראקא, ברוך כהנא רפאפורט, יחזקאל קצנאלבוגן, אלעזר מקראקא. צבי הירש הלברשטט, שמואל הילמן דק"ק מנהיים.

קולופון: נשלם ביום ג' י"ט אלול לסדר **השירה הזאת עד** תומם [תצ"ט].

חלק ב: נשים — קדושה. לסדר **ויכתוב** משה **את כל** דברי ה' [ת"ק]. [1], קמ"ח, קי"ב [2] דף.

חלק ג: הפלאה — טהרה. לסדר **ולכל היד החזקה** ולכל המורא הגדול אשר עשה **משה** לעיני כל ישראל [תק"א]. [1], רכ"א, קס"ט דף.

הסכ' הר' אריה ליב דק"ק לבוב, מרדכי ב"ר צבי הירש דק"ק ליסא, גרשון ב"ר יחיאל מלצנברג ומשה ב"ר אהרן.

חלק ד: נזיקין — שופטים. לסדר ויהי ביום השמיני קרא **משה מיימון** [תק"א]. [1], קלה, קלח—קנד; קנז, [1] דף.

הס' הר' יצחק זעליג ב"ר ארי' יהודא ליב קרא מגלוגא, ישראל דק"ק הענא.

חלק א נדפס שנית בשינויים ובתבנית מוגדלת בשנת תק"א. קע"ב; פ"ז, [5] דף. חלק ב—ד יצא גם בתבנית מוגדלת כדי לצרפם לחלק א' הנ"ל.

על הוצאה זו והמו"ל עיין:

Max Freudenthal, "Aus der Heimat Mendelsohns. Moses Benjamin Wulff und seine Familie", Berlin, J. G. Lederer, 1900, pp 214–219; 261–263.

תקכ"ה (1765)

13. משנה תורה הוא היד החזקה להנשר... רבינו משה בר מיימון... עם השגות הראב"ד... ופירוש הרב המגיד משנה וכסף משנה להגאון... יוסף קארו... ופירוש מגדל עוז והגהות מיימוניות ועם פירוש רבינו עובדיה והרב המוסמך מהר"ל ן' חביב על הלכות קידוש החדש עם כל הצורות השייכות להלכות אלו ולהלכות שבת וסוכה ועם מורה מקום על דברי הרב המגיד וכסף משנה ועם שתי מפתחות... אחת על סדר הפרקים ואחת על דרך אלפ"א בית"א כפי אשר נדפסו בק"ק אמשטרדם... ועוד ניתוסף עליהם ספר לחם משנה מהרב... יהודה רוזאניס... גם ניתוסף על הראשונים תשובת הכסף משנה על השגת הראב"ד שבמנין המצות...

פיורדא: בדפוס חיים ב"ר צבי הירש [וחלק ב' וג': בדפוס איצק ב"ר ליב]. 2°.

חלק א. [תקכ"ה]. [7], רע"ו [צ"ל: רעג ?] דף. הפגינציה משובשת.

הסכ' הר' יוסף שטיין הרט דק"ק פיורדא (ר"ח אדר תקכ"ג), ארי' ליב דק"ק הייצפעלד

(ר"ח טבת תקכ"ג), נתנאל אשכנזי דק"ק קארלסרוא (ר"ח טבת תקכ"ג).

חלק ב. [תקכ"ה]. [1], רס"א, [1] דף. העימוד לא בסדר.

הסכ' הר' שמואל הילמן דק"ק מיץ (י"ט שבט תקכ"ג), יושע העשיל דק"ק שוואבאך (כ"ה שבט תקכ"ג), אליעזר ב"ר משה דק"ק האגנויא (ר"ח ניסן תקכ"ג).

חלק ג. [תקכ"ז]. [1], רכ"א, קס"ו [צ"ל: קס"ט] דף.

הסכ' הר' נפתלי הירש דק"ק מארגיטהאל (ח' אלול תקכ"ג), צבי הירש דק"ק וואלרשטיין (ר"ח כסלו תקכ"ג), יצחק דק"ק וואלרשטיין (ר"ח תמוז תקכ"ו).

חלק ד. [תקכ"ז]. [1], קל"ה, קלח—רצ"ח, [10], רצ"ט—ש"ב דף.

המפתח "על דרך אלפא ביתא" המרומז למעלה לא נדפס בהוצאה זו.

תקס"ח (1808)

14. ספר משנה תורה הוא היד החזקה להנשר... רבינו משה בר מימון זצ"ל עם... השגות הראב"ד... מגיד משנה וכסף משנה להגאון... רבינו יוסף קארו זצ"ל ופירוש מגדל עוז והגהות מימוניות ובחלק הראשון על קידוש החדש פירוש רבינו עובדיה והרב המוסמך מהר"ל ן' חביב... ואלה מוסיף... לחם משנה... להגאון... אברהם די בוטון... משנה למלך מהגאון... יהודה רוזאניס... עלה לפני במחשבה לאדפוסי אדרא... עם... שלשה מטיבי סעד לתמוך אשורי ה"ה... יהודא ליב ב... יואל מק"ק אוסטרהא... אברהם ב... צבי מק"ק ברדיטשוב... זאב וואלף בהרב... יהודה שמשון שפירא זצוק"ל מ"מ דק"ק טארניפאל... דברי... מרדכי בא"א... צבי... מק"ק ברדיטשוב יצ"ו. נדפס פה ק"ק ברדיטשוב בגובערני וואלינסקי ברשיון הצענזור דאקדעמיע דק"ק ווילנא... תחת ממשלת... אלעקסנדר פאוולוויטש... בבית ובדפוס... שמואל במהור"ר ישכר בער סג"ל מדפיס דפה ודק"ק אוסטרהא הבירה... 2°.

חלק ראשון. תקס"ח. [8], רע"ח דף.

חלק שני. תקס"ח. [4], ר"ס דף.

חלק שלישי. תקס"ט. [2], שפ"ט, [1] דף.

חלק רביעי. תקס"ט. [2], ש"י דף. (אותיות מרובעות ואותיות רש"י).

המגיה של שני החלקים הראשונים הוא זאב ברבי יהודה שמשון שפירא מ"מ דק"ק טרניפאל. בחלק שלישי לא נזכר שמו של המגיה. בחלק רביעי חתומים כמגיהים יוסף בן אריה ז"ל מברדיטשב ועקיבה בן משה מסאטנאב.

הקולופון בסוף ח"א: "על ידי המסדר אותיות... אפרים ב... אביגדור... מק"ק פולנאי ולע"ע עוסק פה בק"ק ברדיטשב; ועל ידי... שלמה בן... יואל מק"ק אוסטרהא; ועל ידי המסדר אותיות... הבחור שמעון ב... זאב וואלף... מק"ק סלאפקאוויץ ולע"ע עוסק פה עיר ק"ק ברדיטשב; ועל [ידי] הפועל... במכבש הדפוס... יוסף ב... דובר בער ז"ל מק"ק פולנאי ולע"ע עוסק פה ק"ק ברדיטשב; ועל ידי העוסק... במכבש הדפוס שמשון גדלי' ב... חיים... מק"ק אוסטרהא ולע"ע עוסק פה ק"ק ברדיטשב, ועל ידי... העוסק במכבש הדפוס חיים בן... עקיבא... מק"ק אוסטרהא ולע"ע עוסק פה ק"ק ברדיטשב יצ"ו".

בקולופון שבסוף חלק ב' נזכרו כל הנ"ל מלבד האחרון, ונוספו: "ועל ידי המסדר אותיות... גרשון ב... אליעזר... מק"ק סלאפקאוויץ ולע"ע עוסק פה ק"ק ברדיטשב;

ועל ידי העוסק... במכבש הדפוס... משה אליקום ב... אלעזר.. מק"ק סלאפקאוויץ ולע"ע עוסק פה ק"ק ברדיטשב; על ידי עוסק... במכבש הדפוס... יהודה לוי ב... דוב בער... מק"ק יאנוב לע"ע עוסק פה ק"ק ברדיטשב".

בשערי ח"ג וח"ד נדפס על השער דגל המדפיס.

עם הסכמות אלה שנתנו כולן לשמואל המדפיס: הסכמת ר' לוי יצחק אב"ד ברדיטשב, מיום ו' אלול תקס"ב; הסכמת ר' בצלאל ב"ר מאיר מרגליות אב"ד אוסטרהא, מיום ה' שבט תקס"ב; הסכמת ר' אשר צבי ב"ר ראב"ד ומ"מ דק"ק אוסטרהא, מיום ער"ח אלול תקס"ב; הסכמת ר' אלכסנדר סענדר מרגליות מבראד אב"ד סאטנאב, מיום ז' חשון תקס"ב; הסכמת ר' דוד צבי ב"ר אריה ליבוש אווערבך אב"ד קרעמניץ, בלי תאריך; הסכמת ר' מנחם מענדיל אב"ד רוואני, מיום כ"ה אב תקס"ב; הסכמת בית דין ברדיטשב, מיום כ"ג שבט תקס"ח, חתומה ע"י אברהם עקיבא ב"ר מנחם מענדל אב"ד טראינוב, יעקב קאפל ב"ר משה, יוסף ב"ר אבא; הסכמת ר' שמחה הכהן ראפפורט אב"ד פאדהייץ ולע"ע אב"ד ראדמישלא, בלי תאריך; הסכמת ר' משלם הכהן צדק ומ"מ ומ"צ לבוב, מיום ט"ו אלול תקס"ז; הסכמת ר' מרדכי ב"ר סענדר אב"ד סאטנוב, בלי תאריך; הסכמת רבני אוסטרהא, מיום ב' דר"ח אלול תקס"ב, חתומה על ידי: נתן נטע ב"ר שמואל שמעלקא אב"ד טרטקאב, מרדכי ספרא ודיינא אוסטרהא וראב"ד אלעקסניץ, יהודה ב"ר צבי הירש ספרא ודיינא אוסטרהא, יהודה ליב ב"ר אברהם אבלי מקרעמניץ, ישראל יעקב ב"ר משה יהודה סג"ל..

(יערי: הדפוס העברי בברדיטשב, ק"ס 21 [תש"ה] עמ' 106—107).

מצאתי עותקים שישנם בהם שינויים בשערים של חלק א' ב. וד'.

תקס"ט ? (1809))

14א. ה מ ש נ ה ת ו ר ה הוא היד החזקה להנשר הגדול... משה בר מימון זצ"ל עם... השגות הראב"ד... מגיד משנה וכסף משנה להגאון... רבינו יוסף קארו זצ"ל ופירוש מגדל עוז והגהות מימוניות ובחלק הראשון על קידוש החודש פירוש רבינו עובדיה והרב המוסמך המר"ל ן' חביב... ואלה מוסיף... לחם משנה... להגאון... אברהם די בוטון... משנה למלך מהגאון... יהודה רוזאנים... גם זה ניתוסף מה שנשמט מהראשונים תשובת הכסף משנה על השגת הראב"ד שבמנין המצוות גם סימני ההלכות שברמב"ם הצבנו גם בפירושים הנ"ל... תחת ממשלת... אלעקסנדר פאוו־לוויטש... בגובערני ווֹאלינסקי ברשיון הצענזור דאקדעמיע דק"ק ווילנא... נדפס פה ק"ק ברדיטשב... בבית ובדפוס של... שמואל במהור"ר ישכר סג"ל מדפיס דפה ודק"ק אוסטרהא הבירה. בשנת ולכל הי"ד החזקה ולכל המורה הגדול אשר עשה **משה בן** מיימוני לעיני כל ישראל לפ"ק [תקס"ט]. 2°.

חלק ראשון. [8], רע"ח דף.

חלק שלישי. [2], שפ"ט, [1] דף.

חלק רביעי. [2], ש"ט [צ"ל: ש"י] דף.

חלק שני לא היה לפני.

דפוס זה מצאתי בספריות שונות:

חלק א' בספריה הלאומית, בירושלים; חלק ג' בייווא, ניו יורק; חלק ד' בייווא ובספריה הצבורית בניו־יורק. בכרך ד' ישנם שמות המגיהים (מעבר לדף התיקונים): יוסף ב"ר

ארי׳ מברדיטשוב ועקיבא ב״ר משה מסאטנאב. ובעותק שני בייווא מכרך ד׳ ישנם עוד [2] דפים: ״תיקון כמה טעויות שנפלו בדפוסים הראשונים״ והן שונות מהדף הרגיל שנדפסו בו תיקונים (ואולי זה מדפוס אחר שנכלל בכריכה). אין בהוצאה זו הסכמות וקולפון. דגל המדפיס על השלשה חלקים שראיתי.

הפרט הנ״ל בהוצאה זו מסובך; אות ה̊ (עם כוכב) מרומז לה׳ אלפים, אז הפרט הוא: תקס״ד לפ״ק. אולם, לפי יערי (שם, עמ׳ 100) נפתח בית הדפוס בברדיטשוב בשנת תקס״ז. אם נוסף אות ה למספר, יהיה התאריך תקס״ט. אינו מתקבל על הלב שבשנה שגמר המדפיס את הוצאתו הנ״ל (תקס״ח—תקס״ט) ידפיס מחדש את הרמב״ם בהשמטת ההסכמות שרבים מהן היה כבר בידו בשנת תקס״ב.

תקס״ט (1809)

15. משנה תורה הוא היד החזקה להנשר... רבינו משה בר מיימון... עם השגת הראב״ד... ופירוש הרב מגיד משנה, וכסף משנה להגאון... רבינו יוסף קארו, ומגדל עוז, והגהות מימוניות, ופירוש רבינו עובדיה, והרב... מהרי״ל ן׳ חביב על הלכות קידוש החדש עם כל הצורות השייכות להלכות אלו ולהלכות שבת וסוכה, ועם מורה מקום על דברי הרב המגיד וכסף משנה, גם שתי מפתחות... אחת על סדר הפרקים ואחת על דרך אלפי ביתא... כפי אשר נדפס באמשטרדם. גם מה שנשמט מדפוס אמשטרדם הלא המה תשובת כסף משנה על השגת הראב״ד שבמנין המצוות, וסימני הלכות בכמה פירושים שברמב״ם, ושני הפירושים... ה״ה ספר לחם משנה וספר משנה למלך, הראשון מהגאון... אברהם די בוטון... והשני מהגאון... יהודה רוזאניש...

ונתתי להם יתרון ומעלה על ספרי הרמב״ם דפוס יעסניץ להדפיס ההגהות אשר נמצאו נכתבות בצידי ספרי הרמב״ם של הגאון... יחזקאל סג״ל לנדא האב״ד דק״ק פראג. והגהות... מהגאון... זלמן מווילנא.

[לעמבערג]. 2°.

חלק א׳: (בדפוס נ״ה גרושמאן): תק״ע. [1], רס״ו דף.

חלק ב׳: (בדפוס רובינשטיין): תקס״ט. [1], קמח, קי״ב, [2] דף.

חלק ג׳: (בדפוס רפופורט): תקע״א. שי״א דף.

חלק ד׳: (בדפוס ש. יאריש [— רפפורט]): תקע״א. [1], ש״י דף.

לא מצאתי מפתח אלפא ביתי.

שמות מסדרי הדפוס: יצחק ב״ר צבי מק״ק לבוב; מרדכי שמואל ב״ר יצחק אייזיק מק״ק פאריצק ולע״ע בק״ק לבוב; יחיאל מיכל ב״ר אברהם מק״ק פרעמסלא ולע״ע בק״ק לבוב; ישראל ב״ר מנחם צבי מק״ק לבוב; יוסף יהודא ב״ר נטע מק״ק לבוב; אלעזר ב״ר יהושע מלבוב; משה ב״ר יהודא ליב.

תקס״ט (1809)

16. משנה תורה הוא היד החזקה להנשר הגדול רבינו משה בר מיימון... עם השגות הראב״ד... ופירוש הרב מגיד משנה וגם הכסף משנה להגאון יוסף קארו... ומחובר לזה המגדל עוז והגהות מיימוניות ופירוש על הלכות קידוש החודש מהרב... עובדיה והרב... מהר״ל בן חביב. עם כל הצורות השייכים להלכות אלו וכן להלכות

שבת וסוכה ושמנו אותם בסוף הספר קונטרוס לבדו. גם המפתחות להרמב"ם על סדר המצוות וכן על סדר הפוסקים. הכל באותיות גדולות כמו שנדפס באמשטרדם. ואלה מוסיף עליהם פירוש הלחם משנה להגאון... אברהם די בוטון... ומשנה למלך להגאון... יהודה רוזאניס... גם תשובת בעל הכסף משנה על השגת הראב"ד על מנין המצוות. וסימני אותות להלכות שבהרמב"ם בכל הפירושים הכל כפי אשר נמצא בספרי רמב"ם דפוס יעסניץ... וניתוספו עוד על אלה כמה מעלות טובות ככל אשר יבואר בהקדמת המדפיס...

דיהרנפורט: בדפוס יוסף מייא. 2°.

חלק ראשון: (מדע — זמנים). תקס"ט. [7], קט"ז, קנ"ז דף.

בראשו "כללי הרמב"ם" ובסוף ספר אהבה (דף קטז ב) נדפסו "חידושים הנמצאים בגליון הרמב"ם של הגאון... ישעיה ברלין..."

חלק שני: (נשים — קדושה). תק"ע [2] רמג, [2] דף.

הסכמות הר' יעקב ליסא (ליסא, ח"י שבט תק"ע), אברהם ראב"ד דק"ק גלוגא (גלוגא י"ב שבט, תק"ע).

חלק שלישי: (הפלאה — טהרה). תקע"א. [2], קלא, קמא, צו דף.

הסכ' ה"ר מאיר וויל וב"ד הצדק ה"ר שמעיה לאנצבורג וליזר סג"ל הורוויץ.

(ברלין כ"ד אלול תק"ע); ר' עקיבא איגר אב"ד ור"מ דק"ק פרידלאנד (בעברו ק"ק ברעסלויא "יום ב' ל"ט למב"י תק"ע". חתום "עקיבא במוהר"מ גינז ז"ל מא"ש").

הגהות ר' ישעיה ברלין מעבר לשער.

חלק רביעי: (נזיקין — שופטים). תקע"ד. [2], קמא, קסט דף. המו"ל ר' יוסף מייא היה חתן ר' ישעיה ברלין.

תקע"ח (1818)

17. משנה תורה הוא היד החזקה להנשר הגדול רבינו משה בר מיימון זצ"ל עם... השגות הראב"ד... מגיד משנה וכסף משנה להגאון... רבינו יוסף קארו... ופירוש מגדל עוז והגהות מימוניות ובחלק הראשון על קידוש החדש פירוש רבינו עובדיה והרב המוסמך מהר"ל ן' חביב... עם מורה מקום על דברי הרב המגיד וכסף משנה. גם עשינו שתי מפתחות גדולות... אחת על סדר הפרקים ואחת על דרך אלפא ביתא, כפי אשר כבר נדפסו בק"ק אמשטרדם... ואלה מוסיף על הראשונים: לחם משנה... להגאון... אברהם די בוטון... משנה למלך מהגאון... יהודה רוזאניס... גם זה ניתוסף מה שנשמט מהראשונים תשובת הכסף משנה על השגת הראב"ד שבמנין המצות גם סימני ההלכות שברמב"ם הצבנו גם בפירושים הנ"ל לתועלת המעיינים...

נדפס פה ק"ק ברדיטשוב ברשיון הצענזור אשר באקדעמיא דווילנא... תחת ממשלת... אלכסנדר פאוולאוויטש. 2°.

חלק ראשון (הובא לבית הדפוס ע"י אלכסנדר סענדיר ב"ר שלמה מסדילקוב): מדע — זמנים. לפרט וזאת התורה אשר שם משה לפני [תקע"ח]. [7], רע"ח דף.

הסכמות מעבר לשער מאת הר' ר' לוי יצחק מברדיטשוב (ו' אלול, תקס"ב), ר' בצלאל ב"ר מאיר מרגליות (ה' שבט תקס"ב), אשר צבי ב"ר דוד מאוסטרא (ער"ח אלול תקס"ב); רבני דק"ק ברדיטשוב: אברהם עקיבא ב"ר מנחם מענדיל אב"ד דק"ק טריאנוב; יעקב קאפיל ב"ר משה: יוסף ב"ר אבא (כ"ג שבט (תקס"ח); נוסח שטר מכירה.

דגל המדפיס מהוצאה זו (כעין כתר תורה) חסר בספר "דגלי המדפיסים העבריים" ליערי.

חלק שני (הובא לבית הדפוס ע"י תרי שותפי אלכסנדר סענדר ב"ר שלמה ור' יצחק ב"ר אשר): נשים — קדושה. לפרט וזאת התורה אשר שם משה לפני [תקע"ט]. [4] ר"ס דף.

הסכ' הרבנים הנ"ל והר"א סענדר מרגליות אב"ד סאטנאב (ז' חשון, תקס"ב), ר' דוד צבי ב"ר אריה ליבוש אווערבך אב"ד קרעמניץ (בלי תאריך); ר' מנחם מענדיל אב"ד ראווני (כ"ה אב תקס"ב); הסכמת בית דין ברדיטשוב מיום כ"ג שבט תקס"ח, חתומה ע"י אברהם עקיבא ב"ר מנחם מענדל אב"ד טראינוב; יעקב קאפל ב"ר משה; יוסף ב"ר אבא; מרדכי ב"ר צבי הירש; הסכמות ר' שמחה הכהן ראפפורט, ראדמישלא (בלי תאריך); ר' מרדכי ב"ר סענדר אב"ד סטאנוב (בלי תאריך); משלם הכהן צדק מ"מ ומ"צ לבוב, מיום ט"ו אלול תקס"ז.

נוסח שטר מכירה.

חלק שלישי (חש"מ): הפלאה — טהרה. בשנת ולכל הי"ד החזקה ולכל המורה הגדול אשר עשה משה בן מיימוני לעיני כל ישראל [תקצ"א]. [2] שפ"ט, [1] ד.

שנת דפוס של חלק זה מסופק הוא כפי שהעירני ידידי החוקר והביבליוגראף ר' חיים ליברמן שליט"א, היות וכתוב על השער, כביתר החלקים: תחת ממשלת אדונינו הקיסר... אלעקסנדר פאוולוויטש שנפטר שש שנה לפני תקצ"א (תקפ"ה).

הסכ' רבני ברדיטשוב: יעקב קאפל ב"ר משה, מאיר במהרש"ז סגל מליטא ור' יוסף במהרש"ז (חשון תקע"ז); יצחק אייזיק ב"ר בצלאל, יוסף ב"ר אבא, יוסף אב"ד יאנוב, יהודה ב"ר יעקב מ"ץ (ח' כסלו תקע"ז).

(באוניברסיטה העברית ובספריה הציבורית בניו־יורק).

חלק רביעי (חש"מ): נזיקין — שופטים. בשנת ולכל היד החזקה ולכל המורה הגדול אשר עשה משה בן מיימוני לעיני כל ישראל [תקע"ט]. [2], ש"י דף.

(בספריית הסמינר התיאולוגי בניו־יורק). הוצאה זו לא היתה לפני יערי ברשימתו של דפוסי ברדיטשוב (קרית ספר כ"א (תש"ה), עמ' 113—114) וסמך על פרידברג.

תקצ"ה (1835)

18. משנה תורה הוא היד החזקה להנשר... רבינו משה בר מיימון... עם השגות הראב"ד... ופירוש הרב מגיד משנה ופירוש הכסף משנה להגאון... יוסף קארו... הרב בעל מגדל עוז והגהות מימוניות ופירושי הרב עובדיה והרב... מהר"ל בן חביב על הלכות קידוש החדש עם כל הצורות השייכים להם ולהלכות שבת וסוכה. וגם לרבות... הלחם משנה להגאון... אברהם די בוטן... ומשנה למלך להגאון... יהודא רוזאנים...

ואלה מוסיף על הראשונים ספר השרשים והמצות להרמב"ם עם כל הנלוים אליו ה"ה השגות הרמב"ן... ופירושי מגלת אסתר מהגאון... יהודא די ליאון... וחידושי... מרגניתא טבא מהגאון... אריה ליב זיטל... והיו לאחד בכרך מיוחד.

ועתה ראה זה חדש הוא אשר לא הי' עוד בעולמים ספר קובץ על יד החזקה והוא תוספ' מרובה מחידושים וביאורים על הרמב"ם... מהרב... נחום טריביטש... אב"ד

דק"ק נ"ש ומדינת מעהרין... בעל המחבר ספר שלום ירושלים. וויען: אנטאן עדלען פאן שמיד. 2°.

חלק א': מדע — אהבה. 1835. [9], קט"ז, י"ג דף.

עם מכתב ר' משה סופר (כ"ז שבט תקצ"ה) למדפיס שבו הוא מסכים עם הצעתו להוציא לאור את ספר המצוות ביחד עם המשנה תורה (כמו בדפוס ויניציאה שהדפיס מהר"מ פאדואה). וכך נתפרסם הדבר בשער המשנה תורה אולם מפני נימוקים לא ידועים, ספר המצוות לא נדפס בהוצאה זו; הקדמת ר' נחום טריביטש שבה הוא מסכים גם כן להדפיס את ספר המצוות (פורים, תקצ"ה); "מליצת" ר' אלעזר הלוי דק"ק וויען.

ספר קובץ (י"ג דפים האחרונים) עם שער מיוחד.

חלק ב': זמנים. 1835. [1] קנ"ו דף; [2] דפים: צורות השייכות... לקידוש החדש; ט"ו דף: ס' קובץ.

חלק ג': נשים. 1837. [1], ק"מ דף; ונלווה אליו "ספר קובץ". י"ג [צ"ל: ט"ו] דף.

חלק ד': קדושה. 1838. [1], ק"ו דף.

חלק ה': הפלאה. 1839. קל, [2] דף.

חלק ו': עבודה — טהרה. 1840. [1], קמ"א, [1], צ"ה [1] דף.

חלק ז': נזיקין — קנין. 1842. [1], קמ"א, [1] דף.

חלק ח': משפטים-שופטים. 1842. [1], קס"ח דף.

ספר קובץ נדפס גם כן בפני עצמו באותה צורה, ווין 1835.

בדפוסי ברלין ווארשא השמיטו פירוש זה על נשים, אולם בזמן האחרון נדפס או צולם במשנה תורה דפוסי האחים שולזינגר בניו-יורק, תש"ז והוצאת "פרדס", ירושלים תשט"ז ותשכ"ג. צילום ממנו בהשמטת "ספר קובץ" וקצת שינויים בפגינציה, ראה למטה, דפוס צילום מוקטן, ניו-יורק וברלין "חורב", תרפ"ו, מספר 28.

תר"ד ? (1844 ?)

19. משנה תורה הוא הי"ד החזקה אשר עשה רבינו משה בר מיימון... (ספר ראשון והוא ספר המדע).

חמוש"ד. [קניגסברג או: דאנציג, תר"ד ?]. 16°. [2], ס"ג דף.

עם פירוש קצר והשגות הראב"ד.

הפירוש על ד' פרקים הראשונים מהלכות יסודי התורה נעתק מהפירוש האנונימי (המיוחס להריטב"א) ונדפס ברוב הוצאות הרמב"ם על הדף מול פירושו של הכסף משנה.

"... חזיתי לי להדפיס דבריו הקדושים ז"ל בפ"ע ובכרך קטן. לי"ד כרכים. עם השגות הראב"ד, וגם הצבתי המראה מקומות של בעל המגדל עוז ושארי נושא כליו. ולמען יוקל להבין פשטות דבריו ז"ל הדפסתיו עם פי' וביאור הנדפס כבר בספרי הרמב"ם ז"ל ובאיזה מקומות אשר לא מצאתי להם די באר לקטתי ממפרשי הש"ס והאחרונים בלי תוספת וגרעון ח"ו מלבי ועוד ידי נטוי' להדפיס אי"ה עם פי' מספיק ונפלא מגאון קדמון אשר אקבנו בשמו בחלקים הבאים אי"ה..." (הקדמת המביא לבית הדפוס).

המפרש והמו"ל הוא ר' אליהו צבי ב"ר יוסף הלוי סולוביציק, שהו"ל תרגום אשכנזי לס' המדע (1846) ובהקדמתו לתרגום זה הוא מזכירו. העירני על זה החוקר ר' שמואל אשכנזי בעל אוצר ראשי תיבות.

דפוס צלום מזה [מינכן תש"ז], עיין להלן, מספר 35.

תרכ״ב (1862)

20. משנה תורה הוא היד החזקה להנשר...רבינו משה בר מיימון...עם השגת הראב״ד... ופירושי...המגיד משנה, הכסף משנה להגאון... יוסף קארו... בעל מגדל עוז, והגהות מיימוניות, ופירושי הרב... עובדיה והרב... מהר״ל בן חביב על הלכות קדוש החדש עם כל הצורות השייכות להם ולהלכות שבת וסוכה. גם... סביב לו הלחם משנה... להגאון... אברהם די בוטן... ומשנה למלך להגאון... יהודה רוזאניס... כאשר היו מאז וקדם בדפוסי אמשטרדם, יעסניץ ודיהרנפורט וספר קובץ על יד החזקה... מהרב... ר׳ נחום טריביטש... אב״ד דק״ק נ״ש כפי אשר נדפס בווין.

בערלין (בדפוס יוליוס זיטטענפעלד) [תרכ״ב] 1862. 2°.

כרך א׳ — חלק א׳: מדע — אהבה. [2], קכ״ח דף; ספר קובץ (עם שער מיוחד) בדף [קי״ז]—קכ״ח.

חלק ב׳: זמנים. [1], ק״ע דף; קובץ בדף קנ״ז—ק״ע; 2 דפים צורות לקדוש החדש בין דף קנ״ו—קנ״ז.

כרך ב׳ — חלק ג׳: נשים. [1], ק״מ דף; חלק ד׳: קדושה. [1], ק״ה, [1] דף.

כרך ג׳ — חלק ה׳: הפלאה — זרעים. קל״ה דף; חלק ו׳ עבודה — טהרות. [1], קמ״א [1], צ״ה דף.

כרך ד׳ — חלק ז׳: נזיקין — קנין. [1], קמ״ג דף; חלק ח׳: משפטים-שופטים. [1], קס״ח דף.

תרכ״ב (1862)

21. משנה תורה הוא היד החזקה להנשר הגדול רבינו משה בר מיימון... עם השגות הראב״ד... ובאור חדש מספיק מהרב ר׳ שלמה בן... חנוך מבית לוי... גם כללים ומפתחות להרמב״ם על סדר המצות, ותשובות על השגות הראב״ד על מנין המצות. עם כמה מעלות טובות, כמו שיבואר בהקדמת המבאר... לייפציג. 8°.

חלק א׳ כרך א׳: מדע — אהבה (בדפוס קארל ב. לורק). 1862.

[1] דף; XXII עמ׳; קפ״ג דף. עם תמונות הרמב״ם וצלום מחתימת ידו הידועה.

חלק א׳ כרך ב׳: זמנים (בדפוס קארל ב. לורק) 1863. ר״ם דף.

שער נוסף לועזי בדף ר״ם, ב:

Mischneh Thorah d. i. Jad ha-Chasaka des Moses Maimonides. Mit der Polemik des Rabad und Commentar, sowie astronomische Berechnung der Jahre und Monate, sammt Kalender. Von Salomon Levi.
Leipzig: Nies'sche Buchdruckerei (Carl B. Lorck). 1864.

ספר רביעי — חמישי: נשים — קדושה (בדפוס וילהלם בענש). 1867. [1], קע״ה, קמ״ז, [1] דף. [1] דף מכיל שער לועזי:

Mischneh Thorah d. i. Jad ha-Chasaka des Moses Maimonides. Mit der Polemik des Rabad und Commentar, betreffend die rituellen Verordnungen. Bd. IV.: Ueber Trauungen, Ehescheidungen und Entschwägerungen. Bd. V.: Verordnung über Kauscher und Trefa.
Von Rabbi Salomon Levi in Schrimm im Posenschen.

Leipzig: Druck: Wilhelm Baensch. 1867.

אודות הוצאה זו עיין הערותיו של שטיינשניידר, המזכיר, ה (1862), עמ׳ 84—85.

תרכ"ד (1864)

22. משנה תורה הוא היד החזקה להנשר... רבינו משה בר מיימון... עם השגת הראב"ד... ופירושי הרב המגיד משנה. הכסף משנה להגאון... יוסף קארו... מגדל עוז והגהות מיימוניות ופירוש הרב... עובדיה והרב... מהר"ל בן חביב על הלכות קדוש החדש, עם כל הצורות השייכות להם ולהלכות שבת וסוכה. גם... הלחם משנה להגאון... אברהם די בוטן..., ומשנה למלך להגאון... יהודה רוזאניס... הקובץ חדושים ומקורי דינים מהרב... נחום טריביש...

ברלין (בדפוס יוליוס זיטטענפעלד תרכ"ד 1864. 2°. וראיתי מהוצאה זו רק: ספר מדע — אהבה. [7], קכ"ח דף; זמנים. תרכ"ד 1864. [3], ג — ק"ע דף; נשים. תרכ"ו. [2], ק"מ דף. משפטים — שופטים. [1], קס"ח דף.

תרכ"ח (1868)

23. משנה תורה הוא היד החזקה להנשר הגדול... רבינו משה בר מיימון... עם השגת הראב"ד... ופירושי הרב המגיד משנה. הכסף משנה לגאון... יוסף קארו... מגדל עוז, והגהות מיימוניות ופירושי הרב... עובדיה והרב... מהר"ל בן חביב על הלכות קידוש החודש עם כל הצורות השייכות להם ולהלכות שבת וסוכה. גם שני הגבורים סביב לו הלחם משנה להגאון... אברהם די בוטן... ומשנה למלך להגאון... יהודה רוזאניס... כאשר היו... בדפוסי אמסטרדם, יעסניץ ודיהרנפורט. וספר קובץ על יד החזקה... מהרב... ר׳ נחום טריביטש... כפי אשר נדפס בווין...

בערלין: געדרוקט בייא יוליוס זיטטענפעלד [תרכ"ח] 1868. 2°.

כרך א׳ (מדע — זמנים). [7], קכ"ח, [1], ק"ע דף.

כרך ב׳ (נשים — קדושה). [1], ק"מ, [2], ק"ה דף.

כרך ג׳ (הפלאה — טהרה). קל"ה, [1], קמ"א, [1] צ"ה דף.

כרך ד׳ (נזיקין — שופטים). [1], קמ"ג, [1], קס"ח דף.

ד"ס של ברלין תרכ"ב.

תר"ם (1880)

24. משנה תורה הוא היד החזקה להנשר... רבינו משה בר מיימון... עם השגות הראב"ד... ופירושי הרב המגיד משנה, הכסף משנה להגאון... יוסף קארו..., מגדל עוז, הגהות מיימוניות ופירושי הרב... עובדיה והרב... מהר"ל בן חביב על הלכות קדוש החדש, עם כל הצורות השייכות להם ולהלכות שבת וסוכה. גם הלחם משנה להגאון... אברהם די בוטן..., ומשנה למלך להגאון... יהודא רוזאניס... כאשר היו בדפוסי אמסטרדם, יעזניץ ודיהרנפורט וספר קובץ על יד החזקה... חדושים... מהרב׳... נחום טריביטש... אבד"ק נ"ש...

בערלין: הובא לדפוס בהוצאת בית מספר הספרים של הר׳ יהושע גרשון מונק בווארשא (געדרוקט ביי יוליוס זיטטענפעלד), תר"ם 1880. 2°.

ס׳ מדע — אהבה. [7], קכ"ח דף;

ס׳ זמנים. [3], ג—ק״ע דף;

ס׳ נשים. [1], ק״מ דף;

ס׳ קדושה. [1], ק״ה, [1] דף;

ס׳ הפלאה — זרעים. קלה, [1] דף;

ס׳ עבודה — קרבנות. [1], קמ״א, [1] דף;

ס׳ טהרה. צ״ה דף;

ס׳ נזיקין — קנין. [1], קמ״ג דף; [2] לוחות לקידוש החדש;

ס׳ משפטים — שופטים. [1], קס״ח דף.

הוצאת ברלין עברה בשנה זו למוכר הספרים הווארשאי ר׳ יהושע גרשון מונק (לוצקי, סימן כ׳).

תרמ״א (1881)

25. משנה תורה הוא היד החזקה להנשר רבינו משה בר מיימון... עם השגות הראב״ד... ופירוש הרב המגיד משנה, הכסף משנה להגאון... יוסף קארו... מגדל עוז, הגהות מיימוניות גם תשובות מיימוניות, ופירושי הרב... עובדיה, והרב... מהר״ל בן חביב על הלכות קדוש החדש, עם כל הצורות השייכות להם ולהלכות שבת וסוכה. גם... הלחם משנה להגאון... אברהם די בוטן..., ומשנה למלך להגאון... יהודה רוזאניס... כאשר היו מאז ומקדם בדפוסי יעסניץ, דיהרנפורט, וויען וברדיטשוב. ונלוה לו ספר הקובץ חדושים ומקורי דינים מהרב... נחום טריביטש... אבד״ק נ״ש כפי שנדפס בוויען. ועתה הוספנו חדשות אשר לא היו מעולם בכל ספרי הרמב״ם הנדפסים...:

(א) פירוש המגיד משנה על הלכות שחיטה...

(ב) פירוש הרדב״ז על ספר קדושה, הפלאה, זרעים, שופטים, ממלא מקום המגיד משנה שלא נמצא בספרים האלה...

(ג) חדושים ומקורי דינים מהרב... בעל פרי חדש, נקראים בשם מים חיים.

(ד) חדושים ומקורי הדינים מהרב... בעל מחנה אפרים.

(ה) חדושים ומקורי הדינים מהרב... ישעיה פיק...

(ו) באורים על... הלכות בית הבחירה מהרב... יעקב עמדין...

(ז)* חדושים ומקורי דינים מגאונים מפורסמים בדור העבר הכל מכתבי יד...

---

* בין ההוספות בסוף ספר זמנים, נמצא מאמרו של המשכיל חיים זעליג סלונימסקי: ״איזה הגהות ותיקונים בפירוש הלקה״ח לרבינו עובדיה״. והוא מחקר על פירוש לראש השנה המיוחס להרמב״ם והביאו רבנו עובדיה. סלונימסקי רוצה להוכיח שהפירוש ״ייחסוהו בטעות להרמב״ם, כי הרמב״ם עצמו מעתיק פירושו (פ״ב דר״ה) ודוחה דבריו... אבל אחרי שיצא הרמב״ם [דפוס ורשה] מבית הדפוס נודע לי שהמו״ס קרע והשמיט את הדף ההוא מתוך הרמב״ם. אנכי שאלתי מדוע? והשיבני כי בספרי הרמב״ם הנשלחים לליטא נמצא הדף ההוא, ורק בארצנו ידעתי כי רבים ימשכו את ידם מקנותו, בראותו שבאו בין הליקוטים את בקרת ממבקרים החדשים, התחפוץ כי בשבילך אפסיד במסחרי?״ (חז״ס במאמרו ״בדבר איסור קטניות בפסח״ בספרו ״מאמרי חכמה״, חלק ב׳, ווארשא, תרנ״ד, עמ׳ 109 [=הצפירה, שנה 1886, מספר 30]. ואני הכותב בדקתי כמה עותקים של הוצאה זו ודף זה היה חסר. עיין בקרתו החריפה של בעל החזון איש על סלונימסקי (״חזון איש״ על הרמב״ם, ה׳ קידוש החודש, דף כח, ב—כט, א); י״י

פירוש המגיד משנה, והרדב"ז, והמה בכתיבת יד, הגיעו לידינו מיד...המנוח... זוסמאן יעב"ץ... אשר קנה אותם... מאת רבני חכמי ספרד אשר בירושלים... והרשומים באותיות ג׳ ד׳ ה׳ יבואו בסוף כל ספר והרשומים באות ו יבוא בסוף ספר עבודה, והרשום באות ז׳ בסוף כל חלק מד׳ חלקי הרמב"ם..., ווארשא הובא לביה"ד ע"י... ר׳ מרדכי קאלינבערג... ושותפיו (בדפוס האחים ארגעלבראנד ובדפוס ר׳ יצחק גאלדמאן), תרמ"א 1881. 2°.

ס׳ המדע. [1], ח, ס"ו דף;

ס׳ אהבה. פ"ו דף;

ס׳ זמנים. פה, י"א, [1], פ"ו—רי"ב דף; [2] דפים־צורות לקה"ח.

ס׳ נשים. [1], קכ"ח, ל"ו דף;

ס׳ הפלאה, זרעים. [2], קל"ז דף;

ס׳ קדושה. מ"ד, ק"כ דף;

ס׳ עבודה — קרבנות. מד, קל"ב דף;

ס׳ טהרה. קל"ב דף;

ס׳ נזיקין. [2], ע׳ דף;

ס׳ קנין — משפטים. ס"ד, קל"ד, מ"ב דף;

ס׳ שופטים. קכ"ח דף.

תר"ס (1900)

26. משנה תורה הוא היד החזקה להנשר... רבינו משה בר מיימון... עם השגות הראב"ד... ופירוש הרב המגיד משנה, הכסף משנה להגאון... יוסף קארו..., מגדל עוז, הגהות מיימוניות... [עם הוספות הרב... מהר"ם פאדווה...], גם תשובות מיימוניות, ופירושי הרב... עובדיה והרב... מהר"ל בן חביב על הלכות קדוש החדש, עם כל הצורות השייכות להם ולהלכות שבת וסוכה. גם הלחם משנה להגאון... אברהם די בוטן..., ומשנה למלך להגאון... יהודה רוזאנים... כאשר היו בדפוסי יעמניץ, דיהרנפורט, וויען וברדיטשוב. ונלוה לו ספר הקובץ חדושים ומקורי דינים מהרב... נחום טריביטש... אבד"ק נ"ש כפי שנדפס בוויען.

ועתה הוספנו חדשות אשר לא היו מעולם בכל ספרי הרמב"ם הנדפסים...:

(א) פירוש המגיד משנה על הלכות שחיטה.

(ב) פירוש הרדב"ז על ספר קדושה, הפלאה, זרעים, שופטים, ממלא מקום המגיד משנה שלא נמצא בספרים האלה.

(ג) חדושים ומקורי דינים מהרב... בעל פרי חדש, נקראים בשם מים חיים.

(ד) חדושים ומקורי הדינים מהרב... בעל מחנה אפרים.

(ה) חדושים ומקורי הדינים מהרב... ישעיה פיק...

(ו) ביאורים על הלכות בית הבחירה מהרב... יעקב עמדין...

(ז) השמטות מתוספות הגהמי"י, מדפוס וויניציאה, שנת ש"י, שי"א.

(ח) חדושים מהרב... מהר"ם פאדווה...

(ט) חדושים ומקורים מהרב... אברהם... אבד"ק פ"פ דמיין.

דינסטאג בסיני 56 (תשכ"ה), עמ׳ ק"י — קי"א שבו מובאות הערות ביבליוגרפיות בקשר לפולמוס נגד דעתו של סלונימסקי.

(י) חדושים ומקורים מהרב... זלמן... אחי מוהר"ח... מולאזין.

(יא) חדושים ומקורים מהרב... צבי הירש חיות...

(יב) חדושים ומקורים מהרב...יוסף... בעל ספר מנחת חינוך.

(יג) חדושים ומקורים מהרב... אברהם משכיל לאיתן...

(יד) חדושים ומקורים מהרב... שמואל שטראשון...

(טו) חדושים ומקורים מהרב...בצלאל הכהן... מווילנא.

(טז)* חדושים ומקורים מהרב... ר"ש ארינשטיין... אבד"ק אזירקאוו. [והם מחתנו ר' נחום א"ש].

(יז) חדושים ומקורים מהרב... משה נחום... אבד"ק קאמינקא.

(יח) חדושים ומקורים מהרב... אברהם יונה יעוונין... מהוראדנא.

(יט) ביאור בפרק י"ז מקידוש החדש מהרב... התוכן ר' רפאל מק"ק הנובר...

(כ) ע"ד כתיבת שירת הים ושירת האזינו, מס' שתי ידות להרב... ר"מ די לונזאנו.

[(כא) איזה הגהות ותיקונים בפירוש הלק"ח לרבינו עובדיה ז"ל מאת... חיים זעליג סלאנימסקי... (עיין הערתנו למעלה במספר 25)].

ועתה הוספנו עוד ארבע עשרה הוספות כמבואר מעבר לדף:

(א) חידושי רבינו... אליהו... מווילנא.

(ב) טורי אבן, חדושים וביאורים מאת הרב... אלעזר רוקח... אבד"ק ברוד ואמשטרדם (ובתוכם הגהות וציונים ומ"מ מנינו הרב... לוי חיים...דומ"ץ בק"ק ווילנא).

(ג) כתר תורה חידושים והגהות מאת הרב... לוי הקדוש... אבד"ק קאדני. (ונוספו עליהם ציונים ומ"מ מנינו הרב... לוי חיים)...

(ד) בנין שלמה, באורים וחדושים מהרב... שלמה קלוגר... מברוד...

(ה) יד דוד, הערות וציונים מהרב...דוד לוריא... מביחאוו ישן.

(ו) נמוקי הגרי"ב, מהרב יהודה בכרך... אבד"ק סיניי...

(ז) בן אריה, חדושים, הערות וציונים, ומ"מ מהרב... זאב בן אריה... בעהמ"ח הגהות בן אריה על כל הש"ס (ובתוכם הערות וציונים מאת נכדו הרב... אריה ליב...).

(ח) באר אברהם, הערות וציונים מהרב... אברהם שמעון טרויב... אבד"ק קיידאן.

(ט) מעשה ר"ב, חידושים וביאורים מהרב... בצלאל הכהן... מ"ץ דווילנא (ועתה הגיעו לידינו עוד הוספות ע"י אחיו, הרב... שלמה הכהן... מ"ץ דווילנא, ובתוכם גם הערות ממוהר"ש הנ"ל)...

(י) נמוקי מהרא"י, מהרב... יונה יעוונין... מהוראדנא.

(יא) חשק שלמה, חידושים וביאורים מהרב... שלמה הכהן... מ"ץ דווילנא...

(יב) בני בנימין, הערות וציונים מהרב... אלי' דוד ראבינאוויץ... אבד"ק מירא.

---

* חדושים ומקורים (סימן טז) שרשום עליהם שהם מהר"ש ארינשטיין, מחברם הוא חתנו ר' נחום אש. עיין ר' י"ל מימון בסיני 50 (תשכ"ב), עמ' שס"א וספרו של ר' נחום אש: "זכרון מלך" מאמרים ע"ד הרמב"ם וספריו ליום-הולדתו השמונה מאות בצרוף השמטות, תיקונים ומלואים להגהות ציוני מהר"נ שנדפסו בשנת תרמ"א בווארשא, בסוף ד' חלקי הרמב"ם. פיעטרקוב, תרצ"ה. החוקר ד"ר י. ורפל [רפאל] מצא בקונטרס "ציונים תמרורים" מאת אפרים הכהן מוויזנא האשמה מפורשת כי ציונים אלה אינם אלא גניבה ספרותית. (סיני 14 (תש"ד), עמ' קצ"ב).

(ובתוכם הערות וחידושי מר אביו הרב... בנימין... אבד״ק ווילקאמיר, וגם מאחיו הגאון... יהודה צבי... אבד״ק ליגום)...

(יג) הערת... מהרב... דובער קאראסיק... אב״ד דק״ק קראלעוויץ...

(יד) בנין יהושע, חידושים וביאורים מהרב... יהושע לאנג...

(טו) עזוז חיל, מקורות והערות מהל׳ יסודי התורה עד הל׳ שחיטה מאת הרב... חיים יהודה לייב אייגש... מקובנו [ובסוף ימיו בירושלים].

ווילנא: בדפוס אברהם צבי ראזענקראנץ ור׳ מנחם מענדיל שריפטזעטצער, תר״ס, 2°.

ס׳ המדע. [2], ח, ע״ד דף;

ס׳ אהבה. פ״ז דף;

ס׳ זמנים. רכב, [1], י״ד דף;

ס׳ נשים. [2], קכ״ח, ל״ו דף;

ס׳ קדושה. [1], מד, [2], קכ״ג דף;

ס׳ הפלאה, זרעים. [3], קלז, [1], ק׳ דף;

ס׳ עבודה, קרבנות. מד, [1], קל״ב דף;

ס׳ טהרה. [3], ג—קמ״א דף;

ס׳ נזיקין. [3], ע׳ דף;

ס׳ קנין, משפטים. סד, [1], קלד, [2], ב—מ״ב דף;

ס׳ שופטים. קלב, [1], דף.

תרפ״ד (1924)

27.* משנה תורה...

ה׳ כרכים. ווילנא: ראזענקראנץ. 1924

(קטלוג של היברו יוניאון קולג׳ בסינסינטי. כרך 29, עמ׳ 63).

תרפ״ו (1926)

28. משנה תורה הוא ספר הי״ד החזקה להרב רבנו משה ב״ר מימון... עם הקדמת הרמב״ם ומניין המצוות ועם פירושיו ונושאי כליו והם השגות הראב״ד לרבנו אברהם ב״ר דוד ופירוש הרב המגיד הוא מגיד משנה ופירוש כסף משנה להרב ר׳ יוסף קארו ועם מגדל עוז ועם הגהות מימוניות ופירושי הר״ר עובדיה ב״ר דוד והר״ר לוי ן׳ חביב להלכות קדוש החודש ועם לחם משנה להר״ר אברהם די בוטן ועם משנה למלך להר״ר יהודה רוזאנים ונוספו בו הגהות ומראי מקומות לספרי הפוסקים וכן באו בו כללי הרמב״ם והראב״ד ומפרשיהם ומפתחות לספרי הי״ר ולהלכות ועוד הוספות ותיקונים.

ניו־יורק / ברלין: בהוצאת חורב (בדפוס הורב בליפסיאה), תרפ״ו. 8°.

חלק א: מדע, אהבה, זמנים, נשים, קדושה, הפלאה, זרעים.

מדע — אהבה. [8], קט״ז, [1] דף;

זמנים. קנ״ו דף; 2 דפים — צורות לקידוש החדש;

נשים. ק״ם דף;

קדושה. ק״ו דף;

הפלאה — זרעים. [1], ג — [קל״ד] דף;

חלק ב: עבודה, קרבנות, טהרה, נזיקין, קניין, משפטים, שופטים.

עבודה — קרבנות. [1], קמ"א דף;

טהרות. צ"ה, [1] דף;

נזיקין — קנין. [1], קמ"א, [1] דף;

משפטים — שופטים. קס"ח דף;

דפוס צלום מהוצאת ווין (1835—1842, סימן 18 למעלה) בהשמטת ספר קובץ לר' נחום טריביטש וקצת שינויים בפגינציה.

תרפ"ז (1927)

29. ספר משנה תורה הוא היד החזקה לרבינו משה בר מיימון... עם השגת הראב"ד ומראה מקומות נעתק לאנגלית ע"י הרב ישעיהו בר אברהם אליהו גלאזר.

כרך א: ספר המדע. ניו־יורק: הוצאת מימון פובלישינג קא. תרפ"ז. ג"ד, 446, VII עמ'. 8°.

המקור והתרגום טור לעומת טור.

שער נוסף באנגלית:

Book of Mishnah Torah. Yod Ha-Hazakah by... Moses son of Maimon... with RABD'S criticism and references. Translated in English by Rabbi Simon Glazer, Volume I. New York: Maimonides Publishing Co. 1927.

לא נדפס יותר.

בקורת חריפה מאת יהודה דוד אייזנשטיין ב"אוצר זכרונותי", ניו־יורק, תר"ץ, עמ' 189—191.

תרפ"ח (1928)

30. משנה תורה הוא היד החזקה להנשר... רבינו משה בר מיימון... עם השגות הראב"ד... ופירוש הרב המגיד משנה, הכסף משנה להגאון... יוסף קארו..., מגדל עוז הגהות מיימוניות [עם תוספות מדפוס וויניציה ש"י שי"א], [עם הוספות הרב... מהר"ם פאדווה"ה...], גם תשובות מיימוניות, ופירושי הרב... עובדיה והרב... מהר"ל בן חביב על הלכות חדוש החודש, עם כל הצורות השייכות להם ולהלכות שבת וסוכה. גם הלחם משנה להגאון... אברהם די בוטן..., ומשנה למלך להגאון... יהודה רוזאנים... כאשר היו בדפוסי יעסניץ, דיהרנפורט, וויען וברדיטשוב. ונלוה לו ספר הקובץ חדושים ומקורי דינים מהרב... נחום טריביטש... אבד"ק נ"ש כפי שנדפס בוויען.

ועתה הוספנו חדשות אשר לא היו מעולם בכל ספרי הרמב"ם הנדפסים...

(א) פירוש המגיד משנה על הלכות שחיטה...

(ב) פירוש הרדב"ז על ספר קדושה, הפלאה, זרעים, שופטים, ממלא מקום המגיד משנה שלא נמצא בספרים האלה...

(ג) חדושים ומקורי דינים מהרב... בעל פרי חדש, נקראים בשם מים חיים.

(ד) חדושים ומקורי הדינים מהרב... בעל מחנה אפרים.

(ה) חדושים ומקורי הדינים מהרב... ישעיה פיק...

(ו) ביאורים על הלכות בית הבחירה מהרב... יעקב עמדין...

(ז) השמטות מתוספות הגהמי״י, מדפוס וויניציאה, שנת ש״י, שי״א.
(ח) חדושים מהרב... מהר״ם פאדווה...
(ט) חדושים ומקורים מהרב... אברהם... אבד״ק פ״פ דמיין.
(י) חדושים ומקורים מהרב... זלמן... אחי מוהר״ח... מוולאזין.
(יא) חדושים ומקורים מהרב... צבי הירש חיות...
(יב) חדושים ומקורים מהרב... יוסף... בעל ספר מנחת חינוך...
(יג) חדושים ומקורים מהרב... אברהם משכיל לאיתן...
(יד) חדושים ומקורים מהרב... שמואל שטראשון...
(טו) חדושים ומקורים מהרב... בצלאל הכהן מווילנא...
(טז)* חדושים ומקורים הגיעו אלינו מהרב... ר״ש ארינשטיין... אבד״ק אזירקאוו... [והם מחתנו ר׳ נחום א״ש].
(יז) חדושים ומקורים מהרב... משה נחום... אבד״ק קאמינקא...
(יח) חדשום ומקורים מהרב... אברהם יונה יעוונין... מהוראדנא...
(יט) ביאור בפרק י״ז מקידוש החדש מהרב... התוכן ר׳ רפאל מק״ק הנובר...
(כ) ע״ד כתיבת שירת הים ושירת האזינו, מס׳ שתי ידות להרב... ר״מ די לונזאנו.
ועתה הוספנו עוד ארבע עשרה הוספות כמבואר מעבר לדף:
(א) חידושי רבינו... אליהו... מווילנא...
(ב) טורי אבן, חידושים וביאורים מאת הרב... אלעזר רוקח... אבד״ק ברוד ואמשטרדם (ובתוכם הגהות וציונים ומ״מ מנינו הרב... לוי חיים... דומ״ץ בק״ק ווילנא).
(ג) כתר תורה חידושים והגהות... מאת הרב... לוי הקדוש... אבד״ק קאדני... (ונוספו עליהם ציונים ומ״מ מבן נכדו הרב... לוי חיים...).
(ד) בנין שלמה, באורים וחדושים מהרב... שלמה קלוגר... מברוד...
(ה) יד דוד, הערות וציונים מהרב... דוד לוריא... מביחאוו ישן...
(ו) נמוקי הגרי״ב, מהרב...יהודה בכרך... אבד״ק סיניי...
(ז) בן אריה, חדושים, הערות וציונים, ומ״מ מהרב... זאב בן אריה... אבד״ק גאלדינגען וטעלז, בעהמ״ח הגהות בן אריה על כל הש״ס (ובתוכם הערות וציונים מאת נכדו הרב... אריה ליב...)...
(ח) באר אברהם, הערות וציונים מהרב... אברהם שמעון טרויב... אבד״ק קיידאן...
(ט) מעשה ר״ב, חדושים וביאורים מהרב... בצלאל הכהן... מ״ץ דווילנא... ([גם] הוספות ע״י אחיו, הרב... שלמה הכהן... מ״ץ דווילנא... ובתוכם גם הערות ממוהר״ש הנ״ל)...
(י) נמוקי מהרא״י, מהרב... יונה יעוונין... מהוראדנא...
(יא) חשק שלמה, חידושים וביאורים מהרב... שלמה הכהן... מ״ץ דווילנא.
(יב) בני בנימין, הערות וציונים... מהרב... אלי׳ דוד ראבינאוויץ... אבד״ק מירא... (ובתוכם הערות וחידושי מר אביו הרב... בנימין... אבד״ק ווילקומיר, וגם מאחיו הגאון... יהודה צבי... אבד״ק ליגום)...

---

* ראה הערתנו למעלה, בסוף הוצאת ווילנא תר״ס (סימן 26).

(יג) הערות וביאורים מהרב... דובער קאראסיק... אב"ד דק"ק קראלעוויץ...

(יד) בנין יהושע, חידושים וביאורים מהרב... יהושע לאנג...

(טו) עזוז חיל, מקורות והערות מהל' יסודי התורה עד הל' שחיטה מאת הרב... חיים יהודה לייב אייגש... מקובנו, [ובסוף ימיו בירושלים].

ה' כרכים, ווילנא: בדפוס והוצאת ראזענקראנץ ושריפטזעצער, תרפ"ט 1928. 2°.

כרך א: מדע. [1], ח', ע"ד דף;

אהבה. פ"ד [צ"ל: צ"ב] דף;

זמנים. פ"ה, י"ד, [1], פ"ו—רכ"ב, [1] דף;

כרך ב: נשים. [2], קכ"ח, [1], ל"ו דף;

קדושה. מ"ד, [1], קכ"ג דף;

כרך ג: הפלאה וזרעים. [1], קל"ז; [1], ב'—ק' דף;

כרך ד: עבודה וקרבנות. מ"ד; [1], ב'—קל"ב דף;

טהרה. [1], ב'—קמ"א דף;

נזיקין. [1], ע' דף;

קנין. ס"ד דף;

כרך ה: תרפ"ח [!].

קנין (המשך) ומשפטים. קל"ד; ב'—מ"ב דף;

שופטים. קל"ב, [1] דף.

תרצ"ז (1937)

31. משנה תורה לרבינו משה ברבי מימון זצ"ל...

על פי כתב יד בגנזי אקספרד הובא לדפוס בפעם הראשונה עם הקדמה ומראה מקומות והערות ותרגום אנגלי ע"י משה חיים חיימזאהן.

ספר ראשון: ספר המדע, ניו־יארק (ירושלים, דפוס עזריאל), תרצ"ז. XIII ,93a—1a עמ'; [4] דף 8°.

שער נוסף באנגלית:

The Mishneh Torah by Maimonides, Book I, edited according to the Bodleian codex, with... English translation by Moses Hyamson
New York, Bloch, 1937.

בקורת מאת:

Leo Strauss, *Review of Religion*, vol 3 (1939), pp 448–456.

דפוסי צילום בשנות תשכ"ב ותשכ"ה, למטה

ספר שני: ספר אהבה... ומלווה מראי מקומות והערות ע"י הרב חיים מרדכי הכהן ברכר. ניו־יארק, בלאך, תש"ט 1949. 4°.

[3] דף, [1] עמ'; עמ' 93ב—165א, B 93—165א; [2] עמ'.

מהדורה של יד החזקה לפי כ"י אוכספורד 577 (רשימת ניבויאר ע' 113 שהרמב"ם עצמו העיד עליו בסופו בעצם כתב־ידו: "הוגה מספרי אני משה ב"ר מימון זצ"ל". הטכסט העברי נדפס בשורה לפי כה"י ממש, וממול כל עמוד תרגום אנגלי.

דפוסי צילום בשנת תשכ"ב ותשכ"ה, למטה.

לא נדפס יותר.

שער נוסף באנגלית:

The Mishneh Torah by Maimonides. Book II. Edited according to the Bodleian (Oxford) Codex with Biblical and Talmudical references and with and English translation by Moses Hyamson. The Talmudical references and Hebrew footnotes by... Chaim M. Brecher. New York: Bloch Publishing Co., 1949.

תש"ג (1943)

32. משנה תורה הוא היד החזקה להנשר... רבינו משה בר מיימון... עם השגות הראב"ד... ופירוש הרב המגיד משנה, הכסף משנה להגאון... יוסף קארו..., מגדל עוז, הגהות מיימוניות, גם תשובות מיימוניות, ופירושי הרב... עובדיה והרב... מהר"ל בן חביב על הלכות קדוש החדש, עם כל הצורות השייכות להם ולהלכות שבת וסוכה. גם ... הלחם משנה להגאון... אברהם די בוטון...,. ומשנה למלך להגאון... יהודא רוזאניס... כאשר היו... בדפוסי יעסניץ, דיהרנפורט, וויען וברדיטשוב. ונלווה לו ספר הקובץ חדושים ומקורי דינים מהרב... נחום טריביטש... אבד"ק נ"ש כפי שנדפס בוויען...

שנגהי: בהוצאת בית אוצר הספרים "עזרת תורה" שע"י ישיבת מיר. 4°.

מדע, אהבה, זמנים. תש"ד [8], קפ"ט דף; לוחות קדוש החודש.

נשים. קדושה. תש"ה.

נשים. [1] קכ"ח, ל"ו דף;

קדושה. מד, [1], קי"א דף.

הפלאה. תש"ג. ק"ה דף (מפי הרב צבי הכהן זרקובסקי, ניו־יורק).

זרעים. טהרה. תש"ד.

זרעים. צ"ט דף;

טהרה. [ב] — קי"ח דף.

עבודה — קרבנות. תש"ג. ב—מ"ד; ב—קל"ב דף.

נזיקין — קנין. תש"ג. [1] עמ'; [1], ס"ד; ב'—נ"א דף.

משפטים — שופטים. תש"ג [2], נ"ב—ק"ד; ב'—מ"ב, [1], ק"ח דף.

דפוס צלום מהוצאת ורשה — וילנה מחוץ ההוספות בסופי הספרים למרות שנמנו על השערים.

תש"ד (1944)

33. משנה תורה הוא היד החזקה להנשר הגדול רבינו משה בר מיימון... עם כל המפרשים כאשר נדפס בדפוסים הקודמים עם הוספות חדשות וחדושים רבים שלא היו עוד כמבואר בשער הקודם.

ירושלים הוצאת פאג"י (דפוס חורב ע"י "פאגי" ירושלים). 8°.

חלק א: ספר המדע. תש"ד. [4] דף; 367, [4], נב, [5] עמ';

חלק ב: ספר אהבה. תש"ד. [4] דף; 442, [נג] — ק"י עמ';

חלק ג: ספר זמנים, כרך א (הלכות שבת — שביתת עשור). תש״ד. [4] דף; 364, [10], 4—100, [3], [קיא] — קס״ב עמ׳;

ספר זמנים, כרך ב (שביתת יום טוב — חנוכה). תש״ד. [4] דף; 234, [6], 5—338, [6], [קסג]—רכ״ח עמ׳;

חלק ד: ספר נשים, כרך א (הלכות אישות וגירושין). תש״ו. [4], שנ״ג, [5] דף; פ״ח עמ׳.

רשימת הפירושים וההוספות החדשות:

״הראב״ד לרבינו אברהם ב״ר דוד... מגיד משנה להגאון רבינו דון וידאל די טולוזא... כסף משנה להגאון... יוסף קארו... הגהות מיימוניות לרבינו מאיר הכהן... (תלמיד מהר״ם מרוטנבורג). מגדל עוז מהר׳ שם טוב ב״ר אברהם... פירוש הרדב״ז לרבנו דוד בן זמרא... תשובות מיימוניות — רובם למהר״ם בר ברוך... והשאר לר״ת להר״י לרבינו שמחה ועוד). פירוש על ד׳ פרקים הראשונים של יסודי התורה — להריטב״א... (מהר׳ יום טוב בר אשבלי׳...) פירוש על קדוש החדש — להרב רבינו עובדיה... פירוש על קדוש החדש — למהר״ל בן חביב... לחם משנה — להגאון מו״ה אברהם די בוטן... משנה למלך — להגאון מו״ה יהודה רוזאניס... ועתה הוספנו עליהם הוספות חדשות כאשר יראה הקורא מעבר לדף:

שנויי נוסחאות; ספר הלקט [המכיל לקוטים מספרים] ״שלא חוברו בשביל ביאור דברי המחבר אבל דרך אגב מובאים שם פנינים יקרים לברור פשט הדברים ולבירור ההלכה שהרמב״ם ז״ל הביאה ומשום אל תמנע טוב מבעליו עשינו עבודה לאסוף וללקט מכל מה שמצאנו פה ושם דברים שיש בהם תועלת למעיין לפשט להלכה ולבירור מקורות המחבר כדברי חז״ל וקראנו את העבודה הזו בשם ספר הלקט... גם הבאנו ציונים מפסוקי התנ״ך המובאים בפנים, דבר חדש שלא היה בהוצאות הקודמות כל העבודה הגדולה הזאת, לקוט הנוסחאות השונות והביאורים נעשתה ע״י... שמואל הלוי ווזנר... מרבני ירושלים... ואתו חבר רבנים...״

לא נדפס יותר.

הערכה מאת הרב מ. כשר, סיני, כרך 18 (תש״ו), עמ׳ ג׳.

תש״ו (1946)

34. משנה תורה הוא היד החזקה להנשר הגדול רבנו משה בן־מימון... יוצא לאור בפעם הראשונה כולו מנוקד ומפורש, מוגה ומתוקן על פי כתבי־יד ודפוסים ראשונים בצירוף מקורות, מראי מקומות וכו׳.

תל־אביב: הוצאת ״ראשונים״ בע״מ. (בית דפוס אפרים סטרוד ובניו, תל־אביב). 4°.

ספר ראשון והוא ספר המדע עם פירוש תמציתי ממבחר מפרשי הרמב״ם מאת הרב ש[מואל] ת[נחום] רובינשטין. העורך: מ. ד. רבינוביץ. תש״ו. 20, רנ״ז עמ׳; [3] דף. 20 עמודים הראשונים מכילים מלבד השער דברי היוזם ר׳ יחיאל רבינוביץ הסכמות הרבנים והקדמת המפרש; [3] דפים האחרונים מכילים ״מוספים״ שלשלת הקבלה מימי רב אשי עד רבנו משה בן מימון; רשימת הגאונים וארבעת השבויים. כל אלו הושמטו ממהדורת ״רמב״ם לעם״ שיצאה לאור ע״י מוסד הרב קוק, תשי״ז. עיין להלן מספר 44.

יצאה גם הוצאה מוקטנת בתבנית 12°.

ספר שני והוא ספר אהבה עם פירוש תמציתי ממבחר מפרשי הרמב״ם מאת הרב שמואל ת[נחום] רובינשטין. תש״ט.

12, ת״א, [3] עמ׳.

12 עמ׳: מכילים מלבד השער דברי היוזם הנ״ל והקדמת המפרש שהושמטו ממהדורת ״רמב״ם לעם״ שיצאה לאור ע״י מוסד הרב קוק בשנת תשי״ז (סימן 44, להלן).

ממהדורה זו, הוצאת ״ראשונים״ לא נדפס יותר אולם נמשכה בהוצאת מוסד הרב קוק, שם, תשי״ז—תשכ״ה.

תש״ו (1946)

34 א. [משנה תורה עם תרגום ערבי לר׳ יוסף בן גנאסייא].

ג׳רבה (בדפוס חי׳ הדאד). 8°.

מדע (בלי הלכות תשובה). תשי״ח. מעטפה, 172 עמ׳;

אהבה (עד ה׳ ברכות). תשי״ז. [1], מעטפה, 224 עמ׳;

אהבה (עד ה׳ מילה; כולל גם ה׳ שקלים). תשי״ט. מעטפה, 120; 24 עמ׳;

זמנים. ה׳ שבת. תשי״ד. מעטפה, קנ״ז דף;

ה׳ עירובין וקידוש החדש. תשי״ט. מעטפה, 149, [1] עמ׳;

ה׳ חמץ ומצה — מגלה וחנוכה. תשי״ח. מעטפה, 120, 100 עמ׳;

ה׳ שביתות עשור — לולב (וכולל גם ה׳ תשובה שלא נדפס בס׳ המדע הנ״ל). תשט״ו. מעטפה, 14, 84, 64 עמ׳. ונלוה לו בסופו: דרוש תחיית המתים. 48 עמ׳;

נשים. ה׳ אישות. תש״ד [תשי״א ?]. קכ״ז, [1] דף;

חוברת זו מכונה בשם ״סוכה וחופה״.

גירושין, יבום וחליצה, נערה בתולה, סוטה. תשי״ב. מעטפה, קמ״ד דף;

קדושה. איסורי ביאה. [תש״ו]. מעטפה, ק״ט דף;

מאכלות אסורות [תשי״ד ?]. 175 עמ׳;

שחיטה. תשי״ח. מעטפה, 104 עמ׳;

הפלאה. שבועות. [תשי״ד ?]. 88 עמ׳;

נדרים ונזירות. חש״ד. 102, 76 עמ׳;

זרעים. בכורים, שמיטה ויובל (ונלווה לו פרה אדומה). תש״ך. מעטפה, 180, 88 עמ׳;

כלאים, מתנות עניים, תרומות, מעשרות, מעשר עני ונטעי רביעי. תשכ״ב. מעטפה, 440 עמ׳;

עבודה. ה׳ תמידין ומוספין ופסולי המקודשין. תשכ״א. מעטפה, 196 עמ׳;

נזקין.ה׳ נזקי ממון. תש״ו. מעטפה, מ״ו דף; 5 עמ׳;

חוברת זו מכונה ״אורה ושמחה״.

גניבה גזלה ואבדה, חובל ומזיק. חש״ד. כ״ד; נ״ב; כ״ד דף; רוצח ושמירת הנפש. [תש״ו]. ל״ב דף;

קנין. ה׳ מכירה, זכייה ומתנה, שכנים, שלוחין ושותפין, עבדים. חסרים מעטפות. ע״ז, ל״ה, ל״ו, כ״ה, כ״ז דף;

משפטים. ה׳ שכירות — נחלות. תשי״ד. מעטפה, 80, 43, [1], 176, 107, 54 עמ׳;

שופטים. ה׳ סנהדרין. תשי״ד. מעטפה, 129 עמ׳;

ה׳ עדות — ממרים. חש״ד. מעטפה, 93, [1], 41, [1] עמ׳;

ה׳ אבל, תשי״ח. מעטפה, 62, [1] עמ׳;
ה׳ מלכים (ונלוה לו עבודה זרה). תש״ו. מעטפה, 62, [1], 86, [1] עמ׳.

תש״ז (1947)

35. משנה תורה הוא הי״ד החזקה אשר עשה רבינו משה בר מיימון... (ספר ראשון והוא ספר המדע). מינכן, ״סיני״ (תש״ז). [3], ס״ב, [1] דף. 16°.

״את נדרי אשלם. לא פעם אחת התהום פערה פי׳ להבליעני בעמדי בין החיים והמות בטרבלינקי ואשבנצין ועוד, ורק בדרך נס בחסד השי״ת נשארתי בחיים ואז עלה על רעיוני... לקיים את מחשבתי ולהדפיס את ספרי הרמב״ם״ (מדברי המו״ל יצחק מאיר זעמבה).

דפוס צלום של הוצאת [קניגסברג או: דאנציג, תר״ד?] בהוספת דברי המו״ל הנ״ל. עיין למעלה מספר 19.

תש״ז (1947)

36. משנה תורה והוא ספר הי״ד החזקה להרב... משה ב״ר מיימון... עם הקדמת הרמב״ם ומניין המצוות ועם פירושיו ונושאי כליו והם השגות הראב״ד לרבנו אברהם ב״ר דוד ופירוש הרב המגיד הוא מגיד משנה ופירוש כסף משנה להרב ר׳ יוסף קארו ועם מגדל עוז ועם הגהות מימוניות ופירושי הר״ר עובדיה ב״ר דוד והר״ר לוי ן׳ חביב להלכות קדוש החדש ועם לחם משנה להר״ר אברהם די בוטן ועם משנה למלך להר״ר יהודה רוזאניס ונוספו בו הגהות ומראי מקומות לספרי הפוסקים וכן באו בו כללי הרמב״ם והראב״ד ומפרשיהם ומפתחות לספרי הי״ד ולהלכות ועוד הוספות ותיקונים.

ניו־יורק: הוצאת ״בינה״ (בדפוס יהושע קמינסקי), תש״ז. ב׳ כרכים. 8°.

כרך א: מדע. [3], ג—ח, ס״א דף;
אהבה. ע״ט דף;
זמנים. קפ״ט דף;
נשים. קכ״ו, ל״ו דף;
קדושה. [1], מ״ד, [1], קי״א דף;
הפלאה — זרעים. [1], קל״ז דף.
כרך ב: זרעים (המשך). צ״ט, [1] דף;
עבודה — קרבנות. [1], מ״ד; ב׳—קכ״ח דף;
טהרה. קי״ח דף;
נזיקין. [1], ע׳ דף;
קנין — משפטים. ס״ג; ב׳—קל״ד, מ״א דף;
שופטים. [1], ק״ח דף.

צלום מדפוס ווילנא—ורשה בלי ההוספות שבסופי הספרים.

תש״ז (1947)

37. משנה תורה הוא היד החזקה להנשר... רבינו משה בר מיימון... עם השגות הראב״ד... ופירוש הרב המגיד משנה, הכסף משנה להגאון... יוסף קארו..., מגדל עוז לרבינו שם טוב בן גאון הספרדי, הגהות מיימוניות [עם תוספות מדפוס

וויניציה ש״י שי״א), [עם הוספות הרב... מהר״מ פאדווה...], גם תשובות מיימוניות, ופירושי הרב... עובדיה והרב... מהר״ל בן חביב על הלכות קדוש החדש, עם כל הצורות השייכות להם ולהלכות שבת וסוכה. גם הלחם משנה להגאון... אברהם די בוטן..., ומשנה למלך להגאון...יהודא רוזאנים... ונלוה לו ספר הקובץ חדושים ומקורי דינים מהרב... נחום טריביטש...

עם שלושים וארבע הוספות כאשר נדפסו בדפוסי ורשה—ווילנה:

(א) פירוש המגיד משנה על הלכות שחיטה...

(ב) פירוש הרדב״ז על ספר קדושה, הפלאה, זרעים, שופטים, ממלא מקום המגיד משנה שלא נמצא בספרים האלה...

(ג) חדושים ומקורי דינים מהרב בעל פרי חדש, נקראים בשם מים חיים.

(ד) חדושים ומקורי הדינים מהרב... בעל מחנה אפרים.

(ה) חדושים ומקורי הדינים מהרב... ישעיה פיק...

(ו) ביאורים על הלכות בית הבחירה מהרב... יעקב עמדין...

(ז) השמטות מתוספות הגהמי״י, מדפוס וויניציאה, שנת ש״י, שי״א.

(ח) חדושים מהרב... מהר״ם פאדווה...

(ט) חדושים ומקורים מהרב... אברהם...אבד״ק פ״פ דמיין.

(י) חדושים ומקורים מהרב... זלמן אחי מוהר״ח... מוולאזין.

(יא) חדושים ומקורים מהרב... צבי הירש חיות...

(יב) חדושים ומקורים מהרב...יוסף... בעל ספר מנחת חינוך.

(יג) חדושים ומקורים מהרב... אברהם משכיל לאיתן...

(יד) חדושים ומקורים מהרב... שמואל שטראשון...

(טו) חדושים ומקורים מהרב... בצלאל הכהן... מווילנא.

(טז)* חדושים ומקורים מאת הרב... ר״ש אורנשטיין... אבד״ק אזירקאוו [והם מחתנו ר׳ נחום א״ש].

(יז) חידושים ומקורים מהרב... משה נחום... אבד״ק קאמינקא.

(יח) חדושים ומקורים מהרב... אברהם יונה יעווניו... מהוראדנא.

(יט) ביאור בפרק י״ז מקידוש החדש מהרב... התוכן ר׳ רפאל מק״ק הנובר...

(כ) ע״ד כתיבת שירת הים ושירת האזינו, מס׳ שתי ידות להרב... ר״מ די לונזאנו.

(כא) חידושי רבינו... אליהו... מווילנא.

(כב) טורי אבן, חדושים וביאורים מאת הרב... אלעזר רוקח... (ובתוכם הגהות וציונים ומ״מ מנכדו הרב... לוי חיים... דומ״ץ בק״ק ווילנא).

(כג) כתר תורה חידושים והגהות מאת הרב... לוי הקדוש... אבד״ק קאדני. ונוספו עליהם ציונים ומ״מ מנכדו הרב... לוי חיים...

(כד) בנין שלמה, באורים וחדושים מהרב... שלמה קלוגר... מברוד.

(כה) יד דוד, הערות וציונים מהרב... דוד לוריא...

(כו) נמוקי הגרי״ב, מהרב יהודה בכרך... אבד״ק סיניי.

(כז) בן אריה, חדושים, הערות וציונים ומ״מ מהרב... זאב בן אריה... אבד״ק טעלז, בעהמ״ח הגהות בן אריה על כל הש״ס (ובתוכם הערות וציונים מאת נכדו הרב... אריה ליב...).

(כח) באר אברהם, הערות וציונים מהרב... אברהם שמעון טרויב... אבד״ק קיידאן.

(כט) מעשה ר"ב, חדושים וביאורים מהרב... בצלאל הכהן... מ"ץ דווילנא, גם הוספות ע"י אחיו, הרב... שלמה הכהן... מ"ץ דווילנא, ובתוכם גם הערות ממוהר"ש הנ"ל.

(ל) נמוקי מהרא"י, מהרב... יונה יעוונין... מהוראדנא.

(לא) חשק שלמה, חידושים וביאורים מהרב... שלמה הכהן... מ"ץ דווילנא.

(לב) בני בנימין, הערות וציונים מהרב... אלי' דוד ראבינאוויץ... אבד"ק מירא. (ובסוף ימיו נמנה לרב ראשי בירושלם ת"ו) ובתוכם הערות וחדושי מר אביו הרב... בנימין... אבד"ק ווילקומיר, וגם מאחיו הגאון... יהודה צבי... אבד"ק ליגום.

(לג) הערות וביאורים מהרב... דובער קאראסיק... אב"ד דק"ק קראלעוויץ.

(לד) בנין יהושע, חידושים וביאורים מהרב... יהושע לאנג...

[(לה) עזוז חיל, מקורות והערות מהל' יסודי התורה עד הל' שחיטה מאת הרב... חיים יהודה ליב אייגש... מקובנו, ובסוף ימיו בירושלים].

ועתה הוספנו עוד שבע עשרה [צ"ל: עשרים ושתים] הוספות חדשות וחשובות מהן כמה ספרים שלמים מגדולי המפרשים כמבואר בשער הבא:

[(א) כתב יד הרמב"ם זצ"ל. שרידים מספר משנה תורה שנכתבו בעצם כתב יד קדשו של רבינו המחבר בנוסחם הראשון, שנתגלה מתוך הגניזה אשר במצרים עם הערות ושנויי נוסחאות ע"י ר' משה ב"ר פינחס לוצקי כמבואר בשער אשר בסוף כרך ה'.

(ב) קובץ שאלות ותשובות להרמב"ם זצ"ל, שהריצו אליו חכמי דורו, רבנים ודיינים ראשי ישיבה ותלמידים, בתי דין, שהציעו הוראותיהם לפני המושב הגדול של הרמב"ם ושכמה מהן הוקראו ברבים לשם פרסום פסקי הדין, הלכות קשות שבחבורו "משנה תורה", שהרבה מחכמי דורו ובתוכם ר' יהונתן זצ"ל (תלמיד הראב"ד בעל ההשגות) מחכמי לוניל נתקשו בהן. נאספו ונסדרו מתוך ספר "תשובות הרמב"ם" שהו"ל רא"ח פריימאן בהוצאת חברת "מקיצי נרדמים", ירושלים תרצ"ד [מחולקים בכל הכרכים, כרך כרך והחלקים המתאימים לו].

(ג) שאלות ותשובות לרבנו אברהם ב"ר הרמב"ם זצ"ל. בתשובות אלו מברר רבינו כמה הלכות קשות ש"במשנה תורה", ומוסיף נוסחאות נכונות ותקונים שקבל מאביו המחבר ז"ל. נאספו ונסדרו מתוך ספר "תשובות רבינו אברהם בן הרמב"ם", שהו"ל רא"ח פריימאן בתרגומו של רש"ד גויטיין, בהוצאת חברת "מקיצי נרדמים", ירושלים תרצ"ח [מחולקים כנ"ל].

(ד) ברכת אברהם, קובץ של תשובות שהשיב ר' אברהם הנ"ל על שאלותיו והשגותיו של ר' דניאל הבבלי על ספר "משנה תורה". נסדרו ונדפסו מספר "ברכת אברהם", ליק, תר"ך [בסוף כרך א].

(ה) שאלות ותשובות לרבי יהושע הנגיד, ב"ר אברהם הנגיד נכד הרמב"ם זצ"ל, אשר הציעו לפניו חכמי דורו, וביחוד אנשי עדן אשר במדינת תימן. נאספו ונסדרו מתוך ספר "תשובות ר' יהושע הנגיד" שהו"ל רא"ה פריימאן בתרגומו של רי"י ריבלין בהוצאת חברת "מקיצי נרדמים", ירושלים ת"ש [בסוף כרך א].

(ו) ספר המנוחה לרבינו מנוח ב"ר יעקב מנרבונא זצ"ל, פירושים וחידושים על משנה תורה, הל' חמץ ומצה, שופר, שביתת העשור, סוכה ולולב. נדפס בפעם הראשונה בקושטא תע"ח, ועתה נסדר ונדפס מחדש בהגהה מדויקת [בסוף כרך א].

(ז) ללשונות הרמב"ם על כל חלקי "משנה תורה" לרבינו מרן דוד ב"ר שלמה ן'

זמרא זצ"ל (הרדב"ז). נלקטו מכל חלקי "שו"ת הרדב"ז") ונסדרו על פי סדר "משנה תורה" עם מפתח בסופו. על ידי הרב ר' דוב בעריש במוה"ר אהרן ז"ל צוקערמאן.

(ח) ביאור על ספר זרעים ממשנה תורה לרבינו מרן יוסף קורקוס זצ"ל, שנדפס רק פעם אחת (אזמיר תקי"ז) ועתה נסדר מחדש בהגהה מדויקת [בסוף כרך ג']

(ט־י) ביאורי מהר"י קורקוס והרדב"ז זצ"ל על ספר עבודה של "משנה תורה". יוצא לאור בפעם הראשונה מתוך כתב יד ישן עם מראה מקומות והע־ות מאת הרב ר' דוב בעריש במהור"ר אהרן ז"ל צוקערמאן [בסוף כרך ד].

(יא) ביאור מהר"י קורקוס זצ"ל, על ספר קרבנות, חידושים וביאורים שנלקטו מספר חזון נחום לר' אליעזר ב"ר יעקב נחום (נדפס רק פעם אחת בקושטא תק"ח והוא יקר במציאות) ונסדרו עם מראה מקומות והערות על ידי הרב ר' בעריש במוה"ר אהרן ז"ל צוקערמאן [בסוף כרך ד].

(יב) ספר יקר תפארת לרבינו דוד בן זמרא (הרדב"ז על הלכות שלוחין־ושותפין ועבדים עם הערות ומראה מקומות. נסדר מתוך ספר "יקר תפארת" שי"ל בפעם הראשונה מכתב יד שבירושלים ע"י הרב שמואל ברוך ורנר בהוצאת "מוסד הרב קוק", ירושלים תש"ה [בסוף כרך ה].

(יג) שאלות ותשובות למהר"י קורקוס זצ"ל על הלכות שבת, שהרב חיד"א זצ"ל מצא והדפיסן בסוף ספרו חיים שאל (רק בהוצאה הראשונה היקרה במציאות — ליוורנו תקנ"ב) ועתה נסדרו ונדפסו בהגהה מדויקת [בסוף כרך א].

(יד) ספר הקובץ, חידושים ומקורי הדינים על הלכות אישות להרב ר' נחום טריביטש זצ"ל (נדפס רק פעם אחת ב"משנה תורה" הוצאת ווינא) [בסוף כרך ב'].

(טו) הגהות וחידושים על "משנה תורה" ממורנו ורבנו ר' עקיבא איגר זצ"ל [בסוף כרך א].

(טז) קונטרס תשובה מיראה, הערות ומקורות על לשון "יראה לי" שבדברי הרמב"ם, מאת הרב הגאון הגדול ר' אליהו דוד ראבינאוויץ תאומים זצ"ל אב"ד בעיה"ק ירושלים [בסוף כרך ה].

(יז) פרי חיים, באורים וחדושים בספר נזיקין, קנין, משפטים ושופטים מאת הגאון ר' חיים העליר [בסוף כרך ה].

(יח) צורות הנדסיות להלכות קדוש החודש השייכות לפירושו של מהר"ל בן חביב זצ"ל (נמצאות ב"משנה תורה" הוצאת וינא) [בסוף כרך א].

(יט) הגהות כבוד מלכים מאת הרב ר' זאב וואלף לייטער [בסוף כרך ה].

(כ) חדושים והארות על תשובות הרמב"ם מאת הרב ר' יוסף ליב ארנסט [בסוף כרך ה].

(כא) קונטרס אוצר מפרשי משנה תורה, רשימה מפורטת מכל מפרשי הרמב"ם ונושאי כליו מיום הופעת הספר עד ימינו אלה. מאת הרב ר' יהודה רובינשטיין, איש ירושלים [בסוף כרך ה].

(כב) אחרית דבר, ע"ד כ"י הרמב"ם הנדפס פה, רשימה מפורטת מכל ההוצאות השלמות של ספר משנה תורה ונו"כ, השלמת סדר התפילה מנוסח הרמב"ם מתוך כ"י (נדפס בסוף כרך ה'), ואוסף של שנויי נוסחאות מכ"י, מאת ר' משה ב"ר פינחס לוצקי [בסוף כרך ה].

ה' כרכים. ניו־יורק, "עם חי", דפוס שולזינגר, תש"ז. פקסימילים. 2° גדול. צילום

מוגדל של הוצאת ורשא—וילנה האחרונה. בסוף כל כרך נמצאות הוספות בדפוס (לכמה מהם עם שערים מיוחדים).

תכן כל כרך וכרך עם העימוד:

כרך א: ספר המדע. [7], ח, ע״ד דף;

ספר אהבה. פ״ד [צ״ל: צ״ב] דף;

ספר זמנים. רל״ז דף;

נספחים: שו״ת הרמב״ם. [1], 14 דף [עם שער מיוחד];

שו״ת לרבינו אברהם בן הרמב״ם. [2], ג׳ דף [עם שער מיוחד];

ספר ברכת אברהם לר׳ אברהם בן הרמב״ם. [2], י״ד דף [עם שער מיוחד];

שו״ת ר׳ יהושע הנגיד. [2], 3 דף [עם שער מיוחד];

ספר המנוחה על הלכות חמץ ומצה שופר, שביתת העשור סוכה ולולב לרבינו מנוח ב״ר יעקב מנרבונא. כ״ו עמ׳ [עם שער מיוחד].

ספר ללשונות הרמב״ם לר׳ דוד בן שלמה ן׳ זמרא (הרדב״ז). [1], כ״ג דף [עם שער מיוחד].

תשובות חד מקמיא הרב הגדול מה״ר יוסף קורקוס ז״ל (שמביאו מרן בכ״מ) על קצת דיני הרמב״ם ה׳ שבת). ב׳ דף;

הגהות וחידושים על הרמב״ם ממרנא רבינו עקיבא איגר ב׳ דף;

צורות השייכות להלכות שבת וסוכה וקידוש החדש [ב] דף.

כרך ב: נשים. [3] קכ״ח, ל״ו דף;

קדושה. [1], מ״ד, קכ״ג דף.

נספחים: ספר קובץ על יד החזקה, הלכות אישות. ט״ו דף;

שאלות ותשובות הרמב״ם. ט׳ [צ״ל: י״א] דף [עם שער מיוחד];

שאלות ותשובות לרבינו אברהם בן הרמב״ם. [2], ג׳ דף [עם שער מיוחד];

ללשונות הרמב״ם לרבינו דוד בן שלמה ן׳ זמרא (הרדב״ז). י׳ דף. [עם שער מיוחד].

כרך ג: ספר הפלאה. [3], ק״ה דף;

ספר זרעים. ל״ג; ב — ק׳ דף;

נספחים: שו״ת הרמב״ם. [1], ה׳ דף [עם שער מיוחד];

ספר ללשונות הרמב״ם לר׳ דוד בן שלמה ן׳ זמרא (הרדב״ז). י״ב דף [עם שער מיוחד];

ביאור מהר״י קורקוס על ספר זרעים מאת ר׳ יוסף קורקוס. [1], ק״א דף [עם שער מיוחד].

כרך ד: ספר עבודה — קרבנות. [2], מ״ד, [3], קל״ב דף;

ספר טהרה. קמ״א דף;

נספחים: שו״ת הרמב״ם. [1], 3 דף [עם שער מיוחד];

שו״ת ר׳ אברהם בן הרמב״ם. [2], ב דף [עם שער מיוחד].

ספר ללשונות הרמב״ם לרדב״ז. י׳ דף [עם שער מיוחד];

ביאורי מהר״י קורקוס והרדב״ז על ספר עבודה של משנה תורה. [5], ד—ל״ה דף [עם שער מיוחד]

ביאור מהר״י קורקוס... על ספר קרבנות. י״ד דף [עם שער מיוחד].

כרך ה: ספר נזיקין. [3], ע׳ דף;

ספר קנין. משפטים. [1], ס"ד, ב—קל"ד ; ב—מ"ב דף ;
ספר שופטים. [1], קל"ב, [1] דף ;
נספחים : שו"ת הרמב"ם. [1], ג ; ב—ט"ו [וצ"ל : י"ח] דף [עם שער מיוחד] ;
שו"ת ר' אברהם בן הרמב"ם. [2], ה' דף [עם שער מיוחד] ;
ללשונות הרמב"ם לרדב"ז. י"ז דף [עם שער מיוחד] ;
ספר יקר תפארת לרדב"ז על הלכות שלוחין ושותפין והלכות עבדים. [2], ד — י"ז דף ;
קונטרס תשובה מיראה לר' אליהו דוד ראבינוביץ תאומים. ח' דף [עם שער מיוחד] ;
פרי חיים על ספר י"ג וי"ד ממשנה תורה מלקוטים... מתוך ספרי... ר' חיים העליר. ל"ו דף [עם שער מיוחד] ; הגהות כבוד מלכים מאת הרב זאב וואלף לייטער. ב' דף ;
חידושים והארות על תשובות הרמב"ם מאת הרב יוסף ליב ארנסט. ו' דף ;
פרקים מספר משנה תורה שנכתבו בעצם יד קדשו של רבינו המחבר... ערוך ומסודר ע"י משה בן פינחס לוצקי. [14] דפים ופקסימיליות [עם שער מיוחד] ;
אחרית דבר מאת משה לוצקי. י"ח [צ"ל : י"ז] דף.
כולל : א) הנוסח של המשנה תורה ;
ב) כתב יד הרמב"ם המתפרסמים בזה ;
ג) רשימה של ההוצאות השלמות של ספר משנה תורה להרמב"ם ;
ד) השלמה לסדר התפילות שבמשנה תורה ;
ה) לשנויי הנוסחאות שבמשנה תורה ;
קונטרס אוצר מפרשי משנה תורה. ערוך ע"י הרב יהודה רובינשטיין. ו', [1] דף [עם שער מיוחד].
כל ההוספות והנספחים הנ"ל הופיעו גם כן בכרך מיוחד; פרטים במדור החידושים והפירושים על הרמב"ם שברשימתנו, אי"ה במקום אחר.

תשי־? (?־195)

38. משנה תורה הוא היד החזקה להנשר... רבינו משה בר מיימון... עם השגות הראב"ד... ופירוש הרב המגיד משנה, הכסף משנה להגאון... יוסף קארו..., מגדל עוז, הגהות מיימוניות [עם תוספות מדפוס וויניציה ש"י שי"א], [עם הוספות הרב... מהר"ם פאדוו"ה...], גם תשובות מיימוניות, ופירוש הרב... עובדיה והרב... מהר"ל בן חביב על הלכות קדוש החדש, עם כל הצורות השייכות להם ולהלכות שבת וסוכה. גם הלחם משנה להגאון... אברהם די בוטן..., ומשנה למלך להגאון... יהודא רוזאנים... כאשר היו בדפוסי יעסניץ, דיהרנפורט, וויען וברדיטשוב. ונלווה לו ספר הקובץ חדושים ומקורי דינים מהרב... נחום טריביטש... אבד"ק נ"ש כפי שנדפס בוויען.
ועתה הוספנו חדשות אשר לא היו מעולם בכל ספרי הרמב"ם הנדפסים :
(א) פירוש המגיד משנה על הלכות שחיטה...
(ב) פירוש הרדב"ז על ספר קדושה, הפלאה, זרעים, שופטים, ממלא מקום המגיד משנה שלא נמצא בספרים האלה...
(ג) חדושים ומקורי דינים מהרב... בעל פרי חדש, נקראים בשם מים חיים.
(ד) חדושים ומקורי הדינים מהרב... בעל מחנה אפרים.

(ה) חדושים ומקורי הדינים מהרב... ישעיה פיק...

(ו) ביאורים על הלכות בית הבחירה מהרב... יעקב עמדין...

(ז) השמטות מתוספות הגהמי״, מדפוס ויניציאה, שנת ש״י, שי״א.

(ח) חדושים מהרב... מהר״ם פאדווה...

(ט) חדושים ומקורים מהרב... אברהם... אבד״ק פ״פ דמיין...

(י) חדושים ומקורים מהרב... זלמן... אחי מוהר״ח... מוולאזין.

(יא) חדושים ומקורים מהרב... צבי הירש חיות...

(יב) חדושים ומקורים מהרב... יוסף... בעל ספר מנחת חינוך...

(יג) חדושים ומקורים מהרב... אברהם משכיל לאיתן...

(יד) חדושים ומקורים מהרב... שמואל שטראשון...

(טו) חדושים ומקורים מהרב... בצלאל הכהן מווילנא...

*(טז) חדושים ומקורים הגיעו אלינו מהרב... ר״ש ארינשטיין... אבד״ק אזירקאוו [והם מחתנו ר׳ נחום א״ש]

(יז) חדושים ומקורים מהרב... משה נחום... אבד״ק קאמינקא...

(יח) חדושים ומקורים מהרב... אברהם יונה יעווניץ... מהוראדנא...

(יט) ביאור בפרק י״ז מקידוש החדש מהרב... התוכן ר׳ רפאל מק״ק הנובר...

(כ) ע״ד כתיבת שירת הים ושירת האזינו, מס׳ שתי ידות להרב... ר״מ די לונזאנו...

ועתה הוספנו עוד ארבע עשרה הוספות כמבואר מעבר לדף;

(א) חידושי רבינו... אליהו... מווילנא...

(ב) טורי אבן, חדושים וביאורים מאת הרב... אלעזר רוקח... אבד״ק ברוד ואמשטרדם (ובתוכם הגהות וציונים ומ״מ מנינו הרב... לוי חיים... דומ״ץ בק״ק ווילנא).

(ג) כתר תורה חידושים והגהות מאת הרב... לוי הקדוש אבד״ק קאדני. ונוספו עליהם ציונים ומ״מ מנינו הרב... לוי חיים...

(ד) בנין שלמה, באורים וחדושים מהרב... שלמה קלוגר... מברוד...

(ה) יד דוד, הערות וציונים מהרב... דוד לוריא... מביכוב ישן...

(ו) נמוקי הגרי״ב, מהרב יהודה בכרך... אבד״ק סיניי...

(ז) בן אריה, חדושים הערות וציונים, ומ״מ מהרב... זאב בן אריה... אבד״ק גולדינגן מטעלז, בעהמ״ח הגהות בן אריה על כל הש״ס ובתוכם הערות וציונים מאת נכדו הרב... אריה ליב...).

(ח) באר אברהם, הערות וציונים מהרב... אברהם שמעון טרויב... אבד״ק קיידאן...

(ט) מעשה ר״ב, חדושים וביאורים מהרב... בצלאל הכהן... מ״ץ דווילנא... [גם] הוספות על־ידי אחיו, הרב... שלמה הכהן... מ״ץ דווילנא, ובתוכם גם הערות ממוהר״ש הנ״ל...

---

* ראה הערתנו למעלה, בסוף הוצאת וילנה, תר״ס (סימן 26).

(י) נמוקי מהרא"י, מהרב... אברהם יונה יעוונין... מהוראדנא...

(יא) חשק שלמה, חידושים וביאורים מהרב... שלמה הכהן... מ"ץ דווילנא...

(יב) בני בנימין, הערות וציונים מהרב... אלי' דוד ראבינאוויץ... אבד"ק מירא... (ובתוכם הערות וחדושי מר אביו הרב... בנימין... אבד"ק ווילקומיר, וגם מאחיו הגאון... יהודה צבי... אבד"ק ליגום...).

(יג) הערות וציונים מהרב... דובער קאראסיק... אב"ד דק"ק קראלעוויץ...

(יד) בנין יהושע, חידושים וביאורים מהרב... יהושע לאנג...

[(טו) עזוז חיל, מקורות והערות מהל' יסודי התורה עד הל' שחיטה מאת הרב... חיים שהודה לייב אייגש... מקובנו, ובסוף ימיו בירושלים]. ה' כרכים. חמוש"ד [אוסטריה. תש"י — ?]. 4°.

כרך א: ספר מדע. אהבה, זמנים (עד הל' שביתת עשור). [1], ע"ד, פ"ז [צ"ל: צ"ב], פ"ה, י"ד דף.

כרך ב: ספר זמנים [מהל' יום טוב). נשים. קדושה. 2], פ"ו—רכ"ב, [2], קכ"ח, [1], ל"ו, מ"ד, [2], קכ"ג דף.

כרך ג: ספר הפלאה, זרעים. [2], קל"ז, [2], ק' דף.

כרך ד: ספר עבודה. טהרה. [2], קל"ב, [2], [ב]—קמ"א דף.

כרך ה: ספר נזקין, קנין, משפטים, שופטים. [2] ע'; ס"ד, [3], ב—קל"ד. [2], ב—מ"ב, קל"ב, [1] דף.

דפוס צלום מדפוס ווילנא תר"ס, עם השער המקורי.

בשער כל כרך חותם:

Printed in Austria Jüdischer Verlag Ges. M.B.H. Vienna.

תשי"ג (1953)

39. משנה תורה הוא היד החזקה להנשר... רבינו משה בר מיימון... עם השגת הראב"ד ופירוש הרב המגיד משנה, הכסף משנה להגאון... יוסף קארו..., מגדל עוז, הגהות מיימוניות, גם תשובות מיימוניות, ופירושי הרב... עובדיה, והרב... מהר"ל בן חביב על הלכות קדוש החדש, עם כל הצורות השייכות להם ולהלכות שבת וסוכה. גם... הלחם משנה להגאון... אברהם די בוטן... ומשנה למלך להגאון... יהודה רוזאניס... ועתה הוספנו.. פירוש המגיד משנה על הלכות שחיטה.. על מקומות בפנים הספר. פירוש הרדב"ז על ספר קדושה, הפלאה, זרעים, שופטים, ממלא מקום המגיד משנה שלא נמצא בספרים האלה...

ה' כרכים. ניו־יארק: הוצאת פעלדהיים (בדפוס "נאבעל" אפסעט קא. שלום וויינרייך), תשי"ג. 8°.

כרך א': ספר א': מדע. ח', [1], ס"א דף;

ספר ב': אהבה. [1], ע"ט דף;

ספר ג': זמנים. [1], קפ"ט דף;

כרך ב', ספר ד': נשים. [2], קכ"ו, ל"ו דף;

ספר ה': קדושה. [1], מ"ד, [1], קי"א דף;

כרך ג', ספר ו'—ז': הפלאה — זרעים. [2], קל"ז, [1], ב—ק דף;

כרך ד', ספר ח'—ט': עבודה — קרבנות. [2], מ"ד; ב—קכ"ח דף;

ספר י׳: טהרה. קי״ח דף;

כרך ה׳, ספר י״א: נזקין. [2], ע׳ דף;

ספר י״ב—י״ג: קנין — משפטים. [1], ס״ג; ב—קל״ד; ב—מ״א דף;

ספר י״ד: שופטים. [1], ק״ח דף;

דפוס צלום מוקטן מהוצאת ורשה—וילנה בלי ההוספות שבסופי הספרים.

תשי״ד (1954)

40. משנה תורה הוא היד החזקה להנשר... רבינו משה בן מימון... (עם השגות הראב״ד... ופירוש הרב המגיד משנה, הכסף משנה להגאון... יוסף קארו... פירוש הרדב״ז, מגדל עוז, הגהות מיימוניות, גם תשובות מיימוניות, ופירושי הרב רבינו עובדיה והרב הגאון מהר״ל בן חביב על הלכות קדוש החודש, עם כל הצורות השייכות להן ולהלכות שבת וסוכה, גם הלחם משנה להגאון... אברהם די בוטן... ומשנה למלך להגאון המפורסם... יהודה רוזאניס... חידושי הגר״א מווילנא... וחידושי מים חיים מהגאון בעל פרי חדש... וספר הקובץ ומקורי דינים מהגאון רבי נחום טריביטש...

ועתה הוספנו הוספות חדשות:

(א) מפתח על פי אלפא ביתא לכל הענינים שביד החזקה, מוצאו מבית מדרשו של הרב הזקן גדול בדורו כמוהר״ר ברוך עוזיאל חזק... נדפס בוויניציאה של״ד.

(ב) תשובות הרמב״ם... לחכמי דורו נאספו מכתבי־יד ומספרים על־ידי הרה״ח רבי א. ח. פריימן... מסודרות על ידינו על פי הלכות הרמב״ם.

(ג) תשובות רבי אברהם בן הרמב״ם... נאספו מספר ״ברכת אברהם״ ומכת״י על־ידי הנ״ל מסודרות על ידינו על־פי הלכות הרמב״ם.

(ד) חידושים מרבי אברהם בן הרמב״ם ומשאר גאונים קדמונים.

(ה) הגהות הרמ״ך... על הרמב״ם מתוך כתב־יד שלא נדפסו אף פעם בהוצאות הרמב״ם, יבואו בהדפסה מיוחדת.

(ו) תשובות הרשב״א על הרמב״ם מסודרות עפ״י הלכות הרמב״ם.

(ז) הגהות על הרמב״ם לרבינו משולם... בעל ההשלמה וביאורים עליהן מאת... רבי יהודה לובעצקי...

(ח) השלמת הגהות מיימוניות עפ״י הדפוס הראשון שנדפס בקושטא רס״ט מה שהוחסר בכל הדפוסים.

(ט) גליון הרמב״ם להגאון רבי עקיבא אייגר... על הרמב״ם מכתי״ק בגליון הרמב״ם שלו.

(י) ביאורים חדושים והגהות על הרמב״ם מאת גאון דורנו, בעל חזון איש...

ירושלים: הוצאת ״אל המקורות״. 8°.

כרך א. תשי״ד. מדע—אהבה: ל, [1], ס״ו, פ״ו, פ״ד, י׳ דף.

הדפים הראשונים כוללים מלבד ההקדמה, ומנין המצות, גם ״מפתח להרמב״ם על סדר אלפא ביתא מוצא מבית מדרשו של הרב... בתוך עוזיאל חזק...״ (דף כא—ל׳).

כרך ב. תשי״ד. זמנים: [2], קפט, טז, ס״ג, [י״א]—ל״ז, [4], דף; [4] דף: צורות להלכות קדוש החדש.

כרך ג. תשי״ד. נשים: [3], קכ״ז, ל״ו, טו, ס״ד, [לט] — ס״ג דף.

כרך ד. תשט״ו. קדושה־הפלאה: [3], מ״ד, קי״א, [1], ק״ה, צ״ה דף.

כרך ה. תשט"ז. זרעים: [3], [קו]—קלז; ב—צט, כ, צו—קעד דף; [1], דף "לוח הצורות".

כרך ו. תשט"ז. עבודה—קרבנות: [3], מ"ד; ב—קלב, לו, [1], [קע"ה]—רמג דף.

כרך ז. תשי"ז. טהרה־קנין: [3], [ב] — קכ, [1], ע, [1], ס"ד; [ב] — נ"א דף; 16, מא, [4], [יא] — מד עמ'.

כרך ח. תשי"ז, משפטים־שופטים: [2], [נב]—קל"ד; ב—מא, [1], ק"ט, נ"ח, [1], [רמ"ד] — תכ"ד דף.

דפוס — גוף הספר צלום מדפוסי ווארשא — ווילנא בהשמטת רוב החידושים שבסופי הספרים שם; הנספחים (א—י) מסודרים ומודפסים מחדש בפגינציות נפרדות. לרובם שערים או חצאי שערים מיוחדים. רוב ההוספות הנ"ל יצאו לחוד.

בקרת מאת ב. דה־פריס, "מהדורה חדשה של משנה תורה (במלאות 750 שנה לפטירתו של הרמב"ם)". הארץ, שנה ל"ז, יום ו' כ' טבת, תשט"ו [מדור תרבות וספרות], עמ' 1.

תשט"ו (1955)

41. משנה תורה הוא היד החזקה לרבינו משה בן מימון. מהדורה חדשה מצולמת מדפוס רומי ר"מ, עם מבוא מאת הרב יהודה ליב הכהן מימון. ירושלים, מוסד הרב קוק, בהשתתפות משרד הדתות [של ממשלת ישראל], [דפוס אופסט ש. מונזון ודפוס מרכז], תשט"ו. 35, [4], תרצ"ג, X, [1] ע', פקסימילים. 2°. שער נוסף באנגלית:

Mishneh Torah. Being the Yad Hachazakah of Rabbi Moshe Ben Maimon (Maimonides). A new edition photographed from the Rome edition of the year 5240 (1480) with an introduction by Rabbi Yehudah Leib Hakohen Maimon. Published by Mosad Harav Kook with the participation of the Ministry of Religions of the State of Israel. Jerusalem, 5715.

הספר יצא בכ' טבת במלאת 750 שנה לפטירת הרמב"ם, במסגרת התכנית הרחבה של מוסד הרב קוק להוציא את כל כתבי הרמב"ם. מהדורה מצולמת זו של דפוס רומי הידוע כדפוס השלם הראשון של הרמב"ם (עיין למעלה, מספר 1), הוכנה לפי הטופס הנמצא בבית הספרים הלאומי והאוניברסיטאי בירושלים והושלמה על יסוד הטפסים שבספרית בית המדרש לרבנים ניו־יורק, ספרית אוקספורד והחלק שבידי מר שמואל וואהרמן בירושלים. "מלבד המבוא מאת... נשיא מוסדנו הכנסנו גם תיקונים אלה: (א) ציון סימני ההלכות, שאינם בדפוס רומי; (ב) תוכן י"ד הספרים; (ג) מפתח הענינים לפי סדר א"ב, שנדפס במשנה תורה דפוס ויניציאה של"ד—של"ו, תוקן והושלם על ידינו; (ד) פקסימיליות מדפוסים ראשונים". — תוכן המבוא של הרב מימון (ע' 5—35): החיבור, הנוסחאות והשיבושים. המקורות, דרכי הרמב"ם בקביעת ההלכה. הדפוס הראשון של ספר משנה תורה בשלמותו.

על ההצעה להדפיס הוצאה זו, עיין הרב י.ל. מימון "ספר היד־החזקה לנוסחאותיו ומקורותיו", הצופה, כ"ט טבת, תשי"ג, עמ' 4.

ראוי לציין שבהוצאה המקורית, שממנה צולמה מהדורה זו, נשמט מהלכות טומאת מת, חלק מפרק י"ז וראש פרק יח. לאחר שהבחינו המדפיסים בדילוג זה, הדפיסו את החסר על סרט נייר והדביקוהו לתחתית העמוד שם (לוצקי, שם, מספר א'; הרב יהודה

אבידע: לתולדות הדפוס בישראל ודפוסי ספר "משנה תורה" להרמב"ם ז"ל, סיני לד [שבט תשי"ד], עמ' שז—שח).

סרט ההשלמה, כפי שהוא במהדורת צילום שלפנינו, אינו מכיל את כל ההשמטה ועדיין חסרים בו, בפרק יח — חלק אחרון של הלכה ב', הלכה ג' כולה וחלק ראשון של הלכה ד'. עיין: הרב שלמה זלמן הבלין, "משהו לתולדות דפוסי הרמב"ם", קרית ספר, מב (אלול תשכ"ז), עמ' 509—510 המביא נוסח השורות החסרות במהדורת צילום. הרב הבלין, כמו כן, מציין "כי במספר מקומות במהד' הצילום ניכר שאין זה צילום נאמן לחלוטין כי אם צילום שזכה להשלמה מצויירת על־ידי גרפיקאי שהשתדל לחקות את האותיות המקוריות".

תשט"ז (1956)

42. משנה תורה הוא היד החזקה להנשר... רבינו משה בר מיימון... עם השגות הראב"ד... ופירוש הרב המגיד משנה, וכסף משנה להגאון... יוסף קארו... מגדל עוז, הגהות מיימוניות [עם תוספות מדפוס וויניציה ש"י שי"א], גם תשובות מיימוניות, ופירושי הרב... עובדיה והרב... מהר"ל בן חביב על הלכות קדוש החדש, עם כל הצורות השייכות להם ולהלכות שבת וסוכה. גם הלחם משנה להגאון... אברהם די בוטן... ומשנה למלך להגאון... יהודא רוזאנים... כאשר היו בדפוסי יעסניץ, דיהרנפורט, וויען וברדיטשוב, ונלוה לו ספר הקובץ חדושים ומקורי הדינים מהרב... נחום טריביטש... אבד"ק נ"ש כפי שנדפס בוויען.

ועתה הוספנו חדשות אשר לא היו מעולם בכל ספרי הרמב"ם הנדפסים...

(א) פירוש המגיד משנה על הלכות שחיטה...

(ב) פירוש הרדב"ז על ספר קדושה, הפלאה, זרעים, שופטים, ממלא מקום המגיד משנה שלא נמצא בספרים האלה...

(ג) חדושים ומקורי דינים מהרב... בעל פרי חדש, נקראים בשם מים חיים.

(ד) חדושים ומקורי הדינים מהרב... בעל מחנה אפרים.

(ה) חדושים ומקורי הדינים מהרב... ישעיה פיק...

(ו) ביאורים על הלכות בית הבחירה מהרב... יעקב עמדין...

(ז) השמטות מתוספות הגהמי"י, מדפוס וויניציאה, שנת ש"י, שי"א.

(ח) חדושים מהרב... מהר"ם פאדווה...

(ט) חדושים ומקורים מהרב... אבוש... אבד"ק פ"פ דמיין.

(י) חדושים ומקורים מהרב... זלמן... אחי... מוהר"ח... מוולאזין.

(יא) חדושים ומקורים מהרב... צבי הירש חיות...

(יב) חדושים ומקורים מהרב... יוסף... בעל ספר מנחת חינוך.

(יג) חדושים ומקורים מהרב... אברהם משכיל לאיתן...

(י) חדושים ומקורים מהרב... שמואל שטראשון...

(טו) חדושים ומקורים מהרב... בצלאל הכהן... בווילנא.

*(טז) חדושים ומקורים הגיעו אלינו מהרב... ר"ש ארינשטיין... אבד"ק אזרקאוו [מאת חתנו ר' נחום א"ש].

* ראה הערתנו בסוף הוצאת ווילנא, תר"ס מספר 26.

(יז) חדושים ומקורים מהרב... משה נחום... אבד"ק קאמינקא.

(יח) חדושים ומקורים מהרב... אברהם יונה יעוונין... מהוראדנא.

(יט) ביאור בפרק י"ז מקידוש החדש מהרב... התוכן... ר' רפאל מק"ק הנובר...

(כ) ע"ד כתיבת שירת הים ושירת האזינו, מס' שתי ידות להרב... ר"מ די לונזאנו.

ועתה הוספנו עוד הוספות... כמבואר מעבר לדף:

(א) חידושי רבנו... אליהו... מווילנא...

(ב) טורי אבן, חדושים וביאורים מאת הרב... אלעזר רוקח... אבד"ק ברוד ואמשטרדם... (ובתוכם הגהות וציונים ומ"מ מנינו הרב... לוי חיים... דומ"ץ בק"ק ווילנא.

(ג) כתר תורה חידושים והגהות... מאת הרב... לוי הקדוש... אבד"ק קאדני... ונוספו עליהם ציונים ומ"מ מבן נכדו הרב... לוי חיים...

(ד) בנין שלמה, באורים וחדושים מהרב... שלמה קלוגר מברוד...

(ה) יד דוד, הערות וציונים מהרב... דוד לוריא מביכוב ישן.

(ו) נמוקי הגרי"ב, מהרב יהודה בכרך... אבד"ק סיניי.

(ז) בן אריה, חדושים, הערות, וציונים, ומ"מ מהרב... זאב בן אריה... אבד"ק גולדינגן וטעלז, בעהמ"ח הגהות בן אריה על כל הש"ס (ובתוכם הערות וציונים מאת נכדו הרב... אריה ליב...).

(ח) באר אברהם, הערות וציונים מהרב... אברהם שמעון טרויב אבד"ק קיידאן...

(ט) מעשה רב, חדושים וביאורים מהרב... בצלאל הכהן מ"ץ דווילנא... (... הוספות ע"י אחיו, הרב... שלמה הכהן מ"ץ דווילנא... ובתוכם גם הערות ממוהר"ש הנ"ל...).

(י) נמוקרי מהרא"י, מהרב אברהם יונה יעוונין מהוראדנא...

(יא) חשק שלמה, חידושים וביאורים מהרב... שלמה הכהן... מ"ץ דווילנא...

(יב) בני מנימין, הערות וציונים מהרב... אלי' דוד ראבינאוויץ... אבד"ק מירא. ובתוכם הערות וחידושי מר אביו הרב... בנימין... אבד"ק ווילקומיר, וגם מאחיו הגאון... יהודה צבי... אבד"ק ליגום.

(יג) הערות וביאורים מהרב... דובער קאראסיק... אב"ד דק"ק קראלעוויץ...

(יד) בנין יהושע, חידושים וביאורים מהרב... יהושע לאנג...

[(טו) עזוז חיל, מקורות והערות מהל' יסודי התורה עד הל' שחיטה מאת הרב... חיים יהודה לייב אייגש... מקובנו, ובסוף ימיו בירושלים].

ואלה הן ההוספות שאנו נותנים בהוצאה זו:

חידושי אור שמח לרבינו מאיר שמחה הכהן...;

ברכת אברהם לרבנו אברהם בן הרמב"ם, בכרך ב';

בינה לעתים על הלכות יו"ט לר' יהונתן אייבשיץ, בכרך ב';

לשונות הרמב"ם מהגאון בעל אור החיים [לר' חיים עטר]... נדפס מספר ראשון לציון בכרך א';

חידושי קובץ על יד על הלכות אישות [לר' נחום טריביטש שבהוצאת וינה], בכרך ג';

הגהות ישועות להג' ר' יהושע מקוטנא [טרונק], בכרך א;

הגהות אוצר המלך מהגאון...רבנו צדוק הכהן [רבינוביץ];
כללי הרמב״ם מהרש״ם מבערזאן נדפס מספרו דרכי שלום;
מאמר דרכי משה להגאון... ר׳ צ״ה חיות, בכרך א׳.
ניו יורק: הוצאת רמב״ם, תשט״ז. 4°. 6 כרכים.
כרך א: מדע, אהבה, זמנים. [1], ח, עד, פ״ז [צ״ל: צ״ב], פ״ה, י״ד דף.
נספחים: אור שמח. נז דף;
ראשון לציון; אוצר המלך; ישועות מלכו. [4] דף;
מאמר דרכי משה. י״ח דף.
כרך ב: זמנים (המשך). [ב], פו—רכ״ב, [1] דף; 2 דפים: צורות לקידוש החודש;
נספחים: אור שמח. [נז, ב] — צב דף;
ברכת אברהם לר׳ אברהם בן הרמב״ם. [41] דף;
בינה לעתים לר׳ יהונתן. [3], ב—לד דף;
כרך ג: נשים. קדושה (איסורי ביאה). קכ״ח, [1] לו, מד, י״ג [צ״ל: ט״ו] דף;
[= קובץ על היד החזקה הל׳ אישות מדפוס ווין שלא נדפס בהוצאות הרגילות ורשה — וילנה];
נספח: אור שמח. צ״ב דף;
כרך ד: קדושה (מאכלות אסורות — שחיטה). [2], קכ״ג דף:
הפלאה. [1], קלז, [1], ב—ק דף;
נספח: אור שמח. צג—קכד; [ב] — מ״ח דף;
כרך ה: עבודה וקרבנות. [2] מד; ב—קל״ב דף;
טהרה. [2], [ב] — קמא דף;
נספח: אור שמח. [מח, ב] — קכ״ו דף;
כרך ו: נזיקין. [2], ע׳ דף;
קנין. משפטים. ס״ד, קלד, סב דף;
שופטים. [1], קלב, [1] דף;
נספח: אור שמח. [ב] — קכג דף
דפוס צילום של הוצאות ורשה — וילנה; גם הנספחים צולמו.

תשט״ז (1956)

43. משנה תורה הוא היד החזקה להנשר... רבינו משה בר מיימון... עם השגות הראב״ד... ופירוש הרב המגיד משנה, הכסף משנה להגאון... יוסף קארו... מגדל עוז לרבינו שם טוב הספרדי, הגהות מיימוניות [עם תוספות מדפוס ויניציה ש״י שיא], [עם הוספות הרב... מהר״ם פאדוו״ה...], גם תשובות מיימוניות, ופירושי הרב... עובדיה והרב... מהר״ל בן חביב על הלכות קדוש החדש, גם הלחם משנה להגאון... אברהם די בוטן..., ומשנה למלך להגאון... יהודא רוזאנים... ונלווה לו ספר הקובץ חדושים ומקורי דינים מהרב... נחום טריביטש... אבד״ק ניקלשבורג.

עם שלושים וחמש הוספות כפי שנדפסו בדפוסי ווארשה—ווילנה:

(א) פירוש המגיד משנה על הלכות שחיטה...

(ב) פירוש הרדב״ז על ספר קדושה, הפלאה, זרעים, שופטים, ממלא מקום המגיד משנה שלא נמצא בספרים האלה...

(ג) חדושים ומקורי דינים מהרב... בעל פרי חדש, נקראים בשם מים חיים.

(ד) חדושים ומקורי הדינים מהרב... בעל מחנה אפרים.

(ה) חדושים ומקורי הדינים מהרב... ישעיה פיק...

(ו) ביאורים על הלכות בית הבחירה מהרב... יעקב עמדין...

(ז) השמטות מתוספות הגהמי"י, מדפוס ויניציאה, שנת ש"י, שי"א.

(ח) חדושים מהרב... מהר"ם פאקווה...

(ט) חדושים ומקורים מהרב... אברהם... אבד"ק פ"פ דמיין...

(י) חדושים ומקורים מהרב... זלמן... אחי מוהר"ח... מוולאזין.

(יא) חדושים ומקורים מהרב... צבי הירש חיות...

(יב) חדושים ומקורים מהרב... יוסף... בעל ספר מנחת חינוך...

(יג) חדושים ומקורים מהרב... אברהם משכיל לאיתן...

(יד) חדושים ומקורים מהרב... שמואל שטראשון...

(טו) חדושים ומקורים מהרב... בצלאל הכהן... מווילנא...

*(טז) חדושים ומקורים מהרב... ר"ש ארינשטיין... אבד"ק אזירקאוו [והם מחתנו ר' נחום א"ש].

(יז) חדושים ומקורים מהרב... משה נחום... אבד"ק קאמינקא...

(יח) חדושים ומקורים מהרב... אברהם יונה יעוונין... מהוראדנא...

(יט) ביאור בפרק י"ז מקידוש החדש מהרב... התוכן ר' רפאל מק"ק הנובר...

(כ) ע"ד כתיבת שירת הים ושירת האזינו, מס' שתי ידות להרב... ר"מ די לונזאנו...

(כא) חידושי רבינו... אליהו... מווילנא...

(כב) טורי אבן, חדושים וביאורים מאת הרב... אלעזר רוקח... אבד"ק ברוד ואמשטרדם (ובתוכם הגהות וציונים ומ"מ מנינו הרב... לוי חיים... דומ"ץ בק"ק ווילנא).

(כג) כתר תורה חידושים והגהות מאת הרב... לוי הקדוש... אבד"ק קאדני... ונוספו עליהם ציונים ומ"מ מנינו הרב... לוי חיים..

(כד) בנין שלמה, באורים וחדושים מהרב... שלמה קלוגר... מברוד.

(כה) יד דוד, הערות וציונים מהרב... דוד לוריא... מביכוב ישן...

(כו) נמוקי הגרי"ב, מהרב יהודה בכרך... אבד"ק סיניי.

(כז) בן אריה, חדושים, הערות וציונים, ומ"מ מהרב... זאב בן אריה... אבד"ק טעלז, (ובתוכם הערות וציונים מאת נכדו הרב.... אריה ליב...).

(כח) באר אברהם, הערות וציונים מהרב... אברהם שמעון טרויב... אבד"ק קיידאן...

(כט) מעשה ר"ב, חדושים וביאורים מהרב... בצלאל הכהן... מ"ץ דווילנא, ותוספות ע"י אחיו, הרב... שלמה הכהן... מ"ץ דווילנא, ובתוכם גם הערות ממוהר"ש הנ"ל...

(ל) נמוקי מהרא"י, מהרב... יונה יעוונין... מהוראדנא...

(לא) חשק שלמה, חידושים וביאורים מהרב... שלמה הכהן... מ"ץ דווילנא...

(לב) בני בנימין, הערות וציונים מהרב... אלי' דוד ראבינאוויץ... אבד"ק מירא.

---

* ראה הערתנו, למעלה, בסוף הוצאת וילנה, תר"ס (מספר 26).

(ובסוף ימיו לרב ראשי בירושלם ת"ו) ובתוכם הערות וחדושי מר אביו הרב... בנימין... אבד"ק ווילקומיר, וגם מאחיו הגאון... יהודה צבי... אבד"ק ליגום...

(לג) הערות ובאורים מהרב... דובער קאראסיק... אב"ד דק"ק קראלעוויץ...

(לד) בנין יהושע, חידושים וביאורים מהרב... יהושע לאנג...

(לה) עזוז חיל, מקורות והערות מהל' יסודי התורה עד הל' שחיטה מאת הרב... חיים יהודה לייב אייגש... מקובנו, ובסוף ימיו בירושלים.

ועתה במהדורה ישראלית זו הוספנו עוד שתים־עשרה הוספות חדשות... מהן כמה ספרים... מכתבי יד ודפוסים עתיקים כפי שמבואר בשער הבא:

[(א) שאלות ותשובות לרבנו משה בן מיימון... השאלות והתשובות שלוקטו מתוך הספר "תשובות הרמב"ם" ועוד, שייכות כולן לספר משנה תורה, ונדפסו חלקים חלקים, בכל כרך, השו"ת השייכות להלכות שבאותו כרך.

(ב) שאלות ותשובות לרבנו אברהם בן הרמב"ם... גם שו"ת אלו שייכות כולן לספר משנה תורה ולוקטו מתוך הספרים "תשובות רבנו אברהם בן הרמב"ם" (שהו"ל רא"ח פריימן, המו"ל גם של תשובות הרמב"ם הנ"ל, בתרגומו של רש"ד גויטיין, ע"י חברת "מקיצי נרדמים" בירושלים תרצ"ח), "ברכת אברהם", תשובות רבנו אברהם לשאלותיו והשגותיו של רבי דניאל הבבלי על ספר משנה תורה (ליק תר"ך) ועוד.

(ג) ספר המנוחה, לרבנו מנוח בן ר' יעקב מנרבונה... פירושים וחידושים על ספר משנה תורה, הלכות חמץ ומצה, שופר, שביתת העשור, סוכה ולולב. לפי הוצאת קושטא שנת תע"ח...

(ד) בית יעקב והוא פירוש רבנו יעקב בירב... על ספר משנה תורה. ונמצאים בתוך הראשונה מתוך כתב יד, הנמצא בבית הספרים של האוניברסיטה בקמברידג'. הועתק והוגה היטב על ידי קבוצת תלמידי חכמים בירושלים.

(ה) קרית ספר, לרבנו משה מטראני... נדפס חלקים חלקים, בכל כרך הדברים השייכים להלכות הנמצאות בו. הספר הוגה וצולם מתוך הוצאת ווארשה שהיא המדויקת בהוצאות של "קרית ספר".

(ו) שאלות ותשובות רבנו יוסף קורקוס... מיוצאי גירוש ספרד — על הלכות שבת. הוגהו וסודרו מחדש לפי שנדפסו על ידי מרן הרב החיד"א ז"ל, בסוף ספרו חיים שאל, ח"ב בליוורנו שנת תקנ"ב.

(ז) ספר הקובץ, לרבנו נחום טריביטש... — על הלכות אישות. צולם מחדש לפי הוצאת משנה תורה בווינה...

(ח) חידושי רבנו יהונתן אייבשיץ... על הלכות תפלה, איסורי ביאה, ביכורים, נחלות, עדות, מלכים ועוד (לפי הספר חסדי יהונתן). הלכות יום טוב (לפי הספר בינה לעתים). הוגהו בהגהה מדויקת וסודרו מחדש.

(ט) הגהות וחידושי רבינו עקיבא איגר... על משנה תורה. הועתקו מתוך כתי"ק ונדפסו בווארשה בשנת תרפ"ו על ידי הגאון מהר"ר מנחם מנדיל כשר.

(י) צורות הנדסיות להלכות קידוש החודש, השייכות לפירוש רבינו לוי בן חביב... צולמו לפי הצורות שנדפסו בהוצאות משנה תורה באמסטרדם ווינה.

(יא) מפתח הענינים לפי סדר אלף בית של כל ההלכות הנמצאות בי"ד ספרי משנה תורה, כפי שנמצא בבית מדרשו של הרב המובהק כמוהר"ר ברוך עוזיאל חזק... ונדפס בהוצאת משנה תורה וויניציאה שנת של"ו.

(יב) כתב יד הרמב"ם... צילומים של קטעים מספר משנה תורה שנכתבו בעצם כתב יד קדשו של הנשר הגדול רבנו משה בן מיימון... שנתגלה בגניזה במצרים. צילומים של דפים מההוצאות הראשונות יקרות המציאות של משנה תורה, בהן שינויי נוסחאות של ההוצאות האחרונות הנמצאות בידנו. שינויי נוסחאות בסדר התפלה ועוד. כל זה וגם המפתח לפי סדר האלף בית — בכרך האחרון, הששי להוצאה זו].

6 כרכים, ירושלים, פרדס; [תל־אביב], דפוס חברה ישראל־אמריקה להדפסת אופסט), 2°. גוף הספר (לו פירושים הראשונים) דפוס צלום של הוצאת ורשה—וילנה. הנספחים (א—יב הנ"ל) סודרו ונדפסו מחדש לרובם שערים מיוחדים.

התכן: כרך א: ספר מדע, ספר אהבה. תשט"ז. ט, [1], עד, פ"ז [צ"ל: ב"ב], [1] דף. קודם: [1]: הקדמה למהדורה הישראלית ועוד [2] דף; ה', [1] עמ', פקסימיל. [2]: ספר המצוות חלק א—ב [1], ד, פד, נ"ו דף. [3]: ספר מעשה נסים... שאלות ר' דניאל הבבלי על ספר המצוות... ותשובות רבנו אברהם [בן הרמב"ם, לפי דפוס פאריס תרכ"ז, הוכן ע"י הרב קלמן כהנא]. כ"ב עמ' (עם שער מיוחד). [4]: תשובות רבנו אברהם בן הרמב"ם לספר המצוות. השלמה להשגות הרמב"ן (י"ל ע"י ר' חיים הליר מתוך ספר המצות שלו, מהדורה שניה, ירושלים — ניו־יורק, תש"ו); מפתח הענינים של ספר המצות לפי ההלכות בספר משנה תורה להרמב"ם; מפתח הענינים של המצות לפי פרשיות התורה [שניהן מהרב ראובן אליצור]. [5] דף.

הנספחים: [1] שאלות ותשובות הרמב"ם... ובנו רבנו אברהם השייכות לספר משנה תורה ומסודרות לפיו מלוקטות מתוך ספר "שו"ת הרמב"ם, שו"ת רבנו אברהם בן הרמב"ם", "ברכת אברהם" ועוד. עם מפתח השו"ת [עם שער מיוחד] ט' עמ'. [2]: בית יעקב והוא פירוש רבנו יעקב בירב... על ספר משנה תורה להרמב"ם... ועוד ממחבר בלתי נודע, יוצא לאור בפעם הראשונה מתוך כתב יד הנמצא בספריה האוניברסיטאית בקמברידג'. [עם שער מיוחד]. ס"ט עמ'. [3]: הגהות וחידושים מאת רבנו עקיבא איגר... [3] עמ'. [4]: קרית ספר. חברו... רבינו משה מטראנ"י <המבי"ט>... [צלום מדפוס ורשה עם שער מיוחד]. 24 עמ'.

כרך ב: ספר זמנים. תשט"ז. [4], [ג]—רכ"ב, [2] דף;

הנספחים: [1]: שו"ת הרמב"ם ובנו [כנ"ל]. כ' עמ'. [עם שער מיוחד ותאריך: תשי"ז].

[2]: ספר המנוחה פירושים וחידושים על ספר משנה תורה הלכות חמץ ומצה, שופר, שביתת העשור, סוכה ולולב מאת... רבנו מנוח ב"ר יעקב מנרבונה... סודר ונסדר... לפי... דפוס קונשטנטינא... תע"ח. [עם שער מיוחד, ותאריך: תשי"ז]. מ"א עמ', פקסימיל.

[3]: תשובות רבנו יוסף קורקוס... על קצת דיני הרמב"ם הלכות שבת [מתוך ס' חיים שאל לר' חיד"א]. מ"ג—מ"ו עמ'.

[4]: בית יעקב [כנ"ל עם שער מיוחד ותאריך: תשי"ז]. ט"ו עמ'.

[5]: בינה לעתים. חידושים על הרמב"ם הלכות יום טוב שחיבר הרב... יהונתן... אייבשיץ. סודר ונדפס מחדש... לפי הוצאת וינה [עם שער מיוחד. תאריך: תשי"ז]. כ"ז עמ'. [6]: הגהות ר' עקיבא איגר [כנ"ל] [2] עמ'. [7]: ציורים להלכות קדוש החדש [4] עמ'. [8]: קרית ספר [כנ"ל] עם שער מיוחד, תאריך: תשט"ז], [20] עמ'.

כרך ג: ספר נשים. קדושה. תשי״ז.

ספר נשים. [4], קכ״ח, ל״ו דף ונלווה לו: ספר קובץ על היד החזקה ספר נשים... מהרב... נחום טריביטש... לא נדפס במהדורת וארשה — וילנא המשמש יסוד למהדורתנו זו. והוספנו מתוך היד החזקה מהדורת וינה... [עם שער מיוחד]. [1], ט״ו דף.

ספר קדושה. [1], מ״ד, קכ״ג דף.

הנספחים לשני ספרים הנ״ל [1]: שאלות ותשובות הרמב״ם ובנו ר׳ אברהם [כנ״ל עם שער מיוחד]. ט׳ עמ׳. [2]: בית יעקב [כנ״ל עם שער מיוחד]. ל״ו עמ׳.

[3]: הגהות וחידושים לר׳ עקיבא איגר [כנ״ל]. י׳ עמ׳.

[4]: קרית ספר [כנ״ל עם שער מיוחד]. [40] עמ׳.

כרך ד: ספר הפלאה, זרעים, עבודה, תשי״ז.

ספר הפלאה. [ז], ק״ה דף.

ספר זרעים. [1], ק״ו—קל״ז, ק׳ דף.

ספר העבודה. [1], מ״ד, ע״ח.

הנספחים לשלושת הספרים הנ״ל: [1]: קרית ספר [כנ״ל עם שער מיוחד]. [47] דף. [2]: שו״ת הרמב״ם ובנו ר׳ אברהם ועוד [כנ״ל עם שער מיוחד]. ט, [1] עמ׳. [3]: הגהות ר׳ עקיבא איגר [כנ״ל]. [ג] — ט״ו עמ׳ (חידושי ר׳ יעקב בי רב הנ״ל השייכים לכרך רביעי זה יודפסו בכרך הבא).

כרך ה: ספר קרבנות, טהרה, נזיקין, תשי״ז.

ספר הקרבנות. [5], ע״ט — קלב דף.

ספר טהרה. קמ״א [צ״ל קמב] דף.

ספר נזיקין. [1], ע׳ דף.

הנספחים: [1]: קרית ספר [הנ״ל עם שער מיוחד]. 100 עמ׳. [2]: שאלות ותשובות הרמב״ם ובנו רבנו אברהם [כנ״ל עם שער מיוחד. י׳ דף. [3]: בית יעקב [כנ״ל מיוחד לספר הפלאה עם שער מיוחד לספר הפלאה עם שער מיוחד]. נ״א עמ׳. [4]: הגהות וחדושים מר׳ עקיבא איגר [כנ״ל]. י׳ עמ׳.

כרך ו: ספר קנין, משפטים, שופטים, תשי״ז.

ספר קנין — משפטים.

[5], ס״ד, קל״ד מ״ב דף;

ספר שופטים. קל״ב, דף:

הנספחים: [1]: קרית ספר (כנ״ל עם שער מיוחד). [15] דף;

[2]: שאלות ותשובות הרמב״ם ובנו ר׳ אברהם. 7 עמ׳.

[3]: הלכות מלכים ומלחמותיהם פרק י״א. נוסח מלא, בלתי מצונזר על פי כתבי יד ודפוסים ישנים ערוך ע״י הרב קלמן כהנא. [2], ז׳ פקסימיליות. [4]: השלמה לחידושי מהר״ם פדואה על הרמב״ם. [1] עמ׳. [5]: בית יעקב [כנ״ל עם שער מיוחד]. ל״ד עמ׳. [6]: מפתח הענינים לפי סדר אלף בית. ו׳ עמ׳. — [7]: הגהות ר׳ עקיבא איגר מכי״ק בגליון הרמב״ם שלו [דפוס יעסניץ], ו׳ עמ׳. [8]: ספר קרית מלך... ציוני מקורות רבים על פסקי הרמב״ם לר׳ שי״ח קניבסקי [עם שער מיוחד.

התאריך: תשי"ח]. פ"ו עמ׳. [9]: חידושי ר׳ יהונתן אייבשיץ [כנ"ל]. [1] דף. [10]: דפים מספר משנה תורה מהדורה קמא. כתובים בכתב יד קדשו של רבנו הרמב"ם ועוד [לפי הוצאת ר"מ לוצקי ברמב"ם הוצאת שולזינגר עם שער מיוחד. התאריך: תשי"ח]. [2], י"ט, [4] דף, פקסימליות.

תשי"ז (1957)

44. משנה תורה הוא היד החזקה לרבינו משה בן מימון. מהדורה מנוקדת עם פירוש לעם. ניקד מרדכי דב רבינוביץ.

ירושלים, מוסד הרב קוק. 8°.

ספר א: ספר המדע (מפורש על ידי הרב שמואל תנחום רובינשטיין). ירושלים (דפוס ש. וינפלד), תשי"ז. 8, [ה]—ר"ס עמ׳.

בסופו: תשובות הרמב"ם; מהדורה שניה, שנדפסה מאמהות מהד׳ א׳ תל־אביב, הוצאת "ראשונים", תש"ו) עם קצת שינויים, בהשמטת ההקדמה של יוזם ההוצאה, ר׳ יחיאל רבינוביץ, הסכמות הרבנים והקדמת המפרש ושלשלת הקבלה שבסוף הכרך.

ספר ב: ספר אהבה (מפורש על ידי הרב שמואל תנחום רובינשטיין) ירושלים (דפוס טורים) תשי"ח, [9], ת"ד עמ׳.

— ירושלים (דפוס וינפלד) תשי"ט, [9], ת"ד עמ׳.

מהדורה שניה, שנדפסה מאמהות מהדורה א [תל־אביב הוצאת "ראשונים" תש"ט) עם קצת שינויים, בהשמטת הקדמתו של יוזם ההוצאה הנ"ל והקדמת המפרש.

ספר ג: ספר זמנים. כרך א: הלכ׳ שבת — הלכ׳ שביתת־עשור (מפורש על ידי הרב נתן צבי פרידמן, צבי מאיר רבינוביץ בעריכת הרב מרדכי יהודה ליב זק"ש). ירושלים (דפוס טורים), תשי"ז. 11, שלב, 6 עמ׳. בראשו: הקדמת העורך.

ששת עמודים האחרונים, תשובות הרמב"ם.

ספר ג: ספר זמנים, כרך ב: הלכות שביתת יום־טוב — הלכות מגילה וחנכה. (מפורש על ידי הרב נתן צבי פרידמן, הרב ישראל הלוי בארי, אברהם ארזי, בעריכת הרב מרדכי יהודה ליב זק"ש). ירושלים (דפוס תרבות), תשי"ז. 10. [שלג] — תר"ע עמ׳. בסופו: תשובות הרמב"ם.

בקורת מאת יהושע בראנד, סיני מ"ב (תשי"ח). עמ׳ קצ"א—קצ"ב.

ספר ד: ספר נשים (מפורש על ידי הרב שמואל תנחום רובינשטיין, בעריכת הרב מרדכי יהודה ליב זק"ש).

ירושלים (דפוס סלומון), תשי"ח. 10, [2], תע"ו עמ׳.

עיין גם כן הערותיו של המפרש ספר נשים, "הרמב"ם לעם ופירושיו", סיני, מ"ב (תשי"ח), עמ׳ ש"ו—שי"ב.

ספר ה: ספר קדושה. (מפורש על ידי הרב אריה קרלין בעריכת הרב משה רייך). ירושלים (דפוס ר"ח הכהן), תש"ך. 13, שפ"ד עמ׳.

ראה א. קרלין: "הערות לספר הרמב"ם ונושאי כליו": הלכות איסורי ביאה, סיני, כרך כ"ג (תש"ח), עמ׳ רכ"ח—רל"ח; כ"ד (תש"ט), עמ׳ ע"ט—פ"ה; שי"ח—שכד.

ספר ו: ספר הפלאה. מפורש על ידי הרב שמואל תנחום רובינשטיין), ירושלים (דפוס ר"ח הכהן), תשי"ט. 10, [2], שלה, [1] עמ׳. עמ׳ שכ"ט—שלה: תשובות הרמב"ם.

ספר ז: ספר זרעים. (מפורש על ידי הרב אריה קרלין: כלאים—תרומות; הרב חיים הלוי פרדס: מעשר — שמטה ויובל. בעריכת הרב מרדכי יהודה ליב זק״ש).

ירושלים (דפוס רפאל חיים הכהן), תשכ״ב. 16, תרמ״ח עמ׳. בסופו תשובות הרמב״ם.

ספר ח: ספר עבודה. (מפורש על ידי הרב ש. ד. מנדלסון: בית הבחירה, כלי המקדש והעובדים בו, ביאת המקדש; פרקים: א, ב, ה, ו; הרב זבולון זק״ש: ביאת המקדש, פרקים: ג, ד, ז, ח, ט; איסורי המזבח, מעשה הקרבנות, תמידין ומוספין; הרב משה רייך: פסולי המוקדשין, עבודת יום הכפורים, מעילה.

ערך: הרב מרדכי יהודה ליב זק״ש: בית הבחירה — תמידין ומוספין. ירושלים (דפוס ר. ח. הכהן) תשכ״ג. 12, תרמ״ח עמ׳.

ספר ט: ספר קרבנות. (מפורש על ידי הרב זבולון זק״ש בעריכת הרב מרדכי יהודה ליב זק״ש).

ירושלים (״דפוס העשור״), תש״ד. 10, [2], ש״ז עמ׳.

ספר י: ספר טהרה, כרך א: הלכ׳ טומאת מת — מטמאי משכב ומושב. (מפורש על ידי הרב משה רייך).

ירושלים (דפוס לימודי קרית נוער), תשכ״ב. 15, ש״ט, [1], 14 עמ׳.

ספר י: ספר טהרה, כרך ב: הלכ׳ שאר אבות הטומאות — מקואות (פירוש והשלמות מאה הרב משה רייך).

ירושלים (דפוס רפאל חיים הכהן), תשכ״ד. 14, [שי״א] — תשלז, [1] עמ׳.

ההשלמות: עמ׳ תרצח—תשלז.

ספר יא: ספר נזיקין: (מפורש על ידי אברהם ארזי, בעריכת הרב משה רייך).

ירושלים (דפוס רפאל חיים הכהן), תשי״ט. 11, [1], שכ״ו, [2] עמ׳.

בסופו (עמ׳ שכ״ד—שכ״ו) תשובות הרמב״ם.

ראה, אברהם ארזי: ״הרמב״ם כפשוטו״, סיני, מ״ב (תשי״ח), עמ׳ נ״ז—ס״א, המכיל הערות על הלכות גניבה וגזילה.

ספר יב: ספר קנין. (מפורש על ידי הרב שמחה בונם אורבאך. בעריכת הרב מרדכי יהודה ליב זק״ש).

ירושלים (דפוס רפאל חיים הכהן), תשי״ט. 14, [2], תס״ב, [1] עמ׳.

בסופו תשובות הרמב״ם.

ספר יג: ספר משפטים. (מפורש על ידי הרב יעקב כהן: שכירות — מלוה ולוה (פרקים: א—יד); הרב משה רייך: שאלה ופקדון, מלוה ולוה (פרקים: טו—כז), טוען ונטען, נחלות).

ירושלים (דפוס רפאל חיים הכהן), תשכ״ה. 13, תמה עמ׳.

עמ׳ תיז—תלט: תשובות הרמב״ם; תמ—תמה: השלמות מאת הרב רייך.

ספר י״ד: ספר שופטים. (מפורש על ידי הרב שמואל תנחום רובינשטיין).

ירושלים (דפוס העשור תל־אביב), תשכ״ב. 15, תכ״ז עמ׳. בסופו: תשובות הרמב״ם.

תשי״ט (1959)

44 א. משנה תורה הוא היד החזקה להנשר... רבינו משה בן מימון... עם השגות הראב״ד... ופירוש... המגיד משנה, הכסף משנה להגאון... יוסף קארו... מגדל עז, לרבינו שם טוב ב״ר אברהם בן גאון הספרדי, הגהות מיימוניות [עם תוספות

מדפוס וויניציאה ש"י, שי"א], [עם הוספות הרב... מהר"ם פאדווי"ה...], גם תשובות מיימוניות, ופירושי הרב... עובדיה והרב... מהר"ל בן חביב על הלכות קדוש החודש, עם כל הצורות השייכות להם ולהלכות שבת וסוכה. גם הלחם משנה להגאון ר' אברהם די בוטן... ומשנה למלך להגאון ר' יהודא רוזאניס... ונלווה לו ספר הקובץ חדושים... מהרב... ר' נחום טריביטש... עם שלשים וחמש הוספות כאשר נדפסו בדפוסי ורשא—ווילנא [עיין למעלה, סימן 43].

ועתה במהדורה ישראלית זו הוספנו: צורות הנדסיות צולמו לפי הצורות שנדפסו בהוצאת משנה תורה וויניציאה שנת של"ו; כתב יד הרמב"ם ז"ל; צילומים של קטעים מספר משנה תורה שכתבו בעצם ככתב יד קדשו של הנשר... רבנו משה בן מיימון... שנתגלה בגניזה במצרים. צילומים של דפוס מההוצאות הראשונות יקרות המציאות של משנה תורה, בהן שינויי נוסחאות של ההוצאות האחרונות הנמצאות בידנו שינויי נוסחאות בסדר התפלה ועוד. כל זה וגם המפתח לפי סדר אלף־בית בכרך האחרון.

5 כרכים. ירושלים, פרדס; תל־אביב, תשי"ט; כרך ד—ה: תשכ"ח. 2°.

דפוס צלום של הוצאת וילנה. הנספחים סודרו ונדפסו מחדש.

התכן: כרך א: ספר מדע — אהבה. [2], ד—ט, ע"ד, פ"ז [צ"ל צ"ב]),[1] דף. קודם:

[1]: הקדמה למהדורה הישראלית ועוד. [3] דף, פקסימיל. [2]: ספר המצוות חלק א—ב. ד', פ"ד נ"ו דף. [3]: מפתח הענינים של ספר המצוות לפי ההלכות בספר משנה תורה להרמב"ם; מפתח הענינים של ספר המצוות לפי פרשיות התורה [שניהם מהרב ראובן אליצור]. 5 דף.

כרך ב: ספר זמנים. [3], [ב]—רכ"ב, [1], [2] דפים "צורות השייכות להלכות שבת וסוכה וקידוש החודש";

ספר נשים. [1], קכ"ח, ל"ו דף;

כרך ג: ספר קדושה. [3], מ"ד, קכ"ג;

ספר הפלאה. ק"ה דף;

ספר זרעים. [1], [ק"ו]—קל"ז; ב—ק דף;

כרך ד: ספר עבודה. [3], מ"ד; ב—ע"ח, א דף;

ספר קרבנות. ע"ח, ב—קל"ב דף;

ספר טהרה. [1], [ב]—קמ"א דף;

ספר נזיקין. [1], ע' דף;

כרך ה: ספר קנין — משפט. [3], ס"ד, [1] דף: השלמה לחידושי מהר"ם פדואה... על הרמב"ם שהושמטו בדפוסי ווילנא—ורשה ו"השמטות הצנזורה"; [1], ב—קל"ד, [1], ב—מ"ב דף;

ספר שופטים. קל"ב, [1] דף;

מפתח הענינים לפי סדר אלף בית. ו' עמ'; דפים ממשנה תורה מהדורא קמא כתובים בכתב יד קדשו ערוך על־ידי קלמן כהנא. [2], י"ג, [1] דף ופקסימי' (עם שער מיוחד. תאריך: תשי"ח).

דפוס צילום מהוצאת ורשה — ווילנה מלבד הנספחים. רוב הנספחים שהוכנסו בהוצאת פרדס תשט"ז (עיין מספר 43) הושמטו פה.

תשי״ט (1959)

44ב. משנה תורה הוא היד החזקה להנשר הגדול רבינו משה בר מיימון... עם השגות הראב״ד... ופירוש הרב המגיד משנה, הכסף משנה להגאון... יוסף קארו... מגדל עז, לרבינו שם טוב ב״ר אברהם בן גאון הספרדי, הגהות מיימוניות [עם תוספות מדפוס ויניציה ש״י שי״א] [עם הוספות הרב... מהר״ם פאדוו״ה...] גם תשובות מיימוניות, ופירושי הרב... עובדיה והרב... מהר״ל בן חביב על הלכות קדוש החודש, עם כל הצורות השייכות להם ולהלכות שבת וסוכה. גם הלחם משנה להגאון ר׳ אברהם די בוטן... ומשנה למלך להגאון יהודה רוזאניס ונלווה לו ספר הקובץ... מהרב... נחום טריביטש. עם שלשים וחמש הוספות כאשר נדפסו בדפוסי ורשה—וילנה [עיין למעלה סימן 43].

6 כרכים. תל־אביב: הוצאת ״תורה לעם״ (אופסט ישראל—אמריקה), תשי״ט. 2°.
קודם שער מקוצר.

תוכן: כרך א: מדע. [1], ח, ע״ד דף;
אהבה. פ״ד [צ״ל: צ״ב] דף;
זמנים (עד שביתת עשור). פ״ה, י״ד דף;
כרך ב: זמנים (מהל׳ יום טוב). [2], פ״ו—קפ״ט, ל״ז דף; [2] דפים: צורות השייכות להלכות שבת וסוכה וקידוש החודש.
נשים [1], קכ״ח, ל״ו, ט״ו דף;
ט״ו דפים האחרונים: ס׳ קובץ על נשים שהושמט ברוב ההוצאות המיוסדות על הוצאות ווילנא-–ורשה.
כרך ג: קדושה. [2], מ״ד, קכ״ג דף;
הפלאה. [1], ק״ו דף;
כרך ד: זרעים. [2], ב—ל״ג; ב—ק דף;
עבודה — קרבנות. [1], מ״ד; ב—קל״ב דף;
כרך ה: טהרה. [2], ב—קמ״א דף;
נזיקין. ע׳ דף;
קנין. [1], ס״ד; ב—נ״ב דף;
משפטים. [2], נ״ב; ב—קל״ד; ב—מ״ב דף;
שופטים. [1], קל״ב, [1] דף.
דפוס צלום לפי הוצאת וילנה, תר״ס בהוספת שערים מקוצרים.

תשי״ט (1959)

45. משנה תורה הוא היד החזקה להנשר... רבינו משה בן מיימון... עם השגות הראב״ד...ופירוש הרב המגיד משנה, הכסף משנה, להגאון... יוסף קארו..., מגדל עז לרבינו שם טוב ב״ר אברהם בן גאון הספרדי, הגהות מיימוניות (עם תוספות מדפוס וויניציה ש״י שי״א), [עם הוספות הרב...מהר״ם פאדוו״ה...], גם תשובות מיימוניות, ופירושי הרב... עובדיה והרב... מהר״ל בן חביב על הלכות קדוש החדש, עם כל הצורות השייכות להם ולהלכות שבת וסוכה. גם הלחם משנה להגאון... אברהם די בוטן..., ומשנה למלך להגאון... יהודא רוזאניס... כאשר היו בדפוסי יעסניץ, דיהרנפורט, וויען

וברדיטשוב. ונלווה לו ספר הקובץ חדושים ומקורי דינים מהרב... נחום טריביטש... אבד״ק נ״ש כפי שנדפס בוויען.

עם שלושים וחמש הוספות כפי שנדפסו בדפוסי ווארשה—ווילנה... [עיין למעלה, סימן 43].

ועתה במהדורה ישראלית זו הוספנו עוד... הוספות חדשות... כפי שמבואר בשער הבא...

כרך א: ספר מדע ואהבה. ירושלים. (פרדס; [תל-אביב], בדפוס אופסט ישראלי ליצוא). תשי״ט. 2°.

[ט], עד, פ״ז [צ״ל: צ״ב], [1] דף. ט׳, ס״ט, [27] עמ׳.

דפוס צלום מדפוס וילנה מלבד ההוספות: שו״ת הרמב״ם ובנו ר׳ אברהם וס׳ בית יעקב לר׳ יעקב בירב; חידושי ר׳ יהונתן אייבשיץ, ס׳ קרית ספר לר׳ משה מטראני.

קודם לו: ספר המצות חלק א—ב. [1] ד, פ״ד, נ״ו, [6] דף; כ״ב עמ׳. דפוס צלום מדפוס ורשה מלבד [6] דף וכ״ב עמ׳ המכילים מפתחות וס׳ מעשה נסים.

כרך זה זהה עם הוצאות פרדס תשט״ז (עיין למעלה) ותשכ״ג (עיין להלן). כרך ב—ו בסדר זה הם משנת תשכ״ג. אולי חברת פרדס התחילה להוציא לאור הוצאה חדשה בשנת תשי״ט ונפסקה באמצע. ובשנת תשכ״ג הופיעה הוצאה חדשה ונשאר בינתיים כרך א׳ עם התאריך: תשי״ט.

תשי״ט (1959)

46. משנה תורה הוא היד החזקה להנשר הגדול רבינו משה בר מיימון. עם: השגות הראב״ד ופירוש... המגיד משנה, הכסף משנה... מגדל עז... הגהות מיימוניות... תשובות מיימוניות... הלחם משנה... ומשנה למלך... ונלווה לו ספר הקובץ, חדושים... מהרב... נחום טריביטש. עם שלשים וחמש הוספות... א—ו. ירושלים, פרדס, (דפוס מוזנון), תשי״ט. 4°. קודם שער מקוצר. בכריכת כרך א: ״ספרית מעריב״. הכרכים ד—ו נדפסו ע״י דפוס אופסט ישראלי ליצוא, ת״א.

כרך א: מדע — זמנים (עד שביתת עשור). [3], ד—ט, [1], ע״ד, [1], ב—פ״ז [צ״ל: צ״ב), [2], ב—פ״ה, י״ד דף;

כרך ב: זמנים (עד חנוכה) — נשים. [3], פו—רכ״ב, [2], קכ״ח, ל״ו דף;

כרך ג: קדושה — הפלאה. [3], מ״ד, קכ״ג, [1], ק״ה דף;

כרך ד: זרעים — קרבנות. [3], ב—ק, [1], קל״ב דף;

כרך ה: טהרה — קנין. [3], [ב]—קמ״א, [1], ע׳, [1], ס״ד, [1], ב—נ״ב דף;

כרך ו: משפטים — שופטים. [3], נ״ג—קל״ד; ב—מ״ב, קכ״ח דף.

ד״צ לפי הוצאת ווילנה.

תש״ך (1960)

47. משנה תורה הוא היד החזקה להנשר... רבינו משה בר מיימון... עם השגות הראב״ד... ופירוש הרב המגיד משנה, הכסף משנה להגאון... יוסף קארו..., מגדל עוז; הגהות מיימוניות, גם תשובות מיימוניות, ופירושי הרב... עובדיה והרב... מהר״ל בן חביב על הלכות קדוש החדש, עם כל הצורות השייכות להם ולהלכות שבת וסוכה. גם... הלחם משנה להגאון... אברהם די בוטן... ומשנה למלך להגאון... יהודא רוזאניס...

ה׳ כרכים. ניו־יורק : הוצאת גראסמאן, תש״ך. 8°.

כרך א : מדע. [8], ס״א דף ;
אהבה. [ב] — עט, [1] דף ;
זמנים. [ג] — קפ״ט דף ;
כרך ב : נשים. [1], קכ״ו, ל״ו דף ;
קדושה. מ״ד, [2], קי״א דף ;
כרך ג : הפלאה. זרעים. קל״ז, ב—ק דף ;
כרך ד : עבודה. קרבנות. [1], מ״ד ; ב—קכ״ח דף ;
טהרה. [ב] — קי״ח דף ;
כרך ה : נזיקין. [2], ע׳ דף ;
קנין. משפטים. ס״ג ; קל״ד ; ב—מ״א דף ;
שופטים. ק״ח דף.

דפוס צלום מוקטן מהוצאת ורשה—וילנה בלי ההוספות שבסופי הספרים.

תשכ״א (1961)

48. ספר משנה תורה הוא היד החזקה לרבינו משה בר מיימון, עם כל המפרשים... חלק א—ה. ירושלים, ״המאור הגדול״, (דפוס ש. מונזון), תשכ״א. 8°. ספירת העמודים אינה מתאימה תמיד לחלוקת הספרים).

התכן : א : מדע, אהבה, זמנים. [2], ב—ח, ס״א ; ע״ט ; קפ״ט דף ; ב : נשים, קדושה. [2], קכ״ו, ל״ו ; [1], מ״ד, קי״א דף ; — ג : הפלאה זרעים. [2], ק״ה ; [1], ק״ו—קל״ז ; ב—צ״ט דף ; — ד : עבודה, קרבנות טהרה [2], מ״ד ; ב—קכ״ח : קי״ח דף ; — ה : נזיקין, קנין, משפטים, שופטים. [2], ע ; ס״ג ; ב—קל״ד ; ב—מ״א ; ק״ה דף.
ד״צ מוקטן לפי הוצ׳ וילנא תר״ס ואילך. עם שער מפורט לרובם של י״ד הספרים.

תשכ״א (1961)

49. משנה תורה הוא היד החזקה להנשר... רבינו משה בר מיימון... עם השגות הראב״ד... ופירוש הרב המגיד משנה, וכסף משנה להגאון... יוסף קארו..., מגדל עוז הגהות מיימוניות [עם תוספות מדפוס ווינציה ש״י שי״א], גם תשובות מיימוניות, ופירושי הרב... עובדיה והרב... מהר״ל בן חביב על הלכות קדוש החדש, עם כל הצורות השייכות להם ולהלכות שבת וסוכה.. גם הלחם משנה להגאון... אברהם די בוטן... ומשנה למלך הגאון... יהודה רוזאניס... כאשר היו בדפוסי יעסניץ, דיהרנפורט, וויען וברדיטשוב. ונלוה לו ספר הקובץ חדושים ומקורי דינים מהרב... נחום טריביטש... אבד״ק נ״ש כפי שנדפס בוויען.

ה׳ כרכים.

ניו־יורק : דפוס והוצאת סיני אופסעט קא. (ובשערים של כרך ג—ה : דפוס והוצאת אברהם יצחק פריעדמאן). 8°.

כרך א : תשכ״א. מדע. [1], ח׳ ע״ד דף ;
אהבה. פ״ז [צ״ל : צ״ב] דף.
זמנים. קפ״ט דף.
כרך ב : תשכ״א. נשים. [2], קכ״ח, [1], ל״ו דף ;

קדושה. מ"ד, ט"ו דף;

ט"ו דפים האחרונים: ספר קובץ על־יד החזקה על נשים שנדפס בהוצאת ווין ונשמט מהוצאות ברלין, ורשה—וילנה.

כרך ג: תשכ"ג. קדושה (המשך). [1], קי"א דף;
הפלאה. זרעים. [1], קל"ז; ב'—ק' דף;

כרך ד: תשכ"ג. עבודה. קרבנות. [1], מ"ד: ב'—קכ"ח דף;
טהרה. קי"ח דף;

כרך ה: תשכ"ג. נזיקין. [2], ע' דף;
קנין, משפטים. ס"ג; ב'—קל"ד; ב'—מ"א דף;
שופטים. ק"ח דף.

דפוס צלום מוקטן של הוצאת ורשה—וילנה. אולם ההוספות (א'—י') שנמנו בשער כרך א' (כבשערים שבדפוס וילנה) נשמטו מכרך ב'—ה', ונדפסו רק בסוף ספר המדע.

תשכ"ב (1962)

50. משנה תורה הוא היד החזקה להנשר... רבינו משה בר מיימון... עם השגות הראב"ד... ופירוש הרב המגיד משנה, וכסף משנה להגאון... יוסף קארו..., מגדל עוז, הגהות מיימוניות [עם תוספות מדפוס וויניציה ש"י שי"א], גם תשובות מיימוניות, ופירושי הרב... עובדיה והרב... מהר"ל בן חביב על הלכות קדוש החדש, עם כל הצורות השייכות להם ולהלכות שבת וסוכה. גם הלחם משנה להגאון... אברהם די בוטן..., ומשנה למלך להגאון... יהודה רוזאניס... כאשר היו בדפוסי יעסניץ, דיהרנפורט, וויען וברדיטשוב. ונלווה לו ספר הקובץ חדושים ומקורי דינים מהרב... נחום טריביטש... אבד"ק נ"ש כפי שנדפס בוויען.

ועתה הוספנו חדשות אשר לא היו מעולם בכל ספרי הרמב"ם הנדפסים... [עם שלושים וחמש הוספות כפי שנדפסו בדפוסי ווארשה—ווילנה]:

(א) פירוש המגיד משנה על הלכות שחיטה...

(ב) פירוש הרדב"ז על ספר קדושה, הפלאה, זרעים, שופטים, ממלא מקום המגיד משנה שלא נמצא בספרים האלה...

(ג) חדושים ומקורי דינים מהרב... בעל פרי חדש, נקראים בשם מים חיים.

(ד) חדושים ומקורי הדינים מהרב... בעל מחנה אפרים.

(ה) חדושים ומקורי הדינים מהרב... ישעיה פיק...

(ו) ביאורים על הלכות בית הבחירה מהרב... יעקב עמדין...

(ז) השמטות מתוספות הגהמי"י, מדפוס וויניציאה, שנת ש"י, שי"א.

(ח) חדושים מהרב... מהר"ם פאדווה...

(ט) חדושים ומקורים מהרב... אברהם... אבד"ק פ"פ דמיין.

(י) חדושים ומקורים מהרב... זלמן... אחי מוהר"ח... מוולאזין.

(יא) חדושים ומקורים מהרב... צבי הירש חיות...

(יב) חדושים ומקורים מהרב... יוסף... בעל ספר מנחת חינוך.

(יג) חדושים ומקורים מהרב... אברהם משכיל לאיתן...

(יד) חדושים ומקורים מהרב... שמואל שטראשון...

(טו) חדושים ומקורים מהרב... בצלאל הכהן... מווילנא.

*(טז) חדושים ומקורים הגיעו אלינו מהרב... ר"ש ארינשטיין... אבד"ק אזירקאוו [והם מחתנו ר' נחום א"ש]

(יז) חדושים ומקורים מהרב... משה נחום... אבד"ק קאמינקא.

(יח) חדושים ומקורים מהרב... אברהם יונה יעוונין...מהוראדנא.

(יט) ביאור בפרק י"ז מקידוש החדש מהרב... התוכן ר' רפאל מק"ק הנובר...

(כ) ע"ד כתיבת שירת הים ושירת האזינו, מס' שתי ידות להרב... ר"מ די לונזאנו...

עם הרבה הוספות חדשות כמבואר מעבר לדף:

[(א) חידושי רבינו... אליהו... מווילנא...

(ב) טורי אבן, חדושים וביאורים מאת הרב... אלעזר רוקח.. .אב"ד בק"ק בראד ובק"ק אמשטרדם... (ובתוכם הגהות וציונים ומ"מ מנינו ומנכדו הרב... לוי חיים... דומ"ץ בק"ק ווילנא).

(ג) כתר תורה חידושים והגהות... מאת הרב... לוי הקדוש... אבד"ק קאדני... (נוספו עליהם ציונים ומ"מ מבן נכדו הרב... לוי חיים...)...

(ד) בנין שלמה, באורים וחדושים מהרב... שלמה קלוגר...מבראד...

(ה) יד דוד, הערות וציונים מהרב... דוד לוריא... מביחאוו ישן...

(ו) נמוקי הגרי"ב, מהרב יהודה בכרך... אבד"ק סיניי...

(ז) בן אריה, חדושים, הערות וציונים, ומ"מ מהרב... זאב בן אריה... אבד"ק גאלדינגען... וטעלז, בעהמ"ה הגהות בן אריה על כל הש"ס (ובתוכם הערות וציונים מאת נכדו הרב... אריה ליב...)...

(ח) באר אברהם, הערות וציונים מהרב... אברהם שמעון טרויב.. .אבד"ק קיידאן...

(ט) מעשה ר"ב, חדושים וביאורים מהרב... בצלאל הכהן... מ"ץ דווילנא... ועתה הגיעו לידינו עוד הוספות ע"י אחיו, הרב... שלמה הכהן... מ"ץ דווילנא, ובתוכם גם הערות ממוהר"ש הנ"ל...

(י) נמוקי מהרא"י מהרב... אברהם יונה יעוונין... מהוראדנא...

(יא) חשק שלמה, חידושים וביאורים מהרב... שלמה הכהן... מ"ץ דווילנא...

(יב) בני בנימין, הערות וציונים מהרב... אלי' דוד ראבינאוויץ... אבד"ק מירא... (ובתוכם הערות וחידושי מר אביו הרב... בנימין... אבד"ק ווילקומיר, וגם מאחיו הגאון... יהודה צבי... אבד"ק ליגום)...

(יג) הערות וביאורים מהרב...דובער קאראסיק... אב"ד דק"ק קראלעוויץ...

(יד) בנין יהושע, חידושים וביאורים מהרב... יהושע לאנג...

[(טו) עזוז חיל, מקורות והערות מהל' יסודי התורה עד הל' שחיטה מאת הרב... חיים יהודה לייב אייגש... מקובנו, ובסוף ימיו בירושלים].

ואלו הן ההוספות החדשות שאנו נותנים בהוצאה זו:

(א) ספר ברכת אברהם הוא תשו' לרבינו אברהם בן הרמב"ם ז"ל על שאלות והשגות שעשה רבינו דניאל הבבלי ז"ל. בכרך ב'.

(ב) ספר בינה לעתים, על הרמב"ם הל' יו"ט, למרנא ורבנא הרבי ר' יהונתן זצ"ל. בכרך ב'.

---

* ראה הערתנו, למעלה, בסוף הוצאת ווילנא, תר"ס (מספר 26).

(ג) לשונות הרמב"ם מהגאון הקדוש בעל אור החיים זצ"ל, נדפס מספר ראשון לציון. בכרך א'.

(ד) חידושי קובץ על יד על הל' אישות שבהוצאת ווינה. בכרך ג'.

(ה) חידושים מספר שער המלך עם הגהות טעם המלך, ומעשה חושב, והגהות מהרש"ק, והגהות הרב הגאון יוסף שאול נטנזאהן זצ"ל.

(ו) הגהות ישועות מלכו להגאון ר' יהושע ז"ל מקוטנא. בכרך א'.

(ז) הגהות אוצר המלך להגאון הקדוש רבינו צדוק הכהן ז"ל מלובלין.

(ח) כללי הרמב"ם מהגאון האדיר מהרש"ם ז"ל מבערזשאן, נדפס מספר דרכי שלום.

(ט) חידושי רבינו חיים הלוי לרבינו הגאון החסיד רשכבה"ג ר' חיים הלוי זצוק"ל סאלאווייציק.

6 כרכים. ניו־יארק ,הוצאת רמב"ם, דפוס מ. פ. פרעסס, תשכ"ב. 2°.

התוכן:

א: ספר מדע, אהבה, זמנים (עד הל' שביתת עשור). [1], ח, ע"ד, פ"ז [צ"ל: צ"ב]; פה ,י"ד, ט"ו [7] דף.

ב: ספר זמנים (מהל' שביתת יום טוב). [2], פ"ו — רכב, [1, 63] דף, ציורים.

ג: ספר נשים, קדושה (עד הל' אסורי ביאה). [2], קכ"ח, ל"ו, מ"ד, י"ג [צ"ל: ט"ו], [15] דף.

ד: ספר קדושה (מהל' מאכלות אסורות), הפלאה, זרעים. [2], ק"כ; [1], קל"ז; ק, [10] דף.

ה: ספר עבודה, קרבנות, טהרה. [2], מ"ד; קל"ב; קל"ב, [18], קל"ג—קמא, [7] דף, פקס'. ונוסף בכרך זה ספר מעשה רוקח על אהבה וזמנים

ו: ספר נזיקין, קנין, משפטים, שופטים. [3], ע, ס"ד; קל"ד; [2], מ"ב, קל"ב, [17] דף.

ונוסף בכרך זה הגהות עין חנוך מר' חנוך העניך והערות בהרמב"ם מהרב ר' ירוחם לײנער מראדזין ומפתח לספרי והלכות הרמב"ם ע"פ סדר א"ב מאת הרב יוסף כהן.

דפוס צלום מדפוס ווילנא, תר"ס מלבד ט' ההוספות האחרונות.

תשכ"ב (1962)

51. משנה תורה... לרבנו משה ברבי מימון הובא לדפוס בפעם הראשונה על פי כתב יד בגנזי אוקספורד עם הקדמה, מראי מקומות, הערות ותרגום אנגלי ע"י משה חיים חיימזאהן. ירושלים: הוצאת "קריה נאמנה" (דפוס אופסט לימודי קרית נוער), תשכ"ב. 8°.

ספר המדע. [4], xiii,[3], 1 א—93 א, [2] עמ'.

שער נוסף באנגלית:

Mishneh Torah. The Book of Knowledge by Maimonides. Edited according to the Bodleian (Oxford) Codex with Introduction, Biblical and Talmudical references, notes and English translation by Moses Hyamson.

ספר אהבה.. .ומלווה מראי מקומות והערות ע"י הרב חיים מרדכי הכהן ברכר.

[4] דף, [1] עמ', עמ' 93ב—165א, 93 b—165a, [1], עמ'.

שער נוסף באנגלית:

Mishneh Torah. The Book of Adoration by Maimonides Edited according to the Bodleian (Oxford) Codex with an English translation by Moses Hyamson. The Talmudical references and Hebrew footnotes by . . . Chaim M. Brecher.

דפוס צלום לפי הוצאת ניו יארק, תרצ״ז—תש״ט.

תשכ״ג (1963)

52. משנה תורה הוא היד החזקה להנשר... רבינו משה בן מיימון... עם השגות הראב״ד... ופירוש הרב המגיד משנה, הכסף משנה להגאון... יוסף קארו..., מגדל עז לרבינו שם טוב הספרדי, הגהות מיימוניות [עם תוספות מדפוס וויניציה ש״י שי״א], [עם הוספות הרב... מהר״ם פאדוו״ה...], גם תשובות מיימוניות, ופירושי הרב... עובדיה והרב... מהר״ל בן חביב על הלכות קדוש החודש, גם הלחם משנה להגאון... אברהם די בוטן..., ומשנה למלך להגאון... יהודא רוזאניס... ונלוה לו ספר הקובץ חדושים ומקורי הדינים מהרב... נחום טריביטש... אבד״ק ניקלשבורג.

עם שלשים וחמש [צ״ל: ושש] הוספות כפי שנדפסו בדפוסי ווארשה—ווילנה:

(א) פירוש המגיד משנה על הלכות שחיטה...

(ב) פירוש הרדב״ז על ספר קדושה, הפלאה, זרעים, שופטים, ממלא מקום ממגיד משנה שלא נמצא בספרים האלה...

(ג) חדושים ומקורי הדינים מהרב... בעל פרי חדש, נקראים בשם מים חיים.

(ד) חדושים ומקורי הדינים מהרב... בעל מחנה אפרים.

(ה) חדושים ומקורי הדינים מהרב... ישעיה פיק...

(ו) ביאורים על הלכות בית הבחירה מהרב... יעקב עמדין...

(ז) השמטות מתוספות הגהמי״, מדפוס וויניציאה, שנת ש״י, שי״א.

(ח) חדושים מהרב... מהר״ם פאדווה...

(ט) חדושים ומקורים מהרב... אברהם... אבד״ק פ״פ דמיין...

(י) חדושים ומקורים מהרב... זלמן... אחי מוהר״ח... מוולאזין.

(יא) חדושים ומקורים מהרב... צבי הירש חיות...

(יב) חדושים ומקורים מהרב... יוסף... בעל ספר מנחת חינוך...

(יג) חדושים ומקורים מהרב... אברהם משכיל לאיתן...

(יד) חדושים ומקורים מהרב... שמואל שטראשון...

(טו) חדושים ומקורים מהרב... בצלאל הכהן... מווילנא...

*(טז) חדושים ומקורים מהרב... ר״ש ארינשטיין... אבד״ק אזירקאוו [והם מחתנו ר׳ נחום א״ש].

(יז) חדושים ומקורים מהרב... משה נחום... אבד״ק קאמינקא...

(יח) חדושים ומקורים מהרב... אברהם יונה יעוונין... מהוראדנא...

(יט) ביאור בפרק י״ז מקידוש החדש מהרב... התוכן ר׳ רפאל מק״ק הנובר...

(כ) ע״ד כתיבת שירת הים ושירת האזינו, מס׳ שתי ידות להרב... ר״מ די לונזאנו...

(כא) חידושי רבינו... אליהו... מווילנא...

(כב) טורי אבן, חדושים וביאורים מאת הרב... אלעזר רוקח... אבד"ק ברוד ואמשטרדם (ובתוכם הגהות וציונים ומ"מ מנינו הרב... לוי חיים... רומ"ץ בק"ק ווילנא).

(כג) כתר תורה חידושים והגהות מאת הרב... לוי הקדוש... אבד"ק קאדני... ונוספו עליהם ציונים ומ"מ מנינו הרב... לוי חיים...

(כד) בנין שלמה, באורים וחדושים מהרב... שלמה קלוגר... מברוד.

(כה) יד דוד, הערות וציונים מהרב... דוד לוריא... מביכוב ישן...

(כו) נמוקי הגרי"ב, מהרב יהודה בכרך... אבד"ק סיניי.

(כז) בן אריה, חדושים, הערות וציונים, ומ"מ מהרב... זאב בן אריה... אבד"ק טעלז, (ובתוכם הערות וציונים מאת נכדו הרב... אריה ליב...).

(כח) באר אברהם, הערות וציונים מהרב... אברהם שמעון טרויב... אבד"ק קיידאן...

(כט) מעשה ר"ב, חדושים וביאורים מהרב... בצלאל הכהן... מ"ץ דווילנא, והוספות ע"י אחיו, הרב... הרב שלמה הכהן... מ"ץ דווילנא, ובתוכם גם הערות ממוהר"ש הנ"ל...

(ל) נמוקי מהרא"י, מהרב... יונה יעוונין... מהוראדנא...

(לא) חשק שלמה, חידושים וביאורים מהרב... שלמה הכהן... מ"ץ דווילנא...

(לב) בני בנימין, הערות וציונים מהרב... אלי' דוד ראבינאוויץ... אבד"ק מירא. (ובסוף ימיו רב ראשי בירושלים ת"ו) ובתוכם הערות וחידושי מר אביו הרב... בנימין... אבד"ק וילקומיר, וגם מאחיו הגאון... יהודה צבי... אבד"ק ליגום...

(לג) הערות ובאורים מהרב... דובער קאראסיק... אב"ד דק"ק קראלעוויץ...

(לד) בנין יהושע, חידושים וביאורים מהרב... יהושע לאנג...

(לה) עזוז חיל, מקורות והערות מהל' יסודי התורה עד הל' שחיטה מאת הרב... חיים יהודה לייב אייגש... מקובנו, ובסוף ימיו בירושלים.

ועתה במהדורה ישראלית זו הוספנו עוד שתים-עשרה הוספות חדשות... מהן כמה ספרים... מכתבי יד ודפוסים עתיקים כפי שמבואר בשער הבא:

[(א) שאלות ותשובות לרבנו משה בן מיימון... השאלות והתשובות שלוקטו מתוך הספר "תשובות הרמב"ם" ועוד, שייכות כולן לספר משנה תורה, ונדפסו חלקים חלקים חלקים, בכל כרך, השו"ת השייכות להלכות שבאותו כרך.

(ב) שאלות ותשובות לרבנו אברהם בן הרמב"ם... גם שו"ת אלו שייכות כולן לספר משנה תורה ולוקטו מתוך הספרים "תשובות רבנו אברהם בן הרמב"ם" (שהו"ל רא"ח פריימן, המו"ל גם של תשובות הרמב"ם הנ"ל, בתרגומו של רש"ד גויטיין, ע"י חברת "מקיצי נרדמים" בירושלים תרצ"ח), "ברכת אברהם", תשובות רבנו אברהם לשאלותיו והשגותיו של רבי דניאל הבבלי על ספר משנה תורה (ליק תר"ך) ועוד.

(ג) ספר המנוחה, לרבנו מנוח בן ר' יעקב מנרבונה... פירושים וחידושים על ספר משנה תורה, הלכות חמץ ומצה, שופר, שביתת העשור, סוכה ולולב. לפי הוצאת קושטא שנת תע"ח...

(ד) בית יעקב והוא פירוש רבינו יעקב בירב... על ספר משנה תורה. ונמצאים בתוך פירוש זה קטעים שונים ממחבר קדמון בלתי נודע. יוצא לאור בפעם הראשונה מתוך כתב יד, הנמצא בבית הספרים של האוניברסיטה בקמברידג'. הועתק והוגה היטב על ידי קבוצת תלמידי חכמים בירושלים.

(ה) קרית ספר, לרבנו משה מטראני... נדפס חלקים חלקים, בכל כרך הדברים השייכים להלכות הנמצאות בו. הספר הוגה וצולם מתוך הוצאת ווארשה שהיא המדויקת בהוצאות של "קרית ספר".

(ו) שאלות ותשובות רבנו יוסף קורקוס... מיוצאי גירוש ספרד — על הלכות שבת הוגהו וסודרו מחדש לפי שנדפסו על ידי מרן הרב החיד"א ז"ל, בסוף ספרו חיים שאל, ח"ב בליוורנו שנת תקנ"ב.

(ז) ספר הקובץ, לרבנו נחום טריביטש... על הלכות אישות. צולם מחדש לפי הוצאת משנה תורה בווינה...

(ח) חידושי רבינו יהונתן אייבשיץ... על הלכות תפלה, איסורי ביאה, ביכורים, נחלות, עדות, מלכים ועוד (לפי הספר חסדי יהונתן), הלכות יום טוב (לפי הספר בינה לעתים). הוגהו בהגהה מדויקת וסודרו מחדש.

(ט) הגהות וחידושי רבנו עקיבא איגר... על משנה תורה. הועתקו מתוך כתי"ק ונדפסו בווארשה בשנת תרפ"ו על ידי הגאון מוהר"ר מנחם מנדיל כשר.

(י) צורות הנדסיות להלכות קידוש החודש, השייכות לפירוש רבנו לוי בן חביב... צולמו לפי הצורות שנדפסו בהוצאות משנה תורה באמסטרדם ווינה.

(יא) מפתח העינים לפי סדר אלף בית של כל ההלכות הנמצאות בי"ד ספרי משנה תורה, כפי שנמצא בבית מדרשו של הרב המובהק כמוהר"ר ברוך עוזיאל חזק... ונדפס בהוצאת משנה תורה וויניציאה שנת של"ו.

(יב) כתב יד הרמב"ם... צילומים של קטעים מספר משנה תורה שנכתבו בעצם כתב יד קדשו של הנשר הגדול רבנו משה בן מיימון.. .שנתגלה בגניזה במצרים. צילומים של דפים מההוצאות הראשונות יקרות המציאות של משנה תורה, בהן שינויי נוסחאות של ההוצאות האחרונות הנמצאות בידינו. שינויי נוסחאות בסדר התפלה ועוד. כל זה וגם המפתח לפי סדר אלף בית — בכרך האחרון, הששי להוצאה זו.

(יג) הלכות מלכים ומלחמותיהם, פרק י"א, נוסח מלא, בלתי מצונזר, של פרק זה בספר שופטים שבמשנה תורה הוא היד החזקה מאת הרמב"ם... עפ"י כתבי יד ודפוסים ישנים, בצירוף מבוא ושינויי נוסחאות. ערוך ע"י הרב קלמן בן מוהר"ר בנימין זאב... כהנא.

(יד) הערות חשובות בהרמב"ם, מאת הרב הגאון המפורסם רבי ירוחם ליינער... מראדזין.

(טו) ספר קרית מלך, בו ציוני מקורות רבים על פסקי הרמב"ם... במקומות אשר רבותינו נושאי כליו הניחו חלק והניחו מקום להתגדר להבאים אחריהם. גם תקוני טעות סופר אשר בדפוס ווילנא מאת הרב שי"ח בהגרי"י... קניבסקי.

6 כרכים, ירושלים, פרדס; [תל-אביב], דפוס חברה ישראל—אמריקה להדפסת אופסט תשכ"ג. 2°. גוף הספר (לו פירושים הראשונים) דפוס צלום של הוצאת ורשה—ווילנה. הנספחים (א'—ט"ו הנ"ל) סודרו ונדפסו מחדש. לרובם שערים מיוחדים.

התכן: כרך א: ספר מדע, ספר אהבה. [3], ד—ט, עד, פ"ז [צ"ל: צ"ב], [1] דף. קודם: [1]: הקדמה למהדורה הישראלית. ה', [1] עמ'. [2]: ספר המצוות חלק א'—ב'. ד, פד, נ"ו דף. [3]: ספר מעשה נסים... שאלות ר' דניאל הבבלי על ספר המצוות... ותשובות רבנו אברהם [בן הרמב"ם, לפי דפוס פאריס תרכ"ז, הוכן על-ידי הרב קלמן כהנא]. כ"ב עמ' (עם שער מיוחד). [4]: תשובות רבנו אברהם בן הרמב"ם

לספר המצות. השלמה להשגות הרמב"ן (י"ל ע"י ר' חיים הליר מתוך ספר המצות שלו, מהדורה שניה, ירושלים — ניו־יורק, תש"ו); מפתח הענינים של ספר המצות לפי ההלכות בספר משנה תורה להרמב"ם; מפתח הענינים של ספר המצות לפי פרשיות התורה [שניהם מהרב ראובן אליצור]. [6] דף.

הנספחים: [1]: שאלות ותשובות הרמב"ם... ובנו רבנו אברהם השייכות לספר משנה תורה ומסודרות לפיו, מלוקטות מתוך ספר שו"ת הרמב"ם, שו"ת רבנו אברהם בן הרמב"ם, "ברכת אברהם" ועוד. עם מפתח השו"ת [עם שער מיוחד]. ט' עמ'. [2]: בית יעקב והוא פירוש רבנו יעקב בירב... על ספר משנה תורה להרמב"ם... ועוד ממחבר בלתי נודע, יוצא לאור בפעם הראשונה מתוך כתב יד הנמצא בספריה האוניברסיטאית בקמברידג'. [עם שער מיוחד]. ס"ט עמ'. [3]: הגהות וחדושים מאת רבנו עקיבא איגר... [3] עמ'. [4]: קרית ספר. חברו... רבנו משה מטראנ"י [המבי"ט]... [צלום מדפוס ורשה עם שער מיוחד]. 24 עמ'.

כרך ב: ספר זמנים. [3], רכ"ב, [1] דף.

הנספחים: [1]: שו"ת הרמב"ם ובנו [כנ"ל]. כ' עמ' [עם שער מיוחד, בלי תאריך].

[2]: ספר המנוחה פירושים וחידושים על ספר משנה תורה הלכות חמץ ומצה, שופר, שביתות העשור, סוכה ולולה מאת... רבנו מנוח ב"ר יעקב מנרבונה... סודר ונדפס... לפי דפוס קונשטנטינא... תע"ח. [עם שער מיוחד, בלי תאריך]. מ"א עמ', פקסימיל.

[3]: תשובות רבנו יוסף קורקוס... על קצת דיני הרמב"ם הלכות שבת [מתוך ס' חיים שאל לר' חיד"א]. מ"ג—מ"ו עמ'.

[4]: בית יעקב [כנ"ל עם שער מיוחד בלי תאריך]. 15 עמ'.

[5]: בינה לעתים. חידושים על הרמב"ם הלכות יום טוב שחיבר הרב... יהונתן... אייבשיץ. סודר ונדפס מחדש... לפי הוצאת וינה [עם שער מיוחד. בלי תאריך]. כ"ז עמ'.

[6]: הגהות ר' עקיבא איגר [כנ"ל]. [2] עמ'.

[7]: ציורים להלכות קידוש החדש. [4] עמ'.

[8]: קרית ספר [כנ"ל], עם שער מיוחד בלי תאריך. [10] דף.

כרך ג: ספר נשים. קדושה.

ספר נשים. [4], קכ"ח, ל"ו דף ונלוה לו: ספר קובץ על היד החזקה ספר נשים... מהרב... נחום טריביטש... לא נדפס במהדורת וארשה—וילנא המשמש יסוד למהדורתנו זו. והוספנו מתוך היד החזקה מהדורת וינה... [עם שער מיוחד]. [1], ט"ו דף.

ספר קדושה. מ"ד, קכ"ג דף.

הנספחים לשני ספרים הנ"ל: [1]: שאלות ותשובות הרמב"ם ובנו ר' אברהם [כנ"ל עם שער מיוחד]. ט' עמ'. [2]: בית יעקב [כנ"ל עם שער מיוחד]. ל"ו עמ'. [3]: הגהות וחידושים לר' עקיבא איגר, וחידושי ר' יהונתן אייבשיץ. [כנ"ל]. י עמ'. [4]: קרית ספר [כנ"ל עם שער מיוחד]. [20] דף.

כרך ד: ספר הפלאה, זרעים, עבודה.

ספר הפלאה. [4], ק״ה דף.

ספר זרעים. [1], ק״ו—קל״ז; ב—ק דף.

ספר העבודה. [1], מ״ד, ע״ח דף.

הנספחים לשלושת הספרים הנ״ל: [1]: קרית ספר [כנ״ל עם שער מיוחד]. [47] דף. [2]: שו״ת הרמב״ם ובנו ר׳ אברהם ועוד [כנ״ל עם שער מיוחד]. ט, [1] עמ׳. [3]: הגהות ר׳ עקיבא איגר [כנ״ל]. [ג] — ט״ו עמ׳. (חידושי ר׳ יעקב בי רב הנ״ל השייכים לכרך רביעי זה יודפסו בכרך הבא).

כרך ה: ספר קרבנות. טהרה. נזיקין.

ספר הקרבנות. [4], ע״ח, ב—קל״ב דף.

ספר טהרה. קמ״א דף.

ספר נזיקין. [1], ע׳ דף.

הנספחים:

[1]: קרית ספר [הנ״ל עם שער מיוחד]. 100 ע׳.

[2]: שאלות ותשובות הרמב״ם ובנו רבנו אברהם [כנ״ל עם שער מיוחד]. י׳ דף.

[3]: בית יעקב [כנ״ל לספר הפלאה עם שער מיוחד]. נ״א ע׳.

[4]: הגהות וחידושים מר׳ עקיבא איגר [כנ״ל]. י׳ עמ׳.

[5]: הערות ברמב״ם מאת ר׳ ירוחם ליינער מראדזין. 8 עמ׳. (ולא נדפס בהוצאת פרדס, תשט״ז).

[6]: ספר קרית מלך . . . לר׳ שי״ח קניבסקי, עם שער מיוחד. פ״ו עמ׳.

[7]: מפתח הענינים לפי סדר א״ב. ו׳ עמ׳.

כרך ו: ספר קנין, משפטים, שופטים.

ספר קנין — משפטים. [4], ס״ד, קל״ד, מ״ב דף.

ספר שופטים. קל״ב דף; [1] עמ׳.

הנספחים:

[1]: קרית ספר (כנ״ל עם שער מיוחד). [15] דף.

[2]: שאלות ותשובות הרמב״ם ובנו ר׳ אברהם. 7, [1] עמ׳, פקסמיל.

[3]: הלכות מלכים ומלחמותיהם פרק י״א. נוסח מלא, בלתי מצונזר על פי כתבי יד ודפוסים ישנים ערוך על־ידי הרב קלמן כהנא. ו׳, [2] עמ׳, פקסימי׳.

[4]: השלמה חידושי מהר״ם פדואה על הרמב״ם. [1] עמ׳.

[5]: בית יעקב [כנ״ל עם שער מיוחד]. ל״ד עמ׳.

[6]: הגהות ר׳ עקיבא איגר מכי״ק בגליון הרמב״ם שלו [דפוס יעסניץ]. ו׳ עמ׳.

[7]: חידושי ר׳ יהונתן אייבשיץ [כנ״ל]. [1] דף.

[8]: דפים מספר משנה תורה מהדורה קמא. כתובים בכתב יד קדשו של רבינו הרמב״ם ועוד [לפי הוצאת ר״מ לוצקי ברמב״ם הוצאת שולזינגר עם שער מיוחד]. [2], י״ט, [4] עמ׳, פקסימיליות.

[9]: אחרית דבר. [1] עמ׳.

דפוס צילום מהוצאה זו עיין סימן 62 להלן.

---

* ראה הערתנו, למעלה, בסוף הוצאת וילנה, תר״ס (מספר 26).

תשכ"ג (1963)

53. משנה תורה הוא היד החזקה להנשר... רבינו משה בר מיימון... עם השגות הראב"ד... ופירוש הרב המגיד משנה, וכסף משנה להגאון... יוסף קארו..., מגדל עז [עם תוספות מדפוס ויניציאה ש"י שי"א], גם תשובות מיימוניות, ופירושי הרב... עובדיה והרב... מהר"ל בן חביב על הלכות קדוש החדש, עם כל הצורות השייכות להם ולהלכות שבת וסוכה. גם הלחם משנה להגאון... אברהם די בוטן..., ומשנה למלך להגאון... יהודה רוזאניס... כאשר היו בדפוסי יעסניץ, דיהרנפורט, וויען וברדיטשוב. ונלוה לו ספר הקובץ חדושים ומקורי דינים מהרב... נחום טריביטש... אבד"ק נ"ש כפי שנדפס בוויען.

ועתה הוספנו חדשות אשר לא היו מעולם בכל ספרי הרמב"ם הנדפסים... [עם שלשים וחמשה תוספות כפי שנדפסו בדפוסי ווארשה—ווילנה] : *

ואלה הן ההוספות החשובות שאנו נותנים בהוצאה זו :

(א) חידושי אור שמח לרבינו מאיר שמחה הכהן זצ"ל על הרמב"ם.

(ב) ספר ברכת אברהם הוא תשו' לרבינו אברהם בן הרמב"ם ז"ל על שאלות והשגות שעשה רבינו דניאל הבבלי ז"ל. בכרך ב'.

(ג) ספר בינה לעתים, על הרמב"ם הל' יו"ט, למרנא ורבנא הרבי ר' יהונתן ז"ל בכרך ב'.

(ד) לשונות הרמב"ם מהגאון הקדוש בעל אור החיים זצ"ל נדפס מספר ראשון לציון. בכרך א'.

(ה) חידושי קובץ על יד על הל' אישות שבהוצאת ווינה. בכרך ג.

(ו) ביאורים מהגאון ר' יעקב מעמדין ז"ל על הל' בית הבחירה, נדפס מס' לחם שמים. כרך ה'.

(ז) הגהות ישועות מלכו להגאון ר' יהושע ז"ל מקוטנא. בכרך א'.

(ח) הגהות אוצר המלך להגאון הקדוש רבינו צדוק הכהן ז"ל מלובלין.

(ט) כללי הרמב"ם מהגאון האדיר מהרש"ם ז"ל מבערזשאן, נדפס מספר דרכי שלום.

(י) מאמר דרכי משה להגאון מהר"צ חיות ז"ל. בכרך א'.

ואחרון אחרון חביב נספח הספר הכי חשוב מרכבת המשנה להגאון ר' שלמה מחלמא ז"ל על הרמב"ם.

ניו־יורק : דפוס והוצאת סיני (א. י. פריעדמאן). 2°.

התוכן:

א : מדע, אהבה, זמנים (עד הל' שביתת עשור). תשכ"ג. [1], ח, עד ; פ"ו [צ"ל : צ"ב], פ"ה, י"ד, ב"ז דף.

ב : ספר זמנים (מהל' שביתת יום טוב). תשכ"ג. [2], פ"ו—רכ"ב, [3, 20], [1], נח—צב, דף, ציורים.

ג : ספר נשים. קדושה (עד איסורי ביאה). תשכ"ג. [2], קכ"ח, [1], ל"ו, מ"ד, י"ד, [1], צ"ב דף.

ונוסף בו הקובץ על נשים שהושמטו בדפוסי ורשה—וילנה.

---

* עיין למעלה, הוצאת וילנה, תר"ס (מספר 26), שממנה צולמה מהדורה זו מלבד י' ההוספות האחרונות.

ד: ספר קדושה (ממאכלות אסורות). הפלאה. זרעים. תשכ״ג. [2], קכ״ג; [1]. קל״ז; ק; קכ״ד דף.

ה: ספר עבודה. קרבנות. טהרה. תשכ״ג. [2], מ״ד; ב׳—קל״ב; קמ״א; [1], מ״ט—קכ״ו דף.

ו: ספר נזיקין. קנין. משפטים. שופטים. תשכ״ד. [3], ע; ס״ד, קל״ד, מ״ב; קלא, [1]; קכ״ג דף.

ובעותק שלנו לא נמצא ס׳ מרכבת המשנה. ובעותקים אחרים הושמט ס׳ אור שמח ונכרכו בפני עצמם: כרך א—ב. תשכ״ג.

תשכ״ד (1964)

54. משנה תורה הוא היד החזקה להנשר... רבינו משה בר מיימון... עם השגות הראב״ד... ופירוש הרב המגיד משנה, הכסף משנה, להגאון... יוסף קארו..., מגדל עוז לרבינו שם טוב הספרדי, הגהות מיימוניות (עם תוספות מדפוס וויניציה ש״י שי״א), (עם הוספות הרב... מהר״ם פאדוו״ה...), גם תשובות מיימוניות, ופירושי הרב... עובדיה והרב... מהר״ל בן חביב על הלכות קדוש החדש, עם כל הצורות השייכות להם ולהלכות שבת וסוכה. גם הלחם משנה להגאון... אברהם די בוטן..., ומשנה למלך להגאון... יהודא רוזאניס... כאשר היו בדפוסי יעסניץ, דיהרנפורט, וויען וברדיטשוב .ונלווה לו ספר הקובץ חדושים ומקורי דינים מהרב... נחום טריביטש... אבד״ק נ״ש כפי שנדפס בוויען.

ועתה הוספנו חדשות אשר לא היו מעולם בכל ספרי הרמב״ם הנדפסים... [עם שלשים וחמש הוספות כפי שנדפסו בדפוסי ווארשה—ווילנה הנ״ל] *.

ובמהדורה זו נתוספו ההוספות דלהלן:

(א) חידושים, מקורים והגהות מרבינו הגדול מרן משה סופר זצ״ל בעל חתם סופר (מופיע בפעם הראשונה ממה שנלקט מכל חיבוריו ה״ה: שו״ת ז׳ חלקים, חי׳ הש״ס, חי׳ סוגיות, חי׳ עה״ת, דרשות וכו׳ וכן מכתבי יד קודש שטרם ראו אור דפוס).

(ב) חידושים והגהות מרבינו הגדול מרן עקיבא איגר זצ״ל.

(ג) חידושים, מקורים והגהות מרבינו הגדול מרן אברהם שמואל בנימין סופר זצ״ל בעל כתב סופר (מופיע בפעם הראשונה ממה שנלקט מכל חיבוריו ה״ה: שו״ת ד׳ חלקים, חי׳ הש״ס, חי׳ סוגיות וכו׳).

(ד) הגהות ומקורים מהגאון המובהק מוה״ר חזקיה פייבל פלויט זצ״ל אב״ד שוראן בעל דברי חבר בן חיים, מגדולי תלמידי מרן בעל חתם סופר זצ״ל.

6 כרכים. ירושלים (דפוס אופסט ״אסתר״, תל־אביב) תשכ״ד—כ״ה. 4°.

דפוס צלום מהוצאת ווילנא מלבד מד׳ ההוספות האחרונות.

התוכן:

א: מדע. אהבה. זמנים (עד הל׳ שביתת עשור). [1], ח, ע״ד, פז [צ״ל צ״ב]; פ״ה, י״ד דף; כ״ח עמ׳.

ב: ספר זמנים (מהלכות יום טוב). נשים. [2], פ״ו—רכ״ב, [4], קכ״ח, ל״ו, ט״ו דף; נ״ה עמ׳.

---

* עיין למעלה, הוצאה וילנה, תר״ס (מספר 26).

נוסף פה ס' קובץ על נשים שהושמט מרוב הוצאות ווילנא—ורשה והצילומים מהן.

ג: ספר קדושה. הפלאה. [2], מ"ד, קכ"ג; [1], ק"ה דף; פ"ז עמ'.

ד: ספר זרעים. עבודה. קרבנות. [2]; קו—קל"ז; ב—ק; [1]; מ"ד; ב—קל"ב דף; נ"ו עמ'.

ה: ספר אהבה. נזיקין. קנין. [2]; [ב]—קמ"א; [1]; ע'; [1]; ס"ד; ב—נ"ב דף; מ' עמ'.

ו: משפטים. שופטים. [2]; [נב, ב]—קל"ד; ב—מ"ב; [1]; קל"ג; [1] דף; נ' עמ'.

כרך ה—ו נדפסו בשנת תשכ"ה.

תשכ"ד (1964)

55. משנה תורה והוא ספר היד החזקה להרב... משה ב"ר מיימון... עם הקדמת הרמב"ם ומניין המצוות ועם פירושיו ונושאי כליו והם השגות הראב"ד לרבינו אברהם ב"ר דוד ופירוש הרב המגיד הוא מגיד משנה ופירוש כסף משנה להרב יוסף קארו ועם מגדל עוז ועם הגהות מיימוניות ופירושי ה"ר עובדיה ב"ר דוד והר"ר לוי ן' חביב להלכות קדוש החדש ועם לחם משנה לה"ר אברהם די בוטן ועם משנה למלך לה"ר יהודה רוזאניס ונוספו בו הגהות ומראי מקומות לספרי הפוסקים וכן באו בו כללי הרמב"ם והראב"ד ומפרשיהם ומפתחות לספרי הי"ד ולהלכות ועוד הוספות ותיקונים.

ניו יורק: בדפוס והוצאת מ. פ. פרעסס אינק .ע"י האחים פאלאק, תשכ"ד. 2 כרכים. 8°.

כרך א: מדע — זרעים. [2], 16, 122, 158, 378, [2], 251, 72, [1], 87, [1], 221, [1], 274 עמ'.

כרך ב: עבודה — שופטים. [2], 198, [1], 88, 256, 236, [2], 140, 125, 268, 82, 215 עמ'.

צלום מדפוסי ורשא—ווילנא בלי ההוספות שנדפסו בסוף כל כרך.

תשכ"ד (1964)

56. משנה תורה. הוא היד החזקה לרבינו משה בן מיימון. על פי דפוס קושטא רס"ט ושנויי נוסחאות מתוך כתבי־יד ודפוסים ראשונים עם ציוני מקורות (ציוני מקורות... מאת יעקב ב"ר אליעזר כהן; שינויי נוסחאות מאת משה חיים... קצנלנבוגן; עורך ראשי: שאול ליברמן. א: ספר המדע). ירושלים, מוסד הרב קוק; (תל־אביב, דפוס מ. גרינברג, תשכ"ד). [6] דף; [4] דף: פקסימילות; של"ח עמ', [4] דף.

בראש השער: רבינו משה בן מיימון.

שערים נוספים באנגלית:

Mishneh Torah Yad ha-Hazaka of Moshe Ben Maimon (Maimonides). According to the 1489 [! i.e. 1509] Constantinople edition with variae lectiones from unpublished manuscripts and early editions, and annotation of sources (Annotation of sources, notes and elucidations: Jacob Cohen; variae lectiones: Moshe Hayim Katzenelenbogen. Editor in Chief: Saul Lieberman). Jerusalem: Mossad Harav Kook.

לנוסח נוספו: א: מערכת גרסאות מתוך דפוסים ראשונים, מתוך כשלושים כתבי יד,

שביניהם נבדלים כ״י תימניים כקבוצה נפרדת, אבל לא שוחזר טכסט מקורי כביכול. ב: ציוני מקורות לתלמודים ולראשונים, ומשולבים בהם דיונים קצרים לבירור הגרסה וברורים עניניים. — על הצורך בהוצאה בקורתית כבר עמד הרב מיימון בשעתו (״סיני״ כרך ל״ב) ולפנינו ראשית הגשמת תכניתו. (ק״ס, מ׳ [תשכ״ה], עמ׳ 148). בקרת מאת יהושע בראנד, בהארץ [מדור ״תרבות וספרות״] 31 יולי 1964, עמ׳ 10, 15.

תשכ״ה (1965)

57. משנה תורה הוא היד החזקה להנשר... רבינו משה בר מיימון... עם השגת הראב״ד... ופירוש הרב המגיד משנה, הכסף משנה להגאון... יוסף קארו... פירוש הרדב״ז, מגדל עז, הגהות מיימוניות, גם תשובות מיימוניות, ופירושי הרב... עובדיה והרב... מהר״ל בן חביב על הלכות קדוש החודש, עם כל הצורות השייכות להם ולהלכות שבת וסוכה, גם הלחם משנה להגאון... אברהם די בוטן..., ומשנה למלך להגאון... יהודא רוזאניס... חידושי הגר״א מווילנא... וחידושי מים חיים מהגאון בעל פרי חדש... וספר הקובץ ומקורי דינים מהגאון רבי... נחום טריביטש... ועתה הוספנו... מפתח עפ״י אלפא ביתא לכל הענינים שביד החזקה מוצאו מבית מדרשו של הרב... ברוך עוזיאל חזק... נדפס בוויניציה של״ד. ירושלים (בדפוס א. לוין־אפשטיין), תשכ״ה. 8°.

כרך א: מדע. [5], ס״ו דף;
אהבה. פ״ו דף;
זמנים. [2], קפ״ט, ט״ז דף;
כרך ב: נשים. [3], קכ״ז, ל״ו, ט״ו דף;
ט״ו דפים האחרונים: קובץ על ה׳ אישות שלא נדפס בהוצאות הרגילות.
כרך ג: קדושה. [3], מ״ד, קי״א דף;
הפלאה. [1], ק״ה דף;
כרך ד: זרעים. [3], [קו] — קלז; ב—צ״ט דף;
עבודה — קרבנות. [3], מ״ד; ב—קל״ב דף;
כרך ה: טהרה. [3], [ב] — ק״כ דף;
נזיקין. [1], ע׳ דף;
קנין. [1], ס״ד; ב—נ״א דף;
כרך ו: משפטים. [2], נב, ב—קלד; ב—מ״א דף;
שופטים. [1], ק״ט דף.

זהה עם הוצאת ״אל המקורות״ (תשי״ד, עיין למעלה מספר 40), בלי ההוספות.

תשכ״ה (1965)

58. משנה תורה... לרבנו משה ברבי מימון הובא לדפוס בפעם הראשונה על פי כתב יד בגנזי אוקספורד עם הקדמה, מראי מקומות, הערות ותרגום אנגלי ע״י משה חיים חיימזאהן. ירושלים: הוצאת ״קריה נאמנה״ (דפוס אופסט ש. מונזון, ירושלים), תשכ״ה. 8°.

ספר המדע. [3] דף; xiii; [3], 1א—93א; 93a—1a; [2] עמ׳.

שער נוסף באנגלית:

Mishneh Torah. The Book of Knowledge by Maimonides. Edited according to the Bodleian (Oxford) Codex with Introduction, Biblical and Talmudical references, notes and English translation by Moses Hyamson.

ספר אהבה... ומלווה מראי מקומות והערות ע"י הרב חיים מרדכי הכהן ברכר.

[4] דף, [1] עמ'; עמ' 93ב—165א; 165a—93b; [1] עמ'.

שער נוסף באנגלית:

Mishneh Torah. The Book of Adoration by Maimonides Edited according to the Bodleian (Oxford) Codex with an English translation by Moses Hyamson. The Talmudical references and Hebrew footnotes by... Chaim M. Brecher.

דפוס צלום לפי הוצאת ניו יארק, תרצ"ז — תש"ט.
ראה הערתנו שם, למעלה (מספר 31).

תשכ"ה (1965)

59. משנה תורה הוא היד החזקה להנשר... רבנו משה בר מימון... עפ"י דפוס ויניציה של"ד—של"ו. מנוקד, עם השגות הראב"ד ועם פירוש מאת... רבי דוד בן רבי אברהם עראמה נכתב בשנת ש"ה ליצירה (הותקן לדפוס, נוקד והוגה בידי ישעיהו גבריאלי).

ירושלים — תל־אביב, "אלומות"; רמת־גן — גבעתיים, דפוס פלאי). 4°.
כרך א: מדע. אהבה. תשכ"ה. [3] דף, 249 עמ', פקס';
כרך ב: זמנים. תשכ"ה. [249] — 472 עמ';
כרך ג: נשים. קדושה. תשכ"ו. [2] דף; [475]—749 עמ';
כרך ד: הפלאה. זרעים. תשכ"ו. [3] דף; [753]—998 עמ';
כרך ה: עבודה. קרבנות. תשכ"ו. [3] דף, [1001] — 1224 עמ';
כרך ו: טהרה. תשכ"ז. [3] דף, [1229] —1451 עמ';
כרך ז: נזיקין. קנין. תשכ"ז. [2] דף, [1453] — 1656 עמ';
כרך ח: משפטים. שופטים. תשכ"ז. [2] דף, [1657] — 1872 עמ'.

הפירוש של ר' דוד עראמה נדפס על פי מהדורת אמשטרדם תס"ו ביחד עם הסכמות הרבנים עליו. עיין במדור הפירושים, אי"ה, במקום אחר.

תשכ"ח (1968)

60. משנה תורה הוא היד החזקה להנשר... רבינו משה בר מיימון... עם השגות הראב"ד ... ופירוש הרב המגיד משנה, כסף משנה להגאון... יוסף קארו..., מגדל עז לרבינו שם טוב... הספרדי, הגהות מיימוניות [עם תוספות מדפוס וויניציה ש"י שי"א], [עם הוספות הרב... מהר"ם פאדווה"ה...], גם תשובות מיימוניות, ופירושי הרב... עובדיה והרב... מהר"ל בן חביב על הלכות קדוש החודש, עם כל הצורות השייכות להם ולהלכות שבת וסוכה. גם הלחם משנה להגאון... אברהם די בוטן..., ומשנה למלך להגאון... יהודה רוזאניס... ונלווה לו ספר הקובץ חדושים ומקורי הדינים מהרב... נחום טריביטש...

עם שלושים וחמש [צ"ל: וששׁ] הוספות כאשר נדפסו בדפוסי ווארשה—ווילנה:

(א) פירוש המגיד משנה על הלכות שחיטה...

(ב) פירוש הרדב"ז על ספר קדושה, הפלאה, זרעים, שופטים, ממלא מקום המגיד משנה שלא נמצא על הספרים האלה...

(ג) חדושים ומקורי הדינים מהרב... בעל פרי חדש, נקראים בשם מים חיים.

(ד) חדושים ומקורי הדינים מהרב... בעל מחנה אפרים.

(ה) חדושים ומקורי הדינים מהרב... ישעיה פיק...

(ו) ביאורים על הלכות בית הבחירה מהרב... יעקב עמדין...

(ז) השמטות מתוספות הגהמי"י, מדפוס ויניציאה, שנת ש"י, שי"א.

(ח) חדושים מהרב... מהר"ם פאדווה...

(ט) חדושים ומקורים מהרב... אברהם... אבד"ק פ"פ דמיין.

(י) חדושים ומקורים מהרב... זלמן... אחי... מוהר"ח... מוולאזין.

(יא) חדושים ומקורים מהרב... צבי הירש חיות...

(יב) חדושים ומקורים מהרב... יוסף... בעל ספר מנחת חינוך.

(יג) חדושים ומקורים מהרב... אברהם משכיל לאיתן...

(יד) חדושים ומקורים מהרב... שמואל שטראשון...

(טו) חדושים ומקורים מהרב... בצלאל הכהן... מווילנא.

*(טז) חדושים ומקורים מאת הרב... ר"ש ארינשטיין... אבד"ק אזירקאוו [והם מחתנו ר' נחום א"ש].

(יז) חדושים ומקורים מהרב... משה נחום... אבד"ק קאמינקא.

(יח) חדושים ומקורים מהרב... אברהם יונה יעוונין... מהוראדנא.

(יט) ביאור בפרק י"ז מקידוש החדש מהרב... התוכן ר' רפאל מק"ק הנובר...

(כ) ע"ד כתיבת שירת הים ושירת האזינו, מס' שתי ידות להרב... ר"מ די לונזאנו...

(כא) חידושי רבינו.. .אליהו... מווילנא...

(כב) טורי אבן, חדושים וביאורים מאת הרב... אלעזר רוקח... (ובתוכם הגהות וציונים ומ"מ מנכדו הרב... לוי חיים... דומ"ץ בק"ק ווילנא).

(כג) כתר תורה חידושים והגהות מאת הרב... לוי הקדוש... אבד"ק קאדני. ונוספו עליהם ציונים ומ"מ מנינו הרב... לוי חיים...

(כד) בנין שלמה, באורים וחידושים מהרב..., שלמה קלוגר... מבראד.

(כה) יד דוד, הערות וציונים מהרב... דוד לוריא...

(כו) נמוקי הגרי"ב, מהרב יהודה בכרך... אבד"ק סיניי.

(כז) בן אריה, חדושים, הערות וציונים, ומ"מ מהרב... זאב בן אריה... אבד"ק טעלז, בעהמ"ח הגהות בן אריה על כל הש"ס (ובתוכם הערות וציונים מאת נכדו הרב... אריה ליב...).

(כח) באר אברהם, הערות וציונים מהרב... אברהם שמעון טרויב... אבד"ק קיידאן.

(כט) מעשה ר"ב ,חדושים וביאורים מהרב... בצלאל הכהן... מ"ץ דווילנא, גם הוספות ע"י אחיו, הרב... שלמה הכהן... מ"ץ דווילנא, ובתוכם גם הערות ממוהר"ש הנ"ל.

---

* ראה הערתנו, למעלה, בסוף הוצאת וילנה, תר"ס (מספר 26).

(ל) נמוקי מהרא״י, מהרב... אברהם יונה יעוונין... מהוראדנא.

(לא) חשק שלמה, חידושים וביאורים מהרב... שלמה הכהן... מ״ץ דווילנא.

(לב) בני בנימין, הערות וציונים מהרב... אלי׳ דוד ראבינאוויץ... אבד״ק מירא. (ובסוף ימיו נמנה לרב ראשי בירושלם ת״ו) ובתוכם הערות וחדושי מר אביו הרב... בנימין... אבד״ק ווילקומיר, וגם מאחיו הגאון... יהודה צבי... אבד״ק ליגום.

(לג) הערות וציונים מהרב... דובער קאראסיק... אב״ד דק״ק קראלעוויץ.

(לד) בנין יהושע, חידושים וביאורים מהרב... יהושע לאנג...

(לה) עזוז חיל, מקורות והערות מהרה״ג... חיים יהודה לייב אייגעש...

6 כרכים. (תל־אביב): הוצאת עם עולם (דפוס ברודי את כץ), [תשכ״ח]. 4°.

עם שער מפורט לכל ספר וספר. דפוס צלום של הוצאות ווארשא—ווילנא.

התוכן:

כרך א: ספר מדע, אהבה, זמנים (עד הל׳ שביתת עשור). [1], עד; פ״ד [צ״ל: צ״ב]; פה; י״ד דף.

כרך ב: ספר זמנים (מהל׳ יום טוב). נשים. [2], פו—קפ״ט; לז, [2]; [1], קכ״ח, ל״ו, ט״ו דף וציורים. ונוסף פה ס׳ קובץ על נשים שהושמט ברוב הוצאות ווילנא—ורשה והצילומים מהן.

כרך ג: ספר קדושה. הפלאה. [2], מד, קכ״ג; [1], ק״ו דף.

כרך ד: ספר זרעים. עבודה. [1], ל״ג; ב—ק; [1], מד; ב, קל״ב דף.

כרך ה: ספר טהרה. נזיקין. קנין. [1], קמא; [1], ע; [1], ס״ד; ב—נב דף.

כרך ו: ספר משפטים. שופטים, [2], נב, ב—קל״ד; ב—מב; [1], קלב, [1] דף.

שנת הדפוס על פי קרית ספר, כרך 44 (כסלו תשכ״ט), עמ׳ 5—6 (מספר 55).

תשכ״ח (1968)

61. משנה תורה הוא היד החזקה להנשר... רבינו משה בר מיימון... עם השגות הראב״ד... ופירוש הרב המגיד משנה, וכסף משנה להגאון... יוסף קארו..., מגדל עוז, הגהות מיימוניות (עם תוספות מדפוס וויניציה ש״י שי״א), גם תשובות מיימוניות, ופירושי הרב... עובדיה והרב... מהר״ל בן חביב על הלכות קדוש החדש, עם כל הצורות השייכות להם ולהלכות שבת וסוכה. גם הלחם משנה להגאון... אברהם די בוטן..., ומשנה למלך להגאון... יהודא רוזאניס... כאשר היו בדפוסי יעסניץ, דיהרנפורט, וויען וברדיטשוב. ונלוה לו ספר הקובץ חדושים ומקורי דינים מהרב... נחום טריביטש... אבד״ק נ״ש כפי שנדפס בוויען.

ועתה הוספנו חדשות אשר לא היו מעולם בכל ספרי הרמב״ם הנדפסים:

(א) פירוש המגיד משנה על הלכות שחיטה...

(ב) פירוש הרדב״ז על ספר קדושה, הפלאה, זרעים, שופטים, ממלא מקום המגיד משנה שלא נמצא בספרים האלה.

(ג) חדושים ומקורי דינים מהרב... בעל פרי חדש, נקראים בשם מים חיים.

(ד) חדושים ומקורי הדינים מהרב... בעל מחנה אפרים.

(ה) חדושים ומקורי הדינים מהרב... ישעיה פיק...

(ו) ביאורים על הלכות בית הבחירה מהרב... יעקב עמדין...

(ז) השמטות מתוספות הגהמי״י, מדפוס וויניציאה, שנת ש״י, שי״א.

(ח) חדושים מהרב... מהר״ם פאדווה...

(ט) חדושים ומקורים מהרב... אברהם... אבד״ק פ״פ דמיין.

(י) חדושים ומקורים מהרב... זלמן... אחי מוהר״ח... מוולאזין.

(יא) חדושים ומקורים מהרב... צבי הירש חיות...

(יב) חדושים ומקורים מהרב.. .יוסף... בעל ספר מנחת חינוך.

(יג) חדושים ומקורים מהרב... אברהם משכיל לאיתן...

(יד) חדושים ומקורים מהרב... שמואל שטראשון...

(טו) חדושים ומקורים מהרב... בצלאל הכהן... מווילנא.

* (טז) חדושים ומקורים הגיעו אלינו מהרב... ר״ש ארינשטיין... אבד״ק אזירקאוו [מאת חתנו ר׳ נחום א״ש].

(יז) חדושים ומקורים מהרב... משה נחום... אבד״ק קאמינקא.

(יח) חדושים ומקורים מהרב... אברהם יונה יעוונין... מהוראדנא.

(יט) ביאור בפרק י״ז מקידוש החדש מהרב... התוכן ר׳ רפאל מק״ק הנובר...

(כ) ע״ד כתיבת שירת הים ושירת האזינו, מס׳ שתי ידות להרב... ר״מ די לונזאנו.

ועתה הוספנו עוד הוספות כמבואר מעבר לדף.

[(א) חידושי רבינו... אליהו... מווילנא.

(ב) טורי אבן, חדושים וביאורים מאת הרב... אלעזר רוקח... אבד״ק ברוד ואמשטרדם (ובתוכם הגהות וציונים ומ״מ מנינו הרב... לוי חיים... דומ״ץ בק״ק ווילנא.

(ג) כתר תורה חידושים והגהות מאת הרב... לוי הקדוש... אבד״ק קאדני. ונוספו עליהם ציונים ומ״מ מנינו הרב... לוי חיים...

(ד) בנין שלמה, באורים וחדושים מהרב... שלמה קלוגר... מברוד.

(ה) יד דוד, הערות וציונים מהרב... דוד לוריא... מביכוב ישן.

(ו) נמוקי הגרי״ב, מהרב יהודה בכרך... אבד״ק סיניי.

(ז) בן אריה, חדושים, הערות וציונים, ומ״מ מהרב... זאב בן אריה... אבד״ק טעלז, בעהמ״ח הגהות בן אריה על כל הש״ס (ובתוכם הערות וציונים מאת נכדו הרב... אריה ליב...).

(ח) באר אברהם, הערות וציונים מהרב... אברהם שמעון טרויב... אבד״ק קיידאן.

(ט) מעשה רב, חדושים וביאורים מהרב... בצלאל הכהן... מ״ץ דווילנא, גם הוספות ע״י אחיו, הרב... שלמה הכהן... מ״ץ דווילנא, ובתוכם גם הערות ממוהר״ש הנ״ל.

(י) נמוקי מהרא״י, מהרב... אברהם יונה יעוונין... מהוראדנא.

(יא) חשק שלמה, חידושים וביאורים מהרב.. .שלמה כהן... מ״ץ דווילנא...

(יב) בני בנימין, הערות וציונים מהרב... אלי׳ דוד ראבינוביץ... אבד״ק מירא. (ובסוף ימיו נמנה לרב ראשי בירושלם ת״ו) ובתוכם הערות וחדושי מר אביו הרב... בנימין... אבד״ק ווילקומיר, וגם מאחיו הגאון... יהודה צבי... אבד״ק ליגום.

---

* ראה הערתנו, למעלה, בסוף הוצאת ווילנה, תר״ס (מספר 26).

(יג) הערות וציונים מהרב... דובער קאראסיק... אב"ד דק"ק קראלעוויץ...

(יד) בנין יהושע, חידושים וביאורים מהרב... יהושע לאנג...

[(טו) עזוז חיל, מקורות והערות מהל' יסוד התורה עד הל' שחיטה מאת הרב... חיים יהודה לייב אייגש... מקובנו, ובסוף ימיו בירושלים].

ואלה הן ההוספות שאנו נותנים בהוצאה זו:

חידושי אור שמח לרבינו מאיר שמחה כהן...;

ברכת אברהם לרבנו אברהם בן הרמב"ם, בכרך ב';

בינה לעתים על הלכות יו"ט לר' יהונתן אייבשיץ, בכרך ב';

לשונות הרמב"ם מהגאון בעל אור החיים [לר' חיים עטר]... נדפס מספר ראשון לציון בכרך א';

חידושי קובץ על יד על הלכות אישות [לר' נחום טריביטש שבהוצאת וינה], בכרך ג';

הגהות ישועות מלכו להרה"ג ר' יהושע מקוטנא [טרונק], בכרך א';

הגהות אוצר המלך מהגאון... רבנו צדוק הכהן [רבינוביץ];

מאמר דרכי משה להגאון... ר' צ"ה חיות, בכרך א'.

ה' כרכים. ניו-יורק: הוצאת אוצר הספרים. תשכ"ח. 4°.

דפוס צלום של הוצאת ורשה—וילנה; גם הנספחים צולמו.

כרך א: מדע. [1], ח, עד דף;

אהבה. פ"ז [צ"ל: צב] דף;

זמנים. פ"ה; י"ד [=קובץ על היד החזקה לר' נחום טרייביטש ועוד חידושים];

נספחים: אור שמח. נ"ז דף;

ראשון לציון ואוצר המלך. [2] דף.

ישועות מלכו. דף נ"ט—ס;

מאמר דרכי משה. י"ח דף עם שער מיוחד (צלום מהוצאת זאלקווא).

זמנים (המשך). [2], פ"ו—רכ"ב, [1] דף; 2 דפים צורות לקידוש החדש.

נספחים: אור שמח [נז, ב], — צב דף;

ברכת אברהם לר' אברהם בן הרמב"ם. [41] דף;

בינה לעתים לר' יהונתן אייבשיץ. [3], ב — לד דף;

כרך ב: נשים. [1], קכ"ח; [1], לו דף.

קדושה. מג דף; ספר קובץ על הלכות אישות שלא נדפס בהוצאות הרגילות ט"ו דף;

נספח: אור שמח. צ"ב דף.

כרך ג: קדושה (המשך). [2], קכ"ג דף;

הפלאה. זרעים. [1], קלז, [1], ב—ק דף;

נספח: אור שמח. צ"ג—קכ"ד; [ב] — מ"ח דף;

כרך ד': עבודה. קרבנות. [2], מד; ב— קל"ב דף;

טהרה. קמ"א דף;

נספח: אור שמח. מח, ב— קכ"ו דף;

כרך ה: נזיקין. [2], ע' דף;

קנין. משפטים. סד, קל"ד, מ"ב דף;

שופטים. [1], קלב, [1] דף;
נספח: אור שמח. [2], ב—קכ"ג דף.

תשכ"ח (1968)

62. משנה תורה הוא היד החזקה להנשר... רבינו משה בר מיימון... עם השגות הראב"ד... ופירוש הרב המגיד משנה, הכסף משנה להגאון... יוסף קארו... מגדל עז לרבינו שם טוב הספרדי, הגהות מיימוניות [עם תוספות מדפוס וויניציה ש"י שי"א], [עם הוספות הרב... מהר"ם פאדוו"ה...], גם תשובות מיימוניות, ופירושי הרב... עובדיה והרב... מהר"ל בן חביב על הלכות קדוש החדש. גם הלחם משנה להגאון... אברהם די בוטן... ומשנה למלך להגאון... יהודא רוזאניס... ונלווה לו ספר הקובץ חדושים ומקורי דינים מהרב... נחום טריביטש.. אבד"ק ניקלשבורג. עם שלושים וחמש הוספות כפי שנדפסו בדפוסי ווארשה—ווילנה [עיין למעלה סימן 43].

ועתה במהדורה ישראלית זו הוספנו עוד שתים־עשרה הוספות חדשות... מהן כמה ספרים... מכתבי יד ודפוסים עתיקים כפי שמבואר בשער הבא [עיין למעלה סימן 52].

6 כרכים. 2°. ירושלים, פרדס (דפוס אופסט ישראלי ליצוא). תשכ"ח.

זהה עם ירושלים, הוצאת פרדס, סימן 52. דפוס—צילום עם קצת שינויים בפגינציה. התאריך תשכ"ח מופיע בכרך ד—ו.

תש"ל (1970)

63. משנה תורה והוא ספר הי"ד החזקה להרב... משה ב"ר מיימון... עם הקדמת הרמב"ם ומניין המצוות ועם פירושיו ונושאי כליו והם השגות הראב"ד לרבינו אברהם ב"ר דוד ופירוש הרב המגיד הוא מגיד משנה ופירוש כסף משנה להרב ר' יוסף קארו ועם מגדל עז ועם הגהות מיימוניות ופירושי הר"ר עובדיה ב"ר דוד והר"ר לוי ן' חביב להלכות קדוש החדש ועם לחם משנה להר"ר אברהם די בוטן ועם משנה למלך להר"ר יהודה רוזאניס ונוספו בו הגהות ומראה מקומות לספרי הפוסקים וכן באו בו כללי הרמב"ם והראב"ד ומפרשיהם ומפתחות לספרי הי"ד ולהלכות ועוד הוספות ותיקונים.

ג' כרכים. ירושלים: הוצאת "ירושלים", תש"ל. 8°.

כרך א: מדע. [2], [ב']—ח', ס"א דף;
אהבה. ע"ט דף;
זמנים. קפ"ט דף;
נשים. [1], קכ"ו, ל"ו דף;

כרך ב: קדושה. [2], מ"ד, קי"א דף;
הפלאה — זרעים. [1], קל"ז; ב'—ק' דף;
עבודה — קרבנות. [1], מ"ד; ב—קכ"ח דף;

כרך ג: טהרה. קי"ח דף;
נזיקין. [1], ע' דף;
קנין — משפטים. [1], ס"ג; ב'—קל"ד; ב'—מ"א דף;
שופטים. [1], ק"ח דף.

דפוס צלום של הוצאת ורשה—וילנה בהשמטת רוב החידושים שבאו בסופי הספרים. זהה לרוב עם הוצאת "בינה", ניו־יורק, תש"ז (מספר 36).

מפתחות

א. שמות מחברים וחוקרים

ב. שמות הספרים

עיתוניו של מאיר הלוי לעטעריס

א. מ. הברמן
ספרית שוקן
ירושלים

מאיר הלוי לעטעריס (זאלקווא 1800—וינה 1871) היה סופר פורה ביותר בשתי לשונות, בעברית ובגרמנית. הוא היה משורר, מתרגם, עורך, מהדיר, מחבר ספרי לימוד ודברים לעת מצוא. הוא עסק גם בהגהת ספרים, וידועות מהדורות התנ״ך שיצאו על ידי חברת מפיקי כתבי הקודש בלונדון ושמו מופיע בשעריהן.

ברכה לא ראה בעמלו, וכל ימיו היה בבחינת ״נצרך״, המצפה לתמיכה.

ספריו, ובעיקר ספריו הראשונים, אינם מצויים בשוק, והעיתונים שערך הם כיום יקרי המציאות, ואין אדם מוצא אותם אפילו בספריות הגדולות בעולם. מסתבר שלא נדפסו אלא במספר מצומצם, ועל עיתונו הראשון, ״הצפירה״, העיד הוא עצמו, שנדפס רק בשמונים טפסים.

הנני לרשום כאן את עיתוניו לפי סדר זמנם:

(1) הצפירה, חוברת ראשונה [זאלקווא תקפ״ג—1823]. 8°; (8), ק״י עמודים. ב״דבר אל הקורא״ כתב העורך: ״התועלת אשר תצא לנו בקראנו ספר קובץ על יד ענינים שונים, היא: כי בהשתנות והתחלפות הענינים יתן מרגוע ומעדנים לנפש הקורא״. בדבריו הוא מזכיר את ״החכמים בעלי המאסף, בפעלם אשר פעלו לתהלה ותפארת״. והוא מוסיף ואומר: ״וגם אנחנו אמרנו לעשות כדבר הזה בהספר אשר נגד עיניך. וקראנו אותו בשם הצפירה, כי זה ימים מעטים אשר נקבע כשחר גם בארץ הזאת, אור האמת והחכמה״.

ובמאסף זה יבואו סוגים אלה:

״(א) שיר ומליצה. אך בזאת נאות לתת לשירים יד במכתבנו, אם יהיה חדש מצד הרעיון וההמצאה...

(ב) מליצה פשוטה. המליצה פשוטה תהי על שני פנים: או תהי כתובה קלה בלשון המקרא... או אם הענין אשר ידרוש עליו הכותב יהיה על אופן אשר לא תכיל

אותו לשון עבר. אז רשות נתן אל הכותב לתת מקום גם למלות ומליצות תלמידיות (=תלמודיות), אך בתנאי, שיהיו קלים להבין...

והענינים אשר ידוברו במליצה פשוטה הלא המה:

1: ביאורי כתבי קדש. 2: תולדות היהודים ותולדות גדולי ישראל. 3: תולדות עם ועם ותולדות אנשים נפלאים מהעמים... 4: מוסר השכל. 5: כתבים מתנגדים ומערערים על המנהגים הנשחתים אשר צמחו בינינו. 6: בשורת ספרים אשר לא יצאו עוד לאור ואשר כבר יצאו לאור, לשפוט מעלתם וחסרונם ברוח נכון. 7: מכתבים אשר יהיו יקרים מצד ענינם, ודברים שונים".

בראש החוברת בא שירו של העורך "יונה הומיה", שנדפס אחרי כן הרבה פעמים והפך במשך השנים להיות מעין שיר עם.

בטופס הנמצא בבריטיש מוזיאון נאמר בכתב ידו של לעטעריס: "מנחת אזכרה לכבוד ידידי ואוהבי החכם החוקר קדמוניות שפוני קודש וטמוני חול כהו' מ. שטיינשניידר נ"י, בהפרדו ממני ללכת לקרית ברלין. יברך ה' מעשי ידיו ותכונות כפיו וכל חפצו, שלום. כה יבורך מאת אוהבו ומכבדו מאיר הלוי לעטעריס Ph. Dr. M. Letteris. הספר הצפירה הזה חסר השער הכולל אשר זה לשונו: 'הצפירה או המאסף החדש לבני ישראל היושבים בארצות גאליציען פולין ורוסיה וטורקי יצא לאור מאת חברת חכמים על ידי מ. ה. לעטריס'. הוא היה נדפס בבית דפוס אבי זצ"ל [גרשם לעטעריס]. ואלה שמות האנשים הבאים בחוברת הזאת, אשר לא פורש שמם להקרא על מעשי ידיהם באר היטב; הקדמה ממני. גם באור כתבי קדש (ה־ט) ותולדות אלכסנדר וכו' (יג—מב), אגרת התנצלות (מד—נ) מאת החוקר ר' נחמן קראחמאל ז"ל, ו"למנצח לבני לוי" (פה—פט) מאת אבי הרב המנוח מוה"ר גרשם זצ"ל.

מן ס' הצפירה לא נדפס רק פ' ספרים. לכן תיקר מנחתי זאת בעיניך. בס' כרם חמד (ח"א) ובתולדות ר"נ קראחמאל מאת החכם הגדול עומד לנס עמו ועם אחר הוא ל' צונץ יחי', נזכר שם הצפירה.

ע"י מכתב ה' מיזיס [יהודה ליב, לבוב 1748—1831] נאסף אור הצפירה כמעט צאתו, כי התמרמרו עליו רבני לבוב ובראדי וכו'. בהשירים נחסרו הדגושים לרוב, כי לא היו בבית דפוס אבי ז"ל. א. הורוויץ הוא אבי דאק' הורוויץ, חתן קראחמאל, זכרונם לברכה".

בדברי מיזיס הכוונה למאמרו שם "על דבר סיבת העדר החכמות האנושיות בבני עמנו" (עמ' נד—סט). וא. הורוויץ כתב שם "תנחומות אדם" (י—יג).

(2) צפירת תפארה, להיות לוית חן לראש כל אוהב חכמת ישראל ומליצת לשוננו הקדושה ערוכה בכל ושמורה ע"י מאיר הלוי לעטעריס [וינה 1850—1851].

תוספת עברית לעיתון הגרמני שלעטעריס ערך בשם Wiener Blätter. עיתון זה הופיע גם בשם Wiener Mitteilungen, וראה להלן סי' 6. 8°. י"ב חוברות, ולא הופיעו יותר.

בהקדמה נאמר: "אחי ועמי! זה ימים ושנים אשר הוצאתי לאור מכתב העתי בשם הצפירה, בעוד היותי על אדמתי ארץ מולדתי... למן אז ועד עתה פרחו עלי עתים חדשים גם ישנים בלשוננו, העלו נצה הבשילו אשכולותיהם; אמנם ברובם לא האריכו ימיהם, וכאשר באו כן הלכו... ועתה מרחוק ומקרוב פנו אלי אוהבי לשוננו ונפשם בשאלתם, כי אוסיף להוציא לאור את הצפירה... לכן אמרתי אשובה אל פעלי

הראשון... אם יהיו בתומכי ידי די מסת הדפוס, אזי אנופף ידי להביא מדי חדש בחדשו מעט צרי ומעט דבש מזמרת ארץ אבותינו״.

בהקדמה לחוברת 12 הודיע העורך: ״כלו שנים עשרה עלי צפירה תפארה, כמספר חדשי השנה... דעו כי מן הוא והלאה תצא הצפירה לאור ביתר שאת ויתר עז... לכן שמעתי לעצת חכמי לב לתת מעתה בכל משלש חדשים חוברת אחת שלמה... ארבע פעמים בשנה״. השווה הסי׳ הבא.

(3) אבני נזר כוללים דברי חכמה ותושיה, תוספת עברית ל־Wiener Vierteljahrs-schrift [וינה 1853].

נראה כי זהו הרבעון, שעלה בדעתו של העורך להוציא, וממנו לא הופיעו אלא ארבע חוברות בלבד.

(4) המאסף לשנת תקמ״ד כולל שירים ומכתבים אשר נאספו ונקבצו יחד על ידי אנשי חברת דורשי לשון עבר בקאניגסבערג, יצא שנית לאור בהגהה מדויקת עם נוספות חדשות, על ידי מאיר הלוי לעטעריס, וויען תרכ״ב בבית דפוס יוסף הלצוואַרטה, 8°. (4). רלד (4) עמ׳ ו־30 עמודים בגרמנית.

בדבריו אל הקורא מספר לעטעריס, כי בקושי ובהון רב הצליח לאסוף את כרכי ״המאסף״, והוא מסיים ״ואני נדרשתי לאשר שאלוני, והנני להוציאם לאור ברב חן והדר תפארת לרגל המלאכה אשר לפני, כאשר עיניך לנוכח יביטו, ולבי נכון ובטוח, כי המנחה הזאת תמצא חן בעיני משכילי עמנו, ולא ימנעו טוב מבעליו ויהי׳ שכר לפעולתו.

והנה ספרי ״המאסף״ יודפסו אי״ה על ידי בשלמותם ברב הוד והדר ובהגהה מדויקת מאד, לא יחסר בהם דבר, אף שורה אחת (לא לבד ״מבחר המאסף״, אשר נדפסו דוגמאות ממנו לפני ימים ושנים בכה״ע), כי גם דברים קטנים, אשר יקטן ערכם לעת כזאת, לא אמנע מן הקוראים אשר נכספה נפשם להיות בידם ספר המאסף שלם בכל חלקיו וכלול בהדרו, כאשר יצא לאור בעצם וראשונה, בלי לגרוע ממנו דבר או חצי דבר״.

גם לתכנית זו לא האירה ההצלחה את פניה, ו״המאסף״ לא הופיע יותר.

(5) Wiener Vierteljahrsschrift für Wissenschaft und Kunst, Kultur und Literaturgeschichte mit besonderem Hinblick auf israelitische Zustände, Wien 1853.

הרבעון הזה נאסף בשנתו הראשונה.

(6) Wiener Mitteilungen, Zeitschrift für israelitische Kulturzustände, Geschichte und Literatur, Wien 1854–1870.

העיתון הופיע גם בשם Wiener Blätter, והכיל מאמרים שונים, מהם שהזמן גרמם ומהם דברי מדע פופולאריים ותרגומים. עיתון זה היה שבועון, והופיע בכל יום שני בשבוע. באותו עיתון מיום 2.12.57 באה מודעה בסוף הגליון ותרגומה העברי ניתן בזה:

נא לא להסיר עין מזה:

החוברות ״אבני נזר״ ו״צפירה תפארה״ שהוכרז עליהן לפנים, שהן תוספות לא קבועות לעיתוני, שיצאו לאור מעת לעת, הופיעו ונשלחו עד כה בכל 16 המשלוחים, היינו 12 חוברות ״צפירה תפארה״ ו־4 ״אבני נזר״. לצערי ידוע יפה זה שנים רבות, כי ההתעניינות בספרות העברית מצומצמת מאד בתפוצות ישראל, אבל אני הבאתי קרבן על מזבח המדע העברי לשם מספר קטן של חובבי ספרותנו הלאומית. כהוכחה למיעוט

העניין בספרותנו העברית, שרמזתי עליו, אפשר לראות בזה, כי גם מספרי השנה העברים ״בכורי העתים״ ו״כרם חמד״ (וינה ופראג 1820—1843), הנזכרים בפי אנשים בכבוד, לא נדפסו אלא 500 טפסים, ויותר ממחציתם עדיין מונחים כאבן שאין לה הופכים בחנות הספרים של קנפפלמאכר בווינה ושל מ. י. לאנדוי בפראג, וזה מחוץ לכתבי עת אחרים המצויים בשוק וקשה למכרם.

משום יתמותו של ענף ספרותי זה, שקופציו מעטים, הודעתי במודעות שונות, כי תוספותי העבריות תישלחנה רק למנויים שיודיעו במפורש כי רצונם בהן.

מ״אבני נזר״ נמצאים עדיין טפסים שלימים במחסן ויישלחו למנויים חדשים בתשלום דמי המשלוח בלבד, כשיחישו את הזמנתם ולא יאזלו בינתיים, ומ״צפירת תפארה״ נמצאות רק חוברות מעטות, וגם הן אינן שלימות.

בדברי אלה אני מתכוון גם לעניין אחר: ברצוני לתקן ולהעמיד על אמיתתה ידיעה כוזבת עם מסקנה משונה, בקשר לתוספות הנ״ל, שהופיעה באחד העיתונים הזרים: בעתיד, ורק לפי ההשתתפות, יופיעו ״אבני נזר״ מאת לעת, מבלי שאתחייב להוציא מספר מסויים מהן.

וינה דצמבר 1857.

כשם שלא נתמזל מזלם של העיתונים העברים כך גם לא האיר המזל פנים לעיתונים הגרמנים ופעולתו העיתונאית של לעטעריס נפסקה לגמרי בשנת 1870.

קל וכבד
[לדרכו של פתגם]

דב סדן
האוניברסיטה העברית
ירושלים

א

נאַר מיט איין באַדינג: טראָגן לייכט און האָבן גרינג — היא אמירה חרוזה, שתרגומה ללשון עברי אי־אפשר שיהא מדוקדק, שכן גם תיבת לייכט וגם תיבת גרינג מקבילה אחת להן: קל, אבל שיעורה: אך בתנאי אחד, הריון קל ולידה קלה. אמירה זו לא נמצאה לי בדפוס, אך בימי ילדותי שמעתיה כקטע מסיפור־מעשה שכך ענינו: שדכן ביקש לשדך בתולה זקנה וכעורה, שאביה העשיר והשוטה היה בררן כל־כך, שלאחר שהשדכן כבר וויתר לכל חפציותיו, היתנה לסוף כאותו תנאי. השדכן קימט מצחו ואמר: אי לייכט אי גרינג, איז א שווערער באדינג, לאמור: גם [הריון] קל גם [לידה] קלה הוא תנאי כבד [=קשה], והוסיף, כי הוא עצמו אינו יכול, כמובן, להבטיח קיומו של התנאי הכפול, אך ישאל את פי הבחור, שהוא משדכו לאותה בתולה. הוא לא שאל לו לבחור, גזירה שמא יעמוד על טיבו של אותו שוטה, המועמד להיות חותנו, אך העמיד בפני אותו שוטה פנים, כאילו שאל לו לבחור ומשמו אמר, כי אם כך הרי יתנה תנאי לכלה: נאַר מיט איין באדינג: אי שיין אי יינג, כלומר: אך בתנאי אחד [שהיא תהיה] גם יפה גם צעירה, והוא, השדכן, עוד מוסיף משלו: ווייל אַז די כלה איז יינג [= יונג], איז ביי איר אַלץ לייכט און גרינג, כלומר: כשהכלה צעירה, הכל לה קל וקל.

אפשר שאותה הלצה היתה מעיקרה חרוזה כולה, ואולי הוא פזמון מפזמאותיהם של זמרי־ברוד וכדומה, אך תשומת־דעתנו קודם־כל לבחינה השעשועית־טכנית: (1) החריזה העממית; שעל־פיה מתחרזות בי״ת וגי״מל: האָבן—טראָגן; (2) החריזה הרגילה: באדינג—גרינג—יינג; (3) צמד־התארים, בין לשונות נרדפים: לייכט—גרינג, בין לשונות סותרים: לייכט [= גרינג] — שווער.

ב

לפי שגרעינם של כל מיני אמירה אלו הוא, בעצם, צמד־החרוזים: אי לייכט אי גרינג איז א שווערער באַדינג, שניתן לסגלו ולתאמו לעובדות ולמשאלות שונות, דין למנותו במשפחת פתגמים, מימרות, מוטיבים, שבהם בא הניגוד הזה על ביטויו ברוב חידוד וחידודים. אם להסתפק בקצת דוגמאות, הרי לפנינו האימרה: גיב גאָט א גרינג געמיט און א שווערע קעשענע, כלומר: מי יתן רוח קלה [= לב קל] וכיס כבד. ואיפכא אתה מוצא במה שש״י עגנון מספר בסוחר, ר׳ חנן, שנסע לקנות ביריד ואבד כיס ממונו וחזר עם אנשיו הביתה: ״קרונותיו קלים ולבו כבד״ (מעלות ומורדות, אלו ואלו, תש״ך, עמ׳ קמ״ז) והיא בת־לויתה של האמירה: א גרינגע קעשענע און א שווערגעמיט. ההומור מתחדד בשימוש המבודח: אז מען ווערט א שווער ווערט לייכטער, כשתיבת שווער יוצאת לכפל משמע, גם משורש schwer כלומר: כבד, גם משורש Schwäher כלומר חותן, וכאן המכוון למישמע אחרון: כשנעשים חותן נעשה קל, דהיינו משנפטר אדם מבנו, וביחוד מבתו, שקשה היה להשיאם והשיאם, כאילו מעמסה כבדה נגולה מעל לבו והוקל לו. אמירה זו שמעתי מפי דניאל לייבל, ששמעה בעיר־מולדתו דמביץ ובודאי היתה שכיחה גם במקומות אחרים. ויותרת חידוד אתה מוצא באמירה: וואָס לייכטער דער שווער דאָס שווערער דער לייכטער, כשתיבת לייכטער יוצאת לכפל משמע, גם משורש leicht [קל] ויתרונו leichter [=קל יותר] גם משורש Leuchter שפירושו מנורה, נברשת, וכוונת האמירה, כי כל מה שהחותן קל [יד] יותר, כן מתנתו — לבנו ולבתו בחתונתם — ועיקרה נברשת, משקלה מרובה יותר. ושמעתי מפי המשורר מ. מ. שאפיר דרוש של דופי, והוא מעשה בחותן שהבטיח לחתנו זוג פמוטות ויצאו ימים הרבה ולא קיים הבטחתו, כתב לו: ווו זענען דאָס די לייכטער [= היכן הפמוטות], שלח לו שזיפים וכתב לו: מיט פלוימען דאָסטו לייכטער, והוא יוצא לכפל משמע ואין להאריך.

ג

ותיבת שווער שראינוה בשתים הוראות, כשם־עצם (חותן) וכתואר (כבד), פתוחה להוראה שלישית, כלשון ציווי של פועל שווערן שענינו שבועה. וענין זה הניח פתח לתוספת שעשוע בחידוד על החותן והחתן, שנידיינו לפני הרב, ולשון החידוד: זאָגט דער רב צום איידעם: שווער און צום שווער זאָגט ער: איידעם, וכך הוא למשמע־אוזן, שעל־פיו אמר הרב לחתן חותן ולחותן חתן, ובאמת הכוונה שהוא אומר לו לחתן: שווער כלומר: תישבע ולחותן אמר: עדים, כלומר שיביא עדים, ושחוק הניגוד שחסרנו בחידוד זה, בא על תשלומו בתוספתו: שבועה קלה — תרתי דסתרי, שתרגומו: א לייכט שווערן. ואין צריך לומר, שהוא בא על תשלומו באמירה: ביי א שווערן וואגן איז לייכט צו פוס צו גיין, כלומר: ליד עגלה כבדה קל לילך ברגל, משמע מי שעגלתו כבדה, עמוסה רוב פרקמטיה, יגיעה כהליכה על ידה קלה לו. אבל יש גם ניסוח אחר וכן מביא אברהם מנדל מוהר, מאמר חז״ל: בתר מרי נכסי ציבי

משוך (בבא קמא צ״ג ע״א) דהיינו: תמיד טוב היות בבית־עסקו של אדם גדול, שאפילו קטון בתי־העסק של נגיד גדול נושא ריווח גדול יותר מבית־עסקו של בינוני, והוא מזכיר מאמר הבריות: ביי אשווערן וואָגן איז גוט צו פוס צו גיין, והוא מסביר כוונתו, כי ביי אגרינגען וואָגן טאר מען נישט צו פוס גיין, כלומר: ליד עגלה קלה אסור לילך ברגל, שכן אי אפשר לסמוך עליה, כי עד שאתה פונה כה וכה, כבר הפליגה העגלה, וכשאתה מתעייף אין לך היכן תנוח. אבל ביי אשווערן וואָגן מעג מען גאנץ געלאסן צו פוס גיין, כלומר: מותר לילך מתון מתון ברגל, שכן העגלה נוסעת לאטה ואתה תמיד על ידה, וכשאתה מתעייף, אתה יושב בתוכה (בספרו הכתוב יידיש, כתר תורה, לבוב 1862).

ונראה כי הנוסח האחרון: ביי א שווערן וואגן איז גוט וכו׳ קדם לנוסח הראשון: ביי א שווערן וואגן איז לייכט וכו׳, שהנוסח הראשון אינו יוצא מכלל הוראה כדרך פשט והנוסח האחרון נכנס לכלל הוראה כדרך משל, והניגוד: שווער — לייכט מסייעה.

ד

ופלפלת נאה נותנת תיבולה בשימוש צמד־המילות בלשון עברי, וכן לשון אמירה: אין שטוב איז ער א קל, אין שול וויל ער כבוד, ונדרש במי שבצנעה אינו זהיר במצוות, ואדרבה עבירה נוחה לו, אבל בפרהסיא, ועיקרה בית־הכנסת, הוא מבקש גבאות, עליה שמנה וכדומה. ענין קל מתפרש כאן בתחום המוסר (קל שבקלים, קל דעת, קלי עולם וכדומה). ואילו תיבת כבוד הנשמעת בשיגרת הדיבור כתיבת כבד נתפסת כממילא כניגודו של קל. והרי כבד וכבוד שרשם אחד, והוא הדין בתיבת יקר היוצאת להוראת כובד: ״יקר לד׳ המותה לחסידיו״ (תהלים קט״ז, ט״ו) ״וירח יקר הולך״ (איוב ל״א, כ״ו), כשם שהיא יוצאת להוראת כבוד: ״את עושר כבוד מלכותו ואת יקר תפארת גדולתו״ (אסתר א׳, ד׳). ״וכל הנשים יתנו יקר לבעליהן״ (שם, א׳ כ״א) ומפורסמות אינם צריכים תוספת ראיה. הלכך הקל הוא לא בלבד ניגודו של כובד אלא אף ניגודו של כבוד: ״את מכבדי אכבד ובוזי יקלו״ (שמו״א ב׳, ל׳), ״ונקלותי עוד מזאת והייתי שפל בעיני ועם האמהות אשר אמרת עמם אכבדה״ (שמו״ב, י׳ כ״ב).

ותיבת כבד היא לא בלבד תואר שענינו חילופו של קל, אלא שם עצם שענינו אבר באברי הגוף, והחלפתו בתיבת כבוד גרם־של־שעשוע. ולענין הקרבנות נאמר: יותרת־הכבד (שמות כ״ט, כ״ב; ויקרא ח׳, טז כ״ה; ט׳ י״ט) ובתוספת אות נעשתה דרך שעשוע הסמיכות: יותרת הכבוד, כהגדר לכבוד מופלג. ודרש הנתלה בהדיוטות נעזר בהחלפה הפוכה, שדברי הכתוב: ״יעלזו חסידים בכבוד״ וכו׳ (תהלים קמ״ט, ה׳) מיתרגם: חסידים פרעסן זיך אָן מיט לעבער ותרגום המשכו של הכתוב וסיומו יוצא לדרוש של דופי, וודאי המצאת משכיל היא, שתלאו בהדיוט, והצניע החלפה: יעלזו — ילעסו, וככל המשוער הוא סירוסו של דרוש פשוט: יעלזו חסידים בכבוד — ואין כבוד אלא חופה שנאמר: כי על כל כבוד חופה, (ישעיה ב׳ ה׳), שאם יקיימו מצוות נישואין, הרי מצוה גוררת מצוה: ירננו על משכבותם — יקיימו מצות פריה ורביה, ושוב מצוה גוררת מצוה: וחרב פיפיות בידם שיקיימו מצות מילה. ואף תורת פורים לא פסחה על אפשרות השימוש בדרך ההחלפה כבוד — כבד והסמיכה

לו דרך החלפה: כ ב ד — ש ו ו ע ר — ח ו ת ן, וצירפה מיני שעשוע אחרים וכן נדרש לה לשון שיר הכבוד, כפי שגדרו לו לגלב: ״אספרה כבודך ולא ראיתיך אדמך אכנך ולא ידעתיך״, שלשון א ס פ ר ה יוצא להוראת תספורת, לשון כ ב ו ד ך להוראת חותנך, לשון א ד מ ך להקזת דם ולשון א כ נ ך ללשון קאנע [= הרקה, חוקן]. וראה גם דרך תרגום מבודח: ע ר ה אָ ט י ר א ת ה כ ב ו ד [= הכבד], ע ר ה אָ ט מ ו ר א פ א ר ן ש ו ו ע ר [ירא מחותנו].

וראוי להעיר, כי ענין הניגוד כ ב ו ד — ק ל מצוי גם בלשונות אחרות, והרי דוגמה מפליאה בלשון הפולנים, שמשוררה יאן ק ו כ א נ ו ב ס ק י כותב בענין בתולה שמחזרים אחריה (כתביו, מהדורת יוליאן ק ז׳ י ז׳ א נ ו ב ס ק י, 1967, כרך א׳, עמ׳ 186):

a kiedy by chciała
rychlej z nich cześć niż lekkość miała

לאמור: אלו רצתה, היתה זוכה מהם יותר מהר לכבוד מאשר לקלות, כביכול תרגם לשון הניגוד בלשוננו: כ ב ו ד — ק ל ו ן. ואחרון אחרון הפתגם השגור הבנוי שני תארים: ע ר ל ע ך א י ז ש ו ו ע ר ל ע ך שכוונתו לומר כי קשה לו לאדם לקיים ישרו, שורש תארו אחד: ע ר ל ע ך הוא לשון ehrlich, שיסודו Ehre, הוראתו כ ב ו ד ושורש תארו אחר: ש ו ו ע ר ל ע ך הוא ש ו ו ע ר שיסודו, schwer, והוראתו כובד, קושי.

ו

פרשת הניגוד: ש ו ו ע ר — ל י י כ ט היא כבקעה רחבה, ושימושיו הרבה, והרי אמירה: פ א ר ד י נ ע ן א י ז ש ו ו ע ר ו ו י ב ל י י, א ו י ס ג ע ב ן א י ז ל י י כ ט [או: ג ר י נ ג] ו ו י ש פ ר י י, כלומר: להשתכר קשה [=כבד] כעופרת, להוציא קל כמוץ. אמירה מורכבת היא, כי יש בה שלושה צמדי־ניגוד, שניים האחרונים מקבילים ממש, שכך עשויים הם כמשלים ונמשליהם: (1) ל ה ש ת כ ר [= להכניס] — ל ה ו צ י א, (2) כ ב ד [= ק ש ה] — ק ל; (3) ע ו פ ר ת — מ ו ץ, ומשלים מצויים הם.

ולשם האמירה על ריווח ובזבוזו, הנה נוסח אוקראיני, שהיה גם פשוט ברחוב היהודים בגלילות ילדותי ואגפיה: Дай Боже тяжко заробити а лекко пустити ולכאורה עניננו מי יתן להשתכר בקושי [= בכבדות] ולנטוש [= להוציא] בנקל, דהיינו שהשכר או הריווח יבוא ברוב יגיעה, ובאמת הכוונה היא, שהשכר או הריווח יהא כבד, דהיינו שממונו יהא כבד ואילו ההוצאה תהיה קלה, דהיינו בלב קל, בנחת רוח. ודין לזכור כי כשם שהתיבה העברית ק ל יש בה שתי מקבילות ביידיש: ל י י כ ט, ג ר י נ ג כך התיבה ביידיש ש ו ו ע ר יש לה שתי מקבילות בעברית: כ ב ד, ק ש ה והוא הדין בסלאווית, כגון האוקראינית שיש בה שתי תיבות מקבילות לה: тяжко ו־трудно, ראשונה עניינה כובד, ועיקרה משא, אחרונה שרשה בתיבת труд, ועניינה עמל, יגיעה. כן מצוי בה ניב: тяжко нести жалко покинути כלומר: כבד [=קשה] לשאת, צר להשליך, אבל בגליל ילדותי הנוסח היה тяжко нести, трудно иокинутй כלומר: כבד לשאת, קשה לזרוק.

ולשון ק ש ה יוצא, כידוע, גם להוראה אחרת; כניגודו של רך, נוח, ולשון תרגומו ה א ר ט, וראה, למשל: ״אסור ל ד ב ר עם יתום ואלמנה ב ק ו ש י — מען טאר ניט ר י י ד ן ה ר ט י ר י י ד צו איין אלמנה און צו איין יתום״ (הנהגות אדם לר״ד אופנהיים, לבוב, 1862, סעיף מ׳), והוא פרק לגופו.

משמעות "השאלה הנכבדה" לאליעזר בן־יהודה

ג. קרֶסֶל
חולון

מעטים הם המאמרים הפובליציסטיים העבריים שניתן לומר עליהם בפה מלא שפתחו תקופה חדשה בתולדות עמנו ותרבותנו בדורות האחרונים. אחד המעטים האלה הוא ללא כל ספק מאמרו הנודע והמפורסם של אליעזר בן יהודה: "שאלה נכבדה", שנדפס ב"השחר" התשיעי (תרל"ט/1879) [1] ופתח תקופה בתולדות חיבת ציון וישוב ארץ־ישראל, הלשון העברית ודיבורה בארץ, המילונאות העברית ועוד, וכן היה בן־יהודה הרוח החיה בהנחת יסודות ל"ועד הלשון העברית", שהוקם עשר שנים לאחר מכן וממנו צמחה האקדמיה ללשון העברית (החוגגת עתה את שנת השמונים לקיום "ועד הלשון"). לא היה לו מזל מיוחד לבן־יהודה במאמרו זה. הוא שלחו תחילה לעתון "המגיד", העתון שעסק בחיבת ציון וישוב ארץ ישראל בימים ובשנים ששום עתון עברי לא התענין בכך. ואף על פי כן סירב עורך "המגיד" להדפיסו בטענה: "שהמאמר לא יוצלח לדפוס מפאת החלומות והגוזמאות אשר בו". למזלנו לא נהג ככה עורך "השחר" פרץ סמולנסקין, שהדפיסו בשינוי שמו, שהיה תחילה: "שאלה לוהטת".

המאמר הוא על כן בעל חשיבות עצומה ומן הפלא שעל אף הספרות העצומה על בן־יהודה לא זכה עדיין לתשומת לב הראוייה, ביחוד למניעיו ומקורותיו. על אחד המקורות למאמר זה, שהוא ללא כל ספק מהחשובים ביותר, ידובר כאן, הוא המקור השופע רוב אור ובהירות על המחשבה היהודית במערב והתנגדותו הפנימית של בן־יהודה לאורח־חשיבה זה. ברם לפני כן נקדיש כמה מלים לתמונה הכללית של הפתרונות לבעיית ישראל בגולה, בהם נאבק בן־יהודה במאמרו זה.

בן־יהודה ישב באירופה המערבית באותם ימים, שנתיים לפני עלייתו לארץ. כאן שלטו בכיפה, בדרך כלל, שני מהלכי־מחשבה לגבי השאלה היהודית. האחת, המכריעה ברובה הגדול, הקרוייה בפינו היום: המתבוללת ובאותם ימים הריפורמית (ולאחר מכן הלי־ברלית), ראתה בישיבת ישראל בגולה והתערבותה בגויים הפתרון האחד הראוי והמציאותי. בכלל ישיבה זו היה צורך לשבץ את הייחוד היהודי, שהוגבל לתחום הדתי

בלבד ואף הוא בשימוט מכסימאלי של כל הכרוך בערגה לארץ־ישראל והשיבה לציון. גלי האנטישמיות שהחלו אז לשטוף את אירופה וביחוד את גרמניה, מרכזו של זרם זה, לא הפחית במלוא נימה מתיאוריה זו, שאדרבא, היא הנותנת שיש ויש להילחם בה ולהראות את נביבותה. אנו, כך טענו אלה, יושבים בגרמניה מאות בשנים והרגשת הגרמנית שלנו אינה פחותה מאלה הנוצרים. לעומתם היה הזרם האורתודוכסי על גווניו המרובים, בעל זיקה איתנה לארץ ישראל ולמסורת הדתית. הזיקה לארץ־ישראל התבטאה בפעילות פילנטרופית למען מוסדות צדקה וחסד. ברם בתחום ההשתייכות המדינית היו כל אלה האורתודוכסים פטריוטים פרוסים וגרמניים אדוקים לא פחות ממתנגדיהם אנשי הריפורמה. ואכן, הדבר יצא ברבים עם הופעתו של הרצל, שאז יצאו כולם כאחד במחאה עזה וחריפה נגד הציונות המדינית ולא בכדי היו בין "רבני־המחאה" הנודעים מיוצגים שני המחנות האלה, שבדרך כלל לחמו איש ברעהו כל הימים.

בתווך בין שני מחנות מוגדרים אלה ניצב קומץ קטן, שהיה אף הוא מגוון ביותר: רבנים חרדים, משכילים, חלוצי הקומוניזם והסוציאליזם — הם מבשרי חיבת ציון, שלא האמינו בפתרון הנזכר אלא ראו חזות הכל בשיבה לארץ ישראל ולכך חתרו בפעילותם ובהטפותיהם. והנה באותם ימים, שנות השבעים למאה הקודמת אירעו שני מאורעות במערב, שהסעירו לא במעט את העולם היהודי במערב: יצא ספרה של ג׳ורג אליוט "דניאל דירונדה" (1876) ומיד לאחר מכן יצא ציר הפרלמנט ההונגארי ממפלגת־השלטון הליברלית ויקטור אישטוצי (Győző Istóczy, 1842–1915), האיש בעל הזכות המפוקפקת להיות חלוץ האנטישמיות בפרלמנט ההונגארי, בדרישה להקים מחדש את המדינה היהודית בארץ ישראל. ודאי שמרחק תהומי בין הסופרת לבין הצורר היהודי: אולם הצד השווה שביניהם: דרישה להחזיר את היהודים לארץ ישראל והקמת מדינה יהודית בה. לא ייפלא איפוא שדרישה משותפת זו שבין קצוות אלה, עוררה לעג וגם זעם אצל כל אלה, שראו ברעיון זה אבסורד מאין כמותו.

לא נעסוק כאן בתגובות של הימים ההם לשני מאורעות אלה, המצויות בשפע בספרות ובעתונות, הן לשלילה והן לחיוב. לענייננו כאן נדגיש תגובתו של לודוויג פיליפסון, עורך השבועון Allgemeine Zeitung des Judentums שנערך על ידו החל מ־1837 והיה למעשה עתונו המרכזי של האגף המתבולל ביהדות גרמניה במשך שלושה דורות כמעט. לא היה מאורע גדול וקטן בעולם היהודי שעתון זה לא הגיב עליו וביחוד עשה זאת העורך עצמו, בנוסף לידיעות מכל רחבי העולם היהודי, המצויות בכל גליון וגליון (ומבחינה זו הוא עד היום אוצר בלום לידע יהדות המאה הי"ט באירופה ובשאר חלקי העולם). בעיצומה של סערה זו סביב המדינה היהודית, אז ללא כל ספק תכנית דמיונית ביותר, פירסם פיליפסון מאמר מקיף בשם "כינונה מחדש של המדינה היהודית"[2]. מאמר זה ראוי לבחינה הן בשל כך שהוא מגבש למעשה את התיאוריה של ההתבוללות, או כפי שקרא לזה רבי יחיאל מיכל פינס: "התערבות בגויים" וכן בשל כך שאל מאמר זה מכוון בן יהודה את דבריו ב"שאלה נכבדה" שלו, עובדה שכל חוקרי בן־יהודה עד כה לא שמו לבם אליה כלל ועיקר.

המאמר נכתב בגילוי־לב מאין כמוהו ואף בבהירות יתירה, תכונה נדירה ביותר בסגנונו הגרמני של פיליפסון, שהוא בנוסח הדרשני של רב (היה כידוע רב במשך עשרות בשנים). הוא אינו מתפלא שענין אבסורדי זה מעסיק עתה את דעת הקהל, שכן כך דרכו של הפיקנטי והאבסורדי, שהוא שובה לבבות וביחוד לבות העתונאים והעתונות. כמובן,

מוסיף הוא, שהכוונה לארץ־ישראל. הגיון מסויים יש בכך, שרבות המעצמות הלוטשות עין לתורכיה ולחלוקתה וביחוד לארץ הקודש ולירושלים. ומכיוון ששום מעצמה ושום כנסיה לא תוכל להיות בעלת הריבונות הממלכתית על מקום־מריבה זה הרי מובן שהיהודים הם הכתובת הנכונה, בהיותם מחוץ לכל צד (כמה נשתנו הזמנים עתה והתכנית הדמיונית ובעיקר לגבי ירושלים הוגשמה מקץ תשעים שנה במלואה...). אכן, אומר פיליפסון, אפשר היה להתייחס לכל התכנית הזו כאל משחק מדיני תמים, אילולי נתעורר הענין על ידי "דניאל דירונדה", הספר, שבמרכזו רווח הרעיון שכינונה מחדש של המדינה היהודית הוא עיקרו המהותי של היהדות.

ספר זה עורר הדים מרובים באנגליה ומחוצה לה, במידה שנמצאו מחברים אחרים, שתיארו רעיון זה כסותר ומנוגד בתכלית למהות־היסוד של היהדות. אין פיליפסון רוצה להתווכח עם רומן של סופרת, כלומר, שאין הרעיון בר־ויכוח כלל, לפי שהוא פרי דמיון של רומניסט. אולם אין הוא יכול לא להזכיר ולהדגיש את העובדה, שכל צורר־יהודים, שאין ידו משגת לחסל את היהודים בגבולו משלח אותם לארץ־ישראל. לגבי דידם מהווים היהודים גורם זר ומסוכן בארצות אירופה ויש על כן להרחיקם הרחק הרחק לאסיה. כאן מזכיר פיליפסון את הצעתו של אישטוצי[3], שלא תזכה כמובן לתשומת לב רצינית בפרלמנט ההונגארי. מכאן אך כפסע להמשך רעיונו של פיליפסון, שכל שונאי ישראל מוצאים לעצמם רעיון זה לשם גיבוי וכיסוי לשנאתם במעטה של אהבת ישראל כביכול. הוא מספר על הצעה דומה בדבר מדינה יהודית בארץ־ישראל של עתון גרמני, המקדים לכך קצת דברים על תכונת היהודים וגזעם, המוזרה לתכלית לטעם המערב. מכאן משתמע ששנאת ישראל והרעיון על מדינת היהודים בארץ ישראל שלובים ואחוזים זה בזה ולא קשה לפיליפסון להסיק מכך, שכל ההוגה ברעיון זה הוא צורר ישראל, בין הוא בעל כוונות טובות, כג׳ורג׳ אליוט, ומכל שכן אם הוא צורר ישראל כאישטוצי.

לשם גילוי הדבר לכל משמעותו הקדיש פיליפסון מאמרו זה, בו הוא מביע דעת זרמי היהדות, ושל זרם האורתודוכסיה בכללם. אף אורתודוכסיה זו דוחה את רעיון מדינת היהודים, שכן היא הוגה אך בגאולה המופיעה באורח נס ופלא (כידוע נאבקו הרבנים הראשונים שבמחנה חיבת ציון ברעיון זה ויכלו לו). מכאן שיש לדחות רעיון זה מכל וכל ויהא מקורו טהור או נרפש ונאלח ביותר. ואין מסתפק פיליפסון בשלילת הרעיון ומוסיף לטיעונו זה טענה חזקה ביותר, לדעתו, העשויה לבסס את ההבל שבתכנית זו, הוא ענין ה ל ש ו ן. למותר להוסיף שביסוס ההתנגדות למדינה יהודית על סמך ראיה זו ה י א שנתנה דחיפה אחרונה לבן־יהודה ליטול את הענין הזה ולעשותו לאחר מכן, לכל ימי חייו, יסוד מוסד לתחייתנו הלאומית.

לשון משותפת היא, לדעת פיליפסון, עיקר העיקרים לחיים לאומיים במדינתם ואילו ליהודים חסרה שפה כזו. הם מדברים גרמנית, אנגלית, הולנדית — באחת כל הלשונות בעולם. אפילו יידיש, שמכתלי דברי פיליפסון משתמע שאין זו לשון כלל, המדוברת בין יהודי פולין ורוסיה, סופה שתפנה אף היא מקומה ללשון המדינה, רוסית. הנקל להבין איזו צורה תהיה למדינה הזאת בארץ ישראל, כשיתקבצו המוני המונים בעלי לשונות אין קץ. אכן יש לשון ליהודים, היא העברית, המשותפת לכל יהודי העולם והמובנת לכולם, לפחות לאינטליגנציה שבהם. החכמים יודעים וכותבים בלשון זו אבל אין היא עשוייה להיות לשון־דיבור ובנוסף לכך שונה היגוי העברית בכל עדה ועדה. בשל כך

הישוב היהודי בירושלים מפוזר ומפורד לעדות ולשונות ואין בין עדה לעדה כל מכנה משותף. אלה יושבי ירושלים היהודים אינם מסוגלים להתלכד לכלל חטיבה אחת ומכל שכן קיבוצי היהודים בעולם. מכאן מוכיח פיליפסון שהיהודים הם חלק אורגאני של העמים בהם הם יושבים זה מאות דורות ושנים. השוני שבין היהודים לעם סביבו אינו חורג מהמצוי בכמה וכמה מדינות, בהן יושבות יחידות אתנוגרפיות שונות: הבאסקים ועוד, שעם כל זאת הם חלק העמים בהם הם שוכנים. הלשון היא איפוא הקשר האיתן ביותר המלכד את היהודי לעם שבקרבו הוא יושב.

מכאן צועד פיליפסון לקראת החתימה והסיכום: היהודים הושלכו מארצם לאחר ששלטו בה תחילה שמונה מאות שנה ולאחר מכן שש מאות שנה. אחר כך פוזר העם היהודי בעולם כולו, תהליך הנמשך זה אלף ושמונה מאות שנה, היינו תקופת־זמן ארוכה יותר מזו שארכו ימי העצמאות המדינית. במשך הזמן הזה סיגלו לעצמם היהודים ארחות חיים, זרים בתכלית למקום מהם יצאו, דבר העושה את רעיון המדינה היהודית לבלתי־אפשרי כלל ועיקר. ועתה, למרבה הצחוק, רוצים לשלחם לשם. ל א, מדגיש פיליפסון בפסוקים החותמים מאמרו, שכן עתה חייבים וצריכים אנו להשתדל למען שיווי זכויות בני אמונתנו (חלילה לא: "בני עמנו"...) בארצות בהן הם יושבים זה שנות אלף ומחצית האלף (הכוונה כמובן לגרמניה). לכאורה יש בפסוק זה, שלאחר שנות אלף ומחצית האלף יש להשתדל למען שיווי זכויות, מעין ניגוד הגיוני לכל עצמו של בנינו זה של פיליפסון. אולם אין זה מענייננו הפעם, אלא השלכותיו של מאמר זה על "שאלה נכבדה" של בן־יהודה.

אפייני ביותר, שכל עצם מבנה מאמרו של בן־יהודה מזכיר בהרבה את צורת מאמרו הנזכר של פיליפסון. אף כאן צועד בן־יהודה החל בפסוקים הראשונים, לקראת מטרתו, ההפוכה בתכלית לזו של פיליפסון כמובן, לשם ההוכחה שיש ויש לאומיות לעם ישראל והיא יכולה להתבצע אך ורק בארץ ישראל. בימינו אנו אין כמות מאמרו זה של בן־יהודה באנאלי ושיגרתי, כשם שמאמרו של פיליפסון, לאחר ימות השואה, טראגי במסקנותיו. קודם כל הוא מבקש להוכיח שהלאומיות בכלל, ככל שהיא ילידת הזמן החדש באירופה, אינה כה מופרכת, שכפי שהיא נראית בעיני רבים וביחוד בעיני הקוסמופוליטיים למיניהם, החל בנציגי הזרם האידיאליסטי בהגות הגרמנית וכלה בסוציאליסטים וקומוניסטים. הוכחת הלאומיות בכלל, כפי שהיא נעשית על ידי בן־יהודה במאמר זה, אף היא אינה מענייננו הפעם ואף למותר היא ה י ו ם, מקץ תשעים שנה. אולם הנופך של בן יהודה הוא מעניין ביותר וביחוד שהוא משווה לו גוון בלטריסטי־פיוטי. בנוסח זה הוא מדבר על השוני ביצורי האדם, על הכוח המקרב אחד לאחר ובה במידה גם דוחה אחד מהשני. כאן גם המסקנה, שכל מה שמתאים לכלל האנושות נאה ויאה כמובן גם ליהודים.

אך אם באמת הצדקה לכל עם ולאום להגן על לאומתו (הכוונה לאומיות) ולסוכך עליה לבל ימח שמה מתחת השמים, הלא אז גם לנו העברים, כה ישפוט שכל ישר של כל בן־תמותה, הצדקה הזאת; כי מדוע ייגרע חלקנו מחלק כל העמים? במה נופלים אנחנו מהם? אך אהה! לא כל אשר ייטיב בעיני השכל הישר ייטב גם בעיני הפילוסופיה, וגם הפעם נגזר גם עלינו, כי ביחוס אל השאלה הזאת תתנגד הפילוסופיה לשכל כל בן־תמותה. "כבר חדלה העברית מהיות עם" — תשים בפי כוהניה; "כבר נאספה לאומות העברית" ורק דת היהודים והמאמינים בה רק המה נשארו בארץ, ולכן להתבולל עם אחיהם בני מולדתם, רק זה אושר מאמיני בדת היהדות בעתיד — — —

וכאן מגיע בן־יהודה לעיקר ההתדיינות עם פיליפסון, היינו ענין הלשון. מפריך בן־יהודה את קנה המידה הלשוני להגדרתה של אומה, שכן לא לשון אחת ידברו הצרפתים ואף על פי כן הם עם ואומה "ומדוע אם כן, ממשיך לשאול בן־יהודה, יתרצו אחדים מבני עמנו (כח' פיליפזאן במ"ע) [4], כי לא מוכשרים אנחנו לחיי לאום, יען לא שפה אחת נדבר כולנו ?". וכאן אנו מגיעים לפסוק, שניתן לומר עליו, שהוא הוא שקבע את ערכו הגדול של מאמר בן־יהודה, שכן מפסוק זה מתחילה התקופה החדשה של העברית, הדיבור העברי בארץ־ישראל וכל הכרוך בכך. ולא היה נוצר פסוק זה אילולי הפיסקה במאמרו של פיליפסון, שבה הוא דן הרבה בקריטריון הלשון לגבי קביעת מעמד לעם ולאומה.

שתי טענות לו לפיליפסון ליהודים וללשונותיהם: ראשית אין להם לשון משותפת וכל תפוצה מדברת בלשון עם ועם ועל כן אי אפשר ללכד ציבור רב־לשוני ורב־גוני זה לכלל אומה אחת וביחוד בארץ־ישראל. מצד שני. יודע פיליפסון הרב, שקיימת העברית, היא הלשון הלאומית לכל בני ישראל בעולם כולו, לשון התפילה וספרות־הקודש־והחול שלו במשך הדורות ובכל העולם. אולם הוא מודה, שהיא מובנת אך לחכמים ולכן אין היא יכולה להיות לשון־דיבור. בנוסף לכך הוא מספר על שוני־הגייה של ספרדים ואשכנזים וכו'. דן פיליפסון על המציאות בימיו, שהיתה כמובן גם לנגד עיני בן־יהודה. ואף על פי כן מעניין ואף נפלא לראות מסקנות שונות לגבי מציאות אחת. פיליפסון מקבל אותה כקבועה ועומדת ורואה לפיה את משאלות לבו: לראות את עצמו ואת כלל ישראל בגרמניה כגרמנים בני דת משה, עובדה, אותה מוקיע בן־יהודה בכל עוזו בקטע שהבאנו לעיל. לצד טענתו של פיליפסון על הדגשת הדת כמכנה משותף ליהודים בעולם כולו ואילו לגבי הלאום אנו גרמנים, צרפתים, אנגלים וכו', הוא מטיל את הנימוק הבא, שכל כולו בתחום העתיד ולא היה כמותו לדמיון באותם ימים. כל זה הקדמנו לפסוקו המופלא, המעורר השתאות ככל שאנו מתרחקים מעת היכתבו, שכן גלומה בפסוק זה ראיית העתיד היהודי בארץ ישראל על כל ההשלכות בדורות האחרונים. "והלא יתר שאת לנו העברים, טוען בן־יהודה בפסוקו זה, כי יש לנו שפה אשר בה נוכל לכתוב ככל העולה על רוחנו וגם לדבר בה יש לאל ידינו אם אך נחפוץ".

לכאורה ניצב כאן איש בעל דמיון וחזון מול איש המדבר בלשון המציאות. ברם, לא יארכו הימים ובן־יהודה יעלה לארץ־ישראל ויגשים בה, מאז צעדו על אדמת ארץ ישראל, את הצוו הגלום בפסוק זה: ינהיג את הדיבור העברי ויסגל את העברית, אחת הלשונות העתיקות, לצרכי יום יום. הוא יתחיל לאחר זמן קצר של התערות בארץ, להוציא ולערוך את העתון "הצבי" ומאז ועד יום מותו, היינו במשך ארבעים שנה כמעט, ישתמש בעתוניו להפוך את העברית ללשון של יום ויום, יחדש חידושי־לשון וצירופי־לשון לצרכים אלה ולשם כך אף יתחיל עוד לפני עלייתו להגות במילון הגדול ללשון העברית, שיגשימו לאחר מכן בכוחות עצמיים. אף יהא הרוח החיה בהקמת ועד הלשון בירושלים, החוגג עתה את שנת השמונים לקיומו והאקדמיה ללשון העברית העלתה זה מקרוב, בחנוכה תש"ל, תאריך זה ברוב פומבי.

זהו קיצור תולדותיו של מאמר זה ופסוק זה בתוכו. הוא נולד תוך מאבק עם הביטוי הקיצוני ביותר של ההתבוללות היהודית והוא דוגמה מובהקת כיצד נעשה חזון מנוגד למציאות ממשות חיה תוך הגשמה עצמית והתמסרות עד תום לרעיון זה. מקץ עשרות

שנים הפכה מציאות זו של פיליפסון למציאות של דם ודמעות, שההיסטוריה היהודית לא ידעה כמותה. ואילו ביקשנו לסמל את התמורה הכבירה בתולדותינו האחרונים אין לנו אלא להציב מאמר זה של בן־יהודה ופסוק זה בכללו, לעומת מאמרו הנזכר של פיליפסון.

הערות

[1] כונס לאחרונה באסופה: כל כתבי אליעזר בן־יהודה כרך ראשון (1941) מחלקה שניה (פגינציה מיוחדת לכל מחלקה), עמ׳ 3—13.

[2] Die Wiederherstellung des jüdischen Staates. Allgemeine Zeitung des Judentums, Vol. 42, 1878, No 24, pp. 371–373

[3] ראה במפורט על כך בספרו של נתנאל קצבורג: אנטישמיות בהונגריה — 1867—1914 (הוצאת דביר, תל אביב, 1969), עמ׳ 56 ואילך.

[4] במכתב־העתי, המונח לעתון בימים ההם, והכוונה לעתונו הנזכר של פיליפסון.

בקורת יהודית של הברית החדשה מן המאה הי״ג

יהודה רוזנטל
ירושלים

לכבוד יובל ידידי הרב אדוארד יצחק קיוב אני מפרסם בזה בקורת יהודית של הברית החדשה מן המאה הי״ג מתוך כ״י עברי (מס׳ 53) שבספריה הלאומית המרכזית ע״ש ויטוריו עמנואל ברומי [1]. בקורת זו היא מאת המתווכח היהודי ר׳ יוסף ב״ר נתן המקנא או ר׳ יוסף האופיציאל שפעולתו חלה באמצע ובמחצית השניה של המאה הי״ג [2].

הבקורת היהודית של הברית החדשה מתחילה עם הופעתה. שרשיה נעוצים בתלמוד של הכנסיה. לאט לאט מתחילים היהודים לחבר ספרי ויכוח נגד הנצרות; מתחילה לשם ובספרות המדרשית [3]. הספרים האנטי־נוצריים הראשונים בעברית נתחברו בארצות האיסלאם תחת השפעת הספרות האנטי־נוצרית האיסלאמית [4]. באותן הארצות יכלו היהודים לכתוב בחופש גמור על הנצרות ולא פחדו מפני רדיפות. אבל גם באירופה המערבית מוכרחים היו היהודים להלחם נגד השפעת הנצרות ונגד מאמצי התעמולה של הכנסיה. לאט לאט מתחילים היהודים לחבר ספרי וכוח נגד הנצרות; מתחילה לשם צורך פנימי; לשם דחיית הפרושים הכריסטולוגיים של התנ״ך. אחרי כן הם עוברים גם להתקפה; לבקורת הברית החדשה והנצרות [5]. ספר הויכוח הראשון באירופה המערבית שמכיל גם בקורת של הברית החדשה הוא הספר מלחמות השם ליעקב בן ראובן (מאה י״ב; ספרד) [6]. גם ספר נצחון ישן שפורסם ע״י ואגנזייל בספרו ״חיצי האש של השטן״ [7] מכיל בקורת של הברית החדשה; כמו כן הספר ״יוסף המקנא״ ליוסף בן נתן המקנא מכיל בסופו בקורת על הברית החדשה [8]. כ״י רומא מס. 53 שהזכרתי למעלה ושמכיל חלק גדול של הספר יוסף המקנא מכיל שני פרקים מוקדשים לבקורת הברית החדשה.

המחברים של בקורות אלה עוברים על חייו ותורותיו של ישו כמו שהם מובאים בבשורות ובעיקר בבשורה של מתי ושואלים קושיות חמורות בכדי להפריך את הספורים עפ״י השכל ומבליטים את הסתירות שהם מוצאים בהם.

אפייני בבקורת הוא ההומור העוקץ שלפעמים הוא בא לידי ביטוי אפילו בצורה

גסה [9]. מזה יש לראות שהיתה מופנית כלפי פנים ולא כלפי חוץ. מחברי הבקורות ידעו את הברית החדשה מתוך התרגום הלאטיני. אבל מצוטט גם התרגום הלועזי ז"א הצרפתי [10]. נמצאים בבקורת גם שינויי נוסחאות אחדים כלפי הנוסחא המקובלת [11]. המחברים ידעו את הפולחן הנוצרי. בדרך כלל יש לעמוד מתוך הבקורת על קשרי היחס התרבותיים שבין היהודים והנוצרים של התקופה.

השפעת הגומלין בין בקורת הברית החדשה היהודית ובין בקורת הברית ההדשה של הכתות האפיקורסיות השונות דורשת בדיקה מדוייקת מיוחדת.

[13 ב] אתחיל תחילת התשובה שהשיב הר' יוסף [1] על השמד [2].

כתוב להם, אז יבאו אל יוחנן יושבי ירושלים וכל יודא וכל הממלכות עד הירדן והיו מטבילין בירדן [מתי ג. 5—6] ואותה טבילה קורין בשטיטור [3], וכל כך למה, מי צוה ליוחנן זו הטבילה, ועוד הא [4] הגויים אין עושין לא כישנה ולא כחדשה כי טבילת יוחנן היה בירדן והם משמדין [5] במים שאובין.

כ"ל [כתוב להם], אז בא ישו אל המחנה ויטבילהו יוחנן ובעלותו מהמים נפתחו השמים וירא רוח בת קול יורד ובאה עליו ועגה בדמות יונה מן השמים, זה בני בכורי בחירי רצתה נפשי [מתי ג, 16—17] וכ"כ [וכל כך] למה, וכי יש אלוה צריך לקדשו מטומאת בשר ודם. ועוד כ"ל [כתוב להם] במקום אחר כי רוח הקדש נכנס במרים כשנתעברה [6], אותו רוח היכן היה וא"ת נטמאה בידיעה הכי נטמאה כשאר נשים, אין זה בתורתם.

ועוד מצינו בתורתם שהממאן מלהטבילם רק פעם אחת והשונה בטבילה נקרא מין [7], ואם נקדש מאלהותו מה לו להטביל. ועוד הצלמים למה מטבילים כי אומרים גם האדם לא מטבילים רק על הנפש כי גוף האדם קורין כלי ריק [8].

שאלתי למינים מהו שכתוב, דור טהור בעיניו ומצואתו לא רוחץ [משלי ל. יב]. עוד מהו, לולי ה' שהיה לנו בע"א [בקום עלינו אדם, תהלים קכד. ב], וכתיב, אזי עבר על נפשנו המים הזדונים [שם שם ה] [9], וכתיב ברוך ה' אשר לא נתננו טרף לשיניהם [שם שם ז], לא היה אדם שהשיבני דבר.

פעם אחת הייתי לפני שלטון דוטרו [10] איש חיל ויודע תורתנו וגם אשתו ביותר והיו גלחים מתווכחים עמי בדבר והשגל [11] יושבת אצלו, הקשיתי להם, לולי ה' [תהלים קכד. ב—ד] וכל הענין, אשתק, וענתה השגל כתוב, בקום עלינו אדם זה פרעה, המים הזדונים זה מי ים סוף [12]. אמרתי להם חס לו לבן ישי ולנביא ולגדול כמוהו לחרף ולגדף המים אשר עשו לו טובה כזאת, היה לו לקרותם מים אדירים כמו משה רבינו [שמות טז, י].

עוד שאלתי אם השמד מטהר ומנקה למה לא נכנס בגוייה [13] שהרי השמד קדם לו מימי יוחנן המטביל, ולמה לא השמיד אותה בתחילה לטהרה ולנקותה.

עוד שאלתי מי צוה ליוחנן להטביל את ישו הרי כבר הטביל רבים קודם שמועת שיו שכן כתוב להם, אז הלך ישו מגליל אליו [מתי ג, 13], וכך נמצא שבדאו יוחנן מלבו והיה ראש האמנה ולא ישו וממנו היה להם לעשות אלהות.

ועוד משביעין בשעת השמד שלא ישלוט בהן עין הרע ולא שד ולא פגע רע [14], ומצינו ששלטו ברבים מחלות וחלאים, למה הדבר דומה היוצא ואומר אדם לחברו מי תקן המטבע הזאת וא"ל מלך פלוני נסתכל בצורה ובדמות ובאותן הרשומות מסביב ומצא בו שם אחר א"ל שקר אמרת.

עוד שאלתי אתם אומרים השמד לטהר הגוף הוא בא ולמה תטביל[ו]הו מיד כשנולד קודם שחטא ורוחצים הבגד קודם טנופו, ועוד הכי טוב מדעת או שלא מדעת. עוד שאלתי כשנשתמד ישו מיודי לגיות למה לא החליף שמו ואם לא נשתמד לשם גיות א׳כ עדיין הוא יודי ואינכם עמו [15].

עוד שאלתי לדבריכם כי מאת אלהיכם השמד ויש בו ממש למה אינו מרפא חולים ומצורעים, ועוד למה לא נשתמדה אמו מרים ויש דוחים לומר כי בכניסתו בה נשתמדה ועלתה בה טבילה עכ״ז [עם כל זה] אם יצאת לגיות למה לא נתחלף שמה.

כתוב להם שהלך ישו במקום אחד ומצא שם חולה שחלה שנה אחת א״ל ישו רצונך להרפא א״ל אדוני בך אני רוצה א״ל קח מיטתך ולך ונרפא מיד ויקח מטתו וילך [מתי ט. 6—7] [16] ובאותו היום שבת היה ולכך באו היודים ואמרו שבת היום ואסור בעשיית מלאכה ולישא משא ביום השבת, ואיך צוה לחלל שבת, הלא כתוב בירמיה, לא תוציאו משא ביום השבת [יז, כב].

כתוב להם שאמר ישו לבן השידים השוכב על המטה קום לך למען תדע כי בן אדם שולט בארץ סולח חטאים אז אמר ישו לבעל השידים שא מיטתך ולך אל ביתך [מתי ט, 1—7].

עוד **[14 א]** כ״ל [כתוב להם] במקום אחר, וירא ישו כתות סביבותיו וילך מעבר לנהר פרת ויבא סופר אחד ויאמר לו רבי אלך אחריך אל אשר תלך, ענה ישו, שועלים חפורות יש להם ולעופות השמים קנים ואני בן אדם אין לי קרקע במה שאוכל להשים ראשי [מתי ח, 1—20], ואם אלוה הוא לא [נ]קרא ב״א [בן אדם]. ועוד אם עשה אות הזה להודיע כחו וגבורתו שהוא אלוה כשמצא בעל השד למה אמר לסופר תדע שבן אדם שולט בארץ [מרקוס ב, 10] ה״ל [היה לו] להשיב אלוה שליט בארץ, ועוד אם אלוה הוא למה ענה שקר לאותו סופר שאמר אין לי קרקע להשים ראשי הא כתוב, לה׳ הארץ ומלואה תו״ב [תבל ויושבי בה, תהלים כד, א] וכן, הארץ לא תמכר לצמיתות כי לי כל הארץ [ויקרא כה, כג], וכתוב, לא איש אל ויכזב [במדבר כג, יט] ואומר ע״כ [על כן] שאינו מכזב ואינו בן אדם, ואם היה בן אדם כתוב, ארור (האיש) [הגבר] אשר יבטח באדם [ירמיהו יז, ה] וכתוב, אל אנכי ולא איש [הושע יא, ט].

כתוב להם, ובמלאת ימי טהרה ככתוב בתורת משה והביאה עמה בירושלים ב׳ בני יונה [לוקס ב, 22—24], משמע שהיתה טמאה כשאר יולדת, והם אומרים שלא נטמאה.

כ״ל [כתוב להם], ובשעה הששית החשיך העולם ובתשיעי צעק אלי אלי למה עזבתני [מתי כז, 45—46], ואם אלוה הוא למה צעק ולמה עזבתני, הרי כל הצרות ישרו בעיניו.

כ״ל [כתוב להם] בפ [17] (מרקוש) [לוקס] שבא מלאך למרים לבשר לה הנך הרה ויולדת בן וקראת שמו ישו ויהי גדול ובן עליון יקרא ויתן לו ה׳ כסא דוד אביו וימלוך בבית יעקב לעולם ובמלכותו אין סוף [לוקס א, 31—33], ואם אלוה הוא מי נתנו לו, הא הכל שלו ודוד לא מלך על כל העולם, ועוד שקוראו דוד אביו. מי נברא ראשון האב או הבן ?

כ״ל [כתוב להם] בפ׳ לוקס, בהיות ישו בן יב שנים הלך לירושלים עם אבותיו לחג הפסח וישובו אבותיו ויוותר ישו לבדו בירושלים ויראו אמו ואבותיו ויתמהו כי לא חזר עמהם וישובו לירושלים ובקשוהו בין יודעיו וימצאוהו בין התלמידים ותאמר לו אמו למה עשית זאת כי אני ואביך עצבים וכואבים בקשנוך [לוקס ב, 42—48], אם נקרא [18] יוסף א״כ לא אלוה הוא ואם אביו שבשמים נמצא הכעיס בוראו, ועוד אם אביו שבשמים מדוע לא מצאוהו אין דבר נעלם ממנו.

כ"ל [כתוב להם] ויהי בערב ויצא ישו אל בית תנא עם י"ב תלמידיו; **בצאת אל בי** תנא נרעב ישו וירא מרחוק עץ תאנה טעין עליה ויבא שם לראות היש בה תאנה ולא מצא בו רק עלים לבדם כי לא היה עת תאנים ויאמר לא יצא ממיך פרי לאכול [מתי כא, 17—19]. ולמה נרעב, וא"ת מפני הבשר הלא משה צם מ' יום ומ' לילה מזיו שכינה, וא"ת שהרוח נרעב, היתכן זה הלא אינו אוכל כלום, ועוד למה הלך לתאנה לראות היש בו תאנים, הלא ידע מרחוק וא"ת כנגד הבשר דיבר הלא גלוי לכל שאינו יודע מאומה כי אם הרוח ולמה קללו ומה חטא האילן אם בשביל שהטריח אותו כעס עליו הלא צוה לאפושטל, הם תלמידיו, אהבו שונאיכם והתפללו בעד עושקיכם והטיבו לאויביכם וברכו לאורריכם [מתי ה, 44], ואלון זה שלא פשע כלום ולא שלח בעדו לאמר בא ואכול מפירותי, למה קללו בלא משפט[19]?

כ"ל [כתוב להם] **[14 ב]** ויקח ישו תינוק אחד ויעמידהו בתוך י"ב תלמידיו ויאמר להם כל מי שיקבל בשמי קטן זה כאילו מקבל אותי והמקבלו לא יקבלנו כ"א אותי שכן למדתי מן הנערים ס"א [סברה אחרת] אותו מקבל[20], והמקבל אותי אינו מקבל אותי אלא אותו ששלחני [מרקוס ט, 36—37], ויען לו יוחנן ויאמר רבי ראינו אנשים שהוציאו שדים בשמך שהם אינם הולכים אחריך, ואם נאמין[21] אליהם ויאמר ישו אל תאמינו בם[22] אין אדם עושה גבורה בשמי [מרקוס ט, 38—39]. מה הדבר הזה והמקבל אותי אינו מקבל (אנכי) [אותי], מה החידה הזאת? ועוד שאמר ישו ליוחנן אל תאמינו לאותם המוציאים שדים בטומאה[23], מכלל שהיה להם לעשות גבורה ע"י כשוף[24].

כ"ל [כתוב להם] ויעזוב ישו את ארץ יודה וילך בגליל והיה רצונו לעבור שומרון ויבא במדינת שומרון הנקראת שמר אצל החלקה אשר נתן יעקב ליוסף בנו ויהי שם מעיין וישו יעף וישב על המעיין ובשעה הששית באה אשה משומרון לשאוב מים ואמר לה ישו תן לי מים לשתות ותלמידיו היו במדינה לקנות להם מאכל, ותאמר להם האשה השומרונית איך תוכל לשתות עמי שאתה יודי ואנכי אשה שומרונית ואין היודים אוכלים עם השומרונים. [יוחנן ד, 3—9], ואם הוא אלוה למה יעף ולמה היה צריך לשתות מים וא"ת (הנשמה) [הבשר] היה יעף וזאת לא יהיה לעולם בלי רוח חומד בני אדם, כשהבשר מחובר עם הרוח בן אדם יעף אבל בשר שרוח הקדש בתוכו אינו יעף.

כ"ל [כתוב להם] חופה נעשית בכנען[25] בגליל והיה שם ישו נקרא לחופה עם תלמידיו וחסר היין ותאמר אם ישו אליו אין להם יין ויאמר אליה מה לי ולך אשה עדיין לא הגיע שעתי וא"כ [ואחר כך] ירד אל כפר נחום ישו ואמו ואחיו ותלמידיו ושם ישבו מעט ימים היה קרוב לפסח [יוחנן ב, 1—4, 12]. והם אומרים אם ישו אינה נקראת אשה שאין נקרא בתורה עד שתהא בעולה לאיש, ועכשיו כאן מצינו שבנה קראה אשה שאמר, מה לי ולך אשה ואם הוא אלוה לעולם לא היה אומר שקר וכזב. כך אנו שואלים מפני מה (נתארח) [נתארס] יוסף עם מרים כשהוא בעלה, והם משיבים לנו מפני שכתוב בתורה שכל אשה זונה תסקל ולכך נצטווה יוסף להיות עם מרים כשהוא בעלה כשיראו היודים שהיא מעוברת שלא יסקלוהו ועכשיו אני אומר שאין כתוב לסקל אשה על זנותה כ"א אשת איש וארוסה אבל אחרת לא[26] ועוד שהם אומרים שישעיה הנביא ניבא עליו שיהא נולד בנערה בתולה שנאמר, הנה העלמה הרה (בן) וילדת בן וקראת שמו עמנו אל [ישעיה ז, יד], ואם פסוק זה נאמר על ישו, מדוע עשו לו אב (כנגד עשני)[27] על מה היודים תמהים על הפליאה והלא אחרי שיודעי הדבר יכולים לומר

שהם שוטים. אל תתמהו מזאת המעוברת שזאת משלמת דברי הנביא שאמר, הנה העלמה הרה, ועוד שכך אומרים שנקרא עמנו אל מדוע לא היה שמו כן והלא לא נקרא בתורתם כ"א ישו לבדו ועמנו אל לא נקרא מעולם. ועוד אם הוא [15 א] אלוה מדוע לא הציל אמו וכי כבוד היה לו שעשו לו אב, ועוד מי הם אילו האחים שירדו עמו לכפר נחום וא"ת כל ישראל נקראו אחים[28], על שמם, שכן כתוב כשראו ישראל האותות תהו ואמרו זה לזה מאין חכמה וגבורה לזה ולא היה זה בן נפחא ואמו מרים ואחיו יעקב ויוסף ושמעון ויוד ואחיותיו הלא עמנו הם [מתי יג, 54—56].

כ"ל [כתוב להם] שאמר לו אדם אמך ואביך עומדים בחוץ לבקש אותך וישב אל שפת הים ויתקבצו לו כתות כתות ויכנס באניה וכל הכתות עומדות על שפת הים וידבר אליהם משלים הרבה ויאמר הנה יצא הזורע לזרוע ונפל מן הזרע קצת בדרך ויבואו עופות ויאכלו אותו הזרע, וקצת אותו הזרע נפל במקום אבנים שלא היה שם לחלוחית מן הארץ ויבש אותו זרע, וקצת מאותו זרע נפל באדמה שמינה ונתקבלה התבואה מידה אחת למאה ומידה אחת לשלושים ומידה אחת לששים, ומי שיש לו אזנים ישמע שמוע, ויקרבו תלמידיו ויאמרו אליו למה תדבר משלים עם הכתות ויען ישו ויאמר להם לכם ניתן לב להבין רזי מלכות שמים ולהם לא ניתן להבין, מי שיש לו חכמה יושפע לו ומי שאין לו מה שיש לו יקח ממנו ע"כ [על כן] אני מדבר להם משלים כי הם אינם רואים ושומעים ואינם מבינים לקיים מה שנאמר, שמעו ולא תבינו וראו ואל תדעו השמן לב העם וגו' ושב ורפא לו [ישעיה ו, י] ואשרי עינים הרואות ואזנים השומעות ועכשיו אפרש לכם המשלים ואתם שמעו כך זה אמר וכך זה ופירש להם כל דבר ודבר [מתי, יב, 47; יג, 1—17], ועכשיו שפעם הזה לא דבר נכונה שדבר לעם ברוח שלא יוכלו להבין היה לו להחכים ועוד שקללם, השמן לב וגו'.

כ"ל [כתוב להם] באותו מקום שאמר לו הסופר ר' אלך אחריך א"ל אחד מתלמידיו הניחני עד שאקבור את אבי א"ל ישו בא אחרי והנח מלקבור את אביך [מתי ח, 21—22] ונכנס בספינה ולקח עמו תלמידיו והנה רוח סערה בים והאניה חשבה להשבר ותבא הרוח בעבר הים גדולה וחזקה ויישן ישו ויבואו תלמידיו ויעוררוהו [מתי ח, 21—25], וכי יש רעה גדולה מזו שאמר לאותו תלמיד הנח מלקבור את אביך (והלא אין מצוה גדולה מזו שאמר לאותו תלמיד הנח מלקבור את אביך) והלא אין מצוה גדולה מלקבור מתים נכרים[29] וכ"ש כמו אביו של אדם, ועוד שהוא אמר שהוא ישן, אם אלוה הוא היאך ישן, הלא כתיב, הנה לא ינום ולא ישן ש"י [שומר ישראל, תהלים קכא, ד].

כ"ל [כתוב להם], ויהי כאשר שבו המלאכים אשר הלכו לבקש את ישו היה מלאך נראה אל יוסף וא"ל קום קח הנער ואמו ולך וברח למצרים ושב שם עד אשר אלך, קום [15 ב] שעתיד הורדוס לבקש הנער ולאבדו ויברח יוסף למצרים [מתי ב, 13—14] וכ"כ [וכל כך] למה היה ירא מן המלך הלא אנו רואים ממלאכי אלהינו וממשרתיו שאינם מתיראים מבשר ודם ועשו משלחתו של מקום בגלוי ולא היה כח באדם ליגע בהם וליזק בהם כלום שכך כתוב בלוט, והאנשים אשר פתח הבית הוכו וגו' [בראשית יט, יא], ובאלישע כתוב, ויתפללו אלישע אל ה' ויאמר הך נא את הגוי הזה בסנורים ויכם כדבר אלישע [מ"ב ו, יח] וכתוב, וישלח המלך ידו לאמר תפשוהו ויבש ידו ולא היה יכול להשיבו אל פניו [מ"א יג, ד].

כ"ל [כתוב להם], ויעבר משם ישו וילך אל צור ואל צידון; והנה אשה כנענית הולכת אחריו וצועקת ואומרת חונינו חנינו אדוני בן דוד בתי מלאה שדים וישו לא

עזר לה כלום; ויקראו אליו תלמידיו וידרשו ממנו ויאמרו לו, רחם על שהיא צועקת אחרינו; ויען ויאמר להם איני שלוח כ״א אל צאן אובדות בית ישראל; והאשה באה ותשתחוה לו ותאמר, אדוני הושיעני; ויען ישו ויאמר לה, אין לגזול לחם מן הבנים ולתתו לכלבים; ותען האשה הכלבים אוכלים מן הפתותים הנופלות משולחן אדוניהם; ויען ישו ויאמר אי אשה גדולה אמונתך יהי לך כאשר תחפצי ותרפא בתה בשעה ההיא [מתי טו, 21—28], כך ענה להם ישו איני שלוח כי אם אל צאן אובדות בית ישראל כלומר שהוא לא בא לארץ כ״א למחול לפושעי ישראל וחטאותיהם, הואיל שבא למחול, מדוע הפשיעם ועיורם שהיו נכשלים במיתתו וכי לא מצא אומה בעולם שהיה יכול להכשיל בו כ״א אותם שבא לפדות ולהושיע.

ועוד אם הוא אלוה או נביא היה לרפאותו מיד להודיע כחו בשאר אומות כאשר עשה אלישע שרפא נעמן מצרעתו להודיע כי יש נביא בישראל [מ״ב, ה, ח], ואף שלמה מלך ישראל התפלל לפני המקום על ישראל, ונתת לאיש כדרכו ככל דרכיו [מ״א ח, לט] וגם אל הנכרי אשר לא מעמך הוא [שם, „שם, מא] כך התפלל וגם (הנביא) הנכרי שבא והניח ע״ז שלו ובא להתפלל בבית הזה לא ישוב ריקם ואתה תשמע השמים את תפלתו ואת תחנתו [שם, שם, לח] כדי ש... על כחך וגבורתך.

ועוד שאמר אל הכנענית, אין טוב לגזול לחם מהבנים לתת לכלבים, תמה [30] הא לא אמר אלא כלומר אין טוב לגזול החסד שיש לי ליתן לישראל ואתננו לשאר אומות כלומר לזו הכנענית שנקראת כלבים [31].

כך אני שואל להם מאחר שאדם מת בלא טבילה אותה טבילה יכול אדם להטבילו כדי שיכנס לג״ע בעד אותה טבילה. והם אומרים לעולם לא יכנס הואיל ובחייו לא נטבל. כ״ל [כתוב להם] איך אמר להם גריגוריש קדוש שלהם שפעם אחת היה הולך בקברי הישמעאלים מצא בקבר אחת כתוב בחרט אנוש, כמה מספר החיות של אותו הישמעאלי. **[16 א]** כמה היה רחמן ואוהב משפט וחסד שעשה עם אשה ענייה, שפעם אחת פגע אחד מעבדיו בבנה של אותה האשה וכעס עליו והרגו וא״כ באתה האשה צועקת אל אותו ישמעאל, ואותה אשה שבאה לפניו בכתה על מיתת בנה ואמרה לו כך וכך עשה לי עבדך, מיד לקח אותו העבד וצוה לו בנפשו לילך עם האשה ולהיות עמה כל ימי חייה כאילו היתה אמו ומיד הלך לדרכו בחיל אותו שר ונהרג, וכשראה גריגוריש מעשה הזה ונתגלגלו רחמיו ובכה על הקבר ובקש רחמים שיסלחו לו חטאותיו ותהי נפשו בג״ע וכאשר שאל כן היה ואמרו שמן הדמעות שנפלו בקבר היה נטבל לקיים מה שכתב בתורתו שאין אדם יכול ליכנס בג״ע אא״כ נטבל ואח״כ אמרו בקול מן השמים לגריגוריש, אני מתרה בך שלא תבקש ולא תשאל מחילה כזאת שמחלתי לך מזה ישמעאל לעולם לא אעלה לך (אדם) משום אדם בעולם מחילה זאת ומזאת המחילה שמחלתי לך תהא חולה עד רוב ימים וכן היה ואחזתו חמה, ומן המעשה נפלא לי מאד שאני יודע שנאמר בתורתכם מתחילה שאין יכול אדם ליכנס לג״ע אם לא נטבל וזה היאך נכנס בג״ע שמהדמעות הללו לא נטבל אפילו חצי רביע מהאבר [32] אשר על הגוף [33].

ועוד כיון שאין בו רוח אם הוא נטבל אלף פעמים בק׳ מודיאות [34] מים מה הוא יש לו עוד לדבריך שאתה אומר הטבילה הזאת טבילה מעולה היא מהדמעות אלא שלא יעלה בדעתו לעשות מעשה כזה לבקש רחמים משום אדם בעולם לא בדמעות ולא בע״א [בענין אחר] וכי לא היה לו לשמוח על אותו גריגוריש ולהכריעו לכף זכות שהשלים לו נפשו אחרת.

ועוד אם תדחני שישמעאלי זה לא נכנס תחת כנפי אלהי שמים אלא לא היה לו צרת גיהנום מפני תפילה של גריגוריש ולהכריעו לכף זכות היה נטבל, היה יכול לומר שבעד התפלה ובעד הדמעות נמחלו עוונותיו אבל הואיל שנזכר הטבילה נמצא שכל המחילה תולה באותה הטבילה.

כ״ל [כתוב להם] שתבוא השעה שכל מי שבקברים ישמעו קולו ויקומו טובים לתקומת חיים ורשעים יעמיד במשפט, איני יכול לעשות כלום מלבי ומעצמי אבל כשאני שומע אני שופט, ומשפטי ישר שאיני מבקש חפצי כ״א חפץ אשר שלחני [יוחנן ח, 28—32], וכי יש להם ברצונות מה שרוצה זה אין רוצה זה, והלא שניהם רשות אחת לדבריך, והאחד אומר איני מבקש חפצי לא היית חפצו באותו משפט אבל חפץ אביו הוא. ועוד אם הם אומרים שזהו ישו שהיה, מפני מה כתיב, ונחה עליו רוח ה׳ רוח חכמה ובינה רוח עצה וגבורה רוח דעת ויראת ה׳ [ישעיה יא, ב], היאך יכול לומר איני יכול לעשות כלום מעצמי אבל כשאני שומע אני שופט, והלא כתיב אחר המקרא הזה, והריחו ביראת ה׳ לא למראה עיניו ישפוט ולא למשמע (אוזן) (אזניו) יוכיח ושפט בצדק דלים והוכיח במישור ענוי ארץ והכה ארץ בשבט פיו וברוח (שיר) שפתיו ימית רשע [שם, שם, ג—ה], וזה לא יהיה יכול לעשות רצונו [16 ב] כמו רצון ששלחו. ועוד אם אומר שזה משיח שאנו מקוים כבר עבר ובא והלא כתוב בפ[רשה] זו אחר כל הדברים האלה, וגר זאב עם כבש ונמר עם גדי ירבץ ופרה ודוב תרעינה ושעשע יונק על חור פתן [ישעיה יא, ו—ח] ואח״כ לא יריעו ולא ישחיתו בכל הר קדשי כי מלא כל הארץ דעת ה׳ כמים לים מכסים [שם שם, ט], וכל ימיו של ישו לא היה שלום כ״א פורענות וקללה.

ועוד שכתוב על משיחנו, לא ישא גוי אל גוי חרב ולא ילמדו עוד מלחמה וכתתו חרבותיהם לאתים וחניתותיהם למזמרות [שם ב, ד] ובימיו לא היה כן ועדיין לא נשלמו הפסוקים שאמרם הנביא הן על האומות הן על ישראל ועדיין לא נבנה בית המקדש כאשר אמר הנביא באחרית הימים, נכון יהיה הר בית י״י בראש ההרים [שם ב, ב] ע״כ אני אומר שדבריהם דברי בדאי הבל המה מעשה תעתועים בעת פקודתם יאבדו, כי אין חרצובות למותם ובריא אולם [תהלים עג, ד].

כ״ל [כתוב להם] ברדת ישו מן ההר הלכו אחריו רב עם והנה מצורע אחד בא וישתחו לו ויאמר אדני אם תחפוץ תוכל לאספיני מצרעתי וישלח ישו ידו ויגע בו ונרפא ויאמר אליו ישו אל תדאג ותאמר לאדם אלא הראה לכהן והבא אליו קרבנך על טהרתך כאשר צוה משה בתורתו [מתי ח, 1—4], עכשיו נפלא הדבר מדוע יצוה לאותו מצורע לילך אל הכהן להביא קרבן כיון שרפא אותו למה צריך אל הכהן ועוד אין אנו רואים כל שאר מצות שבתורה אפילו אחת נעשית על פיו מאחר שנולד מן האשה כגון שבת ומילה ובשר חזיר ואחרות כג[ון] וכג[ון] שהתיר אחר ביאתו ואת עצמה לא נעשית מאותו יום והלאה.

כ״ל [כתוב להם] שאמר ישו, אל תחשבו שבאתי לעקור התורה והנביאים לא באתי כ״א לקיים, אמת אני אומר לכם עד שיכלו שמים וארץ, היו״ד שבתורה לא יעקר ונקוד שבתורה לא יעקר בעוד שהעולם קיים, שמים וארץ יעבורו ודברי לא יעבורו. ומי שהתיר אחת ממצות קלות וילמד כן לבני אדם יהא נדון במלכות שמים וחייב הוא בדין [מתי ח, 17—22] שמעתם מה שאומר מקרא לא תרצח והמרצח חייב הוא בדין ומי שיאמר על אחיו רעה [שם שם,21—22] הוא חייב בדין והאומר בזוי וקלון על חברו חייב

הוא לאשו של גיהנום, ואתם איך תאמרו אשר אינו דין ליטול עין בעין והלא ענשו לגיהנום אפילו האומר קלון על חברו, וא״ת בידי שמים חייב בידי אדם לא, והלא אמר לא באתי לעקור אפילו יו״ד ואפילו נקוד כ״א לקיים מה שכתוב בתחלה עין בעין שן בשן חס וחלילה להוסיף על מצות הראשונות הוא בא שהרי אמר כשם שהמרצח הוא חייב כך האומר רעה על אחיו חייב. ועוד מה שאמר מה שנאמר מקדם, ואהבת לרעך כמוך ותשנא את שונאיך אבל אני אומר אהבו אוהביכם ושנאו שונאיכם [שם שם 43—44], אין לך שקר גדול מזה שהרי בכל **[17 א]** התורה לא תמצא שיהא אדם לבנו שונא שכך כתוב, כי תראה שור אויבך או חמורו תועה הת״ל [השב תשיבנו לו, שמות כג, ד]; הסכת היטב לדברי ישו ועיין בהם לא תמצא בהם כ״א תוספות ולא מגרעות כי גם אחר שכתב מה שנאמר מקדם לא תשבעו בשמי לשקר עתה אני אומר לכם לא תשבעו, אתה בן אדם לא תשבעו שמים כי כס אלוה הוא לא תשבעו ירושלים כי קרית מלך רב הוא לא תשבעו ראשו כי שלא תוכל לעשות בו אפילו שער אחת לבן [מתי ה, 33—36]; ס״ס [סוף סוף] להוסיף בא ועתה דבריו סותרין זה את זה שהרי אחר מה שנאמר מקדם, עין תחת עין אני אומר לכם שלא תשלם לאדם כרעתו.

אומרים אב ובן ורוח הוא, בשלמא אב ורוח זה אינו אוכל וזה אינו אוכל, זה אינו ישן כו׳, זה אינו יעף וזה כו׳, זה אינו מפחיד וזה אינו מפחיד אבל הבן היכי משכחת לה שהוא כאב וכרוח הקודש הלוא הוא אוכל והוא יעף ונפחד, יעף שהרי כתוב בתורתכם וישב על המעין ושאל מים מהשומרונית [יוחנן ד, 7], נפחד דכתיב, אלי אלי למה עזבתני [מתי כז, 48], ישן דכתיב ותבא הרוח בעבר לים גדול וחזק ויישן ישו ויבאו תלמידיו ויעוררוהו [מתי ח, 24—25], וא״ת לפי שהיה רוח הקודש אומר אני שהוא בן אלהים וגם אדם הראשון אשר נפח באפיו נשמת רוח חיים קורא אני כן, וא״ת אדם הראשון לא עשה גבורה כמו זה הנה אליהו הנה אלישע שעשו כמה גבורות, ועוד אפילו לדבריך בשעה שפרח רוח הקודש ממנו מיד מת הבשר ומודה אתה לי שלאחר שמת לא יוכל הבשר לעשות לא טוב ולא רע ולאחר מיתה היאך שלשתן דבר אחד.

ועוד שהמעשים אשר עשה ובכל הדברים אשר ידבר אין דרכו של הק׳ [ב״ה], ומיד אתה מדחני בקש לומר כנגד הבשר וא״כ הבשר ורוח הקודש דבר אחד. אודיע לך שאין הבשר יודע כלום לא טוב ולא רע כי הרוח הוא יודע, הוא מחשב, הוא חוטא, הוא מתאוה וכתוב לא (תחמוד) [תתאוה] בית ריעיך ולא (תתאוה) [תחמוד] אשת ריעיך [דברים ה, יח], ומאחר שהזהיר הכתוב לא תחמוד ולא תתאוה מכלל שחומד ומתאוה ממש הוא ואיזהו חומד ומתאוה הוי אומר זה הנפש, וא״ת הבשר חומד ומתאוה הרי הוא אומר, כלתי נפשי לישועתך ה׳ [תהלים קיט, פא], הנפש החוטאת היא תמות [יחזקאל יח, ד] כלומר תפול בגיהנום, וא״ת תמות נפשי עם פלישתים [שופטים טז, ל] ונפש שמשון מי נפלה בגיהנום, אה״נ [אין הכי נמי] שחבל בגופו והחובל בגופו נופל בגיהנום[36] ועוד ראיה לדבר שהבשר אינו יודע כלום כ״א הנפש שהרי אמר פולוש באוגילש איגנייליש[36א], אשר הנפש מזהרה כל שעה לגוף שלא לחטוא[37] ועוד כתוב בתורתכם אל תכנסו במשכני בידים מרומות[38], שאם יש אדם ששונא רעהו וחושב בדעתו להרגו, בזה קורא ידים מרומות (נוא), ואע״פ שלא הרגו מעלה עליו בתורת[ם] כאילו הרגו לענשו עליו מלהכנס למשכן, ומי הוא זה שחושב להורגו הוי אומר זה הרוח, וא״ת הלב שהוא הבשר חושב להורגו דכתיב, רבות מחשבות בלב איש [משלי יט, כא], כבר הוא אומר, כלתה נפשי (לישועתך) לתשועתך [תהלים קיט, פא], ואומר, נפשי אויתיך

בלילה [ישעיה כו, ט] ואומר, כל עמל אדם לפיהו [קהלת ו, ז] וגם הנפש לא תמלא ויאמר, טוב מראה עינים מהלוך נפש [שם שם, ט], ואומר אם יש נפשכם לקבור את מתי מלפניך [בראשית כג, ח] שכל רצונות תלויות בנפש, ועוד אם הבשר חוטאת בלוא רוח מדוע הנפש נענשה וכי זה חוטא וזה נענש אלא עיקר הדבר כך הוא שניהם חוטאים כאחד משל לחגר וסומא [39] ועוד משל לאדם נרדם [40].

אמר מאמין. למה לו לישו צורך להיוולד מאשה ולסבול כל הטרחים הללו וכל שנעשו לו ולמה טעם טעם מיתה, והם משיבים בעון אדם הראשון היית כל זאת שבעברו על מצות הבורא מיד היה נמסר לידי השטן, וכן כל הנולדים אחריו בין טובים בין רעים נמסרים ליד השטן [41], וחלילה לו לעשות שום רע גזל ועוולה לא לשטן ולא לאחרים עד שכבשו רחמיו של בורא וחס על בריותיו שהלכו לגיהנום ואמר ארד ואפדה אותם הנמסרים לשטן ובאיזה ענין עשה עול אדם אחד ממנו שעשה מעצמו זהו של ישו שקורא בן אלהים ושלחו בארץ במעי אשה אחת כשאר אנשים, אותו אדם היה נקי מחטא ומעוון ורצה לפדות העולם ע"י אשה, וכשראהו השטן לקח בדעתו שמתעלה אותו לחלקו כמו שעשה מן החוטא. אחרים אומרים הבורא הואיל שהחזקת על אותו נקי שאין לך עליו בדין וכתורה שאגזול ממך הפושעים שמסורים בידך וכן עשה וירד לגיהנום ויוציא משם הנמסרים ביד השטן ולכך עשה כל זאת. והיאך עשה זאת הרי מחל מיתתו [17 ב] לאותן שהרגוהו שבשעת מותו אמר, אבי כפר להם כי אינם יודעים מה הם עושים [לוקס כג, 34] כ"ש שימחול לשטן שלא עשה לו שום רע אלא רצה לעשות בשוגג, ועכשיו אני אומר אם אמת היה הדבר הזה תמהני, היתכן לעשות כל זאת והלא יודעים כל העולם שהשטן מלאך רע ובכל יום עולה ומקטרג לפני הקב"ה בתוך מלאכים טובים אולי ימצא חן בעיני אלהים לקחת לו חוטא במתנתו שנתן לו הבורא וכתוב באיוב, ויבואו בני האלהים להתיצב על ה' ויבא גם השטן בתוכם ויאמר ה' אל השטן אי מזה תבא ויען השטן את ה' משוט בארץ ומהתהלך בה [איוב א, ו—ז], כלומר לדעת לי בארץ חוטאים שאקח במתנתי לי וכיון שהשטן עולה למעלה ומדבר עם הבורא יודע מה היה ויהיה, והיאך את אומ' שכך כסה ממנו הקב"ה ולא הכיר בנו בארץ ובא לנסותו פעמים כאשר כתוב באיונייליא. ועוד לדבריך שכסה ממנו ולא הכיר השטן את בוראו מפני שראוהו שנעשה מלובש כשאר אנשים מה פשע השטן בכך, כלומר שעשה לא עשה אלא כי שכח הוא ליכנס עם בריותיו בעורמות ובמרמה ובתחבולות, זה אינו נכון אפי' מבשר ודם שאין נוהגין זה עם זה כשורה, ואם אדם עשה שלא כדין נגד אדונו אם עושה בשוגג יכול האדון לאנס [42] מתנתו וכ"ש הבורא שמכריע לכף זכות עם בריותיו ונכנס להם לפנים משורת הדין וזהו שבחו. ועוד שאנו מוצאים בכמה מקומות בעון יילגא שישו הוציא כמה שדים מכמה בני אדם, בדבר זה גזל לו מתנתו בחנם, קדם ששלט לו השטן ועדיין לא מצא בו משום עול ולמה גזל מתנתו שנתן לו מתחלה, ולמה הוציאו מהגוף הרי שהכריחו בלא דין ודברים, ואומר אני שקודם לכן היה יכול לעשות לו בתחלה כששלט באדם הראשון היה יכול לומר אל תגע באדם שאיני רוצה כאשר אמר לאותו שד (ים) שהוציא מכמה גופים כשעשה נפלאות בארץ. ועוד מדוע עכב כל כך הפדות הזה ואי אתה מודה אם היה אחד מאוהביך חבוש בבית הא(י)סורים ואם היה יכולת בידך להוציאו היית מזרז להוציאו מיד א"כ למה עכב כ"כ [כל כך] ולמה נתן להם התורה קודם לכן הואיל ואין להם שכר טוב עליה כי כך אתם אומרים שכולם הולכים לגיהנום בין טובים בין רעים, ואומר אני שיפה היה מתחילה לפדות העם מגיהנום ואח"כ

ליתן להם התורה. ועוד שהם אומרים שכל [18 א] הבריות הולכים לגיהנום בין טובים בין רעים והלא אתם רואים קודם שבא אותו ישו בארץ היה מעשה מן לזרוש שהוא שוכב בפני פתח בית העשיר וצועק כל שעה לעשיר לעשות לו חסד ולא רוצה לסוף מתו שניהם. העשיר הלך לגיהנום ולזרוש הלך בחיקו של אברהם בנחת רוח ובגיל רב ובחדוה והוא בצער גדול נדון באש להבה בתוך פיו אמר, אברהם הנני ואמור ללזרוש שיטבול אצבעו הקטן בתוך המים ויטיל לפי מפני להבה שיוצא מפ(נ)י[43] ועכשיו משמע שאברהם ואותו לזרוש לא היה בגיהנום ואיך אומר שכולם הלכו לגיהנום.

תשובה אחרת לדבריכם שאתם בודים מלבבכם שבאותו עון נתן כל הנשמות (לגיהנום) [לשטן] לתתו לגיהנום הן טובים הן רעים עד בית שני שירד ישו ונתעלה[44] כדי לכפר על עון שלא רצה לכפר לעשות עולה לשטן, תקשי לכם חנוך שכתב בו, כי לקח אותו (ה)אלהים [בראשית ה, כד] ומאליהו שגזלם לו. ועוד כתוב, מי זה האיש ירא ה׳ יורנו בדרך יבחר נפשו בטוב תלין וזי״א [וזרעו יירש ארץ, תהלים כה, יב—יג] מי אמרו דוד, הרי שקודם ישו אין נפש טובים בגיהנום, ועוד כתוב, אל תמנע מנער מוסר כי תכנו בשבט לא ימות, אתה בשבט תכנו ונפשו משאול תציל [משלי כג, יג—יד]. והם קורין שאול גיהנום בכל מקום הרי שבמוסר נוטל משאול טרם שבא ישו.

יש להקשות למינים בשלמא לדידן סם המות אכל וטרף כן יוצאי יריכו טריפא כמוהו, וראיה לדבר שריחקם מעץ החיים שלא יתרפאו[45], אבל לדבריכם שתאמרו שאותו עון מגיע לכל דור, ואתם אומרים שכל אדם גם בשעה שנולד כבר הוא בחטא ואתם מפרשין, הן בעון חוללתי ובחטא יחמתני אמי [תהלים נא, ז], זה חטא של אדם הראשון, א״כ מהו פוקד עון אבות על בנים וכו׳ ועל רבעים לשונאי [שמות כ, ה] וק״ו לאוהביו שאינו מגיע עד רביעי והרי מגיע הוא, מגיע הן בגוף הן בנשמה לדורות הרבה הן לטובים הן לרעים ,וגם אם היה רוצה להציל מדור רביעי היה לו להציל כמו שהציל עכשיו.

ויש להקשות אתם אומרים ששבר שערי גיהנום להוציא מהם טובים ורעים א״כ אתם מרפים ידיהם של יראי חטא וכול בעלי תשובה שאין עוד דאגת פחד גיהנום עליהם, וא״ת עדיין גיהנום ושעריו קיימין א״כ לא הועילו תחנתו לדורות שעדיין יהיו רשעים בגיהנום א״כ לא מת להציל היודי׳ כי עדיין (לא) יודי׳ בעולם, וא״ת הועילו בתקנתו לדורות שיהיו כלן טובים בגיהנום כלפנים י״ל הלא הוציא אז רק ביוד׳ אבות ומשה וכל הנביאים מלכי בית דוד אבותיו עד אמו ועוד שעשה להם טובה גדולה וטובה גדולה מה שנולד מיודי׳ ונמול להציל מגלות למה נכשלו בדבר משכבר, כי לפני׳ היה שרים גדולים בארצינו והיום אנחנו בגלות עניים ודע.

עוד תשובה ע״ז לדבריכם שאתם אומרים כי באכול אדם מן העץ אז נתן הקב׳ה כל הנשמות לשטן להוליכם בגיהנום זה לא תמצא בפסוק[46] ואת״ל [ואם תמצא לומר] שכן הוא א״כ כשירד ישו לכפר עונשים הכתובים כגון קללות אדמה, קוץ ודרדר תצמיח לך, בזיעת אפיך תאכל לחם [בראשית ג. יח—יט] וכן עונשי אשה, הרבה ארבה עצבונך והרונך בת״ב [בעצב תלדי בנים, שם שם טז], כי כל אילו העונשין עדיין קיימים ועונש הנפש בגיהנום שלא [18, ב]. נתפרש ואינו אלא דעת הכרס בזה תאמרו שכפר, מי הוכיח ומי יעיד עליכם אך אם היו אותות המפורשים בפסוק נעזבים בביאת ישו אז היו נסיוני דבריכם כנים, ארורה האדמה ומדבר מקולל יצא גוף התלוי.

כ״ל [כתוב להם] כמו שהיה יונה ג׳ ימים וג׳ לילות במעי הדגה כך היה התלוי ג׳

ימים וג׳ לילות [מתי יב. 40] כל א[46]. והיאך יכול להיות אם היה נקבר ביום ו׳ מקולל[47] כמו שהם אומרים ויצא ממנו ביום א׳ שלאחריו שהוא יום אידם שקורים (מיצח) קצח[48] א״כ לא היה כ״א יום אחד וב׳ לילות ואם תאמר מקצת היום ככולו[49] מ״מ יחסר לילה אחת.

שאל הגמון משאנץ למה תקראו ליום ו׳ שלפני פסח יום ששי מקולל, השיב ודאי אמת הוא שהוא מקולל אלינו לדבריכם, אבל אם היה אלוה ואתם מאמינים בו מפני שנעשה אליכם מה או דבר אליכם דברים אשר לא כן א״כ מקולל הוא אליכם שתאמינו באדם הנתלה ואומרים שהוא אלוה[50], ובלעם נביאיכם אמר לא איש אל ויכזב [במדבר כג. יט] כלומר מי שאומר שהוא (אדם) [אל] מכזב הוא[51] ושתק ההגמון.

שאל פרש אחד ליודי איך תוכל לדבר עמנו הלא תליתם יראתי, והשיב היודי ואמר ומה היה לנו לעשות כי העליונים היו קובלים אותו ואומרים לתחתונים למסור להם האלהים השייך למעלה וענו התחתונים אתנו יהיה כי קבל בו הבשר שהוא מהתחתונים וכך היו חלוקים חלוק גדול באנו לעשות פשרה ביניהם ותלינוהו באויר בין עליונים לתחתונים[52].

תשובה על שאומרים לכך לקח בשר מן האשה כדי לכסות שלא ליוודע לשטן שהוא אלוה כמו שהשטן רצה לשלוט בנפשו חרה אפו עליו וגזל לו את כל אשר (כ) הנשמות האחרות שהיו לו תחת ידיו, י״ל להם הלא מחל לאותן שהרגוהו ועשו לו צרות והשטן שלא נגע בו ולא עשה לו כלום היזק אלא בשוגג שלא הכירו רצה לשלוט למה גזל מתנתו.

אומרים המינים שעדיין לא נפקד עלינו עון התלוי ולכך נחנו בגלות, י״ל הלא קודם מיתתו היינו בגלות בבל, ועוד לדבריכם שחטאנו בו לא היינו בכך לוקים שהרי עברו עלינו ק׳ דורות משנצלב והתורה אמרה, פוקד עון אבות על בנים וכו׳ ועל רבעים [שמות כ. ה] לכל היותר א״כ לא בשבילו הוא. ועוד לדבריכם לכך נולד ולכך בא למסור עצמו למיתה, ועוד תשובה שלא מצינו מלך ישראל מיום שגלו גלות בבל יותר מת׳ שנים כדלקמן בתשובה, לא יסור שבט מיודה [בראשית מט. י] ועוד יצא שלא תוכלו לומר שגלינו מחמת אותו עון שכן בשעת מיתתו של ישו היה מבקש מאביו ואמר לו, אדוני מחל להם כי אינם יודעים מה הם עושים [לוקס כג. 34] ועכשיו אני תמה אם הבן והאב דבר אחד ורצון אחד להם שכל העון הזה נמחל להם. והשואלים למה הארכנו בגלות זה כ״כ שלא עשינו בגלות בבל ובגלות מצרים י״ל שלא יתן לנו הק[ב״ה] העולם הבא שהוא גדול כ״כ עד אין קץ אלא א״כ נקבל בעדו הרבה יסורים קודם.

עוד י״ל מדכתיב בספר הושע, ואומר אליה ימים רבים תשבי לי לא תהיי לאיש וגם אני אליך [הושע ג. ג] וכתיב, כי ימים רבים ישבו בני ישראל אין מלך ואין שר ואין זבח ואין מצבה אחר ישובו בני ישראל ובקשו את ה׳ אלהיהם ואת דוד מלכם ופחדו אל ה׳ ואל טובו באחרית הימים [הושע שם]. אלמא שכבר נבא הנביא שנשהא בגלות ימים רבים שאין לנו לא מלך ולא שר, אך לא כל הימים כן משמע ימים רבים וכתוב, אחר ישובו בני ישראל וגו׳ אלמא בתשובה תלויה מילתא וכשישובו ישוב.

[19. א] כתוב להם בעון גליון כל מי שאינו נמול מעור ומבשר אינו יכול ליכנס בגן החיים, בלעטיין קי נון פואיריט שרקונניאריש די קארני פיליש נון פוטיש אינטררי איני ביאא[53], ערל בשר אינו ראוי לעבודה הקדושה ופסול לכך, דכתיב, בהביאכם בני נכר ערלי לב וערלי בשר להיות במקדשי לחלל[ו את] ביתי בהקריבכם את לחמי חלב ודם

ויפרו את בריתי וגו׳ לכן כה אמר ה׳ אלהים ערל לב וערל בשר לא יבא אל מקדשי [יחזקאל מד. ז—ט], אלמא ערל בשר אינו ראוי לעבודה הקדושה שהרי קראו הכתוב ערל טמא, בא להתווכח על המילה וזה לשונן ניזי צירקוס ציזי פואיריט נון אינטרבטיש אינטרגנום צילורום [54] פי׳ אם אין אתם נמולים כמונו אתם לא רואים פני אדונינו וכן, כל בן אדם זכר אומניש משקוליש אשר ערלתו בשרו מילה קוויש פריפוסיא קארו שירקומסיא לא תהיה נכרתה נשמה שלו, נון פואיריט די ליביטור אנימה איליאוש, מעם שלו ד פופולו שואו [55], א״כ למה אינכם נימולים והרי חייב כרת כל מי שאינו נימול, וא״ת ישו בטל מילה ונתן שמד תחתיו י״ל והא אמרתם שלא בא לגרוע [56] ועוד הכתיב לדורות(יכ)ם לברית עולם [בראשית יז, ז] כמו בשבת כתיב, לדורותם ברית עולם [שמות לא, טז], וכן באות הקשת כתיב, לדורות עולם [בראשית ט, יב], וגם בשלשתם נאמר אות ומה קשת אנו רואים שאינן מופר לעולם כך מילה ושבת אינו מופר כי פי ה׳ דבר.

מה ששואלין במה הנשים נכנסות ליהדות שאינן בני מילה וי״ל בעליהן פוטרות אותן [57], משל למה הדבר דומה לב׳ שותפין הבאים במכס האחד פוטר את חברו כך שהאיש נמול כל גופו פטור והאשה באה מצלעו, וכן מצינו בדוד שקרא לאשתו צלע שאמר, ובצלעי שמחו ונאספו [תהלים לה, טו], בשל[מ]א נשואות, שאינן נשואות מאי איכא למימר וי״ל אביה פוטר אותה כמו שמצינו שכל זמן שהבת אינה נשואה רשות וכח האב בה הן בנדרים הן בעונשים ובכל ענין ואפילו בדבר ששאר ישראל אסור כגון בתרומה שנאמר, וכל זר לא יאכל [ויקרא כב, י] כל זמן שאינן נשואות היא אוכלת וכשנשאת שוב אינה אוכלת [58]. נאום הגבר מנחם [59].

נשאלה שאלה לגוים כתוב (בירמיה) [בישעיה], העם המכעיסים אותי על פני תמיד הזובחים בגנות ומקטרים על הלבנים, היושבים בקברים ובנצורים ילינו האוכלים בשר חזיר ומרק פיגולים כליהם [ישעיה סה, ג—ד] פי׳ מקטרים על הלבנים הרי מקטרים בכל יום על הלבנים על קבריהם היושבים בקברים שקוברים פגריהם בבית ע״ז שלהם ומטמאים עצמם באוהל המת, ובנצורים ילינו מלינים פגריהם ומי הם האוכלים בשר חזיר ומרק פיגולים כליהם וכל העניין עד הנה כתובה לפני לא אחשה (עד) כי אם שלמתי אל חיקם [שם שם, ו] ש״מ [שמע מינה] לא יחשה הק[ב״ה] עד שינקום מאוכלי בשר החזיר ובספר ישעיה כתוב, אוכלי בשר החזיר השקץ והעכבר יחדיו — יסופו נאום ה׳ [ישעיה סו, יז]. וזה הלאטין ממנו קוי קומיטאט קארנס שואילס איט אבומינטס שימול קונשימנטור דיציט דומינוס [60].

הר׳ אשר [61] שאל מין אחד מדוע אתם אוכלים בשר חזיר ושאר בהמות וחיות ועופות שאסר הכתוב א״ל כבר נטהרו והותרו וסיפר לו כי כתוב להם (בספר יוהנש), פ״א [פעם אחת] פתח פתחון ונראה לו בחזיון והנה יריעה יורדת לפניו ובה ראה תמונת כל אשר בו רוח חיים והנה אליו קול, את אשר לפניך אכול והוא השיב, רשע הן נפשי לא מטומאה ולא בא **[19 ב]** בפי בשר פיגול והרי לפני בהמות חיות ועופות טמאים ומשמים הושב לו שנית, הכל טהורים והתרתי [62], והשיבו(ם) גם באותה יריעה ראה נחשים ועקרבים גם שקצים ורמשים. א״ל ומדוע לא תאכלום א״ל הרשות בידינו א״ל והלא מסוכן בנפשו הוא ואתם דנים למיתה למתחייב בנפשו, ושתק.

עוד השיב הרי טפשים שבכם אומרים שלא נאסרו מעולם ומה שנכתב אינו אלא משל ודוגמא וראיה, כירק עשב נתתי לכם את כל וגו׳ [בראשית ט, ג] ועכשיו תקשי לך

כיון שלא נאסרו מה לו להתירם ע"י יוהנש, אך יש אומרים לא נאסר וי"א נאסר והותר [63]. וי"א עיצה טובה קא"ל להבדל מהן להבראת הגוף [64], לדבריכם מותרים זה את זה. אמר המין הלא תדע, כי מי שחטא נגד האב יש לו כפרה אם ישוב בתשובה וכו' מי שחטא נגד הבן יש לו מחילה והחוטא נגד רוח הקודש אין לא מחילה לא בעולם הזה ולא בעולם הבא. וזה לשונו בלעטין, מי שחוטא באב יש לו מחילה קווי פיקטו אָ פטרס רימיטיטור [מחילה] יש לו, מי שחוטא בבן אי אי קווי אינ פיליאו מחילה יש לו, מי שחוטא רימיטיטור אי אי קווי פיקטו ברוח הקדש לא מחילה, אין שפיריטום שנטוס נון רימיטיטור (יש) [אין] לו בעולם הזה ולעולם הבא, אי איאוק שקולו ניקווי אין פוטורו [65], וי"ל אתם אומרים שהג' אחד הן, מי שמע מעולם מי שיחטא נגד הבן קשה מאשר יחטא נגד הבורא, והבורא יתרצה והבן לא יתרצה, משמע שהבורא מוחל ולא מוחל, שהרי שמת לו ב לבבות וב מחשבות ונתת לו ב מדרגות במחילה זה מוחל וזה אינו מוחל, ולא יתכן שהרי הוא מכריז ע"י נביאיו, שובו אלי ואשובה אליכם [זכריה א, ג], אם הוא אינו מוחל א"כ לא של זהו המכריז שובו; ואם אינו זה הבורא ואינו אחד כאשר תאמר ג פארשונ שונטא אונא [66] אחת כדלעיל הלאטיין עד פיקטו אינ פיליא נון רימונטיטור [67] וזה הלעז קפיקא ויל לופיר אי לו פאתא פאדנא קוביק ויר לפריטא שייטא איי לו פרדונא. קי פיקטו ויר לופישנון לא פרדונא [68]. מפי ה"ר יצחק האשכנזי [69].

שאל גוי אחד למה אין הקב"ה מכה אתכם ברעמים ובברד ואין אתם יראים מהם כמו הכלבים [70] שגם אין הקב"ה מכה אותם ואין שולח את הברד אלא בדבר קודש כמו בית תרפותינו והשיב המשיב אדרבא אינו מכה אלא דבר שקר וכזב כדכתיב, ויעה ברד מחסה כזב [ישעיה כח, יז] והק' שונא בית תרפותיכם וגם אתכם לכך אתם צריכים לירוא מהם ולכך מכה בית תרפותכם, משל למה הדבר דומה למלך שצר והקיף כרכום על עיר הופך הקלע לצד אויביו ולא לצד אוהביו כך קלעו של הקב"ה הן הרעמים והופך אותו לנגד אויביו שאין מכירים אותו כמוכם שנאמר, שפוך חמתך על הגויים ועל הממלכות אשר בשמך לא קראו [ירמיהו י, כה] ועוד כתוב בירמיהו, מאותות השמים אל תחתו כי יחתו הגוים מהם כי חוקת העמים הבל הוא [שם, שם ב—ג] א"כ לחוקותיהם קורא הקדוש הבל, לכן תצטרכו לירוא אבל לנו יפה הפסוק שלא לירוא. סליק תשובות להמינים. מן (אותיות מטושטשות).

הערות

1 עיין Angelo di Capua, Catalogo Biblioteca nazionale centrale Vittorio Emanuele dei codici ebraici della Biblioteca Emanuele, Firenze 1876, no. 8; נתוח מפורט של כ״י זה פרסם פרופ׳ א. א. אורבך ב־REJ ק (1935), 49—77.

2 עיין במבוא למהדורה שלי של ספר זה בהוצאת מקיצי נרדמים, ירושלים, תש״ל.

3 עיין Robert Travers Herford, *Christianity in Talmud and Midrash*, 1903.

4 I. Goldziher, *ZDMG* 72 (1878), 341 ff.

5 עיין במחקרי ׳הגנה והתקפה בספרות הויכוח של ימי הביניים׳, פרק: בקורת הברית החדשה; המחקר עומד להופיע בדברי הקונגרס העולמי החמישי למדעי היהודות.

6 עיין יעקב בן ראובן, מלחמות השם, מהדורת י. רוזנטל, תשכ״ג, 141—156.

7 *Tela ignea satanae*, Altdorf 1681

8 עיין ספר יוסף המקנא, עמ׳ 125—138.

9 עיין בפרק ׳לגלוג ולעג דוקר בבקורת׳ במחקר הנזכר בהערה 5.

10 עיין הערה 68 למטה.

11 עיין הערות 21, 38, 53 למטה.

1 זהו ר׳ יוסף ב״ר נתן המקנא או האופיציאל.

2 ז״א על הטבילה.

3 "Baptisma" צורות שונות למלה זו במקורות. עיין בפרק האחרון של ספר יוסף המקנא במהדורה שלי, עמ׳... יאהן בפטישטל; בכ״י רומא: יוהנש בפטישט, יאהן בפטישט. ע״ג *REJ* ג, 30, הערה 1.

4 ז״א הלא.

5 עיין ספר יוסף המקנא, עמ׳ 131.

6 עיין מתי א, 18.

7 עיין בערך "Baptism" באנציקלופדיה הקאטולית ב, 282, טור ב. ע״ג נצחון ישן הוצאת ואנגזייל, 196.

8 *Vasa Vacuum*; עיין נצחון ישן, שם.

9 בעל הויכוח דרש את כל הפרק קכד בתהלים על ישו והנצרות. אדם — ישו, המים הזדונים — מי הטבילה.

10 ז״א השר של העיר ויטרי. עיין *REJ* ק (1935), 55.

11 ז״א אשת השר, עיין נחמיה ב, ו.

12 עיין זוהר ב, 544.

13 ז״א במרים, אמו של ישו.

14 בפולחן של הטבילה אומר הכומר פעמים אחדות את התפלה הבאה: Exorcizo te, immunde spiritus; Exi ab eo (ea) spiritus immunde et da locum Spirito Sancto Paraclito. Disrumpe omnes laqueas satanae. Ergo maledice diabole, recognosce senetentiam tuam. Exorcizo te omnis spiritus immunde.... עיין *The Roman Ritual. In Latin and English*. Translated and Edited by Philip T. Weller, I, 38, 52, 90.

15 כאן נמצאת ההערה הבאה על השוליים: ועוד המנובלים אומרים. ההמשך חסר.

16 ע"ג מרקוס ז, 6—21; לוקס ה, 17—26. בברית החדשה כתוב רק שההמון השתומם.

17 בפרק במובן של הספר.

18 ז"א אביו.

19 עיין יעקב בן ראובן, מלחמות השם, מהדורת י. רוזנטאל, 151.

20 ז"א את ד'. עיין מרקוס ט, 36—37.

21 כפי הנראה טעות המעתיק. תלמידיו שאלו את ישו אם עליהם לאסור על האנשים להוציא שדים בשמו. ישו ענה שלא לאסור. עיין מרקוס ט, 38.

22 עיין הערה קודמת.

23 עיין הערה 21.

24 כבר בתלמוד כתוב שישו כישף. עיין סנהדרין קז, ב: אמר מר ישו הנוצרי כישף והדיח את ישראל. עיין דקדוקי סופרים על אתר.

25 עיין נצחון ישן, 222. בוולגאטה: Cana.

26 עיין דברים כב, כג. לפי המשנה, סנהדרין ז, ד: אשה שזנתה היא בחנק. ע"ג ספר יוסף המקנא במהדורה שלי, עמ' 135.

27 מעל למלים כנגד עשני בכ"י גרשיים. כפי הנראה לסימן שיש למחוק אותן.

28 עיין מדרש תנחומא נשא, א: שכל ישראל אחים ורעים הם. זאת היתה כפי הנראה אחת התשובות אשר התיאולוגים הנוצרים נתנו לבעיית אחיו של ישו. עיין: Maurice Goguel, *The Life of Jesus*, 1954, 260.

29 עיין על מת מצוה מגילה ג, א—ב.

30 מלה אחת בת שלש אותיות מטושטשת.

31 בספרות המדרשית נדמו אוה"ע לכלבים. עיין בתרגום על תהלים כב, יז; ע"ג בפרוש רש"י על שה"ש ז, ו.

32 ז"א מאבר הזכרות.

33 עיין נצחון ישן, 197—198. עפ"י הנוסחא הרווחת של אותה האגדה הישמעאלי הוא הקיסר טריאנוס. עיין: Charles W. Jones, *Saints' Lives* and *Chronicles in Early England* (1947), 116f.

34 מודיא — מדת היבש. עיין במלונים הארמיים על התלמוד.

35 המלה "לדברי" היא הוספה על השולים.

36 עיין בבא קמא צא, ב.

36א שבוש מאיוון גיליון. עיין נצחון ישן, 225.

37 בנצחון ישן (עמ' 225) כתוב: הנפש מזהרה לגוף כל שעה לחטוא, והתרגום הלטיני הוא: Anima semper corpus ad peccandum incitat.

38 צ"ל מדומדמות. עיין נצחון ישן, שם. (Cubans) in lecto meo manibus cruentis. שני המא־מרים האלה אינם נמצאים בברית החדשה. המאמר האחרון מבוסס על ישעיהו א, יב, טו. ע"ג שמות כא, יד. ע"ג רמב"ם, משנה תורה, הלכות רוצח ושמירת הנפש ה, יב: אסור לרוצח להכנס אל בית המקדש.

39 עיין סנהדרין צא. א—ב; ע"ג מדרש ויקרא רבא, מהד. מרגליות, פז ואילך.

40 המקור הוא בלתי ידוע לי.

41 עיין י. רוזנטל, מחקרים, 435, הערה 3.

42 ז"א לקחת בחוזק. עיין בן יהודה, מלון א, 321.

43 עיין לוקס, טז, 19—24.

44 עיין הערה 41.

45 לפי רב סעדיה גאון עץ החיים שבגן עדן היה עץ מרפא. עיין משה צוקר, על תרגום רב סעדיה גאון לתורה. 296; יוסף קאפח, פרושי רבינו סעדיה גאון על התורה, יד.

46 בפסוק במובן של המקרא בכללו. עיין בן יהודה, מלון, 5023, טור ב.

46א אחר המלה כל רווח למלה בת אותיות אחדות.

47 על שמות גנאי של קדושי וחגי הנוצרים עיין: L. Zunz, *Die synagogale Poesie des Mittel-alters* (1920), 468ff.

48 ז"א הפסחא של הנוצרים עיין: *REJ* (1884), 194

49 עיין פסחים ד, א.

50 בספר יוסף המקנא (פרק כט) הנוסחא של וכוח זה היא: נשאל מעולם מקולל, למה נקרא מקולל יותר מאדם אחר... והשיב מכל צד נקרא מקולל אם לדידכם אם לדידינו, לדידכם נקרא מקולל כי אלקיכם היה תלוי וגם לדידנו נקרא מקולל עבור גלוית אשר גלל עלינו על כי תלינו אותו כי אתם אומרים.

51 עיין ירושלמי תענית ב, א; (הוצאת קרוטושין סה, ב); ע"ג ילינק, בית המדרש ה, 207—208. י. רוזנטל, מחקרים 203—204.

52 יש בה בתשובה זו הומור דוקר.

53 Qui non fuerit circumcideretur de carno Filius non potest introire in hortum vitae. מאמר זה לא נמצא בברית החדשה, בספר נצחון ליום טוב ליפמן מיהלהויזן (מס. רי"ח) הוא מובא בשם ספר גרגריאות (גרגוריוס). עיין יהודה קויפמאן, ר' יום טוב ליפמן מיהלהויזן, 55: Qui non circomcisus est sicut Abraham, Isaac, Jacob non potest introire in regnum coeli. לא יכולתי למצוא את המקום המדויק בכתבי גריגוריוס. P.L. כרכים 75—79.

54 Nisi circumcisi fueritis non intrabitis intra regnum coelorum במעשי השליחים (טו. 1) כתוב: Quia nisi circumcidamini secundum morem Moysi, non potesis salvari.

55 Omnis masculus cuius preputii caro circumcisa non fuerit delebitur anima illius de populo suo (עיין בראשית יז, יד).

56 עיין מתי ה, 17—18.

57 התלמוד דן בבעיה זו. עיין ברכות יז, א: נשים במאי זכיין, והתשובה היא: באקרויי בנייהו לבי כנישתא.

58 עיין ויקרא כב, יב.

59 איננו זהה עם ר' מנחם בן פרץ מיואני שהיה בן דורם של רבנו תם והרשב"ם. ר' מנחם המתווכח חי במחצית השניה של המאה הי"ג. הוא התווכח עם המומר הידוע פאבלו כריסטיאני בשנת 1269 בפאריס. עיין במחקרי "ויכוח דתי בין חכם בשם מנחם ובין המומר והנזיר הדומיניקאני פאבלו כריסטיאני" שעומד להופיע במאסף הגות עברית באמריקה בהוצאת הברית העברית העולמית.

60 Qui comedebat carnem suillam et abominationem simul consummentur dicit Dominus.

61 ר' אשר זה הוא אחיו של ר' יוסף המקנא. עיין עליו במבוא למהדורה שלי לספר יוסף המקנא, עמ' כ, ע"ג, שם, עמ' 60, 90, 141.

62 עיין מעשי השליחים י, 12—16.

63 עיין במחקרי ב- *HUCA* כא, חלק עברי, עמ' נח. ע"ג המפרשים על בראשית א, כט.

64 עיין ברלב"ג על ויקרא יא; ע"ג יצחק היינמאן, טעמי המצוות בספרות ישראל.

65 Qui peccatus a patre remittetur ei, qui in filium remittetur ei, qui peccatus in Spiritum Sanctum non remittetur ei (et) neque in hoc seculo neque in futuro. עיין מתי יב. 30—32; לוקס יב. 10; מרקוס ג. 28.

66 זאת היא הדוגמא הנוצרית: tres personae una substantia. עיין יעקב בן ראובן, מלחמות השם, מהדורת י. רוזנטל, 40, הערה 26.

67 עיין הערה 65.

68 המקור הצרפתי של תעתיק זה הוא בלתי ידוע לי.

69 קשה לזהות אותו. עיין *REJ* ק. 54.

70 היהודים דימו את עע"ז ואת שונאי ישראל לכלבים והנוצרים את היהודים. עיין הערה 31 למעלה. הכנסיה הנוצרית הסבה את המלה כלבים בתהלים כב, יז על היהודים. עיין יוסטין מארטיר, שיחה עם טריפון, פרק צז.

נספח

על השוליים בעמ׳ 17 ב מלמטה של כה״י נמצאת ההוספה הבאה:

עוד י״ל אם כדבריהם שכל הנשמות נתן לשטן בשביל עון אדם א״כ עשה הקב״ה כביכול לשטן שלקח לו חנוך ואליהו חיים ולא המיתן [1], וגם הנשמות לא נתן לשטן אלא ודאי לא נקנס מות תמות אלא באדם וחוה בלבד [2], כי כל אדם בחטאו מת דכתיב גבי צלפחד, כי בחטאו מת [במדבר כז, ג] וכתוב, לא יומתו אבות על בנים וגו׳ [דברים ה ט], ואם יאמר ולמה לא מתו חנוך ואליהו [3] י״ל כי אמרו להקב״ה אדם לא עבר כי לא צוית לו רק ומעץ הדעת והוא לא אכל העץ אלא מן הפרי [4], ודו״ק. עוד י״ל ממה שאמר הב״ה לאברהם ואתה תבא אל אבותיך בשלום [בראשית טו, טו] וכי זה שלום שירד לגיהנום [5], ואומר למשה, הנך שוכב עם אבותיך [דברים לא, טז] לגיהנום או לכן שמח לבי ויגל כבודי [תהלים טז, ט] כן עד, לא תעזוב נפשי לשאול וגו׳ תודיעני אורח חיים [שם, שם י, יא] [6].

[1] הלשון כאן היא מגומגמת, יתכן שחסרה כאן מלה אבל הכוונה היא ברורה והיא להוכיח מזה שחנוך ואליהו עלו חיים שמימה ושהקב״ה לא מסר נשמותיהם לשטן.

[2] עיין שבת נה, א—ב. ע״ג י. רוזנטל, מחקרים, 436, הערה 12. (בעיית החטא הקדמון ביהדות).

[3] עיין במחקרי בספר יובל יהושע פינקל.

[4] הרמב״ן שמודה בתורת החטא הקדמון מתווכח נגד הסבר זה. עיין ברמב״ן על בראשית ב, יז.

[5] עיין יעקב בן ראובן, מלחמות השם, מהדורת י. רוזנטל, 51 ואילך.

[6] מן הצלום יש לראות שחסרה עוד שורה שלמה.